Fenwick on Civil Liberties and Human Rights

More than merely describing the evolution of human rights and civil liberties law, this classic textbook provides students with detailed and thought-provoking coverage of the most crucial developments in the field, clearly explaining the law in context and practice.

Updated throughout for this new edition, *Fenwick on Civil Liberties and Human Rights* considers a number of recent major changes in the law – in particular proposals to replace the Human Rights Act with a British Bill of Rights, and the Counter-Terrorism and Security Act 2015 – whilst also contextualising the impact of reforms on hate speech and contempt due to advances in new media.

Comprehensive and authoritative, this textbook offers an essential resource for students on human rights or civil liberties courses, as well as a useful reference for students and scholars of UK Public Law.

Helen Fenwick is a Professor of Law at Durham University, specialising in human rights, counter-terrorism law and policy, and media freedom.

Fenwick on Civil Liberties and Human Rights

Fifth Edition

Helen Fenwick

With contributions from
Aaron Baker, Richard Edwards,
Daniel Fenwick, Michael Hamilton,
Paul Wragg and Alison Young

R Routledge
Taylor & Francis Group

LONDON AND NEW YORK

Fifth edition published 2017
by Routledge
2 Park Square, Milton Park, Abingdon, Oxon, OX14 4RN

and by Routledge
711 Third Avenue, New York, NY 10017

Routledge is an imprint of the Taylor & Francis Group, an informa business

First edition published 1994
Fourth edition published 2007

British Library Cataloguing in Publication Data
A catalogue record for this book is available from the British Library

Library of Congress Cataloging-in-Publication Data
Names: Fenwick, Helen, author.
Title: Fenwick on civil liberties and human rights / Helen Fenwick.
Other titles: Civil liberties and human rights
Description: Fifth edition. | New York, NY : Routledge, 2016. |
    Includes bibliographical references and index.
Identifiers: LCCN 2016014921 | ISBN 9781138837942 (hbk) |
    ISBN 9781138837935 (pbk) | ISBN 9781315734767 (ebk)
Subjects: LCSH: Civil rights—Great Britain.
Classification: LCC KD4080. F46 2016 | DDC 342.4108/5—dc23
LC record available at https://lccn.loc.gov/2016014921

ISBN: 978-1-138-83794-2 (hbk)
ISBN: 978-1-138-83793-5 (pbk)
ISBN: 978-1-315-73476-7 (ebk)

Typeset in Times New Roman
by Apex CoVantage, LLC

Printed and bound in Great Britain by Ashford Colour Press Ltd, Gosport, Hampshire.

Contents

Preface

This fifth edition was completed eight years after the fourth. The delay was partly due to the great changes that occurred in the legal landscape in this field over that period of time, which made completing this edition a daunting task. It is now almost impossible for a single author to cover the developments that have occurred, so reliance on a team of academics to up-date certain chapters has been both necessary and very beneficial. In writing this edition the contradictions surrounding the Human Rights Act have been thrown into sharp relief. On the one hand, it has, to an extent, bedded down, and there has been, since the *Belmarsh* case in 2004 in the House of Lords, a sea change in the judicial attitude towards it. The judges have, for the last ten years, quite often shown that they treat the duty under s 6 HRA with a seriousness that was not apparent in the first few years of the HRA's life. In a series of cases, often related to counter-terrorism law, the judges have departed from the government's view as to justifiable infringements of liberty. On the other hand, since 9/11, the Human Rights Act has obviously come under threat. For almost the whole of its existence it has been under attack, from the previous Labour government, the Conservatives as part of the Coalition government 2010–15, and now from a Conservative government untrammelled by the influence of the Liberal Democrats. It has also been attacked in vitriolic fashion by parts of the media, partly on the ground that it protects criminals and stands in the way of an effective counter-terrorist policy. The tensions between the HRA and the main counter-terrorist statutes introduced since 2000 are explored in particular in Chapter 15.

The second and third editions of this book were written during the early stage of the Blair Government, when a new era seemed to be dawning in Britain in human rights terms. In contrast, this edition was completed after the Conservative government took power in 2015, albeit with a very small majority. At this point in time the future of the Human Rights Act looks highly uncertain in Britain. It is perhaps somewhat ironic that once the HRA became in effect a Bill of Rights for Britain, plans to repeal and replace it with a 'British Bill of Rights' were put forward by the Conservative government, and repeal may occur some time between 2017–2021. Further, given that the British people voted in favour of 'Brexit' in the EU Referendum in June 2016, the influence of the EU, and in particular of the Fundamental Charter of Rights will, presumably, cease as a means of protecting human rights in Britain, once withdrawal from the EU occurs.

But the future of human rights in Britain clearly does not depend only on the HRA, or on the EU; Britain would remain bound to the ECHR rights at the international level unless the Conservative government pursues the possibility that has been previously mooted of withdrawal from the ECHR. Moreover, this book, especially in Chapter 3, charts the extent to which there has recently been a resurgence in the protection of rights offered by the common law. But in some contexts, such as public protest and counter-terrorist powers, the ECHR as scheduled in the HRA has proved crucial in protecting rights. The case for the HRA has not been made to the British public; instead it has been portrayed as a charter for criminals and terrorists, allowing the Conservative party to pass off the plan to repeal the HRA as aiding in deporting foreign criminals, furthering counter-terrorist strategy, and representing a return to 'British values'. The less responsible sections of the media have been and will present it in that way, playing on the ignorance of the British people as to the relationship between the HRA and the European Convention on Human Rights. Attempts to sell it to them as the protector of vulnerable persons, such as old people in care homes, do not appear to have taken hold, given the counter-narrative presented by much of the press.

Contradictions are also evident in the judicial attitude to the HRA. This book traces the signs of the judicial acceptance of a constitutional human rights jurisdiction, held back to an extent by the House of Lords' decision in *Ullah*. As Chapter 4 in particular indicates, *Ullah* has been circumvented and in any event is in tension with the whole enterprise of the HRA and the general approach in Britain to constitutional instruments. The tension between the approach that sees the HRA merely as a vehicle for giving easier access to the Convention domestically, and with the one that sees it as a constitutional human rights instrument forms an important theme in this book, but it is now overshadowed by the prospect of repeal of the HRA and reliance at the domestic level on a British Bill of Rights.

The decision was taken in writing this new edition to reach for depth rather than breadth, and to that end certain chapters were shortened, in particular the chapter on equality. If this discipline is to retain some coherence and to move forward in a way that continues to appeal to academics, students and others, it needs to be selective and to recognise how far it overlaps with other disciplines, such as employment law. Detailed discussion of domestic law on anti-discrimination is better found in specialist texts.

As mentioned, certain chapters in this edition have been revised by a number of authors who have updated particular chapters falling within their special areas of expertise, although I have updated Chapters 2, 3, 12 and 14. I also had some involvement in updating Chapter 10, and in finalising updates for Chapters 13 and 14. The contributor authors are listed at the beginning of relevant chapters.

I must also acknowledge the contribution of those who helped in formulating the ideas expressed in this book. In relation to the fourth edition my thanks are due to Aaron Baker, Senior Lecturer (now Reader) at Durham University, for reading and commenting on Chapter 15 (now Chapter 5) and to Professor Gavin Phillipson of Durham University who commented on Chapter 4 in that edition. Professor Colin Warbrick offered helpful comments on early drafts of Chapters 2 and 3 of the first edition. I have drawn on certain of my articles as indicated at various points.

The main body of the text was completed by September 2015, but it was possible to add some later material in 2016. So some small additions were made at proof stage. Also, when a team is involved, completion rates for different chapters differ, and certain chapters were completed by December 2015.

The book is dedicated with love and affection to my family.

Durham
August 2016

Postscript

As anyone reading this book will know, on 23rd June 2016 the UK voted in a referendum to leave the EU, common referred to as voting in favour of 'Brexit'. That occurred some months after this book was completed, but this postscript is being added to explain very briefly the implications of so-called 'Brexit' for the purposes of references to EU law in certain chapters. Clearly, this book is largely concerned with the impact of the European Convention on Human Rights (ECHR) on UK law. The ECHR and EU legal systems are distinct; a state can remain within the ECHR system, as Chapter 2 explains, without being a member of the EU. So at present the relationship between the ECHR and the UK remains as described in that chapter and may continue unchanged. That chapter, and Chapter 3, referred to the possibility that a draft British Bill of Rights (BBoR) would be introduced after the EU Referendum. But given the current turmoil in the Conservative Party after the referendum, which for some time will be focused on the election of a new leader, it is probable that such publication will be further delayed, and the question of repeal of the HRA and of introduction of a BBoR will not be resolved until after a new leader is in place. Obviously if there is a General Election in 2016 the fate of the HRA would be likely to depend on its result.

As far as the EU is concerned, the result of the referendum does not in itself formally change the relationship between the UK and the EU since as a referendum it is not legally binding. Article 50 of the Lisbon Treaty sets out the way in which an EU country might voluntarily leave the Union. Article 50 says: "Any member state may decide to withdraw from the union in accordance with its own constitutional requirements." The Article provides that a state intending to leave should notify the European Council of its intention; it should negotiate an agreement setting out the arrangements as to its withdrawal and establishing a framework for its future relationship with the EU. That agreement will then be concluded on behalf of the Union by the Council acting by a qualified majority of member states in the Council after the consent of the European Parliament.

David Cameron as the current Prime Minister has stated that he is not going to invoke Article 50; he has resigned but will serve until the new leader of the Conservative Party is in place, who will presumably – unless a snap General Election is called – also be Prime Minister. That person will be expected then, according to Cameron, to invoke Article 50. Once formal Article 50 notification has occurred the negotiators have two years from that date under Article 50 to conclude the new arrangements.

As far as references to EU law in this book are concerned, then, it is not expected that any change resulting from 'Brexit' will occur till late 2018.

Table of cases

Table of UK statutes

Table of UK statutory instruments

Table of national legislation from other jurisdictions

Table of treaties and conventions

Table of EU legislation

Part I

Rights and liberties; their legal protection in the UK

In many Western democracies the rights of citizens are enshrined in a constitutional document usually known as a Bill or Charter of Rights. As Chapter 3 will explain, the rights protected under such a constitutional document are often given a special status; in a number of countries they are entrenched. Until the inception of the Human Rights Act 1998 (HRA), the UK had no similar charter of rights. The Magna Carta 1215, while influential as a very early statement of rights, is not comparable to a modern Bill of Rights in terms of extent or impact on current law.[1] In 2000, the HRA afforded further domestic effect to the European Convention on Human Rights (ECHR), as discussed in Chapter 4. But even under the HRA, the rights are not entrenched, meaning that the HRA or parts of it could be repealed just as any other statute can be. However, as Chapter 1 explains, the inception of the HRA means that protections previously recognised as liberties are now recognised as rights.

Traditionally, pre-HRA, in order to discover which freedoms were protected and the extent of that protection, it was necessary to examine the common law, statutes and the influence of treaties to which the UK is a party, especially the European Convention on Human Rights. Civil liberties were traditionally defined as residual, not entrenched as in other countries. In other words, once the restrictions had been defined the area of liberty was the residue that could be recognised as remaining. Thus, traditional judicial reasoning in civil liberties cases quite often consisted merely of the application of the law deriving from statute and common law precedents; the negative liberty was simply what was left over after the scope of the restrictions had been determined. Often there was an application of common law precedents or a mechanistic approach to statutory interpretation, which was devoid of principle in the sense of recognising that any important issues were at stake requiring a departure from that normal judicial technique. This approach was very marked in freedom of assembly cases.[2] In the first edition of this book it was necessary to confront a mass of common law and statutory restrictions on liberties to consider the width of these restrictions in order to determine the size of the residual area left within which liberty could be exercised.[3] This did not mean that civil liberties were without protection, and in the late 1990s, the immediate pre-HRA era,

---

1 See Fenwick, H, 'Origins of Rights and Freedoms', in Lord Mackay of Clashfern and Falkowski, D (eds), *Halsbury's Laws*, 2013, LexisNexis.
2 See Chapter 9, p 608 *et seq*.
3 See further: Gearty, C and Ewing, K, *Freedom under Thatcher*, 1990, OUP; Feldman, D, *Civil Liberties*, 1st edn, 1993, Clarendon; Gearty, C and Ewing, K, *The Struggle for Civil Liberties*, 2000, Clarendon.

certain common law 'rights' found recognition, as Chapter 3 explains. Thus, it was often said that civil liberties in the UK were in a more precarious position than they were in other democracies with Bills of Rights, although this clearly did not necessarily mean that they were inevitably less well protected: some Bills of Rights offered only a theoretical protection to freedoms, which was far from being reflected in practice. As Chapter 3 explains, freedoms obtained significant recognition under the common law pre-HRA, and continue to do so in the HRA era. The mere fact that a freedom falls within the area of an ECHR right, does not mean that further enquiry as to its protection under the common law should be abandoned.[4]

Certain characteristics of the UK Constitution have determined and, under the HRA, are continuing to determine – albeit with some modification – the means of protecting fundamental freedoms in the UK. The doctrine of the supremacy of Parliament means that constitutional law can be changed in the ordinary way – by Act of Parliament. As every student of constitutional law knows, Parliament has the power to abridge free-doms that in other countries are seen as fundamental rights. It follows from this that, aside from EU law, all parts of the law are equal – there is no hierarchy of laws and therefore constitutional law cannot constrain other laws. In general there is no judicial review of Acts of Parliament. If, for example, a statute is passed containing a provision that in some way limits freedom of speech, a judge must apply it, whereas in a country with an entrenched Bill of Rights the provision might be struck down as unconstitu-tional. As Chapter 4 explains, s 3 HRA has placed significant pressure on this traditional position, but technically it still subsists. Under the HRA, a judge is not able to declare a statutory provision invalid because it conflicts with a Convention right protected by the Act. These constitutional arrangements have not been fundamentally changed by the HRA but, as Chapter 4 indicates, they have been placed under considerable pressure because the HRA effected a difficult compromise between protecting parliamentary sovereignty and achieving effective rights protection.

However, where fundamental rights are protected by EU law, which also reflects the principles of the European Convention on Human Rights, they take precedence over statutory provisions due to the supremacy of EU law. Thus if a domestic provision comes into conflict with an EU provision, the judge will decide to 'disapply' it, unless the conflict can be resolved. Parliamentary sovereignty has therefore suffered some limitation. Where EU law does have an impact on fundamental freedoms, it provides a protection which may broadly be said to remove certain freedoms, or aspects of them, from the reach of Parliament, at least while the UK is a member of the EU.

That is the constitutional background to the HRA. It is still of great significance since it is crucial in the development of civil liberties in this country and because the HRA has been greatly influenced by the domestic constitutional traditions. This Part will seek to show that although the HRA is of immense constitutional significance, it has not brought about a fundamental constitutional transformation. It has allowed the European Convention on Human Rights to be relied on directly in domestic courts, and in the 15 years that the HRA has been in force there have been some signs – but not many – that the judiciary are prepared to give a domestic effect to the rights that affords them a broader scope than they have been afforded at the Strasbourg Court (the European

---

4 See Chapter 3, pp 108–09.

Court of Human Rights).[5] Further, although under the HRA judges cannot strike down legislation, they can change its provisions through interpretation, which includes implying 'missing' words into it, or declare the incompatibility between such provisions and one or more ECHR rights. Where they take the latter course, the government, as Chapter 4 shows, normally tends to respond.[6] Thus the HRA has shown a resemblance to a Bill of Rights, despite its limitations, which were imposed on it in accordance with British constitutional traditions.[7] This notion of the transition over the last 15 years from an instrument giving an international instrument domestic effect to something resembling a Bill of Rights forms a key theme in this part, and indeed in this book as a whole. But this edition of this book is written at a time when pressure to repeal the HRA is apparent, partly due to the rising fear of Islamic terrorism.

The HRA was introduced by the Labour government in 1998 on the basis that the Convention rights were, finally, to be 'brought home'.[8] There were expectations at that time that the HRA would revive the civil liberties tradition – there was a sense of a break with the erosions of liberty of the past. But before the HRA had had a chance to gain acceptance among politicians and the British people generally, the world was hit by the devastating 9/11 attacks. The same Labour government that passed the HRA was then responsible for an unprecedented incursion into peacetime civil liberties in an effort to address the terrorist threat. The legislative response began only one year after the HRA came into force, in 2001, when the Labour Government derogated from one of the most fundamental freedoms – the right to liberty.[9] The Labour government followed this derogation with further legislation that curbed freedoms that had long been entrenched as civil liberties before the inception of the HRA, including the Regulation of Investigatory Powers Act 2000 (see Chapter 11), the Serious and Organised Crime Act 2005 (see Chapter 13) and, in response to the 7/7 bombings, the Terrorism Act 2006 (see Chapter 15). The Coalition government of 2010–15 built on that legislation in passing the Counter-Terrorism and Security Act 2015, and the current Conservative government proposes to introduce further legislation to combat extremism, in response to the spread of Isis and various terrorist incidents, including the shooting of 30 Britons in Tunisia on 26 June 2015, the greatest loss of British life in a terrorist attack since the 7/7 bombings.

Thus, a key aim of this book is to consider the impact which the HRA has had in enhancing the protection for liberty in the face of a range of statutes enhancing state power very significantly since 9/11. At the same time it will examine the extent to which

---

5 See p 237 et seq.
6 See p 169 et seq.
7 See Klug, F, *A Magna Carta for all humanity: homing in on human rights*, 2015, Routledge; Klug, F, 'The Human Rights Act: a "third way" or "third wave" bill of rights?' (2001) EHRLR 361; Klug, F and Starmer, K, 'Incorporation through the front door, an evaluation of the Human Rights Act in the courts' [2001] PL 654; Klug, F, *Values for a Godless Age, the story of the UK's new bill of rights*, 2000, Penguin.
8 See *Bringing Rights Home: Labour's plans to incorporate the ECHR into UK Law*, December 1996, published as Straw, J and Boateng, P, 'Bringing Rights Home: Labour's plan to incorporate the European Convention on Human Rights into UK law' (1997) 1 EHRLR 71; see also the White Paper *Rights Brought Home*, Cm 3782, October 1997.
9 See Lord Cooke, 'The British embracement of human rights' (1999) 3 EHRLR 243; Feldman, D, 'The Human Rights Act and constitutional principles' (1999) 19(2) LS 165.

expansive interpretations of Convention rights are currently being retreated from at Strasbourg, in Parliament and in the courts. There is the possibility that, in Parliament, the rights have at times been treated as guarantees partly emptied of content which cast a legitimising cloak over rights-abridging legislation and executive action.

This book will argue that the core values that human rights protect – whether recognised under the ECHR, the common law or in future under a British Bill of Rights – should be afforded a genuine efficacy, since the alternative would be likely to lead to a *decrease* in state accountability and an obscuring of political discourse as to the nature of state power and countervailing rights. The fact that the UK may in future have a British Bill of Rights and at present relies on a measure – the HRA – that looks something like a Bill of Rights, in the tradition of other democracies, should not necessarily be taken to suggest that rights protection is secured. Countervailing concerns are especially pressing at the present time, in 2015, after a number of terrorist incidents, including the murder of Lee Rigby in 2013, and the foiling of a range of terrorist plots. Indeed, such concerns are leading to the current demand for departure from ECHR standards. The interaction between the HRA and the interests of unpopular minority groups, including suspected terrorists and prisoners, has fuelled the move to repeal the HRA. The perception that the HRA stands in the way of adopting necessary security measures, in addition to various concerns that the Act is overly generous towards the morally culpable (such as prisoners and terrorists) has gradually become established in the popular consciousness. After 15 years of the HRA, the Conservative government, now unrestrained by being part of a Coalition (albeit with a limited majority), and threatened by the anti-HRA rhetoric of UKIP, has stated that it intends to consult on repeal of the HRA and its replacement with a British Bill of Rights.[10]

It is argued in this book that the popular assessment of the HRA is largely unfounded and is the result of the failure of the British public to grasp its real nature and significance. The lack of popular support is a result of various problems with the popular image of human rights and with their operation in the UK under the HRA specifically. Human rights represent complex requirements whose specific content is often controversial (see Chapter 1). Furthermore, they create a profound legal challenge that redefines the role legal institutions play in developing the law in a common law jurisdiction, such as the UK. Finally, as discussed in Chapter 2, the practical enforcement of human rights in the UK is parasitic upon an international legal instrument (the European Convention of Human Rights). The rights are not 'owned' by the British people in the way that Canadians appear to own their Charter or US citizens their Constitution.

All these difficulties with the popular image of human rights in the UK have been fostered and preyed upon by the British news media, which has been almost uniformly hostile to the HRA. This is a striking feature of the UK human rights debate (and the Bill of Rights debate, discussed in Chapter 3) since the news media are the traditional guardians of and even *recipients* of civil liberties and human rights (in particular, the right to free expression; see Part II). The reason for such hostility, in addition to the fertile ground for misunderstandings about the protection of human rights, is perhaps

---

10   See e.g., Michael Gove the Secretary of State for Justice HC Deb, 28 May 2015 Vol 596 col 291. The implications of the current proposal from the Conservative government to consider repealing the HRA and replace it with a British Bill of Rights are considered at a number of points, and specifically in Chapter 3, p 122 *et seq.*

that the traditional conception of civil liberties in the UK undoubtedly gave greater weight to the right to free expression relative to the countervailing right to privacy (see Chapter 10).

So the HRA is under immense pressure at the present time, a time when, ironically, in a number of respects it has shown its ability to change the face of rights protection in the UK. This is an age in which counter-terrorist and organised crime concerns dominate the political agenda, and when the need for an instrument that can curb executive tendencies to introduce in response hasty, over-broad rights-abridging measures is especially pressing. But at the same time it will be acknowledged that the maintenance of security is an essential prerequisite for the enjoyment in practice of the benefits of rights.

In this Part, Chapter 1 will offer an indication of the theoretical basis of rights and liberties and of the distinction between them, seeking to demonstrate that a shift from liberties to rights has occurred in the UK. Chapter 2 will undertake analysis of the treaty which has been afforded further effect in domestic law and which is currently tending to act, in effect, as the basis of a UK Bill of Rights – the European Convention on Human Rights (ECHR). Chapter 3 will consider the nature and adequacy of the traditional domestic arrangements which protected fundamental freedoms mainly as liberties and the extent to which the Convention influenced the domestic protection of civil liberties in the pre-HRA era; it will also consider the current resurgence in 2013–15 of common law rights, not reliant on the HRA.[11] It will also discuss the proposal for the future replacement of the HRA with a British Bill of Rights. Chapter 4 will consider the nature of the instrument that has received the Convention into domestic law – the HRA. Chapter 5 will consider the influence of the ECHR upon anti-discrimination law, and the protection of equality in the UK.

11 Masterman, R and Se-shauna, W, 'A common law resurgence in rights protection?' (2015) EHRLR 57.

Chapter 1

An introduction to the nature of rights and liberties

This chapter has been updated and revised for this edition by Daniel Fenwick, Lecturer in Law, University of Northumbria, UK.

1 Introduction

This book is intended to provide an analysis of the legal protection given to civil liberties and human rights in the UK.[1] The term 'civil liberties' denotes the broad class of liberties often referred to as civil and political liberties as they are traditionally recognised in the UK,[2] while the term 'human rights' broadly refers to rights that can be claimed against state bodies, recognised internationally in the Universal Declaration on Human Rights. In order to develop a conception of these requirements a theoretical position will be outlined from which to mount an internally consistent critique of the state of civil liberties and human rights in the UK today.[3] This chapter will therefore aim to provide an outline account of the nature of and underlying justification for state acceptance of civil liberties and human rights.

1　Texts referred to throughout this book: Klug, F, *A Magna Carta for all Humanity: Homing in on Human Rights*, 2015, Routledge; Feldman, D, *Civil Liberties and Human Rights in England and Wales*, 2002; Klug, F, Starmer, K and Weir, S, *The Three Pillars of Liberty: Political Rights and Freedoms in the UK*, 1996, Routledge; Gordon, R and Wilmot-Smith, R (eds), *Human Rights in the UK*, 1997, OUP; Van Dijk, P and Van Hoof, F, Van Rijn, A, Zwask, L, *Theory and Practice of the European Convention on Human Rights*, 4th edn, 2006, Intersentia; Mowbray, A, *Cases and Materials on the European Convention on Human Rights*, 3rd edn, 2012, OUP; Janis, M, Kay, R and Bradley, A, *European Human Rights Law*, 3rd edn, 2008, OUP; Harris, D, O'Boyle, K, Bates, E and Buckley, C, *Law of the European Convention on Human Rights*, 2014, OUP; Dickson, B (ed), and Connelly, A, *Human Rights and the European Convention*, 1996, Sweet and Maxwell; Farran, S, *The UK before the European Court of Human Rights*, 1996, Blackstone. Background: Beddard, R, *Human Rights and Europe*, 3rd edn, 1980, CUP; Fawcett, JES, *The Application of the European Convention on Human Rights*, 2nd edn, 1987, Clarendon; Jacobs, F, *The European Convention on Human Rights*, 1975, OUP; Nedjati, ZM, *Human Rights under the European Convention*, 1978, Elsevier; Merrills, JG and Robertson, AH, *Human Rights in Europe*, 4th edn, 2001, Juris Publishing.

2　The term 'civil and political rights' is used in contradistinction to the term 'economic and social rights' to denote first generation rights – those which have long been recognised in the Western democracies from the time of the French and American Declarations of the 'Rights of Man' in the eighteenth century.

3　The literature is immense, but the following are of particular importance. Simmonds, NE, *Central Issues in Jurisprudence*, 1986, Sweet and Maxwell, provides a brief but extremely lucid introduction to relevant jurisprudential issues. Substantive texts: Rawls, J, *A Theory of Justice*, 1972, Clarendon; Dworkin, R, *Taking Rights Seriously*, 1977, Duckworth, and *A Matter of Principle*, 1985, Clarendon; Hart, HLA, *The Concept of Law*, 1961, Clarendon, and *Essays in Jurisprudence and Philosophy*, 1983, Clarendon; Waldron, J (ed), *Theories of Rights*, 1984, OUP.

2 The nature of civil liberties and human rights

Both rights and liberties are fundamentally *requirements*. To have a right is to be able to (validly) require another person/institution to do or not do something. As requirements they can be broken down into various elements: firstly the requirement must have an object, i.e. it must be about some thing or action (e.g., not to be killed); secondly the requirement must have a subject, a person (S) who is owed the object; thirdly it must have a respondent (R), who owes S the object.

   This section will provide an outline account of the constituent elements and relations that define rights and liberties as requirements. This outline will be used to define the nature and operation of human rights and civil liberties which as pertaining to the UK is the focal concern of this book.

Legal rights and moral rights

Before considering the content of rights as requirements it is first necessary to establish their validity. In other words, why should a respondent state accept that it owes a duty towards an individual who is the subject of a right? Validity is at the essence of the distinction between a legal and a moral right. The endeavour to distinguish legal from moral rights involves a central issue in jurisprudence, namely the relationship between law and morality, on which there is a vast literature and a number of clearly defined schools of thought. Only the barest indications of the various positions on this tendentious issue are possible here.

   There are two familiar scenarios within which 'rights' and 'liberties' are commonly referred to. The first such scenario is one where an individual makes a claim that he has a right/liberty from the state by virtue of a specific legal authority, such as a statute. For example, if an individual who will be called Sam is arrested by police with no given reason and attacked by the same officers while in custody, he could claim that the state has violated a number of his rights (including his rights to privacy and liberty; see Chapters 10 and 12). Sam could refer to the various relevant legal authorities proscribing the actions of the police, such as the offence of assault.[4] Thus Sam's rights would be vindicated in a legal sense. The second scenario arises where the individual claims that his rights/liberties are infringed, but there is no such legal authority vindicating his rights. For example, if pre-HRA Shirley, a male to female transsexual teacher seeking to receive social acceptance for her transition, finds that her personal life is exposed in various newspapers in lurid terms, with intimate details obtained by secret filming, before she can talk to her pupils about her transition, she would not be able to refer to authorities proscribing the newspapers' actions, as Sam could. Prior to the developments that occurred after the passing of the Human Rights Act she would not have been able to vindicate her right to private life in UK law in this situation.[5] She could still argue that the newspaper had infringed her right to privacy, but her putative right would not be enforced in UK law.

   The two scenarios represent – very crudely – the division between a legal and moral right put forward by the school of jurisprudence known as legal positivism, whose

4   Criminal Justice Act 1988, s 39.
5   See Chapter 10, p 725 *et seq.*

central insistence is that there is no *necessary* connection between law and morality.[6] A positivist would argue that in the second scenario there is no *law* justifying Shirley's claim and, instead, that she is merely asserting a moral right. A positivist would argue that while Shirley could argue that her claim *ought* to be given legal force through the enactment of a specific legal right, that is in no respect equivalent to her possession of a legal right.

To a member of the natural law school in its traditional form,[7] by contrast, the question of whether Shirley's claim was moral or legal would not be decided empirically (e.g., by consulting the statute book), but rather by examining the normative claim made by her. If her claim was supported by *moral* law, then an empirical authority purporting to deny her claim would not be accepted as a valid law since it would be unjust. The approach sounds extreme, but was employed during the Nuremberg trials as the underlying justification for what might otherwise have been seen as the retrospective criminalisation of those who committed their crimes under the Nazi laws thought valid at the time.

The views of Ronald Dworkin[8] provide a middle ground between these two theories – a 'third theory of law'.[9] His theory is highly complex, but in essence it is more inclusive than the positivist theory; recognising rights set forth by empirical authorities,[10] it insists that the law may contain *further* rights which have never yet been recognised by a statute or in any judicial decision. Thus, Shirley could correctly claim she had a right, on Dworkin's account, if (a) the right would be consistent with the bulk of existing empirical authority and (b) it would figure in the best possible interpretation of those authorities. By this, Dworkin means that the relevant past judicial decisions would be most satisfactorily justified by showing them all to have been concerned with protecting the right at issue, even if previous individual judgments did not explicitly recognise its existence. This exercise involves *moral* analysis in that the criteria for determining the 'best interpretation' consist of an evaluation of how far the relevant laws adhere to a principle of equal concern and respect. Such a claim might well, of course, be controversial, but it is precisely this that is at the root of Dworkin's disagreement with the positivists: finding out what the law is, he argues, will require not merely an empirical test of the law's *pedigree* (does it emanate from a particular institution?), but rather a complex inquiry which will, as he puts it, carry the lawyer 'very deep into moral and political theory'.[11]

If one is convinced by Dworkin's ingenious argument, the existence of a legal right can be adduced through interpretation (at least in common law jurisdictions) that is

6 For a full discussion of this issue, see Hart, HLA (ed), 'Positivism and the separation of law and morals', in *Essays in Jurisprudence and Philosophy*, 1983, Clarendon.

7 For the classical exposition of this theory, see Aquinas, T, '*Summa theologica*', in d'Entreves, P (ed), *Selected Political Writings*, 1970, Blackwell.

8 See Dworkin, R, *Taking Rights Seriously*, 1977, Duckworth. Dworkin sets out his account of judicial adjudication in Chapters 2–4, in which his theory is cast mainly in the form of a critique of legal positivism. For a fuller development of the theory, see *Law's Empire*, 1986, Fontana.

9 The term was coined by Mackie, J, 'The third theory of law', in Cohen, M (ed), *Ronald Dworkin and Contemporary Jurisprudence*, 1984, Duckworth.

10 For criticism of this position, see e.g., Simmonds, NE, 'Imperial visions and mundane practices' [1987] CLJ 465 and Cotterell, R, *The Politics of Jurisprudence*, 1989, Butterworths, pp 172–81.

11 Dworkin, R, *Taking Rights Seriously*, 1977, Duckworth, p 67.

partially moral in character. The resulting laws thus posited are 'legal-moral' in that they amount to authoritative determinations whose authority stems from moral *and* empirical law. Returning to Shirley's situation above, a judge deciding on the validity of her claim should, on Dworkin's view, seek to identify a consistent line of authority valuing analogous rights and then adopt the 'best' interpretation of such authorities in order to determine whether Shirley possesses the relevant right. By 'best' is meant very broadly that the judge adjudicating on Shirley's claim, which might be loosely based on an existing but doubtfully applicable cause of action, could take account of counter-vailing legal considerations but also the recognition of the right in international human rights treaties and in the bills of rights of comparable democracies.[12]

The Hohfeldian conception of rights and liberties

Having given an account, in general terms, of the nature of rights and liberties as legal and moral requirements it is now necessary to consider the content of such requirements. Their content is fundamentally derived from the relationship of obligation between the subject (e.g., an individual) and the respondent (usually the state or an emanation of it, such as the police service) involved in the assertion of a right or liberty. One of the more influential attempts to analyse closely the nature of a right or a liberty was made by the American jurist Wesley Hohfeld.[13] Hohfeld attempted to demonstrate that claims of rights in everyday language can in fact be broken down into four more specific claims: a claim-right, a liberty, an immunity and a power.[14]

Claim-right

If it is claimed that the subject, an individual (e.g., Sam) has a right proper or a 'claim-right' to the object of the right, then this means that the respondent (e.g., a state or 'public' body)[15] is under a specific corresponding duty to ensure that Sam has access to that object. These rights are among the most 'powerful' rights to possess since the duties typically require the respondent to act to fulfil its duty to the subject. An example would be the right to freedom of expression recognised by Art 10 of the European Convention of Human Rights. If for example Sam was fined or imprisoned for publishing material which was deemed an 'obscene publication'[16] then he could claim that this interference was contrary to his Art 10 right.

Liberty

If Sam has only a liberty (what Hohfeld calls a privilege) to enjoy the object of his right, this far weaker claim merely means that he does no wrong in doing so. The state

---

12   Dworkin, R, *Law's Empire*, 1986, Fontana Press.
13   Hohfeld, W, *Fundamental Legal Concepts as Applied in Judicial Reasoning*, 1920, Yale University Press, particularly pp 35–41.
14   While Hohfeld referred to a power, that concept is not of relevance to the discussions in this book.
15   See Chapter 4, p 189 *et seq.*
16   Under the Obscene Publications Acts 1959 and 1964. See Chapter 7, p 402 *et seq.*

has no duty to enable him to achieve the object of his liberty. Thus if a statute bans all assemblies in public places consisting of more than ten people whereas persons did no wrong in assembling in any numbers in public, then a liberty of persons to assemble has been severely encroached upon. Since individuals cannot claim a right to assemble, they have no clear means of challenging the new statutory power when applied by the police to arrest persons assembling in a group of more than ten. On the other hand, persons representing the state, such as the police, need a specific power to encroach on a liberty. Liberties are assumed to exist unless specifically curtailed by legal powers. A historical example, which could have arisen in Britain prior to the general statutory power of stop and search created by the Police and Criminal Evidence Act 1984 (PACE), is provided by the lack of a general statutory power for police to detain and search individuals.[17] If the police were to seek to stop and search a hypothetical suspect, Sam, in the absence of specific common law or statutory authority – he could assert that he was under no duty to consent to their search. Obviously, by asserting his liberty he is not asserting a claim-right (e.g., to non-interference with his person), but he is asserting that there is no power to interfere with his liberty. In that instance in the absence of a specific power of stop and search, the assertion of a claim-right or of a liberty would lead to the same legal result – that the police would be found to have acted unlawfully. But the creation of a general statutory power of stop and search would obviously destroy Sam's liberty to go about his business in public free from police interference, assuming that he satisfied the conditions in the statute allowing the police to stop and search him. If however he had a claim-right to non-detention by police, even for the brief period of a stop and search, then he could challenge the stop and search on the basis of non-compliance with the terms of that right (as set out in the relevant Bill of Rights), even if the terms of the statute allowing the police to stop and search him were fulfilled.

Immunity

Both the previous requirements considered so far, claim-rights and liberties, are *primary* rules that directly require the respondent to do something (claims) or that the subject has no duty not to do something (liberties). An immunity, in contrast, is a *secondary* rule. Rather than refer to rules requiring action directly (claims/liberties), the immunity refers to the right to *change* such rules. More specifically, if one has an immunity, then the respondent (e.g., a public authority) is disabled from creating a rule requiring the subject to act contrary to the object of the immunity. An immunity has a corollary – a power – which, rather than disable the alteration of primary rules, enables such alteration; however, unlike an immunity, a power is not a feature of the civil liberties or human rights considered in this work and is therefore not considered further in this chapter.[18]

---

17 See Chapter 12, p 842.
18 Civil liberties and human rights are very rarely framed as powers, since these must typically be earned and are associated with individuals in a position of power, while civil liberties and human rights are typically conceived of as restraints on the (illegitimate) use of power by the state. An example of a power that is also protected as a human right is the power to transfer one's property (an aspect of the protection of property, ECHR Protocol 1, Art 1). This is a power because the subject of such a power has the right to alter the claim-rights/liberties associated with his property ownership (such as to exclude others from it) by transferring them to another who will then benefit those claim-rights/liberties.

An immunity works most effectively in tandem with a liberty; that is because a liberty refers to the absence of a duty to act contrary to its object (e.g., above Sam had no duty to acquiesce to a police stop and search in the absence of a statutory provision allowing such police action), while an immunity disables the creation of a duty contrary to the object of the immunity (e.g., no statutory provision can be created authorising police stop and search). In general the UK does not recognise immunities in its constitutional arrangements, since Parliament can in theory legislate to abridge any human right. However, an example of a de facto immunity in the UK is the right to silence since, while Parliament is free to abolish it completely,[19] it has such a long pedigree in the UK that such an eventuality is unlikely. This right could be said to operate currently as an immunity in the sense that it is a requirement that a court is disabled from exercising its authority to convict a suspect purely on the basis of remaining silent in court or in the face of police questioning since that would fundamentally violate his right to silence (which is the object of the immunity). To return to the example of Sam, his right to silence means that while adverse inferences could be drawn in court from his refusal to answer police questions about a suspected offence, he can nevertheless refuse to answer such questions. His immunity provides that he will only be convicted if a court finds him guilty of the offence without relying solely on such adverse inferences.

Conclusions on the Hohfeldian framework

The above outline emphasises two significant distinctions. Firstly, and most straightforwardly, claim-rights impose an obligation upon the respondent (the state) to act, while liberties do not and instead indicate that there is no obligation upon the subject (an individual) to do anything in the absence of a legal rule preventing a particular exercise of a liberty. Secondly, rights involve two basic *types* of rules: primary rules that establish the existence of an obligation upon the respondent to secure the individual's right – a claim-right, or in the case of a liberty of no-obligation upon the subject to act contrary to his liberty, and secondary rules that disable the creation or alteration of the individual's claims or liberties (an immunity). These two, basic, distinctions are important when considering the practical implementation of human rights, since it is human *claim*-rights as primary rules requiring the state to act or not to act where it otherwise would that cause the greatest difficulty in deploying rights in practice. For example the right of access to legal advice captured in Art 6(3) requires the state to ensure that such provision is made (see Chapter 2), regardless of the financial cost.[20] The claim-right to freedom from torture or inhuman and degrading treatment (Article 3 ECHR, scheduled in the HRA) has been applied to suspected Islamic terrorists so as to prevent deportation to their country of origin on the basis that they might be subject to treatment contrary to that article.[21] This application of Article 3 is controversial due to the burden it places upon the UK government, especially given its responsibility to safeguard the lives of its citizens from the actions of such suspects.

---

19 See PACE Code C, Annex C; the right has already been undermined but not abolished in the Criminal Justice and Public Order Act 1994; see Chapter 13, p 939 *et seq.*
20 See p 63.
21 See *Othman v UK* (2012) 55 EHRR 1; *MT (Algeria) v Secretary of State for the Home Department* [2007] EWCA 808; *Chahal v UK* (1996) 23 EHRR 413.

What are 'human rights' and 'civil liberties'?

To address this question it is useful to summarise briefly what has already been established. Rights are requirements with an individual subject, object, respondent, which are justified by reference to both moral and legal principle on Dworkinian lines, as discussed above. The word 'right' can denote a primary rule requiring a respondent to act to secure the right (a claim-right) or merely the absence of a duty upon the subject to act or refrain from acting (a liberty). Secondary rules can affect the respondent's ability to alter the subject's claim-rights or liberties (powers/immunities), but they are not of significance in the UK context. This section will therefore outline the areas of consensus and division as to what is generally accepted to constitute the subject, object, respondent of civil liberties and human rights as relevant to this work. The relations between civil liberties and human rights will also be considered.

Civil liberties and rights

Liberties are termed 'civil' liberties in the UK because they refer to freedoms of citizens within the civic state. The term civil is also used in contrast to the term 'social and economic', referring to matters such as 'a right to housing', which would fall within the area of social and economic rights.[22] The subjects of civil liberties are straightforwardly citizens, and the respondent is the 'state', meaning an emanation of the state (public authorities, such as the police or prison service). The object of civil liberties is the freedom to act except as is prohibited by law (e.g., to take part in a protest or go about one's everyday life without interference from the police except as designated in legal rules governing police powers). The basis of civil liberties is the existence of laws which impliedly designate the areas of freedom that citizens can enjoy. In other words, it is clear that the existence of a civil liberty depends on the non-existence of a conflicting legal enactment (e.g., a statute). The relationship between the citizen and the state is that of a Hohfeldian liberty: only when a citizen is not placed under a duty to refrain from exercising the liberty, such as his freedom of expression, does he have a civil liberty. Thus, he has an area within which the liberty in question can be exercised, delineated by laws that designate the extent of the area. That notion is explored in particular in Part II in relation to freedom of expression.[23]

From the seventeenth century onwards, liberal theorists and politicians have argued that citizens should be able to benefit from claim-rights rather than civil liberties.[24] Rather than enjoying freedoms to act in ways not proscribed by law, there was increasing pressure post-Enlightenment to recognise civil liberties as legal rights. Virtually all Western democracies have introduced bills or charters of rights which usually accord citizens claim-rights. But, as mentioned at the beginning of this part, the UK only recognised such rights as civil liberties, aside from narrow, specific statutory rights acting as claim-rights[25] or aside from certain protection of rights under the common law,

---

22 See Chapter 2, pp 28–29.
23 See e.g. p 289 *et seq.*
24 See e.g., Mahoney, J, *The Challenge of Human Rights*, 2007, Blackwell, Chapter 1.
25 Such as access to legal advice in police custody under s 58 Police and Criminal Evidence Act 1984; see Chapter 13, p 924 *et seq.*

coming close to attaining the position of claim-rights,[26] until the inception of the Human Rights Act 1998.

Human rights

The subjects implied by 'human rights' would appear straightforwardly to be 'humans'. However, it is not generally accepted that humans at all stages of development are the subject of human rights. There is no consensus as to whether a foetus counts as a subject of human rights[27] and it is not accepted that infants should possess certain rights, such as to marry.[28] Similarly, it is not generally accepted that humans who lack certain capacities can benefit from certain rights, so that the mentally disordered may not be able to benefit in certain circumstances from the right to personal autonomy, an aspect of the right to respect for private life (Art 8 ECHR), since in relation to certain decisions that Art 8 might potentially protect broadly only those decisions taken with the capacity to be rational and self-oriented should be respected.[29]

One interpretation of the subject of human rights espoused by Gewirth is that the subject of certain 'human' rights is more aptly defined as relating to beings with the capacity for autonomous self-determination which is, so far as we know, unique to human beings.[30] Without going into detail, this view did not lead to determining that young children, the mentally ill or unconscious humans (e.g., in a persistent vegetative state) would be excluded from enjoying the benefits of a range of rights. For example, very young children would obviously be able to benefit from a range of human rights, such as the right to be free from torture or inhuman or degrading treatment (see Article 3 ECHR). But this Gewirthian view is disputed by those who argue that it could deny the protection of human rights to a far greater range of human beings than is generally considered to be morally acceptable.[31] The better view is that all humans (except the foetus up to a certain stage of development) are the subject of human rights.

There is a general agreement among legal scholars that the respondent to human rights is the state (under the HRA the respondents are 'public authorities' as representing emanations of the state).[32] Human rights instruments, such as the ECHR, refer to the obligations that fall upon the 'contracting parties' and not upon individuals within those states. However, even this matter is not entirely without controversy. As this book discusses in relation to the right to privacy (see Chapter 10) there are a range of instances in which individual citizens are affixed with an obligation to respect the human rights of others. This position may be referred to as the 'indirect horizontal effect' of a human rights instrument.[33] As explained in Chapter 10, the creation of rights *between* individuals is considered to be an aspect of the UK's obligation to secure the Art 8 right to

---

26 See Chapter 3, pp 117–20.
27 See e.g., in relation to the ECHR *Vo v France* (2005) 40 EHRR 12, especially para 82.
28 Art 12 ECHR states that 'men and women of marriageable age have the right to marry'.
29 See e.g., in relation to assisted suicide and refusal of vital medical treatment, *Pretty v UK* (2002) 35 EHRR 1, para 63.
30 Gewirth, A, *Reason and Morality*, 1978, Chicago University Press, 64 *et seq.*
31 See for discussion e.g., Griffin, J, *On Human Rights*, 2008, OUP, 32 *et seq.*
32 See Chapter 4, p 189 *et seq.*
33 See Chapter 4, p 211 *et seq* and Chapter 10, p 728 *et seq.*

respect for private life effectively. For instance, in the example given as regards Shirley above in relation to claim-rights, the invasion of her privacy was not undertaken by the state but by a newspaper, but the state has an obligation under Art 8 scheduled in the HRA to ensure that her privacy is protected from private actors as well as from the state. In practice the state becomes involved when a *court* is asked to interpret the rights and obligations of Shirley and the newspaper if she brings an action against the newspaper.[34]

As regards the proper object of human rights there is arguably little agreement between theorists.[35] This book considers human rights to expression (Part II), privacy (Part III) and liberty (Part IV). One view is that human rights should be understood to be most fundamentally claims to the conditions that are necessary for 'humans' to live freely and with dignity; human rights that reflect this rationale are the rights to life (Article 2 ECHR) and freedom from torture (Article 3 ECHR).[36] But civil human rights are mainly though not solely aimed at enabling full participation in the political life of civil society (rights to freedoms of expression, assembly, association and to vote). The human right to privacy generates by far the greatest controversy; for example, the tabloid media has (with dubious good faith) ridiculed the idea that this human right extends to a spectrum of further human rights, such as the right of a prisoner to receive IVF.[37] There is also controversy over the validity of claims by certain treaties to establish economic and social human rights as well as civil and political rights since the former depart from traditional enlightenment ideas of the object of human rights.

To describe the rights considered in this book in terms of their Hohfeldian incidents, the rights to freedom of expression, liberty and privacy are straightforwardly understood as Hohfeldian claim-rights, due to the operation of the Human Rights Act, which places obligations on public authorities to abide by those rights.

The above provides an outline of the basic nature of human rights. However, the theoretical disputes as to their nature are somewhat removed from the immediate concerns generated by the legal application of such rights. Rather, it is the *operation* of such rights that form the primary concern of this book, and in particular the scope of the rights and the exceptions to them. This is particularly the case as regards the operation of human *claim-rights*. Therefore it is to this aspect of the nature of human rights that this chapter will now turn.

The operation of human claim-rights: conflicts with other claims

There are many situations where an individual has a claim to a right but it is justifiable for the respondent state not to fulfil its obligation to deliver the right. The right may

---

34 A significant limitation on the operation of indirect horizontal effect is that there must be an existing cause of action that is unable to vindicate the right in question, but is sufficiently relevant to the vindication of the human right in question that it can be developed by the court so as to do so. However, this issue goes beyond the scope of the current chapter; see further Chapter 10, pp 728–30.

35 Griffin, J, *On Human Rights*, 2008, OUP, pp 14 *et seq*.

36 See e.g., Gewirth, A, *Reason and Morality*, 1978, Chicago University Press, 64 *et seq*.

37 Doyle, J, 'Murderers and drug dealer to get IVF in prison and you'll be paying! Criminals using European Human Rights laws to start families at taxpayers expense', *Daily Mail*, 27 December 2012; see http://www.dailymail.co.uk/news/article-2253943/Murderers-drug-dealer-IVF-prison-youll-paying-Criminals-using-Human-Rights-laws-start-family-taxpayers-expense.html.

come into conflict with the claims of society, such as that a certain standard of morality should be upheld. Clearly, in resolving such a conflict, a judge will inevitably draw
upon his or her background political theory. If, for example, a judge in the European
Court of Human Rights, who is a utilitarian by conviction, has to consider a convincing
demonstration by a defendant government that the particular application of the right to
free speech claimed by the applicant will, on balance, make society worse off as a whole,
he or she will be inclined to find for the government and allow the infringement of the
right. Such infringement will, of course, be more readily allowable if the right is framed
or has developed in such a way as to be open-ended in scope with in-built exceptions.

Both Dworkin and Rawls have argued persuasively against making rights vulnerable
to utilitarian considerations in this way. The idea that '[e]ach person possesses an inviolability founded on justice that even the welfare of society as a whole cannot override'[38]
lies at the centre of Rawls's political thought. The idea of such inviolable rights may
seem extreme, but is in fact accepted by all civilised countries in the case, for example,
of torture. It is not thought to be a sound argument for a government to assert that it is
justified in torturing certain of its citizens on the grounds that it can increase the general
welfare thereby. The acceptance of this principle is attested to by the non-derogability
of the right to freedom from torture in all international human rights treaties, including
the European Convention on Human Rights (Article 15(2)).

Dworkin has addressed the specific question as to the means of understanding a legal
right in an adjudicative context in some detail. Earlier, the distinction between moral
and legal rights was discussed. Here it should be noted that Dworkin also distinguishes
between rights that have 'trump' status and those that do not. He gives as an example
of the latter a legal right to drive either way on a two-way road: such a right is a 'weak'
legal right, because it is not an important human interest which is likely to be denied to
certain groups through the influence of external preferences. It follows that such a right
could justifiably be overridden by the government (through making the road one-way)
if it thought it in the general interest to do so. By contrast, his conception of the strength
of 'trump' rights leads to his insistence that an assertion of (for example) a right to free
speech held by citizens 'must imply that it would be wrong for the government to stop
them from speaking, even when the government believes that what they say will cause
more harm than good'.[39]

It can be seen, then, that Dworkin gives us a very clear prescription for the approach
that a judge should take in weighing strong or 'trump' rights against the general welfare
of society. He roundly condemns the idea that a judge, in adjudicating upon a right or
a government in framing it, should carefully weigh up the right of the citizen against
the possible adverse social consequences, accepting that it is sometimes preferable to
err on the side of society, sometimes on the side of the individual, but on the whole
getting the balance about right. 'It must be wrong', he argues, to consider that 'inflat-
ing rights is as serious as invading them'. For to *invade* a right is to affront human
dignity or treat certain citizens as less worthy of respect than others, while to *inflate* a
right is simply to pay 'a little more in social efficiency'[40] than the government *already*

38 Rawls, *A Theory of Justice*, 1972, Harvard University Press, p 3.
39 Dworkin, R, *Taking Rights Seriously*, 1977, Harvard University Press, p 191.
40 *Ibid*, p 199.

has to pay in allowing the right at all. Thus, for Dworkin, if one asserts a 'trump' right, ordinary counter-arguments about a decrease in the welfare of society as a whole are simply irrelevant.

In what circumstances, then, may a strong individual right be overridden? Dworkin has argued[41] that there are three general justifications for infringement and these appear to be generally accepted by liberal thought. This section will consider the three common situations in which rights may be overridden, but will indicate that Dworkin's stringent view as to the means of resolving clashes between rights and societal interests has not been accepted, either in the Strasbourg Court or domestically. Firstly, there are clash of rights situations in which a state's right-based duty conflicts with another duty under a conflicting claim-right. Secondly, there is the situation in which its duty conflicts with another duty under a conflicting non-rights-requirement (i.e. a societal interest such as the protection of national security). Thirdly, a situation may arise in which the state is unable to fulfil its duty because it lacks the resources to do so.

Before considering the operation of human claim-rights in these situations it is useful to consider a preliminary point briefly. Does a respondent state retain its obligation even if it is unable to fulfil it? A maxim of practical ethics is that 'ought implies can',[42] by which is meant that an impossible to fulfil requirement cannot be a moral requirement. That is because a moral requirement fundamentally refers to an individual able to exercise a capacity to act that he currently possesses. Human claim-rights must respect this maxim if they are to be rationally defensible as practical requirements, and therefore modern treaties of human rights include limitations on certain rights. For example, Art 8 (ECHR) sets out the right to respect for private and family life in the first paragraph, but accepts that a public authority may justifiably interfere with an individual's right where that interference is prescribed by law and is 'necessary in a democratic society' to protect the rights of others or to secure various important public interests (such as national security or health).

Conflicts between rights

Rights conflict occurs where there is a clear competing individual claim, so that the exercise of the original right will directly infringe the competing right. A paradigmatic example of such a collision of rights, considered in Chapter 10, arises where one individual (e.g., Albert as a newspaper editor) exercises his right of free speech to invade the right to privacy of another (e.g., Brenda). Another is where Albert uses his right to free speech to incite violence against Brenda, thus infringing her right to security of the person. In such cases rights theorists divide as to the way in which this conflict could be resolved. On the most commonly held view it may be possible to resolve the conflict by undertaking a balancing act between the two rights based on proportionality,[43] the result of which is determined by reference to the rule/principle justifying the existence of the

---

41 *Ibid*, p 200.
42 See for discussion in relation to human rights e.g., Gewirth, A, *Reason and Morality*, 1978, Chicago University Press, pp 64, 263.
43 See e.g., Chapter 2, pp 65–66.

right. This may be termed the conflict view of rights.[44] In most of the instances of a clash of rights covered in this book, that is the way that the conflict is resolved.[45]

If avoidance of conflict was impossible, a determination might be made as to the damage inflicted on each right if the other is allowed to prevail. In the case of incitement to violence, the damage inflicted if free speech was allowed to prevail might be almost irretrievable, since the group affected might be placed at great risk for a period of time. In contrast, the damage to free speech created by avoidance of the risk might be of a lesser nature, although undesirable: the speech could be uttered in another form or another forum, so that its meaning was not lost, but it was rendered less inflammatory. Alternatively, utterance of the speech could be delayed until the situation had become less volatile. The words advocating immediate violence might be perceived as outside the area of protected speech and so might be severed from the accompanying words which could be permitted.

On another view the conflict can be resolved by redefining the scope of the right, or applying a limiting definition to its scope where a more expansive one could have been available, so that either Albert or Brenda are unable to claim that they can validly exercise their right in a way that infringes the other's exercise of their right. The question of whose right is to be non-expansively defined or redefined to allow for the other's exercise can similarly be resolved by reference to the rule/principle justifying the existence of the right. This may be termed the non-conflict view of rights,[46] but it is rarely invoked in the clash of rights instances covered in this book. Deploying a limiting redefinition of the scope of a right is much more relevant to a potential clash between a right and a societal interest, considered below, where deploying such a redefinition allows the societal interest to prevail.[47] That may occur in relation to human rights that are expressed as absolute requirements (e.g., Article 3 ECHR, the prohibition on torture).[48]

However, the influence of a non-conflict view of rights can be discerned when courts adopt strategies to find that in the instant case the values underlying the right in question are not fully at stake. This strategy finds that rights have a 'core', the invasion of which will constitute an actual overriding of the right which cannot be tolerated, but they also have a 'penumbra' – an area in which the value the right protects is present only in a weaker form.[49] An invasion of the penumbra may be said to constitute only an *infringement* of the right and may therefore be more readily justified, whether in relation to a clash with another right or with a societal interest. The argument that commercial speech

---

44 Green, A, 'An absolute theory of Convention rights: why the ECHR gives rise to legal rights that cannot conflict with each other' (2010) UCL Jurisprudence Review 75.

45 See in particular Chapter 10, p 747 *et seq.*

46 Green, *op cit.*

47 See e.g., *Othman v UK* (2012) 55 EHRR 1; *Austin v UK* (2012) 55 EHRR 14.

48 See e.g., Mavronicola, N, 'What is an "absolute right"? Deciphering absoluteness in the context of article 3 of the European Convention on Human Rights' (2012) 12(4) HRL Rev 723.

49 This view is not attributed to Dworkin, although he does accept that there will be situations in which the core value of the right will not be at stake. Dworkin has comprehensively rejected Hart's theory of statutory construction and application of the rules from past cases based around the notion of a core of certainty and a penumbra of uncertainty (for Hart's position, see *The Concept of Law*, 1961, Clarendon; for Dworkin's critique, *op cit*, fn 3, Chapters 2–4). Dworkin argues that the areas of a rule which form the core and those which fall in the penumbra can only be elucidated through a judge's interpretation, which will carry him or her far from the specific words of the statute.

should not be afforded the same protection as other kinds of speech would appear to rest precisely on the argument that it is in the penumbra of free speech;[50] by contrast, political speech is clearly in the 'core' of free speech.[51] Clashes between Art 8 (the right to respect for private life) and Art 10 protecting freedom of expression have been resolved by finding that celebrity gossip in newspapers – i.e. privacy-invading expression – is not in the core of free expression since it has very little speech-value.[52] Therefore while Articles 8 and 10 are balanced against each other in such a situation, the Art 10-based argument will tend to be quite readily overcome.

Conflicts between rights and societal interests

The operation of rights-requirements in practice will frequently involve conflict with societal interests (which however may also be linked, broadly speaking, to certain rights-based requirements), particularly important matters of public policy. An obvious instance arises where the exercise of a right may pose a real danger to society. In such instances, liberals are unwilling to take danger to mean danger to some abstract attribute to society, such as its moral health, but rather insist that the danger must ultimately amount to a threat to some concrete aspect of its citizens' well-being. Thus, typically, liberals are hostile to characterising the likelihood of shocking or offending citizens as a concrete harm justifying the suppression of the right of free speech. Dworkin's own, rather unrealistically stringent, test is that the 'risk to society' justification for overriding rights is only made out if the state demonstrates 'a clear and substantial risk' that exercise of the right 'will do great damage to the person or property of others'. It seems unlikely that governments would be prepared to accept such a test; the criterion laid down, for example, by the European Court of Human Rights for curtailing the right of free expression as set out in Art 10 does not even approach Dworkin's prescription in either stringency or clarity; instead, it has adopted the somewhat weak and uncertain phrase, 'a pressing social need'. Dworkin's rights analysis should not, therefore, be taken as a description of the way rights and liberties are *actually* treated in the UK under the ECHR.

The rights-as-trumps view finds that it is only meaningful to describe an individual as having a right when the justification for his claim is a value that is fundamental to the legal system. The fundamental status of these values means that the legal system can only condone their abrogation when similarly fundamental values are at stake. This view is one that is associated with liberal political theory, since rights are individually oriented requirements, and thus when a society accepts that the protection of rights is among its fundamental legal values it has committed itself to demonstrating respect for the liberty of individuals. However, the competing societal interest at stake may also relate in a general sense to the liberty, security and well-being of individuals in the

---

50 See e.g., the Judgment of US Supreme Court, *Bolger v Youngs Drug Products Ltd* (1983) 103 Ct 2875, 2880–81.

51 The House of Lords recognised the central importance of free political speech in their pre-HRA decision that neither local nor central government could pursue an action in defamation: *Derbyshire CC v Times Newspapers* [1993] 1 All ER 1011.

52 See *Von Hannover v Germany* (2005) 40 EHRR 1.

society in question, even if it cannot be said or is not claimed that a specific clash of rights is present.[53] For example, a mass public protest may significantly impede the use of the highway by passers-by; it may also be threatening or harassing to such persons.[54] The use of anti-terrorist legislation may reduce the scope for terrorist attacks and may lead to a reduction in the need to use security measures in a range of circumstances, impeding free movement of persons generally. Refusal to rely on hearsay evidence where the victim-witness in question is too intimidated to come to court, or too badly injured to do so may be detrimental to the interests of that victim and potential victims.[55] Thus respect for liberty in the society in general does not depend only on elevating respect for individual rights on the Dworkinian model above societal concerns that also relate to liberty.

Thus, the approach to such conflicts under the ECHR, whether domestically under the HRA or at the Strasbourg Court, rely on balancing/proportionality approaches rather than the more absolutist Dworkinian approach. The view taken is that rights should be treated as particularly weighty requirements, but that sometimes public policy concerns can outweigh the right, as discussed in Chapter 2.

Respondent unable to fulfil duty due to lack of resources

A respondent state may be able to respect an individual's human claim-rights in *isolation*, but a state such as the UK has many similar claims upon its actions and, in their totality, the state may be unable to fulfil them.[56] It is therefore necessary in practice for such a respondent to recognise a hierarchy of obligations if it is to act to fulfil them. The nature of this hierarchy will depend upon the *justification* for the right, since the courts or legislative bodies must determine which obligations are more 'weighty';[57] such a determination requires an analysis of the relationship between the various obligations and their justifying basis.

The rights discussed in this book refer to state actors with extensive responsibilities and limited resources. The *object* of these rights – even seemingly basic rights, such as the right to life – can require extensive action in certain situations. Furthermore, if a legal regime that respects these rights is to be administered effectively, then resources must be deployed to enable legal officials to prioritise the differing obligations. All of these considerations have resulted in a consensus among rights-theorists that human claim-rights must impose *minimal* or even entirely *negative* obligations.[58] Negative obligations require individuals merely to refrain from acting to interfere with another's right depending upon the justification advanced for its existence; they are contrasted

53 An example in the context of assisted suicide is the ECtHR's treatment of the right to personal autonomy balanced against the state interest in preservation of life (e.g., *Pretty v UK* (2002) 35 EHRR 1 para 74).
54 See the discussion of balancing crowd control measures against the individual right of protest in *Austin v UK* (2012) 55 EHRR 14.
55 See *Horncastle v UK* (2015) 60 EHRR 31.
56 See e.g., Gewirth, A, *Reason and Morality*, 1978, University of Chicago Press, 223 *et seq*.
57 An example is arguably provided by *Firth v UK*, Appl 47784/09, judgment of 12 August 2014, which concerned compensation for prisoners who were denied the right to vote (protected by the ECHR Protocol 1, para 1).
58 See e.g., Griffin, J, *On Human Rights*, 2008, OUP, p 191.

with (minimal) positive obligations that do require the state to secure the right by positive action, although not all obligations deemed 'positive' do require the expenditure of significant resources.[59]

A separate problem in respect of positive obligations is raised by libertarian theorists. Libertarians consider that natural rights exceed their justificatory basis when they require another to act to further the purposes of the rights-holder.[60] This view has not found purchase in European human rights law. The European approach reflects a social liberal approach that is closer to the views of theorists, such as Gewirth, who do not recognise an absolute limitation on positive rights.[61]

3 The justifications for human rights

This section will discuss the main criticisms of, and justifications for, the existence of a duty upon the state to protect human rights. The section will begin by setting out key criticisms of human rights from utilitarian, Marxist and critical legal studies perspectives. The chapter will then turn to the justification for human rights; the position adopted will reflect the particular brand of political liberalism expounded by John Rawls and Ronald Dworkin, in so far as their theories converge.

Opposition to the liberal conception of human rights

Utilitarianism

Utilitarianism has historically been generally hostile to the idea of rights, most famously to the notion of natural and inalienable human rights as set out, for example, in the American Declaration of Independence, which was characterised by Jeremy Bentham as merely so much 'bawling upon paper'.[62] The opposition of utilitarians to the notion of *natural* rights sprang mainly from their legal positivism – their belief that a legal right only exists if there is a specific 'black letter' provision guaranteeing it. But in general, since utilitarianism sets out one supreme goal of happiness or, in its more modern version, preference maximisation, it would clearly follow that rights under utilitarianism can have only a contingent justification.[63] In other words, they are to be respected if they help bring about the goal of maximum satisfaction of preferences, but not otherwise. It may seem odd to postulate an opposition between utilitarianism and human rights, bearing in mind that JS Mill combined utilitarianism with a passionate belief in the desirability of

59 See e.g., *Hamalainen v Finland* [2015] 1 FCR 379; the claim was deemed to concern a positive obligation but would have involved minimal resources to satisfy it.
60 See e.g., Nozick, R, *Anarchy, State and Utopia*, 1974, Basic Books.
61 See e.g., Gewirth, A, *The Community of Rights*, 1996, University of Chicago Press.
62 Bentham, J, 'Anarchical fallacies', in Bowring, J (ed), *Collected Works of Jeremy Bentham*, 1843, William Tait, p 494.
63 Utilitarianism is a major political philosophy. The original conception of utilitarianism espoused by Jeremy Bentham saw the aim of government as being to promote the greatest happiness of the greatest number of people (see Burns (ed), *Collected Works of Jeremy Bentham*, 1970). A more recent and fashionable version states that an ideal society is one in which there is the maximum amount of preference satisfaction (see, generally, Smart, C and Williams, B, *Utilitarianism: For and Against*, 1973, CUP). References in the text will be to this latter version, known as 'preference utilitarianism'.

free expression and civil rights generally. It should be noted, however, that Mill's arguments for free speech depend essentially on a belief that allowing free speech will, in the long term, have good effects – such as increasing the likelihood that the truth will be discovered – rather than on a belief that free expression is a good in itself or something to which human beings are entitled without reference to its likely effects. A utilitarian, confronted with a situation in which infringing a right would undeniably benefit society as a whole, would have no reason to support the inviolability of the right; for example, he or she would find it hard to explain why criminal suspects should not be tortured if it were proved that reliable evidence would be derived thereby, leading to increased convictions, deterrence of crime and substantial consequential benefit to society.

A further variant of the theory which has sometimes been termed 'rule utilitarianism', however, states that the goals of utilitarianism can best be reached by constructing rules which it is thought will, in general, further the goal of happiness or 'preference maximisation' and then applying these rules to situations as absolutes rather than considering in each individual situation what can best further the goal (for discussion, see Smart and Williams[64]). Such rules could, of course, consist, at least in part, of a set of human rights. In relation to the example of torture given in the text, a rule utilitarian could plausibly maintain that a general rule of humane treatment of citizens is likely to lead to the greatest happiness. In deciding whether to torture an individual suspect, this would mean that instead of considering whether in this case overall utility would be increased thereby, the state should apply the rule of humane treatment, even if in the particular case it would lead to a decrease in utility. It can be seen that for rule utilitarians, the good (the goal of preference maximisation or greatest happiness) is prior to the right, in opposition to Rawls's clearly expressed conviction that the right (a system of just entitlements of citizens) is prior to any conceptions of the good – the substantive moral convictions by which individuals will live their lives (see below).

Marxism

The former socialist bloc of states – the Soviet Union and Eastern Europe – was the driving force behind the international recognition of economic, social and cultural rights. This was at least partly due to the fact that there is a measure of hostility within Marxist thought to civil and political rights.[65] Such hostility exists mainly because Marxism advocates establishing a state which, far from being neutral amongst its citizens' varying conceptions of the good and guaranteeing them the liberties necessary to pursue their private goals, instead imposes a particular conception of the good upon society. Since it regards the protection of this conception (the achievements of the revolution) as the supreme value and duty of the state, the exercise of liberties which threaten this achievement can be justifiably curtailed; hence the consistently poor record of the former Soviet bloc states and Communist China on such civil rights as freedom of speech. A theoretically related, but more moderate, critique of the Western liberal conception of human rights can be found in the writings of the so-called communitarians.[66]

---

64 Smart, C and Williams, B, *Utilitarianism: For and Against*, 1973, CUP.
65 See e.g., Marx, K, *On the Jewish Question*, 1843.
66 See, e.g., Sandel, M, *Liberalism and the Limits of Justice*, 1982, CUP.

Critical Legal Studies

The Critical Legal Studies movement (CLS) attacks the whole liberal conception of law as neutral, objective and rational. It seeks to expose the value judgments, internal inconsistencies and ideological conflicts that it sees as concealed under law's benevolent exterior of impartial justice.[67] Since the whole structure of legally guaranteed human rights is a creature of the liberal conception of law, the CLS attack fastens by extension onto the liberal notion of rights. Mark Tushnet, for example, has made four main criticisms of the liberal theory of rights in what he calls 'a Schumpeterian act of creative destruction'. He asserts that rights are: first, unstable – that is, meaningful only in a particular social setting; secondly, they produce 'no determinate consequences if claimed'; thirdly, 'rights talk . . . falsely converts into empty abstractions . . . real experiences that we ought to value for their own sake'; and fourthly, if conceded a dominant position in contemporary discourse, rights threaten to 'impede advances by progressive social forces'.[68] It would be inappropriate to attempt a detailed refutation of the CLS position here. Perhaps the most important weakness in its critique of rights is that, as many writers have pointed out, it offers no guidance whatsoever as to how the interests of vulnerable minorities are to be protected without the institution of legal rights.

The liberal justification for human rights

The liberal conception of human rights and civil liberties can be seen to owe its antecedents to the school of so-called social contractarians which found perhaps its earliest advocate in the writings of John Locke.[69] Locke imagined an actual social contract between individuals and the state at the setting up of civil society in which citizens, in order to secure the protection of their property, handed over certain powers (most importantly, a monopoly of coercive force) to the government in return for the guarantee of certain rights to 'lives, liberties and estates'. Locke thus introduced the idea, which is still central to liberalism today, that the overriding purpose of the state is the securing and protection of its citizens' basic liberties.

The idea of the social contract is clearly an immensely potent one and it is John Rawls's revival and radical revision of the idea in his *A Theory of Justice*[70] which has almost single-handedly transformed the face of political theory; as HLA Hart has commented, rights-based theories have replaced utilitarianism as the primary focus of attention.[71] Robert Nozick, a right-wing critic of Rawls whose work *Anarchy, State and Utopia* mounts a sustained attack upon Rawls's theory, has written: 'Political philosophers now must either work within Rawls's theory or explain why not.'[72]

---

67 Unger, R, *The Critical Legal Studies Movement*, 1986, HUP.
68 Tushnet, M, 'An essay on rights' (1984) 62(18) Texas L Rev 1363.
69 Locke, J, *The Second Treatise of Government*, 1698.
70 Rawls, J, *A Theory of Justice*, 1972, HUP.
71 See Hart's comments on this phenomenon generally in 'Between utility and rights', in Cohen, M (ed), *Ronald Dworkin and Contemporary Jurisprudence*, 1984, Duckworth.
72 Nozick, R, *Anarchy, State and Utopia*, 1974, Blackwell, p 183.

Rawls imagines not an actual, but a hypothetical, social contract taking place in what he terms 'the original position'. The essential feature of this position is that the contractors (Rawls's men) are devising amongst themselves the outlines of 'the foundation charter of their society' whilst behind 'the veil of ignorance'. The men are ignorant not only of what will be their positions in the future social hierarchy, but also of their skills, weaknesses, preferences and conceptions of the good life – whether, for example, they will be strict Muslims or humanist academics. Since none of the contractors knows what mode of life he will wish to pursue, he is bound (if he is rational) to choose a tolerant society and one which guarantees him the rights necessary to pursue any individual goals he may in future choose. In other words, the men will wish to put in place the means whereby they will, in future, be able to pursue their goals rather than adopting structures which might in future prevent them from doing so. Thus, almost any conception of the good life will require, for example, freedom from arbitrary arrest, the right to a fair trial and freedom from inhuman treatment. In addition, the man who will become a Muslim might *in future* wish to restrict freedom of speech on religious matters but, *at present*, self-interest dictates that he consider the possibility that his conception of the good life might necessarily include the exercise of freedom of speech. Thus Rawls's men adopt, *inter alia*, 'the first principle', stating that 'each person is to have an equal right to the most extensive, total system of equal basic liberties compatible with a similar system of liberty for all'.[73] These basic liberties are identical with any familiar list of civil and political rights in a human rights treaty such as the ECHR or in a domestic bill or charter of rights.

Although similar to Rawls in political outlook, Ronald Dworkin offers a theoretical construct which derives rights in a different manner, and indeed has criticised Rawls's theory, arguing that a *hypothetical*, unlike an *actual*, contract provides no grounds for binding actual people to its terms.[74] Dworkin attempts to derive rights from the premise, to which he hopes all will agree, that the state owes a duty to treat all of its citizens with equal concern and respect – a premise which he argues persuasively is the deep assumption underlying Rawls's use of the contract device. Dworkin is not concerned with defending rights from despotic and repressive governments and indeed he sees no need to protect – by designating them as rights – those individual interests which the *majority* would like to see protected, since these will in any case be ensured by the democratic process which he assumes as a background to his theory. Dworkin's particular concern is to justify the protection of *unpopular* or minority rights – or those whose exercise may on occasion threaten the overall well-being of the community – because such rights would potentially be put at risk if their validity were to be determined through a democratic vote.

Clearly, the institution of democracy and most familiar sets of political policies, such as seeking the economic betterment of the majority, seem to be satisfactorily explained by an underpinning utilitarianism. Dworkin hypothesises that the great appeal of utilitarianism is owed at least in part to its appearance of egalitarianism through its promise to 'treat the wishes of each member of the community on a par with the wishes of

---

73 For this reference and a brief summary of the theory, see Rawls, J, *A Theory of Justice*, 1972, HUP, pp 11–15.
74 Dworkin, *Taking Rights Seriously*, Chapter 6.

any other',[75] taking into account only the intensity of the preference and the number of people who hold it. This appeal is evinced in the utilitarian maxim: 'everybody to count for one, nobody for more than one'. Dworkin finds, however, that raw utilitarianism betrays this promise, since it fails to distinguish between what he denotes external and personal preferences. For example, if the question of whether homosexual partners should be able to contract marriage were to be decided by a majority vote (*preference maximisation*) in certain states, many homosexuals would probably express their personal preference for freedom to choose to marry. Certain heterosexuals, however, might vote against allowing this freedom, because their external preference is that homosexuals should not be free to marry.

Thus, resolution of the question could be affected by the fact that certain citizens think that the homosexual way of leading family life is not deserving of equal respect; a decision would therefore have been made at least partly on the basis that the way of life of certain citizens was in some way contemptible. If the government enforced this decision through the use of coercive force (the criminal law), it would clearly have failed in its central duty to treat its citizens with equal concern and respect. In other words, utilitarianism – and therefore democracy – has an in-built means of undermining its own promise of equality. Since for Dworkin protecting this promise of equality is the central postulate of political morality, he finds that homosexuals should be granted a right to moral autonomy that cannot be overridden even by a majority decision-making process.

Conclusion on the liberal justification for human rights

The fundamental basis of the liberal justification for human rights presented in this section is the equal intrinsic value of individuals. This is reflected in Rawls's 'original position' device and the fundamental value of 'equal concern and respect' alluded to by Dworkin. Both theories seek to address criticisms of the individualism of human rights by emphasising that majority preferences to protect majority-rights are a primary goal of liberal theory, but seek to adjust such rights via rationalism. However, Dworkin goes further than Rawls by imposing a *moral* adjustment in favour of equal concern and respect. It is the development of a rational and moral theory in favour of *substantive* rights for individuals that provides a justification for human rights.

The outline of the liberal justificatory approach to human rights set out in this chapter provides the foundation for the evaluation of the relevant law discussed in this work. It is important to emphasise that this evaluation does not assume that the responsibility for protecting human rights is mainly a judicial responsibility. Obviously, the responsibility of Parliament should be emphasised since it is the democratically accountable institution. However, to underemphasise judicial responsibility risks undermining underrepresented minority rights in favour of majority rights. In the current climate of popular hostility to human rights which sometimes assumes that judges, especially judges in the Strasbourg Court, are imposing alien, anti-common-sense standards of rights' protection in Britain, it is more important than ever for those engaging with law to appreciate these concerns.

---

75 Dworkin, *Taking Rights Seriously*, p 275.

4 Challenges for the legal protection of human rights in the UK

The most significant challenges created by the legal protection of human rights are that the obligations imposed upon the state by claim-rights can be particularly onerous and the reasons for the imposition of such obligations can be complex. These challenges contrast with the relatively weaker, and more straightforward, traditional approach to civil liberties in the UK prior to the Human Rights Act (HRA).[76] When the HRA came fully into force many of the British Hohfeldian liberties became rights in Hohfeldian terms since, as Chapter 4 explains, public authorities were laid under a positive duty to respect them and are acting unlawfully if they do not (s 6(1)).[77]

The HRA clearly represented a dramatic shift in rights protection in the UK, away from residual freedoms towards positive rights. The liberal ideal was therefore realised to an extent under the HRA, and – as this book discusses – the legal protection of human rights has been bolstered in a number of respects. However, crucially for the continued protection of human rights in the UK, various criticisms of its operation have gained considerable traction with the current Conservative government and the voting public, who support the current government's anti-HRA stance. To an extent these criticisms stem from the difficulties with the operation of human rights discussed in this chapter.

The most powerful criticism is that judges usually in the Strasbourg Court, but also at times in domestic courts under the HRA, have failed to balance individual rights with the rights of others and societal interests correctly. This general criticism is made most forcefully in relation to the legal protection of human rights in the terrorism context; for example, in respect of Abu Qatada whose deportation to face terrorism charges in Jordan was successfully challenged (under Art 6 ECHR), due to concerns that he would not receive a fair trial.[78] Another criticism is that the administrative burden of securing human rights in law is disproportionately great. Again, this criticism is made particularly as regards rights-protection in the terrorist context, where challenges to the detention of a small number of suspected terrorists have resulted in prolonged and extremely costly litigation.[79] However, while both criticisms raise important challenges that any legal system seeking to protect human rights must face, it is not the case that in

---

76 Prior to the HRA most freedoms were merely liberties; one did no wrong to exercise them, but there was no positive duty on any organ of the state to allow or facilitate them. For example, the Public Order Act 1986 nowhere placed upon chief constables a duty to ensure freedom of assembly and speech. It should be noted that some of our entitlements clearly had and have the quality of Hohfeldian claim-rights in that they are protected by a positive correlative duty, such as the right of access to a solicitor while in police custody (s 58 of the Police and Criminal Evidence Act 1984). Similarly equal treatment in certain contexts is provided for under domestic and EU instruments. Even when a citizen held a right, there were – under domestic law – no *legal* guarantees that the legislation providing the positive protection would not be repealed. Similarly, a citizen enjoying a liberty could not be certain that legislation would not be introduced into a previously unregulated area, thus destroying or limiting that liberty.

77 Unless the only possible reading of contrary primary legislation is that the right must be infringed. Even in that instance, a court may issue a non-binding declaration that the law is incompatible with the claimed human right (s 4), and the protection of human rights in law has then been secured by introducing remedial legislation (which has happened in almost all such instances of a declaration of incompatibility).

78 *Othman v UK* (2012) 55 EHRR 1, see Chapter 15.

79 See Chapter 15, p 1117.

other democratic societies where such rights receive legal protection there is a popular movement to repeal such protections. In the USA, for example, the Constitution retains support from voters and politicians on both sides of the political spectrum, despite leading to the protection of rights – such as abortion[80] and gay marriage[81] – which were, at the times in question, hugely unpopular with large sections of its population. The HRA faces an objection that goes deeper than the practical operation of human rights in that the rights-settlement that the HRA represents is not the product of a popular revolution, as occurred in European countries, but was instead created by a standard legislative process and was not 'sold' to the British people via some form of educational programme.

The cultural transition from liberties to human rights has therefore not taken a favourable hold in the popular imagination; instead, human rights are associated with European institutions, such as the European Court of Human Rights. Judicial reasoning has confirmed the impression that the divergence between civil liberties and human rights amounts to a European imposition. Judges have had limited success in developing a *domestic* interpretation of human rights and have sought rather to *mirror* Strasbourg.[82] As Chapter 3 discusses, repeal and replacement with a British Bill of Rights creates an opportunity to create a new *popular* British rights-settlement, building from the traditional protection of civil liberties. However, Conservative proposals to repeal the HRA in tandem with the creation of a neutered Bill of Rights might simply return the UK to the inferior protections of the previous rights-settlement in the UK, partially removing effective judicial opposition to legislative incursions into the various rights discussed in this work, and failing to call the executive fully to account.

---

80 *Roe v Wade* (1973) 410 US 113.
81 *Obergefell v Hodges*, Dockett No 14–556, Supreme Court judgment of 26 June 2015.
82 See e.g., *R (on the application of Ullah) v Special Adjudicator* [2004] 2 AC 323; see further Chapter 3 p 124.

Chapter 2

The European Convention on Human Rights

1 Introduction[1]

The impetus for development of intergovernmental organisations and development of international human rights law after World War II came from the manner in which Nazi Germany had treated its own citizens, in particular Jews via the Holocaust. No international human rights mechanisms had existed prior to and during the war that could have allowed interference between a state and its citizens in relation to even extreme human rights' abuses. The result was the setting up of the UN which introduced the Universal Declaration of Human Rights (UDHR). The same impetus lay behind the establishment of the Council of Europe, which was founded by the Statute of the Council of Europe in 1949. The UDHR was specifically concerned with the relations between governments and their own subjects. The European Convention on Human Rights was based on the UDHR and was intended to prevent the kind of extreme violation of human rights seen in Germany during and before the war, by providing an early warning system that such violations were beginning to occur. It came into force in 1953.[2] The Council of Europe – which now has 47 member states – was set up in the course of the post-war attempt to unify Europe in order to safeguard common ideals, which included creating greater recognition of the importance of human rights.

The ECHR was only intended to provide basic protection for human rights, subsidiary to the protection provided in the member states. It has not generally been invoked in relation to large-scale violations of rights, but instead has addressed particular

1 Texts referred to below: Clayton, R and Tomlinson, H, *The Law of Human Rights*, 2nd edn, 2009, OUP; Ovey, C and White, R, *Jacobs and White European Convention on Human Rights*, 6th edn, 2014, OUP; Bailey, SH, Harris, DJ and Jones, BL, *Civil Liberties: Cases and Materials*, 6th edn, 2009, OUP; Feldman, D, *Civil Liberties and Human Rights in England and Wales*, 2002; Van Dijk, P and Van Hoof, F, Van Rijn, A, Zwaska, L, *Theory and Practice of the European Convention on Human Rights*, 4th edn, 2006, Intersentia; Mowbray, A, *Cases and Materials on the European Convention on Human Rights*, 3rd edn, 2012, OUP; Janis, M, Kay, R and Bradley, A, *European Human Rights Law*, 3rd edn, 2008, OUP; Harris, D, O'Boyle, K, Bates, E and Buckley, C, *Harris, O'Boyle, and Warbrick: Law of the European Convention on Human Rights*, 2014, OUP; Dickson, B (ed), and Connelly, A, *Human Rights and the European Convention*, 1996, Sweet and Maxwell; Farran, S, *The UK before the European Court of Human Rights*, 1996, Blackstone. Background: Beddard, R, *Human Rights and Europe*, 3rd edn, 1980, CUP; Clarendon; Jacobs, F, *The European Convention on Human Rights*, 1975, OUP; Nedjati, ZM, *Human Rights under the European Convention*, 1978, Elsevier; Merrills, JG and Robertson, AH, *Human Rights in Europe*, 4th edn, 2001, Juris Publishing.

2 On the history of the Convention, see Lord Lester, 'European Human Rights and the British Constitution', in Jowell, J and Oliver, D (eds), *The Changing Constitution*, 4th edn, 2000 (current edn, 2014).

deficiencies in the legal systems of the member states, most of which create regimes of human rights in conformity with it. Drafted in 1949 by the Council of Europe, it was based on the United Nations Declaration of Human Rights,[3] and partly for that reason and partly because it was only intended to provide basic protection for human rights, it appears today as quite a cautious document, less far reaching than the International Covenant on Civil and Political Rights.[4] Nevertheless, it has had far more effect on UK law than any other human rights treaty due to its machinery for enforcement, which includes the European Court of Human Rights, with the power to deliver a ruling adverse to the governments of member states. Moreover, the Court insists upon the dynamic nature of the Convention and adopts a teleological or purpose-based approach to its interpretation which has allowed the substantive rights to develop until they may cover situations unthought of in 1949. Had it been a more radical document, the Convention might have been self-defeating because it might have failed to secure the necessary acceptance from member states, both in terms of ratifying various parts of it, such as the right of individual petition, and in terms of responding to adverse judgments.

Although the European Court of Human Rights may rule against the governments of member states, its approach – which is reflected throughout the machinery for the supervision of the Convention – is not ultimately coercive. A persuasive or consensus-based approach is evident at every stage through which an application may pass. A friendly settlement may well be reached before the case comes before the Court; even if it does not, and the case reaches the stage of a final ruling adverse to the government in question, the government is in effect free to determine the extent of the changes needed in order to respond, although the possibility of future adverse rulings at Strasbourg may exercise an influence on its decision. This approach is also reflected in the doctrine of the 'margin of appreciation' which has been developed by the Strasbourg authorities. This doctrine, to which we will return below,[5] involves allowing the domestic authorities a degree of discretion in deciding what is needed to protect various public interests in their own countries, even though such interests have an impact on protection for Convention rights. The use of this doctrine allows evasion of conflict over very sensitive issues between Strasbourg and the member state. Clearly, its use may lead at times to an acceptance of a lower standard of human rights than some liberal critics would advocate,[6] but some commentators have suggested that it can be an appropriate influence on the dealings between Strasbourg and democracies with generally sound human rights records.[7]

---

3 The Declaration was adopted on 10 December 1948 by the General Assembly of the UN.
4 1966.
5 See pp 95–98.
6 See: Letsas, G, 'Two concepts of the margin of appreciation' (2006) 26(4) OJLS 705–32; McDonald, RJ, 'The margin of appreciation in the jurisprudence of the European Court of Human Rights', *International Law and the Time of its Codification*, 1987, pp 187–208; Van Dijk, P and Van Hoof, F, *Theory and Practice of the European Convention on Human Rights*, 3rd edn, 1998, p 82 *et seq*; O'Donnell, T, 'The margin of appreciation doctrine: standards in the jurisprudence of the European Court of Human Rights' (1982) 4 Human Rights Q 474; Jones, T, 'The devaluation of human rights under the European Convention' [1995] PL 430; Mahoney, P, 'Marvellous richness or invidious cultural relativism?' (1998) 19 Human Rights LJ 1.
7 See Gearty, C, 'Democracy and human rights in the European Court of Human Rights: a critical appraisal' (2000) 51(3) NILQ 381, esp p 387.

When examining the substantive rights, they may be said to fall into two groups: Articles 2–7, covering the most fundamental human rights and containing, broadly, no express exceptions,[8] or narrow express exceptions; and Articles 8–12, which may be said to cover a more sophisticated or developed conception of human rights and which are subject to a broad range of express exceptions. Thus, under Articles 2–7, argument will tend to concentrate on the question of whether a particular situation falls within the scope of the right in question, whereas under Articles 8–11 it will largely concentrate on determining whether the interference with the guarantee can be justified (Article 12 contains only one exception, but of a very broad nature). There is an enormous amount of overlap between the articles and it may be found that weaknesses or gaps in one can be remedied by another, although the Convention will be interpreted as a harmonious whole.[9] It will also be found that invocation of a substantive right in order to attack a decision in the national courts on its merits may sometimes fail, but that a challenge to the *procedure* may succeed under one of the articles explicitly concerned with fairness in the adjudicative process – Articles 5, 6 and 7.[10] The rights and freedoms are largely concerned with civil and political rather than social and economic matters; the latter are governed by the 1961 European Social Charter and the 1966 International Covenant on Economic, Social and Cultural Rights.[11]

The Convention has grown by way of additional protocols so that it now creates a more advanced human rights regime based on Articles 2–14 with the First Protocol[12] in conjunction with the Fourth,[13] Sixth[14] and Seventh[15] Protocols. The very significant Protocol 12 was opened for ratification in November 2000.[16] The UK has not yet ratified the rights

---

8   Art 6 provides that trial judgments should be pronounced publicly except where, *inter alia*, the interest of morals, public order or national security demand otherwise but the primary right – to a fair hearing – is not subject to these exceptions.

9   Van Dijk etc, *op cit*, fn 1, Chapter 2.

10   This point is developed below; see p 58. See Gearty, C, 'The European Court of Human Rights and the protection of civil liberties: an overview' [1993] CLJ 89 for argument that the Convention as a whole is largely concerned with *procedural* rights.

11   (1965) Cmnd 2643; see Harris, D, *The European Social Charter*, 1984, University of Virginia Press. The charter does not have a system of petitions. On an international level, the UK is also party to the 1966 International Covenant on Economic, Social and Cultural Rights, Cmnd 6702. It is not enforceable as regards the UK by individual petition.

12   Cmnd 9221. All the parties to the Convention except Switzerland are parties to this protocol, which came into force in 1954.

13   Cmnd 2309. It came into force in 1968; the UK is not a party. It contains rights relating to the field of immigration law, which have raised governmental concerns regarding the nature of the obligations created: see the White Paper, *Rights Brought Home: The Human Rights Bill*, Cm 3782, 1997, paras 4.10–4.11. The then Labour government considered the possibility of future ratification with reservations: the *Home Office Review of Human Rights Instruments* (amended), 26 August 1999. See below, pp 140–41.

14   (1983) 5 EHRR 167. It came into force in 1985. The UK is now a party to it and it is included in the Human Rights Act, Sched 1. See below, Chapter 4, p 141.

15   (1984) 7 EHRR 1. It came into force in 1988. The UK is not a party but proposes to ratify imminently: see the White Paper, *Rights Brought Home: The Human Rights Bill*, Cm 3782, 1997, paras 4.14–4.15, and the *Home Office Review of Human Rights Instruments* (amended) 26 August 1999. Note that the other protocols are concerned with the procedural machinery of the Convention.

16   See Chapter 4, p 141, and Chapter 5, pp 271–2 and see below, p 92.

contained in the Fourth and Seventh Protocols, and at present does not intend to ratify the Twelfth Protocol, suggesting that although there is a measure of harmony between the basic Convention regime and the UK legal system, this is not the case as far as aspects of the more advanced regime is concerned. The UK has ratified Protocol 13 which abolishes the death penalty in all circumstances. The Joint Committee on Human Rights in 2005 recommended that the government should ratify the Fourth and Twelfth Protocols.[17]

In considering the operation of the Convention in practice, it should be remembered that it was not intended to mimic the working of a domestic legal system. Thus, individuals could not, until fairly recently, take a case directly to the European Court of Human Rights in Strasbourg[18] and, in fact, it is a feature of the Court that it hears very few cases in comparison with the number of applications made.[19] However, its jurisprudence has had an enormous impact, not merely through the outcome of specific cases, but in a general symbolic, educative and preventive sense. Its function in raising awareness of human rights was of particular significance in the UK since, until the enactment of the HRA, no equivalent domestic instrument had the role of doing so. Since the HRA has afforded the Convention further effect in UK law, its interpretation, the values it encapsulates and the development of the control machinery have become of even greater significance. An understanding of the workings of the Convention is now crucial since the jurisprudence is now being very frequently relied on in the domestic courts.

The enormous increase in the number of applications from the UK since the early days of the Convention suggests that, before the Human Rights Act was enacted, it was seen as a guardian of human rights by UK citizens, although to an extent it held out a promise that it could not fulfil. The immensely slow and difficult route to Strasbourg discouraged applicants from using it. It is still a slow and cumbersome route owing to the number of applications, despite improvements in the mechanisms for considering them.[20] Further reforms were introduced under Protocol 11, intended to address the increasing backlog of cases. That aim does not appear to have been realised; Protocol 14 is also intended to speed up the process and deal with the backlog; it came into force in 2010 and has had an impact in diminishing the backlog. The fact that an application may take, at present, five years to be heard is perhaps one of the main deficiencies of the Convention enforcement machinery.[21] This chapter therefore devotes some time to explaining that process and the significant part which was, until fairly recently, played in it by the European Commission on Human Rights,[22] before going on to consider the substantive rights. This chapter only provides an overview of selected substantive rights and of selected aspects of the jurisprudence. The selections have been made on the basis

17 Seventeenth Report of Session 2004–5 HL Paper 99, HC 264, paras 34 and 37.
18 Once the Eleventh Protocol came into force, individuals acquired the right to take a case directly to the Court; see below, p 34 *et seq.*
19 E.g., in 1991, the Commission registered 1,648 applications; it referred 93 cases to the Court, which gave judgment in 72: European Court of Human Rights, Survey of Activities 1959–91.
20 E.g., procedures were introduced under the Eighth Protocol, including a summary procedure for rejecting straightforward cases.
21 The *average* time is a little over four years: see e.g., 'Reform of the control systems of the European Court of Human Rights' (1993) 14 Human Rights LJ 31.
22 See further Bratza, N and O'Boyle, M, 'Opinion: the legacy of the Commission to the new Court under the 11th Protocol' (1997) EHRLR 211.

that those aspects have had a particular impact in domestic law; the more recent cases are referred to at relevant points in the succeeding chapters.

When the Conservative Party was able to form a government without reliance on the Liberal Democrats in 2015 David Cameron, then Prime Minister, made it clear immediately after the general election that the Human Rights Act (HRA) would be repealed, but it is now apparent that such repeal is unlikely until 2017 or 2018, if then. It was also made clear that withdrawal from the ECHR remained a possibility. During the period of Coalition government, 2010–15, Conservative hostility to the European Court of Human Rights' application of the ECHR increased markedly and was traceable mainly to a number of decisions against the UK, especially in the context of counter-terrorism, and prisoners' voting rights.[23] Aspects of a number of these decisions are considered below. Assuming that repeal of the HRA eventually does occur, it would be expected that there would be an increase in cases coming from the UK to Strasbourg. So from the perspective of the Conservative government, opposed to the impact of the ECHR in the UK, it would appear to be pointless to repeal the HRA, but allow UK citizens to bring cases to Strasbourg. At present the rights the Convention provides, depending on the Strasbourg Court's interpretation of them, can be claimed in Britain by individuals against public authorities under the HRA.[24] If such a claim does not succeed in Britain under the HRA, it can still be pursued at Strasbourg.

2 The supervisory procedure for the Convention

Introduction

The Convention's procedural machinery has been altered several times by various protocols. A key reform of the procedure arose from a recommendation of the Parliamentary Assembly of the Council of Europe that the Commission should be abolished and its function merged with that of the Court, so that there would only be one body – the single Court. It was proposed[25] that the new Court would come into operation in 1995 and that there would be a transitional period from 1995 to 2000 during which the old Commission and Court would hear cases already referred to them while new cases would be referred to the new Court. This established a fundamental change in the machinery of the Convention. The arrangements governing the control mechanism[26] were set out in Protocol 11.[27] The single, restructured, Court[28] sits full-time in place of

---

23 In the wake of the decision in *Firth and others v UK*, Appls 44784/09 etc, judgment of 14 August 2014, the then Home Secretary, Theresa May, on 13 August 2014 called for Britain to withdraw from the European Convention on Human Rights.
24 See Chapter 4.
25 Recommendation 1194 adopted on 6 October 1992 by the Parliamentary Assembly of the Council of Europe.
26 See 'Reform of the control systems of the European Court of Human Rights' (1993) 14 Human Rights LJ, 31. For comment, see Mowbray, A, 'The reform of the control system of the ECHR' [1993] PL 419.
27 Protocol 11 came into force on 1 November 1998 under Art 5 of the Protocol. See (1994) 15 HRLJ 86. The merger procedure was completed in November 1998 when the Commission was abolished. For discussion see, e.g., Schermers, H, 'The Eleventh Protocol to the European Convention on Human Rights' (1994) 19 EL Rev 367, at p 378 and (1995) EL Rev 3; Lord Lester of Herne Hill QC, 'The European Convention in the new architecture of Europe' [1996] PL 5.
28 See 'Reform of the control systems of the European Court of Human Rights' (1993) 14 Human Rights LJ 31.

the Court and Commission (under Article 19). Once the Court and Commission merged, the authority of the Convention increased because its jurisprudence was no longer influenced by the decisions of an administrative body. Protocol 11 also abolished the judicial functions of the Committee of Ministers.[29]

The previous role of the European Commission on Human Rights

Originally, under Article 19, the Convention set up the European Commission on Human Rights (hereafter referred to as 'the Commission') and the European Court of Human Rights (hereafter referred to as 'the Court'). Thus, the machinery for the enforcement of the Convention was and is impressive compared to that used in respect of other human rights treaties, particularly the 1966 International Covenant on Civil and Political Rights, which, as far as the UK is concerned, has been enforceable only through a system of assessment of national reports.[30]

The role of the Commission evolved over time. It was conceived of as an advisory body which provided assistance for the Committee of Ministers (see below), composed of the Foreign Affairs Ministers of each state, who had the key role in supervising the Convention. The idea of an independent body interfering in the use of governmental powers in relation to their own citizens gained gradual acceptance, and the Commission became less of an administrative and more of a judicial body, giving opinions on the law, albeit without the ability to take binding decisions except in relation to inadmissibility (see below). Broadly, creation of the Commission represented a compromise: it was previously seen as too controversial merely to allow citizens to take their governments before the Court. There was a feeling that an administrative body might be more sympathetic to member states' cases and the member state might feel less on trial than in the Court.[31] Therefore, the Commission was created as an administrative barrier between the individual and the Court and was used as a means of filtering out a very high proportion of cases, thus considering far more cases than the Court.

The main role of the Commission was to filter out cases as inadmissible, thereby reducing the workload of the Court. However, it also had another role: it tried to reach a friendly settlement between the parties and could give its opinion on the merits of the case if it was not intended that a final judgment should be given. It could also refer the case to the Court or the Committee of Ministers[32] for the final judgment.

The European Court of Human Rights[33]

The Court has increased enormously in standing and efficacy over the last 35 years, partly due to its activism and creativity in interpreting the Convention and its willingness

---

29 Protocols 2, 3, 5, 8, 9 and 10 were superseded by Protocol 11.
30 The Optional Protocol to the Covenant governs the right of individual petition; but it has not been ratified by the UK. For comment on the general efficacy of the reporting system, see (1980) HRLJ 136–70.
31 See Janis, M, Kay, R and Bradley, A, *European Human Rights Law*, 2nd edn, 2000, OUP, p 27.
32 For the composition and functioning of this body, see pp 40–41.
33 For discussion of the role of the Court in interpreting the Convention, see Gearty, C, 'The European Court of Human Rights and the protection of civil liberties' [1993] CLJ 89. The Court's constitution and jurisdiction were governed by the Convention Arts 19–56, but under Protocol 11 these articles were replaced by a revised Section II of the Convention (Arts 19–51).

to find that member states have violated the rights of individuals. It has been pointed out that an explosion in the number of cases it considered occurred in the 1980s as lawyers in the different European countries realised that it held out the possibility of a remedy for their clients and also of bringing about important legal change.[34] It may be considered the European constitutional court as far as human rights matters are concerned.

As originally set up, however, the Court did not bear a great resemblance to a domestic supreme or higher court in a number of respects. In particular, individuals previously could not take a case directly to it and its role was restricted because of the likelihood that the European Commission on Human Rights would find a case inadmissible. Protocol 11 amended the right of individual petition under the Convention (Article 34). From 1998, under Protocol 11, the admissibility and the examination of the merits with a view to reaching a friendly settlement were undertaken by the Court.

The terms of membership of the Court, governed by Articles 19–24 of the Convention, are intended to ensure that the judges will act independently of their own governments. Under Article 20, each member state sends to the Court[35] one judge, who must be 'of high moral character and must either possess the qualifications required for appointment to high judicial office or be jurisconsults of recognised competence' (Article 21). Under the Protocol 11 reforms, the Court sits in committees of three judges, chambers of seven judges and in a Grand Chamber of 17 judges (Article 26). Chambers designate judge rapporteurs to examine applications. The Plenary Court does not perform a judicial function; it elects its president and vice-president for three-year terms and sets up Chambers, constituted for three years.[36] Under Article 43, a party to a case may request that it be referred to the Grand Chamber within a period of three months from the date of the judgment of the Chamber. A panel of five judges from the Grand Chamber will accept the request if it raises a serious issue regarding the interpretation of the Convention or an issue of general importance. This procedure represents a further significant improvement brought about by the Eleventh Protocol since it seemed anomalous that a human rights convention should make no provision for appeals. In general, adoption of the Eleventh Protocol has brought about quite radical changes in the role of the Court, changes that have not been welcomed wholeheartedly by some critics.[37]

The right of complaint: inter-state applications

Under Article 33 any contracting party may refer to the Court any alleged breach of the provisions of the Convention by another contracting party. The violation in question may be against any person; it need not be a national of the complainant state. Further, it can be an abstract application: one that does not allege a violation against any specified person but concerns incompatibility of a state's legislation or administrative practices

---

34 See Harris, D, O'Boyle, K and Warbrick, C, *Law of the European Convention on Human Rights*, 1995, Butterworths, p 648 (current edn, 2014; see n 1 above).

35 A list of persons is nominated by the Members of the Council of Europe and they are then elected by the Consultative Assembly. Under Art 22, each member shall nominate three candidates, of whom two at least shall be its nationals.

36 Rule 25(1).

37 See, e.g., Schermers, H, 'The Eleventh Protocol to the European Convention on Human Rights' (1994) 19 EL Rev 367, p 378.

with the Convention. There have been 19 inter-state applications so far, but more than one complaint has sprung from the same situation; only six situations have, in fact, given rise to complaints.[38] Thus this right has not proved effective; generally, states prefer not to sour their relations with other states if no interest of their own is involved. Therefore, inter-state complaints have had a much less significant impact on human rights in the member states than the individual's right of petition.

The right of complaint: individual applications

Article 34 is widely viewed as one of the most important articles in the Convention since it governs the right of individual complaint, enabling citizens of member states to seek a remedy for a breach of Convention rights by petitioning the European Court of Human Rights. Under Article 34, the Court can receive petitions from any person, non-governmental organisation or group of individuals claiming to be the victim of a violation of one or more of the rights set forth in the Convention.

The individual need not be a national of the state in question, but must be in some way subject to its jurisdiction. The Court has established that the applicant must have been personally affected by the particular violation; it is not possible to bring an abstract complaint.[39] Therefore, an application alleging that Norwegian abortion legislation conflicted with Article 2 (guaranteeing protection of life) failed because the applicant did not allege that he had been personally affected by it (*X v Norway*).[40] However, there are two exceptions to this principle. First, the application can have a mixed nature: it can be partly abstract so long as there has been some personal impact on the applicant. In *Donnelly v UK*[41] the complaint concerned the allegation that the applicants had been tortured during their detention in Northern Ireland. They also wanted a full investigation of the whole system of interrogation employed by the security forces. It was found that, so long as the applicants had been *affected*, a more wide ranging review was possible in the public interest, and the complaint was admissible on that basis. Second, a potential victim may make a complaint if the circumstances are such that the complainant is unsure whether or not he or she is a victim of a violation of a Convention right. This was found to be the case in a complaint concerning the possibility that the applicants' telephones were being tapped (*Klass v Federal Republic of Germany*)[42] where, by virtue of the very nature of the action complained of, it was impossible for the applicants to be certain that they had been affected.

Individual applications – procedure

The process of making a complaint remained a long drawn out one and was extremely cumbersome; there are a very large number of hurdles to be overcome which arise, in particular, from the question of admissibility. A number of stages can be identified.

---

38 See Van Dijk and Van Hoof, *op cit*, fn 1, p 43.
39 *Klass v Federal Republic of Germany* (1978) 2 EHRR 214.
40 Appl 867/60, 4 YB 270, 276; see also *Vijayanathan v France* (1992) 15 EHRR 62.
41 Appl 5577–82/72, Yearbook XVI.
42 Judgment of 6 September 1978 A 28 (1979–80); 2 EHRR 214 (see (1980) 130 NLJ 999).

Determination of the admissibility of the complaint

Determining the question of admissibility is the main method of filtering out applications. A Chamber of the Court can decide on admissibility and, if the application is found to be admissible, proceeds to consideration of the merits.[43] Under Article 26 a single judge may declare inadmissible or strike out of the Court's list of cases an application submitted under Article 34, where such a decision can be taken without further examination.

The complaint must satisfy the admissibility conditions as follows:

(a) The application must not constitute an abuse of the right of complaint.[44] This condition is not often used; it concerns either the aim of the applicant – it may appear that the case is obviously being brought for political propaganda purposes – or his or her conduct.

(b) Under Article 35(2)(b), the matter must not be the same as a matter already examined.[45] This means that unless it contains relevant new information, the complaint must not concern a matter 'which is substantially the same as a matter which has already been examined by the Court or has already been submitted to another procedure or international investigation or settlement or contains no relevant new information'.[46] The limitation in respect of complaints submitted to another international organ has not, in practice, been of significance; no UK complaints have been rejected on this basis. This is mainly because the UK has not accepted the individual right of complaint to the UN Covenant on Civil and Political Rights. The limitation in respect of previous complaints made to the Court refers to substantially similar applications. If the same applicant makes a complaint, new *facts* are needed if it is not to be rejected.[47]

(c) The application must not be incompatible with the provisions of the Convention.[48] This provision encompasses a number of aspects. Incompatibility will occur if:

  • the application claims violation of a right not guaranteed by the Convention. This includes the substantive rights of Section 1 (Articles 2–14) and, as far as the UK is concerned, the First and Sixth Protocols. However, it may be that the right in question does not appear in the Convention, but that if the claim is not granted, violation of one of the Convention rights might then occur; the right claimed may thereby acquire indirect protection;

  • the application claims violation of a right which is the subject of a derogation (Article 15) or reservation (Article 64) by the relevant member state.[49] Thus, the right does appear in the Convention, but the state in question is not, at present, bound to abide by it. A reservation is made when a state ratifies the Convention, while a derogation may be made if an emergency arises, thus suspending part

---

43 Article 29(1).
44 Article 35(3) (previously Art 27(2)).
45 Previously Art 27(b).
46 Article 32(2)(b).
47 *X v UK* (1981) 25 DR 147.
48 Article 27(2).
49 These provisions are discussed below, pp 99–100.

of the state's Convention obligations. Some rights, as will be seen, are non-derogable, because they are viewed as particularly fundamental;

- the applicant or respondent are persons or states incompetent to appear before the Commission. An application from an individual can only be directed against those states which are contracting parties. Further, the complaint must be directed against an organ of government, not against individuals.[50] However, the violation of the Convention by an individual may involve the responsibility of the state. The state may have encouraged the acts in question or failed to prevent or remedy them. Thus, the condition will be fulfilled if the state is in some way responsible for the alleged violation. This is an aspect of the phenomenon known as *Drittwirkung*, which means that human rights provisions can affect the legal relations between private individuals, not only between individuals and the public authorities;[51]
- the application is aimed at the destruction or limitation of one of the rights or freedoms guaranteed by the Convention and therefore conflicts with Article 17. The intention is to prevent an applicant claiming a right which would enable him or her to carry out activities which ultimately would lead to the destruction of the guaranteed rights. Therefore, the Commission rejected the application of the banned German Communist party due to its aims (*Kommunistische Partei Deutschland v Federal Republic of Germany*[52]). This provision suggests that the Convention adopts a teleological view of freedom; in other words, freedom is valued instrumentally as something that will lead to benefit for society as a whole, rather than as being a good in itself.

(d) Domestic remedies must have been exhausted.[53] In brief, this means that the applicant must provide prima facie evidence of exhaustion of remedies. The burden then shifts to the state to show that a remedy was reasonably ascertainable by the applicant, that the remedy does exist and has not been exhausted and that the remedy is effective. The requirement that domestic remedies must have been exhausted refers to: the 'legal remedies available under the local law which are in principle capable of providing an effective and sufficient means of redressing the wrongs for which the Respondent state is said to be responsible'.[54] If there is a doubt as to whether a remedy is available, Article 35 will not be satisfied unless the applicant has taken proceedings in which that doubt can be resolved.[55] This generally means that judicial procedures must be instituted up to the highest court which can affect the decision but also, if applicable, appeal must be made to administrative bodies. However, the applicant only needs to exhaust those possibilities which offer an *effective* remedy, so if part of the complaint is the lack of a

---

50 See, e.g., *Nielsen v Denmark* (1988) 11 EHRR 175.
51 See Van Dijk and Van Hoof, *op cit*, fn 1, Chapter 1, Part 6. For commentary on *Drittwirkung*, see Alkema, E, 'The third party applicability or *Drittwirkung* of the ECHR in protecting human rights', in *The European Dimension*, 1988, pp 33–45.
52 Appl 250/57, Yearbook I (1955–57), Vol 6, p 222.
53 Article 35(1) (previously Arts 26 and 27(3)).
54 *Nielsen v Denmark* Appl No 343/57; (1958–59) 2 YB 412, p 412.
55 *De Vargattirgah v France* (1981), Appl 9559/81.

remedy under Article 13, then the application is not likely to be ruled inadmissible on this ground.[56] A remedy will be ineffective if, according to established case law, there appears to be no chance of success,[57] and the Court will decide whether a remedy did in fact offer the applicant the possibility of sufficient redress. If there is a doubt as to whether a given remedy is able to offer a real chance of success, that doubt must be resolved in the national court itself.[58] Until fairly recently, the Court viewed judicial review as a sufficient remedy,[59] but this is no longer necessarily the case, as explained below.[60] If it can be said that the state practice complained of is a repetition of one that is in breach of the Convention, but tolerated by the state authorities, it may be argued that taking the proceedings available would be ineffective.[61]

The application must have been submitted within a period of six months from the date on which the final national decision was taken (Article 35(1)). Time runs from the decision taken by the last national authority that had to be used and after the point when the decision has been notified to the applicant; ineffective remedies will not be taken into account in assessing the point from which time runs.

(e) The application must not be manifestly ill-founded (Article 35(3)(a)). Under the current procedure, the Committee or a Chamber of the Court finds this condition unfulfilled if the facts obviously fail to disclose a violation.

In theory, this ground should only operate if the ill-founded character of the application is clearly manifest. It has been said that the task involved is not to 'determine whether an examination of the case submitted by the applicant discloses the actual violation of one of the rights and freedoms guaranteed by the Convention but only to determine whether it includes any possibility of the existence of such a determination'.[62] In practice, ill-foundedness has not always been clearly manifest.

(f) Once Protocol 14 was in force it changed para 3 of Article 35 so that it reads:

The Court shall declare inadmissible any individual application submitted under Article 34 if 'it considers that:

b. the applicant has not suffered a significant disadvantage, unless respect for human rights as defined in the Convention and the Protocols thereto requires an examination of the application on the merits and provided that no case may be rejected on this ground which has not been duly considered by a domestic tribunal'.

Under this provision cases are 'filtered' out that have less chance of succeeding, as are those that are broadly similar to cases brought previously against the same

---

56 *X v UK* (1981) Appl 7990/77; 24 D & R 77.
57 Appl 5874/172, Yearbook XVII (1974). See *H v UK* 33 D & R 247(1983) (Counsel's opinion as to inefficacy sufficient). Cf *K, F and P v UK* 40 D & R 298 (1984).
58 *Spencer v UK* (1998) 25 EHRR CD 105.
59 See *Vilvarajah and Four Others v UK* (1991) Judgment of 30 October 1991; Appl 12 (1991).
60 See below, pp 92–93.
61 *Akdivar v Turkey* (1997) 23 EHRR 143, paras 66–67.
62 *Pataki*, Appl 596/59, Yearbook III (1960).

Member State. Moreover, a case will not be considered admissible where an applicant has not suffered a 'significant disadvantage'. The UK Joint Committee on Human Rights broadly welcomed Protocol 14, since it considered that it included many positive aspects which should improve the functioning of the control system of the Convention. But it found that the introduction of a new requirement that an applicant to the European Court of Human Rights must have suffered a 'significant disadvantage', was 'very controversial' because it restricts the right of individual petition.[63]

The examination of the application and friendly settlements under Article 39(1)

If the application is declared admissible, the Court places itself at the disposal of the parties under Article 39 with a view to securing a friendly settlement between the parties. If both parties are willing, they can reach a friendly settlement straight after the application has been declared admissible.[64] If the application is declared admissible and no friendly settlement is reached, it is examined under Article 38.

The judgment of the Court

Under the current procedure, the proceedings before the chamber of seven judges will consist of a written stage, followed by a hearing.[65] The chamber may appoint one or more of its members to conduct the initial examination. The arrangements are characterised by their flexibility: within the Rules, the Court is free to decide on a procedure which can be tailored to the nature of a particular application[66] and this may include visiting a particular place, such as a prison. An on-the-spot inquiry can be conducted by a delegate of the Court. The Court can also order a report from an expert on any matter. After this initial stage, the Chamber will normally conduct an oral hearing if there has been no oral admissibility hearing.

Each of the parties can address the Court; in practice, hearings take half a day and each party is given 45 minutes to make oral submissions. If a violation appears to be established, the state must attempt to demonstrate that the case falls within an exception to the right in question. The Court is not bound by its own judgments.[67] Nevertheless, it usually follows and applies its own precedents unless departure from them is indicated in order to ensure that interpretation of the Convention reflects social change.

The judgment does not state what remedial measures should be taken; it is up to the state to amend its legislation or make other changes in order to conform with the

---

63 1st Report Session, 2004–05.
64 If a friendly settlement is reached, a report will be drawn up stating the facts and solution reached.
65 Under Art 55, the Court shall draw up its own rules and determine its own procedure.
66 See Rule 42(2).
67 Rule 51, para 1 of the Rules of the Court. See Feldman, D, 'Precedent and the European Court of Human Rights' Law Com Consultation Paper No 157 (1999), Appl C.

judgment. Thus, a response may well be in doubtful conformity with the Convention.[68] The Court is not ultimately a coercive body and relies for acceptance of its judgments on the willingness of states to abide by the Convention. Under Article 45, reasons must be given for the judgment of the Court and if the judgment does not represent in whole or in part the unanimous opinion of the judges, any judge shall be entitled to deliver a separate opinion. Under Article 43 the judgment can be referred to the Grand Chamber 'in exceptional cases' for judgment. Under Article 44, the judgment of the Grand Chamber is final, while a judgment of a chamber will become final: when the parties declare that they will not request referral to the Grand Chamber; or where after three months no such request has been made; or where the panel of the Grand Chamber rejects the request. Under Article 46, very significantly, the judgment of the Court is binding on the state party involved.

The Court can award compensation under Article 41. The purpose of the reparation is to place the applicant in the position he would have been in had the violation not taken place. It will include costs unless the applicant has received legal aid. It can also include loss of earnings, travel costs, fines and costs unjustly awarded against the applicant. It can also include intangible or non-pecuniary losses which may be awarded due to unjust imprisonment or stress.[69]

Protocol 16, which is not yet in force, makes provision for advisory opinions to be sought from the Grand Chamber, which will be non-binding on the state and which must be sought in the context of a case before a domestic court or tribunal.[70] That provision has the potential to allow disputes concerning the ECHR to be resolved at the domestic level, which might alleviate the pressure on the Court, but probably only to a small extent.

Supervision of the judgment by the Committee of Ministers

The Committee of Ministers was not set up by the Convention; its composition and functions are regulated in the statute of the Council of Europe (Articles 13–21). The Committee consists of one representative from the government of each member state of the Council of Europe, usually the Minister for Foreign Affairs.[71] Under Article 46, as amended under Protocol 14, the Committee is charged with supervising the execution of the Court's judgment. This includes both the judgment on the merits and on compensation. The Committee notes the action taken to redress the violation on the basis of information given by the state in question. If the state fails to execute the judgment,

---

68 The Contempt of Court Act 1981 may be said to represent such a response to the ruling that UK contempt law violated Art 10 in that it preserved common law contempt, which appears, especially since the decision in *Attorney General v Punch* (see Chapter 6, pp 343–50), to give insufficient weight to freedom of speech.

69 E.g., in the *Young, James and Webster* case (1981) judgment of 13 August 1981, Appl 44; (1981) 4 EHRR 38, pecuniary and non-pecuniary costs were awarded: the Court ordered £65,000 to be paid. See further Chapter 4, pp 208–11.

70 See N O'Meara, 'Advisory jurisdiction and the European Court of Human Rights: a magic bullet for dialogue and docket-control?' (2014) 34(3) *Legal Studies* 444.

71 If an alternative is nominated, he or she should also be a member of the government (Art 14).

the Committee decides what measures to take: it can bring political pressure to bear, including suspension or even, as a final sanction, expulsion from the Council of Europe. A new mechanism was introduced with Protocol 14 to assist enforcement of judgments by the Committee of Ministers. Under it, the Committee can ask the Court for an interpretation of a judgment and can even bring a member state before the Court for non-compliance of a previous judgment against that state. Thus adverse judgments against member states will have a higher chance of being implemented.

Doubts have been raised over the fitness of the Committee to oversee one of the key stages in the whole Convention process, namely the implementation of national law to bring it into line with the findings of the Court.[72] It is apparent that a rigorous analysis of the changes that the offending state has made in its law would be desirable, to ensure that the judgment is fully implemented and to make future similar breaches of the Convention by that state impossible.

3 The substantive rights and freedoms – selected aspects

In what follows, an outline will be given of the scope of the Articles covering the substantive rights and freedoms. In the case of Articles 3, 5, 6 and 8–11, much more detailed treatment of decisions which are relevant to particular areas of UK law will be undertaken in later chapters when those areas of domestic law are considered.

Article 2: protection of life

(1) Everyone's right to life shall be protected by law. No one shall be deprived of his life intentionally save in the execution of a sentence of a court following his conviction of a crime for which this penalty is provided by law.

(2) Deprivation of life shall not be regarded as inflicted in contravention of this article when it results from the use of force which is no more than absolutely necessary:

   (a) in defence of any person from unlawful violence;
   (b) in order to effect a lawful arrest or to prevent the escape of a person lawfully detained;
   (c) in action lawfully taken for the purpose of quelling a riot or insurrection.

The right to life can be viewed as the most fundamental of all human rights. Its significance receives recognition under all human rights' instruments[73] and its vital importance is recognised under UK common law.[74]

---

72 See Leuptracht, P, 'The protection of human rights by political bodies', in Nowak, M, Steurer, P and Tretter, H (eds), *Progress in the Spirit of Human Rights*, 1988, Strasbourg, pp 95–107.

73 Although in, for example, the US and India, the right is protected only on a 'due process' basis. Deprivation of life can occur, but it must be in accordance with the due process of the law.

74 It is recognised in the crimes of murder, manslaughter and infanticide. The deliberate killing of another human being is viewed as requiring to be marked out from other crimes by means of the mandatory life sentence penalty. For an early response of the UK courts to Art 2 under the HRA, see R (on the app of Pretty) v Secretary of State for the Home Dept [2001] UKHL 61. For a full discussion, see Clayton and Tomlinson, *op cit*, fn 1, Chapter 7.

Scope of the right

Article 2 provides non-derogable protection of the right to life.[75] This might seem straightforward – governments are enjoined to refrain from the wanton killing of their subjects – but aside from that instance, it is not a straightforward matter to determine what the guarantee under Article 2 encompasses. The Court has said: 'the first sentence of Article 2 enjoins the state not only to refrain from the intentional and unlawful taking of life, but also to take appropriate steps to safeguard the lives of those within its juris-diction'.[76] Thus, while the state must not order or empower its agents to kill its subjects, except within the specified exceptions, it also has further responsibilities under Article 2 to protect the right to life by law. But clearly, it is difficult to pinpoint the stage at which it may be said that the responsibility of a state for a person's death is so clear, the causal potency between the state's action or omission and the death so strong, that it is possible to find that the right to life has been violated.[77]

Decisions under Article 2 have not yet entirely clarified this issue, but they do sug-gest that two, usually distinct, duties are placed on the national authorities, although their scope is unclear. First, as indicated, Article 2 places the public authorities under a duty not to take life except in certain specified circumstances. This duty covers inten-tional, officially sanctioned killings (executions, deliberate killing to save life) and unintentional killings (where the risk of killing is taken by using lethal force in a riot situation). Where state agents do take life, the obligation to protect the right to life by law requires that 'there should be some form of effective official investigation'.[78] This requirement was found to be breached in *Jordan, Kelly, Arthurs, Donelly and Others v UK*[79] in respect of the killing of eight IRA members by the SAS in 1987. Second, Article 2 places a positive obligation on the state authorities to protect the right to life by law. This positive obligation may take a number of forms. It requires that reason-able steps be taken in order to enforce the law in order to protect citizens (*X v UK and Ireland*[80]). It was held in *W v UK*[81] that these measures will not be scrutinised in detail. Clearly, the state may not be able to prevent every attack on an individual without an enormous expenditure of resources.[82] Therefore, the Convention will leave a wide margin of discretion to the national authorities in this regard, although the state will be under some duty to maintain reasonable public security.[83] Where state agents' actions are very closely linked to the preservation of a known individual's life as, for example, the actions of police officers are during a hostage situation, the state will be under a

---

75 See Art 15(2). Derogation is not allowed in times of emergency or war; derogation is only possible in respect of death resulting from acts of war themselves.

76 *LCB v UK* (1998) 27 EHRR 212, para 36.

77 See further Sieghart, P, *The Lawful Rights of Mankind*, 1986, Clarendon, Chapter 11.

78 *McCann v UK* (1995) 21 EHRR 97, para 161.

79 (2001) *The Times*, 18 May.

80 Appl 9829/82 (not published).

81 Appl 9348/81, 32 DR 190 (1983).

82 It was accepted in *Osman v UK* (1998) 29 EHRR 245 that the obligation to protect the right to life had to be interpreted 'in a way that does not impose an impossible or disproportionate burden on the authori-ties' (para 116). In that instance, the police had failed to take measures to prevent a murder taking place despite very strong indications that the victim was in imminent danger. See further below, on the Art 6 issue in the case, p 60.

83 *Association X v UK*, Appl 7154/75; 14 DR 31 (1978).

positive obligation not only to seek to preserve life, but also to act reasonably in so doing. The need to preserve life in the immediate situation would appear to override the general duty to maintain state security and prevent crime. These notions seem to under-lie the findings of the Commission in *Andronicou and Constantinou v Cyprus*.[84] Article 2 was found to have been violated by Cypriot police when, in attempting to deal with a siege situation in which a hostage had been taken, they fired a number of times at the hostage taker, killing the hostage. The number of bullets fired reflected, it was found, a response which lacked caution.

Similarly, situations may arise in which, while state agents do not directly take life, the state is responsible for creating a life-threatening situation. Where the state has directly created such a situation, its responsibility will arguably be greater. In *LCB v UK*,[85] the applicant had contracted leukaemia; her father had been present during Brit-ish nuclear tests on Christmas Island. She complained of a breach of Article 2 since the state had not advised her parents to monitor her health. In deciding that no breach had occurred, the Court found, taking into account the information that was available at the time, that the state had done all it was required to do to prevent an avoidable risk to her life. Had the information regarding the risk been available at the time, the decision might well have gone the other way, implying that the Court is prepared in principle to hold the state responsible in such instances.

Such an instance may be distinguished from a situation created by others, or by natu-ral causes but in which it may be said that the state still has some responsibility. The positive obligation may entail the taking of appropriate steps to safeguard life[86] where state agents do not themselves unintentionally take life and/or the state itself has not created the life-threatening situation, but the breadth of this duty is unclear. It seems that it will include the provision of adequate medical care in prisons[87] since, in this instance, the state is directly responsible for the welfare of citizens during their impris-onment. However, it is unclear how far the individual should have a right to secure the expenditure of resources so that the state can save or preserve his or her life. The state may bear some responsibility in a number of instances. For example, a person might die due to poor housing conditions after repeated pleas for re-housing, or due to deficien-cies in health care such as a lack of a vaccination programme or poor implementation of the programme,[88] or to exposure to bacteria in certain parts of a hospital while suffer-ing from a condition weakening the immune system. Road traffic regulations and their implementation engage the state's responsibility; life might be put at risk, for example, due to a failure to impose a particular speed limit in poor driving conditions.

The Court is proceeding cautiously in relation to the state's positive obligations under Article 2. It has shown some reluctance to read Article 2 so widely as to cover such situations, although there are indications that this stance may be changing. In *Guerra v Italy*,[89] it was said that the time may be ripe for 'the court's case law on Article 2 . . .

---

84 (1996) 22 EHRR CD 18.
85 (1998) 27 EHRR 212.
86 *X v UK*, Appl 7154/75, 14 DR 31 (1978).
87 *Simon-Herald v Austria*, Appl 430/69, 14 YB 351 (1971) (the application was declared admissible and a friendly settlement was later reached).
88 See *Association X v UK* Appl 7154/75; 14 DR 31 (1978).
89 (1998) 26 EHRR 357, p 387.

to start evolving, to develop the respective implied rights, articulate situations of real and serious risk to life or different aspects of the right to life'. The obligation to provide health care in order to save life and to regulate hospitals in such a way as to protect life has been recognised.[90]

The question has arisen in the context of national legislation on abortion whether the foetus can fall within the interpretation of 'everyone', but it has been determined that even if the foetus is protected, its right to life will be weighed against the mother's life and physical and mental health.[91] In *Paton v UK*[92] it was found by the Commission that Article 2 applies only to persons who have been born. Had the Commission found otherwise, all national legislation in the member states permitting abortion would have been in breach of Article 2, since abortion even to save the mother's life would not appear to be covered by any of the exceptions. *H v Norway*[93] clarified the position. The Commission found that the lawful abortion of a 14-week foetus on social grounds did not breach Article 2. It took this stance on the basis that since the state parties' laws on abortion differ considerably from each other, a wide margin of discretion should be allowed. It appears that the abortion laws within the member states probably comply with Article 2, although in *Open Door Counselling v Ireland* the Court left open the possibility that Article 2 might place some restrictions on abortion.[94]

Exceptions

A very significant express exception to Article 2, limiting the scope of para 1, is in respect of the death penalty, which also includes extradition to a country where the death penalty is in force.[95] Protocol 6 has now removed the death penalty exception and it was ratified by the UK on 27 January 1999. It may be possible to challenge use of the death penalty in countries that have not ratified Protocol 6 under other Convention rights, such as Article 3.[96]

Generally, the para 2 exceptions are reasonably straightforward and are aimed mainly at unintentional deprivation of life. This was explained in *Stewart v UK*,[97] which concerned the use of plastic bullets in a riot. It was found that para 2 is concerned with situations where the use of violence is allowed as necessary force and may, as an unintended consequence, result in loss of life. On this basis, the use of plastic bullets was found to fall within its terms. However, paras 2(a), (b) and (c) also cover instances where the force used was bound to endanger life and was intended to do so, but was necessary in the circumstances. Thus, national laws recognising the right to use self-defence are, in

---

90 *Scialacqua v Italy* (1998) 26 EHRR CD 164; and *Erikson v Italy*, Appl 37900/97, judgment of 26 October 1999.
91 *X v UK*, Appl 8416/78, 19 DR 244 (1980).
92 (1981) 3 EHRR 408. It has been argued that a woman's right to an abortion must therefore have been impliedly accepted: Rendel, M (1991) 141 NLJ 1270, but that is not at present the case: *ABC v Ireland* [2010] ECHR 2032.
93 No 17004/90, 73 DR 155 (1992).
94 Judgment of 29 October 1992; (1992) 15 EHRR 244. For comment, see K Ewing and C Gearty 'Terminating abortion rights?' (1992) 142 NLJ 1696.
95 *X v Spain*, Appl 10227/82, 37 DR 93 (1984).
96 See *Soering v UK* (1989) 11 EHRR 439, pp 46–47, 59–60 in relation to Art 3.
97 (1985) 7 EHRR 453; see also *Kelly v UK* (1993) 16 EHRR 20, in which the European Commission found that the use of force to prevent future terrorist acts was allowable. For criticism of the decision in *Kelly*, see (1994) 144 NLJ 354.

principle, in harmony with para 2(a). Clearly, the state can use lethal force where absolutely necessary in order to quell a riot. But, the necessity will be carefully scrutinised: state agents must act with caution in resorting to lethal force.[98]

Also, in certain circumstances, the state can sanction the use of force with the intention of killing. It can do so, however, only when such force is absolutely necessary for the fulfilment of one of the para 2 purposes. This issue was considered by the Commission in *Kelly v UK*,[99] in which a young joyrider was shot dead by soldiers in Northern Ireland when he tried to evade an army checkpoint. It was found that the application was manifestly ill-founded, since the use of force was justified. However, it can be argued that this finding does not represent a strict application of a strict proportionality test. Kelly was apparently shot in order to prevent him escaping, but it would not appear that it was 'absolutely necessary' to shoot to kill in the circumstances, since it might well have been possible to arrest him later.

The Court addressed the question of the strictness of the 'absolutely necessary' test in *McCann, Farrell and Savage v UK*,[100] the first judgment of the Court to find a breach of Article 2. The case concerned the shooting by SAS soldiers of three IRA members on the street in Gibraltar. The UK argued that this was justified on the basis that they apparently had with them a remote control device which they might have used to detonate a bomb. The Court found that para 2 primarily describes situations 'where it is permitted to use force which may result, as an unintended outcome in the deprivation of life', but that para 2 would also cover the intentional deprivation of life. However, the use of force must be no more than absolutely necessary for the achievement of one of the para 2 purposes and the test of necessity to be used was stricter than that used in respect of the test under paragraph 2 of Articles 8–11. The main question for the Court was the extent to which the state's response to the perceived threat posed by the IRA members was proportionate to that threat. The Court found that the use of force could be justified where 'it is based on an honest belief which is perceived for good reason to be valid at the time but which subsequently turns out to be mistaken. To hold otherwise would be to impose an unrealistic burden on the state and its law enforcement personnel.' Following this finding, the Court found that the actions of the soldiers who carried out the shooting did not amount to a violation of Article 2.

However, the organisation and planning of the whole operation had to be considered in order to discover whether the requirements of Article 2 had been respected. The Court focused on the decision not to arrest the suspects when they entered Gibraltar. This decision was taken because it was thought that there might have been insufficient evidence against them to warrant their charge and trial. However, this decision subjected the population of Gibraltar to possible danger. The Court considered that taking this factor into account and bearing in mind that they had been shadowed by the SAS soldiers for some time, the suspects could have been arrested at that point. Further, there was quite a high probability that the suspects were on a reconnaissance mission at the time of the shootings and not a bombing mission. This possibility, that there was no car

---

98   A breach of Art 2 was found in *Gulec v Turkey* (1999) 28 EHRR 121: gendarmes had fired into a crowd to disperse it; less forceful means could have been used.

99   (1993) 16 EHRR CD 20.

100 (1995) 21 EHRR 97, A 324, Council of Europe Report.

bomb or that the suspects had no detonator, was not conveyed to the soldiers and since they were trained to shoot to kill, the killings were rendered almost inevitable. All these factors were taken into account in finding that the killing of the three constituted a use of force which was more than absolutely necessary in defence of persons from unlawful violence within the meaning of para 2(a) of Article 2. The state had sanctioned killing by state agents in circumstances which gave rise to a breach of Article 2.

This was a bold decision which departs from the stance taken in *Kelly*. It emphasises that a strict proportionality test must be used in determining issues under para 2 of Article 2. Applying this test, it would appear that where an alternative to the deliberate use of deadly force exists, it should always be taken. It would therefore seem that the use of such force to effect an arrest would never be justified except where, in the circumstances, there was near-certainty that the suspect would kill if allowed to escape. This might apply, for example, in situations where hostages had been taken and threats against them issued. It would also apply in circumstances similar to those arising in *McCann*, but where no opportunity for apprehension had previously arisen and where there was a stronger likelihood that a bomb might be about to be detonated. In such instances, of course, both sub-paras (a) and (b) of Article 2(2) would be in question and it therefore appears that the *McCann* judgment leaves little room for the operation of sub-para (b) independently of sub-para (a) *McCann* and *Kelly* make clear the partially subjective nature of the judgment as to when the use of deadly force is 'absolutely necessary'.

Article 3: freedom from inhuman treatment

'No one shall be subjected to torture or to inhuman or degrading treatment or punishment.'

The right to freedom from torture or inhuman or degrading treatment or punishment is recognised in international human rights treaties[101] and in many, although not all, domestic human rights instruments.[102] The right is also protected by specific conventions, the United Nations Convention Against Torture and Other Cruel, Inhuman or Degrading Treatment or Punishment 1984[103] and the European Convention for the Prevention of Torture and Inhuman and Degrading Treatment or Punishment 1987.[104] Torture is a crime under international law.[105] Thus, there is strong international recognition of the fundamental values enshrined in this right.

Article 3 contains no exceptions and it is also non-derogable. Thus, on the face of it, once a state has been found to have fallen within its terms, no justification is possible.[106] However, it has been suggested that the exceptions to Article 2 must be taken as applying also to Article 3 since, if the state in certain circumstances may justifiably take life, it must be justifiable *a fortiori* to inflict lesser harm on citizens in the same

---

101 Article 5 of the Universal Declaration and Art 7 of the ICCPR.
102 For discussion of this right as recognised in other jurisdictions, see Clayton and Tomlinson, *op cit*, fn 1, Chapter 8, esp pp 412–29.
103 Cmnd 9593, 1985; it came into force in 1987 and it was ratified by the UK in December 1988.
104 Cm 1634, 1991; it was ratified by the UK in June 1988. For discussion, see Evans, M, and Morgan, R, *Preventing Torture: A Study of the European Convention for the Prevention of Torture*, 1998, OUP.
105 See *R v Bow Street Stipendiary Magistrate ex p Pinochet Ugarte (No 3)* [1999] 2 WLR 827.
106 *Ireland v UK* (1978) 2 EHRR 25.

circumstances.[107] This may be correct, but clearly it is not intended to be taken to mean that all the exceptions to Article 2 apply to all forms of Article 3 treatment. The Article 2 exceptions suggest elements of immediacy which would be applicable to severe wounding but not usually to, for example, the form of torture, severe beating of all parts of the body to extract information, which occurred in the *Greek* case.[108] Similarly, state laws allowing wounding by private individuals in self-defence would not appear to be in breach of Article 3 so long as they were in accord with para 2 of Article 2. The Court has made it clear that the use of forms of Article 3 treatment in order to extract information, even in order to combat terrorism, is unjustifiable.[109]

The responsibility of the state extends beyond prohibiting the use of Article 3 treatment by state agents. It includes a duty to ensure that individuals within their jurisdiction are not subjected to Article 3 treatment by other individuals.[110] It also includes an obligation not to deport a person who needs medical treatment to a country where he will not receive it.[111] The state also has a positive obligation to carry out an effective investigation into allegations of breaches of Article 3.[112]

In determining the standard of treatment applicable below which a state will be in breach of Article 3, a common European standard is applied, but also all the factors in the situation are taken into account.[113] The Court has found that such factors include: 'the nature and context of the treatment, its duration, its mental and physical effects and, in some instances, the sex, age and state of health of the victim'.[114] Thus, it does not connote an absolute standard and, in its application, it allows for a measure of discretion. It is clear that, in order to determine this issue, *present* views must be considered rather than the views at the time when the Convention was drawn up. The three forms of treatment mentioned represent three different levels of seriousness. Thus, torture, unlike degrading treatment, has been quite narrowly defined to include 'deliberate inhuman treatment causing very serious and cruel suffering'.[115] In a number of cases, there has been a finding of torture against Turkey. In *Aksoy v Turkey*,[116] the applicant had been stripped naked, his arms had been tied behind his back and he had then been hung from his arms. In *Aydin v Turkey*,[117] the rape of a young girl by a military official was found to amount to torture; the other forms of ill treatment to which she was subjected, including beating for an hour, also amounted to torture. In *Selmouni v France*,[118] the Court found

---

107 See Harris, D, O'Boyle, K and Warbrick, C, *Law of the European Convention on Human Rights*, 1995, Butterworths, p 56.
108 (1969) Yearbook XII 1, p 504, Com Rep; CM Res DH (70) 1.
109 *Tomasi v France* (1992) 15 EHRR 1.
110 In *A v UK* (1999) 27 EHRR 611, a violation of Art 3 was found since the law had failed to protect a child from excessive chastisement by his stepfather.
111 In *D v UK* (1998) 24 EHRR 423, a violation of Art 3 was found since the UK proposed sending D back to the West Indies after he had contracted AIDS, where he would not receive appropriate treatment for his condition.
112 *Aksoy v Turkey* (1996) 23 EHRR 533; *Selmouni v France* (2000) 29 EHRR 403.
113 *Netherlands v Greece* (1969) 12 YB 1.
114 *A v UK* (1998) 27 EHRR 611, para 20.
115 *Ireland v UK* (1978) 2 EHRR 25.
116 (1996) 23 EHRR 553.
117 (1997) 25 EHRR 251. See also *Salman v Turkey* (2000) 54 EHRR 17 (beatings in custody with rifle butts and sticks amounted to torture).
118 (2000) 29 EHRR 403.

that beatings and humiliation in custody amounted to torture rather than inhuman or degrading treatment, bearing in mind the fact that 'the increasingly high standard being required in the area of protection of human rights and fundamental liberties correspondingly and inevitably requires greater firmness in assessing breaches of the fundamental values of democratic societies'.[119]

Clearly, treatment which could not come within the restricted definition of torture could still fall within one of the other two heads, especially the broad head – 'degrading treatment'. In order to characterise treatment as inhuman, it must reach a minimum level of severity.[120] Physical assault,[121] the immediate threat of torture[122] and interrogation techniques causing psychological disorientation[123] have all been found to amount to inhuman treatment.

Treatment may be both inhuman and degrading, but degrading treatment may not also amount to inhuman treatment.[124] Degrading treatment is treatment that is grossly humiliating.[125] Degrading punishment does not inevitably include all forms of physical punishment, although it can include certain forms of corporal punishment, including caning,[126] which have been found not to amount to torture or inhuman punishment. Corporal punishment which could be said to be of a 'normal' type may be distinguished, it seems, from degrading corporal punishment.[127] Thus, the mere fact that physical punishment is administered will not, without more, necessarily involve a breach of Article 3 and nor will the mere threat of such punishment.[128]

A number of cases have arisen concerning the position of detainees. It is now clear that if a person enters police custody in a sound physical condition but, on release, is found to have sustained injuries such as bruising, the state must provide a plausible explanation.[129] In determining whether a particular treatment, such as solitary confinement, amounts to a violation of Article 3, a number of factors must be taken into account. These will include the stringency and duration of the measure,[130] the objective pursued – such as the need for special security measures for the prisoner in question[131] or the fear of stirring up discontent among other prisoners[132] – and the effect on the person concerned. The applicant will need to submit medical evidence showing the causal

---

119 *Ibid*, para 101.
120 *A v UK* (1998) 27 EHRR 611, para 20.
121 *Ireland v UK* (1978) 2 EHRR 25.
122 *Campbell and Cosans v UK* (1982) 4 EHRR 293.
123 *Ireland v UK* (1978) 2 EHRR 25.
124 *Tyrer v UK* (1978) 2 EHRR 1.
125 *Netherlands v Greece* (1969) 12 YB 1.
126 *Tyrer v UK* (1978) 2 EHRR 1. In *Warwick v UK*, Eur Comm HR Report of 15 June 1986, the Commission considered that corporal punishment in schools amounted to degrading treatment.
127 *Costello-Roberts v UK* (1995) 19 EHRR 112. It may be noted that the School Standards and Framework Act 1998 has abolished corporal punishment in the independent sector; it had already been abolished in the state sector.
128 *Campbell and Cosans* (1982) 4 EHRR 293.
129 *Tomasi v France* (1992) 15 EHRR 1; *Ribbitsch v Austria* (1992) 21 EHRR 573.
130 Complete sensory isolation is likely to amount to Art 3 treatment: *Ensslin, Bader and Raspe v Germany* (1978) 14 DR 64, p 109.
131 In *Kröcher and Möller v Switzerland* (1984) 6 EHRR 345 it was found that harsh conditions imposed to ensure security may not constitute a violation of Art 3.
132 *X v UK* Appl 8324/78 (not published) (the ability to encourage other prisoners to acts of indiscipline was taken into account).

relationship between the prison conditions complained of and his or her deterioration in mental and physical health. If the adverse treatment has been adopted as a result of the claimant's own uncooperative behaviour, it is probable that no breach will be found.[133]

Article 3 has been interpreted widely as to the forms of treatment it covers, which include some not readily associated with the terms it uses. It could probably be used, for example, in relation to involuntary medical intervention such as sterilisation or Caesarean section,[134] and, as indicated below, racial discrimination can amount to degrading treatment. Article 3 has been used to bring rights within the scope of the Convention which are not expressly included. Thus, Article 3 could be invoked in relation to discriminatory treatment on the basis of race and possibly on the basis of sex or sexual orientation, because such treatment can be termed degrading according to the Commission in the *East African Asians* cases.[135] This possibility could help to compensate for the weakness of the Article 14 guarantee against discrimination which does not create an independent right.[136]

Other rights which otherwise would not be recognised under the Convention include under Article 3, in certain circumstances, the right to remain in a certain country. Violation of Article 3 may occur because of the treatment a person may receive when returning to his or her own country having been expelled or refused admission. It will have to be clearly established that the danger of such treatment is really present. The question arose in *Soering v UK*[137] whether expulsion to a country (the US) where the applicant risked the death penalty would be compatible with Article 3 because it would subject him to conditions on Death Row likely to cause him acute mental anguish. Of course, since Article 2 specifically excludes the death penalty from its guarantee, the possibility of its use cannot in itself create a violation of Article 3 because that would render those words of Article 2 otiose. The Convention must be read as a whole. However, the Court found that the manner and circumstances of the implementation of the death penalty could give rise to an issue under Article 3. The Court held that it had to consider the length of detention prior to the execution, the conditions on Death Row, the applicant's age and his mental state. Bearing these factors in mind, especially the very long period of time spent on Death Row and the mounting anguish as execution was awaited, it was found that expulsion would constitute a breach of Article 3. (In response to this ruling, the UK and the US agreed to drop the charges to non-capital murder and then extradite the applicant.)

The principle laid down in *Soering* was followed in *Chahal v UK*.[138] Originally an illegal immigrant, Mr Chahal obtained leave to remain in Britain indefinitely in 1974. In 1984, he visited the Punjab for a family wedding and met the chief advocate of creating an independent Sikh state. Later, he was arrested by Indian police and allegedly tortured. He escaped from India and became the founder of the International Sikh Youth Federation in the UK. In 1990, he was arrested after a meeting at a Southall temple. The

---

133   *M v UK* Appl 9907/82, 35 DR 130 (1983) (dangerous behaviour of detainee taken into account in considering conditions).

134   See *X v Denmark* (1983) 32 DR 282.

135   (1973) 3 EHRR 76.

136   See below, pp 93–94.

137   (1989) 11 EHRR 439. For discussion, see Schabas, W 'Soering's "Legacy: the Human Rights Committee and the Judicial Committee of the Privy Council take a walk down death row"' (1994) 43 ICLQ 913.

138   (1997) 23 EHRR 413.

Home Office accused him of involvement in Sikh terrorism and decided to deport him on national security grounds. He sought asylum on the ground that he would be tortured if sent back to India and applied to the European Commission, alleging, *inter alia*, a breach of Article 3. The Court found that since there were strong grounds for believing that Mr Chahal would indeed have been tortured had he been returned to India, a breach of Article 3 had occurred.[139]

In *Othman (Abu Qatada) v UK*[140] the Court found that assurances given by the Jordanian government to the UK in a Memorandum of Understanding (MOU) that Qatada would not be subjected to Article 3 treatment if deported from the UK to Jordan were of sufficient quality to be relied on to obviate the risk of such treatment. Thus he could be deported to Jordan, without breaching Article 3. (However, the Court also found that he faced a flagrant denial of his Art 6 right to a fair trial if deported, and therefore his deportation would breach Art 6; on that basis he could not be deported.)

For a breach of Article 3 to be established in the context of deportation or extradition cases, there must be a clear risk of ill treatment; a 'mere possibility' will be insufficient. In *Vilvarajah and Four Others v UK*,[141] the applicants, Sri Lankan Tamils, arrived in the UK in 1987 and applied for political asylum under the UN Convention of 1951 Relating to the Status of Refugees, contending that they had a well-founded fear of persecution if returned to Sri Lanka. The Home Secretary rejected the applications and the applicants sought unsuccessfully to challenge the rejection by means of judicial review. The applicants were then returned to Sri Lanka where, they alleged, four of them were arrested and ill-treated. They claimed that their deportation constituted breaches of Articles 3 and 13 of the European Convention. The Court considered whether the situation in Sri Lanka at the time the applicants were deported provided substantial support for the view that they would be at risk of Article 3 treatment. The Court determined that the general unsettled situation in Sri Lanka at the time did not establish that they were at greater risk than other young male Tamils who were returning there; it established only a possibility rather than a clear risk of ill treatment. No breach of Article 3 could therefore be established.[142] Arguably, this decision suggests that although an Article 3 issue may arise in asylum cases, the Convention cannot be viewed as a substitute for an effective domestic means of determining refugee claims. (It should be noted that Art 8 issues may also arise in some immigration claims; this possibility will be discussed below.)

Article 3 is considered further in relation to police powers and anti-terrorism law.[143]

Article 4: freedom from slavery, servitude and forced or compulsory labour

It is necessary to distinguish between slavery and servitude under Article 4(1) and forced or compulsory labour under Article 4(2). Slavery denotes total ownership, whereas servitude denotes less far-reaching restraints; it is concerned with the labour conditions and the inescapable nature of the service. Article 4(1) contains no express exceptions

---

139   The Art 5 issue is considered below, p 57.
140   [2012] ECHR 56.
141   (1991) 14 EHRR 248.
142   See further for comment on this case, Warbrick, C, *Yearbook of European Law*, 1991, OUP, pp 545–53.
143   See Chapter 12, pp 903–4 and 1180–1 and Chapter 15, pp 1039–42 and 1082–83.

and is also non-derogable. Forced or compulsory labour has been held to denote the following: 'first that the work or service is performed by the worker against his will and, secondly, that the requirement that the work or service be performed is unjust or oppressive or the work or service itself involves avoidable hardship'.[144]

Article 5: right to liberty and security of person

(1) Everyone has the right to liberty and security of person. No one shall be deprived of his liberty save in the following cases and in accordance with a procedure prescribed by law.

The instances in which a person can be deprived of liberty are indicated below, as are the procedures that must be followed to avoid a breach of Art 5. Although Art 5 speaks of liberty *and* security as though they could be distinguished, they are not treated in the case law as though there is any significant distinction between them. The use of the term 'security' does not appear to add anything to the term 'liberty'. The guarantee refers to protection from deprivation of physical liberty, not to protection for physical safety.[145] The presumption embodied in the article is that liberty and security must be maintained. However, it then sets out the two tests that must be satisfied if it is to be removed. First, exceptions are set out where liberty can be taken away; second, under paras 2–4, the procedure is set out which must be followed when a person is deprived of liberty. Thus, if the correct procedure is followed, but an exception does not apply, Art 5 will be breached, as, conversely, it will if an individual falls within an exception but, in detaining him or her, the correct procedure is not followed. It will be found that a number of successful applications have been brought under Art 5 with the result that the position of detainees in Europe has undergone improvement. It should be noted that Art 5 is concerned with total deprivation of liberty, not restriction of movement, which is covered by Article 2 of Protocol 4 (at the time of writing, the UK is not a party to Protocol 4).

In general, the case law of the Court discussed below suggests that the circumstances in which liberty can be taken away under Art 5(1)(a)–(f) will be restrictively interpreted, although the instances included are potentially wide. Art 5(1) not only provides that deprivation of liberty is only permitted within these exceptions, it also requires that it should be 'in accordance with a procedure prescribed by law'. In *Winterwerp v Netherlands*,[146] the Court found that this meant that the procedure in question must be in accordance with national and Convention law, taking into account the general principles on which the Convention is based, and it must not be arbitrary. In *Chahal v UK*,[147] the applicant complained, *inter alia*, that he had been detained although there had been no court hearing. The Home Office decided to deport him on national security grounds, but he applied for asylum. He was then imprisoned for over six years. He applied to the

---

144 *X v Federal Republic of Germany* Appl 8410/78, decision of 13 December 1979.
145 *X v Ireland* (1973) 16 YB 388.
146 Judgment of 24 October 1979 (1979) 2 EHRR 387.
147 (1997) 23 EHRR 413.

European Commission on Human Rights, alleging, *inter alia*, a breach of Art 5, which guarantees judicial control over loss of liberty. The Court found that a breach of Art 5 had occurred, since his detention should have been subject to scrutiny in court. It had been considered by an advisory panel, but that did not provide sufficient procedural safeguards to qualify as a court.

Article 5(1)(a): detention after conviction

This exception covers lawful detention after conviction by a competent court. Thus, the detention must flow from the conviction. This calls into question the revocation of life licences because, in such instances, a person is being deprived of liberty without a fresh conviction. In *Weeks*[148] the Court considered the causal connection with the original sentence when a life licence was revoked after the applicant was released. The Court accepted a very loose link between the original sentence and the revocation of the life licence on the basis that the sentencing judge must be taken to have known and intended that it was inherent in the life sentence that the claimant's liberty would hereafter be at the mercy of the executive. The Court declined to review the appropriateness of the original sentence.

Article 5(1)(b): detention to fulfil an obligation

This exception refers to deprivation of liberty in order to 'secure fulfilment of an obligation prescribed by law'. This phrase raises difficulties of interpretation and is clearly not so straightforward as the first form of such deprivation permitted under Art 5(1)(a). It is very wide and appears to allow deprivation of liberty in many instances without intervention by a court. It might even allow preventive action before violation of a legal obligation. However, it has been narrowed down; in *Lawless*[149] it was found that a specific and concrete obligation must be identified. Once it has been identified, detention can in principle be used to secure its fulfilment.

   The obligation includes a requirement that specific circumstances, such as the possibility of danger to the public, must be present in order to warrant the use of detention. A requirement to submit to an examination on entering the UK has been found to be specific enough.[150] Moreover, it must be apparent why detention rather than some lesser measure is needed to secure compliance with the obligation. Thus, the width of Art 5(1)(b) has been narrowed down by the use of restrictive interpretation in line with furthering the aims of the Convention.

Article 5(1)(c): detention after arrest but before conviction

This provision refers to persons held on remand or detained after arrest. Art 5(3) requires that, in such an instance, a person should be brought 'promptly' to trial; in other words,

---

148 (1987) 10 EHRR 293.
149 (1961) 1 EHRR 15.
150 *McVeigh, O'Neill and Evans v UK* (1981) 5 EHRR 71.

the trial should occur in *reasonable* time. The part of Art 5(1)(c) which causes concern is the ground 'arrest or detention to prevent him committing an offence'. This is an alternative to the holding of the detainee under reasonable suspicion of committing an offence; arguably, the two should have been cumulative. This ground would permit internment of persons even if the facts which showed the intention to commit a crime did not, in themselves, constitute a criminal offence. In *Lawless*[151] the Court narrowed this ground down on the basis that internment in such circumstances might well not fulfil the other requirement in Art 5(1)(c) that the arrest or detention would be effected for the purpose of bringing the person before a competent legal authority. This interpretation was warranted because all of Art 5 must be read together.

A level of suspicion below 'reasonable suspicion' will not be sufficient; in *Fox, Campbell and Hartley*,[152] the Court found that Art 5(1)(c) had been violated on the basis that no reasonable suspicion of committing an offence had arisen, only an honest belief (which was all that was needed under s 11 of the Northern Ireland (Emergency Provisions) Act 1978). The only evidence put forward by the government for the presence of reasonable suspicion was that the applicants had convictions for terrorist offences and that, when arrested, they were asked about particular terrorist acts. The government said that further evidence could not be disclosed for fear of endangering life. The Court said that reasonable suspicion arises from 'facts or information which would satisfy an objective observer that the person concerned may have committed the offence'. It went on to find that the government had not established that reasonable suspicion was present in justifying the arrests in question. The Court took into account the exigencies of the situation and the need to prevent terrorism; however, it found that the state party in question must be able to provide some information which an objective observer would consider justified the arrest. It was found that the information provided was insufficient and therefore a breach of Art 5 had occurred. This ruling suggests that in terrorist cases a low level of reasonable suspicion is required, and this test was applied in *Murray v UK*.[153] The Court found that no breach of Art 5(1)(c) had occurred, even though the relevant legislation (s 14 of the Northern Ireland (Emergency Provisions) Act 1987) required only suspicion, not reasonable suspicion, since there was some evidence which provided a basis for the suspicion in question.

Article 5(1)(d): detention of minors

This provision confers far-reaching powers on national authorities with regard to those under 18 years of age. This has led the Court to interpret the term 'educational purpose' restrictively. In *Bouamar v Belgium*[154] it was found that mere detention without educational facilities would not fulfil Art 5(1)(d); there had to be educational facilities in the institution and trained staff.

---

151 (1961) 1 EHRR 15.
152 (1990) 13 EHRR 157.
153 (1994) 19 EHRR 193.
154 (1988) 11 EHRR 1.

Article 5(1)(e): detention of non-criminals for the protection of society

This sub-paragraph must, of course, be read in conjunction with Art 5(4) – all the persons mentioned have the right to have the lawfulness of their detention determined by a Court. The width of Art 5(1)(e) was narrowed down in the *Vagrancy* cases, in which the question arose of the current application of the term 'vagrant'.[155] The term had been applied to the applicants who had, therefore, been detained. The Court considered whether the applicant was correctly brought within the ambit of the term in the relevant Belgian legislation, but it refused to conduct a more than marginal review of municipal law; the question of the interpretation of national law was separated from the application of the Convention. However the Court did then turn to the Convention and conduct a far-reaching review of the meaning of 'vagrant' in accordance with the Convention on the basis of a common European standard; it then found that the applicants had not been correctly brought within that term. Thus, ultimately, the margin of appreciation allowed was narrow. This stance prevents too wide an interpretation of the application of the categories of Art 5(1)(e).

In *Winterwerp v Netherlands*[156] the Court found that the detention of the mentally disordered or handicapped could be justified only where there was reliable medical evidence of the mental disorder; it must be of a type justifying compulsory detention; and the condition in question must persist throughout the period of detention. In *Kay v UK*[157] a breach of Art 5(1)(e) was found since the first of these conditions had not been complied with; *current* medical information had not been considered.

Article 5(1)(f): detention of aliens and deportees

The importance of this provision is that the Convention does not grant aliens a right of admission or residence in contracting states, but Art 5(1)(f) ensures that an alien who is detained pending deportation or admission has certain guarantees; there must be review of the detention by an independent body[158] and the arrest must be in accordance with national law.[159] The nature of the measures taken, including the period of detention before review, must ensure that the detention is not arbitrary.[160] Also, because the lawfulness of the detention may depend on the lawfulness of the deportation itself, the lawfulness of the deportation may often be in issue.[161]

Safeguards of paras 2–4: general

Paragraphs 2–4 reiterate the principle that the liberty of the person is the overriding concern; if one of the exceptions mentioned in Art 5(1) applies, the safeguards of paras

155   *De Wilde, Ooms and Versyp v Belgium* (1971) 1 EHRR 373.
156   (1979) 2 EHRR 387.
157   (1998) 40 BMLR 20.
158   In *Chahal v UK* (1996) 23 EHRR 413, review by the immigration advisory panel procedure was found to be sufficient to guard against arbitrariness.
159   In *Bozano v France* (1986) 9 EHRR 297, a French deportation order was found to be invalid under national law since it was – in effect – a disguised extradition order. A violation of Art 5(1)(f) was found.
160   *Guzzardi v Italy* (1980) 3 EHRR 333; *Amuur v France* (1996) 22 EHRR 533.
161   *Zamir v UK*, Report of 11 October 1983; 40 DR 42 (1983).

2–4 must still be complied with. If they are not, the deprivation of liberty will be unlaw-ful even if it comes within the exceptions. Paragraphs 2–4 provide a minimum standard for arrest and detention.

Promptly informing of the reason for arrest

Art 5(2) provides that a detainee or arrestee must be informed promptly of the reason for arrest. This information is needed so that it is possible to judge from the moment of its inception whether the arrest is in accordance with the law so that the detainee could theoretically take action straight away to be released. All the necessary information – the factual and legal grounds for the arrest – need not be given at the point of arrest; it can be conveyed over a period of time, depending on the circumstances. A period of two days between the arrest and the conveying of the information has been found not to breach Art 5(2).[162] The Commission's view is that this information need not be as detailed and specific as that guaranteed by Art 6(3) in connection with the right to a fair trial.[163]

In *Fox, Campbell and Hartley v UK*[164] the applicants, who were arrested on suspicion of terrorist offences, were not informed of the reason for the arrest at the time of it, but were told that they were being arrested under a particular statutory provision. Clearly, this could not convey the reason to them at that time. At a later point, during interroga-tion, they were asked about specific criminal offences. The European Court of Human Rights found that Art 5(2) was not satisfied at the time of the arrest, but that this breach was healed by the later indications made during interrogation of the offences for which they had been arrested. Clayton and Tomlinson comment that this finding was 'an unac-ceptable dilution of a basic guarantee'.[165]

In *Murray v UK*[166] soldiers had occupied the applicant's house, thus clearly taking her into detention, but she was not informed of the fact of arrest for half an hour. The question arose whether she was falsely imprisoned during that half hour. The Court found that no breach of Art 5(2) had occurred in those circumstances. Mrs Murray was eventually informed during interrogation of the reason for the arrest and, although an interval of a few hours had elapsed between the arrest and informing her of the reason for it, this could still be termed prompt.

Both these decisions were influenced by the terrorist context in which they occurred and provide examples of the Court's tenderness to claims of a threat to national security made by governments of member states. In both, a very wide margin of appreciation was allowed. It would appear that both were influenced by the crime control consid-eration of allowing leeway to the police to resort to doubtful practices in relation to terrorist suspects and both exhibit, it is suggested, a lack of rigour in relation to due process. Such lack of rigour might be acceptable if there was a real connection between a failure to give information to suspects and an advantage to be gained in an emergency

---

162 *Skoogstrom v Sweden* (1984) 83 A 190.
163 It was determined in *X v Denmark* Appl 8828/79, 20 DR 93 (1983), p 93 that para 5(2) does not include a right to contact a lawyer.
164 (1990) 13 EHRR 157.
165 *Ibid*, n 1, above, p 498.
166 (1994) 19 EHRR 193.

situation, since the principle of proportionality would then be satisfied. However, in Mrs Murray's case, for example, once she was in detention and her house in effect sealed off from the outside world, it is not clear that telling her of the fact of the arrest could have created or exacerbated the unsettled situation. Thus, the Court has allowed some departure from the principle that there should be a clear demarcation between the point at which the citizen is at liberty and the point at which his or her liberty is restrained.

Promptness of judicial hearing

Art 5(3) confers a right to be brought promptly before the judicial authorities; in other words, not to be held in detention for long periods without an independent hearing. It refers to persons detained in accordance with Art 5(1)(c) and therefore covers both arrest and detention, and detainees held on remand. The significance of Art 5(3) rests on its strong link to the purpose of Art 5 itself.[167] There will be some allowable delay in both situations; the question is, therefore, what is meant by 'promptly'. Its meaning was considered in *Brogan v UK*[168] in relation to an arrest and detention arising by virtue of the special powers under s 12 of the Prevention of Terrorism (Temporary Provisions) Act 1989. The UK had entered a derogation under Article 15 against the applicability of Art 5 to Northern Ireland, but withdrew that derogation in August 1984. Two months later, the *Brogan* case was filed. The applicants complained, *inter alia*, of the length of time they were held in detention without coming before a judge, on the basis that it could not be termed prompt. The Court took into account the need for special measures to combat terrorism; such measures had to be balanced against individual rights. However, it found that detention for four days and six hours was too long. The Court did not specify how long was acceptable; previously, the Commission had seen four days (in ordinary criminal cases) as the limit.[169] Following this decision, the UK Government ultimately chose to derogate from Art 5 and this decision was eventually found to be lawful by the European Court of Human Rights.[170]

The question whether detainees on remand have been brought to trial or released in a reasonable time has also been considered. The word 'reasonable' is not associated with the processing of the prosecution and trial, but with the detention itself. Obviously, if the trial takes a long time to prepare for, there will be a longer delay, but it does not follow that detention for all that time will be reasonable. In the *Neumeister* case,[171] the Court rejected an interpretation of 'reasonable' which associated it only with the preparation of the trial. Thus, continued detention on remand will be reasonable only so long as the reasonable suspicion of Art 5(1)(c) continues to exist. But, grounds for continued detention other than those expressly mentioned in Art 5(1)(c) could be considered, such as suppression of evidence or the possibility that the detainee will abscond. However, it is clear from *Letellier v France*[172] that such dangers must persist throughout the period

---

167 See *Bozano v France* (1986) 9 EHRR 297; *Assenov v Belgium* (1999) 28 EHRR 652; *T v Malta* (1999) 29 EHRR 185.
168 (1989) 11 EHRR 117.
169 *X v Netherlands* (1966) 9 YB 564.
170 *Brannigan and McBride v UK* (1993) 17 EHRR 594.
171 (1979–80) 1 EHRR 91.
172 (1992) 14 EHRR 83.

of detention; when they cease, specific reasons for continued detention which have been properly scrutinised must be apparent. Once the accused has been released on bail, Art 5(3) does not apply, but Art 6(1) does, as will be seen later. The question of a reasonable time for preparing for the trial can also be considered under Art 6(1).

There is no absolute right to bail under Art 5(3), but the authorities must consider whether bail can achieve the same purpose as detention on remand.[173] It is also clear that detention after demand of an excessively large sum for bail will be unreasonable if a lesser sum would have achieved the same objective.[174]

Review of detention

Art 5(4) provides a right to review of detention, whatever the basis of the detention. The detainee must be able to take court proceedings in order to determine whether a detention is unlawful. This is an independent provision: even if it is determined in a particular case by the Commission that the detention was lawful, there could still be a breach of Art 5(4) if no possibility of review of the lawfulness of the detention by the domestic courts arose. The review must be by a court and it must be adequate to test the lawfulness of the detention. This requirement was found not to have been satisfied by judicial review proceedings or by habeas corpus in *Chahal v UK*:[175] neither procedure provided a sufficient basis for challenging a deportation decision.

Art 5(4) also applies to remand prisoners. It was found in *De Jong, Baljet and Van de Brink*[176] that it grants to a person on remand a right of access to a court after the decision (in accordance with Art 5(3)) to detain him or prolong detention has been taken. It also allows access to the files used in coming to the decision on remand.[177]

Compensation

Art 5(5) provides for compensation if the arrest or detention contravenes the other provisions of Art 5.[178] This provision differs from the general right to compensation under Art 50[179] because it exists as an independent right: if a person is found to have been unlawfully arrested under domestic law in the domestic court, but no compensation is available, he or she can apply to the European Court of Human Rights on the basis of the lack of compensation. As far as other Convention rights are concerned, if a violation of a right occurs which is found unlawful by the national courts, but no compensation is granted, the applicant cannot allege breach of the right at Strasbourg.[180]

Article 6: right to a fair and public hearing

(1) In the determination of his civil rights and obligations or of any criminal charge against him, everyone is entitled to a fair and public hearing within a reasonable

---

173 *Wemhoff v Germany* (1968) 1 EHRR 55.
174 *Neumeister v Austria* (1979–80) 1 EHRR 91.
175 (1997) 23 EHRR 413.
176 Judgment of 22 May 1984, A 77, pp 25–26; (1984) 8 EHRR 20.
177 *Lamy v Belgium* (1989) 11 EHRR 529.
178 See the reference to Art 5(5) in HRA, s 9(3).
179 *Huber v Austria* Appl 6821/74, 6 DR 65 (1977).
180 See further Chapter 4, pp 208–11.

time by an independent and impartial tribunal established by law. Judgment shall be pronounced publicly but the press and public may be excluded from all or part of the trial in the interest of morals, public order or national security in a democratic society, where the interest of juveniles or the protection of the private life of the parties so require, or to the extent strictly necessary in the opinion of the court in special circumstances where publicity would prejudice the interests of justice.

The specific safeguards in Art 6(2) and (3) are indicated below. Art 6 is one of the most significant Convention articles and the one which is most frequently found to have been violated. This is partly due to the width of Art 6(1), which may cover numerous circumstances in which rights are affected in the absence of a judicial hearing. This may mean that even where a substantive claim under another article fails, the Art 6(1) claim succeeds because the procedure used in making the determination affecting the applicant was defective.[181] In order to appreciate the way it operates, it is crucial to understand the relationship between paras 1 and 3. Paragraph 1 imports a general requirement of a fair hearing applying to criminal and civil hearings which covers all aspects of a fair hearing. Paragraph 3 lists minimum guarantees of a fair hearing in the criminal context only. If para 3 had been omitted, the guarantees contained in it could have arisen from para 1, but it was included on the basis that it is important to declare a minimum standard for a fair hearing. In practice, then, paras 1 and 3 may often both be in question in respect of a criminal charge.

Since para 3 contains *minimum* guarantees, the para 1 protection of a fair hearing goes beyond para 3. In investigating a fair hearing, the Commission is not confined to the para 3 guarantees; it can consider further requirements of fairness. Thus, if para 1 is not violated, it will be superfluous to consider para 3 and if one of the para 3 guarantees is violated, there will be no need to look at para 1. However, if para 3 is not violated, it will still be worth considering para 1. It follows that although civil hearings are expressly affected only by para 1, the minimum guarantees may also apply to such hearings too.

Article 6(1): fair hearing

Field of application

The term 'criminal charge' has an autonomous Convention meaning. The question of what is meant by 'a criminal charge' has generated quite a lot of case law. 'Charge' has been described as 'the official notification given to an individual by the competent authority of an allegation that he has committed a criminal offence'.[182] The proceedings in question must be *determinative* of the charge. Therefore, proceedings *ancillary* to the determination of the charge do not fall within Art 6.[183]

---

181 E.g., in *Mats Jacobson v Sweden* (1990) 13 EHRR 79, the applicant was prevented from making changes to his property. His substantive claim under Art 1 of Protocol 1 failed, but his Art 6(1) claim succeeded, since he was allowed no adequate access to a court to challenge the prohibition.
182 *Eckle v Germany* (1982) 5 EHRR 1, p 33.
183 See, e.g., *X v UK* (1982) 5 EHRR 273 (appointment of a legal aid lawyer was found to fall outside Art 6).

Offences under criminal law must be distinguished from those arising only under *disciplinary law*. In order to determine whether, whatever the classification of an 'offence' in national law, it should be viewed as criminal in nature, the Court will consider the nature of the offence and the nature and severity of the penalty the person is threatened with.[184] In *Campbell and Fell v UK*,[185] the Court had to consider whether prison discipline could fall within Art 6(1) as the determination of a criminal charge. The applicants, prisoners, were sentenced to a substantial loss of remission. This was such a serious consequence that the procedure in question could be considered as of a criminal character, but the Court considered that not all disciplinary offences in prison which in fact had an equivalent in the ordinary criminal law would be treated as of a criminal character. In general, disciplinary offences will not be viewed as criminal since they are a matter of concern to the particular profession, not a matter regulated by the law in general.[186]

'Regulatory' offences are also, in general, viewed as matters that relate to a specific group rather than to persons in general.[187] But, classification of a petty offence as 'regulatory' rather than criminal will not be decisive for Art 6(1) purposes; Strasbourg may yet determine that the offence is of a criminal character.[188] Otherwise, by reclassifying offences, the state in question could minimise the application of the Convention.

The term 'civil rights and obligations' also has an autonomous Convention meaning and therefore cannot merely be assigned the meaning of 'private' as understood in UK administrative law. Thus, the meaning of 'civil rights and obligations' does not depend upon the legal classification afforded the right or obligation in question by the national legislator; the question is whether the content and effect of the right or obligation (taking into account the legal systems of all the contracting states) allows the meaning 'civil right' or 'civil obligation' to be assigned to it.[189] This wide provision allows challenge to decisions taken in the absence of legal procedures in a disparate range of circumstances.[190] The civil right must have some legal basis as established in the state in question, but assuming that there is such a basis, Art 6 may apply to immunities or procedural constraints preventing the bringing of claims to court.[191]

In *Tinnelly v UK*[192] the Court found that a clearly defined statutory right aimed at freedom from discrimination should be viewed as a civil right. Strasbourg may be moving towards a position in which 'all those rights which are individual rights under the national legal system and fall into the sphere of general freedom . . . must be seen as civil rights'.[193] Clearly, this question remains a problematic one. It is clear that there

---

184   *Campbell and Fell* (1985) 7 EHRR 165; *Garyfallou AEBE v Greece* (1999) 28 EHRR 344, para 33; *Lauko v Slovakia* [1999] EHRLR 105, para 56.

185   *Ibid.*

186   *Wickramsinghe v UK* [1998] EHRLR 338.

187   See *X v UK* (1998) 25 EHRR CD 88.

188   *Öztürk v Germany* (1984) 6 EHRR 409.

189   *Ringeisen v Austria* (1971) 1 EHRR 455.

190   E.g., *O v UK* (1987) 10 EHRR 82 concerned a decision to terminate access to a child in care although no legal procedure was in place allowing consideration of its merits.

191   See *Osman v UK* (1998) 5 BHRC 293; *Fayed v UK* (1994) 18 EHRR 393.

192   (1998) 27 EHRR 249.

193   *Benthem v Netherlands*, Decision of 8 October 1983, A 97, 9, Dissenting opinion of Mr Melcior etc.

must be a dispute between the parties, but the extent to which this is the case is not entirely settled. In *Fayed v UK*[194] it was found that although, strictly, there was no legal basis for the action and so no dispute to trigger Art 6, Art 6 applied to blanket immunities preventing access to a court.

A right of access to a court

Besides the procedural guarantees, Art 6(1) has been found to provide, impliedly, a right of access to a court whether the domestic legal system allows access to a court in a particular case or not. The right is not absolute, but restrictions must not impair the essence of the right.[195] Restrictions must have a legitimate aim and be proportionate to the aim pursued. The test is, therefore, the same as that used in respect of that under para 2 of Articles 8–11.[196] In *Osman v UK*[197] the Court found, controversially, that the immunity of the police from actions in negligence breached this right of access to a court.[198] Other public policy based immunities have subsequently been found not to breach this right,[199] in pursuit of what may arguably be termed a retreat from *Osman*, and not all other constraints will do so.[200]

Once it has been determined that a particular instance falls within Art 6(1), it must be determined whether the claim in question is covered by the right of access to a court. It seems that, for example, Art 6(1) does not confer a right of appeal to a higher court.[201] It may include access to legal advice and, by implication, legal aid. These issues arise in relation both to access to a court hearing and the *fairness* of the hearing. In the very significant decision in *Golder*,[202] it was found that a refusal to allow a detainee to correspond with his legal advisor would be contrary to Art 6(1), since in preventing him even initiating proceedings, it hindered his right of access to a court. In other words, the right of access to a court must be an *effective* one.

Access to legal advice in order to obtain access to a court may not always imply a right to legal aid. The circumstances in which it will do so were considered in *Granger v UK*.[203] The applicant had been refused legal aid and so did not have counsel at appeal; he only had notes from his solicitor which he read out, but clearly did not understand. In particular, there was one especially complex ground of appeal which he was unable to deal with.

194 (1994) 18 EHRR 393.
195 *Tinnelly and McElduff v UK* (1998) 27 EHRR 249; *Fayed v UK* (1994) 18 EHRR 393.
196 See *Fayed v UK* (1994) 18 EHRR 393, para 67. See also below, pp 65–66.
197 (1998) 5 BHRC 293.
198 The decision was severely criticised by Lord Browne-Wilkinson in *Barrett v Enfield London LBC* [1999] 3 All ER 193 on the ground that there was no immunity, but in fact no right to make a claim at all. See also the criticisms of Lord Hoffmann in 'Human rights and the House of Lords' (1999) 62 MLR 159.
199 See *Z and Others v UK* (2002) 34 EHRR 3; the case resulted from a decision of the House of Lords in *X v Bedfordshire CC* [1995] 2 AC 633 that the plaintiff could not bring an action in negligence against the local authority.
200 In *Fayed v UK* (1994) 18 EHRR 393, the Court found that a limitation on the ability of the applicants to take legal proceedings to challenge the findings of a governmental inquiry into the applicants' business affairs did not constitute an unjustified denial of access to a court.
201 *Case relating to Certain aspects of the laws on the use of language in Belgium (No 2)* (1968) 1 EHRR 252 ('Belgian Linguistics case').
202 Judgment of 23 November 1983, A 70.
203 Judgment of 28 March 1990, A 174.

In view of the complexity of the appeal and his inability to deal with it, legal aid should have been granted. It was found that Art 6(1) and Art 6 (3)(c) should be read together and, if it would be apparent to an objective observer that a fair hearing could not take place without legal advice, then both would be violated. *Granger* was concerned with the fairness of the hearing rather than with the ability to obtain access to a court at all. However, in some instances, a person unable to obtain legal aid would be unable to obtain legal advice and therefore might be unable to initiate proceedings. In such instances, access to a court would be the main issue.[204] But, in civil proceedings, legal aid is not fully guaranteed, as it is in Art 6(3); circumstances have been accepted in which legal aid can be denied.[205]

An independent and impartial tribunal established by law

All courts and tribunals falling within Art 6 must meet this requirement. The tribunal must be established by law[206] and be independent of the executive.[207] Factors to be taken into account will include the appointment of its members, their terms of office, and guarantees against outside influence.[208] Impartiality is judged both subjectively and objectively.[209] In other words, actual bias must be shown, but also the existence of guarantees against bias.[210] The decision in *McGonnell v UK*[211] left open the question whether a judge having both legislative and executive functions could be viewed as independent and impartial. In a number of cases against the UK, military discipline as exercised by way of courts martial has not been found to satisfy the requirement of impartiality.[212]

Hearing within a reasonable time

The hearing must take place within a reasonable time. These are the same words as are used in Art 5(3), but here, the point is to put an end to the insecurity of the applicant who is uncertain of the outcome of the civil action or charge against him or her rather than with the deprivation of liberty.[213] Thus, the ending point comes when the uncertainty is resolved either at the court of highest instance or by expiry of the time limit for appeal. In determining what is meant by 'reasonable', fairly wide time limits have been applied so, that in some circumstances, as much as seven or eight[214] years may be reasonable. The Court has approved a period of nearly five years[215] and the Commission a period

---

204 See *Airey v Ireland* (1979) 2 EHRR 305; *Aerts v Belgium* [1998] EHRLR 777.
205 In *Andronicou and Constantinou v Cyprus* (1998) 25 EHRR 491, it was found that *ex gratia* assistance was sufficient.
206 *Zand v Austria* (1978) 15 DR 70 (this means law emanating from Parliament, although aspects of the judicial organisation may be delegated to the executive).
207 *Benthem v Netherlands* (1985) 8 EHRR 1.
208 *Bryan v UK* (1995) 21 EHRR 342.
209 *Fey v Austria* (1993) 16 EHRR 387; *Pullar v UK* (1996) 22 EHRR 391.
210 *Remli v France* (1996) 22 EHRR 253.
211 (2000) 8 BHRC 56.
212 See *Findlay v UK* (1997) 24 EHRR 221; *Hood v UK* (2000) 29 EHRR 365; see also *Coyne v UK* [1997] ECHR 73; *Cable et al v UK*, Appl 24436/94, judgment of 18 Feb 1999.
213 See, generally, Van Dijk, P and Van Hoof, F, *Theory and Practice of the European Convention on Human Rights*, 3rd edn, 1998, pp 446–47.
214 In *Vernillo v France* (1991) 13 EHRR 880, seven and a half years in respect of civil proceedings was not found to be too long owing to the special responsibilities of the parties.
215 *Buchholz v Germany* (1981) 3 EHRR 597.

of seven and a half.[216] It will take into account the conduct of the accused (which may have contributed to the delay) and the need for proper preparation of the case, bearing in mind any special circumstances such as those which might arise in childcare cases. In order to determine how long the delay has been, the point from which time will run must be identified. In criminal cases, it will be 'the stage at which the situation of the person concerned has been substantially affected as a result of a suspicion against him'.[217] In civil cases, it will be the moment when the proceedings concerned are initiated, not including pre-trial negotiations.[218]

Other aspects of fairness

Apart from access to legal advice and the other minimal guarantees of Art 6(3), what other rights are implied by the term a 'fair hearing'? It has been found to connote equality between the parties,[219] and in principle, entails the right of the parties to be present in person,[220] although criminal trial in *absentia* does not automatically violate Art 6: the right can be waived[221] and does not normally extend to appeals.[222] The hearing should be adversarial[223] in the sense that both parties are given an opportunity to comment on all the evidence that is adduced.[224] A refusal to summon a witness may constitute unfairness,[225] as may a failure to disclose evidence.[226] The court must give a reasoned judgment.[227] These and further significant aspects of fairness are discussed further at relevant points in the following chapters, especially Chapter 14.[228]

Article 6(2): the presumption of innocence in criminal cases

Paragraph 2 requires *inter alia* that when carrying out their duties, members of a court should not start with the preconceived idea that the accused has committed the offence charged; the burden of proof is on the prosecution and any doubt should benefit the accused.[229]

---

216 *Haase v Germany*, Report of 12 July 1977, 11 DR 78 (1978).
217 *Neumeister v Austria* (1979–80) 1 EHRR 91.
218 *Lithgow v UK* (1986) 8 EHRR 335.
219 *Neumeister v Austria* (1979–80) 1 EHRR 91; *De Haes and Gijsels v Belgium* (1997) 25 EHRR 1.
220 *Colloza v Italy* (1985) 7 EHRR 516; *Zana v Turkey* (1998) 4 BHRC 242.
221 *Colloza v Italy* n 220 above.
222 *Ekbatani v Sweden* (1988) 13 EHRR 504, *cf Monnell and Morris v UK* (1987) 10 EHRR 205.
223 *Ruiz-Mateos v Spain* (1993) 16 EHRR 505.
224 *Mantovanelli v France* (1997) 24 EHRR 370.
225 *X v Austria* Appl 5362/72, 42 CD 145 (1972).
226 *Edwards v UK* (1992) 15 EHRR 417 (it was found that the hearing in the Court of Appeal remedied this failure). In *Rowe and Davis v UK* (2000) 30 EHRR 1, the failure of the prosecution to make an application to the trial judge to withhold material caused a breach of Art 6. Review of the material later by the Court of Appeal could not remedy the breach.
227 *Hadjianastassiou v Greece* (1992) 16 EHRR 219, para 33.
228 See pp 960–63. Also, for further discussion, see Ashworth, A, 'Article 6 and the fairness of trials' [1999] Crim LR 261.
229 *Barbéra, Messegué and Jabardo v Spain* J (1988) 11 EHRR 360. See also *Salabiaku v France* (1988) 13 EHRR 379.

It follows from the presumption of innocence that the court must base its conviction exclusively on evidence put forward at trial.[230] The expectation that the state bears the burden of establishing guilt requires that the accused should not be expected to provide involuntary assistance by way of a confession. Thus, the presumption of innocence under Art 6(2) is closely linked to the right to freedom from self-incrimination which the Court has found to be covered by the right to a fair hearing under Art 6(1) (*Funke v France*[231]). In *Murray (John) v UK*,[232] on the other hand, the Commission did not find that Art 6(1) had been breached where inferences had been drawn at trial from the applicant's refusal to give evidence. The Court also found no breach of Art 6 due to such drawing of inferences in the particular circumstances of the case, taking into account the fact that 'the right to silence' could not be treated as absolute, the degree of compulsion exerted on the applicant and the weight of the evidence against him.[233] However, the Court did find that Art 6(1) had been breached by the denial of access to a lawyer since such access was essential where there was a likelihood that adverse inferences would be drawn from silence. In *Saunders v UK*[234] the Commission found that the applicant's right to freedom from self-incrimination had been infringed in that he had been forced to answer questions put to him by inspectors investigating a company takeover or risk the imposition of a criminal sanction. The ruling of the Court was to the same effect, taking into account the special compulsive regime in question for Department of Trade and Industry inspections.[235]

Articles 6(3)(a), (b) and (c): time, facilities and legal representation in criminal cases

These sub-paragraphs are closely related due to the word 'facilities' used in sub-para (b). Sub-paragraphs (b) and (c) may often be invoked together: (c) in respect of the assignment of a lawyer, and (b) in respect of the time allowed for such assignment. It is not enough that a lawyer should be assigned; he or she should be appointed in good time in order to give time to prepare the defence and familiarise herself or himself with the case.[236] Both sub-paragraphs also arise in relation to notification of the right of access to legal advice and it has been held that an oral translation of the requisite information is insufficient.[237] As has already been noted in relation to *Granger*, the legal advice provisions must be read in conjunction with the right to a fair trial. A lawyer must be assigned if, otherwise, an objective observer would consider that a fair hearing would not occur. In *Poitrimol v France*[238] the Court stated: 'Although not absolute, the right . . . to be effectively defended by a lawyer, assigned officially if need be, is one of the fundamental features of a fair trial.' In furtherance of the notion of providing effective legal

---

230 *X v Federal Republic of Germany* 17 DR 231 (1980).
231 (1993) 16 EHRR 297.
232 (1996) 22 EHRR 29. For comment, see Munday, R 'Inferences from silence and European human rights law' [1996] Crim LR 370.
233 *Murray (John) v UK* (1996) 22 EHRR 29. See also *Averill v UK* (2001) 31 EHRR 36.
234 Appl 19187/91 Com Rep paras 69–75.
235 *Saunders v UK* (1997) 23 EHRR 313. See further Chapter 13, pp 944–46.
236 *X and Y v Austria*, Appl 7909/74; 15 DR 160 (1979).
237 *Kamasinski v Austria* (1991) 13 EHRR 36 para 138.
238 (1993) 18 EHRR 130.

representation, it has been found that para 6(3)(c) does not merely import a right to have legal assistance, but rather it includes three rights:[239]

(a) to have recourse, if desired, to legal assistance;
(b) to choose that assistance;
(c) if the defendant has insufficient means to pay, for that assistance to be given it free if the interest of justice so require.[240]

Article 6(3)(d): cross-examination in criminal cases

The Strasbourg case law has left a wide discretion to the national court[241] as to the interpretation of the first limb of Art 6(3)(d) – the right to cross-examine witnesses – and so has deprived this right of some of its effect.[242] The second limb – the right to call witnesses and have them examined under the same conditions as witnesses for the other side – obviously allows for a wide discretion as it only requires that the prosecution and defence should be treated equally as regards summoning witnesses.[243]

   Art 6 is considered at various points in this book, and extensively in Chapters 12–15, especially in relation to its impact on pre-trial procedures.

Article 7: freedom from retrospective effect of penal legislation

Article 7 contains an important principle and it is, therefore, non-derogable, although it is subject to the single exception contained in para 2. It divides into two separate principles:

(a) the law in question must have existed at the time of the act in question for the conviction to be based on it;
(b) no heavier penalty for the infringement of the law may be imposed than was in force at the time the act was committed.

As far as the first principle is concerned, this also means that an existing part of the criminal law cannot be applied by analogy to acts it was not intended for.[244] Allowing such extension would fall foul of the general principle that the law must be unambiguous, which is part of the principle that someone should not be convicted if he or she could not have known beforehand that the act in question was criminal. In order to determine whether these requirements have been met, the Strasbourg authorities are prepared to interpret domestic law,[245] although normally they would not be prepared to

---

239 From *Golder v UK* (1975) 1 EHRR 524; see also *Silver v UK* (1983) 5 EHRR 347.
240 *Pakelli v Germany* (1983) 6 EHRR 1.
241 See e.g., *Asch v Austria* (1991) 15 EHRR 597.
242 Such an assertion was made in *Kostovski v Netherlands* (1989) 12 EHRR 434 and *Windisch v Austria* (1990) 13 EHRR 281. However, these decisions were not followed in *Isgro v Italy*, Appl 11339/85, A 194 (1991).
243 *X v Austria*, Appl 4428/70 15 YB 264 (1972).
244 *X v Austria*, Appl 1852/63, 8 YB 190 (1965).
245 *Ibid.*

do so. Article 7 was found to have been breached in *Welch v UK*.[246] Before the trial of the applicant for drug offences, a new provision came into force under the Drug Trafficking Offences Act 1986, making provision for confiscation orders. This was imposed on the applicant, although the legislation was not in force at the time when he committed the offences in question. It clearly had retrospective effect and was found to constitute a 'penalty' within Article 7(1). In *SW v UK* and *C v UK*[247] the applicants claimed that marital rape had been retrospectively outlawed and that, therefore, their criminalisation for forced sexual intercourse with their wives created a breach of Article 7. Their convictions were based on the ruling of the House of Lords in *R*,[248] which removed the marital exemption. The Court found that the anticipated reform of the law undertaken in *R* was almost inevitable and that, therefore, the applicants should have foreseen that their conduct would be found to be criminal. Thus, no breach of Article 7 was found.

General restrictions on the rights and freedoms contained in Articles 8–11

These Articles have a second paragraph enumerating certain restrictions on the primary right. The interests covered by the restrictions are largely the same: national security, protection of morals, the rights of others, public safety. As indicated below, the state is allowed a 'margin of appreciation' – a degree of discretion – as to the measures needed to protect the particular interest.[249]

To be justified under the second para, state interference with Articles 8–11 guarantees must be prescribed by law, have a legitimate aim, be necessary in a democratic society and be applied in a non-discriminatory fashion. In most cases under these articles, Strasbourg's main concern has been with the 'necessary in a democratic society' requirement; the notion of 'prescribed by law' has been focused upon to some extent, but always with the result that it has been found to be satisfied. The 'legitimate aim' requirement will normally be readily satisfied; as Harris, O'Boyle and Warbrick point out, the grounds for interference are so wide that 'the state can usually make a plausible case that it did have a good reason for interfering with the right'.[250] The provision against non-discrimination arises under Art 14 and it is potentially very significant.[251]

The 'prescribed by law' requirement means that the restriction must be in accordance with a rule of national law which satisfies the Convention meaning of 'law'. Also, the law on which the restriction is based is aimed at protecting one of the interests listed in para 2; in other words, the restriction falls within one of the exceptions. Interpreting 'prescribed by law' in *Sunday Times v UK*,[252] the European Court of Human Rights found that 'the law must be adequately accessible' and 'a norm cannot be regarded as

---

246 (1995) 20 EHRR 247.
247 (1995) 21 EHRR 404.
248 [1991] 3 WLR 767.
249 See pp 95–98.
250 See Harris, D, O'Boyle, K and Warbrick, C, *Law of the European Convention on Human Rights*, 1995, Butterworths, p 290.
251 See pp 93–94.
252 (1980) 2 EHRR 245.

a "law" unless it is formulated with sufficient precision to enable the citizen to regulate his conduct'. In *Steel and Others v UK*[253] the Commission introduced a very significant qualification: 'The level of precision required depends to a considerable degree on the content of the instrument, the field it is designed to cover, and the number and status of those to whom it is addressed.'[254] Although the term 'margin of appreciation' was not used, this finding appears to allow the member state a certain leeway in relation to the 'prescribed by law' requirement.

The Court has interpreted 'necessary in a democratic society' as meaning that: 'an interference corresponds to a pressing social need and, in particular, that it is proportionate to the legitimate aim pursued'.[255] Thus, in the particular instance, it can be said that the interference is necessary in the sense that it is concerned with a particular restriction such as the protection of morals, and in the particular case, there is a real need to protect morals – a pressing social need – as opposed to an unclear or weak danger to morals. Further, the interference is in proportion to the aim pursued; in other words, it does not go further than is needed, bearing in mind the objective in question.

But the doctrine of proportionality is strongly linked to the principle of the margin of appreciation: the Court has stated that the role of the Convention in protecting human rights is subsidiary to the role of the national legal system[256] and that since the state is better placed than the international judge to balance individual rights against general societal interests, Strasbourg will operate a restrained review of the balance struck. The notion of a margin of appreciation conceded to states permeates the Arts 8(2), 9(2), 10(2) and 11(2) jurisprudence, although it has not influenced the interpretation of the substantive rights.

Article 8: right to respect for 'privacy'

(1) Everyone has the right to respect for his private and family life, his home and his correspondence.
(2) There shall be no interference by a public authority with the exercise of this right except such as is in accordance with the law and is necessary in a democratic society in the interests of national security, public safety or the economic well-being of the country, for the prevention of disorder or crime, for the protection of health or morals, or for the protection of the rights and freedoms of others.

Art 8 covers four different areas, suggesting that, for example, private life can be distinguished from family life. The inclusion of the wide (and undefined) term 'private' means that rights other than those arising from the home, family life and correspondence may fall within Art 8. It should be noted that Art 8 only provides a right to *respect* for private life, etc. Thus, the extent of the respect required can vary to an extent in view of the various practices in the different states. In contrast to Art 10, finding that a

253 (1998) 28 EHRR 603.
254 Para 145. The Commission based these findings on the judgments of the Court in *Chorherr v Austria* (1994) 17 EHRR 358, para 23 and in *Cantoni v France* (1996) 96 ECHR 52, para 35.
255 *Olsson v Sweden* (1989) 11 EHRR 259 para 67.
256 *Handyside v UK* (1976) 1 EHRR 737 para 48.

claim is covered by para 1 is not a simple matter: attention cannot merely focus on the exceptions. The negative obligation – to refrain from interference – is central,[257] but a number of requirements to take positive action have been accommodated within Art 8. Clayton and Tomlinson posit a number of different forms of such positive action.[258] The first arises where the applicant suffers from state inaction.[259] In *McGinley and Egan v UK*[260] the government was engaging in activities inherently dangerous to the health of the applicant. It was found that Art 8 requires that effective procedures should be in place to ensure that all the relevant information was made available.

A wide range of issues may be accommodated within the right to respect for private life. Other Convention guarantees, particularly those of Article 3, may also be relevant. The right to respect for family life, as the discussion below indicates, is a narrower concept, with which the right to respect for private life overlaps. The European Court of Human Rights has clearly recognised that private life covers individual, personal choices: *Dudgeon v UK*.[261] Equally, respect for family life covers freedom of parental choice,[262] within limits created by the opposing interests of the child.[263] Thus, the interest of individuals in exercising freedom of choice in decisions as to the disposal of or control over the body may be protected. Usually the individual is, in effect, asking the state to leave him or her alone to make such decisions in order to preserve autonomy. This is a negative obligation which is clearly within the scope of Art 8 where the interference can be viewed as arbitrary.[264]

In some instances, however, the individual will be requiring the assistance of the authorities in ensuring that he or she is able to exercise autonomy. The scope for the acceptance of positive obligations as an aspect of respect for private or family life is less wide. But the European Court has characterised claims that the state is under an obligation to provide such assistance as necessary in order to demonstrate respect for private or family life.[265] In other words, the state may be obliged to provide legal protection for the individual even when the public authorities are not themselves responsible for an interference with the Art 8 right, although given that the state merely has to show 'respect', its discretion in determining the means of so doing tends to be increased.[266]

---

257 See, e.g., *Gul v Switzerland* (1996) 22 EHRR 93, para 38.
258 Clayton, R and Tomlinson, H, *The Law of Human Rights*, 2000, OUP, pp 822–24.
259 The transsexual cases in which applicants have argued that they should be allowed to have their birth certificates changed to indicate their current gender provide an example; those against the UK failed until *Goodwin v UK* in 2002, discussed below. The finding of a breach in *B v France* (1992) 16 EHRR 1 occurred since the Court took into account the fact that the applicant was likely to be asked to reveal her birth certificate more often than in the UK.
260 (1998) 27 EHRR 1.
261 (1982) 4 EHRR 149.
262 See *Hoffman v Austria* (1993) 17 EHRR 293; *X v Netherlands* (1974) 2 DR 118.
263 See *Rieme v Sweden* (1992) 16 EHRR 155.
264 See *Case relating to certain aspects of the laws on the use of language in Belgium (No 2)* (1968) 1 EHRR 252 ('Belgian Linguistics case'), para 7; *X and Y v Netherlands* (1985) 8 EHRR 235; *Hokkanen v Finland* (1994) 19 EHRR 139.
265 *X v UK*, Appl 7154/75; 14 DR 31, 32 (1978); *Marckx v Belgium* (1979) 2 EHRR 330, para 31. See also Chapter 10, pp 695 *et seq*.
266 See *JS v UK*, Appl No 191173/91, decision of 3 January 1993. The Commission rejected an application in which it was alleged that an insurance company had carried out a clandestine surveillance in investigating a claim.

Where a positive obligation is claimed, Strasbourg will afford a wide margin of appreciation. The margin can widen or narrow depending on the circumstances of the case, resulting in a variation of the intensity of the Court's review of the state's actions. Two further factors may also be present in this context and may influence Strasbourg in conceding a particularly wide margin of appreciation where a complainant seeks to lay a positive obligation on the state. First, where the harm complained of flows from the action of a private party, rather than the state itself, so that the so-called 'horizontal effect' of the Convention is in issue and, second, where there is a potential conflict with another Convention right. Clearly, these factors may arise independently of each other. In a number of key decisions under Art 8 discussed in Chapter 10, all three were present,[267] which may explain the somewhat unsatisfactory and misleading nature of some of the judgments given, although as Chapter 10 makes clear, a change of stance became evident some years ago.[268] These factors may also arise in this context and may explain the cautious nature of certain of the decisions.

Thus the state may be found to be under a duty to act positively to prevent an interference with the Art 8 guarantees by another private individual. The pollution cases mentioned below[269] provide examples in which it was found that the state had a duty to act to prevent or curb the pollution and to ensure that information regarding the dangers was available. Further, the positive obligation may require a positive act by private persons.[270]

The question of the extent to which positive obligations are recognised under Art 8 is pursued further in this book, especially in Chapter 10.[271] But clearly, there will be limitations. In *Botta v Italy*[272] it was found that although a positive obligation might arise in the circumstances, a fair balance had to be struck: the obligations did not extend to providing a disabled person with access to the beach and sea distant from a holiday residence. In *Barreto v Portugal*[273] no breach was found where each family was not provided with its own home or where a landlord could not recover the possession of rented accommodation.

Exceptions and justification under Art 8(2)

There must be an 'interference' by the public authorities with private life etc. But, as the discussion above indicates, this can include the failure to carry out a positive obligation. In the absence of a positive obligation, however, a failure to act would not constitute

---

267 All three were present in: *Winer v UK* (1986) 48 IR 154; *Spencer v UK* (1998) 25 EHRR CD 105, and *N v Portugal*, Appl 20683/92, Judgment of 20 February 1995; however, the third was influential only in *Winer*.
268 See *Von Hannover v Germany* (2005) 40 EHRR 1.
269 See the cases of *Guerra v Italy* (1998) 26 EHRR 375 and *Lopez Ostra v Spain* (1994) 20 EHRR 277.
270 In *Hokkanen v Finland* (1994) 19 EHRLR 139, it was found that a private data collection firm must grant access to its records.
271 See pp 695–99.
272 (1998) 26 EHRR 241.
273 (1996) 26 EHRLR 214.

an interference.[274] Where an interference occurs, proper safeguards must be in place to protect individuals from arbitrary interference; there must be a legal framework that satisfies the 'in accordance with the law' test and strict limits must be placed on the power conferred.[275] Where very intimate aspects of private life are involved, very particular reasons for the interference must be adduced.[276]

If the exception in respect of national security is invoked, the state may find that it is relatively easy to justify the interference.[277] But where interferences, such as searches or surveillance, occur in respect of criminal activity, a higher standard will be required. Thus, judicial authorisation of searches or surveillance may be required.[278] Where a grave invasion of privacy has occurred, judicial authorisation and a warrant may not be enough.[279] This matter is pursued in Chapter 11.[280]

The head 'the economic well-being of the country' is unusual; it does not appear in para 2 of Art 8's companion articles, Articles 9–11. A number of interferences have been found to be justified under this head.[281] In *MS v Sweden*[282] the obtaining of access to medical records in order to assess a social security claim was found to be justified.

Justification under the heads 'for the prevention of disorder or crime' depends on the seriousness of the crime or threat to disorder, the nature and extent of the interference and the question whether a judicial warrant has been obtained. In *Camenzind*[283] the limited scope of the search and the procedures in place meant that the search was proportionate to the aim of preventing crime. In *Murray v UK*[284] the entry and search of Mrs Murray's home was not disproportionate to that aim, bearing in mind her links to terrorism.

In contrast to the stance taken under Art 10(2),[285] the exception for the protection of morals has received a restrictive interpretation. The Court has required an especially significant justification in order to be satisfied as to proportionality.[286] This exception is sometimes also raised where the exception in respect of the rights of others is invoked especially in relation to family life, where the protection of health may also be in issue. For example, in *Olsson v Sweden*,[287] the decision to take three children into care was an interference with family life. However, it could be justified as being for the protection of the health and the rights of the children.

---

274 *Airey v Ireland* (1979) 2 EHRR 305.
275 *Camenzind v Switzerland* (1999) 28 EHRR 458.
276 *Lustig-Prean v UK* (1999) 7 BHRC 65; *Smith and Grady v UK* (2000) 29 EHRLR 493.
277 See *Leander v Sweden* (1987) 9 EHRR 433.
278 *Funke v France* (1993) 16 EHRR 297.
279 *Niemietz v Germany* (1992) 16 EHRR 97.
280 See pp 793–98.
281 E.g., *Powell v UK* (1990) 12 EHRR 355.
282 (1999) 28 EHRR 313.
283 *Camenzind v Switzerland* (1999) 28 EHRR 458.
284 (1994) 19 EHRR 193.
285 See Chapter 7, pp 403–07.
286 See *Norris v Ireland* (1988) 13 EHRR 186 and *Dudgeon v UK* (1981) 4 EHRR 149.
287 (1988) 11 EHRR 259.

The concept of respect for private life

In *Niemietz v Germany*,[288] the Court said:

> It would be too restrictive to limit the notion [of private life] to an 'inner circle' in which the individual may live his own personal life as he chooses and to exclude therefrom entirely the outside world not encompassed within that circle. Respect for private life must also comprise to a certain degree the right to establish and develop relationships with other human beings.

As Harris, O'Boyle and Warbrick observe: 'this extends the concept of private life beyond the narrower confines of the Anglo-American idea of privacy, with its emphasis on the secrecy of personal information and seclusion'.[289] Thus, 'private life' appears to encompass a widening range of protected interests, but this development has been accompanied by a reluctance of the Court to insist on a narrow margin of appreciation when considering what is demanded of states by the notions of 'respect' for private life and by the necessity of interferences with privacy.

Privacy of personal information

Respect for the privacy of personal information clearly falls within the notion of private life, but the Court has approached this aspect cautiously, tending to be satisfied if a procedure is in place allowing the interest in such control to be weighed up against a competing interest. Thus, in *Gaskin v UK*,[290] the interest of the applicant in obtaining access to the files relating to his childhood in care had to be weighed up against the interest of the contributors to it in maintaining confidentiality, because this interference with privacy had a legitimate aim under the 'rights of others' exception. It was held that the responsible authority did not have a procedure available for weighing the two. Consequently, the procedure automatically preferred the contributors and that was disproportionate to the aim of protecting confidentiality and therefore could not be 'necessary in a democratic society'.

The opposite result was reached, but by a similar route, in *Klass v Federal Republic of Germany*,[291] brought in respect of telephone tapping. It was found that although telephone tapping constituted an interference with a person's private life, it could be justified as being in the interests of national security and there were sufficient controls in place (permission had to be given by a minister applying certain criteria including that of 'reasonable suspicion') to ensure that the power was not abused. In the similar *Malone* case,[292] however, there were no such controls in place and a breach of Art 8 was therefore found, which led to the introduction of the Interception of Communications Act 1985. A similar path was followed in *Leander v Sweden*[293] in respect of a complaint

---

288 (1992) 16 EHRR 97.
289 Harris, D, O'Boyle, K and Warbrick, C, *Law of the European Convention on Human Rights*, 1995, Butterworths, p 304.
290 (1990) 12 EHRR 36.
291 (1978) 2 EHRR 214; see also *Ludi v Switzerland* (1993) 15 EHRR 173.
292 (1984) 7 EHRR 14.
293 (1987) 9 EHRR 443. See also to similar effect *Ebchester v UK* (1993) 18 EHRR CD 72.

that information about the applicant had been stored on a secret police register for national security purposes and released to the navy so that it could vet persons who might be subversive. The applicant complained that he had had no opportunity of challenging the information, but the Court found that as there were remedies in place, albeit of a limited nature, to address such grievances, Art 8 had not been breached because the national security exception could apply. Again, in *Harman and Hewitt v UK*[294] a breach of Art 8 was found as there was no means of challenging the secret directive which had allowed the storage of information on the applicants. In *Murray v UK*,[295] the taking of a photo of the applicant after arrest at an army centre was found to constitute an interference with her Art 8 right to respect for her private life. The notion that personal information should remain private even outside obviously private spaces was strongly indicated in *Niemietz v Germany*.[296]

Bodily integrity and autonomy

Under Art 8, bodily privacy has a number of aspects. The European Court of Human Rights adopted a broad definition of privacy in *X and Y v Netherlands*:[297]

> [the concept of] private life . . . covers the physical integrity . . . of the person . . . Art 8 does not merely compel the State to abstain from . . . interference [with the individual]: in addition to this primarily negative undertaking, there may be positive obligations inherent in effective respect for private . . . life.[298]

Thus, Art 8 recognises that individuals have an interest in preventing or controlling physical intrusions on the body and they may therefore lay claim to a negative right to be 'left alone' in a physical sense. Such a right might also encompass positive claims on the state to ensure that bodily integrity is not infringed. Thus, the state may fail to respect privacy if it fails to prevent infringement of it by others or if in itself it allows such infringement.

Interference with bodily integrity may breach the guarantee of freedom from degrading punishment under Article 3 ECHR and the guarantee of respect for privacy under Art 8. In general, any compulsory physical treatment of an individual will constitute an interference with respect for private life.[299] We will return below to the question as to the level of consensual bodily harm which will be forbidden.

Certain forms of physical punishment may be seen as an unjustified intrusion into bodily integrity. Corporal punishment was outlawed in UK state schools[300] after the decision of the European Court of Human Rights in *Campbell and Cosans v UK*,[301] which was determined not on the basis of Articles 3 or 8 but under Article 2 of the First

---

294 (1992) 14 EHRR 657.
295 (1994) 19 EHRR 193; *cf Friedl v Austria* (1995) 21 EHRR 83.
296 (1992) 16 EHRR 97. The case concerned a search of a lawyer's office.
297 (1985) 8 EHRR 235.
298 *Ibid*, paras 22 and 23.
299 *X v Austria* 18 DR 154 (1979).
300 Under the Education (No 2) Act 1986.
301 (1984) 2 EHRR 293.

Protocol, which protects the right of parents to have their children educated according to their own philosophical convictions. However, corporal punishment in private schools was not outlawed, and in *Costello-Roberts v UK*[302] the European Court of Human Rights found that the UK had a responsibility to ensure that school discipline was compatible with the Convention even though the treatment in question was administered in an institution independent of the state. However, although the Court considered that there might be circumstances in which Art 8 could be regarded as affording protection to physical integrity, which would be broader than that afforded by Article 3, in the particular circumstances the adverse effect on the complainant was insufficient to amount to an invasion of privacy. The Court took into account the 'public' context in which the punishment had occurred and its relatively trivial nature. Corporal punishment in both private and public sector schools was abolished in the UK.[303]

Parents or persons with parental responsibility may also use force to discipline a child. In *A v UK*[304] the applicant was a nine-year-old who had been beaten by his stepfather with a garden cane. The stepfather was acquitted of assault causing bodily harm after the jury were instructed that the crime did not include reasonable chastisement by a parent. It was found that the beating fell within Article 3 and that it was incumbent on states to take measures to ensure that individuals within their jurisdiction are not subject to Article 3 treatment. Had the beating been less severe, a breach of Art 8 rather than Article 3 might have been found. It is clear that, by definition, beating amounting to Article 3 treatment cannot be viewed as reasonable and therefore, in future, the defence of reasonable chastisement could not cover the degree of force used in *A*.

Under Art 8, physical intrusions on the bodily integrity of individuals by state agents may be justified if the requirements of Art 8(2) are satisfied. Equally, UK law also recognises a need to create a balance between the interest of the state in allowing physical interference with individuals for various purposes, including the prevention of crime and the interest of the individual in preserving his or her bodily integrity. UK law determines that, in certain circumstances, bodily privacy may give way to other interests. Articles 3 and 8 together provide substantive guarantees against certain types of custodial ill-treatment. But, clearly, Article 3 will cover only the grossest instances of ill-treatment. It is notable that the Convention contains no provision equivalent to that under Art 10 of the International Covenant on Civil and Political Rights which provides 'persons deprived of their liberty shall be treated with humanity and with respect for the inherent dignity of the human person'.

In the *Greek* case,[305] the conditions of detention were found to amount to inhuman treatment due to overcrowding, inadequate food, sleeping arrangements, heating, toilets and provision for external contacts. Failure to obtain medical treatment after a forcible arrest was found to infringe Article 3 in *Hurtado v Switzerland*.[306] Conduct that grossly humiliates is degrading treatment contrary to Article 3.[307] Art 8 may be viewed

---

302 (1993) 19 EHRR 112; A 247–C.
303 Education Act 1996, s 548, as substituted by School Standards and Framework Act 1998, s 131.
304 (1999) 27 EHRR 611.
305 12 YB 1 (1969).
306 A 280-A (1994) Com Rep.
307 *Greece v Netherlands* (1969) 12 YB 1.

as overlapping, to an extent, with Article 3, but it also covers some matters which would not be serious enough to amount to Article 3 treatment.[308] In order to bring Art 8 into play, it must be found that its protection extends to the matter in question – in this context, it would probably be that 'private or family life' is affected.[309] Certain conditions or incidents of detention may fall outside Art 8, such as a failure to provide an interpreter. But a failure to allow a juvenile or a mentally disturbed person to consult privately with a member of his or her family, acting as an appropriate adult, might be viewed as an interference with either private or family life.

Personal autonomy has been recognised for some time in the USA as strongly linked to privacy. In *Doe v Bolton*,[310] Douglas J said that 'the right to privacy means freedom of choice in the basic decisions of one's life respecting marriage, divorce, procreation, contraception, education and upbringing of children'. At Strasbourg, the value of personal autonomy has also received quite clear recognition.[311] Personal autonomy connotes an interest not only in preventing physical intrusion by others, but also with the extent to which the law allows an individual a degree of control over his or her own body.

Sexual autonomy

Protection for personal information may be regarded as part of the 'core' of the concept of respect for private life, but as the Court has made clear in a number of decisions, aspects of relations with others will also fall within the concept. The Court has made it clear that the choice to have sexual relations with others falls within Art 8. In this sphere, it is suggested that the Court has gradually abandoned its initially cautious approach. In *Dudgeon*,[312] the Northern Ireland prohibition of homosexual intercourse was found to breach Art 8: however, this case concerned a gross interference with privacy since it allowed the applicant no means at all of expressing his sexual preference without committing a criminal offence. In 1984,[313] the Commission declared inadmissible an application challenging s 66 of the Army Act 1955, which governs conviction for homosexual practices in the armed forces, on the basis that it could be justified under the prevention of disorder or protection of morals clauses.[314] That stance has now been

---

308 See the findings in the corporal punishment case of *Costello-Roberts v UK* (1993) 19 EHRR 112 (above). The Court found that the treatment was not severe enough to fall within Art 3; in the particular circumstances it did not fall within Art 8, but the Court considered that there might be circumstances in which Art 8 could be viewed as affording a wider protection to physical integrity than that which is afforded by Art 3.

309 Code of Practice A made under the Police and Criminal Evidence Act 1984 (PACE), provides safeguards for a search by police officers of more than outer clothing which appear to be coterminous with the right to respect for private life under Art 8. There are also Code provisions protecting persons during intimate and strip searches. The domestic relationship between Code provisions and Art 8 is discussed in Chapter 12, pp 837, 903.

310 (1973) 410 US 179; (1973) 35 L E 2d 201.

311 *Dudgeon v UK* (1982) 4 EHRR 149; *Lustig-Prean v UK* (1999) 7 BHRC 65. For discussion, see Feldman, *op cit*, fn 1.

312 (1982) 4 EHRR 149.

313 *B v UK* (1983) 6 EHRR 354.

314 The charges had involved a soldier under 21. Note that the Select Committee on the Armed Forces Bill 1990–91 had recommended that s 66 should be replaced (para 41, p xiv). See, now, *Smith and Grady v UK* (2000) 29 EHRR 493 in which it was found that the ban breached Art 8.

abandoned, and the Court has taken a much more interventionist stance in relation to the sexual autonomy of homosexuals.[315]

Dudgeon v UK[316] concerned the law in Northern Ireland (Offences Against the Person Act 1861), which made buggery between consenting males of any age a crime. Dudgeon, who was suspected of homosexual activities, was arrested on that basis and questioned, but the police decided not to prosecute. He applied to the European Commission on the grounds of a breach of the right of respect for private life under Art 8. The European Court of Human Rights held that the legislation in question constituted a continuing interference with his private life, which included his sexual life. He was forced either to abstain from sexual relations completely, or to commit a crime. Clearly, there had been an interference with his private life; the question was whether the interference was necessary in order to protect morals. The Court considered that some regulation of homosexual activity was acceptable; the question was what was necessary in a democratic society. The Court took into account the doctrine of the margin of appreciation, as considered in the *Handyside* case,[317] where it was held that state authorities were in the best position to judge the requirements of morals. However, the Court found that the instant case concerned a very intimate aspect of private life. A restriction on a Convention right cannot be regarded as necessary unless it is proportionate to the aim pursued. In the instant case, there was a grave detrimental interference with the applicant's private life while, on the other hand, there was little evidence of damage to morals. The law had not been enforced and no evidence had been adduced to show that this had been harmful to moral standards. So the aim of the restriction was not proportional to the damage done to the applicant's privacy and, therefore, the invasion of privacy went beyond what was needed. It was found unnecessary since the prohibition had not in fact been used in recent times and no detriment to morals had apparently resulted. Northern Ireland amended the relevant legislation in consequence,[318] allowing intercourse between consenting males over 21. *Dudgeon* demonstrates that the European Court of Human Rights is prepared to uphold the right of the individual to choose to indulge in homosexual practices[319] and suggests that the term 'private life' in Art 8 may be used to cover a wide range of situations where bodily or sexual privacy is in question.

In the UK s 143 of the Criminal Justice and Public Order Act 1994 amended s 1 of the Sexual Offences Act 1967 to lower the age of consent for homosexual intercourse to 18. The differential ages of consent under s 143 continued to allow discrimination between homosexuals and heterosexuals and between male and female homosexuals. In *Sutherland v UK*[320] s 143 of the 1994 Act was successfully challenged under Art 8 in conjunction with Art 14 on the basis that it allowed discrimination between male and

---

315 See Chapter 12, p 903, n 319, and *Sutherland v UK* [1997] EHRLR 117, in which an application regarding the age of consent for homosexual relations (8.9.1999) was postponed since the government assured the Commission that the Sexual Offences (Amendment) Bill would proceed, equalising the age of consent (see, now, Sexual Offences (Amendment) Act 2000, s 1).

316 (1982) 4 EHRR 149.

317 (1976) 1 EHRR 737.

318 Homosexual Offences (Northern Ireland) Order 1982. See also *Norris v Ireland* (1991) 13 EHRR 186, which followed *Dudgeon v UK* (1982) 4 EHRR 149.

319 *Cf* the stance of the US Supreme Court in *Bowers v Hardwick* (1986) 478 US 186; for comment see (1988) 138 NLJ 831.

320 [1997] EHRLR 117.

female homosexuals, since the age of consent for female homosexual intercourse was 16. The Commission found by 14 votes to four that the fixing of a minimum age of consent at 18 as opposed to 16 was a violation of Art 8 and was discriminatory treatment under Art 14. It took into account the fact that many other states have equalised the ages of consent for homosexual and heterosexual acts and further found that the interference could not be justified on the grounds, including that of protecting public morality, put forward under Art 8(2). It appeared that the European Court of Human Rights was prepared to reconsider its remarks on the point in *Dudgeon* since, as indicated above, it tends to take the view that in sensitive matters of this nature, it should hold back until a clear European consensus on the matter is apparent; at the stage when a trend is clear, but no such standard has emerged, it will tend to invoke the margin of appreciation.[321] Given the changes in the law on this matter in the different member states, it seemed that such a standard was emerging regarding equalisation of the ages of consent. The decision was postponed when the government assured the Commission that the Sexual Offences (Amendment) Bill would proceed with equalising the age of consent.[322] This was eventually achieved under s 1 of the Sexual Offences (Amendment) Act 2000; the government had to use the Parliament Act 1911 (as amended) procedure in order to pass the Bill against the opposition of the House of Lords.

Despite these changes, the law governing the sexual freedom of homosexuals was still not in accord with Art 8 due to the restrictions on homosexual intercourse which did not apply to heterosexuals.[323] In particular, the law had to be changed so as to allow consenting homosexual intercourse in private between more than two men as a result of the '*Bolton Seven*' case brought against the UK.[324] The applicants were prosecuted in 1998 on the basis of a video which showed them engaging in consensual group sex. They were convicted of gross indecency. One of the men, Williams, and another, Connell, admitted to having had sex with one of the other five who was, at the time, six months under 18, the then age of consent. Williams was convicted of buggery, although his suspended sentence was later revoked by the Court of Appeal. At the time of the convictions, the Court was warned that the prosecutions breached Art 8. Five of the men applied to the European Court of Human Rights and, in July 2001, in order to avoid defeat in the Court, the government offered each of them compensation in an out-of-court settlement. The Sexual Offence Act 2003 brought about equalisation of the position. By these incremental steps, legal acceptance of the sexual autonomy of homosexuals was brought about, in the sense of achieving equality with heterosexuals.

In the case of *Brown*,[325] the House of Lords found that a person cannot consent to the infliction of harm amounting to actual bodily harm. However, consent to such harm may negate liability if there is good reason for the harm to be caused. There are a number of activities involving the causing of, or the risk of, consensual harm which

---

321 See discussion on this point in relation to transsexuals, below, pp 77–79.
322 On 8 September 1999.
323 See further Chapter 7, pp 459–61. For discussion, see Wintemute, R, *Sexual Orientation and Human Rights*, 1995, Clarendon, Chapter 4.
324 *ADT v UK* (2000) 2 FLR 697; see the *Guardian*, 27 July 2001.
325 [1993] 2 WLR 556; for comment, see Bix, B, 'Assault sadomasochism and consent' (1993) 109 LQR 540; Bibbings, L and Aldridge, P, 'Sexual expression, body alteration and the defence of consent' (1994) 20(3) JLS 356.

have been found to be justified as in the public interest. In *Brown*, a group of sado-masochistic homosexuals had regularly over a period of ten years willingly participated in acts of violence against each other for the sexual pleasure engendered in the giving and receiving of pain. They were charged with causing actual bodily harm contrary to s 47 and with wounding contrary to s 20 of the Offences Against the Person Act 1861 and were convicted. The convictions were upheld by the Court of Appeal which certified the following point of law of general public importance:

> Where A wounds or assaults B occasioning him actual bodily harm in the course
> of a sado-masochistic encounter, does the prosecution have to prove lack of con-
> sent on the part of B before they can establish A's guilt under s 20 and s 47 of the
> Offences Against the Person Act 1861.

The House of Lords, by a majority of three to two, answered this question in the neg-ative, finding, therefore, that consent could operate only as a defence and would be allowed so to operate only where the public interest would thereby be served. It was found that in a sado-masochistic context, the inflicting of injuries amounting to actual bodily harm could not fall within the category of 'good reason' and therefore, despite the consent of all the participants, the convictions of the defendants were upheld.

The judgments of the majority in the House of Lords are couched in terms which suggest that distaste for the activities in question was a significant influencing factor. Lord Mustill, in the minority in the House of Lords, considered each of the grounds considered by the majority to be in favour of criminalising the activities in question and discounted each of them. These included fear of the spread of AIDS and the possibility that things might get out of hand if activities such as these were allowed. AIDS, as Lord Mustill pointed out, may be spread by consensual buggery, which is legal, rather than by the activities in question. If a person consents to a lesser harm than that which is actually inflicted, the existing law could be used to punish the perpetrator.

Three of the men who were convicted in *Brown* applied to the European Commis-sion on Human Rights, arguing that their convictions were in breach of Art 8 of the Convention,[326] since they constituted an interference with their private life. The Com-mission found that no violation of Art 8 had occurred and referred the case to the Court, which came to the same conclusion: *Laskey, Jaggard and Brown v UK*.[327] The Court considered that the activities in question could be seen as occurring outside the private sphere: many persons were involved and videos had been taken. However, as the issue of privacy was not in dispute, the Court accepted that an interference with respect for the applicants' private life had occurred.

The question was whether the interference was necessary in a democratic society under Art 8(2). The Court found that the harm was serious, since it concerned genital torture. The state is entitled to regulate the infliction of physical harm, and the level of harm to be tolerated by the state where the victim consents is in the first instance a mat-ter for the state concerned. The activities had the potential to cause harm in the sense that, if encouraged, harm, including the spread of AIDS, might occur in future. Was

---

326   *Laskey, Jaggard and Brown v UK* (1997) 24 EHRR 39.
327   (1997) 24 EHRR 39.

the interference proportionate to the aim pursued? Numerous charges could have been preferred, but only a few were selected. The level of sentencing reflected the perception that the activities were rendered less serious by the consent of the 'victims'. The Court, therefore, found that the state had not overstepped its margin of appreciation, taking into account the need for regulation of such harm and the proportionate response of the authorities. Thus, no violation of Art 8 was found. The partly dissenting judgment of Judge Pettiti is of interest. He reasoned that the case did not fall within Art 8 at all, since Art 8 provides protection for a person's intimacy and dignity, not for a person's baseness or criminal immorality. The wording of this judgment echoes the wording of parts of the majority judgments of the House of Lords in allowing distaste and lack of sympathy for the activities in question to have some bearing.

The judgment of the Court reflects, it is suggested, the tendency of the operation of the margin of appreciation to dilute the Convention standards. As suggested elsewhere in this book,[328] a strong justification for trusting human rights and freedoms to the judicial as opposed to the democratic process is that the interests of minorities (including sexual minorities) may thereby be safeguarded, whereas, if they were at the mercy of majoritarianism, they might be at risk. However, this judgment lends credibility to the arguments of those who view the Convention as ineffective as a protector of minorities who stray too far from conventional forms of sexual expression, even where all involved are consenting adults. Clearly, if a similar prosecution is brought in future, Art 8 arguments might be raised with more success, bearing in mind the fact that the margin of appreciation doctrine has no application in domestic law.

Sexual identity

UK law did not give full expression to the fundamental interest of individuals in determining their own identity. This significant aspect of private life arose in a number of cases brought under the European Convention on Human Rights against the UK by transsexuals. In *Rees v UK*[329] the applicant, who was born a woman but had had a gender re-assignment operation, complained that he could not have his birth certificate altered to record his new sex, thereby causing him difficulty in applying for employment. However, the Court refused to find a breach of Art 8, because it was reluctant to accept the claim that the UK was under a positive obligation to change its procedures in order to recognise the applicant's identity for social purposes. It followed a similar route in *Cossey v UK*,[330] although it did consider whether it should depart from its judgment in *Rees* in order to ensure that the Convention might reflect societal changes. However, it decided not to do so because developments in this area in the member states were not consistent and still reflected a diversity of practices. In *B v France*[331] it was found that although there had been development in the area, no broad consensus among member states had emerged. Nevertheless, the civil position of the applicant in terms of her

---

328 See Chapter 1, pp 24–25.
329 (1986) 9 EHRR 56.
330 (1990) 13 EHRR 622. A similar application also failed in *Sheffield and Horsham v UK* (1999) 27 EHRR 163.
331 (1992) 13 HRLJ 358; for comment, see Milns, S, 'Transsexuality and the European Court of Human Rights' [1992] PL 559.

sexual identity was worse than that of transsexuals in the UK and, on that basis, a breach of Art 8 could be found.

In *Goodwin v UK*[332] the Court finally took the step of affording that full recognition to the status of transsexuals under Art 8. In *Goodwin* the applicant complained about the lack of legal recognition of her post-operative sex and about the legal status of transsexuals in the United Kingdom. She complained, in particular, about her treatment in relation to employment, social security and pensions and her inability to marry. She relied on Articles 8, 12, 13 and 14 of the Convention. The Court found under Art 8 that although the applicant had undergone gender re-assignment surgery provided by the national health service and lived in society as a female, she remained for legal purposes a male. This had effects on her life where sex was of legal relevance, such as in the area of pensions, retirement age, etc. The Court noted that there was clear and uncontested evidence of a continuing international trend in favour of not only increased social acceptance of transsexuals but also of legal recognition of the new sexual identity of post-operative transsexuals. It was also noted that the UK Government was currently discussing proposals for reform of the registration system in order to allow ongoing amendment of civil status data.

The Court found that although the difficulties and anomalies of the applicant's situation as a post-operative transsexual did not attain the level of daily interference suffered by the applicant in *B v France*[333] the Court emphasised that the very essence of the Convention was respect for human dignity and human freedom. Under Art 8 of the Convention in particular, where the notion of personal autonomy was an important principle underlying the interpretation of its guarantees, protection was given to the personal sphere of each individual, including the right to establish details of their identity as individual human beings. In the twenty-first century, the Court found, the right of transsexuals to personal development and to physical and moral security in the full sense enjoyed by others in society could no longer be regarded as a matter of controversy requiring the lapse of time to cast clearer light on the issues involved.[334] Although the Court did not underestimate the important repercussions which any major change in the system would inevitably have, not only in the field of birth registration, but also for example in the areas of access to records, family law, affiliation, inheritance, social security and insurance, these problems were far from insuperable. The Court also considered that society might reasonably be expected to tolerate a certain inconvenience to enable individuals to live in dignity and worth in accordance with the sexual identity chosen by them at great personal cost.

The Court also noted that despite its reiteration since 1986 and most recently in 1998 of the importance of keeping the need for appropriate legal measures under review having regard to scientific and societal developments, nothing had effectively been done by the respondent government. Having regard to the above considerations, the Court found that the respondent government could no longer claim that the matter fell within their

332 [2002] ECHR 583.
333 (1992) 13 HRLJ 358.
334 Domestic recognition of this evaluation could be found, the Court noted, in the report of the Interdepartmental Working Group on Transsexual People and the Court of Appeal's judgment in *Bellinger v Bellinger* [2001] EWCA Civ 1140.

margin of appreciation, save as regards the appropriate means of achieving recognition of the right protected under the Convention. It concluded that the fair balance that was inherent in the Convention now tilted decisively in favour of the applicant. There had, it found, accordingly, been a failure to respect her right to private life in breach of Art 8.

As regards Art 14 the Court considered that the lack of legal recognition of the change of gender of a post-operative transsexual lay at the heart of the applicant's complaints under Art 14 of the Convention. These issues had been examined under Art 8 and resulted in the finding of a violation of that provision. In the circumstances, the Court found that no separate issue arose under Art 14 and made no separate finding.

The Court found that while it was true that Article 12 referred in express terms to the right of a man and woman to marry, the Court was not persuaded that at the date of this case these terms restricted the determination of gender to purely biological criteria. The Court went on to consider whether the allocation of sex in national law to that registered at birth was a limitation impairing the very essence of the right to marry in this case. In that regard, it found that it was artificial to assert that post-operative transsexuals had not been deprived of the right to marry as, according to law, they remained able to marry a person of their former opposite sex. The applicant in this case lived as a woman and would only wish to marry a man. As she had no possibility of doing so, she could therefore claim that the very essence of her right to marry had been infringed. Though fewer countries permitted the marriage of transsexuals in their assigned gender than recognised the change of gender itself, the Court did not find that this supported an argument for leaving the matter entirely within the contracting states' margin of appreciation. This would be tantamount to finding that the range of options open to a contracting state included an effective bar on any exercise of the right to marry. The margin of appreciation could not extend so far. While it was for the contracting state to determine, *inter alia*, the conditions under which a person claiming legal recognition as a transsexual established that gender re-assignment has been properly effected and the formalities applicable to future marriages (including, for example, the information to be furnished to intended spouses), the Court found no justification for barring the transsexual from enjoying the right to marry under any circumstances. It concluded that there had been a breach of Article 12.

Respect for family life

The concept of 'family life'

This concept under Art 8 may encompass many types of 'family' – formal or informal – but if the 'family' in question might not fall within the term as, for example, a foster parent might not do, there might still be an interference with private life.[335] Generally, a close relationship falling within the term will be presumed where close ties such as those between parent and child exist; for other relations, the presumption will be the other way. In *X, Y and Z v UK*[336] the Court considered that no breach of Art 8 had arisen

---

335 See generally Liddy, J, 'The concept of family life under the ECHR' [1998] EHRLR 15; Kilkelly, U, *The Child and the ECHR*, 1999, Ashgate, Chapter 9.

336 (1997) 24 EHRR 143.

where the UK refused to recognise a female to male transsexual as the father of a child born after artificial insemination by a donor. The father had lived with the mother in a stable relationship for ten years and acted as the child's father after the birth. Nevertheless, the Court did find that a family relationship existed between the 'father' and the child, taking into account his involvement with the child before and after the birth.

There are signs that Art 8 jurisprudence has rejected the notion that respect for family life, and perhaps for privacy generally, entails failure to interfere in the family when other rights or freedoms are in danger of abuse. In *Marckx v Belgium*,[337] the applicant complained under Art 8 in conjunction with Art 14 that an illegitimate child was not recognised as the child of his or her mother until the latter had formally recognised the child as such. Also, the child was treated under Belgian law as, in principle, a stranger to the parents' families. In finding that the state was under an obligation to ensure the child's integration in the family and, therefore, that Art 8 applied, the Court impliedly rejected the view put forward by the UK judge, Sir Gerald Fitzmaurice:

> It is abundantly clear that the main if not indeed the sole object and intended sphere of application of Art 8 was that of what I will call the 'domiciliary protection' of the individual. He (*sic*) and his family were no longer to be subjected to domestic law. Such and not the internal regulation of family relationships was the object of Art 8.

It is reasonably clear that this notion of the meaning of respect for family life represents an impoverished view of the Convention requirements. Respect for family life means, negatively, that the state should abstain from interference except where to do so would mean failing to adhere to the requirements of respect for the private life of the child or to the requirements of another Convention article.[338] The requirement of respect for family life also places positive obligations on the authorities to 'allow those concerned to lead a normal family life'.[339]

Although the term 'family' may receive a broad interpretation, this has not consistently been the case with respect to the requirements arising from the need to respect family life. In *X v UK*,[340] which was found inadmissible by the Commission, it was determined that 'family life' cannot be interpreted so broadly as to encompass a father's right to be consulted in respect of an abortion. The Commission could have rested the decision on para 2 – the 'rights of others' exception – by taking the rights of the woman in question into account, but it preferred to interpret the primary right restrictively. Had it not adopted such an interpretation, 'family life' might have come into conflict with 'private life' since pregnancy and its management has been accepted as an aspect of a mother's private life, although not to be divorced entirely from consideration of the life of the foetus.[341] Family life has also received a narrow interpretation in immigration

---

337 (1979) 2 EHRR 330.
338 See *Riem v Sweden* (1992) 16 EHRR 155.
339 See Ovey, C and White Jacobs, R, *The European Convention on Human Rights*, 4th edn, 2006, OUP, Chapter 11; Bainham, A, 'Can we protect children and protect their rights?' [2002] Fam Law 279.
340 Appl No 8416/78; 19 D & R 244 (1980).
341 *Brüggemann and Scheuten v Federal Republic of Germany* Appl No 6959/75, 10 D & R 100 (1975), Eur Comm HR, Report of 12 July 1977. See also *Vo v France* (2005) 40 *EHRR* 12. See further Gher, JM and Zampas, C, 'Abortion as a human right' (2008) HRLR 249.

cases in respect of a right to enter a country. In *Abdulaziz, Cabales and Balkandali v UK*[342] it was found that:

> The duty imposed by Art 8 cannot be considered as extending to a general obliga-tion . . . to respect the choice by married couples of the country of their matrimonial residence and to accept the non-national spouses for settlement in that country.

However, in contrast, where an alien is faced with expulsion from a country in which he or she has lived for some time and where members of the family are established, the Court has shown itself willing to uphold the right to maintain family ties if satisfied that the ties are clearly in existence.[343]

Respect for the home

In this area, the Strasbourg authorities have adopted a cautious attitude and tend to prac-tise only marginal review of the justification of restrictions. At the core of the right to respect for the home is the right to occupy the home and a right not to be expelled from it. Thus, a violation of Art 8 was established in *Cyprus v Turkey*[344] which concerned occupying forces expelling citizens and making their return to their homes impossible. This was a very clear violation of the right. A contrasting result was reached in *Buckley v UK*.[345] A gipsy, who had lived in her home for five years without planning permission, was still entitled to respect for her home – the concept was not found only to cover homes lawfully established. However, no violation of this right was found where plan-ning permission for retaining the applicant's caravan on her own land was refused. The refusal was partly based on the planning authority's policy in controlling the sites on which gipsies could live. The Court found that a wide margin of appreciation should be allowed to the member state and that such margin had not been exceeded since procedural safeguards were in place which allowed for the weighing up of the interests involved: the interest of the applicant in her traditional lifestyle in a caravan and the interest of the planning authority in regulating the use of the land in the area for the benefit of the local community.

So, the concept of the home is quite broad, although it does not cover a future home which is not yet built.[346] Further, the right to respect for the home does not include a right to a home; nor does it extend to providing a decent home,[347] nor to providing alternative accommodation.[348] Interference can arise due to a direct interference such as a seizure order,[349] or to the use of a compulsory purchase order threatening the actual home.[350]

---

342 (1985) 7 EHRR 471. A breach of the Convention was found when Art 8 was read in conjunction with Art 14 (see below, p 94).
343 See *Moustaquim v Belgium* (1991) 13 EHRR 802 and *Djeroud v France* (1992) 14 EHRR 68.
344 (1976) 3 EHRR 482.
345 (1997) 23 EHRR 101.
346 *Loizidou v Turkey* (1996) 23 EHRR 513.
347 *X v Germany* (1956) 1 YB 202.
348 *Burton v UK* (1996) 22 EHRR 135 CD.
349 *Chappel v UK* (1989) 12 EHRR 1.
350 *Howard v UK* (1987) 52 DR 198.

The concept does not cover merely proprietorial rights; it includes the ability to live freely in the home and enjoy the home.[351] The peaceful enjoyment of the home is established as an aspect of respect of the home,[352] and this notion has been extended to cover various forms of interference with the enjoyment of the home, such as pollution by traffic fumes on the basis that the right implies that the home is private space to be enjoyed free from the covert or overt blight of pollution. A number of cases have concerned noise pollution. In *Powell v UK*,[353] a claim in respect of airport noise was rejected on the basis that a fair balance had to be struck between the interests of the individual and of the community. In *Lopez Ostra v Spain*,[354] a breach of Art 8 was found after considering the fair balance to be struck, in respect of a failure to prevent a waste treatment plant releasing fumes and smells. Failure to prevent the risk of serious pollution was also found to breach Art 8 in *Guerra v Italy*.[355] Where applications in such instances fail under Art 8 owing to the caution evinced in Strasbourg when dealing with this substantive right, they may succeed under Art 6(1) if the procedure allowing challenge to such interference is non-existent or defective.[356]

Correspondence

The case law in this area has concerned the right of a detainee to correspond with the outside world and, in the UK, has led to a steady relaxation of the rules relating to preventing, stopping and censoring of prisoners' correspondence.[357] In general, the supervision *per se* of prisoners' letters is not in breach of Art 8, but particular instances, such as stopping a purely personal letter, may be.[358] It does not have to be personal: in *Campbell v UK*,[359] correspondence with the applicant's solicitor was read; that was a restriction on correspondence that amounted to a breach of Art 8. Supervision of correspondence during detention has also, to an extent, been found to breach Art 8.[360] It should be noted that an Art 10 issue may also arise in such circumstances since the detainee's right to receive or impart information is affected.[361] Searches and seizures fall within the head of 'correspondence' and, indeed, within all the rights except the right to respect for family life.[362]

Article 9: freedom of thought, conscience and religion

(1) Everyone has the right to freedom of thought, conscience and religion; this right includes freedom to change his religion or belief and freedom, either alone or in

---

351 *Howard v UK* (1987) 52 DR 198.
352 *Arrondelle v UK*, No 7889/77; 26 DR 5 (1982).
353 (1990) 12 EHRR 355. See also *Baggs v UK* (1987) 52 DR 29.
354 (1994) 20 EHRR; for comment, see Sands, P, 'Human rights, environment and the *Lopez Ostra* case' [1996] EHRLR 597.
355 (1998) 26 EHRR 375.
356 See, e.g., *Zimmermann and Steiner v Switzerland* (1983) 6 EHRR 17.
357 See, e.g., *Silver v UK* (1983) 5 EHRR 347.
358 *Boyle and Rice v UK* (1988) 10 EHRR 425.
359 (1992) 15 EHRR 137.
360 *De Wilde, Ooms and Versyp v Belgium* (1971) 1 EHRR 373.
361 See *Herczegfalvy v Austria* (1993) 15 EHRR 437.
362 *Funke v France* (1993) 16 EHRR 297; *Mialhe v France* (1993) 16 EHRR 332; *Crémieux v France* (1993) 16 EHRR 357. For further discussion, see Chapter 12.

community with others and in public or private, to manifest his religion or belief, worship, teaching, practice and observance.

(2) Freedom to manifest one's religion or beliefs shall be subject only to such limitations as are prescribed by law and are necessary in a democratic society in the interests of public safety, for the protection of public order, health or morals or for the protection of the rights and freedoms of others.

The right under Art 9 of possessing certain convictions is unrestricted. Restrictions are only placed on the *expression* of thought under Art 10, and the manifestation of religious belief in Art 9(2). Of course, in general, unless thoughts can be expressed, they cannot have much impact. However, Art 9 provides a valuable guarantee against using compulsion to change an opinion[363] or prohibiting someone from entering a profession due to their convictions. In the latter instance, Article 17 (which allows restrictions where a person's ultimate aim is the destruction of Convention rights)[364] might, however, come into play if someone of fascist or perhaps communist sympathies was debarred from a profession.

Freedom of religion will include the freedom not to take part in religious services, thus particularly affecting persons such as prisoners, but it may also include the opposite obligation – to provide prisoners with a means of practising their religion. However, in such instances, Strasbourg has been very ready to assume that restrictions are inherent in the detention of prisoners or are justified under para 2. For example, in *Huber v Austria*,[365] broad 'inherent limitations' on a prisoner's right to practise religion were accepted. Similarly, in *X v Austria*,[366] the Commission found no violation in respect of a refusal to allow a Buddhist prisoner to grow a beard. It is arguable, however, that inherent limitations should not be assumed in relation to a right which admits express exceptions.

Article 10: freedom of expression

(1) Everyone has the right to freedom of expression. This right shall include freedom to hold opinions and to receive and impart information and ideas without interference by public authority and regardless of frontiers. This article shall not prevent states from requiring the licensing of broadcasting, television or cinema enterprises.

(2) The exercise of these freedoms, since it carries with it duties and responsibilities, may be subject to such formalities, conditions, restrictions or penalties as are prescribed by law and are necessary in a democratic society, in the interests of national security, territorial integrity or public safety, for the prevention of disorder or crime, for the protection of health or morals, for the protection of the reputation or rights of others, for preventing the disclosure of information received in confidence or for maintaining the authority and impartiality of the judiciary.

Art 10 obviously overlaps with Art 9, but it is broader, since it protects the means of ensuring freedom of expression; even if the person who provides such means is not

---

363 Such action would normally also involve a violation of Art 3.
364 See below, p 101.
365 (1971) 14 YB 548.
366 Appl No 1753/63, (1965) 8 YB 174.

the holder of the opinion in question, she or he will be protected. The words 'freedom to hold opinion' used in Art 10 cannot be distinguished from the phrase 'freedom of thought' used in Art 9. There is also an obvious overlap with Article 11 which protects freedom of association and assembly.

Scope of the primary right

The stance taken under Art 10 is that while almost all forms of expression will fall within the primary right, all expression is not equally valuable. It was found in *X and Church of Scientology v Sweden*[367] that commercial speech is protected by Art 10, but that the level of protection should be less than that accorded to the expression of political ideas, thereby implying that political speech should receive special protection. In *Markt Intern Verlag v Federal Republic of Germany*,[368] the Court found: 'the European Court of Human Rights should not substitute its own evaluation for that of the national courts in the instant case, where those courts, on reasonable grounds, had considered the restrictions to be necessary', an extreme statement of the extent to which Strasbourg should defer to the national decision. It appears to have been affected by the fact that the Court was dealing with commercial speech, which it views as of much less significance than political speech.[369] As Harris, O'Boyle and Warbrick put it in *Law of the European Convention on Human Rights*:[370] 'The privileged position of political speech derives from the Court's conception of it as a central feature of a democratic society . . . .'

The motive of the speaker may be significant; if it is to stimulate debate on a particular subject, Art 10 will be more readily applicable.[371] The Court has stressed that Art 10 applies not only to speech which is favourably received, but also to speech which shocks and offends. In *Jersild v Denmark*,[372] the Commission accepted that this may include aiding in the dissemination of racist ideas. In this instance, the applicant had not himself expressed such views; his conviction had arisen due to his responsibility as a television interviewer for their dissemination. This factor was also taken into account by the Court in finding that the conviction constituted an interference with freedom of expression in breach of Art 10.[373] The television programme in question had included an interview with an extreme racist group, the Greenjackets; such interviews were found to constitute an important means whereby 'the press is able to play its vital role as public watchdog' and therefore strong reasons would have to be adduced for punishing a journalist who had assisted in the dissemination of racist statements by conducting the interview, bearing in mind that the feature taken as a whole was not found by the Court to have as its object the propagation of racist views. The Court pointed out that the racist remarks which led to the convictions of members of the Greenjackets did not have the protection of Art 10.

---

367 Appl No 7805/77, 16 DR 109 (1979).
368 In *Markt Intern Verlag GmBH and Beerman v Germany* (1990) 12 EHRR 161, para 47.
369 See the statements regarding the significance of political speech in *Lingens v Austria* (1986) 8 EHRR 103; *Jersild v Denmark* (1994) 19 EHRR 1; *Oberschlick v Austria* (1997) 25 EHRR 357.
370 1st edn, 1995, Butterworths, p 397.
371 See *Thorgeir Thorgeirson v Iceland* (1992) 14 EHRR 843.
372 (1992) 14 HRLJ 74; see also *Open Door Counselling and Dublin Well Woman Centre Ltd v Ireland* (1992) 15 EHRR 244 (below, p 87).
373 (1994) 19 EHRR 1.

There is some evidence that the Court is reluctant to intervene in instances which may not be perceived as constituting a direct interference with freedom of expression by the domestic authorities. If, as in *Glasenapp v Federal Republic of Germany*,[374] the interference can be seen as in some way indirect or as largely concerned with another interest, it may find that the Art 10 guarantee is inapplicable. The case concerned a German schoolteacher who had written a letter to a newspaper indicating her sympathy with the German Communist party. This was found to be contrary to legislation controlling the employment of people with extreme political views and her appointment as a teacher was revoked. Her claim that this constituted an interference with her freedom of expression failed since the Court characterised the claim as largely concerned with a right of access to the civil service rather than with freedom of speech. In *Bowman v UK*,[375] restrictions imposed on persons spending money in support of parliamentary candidates was found to be a disproportionate interference with freedom of expression. In *Ahmed v UK*,[376] the Court upheld restrictions preventing certain local government officers holding political office. The Court took into account the need to protect the rights of others to effective political democracy which was answered by seeking to ensure the neutrality of local government officers.

Art 10 includes an additional guarantee of the freedom to receive and impart information. However, the seeking of information does not appear to connote an obligation on the part of the government to make information available; the words 'without restriction by public authority' do not imply a positive obligation on the part of the authority to ensure that information can be received. So, the right is restricted in situations where there is no willing speaker. Art 10 is not, therefore, a full freedom of information measure.[377] In fact, the freedom to seek information was deliberately omitted from Art 10 – although it appears in the Universal Declaration of Human Rights – in order to avoid placing a clear positive obligation on the member states to communicate information.

A number of aspects of Art 10 and its impact on domestic law are discussed extensively in Part II.

Restrictions and exceptions

Mediums other than written publications can be subjected to a licensing system under Art 10(1) and because this restriction is mentioned in para 1, it appears on its face that a licensing system can be imposed on grounds other than those outlined in para 2, thereby broadening the possible exceptions. This is discussed further in Chapter 7.[378] But this provision has been restrictively interpreted and also any such exceptions must, of course, be considered in conjunction with the safeguard against discrimination under Art 14: for example, if the state has a monopoly on a medium, it must not discriminate in granting air time to different groups.

The restrictions of Art 10(2) are wide, and two, 'maintaining the authority of the judiciary' and 'preventing the disclosure of information received in confidence', are

---

374 (1986) 9 EHRR 25. See, to the same effect, *Kosiek v Germany* (1987) 9 EHRR 328.
375 (1998) 25 EHRR 1.
376 (1998) 5 BHRC 111.
377 This was supported in the *Gaskin* case (1990) 12 EHRR 36 (see above, p 70): the Art 10 claim failed on this basis. But a right of such access was later found in *Gillberg v Sweden* (2012) 34 BHRC 247, *Shapovalov v Ukraine*, Judgment 32 July 2012.
378 See p 403.

not mentioned in Art 10's companion articles, Articles 8, 9 and 11. The first of these exceptions was included bearing in mind the contempt law of the UK, but it was made clear, in the well-known *Sunday Times* case,[379] that in relation to such law, the margin of appreciation should be narrow due to its 'objective' nature. In other words, what was needed to maintain the authority of the judiciary could be more readily evaluated by an objective observer than could measures needed to protect morals. The case in question concerned reporting on a matter of great public interest – the Thalidomide tragedy – and therefore, only very compelling reasons for preventing the information being imparted could be justified. It was held that because Art 10 is a particularly important right and the particular instance touched on its essence, a breach could be found; in response, the Contempt of Court Act 1981 was passed. The 'rights of others' exception may also receive a narrow interpretation – at least in cases of defamation against a public body or person where the applicant was acting in good faith and was attempting to stimulate debate on a matter of serious public concern.[380]

A very different approach was taken in the *Handyside* case[381] arising from a conviction under the Obscene Publications Act 1959 and concerning the more subjective nature of the 'protection of morals' exception. The applicant put forward certain special circumstances – that the prohibited material in question was circulating in most other countries and so suppression could not be very evidently necessary in a democratic society – but such circumstances were barely discussed. A wide margin of appreciation was left to the national authorities as to what was 'necessary'. One possible reason for this was that the authority of the judiciary is a more objective notion than the protection of morals and this may have led to a variation of the necessity test. A similar approach was taken in *Müller v Switzerland*,[382] the Court stating:

> [I]t is not possible to find in the legal and social orders of the contracting states a uniform European conception of morals. By reason of their direct and continuous contact with the vital forces of their countries state authorities are in a better position than the international judge to give an opinion on the exact content of these requirements.

The lack of a uniform standard was also the key factor in the ruling in *Otto-Preminger Institut v Austria*.[383] The decision concerned the showing of a satirical film depicting God as a senile old man and Jesus as a mental defective erotically attracted to the Virgin Mary. Criminal proceedings for the offence of disparaging religious doctrines were brought against the manager of the Institute which had scheduled the showings of the film. The film was seized by the Austrian authorities while criminal proceedings were pending. The European Court of Human Rights found that the seizure of the film could be seen as furthering the aims of Art 9 of the Convention and therefore it fell within the

---

379 (1979) 2 EHRR 245 (discussed in full in Chapter 6, pp 313–14).
380 See *Thorgeir Thorgeirson v Iceland* (1992) 14 EHRR 843; *Castells v Spain* (1992) 14 EHRR 445; *Schwabe v Austria* (1992) 14 HRLJ 26.
381 (1976) 1 EHRR 737. See further Chapter 7, pp 404–05.
382 (1991) 13 EHRR 212.
383 (1994) 19 EHRR 34.

'rights of others' exception. In considering whether the seizure and forfeiture of the film was 'necessary in a democratic society' in order to protect the rights of others to respect for their religious views, the Court took into account the lack of a discernible common conception within the member states of the significance of religion, and therefore considered that the national authorities should have a wide margin of appreciation in assessing what was necessary to protect religious feeling. In ordering the seizure of the film, the Austrian authorities had taken its artistic value into account, but had not found that it outweighed its offensive features. The Court found that the national authorities had not overstepped their margin of appreciation and therefore decided that no breach of Art 10 had occurred. This decision left a very wide discretion to the member state, a discretion which the dissenting judges considered to be too wide.

The stance taken in *Otto-Preminger* and in *Müller* echoes the view expressed in *Cossey v UK*[384] that where a clear European view does emerge, the Court may well be influenced by it, but it also suggests a particularly strong reluctance to intervene in this very contentious area. The margin of appreciation in respect of the protection of morals will not be unlimited, however, even in the absence of a broad consensus. The Court so held in *Open Door Counselling and Dublin Well Woman v Ireland*,[385] ruling that an injunction which prevented the dissemination of any information at all about abortion amounted to a breach of Art 10. This accords with the view expressed in *B v France*[386] that what can be termed the common standards principle is only one factor to be taken into account and must be weighed against the severity of the infringement of rights in question.

The exception in respect of confidential information overlaps with others, including national security and the rights of others, but a situation could be envisaged in which a disclosure of information did not fall within those categories and could therefore be caught only by this extra exception. This might arise in respect of a disclosure by a civil servant that did not threaten national security or any person's individual rights, such as that made in the *Tisdall* case.[387]

Actions in respect of both prior and subsequent restraints on freedom of expression may be brought under Art 10, but pre-publication sanctions will be regarded as more pernicious and thus harder to justify as necessary (*Observer and Guardian v UK*[388]). In relation to post-publication sanctions, criminal actions will be regarded as having a grave impact on freedom of expression, but civil actions which have severe consequences for the individual may also be hard to justify. In *Tolstoy Miloslavsky v UK*,[389] the European Court of Human Rights considered the level of libel damages that can be awarded in UK courts. Libel damages of £1.5 million had been awarded against Count Tolstoy Miloslavsky in the UK in respect of a pamphlet he had written which alleged that Lord Aldington, a high-ranking British army officer, had been responsible for handing over 70,000 people to the Soviet authorities without authorisation, knowing that they would meet a cruel fate. The Count argued that this very large award constituted

384 (1990) 13 EHRR 622.
385 (1992) 15 EHRR 244.
386 (1992) 13 HRLJ 358.
387 (1984) *The Times* 26 March.
388 (1991) 14 EHRR 153.
389 (1995) 20 EHRR 422.

a breach of Art 10. Was the award necessary in a democratic society as required by Art 10? The Court found that it was not, having regard to the fact that the scope of judicial control at the trial could not offer an adequate safeguard against a disproportionately large award. Thus, a violation of the applicant's rights under Art 10 was found.

Article 11: freedom of association and assembly

(1) Everyone has the right to freedom of peaceful assembly and to freedom of associa-
    tion with others, including the right to form and to join trade unions for the protec-
    tion of his interests.
(2) No restrictions shall be placed on the exercise of these rights other than such as
    are prescribed by law and are necessary in a democratic society in the interests of
    national security or public safety, for the prevention of disorder or crime, for the
    protection of health or morals or for the protection of the rights and freedoms of
    others. This article shall not prevent the imposition of lawful restrictions on the
    exercise of these rights by members of the armed forces, of the police or of the
    administration of the state.

Assembly

The addition of the word 'peaceful' has restricted the scope of para 1: there will be no need to invoke the para 2 exceptions if the authorities concerned could reasonably believe that a planned assembly would not be peaceful. Thus, assemblies can be subject to permits so long as the permits relate to the peacefulness of the assembly and not to the right of assembly itself. However, a restriction of a very wide character relating to peacefulness might affect the right to assemble itself and might therefore constitute a violation of Article 11 if it did not fall within one of the exceptions.

It should be noted that freedom of assembly may not merely be secured by a lack of interference by the public authorities; they may have positive obligations to intervene in order to prevent an interference with freedom of assembly by private individuals, although they will have a very wide margin of appreciation in this regard.[390] It has been held in respect of the guarantees of other articles that states must secure to individuals the rights and freedoms of the Convention by preventing or remedying any breach thereof. If no duty was placed on the authorities to provide such protection, then some assemblies could not take place.

It will be argued in Chapter 9 that the freedom of assembly jurisprudence under Article 11 is cautious. In finding that applications are manifestly ill-founded, the Commission has been readily satisfied that decisions of the national authorities to adopt quite far-reaching measures, including complete bans, in order to prevent disorder are within their margin of appreciation.[391] The Court has also found 'the margin of appreciation

390 *Plattform 'Ärzte für Das Leben' v Austria* (1988) 13 EHRR 204 (it was not found that Austria had
    failed in its obligation to prevent counter-demonstrators interfering with an anti-abortion demonstration).
391 See *Christians against Racism and Fascism v UK* Appl 8440/78, 21 DR 138 (1980); *Friedl v Austria*
    (1995) 21 EHRR 83.

extends in particular to the choice of the reasonable and appropriate means to be used by the authority to ensure that lawful manifestations can take place peacefully'.[392]

Association

'Association' need not be assigned its national meaning. Even if a group such as a trade union is not an 'association' according to the definition of national law, it may fall within Article 11. The term connotes a voluntary association, not a professional organisation established by the government. It should be noted that it is only with respect to trade unions that the right to form an association is expressly mentioned, albeit non-exhaustively. Such a right in respect of other types of association is clearly implicit – a necessary part of freedom of association. The key rights protected by Article 11 include the basic right to form associations[393] and the right to autonomy of an association.[394] An association itself can exercise Convention rights, including freedom of expression (*Socialist Party and Others v Turkey*[395]).

The earlier Strasbourg jurisprudence tended to be protective of state interests,[396] but the more recent 'association' jurisprudence of the Court is more interventionist. In *Socialist Party and Others v Turkey*,[397] the Court allowed only a very narrow margin of appreciation in finding that the dissolution of the Socialist Party of Turkey had breached Article 11. The Court linked the three freedoms of expression, association and assembly together in finding that democracy demands that diverse political programmes should be debated, 'even those that call into question the way a state is currently organised'. The Court did not accept that the message of the group that a federal system should be put in place, which would ensure that Kurds would be put on an equal footing with Turkish citizens generally, amounted to incitement to violence. The dissolution of the party was disproportionate to the aim in view – the preservation of national security. This stance is in accordance with the Convention jurisprudence, which has quite consistently recognised the need to protect the interests of minority and excluded groups.[398]

Similar findings were made in *Sidiropoulos v Greece*[399] in respect of an association formed to promote the interests of the Macedonian minority in Greece. The Court said that one of the most important aspects of freedom of association was that citizens should be able to form a legal group with the aim of acting collectively in their mutual interest. In *Vogt v Germany*[400] the Court held that a woman who was dismissed from her

392 *Chorherr v Austria* (1994) 17 EHRR 358.
393 *X v Belgium* (1961) 4 YB 324.
394 *Cheall v UK* (1985) 8 EHRR 74.
395 (1999) 27 EHRR 51, paras 41, 47 and 50.
396 See *Glasenapp v Germany* (1986) 9 EHRR 25; *Kosiek v Germany* (1987) 9 EHRR 328; *CCSU v UK* (1988) 10 EHRR 269.
397 (1999) 27 EHRR 51, paras 41, 47, and 50.
398 Such groups have included criminals: *Soering v UK* (1989) 11 EHRR 439; prisoners: *Ireland v UK* (1978) 2 EHRR 25, *Golder v UK* (1975) 1 EHRR 524; racial minorities: *East African Asians v UK* (1973) 3 EHRR 76, *Hilton v UK* Appl No 5613/72, 4 DR 177 (1976) (no breach found on facts); sexual minorities: *Dudgeon v UK* (1982) 4 EHRR 149, *B v France* (1992) 16 EHRR 1; political minorities: *Arrowsmith v UK* Appl No 7050/75, 19 DR 5 (1978); religious minorities: *Kokkinakis v Greece* (1993) 17 EHRR 397.
399 (1999) 27 EHRR 633.
400 (1995) 21 EHRR 205.

teaching post because of her membership of an extreme left-wing group had suffered a violation of both Articles 10 and 11. These decisions suggest that where political associations are in question, the Court will take a strict stance, in accordance with its stance on political expression.[401]

Article 12: the right to marry and to found a family

> Men and women of marriageable age have the right to marry and to found a family, according to the national laws governing the exercise of this right.

Article 12 contains no second paragraph setting out restrictions, but it obviously does not confer an absolute right due to the words 'according to the national laws', which imply the reverse of an absolute right – that Article 12 may be subject to far-reaching limitations in domestic law. The reference to national laws also accepts the possibility that legal systems may vary among contracting states as to, for example, the legally marriageable age. However, this does not mean that the Convention has no role at all; it may not interfere with national law governing the exercise of the right, but may do so where it attacks or erodes its essence.

The Protocols to the Convention

The First, Fourth, Sixth, Seventh, Thirteenth and Twelfth Protocols to the Convention add to it a number of substantive rights. Only the First, Sixth and Thirteenth Protocols have so far been ratified by the UK.

First Protocol

Article 1

> Every natural or legal person is entitled to the peaceful enjoyment of his possessions. No one shall be deprived of his possessions except in the public interest and subject to the conditions provided for by law and by the general principles of international law.

> The preceding provisions shall not, however, in any way impair the right of a state to enforce such laws as it deems necessary to control the use of property in accordance with the general interest or to secure the payment of taxes or other contributions or penalties.

The property article of the First Protocol echoes Article 12 in allowing the national authorities considerable freedom to regulate the exercise of the primary right. The case law has supported this; it was determined in *James and Others*[402] that the margin of appreciation open to the legislature in implementing social and economic policies

---

401 See the Introduction to Part II, pp 277–78, 281–83.
402 (1986) 8 EHRR 123.

should be a wide one.[403] Thus, in this area, the Strasbourg authorities have adopted a cautious attitude to this right and tend to practise only marginal review of the justification of restrictions. As mentioned above, claims of interference with property may fail under Protocol 1, Article 1, but succeed under Art 6, where a defective procedure has authorised the interference.[404]

Article 2

No person shall be denied the right to education. In the exercise of any functions which it assumes in relation to education and to teaching, the state shall respect the right of parents to ensure such education and teaching in conformity with their own religious and philosophical convictions.

The UK is a party to the First Protocol, but has made the following reservation to Article 2:

[I]in view of certain provisions of the Education Acts in force in the United Kingdom, the principle affirmed in the second sentence of Article 2 is accepted by the United Kingdom only so far as it is compatible with the provision of efficient instruction and training and the avoidance of unreasonable public expenditure.

Article 3

The High Contracting Parties undertake to hold free elections at reasonable intervals by secret ballot, under conditions which will ensure the free expression of the opinion of the people in the choice of the legislature.

Article 3 provides an undertaking (not formally expressed as a right) which is clearly central to a democratic society.[405] However, it does refer to a right that individuals can invoke.[406] Article 3 does not imply an absolute right to vote, but that elections should be held at regular intervals, should be secret, free from pressure on the electorate and the choice between candidates should be genuine. It does not confer a right to a particular form of electoral system.[407]

Further Protocols

Articles 1 and 2 of the Sixth Protocol abolish the death penalty except in time of war or the threat of war. Protocol 13 abolishes it in all circumstances, including in wartime.

---

403 See further Harris, D, O'Boyle, K and Warbrick, C, *Law of the European Convention on Human Rights*, 1995, Butterworths, p 516; Clayton, R and Tomlinson, H, *The Law of Human Rights*, 2000, OUP, pp 1301–20.

404 *Mats Jacobson v Sweden* (1990) 13 EHRR 79. See above, p 58, n 181.

405 For discussion, see Clayton and Tomlinson, *op cit*, fn 1, Chapter 18.

406 *Mathieu-Mohin v Belgium* (1987) 10 EHRR 1, para 50.

407 *Liberal Party v UK* (1980) 21 DR 211. Complete disenfranchisement of prisoners is not compatible with Article 3: *Hirst v UK (No 2)* [2005] ECHR 681. For discussion of the long-running (and unresolved) battle between the UK and Strasbourg, pp 170–71.

The Fourth and Seventh Protocols cover, broadly: freedom of movement (Protocol 4); the right of an alien lawfully resident in a state to full review of his or her case before expulsion, rights of appeal, compensation for miscarriages of justice, the right not to be subjected to double jeopardy and sexual equality between spouses as regards private law rights and responsibilities (Protocol 7). Protocol 12 provides, very significantly, a freestanding right to equality.[408] The Joint Committee on Human Rights in its review of international human rights legislation in 2005 recommended that the government should ratify the Fourth and Twelfth Protocols with appropriate reservations where necessary.[409]

The other protocols are concerned with the procedural machinery of the Convention.

4 Additional guarantees to the primary rights

Article 13: the right to an effective remedy before a national authority

> Everyone whose rights and freedoms as set forth in this Convention are violated shall have an effective remedy before a national authority notwithstanding that the violation has been committed by persons acting in an official capacity.

In *Leander v Sweden*[410] it was found that 'the requirements of Article 13 will be satisfied if there exists domestic machinery whereby, subject to the inherent limitations of the context, the individual can secure compliance with the relevant laws'. This machinery may include a number of possible remedies. It has been held that judicial review proceedings will be sufficient. In *Vilvarajah and Four Others v UK*,[411] the applicants maintained that judicial review did not satisfy Article 13 since the English courts could not consider the merits of the Home Secretary's decision in this instance, merely the manner in which it was taken. In holding that the power of judicial review satisfied the Article 13 test, the Court took into account the power of the UK courts to quash an administrative decision for unreasonableness, and the fact that these powers were exercisable by the highest tribunal in the UK. Thus, no violation of Article 13 was found. However in *Smith and Grady v UK*,[412] the Court said of the concept of *Wednesbury* unreasonableness: 'the threshold at which the . . . Court of Appeal could find the Ministry of Defence policy irrational was placed so high that it effectively excluded any consideration by the domestic courts of the question whether the interference with the applicants' rights answered a pressing social need or was proportionate to the national security and public order aims pursued, principles which lie at the heart of the Court's analysis of complaints under Art 8 of the Convention'.[413] This is not the last word on

---

408 See Chapter 5, pp 271–72.
409 17th Report of Session 2004–5 HL Paper 99, HC 264, paras 34 and 37.
410 (1987) 9 EHRR 443. Note that if such machinery exists, but is of doubtful efficacy, a challenge under Art 6(1) may be most likely to succeed (*de Geouffre de la Pradelle v France* (1993) HRLJ 276).
411 (1991) 14 EHRR 248.
412 (2000) 29 EHRR 493.
413 *Ibid*, para 138.

the matter. It is arguable that judicial review may provide a sufficient remedy in respect of breaches of Article 1, Protocol 1 especially where a large element of policy-making concerning social and economic matters is at issue.[414] This matter is pursued further at various points in this book.[415]

In *Klass*[416] it was found that 'Art 13 must be interpreted as guaranteeing an effective remedy before a national authority to everyone who claims that his rights and freedoms under the Convention have been violated.' In *Plattform 'Ärzte für das Leben'*[417] it was found that the claim must be arguable. Thus, Article 13 can be invoked only if no procedure is available that can begin to determine whether a violation has occurred. In theory, then, there could be a breach of Article 13 alone and, in that sense, it protects an independent right. In practice, case law tends not to follow this purist approach, and if no violation of the substantive right is found, it is likely that no violation of Article 13 will be found either (as it may be argued occurred in the *Ärzte für das Leben* case).

In the *Klass* case, it was determined that phone tapping did not breach Art 8 since it was found to be in the interests of national security. The applicants claimed that Article 13 could be considered on the basis of their assertion that no effective domestic remedy existed for challenging the decision to tap. The Court accepted that the existing remedy was of limited efficacy: it consisted only of the possibility of review of the case by a parliamentary committee. Nevertheless, it found that in all the circumstances, no more effective remedy was possible. Thus, the Court allowed the doctrine of the margin of appreciation to resolve the difficulty which arose from the fact that the tapping was done in order to combat terrorism in its attack on democracy but the means employed, which included the suspension of judicial remedies, might well be termed undemocratic.

Article 14: prohibition of discrimination

> The enjoyment of the rights and freedoms set forth in this Convention shall be secured without discrimination on any ground such as sex, race, colour, language, religion, political or other opinion, national or social origin, association with a national minority, property, birth or other status.

Art 14 does not provide a *general* right to freedom from discrimination, only that the rights and freedoms of the Convention must be secured without discrimination. Thus, if discrimination occurs in an area which is not covered by the Convention, such as most contractual aspects of employment, Art 14 will be irrelevant. Thus, Art 14 remains of limited value since it is not free standing and does not cover social and economic matters lying outside the protected rights. But, these weaknesses are addressed by Protocol 12, which provides a free-standing right to freedom from discrimination in

---

414 See the decision of the House of Lords in *R (Alconbury) v Secretary of State for the Environment* [2001] 2 All ER 929 (apart from the Art 1 issues, the matter concerned the application of Art 6 under the Human Rights Act).
415 See in particular Chapter 4, p 158.
416 (1978) 2 EHRR 214.
417 (1988) 13 EHRR 204.

relation to rights protected by law.[418] The protection from discrimination under Protocol 12 will render Art 14 redundant but the UK has not ratified it.[419]

However, Art 14 is not the only Convention vehicle that may be used to challenge discriminatory practices. Not only may discrimination be attacked though the medium of one of the other articles, most particularly Article 3,[420] but the Convention may be of particular value as a source of general principles in sex discrimination cases before the European Court of Justice.[421] An applicant may allege violation of a substantive right taken alone and also that he or she has been discriminated against in respect of that right. However, even if no violation of the substantive right taken alone is found and even if that claim is manifestly ill-founded, there could still be a violation of that article and Art 14 taken together so long as the matter at issue is covered by the other article. This was found in *X v Federal Republic of Germany*:[422] 'Art 14 of the Convention has no independent existence; nevertheless a measure which in itself is in conformity with the requirement of the Article enshrining the right or freedom in question, may however infringe this Article when read in conjunction with Art 14 for the reason that it is of a discriminatory nature.' In this sense, the Court has granted more autonomy to Art 14 than appeared to be intended originally.[423]

This ruling allowed more claims to be considered than the 'arguability' principle applying under Article 13. For example, in *Abdulaziz, Cabales and Balkandali*,[424] the female claimants wanted their non-national spouses to enter the UK and alleged a breach of Art 8, which protects family life. That claim was rejected. But a violation of Art 14 was found because the way the rule was applied made it easier for men to bring in their spouses. It was held that: 'Although the application of Art 14 does not necessarily presuppose a breach [of the substantive provisions of the Convention and the Protocols] – and to this extent it is autonomous – there can be no room for its application unless the facts at issue fall within the ambit of one or more of the rights and freedoms.'

Under Art 14, discrimination connotes differential treatment which is unjustifiable. The differential treatment may be unjustifiable either in the sense that it relates to no objective and reasonable aim, or in the sense that there is no reasonable proportionality between the means employed and the aim sought to be realised.[425] In *Abdulaziz*, the aim was to protect the domestic labour market. It was held that this was not enough to justify the differential treatment because the difference in treatment was out of proportion to that aim.

---

418 For further discussion of the Discrimination Protocol, see Grief, N, 'Non-discrimination under the European Convention on Human Rights: a critique of the United Kingdom Government's refusal to sign and ratify Protocol 12' (2002) 27(Supp) EL Rev, 3–18; Moon, G, 'The draft Discrimination Protocol to the European Convention on Human Rights: a progress report' (2000) 1 EHRLR 49.

419 See further Chapter 5, p 271.

420 *East African Asians v UK* (1973) 3 EHRR 76.

421 See, e.g., for an early decision, *Johnstone v Chief Constable of the RUC* [1986] ECR 1651.

422 Appl 4045/69 (1970) 8 YB 698.

423 For comment on the increasing autonomy of Art 14, see Arnardottir, O, 'The differences that make a difference: recent developments on the discrimination grounds and the margin of appreciation under article 14 of the European Convention on Human Rights' (2014) 14(4) HRL Rev 647; Livingstone, S, 'Article 14 and the prevention of discrimination in the ECHR' (1997) 1 EHRR 25.

424 (1985) 7 EHRR 471.

425 *Geïllustreerde Pers NV v Netherlands* Appl 5178/71, 8 DR (1977).

5 The doctrine of the 'margin of appreciation'[426]

The European Court of Human Rights has stated that the role of the Convention in protecting human rights is subsidiary to the role of the national legal system[427] and that since the state is better placed than the international judge to balance individual rights against general societal interests, Strasbourg will operate a restrained review of the balance struck. Under this doctrine, a degree of discretion will be allowed to member states as to legislative, administrative or judicial action in the area of a Convention right. However, Strasbourg will finally determine whether such action is reconcilable with the guarantee in question.

The doctrine of the margin of appreciation conceded to states was first adopted in respect of emergency situations,[428] but it was allowed to affect the application of all the articles although it has a particular application with respect to para 2 of Articles 8–11. It has now reached the stage where it can be said that it permeates the Convention jurisprudence. In different instances, a wider or narrower margin of appreciation has been allowed. The width allowed depends on a number of factors including the aim of the interference in question and its necessity. If a broader margin is allowed, Strasbourg review will be highly circumscribed. For example, the minority in the *Sunday Times* case[429] (nine judges) wanted to confine the role of Strasbourg to asking only whether the discretion in question was exercised in good faith and carefully and whether the measure was reasonable in the circumstances. A narrow margin conceded to the state means that a rigorous or intensive review of the proportionality between the aim of an interference and the extent and nature of the interference will be undertaken. This occurred in the *Sunday Times* case; it was held that Strasbourg review was not limited to asking whether the state had exercised its discretion reasonably, carefully and in good faith; it was found that the state's conduct must also be examined in Strasbourg to see whether it was compatible with the Convention.

Although the doctrine is well established, it has not been applied very consistently. Therefore, it is not always easy to predict when each approach will be taken, but a number of relevant factors may be identified. The nature of the right in question may be relevant. The doctrine is particularly applicable to the Articles 8–11 group of rights since it is used in determining whether an interference with the right is justifiable on

---

426 For general discussion of the doctrine, see, e.g., Letsas, G, 'Two concepts of the margin of appreciation' (2006) 26(4) OJLS 705–32; McDonald, RJ, 'The margin of appreciation in the jurisprudence of the European Court of Human Rights', *International Law and the Time of its Codification*, 1987, pp 187–208; Van Dijk, P and Van Hoof, F, *Theory and Practice of the European Convention on Human Rights*, 3rd edn, 1998, Kluwer, p 82 *et seq*; O'Donnell, T, 'The margin of appreciation doctrine: standards in the jurisprudence of the European Court of Human Rights' (1982) 4 Human Rights Q 474; Jones, T, 'The devaluation of human rights under the European Convention' [1995] PL 430; Mahoney, P, 'Marvellous richness or invidious cultural relativism?' (1998) 19 Human Rights LJ 1.
427 *Handyside v UK* A 24 (1976), para 48.
428 See *Lawless v Ireland* (1961) 1 EHRR 15.
429 Series A 30 (1979); 2 EHRR 245.

grounds of one of the exceptions contained in para 2 of these articles. Within this group, Art 10 may be viewed as particularly fundamental.[430] Also, the particular instance will be considered: does it concern, for example, a very significant need for free expression since there is a strong public interest in the subject matter? The presence of such factors may predispose the Strasbourg authorities to conduct a wide-ranging review. Such review also tends to be applicable under Articles 2[431] and 3,[432] although it may be narrowed where the state claims that the demands of national security justify the measures sought to be challenged under these articles.[433] On the other hand, in considering the imposition of positive obligations placed on the state, a broad margin will be allowed.[434]

The nature of the restriction is significant. Some restrictions are seen as more subjective than others. It is therefore thought more difficult to lay down a common European standard and the Court and Commission have, in such instances, shown a certain willingness to allow the exceptions a wide scope in curtailing the primary rights. For example, Art 10 contains an exception in respect of the protection of morals. This was invoked in the *Handyside* case[435] in respect of suppression of a booklet aimed at schoolchildren that was circulating freely in the rest of Europe. It was held that the UK government was best placed to determine what was needed in its own country in order to protect morals and, therefore, it could make an initial assessment of those requirements, which would then be considered for compatibility with Art 10 by Strasbourg.

The Court and Commission consider that in certain sensitive matters, most notably national security,[436] states are best placed to determine what is needed within their own particular domestic situation. Thus, emergency situations and the invocation of threats to national security invite deference. In *Council of Civil Service Unions v UK*[437] the European Commission, in declaring the Unions' application inadmissible, found that national security interests should prevail over freedom of association even though the national security interest was weak while the infringement of the primary right was very clear: an absolute ban on joining a trade union had been imposed. It is worth noting that the International Labour Organisation (ILO) Committee on Freedom of Association had earlier found that the ban breached the 1947 ILO Freedom of Association Convention. However, in general, if a restriction is very far-reaching, the Strasbourg authorities may be prepared to make a determination as to the need to impose it which differs from that of the state party in question.[438]

The high (or low) point of deference was perhaps reached in *Brannigan and McBride v UK*,[439] in which the European Court of Human Rights upheld a derogation entered by the UK after the decision in the case of *Brogan and Others v UK*.[440] The Court found

430 See, e.g., the judgment of the Court in *Autronic AG v Switzerland* (1990) 12 EHRR 485.
431 *McCann, Farrell and Savage v UK* (1995) 21 EHRR 97.
432 *Soering v UK* (1989) 11 EHRR 439.
433 *Kröcher and Möller v Switzerland* Appl 8463/78, 34 DR 25 (1981).
434 See *Plattform 'Ärzte für Das Leben' v Austria* (1988) 13 EHRR 204.
435 (1976) 1 EHRR 737.
436 See *Leander v Sweden* (1987) 9 EHRR 433, para 67.
437 Appl 11603/85 10 EHRR 269.
438 See, e.g., *Golder v UK* (1975) 1 EHRR 524. Discussed p 60.
439 Series A, 258–B (1993).
440 (1989) 11 EHRR 117. See further Chapter 12, p 897.

'a wide margin of appreciation [on the question] of the presence of an emergency . . . and on the nature and scope of derogations necessary to avert it [should be allowed]'.[441]

The Court is greatly influenced by general practice in the member states as a body and will interpret the Convention to reflect such practice so that a state which is clearly out of conformity with the others may expect an adverse ruling (consensus-based analysis). However, where practice is still in the process of changing and may be said to be at an inchoate stage as far as the member states generally are concerned, the Court may not be prepared to place itself at the forefront of such changes, although it will weigh the lack of a consensus against the degree of detriment to the applicant.[442] Thus, the notion of common standards strongly influences the doctrine of the margin of appreciation. Where a common standard, or a trend towards such a standard, cannot be discerned among member states, greater deference to particular state practice is shown.[443] For example, the lack of a uniform standard was the key factor in the ruling in *Otto-Preminger Institut v Austria*.[444] The decision concerned the seizure of film likely to offend religious feeling. The European Court of Human Rights found that the film would receive protection under Art 10, but that its seizure fell within the 'rights of others' exception. In considering whether its seizure and forfeiture was 'necessary in a democratic society' in order to protect the rights of others to respect for their religious views (under Art 9), the Court took into account the lack of a uniform conception within the member states of the significance of religion in society and therefore considered that the national authorities should have a wide margin of appreciation in assessing what was necessary to protect religious feeling. In this instance, the national authorities had not overstepped that margin and, therefore, the Court found that no breach of Art 10 had occurred. Similarly, in *Wingrove v UK*[445] the Court found that the English common law offence of blasphemy was sufficiently clear and precise. The Court further found: 'there is as yet not sufficient common ground in the legal and social orders of the member states of the Council of Europe to conclude that a system whereby a state can impose restrictions on the propagation of material on the basis that it is blasphemous is in itself unnecessary in a democratic society and incompatible with the Convention'.[446]

On the other hand, where a principle has received general acceptance in the member states and, in particular, where it is closely linked to the notion of democracy, the Court will afford a narrow margin only. For example, in *Socialist Party and Others v Turkey*,[447] the Court found that the dissolution of the Socialist party of Turkey had breached Article 11 since: 'there can be no democracy without pluralism . . . It is of the essence of democracy to allow diverse political programmes to be proposed and debated . . . Taking these matters into account . . . In determining whether a necessity existed, the contracting state was found to possess only a limited margin of appreciation.' The picture is more confused where a principle may be said to have received some general acceptance

---

441 Para 207.
442 *Rees v UK* (1986) 9 EHRR 56.
443 See *Rees v UK, ibid* at para 37. Even where a common European standard (consensus) *can* be shown, a wide margin may be conceded: *ABC v Ireland* [2010] ECHR 2032.
444 (1994) 19 EHRR 34.
445 (1996) 24 EHRR 1.
446 Para 57.
447 (1999) 27 EHRR 51, paras 41, 47 and 50.

within the contracting states and where the Court itself appears to have espoused it in the past, but where it cannot clearly be said that a common standard can be found. Such confusion appears to underlie the remarks in *Cossey v UK*[448] of Judge Martens in his dissenting opinion: 'this caution [in allowing a wide margin of appreciation based on a strict application of the common standards doctrine] is in principle not consistent with the Court's mission to protect the individual against the collectivity[449] . . . in this context [of legal recognition of gender reassignment] there simply is no room for a margin of appreciation'. Thus, even within the Court there is disagreement as to the interferences that fall within the margin conceded to the state. In the only decision of the Court finding a violation of the freedom of assembly guarantee of Article 11, *Ezelin v France*,[450] two of the partly dissenting judges considered that the interference in question fell within that margin,[451] although the majority found that the state had exceeded it.

As the discussion suggests, the margin of appreciation doctrine may tend to undermine the Convention and its growth has therefore attracted criticism. Van Dijk and Van Hoof have written of it as: 'a spreading disease. Not only has the scope of its application been broadened to the point where in principle none of the Convention rights or freedoms are excluded, but also has the illness been intensified in that wider versions of the doctrine have been added to the original concept.'[452] As mentioned at the beginning of this chapter, the doctrine may sometimes be appropriate as part of a general consensus-based approach to the supervision of the Convention. However, an arbitrariness is evident in its application, a theme that is pursued below and at a number of points in this book.

6 Restriction of the rights and freedoms

The system of restrictions

As the discussion of the substantive rights demonstrated, all the articles except Articles 3, 4(1) and 6(2) are subject to certain restrictions, either because certain limitations are inherent in the formulation of the right itself,[453] or because it is expressly stated that particular cases are not covered by the right in question, or because general restrictions on the primary right contained in the first paragraph are enumerated in a second paragraph (Articles 8–11). Certain further general restrictions are allowed

---

448 A 184 (1990).
449 Para 5.6.3.
450 A 202-A (1991).
451 Judges Ryssdal and Pettiti, at pp 26 and 28–30.
452 Van Dijk, P and Van Hoof, F, *The Theory and Practice of the European Convention on Human Rights*, 1990, Kluwer, p 604. For further discussion of the doctrine, see Letsas, G, 'Two concepts of the margin of appreciation' (2006) 26(4) OJLS 705–32; O'Donnell, T, 'The margin of appreciation doctrine: standards in the jurisprudence of the European Court of Human Rights' (1982) 4 Human Rights Q 474; Morrison, J, 'Margin of appreciation in human rights law' (1973) 6 Human Rights J 263; Jones, T, 'The devaluation of human rights under the European Convention' [1995] PL 430; Mahoney, P, 'Marvelous richness or invidious cultural relativism?' (1998) 19 Human Rights LJ 1.
453 E.g., Art 14, which prohibits discrimination, is inherently limited because it operates only in the context of the other Convention rights and freedoms.

under Articles 17, 15 and 57. In considering the restrictions, Article 18 must also be borne in mind. It provides that the motives of the national authority in creating the restrictions must be the same as the aims appearing behind the restrictions when the Convention was drafted.

Article 15: derogation from the rights and freedoms in case of public emergency

(1) In time of war or other public emergency threatening the life of the nation any High Contracting Party may take measures derogating from its obligations under this Convention to the extent strictly required by the exigencies of the situation, provided that such measures are not inconsistent with its other obligations under international law.

(2) No derogation from Article 2, except in respect of deaths resulting from lawful acts of war or from Articles 3, 4 (para 1) and 7 shall be made under this provision.

(3) Any High Contracting Party availing itself of this right of derogation shall keep the Secretary General of the Council of Europe fully informed of the measures which it has taken and the reasons therefore. It shall also inform the Secretary General of the Council of Europe when such measures have ceased to operate and the provisions of the Convention are again being fully executed.

Article 15 allows derogation in respect of most, but not all of the articles. Derogation from Article 2 is not allowed except in respect of death resulting from lawful acts of war, while Articles 3, 4(1) and 7 are entirely non-derogable. Apart from these exceptions, a valid derogation requires the state in question to show that there is a state of war or public emergency and, in order to determine the validity of this claim, two questions should be asked. First, is there an actual or imminent exceptional crisis threatening the organised life of the state? Second, is it really necessary to adopt measures requiring derogation from the articles in question? A margin of discretion is allowed in answering these questions because it is thought that the state in question is best placed to determine the facts, but it is not unlimited; Strasbourg will review it if the state has acted unreasonably. However, the Court has not been very consistent as regards the margin allowed to the state in relation to derogations.[454] In general, if a derogation is entered, it must first be investigated and, if found invalid, the claims in question will then be examined.

The UK entered a derogation in the case of *Brogan*[455] after the European Court of Human Rights had found that a violation of Art 5, which protects liberty, had occurred. At the time of the violation, there was no derogation in force in respect of Art 5 because the UK had withdrawn its derogation. This might suggest either that there was no need for it or that the UK had chosen not to derogate despite the gravity of the situation that would have justified derogation.[456]

---

454 See pp 96–97.
455 (1989) 11 EHRR 117.
456 See Chapter 12, pp 897–98.

However, after the decision in the European Court, the UK entered the derogation, stating that there was an emergency at the time. This was challenged as an invalid derogation,[457] but the claim failed on the basis that the exigencies of the situation did amount to a public emergency and the derogation could not be called into question merely because the government had decided to keep open the possibility of finding a means in the future of ensuring greater conformity with Convention obligations.[458] The fact that the emergency measures had been in place since 1974 did not mean that the emergency was not still in being. However, it may be argued that a state's failure to enter a derogation need not preclude the claim that a state of emergency did exist. If, whenever a state perceived the possibility that an emergency situation might exist, it felt it had to enter a derogation as an 'insurance measure' this would encourage a wider use of derogation, which would clearly be undesirable.

In the *Greek* case,[459] the Commission was prepared to hold an Article 15 derogation invalid. Greece had alleged that the derogation was necessary due to the exigencies of the situation: it was necessary to constrain the activities of communist agitators due to the disruption they were likely to cause. There had been past disruption which had verged on anarchy. Greece, therefore, claimed that it could not abide by the articles in question: Articles 10 and 11. Apart from violations of those articles, violations of Article 3, which is non-derogable, were also alleged. The Commission found that the derogation was not needed; the situation at the decisive moment did not contain all the elements necessary under Article 15. The use of a derogation post 9/11 by the UK is considered in Chap 15.

Article 16: restriction on the political activity of aliens

Nothing in Articles 10, 11 and 14 shall be regarded as preventing the High Contracting Parties from imposing restrictions on the political activity of aliens.

Since Article 16 applies to Articles 10 and 11, it implies that restrictions over and above those already imposed due to the second paragraphs of those Articles can be imposed on aliens in respect of their enjoyment of the freedoms guaranteed, as far as their political activity is concerned. This does not mean that aliens have *no* safeguard of freedom of expression, association or assembly; restrictions can be imposed only if they relate to political activities. Through its effect on Art 14, Article 16 affects all the rights in the Convention, since it means that the national authorities can discriminate in relation to aliens as far as any of the Convention rights are concerned. Article 16 has, therefore, been criticised as creating consequences which 'hardly fit into the system of the Convention'.[460] The fact that discrimination as regards the protection afforded to Convention rights is allowable, would not, however, preclude claims that the substantive rights – other than those arising under Articles 10 and 11 – had been violated.

---

457 *Brannigan and McBride v UK* (1993) 17 EHRR 539.
458 It may be noted that the derogation was withdrawn due to the inception of the Terrorism Act 2000, s 41 and an amendment was made to the Human Rights Act, Sched 3, Part 1, by order, accordingly: Human Rights Act (Amendment) Order 2001, SI 2001/1216.
459 *Greece v Netherlands* (1969) 12 YB 1.
460 See Van Dijk, P and Van Hoof, F, *Theory and Practice of the European Convention on Human Rights*, 3rd edn, 1998, Kluwer, p 410.

Article 17: destruction of convention rights

Nothing in this Convention may be interpreted as implying for any State, group or person any right to engage in any activity or perform any act aimed at the destruction of any of the rights and freedoms set forth herein or at their limitation to a greater extent than is provided for in the Convention.

Article 17 prevents a person relying on a Convention right where his or her ultimate aim is the destruction or limitation of Convention rights. Article 17 is dealt with on the issue of admissibility, but it can be looked at a later stage too. Its 'restriction' applies to all the rights and freedoms. In general, if Article 17 is violated, this may well mean that one of the other restrictions on the freedom in question applies too; thus, Article 17 is of importance only when it appears that some measure allows evasion of a Convention guarantee in a manner not covered by the other restrictions. Thus, Article 17 must be read in conjunction with all the articles as allowing for a new exception. This is of particular importance where the guarantee in question is subject to few or no restrictions.

Making a reservation: Art 57

Art 57 provides that a state can declare when signing the Convention that it cannot abide by a particular provision because domestic law then in force is not in conformity with it. This may be done when the Convention or Protocol is ratified. The Court will review the reservation in order to see whether it is specific enough: it should not be of too general a nature.[461] The UK has only entered a reservation in respect of Protocol 1.[462]

7 Conclusions

It is clear that in one sense, the Convention has been astoundingly successful in creating a standard of human rights which is perceived by so many Europeans as relevant and valuable despite the fact that well over half a century has passed since it was created. The enormous and continuing increase in the number of petitions in the late 1980s, during the 1990s and post-2000 suggest that its potential has only relatively recently been understood. Its influence significantly increased once a number of Eastern European states became signatories to it. Although it was only intended to create a minimum standard of human rights, it has succeeded in revealing basic flaws in UK law in relation to, for example, the decision to maintain or renew the detention of life prisoners.[463]

At the same time, its ability to bring about change in the laws and practices of member states must not be exaggerated. Arguably, the Convention may be termed a largely procedural charter in the sense that a challenge to a flawed procedure is more likely to succeed under it than a claim that a substantive right has been violated.[464] Further,

---

461 In *Belilos v Switzerland* (1988) EHRR 466, it was found that the reservation did not comply with Art 64 because it was too general.
462 The right to education (Art 2) is only accepted if compatible with provision of efficient instruction, training, and avoidance of unreasonable public expenditure.
463 See, e.g., *Thynne, Wilson and Gunnel v UK* (1990) 13 EHRR 666.
464 See, e.g., *Mats Jacobson v Sweden* (1990) 13 EHRR 79, above, p 58, n 181.

it may be argued that the machinery for the enforcement of the Convention is wholly inadequate, particularly in the face of a government unashamedly prepared to breach it for long periods of time.[465] This chapter spent some time dwelling on the stages through which an application will pass if it is pursued all the way through the system. The process means that if an application which is ultimately successful takes five years before the final decision, the individual affected may have to suffer a violation of his or her rights for all that time, although an interim remedy may be available under Rule 39 where the chamber or its president considers that it should be adopted in the interest of the parties or of the proper conduct of the proceedings. Usually, such a remedy would be granted where there is an immediate risk to life or health, in death penalty cases[466] or in deportation or extradition cases.[467] There is no formal mechanism available, such as an interim injunction, to prevent the continuing violation, but a Rule 39 request is normally complied with. Once the Court and Commission merged, some of the overlapping stages, such as the dual consideration of admissibility, disappeared, although the question of admissibility itself still arises. The process is still lengthy, despite the Protocol 14 reforms, especially as the number of petitions increased enormously due to the accession of Eastern European member states.

If a petition comes before the European Court of Human Rights, it may decide that no violation has occurred due to its invocation of the margin of appreciation. If, however, it declares that a breach has indeed occurred, the violation may well subsist for some years while the member state concerned considers the extent to which it will respond. Eventually, a measure may be adopted that may still represent a violation of rights, but of a less pernicious nature.[468] A challenge to such a measure would have to go through the same lengthy process in order to bring about any improvement in the protection afforded in the member state to the right in question.

Thus, it may be concluded that reliance on the Convention has tended to produce only erratic, flawed and fairly weak protection of freedoms in the UK. However, as argued at the beginning of this chapter, the solution does not appear to be adoption of a more coercive process since that might lead to open conflict with Strasbourg and perhaps, ultimately, to withdrawal of some state parties from the Convention. It was intended that the twin problems of the slow procedure and inadequate enforcement would be addressed by the reception of the Convention into UK law under the HRA. The framework of the HRA, as the means of affording the needed further effect to the Convention in domestic law, is considered in Chapter 4. But at the present time the HRA is under threat of repeal, as mentioned above, with probable replacement of the HRA by a British Bill of Rights, and the radical possibility that Britain might withdraw

---

465 The UK Government is quite frequently slow to respond to an adverse ruling, and when the response comes, it may be inadequate or non-existent, as in the prisoners' voting rights ruling in *Hirst* (n 407). See Chapter 4, pp 170–71.

466 *Ocalan v Turkey* (2005) 41 EHRR 45.

467 *Soering v UK* (1989) 11 EHRR 439.

468 The response of the UK Government to the ruling in *Malone v UK* (1984) 7 EHRR 14, which was to place telephone tapping on a statutory footing (under the Interception of Communications Act 1985), may be an example of an inadequate implementation of a ruling since the Act did not require independent authorisation of intercept warrants even in cases unconcerned with national security. The position under the legislation which replaced the 1985 Act – the Regulation of Investigatory Powers Act 2000, Part 1 – is, in essentials, the same. (See further Chapter 11, pp 794–99.)

from the ECHR is being mooted (although it is possible that a Bill of Rights will not be introduced before the next General Election, expected in 2020, and withdrawal from the ECHR would probably only be a possibility if the Conservatives had a more substantial majority after that election). If that occurred the post-war consensus on protecting human rights might well begin to break down and the level of protection of human rights in Britain might tend to diminish. A possible option for the Conservative government, however, would be, rather than withdrawal, to rely on the compromise which in effect is already – broadly speaking – in place since Protocol 15 (not yet in force) emphasised subsidiarity, and the Strasbourg Court itself is showing signs of seeking to appease the UK government,[469] especially where senior judges in the domestic courts have fully considered the ECHR arguments.[470] If a British Bill of Rights (BBoR) replaced the HRA in 2018–20, but citizens could still bring cases against the UK at Strasbourg, that would largely not itself necessarily lead to a greater likelihood of breaches of the ECHR, since the rights protected under the BBoR would largely echo the ECHR ones, and there is no requirement under the ECHR itself that a member state should incorporate the ECHR into domestic law.[471] But the intention of the current Prime Minister, Theresa May, appears to be to create some watering down of the rights under the BBoR as compared with the ECHR as interpreted at Strasbourg. As she appears to accept, that might indeed lead to further challenges to the UK at Strasbourg.

---

469 See further, Fenwick, H, 'Protocol 15, enhanced subsidiarity and a dialogic approach, or appeasement in recent cases at Strasbourg against the UK', in Ziegler, K (ed), *The European Court of Human Rights and the UK – a Strained Relationship*, 2016, Hart.

470 See e.g., in relation to Art 5: *Gillan v UK* (2010) 50 EHRR 45; *Austin v UK* (2012) 55 EHRR 14. See in relation to Art 3: *Ahmad and others v UK* (2013) 56 EHRR 1. See in relation to Art 6: *Horncastle v UK* Appl 4184/10, judgment of 16 December 2014.

471 See e.g., Fenwick, H, 'The Conservative stance in the 2015 election on the UK's relationship with the Strasbourg Court and its jurisprudence – bluff, exit strategy or compromise on both sides?' UK Constitutional law group blog, 10 March 2015; Fenwick, H, 'The Conservative anti-ECHR stance and a British Bill of Rights: rhetoric and reality; Conservative policy on the Human Rights Act: the role of the Bill of Rights' Commission and the aim of handing back autonomy to the UK in human rights matters' UK Constitutional Law Group blog, 1 November 2011; see at http://ukconstitutionallaw. org/2011/11/01/helen-fenwick-the-conservative-anti-echr-stance-and-a-british-bill-of-rights-rhetoric-and-reality/; the *Independent* reports that at present in any event plans to introduce a BBoR may be delayed or even dropped, during the current Parliament: A Cowburn, 11.8.16. See further Chapter 3.

Chapter 3

Methods of protecting civil liberties and human rights in the UK aside from the Human Rights Act

1 Introduction

The premise behind the adoption of Bills of Rights all over the world is that citizens can never be fully assured of the safety of their fundamental civil and political rights unless those rights are afforded protection from state interference. It is thought that such protection can be achieved by enshrining a number of rights in a Bill of Rights, affording it some constitutional protection and entrusting it – in effect – to the judiciary on the basis that a government cannot be expected to keep a satisfactory check on itself; only a source of power independent of it can do so. Democracies across the world that have adopted a bill or charter of rights have entrusted its application largely to the judiciary on the basis that among such sources of power, they are best placed to ensure the delivery of the rights to citizens. Dworkin has argued that under a bill of rights, a government is not free to treat liberty as a commodity of convenience or to ignore rights that the nation is under a moral duty to respect.[1]

In the UK, however, it was thought until relatively recently that the unwritten constitution recognising residual liberties, as maintained by Parliament and the judiciary, provided a sufficiently effective means of ensuring that power was not abused.[2] As discussed in Chapter 1, residual liberties were, however, vulnerable to invasion: the doctrine of parliamentary sovereignty meant that Parliament could legislate in an area of fundamental rights, thereby restricting or even destroying them.[3] Pre-HRA the judiciary could also invade liberties in developing the common law, while unless a right could be said to be recognised by the common law, public authorities could invade it without relying on statute, the prerogative or common law rules, although a successful challenge at the Strasbourg Court could then have arisen.[4]

The argument that residual liberties were ineffective and that the change to a rights-based approach should be brought about gathered momentum during the 1970s and 1980s and gained ascendancy in the 1990s. This change of view was clearly traceable to the development and influence of international human rights law,[5] especially the impact

1 Dworkin, R, *A Bill of Rights for Britain*, 1990, Chatto and Windus, p 23.
2 See Jennings, *WI, The Approach to Self-Governance*, 1958, CUP.
3 Thus, freedom of assembly was severely restricted in the 1990s and beyond; see Chapter 9, esp at pp 620–22.
4 See *Malone v MPC* [1979] Ch 344, p 372.
5 See further Hunt, M, *Using Human Rights Law in English Courts*, 1997, Hart.

of the European Convention on Human Rights. The argument was further fuelled by the invasions of liberty that occurred under the Conservative governments from 1979 to 1997. It was argued that the traditional checks on government power could now be seen as insufficiently effective. These two developments were, it is suggested, interlinked; as Hunt argues: 'no single factor has been more significant in exposing this gap between theory [the traditional account of domestic constitutional arrangements] and practice than the international dimension which [over the last 25 to 30 years] domestic constitutional practice has been forced to accommodate'.[6] This view of the record of those Conservative governments, viewed from the perspective offered by international human rights law, was used to support the introduction of the Human Rights Act 1998 (HRA).[7] The HRA comes as close to creating a Bill of Rights as the UK has ever come. However, the Conservative leadership, as part of the Coalition government from 2010–15, and now leading a Conservative government, views the HRA as having elevated individual rights too far over societal interests, as having been used to protect criminals and terrorists. Thus, while the current government does not appear to dispute that a bill of rights is needed, rather than relying on pre-HRA constitutional arrangements, it considers that an especially tailored British Bill of Rights is now needed.

This chapter begins by considering the traditional methods of protecting civil liberties in the UK, methods that are proving still significant during the Human Rights Act era. Existing established rights and existing rights to bring proceedings are preserved by s 11 of the HRA; therefore, all the existing methods of protecting civil liberties already developed under the law are still highly relevant. The chapter goes on to consider the proposal to enact a British Bill of Rights (BBoR) to replace the HRA at some point between 2018–21: at the present time the Conservative party plans, as mentioned in Chapter 1, to introduce a BBoR and repeal the HRA. Chapter 4 considers the model of protection that was chosen for the Convention, in the Human Rights Act, which at present is still playing a significant role in protecting human rights in the UK.

2 Methods of protecting civil liberties in the UK outside the HRA

The democratic process as the guardian of civil liberties

It has traditionally been thought that Parliament provides a means of allowing the will of the people to influence the government towards the maintenance of liberty[8] through free elections and aided by the operation of a free press. It can react to the needs of civil liberties by providing specific legislative safeguards and, in so doing, can take into account the views and expertise of a range of groups. Moreover, it will govern according to the rule of law, which will include the notion that it will accept certain limits on its powers based on normative ideals.[9]

---

6 *Ibid*, p 1.
7 The HRA received Royal Assent on 9 November 1998.
8 See, e.g., Dicey, AV, *The Law of the Constitution*, 1959, Macmillan, pp 189–90; Hume, D, *Political Discourses*, 1906, Walter Scott (first published 1752), p 203.
9 See, e.g., Wade, W and Bradley, A, *Constitutional and Administrative Law*, 1985, Longman, pp 99–100.

However, commentators such as Ewing and Gearty, evaluating governments in the 1980s, argued that these traditional checks were insufficiently effective as methods of curbing the power of a determined and illiberal governing party: 'Mrs Thatcher has merely utilised to the full the scope for untrammeled power latent in the British Constitution but obscured by the hesitancy and scruples of previous consensus-based political leaders.'[10] In particular, it is clear that when the government in power has a large majority, as the Thatcher government had, it may more readily depart from traditional constitutional principles if it is minded to do so, because Parliament is likely to be ineffective as a check on its activities. Even where the governing party does not have a large majority, it can still introduce legislation abridging basic freedoms, especially where the main opposition party sympathises with its stance. As this book indicates at a number of points, the Major government exemplified this tendency. The Thatcher and Major governments introduced very little legislation protective of civil liberties except where they were forced to do so by a ruling of the European Court of Human Rights, an EC Directive or a ruling of the European Court of Justice. In short, the dangers represented by the doctrine of parliamentary sovereignty in terms of threatening fundamental liberties became more apparent during the Conservative years of 1979–97.

It may also be questioned more generally whether the Westminster Parliament by its nature provides an effective forum for taking the protection of civil liberties into account in passing legislation. A number of writers[11] have noted that Parliament at times displays a readiness to pass emergency legislation which may go further than necessary in curtailing civil liberties and which is apt to remain on the statute book long after the emergency is over. MPs, whether in government or out of it, tend to respond in an unconsidered fashion to emergencies, apparent or real. Governments wish to be perceived as acting quickly and decisively, while members of the opposition parties, mindful of their popularity, may not wish to oppose measures adopted in the face of scares whipped up by some sections of the media. Such reactions were seen in relation to the original Official Secrets Act 1911, passed in one day with all-party support in response to a spy scare. The far-reaching s 2, which was never debated at all, remained on the statute book for 78 years. Similarly, the Birmingham pub bombings on 21 November 1974 led, four days later, to the announcement of the Prevention of Terrorism Bill,[12] which was passed by 29 November virtually without amendment or dissent. But some examples can be found to support the other side in this debate. It is generally agreed that the democratic process worked well in creating the Police and Criminal Evidence Act 1984,[13] and it is fair to say that it had at least some impact, as suggested above, on the Police Act 1997.

In the 1990s, Parliament quite frequently showed a marked readiness to accept claims that a number of proposed statutory measures would lead to the curbing of terrorist or criminal activity. A number of political scientists observed that in the 1990s there was a general policy convergence, with the frontbenchers of the Labour and Conservative

10 Ewing, KD and Gearty, CA, *Freedom under Thatcher*, 1989, Clarendon, p 7.
11 E.g., Robertson, G, *Freedom, the Individual and the Law*, 1993, Penguin, p 506; Walker, C, *The Prevention of Terrorism in British Law*, 2nd edn, 1992, Manchester University Press, Chapter 4, p 32.
12 HC Debs Vol 882 col 35.
13 See Zander, M, *The Police and Criminal Evidence Act 1984*, 1995, Sweet and Maxwell, p xi: 'there can be no denying that the whole exercise was an example of the democratic process working'.

parties closer on many issues than at any point since the 1970s.[14] In the civil liberties context, two key examples were provided by the opposition impact on the Criminal Justice and Public Order Act 1994 and the Police Act 1997. Many pressure groups protested against the 1994 Bill: it probably attracted more public opposition than any other measure during the Conservative years in government from 1979 to 1997, apart from the 'poll tax'. But, despite protests against the Bill and the far-reaching nature of many of the new provisions, it went through Parliament relatively intact.[15] Similarly, the debate in the House of Commons on the Prevention of Terrorism (Additional Powers) Act 1996, which was guillotined, failed to consider in depth either the efficacy of the measure in terms of curbing terrorist activity or its likely impact on civil liberties.

The change of government in 1997, when Labour came to power after 18 years of Conservative rule, heralded the introduction of two key pieces of liberal legislation – the HRA 1998 and the Freedom of Information (FoI) Act 2000 (see Chapters 4 and 8). However, shortly after those Acts were introduced, the terrorist attacks of 9/11 occurred, heralding an era in which the prevention of terrorism became the prevailing concern. At the present time, 2016, due to the actions of ISIS/Daesh, that concern is even more influential than in 2001.

The prevailing stance on both government and opposition benches post-2001 remained a largely anti-liberal one during the following nine years of Labour rule. The central measures enhancing state power introduced in the first term of the Blair Government – the Terrorism Act 2000, the Regulation of Investigatory Powers Act 2000, the Anti-Terrorism Crime and Security Act 2001, showed, it is argued in this book, even less respect for human rights than measures such as the Police Act 1997. The stances of the then Labour Government, the subsequent Coalition government (2010–15) and the current Conservative government that took office in 2015 are indicated at various points in the following chapters. As Chapters 15, 13 and 9 in particular point out, post 9/11, criminal justice, anti-terrorism and public order legislation became markedly authoritarian.

Little changed once Labour was in opposition from 2010 onwards. For example, the Counter-terrorism and Security Bill 2015 was rushed through Parliament with limited scrutiny or public consultation on most of its provisions – a speed justified by the increased terror threat posed by the return of radicalised Muslims from Syria and Iraq after training with ISIS. Introduced at the end of November 2014, it finished its Commons stages on 7 January 2015 and had its second Lords reading on 13 January. It may be argued, then, that there was limited effective opposition in the Commons on counter-terror measures and human rights from the mid-1990s onwards, but especially post-9/11. However, the Liberal Democrats as part of the Coalition government from 2010 to 2015 did oppose certain measures, especially as to the mass collection of communications data.[16]

The House of Lords has had an impact on the protection of rights, notably its influence on the incorporation into the Police and Criminal Evidence Act 1984 of a provision with clear potential to safeguard the liberty of the citizen – s 78.[17] Crucial amendments to

---

14 Seldon, A, 'The consensus debate' (1994) 14 *Parliamentary Affairs* 512.
15 Smith, ATH, 'The Criminal Justice and Public Order Act 1994 – the public order elements', [1995] Crim LR 19, p 27.
16 See Chapter 11, pp 828–29.
17 House of Lords, *Hansard*, 31 July 1984, cols 635–75. See Chapter 14, p 979 *et seq.*

the Terrorism Act 2000, which narrowed the definition of 'terrorism' in cl 1, were passed in the Lords.[18] The Lords also expressed opposition to aspects of the Counter-terrorism Bill 2015; the government had to accept a partial amendment relating to a proposal to exempt universities and other academic institutions from anti-radicalisation measures.

However, the powers of the Lords to thwart the wishes of the Commons are limited. Section 2 of the Parliament Act 1911 makes various provisions for presenting a Bill for the royal assent against the opposition of the Lords. When a Bill has been passed by the Commons in two successive sessions and it is rejected for a second time by the Lords, it can be presented on its second rejection for the Royal Assent. The very existence of this power means that the need to invoke it is unlikely to arise because the Lords will wish to avoid the need for the Commons to use it.[19]

It may be concluded that Parliament has demonstrated that it is willing to move quickly to cut down freedoms, but it is, at the same time, slow to bring in measures to protect them, because civil liberties and human rights issues tend to be perceived as difficult to handle and as doubtful vote-winners. Under the HRA, the Westminster Parliament is still dominated by the executive and, aside from the impact of EU law, (at present) still has in theory an untrammelled power to introduce rights-abridging legislation throughout the UK.[20] During the HRA years, Parliament appeared to accept quite readily that when Bills were presented to it and were declared to be compatible with the Convention rights under s 19 of the HRA,[21] that meant that a process of human rights auditing had already occurred and that, therefore, concerns about the effect on human rights of the provisions in question could be allayed.[22] So it is clearly pertinent to ask whether the democratic process can be trusted to safeguard civil liberties and human rights in the context of the doctrine of parliamentary sovereignty. In so far as the Strasbourg Court decisions have influenced domestic law via the domestic courts, a future British Bill of Rights might ensure that such impact was diminished, removing some indirect trammelling impact on parliamentary decisions to diminish the scope of human rights.

Common law protection of civil liberties and human rights: current relevance of the traditional constitutional position

Judicial protection for liberties

Under the traditional view of the constitution, the judges will interpret common law doctrines so that fundamental freedoms are protected.[23] Judicial activism in the 1990s

---

18   The amendments resulted in s1(1)(b). See Chapter 15, pp 1048–49. But narrowing amendments in the Commons were rejected: HC Debs 15.3.2000, cols 399, 394.

19   The House of Lords will, however, on occasion use its powers of suspension fully as it did in relation to the Trade Union and Labour Relations (Amendment) Bill 1974–75.

20   See Chapter 4, p 147. Further, the government can, of course, use the Parliament Act procedure in order to get its legislation through the Lords, as it did in respect of the Sexual Offences (Amendment) Bill 2000. In practice, if the government has a small majority in Parliament, as the current Conservative government (post-2015) has, it may not risk seeking to persuade Parliament to pass controversial legislation affecting the whole of the UK, such as a Bill of Rights which also repealed the Human Rights Act, since the SNP and Labour MPs, together with MPs from other parties, might well combine to reject it.

21   See Chapter 4, pp 180–83.

22   In particular, although Parliament accepted a number of post-2000 counter-terror measures as ECHR-compatible, the judicial response in certain significant instances differed. See further Chapter 14, p 1027 *et seq.*

23   See *Entinck v Carrington* [1765] 19 state Tr 1029.

led to a number of significant decisions protective of liberty. They were influenced by international human rights law, and more specifically by the European Convention on Human Rights, in the sense that pre-HRA the judiciary began to demonstrate a strong inclination to show that the common law had long recognised the values encapsulated in the Convention.

The decision of *Derbyshire v Times Newspapers*,[24] which has been acclaimed as 'a legal landmark',[25] provides an important example of this tendency. The House of Lords found, without referring to Art 10 of the European Convention, that the importance the common law attached to free speech was such that defamation could not be available as an action to local (or central) government.[26] In the House of Lords, Lord Keith said: 'I find it satisfactory to be able to conclude that the common law of England is consistent with the [freedom of expression] obligations assumed under [the Convention].'[27] Butler-Sloss LJ said in the Court of Appeal: 'I can see no inconsistency between English law upon this subject and Art 10 . . . This is scarcely surprising, since we may pride ourselves on the fact that freedom of speech has existed in this country perhaps as long, if not longer than . . . in any other country in the world.'[28]

But, while an attachment to free speech values that is arguably consonant with the value it is accorded at Strasbourg is clearly evident in these decisions, this book discusses a number of decisions taken in the mid- to late-1990s affecting equally fundamental rights, in the fields of public protest,[29] police powers and fair trial rights,[30] which took a very ungenerous approach to rights and liberties. Thus, it can be said that over the last three decades, prior to the introduction of the HRA, the judiciary did not develop a coherent approach to the protection of civil rights and liberties, although the influence of the European Convention on Human Rights became very marked, especially in the field of freedom of expression, in the 1990s. The dualist approach became 'in reality a matter of degree'.[31] But the difference of degree was sometimes quite remarkable.

Judicial review

It may be said that, before the 1990s, when fundamental human rights became an increasingly significant factor in judicial review, strong deference was shown to executive decision-making in the politically important areas of executive action. The reluctance of judges to intervene in such areas, including those of public security or deportation,

---

24 [1993] AC 534; [1993] 1 All ER 1011; [1992] 3 WLR 28, HL.
25 See Laws, J (Sir), 'Is the High Court the guardian of fundamental constitutional rights?' [1993] PL 67.
26 *Derbyshire* was followed and its principle extended in *Goldsmith and Another v Bhoyrul and Others* [1997] 4 All ER 268; (1997) *The Times*, 20 June. It was found that a political party cannot sue in libel, although individual candidates would be able to.
27 [1993] AC 534, p 551.
28 [1992] 3 WLR 28, p 60.
29 Examples of such decisions discussed in this book include: the Divisional Court and House of Lords decisions in *DPP v Jones* and *Lloyd v DPP* [1999] 2 AC 240; [1997] 2 All ER 119 (for comment, see Fenwick, H, and Phillipson, G, 'Public protest, the Human Rights Act and judicial responses to political expression' [2000] PL 627) and *DPP v Moseley, Woodling and Selvanayagam*, Judgment of 9 June 1999; reported [1999] J Civ Lib 390, (Chapter 9, p 621 *et seq* and p 673, respectively).
30 *Khan* [1996] 3 WLR 162; *Chalkley* [1998] 2 Cr App R 79.
31 Hunt, M, *Using Human Rights Law in English Courts*, 1997, Hart Publishing, p 41.

was evident in a number of decisions. Those in *Secretary of State for the Home Depart-*
ment ex p Northumbria Police Authority[32] and *Secretary of State for the Home Depart-*
ment ex p Hosenball[33] showed this tendency to a particularly marked degree. Thus,
traditionally, the doctrine remained fundamentally limited in that as long as a minister
appeared to have followed a correct and fair procedure, to have acted within his or her
powers and to have made a decision that was not clearly unreasonable under the traditional *Wednesbury* test, the decision had to stand regardless of its potentially harmful
impact on civil liberties. The fact that basic liberties were curtailed in, for example,
the *GCHQ*[34] case did not, in itself, provide a ground for review. In cases that touched
directly on national security, so sensitive were the judges to the executive's duty to
uphold the safety of the realm, that they tended to define their powers even to look back
on the decision as almost non-existent.[35]

A development in the stance the judiciary was prepared to take when an administrative decision infringed human rights was evident in *Secretary of State for the Home*
Department ex p Brind.[36] The change was explained by Lord Bridge. He rejected the
argument that state officials must take the European Convention on Human Rights into
account in exercising discretionary power, and thus the possibility of extending the role
of the Convention in domestic law by importing it into administrative law was rejected.
The decision in *Brind* reaffirmed the accepted principle that the Convention should be
taken into account where domestic legislation was ambiguous. It also determined that
state officials were not bound by the Convention in exercising discretionary power.[37]
Lord Bridge, reflecting the view of the majority, accepted nevertheless that where fundamental rights are in issue they will affect the review of the exercise of such power.
He said:

> we are entitled to start from the premise that any restriction of the right of freedom
> of expression requires to be justified and nothing less than an important competing
> public interest will be sufficient to justify it. The primary judgment as to whether
> the particular competing public interest justifies the particular restriction . . . falls
> to be exercised by the Secretary of State . . . But we are entitled to exercise a sec-
> ondary judgment by asking whether a reasonable Secretary of State on the material
> before him could reasonably make that primary judgment.[38]

Thus, where fundamental human rights were in question, the *Wednesbury* test had to be
refined. This argument was applied and taken further in *Ministry for Defence ex p Smith*

32 [1989] QB 26; [1988] 2 WLR 590; [1988] 1 All ER 556, CA.
33 [1977] 1 WLR 766.
34 *Council of Civil Service Unions v Minister for Civil Service* [1985] AC 374; [1985] 3 WLR 1174; [1984]
    3 All ER 935, HL (the Prime Minister's decision struck directly at freedom of association).
35 See *Secretary of State for Home Affairs ex p Stitt* (1987) *The Times*, 3 February.
36 [1991] 1 AC 696; [1991] 1 All ER 720; [1991] 2 WLR 588, HL (political speech was directly curtailed);
    [1990] 1 All ER 469, CA.
37 It may be noted that the then Conservative government subsequently accepted that state officials exer-
    cising such powers should comply with the Convention: HL Deb 559 WA 7 December 1994 col 84 and
    WA 9 January 1995 Vol 560 col 1.
38 [1991] 1 All ER 720, p 723.

and Others.[39] The case concerned the legality of the policy of the Ministry of Defence in maintaining a ban on homosexuals in the armed forces. The applicants, homosexuals who had been dismissed due to the existence of the ban, applied for review of the policy. The court applied the usual *Wednesbury* principles. This meant that it could not interfere with the exercise of an administrative discretion on substantive grounds save where it was satisfied that the decision was unreasonable in the sense that it was beyond the range of responses open to a reasonable decision maker. But, in judging whether the decision maker had exceeded that margin of appreciation, the human rights context was important: 'the more substantial the interference with human rights, the more the court will require by way of justification before it will be satisfied that the decision was reasonable'.[40] Applying such principles and taking into account the support of the policy in both Houses of Parliament, it could not be said that the policy crossed the threshold of irrationality. The concept of proportionality, as considered by the Master of the Rolls in this instance, was not viewed as a separate head of challenge, but merely as an aspect of *Wednesbury* unreasonableness.[41]

The significance of this decision lay in the meaning attributed to the word 'reasonable'; it denoted only a decision which was 'within the range of responses open to a reasonable decision-maker'.[42] But, the decision maker was required to take account of human rights in appropriate cases and she had to have a more convincing justification the more her decision was likely to trespass on those rights. That decision, however, remained primarily one for the decision maker. The courts would only intervene if the decider had come up with a justification which no reasonable person could consider trumped the human rights considerations – a position that was akin to classic *GCHQ* irrationality.[43] However, *Smith* did require a variable standard of review, depending on the human rights context.

A further, linked, factor of significance in *Smith* was the determination as to which policy considerations were to be allowed to override rights and which were not. It appeared that in making this determination, easily satisfied criteria were adopted. The policy factors were not required to satisfy the test of meeting a 'pressing social need',[44] since satisfying a lesser test nevertheless brought the decision within the range of responses open to a reasonable decision maker. This decision echoed that of Lord Bridge in *Brind* in relation to determinations as to overriding individual rights as guaranteed in the European Convention on Human Rights.[45]

---

39 [1996] 1 All ER 257; [1996] ICR 740. See also *Secretary of State for the Home Department ex p McQuillan* [1995] 3 All ER 400; (1994) *Independent*, 23 September, in which Laws J's approach was expressly followed. Sedley J was unable to find for the applicant due to the particular statutory framework in question.

40 [1996] 1 All ER 257, p 263. See also *Bugdaycay v Secretary of State for the Home Dept* [1987] AC 514, p 531. For comment, see Fordham, M, 'What is anxious scrutiny?' [1996] JR 81.

41 For further argument as to the notion of proportionality, see Himsworth, C, 'Legitimately expecting proportionality' [1996] PL 46; his argument that the notion of proportionality as a separate head of review remains a possibility rests on an examination of *Ministry of Agriculture, Fisheries and Food ex p Hamble* [1995] 2 All ER 714.

42 *Ibid.*

43 Fenwick, H and Phillipson, G, *Sourcebook on Public Law*, 1997, Cavendish (2nd edn, 2002), p 803.

44 See Chapter 2, pp 92–93.

45 See *Brind* case [1991] 1 AC 696.

In 1993, Sir John Laws, in an important article,[46] suggested a method of developing judicial review so that it could afford greater protection to liberties. It was proposed that a stringent presumption could be imposed – namely, that no statute's purpose could include interference with fundamental rights embedded in the common law and that such interference would only be allowed if it was demonstrated that reading the statute to permit such interference was the only interpretation possible. To assume that power is never granted to infringe basic liberties is to make a substantive claim – and until the late 1990s, the courts were not prepared to make it. Preparedness to impose such a presumption in all cases implied the kind of unified, purposeful determination to protect civil liberties that most commentators failed to perceive in the judiciary during most of the 1980s and 1990s.[47]

This aspect of the thesis, concerning statutory interpretation in relation to fundamental human rights, found expression in a number of decisions in the immediate pre-HRA era. In this sense, s 3 of the HRA (see Chapter 4 below) was prefigured in certain decisions that recognised common law rights that cannot be abrogated except by express words or necessary implication – where there is only one way of reading the legislation in question. They included the rights of access to the courts,[48] to free speech[49] and to basic subsistence,[50] and certain of these decisions are discussed further below.[51] The rule of construction in these instances was described in one of the most significant of these decisions, *Ex p Simms*,[52] by Lord Hoffmann, as follows:

> Parliamentary sovereignty means that Parliament can if it chooses legislate contrary to fundamental principles of human rights . . . But the principle of legality means that Parliament must squarely confront what it is doing and count the political cost. Fundamental rights cannot be overridden by general or ambiguous words . . . because there is too great a risk that the full implications of their unqualified meaning may have passed unnoticed in the democratic process . . .[53]

In *Ex p Witham*,[54] Laws J found that the power of the Lord Chancellor to prescribe court fees was not based on sufficiently precise words to allow him to deny the right of access to a court by preventing an applicant on income support from issuing proceedings for defamation.

The second aspect of Sir John Laws' proposed thesis was as follows: in the pre-HRA era, the courts insisted that relevant considerations should be taken into account

---

46 Laws [1993] PL 59–79.
47 See, e.g., Oliver, D, 'A Bill of Rights for the United Kingdom' in D. Oliver (ed.), *Government in the United Kingdom* (1991), pp 151, 163; Ewing, KD, and Gearty, C, *Freedom under Thatcher*, 1989, Clarendon, generally and pp 64, 111, 157–60, 270–71 for particular criticisms of *anti-libertarian* judicial decisions and attitudes; Lester, A, 'Fundamental rights: the United Kingdom isolated?' [1984] PL 46.
48 *R v Lord Chancellor ex p Witham* [1998] QB 575. But *cf R v Lord Chancellor ex p Lightfoot* [2000] 2 WLR 318. For comment on the first instance decision [1998] 4 All ER 764, see Elliott, M, 'Lightfoot: tracing the perimeter of constitutional rights' [1998] JR 217.
49 *R v Secretary of State for the Home Dept ex p Simms* [1999] 3 All ER 400, CA; [1999] 3 WLR 328, HL.
50 89 *R v Secretary of State for Social Security ex p Joint Council of Welfare of Immigrants* [1996] 4 All ER 835; *Lord Saville ex p A* [1999] 4 All ER 860.
51 See Part II, p 289.
52 *R v Secretary of State for the Home Dept ex p Simms* [1999] 3 All ER 400, CA; [1999] 3 WLR 328, HL.
53 [1999] 3 All ER 400, p 412.
54 [1998] QB 575.

when making a decision, but held that the weight to be given to those considerations was entirely for the decision maker to determine. Laws argued that, on principle, while this might be a reasonable approach when the matter under consideration involved such issues as economic policy, this was far from the case where fundamental rights were at stake, since it meant that the decision maker would be free 'to accord a high or low importance to the right in question, as he chooses' which 'cannot be right'. The Laws approach was applied in order to reach an outcome protective of individual rights in *Cambridge HA ex p B*[55] in which Laws J himself was presiding; his decision was immediately overturned by the Court of Appeal.[56] In contrast to that decision, the decision in *R v Lord Saville ex p A*[57] arguably prefigured the introduction of the proportionality test under the HRA and was consistent with that of Laws in *Ex p B*. The Court of Appeal subjected the decision not to afford anonymity to witnesses in the 'Bloody Sunday' inquiry to anxious scrutiny and went on to find that the inquiry had acted irrationally in so doing since it had failed to attach sufficient importance to the right to life.

This discussion of judicial review in the immediate pre-HRA era indicates that it is possible to identify a common law tradition of upholding fundamental rights in certain limited, but central, areas. That development is very clearly continuing in the HRA era[58] as discussed below, since the common law is being affected by the values of the Convention rights. The decisions considered, together with a number of others of a similar nature,[59] reaffirm, it is suggested, the value of judicial review as a means of ensuring that some harmony between UK executive practice and the standards laid down by the European Convention on Human Rights is achieved, and this was the case even in the pre-HRA era. Murray Hunt has argued that a common law tradition of developing human rights that reflected those enshrined in international human rights treaties was well established.[60] Judicial review had already shown its potential to play a much greater part in the protection of human rights in the UK in the areas of activity affected by EU law.[61] In such areas, the merits of the decision were relevant and express words used in a statute could not overcome EU provisions.[62]

55 [1995] TLR 159; [1995] WLR 898, CA.
56 [1995] 1 WLR 898.
57 [1999] 4 All ER 860.
58 See *Secretary of State for the Home Dept ex p Daly* [2001] 3 All ER 433; [2001] UKHL 26, HL. The case concerned the examination of legal correspondence between a prisoner and his solicitor. The applicant claimed that he should be able to be present while his correspondence was being read. The House of Lords upheld his claim on the basis that the policy was disproportionate to the aim in view. Lord Steyn said: 'it is of great importance . . . that the common law itself is recognised as a sufficient source of the confidential right to confidential communication with a legal advisor for the purpose of obtaining legal advice' (para 30).
59 See, e.g., *Secretary of State for Social Security ex p Joint Council for the Welfare of Immigrants* [1996] 4 All ER 385; *Secretary of State for the Home Dept and Another ex p Norney and Others* (1995) *The Times*, 6 October.
60 Hunt, M, *Using Human Rights Law in English Courts*, 1997, Hart Publishing, p 5.
61 See *Secretary of State for Employment ex p EOC* [1994] 2 WLR 409, HL.
62 For the pre-HRA view that the direct influence of the Convention in the UK due to its significance as a source of general principles of EU law is not confined only to those areas of activity affected by EU law: see Beyleveld, D, 'The concept of a human right and incorporation of the ECHR' [1995] PL 577.

Resurgence of the notion of common law rights in the HRA era[63]

During the HRA era, and especially once Conservative proposals to repeal the HRA gained traction, it became apparent that a growing reanimation of common law constitutional rights was occurring post-2010. Richard Clayton dubbed this tendency 'The Empire strikes back: Common law rights and the Human Rights Act'[64] – the Empire representing the common law. When Lady Hale referred to this analogy in a recent speech,[65] it was immediately seized on by parts of the right-wing media to mean – in their words – that Britain's 'top woman lawyer' was advocating a fight back of the common law against the Europeanised HRA.[66] Perhaps wisely, Lady Hale did not herself rely on that analogy – she termed this tendency in her speech 'UK Constitutionalism on the March'. She said on this: 'there is a growing awareness of the extent to which the UK's constitutional principles should be at the forefront of the court's analysis'. She was referring in particular to a number of recent cases in the Supreme Court – *Osborn*,[67] *Kennedy*[68] and *A v BBC*.[69]

Broadly speaking, the Supreme Court in these instances found that in the HRA era where a dispute falls within the area of a Convention right, it does not follow that the Convention should be considered first without considering the common law. In these decisions common law principles of open justice, fair process and accountability were focused upon, and in *Kennedy* and *Osborn* were determinative of the issues, rather than the Convention rights in question.

A number of key points can be made as to these decisions regarding the relationship senior judges currently perceive between the common law and the ECHR, under the HRA. In *Osborn v Parole Board* Lord Reed was concerned that the submissions on behalf of the appellants focused on Art 5(4) ECHR, and paid comparatively little attention to domestic administrative law. He said that that approach did not properly reflect the relationship between domestic law (considered apart from the Human Rights Act) and Convention rights. He said that where an issue fell within the ambit of a Convention guarantee, it did not follow that the legal analysis of the problem should begin and end with the Strasbourg case law

Similarly, in the Supreme Court in *Kennedy* criticism of the arguments put on behalf of a journalist arose since the argument centred purely on use of Art 10 and s 3 HRA to 'read down' an absolute exemption from the Freedom of Information (FoI) Act 2000, covering inquiries by the Charities Commission. Again the lack of argument based on the common law was criticised. Lord Toulson said: 'since the enactment of HRA there has sometimes been a baleful and unnecessary tendency to overlook the common law'. The duties placed on the Commission under the Charities Act 2011 were, it was found,

---

63   See Masterman, R and Wheatle, S, 'A common law resurgence in rights protection?' [2015] EHRLR 57.
64   Paper given at the Oxford University Public Law Discussion Group; see [2015] (1) PL 3-12.
65   Keynote address to the Constitutional and Administrative Law Bar Association Conference 2014.
66   'Judges are increasingly using British common law to settle human rights cases because they are 'irritated' by the rising creep of the European Courts': *Daily Telegraph*, August 2014.
67   *Osborn v Parole Board* [2013] UKSC 61.
68   *Kennedy v Information Commissioner* [2014] UKSC 20.
69   *A v BBC* [2014] UKSC 25.

underpinned by a common law presumption in favour of openness in judicial proceedings and so would have to be interpreted in the light of that presumption.

In *A v BBC* the argument put on behalf of the BBC was that the Convention as received into domestic law under the HRA had superseded common law rights. That stance was roundly rejected. Lord Reed said that the common law principle of open justice is still vigorous, even when Convention rights are also applicable. He reaffirmed that the approach to the relationship between common law and the ECHR under the HRA in the two previous decisions mentioned above was correct.

So the key message from these decisions is that the common law must not sink into insignificance in the HRA era – it is still robust and vibrant, and capable of development. It was emphasised that rights recognised at common law should be the first port of call in instances such as these. That is partly an issue of chronology – the decisions do not suggest that the common law should take primacy over the Convention within the area of a Convention right. But in terms of the sequence of the argument, the common law should be considered first. But *Kennedy* went further – the majority found that reliance on Art 10 would not in any event clearly mean that there would be a right to receive the information in question, but that the Charities Act, interpreted under common law principles of open justice, could allow it to be received. In other words, *Kennedy* can be taken to imply that certain common law rights are more extensive than their ECHR counterparts.

It was also made clear in all three decisions that having considered the common law it might be found to fail to reflect fully the requirements of the Convention and might require development in order to do so. Lord Reed also said in *A v BBC* that if the balance between competing values is struck differently under the ECHR than under the common law, then primacy would be given to the ECHR – due to s 6 HRA.

But this current tendency also has limits. Lady Hale also pointed out that if a renaissance of common law constitutional rights was occurring its reach should not be overstated. If this is seen as a renaissance of UK constitutional rights, it is important not to overstate its reach. The limits of common law protection for rights are of course yet to be fully explored. The common law conception of rights differs from that of the ECHR as interpreted at Strasbourg, partly due to its origins, and is in some respects less expansive, less focused on individual situations, more pragmatic and flexible. It is no coincidence that the cases in question concerned fair process and open justice since those are long-recognised common law principles. To them should also be added respect for life, and in that context the recent decision also in the Supreme Court in *Nicklinson*,[70] concerning allowing assisted suicide in some circumstances, should be considered. Lord Wilson spoke of 'the sanctity of life which, for obvious reasons, is hard-wired into the minds of every living person and lies at the heart of the common law'. But rights based on the concepts of autonomy and of non-discrimination – which were argued for to support acceptance of assisted suicide – would not tend to receive the same protection as under the ECHR, as the Court of Appeal made clear in *Nicklinson*. The Supreme Court decision found that the common law was not allowed or was deemed unable to play any part in furthering a right of assisted suicide in the UK – Art 8 ECHR was instead relied on. This decision, which post-dated the other three decisions mentioned above, illustrates in various respects

---

70 *R (on the application of Nicklinson and another) (Appellants) v Ministry of Justice (Respondent)* [2014] UKSC 38.

the limitations of relying on the common law if the HRA were repealed (and the position would of course be exacerbated if the UK also withdrew from the ECHR as has been mooted by the current Conservative leadership, although not in 2016).

The list of rights recognised by the common law would not, it is argued, be as extensive as the list contained in the ECHR. The list would also be uncertain and contestable; as Lady Hale said: 'It is true that no two lists of common law rights would be the same.' Also, in the general sense of developing protection for rights, the mechanisms of the HRA are not available to the judges when relying on common law principles. Where s 3 HRA gives Parliamentary permission to the judges to remould statutes to accord with the ECHR,[71] the same obviously cannot be said in relation to the common law. So the judges are unlikely to depart from clear words in an Act of Parliament by reading down wording to protect rights under common law principles. Further, the use of s 4 HRA to promote dialogue with Parliament – pivotal in *Nicklinson* – would not be available.

Conclusions

It is reasonably clear that, in the pre-HRA era, the judiciary did not seem to be united around a clear conception of their role. No compelling evidence emerged of a common understanding that they should form a bulwark to protect the citizens' liberties against the burgeoning power of the executive. While decisions in the field of free speech suggested an acceptance that Convention values were recognised as common law principles, decisions in the areas in which the common law had traditionally taken a non-rights-based stance, such as public order and exclusion of physical evidence unlawfully obtained, showed a persistence of that tradition. Second, even in the area in which a clear acceptance of the role of the common law in protecting fundamental human rights was present – judicial review – the courts seemed to lack the determination to continue pushing the limits of the doctrine outwards in order to ensure greater protection. They stopped short of introducing a full proportionality test.

It may be persuasively argued that since the judiciary had no 'textual anchor for their decisions' pre-HRA and had to 'rely on an appeal to normative ideals that lack any mooring in the common law',[72] it is unsurprising that common practice as regards fundamental freedoms did not emerge. Dawn Oliver points out that what has been termed the 'ethical aimlessness' of the common law – its lack of a sense of clear direction – means that because the judiciary as a body has no clear conception of the way the law should develop, they have not framed any set of 'guiding principles or priorities where civil and political rights clash with public interests'.[73] Thus, the judges in general showed, at times, uncertainty as to the weight to afford to a particular liberty, while the more executive-minded amongst them could take advantage of this uncertainty to grant it little or no weight. These tendencies meant that debate as to the principles underlying civil liberties was stifled and only the most obvious instances of their infringement received attention – where very basic rights were in question.

71 See Chapter 4 p 149, *et seq*.
72 Justice William Brennan of the US Supreme Court in Hart, *Lectures on Jurisprudence and Moral Philosophy*, p 12, 24 May 1989.
73 Oliver, D, 'A Bill of Rights for the United Kingdom', p 151, n 47 above.

In the years immediately preceding the coming fully into force of the HRA, there was, as indicated, an emergence of common law rights going well beyond those rights, particularly to property, that the common law had traditionally recognised. However, it is arguable that without a constitutional document such as the ECHR, with its accumulated jurisprudence, to give them substance and depth, they might have remained at an uncertain and early stage of development, especially as there was some reluctance on the part of the judiciary to import ECHR principles and a preference for relying on a coincidence between such principles and those apparently already embedded in the common law.

Once the judges had a 'textual anchor' in the form of the European Convention on Human Rights, applied domestically under the HRA, an increase in unity amongst domestic judges became apparent on issues of rights; while different judges gave different weights to rights and freedoms, at the very least all were certain about when they had to be taken into account. In particular, it is clear that the structure of judicial reasoning changed under the HRA.[74] It may plausibly be argued that in the last century the judiciary as a body were not able to construct for themselves a clear justification for increasing their powers over government, although signs of judicial activism in the 1990s suggested that some of them considered that they should do so. The reception of the European Convention on Human Rights into domestic law, which may be viewed as a public statement from the nation as a whole of the importance that they attach to human rights, gave the judges a clearer mandate to develop a domestic human rights jurisprudence. On the other hand, opposition to the HRA, which became most apparent in the years leading up to the 2010 General Election, may have persuaded some judges to turn back towards the concept of common law rights. But if a resurgence of common law rights is currently apparent it may be of a more limited nature than some of the rhetoric surrounding this development might suggest, although it is obviously an important development in relation to possible HRA repeal. The judges are currently demonstrating, as they did in 1999, that human rights can be preserved outside the HRA.

The influence of the European Convention on Human Rights in the pre-HRA era

Under Article 1 of the European Convention on Human Rights, the member states[75] must secure the rights and freedoms to their subjects, but they are free to decide how this should be done.[76] Each state decides on the status the Convention enjoys in national law; there is no obligation under Article 1 to allow individuals to rely on it in national courts. In some states, it has the status of constitutional law;[77] in others, of ordinary law.[78]

---

74 See Chapter 4, esp pp 227–28.

75 Currently, the Western European members include: Albania, Andorra, Austria, Belgium, Cyprus, Denmark, Finland, France, Germany, Greece, Iceland, Ireland, Italy, Liechtenstein, Luxembourg, Malta, the Netherlands, Norway, Portugal, San Marino, Spain, Sweden, Switzerland, UK. Eastern European members include: Bulgaria, Croatia, the Czech Republic, Estonia, Georgia, Hungary, Latvia, Lithuania, Macedonia, Moldova, Poland, Romania, Russia, Slovakia, Slovenia, Turkey, Ukraine. The numbers increased owing to the disintegration of the Soviet Union and Yugoslavia.

76 This was affirmed by the Irish Supreme Court in *The State (Lawless) v O'Sullivan and the Minister for Justice*; see *Yearbook of the Convention on Human Rights Vol II* (1958–59), pp 608–22.

77 E.g., Austria.

78 This includes Belgium, France, Italy, Luxembourg and Germany.

In the pre-HRA era, rulings of the European Court of Human Rights led to better protection of human rights in such areas as prisoners' rights,[79] freedom of expression[80] and privacy.[81] But, as an external force, the influence of the Convention was limited. In contrast to the influence of European Union law, discussed below, the influence of the European Convention was, and is, procedurally rather than substantively limited. As pointed out in Chapter 2, the effect at the international level of a ruling of the European Court of Human Rights is dependent on the government in question making a change in the law. The pre- and post-HRA UK government has been able to minimise the impact of an adverse judgment by interpreting defeat narrowly,[82] by avoiding implementation of a ruling (most obviously, in relation to prisoners' voting rights),[83] or by obeying the letter of the article in question, but ignoring its spirit.[84] The impact of the Convention at the international level was, and is, diminished since the process of invoking it, considered in Chapter 2, is still, despite the reforms discussed in Chapter 2, extremely cumbersome, lengthy[85] and expensive.[86] Under the HRA, litigants can and do still take cases to Strasbourg as a last resort, but, as Chapter 2 demonstrated, while the system of the long trek to Strasbourg (starting with the exhaustion of domestic remedies) remains substantially, as at present, only the most exceptionally determined and resourceful litigants are likely to pursue it.[87]

In the UK, prior to the introduction of the HRA, the Convention had no domestic binding force. Thus, until 2000, a UK citizen could not go before a UK court and simply argue that a Convention right had been violated by a public authority. Nevertheless, before the HRA came fully into force, the influence of the Convention was rapidly becoming more significant in domestic law through rulings in UK courts and in the European Court of Human Rights. As indicated below, the Convention also had an increasing significance in human rights-related rulings of the European Court of Justice. It may be said that the Convention was encroaching steadily on UK law from every direction,[88] and that its direct domestic reception under the HRA was merely the culmination of that process.[89]

---

79 E.g., *Golder*, Eur Court HR, A 18, Judgment of 21 February 1975.
80 *Sunday Times*, Judgment of 26 April 1979; (1979) 2 EHRR 245. See further Chapter 6, pp 312–14.
81 E.g., *Gaskin v UK* (1990) 12 EHRR 36. See further Chapter 8, p 526. See further Farren, S, *The UK before the European Court of Human Rights*, Blackstone, 1996.
82 As in *Golder*, Eur Court HR, A 18, judgment of 21 February 1975.
83 The ruling on such voting rights: *Hirst v UK (no 2)* [2005] ECHR 681 is still, in 2016, unimplemented. See G. Cowie, 'Prisoners to Devolved Fortune? The Right to Vote and the Scotland Act 2016', U.K. Const. L. Blog (2016). See further Chapter 2, p 91.
84 *Abdulaziz, Cabales and Balkandali v UK* (1985) 7 EHRR 471. To implement the ruling, the UK 'equalised down'. See further Chapter 2, p 94.
85 The Commission used to make over 3,000 provisional files a year. The average petition took five years and nine months between 1982 and 1987 if it went all the way through the system – four years before the Commission, nearly two before the Court (15 EHRR 321, p 327). Petitions can take nine years. When the Commission was abolished admissibility was then determined by a Chamber of the Court, as Chapter 2 explains. The average time is around four years; for some years the Court has had around 69,000 cases pending. See further 'European Court of Human Rights: Applications pending before a Judicial Formation' 31.12.14.
86 Legal aid is not available until after the complaint has been held admissible.
87 See Chapter 2, pp 29, 31, 35–39.
88 For the argument that the extent of such encroachment has been exaggerated, see Klug, F and Starmer, K, 'Incorporation through the back door?' [1997] PL 223.
89 See esp below, pp 119–20.

The discussion above regarding the influence of human rights values in the common law pre-HRA demonstrated that the courts in a number of significant decisions tended to prefer to refer to common law principle rather than explicitly to the Convention in respect both of statutory interpretation and the development of the common law. However, in both respects, a strand of thinking became very evident to the effect that the Convention itself should be explicitly relied upon. It had an impact through domestic courts in the pre-HRA era in the following ways.

The domestic impact of the ECHR in the pre-HRA era: statutory construction

It became a general principle of construction that statutes would be interpreted if possible so as to conform with international human rights treaties to which the UK is a party, on the basis that the government is aware of its international obligations and would not intend to legislate contrary to them.[90] A legal presumption developed that 'Parliament does not intend to act in breach of international law' (per Diplock LJ in *Saloman v Commissioners of Custom and Excise*),[91] so that a reading of the relevant legislation that did not create a breach of rights would be adopted by the courts if such a reading was possible. Other international human rights treaties to which the UK is a party, including the International Covenant on Civil and Political Rights, had much less influence, as indicated above.[92] The interpretation of ambiguous provisions in conformity with the Convention thus left it great scope to influence domestic law even before the introduction of the HRA, and such an influence would still arise if the HRA were repealed in around 2019–20.

The domestic impact of the ECHR in the pre-HRA era: influence on the common law

Lord Scarman, in *AG v BBC*,[93] considered that the Convention could also influence the common law. He said that where there was some leeway to do so, a court which must adjudicate on the relative weight to be given to different public interests under the common law should try to strike a balance in a manner consistent with the treaty obligations accepted by the government. This approach was endorsed by the House of Lords in *AG v Guardian Newspapers (No 2)*,[94] Lord Goff stating that he considered it to be his duty, where free to do so, to interpret the law in accordance with Convention obligations.

The need to take the Convention into account was emphasised even more strongly by the Court of Appeal in *Derbyshire CC v Times Newspapers Ltd*,[95] Ralph Gibson LJ ruling that where a matter 'was not clear [by reference to] established principles of our law . . . the court must . . . have regard to the principles stated in the Convention'. Butler-Sloss LJ put the matter even more strongly: 'where there is an ambiguity or the

---

90 See the judgment of Lord Brandon of Oakbrook in *re M and H (Minors)* [1990] 1 AC 686; [1988] 3 WLR 485, HL, p 498; [1990] 1 AC 686.
91 [1967] 2 QB 116, p 143.
92 See p 29. See further Clayton, R and Tomlinson, H, *The Law of Human Rights*, 2000, OUP, pp 89–103.
93 [1981] AC 303, 354; [1980] 3 WLR 109, p 130, HL.
94 [1990] 1 AC 109, p 283.
95 [1993] AC 534; [1993] 1 All ER 1011; [1992] 3 WLR 28, HL.

law is otherwise unclear or so far undeclared by an appellate court, the English court is not only entitled but . . . obliged to consider the implications of Art 10'. It may, therefore, have been the case that all areas of the common law which were not clearly settled in the House of Lords and which affected Convention rights were expected to reflect Convention principles even before the HRA came into force.

The influence of European Union law

It is clear that membership of the European Union has had a dramatic impact on civil liberties and human rights in the UK over the last five decades. This is despite the fact that EU law is concerned more with social and economic than civil rights. The influence of the Convention in EU law became increasingly important due to acceptance of the principle enunciated in *Amministrazione delle Finanze dello Stato v Simmenthal*[96] and *Nold v Commission*,[97] namely, that respect for fundamental rights should be ensured within the context of the EU. The ECHR has come into a closer relationship with EU law as the process of European integration has continued. The influence of EU human rights law increased, after the Amsterdam Treaty came into force.[98] The doctrine of respect for fundamental rights, as guaranteed by the European Convention and as resulting from the constitutional traditions common to member states, was embodied in Article F(2)(6)(2) of the Treaty on European Union.[99] Under the Treaty of Amsterdam, Article F1, voting rights of member states who fail to observe the principle embodied by Article F(2)(6)(2) can be suspended.

The result of these developments is that, in all the member states, implementation of EU measures in national law is clearly subject to respect for the Convention rights, although an individual cannot at present make an application to Strasbourg against the Union alleging that the Union has violated the Convention. Even though formal accession of the Union to the Convention has not yet occurred,[100] the Convention affects Union conduct. Thus, the decision of the ECHR in *Rees*[101] was relied upon by the ECJ in deciding, in *P v S and Cornwall CC*,[102] that transsexuals fall within the Equal Treatment Directive. This was found on the basis that the Directive is simply the expression of the principle of equality, which is one of the fundamental principles of European law.

---

96 Case 106/77 [1978] ECR 629.
97 [1974] ECR 481.
98 The Treaty came into force in 1999. It extended a number of existing rights under EU law and amended the Social Charter, which laid down minimum rights for workers in the Community countries. The then Conservative government failed to ratify it, but in the agreement annexed to the Protocol on Social Policy in the Treaty of Maastricht the other member states recorded their agreement to 'continue along the path' laid down in it. The then Labour government withdrew the opt-out.
99 For enforcement of the Convention by this means, see Craig, P and De Burca, G, *European Law: Text and Materials*, 2nd edn, 1998, OUP.
100 The Court of Justice of the European Union issued its long-awaited Opinion on 18 December 2014 (Opinion 2/13 of the Court) in which it held that the Draft Agreement on the Accession of the European Union to the ECHR is incompatible with EU law.
101 (1986) 9 EHRR 56.
102 [1996] ECR I-2143; [1996] 2 CMLR 247; [1996] All ER(EC) 397.

Until after the 2016 EU Referendum, which will usher in 'Brexit' around 2019/2020, it appeared probable that, as the influence of the Convention on EU law became more significant and the impact of EU law became greater in the UK, the Convention may also have more domestic influence, indirectly, aside from the HRA. If the HRA was repealed this influence would continue. The position was set out in the case *Elliniki Rasdio Phonia Tiles Rassi AE v Dimotiki Etaria*:[103] 'as soon as any [national] legislation enters the field of application of Community law, the [ECJ] as the sole arbiter in this matter, must provide the national court with all the elements of interpretation which are necessary in order to enable it to assess the compatibility of that legislation with the fundamental rights – as laid down particularly in the ECHR – the observance of which the Court ensures'. Thus, any national law within the field of application of EU law can be assessed as to its compliance with the Convention rights. But, as a matter of EU law, the Convention rights are not directly justiciable since they are not freestanding rights. The position under *Elliniki* was not, therefore, changed by Article F(2)(6)(2). The domestic courts can disapply legislative provisions which appear to conflict with EU law as interpreted in reliance on those rights. Certain Convention principles have therefore come to be of limited binding force in the UK as forming part of EU law. However, the potential impact of the Convention in the UK by this means is unlikely to be realised once the UK withdraws from the EU.[104]

EU law has already had an important impact, as this book will demonstrate, in the areas of sex discrimination,[105] surveillance, data protection[106] and race discrimination.[107] Where national measures come within the scope of EU law, they must comply with the human rights standards it maintains.[108] EU law can, of course, have direct effect in UK courts and can even override a UK statute.[109] The ability of Parliament to infringe rights under the HRA, as discussed below, is therefore subject to the ability of the judiciary to disapply domestic law which is incompatible with EU law. As this book indicates at a number of points, EU human rights law has increasingly become a powerful force both in terms of the protection offered by the ECJ, and of its domestic implications.[110] The EU Charter of Fundamental Rights aids in the interpretation of EU law[111] and following the entry into force of the Lisbon Treaty in 2009 the fundamental rights charter has the same legal value as the European Union treaties.

---

103 [1991] ECR I-2925.
104 See further on this issue, Van Dijk and Van Hoof, *Theory and Practice of the ECHR*, 3rd edn, 2006, Intersentia Publishers, Chapter 8; Adenitire, J, 'The Executive Cannot Abrogate Fundamental Rights without Specific Parliamentary Mandate – The Implications of the EU Charter of Fundamental Rights for Triggering Art 50' U.K. Const. L. Blog (21st July 2016); O'Leary, S, 'Accession by the EC to the ECHR' (1996) 4 EHRR 362.
105 See, e.g., *Marshall (No 2)* [1993] 4 All ER 586. See further Chapter 5, p 258 *et seq.*
106 For example, the Data Protection Act 1984 (now 1998) derived from the European Convention for the Protection of Individuals with regard to the Automatic Protection of Data, 17 September 1980. See further Chapter 10, p 763 *et seq.*
107 See Chapter 5, p 258 *et seq.*
108 See, e.g., *R v Secretary of State for the Home Dept ex p Adams* [1995] All ER (EC) 177.
109 See *Factortame Ltd v Secretary of State for Transport* [1991] 1 All ER 70, HL.
110 See further Betten, L and Grief, N, *EU Law and Human Rights*, 1998, Longman; Neuwahl, N and Rosas, A, *The EU and Human Rights*, 1995, Martinus Nijhoff; Jacobs, F, 'Human rights in the EU: the role of the ECJ' [2001] 26(4) ELR 331.
111 The Charter, published in May 2000 (available from the European Commission website and from the website of the House of Lords Select Committee on the European Parliament) contains those rights recognised under the European Convention on Human Rights together with a number of new social

However, Britain opted out of the Charter of Fundamental Rights as part of the Lisbon treaty negotiations, although the precise effect of the opt-out (Protocol 30) remained unclear for a time. But in *R (on the application of Davis et al) v Secretary of State for Home Department*[112] it was found that s 1 of the Data Retention and Investigatory Powers Act 2014 was unlawful under EU law. The case was important since it involved a British court using the Charter to invalidate an Act of Parliament (although it suspended that invalidation until March 2016). Lawyers for the Home Secretary sought to limit the effect of the Charter by arguing that the Court should follow the less stringent European Convention case law. That argument failed since the judges held that: 'Art 8 of the Charter goes further . . . and has no counterpart in the ECHR.' The opt-out did not preclude this finding; it was found: 'the precise scope of Protocol 30 is far from clear, since it only precludes the extension by the CJEU or domestic courts of their existing powers to find that UK laws are not in accordance with the Charter. It cannot be used to prevent the court from defining the extent of rights contained in the Charter which set out provisions within the material scope of EU law.'

Also Art 51 of the Charter appears to limit its effect considerably in providing: 'The provisions of this Charter are addressed to the institutions, bodies, offices and agencies of the Union . . . and to the Member States only when they are implementing Union law.' However the Court in *Davis* reiterated that this applies whenever a member state is acting 'within the material scope of EU law'. Thus once the matter at issue is within the scope of EU law, then an individual can rely on a right conferred by the Charter.[113]

3 Relying on a new 'British Bill of Rights'?

Introduction[114]

In 2020 or earlier it is possible that the HRA will be repealed and replaced by a new BBoR. What underlies this change? Under Duncan-Smith and then under David Cameron the Conservatives favoured repeal of the HRA, and that remained the stance in the

---

rights, including the right to strike, guarantees of maximum working hours, worker consultation and trade union membership. On 1 December 2009, with the entry into force of the Treaty of Lisbon, the Charter became legally binding on the EU institutions and on national governments, like the EU Treaties themselves. See for discussion, M Wheeler 'Cavalier with our Constitution: a Charter too far' UK Human Rights blog, 9.2.16; Wicks, E [2001] PL 527.

112 [2015] EWHC 2092, 17 July 2015.

113 See further Chalmers, D et al, *European Union Law Text and Materials*, 3rd edn, 2014, Cambridge University Press.

114 For discussion as to replacing the HRA with a BBoR, see: Fenwick, H, 'The Human Rights Act or a British Bill of Rights: Creating a down-grading recalibration of rights against the counter-terror backdrop?' (2012) Public Law 468–490; Wadham, J, 'The Conservative Party's Proposals for human rights' UK Human Rights blog 2.6.15. For general background reading on the debate as to enacting a Bill of Rights in Britain prior to the inception of the HRA, see: Lord Scarman, *English Law: The New Dimension*, 1974; Wallington, P and McBride, J, *Civil Liberties and a Bill of Rights*, 1976, Blackwell; Bailey, SH, Harris, DJ and Jones, BL, *Civil Liberties: Cases and Materials*, 5th edn, 2002, OUP, Chapter 1; Feldman, D, *Civil Liberties and Human Rights in England and Wales*, 2002, OUP, Chapter 2; Clayton, R and Tomlinson, H, *The Law of Human Rights*, 2nd edn, 2006, Cambridge University Press, Chapter 1; Jaconelli, J, *Enacting a Bill of Rights*, 1980, Clarendon; Zander, M, *A Bill of Rights*, 4th edn, 1997, Sweet and Maxwell; Dworkin, R, *A Bill of Rights for Britain*, 1990, Chatto and Windus; Ewing, KD, *A Bill of Rights for Britain*, 1990, Institute of Employment Rights; Lord Lloyd of Hampstead, 'Fundamental rights: the UK isolated?' [1984] PL 46; Craig, PP, *Public Law and Democracy in the United Kingdom and the United States of America*, 1990, Clarendon; Waldron, J,

2010 and 2015 General Elections. As indicated above, the plan is to replace the HRA with a 'British Bill of Rights'. As David Cameron said in an article in 2007: 'under my leadership, we have opposed ID cards and will replace the Human Rights Act with a British Bill of Rights that better protects both our security and our freedom'.[115]

The Conservatives pledged, in their 2015 General Election manifesto, to abolish the HRA and replace it with a British Bill of Rights (BBoR). The Queen's Speech 2015, however, did not refer to legislation, but merely to proposals to introduce such a Bill that would effect such repeal.[116] No draft BBoR made its appearance before the election. It is clear that a lengthy consultation period is about to be embarked upon, and that the BBoR will not be introduced until some considerable time after the EU referendum in 2016 (possibly after the 2020 General Election, if the Conservatives have a larger majority, if it is to be introduced at all). The Conservative pledge, in their 2015 manifesto, was to 'break the formal link between British courts and the European Court of Human Rights, and make our own Supreme Court the ultimate arbiter of human rights matters in the UK'.[117] It was notable, however, that the possibility of withdrawal from the European Convention on Human Rights (the Convention) was not mentioned in the manifesto, although it was in the Conservative policy document on a BBoR published in 2014.[118] The implications of repealing the HRA in terms of the devolved institutions have not been addressed and are likely to prove problematic.

But although the Conservatives won a majority in 2015, it was paper thin. A Queen's Speech that had included a legislative measure intended to repeal the HRA would have been highly controversial. It would have been opposed by the MPs of all other parties (apart, presumably, from the single UKIP MP) and probably by Conservative supporters of the HRA. In the face of that opposition, David Cameron backed down – hence the replacement of a reference to legislation by reference to proposals and the expression of an intention to embark on a lengthy consultation period, defended, in commenting on the Queen's Speech, by Priti Patel (the then employment minister) as important in order to ensure that the eventual draft bill is fully thought through.[119] Predictably, various newspapers fiercely attacked Cameron for pusillanimity on the issue.[120] The *Times'* reporting on the issue on the morning of the speech was to the effect that plans to introduce a BBoR to 'limit abuse of human rights laws' had faced a backlash.[121]

'A rights-based critique of constitutional rights' (1993) 13 OJLS 18; Adjei, C, 'Human rights theory and the Bill of Rights debate' (1995) 58 MLR 17; Oliver, D, 'A Bill of Rights for the United Kingdom', in *Government in the United Kingdom*, 1991, Open University Press; Lester, A, 'The judges as law-makers' [1993] PL 269.

115 *Daily Telegraph*, 15 January 2007.
116 The Conservatives have a majority of only 12. It appeared that legislative proposals would have been opposed by the MPs of all other parties (apart from the single UKIP MP) and probably by 'Runnymede' Conservative MPs as supporters of the HRA.
117 *Strong leadership. A clear economic plan. A brighter, more secure future*, available at: https://s3-eu-west-1.amazonaws.com/manifesto2015/ConservativeManifesto2015.pdf (p 60).
118 *Protecting human rights in the UK: the Conservatives' proposals for changing Britain's human rights laws*, available at: https://s3.amazonaws.com/s3.documentcloud.org/documents/1308198/protecting-human-rights-in-the-uk.pdf.
119 Nicholas Watt, 'Threat to exit human rights convention must be dropped, Tories tell Cameron', *The Guardian*, 27 May 2015.
120 'European Court puts terrorists & murderers first. Why is Cameron dithering over ending this farce? Their rights . . . or yours', *The Sun*, 27 May 2015.
121 Sam Coates, 'Cameron blinks first in human rights row', *The Times*, 27 May 2015.

Below, the nature of the probable BBoR will be considered, taking account of previous proposals from senior Conservatives, and some tentative comparisons will be made with the method of protection for human rights effected in the HRA.

'Breaking the link between the domestic courts and the Strasbourg Court'

The new BBoR would be intended to seek to break the link between the courts and Strasbourg – and, of course, creation of such a link is not required under the Convention itself. At present, in seeking to interpret the Convention rights under the Human Rights Act, the domestic judiciary must merely 'take into account' any relevant Strasbourg jurisprudence, under s 2; it was clearly the intention underlying s 2 that the jurisprudence would not be viewed as, in effect, binding.[122] The problem from the Conservative perspective stems from the finding in *Ullah*[123] in the House of Lords that the judges should follow any clear and constant jurisprudence of the Strasbourg Court, a finding generally referred to as 'the mirror principle'[124] (that domestic courts should 'mirror' the Strasbourg Court's jurisprudence in HRA judgments), which until fairly recently remained the dominant approach.[125]

The reason expressed in the 2014 Conservative document for seeking this change is that 'over the past 20 years, there have been significant developments which have undermined public confidence in the human rights framework in the UK'. It states that the European Court of Human Rights has developed 'mission creep' on the basis that Strasbourg adopts 'a principle of interpretation that regards the Convention as a living instrument'. The 'living instrument' approach has been criticised as giving rise to unpredictability when creative decisions have an unexpected effect in areas of domestic law, via s 2 HRA.

The Commission on a Bill of Rights (was set up by the Coalition government to consider the introduction of a Bill of Rights (BoR). It delivered its report – *A UK Bill of Rights? – The Choice Before Us* – to the government in December 2012. The report was unsurprisingly affected by the lack of agreement between the Liberal Democrats and the Conservatives in government – and on the Commission – as to the role that any human rights' instrument in Britain should play. The Coalition partners appeared to want it to play two different roles – defending or attacking the Human Rights Act. The Commission's membership was evenly split between Conservative and Liberal Democrat nominees and obviously represented a compromise between the Liberal Democrats and the Conservatives.[126] Its terms of reference

---

122 See further Klug, F and Wildbore, H, 'Follow or lead? The Human Rights Act and the European Court of Human Rights' (2010) 6 EHRLR 621–30.

123 *R (on the application of Ullah) v Special Adjudicator* [2004] UKHL 26. See also *Kay v Lambeth London Borough Council* [2006] 2 AC 465 para [88]; Lord Hope found that the national courts should not 'outpace' the ECtHR.

124 See Lewis, J, 'The European ceiling on human rights' (2007) PL 720. See Chapter, p 157 *et seq.*

125 See *Manchester City Council v Pinnock (Secretary of State for Communities and Local Government and another intervening)* [2010] UKSC 45. See further Mahoney, P, 'The relationship between the Strasbourg court and the national courts' (2014) 130 LQR 568. See further Chapter 4, pp 164–66.

126 The Commission was headed by former Permanent Secretary, Sir Leigh Lewis. The eight members were: Martin Howe QC, Anthony Lester QC, Jonathan Fisher QC, Helena Kennedy QC, Anthony Speaight QC, Philippe Sands QC, Michael Pinto-Duschinsky (who resigned from it), Sir David Edward.

were to: 'investigate the creation of a UK Bill of Rights that incorporates and builds on all our obligations under the European Convention on Human Rights, ensures that these rights continue to be enshrined in UK law . . .'. The BoR Commission did not meet the current Conservative concerns as to s 2 HRA since it proposed no change to s 2.

The Commission noted that there was a substantial body of opinion that wanted to enable it to be made clearer that courts were free to depart from Strasbourg[127] under s 2 HRA. But although, as they noted, it could not be said that the judges had confined themselves only to 'taking account' of the Strasbourg jurisprudence, the Commission did not propose a change to the position under s 2 on the basis that they found a clear majority of respondents to their consultation in favour of maintaining the requirement in the Human Rights Act on UK courts to 'take into account' relevant judgments of the European Court of Human Rights. But they said that a number of those taking that view only did so on the basis that our courts were now '*correctly* interpreting the Act's wording in this respect having failed on some occasions to do so in the past'.[128] So on the basis that a majority of respondents considered that s 2 was now being interpreted as it should have been originally – i.e. 'the mirror principle' was being abandoned – the majority recommended no change to s 2.

The current Conservative proposal entirely ignores that put forward by the Bill of Rights Commission in 2012. The Conservative proposals as to a BBoR in 2014 were fore-shadowed in 2009 by Dominic Grieve who said that the equivalent of s 2 HRA in a new BBoR should allow or require the domestic courts to take a different stance from Strasbourg in a wider range of circumstances than those currently accepted. Grieve argued that the HRA had been 'interpreted as requiring a degree of deference to Strasbourg that I believe was and should be neither required nor intended'. According to Dominic Grieve – and now reflected in the 2014 Conservative document – s 2 as interpreted post-HRA needs to be drastically reined in, not just returned to its original conception[129] since it has gone far too far in allowing Strasbourg decisions to re-shape domestic law (combined with ss 3 and 6). The problem, from the anti-HRA viewpoint espoused by a number of senior Conservatives, is partly that the interpretations of the Convention rights at Strasbourg on a number of contentious issues – in particular prisoners' voting rights, aspects of counter-terrorism law and deportation of non-citizens – are ones that are not assented to by the Westminster Parliament, or in some instances by judges in the House of Lords/Supreme Court,[130] but which may have effect in UK law[131] or constrain Parliament.[132]

Dominic Grieve proposed in 2009 that a new bill of rights, which would replace the Human Rights Act, would make it clear that British courts could allow for UK common law to take precedence over decisions by the Strasbourg Court. He said: 'We would

---

127 At paras 56 and 57.

128 Para 58.

129 Speech by Dominic Grieve QC, Attorney General: *European Convention on Human Rights – Current Challenges*, 24 October 2011, at Lincoln's Inn, London.

130 See the judgments in *Secretary of State for the Home Department v AF (No 3)* [2009] UKHL 28, especially that of Lord Hoffmann.

131 See, for example, the Home Secretary's (Mrs Theresa May) speech to the Conservative party conference on 4 October 2011 on this point.

132 See HC Deb 24 October 2012 cols 922–23, on prisoners' voting rights. See also n 83 above.

want to reword it to emphasise the leeway of our national courts to have regard to our own national jurisprudence and traditions and to other common law precedents while still acknowledging the relevance of Strasbourg Court decisions.'[133] He has also said: 'there is no duty in the ECHR to follow Strasbourg case-law'.[134]

BoR Commission member Anthony Speaight said on this in evidence to the Constitutional Reform Select Committee in 2011: 'the court . . . makes decisions that something or other is a human right that would not by the average Briton be regarded as a human right . . .'.[135] Grieve's key speech on the ECHR in 2011[136] targeted s 2 HRA as a failing section on the basis that it allows Strasbourg interpretations of the ECHR too much purchase in domestic law.[137] Martin Howe, in his individual paper, took a similar view, arguing that domestic courts, adjudicating under a UK Bill of Rights, should not 'slavishly follow every twist and turn of the doctrines formulated in the decisions of the Strasbourg Court'.[138]

From this viewpoint the effects of ss 2 and 3 HRA combined, or of ss 2 and 6, are part of the problem (as 'gold-plating' the Strasbourg decisions in the UK). As discussed in Chapter 4, s 2 HRA can operate in conjunction with ss 3 or 6 to allow a Strasbourg decision, that happens to bear on a matter currently in front of a domestic court, to have legal effect in domestic law (as occurred most obviously in *AF no3*[139]), before the executive has a chance to react to the decision. The executive might well prefer to delay and procrastinate, or to bring forward legislation to Parliament which might represent a more minimal response to the Strasbourg decision than the court-based findings did. That may not have been the case in *AF* itself, but the decision illustrated the potential of ss 2 and 3 HRA combined.

The Conservative plan in the 2014 document and expressed in the 2015 manifesto is to ensure that 'the European Court of Human Rights is no longer binding over the UK Supreme Court'. In so stating it echoed the 2014 document which stated that:

> Labour's Human Rights Act undermines the role of UK courts in deciding on human rights issues in this country. Section 2 of the HRA requires UK courts to 'take into account' rulings of the Strasbourg Court when they are interpreting Convention rights. This means that problematic Strasbourg jurisprudence is often being applied in UK law. Strasbourg jurisprudence includes the doctrine of 'proportionality', and the application of this doctrine has led judges to question whether provisions of legislation and decisions of public authorities are 'proportionate' to their objectives, which can amount to an essentially political evaluation of different policy considerations.

---

133 Dominic Grieve's Guest Lecture, Middle Temple Hall, 30 November 2009.
134 Article published on the Conservativehome website 2009.
135 In reply to Q36.
136 *European Convention on Human Rights – Current Challenges*, 24 October 2011, Dominic Grieve speaking at Lincoln's Inn, London.
137 See also 'It's the interpretation of the Human Rights Act that's the problem – not the ECHR itself', Dominic Grieve, Conservativehome blog 14 April 2009.
138 Commission on a Bill of Rights, *A UK Bill of Rights? – The Choice Before Us, Vol 1* (2012), 218.
139 *Secretary of State for the Home Department v AF (No 3)* [2009] UKHL 28. *A v UK* [2010] HRLR 5, [2010] ICR 223 was absorbed directly into law.

So it proposes to 'break the formal link between British courts and the European Court of Human Rights. In future Britain's courts will no longer be required to take into account rulings from the Court in Strasbourg. The UK courts, not Strasbourg, will have the final say in interpreting Convention rights, as clarified by Parliament'.

As is well known, in *R v Horncastle*,[140] in the context of Art 6, the Supreme Court considered that departure even from clear jurisprudence was exceptionally acceptable under s 2 HRA, as s 2 originally intended. The Supreme Court decided that the European Court's decision (*Al-Khawaja*)[141] insufficiently appreciated or accommodated particular aspects of the domestic process, and determined that in those rare circumstances it could decline to follow the decision, as it did. The domestic provisions in question, the Court found, struck the right balance between the imperative that a trial must be fair and the interests of victims in particular and society in general. The Strasbourg test, it was found, did not strike the right balance since it gave a higher value to Art 6 standards than those provisions did, and therefore was not applied.

The idea as expressed in the 2014 Conservative document and in the manifesto is to make provision in the BBoR that would allow or require the judges, in effect, to apply the *Horncastle* principle in a range of circumstances, and as the normal approach, *not* exceptionally. That would appear to avoid the situation that arose in *AF (No 3)*, in which s 2 HRA was taken to require immediate acceptance into law of the *A v UK* minimum disclosure principle.[142] *AF* then had the result – obviously, in terms of its general implications, unwelcome to the executive – of affecting the use of the counter-terror control orders system.

The Human Rights Act 1998 (Repeal and Substitution) Bill, introduced in 2012 by Conservative MP Charlie Elphicke,[143] was withdrawn before its second reading. But it can be taken as affording a possible indication as to the nature of forthcoming Conservative proposals for the BBoR as to a replacement for s 2.[144] Its clause 2 provides that a court or tribunal determining a question that has arisen in connection with a protected right 'may', not 'must', take into account a judgment of the ECtHR.[145] It further provided that 'a court may take account of a judgment of a court in Australia, Canada, New Zealand, the USA or any country having a common law-based judicial system; of the European Court of Human Rights; or a court in any other jurisdiction which may be relevant to the UK right under consideration'.

---

140 [2010] 2 WLR 47. See also *R v Spear* [2003] 1 AC 734.
141 (2009) 49 EHRR 1. See also *Horncastle v UK* [2014] ECHR 1394.
142 (2009) 49 EHRR 29.
143 Available at http://www.publications.parliament.uk/pa/bills/cbill/2012–2013/0031/2013031.pdf.
144 Charlie Elphicke MP is a member of the committee which was working on the Conservative proposals for a Bill of Rights prior to the general election.
145 The full text of cl 2 read: Interpretation of UK rights
    (1)   A court or tribunal determining a question which has arisen in connection with a UK right may take account of a judgment of –
        (a)   a court in Australia, Canada, New Zealand, the United States of America or any country having a common law-based judicial system;
        (b)   the European Court of Human Rights; or
        (c)   a court in any other jurisdiction which may be relevant to the UK right under consideration, but shall be bound to follow the judgments of higher courts in the United Kingdom, in accordance with the usual rules of precedent (though, for the avoidance of doubt, precedent relating to rights under the Convention shall not be binding when determining a question in connection with a UK right).

It would also be possible to provide in the BBoR that relevant clear and constant Strasbourg jurisprudence against the UK (or another member state) should be treated as of no more significance in interpreting the BBoR rights than jurisprudence from other national Supreme Courts (listed as in the Elphicke Bill). Or, most simply, reference to the Strasbourg jurisprudence could be omitted altogether from the new Bill.

The rights to be protected in the BBoR

The attempt to diminish the domestic impact of the Strasbourg Court is not – at first glance – reflected in the 2014 Conservative proposals as to the list of rights to appear in the BBoR; it is to 'Put the text of the original Human Rights Convention into primary legislation.' The document proceeds:

> There is nothing wrong with that original document, which contains a sensible mix of checks and balances alongside the rights it sets out, and is a laudable statement of the principles for a modern democratic nation. We will not introduce new basic rights through this reform; our aim is to restore common sense, and to tackle the misuse of the rights contained in the Convention.

So it appears that the aim expressed by Cameron and in the 2015 manifesto of seeking to weaken the ties to Strasbourg via a BBoR is not to be realised via changes to the listed rights. That was also reflected in the BoR Commission's remit. When the Commission referred to listed rights, the reference was to the list of ECHR rights in Sched 1 HRA, with some additions, most obviously a right to jury trial, and possibly the creation of limits on the power of the state to impose administrative sanctions without due process of law, such as fines for speeding.[146]

However, the 2014 Conservative document also proposed to:

> Clarify the Convention rights, to reflect a proper balance between rights and responsi-
> bilities. This will ensure that they are applied in accordance with the original intentions
> for the Convention and the mainstream understanding of these rights. We will set out a
> clearer test in how some of the inalienable rights apply to cases of deportation and other

---

(2)   A court or tribunal determining a question which has arisen in connection with a UK right shall take into account all the facts and circumstances of the case, including the conduct of the person seeking to assert the UK right (including his adherence to the responsibilities set out in Article 23 of Schedule 1) and whether it is fair, equitable and in the interests of justice for such UK right to be applied in relation to the question at hand.

(3)   Evidence of any judgment of which account may be taken under this section is to be given in proceedings before any court or tribunal in such manner as may be provided by the rules.

(4)   In this section 'rules' means rules of court or, in the case of proceedings before a tribunal, rules made for the purposes of this section –
   (a)   by the Lord Chancellor or the Secretary of State, in relation to any proceedings outside Scotland;
   (b)   by the Secretary of State, in relation to proceedings in Scotland; or
   (c)   by a Northern Ireland department, in relation to proceedings before a tribunal in Northern Ireland –
      (i)   which deals with transferred matters; and
      (ii)   for which no rules made under paragraph (a) are in force.

146 *Proposals for a British Bill of Rights* (A British Academy/AHRC Forum 8 March 2010).

removal of persons from the United Kingdom. The ECtHR has ruled that if there is any 'real risk' (by no means even a likelihood) of a person being treated in a way contrary to these rights in the destination country, there is a bar on them being sent there, giving them in substance an absolute right to stay in the UK. Our new Bill will clarify what the test should be, in line with our commitment to prevent torture and in keeping with the approach taken by other developed nations. The Convention recognises that people have civic responsibilities, and allows some of its rights to be restricted to uphold the rights and interests of other people. Our new Bill will clarify these limitations on individual rights in certain circumstances. So for example a foreign national who takes the life of another person will not be able to use a defence based on Art 8 to prevent the state deporting them after they have served their sentence.

This appears to mean that 'interpretation' or re-balancing clauses could be introduced in a BBoR, creating exceptions going beyond those expressly present in the ECHR. That could mean introducing exceptions in cases of deportation into non-materially qualified rights, limiting the scope and effect of the right. Such provision, it appears, could affect Articles 2 and 3 ECHR, and would be likely to apply to Articles 5 and 6. Articles 8–11 already contain exceptions based on a broad range of societal interests if the interference is necessary and proportionate, but the proposal would include creating broader exceptions to Art 8 (as has occurred already in the Immigration Act 2014) or provision to disapply it in the circumstances envisaged. Jean-Paul Costa, President of the ECtHR, said in 2010 of this aspect of the previous BoR proposal from the Conservatives:

> Introducing a British bill of rights could create a complex situation . . . it could mean that most rights [in the Convention] are protected to more or less the same extent, but not 100% of them. This could create divergences between the case law [from Strasbourg] and the law in the UK.[147]

Constitutional status of the BBoR

The constitutional status of the BBoR will obviously have to be determined. As indicated above, the constitutional status of Bills or Charters of Rights varies from jurisdiction to jurisdiction. Such instruments may have no special status or they may be afforded (or may acquire) some special protection from express or implied repeal which may, at its highest, involve their entrenchment.[148] A variety of models was available to choose from in considering the model to be used in order to protect the Convention under the HRA. The choice arrived at, which is discussed in Chapter 4, was extremely significant, in terms of the allocation of power between the judiciary, parliament and the government.

There is the possibility of using a so-called 'notwithstanding' clause for the BBoR. Based on the model of the Canadian Charter, the clause could state that subsequent legislation would only override the Convention if the intention of doing so were expressly stated in such legislation. Under a 'notwithstanding' clause, the judiciary would not be required to strike down legislation without a mandate from the democratically elected government. If that government did not include the clause in any legislative provision that

---

147 Quoted in Hirsch, A, 'UK bill of rights plan a "bad idea", warns head of European Court' *The Guardian*, 27 June 2010.
148 See Jaconelli, J, *Enacting a Bill of Rights*, 1980, for a full discussion of this issue.

subsequently was found to infringe the Convention, the government could impliedly be taken to be mandating the judiciary, by its omission, to strike down the offending legislation. Thus, although under such a model the judiciary are required to disapply provisions in Acts of Parliament, a role that the domestic judiciary might find constitutionally problematic, they are not required to act against the wishes of the democratically elected government. Dworkin has observed, in relation to such a clause, that: 'In practice this technically weaker version of incorporation would probably provide almost as much protection as [formal entrenchment].'[149] However, this model accepts the possibility that clearly arises that future governments might come to use the clause more frequently, but it is more likely to commend itself to the Conservative leadership than a form of entrenchment.

Withdrawal from the ECHR?

The new BBoR would not, in itself, be able to address fully the key objective of the Conservative leadership, without the prospect of withdrawal from the Convention, which is to break the link between the Strasbourg Court and the state – to allow Parliament to disregard rulings of the Strasbourg Court against the UK by making the judgments 'advisory' only. The UK is bound under Article 46 of the Convention to respond to adverse judgments of the Court against itself: it is hard to see that it could remain within the Convention system if it openly refused so to respond. In any event, while the bill could purport to render the judgments advisory only, it probably could not pass the Commons over the life of this administration. So that aspect of the BBoR will probably have to be dropped, at least until the next General Election in 2020.

A number of senior Tories (so-called 'Runnymede Tories') reportedly told David Cameron after the 2015 Queen's Speech that he must abandon a 'deeply offensive' threat to withdraw from the Convention if he is to gain support for the plans to repeal the HRA.[150] Dominic Grieve QC also warned in the *Times* that withdrawal from the Convention could mean that if individuals could not obtain a satisfactory level of redress for rights violations domestically or at Strasbourg that would be likely to lead to mission creep at the European Court of Justice (ECJ), rather than at Strasbourg, under the Convention.[151] However, the Conservative leadership would now respond by pointing out that the UK's exit from the EU will (eventually) solve that problem. Given 'Brexit' (probably in the period 2019–21) protection for human rights may eventually have to rely on the application of the ECHR at Strasbourg and on a BBoR. The level of redress provided by the Supreme Court, either under a BBoR or possibly under common law protection for rights, might be as high as that to be obtained at Strasbourg, but differences might emerge, prompting recourse to the Strasbourg Court.)

The possibility of withdrawal from the European Convention on Human Rights was not mentioned in the 2015 manifesto, although it was in the Conservative policy document on a BBoR published in 2014.[152] The 2014 Conservative plan addresses the

---

149 Dworkin, R, *op cit*, fn 1.
150 See 'Threat to exit human rights convention must be dropped', Watts, N, in *The Guardian* 27.5.15.
151 See Dominic Grieve, 'This UK bill of rights is a recipe for disaster', *The Times*, 28 May 2015.
152 *Protecting human rights in the UK: the Conservatives' proposals for changing Britain's human rights laws*, available at: https://s3.amazonaws.com/s3.documentcloud.org/documents/1308198/protecting-human-rights-in-the-uk.pdf.

separate issue of the relationship between the Strasbourg Court and the UK state. It proposes that the European Court of Human Rights 'is no longer able to order a change in UK law and becomes an advisory body only'.[153] That is intended to 'end the ability of the Strasbourg Court to force the UK to change the law'. It is intended to mean that 'every judgement that UK law is incompatible with the Convention will be treated as advisory and we will introduce a new Parliamentary procedure to formally consider the judgement. It will only be binding in UK law if Parliament agrees to enact it.' The issues of prisoners' voting rights,[154] deportation of foreign criminals,[155] and sex offenders[156] would be the type of issues that the document is referring to. At the time of writing it is unclear whether this aspect of the plan will be taken forward; Theresa May, the current Prime Minister, clearly does not view the government as bound by Grayling's document.

That aspect of the plan would obviously oppose Article 46 ECHR, which provides that states agree to adhere to final judgments against themselves. If it was implemented in a BBoR it would mean that sensitive rights-based issues would be determined by Parliament, not the Strasbourg Court. Parliament would have the key responsibility for protecting the ECHR rights. However, the document does not explain how the aim of treating the Strasbourg Court as an advisory body only, and open defiance of Strasbourg decisions in legislation, could be reconciled with Article 46 or with the UK's continued adherence to the ECHR. The proposals are unlikely to be seriously pursued over the next two years given the possibility that they would not pass the Commons due to opposition from the SNP, Labour and the Liberal Democrats, combined with some pre-ECHR Conservative MPs. They would represent the first steps on the way to withdrawal from the Convention. That prospect has disappointed a number of senior Conservatives and a number of newspapers. But Theresa May could take comfort from a degree of appeasement of the UK that appears to be occurring recently at Strasbourg.[157]

153 p 14 of the 2014 document.
154 This issue continues to be of especial significance at the time of writing. See *Greens and M.T. v United Kingdom* (23 November 2010); Firth, n 158 below, and the subsequent developments: see pp 170–71, below.
155 An Iraqi asylum-seeker, Aso Mohammed Ibrahim, brought about the death of a child in a driving accident and fled the scene. An immigration tribunal refused the application to deport him on the basis of his right to respect for his family life under Art 8 ECHR, a decision upheld on appeal (*SSHD v Respondent* [2010] UKUT B1 Upper Tribunal (Immigration and Asylum Chamber) Appeal Number: IA/13542/2009). In a letter to the father of the girl in January 2010, Cameron promised that a future Conservative government would repeal the HRA which he held responsible for the decision; see *The Guardian*, 28 December 2010. The Court of Appeal refused leave to appeal the decision. The role played by Art 8 in relation to refusal of deportation in *EM (Lebanon) v Secretary of State for the Home Dept* [2008] UKHL 64 was highlighted by Dominic Grieve in 2010 as a matter requiring a change of balance away from protection for the individual.
156 Theresa May, the then Home Secretary, wrote in *The Sun*, 10 May 2011: 'We need to bring sanity back to the law. That's why this Government is setting up a commission to look into creating a UK Bill of Rights. This will put the rights of the public ahead of the rights of paedophiles, rapists and criminals.' http://www.thesun.co.uk/sol/homepage/news/3416421/David-Cameron-is-under-pressure-after-judges-rule-that-paedophiles-and-rapists-can-apply-to-have-their-names-removed-from-the-Sex-Offenders-Register.html#ixzz1LwL7j1P1.
157 See Chapter 2, n 469.

In other words, the Court seems, in more sensitive areas of rights' interpretation, to be abandoning an approach often referred to as a 'living instrument' one, one that can be viewed as exemplifying 'mission creep'. That was most evident in the decision not to award compensation to prisoners deprived of voting rights.[158]

4 Conclusions

At the present time still, as discussed, it is Conservative party policy to repeal the Human Rights Act and replace it with a 'British Bill of Rights'. The problem that the HRA faces in terms of its image in the popular consciousness is two-fold. It was never really 'sold' to the people of the UK in 1998. Further, it is perceived as a European instrument, as something imposed from outside, and as associated with the EU and over-regulation. A British Bill of Rights could fulfil the role played currently by the HRA, and could be based on it and on the European Convention, but could be presented to the British public as an instrument based more firmly on core British values. If (but clearly this is the very problem the BBoR might present) the Bill of Rights did not deliver *less* than the Convention in terms of rights, it would still satisfy the goal of allowing British people to rely on the Convention rights in domestic courts. But it might also hold out the possibility of dealing with some of the gaps and inadequacies inherent in the HRA, which are explored in Chapters 2 and 4. They include the narrow definition of 'public function' that has been adopted under s 6 HRA, the problems created by the doctrine of indirect horizontal effect and the inadequacies of the Convention itself. On the other hand, as indicated, the Conservative policy as regards human rights does not demonstrate a determination to *increase* their protection in a BBoR as compared to the HRA – far from it. The proposal as regards the treatment of the Strasbourg Court's jurisprudence indicates an intention to maintain in some respects a different (arguably, lower) standard of rights protection domestically than at Strasbourg.

If the HRA is repealed, then, as discussed, human rights may still be protected by a range of means, and in particular via the ECHR and the Strasbourg Court, and under common law principle. In principle, supporters of the HRA would not be likely to object to the introduction instead of a Bill of Rights. Labour should have introduced one in place of the HRA originally, in part to avoid the accusations from parts of the media and senior Conservatives that Europe is imposing alien, anti-common sense measures on the UK. But to use one as a method of escaping from the impact of the Convention, rather than as a domestic means of seeking to ensure that recourse to Strasbourg to vindicate rights is unnecessary, is a clearly retrograde step, opposing the notion, on the international stage, that the UK's human rights' record is one that is overall to be respected.

158 *Firth and others v UK* App No 47784/09, judgment of 14 August 2014.

Chapter 4

The Human Rights Act

This chapter has been updated and revised for this edition by Alison Young, Professor of Law at Hertford College, University of Oxford, UK.

I Introduction[1]

The Labour Government came to power in 1997 with a manifesto that promised a radical programme of constitutional change and, most significantly, the introduction of the Human Rights Act 1998 as the means of receiving the European Convention on Human Rights into domestic law, nearly 50 years after it was signed. Finally, rights were, in the government's words, to be 'brought home'.[2] It would not be too much of an exaggeration to say that the advent of the HRA appeared at the time to herald a new dawn for civil liberties. Relief seemed to be at hand, after many years of seeing the country condemned at Strasbourg and elsewhere, during the Conservative years, for its human

1 Texts referred to below and background: Clayton, R and Tomlinson, H, *The Law of Human Rights*, 2nd edn, 2009, OUP; Singh, R, and Hunt, M, *Assessing the Impact of the Human Rights Act*, 2003, Hart; Jowell, J, and Cooper, J, (eds), *Delivering Rights? How the HRA is Working and for Whom*, 2003, Hart; Fenwick, Masterman, Phillipson (eds), *Judicial Reasoning under the HRA*, 2007, CUP; Hoffman, D, and Rowe, J, *Human Rights in the UK*, 4th edn, 2013, Longman; Pannick, D and Lester of Herne Hill QC, Lord, *Human Rights Law and Practice*, 3rd edn, 2009, Butterworths; Gearty, C, *Principles of Human Rights Adjudication*, 2004, OUP; Wadham, J, Mountfield, H and Desai R, *Blackstone's Guide to The Human Rights Act*, 7th edn, 2015, OUP; Smith, R, *Textbook on International Human Rights*, 6th edn, 2014, OUP; Steiner, H, Alston, P and Goodman, R, *International Human Rights in Context: Law, Politics, Morals*, 3rd edn, 2008, OUP; Hunt, M, *Using Human Rights Law in English Courts*, 1997, Hart; Singh, R and Hunt, M, *A Practitioner's Guide to the Impact of the Human Rights Act*, 1999, Hart; Grosz, S, Beatson, J, and Duffy, P, *Human Rights: The 1998 Act and the European Convention*, 2000, Sweet and Maxwell; Fenwick, H, *Civil Rights: New Labour, Freedom and the Human Rights Act*, 2000, Longman Chapter 2; Clements and Thomas (eds), *The HRA: A Success Story?* 2005, Blackwell; Irvine, Lord, 'The impact of the Human Rights Act: parliament, the courts and the executive' (2003) *Public Law*, Sum, 308–25; Klug, F, 'Judicial deference under the Human Rights Act 1998' (2003) EHRLR 2, 125–33; Klug, F, 'Standing back from the Human Rights Act: how effective is it five years on' (2005) *Public Law*, Win, 716–28; Lester of Herne Hill, Lord, 'The Human Rights Act – five years on' [2004] EHRLR 259; Steyn, Lord, 'Deference: a tangled story' (2005) Public Law 346; Kavanagh, A, 'Statutory interpretation and human rights after Anderson: a more contextual approach' [2004] *Public Law* 537; Steyn, Lord, '2000–2005: laying the foundations of human rights law in the United Kingdom' (2005) EHRLR, 4, 349–62; Sunkin, M, 'Pushing forward the frontiers of human rights protection: the meaning of public authority under the HRA' [2004] *Public Law* 643; Leigh, I, 'Taking rights proportionately, judicial review, the HRA and Strasbourg' [2002] *Public Law* 265; Klug, F and Starmer, K, 'Incorporation through the "from door": the first year of the Human Rights Act' [2001] *Public Law* 654; McGoldrick, D, 'The HRA in theory and practice' (2001) 50(4) ICLQ 901.

2 See: *Bringing Rights Home: Labour's Plans to Incorporate the ECHR into UK Law: A Consultation Paper*, December 1996 (1997) and the White Paper: *Rights Brought Home*, October 1997 Cm 3782; see also Straw, J and Boateng, P, 'Bringing Rights Home: Labour's Plans to Incorporate the European Convention on Human Rights into UK Law' (1997) 1 EHRLR 71.

rights' record. Ronald Dworkin said, famously, of the Thatcher years, 'Liberty is ill in Britain'.[3] Ewing and Gearty wrote in 1989: 'It should now be clear that civil liberties in Britain are in a state of crisis.'[4] There were expectations that the HRA would prove to be something akin to a panacea for all that was wrong with fundamental freedoms in Britain or, at the least, commentators perceived that civil liberties had been re-energised.

Under the Diceyan model of the constitution, discussed in Chapter 3, civil liberties are protected by individual judicial decisions; a document termed a Bill or Charter of Rights is both unnecessary and undesirable as a means of protecting them.[5] Under this model, citizens in a state in which everyone is free to do all which the law does not forbid, enjoy, Dicey argued, greater liberty than those whose liberty is protected by such a document because, by being delineated, rights would be more limited. The Diceyan model underpinned the view expressed in the post-war years that a constitution embodying a presumption of liberty provided a protection for rights that could not be achieved by basing them on a constitutional document such as a Bill of Rights. From the perspective of the post-war, pre-1979 era, there appeared to be some basis for that view. Although it would be problematic to argue that there was ever a 'golden age' of civil liberties in Britain,[6] the post-war years appeared to a number of commentators to come closer to one than the Thatcher and Major years,[7] in comparison with the records in other European countries.

It has been argued that there was a post-war understanding as to the use of parliamentary power in British politics until the Thatcher Government 'dismantled much of the consensus'.[8] Under this view of the consensus, high Tory values underpinned respect for political freedoms, but under Conservative rule since 1979 liberty suffered and Britain began to lag behind many other democracies in respect of her human rights' record. The Thatcher Government was said to have demonstrated a 'mundane and corrupting insensitivity to liberty'.[9] Although the Major Government showed in certain respects a greater awareness of the value of individual rights,[10] in its central criminal justice Act, the Criminal Justice and Public Order Act 1994, it demonstrated, as Chapter 9 argues, a similar insensitivity. The Conservative years from 1979 to 1997 were marked by the

---

3   Dworkin, R, *Index on Censorship*, 1988, pp 7–8 (Index on Censorship magazine).
4   *Freedom under Thatcher*, 1989, OUP, p 255.
5   Dicey, AV, *The Law of the Constitution*, 8th edn, 1959.
6   Ewing and Gearty argue that there is a misconception that the first half of the twentieth century constituted such an age in *The Struggle for Civil Liberties: Political Freedom and the Rule of Law in Britain 1914–1945*, 1999, OUP.
7   See Thornton, P, *Decade of Decline: Civil Liberties in the Thatcher Years*, 1989, National Council for Civil Liberties. Ewing and Gearty, writing in 1989, found: 'In recent years there has been a marked decline in the level of political freedom enjoyed in Britain.' They found that the turning point and beginning of the decline might be said to have occurred in the 1970s but that 'the process of erosion became more pronounced' after the Conservative election victory in 1979 (Preface to *Freedom under Thatcher*, 1989, OUP).
8   Fraser, D, 'Post-war consensus: a debate not long enough' [2000] 53(2) *Parliamentary Affairs* 347.
9   Dworkin, R, *Index on Censorship*, 1988, pp 7–8. See also Thornton, P, *Decade of Decline: Civil Liberties in the Thatcher Years*, 1989, National Council for Civil Liberties.
10 The 'Open Government' initiatives were introduced under the Major Government: see The White Paper: *Open Government*, Cm 2290 and the *Code of Practice on Access to Government Information*. The Intelligence Service was placed on a statutory basis under the Intelligence Services Act 1994 (see Chapter 11, pp 810–14).

attempts of outside bodies – the European Court of Justice and the European Court of Human Rights – to protect liberties in the UK, attempts that were met, increasingly, by hostility among sections of the Conservative party.[11]

Contrary to the Diceyan thesis, liberty was receiving a significant measure of protection as a result of the impact of the European Convention on Human Rights at the international level, rather than being the result of decisions of the judiciary applying the common law. In *Freedom under Thatcher*[12] Ewing and Gearty pointed out that Thatcher had exposed the precarious nature of the constitutional means of protecting liberty. Their central criticism was not that she had changed the constitutional structures to her advantage, but that she 'merely utilised to the full the scope for untrammelled power latent in the British constitution but obscured by the hesitancy and scruples of previous, consensus-based political leaders'.[13] In other words, she exposed and exploited the weaknesses of the British constitution.

In the context of fundamental rights, Thatcherism exposed the flawed nature of the Diceyan constitutional model.[14] Since under that model the Constitution provides no effective check to untrammelled parliamentary sovereignty, a government determined to push through a legislative programme extending the reach of state power which, perhaps almost incidentally, erodes the residual areas of liberty, is able to do so. Despite strong common law traditions of upholding certain fundamental rights, constitutional inadequacy became, inevitably, apparent.

Thatcherism therefore influenced the long-running debate between those commentators and policy-makers who had always wanted to leave liberties to the protection of that process[15] and those in the liberal tradition who had wished to entrust them, for the most part, to the judiciary.[16] The Labour opposition of the time changed sides in that debate,[17] apparently in the main as a response to Thatcherism. The Labour Green Paper: *Bringing Rights Home*,[18] published in 1997, concluded: 'We aim to change the relationship between the state and the citizen, and to redress the dilution of individual rights by an over-centralising government that has taken place over the past two decades.' This aim was to be achieved through the introduction of the European Convention on Human Rights into domestic law. Once Labour came to power in 1997 the White Paper: *Rights Brought Home* was published[19] and the Human Rights Bill was introduced into

---

11 The reaction of senior cabinet members at the time, particularly Michael Heseltine, to the decision of the European Court of Human Rights in *McCann v UK* (1995) 21 EHRR 97 that the UK had breached Art 2 (right to life) was particularly hostile.

12 1989.

13 *Ibid*, at p 7.

14 Dicey, *The Law of the Constitution*, 8th edn, 1959.

15 See, e.g., Griffith, JAG, 'The political constitution' [1979] MLR 1; Loughlin, M, *Public Law and Political Theory*, 1992, OUP.

16 Leading exponents of this position included: Zander, M, *A Bill of Rights?* 1996, Sweet and Maxwell; Robertson, G, *Freedom, the Individual and the Law*, 1993; Lord Lester of Herne Hill QC, 'Fundamental rights: the UK isolated?' [1994] PL 70; Lord Scarman, *English Law: The New Dimension*, 1974.

17 See Chapter 3, pp 144–45.

18 Straw, J and Boateng, P, *Bringing Rights Home: Labour's Plans to Incorporate the ECHR into UK Law: A Consultation Paper*, 1997.

19 October 1997 Cm 3782.

Parliament. The Act came fully into force on 2 October 2000. The Convention thus received into domestic law created a constitutional transformation, not only in terms of rights-protection, but also in terms of judicial reasoning.[20] Since, traditionally, the constitution recognised only negative liberties as opposed to positive rights, the judicial focus of concern always tended to be on the content and nature of the restrictions in question rather than on the value and extent of the right.

While the Diceyan tradition demanded a basis in law for interference with liberties by public authorities, under the HRA this demand was clarified and confirmed in respect of interferences with the guarantees.[21] The Act obliges public authorities, in particular the police, not only to discharge duties such as the duty to keep the peace, but to uphold human rights. It asks the judiciary to examine the necessity in a democracy of interfering with a right, the proportionality of the means used with the aim in question, and, if necessary, it asks them to inform Parliament that on one or more of these matters it has breached the Convention. Placing the judges in a position where they need to consider the proportionality of a restriction on a Convention right with its aim changed the role of the judges; it brought them into the constitutional sphere previously occupied only by Parliament and covered by the doctrine of parliamentary sovereignty. For the first time the judges were invited to consider the compatibility of primary legislation with the Convention rights, and to take the responsibility for determining how far into the contracted-out sector the Convention rights should reach, and on what basis. The previous divergence of constitutional role between Parliament and the judiciary was narrowed down, and that doctrine itself came under very strong pressure. These were bold, imaginative constitutional changes. However, such boldness had apparent limits, which are reflected in the HRA.

A seminal constitutional decision involving a choice between judicial and parliamentary checks on executive power, and therefore as to the allocation of power, had to be taken regarding the choice of model for the enforcement of the Convention. The choice made was to afford the HRA no special constitutional protection and to leave the ultimate task of curbing executive power to Parliament; so judicial rulings remain (at least as a matter of constitutional theory) subject to primary legislation. The HRA therefore sought to reconcile rights protection placed to a significant extent in the hands of the courts with parliamentary sovereignty. Although the Convention contains the familiar list of rights usually found in a number of bills or charters of rights, the HRA was not intended to be a Bill of Rights in the way that the US Amendments to the Constitution or the Canadian Charter are Bills of Rights, in the sense that those rights have a higher status than other laws: laws that conflict with the rights can be struck down. Further, unlike the German Basic Law or the US Amendments, the HRA can simply be repealed or amended like any ordinary statute and it is, therefore, in a far more precarious position.

So although there was a significant transfer of power to the judiciary, the HRA imposed limitations on its use. On a face-value reading of the HRA, legislation incompatible with the Convention can be passed and legislation declared incompatible remains

20 See Sir Stephen Sedley on this point (2005) 32 JLS 3, p 9.
21 See Chapter 2, esp pp 65–66.

valid. It is readily apparent, then, that there is a contradiction between the liberal aim of affording the Convention rights efficacy in domestic law in order to aid in reversing the effects of the over-centralisation of power, and the aim of preserving the key feature of the constitution that gave rein to that power. The factors underlying this contradiction form one of the central themes explored throughout this book – the search for a means of giving efficacy to the rights in the face of hostile legislation.

But this chapter will argue that while the tension between government criminal justice and counter-terrorist policy and the Convention rights in 2000–16 is indeed a key theme of this book, the particular resolution of the contradiction created by the HRA has not been the determining factor in settling the rules of engagement. As explored in this chapter, and in the following ones, the particular constitutional choices reflected in the HRA have on the whole *not* been exploited to allow the government, as dominant within Parliament, to disregard or limit the Convention rights to an extent that the Convention itself does not allow. As Keith Ewing wrote in 1999, 'we should be careful about distinguishing form from substance, principle from practice. As a matter of constitutional legality, Parliament may well be sovereign, but as a matter of constitutional practice, it has transferred significant power to the judiciary [under the HRA].'[22] A doctrinal analysis of the status of the Convention in domestic law is inadequate to explain its impact, since such an analysis has been superseded by the political stance that the government has taken.

This chapter thus attempts a doctrinal analysis of the HRA mechanisms that takes account of a political reality in which overt disregard of the Convention has largely been avoided, with the notable exception of the UK's continued avoidance of implementing the judgment of the Grand Chamber of the Strasbourg Court that a blanket ban on prisoner voting breached Article 3 of the First Protocol. Moreover, there has been increasing criticism of the Act in recent years, particularly from the Conservative Party, leading to their pre-election proposal and manifesto pledge to replace the Act with a British Bill of Rights and Responsibilities. The 2015 and the 2016 Queen's Speech contained a commitment to 'bring forward proposals for a British Bill of Rights', however no promised consultation paper has yet appeared.

The proposals do not propose to remove the court's interpretative obligation or its power to issue declarations of incompatibility, although the interpretative obligation may be weakened, with the Conservative party's proposals aiming to ensure that such interpretations do not contradict the ordinary meaning of legislation. The concern is to constrain the influence of the Strasbourg Court and to 'repatriate' human rights. In particular, the Conservatives intend to make decisions of the Strasbourg Court advisory only as a means of moving away from the court's approach to Convention rights as a 'living instrument', which has allowed the Court to develop the content of Convention rights so as to better reflect a pan-European consensus on human rights found in the twenty-first century, as opposed to the 1950s, instead returning the content of Convention rights to their original meaning as intended by the signatories to the Convention. If the desire to ensure that decisions are advisory only extends to judgments

---

22 'The HRA and parliamentary democracy' [1999] 62(1) MLR 79, p 92.

of the Strasbourg Court concluding that the UK has breached Convention rights, then this would be unable to be achieved without withdrawing from the ECHR – which David Cameron appeared recently to reject, it being his intention to 'pass a British Bill of Rights which we believe is compatible with our membership of the Council of Europe',[23] but which was not ruled out by Michael Gove. The new Prime Minister, Theresa May, also appears to have indicated that it is not her intention for the UK to withdraw from the ECHR. The doctrinal analysis will bear these concerns in mind, evaluating, where relevant, the current reform proposals.

It also takes account of the status of the Convention in the popular consciousness since it poses a continuing problem for human rights advocates in the UK. The inception of the HRA was not accompanied by the kind of popular debate that preceded the US Bill of Rights in 1789, or that accompanied the adoption of the Canadian Charter of Fundamental Rights and Freedoms as part of the patriation of the Canadian constitution in 1982. Thus, although at the time the new Labour government commanded widespread popular support, and the HRA was passed during its honeymoon period, it did not seek to make the case for the HRA to the British people. That proved eventually to create problems, when the HRA came under pressure in relation to counter-terrorist strategy, and the war in Iraq led to a rapid diminution of the Labour government's popularity.

Previous editions of this book drew attention to the *Review of the Implementation of the Human Rights Act* conducted in 2006 by the Department of Constitutional Affairs,[24] which expressed concerns as to the existence of myths concerning the role of the Human Rights Act that often arose from the way in which cases were reported, or partially reported.

The key question that the Review set out to answer was whether the HRA had impeded the achievement of the government's objectives on crime and terrorism and so led to the public being exposed to additional and unnecessary risk. The Review answered this question in the negative, finding that while the security agencies had stated that significant resource implications are involved in servicing the structures set up to deal with dangerous terrorist suspects, these result not from the HRA, but from the decisions of the Strasbourg Court in cases such as *Chahal*.[25] But the perception created by the media that the HRA is hindering counter-terrorist and crime-control measures remains, and the appeal to the fear of terrorism has been effective in creating a false image of the HRA. Sadly, as noted by the Joint Committee of Human Rights, this tendency has continued.[26] For example, the Committee drew attention to a criticism found in the *Daily Mail* of the extent to which Strasbourg decisions are overriding the decisions of British judges, despite statistical evidence demonstrating that the Strasbourg Court decided against the UK in only 1% of cases in 2011, and 0.6% of cases in 2012 and

---

23   Hansard HC vol 598 col 311, 8 July 2015.

24   Published, DCA, July 2006. http://webarchive.nationalarchives.gov.uk/+/http:/www.dca.gov.uk/peoples-rights/human-rights/pdf/full_review.pdf.

25   *Ibid*, p 34.

26   Joint Committee of Human Rights, 'Human rights judgments' (7th Report of Session 2014–15) HL Paper 130, HC 1088.

2013.[27] The reactions of the British media have also been criticised by the European Court of Human Rights.[28] There are other reasons why a narrow doctrinal legal analysis is at best incomplete and, at worst, positively misleading. Critical analysis of, for example, the theoretical protection for individuals under the HRA is of little value without an awareness of the influence of wider societal factors. There should be an awareness of how much that theoretical protection is in reality available to the underprivileged individuals who are often in most need of asserting their rights (in particular, working class black men, the most likely target of police harassment or misuse of police powers, such as stop and search).

The main concern of this book is with the years 2000–15: the Human Rights Act years. It seeks to evaluate the impact the HRA has actually had in various areas of fundamental rights and asks how far the expectations it aroused in 1998 have been answered. It will be argued that at times the Convention rights have been minimised and undermined in Parliament and in the courts.[29] In Parliament, the rights have at times been treated as almost empty guarantees that cast a legitimising cloak over rights-abridging legislation and executive action.[30] Under the model termed 'minimalist', judges have at times been able to duck the hard issues, purporting to review government actions under the Convention standards, but adopting a deferential stance that fails to create any real accountability.[31] An appearance of human rights auditing has sometimes been created which is belied by the reality. But it will be argued throughout this book that there are signs that the HRA in 2015 has bedded down; the senior judges are taking their role as the guardians of human rights seriously; a fusion between Strasbourg principles and common law ones is now successfully occurring.[32],[33] It will further be argued that the HRA has indeed had an impact on executive power, and has had an effect in protecting the rights of vulnerable and minority groups.

The HRA has proved to be a more controversial piece of legislation than its sponsors can have predicted. After it had been in force only a year, terrorists flew planes into the Twin Towers in New York, triggering a global 'war on terrorism' that has placed the HRA under pressure during almost the whole of its existence. The years 2001 to 2015 saw increasing attempts by the right-wing press and by the Conservative party to discredit the HRA on the basis that it is a bar to the use of effective counter-terrorist measures and focuses too greatly on protecting the rights of prisoners and criminals. In October 2013, for example, the *Daily Mail* ran a story claiming that British taxpayers were paying the bill for Strasbourg Court payouts to 'murderers, terrorists and traitors'.[34] The HRA is in an extremely precarious position. As Chapter 15 argues, the idea

---

27 *Ibid*, paras 2.1–2.4.
28 http://www.humanrightseurope.org/2013/10/court-concern-at-seriously-misleading-uk-news-articles/?utm_source=twitterfeed&utm_medium=twitter.
29 See, e.g., Chapter 6 at p 347 *et seq* and Chapter 8, p 507 *et seq*.
30 This danger was pointed out by Conor Gearty in 'Terrorism and human rights: a case study in impending legal realities' (1999) 19(3) LS 367, p 379.
31 See below pp 226–37.
32 See, e.g., Chapter 10, pp 695–99.
33 4 March 2005.
34 http://www.dailymail.co.uk/news/article-2449256/Human-right-make-killing-Damning-dossier-reveals-taxpayers-European-court-payouts-murderers-terrorists-traitors.html).

that the HRA bars the way to effective counter-terrorist action is misconceived. But it is obscuring, at least in the popular consciousness, the more general 'endeavour' of the HRA – to provide UK citizens with a guarantee of a range of fundamental rights, enforceable in their own courts, rather than at Strasbourg.

This chapter, which considers and analyses the HRA and certain very significant decisions taken under it in the first 15 years of its life, is intended to provide a framework for the discussion of the impact of the Act, which pervades the whole book. The discussion embarks on a doctrinal analysis of the central aspects of the Act, but also argues that such an analysis is inadequate to explain the operation of the Act in practice. In certain respects, explored below, the deliberate choice was made in a number of the areas, especially the question of indirect horizontal effect in s 6, to leave options open, requiring political and moral choices to be made by the judiciary in adjudicating on the HRA. It will also be argued that certain choices were made in settling on the wording of the key sections of the Act, in particular ss 3(2) and 6(2), creating exceptions to Convention adherence, which did not reflect the political reality of the involvement of Britain in the Convention system, or the acceptance of the implications of transferring power to the judiciary. That reality then became apparent over the early HRA years. Earlier editions of this book focused on the preference shown by the government and the judiciary for accepting the limitations on the rights afforded by the Convention, *not* those provided by the HRA. Although this concern remains, it has been lessened as there are signs that the domestic courts are both more willing to lead as opposed to merely follow Strasbourg decisions, although such instances are still relatively rare. Moreover, the courts have continued to develop the common law, with recent decisions showing a move towards recognising common law rights that go further than those contained in the ECHR.

2 The choice of rights

The rights protected under the HRA

As Chapter 2 demonstrated, the Convention continues to grow by means of additional protocols, reflecting more developed conceptions of human rights. However the UK has not ratified all of them. Ratification decisions have affected the choice of rights received into domestic law under the HRA. But also the decision was taken to omit Article 13, requiring that an effective remedy should be available in national law for breach of the Convention rights,[35] and Article 1 which provides for the state to secure to everyone within its jurisdiction the Convention rights and freedoms. The rights received into domestic law are, under s 1(1) HRA, Articles 2–12 and 14 of the Convention, Articles 1–3 of the First Protocol, Article 1 of the Thirteenth Protocol and Articles 1 and 2 of the Sixth Protocol[36] as read with Articles 16–18 of the Convention. The rights are set out in Sched 1 of the HRA; further protocols could be added by the Secretary of State, by order, under s 1(4). Equally, rights could be removed and any other amendments to the Act could be made, by the same route in order to 'reflect the effect, in relation to the UK, of a Protocol'.

---

35 See Chapter 2, pp 91–2.
36 (1983) 5 EHRR 167. It came into force in 1985.

The omission of Art 13 is particularly significant. The idea behind it is that the function of that article will be carried out by s 8 of the HRA (see below) and that its inclusion might have encouraged the judiciary to provide new remedies, going beyond those that could be provided under s 8. Possibly, Art 13 could have been utilised in an attempt to create new free-standing causes of action between private parties – direct horizontal effect. As indicated below, ss 6 and 7 seek to ensure that the creation of a new cause of action under the HRA confines it to use against public authorities. Arguably, the Art 13 jurisprudence can, however, be taken into account by the judiciary under s 2 of the HRA.[37]

This choice of rights in Sched 1 is significant and obviously in part reflects UK decisions as to ratification. It is clearly a deficiency of the international record of the UK in human rights matters that it has not ratified all the protocols. The most satisfactory course would have been their ratification and then inclusion in the list of rights in Sched 1. As Chapter 2 indicated, the government has considered the question of ratifying the Fourth[38] and Seventh Protocols. It has declared an intention to ratify the Seventh Protocol,[39] although ratification has still not taken place, but has not yet decided to ratify the Fourth, which would require changes to immigration legislation or the entry of a reservation.[40] The very significant Anti-Discrimination Protocol, Protocol 12, was opened for ratification in November 2000.[41] As explained in Chapter 2 it provides a guarantee of freedom from discrimination extending beyond the civil rights' arena since, unlike Art 14, it does not depend on the engagement of another Convention right.[42] The UK at present does not intend to ratify the Twelfth Protocol. Clearly there are concerns that while there is reasonable harmony between the basic Convention regime and the UK legal system, that is not fully the case as far as aspects of the more advanced Protocol-based regime is concerned. The Joint Committee on Human Rights in 2005 recommended that the government should ratify the Fourth and Twelfth Protocols.[43] The question of extending the scope of the Convention in this way is of particular significance in relation to Protocol 12, but at the present time, the government has not yet ratified it[44] and clearly is not therefore at present minded to include it in Sched 1.

---

37 See Grosz, Beatson and Duffy, *op cit*, fn 1, para 1–6; see also Feldman, D, 'Remedies for violation of Convention rights under the HRA' [1998] EHRLR 691.
38 Cmnd 2309. It came into force in 1968; the UK is not yet a party.
39 (1984) 7 EHRR 1. It came into force in 1988. The UK is not a party but has proposed ratification: see the White Paper: *Rights Brought Home: The Human Rights Bill*, Cm 3782, 1997, paras 4.14–4.15, and the Home Office Review of Human Rights Instruments (amended) 26 August 1999.
40 It contains rights relating to the field of immigration law, which have raised governmental concerns regarding the nature of the obligations created and the government indicated in 1997 that it did not intend to ratify it at that time: see the White Paper: *Rights Brought Home: The Human Rights Bill*, Cm 3782, 1997, paras 4.10–4.11. It has, however, considered the possibility of future ratification with reservations: the Home Office Review of Human Rights Instruments (amended), 26 August 1999. In a written answer to the Commons of 10 June 2002 it was stated that there were no plans to ratify it: 'To ask the Secretary of State for the Home Department what plans he has to introduce legislation to enable the UK to ratify the Fourth Protocol to the ECHR. [58371]. Beverley Hughes: None at the present time.' See further Chapter 2, p 91.
41 See Chapter 2, p 93.
42 See Chapter 2, p 91–92 and Chapter 5, pp 269–72.
43 Seventeenth Report of Session 2004–5 HL Paper 99, HC 264, paras 34 and 37.
44 It was opened for signature in November 2000.

The recent Brighton Convention gave rise to Protocols 15 and 16, which are designed not to expand Convention rights, but to reform the Strasbourg Court in the face of an ever-expanding caseload. Article 1 of Protocol 15 affirms that the signatories to the Convention have the primary responsibility for upholding Convention rights 'in accordance with the principle of subsidiarity' and that in doing so they 'enjoy a margin of appreciation'. This is not to be understood as a means of giving way to national parliaments, but as respecting national human rights mechanisms as a whole. The time limit is also reduced from six months to four months and it aims to remove trivial cases by removing the exception to the need to show 'significant disadvantage', which permitted individuals to petition when the issue had not been duly considered by a domestic court. Protocol 16 empowers domestic courts to ask the Strasbourg Court for an advisory opinion. The UK has ratified Protocol 15, despite some concerns expressed by the Joint Committee on Human Rights over the reduction in time limits and the restriction of standing,[45] although this is not yet in force, and has adopted a wait and see policy as regards Protocol 16.

Deficiencies and limitations of the Convention

It must be asked why the decision was made in the HRA to provide protection for parts of the European Convention on Human Rights, as opposed to introducing a tailor-made UK Bill of Rights or incorporating the International Covenant on Civil and Political Rights. In taking this course, the Labour government followed a long UK tradition of proposals for a Bill of Rights that favoured the Convention over other instruments. The overwhelming majority of human rights bills considered by Parliament over the years have simply advocated incorporation of the European Convention on Human Rights[46] into UK law. The House of Lords Select Committee on a Bill of Rights was unanimous on the question of creating a tailor-made Bill of Rights: 'To attempt to formulate *de novo* a set of fundamental rights which would command the necessary general assent would be a fruitless exercise.'[47] Starting from scratch and developing a Bill of Rights for the UK would have been a burdensome task because the political parties (and the various pressure groups) would have had great difficulty in reaching agreement on it, while the process of hearing and considering all the representations made by interested parties would have been extremely lengthy.

Zander has argued that it was politically and psychologically easier to incorporate the Convention,[48] since it was already binding on the UK internationally, and both major parties when in power have accepted the jurisdiction of the European Court of Human Rights and the right of individual petition.[49] A key argument put forward by supporters of the Convention was that the advantage to be gained by adopting the course

---

45 Joint Committee on Human Rights, 'Protocol 15 to the European Convention on Human Rights' (Fourth Report of Session 2014–15) HL Paper 71, HC 837.
46 This reference to incorporation of the Convention refers to Arts 2–18 and the First Protocol – the course advocated by the House of Lords Select Committee on Human Rights in 1978.
47 Report of Select Committee, HL Paper 176, June 1978.
48 Zander, M, *A Bill of Rights?*, 1996, Sweet and Maxwell p 83.
49 It may be noted that under the changes made by Protocol 11, the right of individual petition can no longer be withdrawn; see Chapter 2, pp 35–6.

of creating a home-grown Bill of Rights would have had to be weighed up against the possible detriment caused if the jurisprudence of the European Court of Human Rights had been seen as less directly applicable. The British judiciary might have felt that they had lost the 'anchor' of the authority of the Court and the constraint of the need to apply a reasonably uniform European standard of human rights.

Arguments against relying on the Convention were based partly on its defects of both form and content, which have often been criticised.[50] It is a cautious document: it is not as open-textured as the American Bill of Rights, and contains long lists of exceptions to the primary rights – exceptions which suggest a strong respect for the institutions of the state. Perhaps the most outstanding example of inadequacy is the limited scope of Art 14.[51] There is also the dangerous potential of Art 17.[52] From today's perspective, the nearly 60-year-old Convention looks very much like a creature of its period,[53] with its provision against slavery[54] and its long lists of exceptions to certain fundamental rights. Its out-of-date feel has led a number of commentators to echo the plea put forward some years ago by Tomkins and Rix for 'a document of principle for the 1990s and not a document of exceptions from the 1950s'.[55]

It could be argued that at first glance in its present manifestation the Convention is simply not adequate to the task of bringing about far-reaching reforms, and thereby fulfilling the constitutional role that a number of commentators had enthusiastically mapped out for it pre-HRA.[56] As Feldman puts it, the Convention rights are 'by no means a comprehensive basis for a modern system of protection for [individualistic and public] values'.[57] The far more thorough South African Bill of Rights, which covers certain social, economic and environmental rights, provides an example of such a system. The pressure group Liberty's *Manifesto for Human Rights* proposed that a domestic Bill of Rights could be drawn up, based on the Convention, but using more up-to-date language and addressing certain of the inadequacies indicated in Chapter 2.[58] In particular, Liberty criticised the lack of minimum conditions for detention outside Art 3, and the lack of a right to jury trial. It has also often been pointed out that the Convention

---

50 See, e.g., Hewitt, P, *The Abuse of Power*, 1982, Martin Robertson, pp 232–40; Gearty, C [1993] CLJ 89.

51 Art 14 provides a guarantee of freedom from discrimination, but only in the context of the substantive rights. See further Chapter 2, pp 93–94.

52 It was used by the Commission to allow the banning of the German Communist party: *Kommunistische Partei Deutschland v Federal Republic of Germany*, Application 250/57 Yearbook I (1955–57), Vol 6, p 222.

53 The Convention was drafted in 1949 and based on the United Nations Declaration of Human Rights. The Declaration was adopted on 10 December 1948 by the General Assembly of the UN.

54 Although slavery in the sense of human trafficking is still a live issue in Europe. See eg 26th Report of the JCHR on human trafficking 2005–06, HL Paper 245–1, HC Paper 1127–1, published 13 October 2006. See also *Guardian*, 23 March 2007.

55 'Unconventional use of the Convention' (1992) 55(5) MLR 721, p 725. See also Ashworth, A, 'The European Convention on Human Rights and English criminal justice: ships which pass in the night?', in Andenas, M (ed), *English Public Law and the Common Law of Europe*, 1998, Key Haven, p 215.

56 See, e.g., Feldman, D, 'The Human Rights Act 1998 and constitutional principles' (1999) 19(2) LS 165; Lord Lester of Herne Hill QC, 'First steps towards a constitutional bill of rights' (1997) 2 EHRLR 124.

57 *Op cit*, Feldman, (1999) p 170.

58 National Council for Civil Liberties 1997 (now *Liberty*). See also the Bill drawn up by the Institute for Public Policy Research: Constitution Paper No 1, 'A British Bill of Rights', 1990.

contains no specific rights for children.[59] The HRA can also be criticised on the basis that the opportunity was lost to include certain social and economic rights,[60] including some of those protected under the International Covenant on Social, Economic and Cultural Rights. The dynamic approach of the Strasbourg Court can only marginally address the failure to provide second or third generation rights under the HRA, although, as Chapter 2 pointed out, there are signs of a change of approach in this respect.[61]

The decisions of the European Court of Human Rights documented in this book make it clear, however, that the Convention is sufficiently open-textured to be able to cover circumstances not envisaged when it was created[62] and to adapt to changing social values. Indeed, it is the way in which the Convention is interpreted as a 'living instrument', taking it away from the original intentions of the framers of the Convention, which has prompted recent calls for its reform by the Conservatives. For example, although a right of access to legal advice in police custody is not expressly included, the Court has – in effect – read one into Art 6, arising in a number of circumstances.[63] The Convention, with its associated jurisprudence, comes close to comprising a modern 'document of principles' thanks largely to the enterprise of the Court, which has insisted upon the dynamic nature of the Convention and has adopted a teleological or purpose-based approach to interpretation which has allowed the substantive rights to develop.[64] Those principles cannot always be sought in the *outcomes* of applications, especially in older Commission admissibility decisions.[65] But Strasbourg decisions are not binding on domestic courts. The traditional approach of the doctrine of precedent in UK courts has not been applied to Strasbourg decisions under s 2 HRA, giving the courts some leeway, as discussed below, in developing the domestic Convention jurisprudence.[66]

But it remains legitimate to attack the HRA as an instrument that has selected and elevated 'first generation' civil rights, ignoring the social and economic ones that would have aided in giving those civil rights some substantive rather than formal value.[67] That argument could possibly, however, be utilised in future to press for introducing second generation rights to future protocols to the Convention,[68] for including Protocol 12 in Sched 1 and for giving consideration to the reception of other unincorporated treaties into domestic law. As Ewing has put it: 'the HRA provides a valuable template for other international treaties . . .'.[69] At the present time, however, when the very existence of the HRA is under threat, there is little likelihood of persuading the government that further rights should be included in the list of those protected.

Some of these problems have been mitigated to a limited extent following the ratification of the Lisbon Treaty,[70] which gave legal force to the EU's Charter of Fundamental

59 Fortin, J, 'Rights brought home for children' (1999) 62 MLR 350.
60 See Ewing, KD and Gearty, CA, 'Rocky foundations for Labour's new rights' (1997) 2 EHRLR 149.
61 See Chapter 2, p 43.
62 See, e.g., *Soering v UK*, judgment of 7 July 1989, A 161; (1989) 11 EHRR 439.
63 See Chapter 13, p 925.
64 See: Van Dijk, P and Van Hoof, F, *Theory and Practice of the European Convention on Human Rights*, 3rd edn, 1998.
65 See Chapter 2, p 33.
66 See pp 16–68.
67 See further Ewing, KD, 'Social rights and constitutional law' [1999] PL 104.
68 With a view to adding such Protocols to Sched 1 to the HRA 1998.
69 Ewing, 'Social rights and constitutional law' [1999] PL 104, p 110.
70 EU 2007/C 306/01.

Rights.[71] The Charter includes rights which mirror the provisions of the ECHR, as well as including equality rights, socio-economic rights and citizen's rights. The Charter can be relied upon in English courts when the UK is acting within the scope of European Union law: i.e. when it is implementing EU law, acting as an agent of the European Union, derogating from directive effectively provisions of EU law and, more controversially, when enacting law in an area where there is existing European Union law.[72] As well as providing for a broader scope of rights, the EU Charter may also provide a better remedy, with one recent Court of Appeal decision suspending the application of legislation[73] and a recent High Court decision granting a declaration of incompatibility against the Data Retention and Investigatory Powers Act 2013, suspending its disapplication in order to enable the government to provide a legislative response to the declaration of incompatibility.[74]

In addition, the courts have been willing to draw on the common law, either to protect rights that are not currently clearly protected by the Convention, or to rely on the common law approach to rights, recognising that such rights mirror the rights found in the ECHR. In *Osborn v Parole Board* the Supreme Court used the common law standards of procedural fairness to determine whether the Parole Board should hold oral hearings before deciding whether to grant an application for release or a transfer to open conditions, concluding that its assessment of this issue was in line with Art 6 ECHR.[75] In *Kennedy v Charity Commissioner*, a UK journalist challenged the decision of the Charity Commission to refuse a request for information, made under the Freedom of Information Act 2000, about the Commission's inquiry into a charity run by George Galloway, who was then an MP.[76] Section 32 of the Act provided for an absolute exemption for Charity Commission inquiries and it would not have been possible to interpret this provision in a manner compatible with Convention rights. There was also disagreement as to whether the direction of travel of Strasbourg decisions would extend Art 10 to include a right to information in these circumstances. Nevertheless, s 78 of the Act permitted disclosure either under the common law or through other statutory powers, specifically the Charities Act 1993. The Supreme Court recognised the common law principle of 'open justice' which required 'the disclosure to a newspaper for serious journalistic purposes of documents placed before a judge and referred to in open court'.[77] Although this would not apply automatically to inquiries of the Charities Commission, it would apply in this case where the Charity Commission had published a report and where the journalist was requesting additional information where a journalist had demonstrated that the report raised unanswered questions of real public interest. Lord Mance remarked that:

> Since the passing of the Human Rights Act 1998, there has too often been a tendency to see the law in areas touched by the Convention solely in terms of Convention rights. But the Convention rights represent a threshold protection; and,

71 EU 2000/C 364/01.
72 C-671/10 *Aklagaren v Hans Akerberg-Fransson* [2013] 2 CMLR 1273.
73 *Benkharbouche v Republic of Sudan* [2015] EWCA Civ 33; [2015] 2 CMLR 528.
74 *Davis v Secretary of State for the Home Department* [2015] EWHC 2092 (Admin). The Court of Appeal subsequently referred the issue to the European Court of Justice. *R (Davis) v. Secretary of State for the Home Department* [2015] EWCA Civ 1185.
75 [2013] UKSC 61; [2014] AC 1115.
76 *Kennedy v Charity Commission* [2014] UKSC 20; [2014] 2 All ER 847.
77 *Ibid*, [47] (Lord Mance).

especially in the view of the contribution which common lawyers made to the Convention's inception, they may be expected, at least generally even if not always, to reflect and to find their homologue in the common or domestic statute law.[78]

There are nevertheless limits to the ability of the common law to expand the list of rights protected under the Human Rights Act, as illustrated in *Moohan* where the Supreme Court concluded that the common law did not provide for a general right to vote, such that the exclusion of prisoners from taking part in the Scottish referendum was contrary to the common law.[79] Although Lord Hodge had 'no difficulty in recognizing the right to vote as a basic or constitutional right' he did not think that 'the common law has been developed so as to recognise a right of universal and equal suffrage from which any derogation must be provided for by law and must be proportionate'.[80] This is because it has been legislation and not the common law which, historically, has granted the right to vote and which has expanded the franchise over time. Similarly, Lady Hale concluded that 'it would be wonderful if the common law had recognized a right of universal suffrage' but that as the creation and expansion of the franchise had been created by Parliament: '[i]t makes no more sense to say that sentenced prisoners have a common law right to vote than it makes to say that women have a common law right to vote, which is clearly absurd'.[81] Only Lord Kerr was prepared to conclude that it was 'at least arguable that the exclusion of all prisoners from the right to vote is incompatible with the common law' given that the 'common law can certainly evolve alongside statutory developments'.[82]

3 The interpretative obligation under s 3: the remedial process and pre-legislative scrutiny

Introduction

The HRA does *not* 'incorporate' the Convention rights into substantive domestic law, since it does not provide that they are to have the 'force of law', the usual form of words used when international treaties are incorporated into domestic law.[83] Instead, under s 1(2) of the HRA, certain of the rights discussed in Chapter 2 are to 'have effect for the purposes of this Act'.[84] The rights are not directly enforceable between private parties. But the rights are in a sense incorporated into domestic law when asserted against public authorities.

The key mechanism affording the Convention under the HRA a higher status than other laws is s 3, which requires the judiciary to 'read and give effect' to legislative provisions compatibly with the Convention rights 'so far as it is possible to do so'. This

---

78 *Ibid*, [46].
79 [2014] UKSC 67; [2015] AC 901.
80 *Ibid*, [33]–[34].
81 *Ibid*, [56].
82 *Ibid*, [86]–[87].
83 See, e.g., the Carriage of Goods by Sea Act 1971, s 1(2).
84 According to the then Lord Chancellor, the rights are a form of common law and, in that sense, they are part of domestic law: HL, Third Reading, col 840, 5 February 1998.

means that although the judges cannot strike down a provision as incompatible with the rights, s 3 can be relied upon to bring the provision into conformity with them if possible. The judges, as will be seen below, have adopted a robust stance under s 3, coming very close to, or even crossing, the boundary between legislating and interpreting in so doing. If a provision cannot be rendered compatible with the Convention, the incompatibility can be declared, under s 4, leaving the government to introduce remedial legislation. In this way a delicate compromise was struck between creating greater rights protection and preserving parliamentary sovereignty. The HRA also preserved the possibility that Parliament might deliberately introduce legislation that was incompatible with the Convention. This is implicit in s 19, as discussed below. If this occurred, and the legislation could not be rendered compatible through the use of s 3, it would remain valid and could be applied, under s 3(2).

The HRA is frequently referred to as a 'Commonwealth model' of rights protections[85] or as a Parliamentary Bill of Rights,[86] along with the Canadian Charter of Fundamental Rights and Freedoms, the New Zealand Bill of Rights Act 1990 and the human rights provisions found in the Australian Capital Territories[87] and in Victoria.[88] At the time of its enactment, both the Canadian Charter and the New Zealand Bill of Rights provided a possible model of achieving the HRA's aim of ensuring a stronger protection of human rights whilst preserving parliamentary sovereignty. The HRA is closer to the New Zealand model, as opposed to the Canadian model, where the Canadian Supreme Court may strike down legislation that contravenes Charter rights, with the legislatures being empowered to legislate contrary to most Charter rights by including a clause stating that the legislation takes effect 'notwithstanding' the Charter. Despite its similarities, the HRA differs from the New Zealand model by providing a stronger interpretative obligation than is found in New Zealand, as well as including the power to issue a declaration of incompatibility. The current reform proposals show no intention of moving from a Commonwealth model to a stronger protection of rights. Rather, there is the suggestion that Parliament's role should be strengthened and that of the courts weakened through weakening the interpretative obligation based on an assessment that the courts have gone too far, undermining the sovereignty of Parliament in practice. Rather, there is a proposal to ensure that courts interpret legislation according to its 'normal meaning and the clear intention of Parliament'.[89] An analysis of the case law on s 3, however, demonstrates that courts are acutely aware of the need to ensure that interpretation does not slide into repeal. However, it can be difficult to determine the precise intention of Parliament. As such, it is difficult to know what difference any reform of s 3 would make in practice.

---

85 See Gardbaum, S, *The Commonwealth Model of Rights Protections*, 2013, CUP.
86 Hiebert, JL and Kelly, JB, *Parliamentary Bills of Rights: The Experiences of New Zealand and the United Kingdom*, 2015, CUP.
87 Human Rights Act (Australian Capital Territories) 2004.
88 The Charter of Human Rights and Responsibilities Act (Victoria) 2006.
89 'Protecting Human Rights in the UK: The Conservatives' Proposals for Changing Britain's Human Rights Laws', page 6.

The interpretative obligation under s 3[90]

Introduction

Under the HRA 1998, which largely reflects the proposals in Labour's consultation paper on the matter,[91] the Convention[92] receives a subtle form of constitutional protection. The key provision in creating this form of protection for the Convention under the HRA is s 3(1), which reads: 'So far as it is possible to do so, primary and subordinate legislation must be read and given effect in a way which is compatible with the Convention rights . . .'. Section 3(2)(b) reads: 'this section does not affect the validity, continuing operation or enforcement of any incompatible primary legislation; and (c) does not affect the validity, continuing operation or enforcement of any incompatible subordinate legislation if . . . primary legislation prevents the removal of the incompatibility'. Significantly, s 3(2)(a) makes it clear that the obligation imposed by s 3 arises in relation to both previous and subsequent enactments.

It is clear from s 3 that the Convention has, in one sense, a lower status than ordinary statutes in that it cannot *automatically* override pre-existing law. But, more significantly, s 3 demands that all statutory provisions should be rendered, if possible, compatible with the Convention rights. Therefore, by imposing this interpretative obligation on the courts, the rights become capable of affecting subsequent legislation in a way that is not normally possible.[93] If legislation cannot be rendered compatible with the rights, a declaration of incompatibility can be made under s 4;[94] remedial legislation can then be introduced into Parliament to modify or repeal the offending provisions under s 10.[95] This subtle form of protection avoids entrenchment and therefore creates a compromise between leaving the protection of rights to the democratic process and entrusting them fully to the judiciary.

Use of this model for the Convention obviously places protection for human rights very much at the mercy of judicial interpretation of statutes. It means that a more liberal-minded judge can find that most, if not almost all, statutory provisions, even if unambiguous, can be modified through interpretative techniques in order to achieve harmony with the Convention. The requirement to construe legislation 'so far as it is *possible* to do so' consistently with the Convention (emphasis added) makes it clear that such a

---

90   For discussion in the very early post-HRA years, see Elliott, MC, 'Fundamental rights as interpretative constructs: the constitutional logic of the HRA', in Forsyth, C (ed), *Judicial Review and the Constitution*, 2001, Hart; Lester, A, 'The article of the possible – interpreting statutes under the Human Rights Act' [2000] EHRLR 665; Bennion, 'What Interpretation is 'Possible' under Section 3(1) of the Human Rights Act' [2000] PL 77; Edwards, 'Reading down legislation under the Human Rights Act' (2000) 20 LS 353.

91   Bringing Rights Home: Labour's Plans to Incorporate the ECHR into UK Law. See Straw and Boateng (1997) 1 EHRR 71. For discussion, see Lyell, N (Sir) (1997) 2 EHRR 132; Wadham, J (1997) 2 EHRLR 141; Ewing, *op cit*, fn 72.

92   The term 'the Convention' will be used to refer to the Convention rights currently included in Sched 1 to the HRA 1998.

93   For extensive consideration of this point, see Clayton and Tomlinson, *op cit*, fn 1.

94   See below, pp 169–78.

95   See below, pp 178–09.

stance best reflects the intention of Parliament, although it may also be pointed out that since Parliament has enacted s 4, it clearly contemplated *some* limits on what could be achieved by means of s 3. At the Committee stage of the Human Rights Bill Lord Irvine said:

> We want the courts to strive to find an interpretation of legislation which is consistent with Convention rights so far as the language of the legislation allows, and only in the last resort to conclude that the legislation is so clearly incompatible with the Convention that it is impossible to do so.[96]

Clearly, however, a very bold approach to s 3, going well beyond use of an interpretative technique, would not have democratic legitimacy and would encroach on the role of Parliament. The question that faced the judges at the inception of the HRA was as to the line that should be drawn under s 3 between interpreting and legislating.

Interpretative techniques adopted under s 3[97]

The leading case on the application of this section is *Ghaidan v Godin-Mendoza*.[98] The Court of Appeal found that Sched 1, para 2 of the Rent Act 1977 was incompatible with Art 14 read with Art 8. But it found that the potential incompatibility could be remedied under s 3 HRA by construing the words 'as his or her wife or husband' in Sched 1, para 2 as if they meant 'as if they were his or her wife or husband'. The House of Lords in *Ghaidan v Godin-Mendoza* agreed with the Court of Appeal, and used s 3 HRA to interpret the statute to avoid the discrimination against homosexuals so that they had the same rights to succeed to tenancies upon the death of their partner as were enjoyed by heterosexual couples. This meant not merely changing the meaning given to certain words, but the addition of (a few) words that were not included in the provision.

Lord Nicholls made a number of very significant points on s 3 which are worth quoting in full:[99]

> [T]he first point to be considered is how far, when enacting section 3, Parliament intended that the actual language of a statute, as distinct from the concept expressed

---

96 *Hansard*, HL Deb col 535, 18 November 1997. The Lord Chancellor further observed that 'in 99 per cent of the cases that will arise, there will be no need for judicial declarations of incompatibility' and the Home Secretary said 'We expect that, in almost all cases, the courts will be able to interpret the legislation compatibly with the Convention': Hansard (HL Debates,) 5 February 1998, col 840 (3rd reading) and Hansard (HC Debates,) 16 February 1998, col 778 (2nd reading).

97 For comment on s 3(1) generally in the first three years of the HRA, see further: Lester, A, 'The Art of the Possible – Interpreting Statutes under the Human Rights Act' [1999] EHRLR 665; Bennion, F, 'What Interpretation is 'Possible' under Section 3(1) of the Human Rights Act' [2000] PL 77; Edwards, R, 'Reading down Legislation under the Human Rights Act' (2000) 20 LS 353; Gearty, C, 'Reconciling Parliamentary Democracy and Human Rights' (2002) 118 LQR 248; Phillipson, G, '(Mis)Reading Section 3(1) of the Human Rights Act' (2003) LQR 183.

98 [2003] 2 WLR 478; [2002] 4 All ER 1162; [2004] 2 AC 557 (HL).

99 [2004] UKHL 30; [2004] 2 AC 557; [2004] 3 WLR 113, HL paras 31–34.

in that language, should be determinative. Since section 3 relates to the 'interpretation' of legislation, it is natural to focus attention initially on the language used in the legislative provision being considered. But once it is accepted that section 3 may require legislation to bear a meaning which departs from the unambiguous meaning the legislation would otherwise bear, it becomes impossible to suppose Parliament intended that the operation of section 3 should depend critically upon the particular form of words adopted by the parliamentary draftsman in the statutory provision under consideration. That would make the application of section 3 something of a semantic lottery. If the draftsman chose to express the *concept being enacted* in one form of words, section 3 would be available to achieve Convention-compliance. If he chose a different form of words, section 3 would be impotent. [emphasis added]

From this the conclusion which seems inescapable is that the mere fact the language under consideration is inconsistent with a Convention-compliant meaning does not of itself make a Convention-compliant interpretation under section 3 impossible. Section 3 enables language to be interpreted restrictively or expansively. But section 3 goes further than this. It is also apt to require a court to read in words which change the meaning of the enacted legislation, so as to make it Convention-compliant. In other words, the intention of Parliament in enacting section 3 was that, to an extent bounded only by what is 'possible', a court can modify the meaning, and hence the effect, of primary and secondary legislation.

Parliament, however, cannot have intended that in the discharge of this extended interpretative function the courts should adopt a meaning inconsistent with a fundamental feature of legislation. That would be to cross the constitutional boundary section 3 seeks to demarcate and preserve. Parliament has retained the right to enact legislation in terms which are not Convention-compliant. The meaning imported by application of section 3 must be compatible with the underlying thrust of the legislation being construed. Words implied must, in the phrase of my noble and learned friend Lord Rodger of Earlsferry, 'go with the grain of the legislation'. Nor can Parliament have intended that section 3 should require courts to make decisions for which they are not equipped. There may be several ways of making a provision Convention-compliant, and the choice may involve issues calling for *legislative deliberation* (emphasis added).

Both these features were present in *In re S (Minors)(Care Order: Implementation of Care Plan)* [2002] 2 AC 291. There the proposed 'starring system' was inconsistent in an important respect with the scheme of the Children Act 1989, and the proposed system had far-reaching practical ramifications for local authorities. Again, in *R (Anderson) v Secretary of State for the Home Department* [2003] 1 AC 837 section 29 of the Crime (Sentences) Act 1997 could not be read in a Convention-compliant way without giving the section a meaning inconsistent with an important feature expressed clearly in the legislation. In *Bellinger v Bellinger* [2003] 2 AC 467 recognition of Mrs Bellinger as female for the purposes of section 11(c) of the Matrimonial Causes Act 1973 would have had exceedingly wide ramifications, raising issues ill-suited for determination by the courts or court procedures.

The majority in the Lords took a broadly similar view.[100] We can draw three conclusions from Lord Nicholls's account. First, s 3 may require legislation to bear a meaning that departs from the unambiguous meaning the legislation would otherwise bear, since the particular form of words used by the draftsman to express the concept of the statute – its underlying policy – should not be allowed to prevent the courts from achieving Convention compliance. Second, to ensure a Convention-compatible interpretation, courts may read words in to legislation, as well as reading down legislative provisions – i.e. making it clear that a broad provision only applies to certain specific situations where its application would not breach Convention rights. Third, there are nevertheless limits to the court's duty under s 3. A meaning cannot be adopted that goes against a fundamental feature of the legislation or that requires legislative deliberation.

Ghaidan itself provides an example of the extent to which courts may read words in to legislation. The House of Lords thus adopted the course taken in the Court of Appeal, and found that the words 'living with the tenant as his or her wife or husband' could be read as: 'living with the tenant, as *if they were* his or her wife or husband'. A further, more recent, example of the extent to which the courts may be prepared to read words in to legislation in order to read down a general provision is found in litigation concerning the legality of non-derogating control orders. Section 2 of the Prevention of Terrorism Act 2005 empowered the Secretary of State to make a non-derogating control order when she has reasonable grounds to suspect that an individual is or has been involved in a terrorism related activity and where she considers that the control order is necessary for the purpose of preventing a risk of terrorism. The imposition of control orders is subject to court oversight and the Schedule to the Act provides an outline of the procedures to be applied in such court hearings, including para 4(3)(d) that provides that 'the relevant court is required to give permission for material not to be disclosed where it considers that the disclosure of the material would be contrary to the public interest' – closed material. The Grand Chamber of the Strasbourg Court in *A v UK* concluded that hearings as to legality of the imposition of a non-derogating control order must provide sufficient information to the individual as to enable him to give effective instructions against the allegations on which the non-derogating control order was based. In particular, Art 6 would be breached where the open material – i.e. the material disclosed in court – consisted of purely general assertions and the case against the individual was based solely or to a decisive degree on closed materials. To achieve a Convention-compatible interpretation of the legislation, the Supreme Court in *AF* adhered to the Convention-compatible reading of this section in the earlier Supreme Court decision of *MB*, reading into para 4(3)(d) the words 'except where to do so would be incompatible with the right of a controlled person to a fair trial'. These words effectively read down a general requirement that the court *must* permit material not to be disclosed into a conditional requirement – the material must be disclosed *unless doing so breaches the right to a fair hearing.*

Nevertheless, it is not possible to read legislation so as to comply with Convention rights where to do so would undermine a fundamental feature of legislation.

---

100 For discussion of the other judgments, including the dissenting judgment of Lord Millett, see Kavanagh, A, in *Judicial Reasoning under the HRA* (2007) fn 1 above, Chapter 5.

In *Anderson*, for example, the incompatibility lay in the involvement of the Secretary of State in sentencing adult life prisoners.[101] A pervasive feature of s 29 of the Crime (Sentencing) Act 1997 provides for the Secretary of State's role in determining the mandatory component of life sentences. However, this power was inconsistent with the right to have a sentence imposed by 'an independent and impartial tribunal', under Art 6 ECHR. A declaration of incompatibility was made rather than seeking to use s 3(1) since the Secretary of State's role was such a fundamental feature of the statute as a whole – any other approach would have been against the grain of the statute.

Nor is such an interpretation possible where reading the legislation so as to comply with Convention rights would require legislative deliberation. In *Bellinger v Bellinger*,[102] for example, W, a post-operative transsexual, appealed against a decision under the Matrimonial Causes Act 1973 that she was not lawfully married to her husband, H, because she, W, was not female. Section 11 of the 1973 Act states: 'A marriage . . . shall be void on the following grounds only, that is to say . . . that the parties are not respectively male and female'. W argued that the word 'female' should be interpreted as including her and other post-operative transsexuals, relying on her right to private and family life under Art 8 ECHR. As Phillipson has argued, 'All that was required was the re-interpretation of the single word "female", to reflect modern understandings of the protean nature of gender, so that it included post-operative male to female transsexuals.'[103] However, the House of Lords refused to reinterpret the word 'female' to include transsexuals as had been argued for. They were influenced by the fact that the government had already accepted that the area of law in question had become incompatible with Art 8 and had stated that it intended to bring legislation before Parliament to remedy the matter. In those circumstances, it appeared that the Lords preferred to leave reform of the law to Parliament which would be able to take a far more comprehensive and systematic view of the issue. A range of policy matters were involved; as Kavanagh observes: 'the resulting change in the law would have [had] far-reaching practical ramifications, raising issues whose solution calls for extensive inquiry and the widest public consultation and discussion which was more appropriate for Parliament than the courts'.[104]

Although *Ghadan v Godin-Mendoza* provides clarity as to when it is and is not possible to read and give effect to legislation so as to comply with Convention rights, it can be difficult to apply these criteria to any particular case, as illustrated by the *GC* case concerning the retention of DNA and fingerprint evidence. Section 64(1A) of the Police and Criminal Evidence Act 1984 stated that fingerprints and samples 'may be retained after they have fulfilled the purposes for which they were taken' in circumstances where there was no legislative requirement to destroy them. The practice had been to retain fingerprints and samples indefinitely. However, in *S and Marper v UK*, the Strasbourg Court concluded that Art 8 ECHR was breached when fingerprints and DNA samples were indefinitely retained from those who were arrested and then either later acquitted of the offence, or where charges had been dropped. The question arose as to whether the legislative provision could be read compatibly with Convention rights. The majority

---

101 *R (on the application of Anderson) v Secretary of State for the Home Department* [2003] 1 AC 837.
102 [2003] 2 AC 467 (HL).
103 Phillipson, G, 'Deference, Discretion and Democracy in the Human Rights Act Era' (2007) CLP 40 at p 65.
104 'Statutory interpretation and human rights after Anderson: a more contextual approach' [2004] PL 537 at 541.

concluded that this was possible as s 64, through the use of the word 'may' clearly gave a wide discretion to the police. Although the practice had been to retain information indefinitely, this was not required by the statute. Indeed, had Parliament wished this information to have been retained indefinitely it would have said so. Therefore, it was possible to read s 64 in a manner that complied with Convention rights, with the police exercising their discretion in a manner that did not lead to the retention of samples and fingerprints from those acquitted or where charges had been dropped. Indeed the majority concluded that this was possible through an application of the ordinary principles of legislative interpretation, without needing to apply the stronger interpretative obligation found under s 3. The minority, however, argued that the policy and objective of Parliament when enacting s 64(1A) had been to retain data indefinitely so as to aid the creation of a large database to help in the detection and prosecution of crimes. This aim and purpose was a fundamental feature of the legislation and, as such, to interpret s 64(1A) so as to prevent the retention of data and fingerprints from the acquitted would undermine a fundamental feature. Furthermore, it would require a legislative choice to determine how to bring English law in line with Convention rights, as illustrated by the fact that Parliament, at the time, had introduced a Bill to deal with this issue. The disagreement between the majority and minority here turned upon how they interpreted legislative provisions, particularly as to whether the court focused on the specific wording of the legislative provision, or looked to broader information concerning the legislation's purpose.

Summing-up the current approach to s 3[105]

Section 3 may be used in a very creative fashion, as indicated by Lord Nicholls in *Ghaidan*, in order to avoid a finding of incompatibility, unless so doing would mean crossing the

---

105 Texts referred to below and background: Clayton, R and Tomlinson, H, *The Law of Human Rights*, 2nd edn, 2009; Singh and Hunt, *Assessing the Impact of the Human Rights Act*, (2003), Hart; Jowell and Cooper (eds), *Delivering Rights? How the HRA is working and for whom*, 2003, Hart; Fenwick, Masterman, Phillipson (eds), *Judicial Reasoning under the HRA*, 2007, CUP; Hoffman and Rowe, *Human Rights in the UK*, 4th edn, 2013, Longman; Pannick, D and Lester of Herne Hill QC, Lord, *Human Rights Law and Practice*, 3rd edn, 2009, Butterworths; Gearty, C, *Principles of Human Rights Adjudication*, 2004, OUP; Wadham, J, Mountfield, H and Desai R, *Blackstone's Guide to The Human Rights Act*, 7th edn, 2015; Smith, R, *Textbook on International Human Rights*, 6th edn, 2014, OUP; Steiner H, Alston P and Goodman R, *International Human Rights in Context: Law, Politics, Morals*, 3rd edn, 2008, OUP; Hunt, M, *Using Human Rights Law in English Courts*, 1997; Singh, R and Hunt, M, *A Practitioner's Guide to the Impact of the Human Rights Act*, 1999; Grosz, Beatson and Duffy, *Human Rights: The 1998 Act and the European Convention*, 2000, Sweet and Maxwell; Fenwick, H, *Civil Rights: New Labour, Freedom and the Human Rights Act, 2000*, Chapter 2; Clements and Thomas (eds), *The HRA: A Success Story?* 2005, Blackwell; Irvine, Lord, 'The impact of The Human Rights Act: Parliament, The Courts and The Executive' (2003) *Public Law*, Sum, 308–25; Klug, F, 'Judicial Deference Under the Human Rights Act 1998' (2003) EHRLR 2, 125–33; Klug F, 'Standing Back From The Human Rights Act: How Effective is it Five Years On' (2005) *Public Law*, Win, 716–28; Lester of Herne Hill, Lord 'The Human Rights Act – five years on' [2004] EHLR 259; Steyn, Lord, 'Deference: A Tangled Story' (2005) Public Law 346; Kavanagh, A, 'Statutory interpretation and human rights after Anderson: a more contextual approach' [2004] PL 537; Steyn, Lord, '2000–2005: Laying The Foundations Of Human Rights Law In The United Kingdom' (2005) EHRLR, 4, 349–62; Sunkin, M, 'Pushing Forward the Frontiers of Human Rights Protection: the meaning of public authority under the HRA' [2004] PL 643; Leigh, I, 'Taking Rights Proportionately, Judicial Review, the HRA and Strasbourg' [2002] PL 265; Klug, F and Starmer, K [2001] PL 654; McGoldrick, D, 'The HRA in theory and practice' (2001) 50(4) ICLQ 901.

boundary between interpreting and legislating. *Bellinger* and *Ghaidan* indicate that the word 'possible' in s 3(1) relates to matters ranging well beyond linguistic possibility. Clearly, they appear to view it as denoting something that is possible linguistically but that may be undesirable, for a range of reasons. So when will the courts be prepared to read words into a statute, or to reinterpret an existing word, in order to avoid incompatibility? In other words, which factors will persuade them to the more radical approach adopted in *AF* and in *Ghaidan*? Their approach appears to be that they will adopt that more radical approach where it appears to them to be proper and desirable to do so. What factors will strike them as bringing a particular instance into that category of desirableness?

The following discussion is based on Dr Kavanagh's analysis of the s 3(1) cases[106] which the author finds compelling in the sense that it is the most accurate analysis of the wide range of factors that the courts are relying on in determining how radical their approach should be in particular instances under s 3. Clearly, the courts are concerned that they should not cross the line between interpretation and legislation. Kavanagh argues that the decision in *Re S and re W*,[107] shows that, while the courts are prepared to read words into statutes, as in *R v A* or *Ghaidan*, they will not do so, 'as a way of radically reforming a whole statute or writing a quasi-legislative code granting new powers and setting out new procedures to replace that statute'.[108]

Another aspect of this stance is to find that the change proposed, to ensure compatibility, will probably be rejected where it would run counter to a pervasive feature of the statute – where the objectionable provisions permeate the statute. This factor was decisive in *Anderson*.[109] In *Ghaidan* the objected-to provision was not viewed as fundamental to the statute as a whole or a substantial part of it. Where the change is viewed as fundamental it would probably require extensive statutory modification to achieve compatibility. Clearly, different views could be taken as to the fundamental nature or otherwise of a provision.

The subject matter of the provision at issue is relevant. If it relates to matters peculiarly within the judicial domain, including the ordering of the criminal or civil justice system, in matters of sentencing, or admissibility of evidence, the judges are more likely to be prepared to take a radical approach, as they did in *R v A* and in *R v Offen*.[110] In taking such a stance in that context they would not view themselves as stepping outside their own area of constitutional responsibility.

If, however, a case involves issues of social policy or resource allocation, the courts are much less likely to be bold. This factor was of relevance in *Re S*: the proposed 'interpretation' of the statute that had been accepted in the Court of Appeal would also

---

106 See Kavanagh, A, 'Unlocking the Human Rights Act: the 'radical approach' to section 3(1) revisited' (2005) 3 EHRLR 259; see in particular 'The elusive divide between interpretation and legislation under the HRA' (2004) 24(2) OJLS 259; and 'Statutory interpretation and human rights after Anderson: a more contextual approach' [2004] P.L. 537, which is a response, in part, to Nicol, D, 'Statutory interpretation and human rights after Anderson' [2004] PL 273. The analysis below (pp 154–55) partially follows my co-author's in *Media Freedom under the Human Rights Act*, pp 161–62.
107 [2002] 2 AC 291. This decision was reversed unanimously by the House of Lords.
108 'Statutory interpretation and human rights after *Anderson*: a more contextual approach' [2004] PL 537 at p 540.
109 *R (on the application of Anderson) v Secretary of State for the Home Department* [2003] 1 AC 837.
110 [2001] 1 WLR 253. The case concerned the 'reading down' of provisions governing mandatory sentences for repeat offenders.

have had 'far-reaching practical ramifications for local authorities and their care of children, including the authority's allocation of scarce financial and other resources'.[111] Those policy and resource factors were also of relevance, as indicated above, in *Bellinger v Bellinger* and persuaded the court to take a cautious approach to s 3.[112] As discussed, the change brought about in *Ghaidan v Godin-Mendoza*[113] did not engage significant countervailing policy or resource-based factors.

Kavanagh further argues, referring to Lord Steyn's judgment in *Ghaidan*, that the key to understanding the various uses of s 3 is to see it as a remedial provision.[114] In other words, where the use of s 3 rather than s 4 is the only means of providing a remedy in the particular situation, the judges will tend to employ s 3. As she notes, in *Bellinger*, a remedy was about to be provided for the applicant by planned legislation, whereas in *Ghaidan* Mr Mendoza would have had no means of succeeding to a statutory tenancy had s 3 not been employed as it was. In addition, as *AF* perhaps suggests, the courts may be more willing to reach a radical interpretation when faced with a series of decisions from the Grand Chamber of the Strasbourg Court.

As a final step, if one or more of the other countervailing factors discussed are present, so that the use of s 3 is viewed as inappropriate in order to find compatibility, a declaration of the incompatibility may have to be made, when and if the matter reaches a court able to make such a declaration, under s 4.[115] It now appears that the courts tend to view s 3, not s 4, as the main remedial mechanism of the HRA, only turning to s 4 exceptionally as a last resort, so normally this fourth step will not be needed.[116] If no remedy is available or in prospect, except by way of s 3, it appears that the courts may be strongly inclined towards the more radical use of s 3.

Conclusions

It is argued that the approach being taken to s 3, especially the stance taken in *AF*, is not one that it is entirely easy to feel comfortable with in terms of the doctrine of parliamentary sovereignty.

It is argued that a hierarchy of factors should be identified, founded strongly on the differing constitutional roles and competences of the courts and Parliament, and that the two most significant are the demands of the Convention, taking the jurisprudence into account, and the difficulty of bringing about the change in question in the sense that it opposes a fundamental feature of the statute. In terms of weighing up what is to count as a 'fundamental feature', it is argued that a number of factors might be relevant. Where a provision in a Bill is the product of wide-ranging consultation with interested parties, and Parliament, after weighing up the issues fully, clearly intended the provision in question to have the effect that it has, as opposed to an instance in which the effect is merely

---

111 Kavanagh, A, 'Statutory interpretation and human rights after *Anderson*: a more contextual approach' [2004] PL 537 at p 540.
112 [2003] 2 AC 467 (HL).
113 [2004] 2 AC 557 (HL).
114 See *Judicial Reasoning under the HRA* (2007) fn 1 above, Chapter 5.
115 As in *Wilson v First County Trust Ltd* [2001] 3 All ER 229; [2001] EWCA Civ 633, although arguably, it is unclear that the Court's interpretation of the Convention absolutely demanded this result.
116 See Lord Steyn's remarks on this point in *Ghaidan* [2004] 2 AC 557 (HL) at para 50.

incidental, the courts should be more inclined to accept that interference goes against the grain of the statute. Where the converse is the case, interference is more readily justifiable.

The use of the range of factors identified clearly allows the senior judiciary a great deal of leeway to allow their own values to have an influence on legislation, under the cloak of deploying neutral factors and using interpretative techniques. Reliance mainly on s 3 tends to marginalise the democratic process: if s 3 is used, even if it emasculates a legislative provision, Parliament will not have been asked – under the s 4 procedure – to amend the provision. The whole process remains in the hands of the judiciary. The tensions inherent in the scheme have been explored and heightened, since it appears that s 3 will almost always be used to outflank s 4 and s 10. The idea, which seemed to be inherent in s 4, that declarations of incompatibility would be made, even in criminal cases, seems to have been shown to be misconceived.

Under the HRA there is nothing theoretically to prevent the overturning of what may be perceived by the legislature to be radical interpretations. In *Ghaidan*, for example, Parliament could have enacted a statute with one single, overriding purpose – to discriminate against homosexual couples in the provision of housing.[117] Not only could a government commanding a majority in Parliament probably ensure that such legislation was passed (it certainly could as far as the HRA itself is concerned), but the judges would have to apply it so long as the provisions incompatible with Arts 8 and 14 were pervasive enough to be viewed as a fundamental feature of the statute. It is perhaps somewhat ironic that the more pervasive and clear the incompatibility, the less that can be done in response to it in remedial terms under s 3. But as a matter of constitutional practice a government would be very unlikely to seek to reinstate provisions found authoritatively by the Supreme Court to be in breach of the Convention. Seeking to do so would not only breach the UK's obligations at the international level, it would also undermine the judges' constitutional role as the guardian of human rights. Further, although this is a less significant point, the HRA as currently conceived is quite a blunt instrument to be used for the purpose of passing legislative provisions already found at the domestic level to have breached the Convention (although of course on a face-value reading it appeared to be intended that it could be used for that purpose). It itself contains no safeguards against passing such legislation – such as a demand that if such legislation is passed it must be in response to a particular pressing social need (a requirement that would not be as demanding as the requirements of Art 15,[118] but that would at least place an express burden on government to justify the introduction of apparently incompatible legislation into Parliament). These points illustrate not only the constitutional realities of the HRA, but also the obvious difference between the position in other Commonwealth models and that in the UK – Canada is dealing with its own Charter, while the UK is adhering domestically to an international human rights instrument that also binds it at the international level.

The conclusion must be, then, that s 3 provides the judges with a powerful tool, and it is arguable that a factor determining their choice of approach may be their view of the desirableness of the outcome, in social policy rather than legal terms.[119] The strength

---

117 See above, Chapter 5, p 149.
118 See Chapter 2, pp 99–100.
119 They may favour a legislative regime that aids in the maintenance of road safety, whereas their 'common sense' may inform them that a woman who has allegedly had sex with a man on one occasion may

of the obligation under s 3 is not, it is suggested, without its dangers. The strong interpretative obligation on the judiciary can be viewed as a double-edged sword. They are
enjoined to strive to find a Convention-friendly interpretation, but in certain instances
the Convention standards are diluted as courts adopt the least liberal interpretation of
the Convention right in order to make it harmonise with UK legislation. An interpretative approach that leads to the dilution of Convention standards can be avoided only if
a vigorous, activist approach is taken, not only to foisting Convention-based interpretations onto statutory language, but also to ensuring that Convention standards are fully
upheld by means of that interpretation. But there is a strong argument for using the
declaration of incompatibility procedure where a clash of rights concerning an arguably incommensurable moral issue is in question, one that has been consciously and
systematically addressed by Parliament after full and wide-ranging consultation with
the groups representing those directly affected by the provision in question.[120]

The effect of s 2

Introduction

In seeking to interpret statutory provisions compatibly with the Convention rights under
the HRA, the domestic judiciary 'must take into account' any relevant Strasbourg jurisprudence,[121] under s 2. Section 2 creates on its face quite a weak obligation. UK courts
are not bound by decisions of the Strasbourg Court. It is open to the judiciary to consider but disapply a particular decision. This interpretation of s 2 finds support in the
opinion of the Lord Chancellor when introducing and debating the Bill in the House of
Lords.[122] Nevertheless, following the development of the *Ullah*[123] principle, one would
be forgiven for thinking that the courts had interpreted 'take into account' as coming
close to 'consider as if a binding precedent'.[124] In the words of Lord Rodger: *'[a]rgen-
toratum locutum: iudicium finitum* – Strasbourg has spoken, the case is closed'.[125]

---

be likely to consent to have sex with him on another. The implications of this latter issue are pursued
below, pp 229–30.

120 This very difficult issue is discussed further below in relation to judicial activism; see pp 266–7.

121 The term exhaustively covers any 'judgment, decision, declaration or advisory opinion of the Court',
any 'opinion of the Commission given in a report adopted under Art 31', any 'decision of the Commission in connection with Art 26 or 27(2)' or any 'decision of the Committee of Ministers taken under Art
46'. The words 'in connection with' appear to mean that all findings which may be said to be linked to
the admissibility procedure, including reports prepared during the preliminary examination of a case,
could be taken into account.

122 583 HL 514, 515, 8 November 1997. 583 HL 514, 515, 8 November 1997 and 484 HL 1270, 1271,
9 January 1998.

123 *R (Ullah) v Special Adjudicator* [2004] UKHL 26; [2004] 2 AC 323.

124 See Kavanagh, A, *Constitutional Review under the Human Rights Act*, 2009, CUP, 144–64;Amos, M,
'The Impact of the Human Rights Act on the United Kingdom's Performance before the European
Court of Human Rights' (2007) Public Law 655, Masterman, R, 'Aspiration or Foundation? The Status
of the Strasbourg Jurisprudence and the "Convention Rights" in Domestic Law in Fenwick, H, Phillipson, G and Masterman, R (eds), *Judicial Reasoning under the UK Human Rights Act*, 2007, CUP, 57
and previous editions of this book.

125 *Secretary of State for the Home Department v AF* [2009] UKHL 28; [2010] 2 AC 269, [98] (Lord
Rodger).

This close connection to the decisions of the Strasbourg Court enables the Convention rights to evolve as the Strasbourg Court treats the Convention as a living instrument, extending and clarifying the content of Convention rights. However, the effect of the margin of appreciation doctrine may sometimes have the effect of 'reading down' the right.[126] The interpretation of s 2, therefore, plays a pivotal role in determining the extent to which human rights are protected in the UK. So much so that the modification of s 2 is one of the key proposals of the current Conservative Government's plans to replace the HRA 1998. The Conservatives are concerned that the Strasbourg Court has engaged in 'mission creep', providing a more extensive protection of rights than found in the Convention. These expansive interpretations are then incorporated into domestic law as the UK courts adhere to the judgments of Strasbourg.[127] To combat this danger, the Conservatives wish to make the decisions of Strasbourg advisory only, although it remains to be seen how they propose to modify s 2 in order to achieve this aim.

Since *Ullah*, there has been a significant tempering of the extent to which UK courts are bound to adhere to Strasbourg, with examples of UK courts both refusing to follow decisions of the Strasbourg Court and going beyond current case law, facilitating dialogue between the domestic and Strasbourg Courts.

Legal status of the jurisprudence and the role of the judges under the HRA?

The Lords' acceptance that they should rely heavily on Strasbourg decisions was made apparent in the early post-HRA decision of *R (on the application of Alconbury) v Secretary of State for the Environment*.[128] The Divisional Court made a declaration of incompatibility in relation to planning law provisions, finding them incompatible with Art 6 since the Secretary of State for the Environment, in determining a planning appeal, is acting in a dual capacity in both hearing the appeal and applying his or her own policy guidelines.

On appeal to the House of Lords the declaration was overturned;[129] reliance on the Strasbourg jurisprudence was crucial to this decision. The House of Lords found that the requirements of Art 6 can be satisfied by the possibility of judicial review. If the minister does not act impartially, his or her decision can be judicially reviewed. Therefore, it was found, a remedy was available. The House considered the question whether judicial review could be viewed as providing a sufficient remedy, bearing in mind the findings that it could not in *Lustig-Prean v UK*[130] and *Kingsley v UK*.[131] It came to the view, after extensively reviewing the Strasbourg jurisprudence in planning cases, that judicial review could now be viewed as providing a sufficient remedy, owing to the need to consider proportionality under the HRA. Lord Slynn found that the domestic

---

126 See *Salabiaku v France* (A 141-A) (1988) and see further pp 228–31, below. See also the discussion of the margin of appreciation doctrine in Chapter 2, pp 95–98.

127 'Protecting Human Rights in the UK: The Conservatives' Proposals for Changing Britain's Human Rights Laws', p 4.

128 [2001] 2 All ER 929; (2001) *The Times*, 24 January.

129 *R (on the application of Alconbury Ltd) v Secretary of State for the Environment, Transport and the Regions and* other cases [2001] 2 All ER 929; (2001) NLJ 135.

130 (1999) 29 EHRR 548.

131 (2001) *The Times*, 9 January.

courts should follow any 'clear and constant' Strasbourg jurisprudence, except in special circumstances.[132] This stance was reinforced in *R (on the application of Ullah) v Special Adjudicator*.[133] In the context of s 2, Lord Bingham said: 'In determining the present question, the House is required by section 2(1) of the Human Rights Act 1998 to take into account any relevant Strasbourg case law. While such case law is not strictly binding, it has been held that courts should, in the absence of some special circumstances, follow any clear and constant jurisprudence' of the Strasbourg Court;[134] 'The duty of national courts is to keep pace with the Strasbourg jurisprudence as it evolves over time: no more, but certainly no less.'[135] Klug and Wildbore categorise this approach as the 'mirror approach', contrasting it with later case law that provides evidence of a 'dynamic' and a 'municipal' approach. The mirror approach arises in the sense that domestic courts are bound to follow a clear and consistent line of the Strasbourg Court. It stems from the recognition that it is the role of the Strasbourg Court to determine the content of Convention rights as well as the fact that, if the domestic court under-protects rights through relying on current Strasbourg jurisprudence, an individual may go to the Strasbourg Court, arguing that the court should provide a more extensive interpretation of a Convention right. This option is not open to the state should a domestic court over-protect rights by going beyond current Strasbourg jurisprudence. The dynamic approach is where UK courts go beyond current Strasbourg jurisprudence, either where there is no clear line of case law or where there is a large margin of appreciation. The municipal approach is where national courts depart from Strasbourg jurisprudence. To appreciate the extent to which national courts have retreated from the *Ullah* principle we need to scrutinise recent case law.[136]

First, it is clear that UK courts are not bound to follow decisions of the Strasbourg Court but that they will normally follow a 'clear and constant' line of cases from the Strasbourg Court. This is most clearly expressed in *Pinnock* concerning whether, when dealing with possession orders for demoted tenancies with a public authority landlord, courts must allow the evicted tenant to plead before the court that the eviction was 'necessary in a democratic society' in accordance with Art 8 ECHR.[137] Lord Neuberger, delivering a judgment to which all members of the Supreme Court had contributed, asserted that:

> Of course we should usually follow a clear and constant line of decisions by the EurCtHR: *R (Ullah) v Special Adjudicator* [2004] UKHL 26; [2004] 2 AC 323. But we are not actually bound to do so or (in theory, at least) to follow a decision of the Grand Chamber. As Lord Mance pointed out in *Doherty v Birmingham* [2009] 1 AC 367, para 126, section 2 of the HRA requires our courts to 'take into account' EurCtHR decisions, not necessarily to follow them. Where, however, there

---

132 At para 26.
133 [2004] UKHL 26.
134 He relied on *R (Alconbury Developments Ltd) v Secretary of State for the Environment, Transport and the Regions* [2001] UKHL 23, [2003] 2 AC 295, at para 26.
135 At para 20.
136 See *Moohan v Lord Advocate* [2014] UKSC 67; [2015] AC 901, particularly [104]–[105] (Lord Wilson).
137 *Manchester City Council v Pinnock* [2010] UKSC 45;[2010] 3 WLR 1441.

is a clear and constant line of decisions whose effect is not inconsistent with some fundamental substantive or procedural aspect of our law, and whose reasoning does not appear to overlook or misunderstand some argument or point of principle, we consider that it would be wrong for this Court not to follow that line.

The need for a 'clear and constant' line of case law can provide national courts with a degree of leeway when determining the content of Convention rights. The Strasbourg Court is not bound by precedent in the same manner as UK courts and determines cases by assessing whether, on the facts before the court, there has been a breach of a Convention right. As well as providing flexibility as to the determination of a 'clear and constant' line of cases, this provides the UK courts with the ability to not follow a clear decision of the Strasbourg Court that is specifically on point as regards the matter before the UK court. Two examples of this can be provided. First, in *Animal Defenders International*, the House of Lords was required to determine whether ss 319 and 321 of the Communications Act 2003, which prohibited the televisual and radio broadcasting of political advertising, was contrary to the right to freedom of expression found in Art 10 ECHR.[138] In the *VgT* case, the European Court of Human Rights had concluded that a similar ban on the broadcasting of political advertising was contrary to Art 10.[139] Nevertheless, the House of Lords concluded that ss 319 and 321 did not contravene Convention rights. Although recognising the similarities between the two cases, Lord Bingham was nevertheless able to distinguish the *VgT* case, drawing on cases of the Strasbourg Court decided after *VgT*. He did not consider that the Strasbourg Court in *VgT* had paid enough attention to the fundamental rationale of the restriction on political advertising – the need to ensure fairness of the political process where the public were presented with a full range of differentiating views on an impartial manner. Political advertising can undermine this objective, where opinions are persuasive 'by dint of constant repetition' and where those with more money can sway political debate.[140] The justification for a ban on the broadcast of political advertisements, whilst preserving print and cinema advertising, was found in the immediacy of television and radio, as recognised by the Strasbourg Court.[141] Also, Bingham felt the Strasbourg Court in *VgT* had attached too little weight to the fact that there were other media open to those wishing to place political advertisements; again an interest that was taken in the later *Murphy* case. Lord Bingham also concluded that there was a wide margin of appreciation, there being no European consensus regarding the balance to be made between Art 10 and the protection of the integrity of the democratic process.

Similarly, the Court of Appeal in *Hicks* declined to follow a recent decision of the Strasbourg Court as the decision did not fit with the interpretation of that Convention right provided in earlier decisions of the Strasbourg Court.[142] *Hicks* concerned arrests made to detain individuals who the police suspected would give rise to an imminent

138 R (Animal Defenders International) v Secretary of State for Culture, Media and Sport [2008] UKHL 15.
139 Verein gegen Tierfabriken v Switzerland (2001) 34 EHRR 159; [2001] ECHR 24699/94.
140 R (Animal Defenders International) v Secretary of State for Culture, Media and Sport [2008] UKHL 15, [28].
141 Murphy v Ireland (2003) 38 EHRR 212.
142 R (Hicks) v Commissioner of the Police of the Metropolis [2014] EWCA Civ 3; [2014] 1 WLR 2152.

breach of the peace during the royal wedding of Prince William and Kate Middleton, including Hicks, who was arrested on his way to attend the 'Not the Royal Wedding' street party, and individuals dressed as zombies who were planning to attend a zombie picnic. All had been arrested, detained at a police station and then released following the completion of the wedding celebrations. In *Ostendorf v Germany*, the Strasbourg Court had concluded that Art 5(1)(c) ECHR had been breached when Mr Ostendorf was arrested in a pub and detained until the completion of a football match where it was suspected that he may have caused a breach of the peace. The Strasbourg Court concluded that Art 5(1)(c) did not endorse a general principle of detention for those who were rightly or wrongly perceived to be dangerous or had the propensity to commit an unlawful act and that it required that any arrest or detention must require that the individual is taken before a legal authority. As Ostendorf was taken to a police station and later released, this requirement had not been fulfilled and his arrest breached Convention rights. If applied to the situation in *Hicks, Ostendorf* would also require that these arrests breached Convention rights. However, the Court of Appeal did not feel bound to follow the decision of the Strasbourg Court, concluding that *Ostendorf* was not compatible with a clear and constant line of cases prior to this decision, which concluded that Art 5(1)(c) would be satisfied where there was the intention at the time of arrest for the individual to be taken before a lawful authority, even if the individual was later released without charge. The Court of Appeal also concluded that this was the better interpretation of Art 5, given its wording and the extent to which Art 5(1) and (3) provided an adequate safeguard of the rights of those arrested and detained.

It is clear, therefore, that domestic courts can refuse to follow specific decisions of the Strasbourg Court when they are not representative of a 'clear and constant' line of case law. The question remains, however, as to what domestic courts should do in that situation. This question also arises when the UK courts, having examined a range of Strasbourg decisions, are unable to find a clear and constant line of cases which decide the issue before the court. Should the UK courts merely provide their own interpretation of the case law, perhaps focusing on the principles underpinning Strasbourg cases as opposed to precise outcomes,[143] or may the court go beyond current Strasbourg case law? If so, are UK courts only able to go beyond current interpretations of Convention rights if this is in line with a developing line of case law in the Strasbourg Court, or does the UK court have free reign to decide the case as a domestic interpretation of the scope of the Convention right, regardless of case law of the Strasbourg Court?

This issue arose in *Ambrose v Harris* where the Supreme Court had to determine whether Convention rights would be breached where an individual was prosecuted for an offence based on evidence the individual had provided whilst a search had been carried out under a police caution, but where the individual in question had not had access to a lawyer during this questioning.[144] There was no specific Strasbourg case on point as to whether access to a lawyer was required by the Convention and no clear and constant line of cases to follow. Lord Hope concluded that the UK court had to decide the case as best it could, looking for principles from Strasbourg decisions. He reasoned

---

143 Bjorge, E, 'The Courts and the ECHR: A Principled Approach to the Strasbourg Jurisprudence' (2013) 72 Cambridge Law Journal 289.

144 *Ambrose v Harris* [2011] UKSC 43; [2011] 1 WLR 2435.

that Parliament had not intended to give UK courts the power to give a more generous scope to Convention rights than that found in decisions of the Strasbourg Court given that Convention rights are not freestanding human rights, but rights found in an international treaty that falls to be interpreted by the Strasbourg Court.[145] Lord Kerr, however, argued that the UK courts could not be agnostic in situations where there was no clear and constant line of case law. Rather, it fell to the UK courts to analyse the provisions of the Convention and determine for themselves how a Convention right would apply to a situation that had not yet been decided at Strasbourg, even if this meant recognising a right where Strasbourg had not yet spoken. He provided three reasons for this conclusion. First, as a point of practical reality, it was likely that novel situations would arise in national courts before they did in Strasbourg. Second, as a point of principle, it was the duty of the UK courts to determine these issues, given that the point of the Human Rights Act was to provide UK citizens with 'direct access to the rights which the Convention enshrines through their enforcement by courts of this country'.[146] Third, it was the statutory obligation of the courts under s 6 of the Act to act in manner compatible with Convention rights. This included the obligation to determine the meaning of Convention rights, regardless of whether Strasbourg had pronounced upon the meaning of the right.[147] Lord Dyson steered a middle path between these two extremes, arguing that the UK courts had a choice as to whether to conclude that a Convention right had not been breached, given that there was no case on point concluding a breach of a Convention right in these circumstances, or to go beyond current case law and conclude that the Convention had been breached. How the court should exercise this choice depended on the specific circumstances of the case. In this instance, where expanding the Convention right would raise issues of policy and judgment, Lord Dyson urged caution in the approach of the court, concluding that the UK courts should not interpret the right as applying beyond the circumstances of current Strasbourg case law.[148]

A consensus is emerging in later cases that the UK courts, when there is no clear and constant line of cases, will seek to apply principles from decisions of the Strasbourg Court, recognising that the courts enjoy a choice as to whether to define a right beyond its current definition in Strasbourg, or not,[149] and there are examples both of where the UK courts have been prepared to go beyond Strasbourg case law[150] and when they have refrained from doing so,[151] even, as discussed above, when this requires refraining from following a relevant decision from the Strasbourg Court that can be distinguished or that is out of line with earlier Strasbourg decisions. The courts will be more

145 *Ambrose v Harris* [2011] UKSC 43; [2011] 1 WLR 2435, [18]–[20].
146 *Ibid*, [129].
147 *Ibid*, [128]–[129].
148 *Ibid*, [100]–[105].
149 See *Moohan v Lord Advocate* [2014] UKSC 67; [2015] AC 901, *Rabone v Pennine Care NHS Foundation Trust* [2012] UKSC 2; [2012] 2 AC 72 and *R (Hicks) v Commissioner of the Police of the Metropolis* [2014] EWCA Civ 3; [2014] 1 WLR 2152.
150 *EM (Lebanon) v Secretary of State for the Home Department* [2008] UKHL 64; [2009] AC 1198; *R (Limbuela) v Secretary of State for the Home Department* [2005] UKHL 66; [2006] 1 AC 396; and *Re P* [2008] UKHL 38; [2009] AC 173.
151 *P v Surrey County Council* [2014] UKSC 19 [2014] AC 896, *Rabone v Pennine Care NHS Foundation Trust* [2012] UKSC 2; [2012] 2 AC 72 and *Secretary of State for the Home Department v JJ* [2007] UKHL 45.

likely to develop Convention rights when this is in line with other earlier Strasbourg case law – indeed some members of the judiciary believe that UK courts may only go beyond current Strasbourg case law in these circumstances.[152] For example, in *Re P* the Supreme Court had to determine whether Northern Ireland regulations that prohibited unmarried couples from adopting a child together were contrary to Convention rights. Although there was no clear Strasbourg decision that Art 8 ECHR required unmarried couples to adopt, Lords Hoffmann and Hope drew on earlier Strasbourg decisions, particularly those protecting rights of homosexuals, and concluded that it was likely that Strasbourg would conclude that Art 8 had been breached. They were therefore prepared to go further than currently required by decisions of the Strasbourg Court.[153] UK courts are also likely to move Convention rights beyond current decisions of the Strasbourg Court when there is evidence of parliamentary support. Again, this can be illustrated by *Re P* where Lord Hoffmann recognised that the Joint Committee of Human Rights had recently reached the same conclusion; that legislation had been enacted to achieve this objective in England and Wales and Scotland.[154]

UK courts are less likely to develop Convention rights beyond current decisions in Strasbourg when dealing with a sensitive area where a development of Convention rights may raise policy issues. In *Ambrose*, Lord Dyson decided not to extend case law to require individuals to have access to a lawyer whilst answering questions during a police search. His caution was motivated by recognising that this extension was a matter of policy and judgment, where opinions might reasonably differ, illustrating this through the contrasting approaches taken to this issue in the USA and Canada. As such, it was better resolved by the Strasbourg Court.

These factors can pull in different directions, leading to contradictory conclusions both as to the application of Strasbourg case law to the facts of the case and as to scope of the *Ullah* principle. In *P v Surrey*, for example, the Supreme Court had to determine whether the detention of individuals in a small group setting, which placed restrictions on the liberty of its residents, as opposed to a hospital or care home, where individuals did not have the capacity for themselves to consent to remain in the home and where the initial placement was originally made in the best interests of all concerned, was a breach of Art 5 ECHR.[155] There was no specific case from the Strasbourg court concluding that Art 5 ECHR had been breached in this situation. Nevertheless, the majority concluded that a breach had occurred, drawing on other decisions of the Strasbourg Court pointing to a justification for the adoption of a general test as to a deprivation of liberty, given the importance of this right. The minority argued that this was to take the case law too far, focusing in particular on the specific nature of the detention in question – in a small group setting as opposed to a hospital or care home – and concluding that there was not enough evidence in the case law was reluctant to extend Strasbourg case law away from a case-specific to a general test. In *Moohan* the Supreme Court had to determine whether the right to vote, included in Art 3 of the First Protocol, extended to the right to vote in the referendum on Scottish independence, such that a blanket ban on prisoners

152 See, Lord Hodge and Lord Wilson in *Moohan v Lord Advocate* [2014] UKSC 67; [2015] AC 901 and Lord Brown in *Rabone v Pennine Care NHS Foundation Trust* [2012] UKSC 2; [2012] 2 AC 72.
153 *Re P* [2008] UKHL 38; [2009] AC 173, [21]–[28] (Lord Hoffmann) and [53] (Lord Hope).
154 *Re P* [2008] UKHL 38; [2009] AC 173, [21]–[28] (Lord Hoffmann).
155 *P v Surrey County Council* [2014] UKSC 19; [2014] AC 896.

voting in the referendum would contravene Convention rights.[156] The majority concluded that the Convention right did not extend this far, focusing on the lack of a general indication in earlier case law in the Strasbourg Court to interpret Art 3 of the First Protocol in this manner, and the extent to which this appeared to stretch the language of the Convention.[157] Lord Kerr and Lord Hodge, however, concluded (Lady that the Convention would extend the right to vote to the Scottish independence referendum, given the way in which the Strasbourg Court interprets the Convention as a living instrument and how this extension could be said to be in line with other Strasbourg decisions.[158] Although Lord Kerr did not discuss *Ullah* in *Moohan*, his views in *Ambrose*, discussed above, and extra-judicial writing illustrate that he is more willing to develop UK interpretations of Convention rights beyond Strasbourg decisions, even when there is no clear indication that this is how the Strasbourg Court would have decided this matter were it to hear the case.[159] Lord Hodge gave a detailed account of the historical move away from the *Ullah* principle. Whilst there is no evidence in his judgment that he would adopt the same ability of going further than Strasbourg as Lord Kerr, he nevertheless concluded that:

> where there is no directly relevant decision of the ECtHR with which it would be possible (even if appropriate) to keep pace, we can and must do more. We must determine for ourselves the existence or otherwise of an alleged Convention right. And, in doing so, we must take account of all indirectly relevant decisions of the ECtHR and, in particular, of such principles underlying them as might, whether as currently expressed or as subject to the natural development apt to a living instrument, inform our determination.[160]

It is also clear that, although UK courts will usually follow a clear and constant line of case law, this is not the case when the decision is inconsistent with 'some fundamental substantive or procedural aspect of our law' or when the reasoning of the Strasbourg Court appears to overlook or misunderstand some argument or point of principle.[161] Lord Sumption's assessment of s 2(1) in *Chester* appears to add on a possible further restriction, that the inconsistency, oversight or misunderstanding 'may, when properly explained, lead to the decision being reviewed by the Strasbourg Court'.[162] It is clear that the courts are reluctant to refrain from following a clear decision of Strasbourg; it definitely does not extend as far as suggested by Lord Irvine, who advocates that UK courts should determine Convention rights for themselves, according to domestic principles.[163] The clearest example of a court refusing to follow a Strasbourg decision is

---

156 [2014] UKSC 67; [2015] AC 901.
157 *Ibid*, [13]–[19](Lord Hodge); [40]–[49] (Lord Neuberger) and [53]–[54](Lady Hale).
158 *Ibid*, [63]–[65](Lord Kerr).
159 Lord Kerr 'The Conversation between Strasbourg and national courts: Dialogue or Dictation?' John Maurice Kelly Memorial Lecture, University College Dublin, 20 November 2009 and 'The UK Supreme Court: The modest underworker of Strasbourg?' Clifford Chance Lecture, 25 January 2012.
160 *R (Chester) v Secretary of State for Justice* [2013] UKSC 63; [2014] AC 271, [105].
161 *Manchester City Council v Pinnock* [2010] UKSC 45; [2011] 1 All ER 285, [48] (Lord Neuberger).
162 *R (Chester) v Secretary of State for Justice* [2013] UKSC 63; [2014] AC 271, [121] (Sumption).
163 Lord Irvine of Lairg 'A British Interpretation of Convention Rights' [2012] Public Law 237.

Horncastle, where the Supreme Court declined to follow the Strasbourg Court concerning breaches of Art 6 relating to the admission of 'hearsay evidence'. *Al Khawaja v UK* concluded that Art 6 was breached when a conviction was based solely or to a decisive extent on the statement of a witness that the defendant had not had the chance to cross-examine. Lord Phillips, giving the judgment for the Supreme Court, argued the 'sole and decisive element' test failed to distinguish situations in which it was impossible to cross-examine the witness – e.g., when the witness had died – and also that the test, whilst devised to safeguard against unsafe convictions, failed to take account of the way in which the common law provided for sufficient safeguards in the exceptional circumstances under which hearsay evidence was relied upon in criminal cases. Consequently, Lord Phillips did not follow the Strasbourg Court. It is important to note here that *Al Khawaja* was on appeal before the Grand Chamber, based upon the argument that the Strasbourg Court had failed to understand common law safeguards.

UK courts are less willing to refuse to follow a decision of the Grand Chamber in Strasbourg. Lord Mance in *Chester* makes it clear that the UK courts should only refuse to follow a clear, on point decision of the Grand Chamber if it were to 'ignore a truly fundamental principle of our law' or demonstrate a 'most egregious oversight or misunderstanding'.[164] One example of this is the Court of Appeal decision in *McLoughlin*.[165] The Court of Appeal 'disagreed' with the findings of the Grand Chamber of the Strasbourg Court in *Vinter v UK* concerning the legality of life sentences. The Grand Chamber had concluded that life sentences were compatible with Art 3 ECHR, even if this meant that a prisoner spent the whole of the rest of his life in prison, provided that prisoners be provided with a realistic prospect of release and the possibility of review. Although English law did provide for the release of those serving life sentences, the Grand Chamber concluded that English law was insufficiently clear surrounding the existence of a realistic possibility of release. The 'Lifers' Manual' established a narrow set of exceptional circumstances of release on compassionate grounds. These had been interpreted broadly in *R v Bieber* so as to provide for the possibility of release that would comply with Art 3. Nevertheless, the Grand Chamber concluded that the disparity between the Lifers' Manual, and the principles of interpretation, meant that the law in England and Wales was insufficiently clear to satisfy Art 3. The Court of Appeal disagreed with this assessment, pointing to how English law was clear that the Home Secretary could not fetter her discretion by rigidly sticking to the policy found in the Lifers' Manual, that the 'compassionate grounds' giving rise to a possibility of release would be interpreted in line with s 3 HRA and in accordance with the criteria established in *R v Bieber*. It is important to recognise here that the Court of Appeal was not disagreeing with the scope of a Convention right. Rather, the disagreement concerned the evaluation of English law and its ability to satisfy the requirements of Art 3. This assessment of English law was later accepted by the Strasbourg Court, although this case is now on appeal to the Grand Chamber.[166]

It is clear that the UK courts have moved on considerably from the mirror principle. UK courts actively engage in a detailed evaluation of Strasbourg case law, looking

---

164 *R (Chester) v Secretary of State for Justice* [2013] UKSC 63; [2014] AC 271, [27].
165 *AG's Reference No 69 of 2013, R v McLoughlin: R v Newell* [2014] EWCA Crim 188; [2014] 1 WLR 3964.
166 *Hutchinson v UK* (App. No 57592/08); (2015) ECHR 57592/08.

for a clear and constant line of case law and focusing on the principles underpinning Strasbourg decisions as opposed to merely adhering to cases that appear to be directly on point. Courts are more willing to go beyond Strasbourg, particularly when this is based on an evaluation of principles and is in the direction of travel of the Strasbourg Court and when there is a wide margin of appreciation as applied to Arts 8 to 11 and 14, or when determining limitations on Arts 5 and 6 or when recognising that the application of a Convention right is a matter of degree.[167] They are also willing, in exceptional circumstances, to refuse to follow decisions of the Strasbourg Court. In both instances, the UK courts are sensitive to the tension as to the purposes of the HRA, moving away from merely regarding the Act as a means of securing remedies in domestic courts as opposed to requiring applicants to travel to Strasbourg as well as recognising that some issues are best left to Parliament to develop as opposed to the courts, with the UK courts being reluctant to take Convention rights further in the face of recent UK parliamentary decisions to the contrary.[168] This development has been generally welcomed by academic commentary,[169] and in the extra-judicial commentary of the members of the Supreme Court, with emphasis being placed on the ability of this modification of the mirror principle to stimulate dialogue between Strasbourg and the UK courts.[170]

The modification of the mirror principle calls into question the calls for reform of s 2(1) by the Conservative government. It is not the case that the UK courts have slavishly followed decisions of the Strasbourg Court, extending the concept of Convention rights beyond their original intentions. Instead, UK courts have refused to follow decisions at Strasbourg that fail to understand the nature of the common law and have reserved the power to refuse to follow decisions that are inconsistent with fundamental features of English law. Where courts have gone beyond current Strasbourg decisions they have been sensitive of their proper constitutional role. In doing so, the UK courts have influenced the development of law in Strasbourg. Moreover, even if the Conservative proposals were able to succeed in granting decisions of the Strasbourg Court advisory status only, it is not clear that this would limit the ability of UK courts to develop Convention rights in line with the 'living instrument' approach found in Strasbourg. UK courts also draw on decisions from other common law jurisdictions that adopt a living instrument approach. Moreover, it is welcome that UK courts adopt this approach to interpreting Convention rights, ensuring that human rights protections develop as society evolves while being sensitive to the greater legitimacy of democratic resolution of complex policy issues.

---

167 Malkani, B, 'A Rights-Specific Approach to Section 2 of the Human Rights Act' [2012] European Human Rights Law Review 516.

168 See *R (Animal Defenders International) v Secretary of State for Culture, Media and Sport* [2008] UKHL 15, *R (Chester) v Secretary of State for Justice* [2013] UKSC 63; [2014] AC 271 and *Moohan v Lord Advocate* [2014] UKSC 67; [2015] AC 901.

169 See Clayton, R, 'Smoke and Mirrors: the Human Rights Act and the Impact of Strasbourg Law' [2012] Public Law 639, Sales, P, 'Strasbourg Jurisprudence and the Human Rights Act: a Response to Lord Irvine' [2012] Public Law 253 and Andenas, M and Bjorge, E, 'Ambrose: Is the *Ullah* Principle Wrong?' [2012] LQR 319.

170 Hale, B, '*Argentoratum Locutum:*, Is Strasbourg or the Supreme Court Supreme?' [2012] European Human Rights Law Review 65, Lord Neuberger 'The role of Judges in Human Rights Jurisprudence: A Comparison of the Australian and UK experience' 8 August 2014, with Lord Kerr going further and granting greater freedom to the UK Supreme Court in 'The Supreme Court: The Modest Underworker of Strasbourg?' 25 January 2012.

Conflict with domestic precedents

If clear and constant jurisprudence is apparent it must be followed, although not strictly binding, except where a domestic precedent stands in the way. This was made clear by the House of Lords in *Kay v London Borough of Lambeth; Leeds City Council v Price*.[171] The case concerned rights to possession of property in domestic law which appeared to violate Art 8. The Court of Appeal in the *Leeds* case had concluded that the decision in *Connors v United Kingdom*,[172] which was relied upon by the applicants in resisting possession proceedings, was inconsistent with the earlier House of Lords decision in *Harrow London Borough Council v Qazi*,[173] and that they were bound to apply the House of Lords decision.[174] The later Strasbourg case suggested that the earlier House of Lords decision had not correctly reflected the Convention position. As indicated above, Lord Bingham, with whom the other Law Lords agreed on this issue, said that domestic courts must give effect to the principles expounded by the Strasbourg Court. He pointed out that that court is the highest judicial authority to interpret Convention rights as they are to be understood uniformly by all member states, and domestic courts have to determine initially how the principles it lays down are to be applied in the domestic context. Adherence to precedent, he said, is a cornerstone of the domestic legal system whereby some degree of certainty in legal matters is most effectively achieved. He found that therefore where judges consider that a binding domestic precedent is inconsistent with a Strasbourg decision, they should follow the ordinary rules of precedent, except in an extreme case where the pre-HRA decision of a superior court could not survive the introduction of the HRA 1998.

Lord Hope agreed on the precedent issue. He found that *Connors* was not incompatible with *Qazi*, but that *Qazi* should not in any event be departed from; however, in the light of subsequent Strasbourg cases he found that greater emphasis should be placed on the need for the court to provide a remedy in those special cases not considered in *Qazi* where it was seriously arguable that the right to possession afforded by domestic law violated the Convention right.

The rule from *Price* means that citizens might have to seek the vindication of their Art 8 rights at Strasbourg. This position is in tension, not only with the UK's obligations at Strasbourg under Arts 1, 8 and 13 of the Convention, but with the constitutional status of the Convention in domestic law and with Lord Bingham's finding in *Ullah* that the duty of domestic courts is to keep pace with the Strasbourg jurisprudence as it evolves over time. Therefore, it is argued, the courts should explore methods of marginalising the rule from *Price* in any affected areas of law while technically adhering to domestic precedent. For example, where a statute has been interpreted domestically in a superior court in a post-HRA decision in a manner that conflicts with Strasbourg jurisprudence, the court should strive to find an interpretation of the domestic precedent that avoids the conflict, but if this is impossible it should issue a declaration of the incompatibility, leaving Parliament to overturn the precedent. That course would be preferable to minimising the interpretation of the right in order to avoid the conflict.

171 [2006] UKHL 10.
172 [2006] 40 EHRR 189.
173 [2004] 1 AC 983.
174 See *Price v Leeds CC* [2005] 1 WLR 1825.

Section 2 and the common law

The HRA does not expressly mention the interpretation of the common law. But it is clear that s 2 makes the rights relevant to its interpretation since its application is not confined to statutory interpretation, but to the determination of any question, in a court or tribunal, that has arisen in connection with a Convention right. Further, since the courts themselves are public authorities under s 6, they are expected to ensure, through their interpretation of the common law, that the Convention rights are not breached. As discussed below, the precise duty placed on the courts in this respect is a matter of debate. But it is clear that, where a legislative provision is not in question, but one party in the case before a court is a public authority, or in any event in reliance on the court's own s 6 duty, the court should apply s 2. Section 2 contains no words that limit its application to an instance in which one party before the court is a public authority. The limitation would arise if it was argued in such an instance that a private body does not possess Convention rights as against another private person and therefore that no question has arisen in connection with a Convention right, but that argument was rejected, impliedly, by the courts in early decisions under the HRA.[175]

It is now clear, as Chapter 10 in particular points out,[176] that the Convention rights are as much at issue in private common law disputes as in public law ones, assuming that a cause of action is applicable. In such an instance ss 2 and 6 in combination might be viewed at first glance as placing an interpretative obligation on courts, which is, in one sense, stronger than that created by s 3, since no provision allowing incompatible common law doctrines to override Convention rights appears in the Act. However, this is not the case, for two reasons. As discussed further below, the precise duty placed on the court by s 6 in relation to the development of the common law in private common law adjudication has not yet been fully resolved, and it certainly cannot yet be said that s 6 places a s 3-like interpretative obligation on courts in common law adjudication.[177] Moreover, the decision in *Price* is of particular relevance in common law adjudication since, obviously, such adjudication is reliant on the doctrine of precedent unaffected by statutory intervention. Following *Price*, the odd position has been reached whereby a decision of a superior court inconsistent with Convention principle must be followed, whereas a statutory provision apparently inconsistent with a Convention right can be rendered compatible with it, if possible, even if that means reading words into the statute, under s 3. Therefore, while s 2 is of relevance in common law adjudication as discussed in this section, the Strasbourg jurisprudence may perhaps have a more limited effect in this context in practice. In the key context of privacy, however, in which ss 6 and 2 have had a very significant impact in transforming the common law doctrine of confidence, the problem of incompatibility between common law precedent and Convention principle has not arisen since the key precedents were pre-HRA ones.[178]

---

175 It is clear under s 3 that legislation should be construed compatibly with the Convention rights regardless of the fact that both parties are private bodies. In *Wilson v First County Trust* [2001] 3 All ER 229, the Court of Appeal accepted that s 3 does indeed apply in such instances.

176 See pp 728–30, 735–38.

177 See pp 212–18.

178 It may be noted that the key decision of *Campbell* was taken before *Price*. See further Chapter 10, pp 735–38.

Conclusions

The pursuit of the s 2 endeavour is witnessing the attempt to interweave into a mass of existing statutory and common law provisions the uneven and often flawed jurisprudence of the European Court of Human Rights. In so doing the judges are adopting a more theorised approach to fundamental rights.[179] It is often pointed out that the inception of Bills of Rights tends to have the effect, as in Canada, of requiring courts to grapple with the justification for the limitation of fundamental rights, taking a more philosophical approach to legal reasoning as they attempt to resolve conflicts between rights and competing societal and individual interests. However, the limitations placed on the judicial role under the HRA by both *Price* and *Ullah* create a clear tension, as discussed, with the HRA's constitutional status and with the development of a domestic doctrine of constitutional rights.

Meaning of primary and secondary legislation

Which measures then can override the Convention even if incompatible with it under s 3(2)? Section 21(1) defines 'primary legislation' as used in s 3(2) to include Measures of the General Synod of the Church of England and, most significantly, Orders in Council made under the royal prerogative. Thus, executive power as well as parliamentary sovereignty are preserved under the HRA.[180] This is clearly an anomalous provision, since it renders individual rights subordinate to powers that may be used to infringe them and which cannot claim legitimacy derived from the democratic process.

Subordinate legislation covers Orders in Council not made under the royal prerogative, orders, rules, regulations, bylaws or other instruments made under primary legislation unless 'it operates to bring one or more provisions of that legislation into force or amends any primary legislation'. The last provision is significant, since it means that where provision is made under primary legislation for amendment by executive order, subject to the negative, or even the affirmative resolution procedure, the amendment, which will almost certainly have received virtually no parliamentary attention, will still be able to override Convention provisions. This is of particular importance in relation to, for example, the Terrorism Act 2000 and the Regulation of Investigatory Powers Act 2000, since a number of gaps were left in the provisions, to be filled in this manner.[181]

The 'declaration of incompatibility' under s 4

Section 4(2) applies under s 4(1) when a court is determining in any proceedings whether a provision of primary legislation is incompatible with a Convention right. If a court is satisfied that the provision is incompatible with the right, 'it may make a declaration of that incompatibility' – a declaration that it is not possible to construe the legislation in question to harmonise with the Convention. Section 4(4) applies to incompatible secondary legislation where incompatible primary legislation prevents the removal of

179 See, e.g., Chapter 10, pp 735–38 and below, pp 245–46.
180 For discussion of the effect of treating this exercise of prerogative powers as primary legislation, see Squires, N, 'Judicial review of the prerogative after the HRA' [2000] 116 LQR 572–75.
181 See, e.g., Chapter 11, pp 802 *et seq.*

the incompatibility. Again, the incompatibility can be declared. Thus, s 4 may seem to come close to allowing an infringement of parliamentary sovereignty since, as Feldman observes, 'For the first time Parliament has invited the judges to tell it that it has acted wrongly by legislating incompatibly with a Convention right'.[182] But, as Feldman also notes, the court is not informing Parliament that it has acted unlawfully, since, as explained below, Parliament is not bound by the Convention (s 6(3)).

But only certain courts can make the declaration. Section 4(5) provides that this applies to the Supreme Court, the Judicial Committee of the Privy Council, the Courts-Martial Appeal Court; in Scotland, the High Court of Justiciary sitting otherwise than a trial court, or the Court of Session; in England and Wales, the High Court or the Court of Appeal and the Court of Protection in any matter dealt with by the President of the Family Division, the Vice-Chancellor or a puisne judge of the High Court. Under s 5(1), when a court is considering making a declaration, the Crown must be given notice so that it can, under s 5(2), intervene by being joined as a party to the proceedings.

A court falling within s 4(5) has a *discretion* to make a declaration of incompatibility. Section 4(2) clearly leaves open the possibility that such a court, having found an incompatibility, might nevertheless decide not to make a declaration of it. As indicated above, in *Wilson v First County Trust Ltd*,[183] the Court of Appeal found that s 127(3) of the Consumer Credit Act 1974 was incompatible with Art 6 and with Art 1 of the First Protocol to the Convention. The Court considered that, having found an incompatibility, it should make a declaration of it for three reasons.[184] First, the question of the incompatibility had been fully argued at a hearing appointed for that purpose. Second, the order required by s 127(3) could not lawfully be made on the appeal unless the court was satisfied that the section could not be read in such a way as to give effect to the Convention rights, and that fact should be formally recorded by a declaration that 'gives legitimacy to that order'. Third, a declaration provides a basis for a minister to consider whether the section should be amended under s 10(1) (see below). The Court duly went on to make the declaration. The second reason given is of particular interest, since it suggests that a court would not feel that it could make an order required by an incompatible legislative provision without making a declaration, since the order would lack legitimacy. It may be noted that lower courts, which cannot make a declaration, are being asked under the HRA to do precisely that. This finding indicates the reluctance such courts are likely to feel in this situation. It further suggests, as do the other reasons, that courts within s 4(5) are unlikely to find incompatibility without declaring it. In other words, the discretion under s 4(2) appears to be narrow. It is hard to imagine circumstances in which a higher court would find an incompatibility without declaring it.

Nevertheless, there have been two recent instances when the Supreme Court has declined to make a declaration of incompatibility. In *Chester* the Supreme Court was called upon to make a declaration of incompatibility as regards s 3 of the Representation of the People Act 1983, which disenfranchises prisoners. A series of Strasbourg Court decisions of the Grand Chamber had concluded that a blanket ban on prisoner

---

182 Feldman, D, 'The Human Rights Act 1998 and constitutional principles' (1999) 19(2) LS 165, p 187.
183 [2001] 3 All ER 229.
184 *Ibid*, para 47.

voting was contrary to Art 1 of the First Protocol ECHR,[185] and the Scottish Court of Session had already issued a declaration of incompatibility.[186] Lord Mance gave three reasons as to why the Supreme Court should not issue a declaration of incompatibility. First, he did not believe a further declaration would serve any useful purpose. The government was aware of the incompatibility and could have chosen to issue a s 10 remedial order but had chosen not to. Moreover, the issue was currently before Parliament and the Attorney General was aware of the fact that the current law was incompatible with a series of decisions of the Grand Chamber of the Strasbourg Court.[187] Second, although a blanket ban on prisoner voting was contrary to Convention rights, the Strasbourg Court had concluded that disenfranchising some prisoners did not breach their Convention rights. Chester was serving a life sentence for murder. Given the Grand Chamber decision in *Scopolla*, which concluded that an Italian law that placed a lifetime ban on voting for those convicted of similarly serious offences was compatible with Convention rights – provided that there was a procedure in place for those subject to this ban to explain why the ban was no longer justified – it was clear that Chester's specific Convention rights had not been breached. As such, there was no need to provide Chester with a remedy in this situation.[188] Third, it was for Parliament to decide how to remedy the Convention incompatibility, choosing from a range of possible options that would differentiate between those prisoners who could and could not vote.[189] Lady Hale justified her choice not to issue a declaration of incompatibility on the argument that there was no need for a remedy for Chester as his specific right to vote was not breached by the legislation.[190]

In *Nicklinson* the Supreme Court was once again called upon to assess whether the law preventing assisted suicide, and the DPP's guidelines on prosecution for this offence, was contrary to the Convention right to life. Of the nine Supreme Court justices hearing the case, five concluded that, although not contrary to Convention rights as currently interpreted by the Strasbourg Court, the issue being within the broad margin of appreciation granted to the UK,[191] it was nevertheless contrary to, or arguably contrary to, Convention rights as interpreted by the Supreme Court. Lady Hale and Lord Kerr would have issued a declaration of incompatibility, whereas Lords Neuberger, Wilson and Mance would not. Four concluded that there was no breach of Convention rights.

Lord Neuberger decided not to issue a declaration of incompatibility in light of the relative constitutional and institutional roles of the legislature and the courts. Assisted suicide raised difficult and sensitive issues with moral and religious dimensions. Moreover, it was not easy to identify whether the current law criminalising assisted suicide had breached Convention rights and, if so, how such a breach should be resolved. These suggested that the issue was more suited to legislative as opposed to judicial

---

185 *Hirst v United Kingdom (2)* (App No 74025/01); 42 EHRR 849, *Greens v United Kingdom* (App No 66041/08); [2010] ECHR 60041/08 and *Scoppola v Italy (No 3)* (App No 126/05); [2009]; 33 BHRC 126.
186 *Smith v Scott* [2007] SCC 345; [2007] CSIH 9.
187 *R (Chester) v Secretary of State for Justice* [2013] UKSC 63; [2014] AC 271, [39].
188 *Ibid*, [40]–[41].
189 *Ibid*, [42].
190 *Ibid*, [99]–[102]. Lady Hale's statement was echoed by Lord Wilson, in *R (T) v Chief Constable of Greater Manchester Police* [2014] UKSC 35; [2015] AC 49, [51].
191 *R (Nicklinson) v Ministry of Justice* [2014] UKSC 38; [2015] AC 657.

resolution.[192] In addition, the legislature were actively debating the issue. Lord Neuberger also recognised that a declaration of incompatibility would be a very quick *volte face* from the decision in *Pretty v DPP*, some 14 years prior to *Nicklinson*, where the House of Lords had concluded that the law did not breach Convention rights.[193] He was also sensitive to different types of dialogue between the legislature and the judiciary. Given the sensitive nature of the issue, it was more productive to seek to persuade the legislature through reasoning rather than using the more drastic measure of issuing a declaration of incompatibility.[194] However, were the legislature to fail to respond, then there would be the possibility of the court issuing a declaration of incompatibility in the future.[195]

Lady Hale, unlike Lord Neuberger, had reached the firm conclusion that the law on assisted suicide breached Convention rights. As such, she saw 'little to be gained and much to be lost' from issuing a declaration of incompatibility. She rightly recognised that Parliament was free to respond to this declaration of incompatibility by using s 10, by initiating legislation or by doing nothing.[196] Lord Kerr agreed, stating that:

> an essential element of the structure of the Human Rights Act 1998 is the call which Parliament has made on the courts to review the legislation which it passes in order to tell it whether the provisions contained in that legislation comply with ECHR. By responding to that call and sending the message to Parliament that a particular provision's is incompatibility with the Convention, the courts do not usurp the role of Parliament, much less offend the separation of powers. A declaration of incompatibility is merely an expression of the court's conclusion as to whether, as enacted, a particular item of legislation cannot be considered compatible with a Convention right. In other words, the courts say to Parliament, 'This particular piece of legislation is incompatible, now it is for you to decide what to do about it.' And under the scheme of the Human Rights Act it is open to Parliament to decide to do nothing.[197]

As such, the courts were not making a 'moral choice which is properly within the province of the democratically elected legislature'.[198]

Nicklinson in particular has been criticised for demonstrating too servile a role on the part of the judiciary, with Elliott referring to this as 'double deference'.[199] Lord Neuberger appeared to be concerned that the courts did not usurp the role of Parliament through its engagement with complex moral issues, ensuring the courts did not substitute their assessment of morality for that of Parliament. Yet, as Lady Hale and Lord

---

192 *Ibid*, [116].
193 *Ibid*, [116].
194 *Ibid*, [117].
195 *Ibid*, [118].
196 *Ibid*, [300].
197 *Ibid*, [343].
198 *Ibid*, [344].
199 Elliott, M, http://publiclawforeveryone.com/2014/06/26/the-right-to-die-deference-dialogue-and-constitutional-authority/. See also, E Wickes, 'The Supreme Court Judgment in *Nicklinson*: One Step Forward on Assist, Two Steps Back on Human Rights.' (2015) 23 Medical Law Review 144.

Kerr trenchantly asserted, a s 4 declaration need not require that Parliament automatically reform the law so as to bring it in line with the judgment of the court. There is no usurpation: the very design of the HRA ensures parliamentary sovereignty, as the courts cannot strike down legislation and Parliament has no legal obligation to modify legislation declared incompatible. However, Lord Neuberger's reticence to make a declaration of incompatibility is understandable. Although in theory Parliament need not respond to a declaration of incompatibility, in practice not only does Parliament respond to nearly all declarations of incompatibility, but the possibility of a future appeal to Strasbourg – which may be likely to agree with the conclusion of the UK courts – may transform a political obligation into an obligation in international law. Moreover, research shows that MPs do regard the courts as providing the definitive account of rights, such that they perceive their role as being to modify legislation so as to comply with legal decisions. Given these facts, and that Lord Neuberger was less certain that a Convention right was breached in these circumstances, his refusal to issue a declaration of incompatibility may be justified as a means of encouraging what s 4 declarations are meant to encourage – a detailed parliamentary debate, taking the reasoning of the courts into account on the basis of the strength of their persuasive ability, as opposed to reading the judgments as a recognition of a clear breach where the only issue left to Parliament is as to the means through which to best ensure compliance with Convention rights. However, these concerns should only arise in extreme circumstances where, as in *Nicklinson*, the UK courts are going beyond Strasbourg decisions in a highly complex and controversial area of religious and moral sensitivity, where the judge also has doubts as to whether Convention rights have been breached.

It is easier to justify the refusal to issue a declaration of incompatibility in *Chester* given that a declaration had already existed and the legislature were well aware of the incompatibility and the need to reform following a series of Grand Chamber judgments of the Supreme Court. Nevertheless, this is an insufficient justification for refusing to issue a declaration. A further declaration of incompatibility may provide further impetus to the government to amend legislation in an area where it has appeared reluctant to do so, despite a clear breach as established by the Grand Chamber. The stronger justification for the refusal to issue a declaration here was the recognition that the Convention rights of the applicant had not been breached. As such, the applicant had no need of a specific remedy. This fact, combined with the existing political and international law pressure on the government to change the legislation, can justify the refusal to issue a declaration of incompatibility.

When a declaration of incompatibility has been made, the legislative provision in question remains valid (s 4(6)). Section 3 provides that the interpretative obligation does not affect the validity, continuing operation or enforcement of any incompatible primary legislation, and this is equally the case under s 4(6) if a declaration of incompatibility is made. The Convention guarantee in question is disapplied by the court in relation to that incompatible provision. Once a declaration has been made, there will be a period of time during which the Convention right can still be utilised in respect of other relevant non-incompatible provisions until and if compatibility is achieved by amendment via the s 10 procedure considered below. The Convention provision does not appear to suffer a diminution of status except, to an extent, in relation to the incompatible legislative provision itself. In other words, it is not impliedly repealed in domestic law.

During the period after the declaration, while amendment of the legislative provision is awaited as a possibility, other courts might have to consider the same issue. Owing to the doctrine of precedent, the lower courts are bound by the declaration. The HRA leaves open the possibility – in a higher court than the one which made the declaration – of eventually finding compatibility in respect of the incompatible legislative provision itself once it is revisited in a subsequent suitable case (assuming that the original dec-laration has not already been overturned on appeal). In other words, a different court can take a different view on incompatibility. Possibly, in so doing, it might be aided by jurisprudential developments occurring at Strasbourg, after the initial finding of incom-patibility. But following the decision of the House of Lords in *Price*,[200] a court in a similar case, raising a similar issue of compatibility, would be bound by a declaration already made in a superior court, despite such development.

If legislation is found to be incompatible with a Convention guarantee in a court that cannot make a declaration of incompatibility or in one that can, but exercises its discre-tion not to do so, the position is broadly the same: the legislative provision remains valid and the Convention guarantee in question is disapplied in relation to the incompatible provision. There is less likelihood that it will be amended until and if a declaration of incompatibility is made, although obviously it could, theoretically, be amended without waiting for a declaration.[201] Clearly, the case might not be appealed up to a court that could make the declaration. Thus, there will probably be a longer period of time during which a Convention guarantee cannot be utilised in relation to that legislative provision than there would be once a declaration had been made. In order to avoid this period of uncertainty, the courts are using fast-track procedures to resolve the issue, as in *R v A*[202] and *Alconbury*.

Since, under s 4(5), only higher courts can make a declaration of incompatibility, the pressure on courts to find compatibility is increased since otherwise a citizen has to suffer a breach of their Convention rights without a remedy.[203] The pressure is particu-larly strong in criminal proceedings. However, where essential, as discussed earlier, it is preferable that a declaration of incompatibility should be made rather than 'reading down' the Convention right in question in order to find compatibility.

The declaration is likely to trigger off amending legislation by means of the s 10 so-called 'fast-track' procedure. However, it need not do so – very significantly, the decla-ration is non-binding. Declarations of incompatibility are playing a part in ensuring that domestic law is being brought into a state of conformity with the human rights norms embodied in the jurisprudence of the European Court of Human Rights.[204] However s 4

---

200 See above p 167.
201 Since such amendment would occur outside the s 10 procedure, the normal time constraints would apply.
202 [2001] 2 WLR 1546.
203 This was very clearly a pressing concern in *R v A* [2001] 2 WLR 1546; the ruling was awaited, not only in that case, but in a number of pending rape cases.
204 Apart from the declarations mentioned a number of other examples may be given: in *R (H) v London North and East Region Mental Health Review Tribunal (Secretary of State for Health intervening)* [2002] QB 1 the Mental Health Act 1983 s 73 was found to be incompatible with Arts 5(1) and 5(4); in *R (D) v Secretary of State for the Home Department* [2003] 1 WLR 1315 the Mental Health Act 1983 s 74 was found to be incompatible with Art 5(4); *R (Uttley) v Secretary of State for the Home Depart-ment* [2003] 1 WLR 2590 the Criminal Justice Act 1991 ss 33(2), 37(4)(a) and s 39 were found to be incompatible with Art 7.

is having less impact in this respect, as discussed above, than s 3 and its impact has been declining. Since October 2000 there have been 30 declarations of incompatibility, of which 20 have not been reversed on appeal. Only three declarations of incompatibility were made during the 2010–15 Parliament, one of which is still subject to appeal.[205] The most well-known and far-reaching declaration was made by the House of Lords in *A v Secretary of State for the Home Department*;[206] it is discussed in full in Chapter 15.[207] The declaration was accepted by the government and the offending provisions in the Anti-Terrorism, Crime and Security Act 2001 were repealed. Whilst it is still the case that most declarations have been remedied, there are two causes for concern: the long drawn-out process of a remedy for the declaration of incompatibility concerning the blanket ban on prisoner voting, which has still not been resolved, and the growing use of fast-track legislation, and one example of retrospective legislation, calling into question the extent to which Parliament is able to effectively scrutinise the proposed remedies for declarations of incompatibility.

Section 3(1) of the Representation of the People Act 1983 was declared incompatible with Convention rights by the Scottish Court of Session, sitting as the Registration Appeal Court in Scotland.[208] Despite the declaration of incompatibility and the criticism of the Joint Committee on Human Rights, no changes to the legislation were made by remedial order.[209] The Joint Committee on Human Rights further criticised the lack of response of the UK government to resolve what it saw as a legally clear, but politically difficult, issue in its report on the Political Parties and Elections Bill in 2008.[210] The issue of prisoner voting was discussed further in the House of Commons on 2 November 2010, in response to an urgent question on prisoner voting placed by Sadiq Khan, the Labour MP for Tooting and then Shadow Justice Secretary, asking the deputy Prime Minister to make a statement on the government's plans to give votes to prisoners.[211] The following day, the Prime Minister was asked whether he agreed that it would be wrong to allow prisoners to vote, to which David Cameron replied that it made him 'physically ill even to contemplate having to give the vote to anyone who is in prison' but that he was required to do so, particularly due to the potentially large cost of settling compensation claims brought by prisoners.[212] In a written ministerial statement on 20 December 2010, the parliamentary secretary of the Cabinet Office, Mr Mark Harper, announced the intention of the government to act to implement the judgment in *Hirst (2)*

---

205 Joint Committee on Human Rights 'Human Rights Judgments' (7th Report of Session 2014–15) HL Paper 130, HC 1088, 17.

206 [2004] QB 335.

207 See pp 1087 *et seq*.

208 *Smith v Scott (Electoral Registration Officer for the areas of Clackmannanshire, Falkirk and Sterling)* [2007] CSIH 9, [2007] SCLR 268.

209 See Joint Committee of Human Rights, 'Monitoring the Government's Response to Court Judgments Finding Breaches of Human Rights' (16th Report on 2006–07 session) HL Paper 128, HC 728, paras 70–78. and 'Monitoring the Government's Response to Court Judgments Finding Breaches of Human Rights: Annual Report 2008' (Thirty-First Report of Session 2007–8), HL Paper 173, HC 1078, paras 48–9, 58 and 62–3.

210 Joint Committee on Human Rights 'Legislative Scrutiny: Political Parties and Elections Bill' (Fourth Report of Session 2008–9) HL Paper 23, HC 204.

211 Hansard HC Deb Vol 514, col 771 (2 November 2010).

212 Hansard HC Deb Vol 517 col 921 (3 November 2010).

on which the declaration of incompatibility had been based.[213] The issue of prisoner voting was raised in a Westminster Hall debate on 11 January 2011, which discussed the issue generally as well as the specific announced intention of the government to grant those serving terms of less than four years the right to vote, and the intention to introduce proposals by 23 August 2011.[214] The issue next returned to the House of Commons on 10 February 2011. Following the backbench debate, the House resolved, by a vote of 234 votes to 22:

> That this House notes the ruling of the European Court of Human Rights in *Hirst v. the United Kingdom* in which it held that there had been no substantive debate by members of the legislature on the continued justification for maintaining a general restriction on the right of prisoners to vote; acknowledges the treaty obligations of the UK; is of the opinion that legislative decisions of this nature should be a matter for democratically-elected lawmakers; and supports the current situation in which no prisoner is able to vote except those imprisoned for contempt, default or on remand.

Following a further decision of the Strasbourg Court confirming that a blanket ban on prisoner voting was contrary to Convention rights,[215] a question was asked of the Prime Minister on 23 May 2012 whether he would give an undertaking that he would not succumb to the diktat of the European Court of Human Rights and would stand by the resolution of the House of Commons concluding that the franchise should be removed from prisoners. David Cameron replied:

> The short answer to that is 'yes'. I have always believed that when someone is sent to prison they lose certain rights, and one of those rights is the right to vote. Crucially, I believe that it should be a matter for Parliament to decide, not a foreign court. Parliament has made its decision, and I completely agree with it.[216]

The Prime Minister confirmed this response in reply to a similar question on 24 October 2012, stating that 'prisoners are not getting the vote under this Government'.[217] On 2 November 2012 the Voting Eligibility (Prisoners) Draft Bill was laid before Parliament, proposing three options: (i) a ban for prisoners sentenced to four years or more, (ii) a ban for prisoners sentenced to more than six months, and (iii) a ban for all convicted prisoners.[218] In 2013, the Joint Committee on the Draft Prisoner Voting Bill was appointed. Its report concluded that legislation be brought forward before the 2015 general election to enfranchise prisoners sentenced to imprisonment of 12 months or less and others in their final six months of their sentence prior to release. The government did not formally respond to this report, no legislation was enacted, and there was

213 Hansard HC Deb Vol 520 col 151WS (20 Dec 2010).
214 Hansard HC Deb Vol 521 col 1WH (11 Jan 2011).
215 *Scoppola v Italy (No 3)* (App No 126/05); [2009]; 33 BHRC 126.
216 Hansard HC Deb Vol 545 col 1127 (23 May 2012).
217 Hansard HC Deb Vol 545 col 922–923 (23 May 2012).
218 Voting Eligibility (Prisoners) Draft Bill Cm 8499.

no mention of a desire to implement such legislation in the Queen's Speech of 2016,[219] despite continued criticism from the Joint Committee on Human Rights.[220]

In *Catt* and *T* the Supreme Court upheld the declaration of incompatibility made by the Court of Appeal, concluding that the blanket disclosure of all cautions and convictions was a disproportionate breach of the right to privacy found in Art 8 ECHR.[221] The government responded to the declaration of incompatibility issued by the Court of Appeal by enacting secondary legislation so as to ensure that some convictions and cautions need not be disclosed.[222] However, this was not drawn to the attention of the Joint Committee on Human Rights, meaning that there was little scrutiny over its provisions as concerns its ability to remedy the declaration of incompatibility made by the Court of Appeal.[223] Of even greater concern is the use of retrospective fast-track legislation. The Court of Appeal quashed certain 'Back to Work Schemes' Regulations, concluding that they were beyond the scope of the power granted to make such Regulations. In response, the government enacted the Jobseekers (Back to Work Schemes) Act 2013, which retrospectively reversed the judgment of the Court of Appeal, whilst an appeal to the Supreme Court was still pending. The High Court issued a declaration of incompatibility, concluding that retrospective legislation to overturn a legal judgment that was currently under appeal breached Art 6 ECHR and the rule of law.[224] This declaration of incompatibility is not yet final. This response to judgments critical of government actions illustrates a worrying trend, with the government being more concerned to achieve its legislative agenda as opposed to ensuring a detailed legislative analysis of, and response to, any possible human rights implications of its proposed legislation.

A declaration is clearly an empty remedy as far as the majority of litigants are concerned. Clearly, it cannot be viewed as an effective remedy in Convention terms;[225] this was reaffirmed in the Chamber judgment in *Burden v United Kingdom*.[226] It was found

219 https://www.gov.uk/government/speeches/queens-speech-2016.

220 Joint Committee on Human Rights 'Human Rights Judgments' (7th Report of Session) 2014–15 HL Paper 130, HC 1088, paras 3.15–3.26.

221 *R (T, JB and AW) v Chief Constable of Greater Manchester, Secretary of State for the Home Department and Secretary of State for* Justice [2013] EWCA Civ 25; [2013] 1 WLR 2515, substantially upheld in *R (Catt) v Commissioner of Police of the Metropolis* and *R (T) v Commissioner of Police of the Metropolis* [2015] UKSC 9; [2015] 2 All ER 727.

222 Rehabilitation of Offenders Act 1974 (Exceptions Order) 1975 (Amendment) (England and Wales) Order 2013.

223 Joint Committee on Human Rights 'Human Rights Judgments' (7th Report of Session 2014–15) HL Paper 130, HC 1088, paras 4.3–4.8.

224 *R (Reilly No 2) v Secretary of State for Work and Pensions* [2014] EWHC 2182 (Admin); [2015] 2 WLR 309. Confirmed by the Court of Appeal, see [2016] EWCA Civ 413.

225 The applicant only needs to exhaust those possibilities which offer an effective remedy, so if part of the complaint is the lack of a remedy under Art 13, then the application is not likely to be ruled inadmissible on this ground: *X v UK* (1981) (Appl 7990/77); 24 D & R 57. A remedy will be ineffective if according to established case law there appears to be no chance of success: Appl 5874 172, Yearbook XVII (1974). Until quite recently (see below) Strasbourg had not had the opportunity to rule on the question whether a Declaration of Incompatibility could amount to an effective remedy, since no analogous procedure exists in the contracting states. Since it offers nothing which has previously been recognised as a remedy to the individual in question, it was clear that there were strong grounds for considering that the system would not be viewed as offering an effective remedy.

226 (2006) App No 93378/05.

that the applicants had not needed to exhaust that remedy. The Court stated that it did not consider that the applicants could have been expected to have brought a claim for a declaration of incompatibility under s 4 of the 1998 Human Rights Act before bringing their application to the European Court of Human Rights, since it was a remedy that was dependent on the discretion of the executive and so ineffective on that ground. The Court expressed the view, however, that it was possible that, at some future date, evidence of a long-standing and established practice of ministers giving effect to the courts' declarations of incompatibility might be sufficient to persuade it of the effectiveness of the procedure. Since the government has so far accepted that declarations should be responded to, albeit with one example of extreme reluctance and delay, it is possible that the Court may find eventually that a declaration amounts to an effective remedy.

Since the ability to make the declaration is confined to certain higher courts, a litigant in a lower court or tribunal, who is affected by incompatible legislation, appears to be completely remediless, since even the empty remedy of a declaration is unavailable. The forum at the next level might be equally powerless. In the circumstances covered by this book, the picture is mixed as regards the ability of litigants to get into a court that can issue a declaration.[227] The litigant has little incentive to appeal in the hope of eventually reaching a court able to make a declaration, especially as there is no provision requiring the Crown to bear its own costs where it intervenes in accordance with s 5(2) of the HRA. In criminal proceedings, however, the courts appear to be taking the view that to convict a defendant in breach of Art 6 of the Convention would be an abuse of process.[228]

It is impossible not to conclude that this aspect of the system of remedial action is inadequate to the task of providing a domestic remedy for violation of Convention rights.[229] If, at the least, legislation is not forthcoming within the next few years to amend s 4 of the HRA with a view to allowing lower courts to make declarations, the pressure on the judiciary to find compatibility, already very high, will become increasingly severe. This pressure may explain the recent fall in s 4 declarations.

The remedial process under s 10

Section 10 provides the remedial process to be followed if a declaration of incompatibility is made. Under s 10(2) if a minister of the Crown considers 'that there are compelling reasons for proceeding under this section, he may by order make such amendments to the legislation as he considers necessary to remove the incompatibility'.[230] In a

227 E.g., an appeal from a magistrates' court to the Crown Court would require a further appeal in order to obtain a declaration. A declaration could be obtained using only one level of appeal if an appeal was by way of case stated to the Divisional Court. Appeals from the Proscribed Organisations Appeal Commission are, by leave, to the Court of Appeal in England and Wales, and to the equivalent courts in Scotland and Northern Ireland (see further Chapter 15, pp 1066–67).

228 See the views of Lord Steyn in *R v DPP ex p Kebilene* [1999] 4 All ER 801.

229 See Leigh, I and Lustgarten, L, 'Making rights real: the courts, remedies and the Human Rights Act' (1999) 58(3) CLJ 509, p 543. They concluded that rights may be less well protected than previously as a result of the HRA.

230 Section 10(1): This section applies if:
   (a) provision of legislation has been declared under section 4 to be incompatible with a Convention right and, if an appeal lies-
      (i) all persons who may appeal have stated in writing that they do not intend to do so;

departure from the New Zealand scheme, s 10 allows a minister to make amendments to the offending legislation by means of a 'fast-track' procedure. Section 10 may also be used where a decision of the European Court of Human Rights suggests that a provision of legislation has become incompatible with the Convention. Therefore, campaigning groups could lobby the government to make amendments under s 10 following any such decision. However, as indicated above, the minister is under no obligation to make the amendment(s), either after any such decision or after a declaration of incompatibility under s 4, and may only do so if he or she considers that there are 'compelling reasons for proceeding under this section'. In other words, the fact that a declaration of incompatibility has been made will not necessarily *in itself* provide a compelling reason, although the circumstances in which it is made may do so.

Schedule 2 provides two procedures for making a 'remedial order' that must, under s 20, be in the form of a statutory instrument. Schedule 2, para 2(a) and para 3 provide for a standard procedure whereby the minister must lay a draft of the order before Parliament, together with the required information – an explanation of the incompatibility and a statement of the reasons for proceeding under s 10 – for at least 60 days, during which time representations can be made to the minister. It must then be laid before Parliament again and does not come into effect until it is approved by a resolution of each House within 60 days after it has been laid for the second time. The emergency procedure under Sched 2, para 2(b) and para 4 follows the same route, apart from the very significant provision for allowing the minister to make the order before laying it before Parliament. Thus, the amendment can be made outside the full parliamentary process, which would be required for primary legislation, but otherwise the responsibility for amending primary legislation remains firmly in parliamentary hands, retaining 'Parliament's authority in the legislative process'.[231]

      (ii) the time for bringing an appeal has expired and no appeal has been brought within that time; or

      (iii) an appeal brought within that time has been determined or abandoned; or

  (b) it appears to a Minister of the Crown or Her Majesty in Council that, having regard to a finding of the European Court of Human Rights made after the coming into force of this section in proceedings against the United Kingdom, a provision of legislation is incompatible with an obligation of the United Kingdom arising from the Convention.

(2) If a Minister of the Crown considers that there are compelling reasons for proceeding under this section, he may by order make such amendments to the legislation as he considers necessary to remove the incompatibility.

(3) If, in the case of subordinate legislation, a Minister of the Crown considers:

  (a) that it is necessary to amend the primary legislation under which the subordinate legislation in question was made, in order to enable the incompatibility to be removed, and

  (b) that there are compelling reasons for proceeding under this section, he may by order make such amendments to the primary legislation as he considers necessary.

(4) This section also applies where the provision in question is in subordinate legislation and has been quashed, or declared invalid, by reason of incompatibility with a Convention right and the Minister proposes to proceed under paragraph 2(b) of Sched 2.

(5) If the legislation is an Order in Council, the power conferred by subsection (2) or (3) is exercisable by Her Majesty in Council.

(6) In this section 'legislation' does not include a Measure of the Church Assembly or of the General Synod of the Church of England.

(7) Schedule 2 makes further provision about remedial orders.

231 Ewing, K, 'The Human Rights Act and parliamentary democracy' (1999) 62(1) MLR 79, p 93.

Declarations as to the compatibility of new Bills with the Convention rights

Under s 19(1)(a) HRA, in introducing legislation into Parliament a minister, before second reading of the bill, must state that the bill is compatible with the Convention or that, while unable to make such a declaration, the government nevertheless wishes to proceed with the bill (s 19(1)(b)). When the relevant minister has made a declaration of compatibility under s 19(1)(a), its effects may be viewed as additional to the duty the courts are already under, arising from s 3(1), to ensure that the legislation is rendered compatible with the guarantees if at all possible. The Lord Chancellor has said: 'Ministerial statements of compatibility will inevitably be a strong spur to the courts to find the means of construing statutes compatibly with the Convention.'[232] The guidance given to ministers is to the effect that for a s 19(1)(a) statement to be made it must be 'more likely than not that the provisions . . . will stand up to challenge on Convention grounds'.[233] But if a s 19(1)(b) statement is made this does not have to be taken to mean that 'the provisions of the Bill are incompatible . . . but that the Minister is unable to make a statement of compatibility'. There is no procedure within the HRA allowing the government or Parliament to declare that the judiciary should not strive to achieve compatibility even when dealing with almost certainly incompatible provisions.

The idea behind s 19 is that governments will not be willing, in general, to introduce incompatible bills, although it does open the door to that possibility. In relation to Bills of Rights in general, Dawn Oliver has offered two reasons why a government would be unwilling to state openly that it was legislating in breach of a Bill of Rights.[234] First, there would be the general political embarrassment that would be caused to the government (this may be termed the 'adverse publicity' type of protection). Second, a declaration of intent to infringe constitutional rights would be tantamount to a declaration of the government's intention to breach its obligations under international law; this would undoubtedly provoke widespread international condemnation, which would be highly embarrassing (this may be termed the 'manifest breach' type of protection). The stance taken towards the Communications Act 2003, which was not accompanied by a statement of compatibility, as discussed below, bears out this prediction.

It may be said that, in one respect, s 19 bears comparison with a 'notwithstanding clause', but there is the very significant difference that, as discussed above, the judiciary are not empowered to strike down legislation that contains no such clause, but that is inconsistent with the Convention. Further, s 19 does not expressly provide for the possibility that the government deliberately wishes to achieve incompatibility with the Convention. It merely leaves open the possibility or – in practice – the strong probability that the legislation, or at least certain of its provisions, are incompatible. But s 19 resembles a 'notwithstanding clause' in the sense that a government that intends to introduce measures that are probably or certainly rights-abridging must be open about the fact – at least in the sense that the relevant minister has to state that a declaration is not being made. The government can nevertheless take the position that, while a statement is not being made, it considers the legislation in question to be compatible with the Convention.

---

232 Lord Irvine 'The development of human rights in Britain under an incorporated ECHR' [1998] PL 221.
233 Department of Constitutional Affairs, *Human Rights Act 1998 Guidance for Ministers* (2nd edn), para.36, www.dca.gov/hract/guidance.htm#how, para.36. See further Feldman, D, 'The Impact of Human Rights on the UK Legislative Process' (2004) 25(2) Stat.LR 91.
234 'A Bill of Rights for the UK', in *Government and the UK*, 1991.

The statement of compatibility does not necessarily indicate that compatibility has been achieved once the legislation comes into force. A declaration under s 19(1)(a) might be made and challenged in Parliament. The opposition parties might argue that the legislation had not achieved compatibility, but their amendments intended to achieve compatibility might be defeated due to the large majority of the government. It could hardly be said of such legislation that Parliament was genuinely satisfied that compatibility had been achieved. Further, Parliament might be misled into believing that the legislation was compatible. The legal advice behind the declaration might be flawed. It is arguable that legislation has been passed that gives an appearance of achieving compatibility only because a minimalist interpretation of the Convention was adopted in drafting it. It is suggested in Chapters 11 and 15 that certain provisions of the Terrorism Act 2000 and the Regulation of Investigatory Powers Act 2000 arguably provide examples of such a tendency.[235] Further, legislation, which was arguably compatible with the Convention when passed, might become incompatible due to the effect of subsequent decisions of the European Court of Human Rights taken before the legislation comes into force. Section 2 HRA requires a court to take such decisions into account 'whenever made or given'.

At the time of the inception of the HRA, it was not necessarily apparent that Bills would almost always be accompanied in future by a declaration of their compatibility with the Convention rights, or that a derogation would be sought where otherwise a declaration could not be made. The response of the Conservative Government in the 1990s to certain decisions of the European Court of Human Rights, in particular to its decision in *McCann, Farrell and Savage v UK*,[236] the first judgment of the Court to find a breach of Art 2, did not suggest that future governments would necessarily be deterred on 'manifest breach' or 'adverse publicity' grounds from passing legislation clearly in breach of the Convention without seeking a derogation.

After the decision in *McCann*, Michael Heseltine, the then deputy Prime Minister, declared that the then Conservative government would not change the administrative policies or rules which had led to the deaths in question in that case; members of the government also voiced strong disapproval of the decision, and their stance was welcomed in the right-wing sections of the UK press. A future government might take the view that passing a certain measure in overt breach of the Convention was necessary on crime-control and/or anti-terrorist grounds.

The Communications Act 2003 is the only Act so far since the Human Rights Act came into force in 2000 not to be accompanied by a statement of compatibility. The view taken by the government in introducing the Communications Bill containing a statutory prohibition on political advertising in broadcasting was that the 2003 Act could not be declared to be compatible with the ECHR. The government was not prepared to modify the section by creating exceptions in order to seek to ensure compatibility. The government was supported in this decision by the parliamentary committees that considered the matter prior to the introduction of the new Act.[237] Sections 319 and 321, it was considered, could not be declared to be compatible with Art 10 and so, in accordance with

235 See Chapter 12, p 850 and Chapter 11, p 807.

236 (1995) 21 EHRR 97, A 324, Council of Europe Report.

237 See Joint Committee on the Draft Communications Bill, *the Draft Communications Bill* HL 169-I/HC876-I (2001–2) para 301; Committee on Standards in Public Life *Fifth Report: the Funding of Political Parties in the UK* Cm 4057 (1998) recommendation 94.

s 19(1)(b) HRA, no statement of compatibility was issued accompanying the Bill; but the point was made in Parliament that the provisions need not be viewed as incompatible and that they would be defended if necessary.[238]

This provision was challenged before the House of Lords in *Animal Defenders International Ltd*, discussed above. It will be recalled that the House of Lords distinguished the decision of the Strasbourg Court in *VgT*, concluding that the legislation was compatible with Convention rights. Lord Bingham noted that the blanket ban on the broadcast of political advertising may cause difficulties for Convention compliance, as noted by the Joint Committee on Human Rights, who had asked the government to find a compromise solution enabling the prohibition of political advertising which might skew the democratic process, whilst permitting more social awareness-raising advertising of campaign groups like Animal Defenders International. The Government had judged that there was no fair and workable solution and Lord Bingham did not see any reason to challenge this assessment.[239] Moreover, Lord Bingham concluded that there were three reasons for giving great weight to the decision of Parliament. First, it was reasonable to expect that Parliament would be 'peculiarly sensitive to the measures necessary to safeguard the integrity of our democracy'.[240] Second, Parliament had concluded that the provisions may possibly, though improbably, breach Art 10 ECHR, but had nevertheless issued a s 19(1)(b) statement and proceeded to enact this provision. This course of action demonstrated that the Government considered it important to maintain the blanket ban and that this assessment should not be taken lightly by the court. Third, Lord Bingham recognised that legislation could not be framed so as to address particular cases.[241]

Animal Defenders International took their case to the Grand Chamber of the Strasbourg Court in 2013, which concluded by a narrow majority of nine votes to eight, that the legislation was a proportionate restriction of Art 10. In reaching this conclusion, the Grand Chamber referred in detail to the decision of the House of Lords and the legislative process of the Communications Bill. It concluded that this was an area where states were granted a wide margin of appreciation, as well as recognising that there remained the possibility of communicating information caught within the general broadcasting ban in other media outlets.

Apart from the Communications Act, all legislation passed since the obligation to make a statement of compatibility came into force[242] has been accompanied by a declaration of its compatibility with the Convention rights, under s 19. But this need not mean that all such legislation is in fact compatible: the mere fact that a declaration is made does not mean that it can be assumed that compatibility was in fact achieved.[243]

Thus, the s 19 procedure should be viewed as the expression of an executive opinion based on legal advice, nothing more. As far as s 3 is concerned, the courts are expected

238 See *Hansard*, HC Vol.395, col 789 (Dec 3, 2002); *Hansard*, HL Vol. 646, cols 658–59 (March 25, 2003).
239 *R (Animal Defenders International) v Secretary of State for Culture, Media and Sport* [2008] UKHL 15, [31].
240 *Ibid*, [33].
241 *Ibid*, [33].
242 The obligation to make a statement of compatibility came into force on 24 November 1998, not on 2 October 2000, under the HRA 1998 (Commencement) Order 1998, SI 1998/2882.
243 See Feldman, D, 'Institutional Roles and meanings of 'compatibility' under the HRA', in Fenwick, Masterman and Phillipson (eds), (2007), fn 1 above.

to satisfy their obligation under s 3 in respect of legislation passed prior to the inception of the HRA in 1998, but are under an even stronger obligation, as indicated above, in respect of legislation accompanied by a statement of compatibility since it can be assumed that Parliament intended that the legislation should be compatible with the Convention. Where no declaration is made, it can be said that the courts are placed in a dilemma. Section 3 still applies, but Parliament's intention can be viewed as being that the legislation in question should not be compatible with the Convention. However, if no derogation from the Convention right is sought, the dilemma could be resolved by adopting the view that Parliament could be presumed not to wish to legislate compatibly with the Convention except where it had expressly stated that such was its intention. A court could then apply s 3 as it would to legislation passed after 1950, but before 1998.

As discussed in Chapter 15, when the Anti-Terrorism Crime and Security Act 2001 was passed the government sought a derogation from Art 5 in respect of the detention without trial provisions of Part 4, rather than seeking to pass them through Parliament unaccompanied by a statement of compatibility.[244] In general it is argued, for obvious reasons, that seeking a derogation from the relevant article in question in order to achieve compatibility is preferable to merely pushing incompatible legislation through Parliament, even though the HRA allows for that latter possibility. A derogation under Art 15, as discussed in Chapters 2 and 15, can only be sought under very limited circumstances that can then be subject to judicial scrutiny.[245] In contrast, the HRA allows for exceptions to the Convention to be made in any circumstances – no limitations at all are contained in the HRA itself, except the limitation that can be implied from the wording of s 3. No requirement of proportionality is imported into the HRA itself in relation to the introduction of incompatible bills. A requirement could have been imposed in the HRA that a detailed explanation for the reasons behind seeking to legislate in breach of the Convention must be given to Parliament and that only in certain circumstances, including emergency ones, should Parliament accept them. But, clearly, such a requirement would have been overtly incompatible with the doctrine of parliamentary sovereignty.

Clearly, legislating in deliberate and overt breach of the Convention would eventually invite a successful challenge to the measure in the European Court of Human Rights, but the government in its legislative programme has not sought to take advantage even of the time lapse that would have occurred.

Special protection for the media and religious freedom?

Protecting religious organisations

The Church of England lobbied fiercely during the passage of the Human Rights Bill to be given special protection for religious freedom. The amendments to the bill adopted in the House of Lords, which would have provided a defence where religious organisations breached human rights in the pursuance of religious belief, suggested that the Church wished to be allowed to disregard human rights values in the name of respect

244 See Chapter 15, pp 1081 *et seq.*
245 See p 99 and pp 1087–90.

for religious belief, and that, while protecting its own Art 9 rights, it was prepared to use them to invade the Convention rights of others.[246] The Church appeared to hope that it would be able to discriminate against persons on the ground, for example, of gender or sexual orientation in respect, *inter alia*, of employment in Church schools. Those amendments were removed in the Commons and s 13 was substituted, on the basis that Church concerns could be met without compromising the integrity of the bill.[247] Section 13 does not allow the Church, and other religious organisations, to disregard human rights, but on its face it appears to give special protection to their Art 9 rights. It provides: 'If a court's determination of any question arising under this Act might affect the exercise by a religious organisation . . . of [its Art 9 rights] the right to freedom of . . . religion, it must have particular regard to the importance of that right.' Arguably, s 13 impliedly accepts, therefore, what some commentators regard as a regrettable dislocation between human rights values and religious ones, which could present judges with problems of interpretation.[248] Ian Loveland has dubbed the amendment 'a substantive obscenity'.[249] However, since, as Chapter 10 indicates, s 12 has not been found to enhance the weight to be given to Art 10 on the basis that Arts 8–11 must be viewed as standing on an equal footing,[250] it is probable that this would also be found to be the case in respect of s 13 in relation to Art 9.

Protecting the media

The press also lobbied for special protection. Press lobbying focused overwhelmingly upon the fear that the Act would introduce a right to privacy against the media 'through the back door', due either to judicial development of the common law in the post-HRA era, or to the probable status of the Press Complaints Commission as a public authority, itself bound to act compatibly with the Convention under s 6 HRA.[251] Sometimes the basic point was missed that the Convention rights would not directly bind newspapers, since they are not public authorities.[252] The amendment became s 12, which applies 'if a court is considering whether to grant any relief [which could] affect the exercise of the Convention right to freedom of expression'.

Section 12(2)–(3) provides special provision against the grant of *ex parte* injunctions, which is discussed further in Chapters 9[253] and 10.[254] Under s 12(3), no relief which, if granted, might affect the exercise of the Convention right to freedom of expression is to be granted so as to restrain publication before trial 'unless the court is satisfied that the applicant is likely to establish that publication should not be allowed'. Section 12(3) therefore affects the grant of interim injunctions generally. The use of injunctions is

---

246 See 585 HL Official Report cols 747–60, 770–90, 805, 812–13, 5 February 1998.
247 The Home Secretary, 312 HC Official Report, col 1019 (1998).
248 See further Cumper, P, 'The protection of religious rights under s 13 of the HRA' [2000] PL 254.
249 Loveland, I, *Constitutional Law*, 2000, p 603.
250 See p 747 *et seq.*
251 See Chapter 10, pp 731–35 on this point.
252 The definition of 'public authority' appears in s 6(1), (3)(b) and (5)) of the Act, discussed in HL Deb Vol 582 cols 1277, 1293–94 and 1309–10, 3 November 1997, and *ibid*, Vol 583, cols 771–811, 24 November 1997.
253 See pp 673, 678.
254 See pp 778 *et seq.*

discussed in Chapter 10 in the context of restraining misuse of private information. The discussion considers in particular the use of s 12 HRA where interim injunctions are sought in civil proceedings against newspapers.[255]

Under s 12(5), the term 'relief' includes 'any remedy or order other than in criminal proceedings'. Section 12(4) provides that the court must have special regard to the Convention right to freedom of expression and, in particular, to the extent to which it is about to become or has become available to the public, the public interest in its publication and 'any relevant privacy code'.[256] Section 12(4) is therefore highly relevant in actions originating under the breach of confidence doctrine. Section 12 has not protected the media from the impact of a privacy law. Media fears that a 'privacy law' would develop under the HRA were not misplaced and are currently in the process of being realised. But there was an enjoyable irony in the fact that it was s 12(4) that was used, at least initially, to provide such a law with impetus, ensnaring the group that lobbied for its inclusion. Clearly, from a human rights perspective, this can be viewed as a welcome development, since it means that a group – media proprietors – with the ability and the evident desire to infringe the rights of others, while protecting its own, can be curbed in its ability to do so.

The position of the Scottish Parliament, the Northern Ireland Assembly and the Welsh Assembly

The devolution legislation places the Scottish Parliament, the Northern Ireland Assembly and the Welsh Assembly in a different position from that of the Westminster Parliament as regards the legal status of the Convention rights. The Welsh Assembly is bound by the Convention under s 81 of the Government of Wales Act 2006. The Scottish Parliament cannot act incompatibly with the Convention under s 29(2)(d) of the Scotland Act 1998. The executive and law officers in Scotland are also bound.[257] Under s 21 HRA, legislation passed by the Scottish Parliament, the Welsh Assembly and by the Northern Ireland Assembly is regarded as secondary legislation. Under s 3 HRA, any primary legislation[258] passed by the Westminster Parliament and applicable to Scotland, Northern Ireland and Wales will be binding, even if it is not compatible with the Convention. These arrangements mean that Scotland and Wales have, in effect, a Bill of Rights in the traditional sense since the Parliament is bound by the Convention and therefore cannot

255 See Chapter 10. E.g., in *R (H) v London North and East Region Mental Health Review Tribunal (Secretary of State for Health intervening)* [2002] QB 1 the Mental Health Act 1983 s 73 was found to be incompatible with Arts 5(1) and 5(4); the Mental Health Act 1983 (Remedial Order) 2001 was introduced to address the incompatibility by way of the fast track procedure. In *A and Others* [2004] QB 335 the House of Lords declared Part 4 ACTSA 2001 incompatible with Art 5 and 14 ECHR; Part 4 was repealed by the Prevention of Terrorism Act 2005, in turn repealed by the Terrorism Prevention and Investigation Measures Act 2011, as discussed further in Chapter 15, p 1035 *et seq.*

256 See further on s 12(4): Griffiths, J and Lewis, T, 'The HRA s 12 – press freedom over privacy' (1999) 10(2) Ent LR 36–41. They argue that s 12(4) did not in fact provide the protection the media had hoped for, although their spokespersons believed that it had.

257 See Scotland Act 1998, s 57. Thus, in Scotland and Wales, the Convention became binding from 1 July 1999, when the devolution legislation came into force, over a year before the HRA came fully into force.

258 Scotland Act 1998, s 29(2)(b) and Sched 5, and Government of Wales Act 1988, Sched 2.

pass primary legislation that conflicts with it.[259] The references to 'legislation' so far, and below, are to legislation emanating from the Westminster Parliament.

Conclusions

It can now be said that the rules of interpretation relating to legislation affecting Convention rights differ, depending on when it was passed. Prior legislation passed before 1950 is subject to a compatible construction rule only, arising under s 3. Prior legislation passed after 1950 is subject to a 'legislative intention plus compatible construction rule'[260] since, as indicated above, Parliament can be presumed not to have intended to legislate incompatibly with the Convention. Subsequent legislation – passed after the inception of the HRA – is subject to the general legislative intention rule, the presumption that may be said to be embodied in the s 19 procedure and to the compatible construction rule under s 3. If no declaration of compatibility is made, subsequent legislation is subject to the compatible construction rule and probably to the legislative intention rule too.

In so far as the possibility of incompatibility arises in either prior or subsequent legislation, the stance taken by the House of Lords in *Ghaidan* is that it should be dealt with under s 3, without resorting to a declaration of incompatibility under s 4, except as a last resort. After *R v A* and *Ghaidan*, Parliament's theoretical ability under the HRA to pass incompatible legislation has been undermined. It may be concluded, therefore, that s 3 places the Convention in a strong position when compared with ordinary legislation, although, in a very technical sense, as a matter of constitutional theory, parliamentary sovereignty is preserved.

But at the same time the HRA is in a weak position compared to, for example, the US Bill of Rights, since it is subject to express repeal or amendment by subsequent enactments. This is a significant weakness, bearing in mind the continuing hostility of the Conservative government to the HRA,[261] and indeed the lack of support for its values exhibited by members of the Labour government. As already indicated, the intention of the Conservative government is to repeal the HRA, replacing it with a British Bill of Rights. Although in terms of express repeal, the doctrine of parliamentary sovereignty is preserved, the other HRA mechanisms apparently intended to show adherence to that doctrine now look tokenistic. The possibilities of passing incompatible legislation, or of disregarding declarations of incompatibility, have not been exploited over the last fifteen years of the HRA's existence. Aside from certain provisions of the Communications Act 2003, Parliament has shown little evidence of an intent to employ the leeway allowed for under the HRA to pass incompatible legislation in the years 2000–15.

Instead, the Convention exceptions system has been deployed domestically so that at the least parity with Strasbourg is maintained. When Part 4 of the Anti-Terrorism Crime and Security Act 2001 was passed, a derogation from Art 5 accompanied it.[262] Otherwise, Parliament and the courts have relied on the doctrine of proportionality in finding that

---

259 See further Tierney, S, 'Devolution issues and s 2(1) of the HRA' (2000) 4 EHRLR 380–92.
260 See Bennion, F, 'What interpretation is possible under s 3(1) of the HRA?' [2000] PL 77.
261 Such hostility became ever more evident once the Conservatives had lost the 2001 General Election, owing to the change of leadership. At the 2005 General Election it was stated that the HRA would be modified if the Conservatives were elected. At the 2010 and 2015 elections it was Conservative policy to repeal the HRA.
262 See Chapter 15, p 1080 *et seq.*

exceptions to the Convention rights can be justified. The stance taken under s 3 appears to be, as discussed, a remedial one. In other words, the courts have shown a determination to take measures to avoid a breach of a Convention right at the domestic level, largely disregarding the possibility of dealing with Convention restraints offered by ss 3(2) and 4 HRA. The government and Parliament have largely followed suit, as the discussion of the use of ss 4, 10 and 19(1)(a) and (b) over the last fifteen years indicates. The stance of the senior judges in the leading s 3 cases is in accordance with the redefinition of their role that the HRA has brought about, and with the status of the HRA as a constitutional instrument. However, as the discussion of the leading s 2 decisions reveals, the traditional constraints of the doctrine of precedent are creating a countervailing pressure that has been holding back the development of a British constitutional rights jurisprudence.[263]

4 The position of public authorities under the HRA

The binding effect of Convention rights

Section 6 is the central provision of the HRA. Section 6(1) provides: 'It is unlawful for a public authority to act in a way which is incompatible with a Convention right.' This is the main provision giving effect to the Convention rights: rather than incorporation of the Convention, it is made binding against public authorities. Under s 6(6), an 'act' includes an omission, but does not include a failure to introduce in or lay before Parliament a proposal for legislation or a failure to make any primary legislation or remedial order. Section 6(6) was included in order to preserve parliamentary sovereignty and prerogative power: in this case, the power of the executive to introduce legislation.

Thus, apart from its impact on legislation, the HRA also creates obligations under s 6 that bear upon 'public authorities'. Such obligations have a number of implications. Independently of litigation, public authorities have had to put procedures in place in order to ensure that they do not breach their duty under s 6. Guidance was issued prior to the coming in to force of the HRA[264] to a number of central government departments by the Human Rights Unit (HRU), now the Human Rights Division of the Department for Constitutional Affairs, and a number of the departments undertook a human rights audit, reporting back to the HRU.[265] However, beyond central government departments, practice was very variable,[266] although certain bodies, including the police, undertook quite extensive preparation before the HRA came fully into force.[267] The Human Rights Task Force was set up by the Home Office to aid in the preparations, and it has received

---

263 See further Masterman, Chapter 3, in Fenwick, Masterman, Phillipson (eds) (2007) fn 1 above.
264 A number of documents have been issued by the HRU, including *Putting Rights into Public Services*, July 1999; *Core Guidance for Public Authorities: A New Era of Rights and Responsibilities; The Human Rights Act 1998: Guidance for Departments*, now *A Guide to the Human Rights Act 1998*, 3rd edn, 2006. https://www.justice.gov.uk/downloads/human-rights/act-studyguide.pdf.
265 See further the Ministry of Justice website: www.justice.gov.uk.
266 See for comment at that time Pleming, 'Assessing the act: a firm foundation or a false start' (2000) 6 EHRLR 560–79. See further Clements and Thomas (eds), *The HRA: A Success Story?* (2005).
267 The Association of Chief Police Officers set up a Human Rights Working Group in November 1998; it appointed a Human Rights Programme Team in 1999. Twelve areas of police work were selected

reports from certain public authorities regarding completion of internal human rights reviews.

Clearly, an exception had to be made under s 6 in order to bring it into harmony with s 3 and to realise the objective of preserving parliamentary sovereignty. Section 6(2) provides:

> sub-section (1) does not apply to an act if, (a) as the result of one or more provisions of primary legislation, the authority could not have acted differently; or (b) in the case of one or more provisions of, or made under, primary legislation which cannot be read or given effect in a way which is compatible with the Convention rights, the authority was acting so as to give effect to or enforce those provisions.

Thus, s 6(2)(a) creates a strong obligation requiring public authorities to do their utmost to act compatibly.

It may be noted that s 6(2)(a) applies to primary legislation only, whereas s 6(2)(b) applies also to subordinate legislation made under incompatible primary legislation. This is implicit in the use of the words 'or made under' used in the latter sub-section, but not the former. The exception under s 6 applies to legislation only (which, as indicated above, includes Orders in Council made under the royal prerogative, under s 21(1)). If a common law provision conflicts with a Convention right binding on a public body under s 6, it appears that the right will prevail. No provision was included in the Act allowing the common law to override the Convention or creating restrictions as to those courts that can find incompatibility between the two.

Relationship between ss 3 and 6

Where legislation is applicable to a public authority, a court, as itself a public authority must, in addition to its duty under s 3, seek to ensure that the Convention is adhered to. It must bear in mind that it is considering the obligations of another public authority that is bound by the rights. But its duty under s 3 relates to its interpretation of the legislation itself, its duty under s 6 to the application of the legislation by the public authority and by itself in relation to the Convention rights. The courts in the post-HRA cases do not always advert expressly to their use of either ss 3 or 6 in applying legislation.[268] A court can first apply s 6 and ask whether the public authority has, by its action or omission, breached the Convention guarantee(s) in question. If it appears that it has, the court should look to the relevant legislation to determine whether, even when the attempt is made to construe it compatibly with the Convention, it remains incompatible and therefore provides the public authority with a loophole under s 6(2). An alternative method is to consider the legislation first in relation to the public authority, affording it a *Convention-friendly* interpretation, and then asking whether, under such an interpretation, it appeared

---

as especially significant in HRA terms, including covert policing, discipline, hate crimes, domestic violence and public order. An audit of those areas was undertaken in order to determine whether procedures and policies required modification.

268 See, e.g., Chapter 9, p 675. In the cases discussed it was not clear whether ss 6 or 3 were being relied upon in applying the Convention.

that the body had the power to do what it had done. If it appeared that it had not, it could be found to have acted ultra vires.

Distinguishing between public authorities and private bodies

'Standard' and 'functional' public authorities

Under s 6, Convention guarantees are binding only against 'public authorities'. The terms 'public authority' and 'public function' were left deliberately undefined in the HRA. Nor was an exhaustive list of public authorities attempted, on the model provided by the Freedom of Information Act 2000.[269] Under s 6(3)(b) the term covers 'any person certain of whose functions are functions of a public nature'. So the crucial question in relation to many bodies concerns the meaning of the term 'functions of a public nature' – if the body is not self-evidently a public authority, as explained below. Only two bodies are categorised under the HRA itself – the courts and Parliament. Under s 6(3)(a), the term 'public authority' includes a court or under sub-s (3)(b) a tribunal. Parliament 'or a person exercising functions in connection with proceedings in Parliament' is expressly excluded from the definition. This refers to the Westminster Parliament, the Scottish Parliament, the Northern Ireland Assembly and the Welsh Assembly.

Not only is the definition under s 6(3) non-exhaustive, it also leaves open room for much debate on the meaning of 'functions of a public nature'. The definition was explained in the notes on clauses accompanying the bill as indicating that where a body is clearly recognisable as a public authority, there is no need to look at the detailed provisions of s 6(3)(a)–(b). Thus, the term 'public authority' includes firstly bodies that are self-evidently of a public nature, such as the police, government departments, the Probation Service, local authorities, the security and intelligence services and the BBC. They are usually referred to as 'standard public authorities'.

Second, certain bodies, which have both public and private functions, are quasi-public or hybrid bodies. They are generally referred to as 'functional public authorities', the terminology used in the notes on clauses accompanying the bill. Under s 6(5), 'in relation to a particular act, a person is not a public authority by virtue only of s 6(3)(b) if the nature of the act is private'. Since, in relation to standard public authorities, there is no need to consider s 6(3)(b), this provision refers to functional public authorities and has the effect of excluding the private acts of functional public authorities from the scope of the HRA (but see the discussion of 'horizontal effect', below). This is a very significant matter, since the private acts of standard public authorities are *not* excluded. So under s 6(5), functional public authorities are bound by the Convention rights in respect of their public functions only. Therefore, for example, assuming that acts relating to employment are private acts, an employee of a standard public authority could use the HRA directly against the authority, as explained below, while the employee of a functional public authority could not. A hospital, for example, might be viewed as exercising a public function in relation to NHS patients and a private one in relation to private patients. But some room was clearly created for debate as to those bodies that should be

---

269 See Chapter 8, pp 530–32.

classified as standard rather than functional.[270] Classic functional bodies include privatised fuel or water companies and other contracted-out services.

Thus, under the generally accepted view of s 6(3) and (5), the provisions create three categories of body in relation to the Convention rights. First, there are standard ('pure') public authorities that can *never* act privately, even in respect of matters governed by private law, such as employment relations. Such bodies are obliged under s 6 to act in accordance with Convention rights in relation to all of their activities, whether they can be accounted public or private functions. Secondly, there are functional (quasi-public) authorities that have a dual function and that can act privately; these are bodies having several functions, some public and some private; they are caught by the Convention in respect of the former functions but not the latter. In other words, they are not bound by the Act to adhere to the Convention rights when engaged in *private* acts. It is possible, it is suggested, that they could operate privately in respect of *aspects* of carrying out their public functions, while they would always act privately in respect of their private functions. Thirdly, there are purely private bodies that have no public function at all. It was accepted in Parliament in debate on the Human Rights Bill that this was the correct reading of s 6.[271]

The discussion below, and in this book in general, proceeds on the basis, therefore, that s 6 creates three categories of bodies – standard, functional and private – and that the private acts of functional bodies are excluded from the scope of the s 6 obligation, while standard public authorities are bound in respect of all their functions. They are not excluded from the effects of the HRA entirely, owing to its creation of indirect horizontal effects (discussed below).

Tests determining core and functional public authority status

The relevant test determining that a public authority is a 'core' authority was considered in detail in the leading decision of the House of Lords in *Aston Cantlow PCC v Wallbank*.[272] The question facing the Lords was whether the action of a parochial church council (PCC) seeking to enforce liability to repair a church was taken as an aspect of a public function. Lord Nicholls first considered whether the PCC should be viewed as a core public authority, finding that no single test was available to determine whether a public body carried out a public function. He said:[273]

> The expression 'public authority' is not defined in the Act, nor is it a recognised term of art in English law, that is, an expression with a specific recognised meaning. The word 'public' is a term of uncertain import, used with many different shades of meaning: public policy, public rights of way, public property, public authority [in the Public Authorities Protection Act 1893], public nuisance, public house, public school, public company. So in the present case the statutory context is all important.

---

270 See Grosz, Beatson and Duffy, *op cit*, fn 1, on this point: para 4–10 et seq.
271 See Straw, HC Official Report, cols 409–10 (1998).
272 [2004] 1 AC 546. For discussion, see Meisel, F, 'The *Aston Cantlow* case: blots on English jurisprudence and the public/private law divide' [2004] PL 2–10.
273 At paras 6–8.

As to that, the broad purpose sought to be achieved by section 6(1) is not in doubt. The purpose is that those bodies for whose acts the state is answerable before the European Court of Human Rights shall in future be subject to a domestic law obligation not to act incompatibly with Convention rights. If they act in breach of this legal obligation victims may henceforth obtain redress from the courts of this country. In future victims should not need to travel to Strasbourg.

Conformably with this purpose, the phrase 'a public authority' in section 6(1) is essentially a reference to a body whose nature is governmental in a broad sense of that expression . . . under the Human Rights Act a body of this nature is required to act compatibly with Convention rights in everything it does. The most obvious examples are government departments, local authorities, the police and the armed forces. Behind the instinctive classification of these organisations as bodies whose nature is governmental lie factors such as the possession of special powers, democratic accountability, public funding in whole or in part, an obligation to act only in the public interest, and a statutory constitution. . . . One consequence of being a 'core' public authority, namely, an authority falling within section 6 without reference to section 6(3), is that the body in question does not itself enjoy Convention rights. . . . A core public authority seems inherently incapable of satisfying the Convention description of a victim: 'any person, *nongovernmental organisation or group of individuals*' (Article 34, with emphasis added). Only victims of an unlawful act may bring proceedings under section 7 of the Human Rights Act, and the Convention description of a victim has been incorporated into the Act, by section 7(7) . . . It must always be relevant to consider whether Parliament can have intended that the body in question should have no Convention rights.

Applying these tests, the House of Lords found that PCCs are not 'core' public authorities. Lord Nicholls noted that the established church, the Church of England, has special links with central government, but he considered that it remains essentially a religious organisation. He found that the constitution and functions of PCCs do not support the view that they should be characterised as core public authorities. Lord Nicholls said that the essential role of a PCC is to provide a formal means, prescribed by the Church of England, whereby ex officio and elected members of the local church promote the mission of the Church and discharge financial responsibilities in respect of their own parish church; he viewed these as acts of self-governance and PCCs as far removed from the type of body whose acts engage the responsibility of the state under the European Convention. As indicated, he further noted that if PCCs could be characterised as core public authorities that would mean that they would not be capable of being victims within the meaning of the HRA and, *inter alia*, would not be able to take advantage of s 13, which gives express mention to the exercise by religious organisations of the Art 9 right of freedom of thought, conscience and religion.[274] Lord Hope noted that the Strasbourg jurisprudence supports this approach.[275] He also considered that the case law on judicial review might not provide much assistance as to functions of a public nature

---

274 See paras 13–15.
275 At para 62. *Holy Monasteries v Greece* (1995) 20 EHRR 1 and *Hautanemi v Sweden* (1996) 22 EHRR CD 156.

because the cases were not decided for the purposes of identifying the liability of the state in international law.[276]

The question of categorising core public bodies has not proved unduly problematic[277] since, as Lord Nicholls stated, such bodies are normally self-evidently governmental. But the tests for determining 'hybrid' public authority status are still less than clear. A clear definition of a 'public' function has proved elusive.[278] Earlier case law appeared to focus more on the extent to which a body was enmeshed with a self-evidentially governmental body. Although the leading Supreme Court case has moved away from this approach, focusing more on an analysis of the functions of a public body, its narrow focus on the nature of a public function arguably does not accord with the spirit of the Convention or with the government's intention in deciding on the wording of s 6.

The focus of earlier case law is illustrated by *Poplar Housing & Regeneration Community Association Ltd v Donoghue*[279] and *R (on the application of Heather) v Leonard Cheshire Foundation.*[280] In *Poplar Housing*, a local authority, Tower Hamlets, was under a statutory duty under s 188 of the Housing Act 1996 to provide or secure the provision of housing to certain homeless people. Donoghue was provided with interim accommodation in council property – a flat – by Tower Hamlets pending the council's decision in relation to her application as a homeless person under the Housing Act. The local council set up a housing association, Poplar Housing and Regeneration Community Association Ltd, as a registered social landlord, with the specific purpose of receiving its housing stock; it then transferred a lot of its property, including the applicant's flat, to the association. By the transfer, the applicant's tenancy became an assured shorthold tenancy. Poplar Housing began possession proceedings; Donoghue claimed that this would violate her right to a home under Art 8 ECHR and that Poplar Housing was bound under s 6 HRA to respect this right because it was a public authority under the Act. Poplar claimed, *inter alia*, that it was not a standard public authority, and the Court of Appeal accepted this. It further claimed that it was not a body performing a function of a public nature. On this point, Lord Woolf said:

> What can make an act, which would otherwise be private, public, is a feature or a combination of features which impose a public character or stamp on the act. Statutory authority for what is done can at least help to mark the act as being public; so can the extent of control over the function exercised by another body which is a public authority. The more closely the acts that could be of a private nature are enmeshed in the activities of a public body, the more likely they are to be public. However, the fact that the acts are supervised by a public regulatory body does

276 *Ibid*, para 52.
277 See further for early comment Oliver, D, 'The Frontiers of the State: Public Authorities and Public Functions under the Human Rights Act', [2000] PL 476; Clayton and Tomlinson, *The Law of Human Rights*, 1st edn, 2000, para 5.08.
278 See Oliver, D, 'Functions of a public nature under the Human Rights Act' [2004] PL 329.
279 [2002] QB 48; [2001] EWCA Civ 595.
280 [2002] 2 All ER 936; [2002] EWCA Civ 366. For discussion see Sachdeva, V [2002] JR Law 249. See for the first instance decision: [2001] EWHC Admin 429 [2001] ACD 75. For discussion see Johnston [2001] JR 250. See also Carss-Frisk QC, M, 'Public Authorities: The Developing Definition' [2002] EHRLR 319.

not necessarily indicate that they are of a public nature. This is analogous to the position in judicial review, where a regulatory body may be deemed public but the activities of the body which is regulated may be categorised private.[281]

The Court concluded that the role of the housing association was so closely intertwined with that of the council that it was to be considered as discharging a public function in relation to the management of the social housing it had taken over from Tower Hamlets: 'in providing accommodation for the defendant and then seeking possession, the association's role was *so closely assimilated* to that of the authority that it was acting as a public authority'.[282] On the other hand, the Court considered that the raising of finance by Poplar was probably a private function. Also, the fact of providing accommodation for rent was not viewed 'without more, a public function',[283] even where the accommodation being provided had been previously the responsibility of a local authority.

In *R (on the application of Heather) v Leonard Cheshire Foundation*, the Foundation (hereafter LCF) was a large charitable trust providing residential care homes for those with disabilities. The claimants, who had been placed in the home run by LCF by social services under s 26 National Assistance Act 1948, were long-stay residents. Their fees were partly paid from their benefits and partly by the local authority. The claimants had been promised that it would be their home for life. LCF decided to close the home, and the claimants sought to challenge this decision by way of judicial review as a breach of their rights under Art 8.

Lord Woolf said:[284]

(i) It is not in issue that it is possible for LCF to perform some public functions and some private functions. In this case it is contended that this was what has been happening in regard to those residents who are privately funded and those residents who are publicly funded. But in this case except for the resources needed to fund the residents of the different occupants of [the home], there is no material distinction between the nature of the services LCF has provided for residents funded by a local authority and those provided to residents funded privately. While the degree of public funding of the activities of an otherwise private body is certainly relevant as to the nature of the functions performed, by itself it is not determinative of whether the functions are public or private.[285] . . . (ii) There is no other evidence of there being a public flavour to the functions of LCF or LCF itself. LCF is not standing in the shoes of the local authorities. Section 26 of the [National Assistance Act 1948] provides statutory authority for the actions of the local authorities but it provides LCF with no powers. LCF is not exercising statutory powers in performing functions for the appellants. (iii) In truth, all that [counsel on behalf of the

281 *Ibid*, at p 69.
282 *Ibid*, at p 70.
283 *Ibid*, at p 69.
284 At para 35.
285 He relied on the case of *R v HM Treasury ex parte Cambridge University* [2000] 1 WLR 2514 (ECJ) at pp 2523 and 2534–35, argued as relevant on behalf of LCF, as an interesting illustration in relation to European Union legislation in different terms to s 6.

applicants] can rely upon is the fact that if LCF is not performing a public function the appellants would not be able to rely upon art 8 as against LCF. However, this is a circular argument. If LCF was performing a public function, that would mean that the appellants could rely in relation to that function on art 8, but, if the situation is otherwise, art 8 cannot change the appropriate classification of the function. On the approach adopted in *Donoghue*, it can be said that LCF is clearly not performing any public function.

A clear difference in these cases was as to the extent to which the function, carried out under statutory authority, was subject to the control by another body, which was a public authority. If there were acts that could be of a private nature – providing accommodation for rent – that were enmeshed in the activities of a public body that would also aid in finding that the function was public, as would the closeness of the relationship with the public body, and that a transfer of responsibilities between the public and private sectors had occurred. The relationship between Tower Hamlets and Poplar Housing was close: five members of Tower Hamlets were on the board of Poplar and it was subject to the guidance of the council as to the manner in which it acted towards its tenants. In *Leonard Cheshire*, the court held that the local authority was trying to divest itself of its obligations under Art 8 by contracting out its obligations under the National Assistance Act 1948. The court identified three decisive factors which led it to the conclusion that LCF's functions were not public. The home was publicly funded, but there was no other evidence of a 'public flavour' to the activities of LCF. It was not, it was found, standing in the shoes of the local authority. It was noted that the nature of the service provided by LCF did not differ between those residents of the home who were publicly funded and those who were privately funded. The fact that the claimants would lose the protection of Art 8 against LCF if it was not viewed as performing a public function was viewed as a circular argument. It was observed that the need to secure the protection of Art 8 could not in itself change the classification of a function.

The purpose behind s 6 was obviously to impose Convention obligations on those carrying out public functions and to disallow the avoidance of those obligations simply because functions had been transferred from the public to the private sector. But in making 'public function' the central criterion under the HRA, the intention was to single out only those functions that should be accounted public – and which therefore should be discharged in a Convention-compliant fashion. So the function in question, *not* the nature of institution discharging it, should be the crucial factor. This is particularly problematic as concerns the outcome in *Leonard Cheshire*. The function in question – the provision of accommodation to a particularly vulnerable group in society – had been placed on a statutory basis in order to address a social need. The local authority's function in addressing that need was taken over by LCF in the sense that persons in the home in the position of the claimants were there due to the discharge by the local authority of its statutory obligations. In that sense LCF *was* standing in the shoes of the local authority. The fact that, in such circumstances, depending on timing in relation to the HRA, residents could protect their rights through a contract with the public body misses the point of s 6 – it should not be necessary to impose contractual obligations on a body due to its institutional status to adhere to the Convention since under s 6 those obligations should be imposed due to the nature of the function in question.

As McDermont observes, this decision 'reject[ed] by implication any "public interest" arguments'.[286]

Dawn Oliver is also critical of the extent to which these decisions concentrate on institutional as opposed to functional factors – in particular the closeness of the relationship between the private and the public body. She argues:

> The problem here is that not all of the considerations and criteria identified by Lord Woolf relate to the nature of the functions or acts in question, which is what s 6 is about, but are institutional (the institutional arrangements of the housing association) and relational (the relationship of the local authority with the housing association and the prior relationship between the local authority and the tenant).[287]

There has now been a decisive move towards a focus on more functional as opposed to institutional factors. Public interest factors were found to be relevant, for example, in the decision of the House of Lords in *Aston Cantlow v Wallbank*.[288] Having decided that a PCC was not a core public authority, as discussed above, the question still remained whether the parish council was to be viewed as a functional public authority acting in a public function. Lord Nicholls said on the general test for 'public authority' under the HRA:

> What, then, is the touchstone to be used in deciding whether a function is public [for the purpose of s 6(3)]? Clearly there is no single test of universal application. There cannot be, given the diverse nature of governmental functions and the variety of means by which these functions are discharged today. Factors to be taken into account include the extent to which in carrying out the relevant function the body is publicly funded, or is exercising statutory powers, or is taking the place of central government or local authorities, or is providing a public service.[289]

In considering the 'public' nature of functions he took account, as noted above, of factors such as 'the possession of special powers, democratic accountability, public funding in whole or in part, an obligation to act only in the public interest, and a statutory constitution'.[290]

The majority of the House of Lords found that the PCC was a functional authority; but went on to decide that the PCC was not carrying out a public function in this particular instance. Lord Hope found that:

> [I]t may be said that, as the church is a historic building which is open to the public, it is in the public interest that these repairs should be carried out. [But] the nature of the act is to be found in the nature of the obligation which the PCC is seeking to enforce. It is seeking to enforce a civil debt. The function which it is

---

286 McDermont, M, 'The Elusive Nature of the 'Public Function': *Poplar Housing and Regeneration Community Association Ltd v Donoghue*' (2003) 66(1) MLR 113, at 121.

287 Oliver, D, 'Functions of a Public Nature under the Human Rights Act [2004] PL, pp 329–51.

288 [2004] 1 AC 546 [2003] 3 WLR 283.

289 *Ibid*, at para 12.

290 *Ibid*, at para 8.

performing has nothing to do with the responsibilities which are owed to the public by the state.[291]

The Court of Appeal had seen the liability as a tax and therefore as pertaining to a public function because it was enforced on people who were not necessarily church members and, using circular reasoning, because it was imposed by a public authority. The House of Lords saw it as a civil liability that arose from occupation of a particular type of land. It was stressed in particular that the liability was taken on with notice – and therefore voluntarily – when purchasing the land. This, it was found, distinguished it from a tax,[292] which would apply generally.

This move was confirmed in the current leading authority on the definition of a public authority, the House of Lord's decision *YL v Birmingham City Council*.[293] In *YL* the court was concerned only with the preliminary issue whether the private care home, Southern Cross, when accommodating the claimant under arrangements made with the council under s 21 of the National Assistance Act 1948, was exercising a public function for the purposes of s 6(3)(b). The House of Lords divided, with three concluding that the care home was not a public authority and two concluding that it was.

The majority focused on the purpose of the Human Rights Act 1998 being to 'bring rights home' by ensuring individuals whose rights had been breached could receive a remedy for that breach in UK courts, without having to go to Strasbourg. There was a need, therefore, for the definition of a body to reflect potential liability of a public body under the ECHR, leading to the conclusion that a public authority was a body performing a governmental function. For Lord Mance, governmental functions are functions normally undertaken for the public interest, where the body performing this function has special powers, democratic accountability, public funding, either in whole or in part, for the activity, an obligation to act in the public interest and a statutory constitution.[294]

When making this assessment, it was not relevant to focus on whether a public authority was paying for the service or not – the requirement of being 'publicly funded' depended on whether the public authority was subsidizing the function.[295] Nor was it relevant to determine whether there were other common law or statutory means of protecting the vulnerable,[296] whether the body was subject to judicial review,[297] nor was it sufficient to show merely that the body was providing a service that was regulated or that was protecting the vulnerable,[298] or that body was providing a function that the core public authority was under an obligation to provide. Instead courts needed to look further

---

291 *Ibid*, at para 64.
292 *Ibid*, at para 66, *per* Lord Hobhouse.
293 [2007] UKHL 27; [2008] 1 AC 95.
294 *Ibid*, [102]–[103] (Lord Mance).
295 *Ibid*, [47] (Lord Scott) and [142] (Lord Neuberger).
296 *Ibid*, [79] (Lord Mance).
297 *Ibid*, [87] (Lord Mance).
298 *Ibid*, [135](Lord Neuberger).

to ask why the body was providing this function[299] and recognise that not all of the functions a public authority was under an obligation to provide were public functions.[300]

The majority concluded that, by providing accommodation, Southern Cross was acting as a commercial business. It was carrying out its activities for profit, through contracts governed by private law, with no public funding and no special powers, free to accept and reject any client who wishes to purchase its services and charge its fees on a commercial basis.[301] In addition, s 21 required the local authority to arrange accommodation for the elderly. The care home was providing this accommodation, the public authority having fulfilled its function through arranging for accommodation to be provided by the private care home.[302] It was therefore not carrying out a governmental function and therefore was not a public authority.

The minority preferred a much broader interpretation of the purpose of the Human Rights Act 1998, leading to a broader interpretation of a public function focusing on the context of the 1948 Act as a whole. The Human Rights Act was designed to 'bring rights home' by providing for a domestic protection of rights in line with Convention rights. [303] Lord Bingham and Lady Hale focused on how the care home was not just providing accommodation, but were providing accommodation for the vulnerable, this duty being imposed on public authorities by the 1948 Act as part of the development of the welfare state.[304] Both argued that the provision of care for vulnerable members of society was a clear public function, with Lady Hale focusing on the underlying rationale that 'a task for which the public, in the form of the state, have assumed responsibility, at public expense if need be, and in the public interest'[305] is a public function; '[t]he contrast is between what is "public" in the sense of being done for or on behalf of the people as a whole and what is "private" in the sense of being done for one's own purposes'.[306] In providing care for the elderly, Southern Cross were stepping into the shoes of a public authority and were performing a public function.

Lord Bingham listed six non-exhaustive factors that were relevant to whether a body was performing a public function or not, all of which were to be interpreted in their contextual setting: (i) the nature of the function; (ii) the role and responsibility of the state towards the provision of this function; (iii) the nature and extent of any statutory power relating to this duty; (iv) the extent to which the state supervises or regulates the activity in question; (v) whether the state is willing to pay for the performance of this function; and (vi) the degree of risk of the infringement of Convention rights by the performance of this function.[307] Lady Hale focused on whether the state had assumed responsibility for the performance of this task; whether it was in the public interest for this function to be performed, whether there was the provision of public funding for this service, whether it involved the coercive power of the state and the connection between

299 *Ibid*, [31] (Lord Mance).
300 *Ibid*, [106] (Lord Neuberger).
301 *Ibid*, [26]–[32] (Lord Scott) and [116] (Lord Mance).
302 *Ibid*, [115] (Lord Mance), and [141] (Neuberger).
303 *Ibid*, [4](Lord Bingham) and [54]–[55] (Lady Hale).
304 *Ibid*, [14]–[19] (Bingham) and [49]–[53] (Lady Hale).
305 *Ibid*, [65].
306 *Ibid*, [62].
307 *Ibid*, [5]–[11] (Lord Bingham).

the provision of the service and the real risk that Convention rights may be harmed by the provision of the service unless steps are taken to protect the Convention right.[308]

The House of Lords reached this conclusion in the face of a series of reports from the Joint Committee on Human Rights criticising both the institutional as opposed to functional focus of the courts in addition to the overly narrow definition of a public authority, citing in particular the need for care homes to be a public authority for the purposes of s 6(3)(b).[309] The Health and Social Care Act 2008 effectively reversed the impact of the judgment in *YL*, with s 145 of the Act providing that those who 'provides accommodation, together with nursing or personal care, in a care home for an individual' where this provision was undertaken on behalf of a public body to fulfil its statutory requirements is a public authority for the purposes of the Human Rights Act. Nevertheless, *YL* remains the leading authority on the approach to be taken to the definition of a public authority with Elias LJ summarising its approach as follows in the Court of Appeal decision of *Weaver v London Quadrant Housing Trust*: (i) that 'the purpose of section 6 is to identify those bodies which are carrying out functions which will engage the responsibility of the United Kingdom before the European Court of Human Rights'; (ii) 'a public body is one whose nature is, in a broad sense, governmental'; and (iii) the courts should adopt a 'factor-based approach', looking at 'all the features or facts which may cast light on whether the particular function under consideration is a public function or not, and weigh them in the round'.[310]

Critiquing the tests for 'public function'

Dawn Oliver has pointed out that a corollary of drawing as many bodies as possible into the category of standard public authorities is that they cannot also be 'victims' and therefore cannot assert rights against other public authorities, possibly resulting, if the 'state pigeon-hole becomes too full' in 'the imposition by the body politic of regulations and checks that could inhibit the development of institutions of civil society'.[311] But this point does not apply to functional public authorities, and there are a number of arguments in favour of drawing bodies within that category.

Earlier editions of this book criticised the predominantly institutional as opposed to functional approach to the definition of a public authority, advocating in particular the need to take a broad approach to the definition of a public authority, as preferred by the minority in *YL*. The broad approach is more in line with the intention underlying the HRA[312] and would be consonant with the general approach taken to human rights

---

308 *Ibid*, [65]–[71].
309 Joint Committee on Human Rights, 'The Meaning of Public Authority under the Human Rights Act' (Seventh Report of Session 2003–4) HL paper 39; HC 382 and 'The Meaning of a Public Authority under the Human Rights Act' (Ninth Report of Session 2006–7) HL paper 77; HC 410.
310 *R (Weaver) v London and Quadrant Housing Trust* [2009] EWCA Civ 587; [2009] 4 All ER 865, [35].
311 D. Oliver 'The frontiers of the State: public authorities and public functions under the HRA' [2000] Autumn PL 476, p 477.
312 The Lord Chancellor said at Second Reading of the Bill in the House of Lords: 'We . . . decided that we should apply the Bill to a wide rather than a narrow range of public authorities so as to provide as much protection as possible for those who claim that their rights have been infringed': HL Official Report cols 1231–32, 3 November 1997.

instruments. It would also mean that the contracting out of public services to the private sector would not result in a failure of that sector to observe Convention standards in respect of such services. This is a very significant matter due to the diminution of the public sector that has occurred over the last 20 years and is still occurring. The majority decision in *YL* has been subjected to intensive criticism: its focus on a narrow inter-pretation of a governmental function undermines the ability of the HRA to facilitate a human rights culture in the UK;[313] undermines the focus on function through examining the nature of the institution providing the service and the reason for providing this ser-vice;[314] creates inequalities between those whose care is provided by a public authority and those living in areas where public authorities have contracted out the provision of care to private bodies[315] placing the latter in a situation where they have to resort to contractual rights, which may not always provide effective protection.[316] Although the legislative reversal reduces the specific impact of the *YL* decision as regards the provision of care in care homes, there are others – e.g., children – who do not benefit from this provision. Although recognising that there could be knock-on consequences of extending the definition of a public authority, e.g., the imposition of unexpected Convention rights, these concerns are better dealt with by treating bodies performing public functions as public authorities for the purpose of s 6(3)(b), whilst recognis-ing that these private bodies also have Convention rights when assessing the extent to which their actions have breached human rights.[317] Nor is it true that the adoption of a broad approach may lead to the judiciary relying too greatly on their own assessment of whether a function should be a public function – both Lord Bingham and Lady Hale in *YL* clearly referred to the context of the 1948 Act and the extent to which the state had assumed responsibility for the performance of a particular function.

Categorising specific bodies

This book is centrally concerned with the relationship between the citizen and the state, and so most of the bodies covered by it are standard public authorities, such as the police. But some bodies are in a slightly more uncertain position.[318] A number of regu-lators or watchdog bodies are considered in this book, including, the Commission for Equality and Human Rights (CEHR)[319] and Ofcom, the broadcast media regulator. As Chapter 7 finds, Ofcom is clearly a public authority for the purposes of the HRA. All these regulators are set up under statute and have been given coercive powers and duties

---

313 Palmer, S, 'Public Functions and Private Services: A gap in Human Rights Protection' (2008) ICON 585.

314 Palmer, S, 'Public, Private and the Human Rights Act 1998: An Ideological Divide' (2007) 66 CLJ 559.

315 *Ibid.*

316 Choudry, S, 'Children in "care" after *YL* – the ineffectiveness of contract as a means of protecting the vulnerable' [2013] Public Law 519.

317 See Williams, A, 'A Fresh Perspective on hybrid public authorities under the Human Rights Act 1998: private contractors, rights-stripping and "Chameleonic" horizontal effect' [2011] Public Law 139.

318 It is possible that many – although not all – of those bodies that are listed in Sched 1 to the Freedom of Information Act 2000, as public authorities (see Chapter 8, pp 530–32) can probably be assumed to be public authorities for HRA purposes. But at present that list can only be viewed as a starting-point.

319 See Chapter 5, p 272.

that are clearly governmental in nature. They are probably standard public authorities since they are statutory government regulators/administrative bodies. In any event they are functional public bodies since in their regulatory functions they are clearly bound by the Convention due to s 6(3)(b). As Chapters 10 and 7 argue, the regulators of the press and the film industry, the Independent Press Standards Organisation,[320] the British Board of Film Classification (BBFC) and the Video Appeals Committee are probably functional public bodies.[321] These bodies are not set up under statute but they have a footing in statutory provisions, as the relevant chapters point out. The BBFC's functions are recognised, for example, in the Video Recordings Act 1984, as amended.

As Chapters 7 and 10 note, the private media bodies, including newspaper companies and broadcasters, such as ITV, Channel 5 and Sky, are clearly not public authorities since they have no public functions. As Chapters 10 and 7 point out, the BBC, and possibly Channel 4, may be considered to be functional public authorities.[322] If so, they are bound to adhere to the Convention rights in their public functions, but not their private ones. The BBC is a 'state broadcaster'; it was created under a Royal Charter – in other words, by a direct act of government. It is also fully funded through state funds – the licence fee. As Chapter 7 notes, as a 'public service' broadcaster it has various duties relating to the contents of its programmes that are designed to ensure that it serves the public interest.[323]

As Chapter 10 will discuss, the BBC is probably not a standard public authority; if it was so deemed it could not also be a victim, a definition that includes: 'any person, non-governmental organisation or group of individuals' or a 'non-governmental organisation' within the terms of Art 34 ECHR.[324] As discussed below, those terms are also used to determine who can be a 'victim' for the purposes of s 7(1)(a) HRA.[325] Clearly, it would be strange if the BBC was unable to resist governmental attempts to curb its freedom of expression on the ground that it is a standard public authority. So, although the point has not finally been settled, that is probably the better view. Channel 4 is set up under statute,[326] but it is funded in the same way as the private broadcasters, through the normal commercial means. However, it receives free spectrum in return for fulfilling its statutory public service obligations. As Chapter 7 notes, it has a particular remit in relation to broadcasting innovative, diverse, creative or educational programmes.[327]

In this book the question whether either body has public functions arises in two areas, discussed in Chapters 7 and 10. First, it is relevant in the kind of context that arose in the *Pro-Life Alliance*[328] case, which is discussed in full in Chapter 7.[329] As

---

320 As Chapter 10 notes, this point appears to have been impliedly accepted in *R (on the application of Ford) v Press Complaints Commission* [2002] EMLR 5; see at p 712.
321 See Chapter 7, p 455.
322 See Chapter 7, pp 447–48 and Chapter 10, pp 712–14.
323 See Chapter 7, at pp 438, 440.
324 In *BBC Scotland v UK*, no 34324/96 (1997) (discussed Chapter 6, pp 303–04); *BBC v UK*, no 25798/94 (1996). In both instances, the cases were found to be inadmissible on other grounds; therefore it was not found necessary to decide the point.
325 See *Leonard Cheshire Foundation* [2002] 2 All ER 936 on this point.
326 By the Broadcasting Act 1990.
327 See s 265(3) of the 2003 Act. See further p 439.
328 [2002] 2 All ER 756 CA; [2004] 1 AC 185, HL.
329 See p 451 *et seq.*

that discussion will make clear, the BBC in that instance acted in its regulatory role; it refused to broadcast a video in the form that Pro-Life had submitted it (Pro-Life's party election broadcast) since it considered that the video offended against good taste and decency. In that instance Art 10 was pleaded directly against the BBC on judicial review of the decision; the House of Lords did not state explicitly that the BBC was acting in its public function when it acted as a regulator, but clearly that was implicit in the decision.

The other situation in which functional public authority status could be of some pertinence would arise where it was alleged that either of these broadcasters had breached the right of privacy of a person in a broadcast, for example by showing him or her engaged in some private activity.[330] This issue is no longer of great significance since, as Chapter 10 points out, there is now quite a comprehensive privacy law in this country, albeit arising from a range of sources. So there would not be many situations in which one of the laws in question – especially the new tort of misuse of private information – would not apply where Art 8 would. Assuming that the new tort would apply, there would probably be no advantage to a litigant to argue as an alternative possibility that, for example, Channel 4 was acting in its public function when it breached the claimant's privacy, since the parameters of Arts 8 and 10 would determine the outcome in any event. The litigant would obviously prefer to pursue the tort measure of damages rather than the Strasbourg measure.[331] It is conceivable, however, that the broadcaster might have harassed a person in a manner not covered by either the new tort or by the Protection from Harassment Act 1997. In that instance it would be worth trying to demonstrate that Channel 4 was a functional public authority and acting in a public function at the time in question.

Phillipson argues that the BBC is probably a functional public authority:

> . . . insofar as institutional factors are still taken into account . . . the fact that the BBC is a creature of the state, rather than having a private status, will increase the chances of its being found to have some public functions, as will its public funding. Channel 4, a private and commercial broadcaster, is much less likely, under these criteria, to be found to have such functions. Although it was created by statute, it is entirely privately funded.

Having noted that it is implicit in *Pro-Life* that the BBC was carrying out a public function in deciding not to broadcast the video, Phillipson goes on to find:

> . . . the least unsatisfactory resolution is to accept the apparent anomaly [of differentiating in this respect between broadcasters] and hold that whenever the BBC decides to broadcast a programme, it is performing a public function, whilst the commercial broadcasters are not . . . Further, it could be argued that since the BBC is a state broadcaster, and benefits from full public funding, it is fair for it to accept obligations that lie upon other organs of the state.[332]

---

330 See Chapter 10, at pp 712–14, 726–28.
331 See pp 207–11.
332 See Fenwick and Phillipson, *Media Freedom under the HRA*, 2006, pp 121–22.

This author agrees, but considers for the reasons given that there are very few situations in which anything would turn on this issue. At the points in this book at which this question does arise, it will be considered further.

Invoking the Convention rights against public authorities

This is a detailed and complex area; extended discussion of the procedural issues involved would not be appropriate in a book of this nature; full discussion is available in Clayton and Tomlinson, *The Law of Human Rights*.[333]

'Victims'

Section 7(1)(a) HRA allows a person who claims that a public authority has acted or proposes to act in breach of a Convention right to bring proceedings against the public authority. Section 7(1)(b) allows a person to rely on the Convention in any legal proceedings against a public authority, including in judicial review proceedings. But in either case, the person relying on the Convention must be (or would be) a 'victim' of the unlawful act. Section 7(7) provides: 'a person is a victim of an unlawful act only if he would be a victim for the purposes of Art 34 of the Convention if proceedings were brought in the European Court of Human Rights in respect of that act'. It was accepted in Parliament that the Strasbourg interpretation of 'victim' would be used, rather than the wider test for standing which, under the UK judicial review doctrine, allows pressure groups to bring actions so long as they satisfy the 'sufficient interest' test.[334] The UK group Liberty had argued for adoption of the latter as the test, since it is broader. But the idea behind s 7(5) is that the HRA should create symmetry with the protection for human rights provided by Strasbourg.[335] In order to obviate the possibility of circumvention of the victim test by use of judicial review outside the HRA but raising Convention points, s 7(3) provides: 'if the proceedings are brought on an application for judicial review, the applicant is taken to have sufficient interest in relation to the unlawful act only if he or she is a victim'.

The Strasbourg test was discussed further in Chapter 3.[336] It is now contained in Art 34 (formerly 25): a person (or group or non-governmental organisation) may not bring an application unless he or she has been personally affected by the alleged violation.[337] This may include those directly affected by a general prohibition, even if it could be the case that their individual Convention rights would not be breached by this general prohibition.[338] As Miles points out, it cannot be said that the concept of 'victim' has been interpreted consistently at Strasbourg, although it is clear that those indirectly affected

---

333 Clayton, R and Tomlinson, H, *The Law of Human Rights*, 2nd edn, 2009, OUP.
334 See the ruling of Rose LJ in *Secretary of State for Foreign Affairs ex p World Development Movement* [1995] 1 All ER 611, pp 618–20.
335 See HC Official Report col 1083, 24 June 1998.
336 For extensive discussion, see Clayton and Tomlinson, *op cit*, fn 1, pp 1484–98.
337 *X v Austria* No 7045/75, 7 DR 87 (1976); *Knudsen v Norway* No 11045/84, 42 DR 247 (1985).
338 See *Hirst v UK (2)* (2005) EHRR 849, where the majority concluded that Hirst was a victim as regards the general prohibition on prisoner voting, even though it was accepted that, as a murderer serving a life sentence, his Convention right to vote had not been breached. This approached was accepted by the Supreme Court in *R (Chester) v Secretary of State for Justice* [2013] UKSC 63; [2014] AC 271.

may be covered.[339] There will, therefore, be substantial room for domestic litigation on this issue. But s 7(3) means that pressure groups cannot in general bring actions claiming breach of Convention rights in reliance on s 7(1)(a), although such groups are able to challenge public bodies by way of judicial review, on the test of 'sufficient interest'.[340] They can use the s 7(1)(a) route if they can demonstrate that although part of a pressure group, they have been directly affected by the violation or intended violation of the right in question.[341]

Thus, although the definition of the bodies covered under s 6 is potentially wide and brings quite a large number of them within its scope, the application of the Convention by using the s 7(1)(a) route is narrowed by adopting quite a limited definition of a 'victim'. But for s 7(3), a non-victim body – normally a pressure group – could challenge executive action relying on judicial review and raising Convention points.[342] Had s 7(3) not been included, a pressure group might have been able to bring an action relying on the wider judicial review standing provisions, but then obtained the stricter scrutiny available when it is argued that a public authority has breached s 6.

Due to s 7(3) non-victim groups with sufficient interest must rely on judicial review only. Thus in a very few instances a dual system of judicial review arises, with more generous standing rules but weaker scrutiny, outside the HRA, while the reverse applies under s 7(1).[343] A court, although bound by s 6, confronted by a Convention issue in such an application, would have to apply traditional review principles only;[344] the Strasbourg proportionality doctrine would not appear to be applicable. There would be very few instances, however, in which this limitation would be of significance since members of a pressure group might also be able to show that they were victims, and moreover public interest groups can support victims, acting as third party intervenors in cases brought under s 7.[345] But this limitation does apply to the Commission for Equality and Human Rights, as discussed below.[346]

When administrative action is purportedly taken under statutory powers, non-victim groups with sufficient interest who wish to challenge it by way of judicial review can rely on s 3 and argue that the action is ultra vires on the basis that the statute does not give powers to the executive to act incompatibly with the Convention rights, unless the statute is irretrievably incompatible with them. This is possible because s 3, as indicated

---

339 Miles, 'Standing under the Human Rights Act: theories of rights enforcement and the nature of public law adjudication' (2000) 59(1) CLJ 133–67, p 137. She further points out that while pressure groups cannot bring actions in their own name, there are other public interest enforcement mechanisms at Strasbourg including the possibility, exceptionally, of third party intervention which can be used to seek to ensure that the rights are secured.

340 It may be noted that s 11 HRA would bar the way to any narrowing of those rules.

341 See Cane [1995] PL 276.

342 Section 11 provides: 'A person's reliance on a Convention right does not restrict . . . (b) his right to make any claim or bring any proceedings which he could make or bring apart from ss 7–9.'

343 See Steyn, K and Wolfe, D, 'Judicial review and the Human Rights Act: some practical considerations' (1999) EHRLR 614.

344 As stated *obiter* in *Alconbury* [2001] 2 All ER 929; (2001) NLJ 135, para 53.

345 See Hannett [2003] PL 128. There is no express right on intervention under the HRA, but it has been allowed by the House of Lords and Court of Appeal. See, e.g., *Sepet v Secretary of State for the Home Dept* [2003] UKHL 15.

346 See pp 249–51.

above, applies to all statutes and is not limited by the s 7(7) test regarding victims. This is a significant matter since it broadens the reach of the Convention rights, possibly in an unintended fashion.[347] If freedom of expression was in issue, in an instance similar to those of *Brind*[348] or *Simms*,[349] s 12, providing special protection for freedom of expression would apply, as well as s 3. In respect of non-statutory actions or decisions s 12 alone would apply if freedom of expression was in issue. If so, the fact that the applicant was a non-victim would be irrelevant.

Relying on s 7(1)

Section 7(1) provides: 'A person who claims that a public authority has acted or proposes to act in a way which is made unlawful by s 6(1) may (a) bring proceedings against the authority under this Act in the appropriate court or tribunal . . . or (b) rely on the Convention right or rights concerned in any legal proceedings . . .'. Section 7(1)(b) allows for Convention points to be raised once an action has begun under an existing cause of action, where the other party is a public authority. Under s 7(1)(b), there are a number of possible instances in which a victim can raise Convention arguments in proceedings in which a public authority is involved. In the contexts covered by this book, the Convention is frequently invoked in criminal proceedings. Questions of exclusion of evidence or abuse of process could be raised in relation to breaches of Convention rights, and these possibilities are pursued in Chapter 14.

The Convention guarantees can also afford a defence in criminal proceedings. They can also be used to afford a defence in common law civil proceedings where the plaintiff is a public authority. Other existing tort actions, such as false imprisonment, which are coterminous with Convention rights (in that instance, Art 5) can be brought against public authorities under s 7(1)(b) with a view to expanding the scope of the action by reference to the right.[350] The possibilities presented by the use of tort actions are discussed at various points in this book, but most extensively in Chapter 14.[351] A litigant would be best advised to rely on an existing action, but seek to persuade the court as a public authority, if necessary, that regard should be had to the Convention principles in determining its scope.

Section 7(1)(a) does not demand reliance on an existing cause of action or claim. It allows a victim of a breach or threatened breach of a Convention right to bring an action against a standard public authority or a functional body acting in its public capacity.[352] Proceedings can be brought in the High Court for breach of statutory duty – the duty under s 6. Under s 7(9), the term 'rules' in s 7(2) means: 'in relation to proceedings in a court

---

347 See further on this point Elliott, M, 'The HRA and the standard of substantive review' (2001) 60 CLJ 301.

348 *R v Secretary of State for the Home Dept ex p Brind* [1991] 1 AC 696.

349 *R v Secretary of State for the Home Department ex p Simms* [1999] 3 WLR 328.

350 Such actions are, of course, also available against purely private bodies; see discussion below of horizontal effects and Chapter 10, pp 728–30. For early comment on this matter see Phillipson, G, 'The Human Rights Act and the common law' [1999] 62 MLR 824, esp pp 834–40. See also Bamforth, N, 'The true 'horizontal effect' of the HRA' (2001) 117 LQR 34.

351 See pp 1006–09.

352 The term 'public authority' will be used to encompass both types of body for the purposes of the rest of the discussion.

or tribunal outside Scotland rules made by the Lord Chancellor or the Secretary of State for the purpose of this section or rules of court . . .'. Claims go to the appropriate court or the tribunal dealing with claims closest in nature to the particular situation in which it is alleged that Convention rights were breached. Claims, relying on Convention rights, not existing causes of action or defences, might take the form of private law claims or counterclaims, or defences in civil or criminal law proceedings. A number of post-HRA statutes have designated certain fora as 'appropriate tribunals'. The most significant of these is the tribunal set up by s 65(2) of the Regulation of Investigatory Powers Act 2000.[353]

The possibility of creating what has been termed a 'constitutional tort' of breach of Convention rights was left open by the HRA and by the Lord Chancellor in parliamentary debate.[354] Section 7(1)(a) is able to encourage the growth of new tort actions. Litigation concerning the private functions of standard public authorities, in relation to matters not tortious under existing tort law, could occur under s 7(1)(a), and could be relevant in, for example, the context of discrimination.[355] In an important early article, Dawn Oliver argues that the creation of such new areas of tortious liability operating against public authorities can also tend to lend an impetus to the creation of tortious liability against private bodies, arising out of existing tort actions.[356] As indicated below and considered fully in Chapter 10, a right to privacy has already arisen from the doctrine of confidence. However, the House of Lords is not receptive to the argument that new causes of action against public authorities should be created outwith the s 7(1)(a) action. In *Watkins (Respondent) v Home Office (Appellants)*[357] Lord Rodger held: 'In general, at least, where the matter is not already covered by the common law but falls within the scope of a Convention right, a claimant can be expected to invoke his remedy under the Human Rights Act rather than to seek to fashion a new common law right.' In finding this, he relied on *Wainwright v Home Office*.[358]

Where actions are brought as judicial review applications, they are brought in the High Court and are subject to the Civil Procedure Rules. Actions can also be brought in the county court where a claim for damages is made.[359] The majority of actions brought under s 6 via s 7(1)(a) against public authorities contemplated in this book raise purely public law issues.

Retrospectivity

Under s 22(4)(b): 'para (b) [of s 7(1)] applies to proceedings brought by or at the instigation of a public authority whenever the act in question took place; but otherwise that sub-section does not apply to an act taking place before the coming into force of that section'. Where the Convention is used as a 'shield' against public authorities, therefore, pre-commencement action is covered if, following *R v Lambert*,[360] the proceedings

---

353 See Chapter 11, pp 814 *et seq.*
354 HL Deb Vol 585 cols 853–56, 24 November 1997.
355 See Chapter 5, pp 269–72.
356 'The HRA and public law/private law divides' (2000) 4 EHRLR 343.
357 [2006] UKHL 17.
358 [2004] 2 AC 406, 423, para 33, *per* Lord Hoffmann.
359 HRA 1998: Rules CP5/00, March 2000, para 12.
360 [2001] 3 All ER 577.

are brought 'by or at the instigation of a public authority'. Thus, before the Act came fully into force, public authorities were seeking to abide by it in bringing proceedings, including prosecutions, against citizens. But it was found in *Lambert* that a decision of a trial judge taken before the HRA came into force was not found to amount to such proceedings.[361]

Lord Woolf CJ observed in *Wainwright v Home Office*[362] that there has been considerable uncertainty as to whether the HRA can apply retrospectively in situations where the conduct complained of occurred before the Act came into force. Lord Hope in *Aston Cantlow*[363] considered that the position could be summarised as follows:

> The only provision in the Act which gives retrospective effect to any of its provisions is section 22(4). It directs attention exclusively to that part of the Act which deals with the acts of public authorities – sections 6 to 9. It has been said that its effect is to enable the Act to be used defensively against public authorities with retrospective effect but not offensively . . .[364] Section 22(4) states that section 7(1)(b) applies to proceedings brought by or at the instigation of a public authority whenever the act in question took place, but that otherwise subsection (1)(b) does not apply to an act taking place before the coming into force of section 7. Section 7(1)(b) enables a person who claims that a public authority has acted in a way which is made unlawful by section 6(1) to rely on his Convention rights in proceedings brought by or at the instigation of the public authority. Section 6(2)(a) provides that section 6(1) does not apply if as a result of one or more provisions of primary legislation the authority could not have acted differently.

He went on to find that, therefore, acts of courts or tribunals which took place before 2 October 2000 which they were required to make by primary legislation and were made according to the meaning that was to be given to the legislation at that time are not affected by s 22(4) (*R v Kansal*).[365] He said that the interpretative obligation in s 3(1) cannot be applied to invalidate a decision that was good at the time when it was made by changing retrospectively the meaning which the court or tribunal previously gave to that legislation. He noted that the same view has been taken where the claim relates to acts of public authorities other than courts or tribunals. It has been held that the Act cannot be relied upon retrospectively by introducing a right of privacy to make unlawful conduct that was lawful at the time when it took place: *Wainwright v Home Office*.[366]

Time limits

If proceedings are brought against a public authority alleging breach of a Convention right, they must be brought, under s 7(5), within one year 'beginning with the date on

---

361 Following the decision of the House of Lords in *R v Lambert* [2001] 3 All ER 577, appeals against pre-commencement convictions are not within s 22(4)(b).
362 [2001] EWCA Civ 208, [2002] QB 1334, p 1344G para 22.
363 [2004] 1 AC 546, at paras 27 and 28.
364 He noted the annotations to the Act by the late Peter Duffy QC in *Current Law Statutes*, vol 3 (1999).
365 [2002] 2 AC 69, 112, para 84; *Wainwright v Home Office* [2002] QB 1334, 1346A-1347C, paras 29–36.
366 [2002] QB 1334, 1347G–H, para 40.

which the act complained of took place' or 'such longer period as the court or tribunal considers equitable having regard to all the circumstances', but that is subject to any rule imposing a stricter time limit in relation to the procedure in question'.

Judicial review proceedings are subject to a stricter rule, since the limitation period of three months for judicial review is applicable.[367] But in certain circumstances, the longer period might apply; a *Pepper v Hart* statement suggests that the one-year period could, exceptionally, apply: 'someone with a genuine grievance will be able to pursue it under s 7(1)(a) whether or not within the judicial review time limit'.[368] *Somerville v Scottish Ministers* confirmed that, when faced with a continuing breach of Convention rights, the one-year time limit begins to run from the date when the breach ended as opposed to when it commenced.[369] When assessing whether a time limit can be extended, the burden of proof rests with the applicant. However, when making this assessment, the court will carry out an 'open-ended examination of the factors that weigh on either side of the argument' to determine whether the court should exercise its discretion to extend the time limit.[370]

Remedies

Under s 8(1) a court that has found that an act or proposed act of a public authority is unlawful is authorised to grant 'such relief or remedy or . . . order within its powers as [the court] considers just and appropriate'. Assuming that a breach of the Convention is found, all the familiar remedies, including damages, certiorari (now a quashing order), a declaration or mandamus (a mandatory order), a prohibiting order (now a prohibition), are available so long as they are within the jurisdiction of the relevant court or tribunal. The remedies include all those available in criminal or civil proceedings. The various remedies are considered at the relevant points in the following chapters. Under s 8(2), damages cannot be awarded in criminal proceedings. Traditionally, the courts have been reluctant to award damages in public law cases and s 8(3) of the HRA encourages the continuance of this tradition in requiring consideration to be given first to any 'other relief or remedy granted or order made', the consequences of the court's decisions and the necessity of making the award. If damages are awarded it is on the basis of 'just satisfaction' (s 8(3)).

A line of authorities seeks to emphasise that a declaration of a breach of human rights should be considered 'just satisfaction' and no more should be required by way of redress. In *Anufrijeva and Another v Southwark London Borough Council; R (Mambakasa) v Secretary of State for the Home Office; R (N) v Secretary of State for the Home Office*[371] it was held that: 'Where an infringement of an individual's human rights has occurred, the concern will usually be to bring the infringement to an end and any question of compensation will be of secondary, if any, importance.' *Anufrijeva* involved

---

367 CPR Sched 1 r 53.4(1). See further on a number of these matters, Supperstone and Coppel, 'Judicial review after the Human Rights Act' (1999) 3 EHRLR 301–29; Nicol, D, 'Limitation periods under the HRA and judicial review' [1999] LQR 216.
368 HC Deb Vol 314 col 1099, 20 May 1998.
369 [2007] UKHL 44; [2007] 1 WLR 2734.
370 *A v Essex County Council* [2010] UKSC 33 [2011] 1 AC 280.
371 [2004] QB 1124; [2004] 2 WLR 603.

three Art 8 claims for damages for maladministration in the handling of housing and asylum applications. The Court of Appeal found that there was a wide discretion as to whether damages should be awarded, and that an award should be made only when it was 'necessary' (s 8(3) HRA) so to do in order to afford just satisfaction. The finding of a violation would often itself be just satisfaction, it found, and damages are to be viewed as a 'remedy of last resort'.[372] The Court further found that the exercise of the discretion as to damages should include consideration of the balance between the interests of the victim and of the public as a whole.[373]

It was reaffirmed in *R (Greenfield) v Home Office*[374] that damages need not be awarded. A prisoner who failed a mandatory drugs test was charged and convicted under the Prison Rules 1999 and ordered to serve an additional 21 days' imprisonment. The prisoner alleged that in being denied legal representation at the hearing before the deputy controller of the prison his right to a fair trial had been infringed. The Divisional Court and Court of Appeal dismissed the prisoner's appeal on the grounds that the offence was a prison disciplinary offence and not a criminal offence for the purposes of Art 6. Following a decision of the ECHR it was conceded that the proceedings did involve a criminal charge; the deputy controller was not an independent tribunal and the prisoner was wrongly denied legal representation. On the prisoner's claim for damages, the Lords held that the approach of the ECHR, that a finding that Art 6 had been violated was, in itself, just satisfaction, should be followed and that there should be no award of damages to the prisoner.

Under s 8(4), the court in deciding to award damages must take into account the principles applied by the European Court of Human Rights. The Court can award compensation under what is now Art 41.[375] The purpose of the reparation is to place the applicant in the position he would have been in had the violation not taken place. Compensation will include costs unless the applicant has received legal aid, although where only part of a claim is upheld, the costs may be diminished accordingly.[376] It can also include loss of earnings, travel costs, fines and costs unjustly awarded against the applicant.[377] Compensation is also available for intangible or non-pecuniary losses such as loss of future earnings[378] or opportunities,[379] unjust imprisonment,[380] stress or loss of personal integrity.[381]

---

372 At para 56.
373 At para 56.
374 [2005] 2 WLR 240.
375 Previously Art 50 under the old numbering of the articles.
376 *Steel v UK* (1999) 28 EHRR 603, para 125.
377 See as to heads of loss Burns, N (2001) NLJ 164.
378 E.g., in *Young, James and Webster v UK*, Judgment of 13 August 1981, A 44 (1981), pecuniary and non-pecuniary costs, taking such loss into account, were awarded: the Court ordered £65,000 to be paid.
379 *Weekes v UK*, A 114-A (1988).
380 In *Steel v UK* (1999) 28 EHRR 603, para 122, the three successful applicants were each imprisoned for seven hours. The Court, without giving reasons, awarded them £500 each in compensation for non-pecuniary damage.
381 See further Mowbray, A, 'The European Court of Human Rights' approach to just satisfaction' [1997] PL 647; Feldman, D, 'Remedies for violation of Convention Rights under the HRA' [1998] EHRLR 691; Amos, M, 'Damages for breach of the Human Rights Act' [1999] EHRLR 178; Fairgrieve, D, 'The Human Rights Act 1998, damages and tort law', PL 2001, pp 695–716; Sir Robert Carnwath, 'ECHR Remedies from a Common Law Perspective' (2000) 49 ICLQ 517. The question of the level of damages is addressed further in Chapter 2, p 40.

But there are difficulties in following the principles of the European Court. One is, as Mowbray has pointed out, that the method of determining the award in any particular judgment is frequently unclear.[382] Also, the Court, prior to the changes introduced under Protocol 11, had no independent fact-finding role[383] and therefore, where it was unclear that the breach had occasioned the effect in question, it has at times refused to award compensation. The October 2000 Law Commission report 'Damages under the Human Rights Act 1998'[384] noted that the Strasbourg Court normally applies a strict causation test that bars the majority of claims for pecuniary loss; it argued that the tort measure should be employed under the HRA. Awards at Strasbourg have tended to be modest and its practice is not to award exemplary damages.[385] This is a clear instance in which domestic courts could have created higher standards than those maintained at Strasbourg, both in terms of dealing with this issue of causality and in creating a clearer rationale for awards, although they are able to derive guidance from post-1998 decisions taken under the Protocol 11 reforms.

However, the Supreme Court has not taken this course, confirming in *R (Faulkner) v Secretary of State for Justice; R (Sturnham) v Parole Board of England and Wales* that the UK courts should be guided primarily by clear and consistent practice of the Strasbourg Court, ensuring that the levels of damages broadly reflected the levels awarded by the Strasbourg Court in cases against the UK, or in cases against countries with similar costs of living, and that disputes as to the facts should be resolved in the usual way.[386] The court was sensitive to the difficulties of determining principles as required by s 8(4), but concluded that UK courts were able to glean such guidance as they could from decisions of the Strasbourg Court, bearing in mind the differences between domestic and the Strasbourg Court. Lord Carnwath suggested a more selective approach to the Strasbourg case law, explaining that:

> while Strasbourg case-law must be the starting point, the primary search in my view should be for cases, which are not only referable to the particular article and type of case under consideration, but are also identifiable as more than simple, one-off decisions on their own facts. This may be, for example, because they are expressed in terms of principle or practice . . . or contain substantive decisions of principle, or can be shown to be part of a recognizable trend applied in a series of cases on the same subject-matter.[387]

Faulkner brought an action for damages in relation to the breach of Art 5(4) given a series of delays regarding the review of his detention by the Parole Board and the Secretary of State. Following an extensive review of the case law, the Supreme Court concluded that the Strasbourg Court did award compensation for frustration and anxiety regarding delays in release, but that there was clear distinction between delays relating to

382 Mowbray, *ibid*, p 650.
383 As Leigh and Lustgarten point out in 'Making rights real: the courts, remedies and the Human Rights Act' (1999) 58(3) CLJ 509, p 529.
384 Report No 266, 2000.
385 *BB v United Kingdom* (2004) 39 EHRR 635, para 36.
386 [2013] UKSC 23; [2013] 2 AC 254.
387 *Ibid*, [114] (Lord Carnwath).

conditional release and delays relating to complete freedom. In cases where there was a considerable delay, for example where detention was prolonged for several months, the Strasbourg Court did award damages that were beyond those awarded merely for anxiety and frustration, but which were lower than those awarded for the loss of unrestricted liberty. Although Faulkner suffered a long delay, this was with regard to conditional release and not full liberty. This led the Supreme Court to reduce the damages award from the £10,000 awarded by the Court of Appeal to £6,500.

It is clear from this approach, affirming the approach of the House of Lords in *R (Greenfield) v Home Office*,[388] that reliance is placed on the measure of damages awarded at Strasbourg and not on the measure of damages found in domestic tort law. In the words of Lord Bingham:

> First, the 1998 Act [HRA] is not a tort statute. Its objects are different and broader. Even in a case where a finding of violation is not judged to afford the applicant just satisfaction, such a finding will be an important part of his remedy and an important vindication of the right he has asserted. Damages need not ordinarily be awarded to encourage high standards of compliance by member states, since they are already bound in international law to perform their duties under the Convention in good faith, although it may be different if there is felt to be a need to encourage compliance by individual officials or classes of official. Secondly, the purpose of incorporating the Convention in domestic law through the 1998 Act was not to give victims better remedies at home than they could recover in Strasbourg but to give them the same remedies without the delay and expense of resort to Strasbourg. Thirdly, section 8(4) requires a domestic court to take into account the principles applied by the European Court under article 41 not only in determining whether to award damages but also in determining the amount of an award. There could be no clearer indication that courts in this country should look to Strasbourg and not to domestic precedents . . . The Court routinely describes its awards as equitable, which I take to mean that they are not precisely calculated but are judged by the Court to be fair in the individual case. Judges in England and Wales must also make a similar judgment in the case before them. They are not inflexibly bound by Strasbourg awards in what may be different cases. But they should not aim to be significantly more or less generous than the Court might be expected to be, in a case where it was willing to make an award at all.[389]

According to the Department of Constitutional Affairs, 2006 *Review of the Implementation of the Human Rights Act*,[390] there are only three reported cases where HRA damages have been awarded: *R (Bernard) v Enfield LBC*[391] where £10,000 was awarded to two claimants to reflect the impact on the profoundly disabled wife of living in unsuitable accommodation; *R (KB) v Mental Health Review Tribunal*[392] where damages of £750 to

388 [2005] 1 WLR 673.
389 At para 19.
390 At p 17.
391 (2003) HRLR 111.
392 [2004] QB 836.

£4,000 were awarded for delays in tribunal hearings and *Van Colle v Chief Constable of Hertfordshire*[393] in which substantial HRA damages were awarded for breaches of Arts 2 and 8. The award was to parents of a witness murdered due to inadequate police protection and despite pleas to the police for greater protection. In assessing HRA damages Cox J took account of the character and conduct of the parties and the extent and seriousness of the breach; this included: the failure of the police to appreciate the escalating pattern of intimidation or to consider the need to protect the witness; and the failure to implement the witness protection protocol. Also relevant was the minor disciplinary sanction imposed on the police officer concerned (a fine of five days' pay); the enormous distress and grief of the parents; and the failure of the police to make a suitable apology. Cox J therefore awarded HRA damages of £15,000 for the son's distress in the weeks leading up to his death and £35,000 for the claimants' own grief and suffering.

The cautious approach of the House of Lords in *R (Greenfield) v Home Office* is clearly of concern, in terms of upholding the Convention rights, given the Strasbourg approach to damages. Further, if applied in relation to other Convention rights, it potentially creates anomalies. In particular, if a public authority breached a claimant's Art 8 right within the context now covered by the new tort of misuse of private information, the claimant could obtain the tort measure of damages. But if the claim fell outside that context, but was still within the ambit of Art 8, and no existing cause of action appeared to be applicable, the claimant would only be entitled to the more meagre Strasbourg measure.

5 Private bodies and indirect horizontal effect

Private bodies

Private bodies are defined as such by virtue of the fact that they have no public function at all. This category covers, for example, individual citizens, newspapers and other private companies, so long as they have no public function, such as discharging contracted-out governmental services. Therefore, they are not directly bound by the Convention guarantees under the HRA. This does not mean, however, that they are entirely unaffected by them; apart from the creation of indirect effects under the HRA, discussed below, any legislation that affects them has to be interpreted compatibly with the Convention under s 3. Functional public bodies acting in their private function are in the same position as purely private bodies, and therefore where the discussion below refers to 'private bodies' it should also be taken to be referring to such bodies but only in relation to their private functions.

The division between public and private bodies under the HRA is immensely significant and s 6 can be said to create an arbitrary division between the two. Bodies such as nursery schools, which have little power or desire to infringe human rights, are covered, while corporate bodies, such as Shell or media oligopolies, which may well have the ability, the will and the means to do so, are not. From this perspective, it may be said that the definition of 'public' authorities does not allow the HRA to have an impact that correlates fully with the location of power in the UK. Where power exists, it may be used in a manner that infringes human rights. But the HRA may be unable to address a number of instances of abuse of rights, while allowing certain powerful bodies to use it to enhance their power. For example, corporate media bodies can use the Act and can continue to rely on rights-based arguments for the enhancement of their power. The Act does not directly limit what has been termed 'the ability of corporate media giants to further their own commercial ends while acting in ways that run counter to maximising the provision of information upon which the claim is premised'.[394] In other words, certain powerful bodies are able to use the Act for rights-abridging ends, or in order to curb the expression of the values that underlie the Convention guarantees. For example, powerful media bodies can rely on their right to freedom of expression under Art 10 as a means of defending their invasion of the privacy of private citizens, protected under Art 8.[395]

Under a purposive approach, a court confronted with a large supranational company as a 'victim' of a breach of a Convention right (for example, a corporate press body invoking Art 10 against a media regulator which is itself a public authority), should take into account the values underlying Art 10 in adjudicating on the claim. This was what, it is suggested, the Supreme Court of Canada failed to do when finding that a ban on tobacco advertising infringed the free expression guarantee,[396] since the arguments underlying freedom of expression were hardly engaged by such advertising.

These criticisms could be and are levelled at bills of rights in general on the basis that they identify the elected government as the enemy, not recognising that the elected government can be the protector of the people, who need protection not from it, but from powerful multinational corporations. While, clearly, the elected government does sometimes act as the enemy, through the agency of the police or intelligence services, there is also a need for the HRA to play a very significant role in protecting rights threatened not by the state, but by powerful rights-holders. This point raises the vexed issue of 'horizontal effect'. The horizontal effect of the HRA means that private bodies also to have to respect the Convention rights in certain circumstances, as discussed below.

'Horizontal effect'

As indicated above, s 6 HRA seeks to prevent the creation of full direct 'horizontal' effect. 'Direct horizontal' effect arises if private bodies are directly bound by the Convention in their legal relations with each other. If direct horizontal effect was available under the HRA, it would mean that a private body or person claiming that his or her Convention rights had been breached by another private body could bring proceedings on that basis directly against that other body. The term 'indirect horizontal' effect is used to refer to effects on the legal relations between private parties arising indirectly – by relying on another cause of action as the vehicle by which the rights can have an impact on the legal relations between the two parties. The term 'vertical effect' is used to refer to the binding effect of the Convention on public authorities. Legal effects between private

---

394 See Feintuck, M, *Media Regulation, Public Interest and the Law*, 1999, Edinburgh University Press, Part 1, Chapter 3.
395 See Chapter 10, p 747 *et seq.*
396 *RJR MacDonald Inc v Canada* (1995) 127 DLR (4th) 1.

parties (for example, citizens, newspapers) are limited to the creation of indirect horizontal effect, that is, the use of the Convention in relation to existing causes of action. A key concern of this book is with vertical liability – the relations between citizen and state – but the question of horizontal effect arises in certain contexts, most notably that of the assertion of privacy rights against the media; this is considered fully in Chapter 10 on the privacy of personal information.

Statutes that affect the legal relations between private parties are affected by s 3 of the HRA and, therefore, in this sense, the Act clearly creates indirect horizontal effects.[397] The position was initially much less clear in relation to the common law. Even before the HRA was fully in force there was a strong consensus that the courts' inclusion under s 6 within the definition of those bodies bound not to infringe Convention rights was the key to the horizontal effect of the Act upon the common law.[398] As regards the precise effect of the courts' status as a public authority under s 6, this created the area of greatest uncertainty under the Act and it therefore proved to be a focus for academic debate.[399] The academic debate was initially polarised, Professor Wade perceiving no distinction between the obligations of private and public bodies (direct horizontal effect)[400] and Buxton LJ taking the stance that no horizontal effects are created.[401] Wade argued that a citizen claiming that a private body had breached her Convention rights could claim that the court as a public authority under s 6 must afford a remedy itself for the breach once she had found a cause of action in order to get into court.[402] But the problem was that even if this were possible (for example, a very weak claim in reliance on an uncertain area of the common law), it was always unlikely that the courts would accept that

397 It could have been argued that as private individuals do not have Convention rights against each other, there is no need to construe the statute in question compatibly with the rights. However, since s 3 applies to itself, it is suggested that it would not have been appropriate to construe it in a fashion which would have led to the denial of such rights where they would have been afforded to the individual at Strasbourg, bearing in mind the purpose of the HRA, to 'bring rights home'. On this point see Bamforth, N, 'The true 'horizontal effect' of the HRA' (2001) 117 LQR 34. See further Chapter 10, esp p 728. It is clear in any event that the courts have not adopted this stance (see pp 211–12 above) so that statutes affecting private parties create horizontal effect for the rights.

398 See Hunt, M, 'The "horizontal" effect of the Human Rights Act' [1998] PL 423; Phillipson, G, 'The Human Rights Act, "horizontal effect" and the common law: a bang or a whimper' (1999) 62 MLR 824.

399 For earlier comment, see Hunt, M, 'The 'horizontal' effect of the Human Rights Act' [1998] PL 423; Graber, CB and Teubner, G, 'Art and money: constitutional rights in the private sphere?' (1998) 18(1) OJLS 61; Leigh, I, 'Horizontal rights, the Human Rights Act and privacy: lessons from the Commonwealth' (1999) 48 ICLQ 57; Wade, 'The United Kingdom's Bill of Rights', 1998, before pp 62–64. See on the horizontal effect of the Convention generally: Clapham, A, *Human Rights in the Private Sphere*, 1993, Clarendon; Clapham, A, *The Privatisation of Human Rights* [1995] EHRLR 20; Phillipson, G, 'The Human Rights Act, "horizontal effect" and the common law: a bang or a whimper?' (1999) 62 MLR 824; Buxton LJ, 'The Human Rights Act and private law' [2000] LQR 48. Clayton and Tomlinson (2006) (*op cit*, fn 1) provide a very full discussion of the various aspects of 'horizontal effect' that also considers the position in a variety of jurisdictions – Part II. See also Hare, I (2001) 5 EHRLR 526.

400 *The United Kingdom's Bill of Rights*, 1998, pp 62–63.

401 'The Human Rights Act and private law' (2000) 116 LQR 48. Wade, having set out his position in favour of full direct horizontal effect, 'The United Kingdom's Bill of Rights', 1998, pp 62–64 as indicated above, then returned to the attack, replying to Buxton in 'Horizons of horizontality' (2000) 116 LQR 217.

402 See further Phillipson, *ibid*, pp 828–29.

Parliament could have intended to allow the distinction between private and public bodies under s 6 to be destroyed by this means.[403]

A consensus has now emerged around the creation of indirect horizontal effect – as advocated in earlier editions of this book. This position was endorsed in certain early decisions under the HRA[404] and by the majority of commentators at that time.[405] Pre-HRA, courts were already under a duty to take account of the Convention where the common law was unclear.[406] The majority of commentators considered, pre-HRA and in the first post-HRA years, that the inclusion of courts as public authorities under s 6 would at the least heighten the impact of the Convention on the common law,[407] but the nature of that impact remained uncertain for some time.

So under the HRA the courts had to answer two questions in relation to private common law disputes. First, did the Convention have indirect horizontal effect under the HRA? In other words, did the courts, as an aspect of their s 6 duty, have to give effect to the Convention in relation to adjudications between two private parties? Second, if so, did they have an absolute duty to render the common law Convention-compliant or were they merely under a duty to have regard to it? Their duty was viewed as a qualified one by Phillipson[408] and an absolute one by Hunt.[409] Phillipson suggested that the obligation would only be to have regard to the Convention rights as guiding principles, having a variable weight depending on the context. Leigh considered that the HRA 'does not formally change the approach to Convention questions in the common law, although there may be a change of atmosphere post-incorporation'.[410]

Sedley LJ made it clear in the important early post-HRA decision in *Douglas and Others v Hello! Ltd*[411] that once a plaintiff is in court presenting an arguable case, based on the existing doctrine of breach of confidence, for an injunction, which would affect freedom of expression, the court clearly has a duty to take account of s 12(4) since s 12 is applicable in all instances in which freedom of expression is in issue, not merely those in which the other party is a public authority. Section 12(4) requires the Court to

---

403 See Hunt, M, 'The 'horizontal' effect of the Human Rights Act' [1998] PL 423. Further, s 9(3) HRA precludes an award of damages in respect of a judicial act done in good faith.

404 *Michael Douglas, Catherine Zeta-Jones, Northern and Shell plc v Hello! Ltd* [2001] 2 WLR 992, CA; *Thompson and Venables v Associated Newspapers and Others* [2001] 1 All ER 908.

405 Hunt, M, 'The 'horizontal' effect of the Human Rights Act' [1998] PL 423; Phillipson, G, 'The Human Rights Act, 'horizontal effect' and the common law: a bang or a whimper?' (1999) 62 MLR 824. Hunt's and Phillipson's positions differ as to the scope of the duty under s 6, but the concept of indirect horizontal effect as argued for by both has been accepted by Lord Lester and Pannick in *op cit*, fn 1, p 32 and by Clayton and Tomlinson, 1st edn, *op cit*, fn 1, pp 236–38.

406 See above, Chapter 3, p 110.

407 See Hunt 'The "horizontal" effect of the Human Rights Act' [1998] PL 423; Phillipson, G, 'The Human Rights Act, "horizontal effect" and the common law: a bang or a whimper?' (1999) 62 MLR 824; Lord Lester and Pannick in *op cit*, fn 1, p 32 and by Clayton and Tomlinson, *op cit*, fn 1, pp 236–38. This was precisely the basis of the findings in the early post-HRA decision in *Thompson and Venables v Associated Newspapers* [2001] 1 All ER 908.

408 Phillipson, G, 'The Human Rights Act, "horizontal effect" and the common law: a bang or a whimper' (1999) 62 MLR 824.

409 'The "horizontal" effect of the Human Rights Act [1998] PL 423.

410 See Leigh, I, 'Horizontal rights, the Human Rights Act and privacy: lessons from the Commonwealth' (1999) 48 ICLQ 57 pp 82–83.

411 *Douglas, Zeta-Jones, Northern and Shell plc v Hello! Ltd* [2001] 2 WLR 992, CA.

have particular regard to Art 10 – the right to freedom of expression. So Art 10 must be applicable as between one private party to litigation and another; in other words, it has indirect horizontal effect. However, Art 10(2) is qualified in respect of the reputation and rights of others and the protection of information received in confidence. Therefore, in having particular regard to Art 10, it is also necessary to have such regard to the other Convention rights, including Art 8. Section 12(4) does not, therefore, merely give freedom of expression priority over the other rights; equal weight must also be given to Art 8 as a right recognised under Art 10(2). In other words, Sedley LJ found that in so far as there is doubt as to the scope of the duty of the court under s 6 of the HRA, s 12(4) makes the matter crystal clear where interference with the right to freedom of expression is in issue.

So from early post-HRA decisions it appeared that once adjudication on an existing cause of action was occurring, and freedom of expression was in question, s 12(4) would apply, thus creating indirect horizontal effect. Section 12 made it clear that the Convention rights indirectly affected the legal relations between private parties. However, it was apparent that anomalies would be created if other Convention rights, such as Art 8, protecting privacy, could be considered in private common law adjudication when freedom of expression was in question, but could not be considered when it was not. So, as discussed in Chapter 10, the courts began more overtly to rely on s 6 in taking all the rights into account in relation to the common law.

The seminal decision in *Campbell*[412] in the House of Lords, discussed fully in Chapter 10,[413] rejected the Buxton and Wade positions, and gave some endorsement to Hunt's argument. Naomi Campbell complained of the publication of details of her treatment at Narcotics Anonymous for drug addiction, including a photograph of her taken outside the clinic. She relied upon an existing cause of action – breach of confidence, however, to provide her with a remedy since the body infringing her privacy was clearly not a public authority; it was a purely private body – a newspaper company. The question to be determined was the duty of the court under s 6 in private common law adjudication. Lady Hale took an unambiguous and clearly stated position on this matter:[414]

> Neither party to this appeal has challenged the basic principles which have emerged from the Court of Appeal in the wake of the Human Rights Act 1998. The 1998 Act does not create any new cause of action between private persons. But if there is a relevant cause of action applicable, the court as a public authority must act compatibly with both parties' Convention rights. In a case such as this, the relevant vehicle will usually be the action for breach of confidence, as Lord Woolf CJ held in *A v B plc*, para 4.[415]

---

412 [2004] 2 WLR 1232. See for discussion Phillipson, G, 'Clarity postponed? Horizontal Effect after *Campbell* and *re S'* in Fenwick, Masterman and Phillipson (eds), (2007), see fn 1 above.

413 At pp 733–35.

414 *Op cit*, at para 132.

415 That paragraph reads: 'Under section 6 of the 1998 Act, the court, as a public authority, is required not to "act in a way which is incompatible with a Convention right". The court is able to achieve this by absorbing the rights which articles 8 and 10 protect into the long-established action for breach of confidence.'

Lord Hope found:

> In the present case it is convenient to begin by looking at the matter from the standpoint of the respondents' assertion of the article 10 right and the court's duty as a public authority under section 6(1) of the Human Rights Act 1998, which section 12(4) reinforces, not to act in a way which is incompatible with that Convention right.[416]

Having considered also Ms Campbell's Art 8 right, and balanced the two against each other as discussed in Chapter 10, Lord Hope concluded:

> Despite the weight that must be given to the right to freedom of expression that the press needs if it is to play its role effectively, I would hold that there was here an infringement of Miss Campbell's right to privacy that cannot be justified.[417]

Lord Carswell agreed with Lord Hope and Lady Hale. Phillipson observes on this:

> . . . both Lord Hope and Lady Hale appear to engage in what can be termed strong indirect horizontal effect reasoning. The difference between the two is that while Lady Hale expressly accepted the application of strong horizontal effect as a duty that must be carried out in each case involving common law actions that are in the sphere of Convention rights, Lord Hope did not.[418]

Thus, it now appears that the courts accept a duty to abide by the Convention rights in private common law adjudication, in the context of misuse of personal information.[419] It cannot yet be said that they have accepted such a duty in other contexts.

In the Court of Appeal in *McKennitt v Ash*[420] Buxton LJ appeared to accept something akin to an absolute duty under s 6 HRA to develop the common law consistently with the Convention rights, at least in the context of Arts 8 and 10. He found:

> . . . difficulty has been experienced in explaining how that state obligation is articulated and enforced in actions between private individuals. However, judges of the highest authority have concluded that that follows from section 6(1) and (3) of the Human Rights Act, placing on the courts the obligations appropriate to a public authority: see Baroness Hale of Richmond in *Campbell* at 132; Lord Phillips of Worth Maltravers in *Douglas v Hello!* at 53; and in particular Lord Woolf in *A v B plc*:[421] Under section 6 of the 1998 Act the court, as a public authority, is required not to act in a way which is incompatible with a Convention right. The court is able to achieve this by absorbing the rights which articles 8 and 10 protect into the long-established action for breach of confidence. This involves giving a new strength

---

416   *Ibid*, at para 114.
417   At para 125.
418   See Fenwick and Phillipson (2006) fn 332 above, Chapter 3 at 136–37.
419   See Chapter 10, pp 697–99.
420   [2006] EWCA Civ 1714 at paras 10 and 11.
421   [2003] QB 195[4].

and breadth to the action so that it accommodates the requirements of those articles. The effect of this guidance is, therefore, that in order to find the rules of the English law of breach of confidence we now have to look in the jurisprudence of articles 8 and 10.

As Chapter 10 argues, although the courts are very reluctant to take an explicit position on this matter, it is implicit in *Campbell* that a form of indirect horizontal effect has been accepted, which appears from *McKennitt* to impose something close to an absolute duty to develop the common law compatibly with the rights rather than a requirement merely to have regard to them.[422] The courts do not appear to have reached this position purely by reference to the extent to which the Convention itself accepts horizontal effect. The House of Lords in *Campbell*[423] considered that it could go beyond the demands of the Convention at Strasbourg in determining that indirect horizontal effect arises under the HRA.[424] But that stance is in harmony with the approach of the Convention since it demands that remedies should be available that can be used against private bodies,[425] not merely against the state. The dramatic alteration, documented in Chapter 10, that has been effected to the domestic doctrine of confidence in order to transform it into a remedy for misuse of private information, suggests that the courts accept implicitly that the s 6 duty is an absolute one – at least in the context of privacy. The demands that the duty imposes appear to be determined by the scope of the Convention rights, at least in the context of Arts 8 and 10, following *McKennitt*.

This clearly does not mean that direct horizontal effect is created – that citizens can simply take another private person or body to court in reliance solely on a claim of breach of a Convention right. But under the HRA litigants can rely on an obligation of the court in respect of the common law under s 6 that is beginning to resemble that under s 3 in respect of legislation. There is still not a complete consensus on this matter, either among academics[426] or the judiciary. But this appears to be the stance that the courts are taking as the HRA beds in. As Chapter 10 argues, the extent to which a duty to develop the common law under the doctrine of indirect horizontal effect has been accepted places pressure on the courts to go further towards accepting *direct* horizontal effect in that context since the gaps and anomalies appear more obvious.[427]

So while the eventual impact of s 6 is not a matter that can be regarded as settled, it is possible that eventually, through the development of the common law, we will arrive at a position that in its effects is equivalent to the creation of direct horizontal effects for the rights. In other words, it is possible that, in the long term, citizens will not be

---

422 See pp 727–30, 734–35.
423 [2004] 2 WLR 1232.
424 See Chapter 10, p 727.
425 See the discussion of *Spencer v UK* (1998) 25 EHRR CD 105; [1998] EHRLR 348 in Chapter 10, p 700. See further *Von Hannover*, discussed Chapter 10, pp 697–99.
426 See: Beatson, J and Grosz, S, 'Horizontality: A Footnote' (2000) 116 LQR 385; Morgan, J, 'Questioning the True Effect of the HRA' (2002) *Legal Studies* 259; see also Morgan, J, 'Privacy, Confidence and Horizontal Effect: "Hello" Trouble' (2003) CLJ 443. Professor Beyleveld and Shaun Pattinson have put forward a sophisticated argument in favour of direct horizontal effect: 'Horizontality applicability and horizontal effect' (2002) 118 LQR, 623. See Fenwick and Phillipson (2006) *op cit* fn 1, Chapter 14 which broadly takes the stance that indirect horizontal effect is being created.
427 See pp 735, 786–87.

deprived of a remedy in respect of a breach of their Convention rights, although the body infringing them is a private one. This point is explored further in Chapter 10.[428] But at present reliance must be placed on an existing cause of action in order to be able to invoke the court's s 6 duty in private common law adjudication. Although it would seem hard for a court to resist the argument that indirect horizontal effect cannot be confined to the context of privacy, the question of the courts' duty in relation to the other Convention rights has not yet been settled.[429] Clearly, either statutory provisions or common law doctrines provide citizens with protection in most of the areas now covered by the Convention rights. The context in which it appeared that indirect horizontal effect might be relevant, apart from privacy, was that of discrimination: in particular, since the Convention offered protection against discrimination on grounds of sexual orientation at Strasbourg,[430] there was a strong case for arguing that such protection should be available under the HRA. The problem was that no existing cause of action was available to rely on since the common law was markedly inadequate in protecting persons from discrimination,[431] which has now been addressed by EU-driven legislation; as Chapter 5 explains.[432]

6 The stance of the judiciary in adjudicating on the Human Rights Act

Introduction

Clearly, the response of the judiciary to the interpretation and application of the Convention rights and HRA provisions is crucial to the success of the human rights project. Lord Hope of Craighead, for example, found: 'everything will depend on the ability of the judges to give effect to its provisions in a clear and consistent manner in a way that matches the intentions of the legislature'.[433] Lord Lester and David Pannick have written: 'The challenge and the opportunities for the judiciary are probably going to be the most dramatic.'[434] Clearly, judicial training is a significant factor in relation to the performance of the judiciary.[435] As indicated above, in the whole discussion of the HRA, a number of areas of uncertainty were created and left for the judges to deal with when the HRA was passed through Parliament. This is clearly true in particular of the interpretation of s 3, the definition of 'public function' and the issue of indirect horizontal effect.

The interpretation of the Convention rights demands that the judges consider both the competing claims of individual rights and societal interests and conflicts between

---

428 See pp 697–99.
429 See Chapter 10, pp 727 *et seq.* on this point.
430 See Chapter 5, p 260.
431 See p 257.
432 See pp 258–60, 269–72.
433 'The HRA 1998: the task of the judges' (1999) 20(3) Statute L Rev pp 185–97, p 185.
434 Preface to Human Rights Law and Practice, 1999. See also Martens, S, 'Incorporating the Convention: the role of the judiciary' [1998] EHRLR 5.
435 The Judicial Studies Board (JSB) held a series of 60 one-day training seminars for all full- and part-time members of the judiciary. Magistrates' training was undertaken by Magistrates' Courts Committees. The JSB also provided training for chairs of tribunals and provided a training pack for chairs and members of tribunals.

individual rights. Under s 2 HRA they have some leeway in using imported principles and relevant doctrines in interpreting and developing the HRA provisions and the rights themselves. The often untheorised Strasbourg jurisprudence and the impact of the margin of appreciation doctrine leaves them quite a lot of room for the interpretation of the rights in applying them to new contexts. Thus both the Convention and the HRA create wide scope for the exercise of judicial discretion and for the development of the law. The extent to which they have discretion in human rights claims raises, it is suggested, a number of issues, which are indicated below and considered further at relevant points in the following chapters.

The composition and independence of the judiciary – reform

At the time of the inception of the HRA, a number of commentators criticised the judicial appointments system,[436] and in particular the role of the Lord Chancellor in relation to it,[437] thereby making the case for its reform in order to create a more objective and impartial system, with a view to changing the composition of the judiciary. In response to such criticisms, the then Labour government accepted that some reform was necessary.[438] The Judicial Appointments and Training Commission was set up in 2000; it oversaw all stages of the appointments process, but had an advisory role only. Following extensive consultation, the then Constitutional Reform Act (CRA) received Royal Assent in March 2005. The Judicial Appointments Commission (JAC) was set up by the Constitutional Reform Act 2005 and launched in 2006.[439] It is an independent Non Departmental Public Body (NDPB) established to select judicial office holders. Its remit is to do so on merit, through fair and open competition, from the widest range of eligible candidates. The intention in setting it up was to maintain and strengthen judicial independence by taking responsibility for selecting candidates for judicial office out of the hands of the Lord Chancellor and making the appointments process clearer and more accountable. Therefore, for the first time in 900 years, the Lord Chancellor no longer has the sole power to select the judges to appoint. Instead, the JAC selects the candidates and makes a recommendation to the Lord Chancellor. He or she can reject that recommendation but is required to provide his or her reasons for doing so to the JAC. The 2005 Act also set up a new Judicial Appointments and Conduct Ombudsman (JACO) responsible for investigating and making recommendations concerning complaints about the judicial appointments process and the handling of judicial conduct complaints

The Act brought about other relevant and fundamental changes. It reformed the post of Lord Chancellor, transferring his or her judicial functions to the Lord Chief Justice, the Head of the Judiciary and President of the Courts of England and Wales and established the independent Supreme Court in 2008. It establishes the Directorate of Judicial

---

436 See, e.g., Fredman, S, 'Bringing rights home' (1998) 114 LQR 538.
437 See Bradley, AW and Ewing, K, *Constitutional Law*, 12th edn, 1997, p 419.
438 See the Peach Report, December 1999, www.open.gov.uk/lcd/judicial/Peach/reportfr.htm. The Judicial Appointments and Training Commission was proposed: see Access to Justice Labour Party, 1995. See further Brazier, 'The judiciary', in Blackburn and Plant (eds), *Constitutional Reform: The Labour Government's Constitutional Reform Agenda*, 1999, Longman, p 329. See also The Rt Hon B Hale [2001] PL 489.
439 The JAC was officially launched on 3 April 2006.

Offices for England and Wales (DJO) comprising the Judicial Office, the Judicial Studies Board and the Judicial Communications Office. The Act also imposes a duty on government ministers to uphold the independence of the judiciary.

The argument for the more radical reform of the appointments system that has occurred has a number of aspects, but centrally it concerns the unrepresentative nature of the judiciary. Apart from the likelihood that the judges' backgrounds and experiences may differ radically from those whose rights they are considering, a matter that can have relevance in a number of circumstances, a system that – in effect – tends to exclude women from the highest office also excludes some of the most meritorious candidates, while arguably overestimating the merits of others. As of April 2015, one of the 12 justices of the Supreme Court, eight of the 38 judges in the Court of Appeal (21%) and twenty-one of the 108 judges of the High Court were women (19%). There are now 146 female circuit judges (23%), giving the overall percentage of female judges in both courts and tribunals as 25.2% in the courts and 43.8% in tribunals.[440] Concerns about the lack of diversity in the judiciary led to the amendment of s 63 of the Constitutional Reform Act 2005 by the Crime and Courts Act 2013, such that the requirement of making selections purely on merit does not prevent the JAC, when there are two candidates of equal merit, from recommending a candidate so as to improve diversity on the bench. However, the effectiveness of this change has been criticised, given that it is only initiated at the final stage and not the short-listing stage and because, to date, the JAC has only applied the provision with regard to race and gender, where under-representation can be demonstrated by published data. There are also concerns as to the extent to which the JAC will be faced with candidates of equal merit.[441]

The primary rationale, as Malleson argues, for promoting gender equality on the bench should be based on principles of equity and legitimacy.[442] She rejects as strategically dangerous and empirically doubtful the argument that women will bring a unique contribution to the bench as a result of their different life experiences, values and attitudes.

Judges are still largely drawn from a tiny minority group: upper-middle class, rich, white, elderly males who were public school and Oxbridge educated. As positions of power in Britain are often filled by persons drawn from this group, it appears incongruous to afford them – in effect – the responsibility under the HRA of protecting the rights of minority groups, who by definition tend to be weak or unpopular. John Griffiths, in *The Politics of the Judiciary*,[443] argues that the senior judges:

> . . . define the public interest, inevitably, from the viewpoint of their own class. And the public interest, so defined, is . . . the interest of others in authority. It includes

---

440 https://www.judiciary.gov.uk/about-the-judiciary/who-are-the-judiciary/diversity/judicial-diversity-what-do-the-latest-figures-show/.

441 See Gee, G, Hazell, R, Malleson, K and O'Brien, P, *The Politics of Judicial Independence in the UK's Changing Constitution*m 2015, CUP.

442 Malleson, K, 'Justifying Gender Equality on the Bench: Why Difference Won't Do' (2003) 11(1) *Feminist Legal Studies* 1–24. She finds that arguments, derived from difference theory, have had a strong appeal since they appear to give legitimacy to the undervalued attributes traditionally associated with the feminine while also promoting the merit principle by claiming to improve the quality of justice. However, the article argues that difference theory arguments are theoretically weak and empirically questionable.

443 4th edn, 1991, p 327.

the maintenance of order, the protection of private property, the containment of the trade union movement.

The Griffiths argument, which is echoed by other leftist commentators, has led the left to view the domestic reception of the Convention as likely to lead to a diminution in the protection of civil liberties in the UK.[444] In particular, it is thought that the judiciary, in the UK and abroad, cannot be trusted to protect the interests of minorities and/or unpopular groups, but tends to protect commercial interests[445] and the interests of those in authority.[446] Therefore, Convention rights may be enforced by powerful bodies, including rich individuals and large corporations. Such enforcement can be to the detriment of civil liberties or to the detriment of general public interests of a social welfare nature.[447] This is a powerful argument even to those who do not accept the conclusion that the left draws from it – that the HRA should never have been introduced.

However, the causal link between the judges' backgrounds and their decisions may not be as clear as Griffiths suggests. Other variables may be present influencing particular decisions, and judges, despite similar backgrounds, sometimes display markedly differing degrees of liberalism. As Lee points out,[448] a number of House of Lords decisions on human rights issues have been reached on a three–two majority,[449] while in others, a unanimous Court of Appeal has been overturned by a unanimous House of Lords.[450] Clearly, judges aspire to objectivity and impartiality, but it is obvious that sometimes they will be influenced, unconsciously or otherwise, by the interests of their class and by their experiences in general, including their sexual experiences.

It is apparent, however, that despite the fact that they largely belong to a particular societal group, they do not always display attitudes that tend to be associated with that group. At the least, it is fair to say that, during the Conservative years 1979–97, the judges demonstrated on the whole a greater eagerness to protect the rights of 'weak' or minority groups than did their counterparts in government. A number of highly significant decisions taken in the 1980s and 1990s relating to the rights of, for example, poorly paid women, asylum seekers or of suspects in police custody are documented in this book, in which judges may be said to have acted against the interests of their class.[451] The 'judicial supremacism' controversy discussed by Loveland illustrates this tendency.[452] As he points out, a number of decisions on immigration policies taken during the second Major government in the early-mid 1990s inflamed Conservative MPs

444 See Ewing and Gearty, (1997) 2 EHRLR 149, on Labour's plans to incorporate the Convention.
445 The Supreme Court of Canada struck down as an unjustifiable restriction on freedom of expression a Canadian statute prohibiting advertising: *RJR MacDonald Inc v Canada (AG), SCC, 21* September 1995, a decision that could support the leftist thesis.
446 See Ewing, K, 'The Futility of the Human Rights Act', Public Law (2004), 829–52.
447 See the conclusions of K Ewing in *The Bonfire of the Liberties: New Labour, Human Rights and the Rule of Law*, 2010, OUP.
448 *Judging Judges*, 1989, p 36.
449 E.g., *Gillick v West Norfolk and Wisbech AHA* [1986] AC 112; [1985] 3 WLR 830, HL.
450 *Mandla v Dowell Lee* [1983] 2 AC 548; [1983] 1 All ER 1062, HL.
451 See Chap 13, p 931 *et seq*. See e.g., *Hayward v Cammell Laird* [1988] 2 All ER 257; *Pickstone v Freemans* [1988] 3 WLR 265.
452 *Constitutional Law*, 2000, pp 587–95.

as well as right-wing commentators.[453] Certain decisions under the HRA, in particular *A and Others*,[454] have had a similar impact. The argument that the judges will almost inevitably be influenced by the interests of those in authority is not, it is suggested, fully supported by the evidence.

How far can it be said that male judges are able to overcome a lack of experience or understanding, or straightforward prejudice, based on gender and particular sexual experiences? Given the current dominance of male judges at the higher levels of the judiciary, this is a very pertinent question. Rights of especial relevance to women have often come before all-male courts under the HRA, raising fears of a lack of impartiality and understanding. In particular, Art 6 has been used to diminish the value of special protections for rape victims within the criminal justice system, considered by the House of Lords in *R v A*.[455] It may be noted that the change in the law had been campaigned for by women's groups over a long period of time, and that one of the most persuasive arguments for its introduction concerned the strong tendency of Crown Court judges to allow humiliating questions regarding the complainant's sexual history even where irrelevant to the issue of consent. Women's groups were allowed to intervene in the appeal by making written representations that the law should be retained. Further, an application was made on behalf of the Fawcett Society, a group campaigning for women's rights, to intervene on the basis that the House of Lords is insufficiently impartial to decide the case. The argument was that an all-male court might be influenced, unconsciously, by their attitudes towards sexuality and therefore would not be able to decide impartially where the balance should lie between the rights of the female complainant and the Art 6 fair trial rights of the male defendant.

The House of Lords refused to accept the case made by the group and went on to find that the provision in question could be rendered compatible with Art 6, since s 3 of the HRA could be used in order to allow for the reading of words into the section, allowing the possibility of the admission of relevant evidence relating to a previous (alleged) sexual relationship between defendant and complainant. This was, as indicated above, an extremely activist interpretation of what s 3 requires. In reaching its decision as to the requirements of s 3, the Lords did not rehearse the relevant Strasbourg jurisprudence in any detail. Therefore, it is arguable that the legislative role being adopted was almost overt. The Art 8 rights of the complainant were not mentioned, although Art 8 concerns were considered. It is suggested that this was an instance in which the House of Lords read up the Convention right in question – and read down the domestic legislative provision – the reverse of the position the Law Lords adopted in *Brown v Stott*.[456] This approach may be termed a selectively activist one.

This example indicates the nature of the problem: it is hard to acquit the male judiciary of lacking understanding of women's experiences and of making decisions that at times appear to be tinged by sexism. Possibly, the practice of accepting interventions

---

453   See, e.g., *Secretary of State for Home Affairs ex p Leech (No 2)* [1993] 4 All ER 539.
454   See Chapter 15, pp 1087 *et seq*.
455   *R v A*, p 176. It is also possible that the current anonymity of rape complainants in the UK might be challenged on similar grounds under Art 6 or possibly under Art 8 in conjunction with Art 14 (on grounds of equal rights to privacy).
456   [2001] 1 WLR 817.

from women's campaigning groups in human rights cases is an interesting development that has the potential to address this problem to a limited extent.[457] Part of a broader solution to the problem is to appoint more women to higher judicial office, especially to the Supreme Court. In the case of the 'rape shield' law, the solution, put forward on behalf of the Fawcett Society, was to appoint two female Law Lords in order to ensure that the decision was not taken by an all-male court. It was not expected that this would occur in this instance, but intervention aided in making the general case for reform. Reform of the appointments system may eventually change the gender make-up of the higher courts.

Learning lessons from the Canadian experience

In adjudication on the HRA, domestic judges at times refer to decisions of courts from other jurisdictions, and Canadian cases have been considered with some frequency,[458] although it cannot be assumed that the judiciary will invariably welcome the use of Canadian precedents.[459] Canadian judges share a similar constitutional background with UK judges and Canada has adopted the Charter of Rights and Freedoms relatively recently.

As indicated below, opinions differ as to the success of the Supreme Court of Canada, as compared to that of other equivalent courts throughout the world, in upholding human rights. As well as taking the Court's jurisprudence into account in human rights cases, lessons can be drawn from the Canadian experience that are relevant to UK judges. It should be pointed out, however, that there had been judicial review of legislation in Canada since before Confederation in 1867. It has been argued that they have adjusted successfully to applying the Canadian Charter of Rights and Freedoms 1982. Professor Russell of the University of Toronto wrote in 1988 (six years after the Charter was adopted): 'In *Skapinker*[460] [the first Charter decision of the Canadian Supreme Court] the Court made it clear that it was prepared to take the Charter seriously, to give its terms a liberal interpretation and to strike down laws and practices of government found to be in conflict with it.'[461] Writing on two decisions in which freedom of expression was upheld under the Charter, Judge Strayer of the Federal Court of Canada has said:

> Such vague paternalistic laws had long been recognised as posing a threat to freedom of expression and they could not survive long in a country which had so recently dedicated itself to guaranteeing that freedom. One can only speculate that such laws would long since have been amended and particularised had inertia not been the line of least political resistance.[462]

In passing, it is worth noting that one of the laws in question was a provincial law dealing with film censorship that did not prescribe standards for such censorship; its

---

457 See Samuels, H, 'Feminist Activism, Third Party Interventions and the Courts' (2005) 13(1) *Feminist Legal Studies* 15–42.

458 See *R v A* [2001] 2 WLR 1546; [2001] UKHL 25, esp paras 76, 77, 100, 101. See also *Montgomery v Lord Advocate* [2001] 2 WLR 779, p 810.

459 See *Brown v Stott* [2001] 2 WLR 817, pp 853–55, *per* Lord Hope of Craighead.

460 [1984] 1 SCR 357.

461 Russell, P [1988] PL 385, p 388.

462 'Canada's Charter of Rights and Freedoms: a political report' [1988] PL 347, p 359.

counterpart can be found at present in the UK in the power of local authorities to license films, which derives from legislation passed in 1909.[463]

Decisions under the Charter have not, however, gone uncriticised from the political left: it has been said that 'the Charter is being used to benefit vested interests in society and to weaken the relative power of the disadvantaged and under-privileged',[464] referring to a decision condoning restriction of the collective bargaining power of unions in *Retail, Wholesale and Department Store Union*.[465] On the other hand, Russell has contended that the Supreme Court 'is sensitive to the left's concerns and is struggling to avoid an approach to the Charter which will give credence to them'.[466] These relatively early favourable evaluations of the impact of the Charter have received mixed support in later analysis. It has been suggested that the Charter 'has transformed the rights' agenda in Canada positively and creatively – sometimes even inspirationally'.[467] There have been, however, a number of suggestions that the record of the Supreme Court of Canada must be viewed as timorous and unflattering since it has failed to take a bold and innovative approach, one that could be viewed as showing the way forward for other such courts throughout the world.[468]

Clearly, any assessment of the record of the Supreme Court must be subject to later revision. A number of decisions of the Supreme Court are considered at various points in this book, since it will be suggested that, despite the reservations expressed, they will provide a very valuable source of jurisprudence. Techniques developed by the Supreme Court in relation to the Charter will also be of relevance. The Court adopts a purposive approach: 'the purpose of the right or freedom is to be sought by reference to the . . . larger objects of the Charter itself, to the historical origins of the concept enshrined and, where applicable, to the meaning and purpose of [other associated rights and freedoms] . . .'.[469]

The Court has also shown a strong tendency to draw upon international human rights law and to consider decisions from other jurisdictions.[470] It is, it is suggested, valuable to adopt a similar approach to the Convention rights under the HRA, bearing in mind the meagre, under-theorised nature of much of the Strasbourg jurisprudence and the fact that it is not binding. By considering Canadian human rights jurisprudence and jurisprudence from other jurisdictions, it is arguable that the judiciary will be able to settle human rights issues in a manner that will not depend on their own personal moral outlook. As Raz puts it, the judges have available 'distancing devices . . . devices the judges can rely on to settle [such issues] in a way that is independent of the personal tastes of the judges'.[471]

---

463 The Cinematograph Act 1909, which was concerned with the fire risk posed by films at that time.
464 (1988) 38 UTLJ 278, p 279.
465 (1986) 33 DLR (4th) 174; [1986] 1 SCR 460; for comment, see also (1987) 37 UTLJ 183.
466 *Op cit*, p 388.
467 Penner, R, 'The Canadian experience with the Charter of Rights' [1996] PL 125. See further Hogg, PW, *Constitutional Law of Canada*, 1996, Carswell.
468 See Beatty, D, 'The Canadian Charter of Rights: lessons and laments' [1997] 60(4) MLR 487.
469 *R v Big M Drug Mart Ltd* (1985) 18 DLR (4th) 321, pp 395–96.
470 See Schabas, W, *International Human Rights Law and the Canadian Charter*, 1991, Carswell; Hogg, PW, *Constitutional Law of Canada*, 1996.
471 Raz, J, 'On the authority and interpretation of constitutions: some preliminaries', in *Constitutionalism: Philosophical Foundations*, 1998, p 190.

Many commentators have remarked on the growing tendency of courts to refer to the human rights jurisprudence of other jurisdictions.[472] However, the legitimacy of relying on such jurisprudence has been doubted. For example, if a Canadian decision is relied upon which has itself been especially heavily influenced by jurisprudence from other jurisdictions (as has that other jurisprudence itself), could that decision be viewed as having a particular legitimacy because it reflects an accepted multinational standard of human rights? Or should it be viewed with suspicion on the basis that without looking more closely at the possible decisions that could have influenced it, it might merely reflect a selective use of jurisprudence in order to reach a desired end? It has been suggested that the invocation of foreign jurisprudence may merely obscure rather than guard against moral arbitrariness.[473] However, it is unlikely that such criticisms will lead to a reversal of such an established trend. What is needed is a deeper understanding of the use of foreign jurisprudence in domestic courts with a view to answering a number of questions, especially regarding its effect on the legitimacy of decisions. As McCrudden argues in an important article, a systematic examination of this complex phenomenon is required so that we could 'at least understand it better'.[474]

Domestic approaches to the margin of appreciation doctrine

The part to be played by the margin of appreciation doctrine, discussed in Chapter 2,[475] in some form in the domestic courts is not fully resolved. A central issue under the HRA from its inception concerned the domestic reception of the doctrine. Since it has probably been the key dilutant of Convention standards, as Chapter 2 indicated,[476] it was clearly essential that UK judges should reject it as a relevant factor in their own decision making under the Convention, although it became clear that there would be instances, as indicated below, when it would be appropriate to recognise a 'discretionary area of judgment'. This is a domestic doctrine with some similarities to the margin of appreciation doctrine, but the two doctrines are distinct, although their effects may not always be. As indicated in Chapter 2, the margin of appreciation doctrine is a distinctively international law doctrine, based on the need to respect the decision making of nation states within defined limits. Therefore, it would not appear to have any application in national law.[477]

The judiciary have accepted that they should not import the doctrine wholesale into domestic law, but they have shown that they are prepared to rely on decisions at Strasbourg that have been influenced by it. However, the courts have developed their own version of the doctrine of the margin of appreciation (under a different name) based upon common law acceptance of judicial deference to Parliament and to aspects of executive power.

472 See Nelken, D, 'Disclosing/invoking legal culture: an introduction' (1995) 4 SLS 435.
473 See Ghai, Y, 'Sentinels of liberty or sheep in Woolf's clothing? Judicial politics and the Hong Kong Bill of Rights' [1997] 60 MLR 459.
474 'A common law of human rights? Transnational judicial conversations on constitutional rights' (2000) 20(4) OJLS 499–532.
475 See pp 95–98.
476 See pp 95–98.
477 As Sir John Laws put it in 1998: 'The margin of appreciation doctrine as it has been developed at Strasbourg will necessarily be inapt to the administration of the Convention in the domestic courts for the very reason that they are domestic; they will not be subject to an objective inhibition generated by any cultural distance between themselves and the state organs whose decisions are impleaded before them.' 'The limitations of human rights' [1998] PL 254, p 258.

Discretionary areas of judgment, deference and proportionality[478]

The Human Rights Act and the Convention itself leave open a great deal of leeway for diverse judicial approaches. This chapter has sought to indicate that the judges are hesitating between accepting a role in developing an autonomous constitutional rights jurisprudence and merely applying Strasbourg standards, often in a traditional deferential fashion – adding in what Phillipson has termed a 'double dose of deference'.[479] The complexity of the position described below is the result of the reliance on an international instrument and thus on a body of jurisprudence affected by the influence of the margin of appreciation doctrine. In public law cases a number of stages can be discerned in judicial decision making, and what occurs at each one can be characterised as minimalist or activist, using those terms as shorthand for a 'constitutional rights' or a 'minimal compliance with Convention standards' approach. Although the discussion is largely concerned with public law cases, some of the points, in particular the use of the Strasbourg jurisprudence, are also applicable in private law and criminal cases, and reference is made to case law outside the public law sphere.

Before moving on and accepting that activism is necessary in order to realise the full benefits of the Convention, it is essential to pause briefly to consider both what activism means and what its effects may be. The main concern of this book is with vertical effects in the classic arenas of state power and therefore it avoids the most problematic issues since activism is usually welcomed by most commentators in such arenas.[480] Indeed, as indicated above, some, although by no means all, commentators looked to the HRA in 1998 as a means of undoing the effects in such contexts of years of untrammelled parliamentary sovereignty.[481] As this book indicates, especially in relation to state surveillance in Chapter 11, counter-terrorist and public order measures in Chapters 15 and 9, the security and intelligence services in Chapter 11, such effects are readily evident.

But unbridled judicial activism can also have the effect, in certain contexts, of imposing particular moral views on individuals and thereby infringing their Convention rights. The proper role of activism is to uphold individual rights in the face of state interference or state neglect of the right, not to substitute judicial for state interference, in intruding on rights, even in the name of upholding competing rights. Judicial activism is justified where it results in an enhancement of the fairness and justice of public policy-making,

---

478 For the notion of respect for a 'discretionary area of judgment' see Pannick, D, 'Principles of interpretation of Convention rights under the Human Rights Act and the discretionary area of judgement' (1998) PL 545. See further also: Craig, P, 'The Courts, the Human Rights Act and Judicial Review' (2001) 117 LQR 589; Edwards, R, 'Judicial Review under the Human Rights Act' (2002) 65 CLJ. See further Edwards, R, 'Judicial Deference under the Human Rights Act' 65(6) MLR 859; Klug, F, 'Judicial Deference under the Human Rights Act' (2003) 2 EHRLR 125; Jowell, J and Lord Steyn, 'Deference: A Tangled Story' [2005] PL 346; Hickman, T, 'Constitutional Dialogue, Constitutional Theories and the Human Rights Act 1998' [2005] PL 306; O'Cinneide, C, 'Democracy and Rights: New Directions in the Human Rights Era' [2004] 57 *Current Legal Problems* XXX.

479 See Fenwick, H and Phillipson, P, *Media Freedom Under the Human Rights Act*, 2006, OUP, Chapter 3, p 149.

480 See, e.g., Ewing, KD and Gearty, CA, *Freedom under Thatcher*, 1989.

481 See Chapter 3, pp 105–08. Some commentators, however, have continued to view the allocation of any further power to the judiciary as a dangerous step and therefore consider that the protection of civil liberties should be left to Parliament; see Griffiths, 'The brave new world of Sir John Laws' [2000] March MLR 159; Ewing, K, 'The Futility of the Human Rights Act', Public Law (2004), 829–52.

rendering public authorities accountable by reference to constitutional principle.[482] The most obvious example of such a stance is that taken by the House of Lords in *A v Secretary of State for the Home Department*,[483] discussed in full in Chapter 15.[484] Activism is unjustified as a means of imposing particular judicial views of morality on individuals. As Sir John Laws puts it, that is a matter 'upon which the judges have no special voice'.[485] This point was canvassed above,[486] and is returned to below.

Three stages in judicial reasoning in public law cases can be identified for the sake of clarity, while readily acknowledging that judicial reasoning in these contexts cannot frequently be so easily pigeonholed, and that aspects of activist or minimalist reasoning are often unconsciously adopted. In some instances of judicial reasoning, two or all of the three stages may collapse into each other. Below, examples are given of minimalist or activist reasoning, using this somewhat artificial staged approach as a deliberate means of seeking to pin down elusive ideas of deference, proportionality and the domestic reception of the margin of appreciation doctrine; these points are then developed in the various human rights contexts covered in this book.

The first stage is to find that the case falls within the ambit of a right and to determine the Strasbourg case law to be applied. In fact, under the post-HRA case law this is not necessarily the first step in the reasoning, but there is normally a point in the judgment at which the relevant Strasbourg jurisprudence is assessed. As discussed above, the court can be more or less deferential when determining the extent to which it will be guided by the Strasbourg case law, where the existence of a margin of appreciation can be used to encourage the English courts to go beyond current Strasbourg case law, as a grounds of demonstrating that there is no clear and consistent line of cases to follow, and as a justification for concluding that a Convention right has not been infringed.

The second stage is to determine whether and how far deference should be paid to the decision maker in the context in question. Under a minimalist approach it may readily be found that the decision maker should be afforded a 'discretionary area of judgment', meaning that the court is minded to adopt a deferential, non-rigorous standard of review. Under an activist approach a court will not readily adopt a deferential stance; it will tease out the factors more properly making for deference – this point is returned to below. The key point is that, once the court has made a determination as to deference or no, and degree of deference, the standard of review it wishes to adopt is then apparent.

At the third stage, the court, having settled on the standard of review it views as appropriate, chooses the proportionality test that will most effectively deliver that standard. In other words, it settles on the test that best reflects the standard of review it deems appropriate. Thus, adopting a soft-edged standard of review, a court might take the stance that the decision maker had not acted unreasonably in interfering with

482 See Feldman, D, 'The Human Rights Act 1998 and constitutional principles' (1999) 19(2) LS 165; Laws LJ, 'The limitations of human rights' [1998] PL 254.
483 [2004] QB 335.
484 See pp 1087 *et seq*.
485 Laws, *ibid*. For the view that the judiciary, and Sir John Laws in particular, are, in effect, claiming the power to determine moral and political matters, see Griffiths, 'The brave new world of Sir John Laws' [2000] 63(2) MLR 159.
486 See pp 156–57.

the guarantee in question. At the other extreme – under a very hard-edged standard – it could be asked whether the interference was entirely necessary in the sense that a less intrusive means was available – one that would have invaded the right more minimally. As Chapter 2 indicated, and as discussed at various points in this book,[487] Strasbourg has employed a range of proportionality tests, some of them allowing for a far from hard-edged scrutiny.

In describing judicial reasoning in this way it is accepted that, clearly, a judge does not necessarily consciously decide that deference is appropriate and then go on to select a proportionality test that will deliver the desired result; moreover, every stage of the reasoning process may be redolent of deference. In *Brown v Stott*,[488] for example, considered below, the reason for adopting a restrained approach to the Strasbourg juris-prudence was that the judges were minded to accord deference to the decision maker. In some instances the second and third stages collapse into each other in the sense that having decided that a decision is outwith the area of judicial competence, a court may proceed to refuse to conduct a proportionality exercise at all; it is suggested that this occurred in *Pro-Life Alliance*, discussed below.[489] But unpacking the stages of the reasoning in this fashion has its uses in seeking to tease out the processes that are in reality occurring.

A minimalist approach

At the first stage, a restrained approach to the ambit of a right may be adopted. For example, in *Pro-Life Alliance*,[490] in relation to the banning of the party's election video from broadcasting, Lord Hoffmann said:

> First, the primary right protected by article 10 is the right of every citizen not to be *prevented* from expressing his opinions. He has the right to 'receive and impart information and ideas without *interference* by public authority'. In the present case, that primary right was not engaged. There was nothing that the Alliance was pre-vented from doing. [emphasis in original]

This narrow view of Art 10(1) is critiqued in Chapter 7.[491]

Similarly, in *R (on the application of Gillan) v Commissioner of Metropolitan Police*,[492] a case concerning a blanket stop and search power introduced as a counter-terrorist measure, Lord Bingham found on the application of Art 5(1) to a stop and search conducted without reasonable suspicion: 'there is no deprivation of liberty. That was regarded by the Court of Appeal as "the better view",[493] and I agree.' In other words, a restrained view of the ambit of Art 5 was adopted, which meant, it appeared,

---

487   See Chapter 6, p 378 and Chapter 7, pp 451–52.
488   [2001] 2 WLR 817, the Judicial Committee of the Privy Council. See, for the Scottish decision, *Stott v Brown* 2000 SLT 379; see also, for discussion, Kerrigan [2000] J Civ Lib 193.
489   See pp 200–01.
490   [2004] 1 AC 185 at paras 55 and 56.
491   See pp 448–49.
492   See [2006] UKHL 12. For full discussion see Chapter 12, pp 846–48.
493   At para 46 of the Court of Appeal judgment.

that stops and searches would be unlikely to fall within it. Article 8(1) was similarly viewed in a restrictive manner:

> I am, however, doubtful whether an ordinary superficial search of the person can be said to show a lack of respect for private life. It is true that 'private life' has been generously construed to embrace wide rights to personal autonomy. But it is clear Convention jurisprudence that intrusions must reach a certain level of seriousness to engage the operation of the Convention, which is, after all, concerned with human rights and fundamental freedoms, and I incline to the view that an ordinary superficial search of the person . . . can scarcely be said to reach that level.[494]

Under this approach, it is not stated bluntly that the primary right is inapplicable; rather, its applicability is doubted, leading to an extremely superficial proportionality review when justification for the interference is considered – for which, in *Gillan*, see below.

If the ambit of the right is not defined in such a way as to exclude, or virtually exclude, the case in question from falling within it, and the justification for interfering with the right is considered, the jurisprudence tends to be applied in an unselective fashion. As Phillipson observes:[495]

> when judges are minded to carry out a minimalist audit of UK law against Convention law, they merely examine the outcomes of particular cases – even when those decisions were heavily influenced by the doctrine and, comparing the two, declare that because UK law cannot be seen clearly to breach findings of law made in the Strasbourg jurisprudence, there is no breach of the Convention.

A minimalist judicial approach to the HRA tends to include a full reliance on the margin of appreciation aspects of the Strasbourg jurisprudence, resulting at the third stage, below, in the operation of a restrained review jurisdiction only, in determining issues covered by any 'relevant' jurisprudence. This does not mean openly importing the margin of appreciation doctrine into domestic decision making; rather, it means applying such aspects regardless of the influence it had had on them. In a sense, it means importing the doctrine by the back door.

In various contexts covered by this book the balance struck in the common law between civil liberties and societal concerns, such as public order, had already been found to accord with the Convention at Strasbourg.[496] Thus the judges are able to find, without adverting to the influence at Strasbourg of the margin of appreciation doctrine, that the national legal system has already achieved the requisite balance within the margin it is allowed at Strasbourg. Under this approach it can be argued that having reviewed aspects of the balance struck in the national law of one or more of the signatory states, Strasbourg is satisfied with it and therefore it is necessary only to ensure that that standard is maintained in any particular instance. A number of examples of this approach in the early post-HRA period are documented in this book.[497] An obvious

---

494 At para 28.
495 Fenwick and Phillipson (2006) *op cit*, fn 332, Chapter 2, p 147.
496 E.g., in the public order and freedom of assembly context: see Chapter 9, pp 580–1.
497 See, e.g., Chapter 7, pp 534–44.

example in which this stance was taken arose in respect of the exclusion of improperly or illegally obtained non-confession evidence, where the *Khan* approach was continued; the common law tradition could be viewed as 'amoral',[498] but it was not out of accord with the Strasbourg one – since Strasbourg had declined to take an interventionist stance to matters of evidence in the member states.[499] Under this approach, a court might ostensibly refuse to apply the margin of appreciation doctrine and yet adopt a restrained stance in some circumstances.

The minimalist approach is most problematic when it is confronted by a much more robust and clearly analogous decision at Strasbourg, adopting a stance opposed to the previous general trend of UK law.[500] This may not arise very frequently, as this book indicates, but it arose in the significant Privy Council decision in *Brown v Stott*,[501] a decision that, it is suggested, exemplified the minimalist approach in the sense that it required a 'reading down' of the Convention right in question. *Brown* is discussed more fully in Chapter 13,[502] but it is used as an example of this approach here. In *Saunders v UK*[503] it was found that, if a penalty formally attaches to silence in questioning by state agents, and the coerced statements are then used in evidence, a breach of Art 6 is almost bound to occur. Section 172 of the Road Traffic Act (RTA) 1988 makes it an offence for motorists not to tell police who was driving their vehicle at the time of an alleged offence. The coerced statement can then be used in evidence at trial for the RTA offence in question.

In *Brown*, the Law Lords found a way of distinguishing the instant case in the particular circumstances from *Saunders*. It was pointed out that s 172 could be distinguished from s 437 of the Companies Act 1985, the provision at issue in *Saunders*, on a number of grounds, including the degree of coercion and the length of questioning. The Lords did not find that s 172 was incompatible with Art 6 and therefore it was not necessary to rely on s 6(2)(b). The Lords also used an equivalent doctrine, that of according a discretionary area of discretion to the legislature, in coming to its decision. Bearing that doctrine in mind, it was further argued that Art 6 itself does not expressly require that coerced statements should be excluded from evidence and that although a right to freedom from self-incrimination could be implied into it, the right had not been treated at Strasbourg as an absolute right. Following *Ex p Kebilene*, the Lords relied on decisions to that effect at Strasbourg that had been influenced by the margin of appreciation doctrine. Lord Bingham found: 'Limited qualification of [Art 6] rights is acceptable if reasonably directed by national authorities towards a clear and proper public objective and if representing no greater qualification than the situation calls for.' The objective in question was the laudable one of curbing traffic accidents. On that basis, by importing a form of balancing test into Art 6, it was found that answers given under s 172 could be adduced in evidence at trial.

---

498 Zander, M, The Police and Criminal Evidence Act 1984, 1995, p 236. See further Chapter 14, pp 991–92.

499 See Chapter 14, pp 992–93.

500 This occurred in *Osman v UK* (2000) 29 EHRR 245. In criticising the Strasbourg decision, at the time, Lord Hoffman made it clear that he viewed the House of Lords as having a limited role in adjudicating on human rights' issues: 'Human rights and the House of Lords' (1999) 62(2) MLR 159, p 161.

501 [2001] 2 WLR 817, the Judicial Committee of the Privy Council.

502 See pp 955–56.

503 (1997) 23 EHRR 313; No 19187/91.

While it is understandable that the Lords wished to find a method of preserving the effect of s 172, with the aim of serving an important societal interest, it is suggested that their decision has the effect of undermining the right not to incriminate oneself in Art 6(1), in a range of circumstances. The combination of the uses of the doctrine of deference to the legislature, combined with the use of Strasbourg decisions affected by the margin of appreciation doctrine, led, it is argued, to a decision that affords the right a lesser significance than Strasbourg has accorded it. If the intention had been to balance the rights in Art 6 against a range of societal interests, a paragraph could have been included, as in Articles 8–11, setting out the exceptions and the tests to be applied in using them. Alternatively, a general exception could have been included, as in s 1 of the Canadian Charter. The decision not to adopt either of these courses implies that there is little or no room for the use of implied exceptions. In so far as Strasbourg has suggested that the Art 6 rights are qualified, the Lords should have considered whether adoption of that stance was due to the use of the doctrine of the margin of appreciation.

Thus, in approaching decisions at Strasbourg not heavily influenced by the doctrine, a court, following notions of common law restraint expressed in a manner similar to the *Kebilene* 'area of discretionary judgment' doctrine, might find that it could adopt a cautious interpretation to Strasbourg decisions if to do so appeared to be in accordance with common law tradition. A further consequence of this approach is that it may, in turn, lead to the acceptance by the Strasbourg court that the approach of the domestic court is within the margin of appreciation. A possible example of this is in *Austin v Metropolitan Police Commissioner* [504] and *Austin v UK*,[505] concerning the 'kettling' of protesters, and anyone else in the vicinity of the protest, during the anti-capitalist protests in 2001. The police cordoned off an area around Oxford Circus, detaining around 3,000 people in a small area for around seven hours. Austin challenged this as a deprivation of her liberty, breaching Art 5. The House of Lords unanimously concluded that there had been no deprivation of liberty to trigger Art 5. Lord Hope stated that such crowd-control measures would not trigger Art 5 if they were not arbitrary, were resorted to in good faith, were proportionate and were not enforced for longer than was reasonably necessary. This reasoning was criticised as contrary to Strasbourg authority and for introducing a weaker form of proportionality balancing to determine whether Art 5 was triggered as opposed to applying Art 5 and focusing on a narrower range of justifications – not including 'crowd control' – with a stricter proportionality balancing exercise than 'reasonably necessary' to determine whether Art 5 had been breached.[506]

Given that this marked a shift from what appeared to be clear Strasbourg authority, it was hoped that the Strasbourg Court would conclude that Art 5 had been breached and would criticise the reasoning in the House of Lords. The Strasbourg Court did conclude that Art 5 did not permit an analysis of the underlying public interest motive in order to determine whether Art 5 had been breached. However, it focused specifically on the facts to conclude that there was no deprivation of liberty where the cordon was the least intrusive and effective means to 'isolate and contain a crowd in volatile and dangerous

---

504 [2009] UKHL 5; [2009] 1 AC 564.
505 (2012) 55 EHRR 14.
506 See D Feldman [2009] CLJ 243 and D Mead [2009] EHRLR 376.

conditions'.[507] As Mead argues, 'it is hard not to view the result as a rewriting of the scope of the Art 5 guarantee'.[508]

At the second stage, the court tends to identify reasons for restraint in the particular context. Signs of judicial adherence to a minimalist approach to the Convention by way of a domestic doctrine of deference were found in *Ex p Kebilene*.[509] Lord Hope said:

> This technique [the margin of appreciation] is not available to the national courts when they are considering Convention issues arising within their own countries [but] . . . In some circumstances it will be appropriate for the courts to recognise that there is an area of judgment within which the judiciary will defer, on democratic grounds, to the considered opinion of [the democratic body or person] whose act or decision is said to be incompatible with the Convention.

In the context of the case, which concerned the compatibility of primary terrorist legislation with the Convention, these findings were used to justify a deferential approach. Indeed, they sought to introduce qualifications into a guarantee which on its face was unqualified. The term used by Lord Hope to describe the area in which choices between individual rights and societal interests might arise was 'the discretionary area of judgment';[510] he found that it would be easier for such an area of judgment to be recognised:

> where the Convention itself requires a balance to be struck, much less so where the right [as in Art 6(2)] is stated in terms which are unqualified . . . But even where the right is stated in [such] terms . . . the courts will need to bear in mind the jurisprudence of the European Court which recognises that due account should be taken of the special nature of terrorist crime and the threat which it poses to a democratic society.[511]

In other words, it is possible to discover a judicial approach under which traditional notions of deference on expertise grounds to executive bodies or to Parliament may be coterminous with the expression of the margin of appreciation doctrine, or that Strasbourg principles happen to yield the same result as *Wednesbury* ones. Thus, a court may find that, having relied on Strasbourg case law, affected by the margin of appreciation doctrine, in order to determine what the law is that is to be applied, still further deference can then be built into the decision at the second stage of reasoning, since it is found to be possible, following Strasbourg principles, to afford the decision maker a 'margin of appreciation'. In the early post-HRA period, it became apparent that the judiciary

---

507 (2012) 55 EHRR 14, para 66.
508 D Mead, 'Kettling Comes to the Boil Before the Strasbourg Court: Is it a Deprivation of Liberty to Contain Prisoners en Masse?' (2012) 71 CLJ 472.
509 [1999] 3 WLR 172; [2000] AC 326. The Lord Chief Justice, Lord Bingham, had found that the provisions in question undermined the presumption of innocence under Art 6(2) 'in a blatant and obvious way' due to the use of presumptions and the possibility of conviction on reasonable suspicion falling short of proof under the PTA, s 16A, as amended. See further Chapter 15, pp 1106–08.
510 First coined by Pannick, D, 'Principles of interpretation of Convention rights under the Human Rights Act and the discretionary area of judgement' [1998] PL 545, pp 549–51.
511 He gave the example of the ruling of the Court in *Murray v UK* (1994) 19 EHRR 193, p 222, para 47.

were continuing to find that certain matters, most obviously those relating to national security, were peculiarly matters for Parliament and the institutional body in question to determine. *Gillan* provides an obvious example of that tendency, in relation to the decision of the police officers on the ground[512] as, it is argued, does *Pro-Life Alliance*[513] in relation to both Parliament and the BBC acting as regulator. In *Pro-Life* the House of Lords had to consider rules on taste and decency contained in the Broadcasting Act 1990 and the BBC's decision, taking account of those rules and acting in its self-regulatory capacity, not to broadcast the video showing graphic pictures of abortion.

In *Pro-Life* Lord Hoffmann began by expounding the legal principles on which, he said, decision-making powers are allocated to different branches of government:

> The courts are the independent branch of government and the legislature and executive are, directly and indirectly respectively, the elected branches of government. Independence makes the courts more suited to deciding some kinds of questions and being elected makes the legislature or executive more suited to deciding others. The allocation of these decision-making responsibilities is based upon recognised principles. The principle that the independence of the courts is necessary for a proper decision of disputed legal rights or claims of violation of human rights is a legal principle. It is reflected in Art 6 of the Convention. On the other hand, the principle that majority approval is necessary for a proper decision on policy or allocation of resources is also a legal principle. Likewise, when a court decides that a decision is within the proper competence of the legislature or executive, it is not showing deference. It is deciding the law.[514]

He went on to find that the decision made by Parliament in imposing standards of taste and decency was an entirely proper decision for it as representative of the people to make. He further found that the decision of the broadcasters was one that they were entitled to make; he said: 'Once one accepts that [they] were entitled to apply generally accepted standards, I do not see how it is possible for a court to say that they were wrong.'[515] Thus Lord Hoffmann insisted that as a matter of law the decision was not within the competence of a court but within that of Parliament. He further appeared to view it as outwith the courts' competence, as a legal principle, to interfere with the decision of the BBC as a regulator. This stance did not, it is argued, take account of the courts' own role under s 6 HRA to ensure that the Convention rights – in this case Art 10 – are not infringed. It also avoided the question whether, assuming that the BBC is a functional public function authority and acting in its public function when it took the decision not to broadcast the video,[516] the BBC had fully adhered to Art 10. It was not enough to note that the BBC had taken account of the value of political expression in deciding to ban the video; the question whether they had adhered to Art 10 was for the court to decide. The decision was so determinedly deferential that the basic point as to the legal effect of s 6 HRA was missed and the courts' role as guardian of the

---

512 See pp 1103–04.
513 [2004] 1 AC 185 at paras 55 and 56.
514 At para 76.
515 At para 79.
516 See above pp 189–90, 199–202.

Convention rights was, it is argued, not discharged. Lord Hoffmann's point that a court, in allocating competencies to different spheres of government, 'is deciding the law' ignores the fact that that determination has already been made by s 6.

A somewhat similar approach was taken in *R (SB) v Denbigh High School*.[517] While, under the activist stance discussed below, the courts are adopting a nuanced approach to the notion of deference to Parliament or the executive, they are prepared to show deference where the decision maker appears to have weighed up the competing considerations in an effective fashion due to its special expertise. In that instance the House of Lords had to consider whether a school had breached Art 9 in refusing to allow the 16-year-old Muslim schoolgirl-claimant to wear the stricter *jilbab* form of dress, which contravened its uniform policy. The Lords concluded that the school was fully justified in maintaining its policy. Lord Bingham found:[518]

> [T]he school . . . had taken immense pains to devise a uniform policy which respected Muslim beliefs but did so in an inclusive, unthreatening and uncompetitive way. The rules laid down were as far from being mindless as uniform rules could ever be. The school had enjoyed a period of harmony and success to which the uniform policy was thought to contribute. On further enquiry it still appeared that the rules were acceptable to mainstream Muslim opinion. It was feared that acceding to the respondent's request would or might have significant adverse repercussions. It would in my opinion be irresponsible of any court, lacking the experience, background and detailed knowledge of the head teacher, staff and governors, to overrule their judgment on a matter as sensitive as this. The power of decision has been given to them for the compelling reason that they are best placed to exercise it, and I see no reason to disturb their decision.

Although it is argued that the House of Lords was right to reject the over-formalistic approach of the Court of Appeal, which had demanded that the school follow a Convention-based procedure in reaching its decision, it is argued that the House of Lords itself still had to decide, under s 6, whether the decision of the school was correct in terms of proportionality under Art 9(2). Lord Bingham's approach, it is suggested, comes too close to abdicating responsibility for making that decision.

At the third stage of the reasoning process, where the Strasbourg jurisprudence applies a weak proportionality review, close to ensuring only that the view taken of the need for a particular restriction was not unreasonable, a domestic court fully applying it, including its margin of appreciation aspects, will find itself able to defer to the judgment of the executive. Clearly, this approach is distinguishable from that of heightened *Wednesbury* unreasonableness,[519] but it may tend to lead to the same

---

517 [2006] 2 WLR 719 para 30. For discussion of the Court of Appeal decision see: Poole, 'Of headscarves and heresies: The *Denbigh High School* case and public authority decision making under the Human Rights Act' [2005] PL 685; Linden and Hetherington, 'Schools and Human Rights' [2005] Educational Law Journal 229; Davies, 'Banning the Jilbab: Reflections on Restricting Religious Clothing in the Light of the Court of Appeal in *SB v Denbigh High School* (2005) 1.3 European Constitutional Law Review 511.

518 At para 34.

519 See *Ministry of Defence ex p Smith and Others* [1996] 1 All ER 257, p 263.

outcome.[520] This, it is suggested, was the approach taken, for example, in *Alconbury*[521] in which it was found that the *Wednesbury* unreasonableness test satisfies the Strasbourg demand for an effective remedy. As discussed above, the House of Lords came to the view that judicial review could now be viewed as providing a sufficient remedy, owing to the need to consider proportionality under the HRA. But it also considered that even without considering proportionality, judicial review could provide a sufficient remedy in the socio-economic context in question.

The 'third' stage of reasoning in *Pro-Life* followed logically from the second one. Having decided that 'deference' was appropriate, although he did not use that term, Lord Hoffmann went on to find that the weaker version of 'proportionality' that is sometimes used by Strasbourg, and is closer to *Wednesbury* or 'heightened' *Wednesbury* review,[522] may be viewed as appropriate in some contexts. He made this clear in *Pro-Life Alliance* in stating:

> The test applied in the letter from the Registrar, namely, whether the restriction on the content of the PEB was 'arbitrary or *unreasonable*', seems to me precisely the test which ought to be applied. It is more in accordance with the jurisprudence of the ECHR and a proper analysis of the nature of the right in question than the fundamentalist approach of the Court of Appeal. [emphasis added][523]

Similarly, Moses J in *Ismet Ala v Secretary of State for the Home Department*[524] said:

> It is the Convention itself and, in particular, the concept of proportionality which confers upon the decision-maker a margin of discretion in deciding where the balance should be struck between the interests of an individual and the interests of the community. A decision-maker may fairly reach one of two opposite conclusions, one in favour of a claimant, the other [against him]. Of neither could it be said that the balance had been struck unfairly. In such circumstances, the mere fact that an alternative but favourable decision could reasonably have been reached will not lead to the conclusion that the decision-maker has acted in breach of the claimant's human rights. Such a breach will only occur where the decision is outwith the range of reasonable responses to the question as to where a fair balance lies between the conflicting interests.

As Chapters 9, 12 and 15 point out, courts have traditionally shown deference to decisions of the police regarding public order and national security.[525] At this third stage the

---

520 It could collapse into it if in some instances a test of 'reasonableness' rather than of necessity and proportionality was adopted under the cloak of using the terminology of proportionality. *Gillan* arguably provides an example of this tendency. Beatty suggests that this has occurred in Canada under the Charter: see Beatty, D, 'The Canadian Charter of Rights: lessons and laments' [1997] 60(4) MLR 487, p 493.

521 *R v Secretary of State for the Environment, Transport and the Regions ex p Holding & Barnes Plc (Alconbury)* [2001] 2 WLR 1389, HL.

522 See Chapter 3, pp 110–11.

523 At para 72.

524 [2003] EWHC 521 at para 44.

525 See, e.g., p 682, 1028, fn 20.

proportionality test chosen by Lord Bingham in *Gillan* in considering the interference with the Art 8 guarantee was strongly reflective of that traditional stance:

> If, again, the lawfulness of the search is assumed at this stage, there can be little question that it is directed to objects recognised by article 8(2). The search must still be necessary in a democratic society, and so proportionate. But if the exercise of the power is duly authorised and confirmed, and if the power is exercised for the only purpose for which it may permissibly be exercised (i.e. to search for articles of a kind which could be used in connection with terrorism: section 45(1)(a)), it would in my opinion be impossible to regard a proper exercise of the power, in accordance with Code A, as other than proportionate when seeking to counter the great danger of terrorism.[526]

Clearly, there is no real proportionality review here.

In *Gillan* Arts 10(2) and 11(2) received an even more cursory treatment, bearing in mind that the stop and search affected persons reporting on or going to a protest at an arms fair. In this instance, even in terms of lip service, proportionality vanished from the analysis completely:

> The power to stop and search under sections 44–45 may, if misused, infringe the Convention rights to free expression and free assembly protected by articles 10 and 11 . . . I find it hard to conceive of circumstances in which the power, properly exercised in accordance with the statute . . . could be held to restrict those rights in a way which infringed either of those articles. But if it did . . . I would expect the restriction to fall within the heads of justification provided in articles 10(2) and 11(2).[527]

As Chapter 12 argues, Lord Bingham was unwilling to constrain the exercise of the police discretion to stop persons, even where there was nothing to suggest a connection with terrorism, in any way.[528] Jeffrey Jowell has described certain *dicta* of Lord Hoffmann as 'heavy with deference'.[529] The findings of Lord Bingham in *Gillan*, at every stage in the reasoning, could equally be described as redolent of deference. This approach was strongly criticized by the Strasbourg Court in *Gillan v UK*, which concluded that Art 8 had been breached.[530]

It might appear that a minimalist approach would provide a little more protection for human rights than was provided under pre-HRA judicial review principles, since the domestic courts in theory have to consider proportionality, not merely *Wednesbury* reasonableness. The court might be expected to ask whether an interference goes beyond the aim in question, or whether evidence of the need for it has been advanced by the state. But Lord Bingham's approach in *Gillan* demonstrates that proportionality review can readily be rendered an empty exercise. Minimalist approaches under the HRA are discussed further in Chapters 6 and 15.[531]

---

526 At para 29.
527 At para 30.
528 See pp 846–47; see also p 228.
529 'Judicial Deference: servility, civility or institutional capacity?' [2004] PL 592, 600.
530 [2010] ECHR 4158/08; 50 EHRR 1105.
531 See, e.g., Chapter 6, pp 348–50.

Activism

An approach that takes a more expansive stance towards the Convention rights may be termed activist. Such an approach might be viewed as continuing the activism shown in developing a common law of human rights in the pre-HRA era, as discussed in Chapter 3.[532] Such an approach assumes that the common law recognises and upholds fundamental human rights[533] and that, therefore, an approach that takes an activist stance towards such rights under the HRA is in accordance with UK legal tradition. But it recognises that a constitutional shift has occurred since the HRA has placed the courts under a legal duty, in s 6, to uphold the Convention rights, even in circumstances in which deference has been accorded.

At the first stage of reasoning, under an activist approach, a court is wary of applying decisions at Strasbourg that are heavily influenced by the margin of appreciation doctrine, looking instead to fundamental Convention principles. Strasbourg has found that the purpose of the Convention is to 'maintain and promote the ideals and values of a democratic society',[534] which include tolerance of views offensive to the majority,[535] and to provide 'rights that are practical and effective' rather than 'rights that are theoretical or illusory'.[536] These concepts have not always found expression in practice, partly due to the diluting effect of the margin of appreciation doctrine. But in support of the 'activist' approach, it can be pointed out that much of the more deferential Strasbourg jurisprudence is heavily influenced by decisions of the Commission, which, as indicated in Chapter 2, was not a judicial body[537] and therefore had less authority than the Court. It is in accordance with the Strasbourg principles to have regard to the balance struck between individual rights and societal interests in other European courts, and perhaps also to that struck by the International Covenant on Civil and Political Rights and in other jurisdictions, including the US or Canada. By so doing, it may be possible to determine what the outcome of a decision at Strasbourg would have been had a lesser or no margin been conceded to the state. Human rights jurisprudence from other jurisdictions can clearly prove valuable where the Strasbourg jurisprudence is exiguous, which is frequently the case. Indeed, the domestic courts showed a willingness pre-HRA to take such jurisprudence into account.[538]

532 See pp 109–13.
533 It may be noted that s 11 HRA affords recognition to the protection for fundamental rights already achieved under the common law, in providing that reliance on a Convention right does not restrict existing rights or freedoms, or a person's right to make any claim 'which he could make or bring apart from ss 7–9'.
534 *Kjeldsen v Denmark* (1976) 1 EHRR 711, p 731; see also the comments of the Court in *Socialist Party v Turkey* (1998) 27 EHRR 51 as to the need for pluralism in a democracy.
535 In *Handyside v UK* (1976) 1 EHRR 737, para 49 the Court said: '[Art 10] . . . is applicable not only to "information" or "ideas" that are favourably received or regarded as inoffensive . . . but also to those which offend, shock or disturb the state or any sector of the population. Such are the demands of that pluralism, tolerance and broadmindedness without which there is no "democratic society".'
536 *Airey v Ireland* (1979) 2 EHRR 305, p 314.
537 Chapter 2, p 33.
538 In *Albert Reynolds v Times Newspapers* [1999] 4 All ER 609, the House of Lords took into account authorities from Canada, Australia and New Zealand, although they found that the Strasbourg jurisprudence was more influential.

A national court that afforded greater protection to the substantive rights than accorded at Strasbourg could not exceed the margin conceded to the state, unless two fundamental Convention rights came into conflict.

Clearly, the leading decisions on s 2 place, as discussed above, a very significant constraint on this possibility. But where no clear and constant Strasbourg jurisprudence stands in the way, the courts have some leeway to give a lead to Strasbourg. Under this approach, judges could regard themselves, where such leeway applies, as able to go somewhat *beyond* the minimal standards applied in the Strasbourg jurisprudence,[539] given that Strasbourg's view of itself as a system of protection firmly subsidiary to that afforded by national courts has led it in certain contexts to intervene only where clear and unequivocal transgressions have occurred. Such a stance recognises that the national authorities have not always been required to demonstrate convincingly that the test of 'pressing social need' has been met, or conducted any meaningful analysis of the proportionality of the particular measures taken to restrict the expression in question.[540] It tends to require consideration to be given primarily to the core principles developed at Strasbourg as underlying the Convention rights, rather than following specific decisions, whether as to admissibility or otherwise. But, in contrast to Lord Hope's approach in *Ex p Kebilene*, it would use such principles to enhance rather than constrain the utilisation of the rights.

As far as the second stage of reasoning under this approach is concerned, it is argued that the courts are developing a nuanced stance towards the notion of deference that, in contrast to the minimalist approach at this stage, allows them to satisfy their role under s 6 HRA, even in relation to matters traditionally viewed as particularly within the purview of the government or Parliament, including matters of national security or social policy. The stance taken in *Pro-Life* by Lord Hoffmann – that certain matters are allocated to different branches of government on the basis of legal principle – has been rejected, although *Pro-Life* has not been expressly overruled. The courts have taken the stance that the democratic quality of the rights-infringing rule can be considered: legislation should be treated with greater deference than executive decisions,[541] but in very recent decisions, as discussed below, they have refined that stance.

The most recent discussion of deference illustrating these tensions is found in the recent Supreme Court decision of *R (Lord Carlile) v Secretary of State for the Home Department*, concerning the decision of the Home Secretary which refused permission to allow Maryam Rajavi, defined as an 'Iranian dissident politician', to enter the UK and address a group of politicians, on the grounds that her presence was not conducive to the public good as it could injure diplomatic relations to Iran and may provoke violent reactions in Iran.[542] The Supreme Court upheld the decision, with a dissent from Lord Kerr. What is of interest is the approach taken to deference. It was clear from the judgments of Lady Hale, Lord Neuberger and Lord Clarke in the majority, and Lord Kerr in the minority, that the application of the proportionality test requires the court to

---

539 In the words of Judge Martens, '[the task of domestic courts] goes further than seeing that the minimum standards laid down in the ECHR are maintained' ('Opinion: Incorporating the Convention: The Role of the Judiciary' [1998] 1 EHRLR 3).

540 See Chapter 2, e.g., at pp 76–77.

541 *See International Transport Roth Gmbh v Secretary of State for the Home Dept* [2002] 3 WLR 344.

542 [2014] UKSC 60; [2014] 3 WLR 1404.

determine for itself whether a decision is a proportionate restriction on a human right. Lord Neuberger and Lord Kerr both criticised the approach of the Court of Appeal for wrongly confining its review to an assessment of whether the Home Secretary had 'approached the matter rationally, lawfully and in a procedurally correct manner'.[543] Lord Sumption, however, appeared to view the role of the court in a different light. Courts scrutinise whether the justifications for restricting a Convention right provided by the executive demonstrate that the restriction was indeed proportionate; it is not their role to 'substitute its own decision for that of the decision-maker'.[544]

There was a consensus that the courts should exercise 'deference' (although the court was critical of the term 'deference'), giving weight to the reasoning of the executive on both constitutional and institutional grounds. The less controversial element was the weight given to the Home Secretary's assessment on institutional grounds. The executive has greater knowledge when determining the extent to which admittance of Maryam Rajavi would lead to potentially violent reactions in Iran that could threaten the safety of individuals. As such there were good reasons for granting great respect to the Home Secretary's assessment.

The more controversial aspect of the case concerned the granting of weight on constitutional grounds – i.e. the acceptance that it is the role of the executive to make these assessments which then, in turn, justifies the giving of weight to assessments of the executive. Lord Sumption placed greater weight on this factor, considering that the Human Rights Act had not significantly altered the constitutional balance between the executive and the judiciary. Although the Human Rights Act had altered the constitutional balance of powers, it 'did not abrogate the constitutional distribution of powers between the organs of the state which the courts had recognised for many years before it was passed'.[545] The Human Rights Act meant that courts were no longer constitutionally barred from scrutinising decisions concerning national security, but this did not mean that great weight could not be given to the executive's assessment here given its constitutional competence as well as its institutional expertise. Lord Neuberger and Lady Hale, whilst recognising the great weight to be given to the decision of the executive on institutional grounds, appeared to place less importance on constitutional grounds for deference.

Lord Kerr, dissenting, felt unable to give such weight to the views of the executive, particularly given that the 'anticipated reaction of the Iranian authorities, if indeed it materialises, would be rooted in profoundly anti-democratic beliefs; would be antithetical to the standards and values of this country and its parliamentary system; and would significantly restrict one of the fundamental freedoms that has been a cornerstone of our democracy must weigh heavily against sanctioning such a drastic interference with the appellant's Art 10 rights'.[546] The other members of the Supreme Court were critical of the relevance of this fact when determining whether the restriction on freedom of expression was proportionate. Lord Clarke in particular was sympathetic to Lord Kerr's views, but felt unable to reach this outcome in the manner done so by Lord Kerr. Lord

543 *Ibid*, [67]–[69] (Lord Neuberger) see also [136]–[137] (Lord Kerr).
544 *Ibid*, [33].
545 *Ibid*, [28].
546 *Ibid*, [172].

Kerr also appeared to place less weight on the constitutional reasons for deferring to the decision of the Home Secretary.

At this point the argument that the HRA itself represents a choice as to the division of responsibility between Parliament and the judiciary for resolving moral and political issues should be considered. Under it, it can be argued, judicial activism is inherently limited as a result of the attempt to reconcile conflicting constitutional aims that lie at the heart of the HRA. Lord Steyn has said: 'It is crystal clear that the carefully and subtly drafted [HRA] preserves the principle of parliamentary sovereignty.'[547] Klug concludes:[548] 'The issue of judicial deference to the legislature was settled through the intersection of [ss 3 and 4]. If they are applied as intended, no further doctrine of judicial deference to the legislature . . . is required.'[549] However, the arguments put forward in this chapter have sought to problematise Lord Steyn's stance, to an extent. If, as argued here, the constitutional reality of the HRA is that in practice the carefully and subtly drafted HRA mechanisms are on the whole *not* being used in a manner that fully preserves the principle of parliamentary sovereignty, then a degree of deference to the legislature does retain a role under it. As already noted, s 3, not s 4, is now accepted as the prime remedial mechanism of the HRA.[550] This point must not be overstated since the power under s 3 does have limits, as described above, but this argument would support the stance that the judges appear to be taking in certain very recent decisions under the activist approach.

Lord Steyn's argument would support a refusal to accord any deference at all to the legislature. The senior judges are not currently taking that stance. Instead, a more subtle and differentiated version of deference is being developed, which builds in safeguards against the excessive servility seen in pre-HRA decisions.

At this point the problem of unbridled judicial activism should be addressed. If the judges are putting their s 6 duty fully into practice, and in reality they are relatively unconstrained by the HRA scheme under ss 3 and 4, over-activism could become apparent. The example of abortion was used by the Lord Chancellor in Parliamentary debate on the Human Rights Bill in order to illustrate the possibilities which might arise. In that scenario, if activism was simply taken to mean a requirement to 'read up' the Convention rights, and if necessary to 'read down' the domestic statute, the ideological views of particular judges could be given expression by means of the HRA. Under the Lord Chancellor's example, that could mean affording the Abortion Act 1967, as amended, a very restrictive interpretation (which would not be difficult, given its potentially limited application) and reading up the right to life under Art 2. The government would probably subsequently bring forward legislation to restore the broader application of the Act,[551] but there might be a period of time during which the social effects of the judgment were strongly apparent.

---

547 *R v DPP ex p Kebilene* [2000] 2 AC 326, 327.
548 'Judicial Deference under the Human Rights Act' (2003) 2 EHRLR 125.
549 *Ibid*, p 128.
550 See p 244 below.
551 It may be noted that if the government brought forward such legislation, it would not need to state that it could not issue a declaration of compatibility under s 19 HRA since it would be overruling a precedent of the House of Lords, not the Convention guarantees themselves. As already argued, it is *not* clear that Art 6 demanded the result in *R v A* – see above p 174.

However, at Strasbourg, Art 2, the right to life guarantee, does not prevent abortion, since the Commission has declined to find that the foetus is protected,[552] and the Court has avoided confronting the issue so far.[553] Strasbourg is clearly taking account of the varying abortion laws in the member states, which would be severely affected if the foetus was brought within Art 2. Further, the stance so far adopted avoids the conflict of rights, between Arts 8 and 2, that could potentially arise. So at present the abortion issue does not involve a clash of Convention rights. Clearly where the underlying principles at stake can be viewed as entirely opposed, and largely incommensurable, as in this instance, so that a moral choice would have to be taken in an area of irreconcilable conflict, Strasbourg prefers to defer to the member states.[554] Where such a difficult choice has to be taken, with such wide-ranging social implications, Strasbourg clearly prefers to leave it to the member states to take it, taking account of particular cultural or religious sensitivities in their own jurisdictions.[555]

At present then, interference with abortion law domestically is unlikely since the duty under s 6 HRA relates to the Convention rights, not to freestanding moral principles. It would be a very radical move to find that Art 2 covered the foetus domestically where Strasbourg had not taken that step. There are reasons for deference to the legislature in the sense that the judiciary is not well placed to assess the wide-ranging social and economic implications of according Art 2 rights to the foetus.[556] But such reasons are currently being rejected in somewhat similar areas of social policy. Adoption of an interventionist stance under s 3 in relation to the Abortion Act is unlikely since the judges would be entering a policy arena, something that they are reluctant to do,

---

552 *Paton v UK* (1981) 3 EHRR 408; *H v Norway*, No 17004/90 (1992) 73 DR 155.

553 See *Vo v France* [GC], judgment of 8 July 2004, No 53924/00 in which on unusual facts, the Grand Chamber avoided the question of a foetal right to life within Art 2. *D v Ireland* No 26499/02, oral hearing on admissibility and merits, 6 September 2005, concerned access to abortion for foetal anomaly, an application made under Arts 3, 8, 10 and 14 of the European Convention. If the case of *D* had been declared admissible, the Court would then have had to consider whether a denial of access to abortion for foetal anomaly constitutes inhuman and degrading treatment contrary to Art 3, or an interference with a pregnant woman's right to respect for private life under Art 8. *D* was declared inadmissible on procedural grounds on 13 June 2006. For discussion see Barbara Hewson 'Dancing on the head of a pin? Foetal life and the European Convention' (2005) 13(3) Feminist Legal Studies 363–75.

554 An example is provided by *Evans v United Kingdom* in which the Grand Chamber gave judgment on 11 April 2007. In *Evans* the claimant and her then partner J commenced fertility treatment when she was told that she had pre-cancerous tumors in both ovaries. She and J signed consent forms to IVF treatment on the understanding that under the Human Fertilisation and Embryology Act 1990, either could withdraw consent at any time before the embryos were implanted in her uterus. The couple then attended a clinic, eggs were harvested and fertilised; six embryos were created and put in storage. She then had an operation to remove her ovaries. The relationship subsequently broke up and when J notified the clinic that he was withdrawing his consent, the clinic informed the claimant that it was under an obligation to destroy the embryos. Evans argued that under Art 8 there exists a positive obligation on the state to ensure that a woman who has embarked on treatment for the specific purpose of giving birth to a genetically related child should be permitted to proceed to the implantation of an embryo even though her former partner had withdrawn his consent. She failed to win her case in the domestic courts (*Evans v Amicus Healthcare* [2005] Fam 1) and also failed at Strasbourg. The Grand Chamber found that an irreconcilable conflict between her interests and those of her partner had arisen and declined to find a breach of Art 8 if the eggs were destroyed on the basis that there is no consensus in the member states on the question when the sperm donor's consent would become irrevocable.

555 See Chapter 2, pp 95–98 and Chapter 7, pp 403–07.

556 See *Wilson v First County Trust Ltd (No 2)* [2003] 3 WLR 568, 589, para 70.

as discussed above. Moreover, they would be out of accord with international human rights standards if they did so.[557] However, if in future Strasbourg does find that the foetus is within the ambit of Art 2, it has to be accepted that under an activist stance interference with abortion law would be a possibility. The approach of the Supreme Court in *Nicklinson*, discussed above, concerning the criminalisation of assisted suicide, demonstrates that the current Supreme Court is aware of, and sensitive to, such considerations.

At the third stage of reasoning under the activist approach the stricter versions of the Strasbourg proportionality tests are adopted. In *Smith and Grady v United Kingdom*[558] the traditional *Wednesbury* approach to judicial review was held to afford inadequate protection for the Convention rights. In *R (Daly) v Secretary of State for the Home Department*[559] it was accepted that the 'domestic courts must themselves form a judgment whether a Convention right has been breached' and that 'the intensity of review is somewhat greater under the proportionality approach'.

In *R (SB) v Denbigh High School*[560] Lord Bingham reiterated this principle:

> the court's approach to an issue of proportionality under the Convention must go beyond that traditionally adopted to judicial review in a domestic setting. The inadequacy of that approach was exposed in *Smith and Grady v United Kingdom*[561] and the new approach required under the 1998 Act was described by Lord Steyn in *R (Daly) v Secretary of State for the Home Department*,[562] in terms which have never to my knowledge been questioned.

There is no shift to a merits review, but the intensity of review is greater than was previously appropriate, and greater even than the heightened scrutiny test adopted by the Court of Appeal in *R v Ministry of Defence ex p Smith*.[563] The domestic court must now make a value judgment, an evaluation, by reference to the circumstances prevailing at the relevant time: *Wilson v First County Trust Ltd (No 2)*.[564] Proportionality must be judged objectively, by the court: *R (Williamson) v Secretary of State for Education and Employment*.[565]

The House of Lords in *Ex p Daly* adopted the relatively rigorous proportionality tests from *de Freitas*.[566] Building on this analysis, the House of Lords in *Huang v Secretary*

---

557 E.g., in *R v Morgentaler* [1988] 1 SCR 30, the decision of the Supreme Court of Canada which found the abortion provision in the Criminal Code to be unconstitutional, since in placing restrictions on access to abortion it violated a woman's right under s 7 of the Canadian Charter of Rights and Freedoms to 'security of person'. Ever since that ruling, there have been no laws regulating abortion in Canada. See 'Abortion: Ensuring Access' (2006) 175(1) CMAJ.

558 (1999) 29 EHRR 493.

559 [2001] UKHL 26; [2001] 2 WLR 1622; [2001] 2 AC 532; [2001] 3 All ER 433; HL, paras 23, 27. The decision concerned rights of privacy of prisoners in respect of correspondence. See further Steyn, Lord, 'Deference: A Tangled Story' (2005) Public Law 346.

560 [2006] 2 WLR 719 para 30.

561 (1999) 29 EHRR 493, para 138.

562 [2001] 2 AC 532, paras 25–28.

563 [1996] QB 556.

564 [2004] 1 AC 816, paras 62–67.

565 [2005] 2 AC 246, para 51.

566 *De Freitas v Permanent Secretary of Ministry of Agriculture, Fisheries, Lands and Housing* [1999] 1 AC 69, 80. This test was also utilized by the Supreme Court of Canada in *R v Oakes* [1986] 1 SCR 103, paras 69–70.

of State for the Home Department[567] developed a four-stage test of proportionality that has become the established test: (i) is the objective sufficiently important to justify limiting a fundamental right? (ii) are the measures designed to meet this objective rationally connected to it? (iii) are the measures no more than necessary to accomplish this objective? and (iv) do they strike a fair balance between the rights of the individual and the interest of the community?[568] However, the Supreme Court will apply this test more or less stringently, depending on the circumstances of the case.

In two of the more activist decisions of the House of Lords under the HRA, *Laporte*[569] and *A and Others*, the key proportionality test adopted was the relatively hard-edged *de Freitas* 'least intrusive means' one. In *A and Others* the second *de Freitas* test – demanding that the state demonstrate a rational connection between the means employed and the aim pursued – was also relevant, and the rights/harm balancing test used in *Goodwin* was also relevant, although *Goodwin* itself was not referred to. *Laporte* concerned the detention of protesters on a coach that had been turned back by the police from an anti-war demonstration. The House of Lords found, in a seminal decision for freedom of protest and assembly, that the actions of the police in preventing the protesters travelling to the site of the protest and detaining them on a coach travelling back to London were disproportionate to the aims pursued, in terms of para 2 of Arts 10 and 11. On the question of proportionality, Lord Bingham declined to take a deferential approach to the decision of the police on the ground:

> I would acknowledge the danger of hindsight, and I would accept that the judgment of the officer on the spot, in the exigency of the moment, deserves respect. But making all allowances, I cannot accept the Chief Constable's argument.[570]

Having rejected a fully deferential approach, he went on to find that less intrusive measures could have been taken in that the detention of the protesters had been premature; arrests if necessary could have been made at a later point:

> Nor was it reasonable to anticipate an outburst of disorder on arrival of these passengers in the assembly area or during the procession to the base, during which time the police would be in close attendance and well able to identify and arrest those who showed a violent propensity or breached the conditions to which the assembly and procession were subject. The focus of any disorder was expected to be in the bell-mouth area outside the base, and the police could arrest trouble-makers then and there . . . There was no reason (other than her refusal to give her name, which however irritating to the police was entirely lawful) to view the claimant as other than a committed, peaceful demonstrator. It was wholly disproportionate to restrict her exercise of her rights under articles 10 and 11 because she was in the company

---

567 [2007] UKHL 11; [2007] 2 AC 167.
568 See also, see *R (Quila) v Secretary of State for the Home Department* [2011] UKSC 45; [2012] 1 AC 621, *Bank Mellat v HM Treasury (2)* [2013] UKSC 38; [2014] AC 700 and *R (Lord Carlile of Berriew) v Secretary of State for the Home Department* [2014] UKSC 60; [2014] 3 WLR 1404.
569 [2006] UKHL 55, para 34. CA: *R (on the application of Laporte) v CC of Gloucester Constabulary* [2004] EWCA Civ 1639. See Chapter 9 for discussion at pp 645–50.
570 At para 55.

of others some of whom might, at some time in the future, breach the peace . . . the claimant was not suspected of having personally committed or of being about to commit any crime, or any breach of the peace.[571]

This was a significantly more intrusive stance than has traditionally been taken in public protest decisions; the common law approach pre-HRA did not fully reflect the Convention since the focus of concern was, broadly, on proprietorial rather than protest rights,[572] and there was a distinct reluctance to interfere with the decisions of police officers unless they were manifestly unreasonable. In *Kent v Metropolitan Police Commissioner*[573] that most attenuated form of *Wednesbury* review was adopted. This decision was taken on the basis of affording the Commissioner a very wide margin of discretion to impose a ban leading to the prohibition of a march expected to be entirely peaceful. Similarly, Slynn J (as he was) said 'if the Commissioner took a view of the circumstances which was wholly untenable I consider that the court could intervene'.[574] Under that standard of review the decision of the police to detain the protesters in *Laporte* could readily have been viewed as not unreasonable.

A and Others, discussed in full in Chapter 15,[575] concerned indefinite detention of non-nationals without trial under ss 21 and 23 of Part 4, Anti-Terrorism, Crime and Security Act 2001, a measure adopted to avert the threat of terrorism, taking account of the fact that the suspects could not be deported due to the risk of Art 3 treatment in the receiving country. Lord Bingham, having found – at the second stage of the reasoning process – that a fully deferential approach would not be appropriate, even in relation to executive decisions taken on grounds of national security in relation to anti-terrorist measures, then went on to adopt a relatively hard-edged proportionality test. Relying on a number of Strasbourg decisions,[576] he noted:[577] 'Even in a terrorist situation the Convention organs have not been willing to relax their residual supervisory role.' He further quoted from *Korematsu v United States*:[578] 'in times of distress the shield of military necessity and national security must not be used to protect governmental actions from close scrutiny and accountability'. He therefore went on to find, at the third reasoning stage,

571 At para 55.
572 See Gray and Gray, 'Civil rights, civil wrongs and quasi-public places' (1999) 1 EHRLR 46, and see further Chapter 9, esp pp 680–81.
573 (1981) *The Times*, 15 May. The court found that it could not say that the Commissioner was at fault in making the order, although the reasons for it seemed meagre.
574 Quoted in Brownlie's *Law of Public Order and National Security*, 2nd edn, 1981, Butterworths, p 52.
575 See pp 1087 *et seq.*
576 He relied on *Brogan v United Kingdom* (1989) 11EHRR 117, para 80; *Fox, Campbell & Hartley v United Kingdom*, (1990) 13 EHRR 157 paras 32–34. In *Aksoy v Turkey* (1996) 23 EHRR 553, para 76, he noted that the Court, clearly referring to national courts as well as the Convention organs, held:
    'The Court would stress the importance of Art 5 in the Convention system: it enshrines a fundamental human right, namely the protection of the individual against arbitrary interference by the state with his or her right to liberty. Judicial control of interferences by the executive with the individual's right to liberty is an essential feature of the guarantee embodied in Art 5(3), which is intended to minimise the risk of arbitrariness and to ensure the rule of law.'
577 At para 41.
578 584 F Supp 1406 (1984) para 21, *per* Judge Patel in relation to the Supreme Court's earlier decision (323 US 214 (1944).

that proportionality review was appropriate, and accepted that a relatively strict proportionality test should be used:

> It follows from this analysis that the appellants are in my opinion entitled to invite the courts to review, on proportionality grounds, the Derogation Order and the compatibility with the Convention of section 23 and the courts are not effectively precluded by any doctrine of deference from scrutinising the issues raised.[579]

The appellants founded on the proportionality principles discussed above, adopted by the Privy Council in *de Freitas v Permanent Secretary of Ministry of Agriculture, Fisheries, Lands and Housing*.[580] As to the second test from *de Freitas*, the appellants argued that ss 21 and 23 of Part 4, Anti-Terrorism, Crime and Security Act 2001 did not rationally address the threat to the security of the UK presented by Al-Qaeda terrorists and their supporters because (a) it did not address the threat presented by UK nationals, (b) it permitted foreign nationals suspected of being Al-Qaeda terrorists or their supporters to pursue their activities abroad if there was any country to which they were able to go, and (c) the sections permitted the certification and detention of persons who were not suspected of presenting any threat to the security of the UK as Al-Qaeda terrorists or supporters.

As to the third test from *de Freitas* – the 'less intrusive means' proportionality test – they argued that if the threat presented to the security of the UK by UK nationals suspected of being Al-Qaeda terrorists or their supporters could be addressed without infringing their right to personal liberty, it had not been shown why similar measures could not adequately address the threat presented by foreign nationals.[581] In other words, less intrusive means were available, and were being used, which could therefore also have been used against foreign nationals suspected of terrorist activity. Lord Bingham viewed these arguments as to the disproportionality of the Part 4 scheme with the aims pursued as sound.

Lord Bingham's stance in relation to indefinite detention of the appellants further recalled that of the Strasbourg Court in *Goodwin* in that he was not prepared to accept that the grave intrusion into liberty represented by indefinite detention could be justified by the harm sought to be averted – the terrorist threat:[582]

> In urging the fundamental importance of the right to personal freedom, as the sixth step in their proportionality argument, the appellants were able to draw on the long libertarian tradition of English law, dating back to chapter 39 of Magna Carta 1215, given effect in the ancient remedy of habeas corpus, declared in the Petition of Right 1628, upheld in a series of landmark decisions down the centuries and embodied in the substance and procedure of the law to our own day . . . The authors of the Siracusa Principles . . . were of the opinion . . . that . . . 'no person shall be detained for an indefinite period of time, whether detained pending judicial investigation or trial or detained without charge . . .'.

579 At para 42.
580 [1999] 1 AC 69, p 80.
581 At para 31.
582 At para 36.

He further referred to the recognition of the 'prime importance of personal freedom' in the Strasbourg jurisprudence, noting: 'the fundamental importance of the guarantees contained in Art 5 for securing the right of individuals in a democracy to be free from arbitrary detention at the hands of the authorities' and the need to interpret narrowly any exception to 'a most basic guarantee of individual freedom'.[583]

Jeffrey Jowell has found that 'the courts are charged by Parliament with delineating the boundaries of a rights-based democracy'.[584] In *A and Others* and in *Laporte* a recognition of the courts' role in relation to the core values of the Convention is evident. A purely tokenistic approach to the review of executive decisions is rejected on the basis that this would be an abrogation of the constitutional role accorded to the judges under the HRA. Lord Bingham referred in *A and Others* to the fact that s 6 of the 1998 Act renders unlawful any act of a public authority, including a court, that is incompatible with a Convention right.[585] Thus, as he found, courts must carry out scrutiny of executive decisions that curtail fundamental rights, even in the sensitive context of national security.

Lord Nicholls captured the role of the courts as the guardians of constitutional rights under the HRA effectively in *A and Others* in finding:

> I see no escape from the conclusion that Parliament must be regarded as having attached insufficient weight to the human rights of non-nationals. The subject matter of the legislation is the needs of national security. This subject matter dictates that, in the ordinary course, substantial latitude should be accorded to the legislature. But the human right in question, the right to individual liberty, is one of the most fundamental of human rights. Indefinite detention without trial wholly negates that right for an indefinite period.[586]

These two decisions make it plain that where common law tradition had diverged from Strasbourg in developing in a less rights-oriented manner, the HRA has provided the impetus for change, under an activist approach. This approach clearly leads to greater interference with executive decision making, and departs, to an extent, from common law tradition in so doing. This approach starts from the premise that the reception of the Convention into UK law represents a decisive break with the past. Activism can occur in accordance with a synthesis of Strasbourg and national constitutional principles. As Beatty puts it:

> the same set of principles and analytical framework . . . are used by [the judiciary] in Washington, Tokyo, New Delhi, Strasbourg, Rome, Karlsruhe . . . [principles] which lie at the core of the concept of constitutional rights that allow judges to act out their role as guardians of the constitution in an objective, determinate and ultimately very democratic way.[587]

583 In *Kurt v Turkey* (1998) 27 EHRR 373, para 122. He also mentioned *Garcia Alva v Germany* (2001) 37 EHRR 335, para 39, where the Court referred to 'the dramatic impact of deprivation of liberty on the fundamental rights of the person concerned'.
584 See 'Judicial Deference: servility, civility or institutional capacity?' [2003] PL 592, 597'. See also Clayton, 'Judicial deference and 'democratic dialogue': the legitimacy of judicial intervention under the Human Rights Act 1998' [2004] PL 33.
585 At para 42.
586 At para 81.
587 See Beatty, D, 'The Canadian Charter of Rights: lessons and laments' [1997] 60(4) MLR 487, p 481.

7 Scrutiny of the workings of the HRA

Under the Green Paper, *Bringing Rights Home*, a very significant aspect of the reception of the Convention into domestic law was to be the eventual setting up of a Human Rights Commission. The consultative paper suggested that such a Commission would probably have a number of roles, which would include: providing guidance and support to those wishing to assert their rights, along the lines of the role of the Equal Opportunities Commission; instituting proceedings in its own name; scrutinising new legislation to ensure that it conforms with the Convention and monitoring the operation of the new Act.[588] Setting up such a Commission would therefore have been a significant step towards ensuring the efficacy of the Convention, in a number of respects. However, it was not provided for under the HRA. The Belfast Agreement 1998 promised that Northern Ireland would have such a Commission and the Northern Ireland Human Rights Commission came into existence in 1999.[589] The experiment in Northern Ireland provides a model, although the Northern Ireland Commissioner has particular concerns regarding religious discrimination, which are not applicable in England and Wales. The decision in the early post-HRA years not to set up a Human Rights Commission, as proposed in the Green Paper, created a clear weakness in the extra-judicial enforcement of the Act.[590]

A Joint Parliamentary Committee on Human Rights (JCHR) was set up under the chairmanship of Professor David Feldman, and now of Murray Hunt, in order, *inter alia*, to advise on legislation.[591] It has fulfilled a very valuable role. But the responsibility for the extra-judicial promotion and enforcement of the HRA was clearly fragmented between 2000–06. Further responsibility for monitoring the compliance of the

---

588 See *Bringing Rights Home: Labour's Plans to Incorporate the ECHR into UK Law: A Consultation Paper*, December 1996 (1997), p 11. For discussion of the possible roles of the Commission, see Spence, S and Bynoe, I (1997) 2 EHRR 152; Spencer, S, 'A Human Rights Commission', in Blackburn, R and Plant, R (eds), *Constitutional Reform: The Labour Government's Constitutional Reform Agenda*, 1999, p 395.

589 It was created by s 68 of the Northern Ireland Act 1998, in compliance with the commitment made by the UK Government in the Belfast (Good Friday) Agreement. The current full-time Chief Commissioner Professor Monica McWilliams, succeeded the first holder of the office, Professor Brice Dickson, in 2005. It has a variable number of part-time Commissioners (currently nine). The NIHRC's role is to promote awareness of the importance of human rights in Northern Ireland, to review existing law and practice and to advise the secretary of state and the Executive Committee of the Northern Ireland Assembly (when it is functioning) on what legislative or other measures ought to be taken to protect human rights in Northern Ireland. The Commission is also able to conduct investigations, and (subject to anticipated legislaton) will soon have new powers to enter places of detention, and to compel individuals and agencies to give oral testimony or to produce documents. The Commission also has the power to assist individuals when they are bringing court proceedings, to intervene in proceedings and to bring court proceedings itself. It receives inquiries from people who believe that their human rights have been violated, and provides training and information on human rights. It is specifically charged with advising on the scope for a Bill of Rights to supplement the European Convention on Human Rights (which is part of the law in Northern Ireland as a result of the passing of the Human Rights Act 1998). It is recognised as a member of the worldwide network of National institutions for human rights. For discussion, see Harvey, C and Livingstone, S, 'Human rights and the Northern Ireland peace process' [1999] EHRLR 162, pp 168–74.

590 See Wadham, 'The HRA: one year on' [2001] EHRLR 620.

591 See Blackburn, R, 'A Parliamentary Committee on Human Rights', in Blackburn and Plant, *ibid*.

key public authorities with the Convention has tended to devolve to existing bodies, all of which are bound by s 6, such as the Police Complaints Authority (now Independent Police Complaints Commission), the Parliamentary Intelligence and Security Committee, the Interception of Communications and Surveillance Commissioners,[592] the EOC, the Commission for Racial Equality and the Disability Rights Commission. It may be argued that the proliferation of such bodies tends to lead to the maintenance of inconsistent standards of human rights.[593]

In March 2003 the JCHR published its report on *The Case for a Human Rights Commission*.[594] In the report the JCHR considered that there had not been a rapid development of awareness of a culture of respect for human rights; instead ill-informed and distorted views of the HRA were apparent. The Committee thought that awareness of human rights was ebbing, rather than developing. It found that:

> the development of a culture of respect for human rights in this country was in danger of stalling, and that there was an urgent need for the momentum to be revived and the project driven forward . . . [the Report] concluded that this task could not be undertaken by the courts alone, and that . . . an independent commission would be the most effective way of achieving the shared aim of bringing about a culture of respect for human rights.[595]

It argued that the original vision that the Human Rights Act should aid in developing a culture of human rights would not be realised through litigation alone. In October 2003 the government announced that it had decided to proceed with the single equality body, and to give it a human rights dimension as well as an equality remit. The government's written statement announced that the new Commission would 'promote a culture of respect for human rights, especially in the delivery of public services'.[596]

As the JCHR pointed out in its Eleventh Report of 2004, the most fundamental issue in relation to the powers and functions of the CEHR is the nature of its human rights remit. The Commission has a broad human rights mandate and has a freestanding power to promote human rights. However, it does not have enforcement powers as part of its human rights remit. In the Lords' debate on the JCHR's Sixth Report, Lord Falconer said:

> human rights include but go beyond equality issues. That is to be reflected in the new body: therefore, human rights will not be a seventh strand but will inform and support the six equality strands. It will be a freestanding subject for the body to promote whether or not there is a linked equality issue.[597]

---

592 See Chapter 11, pp 811–14 for discussion of the current position.
593 See further Beckett, S and Clyde, I, 'A Human Rights Commission for the UK: the Australian Experience' (2000) 2 EHRLR 116.
594 Sixth Report, Session 2002–3, *The Case for a Human Rights Commission*, HL Paper 67-I and II, HC 489-I and II; see also Twenty-second Report, Session 2001–2, *The Case for a Human Rights Commission: Interim Report*, HL Paper 160, HC 1142.
595 Sixth Report, Session 2002–3, *op cit*, para 99.
596 HC Deb, 30 October 2003, cols 18–20WS.
597 On 16 January 2004, HL Deb, 16 January 2004, cols 765–66.

Similarly, in the House of Commons, just prior to publication of the white paper, *Fairness for All: A New Commission for Equality and Human Rights*,[598] the then deputy minister for women and equality, Jacqui Smith MP, said:

> we are putting human rights at the heart of the new politics of equality . . . The new body will be able to work to embed a culture of respect for human rights in public services and help public bodies to understand their obligations under the Human Rights Act . . . human rights values will help the new body to balance one person's rights against another's.[599]

The Commission for Equality and Human Rights (CEHR) was set up as a non-departmental public body (NDPB) under Part 3 of the Equality Act 2006 and came into operation in October 2007.[600] As Chapter 5 explains, the CEHR brings together the work of the three existing equality commissions discussed in that chapter,[601] as well as taking on new responsibilities in relation to the Human Rights Act. The government's intention was that the CEHR will have a promotional rather than coercive role in relation to human rights. It has investigatory powers, but in contrast to its powers in relation to equality matters, it does not have special enforcement powers. The new Commission can launch inquiries, but not investigations, in respect of human rights matters. As discussed in Chapter 5, investigations are more serious matters since they can lead to legal consequences.[602] It has to publish terms of reference before launching an inquiry, and must publish reports at the end of the process, which can include recommendations for changes to policies, practices or legislation.

The CEHR power to carry out general inquiries means that it can promote improved human rights practice in public authorities. If during an inquiry the Commission suspects that an unlawful act has been committed – a breach of a Convention right by a public authority – it must stop the inquiry, but it cannot launch an investigation. The CEHR has not been given additional enforcement powers relating to the HRA on the somewhat doubtful basis that legal aid is available.[603] If an inquiry reveals that a body appears to be engaging in non-Convention-compliant practices, but no victim is willing to bring an action, the CEHR can merely make a recommendation. It does not appear that it could challenge the practices by way of judicial review in its own name, as discussed below. Assuming that it commenced an investigation on grounds of suspected unlawful discrimination in a public authority, it might find that a suspected breach of Art

---

598 May 2004, Cm 6185.
599 On 4 March 2004, HC Deb, 4 March 2004, col 1141.
600 See the Equality Act 2006 (Commencement No 1) Order 2006, SI 2006/1082. It may be noted that Scotland also has a Human Rights Commission. The Justice Minister, Jim Wallace, stated in 1999 that he was in favour of a Scottish Human Rights Commission: *The Scottish Executive: An Open Scotland*, SE/1999/51, November 1999. A Bill to that effect was announced by First Minister Jack McConnell in his statement on the Scottish legislative programme to 2007. The Scottish Commission for Human Rights Act was passed in 2006.
601 See p 273 *et seq.*
602 See pp 272–74.
603 White Paper (2004), para 4.2.

14, probably read with Art 8, was also occurring.[604] That would be of some significance if Art 14 in the particular circumstances had a wider ambit than the relevant domestic anti-discrimination instrument. The CEHR is likely to be placed in a difficult position since it appears that it would be expected to close its eyes to Convention breaches while investigating breaches of such instruments.

The CEHR has an advisory role in relation to individuals and pressure or community groups. Under s 13 of the 2006 Act, which covers its advisory role, it will publish information; undertake research; provide education or training; and give advice or guidance. Its guidance could be about the Convention implications of a proposed bill. The CEHR will also act in an advisory capacity in relation to proposed legislation[605] under s 12. It is intended that it should give ministers advice or make proposals on any aspect of current or proposed law that relates to any part of its remit.

While the CEHR can advise and assist, it cannot take representative actions on behalf of individuals in either equality or human rights matters. However, the EOC and CRE were able to bring about general changes in discriminatory practices by seeking a direct change in domestic law in reliance on European Union law (*Secretary of State for Employment ex p EOC*),[606] and the CEHR will be able to do this in a much wider range of circumstances in the field of discrimination.[607] Clearly, in respect of its human rights remit the CEHR would not have the same role in relation to EU law. However, it could have sought judicial review of executive actions and decisions that arguably breach the Convention rights[608] were it not for the narrow 'victim' provisions of the HRA that seem to preclude this possibility.

The 2010–15 Coalition Government carried out a review on potential reform of the CEHR in 2011, following criticisms of its performance. The government's response to the consultation concluded that the CEHR should have two major roles: (i) as a national expert on equality and human rights issues; and (ii) as a strategic enforcer of the law and a guardian of human rights. In order to achieve these objectives, the government recommended repealing the Equality Act 2006, s 3, changing the reporting requirement from every three years to every five years, repealing the good relations duties found in ss 10 and 18 of the Equality Act 2006 and establishing the Equality Advisory and Support Service to replace the CEHR helpline. These legislative changes were enacted through s 64 of the Enterprise and Regulatory Reform Act 2013, with the Equality Advisory and Support Service being established in 2012. A new Governance Framework Agreement for 2012–15 was also agreed, designed to provide more scrutiny over the CEHR's budget and to strengthen leadership and governance.

The CEHR's most recent annual report (HC 173, 14 July 2015) set out the CEHR's strategic priorities for 2012–15: (i) to promote fairness and equality of opportunity across Britain; (ii) to promote the fair access to public services and the respect for autonomy and dignity in the delivery of these services; and (iii) to promote dignity

---

604　See Chapter 5, pp 269–72.
605　See the White Paper *Fairness for All* (2004) Cm 6185, paras 3.35, 3.36.
606　[1994] All ER 910; [1994] ICR 317.
607　See Chapter 5, pp 272–74.
608　See, e.g., *R (Amin) v Secretary of State for the Home Dept* [2003] 4 All ER 1284 in which a declaration was made that a public inquiry investigation into a death in a young offenders' institution should have been held; the failure of the Home Secretary to do so had created a breach of Art 2.

and respect and to safeguard peoples' safety. The annual report also demonstrates that, although the CEHR's work does focus predominantly on equality, it also works on human rights issues. For example: it led a partnership training programme at the National Police College to embed expertise and good practice in the exercise of stop and search powers; intervened in judicial review to highlight the flaws in the fast-track procedure for vulnerable asylum seekers; argued before the Supreme Court to protect Art 8; and advised Parliament on the Care Bill, the Criminal Justice and Courts Bill, the Modern Slavery Bill, the Immigration Bill and the Counter-Terrorism and Security Bill, as well as launching a new strategic litigation policy.

8 Conclusions

This book examines the impact of the HRA in various contexts. It argues that its impact is immensely variable, depending on the context, but that it provides a means of reversing the erosion of fundamental freedoms which occurred under the Thatcher, Major, Labour and coalition, and now Conservative governments in the contexts of public protest, state surveillance and suspects' rights, especially those of terrorist suspects. The Blair and Brown Labour government in some respects carried on the illiberal traditions of the previous Conservative governments in showing, in its 'state power' legislation, especially counter-terrorist legislation, a 'corrupting insensitivity to liberty'.[609] Whilst the coalition government and the current Conservative government introduced legislation to provide for homosexual partnerships and then marriage, it has continued its criticisms of the extent to which the UK government can counter terrorism and has consistently refused to respond to Strasbourg decisions concluding that blanket disenfranchisement of prisoners breached Convention rights. The HRA has taken a role in providing a basic protection for human rights in the face of ill-thought-out and arguably counterproductive anti-terrorism legislation. In the completely different context of privacy rights asserted against the media, it has provided a very significant impetus to the developments that were already occurring in the pre-HRA era.

The HRA incorporates a set of moral values under the Convention into UK law; the Convention represents a series of moral choices in that some of the rights are absolute, while some have presumptive priority over competing social interests.[610] The Convention jurisprudence employs concepts recognised and developed across the world by judges who may be viewed as defending a particular set of liberal values. These may be employed in a counter-majoritarian fashion in the sense that they aid in the protection of the rights of weak and unpopular groups. But in the case of the HRA, their judicial use is subject, theoretically, to the possibility of using the parliamentary override. Under the ECHR exceptions to the rights can only be utilised if both necessary and proportionate, and a number of the rights are not qualified at all or not materially qualified. The ECHR only allows for derogation from the rights in an emergency situation, and even then not from all of the rights.[611] Under the HRA, ss 3(2) and 6(2) in theory derogation is

---

609 Dworkin, R, *Index on Censorship* (1988) pp 7–8. See also Dworkin, R, *A Bill of Rights for Britain?* (1988) pp 9–10.

610 The rights fall into three groups: those which are absolute: Arts 3, 4, 6(2), 6(3), 14 and First Protocol Art 3; those which are very narrowly qualified: Arts 2, 5, 6(1), 7, Sixth Protocol Art 1 (read with Art 2) and those which are materially qualified: Arts 8–12, First Protocol Art 1. See further Chapter 2, pp 30, 65.

611 See Chapter 2, pp 98–99.

completely unconstrained, in accordance with the theory of Parliamentary sovereignty. Further, it is not required in those sections that the demands of proportionality should be satisfied before rights can be abrogated. On a face-value reading of those sections, Parliament is entirely free to pass rights-abridging legislation and the judges must give effect to it if s 3 cannot be utilised to impose compatibility since the infringement of the right is such a fundamental feature of the statute. So on the face of it the HRA represented a compromise between parliamentary sovereignty and rights protection that left the rights entirely at the mercy of a government that could command a majority in Parliament. As far as the courts were concerned, the s 4 declaration of incompatibility procedure left the rights to the mercy of an unfettered executive discretion. So, as argued above, a contradiction was created between parliamentary sovereignty and rights protection: rights were not, apparently, brought home since Parliament could simply override them and the government could disregard declared incompatibility. The HRA itself on its face appeared to be incompatible with the stated aim of reversing erosions of liberty effected via legislative changes in the Thatcher years.

But although the HRA provided mechanisms supposed to allow for an overt resolution of the contradiction between enhanced rights protection and parliamentary sovereignty – ss 3(2), 6(2), 4, 10, 19 – they have hardly been utilised by the Labour or the coalition or Conservative governments.[612] The battle between parliamentary sovereignty and rights protection is playing out much more subtly, in the interpretation given by the judges to s 3 and in the interpretation of 'public function' under s 6. The question whether Parliament has passed rights-abridging legislation is in essence a determination as to which measures satisfy the demands of proportionality. That decision, as a matter of constitutional practice, is now for the judges, not Parliament, to make. The question whether the government can transfer large amounts of public sector resource to the private sector, without imposing Convention obligations on private sector providers, has arguably resolved itself into an issue as to whether judges take a broad or a narrow interpretation of a public function, with specific legislative amendment in order to ensure private care homes are classified as public authorities. The government has not relied on the HRA to force legislation that is overtly rights-abridging through Parliament, preferring instead to utilise the Convention derogation system.[613] It has only once refused to respond to a declaration of incompatibility, and this may also be regarded as one of delay, given the existence of a Draft Bill and the recommendations of the Joint Committee on the Draft Bill that prisoners sentenced to one year or less and those serving the last six months of their sentences should be granted the right to vote. In relying on the ECHR system for creating exceptions to the rights, rather than the HRA one, successive governments have indicated its acceptance of its ECHR obligations.

Thus the moral values captured in the Convention are filtering into domestic law, essentially without being subject to certain of the overt constraints that the HRA appeared to create. The constraints that are apparent are more subtle. They are arguably largely rooted in common law values that are being imposed on the HRA and Convention by the judiciary. This is apparent, as discussed above, in the post-HRA use of deference. The public function question has to an extent been addressed in a manner

---

612 Except in respect of the Communications Act 2003.
613 See, e.g., Chapter 15, p 1035.

that reflects a reluctance to constrain market values in the private sector, relying on judicial review principles. Thus s 6 has been quite narrowly interpreted, whereas s 3 has received on the whole a wide interpretation where common law principles, such as the presumption of innocence or the admissibility of probative evidence, are at stake. A key area in which the judges have given an appearance of departing from common law values in favour of Convention ones, where the two appeared to be in conflict, is in respect of the creation of indirect horizontal effect. But even in that instance the common law was poised pre-HRA to take the leap in the direction of protecting privacy that was then taken. Perhaps a clearer departure from common law values can be seen in *Laporte* in which the Lords used Convention principle to curb not the effect of rights-abridging legislation, but the effect of their own creation – the common law doctrine of breach of the peace[614] – which has had a far more significant impact in the last 20 years in limiting public protest than have the statutory public order provisions.

In the chapters that follow, then, a doctrinal analysis of the use of the HRA mechanisms in various contexts is accompanied by perspectives that take account of government reluctance to breach the Convention in an overt manner, and of the stances taken by the judiciary as they apply those mechanisms in Convention-based adjudication. These perspectives may aid in explaining, not only why certain Convention values are finding a more ready reception in domestic law than others, but also in revealing why the HRA mechanisms themselves are being deployed in Parliament and in the courts in a manner that does not entirely comport with the expectations of 2000.

Earlier editions of this book pointed to the unresolved choice between whether to regard the HRA as a domestic bill of rights, with its own autonomous constitutional rights, or whether the HRA is merely a means of ensuring that remedies for breaches of Convention rights could now be obtained in domestic courts, without a trip to Strasbourg. This tension remains. The modification of the court's approach to s 2, the greater focus on common law rights that mirror, and may even go beyond, Convention provisions, as well as the willingness, in *Nicklinson* and *Chester*, to assess whether legislation breaches Convention rights more generally, even where there is no breach of the Convention rights of the individual before the court, all point to a willingness to see the HRA as a domestic bill of rights. This can be contrasted with the narrow approach to the definition of a public authority in *YL,* and the clear delineation between s 8 HRA and tort claims suggests a focus more on ensuring the HRA ensures domestic remedies for breaches of Convention rights.

This tension appears to motivate, at least in part, the current Conservative government's proposals to repeal the Human Rights Act and replace it with a British Bill of Rights. To date no specific bill has appeared, with the original promise that such a bill would appear in the first 100 days of government being replaced by the mention in the 2015 Queen's Speech to 'bring forth proposals' to replace the Human Rights Act. This pledge was then repeated in the 2016 Queen's Speech. The promised consultation document on the British Bill of Rights is yet to appear, and its content may well depend upon the nature of the Brexit negotiations following the referendum decision for the UK to leave the European Union.

The likely direction of these proposals can be surmised, as discussed also in Chapter 3, from the Conservative party's policy document drawn up before the general election,

---

614 See Chapter 9, pp 645–50.

the Conservative party manifesto and the statements of Michael Gove following his appointment as Justice Secretary and Lord Chancellor. There would appear to be three main justifications for repealing the Human Rights Act: (i) that Strasbourg judges have taken part in 'mission creep' using the 'living instrument' approach to the interpretation of Convention rights, taking them beyond the original intentions, with these interpretations being then adopted by UK judges who feel bound to apply decisions of the Strasbourg Court; (ii) that rights are abused as the wrong balance has been drawn between rights and responsibilities, particularly as regards the use of the right to family life to prevent the deportation of foreigners who commit crimes in the UK; and (iii) that courts have taken their duty under s 3 too far, undermining the sovereignty of Parliament.

The doctrinal analysis of this chapter demonstrates that some of these allegations are inaccurate. Courts are mindful to ensure that their Convention-compatible interpretations do not undermine fundamental features of legislation, although there may be disagreement as to the determination of these fundamental features. There is as much evidence of courts being deferential and failing to protect rights as there are examples of courts going further to protect rights. There are also examples of UK courts declining to follow decisions of the Strasbourg Court. Nevertheless, the Conservative manifesto commitment to scrap the Human Rights Act and replace it with a British Bill of Rights still remains. It is likely that the Bill of Rights will replicate Convention rights, but making them specific sections of a British Bill of Rights, make decisions of the Strasbourg Court advisory only, restrict the interpretative duty of the courts so as to ensure that human rights compatible interpretations do not contradict the ordinary meaning of legislation and redress the balance between rights and responsibilities.

Of fundamental concern is the desire to make decisions of the Strasbourg Court advisory only. Should this be interpreted generally – such that the UK government is also meant to treat specific decisions of the Strasbourg Court concluding that the UK has breached Convention rights as advisory only – this could not be achieved without either renegotiating the UK's treaty obligations (which would seem unlikely to succeed) or leaving the ECHR. Such an outcome would also require a renegotiation of the Good Friday agreement, as well as amendments to the devolution settlements. It would appear that the current Prime Minister, Theresa May, no longer wishes to pursue the withdrawal of the UK from the ECHR. The Conservative government believes that repealing the HRA would not cause problems given the UK's long-standing reputation for upholding human rights, stemming from the Magna Carta and now found in the common law. It is true that the common law can protect human rights. But the analysis of this chapter has clearly demonstrated the positive influence of the Human Rights Act both as to the empowerment of the court to protect human rights and the creation of a culture of human rights. It remains to be seen whether the proposed British Bill of Rights will provide for a strong domestic bill of rights that empowers the judiciary further to build on the work of the last 15 years, or whether it will undermine the work done by the Human Rights Act.

Chapter 5

Principles of equality

This chapter has been substantially rewritten for this edition by Aaron Baker, Reader in Law at Durham University, UK.

I Introduction

Equality and theories of anti-discrimination laws

One of the main themes in human rights jurisprudence concerns the duty of states to treat citizens with equal concern and respect. This does not mean that no differentiation between citizens should occur, but that inequality of treatment should not be based on factors that do not justify it. Thus, discrimination may be defined as morally unjustifiable as opposed to justifiable differentiation.[1] It may be said that the latter occurs when a difference in treatment is accorded owing to behaviour that is the result of voluntary choice, the former when it is based on an attribute over which the individual has no control, such as sex or skin colour. Thus, in a society that allows or imposes discrimination in this sense, the groups affected will be entirely frustrated in pursuing their objectives in all areas of life because the disadvantage they are under cannot be removed. These statements alone, however, do not explain whether differentiation would be justified if based on behaviour to which a person is morally committed owing to her membership of a certain group. Thus, it should also be argued that morally unjustifiable differentiation would also occur, at least presumptively, if different treatment were based on behaviour over which the individual had little real choice, or where it would be morally unjustifiable to force the individual to choose between disadvantage and adherence to a particular group. In addition, there are arguably immutable characteristics that society sees as perfectly reasonable grounds for distinct treatment, such as intelligence, talent, vision, or physical coordination. Thus, a simple semantic boundary between unchangeable traits and voluntary behaviours will not suffice: society must decide which attributes or choices represent generally unacceptable grounds for distinction.

Once factors that do not justify differentiation are identified, the state can be said to be under a duty to ensure that unequal treatment on the basis of such factors does not occur. However, at different times, and according to different schools of thought, the scope of the duty varies. Under early classic liberal rights theory, the state came under a duty to ensure that no formal discriminatory mechanisms were in place but, once that was done, it was thought that individuals would have equal freedom to exercise their talents.[2] This is the dominant theory underpinning the UK legislative policy on equality:

---

1 See Wallman, S, 'Difference, differentiation, discrimination', 5 *New Community* 1.
2 See Mill, JS, *On the Subjection of Women*, 2nd edn, 1869, Longmans, Green, Reader and Dyer.

it assumes that once people have equal freedoms, they will have equal opportunities and thus all that is needed is to ensure such freedoms. Some egalitarians would go further, insisting that persons should be placed in a similar position, even if in order to do so they are treated unequally. Some forms of liberal thought[3] would now also support treating persons unequally in order to ensure equality of opportunity. Formal equality[4] (or treating like as like) is a limitation that has long been placed upon equality legislation by liberalism; its drawback is that it puts the protection of such legislation beyond the reach of those who are differently situated.[5] For example, if women's domestic and parental roles[6] tend to differ from those of men and those roles interfere with women's role as (cost-efficient) workers, in a formal equality model, which takes the male as the norm and assumes that a woman is like a man, the employer may justifiably expose women to different (usually negative) experiences and outcomes through facially neutral (formally equal) rules or decisions. Similarly, if some persons from minority groups are educationally or socially disadvantaged, their difference of situation cannot be addressed by means of legislation based on a formal equality model.

Substantive equality, on the other hand, demands not merely that persons should be judged on individual merit, but that the real situation of many women and/or members of minority groups that may tend to place them in a weaker position in the market should be addressed by a variety of means, including anti-discrimination legislation. Proponents of this argument recognise that the achievement of substantive equality involves more than a few discrimination claims. Under a substantive equality model, equality legislation would attempt to reflect and further the societal movement towards equality that is taking place in the member states of the EU. Thus, legislation enshrining anti-discrimination measures has moved beyond seeking to ensure formal equality to recognise substantive inequality that results from formally equal treatment: this is reflected in the notion of 'indirect discrimination', where neutral provisions with a substantively unequal effect are proscribed unless proportionate. Although this moves beyond mere formal equality, it can at best achieve rough equality of opportunities, and will not bring about results that are consistently substantively equal. Such an outcome would require a more committed embrace (than heretofore) of positive action, and the kind of reflexive regulation represented by positive duties (discussed further below).

Discrimination and the law

The next section of this chapter begins by considering and evaluating the domestic and European legislation aimed specifically at preventing discrimination based on certain

---

3   See Raz, J, *The Morality of Freedom*, 1986, Clarendon; Dworkin, R, *Taking Rights Seriously*, 1978, p 272.

4   Under classic liberalism as expressed by Mill, *op cit*, fn 2.

5   MacKinnon puts it particularly aptly, 'Why should you have to be the same as a man to get what a man gets simply because he is one?' See MacKinnon, C, 'Difference and dominance: on sex discrimination', in Bartlett, K and Kennedy, R (eds), *Feminist Legal Theory*, 1991; see also MacKinnon, C, 'Reflections on sex equality under law' (1991) 100 Yale LJ 1286–93.

6   Matters belonging to the 'private' sphere, in a liberal conception. Mill's view, as expressed in *op cit*, fn 2, was that formal equality operates in certain 'public' spheres, such as franchise, employment and education.

protected grounds including those of race, sex, religion, sexual orientation, age and disability. The anti-discrimination scheme adopted in respect of disability is compared with those applicable to discrimination on other grounds. The chapter considers the means used in the legislation of distinguishing between relevant and irrelevant factors founding differentiation, since only the former provide a morally justifiable basis for different treatment.

Broadly, the legislation embodies three approaches to challenging direct discrimination and discriminatory practices: under the first, the 'individual' method, the responsibility lies mainly with the victim of discrimination to bring an action against the discriminator; under the second, termed the 'administrative' method, an institution or body uses various methods of seeking to ensure that discrimination is prevented; the third method, 'positive duties', imposes on certain institutions an ongoing obligation to take steps to eliminate discrimination and achieve equality. Section 2 considers the nature, scope, content, and efficacy of the various anti-discrimination protections that can be invoked through the individual method. The potential of the Human Rights Act (HRA) to influence the domestic scheme in both respects is also a significant theme although, owing to the influence of EU law, the HRA is likely to have less influence in this context than in others considered by this book. Section 3 turns to the administrative method and positive duties, setting out the role, powers and effectiveness of the Equality and Human Rights Commission, the workings and impact of positive duties and the possibilities for greater commitment to these avenues of change.

2 Anti-discrimination law: domestic and European[7]

Forty years ago, in the UK, protection from discrimination was only offered under the Race Relations Act 1976 (RRA) and the Sex Discrimination Act 1975 (SDA). Disability as a protected ground was included just 20 years ago through the Disability Discrimination

---

7   See the following sources to flesh out concepts and doctrines that can only be discussed here in overview: Clayton, R and Tomlinson, H, *The Law of Human Rights*, 2006, Chapter 17; Connolly, M, *Discrimination Law*, 2006, Sweet and Maxwell; Feldman, D, *Civil Liberties* 2nd edn, 2002, Chapter 3, (esp 3.4); Fredman, S, *Discrimination Law*, 2002, Clarendon; Connolly, M, *Townshend-Smith on Discrimination Law: Text, Cases and Materials*, 2nd edn, 2004, Routledge; EOC's *Submission to the Discrimination Law Review*, 2006; McColgan, A, *Discrimination Law: Text, Cases and Materials*, 2000, Hart; Ewing, K, Bradley, A and McColgan, A, *Labour Law: Text and Materials*, 2001, Hart; Hepple, B, Coussey, M and Choudhury, T, *Equality: A New Framework – The Independent Review of the Enforcement of UK Anti-Discrimination Legislation*, 2000, Hart; Fredman, S, *The Future of Equality in Britain*, EOC Working Paper No 5, 2002; Baker, A, *The Enjoyment of Rights and Freedoms: a New Conception of the Ambit under Art 14 ECHR* (2006) 69 MLR 714; Baker, A, 'Comparison Tainted by Justification: Against a "Compendious Question" ' 2006 PL 476; Dine, J and Watt, B (eds), *Discrimination Law*, 1996, Longman; Palmer, *Discrimination at Work*, 3rd edn, 1996, Legal Action Group; McCrudden, C (ed), *Anti-Discrimination Law*, 1991, Dartmouth; Hepple, B and Szyszczak, E (eds), *Discrimination and the Limits of the Law*, 1992, Continuum; Collins, H, 'Discrimination, Equality and Social Inclusion' (2003) 66 MLR 16; Fredman, S, 'Equality: A New generation?' [2001] 30(2) ILJ 145–68; Johnes, G, Career Interruptions and Labour Market Outcomes (2006) EOC Paper No 45; von Prondzynski, F and Richards, W, 'Tackling indirect discrimination' [1995] PL 117; Gardner, J, 'Discrimination as injustice' (1996) 16(3) OJLS 353; Livingstone, S, 'Art 14 and the prevention of discrimination in the ECHR' (1997) EHRLR 25; Ewing, KD, 'The HRA and labour law' (1998) 27 ILJ 275; Deakin, S and Morris, J, *Labour Law*, 2nd edn, 1998, Butterworths, Chapter 6; Bindman, *Discrimination Law*, 2000; Gregory, J, *Sex, Race and the Law: Legislating for Equality*, 1987, Sage.

Act 1995 (DDA), and subsequently the grounds on which discrimination is prohibited have greatly increased: new protected grounds were added, including sexual orientation, age, religion and belief. The full list of protected grounds now includes: race, nationality, national origins, colour, gender, disability, gender reassignment, marital status, pregnancy, sexual orientation, age, religion and belief. Although this was done through a range of statutes and regulations since 1975 when the Sex Discrimination Act was introduced, all anti-discrimination law in the UK (except some aspects in Northern Ireland) has been brought together in the Equality Act 2010. In contrast to other areas of civil liberties and human rights considered in this book, such as free speech, the common law had completely failed to provide protection in this area. The judicial culture that lay behind the failure of the common law to create tortious protection from discrimination is now, it is argued, evident in the strong judicial stance taken against affirmative action.

This subject is vast and in a book of this scope selectivity is necessary, so this section can provide little more than an overview of the key sources of anti-discrimination law that apply. In the UK there are three strands of law, deriving from the domestic schemes, the legislation of the European Union and from the European Convention on Human Rights. The Human Rights Act (HRA) has complicated the issue since it has introduced a form of anti-discrimination law into domestic law – Art 14 – but has given it a lesser status than EU law. At the same time, at the international and domestic level, the Convention is a source of general principles for EU law.

European Union law

Anti-discrimination law in the UK cannot be studied without taking into account European Union law, which has been a highly significant influence. EU law has led to the introduction of provisions prohibiting discrimination outside the previously established areas of gender and race. Treaty articles have both direct and horizontal effect and, therefore, Art 157 of the Treaty on the Functioning of the European Union (TFEU), which provides for equal pay for equal work without discrimination on grounds of sex, can be enforced in domestic courts against private and state bodies through the vehicle of the 'Equality of Terms' provisions of the Equality Act 2010 (below).[8] Directives, in contrast, only have vertical effect; they can, if sufficiently precise, clear and unconditional, be enforced against state bodies – emanations of the state.[9] Also, they can have indirect horizontal effect against private bodies through interpretation.[10]

Sex discrimination law was initially the only area directly regulated by EU law. Article 119 of the Treaty of Rome, which was signed by Britain in 1973, governed the principle of equal pay for equal work. It is now Art 157 TFEU (having spent many years as Art 141 of the EC Treaty). It is amplified by the Equal Pay Directive 75/117, while the Equal Treatment Directive 76/207 and the Pregnancy Directive 92/85 govern other aspects of sexual discrimination. Until 2003 domestic race discrimination provisions were influenced indirectly but they were then expressly covered by the Race Directive.[11]

---

8   See *Biggs v Somerset CC* [1996] IRLR 203.
9   See *Francovich v Italy* [1992] 21 IRLR 84; [1991] ECR I-5357; [1995] ICR 722.
10 Through s 2 of the European Communities Act 1972.
11 Dir 2000/43/EC; Com 2000 328 (01), adopted in June 2000 by the Council of Ministers.

There have been a number of further very significant developments, widening and deepening the protection from discrimination. The Race Directive, extending beyond the employment field, which was implemented in 2003, brought race discrimination within the direct coverage of EU law for the first time. Article 45 TFEU covers nationality discrimination in employment. The very significant Framework Directive on equal opportunities in employment, adopted, like the Race Directive, under Art 19 (formerly Art 13 EC Treaty) TFEU,[12] allowed for the extension of anti-discrimination measures into the new areas of discrimination on grounds of sexual orientation, age, religion and belief. The Framework Directive also improved the protection offered by the Sex Discrimination Act. Development in this area continues apace. The Equal Treatment in Goods and Services Directive[13] extends Community discrimination law to the fields of supply of goods and services. Council Directive 2006/54/EC, described as a Directive 'on the implementation of the principle of equal opportunities and equal treatment of men and women in matters of employment and occupation', consolidates a number of previous directives in this area, notably, Directive 76/207/EEC.

The commitment of the EU to equality currently receives its most broad and dramatic expression in the Charter of Fundamental Rights, which provides in Art 21(1):

> Any discrimination based on any ground such as sex, race, colour, ethnic or social origin, genetic features, language, religion or belief, political or any other opinion, membership of a national minority, property, birth, disability, age or sexual orientation shall be prohibited.

This is the broadest anti-discrimination measure in EU law in that it refers to a range of protected grounds and is not confined to the sphere of employment. It was to become part of the EU Constitution, but in 2005 the referenda in both France and the Netherlands rejected adoption of the Constitution. It was nevertheless adopted as a binding EU Charter by the Treaty of Lisbon with effect from 1 December 2009, giving it the same legal status as the treaties. This means that EU institutions and member states must act consistently with, eg, Art 21, but this applies to member states only when they are acting within the scope of the implementation of EU law. Thus the Charter has direct effect with regard to any legislation, regulations or actions of the UK government when its reason for acting is implementation of or compliance with EU law.[14] In 2007, the European Council of Ministers created a new Fundamental Rights Agency (FRA) for the European Union, which has a much more limited remit than the UK's Equality and Human Rights Commission. The FRA's remit covers all areas of equality, but its activities primarily involve data collection and advice on thematic areas selected by the Council, and it does not intervene in individual legal cases.[15]

---

12 For discussion of Art 13, which was added by the Amsterdam Treaty, see Bell [1999] 6 Maastricht J of European and Comp Law 5.

13 Dir 2004/113/EC.

14 Joined Cases C-411/10 and C-493/10, *NS v Home Secretary and ME v Refugee Applications Commissioner* [2011] EUECJ C-411/10 (21 December 2011).

15 'The European Union Agency for Fundamental Rights'. European Commission, available at: http://ec.europa.eu/justice/fundamental-rights/agency/index_en.htm

Domestic anti-discrimination legislation

Discrimination law in the UK moved to a new phase in 2010. Previously anti-discrimination legislation had developed piecemeal, not only in that different grounds of discrimination (e.g., race or sex) were targeted by separate legislative instruments, but in that some pieces of legislation originated domestically while others were clearly driven by European initiatives. Starting with strongly differing domestic approaches to race and sex discrimination in the late 1960s and early 1970s, through a period of EU influence on sex discrimination but not race discrimination in the 1980s, UK discrimination law got ahead of the EU with the Disability Discrimination Act in 1995. It then found itself tasked with implementing the 2000 EU Race and Employment Directives, requiring the UK to prohibit employment discrimination on grounds of religion or belief, sexual orientation and age, and to update several existing protections. By 2003 the student of discrimination law needed to learn four separate statutes and three sets of regulations. The regulations (on age, sexual orientation, and religion or belief discrimination) bore the obvious hallmarks of EU implementation measures, while the sex, race and disability statutes consisted of domestic skeletons with bits of EU-driven flesh fastened on.

The Equality Act 2010 solved at least those problems. It drew all of the grounds of discrimination into one statute, extended anti-discrimination protection to a roughly similar scope of coverage (e.g., employment, services, public bodies, etc) across each ground, and harmonised definitions and concepts throughout. It introduced new provisions as well, allowing greater scope for positive action, strengthening judicially weakened disability protections and empowering the government to require the publication of equal pay audits. Unfortunately, the Act left unaddressed important questions about the meaning of discrimination that have spawned inconsistent case law, made no more comprehensible by the Act. On the positive side, this means that much of the pre-2010 case law still applies. The most beneficial outcome of the Act is that it makes explaining how the statute works vastly more straightforward, when compared to the pre-2010 state of affairs.

Protected characteristics

The Act sets out, at the beginning, the protected characteristics to which it applies: age, disability, gender reassignment, marriage and civil partnership, pregnancy and maternity, race, religion or belief, sex and sexual orientation.[16] The Act then sets out protections in a way that refers back to these characteristics and more or less applies the same prohibitions with regard to each (this is somewhat misleading, however, as 'marriage and civil partnership' is excluded from the 'indirect discrimination' provisions, and almost all of the protected characteristics can boast special provisions that make discrimination on that ground subtly unique). Most provisions can be understood to impose roughly the same prohibitions across all grounds so long as the discrimination occurs because of a protected characteristic (other than 'pregnancy and maternity'). This last characteristic is the subject of a singular provision prohibiting unfavourable treatment during a defined maternity period or arising from the pregnancy.[17] Another

16   Equality Act 2010, s 4.
17   Equality Act 2010, s 18.

characteristic that attracts specialised protection is gender reassignment: a person who is absent from work as a result of undergoing gender reassignment has a right to be treated no less favourably than would be the case if the absence was due to sickness or injury, or to some other cause such that, having regard to the circumstances, it is reasonable for the treatment to be no less favourable.[18]

'Race' in the 2010 Act means colour, nationality, ethnic origin or national origin.[19] Section 9 of the Act allows for the Secretary of State to order the inclusion of 'caste' as part of the definition of 'race'. The coalition government promised for years to do so, but recently announced that it would not take any action on the matter before the 2015 general election, which ushered in a Conservative government and probably put paid to the procrastinated plans.[20] However, the Employment Appeal Tribunal (EAT) even more recently held that caste *can* be considered part of 'race' under the Act, so long as it is sufficiently linked to 'ethnic origins', in the sense that it exists by 'descent'.[21] Disability also enjoys special protections, discussed more below. While age appears to receive protection from all of the core provisions, it is undermined by exceptions and qualifications (these were also present in the predecessor regulation), including the ability to justify direct age discrimination. 'Religion or belief' includes philosophical belief as well as the absence of belief.[22] With regard to marriage or civil partnership, different panels of the EAT have sent contradictory messages as to whether discrimination based on the person with whom the claimant is married or partnered (as opposed to based on the status of being married or partnered) receives protection as discrimination 'because of' marriage or civil partnership.[23] Finally, sexual orientation as a protected characteristic is not so fully protected when to guarantee that protection would require religious groups or employers to modify their leadership rules.[24]

'Discrimination' under the Act

The Equality Act 2010 defines several types of discrimination or 'prohibited conduct': direct discrimination, indirect discrimination and discrimination by way of harassment and victimisation (which is not, strictly speaking, discrimination, and receives no further attention here). Direct discrimination is defined in s 13 as where 'person (A) discriminates against another (B) if, because of a protected characteristic, A treats B less favourably than A treats or would treat others'. This epitomises the 'formal equality'

18 Equality Act 2010, s 16.
19 Equality Act 2010, s 9.
20 *Caste legislation introduction – programme and timetable* (Government Equalities Office July 2013) available at https://www.gov.uk/government/uploads/system/uploads/attachment_data/file/225658/130726-Caste-Discrimination.pdf; 'Government breaks promise over consultation on caste discrimination' *National Secular Society* (11 March 2015) available at http://www.secularism.org.uk/news/2015/03/government-breaks-promise-over-consultation-on-caste-discrimination.
21 *Chandhok v Tirkey* UKEAT/0190/14, [2014] EqLR 183 ('Tirkey' is not a typo).
22 Equality Act 2010, s 10.
23 *Dunn v The Institute of Cemetery and Crematorium Management* UKEAT/0531/10, [2012] All ER (D) 173 (holding that it is); *Hawkins v (1) Atex Group (2) Korsvold (3) Malo de Molina (4) Reardon*, UKEAT/0302/11, [2012] All ER (D) 71 (holding that it is not).
24 Equality Act 2010, Sched 9, s 2(1).

understanding of discrimination: treating people differently for prohibited reasons. The scope of s 13 is wide, particularly as the House of Lords has made clear in the leading case of *James v Eastleigh Borough Council*[25] that in determining whether there has been direct discrimination the motive or purpose or intention of the alleged discriminator is irrelevant. The correct approach is an objective one: 'would the complainant have received the same treatment but for his sex?'

The 'equality of terms' provisions of the Act, which essentially take the place of the previous Equal Pay Act 1970, work on the basis of a comparison between the treatment of the applicant and that of a named comparator. However, the rest of the Equality Act is based on a comparison with a hypothetical comparator ('treats or would treat'), and the comparison must be such that there is 'no material difference between the circumstances relevant to each case'.[26] The identification of the appropriate comparator, and the determination of which circumstances are to be considered as relevant, are key elements in any discrimination claim, often requiring difficult judgments as to which of the differences between any two individuals are relevant and which are irrelevant, and the choice of characteristics 'may itself be determinative of the outcome'.[27]

It is important that judges (and the lawyers who brief them) do not lose sight of the point of this exercise: to determine whether the less favourable treatment was 'because of a protected characteristic'. Obviously, if in a dismissal letter an employer writes, 'you have been dismissed because we do not like homosexuals in this company', the dismissed applicant need hardly produce a comparator to prove the point of less favourable treatment. More problematically, tribunals are sometimes tempted to include, as 'circumstances relevant to each case', facts that actually flow necessarily from the alleged ground of discrimination. Recently, in *Lockwood v Department for Work and Pensions*, the Court of Appeal held that a tribunal treating people over 35 as improper comparators for a 26-year-old woman in an age discrimination case, because younger women can more easily find subsequent employment, completely misconceived the point of the comparison.[28]

Relevant circumstances also must not include facts that did not in reality have any bearing on the challenged decision. A comparison should not be rejected because the comparators have different degrees of work experience if work experience was not a criterion in the challenged decision: because it was not actually a criterion for the impugned decision, the distinction cannot disprove that the decision was based on a protected characteristic. It may be possible to find an actual comparator whose circumstances are the same or not materially different to those of the applicant, in which case that person can perform the role of the statutory comparator, but in most cases this will not be possible, and in such circumstances the court or tribunal must[29] make

---

25 [1990] ICR 554, [1990] IRLR 288, HL; revsg [1989] ICR 423, [1989] IRLR 318, CA.
26 Equality Act 2010, s 23.
27 *Shamoon v Chief Constable of the Royal Ulster Constabulary* [2003] UKHL 11, [2003] IRLR 285 at 292, per Lord Hope.
28 [2013] EWCA Civ 1195 (Rimer, LJ).
29 A tribunal commits an error of law if it does not construct a hypothetical comparator, where one is required, against which to test the alleged discriminatory treatment: *Balamoody v United Kingdom Central Council for Nursing, Midwifery and Health Visiting* [2001] EWCA Civ 2097, [2002] IRLR 288, CA. See also *Chief Constable of West Yorkshire v Vento* [2001] IRLR 124, EAT.

a hypothetical comparison, by considering how the employer would have treated a male employee in comparable circumstances. One way of doing this is to see how the employer acted 'in cases which, while not identical, were also not wholly dissimilar',[30] as that evidence may provide a sound basis for inferring how the employer would have treated another employee in the same circumstances as the applicant.

Prior to the 2010 Act, the SDA 1975 based direct discrimination on the sex of the applicant, and the DDA 1995 based discrimination on the disabled status of the applicant, while other legislation (eg, the RRA 1976 and the 2006 Employment Equality Regulations) addressed direct discrimination 'on grounds of' the protected characteristics of, for example, race or sexual orientation. This meant that some legislation was susceptible to the interpretation that it was discriminatory to treat someone less favourably because of their association with a person of a certain race or sexual orientation, while statutes like the SDA expressly ruled this out. Where possible, case law clarified that such 'association' discrimination was actionable, but discontinuities remained. The 2010 Act clears this up by defining all direct discrimination, whatever the ground, as less favourable treatment 'because of a protected characteristic'. This is intended to make the concept of direct discrimination broad enough to encompass, for example, less favourable treatment for caring for a disabled child or for being married to an Asian man.

A significant difficulty with the requirement of 'less favourable' treatment is that it enables a respondent to argue that, because he or she imposes equally bad treatment on everyone, the treatment of one sex, race or other group is no less favourable than the treatment of another. The courts and tribunals in the past were able to circumvent this line of argument, particularly in sex harassment cases, by holding that conduct that is 'gender-specific' is sexually discriminatory *per se*, without the need for any comparison.[31] However, in *Pearce v Governing Body of Mayfield Secondary School*[32] (a case decided shortly before the new statutory definition of 'harassment' was introduced) the House of Lords rejected this approach: 'The fact that harassment is gender specific in form cannot be regarded as of itself establishing conclusively that the reason for the harassment is gender-based: "on the ground of her sex".'[33] The 2010 Act now defines harassment as unwanted conduct 'related to a protected characteristic' that has the purpose or effect (1) of violating a worker's dignity or (2) of creating an intimidating, hostile, degrading, humiliating or offensive environment for the worker.[34] Another circumstance in which the courts are prepared to find that conduct is discriminatory *per se*, without the need for any comparison, is in the context of pregnancy discrimination, where the comparative approach breaks down because of the absence of an appropriate (actual or hypothetical) male comparator.

Discrimination does not, of course, always consist of a breach of formal equality. In particular, it could consist of a rule, policy, criterion or practice which, while not

---

30 *Balamoody v United Kingdom Central Council for Nursing, Midwifery and Health Visiting* [2001] EWCA Civ 2097, [2002] IRLR 288 at 306, per Lord Rodger.

31 See e.g., *British Telecommunications plc v Williams* [1997] IRLR 668, EAT.

32 [2003] IRLR 512, HL.

33 [2003] IRLR 512 at 516, per Lord Nicholls.

34 Section 26 goes on to cover specifically (1) engaging in unwanted verbal, non-verbal or physical conduct of a sexual nature which has a similar effect and (2) treating an employee less favourably because he or she rejected or submitted to any of this unwanted conduct.

formally differentiating on the ground of a protected characteristic, substantively puts one group at a disadvantage because it has a disproportionate impact on the members of that group. A rule that a candidate for a job should come from a certain neighbourhood could be said to discriminate indirectly on grounds of race or religion. On the other hand, it could be the case that the factor causing the discriminatory effect is in fact necessary for some strong policy or business reason. The statutory compromise is the concept of indirect discrimination, which enables an applicant to raise an inference of discrimination by showing that a provision, criterion or practice of the respondent has an adverse impact on a group defined by a protected characteristic, but then permits the respondent to rebut that inference by showing that there is some objective justification for the application of that rule, etc, despite its adverse impact.

There is indirect discrimination when the following four conditions are satisfied:

(1) the respondent applies a provision, criterion or practice that applies or would apply equally to those who do not share the claimant's protected characteristic;
(2) it puts or would put people with the claimant's protected characteristic at a particular disadvantage when compared with those who do not share it;
(3) it puts the claimant at that disadvantage;
(4) it cannot be shown to be a proportionate means of achieving a legitimate aim.

Although issues can arise in the application of the first three steps, these are highly technical and space forbids their discussion here, especially because the vast majority of cases are decided on the fourth element: the proportionality justification. Although the Equality Act does not use the language of justification, it remains how lawyers and judges talk about s 19(2)(d), which maintains that prima facie indirect discrimination is not unlawful if the provision, criterion or practice (PCP) represents a proportionate means to a legitimate aim.

There has been a long history[35] of UK courts and tribunals applying justification inconsistently with clear authority from the *Bilka-Kaufhaus* case, where the CJEU ruled that indirect discrimination under Art 157 TFEU could satisfy the justification defence only where it 'correspond[s] to a real need on the part of the undertaking' and is 'necessary'.[36] Space again forbids a full discussion of this history, but suffice it to say that recently the Supreme Court clarified, among other things, that the *Bilka* requirement of 'real need' (as opposed to a mere 'legitimate aim') remains vital.[37] Although the language of the Equality Act speaks only of legitimate aim, 'this has to be read in the light of the Directive which it implements'.[38] *Homer* not only cited *Bilka*, but engaged in a careful consideration of the *weight* of the purported 'legitimate aim' in the case. Whether it is called a 'real need' or a 'legitimate aim,' the respondent's objective in applying the PCP must be more than merely something he or she is permitted by law to do, or has an understandable motive for doing.

Another problem with reconciling the Equality Act language of proportionality with *Bilka* lies in the fact that proportionality does not, in its purest sense, turn exclusively

---

35 Baker, A, 'Proportionality and Employment Discrimination in the UK' (2008) 37 ILJ 305.
36 *Bilka-Kaufhaus Case* 170/84 [1987] ICR 110, 126.
37 *Homer v Chief Constable of West Yorkshire Police* [2012] IRLR 601.
38 *Ibid*, at para 22.

on a test of necessity. The classic German expression of proportionality requires that state acts or measures be (1) suitable to achieve a legitimate purpose, (2) necessary to achieve that purpose, and (3) proportional in the narrower sense: they must not impose burdens or 'cause harms to other legitimate interests' that outweigh the objectives achieved.[39] The third of these principles constitutes proportionality in its 'strict sense', while more complicated formulations are essentially structured analyses intended to ensure the observation of the principle. Proportionality *stricto sensu* is also included in the CJEU understanding of justification of indirect discrimination, but is far less emphasised owing to *Bilka*'s adoption of a structured analysis involving 'real need' and necessity.[40] Such a test rests on a presumption that a discriminatory impact has substantial 'weight' in the balancing exercise. A justification cannot outweigh this impact unless at least (1) the respondent has a real need to achieve a particular aim, and (2) the measure it employs to achieve it is necessary, in the sense of representing the least discriminatory alternative available. *Homer* looks likely to have made this point sufficiently clear: it not only emphasised the continuing applicability of the *Bilka* requirements, but it declared that 'the assessment of whether the criterion can be justified entails a comparison of the impact of that criterion upon the affected group as against the importance of the aim to the employer'.[41] Even provisions, criteria or practices necessary to the achievement of legitimate aims should fail the test if the aim is not compelling or the impacts imposed are too strongly inconsistent with the aims of anti-discrimination law.

Finally, the Equality Act 2010 significantly strengthened the possibilities for positive action, without eliminating the greatest obstacle to it. While positive discrimination – treating a member of a disadvantaged group formally more favourably – has traditionally been unlawful and remains so under the Act, positive action is not prohibited. Measures aimed at promoting equal opportunities that fall short of positive discrimination might include the development of policies and practices designed to assist disadvantaged groups (for example 'family-friendly' policies), encouraging applications for jobs, promotions or contracts from under-represented groups, and the setting of targets to reduce under-representation. The 2010 Act introduces for the first time in the UK the right to treat a member of an under-represented or disadvantaged group *more favourably* for hiring or promotion. Section 159(1) permits tie-break discrimination where either (1) persons who share a protected characteristic suffer a disadvantage or (2) those persons are disproportionately represented in an activity. If the s 159(1) threshold is met, an employer may treat persons with the protected characteristic *more favourably* in recruitment or promotion; but this is allowed only where (1) the person thus favoured is 'as qualified' as the other to be recruited or promoted and (2) the employer does not have a policy of favouring the group of which the favoured person is a representative. This last condition is almost certainly intended to ensure that this tie-break permission only applies on a case-by-case basis.

39 Lord Hoffmann, 'The Influence of the European Principle of Proportionality upon UK Law', in Evelyn Ellis (ed), *The Principle of Proportionality in the Laws of Europe* (1999) 107.
40 *Cadman v Health and Safety Executive* [2006] ICR 1623, 1635–9, 1647 (the ECJ referred specifically to the paragraph of Bilka which required that the policy correspond to a 'real need' of the business).
41 See fn 37 at para 24.

Issues associated with specific protected characteristics

Some issues associated with specific protected characteristics – equal pay cases requiring an actual comparator, pregnancy discrimination being expressly asymmetrical and certain idiosyncrasies around protection of gender reassignment and marital/civil partnership status – were mentioned above in connection with broader themes. It remains necessary to mention three other areas of divergence: the unique rules governing disability discrimination, the exceptions to direct age discrimination, and gender-specific dress codes. This discussion will be woefully oversimplified owing to space limitations, but will convey a flavour of the issues.

One way in which disability protections under the Act differ significantly from other protections is that they apply only to disabled people[42] – i.e., those who can satisfy the statutory definition of disability – and are thus not symmetrical as with most of the other protections. The definition of disability in s 6 of the Act states that a disability is a (1) physical or mental impairment that has a (2) substantial and (3) long-term adverse effect on (4) the ability to carry out normal day-to-day activities (the Act itself does not number the elements in this way, but courts and tribunals have separate tests for each of these aspects).[43] The Court of Appeal set out the correct approach to impairment in *McNicol v Balfour Beatty Rail Maintenance Ltd*,[44] holding that the term 'impairment' bears its ordinary and natural meaning, that it 'may result from an illness or it may consist of an illness'[45] and, crucially, that 'it is not necessary to consider how an impairment was caused'.[46] This last point was recently underscored by the CJEU in holding that (1) obesity could be a disability if it constitutes an impairment and has the relevant effects and (2) it does not matter whether the obesity was in some way self-inflicted.[47] 'Substantial' is generally a matter of having an effect which is 'more than minor or trivial'.[48] An impairment will be treated as having a 'long-term' effect if it has lasted, or is likely to last, for at least 12 months, or if it is likely to last for the rest of a person's life (as in the case of a terminal illness).[49] Where the impairment is intermittent or sporadic (for example, epilepsy or multiple sclerosis), it will be treated as continuing to have a long-term adverse effect, even through periods of remission, if it is likely to recur.[50] Finally, 'normal day-to-day activities' are the activities of an ordinary average person, not a person with specialised skills or abilities. However, the guidance states that 'normal

---

42 This is of course only true with respect to rights of action – employers and other institutions have duties to make reasonable adjustments that do not require the existence of a complaint or the associated disabled complainiant.

43 The Act makes it clear that this definition includes past disabilities, and it is assumed that the 'because of' language means that direct discrimination applies to people who are perceived as having a disability.

44 [2002] EWCA Civ 1074, [2002] ICR 1498, [2002] IRLR 711.

45 [2002] IRLR 711 at 713, per Mummery LJ. See to like effect Lindsay J in *College of Ripon & York St John v Hobbs* [2002] IRLR 185 at para 32 and *Millar v Inland Revenue Commissioners* [2006] IRLR 112, Ct of Sess (IH).

46 [2002] EWCA Civ 1074, [2002] ICR 1498, [2002] IRLR 711, citing with approval Part 1 of the Guidance.

47 *Kaltoft v Kommunernes Landsforening* C-354/13 (2014) *Times*, 26 December, CJEU.

48 *Goodwin v Patent Office* [1999] ICR 302, [1999] IRLR 4; *Vicary v British Telecommunications plc* [1999] IRLR 680, EAT.

49 Equality Act 2010, Sched 1, para 2(1).

50 Equality Act 2010, para 2(2).

day-to-day activities' do not include work of any particular form, 'because no particular form of work is "normal" for most people'.[51]

The 2010 Act contains two special kinds of protection afforded only to the protected characteristic of disability: the duty to make adjustments (s 20) and discrimination arising from disability (s 15). The Act essentially makes the legal assumption that all of society represents a state of indirect discrimination against disabled people. It places a duty on employers, service providers, and institutions to make reasonable adjustments where a provision, criterion or practice or any physical feature of premises places the disabled person concerned at a substantial disadvantage in comparison with persons who are not disabled, in order to prevent that effect.[52] Failure to comply with the duty to make reasonable adjustments will constitute unlawful discrimination.[53] Notice that this closely resembles indirect discrimination except for the requirement to demonstrate group disadvantage: that is taken as given. The EHRC Guidance on Disability (para 6.28) makes some suggestions about factors to consider in assessing whether adjustments are 'reasonable': (1) the extent to which taking the step would prevent the effect in question; (2) the extent to which it is practicable for the employer to take the step; (3) the financial and other costs that would be incurred by the employer in taking the step and the extent to which taking it would disrupt any of his activities; (4) the extent of the employer's financial and other resources; (5) the availability to the employer of financial or other assistance; and (6) the nature of the employer's activities and the size of his undertaking. In practice these essentially boil down to a balance between efficacy (extent to which it corrects the disadvantage) and cost/practicability for the employer. The EAT has indicated that cost alone can make an adjustment unreasonable in *Cordell v Foreign and Commonwealth Office*.[54] In this case the adjustment was physical (hiring lip-speakers for deaf employee), but the duty of reasonable adjustments also requires changes to procedures, rules and possibly contractual terms.[55]

Section 15 of the Act provides that a person (A) discriminates against a disabled person (B) if A treats B in a way such that, because of B's disability, the treatment amounts to a detriment, and the treatment is not a proportionate means to a legitimate aim. This kind of discrimination, called 'discrimination arising from a disability' in the Act, takes a completely different approach than direct discrimination, and has a lot in common with indirect discrimination, except that it focuses on the individual, not group, adverse effect. It means, essentially, that if a disabled person suffers a detriment because he or she cannot satisfy a requirement (at work, for example), *even if a non-disabled person would suffer the same detriment for not satisfying the requirement*, it will be discrimination if (a) disability was the reason for not satisfying the requirement and (b) applying the requirement in this instance is not proportionate. And of course proportionality must

---

51 ECHR Guidance, para D5. See e.g., *Quinlan v B & Q plc* (EAT 1386/97) (assistant at garden centre not disabled within the meaning of the Act because, although unable to lift heavy objects following heart surgery, he was capable of lifting everyday objects).

52 Equality Act 2010, s 20.

53 Equality Act 2010, s 21. A complaint of a failure to make a reasonable adjustment does not depend upon showing that there has been less favourable treatment: *Clark v Novacold Ltd* [1998] ICR 1044, [1998] IRLR 420, EAT.

54 [2012] ICR 280, [2012] All ER (D) 97.

55 *Archibald v Fife Council* [2004] ICR 954, [2004] IRLR 651, HL; *Nottinghamshire CC v Meikle* [2004] IRLR 703, CA.

be assessed with the duty to make reasonable adjustments in the background: it could never be proportionate to apply a criterion to the detriment of a disabled person if reasonable (and effective) adjustments could have been made but were not. The result is that, for example, if a double amputee cannot complete her rounds in the time generally required by security guards, and any security guard – disabled or otherwise – would be dismissed for failing to complete rounds in good time, it will be discrimination to dismiss the double amputee if a reasonable adjustment was available (such as a golf cart) that would speed the completion of rounds to the extent that performance was close enough to the general standard to make it disproportionate to dismiss.

With regard to age discrimination, there is one *major* difference from all other heads of illegal discrimination. This is that the Equality Act 2010, s 13(2) prescribes that direct age discrimination is not discrimination if it is a proportionate means of achieving a legitimate aim: direct discrimination can be justified.[56] This justification has so far been used to justify enhanced redundancy schemes,[57] points for long service in a redundancy selection process[58] and retirement.[59] This broad exception is arguably authorised by Art 6 of the EU Framework Directive, which allows member states to derogate from the prohibition on direct discrimination in proportionate pursuit of employment policy, labour market and vocational training objectives. Pursuant to Art 6 the CJEU has approved laws or legally sanctioned sector-wide collective agreements that adopt a default retirement age, but in doing so has subjected them to intense scrutiny in connection with the legitimacy of their aims and the proportionality of the laws in achieving them.[60] However, a broad general exception is not the same thing as a state going through all of the policy research and democratic processes to create a default retirement age, and a single employer deciding that a compulsory retirement age meets its employment policy objectives is not the same thing as a government concluding that a retirement age meets national policy objectives. Unfortunately the Supreme Court seems largely to have missed the difference in *Seldon v Clarkson Wright and Jakes*.[61] There it concluded that individual employers may directly discriminate on the basis of age so long as the aims of the employer are consistent with government-level policy objectives approved by the CJEU. This of course skips the part where the government actually adopts employment policy, labour market and vocational training objectives as envisaged by the Directive. Its policy is apparently to let employers set employment policy piecemeal.

Finally, it is not uncommon for employers to impose different rules on men and women in relation to their dress and appearance while at work. It seems obvious that under the test of direct discrimination approved by the House of Lords in *James v Eastleigh Borough Council*[62] any such differentiation necessarily constitutes discrimination on the grounds of sex, because 'but for' a person's sex, the gender-specific appearance

---

56 Swift, 'Justifying Age Discrimination' (2006) 35 ILJ 228.
57 *MacCulloch v ICI* [2008] All ER (D) 81.
58 *Rolls Royce v UNITE* [2008] All ER (D) 174.
59 *Seldon v Clarkson Wright and Jakes* [2012] UKSC 16.
60 *Fuchs and Kohler v Land Hessen* C-159/10, C-160/10, [2011] All ER (D) 97; *Hörnfeldt v Posten Meddelande* C-141/11, [2012] IRLR 785.
61 [2012] UKSC 16.
62 [1990] IRLR 288, HL.

requirement would not have been applied.[63] Furthermore, given that anti-discrimination legislation seeks to eliminate discrimination that results from gender stereotyping, employing ideas of 'conventional' appearance expectations is inherently sexually discriminatory as it epitomises gender stereotyping. Nevertheless, UK courts and tribunals have maddeningly subverted the legislation by holding that there is no violation of the Act as long as a dress code enforces a common principle of smartness or conventionality, and taken as a whole neither gender is treated less favourably. So, for example, in *Schmidt v Austicks Bookshops Ltd*,[64] the EAT approved a rule that women could not wear trousers at work, while men were not allowed to wear tee-shirts. The *Schmidt* approach was approved by the Court of Appeal in *Smith v Safeway plc*.[65] In that case, the employer's appearance code placed restrictions on hair length that applied to men only; women were allowed to have long hair provided it was tied back. The complainant was dismissed because he refused to cut off his ponytail. The idea that it is not less favourable treatment on the ground of sex to prohibit a woman who wants to wear trousers from wearing them, while allowing a man who wants to wear trousers to wear them, is preposterous. The bizarre fiction that where a woman who wants to wear her hair in a ponytail at work can, but a man who wants to wear a ponytail at work (and outside of work) cannot, does not constitute less favourable treatment on the ground of sex, defies the letter and spirit of the legislation to the extent that one cannot help but question the very ingenuousness of the judges involved. This is what anti-discrimination legislation is up against.

The Human Rights Act and the European Convention on Human Rights[66]

The EU provisions are in many respects more valuable than the guarantee of freedom from discrimination under Art 14 of the European Convention, partly because they may override domestic statutory provisions in domestic courts,[67] and partly because, as Chapter 2 explained, Art 14 only covers areas falling within the scope of the other articles, although the other article may be viewed as having an extended ambit where Art 14 is also argued.[68] This limitation was highlighted in *Botta v Italy*.[69] The European Court of Human Rights considered a claim that the lack of disabled facilities at a seaside resort violated the applicant's right to equal enjoyment of his right to respect for private life under Art 8 read together with Art 14. The claim was rejected on the basis that 'social' rights, such as the participation of disabled people in recreational facilities, fall outside Art 8. Therefore, Art 14 did not apply.

---

63 See Cunningham (1995) 24 ILJ 177; Wintemute (1997) 60 MLR 334.
64 [1978] ICR 85, [1977] IRLR 360, EAT.
65 [1996] ICR 868, [1996] IRLR 456, CA.
66 See also Chapter 2, pp 93–94.
67 It was found in *Francovich v Italy* [1992] 21 IRLR 84; [1991] ECR I-5357; [1995] ICR 722 that an individual who suffers loss at the hands of a private body owing to the state's failure to undertake full implementation of a directive may have a claim against the state.
68 See Baker, A, 'The Enjoyment of Rights and Freedoms: A New Conception of the "Ambit" under Art 14 ECHR' [2006] 89 MLR 714; 'Art 14 ECHR: A Protector, Not a Prosecutor', in Fenwick, H, Phillipson, G and Masterman, R (eds), *Judicial Reasoning and the Human Rights Act 1998*, 2007.
69 (1998) 26 EHRR 241.

Even where Art 14 may apply, Strasbourg has often been reluctant to afford it separate consideration, if a breach of another Convention right is established.[70] Where Art 14 has been considered, it was for some time afforded a narrow interpretation. For example, in *Stedman v UK*[71] a requirement to work on a Sunday led to the dismissal of the applicant, who had religious objections to Sunday working. It was found that a general requirement that has a disproportionate impact on one group is not discriminatory. This decision suggested that Art 14 does not recognise indirect discrimination. However, *Thlimmenos v Greece*[72] first opened the door to indirect discrimination by holding that the failure of a scheme for accrediting accountants to distinguish convictions for conscientious objection to military service from other 'serious offences' constituted religious discrimination. There was some question as to whether this amounted to full-blown indirect discrimination or some distinct 'treat different cases differently' principle, but this was surely a distinction without a difference. The ECtHR appears to have confirmed this view (or at least obviated the controversy) in *DH v Czech Republic*[73] which is now generally accepted to have established indirect discrimination as covered by Art 14.[74]

Further, Art 14 covers discrimination on a wide range of bases and therefore, combined with Art 8 or, in some circumstances, a range of the articles, in particular Arts 5, 6, 10 or 11, it can be used to address discrimination that is currently outside the EU or domestic anti-discrimination schemes. The Court has recognised several kinds of 'other status' that are not covered by EU or UK law, such as marital status,[75] residence[76] and professional or military status.[77] But the HRA itself curbs the effect of the Convention since it only binds public authorities under s 6. As it currently appears that the HRA does not create direct horizontal effect,[78] its impact in this area is subject to certain limitations.

If a standard public authority, or a functional public authority acting in its public function, discriminates in a manner that could be addressed by Art 8 in conjunction with Art 14, or Art 8 alone, a freestanding action could be brought against it under s 7(1)(a) HRA, although not in an employment tribunal (ET), which has no jurisdiction to hear such claims. If a discriminatory measure is contained in a statute, s 3 HRA and Arts 8 (or another relevant article) and 14 can be brought to bear upon the offending provision. Section 3 can apply to the Equality Act 2010 if it appears that there is a potential gap in the provisions where, under Arts 14 and 8 combined, a remedy would be available. By this route, it is possible that gaps in the Act could be narrowed. This could also apply to other statutory provisions, such as those governing unfair dismissal,[79] meaning that Art 14's anti-discrimination protection has a very wide-ranging potential, on both neutral

---

70   See *Dudgeon v UK* (1982) 4 EHRR 149, para 69.
71   (1997) 23 EHRR CD 168.
72   (2000) 31 EHRR 411.
73   (2007) 44 EHRR 3.
74   *AM (Somalia) v Entry Clearance Officer* [2009] EWCA Civ 634, [2009] UKHRR 1073, at [39].
75   *Sahin v Germany (2003)* 36 EHRR 43.
76   *Carson & Ors v UK* (2010) 51 EHRR 369.
77   *Van der Mussele v Belgium* (1983) 6 EHRR 163, *Engel v Netherlands* (1976) 1 EHRR 647 respectively.
78   See Chapter 4, pp 212–18.
79   See *X v Y* [2004] IRLR 471; ICR 1634 in which the Employment Appeals Tribunal (EAT) laid out the way that Art 14 could affect unfair dismissal and other statutory claims in Tribunals.

and overtly discriminatory provisions. A number of discrimination claims are, however, brought in employment tribunals, and an ET's powers to give effect to Convention rights are limited in a number of significant respects, even beyond the limitations already imposed by the HRA. Apart from its inability to hear s 7(1)(a) HRA claims, ETs and the Employment Appeal Tribunal (EAT) have no power to make a declaration of incompatibility.[80] It can merely refer the matter to the Court of Appeal, which does have the power to make a declaration of incompatibility.[81]

Where a provision in itself appears to be compatible with the relevant Convention article(s) that of course does not exhaust the duty of the court/tribunal in relation to the Convention, due to s 6 HRA. When a court or tribunal is applying statutory provisions, including anti-discrimination statutes, in relation to, for example, an employment matter, it must abide by its duty under s 6 HRA, which means *applying* the provision compatibly with Art 14 (assuming that another Convention right touches on the matter at hand). However, the potential of Art 14 domestically is doubly limited – first by its own inherent limitation, since it is non-freestanding, and second by the lack of direct horizontal effect under the HRA. In general, therefore, it is not expected that at present the impact of the HRA in this context will be very great. This is an instance therefore in which EU law is of far more significance than the ECHR in the private sector due to the lack of private common law on which the Convention can bite via s 6 HRA.

Where another article and Art 14 combined cover the same area as EU provisions, they can be used as a source of general principles for the interpretation of the EU law, under Art 6 of the Lisbon Treaty. The EU provisions can override domestic law and, therefore, by this means those Convention articles could be given, in a sense, further effect than the HRA allows them. Thus, for example, an applicant bringing an action against a private body and seeking to rely on the Equality Act in respect of discrimination on grounds of gender reassignment in a context excluded from the Act, could begin by arguing that s 3 of the HRA should be used to broaden the meaning of the Act in reliance on Arts 8 and 14. If this failed, on the basis that such an interpretation would amount to legislating, the applicant could rely on s 2 of the European Communities Act 1972 in arguing that the interpretation in question should be adopted in order to satisfy the demands of the Equal Treatment Directive or any other relevant directive. At that stage, in order to determine the requirements of the directive, Strasbourg jurisprudence on Arts 8 and 14 could re-enter the argument. This possibility could be even more significant in relation to the domestic measures that have been adopted in response to the Framework and Race Directives.

As Chapter 2 explained, Protocol 12 provides a freestanding right to freedom from discrimination.[82] Protocol 12 is evidence of a clear recognition of the weakness of the

---

80 Only those courts listed in s 4(5) HRA (the High Court, Court of Appeal and House of Lords, and the High Court of Justiciary and Court of Session in Scotland) can make such a declaration.

81 In e.g., *Whittaker v P&M Watson Haulage* (EAT 157/01, unreported) both the ET and EAT held that the exclusion then in place in the Disability Discrimination Act 1995 for employers with less than 15 employees was incompatible with Art 6 of the ECHR because it contravened Mr Whittaker's right to have his claim regarding his civil rights heard. However, the EAT could not provide Mr Whittaker with a remedy, because it was not possible to interpret the DDA compatibly with his Convention rights, so it had to apply the DDA as drafted.

82 See pp 90–92 for further discussion; see Khaliq, V, 'Protocol 12 to the ECHR: a step forward or a step too far?' [2001] PL 457.

anti-discrimination measure under Art 14 of the Convention, and its existence may be prompting the European Court of Human Rights to move away from earlier stances under Art 14 in favour of a more developed and determined position on anti-discrimination under that article. If Protocol 12 were eventually ratified by the UK and then included in Sched 1 to the HRA, it would have a far-reaching impact in this context, since a freestanding right to non-discrimination on a wide range of grounds would then be created, which would have direct effect as against public authorities. It might also have an impact on the currently protected grounds since it could be relied upon in an attempt to extend or fill gaps in the legislation. At present, however, Protocol 12 has not been ratified by the UK; it has sat unratified for 15 years, and the government remains opposed to ratification.

3 The Equality and Human Rights Commission and positive duties

Obviously the measures discussed above, which only allow for aggrieved individuals to seek redress for discriminatory wrongs, have a limited capacity to achieve substantive equality. Even actions for indirect discrimination, which afford remedies for breaches of substantive inequality rather than formal inequality, cannot hope to bring about a substantively equal outcome on a societal level through a case-by-case approach. One way to make the legal approach to achieving equality more strategic and overarching is to create an institution or agency with power to drive change, through traditional litigation, education and advice, and large-scale inquiries and investigations. This approach has been attempted in some form for decades, in the form of the Commission for Racial Equality, the Equal Opportunities Commission, and the Disability Rights Commission, now subsumed into the Equality and Human Rights Commission (EHRC), and is arguably on the wane. Another way that has recently grown in popularity, but into whose waters the UK has as yet jabbed only the most tentative toe, is a system of positive equality duties. This section discusses both measures, including their trajectory and possible future, in turn.

The EHRC

The administrative method exemplified by the EHRC represents a more coherent and effective approach than the piecemeal method of bringing individual cases. The aim is to bring about general changes in discriminatory practices rather than waiting for an individual to take on the risk and the burden of bringing a case. To this end it has powers to:[83]

*   provide assistance to those taking legal proceedings in relation to equality
*   take legal cases on behalf of individuals or intervene in litigation to test and extend the right to equality and human rights
*   apply to the court for injunctions and interdicts where we consider it likely that an unlawful act will be committed

83   The list below is taken from the EHRC website because of its greater clarity of expression, but the powers are conferred in ss 13 through 32 of the Equality Act 2006.

- conduct inquiries, investigations and assessments to examine the behaviour of institutions
- enforce the public sector equality duty, issuing compliance notices where we believe the law has been breached
- award grants to organisations
- provide education and training to make individuals and institutions aware of their rights and responsibilities
- produce guidance and statutory codes of practice to support individuals and organisations to comply with the law and promote good practice, and
- use our influence and authority to lead new debates, building our arguments from the evidence we collect and publish.

These powers all apply to equality for all protected characteristics named in the 2010 Act, as well as to human rights where specified.

Obviously significant in terms of achieving equality is the power to conduct a formal investigation into any alleged contraventions, which may result in the issue of an unlawful act notice if the EHRC discovers breaches of the Act; such a notice may require the recipient to prepare an action plan for the purpose of avoiding any repetition, and it may contain requirements to be met by the employer, who has six weeks in which to appeal against it to a tribunal. If there is no appeal, or an appeal is dismissed, the notice becomes final, and any further contraventions of it may be restrained by injunction at the suit of the Commission.[84] The Commission may also enter into legally binding agreements to rectify the situation. There are also further, more specific powers given to the Commission to take action against discriminatory advertisements,[85] and to give practical help to individuals to bring discrimination claims.[86]

The EHRC also has the power to carry out general inquiries, meaning that it can promote improved practice in response to particular areas of concern and can focus on specific sectors. This general inquiries model was developed to build on the model established for the previous Commissions. The EHRC's powers have a much broader base, allowing it to look at issues that might affect two or more protected groups, as well as focusing on one equality strand when appropriate. In order to ensure that it can obtain sufficient information to conduct a thorough and useful investigation, the EHRC may as a last resort apply to the Secretary of State for permission to compel third parties to provide certain information relevant to the inquiry.[87] It can initiate these inquiries either independently or at the request of the Secretary of State. It must publish terms of reference before launching an inquiry, and will publish reports at the end of the process, which could include recommendations for changes to policies, practices or legislation.

---

84 Equality Act 2006 ss 20–24. On the nature of an appeal against a non-discrimination notice, see *Commission for Racial Equality v Amari Plastics Ltd* [1982] ICR 304, [1982] IRLR 252, CA; if the formal investigation is not carried out in accordance with the stipulated procedure, any resulting non-discrimination notice is void: *Re Prestige Group plc, Commission for Racial Equality v Prestige Group plc* [1984] ICR 473, [1984] IRLR 166, HL.
85 Equality Act 2006, s 25.
86 Equality Act 2006, s 28.
87 Equality Act 2006, Sched 2, para 9 *et seq.*

The EHRC has an advisory role in relation to individuals and pressure or community groups. Under s 13 of the 2006 Act, which covers its advisory role, it may:

(a) publish or otherwise disseminate ideas or information;
(b) undertake research;
(c) provide education or training;
(d) give advice or guidance (whether about the effect or operation of an enactment or otherwise) ...

The Commission also engages in strategic litigation, either through taking judicial review actions on its own initiative, intervening in existing cases or putting its weight, funds and expertise behind an individual (equality) case.[88] Finally, and not unimportantly, the EHRC produces guidance and codes of practice on the 2010 Act and on specific protected characteristics.[89]

Although the idea of the EHRC appeals, and suggests more wide-reaching social change than individual actions, the reality of such commissions disappoints. The US Federal counterpart to the EHRC, the Equal Employment Opportunity Commission, has existed for half a century and has for decades been viewed by lawyers and claimants as an obstacle to equality.[90] The sad truth is that for coercive mechanisms like strategic litigation, investigations and compliance notices to work they must attract robust funding and government support. Unfortunately the story of the commissions (the EHRC and its precursors) is riddled with tentative empowering legislation, restrictive interpretation of powers[91] and underfunding. The EHRC has seen its core funding drop from £70 million in 2007 to only £17.1 million by 2015, with staffing reductions of over 70% and the closure of regional offices, such that one commentator has referred to it as a 'deconstruction' of the EHRC.[92] Cuts have led to the closure of the EHRC's helpline, and the Commission's assistance with individual cases has slowed to a trickle. This is not to say that having an EHRC is a bad thing – even a trickle of strategic litigation and investigations can achieve something, and advice and codes of practice will slowly but surely make an impact. However, it is hard to see how the 'administrative method', at least in the current political and economic climate, can hope to make the strides towards substantive equality once hoped for.

Positive duties

'Positive duties' in general refers to a reflexive approach to regulation that imposes duties on public or private entities to take steps to improve equality, and places government institutions – either courts, commissions, departments or some combination thereof – in the role of assessing the success of the steps taken, and consulting about new steps, with

---

88   Equality Act 2006, ss 28–31.
89   Equality Act 2006, ss 14–15.
90   Baker, A, 'A Tale of Two Projects: Emerging Tension between Public and Private Aspects of Employment Discrimination Law' 21 *International Journal of Comparative Labour Law and Industrial Relations* 591 (2005).
91   *Re Prestige Group plc, Commission for Racial Equality v Prestige Group plc* [1984] ICR 473, [1984] IRLR 166, HL.
92   Hepple, B, 'Back to the Future: Employment Law under the Coalition Government,' (2013) 42 ILJ 203 at 207–09.

the expectation of an iterative supervision of ongoing progress.[93] However, this can be done in strong ways and in weak ways, and the Equality Act 2010, as implemented by the coalition government, has adopted a weak approach. It is of course not fair to blame this on the 2010 Act, which inherited a particular conception of positive duties from its predecessor statutes, and essentially recreated them in ss 149–157, except in such a way as to apply to equality across all grounds covered by the Act. This inherited form has three key features. First, the duties apply only to a 'public authority' as defined in the Act (or to other entities exercising 'public functions'). Second, and centrally, the Act imposes a general duty on those authorities to have 'due regard', in the exercise of their functions, to the need to promote equality (as specified below). Third, the Act authorises the government to impose 'specific duties', such as to publish action plans or to involve affected persons (with protected characteristics) in the making of key decisions. Enforcement of the duty is by judicial review, and is to some extent policed by the EHRC.

This represents a weak example of reflexive law for several reasons. Obviously the limitation to public authorities reduces the scope and possible ambition of the scheme. More crucially, however, the 'due regard' requirement has no substance related to equality. The courts are not able to encourage movement towards equality, because equality is not the standard. Instead, the standard is simply that the public decision maker must properly direct itself to the possible equality implications of the decision.[94] This very formal standard was intended to receive support from specific duties that would require public authorities to take concrete steps to improve equality, but the coalition government has pared down the originally envisaged list to just two: to publish information to demonstrate its compliance with the general 'due regard' duty and to publish one or more objectives it thinks it should achieve.[95] Left by the wayside were duties such as to produce plans of action, show the meeting of objectives or involve affected groups in decisions. This feebleness stands in stark contrast to, for example, the specific duties adopted in Scotland.

Each listed authority is required to:

- report on mainstreaming the equality duty;
- publish equality outcomes and report progress;
- assess and review policies and practices;
- gather and use employee information;
- publish gender pay gap information;
- publish statements on equal pay;
- consider award criteria and conditions in relation to public procurement; and
- publish in a manner that is accessible.[96]

The overall effect is to leave the scheme without the capacity to oblige public authorities (much less private entities) to make any substantive change or move in any particular direction. So long as a decision maker can evidence the decision incorporated careful consideration of the need to promote equality, it can in theory act entirely inconsistently with that need.

---

93 Fredman, S, 'The Public Sector Equality Duty' (2011) 40 ILJ 405, 418–19.
94 *Moore v Secretary of State for Communities and Local Government* [2015] EWHC 44 (Admin); [2015] J.P.L. 762 (QBD), [108]–[110] (these paragraphs of the judgment provide a very helpful review of the relevant case law).
95 Fredman, fn 93 at 415–16.
96 Henery, I, 'The public sector equality duty: are employers "measuring up"?' (2015) 126 Emp LB 4–6.

The foregoing does not of course fairly describe the impact of the duties on the ground. Although the scheme has demonstrated only muted effects, its overall influence has been positive.[97] Formal requirements can slowly but surely make headway, because being forced to go through the motions sometimes causes decision makers to rethink. The general duty is described fairly precisely in the Act, and the due regard standard requires that decisions take all of the following into account; the need to:

(a) eliminate discrimination, harassment, victimisation and any other conduct that is prohibited by or under this Act;
(b) advance equality of opportunity between persons who share a relevant protected characteristic and persons who do not share it;
(c) foster good relations between persons who share a relevant protected characteristic and persons who do not share it.

...

(a) remove or minimise disadvantages suffered by persons who share a relevant protected characteristic that are connected to that characteristic;
(b) take steps to meet the needs of persons who share a relevant protected characteristic that are different from the needs of persons who do not share it;
(c) encourage persons who share a relevant protected characteristic to participate in public life or in any other activity in which participation by such persons is disproportionately low.

...

(a) tackle prejudice, and
(b) promote understanding.[98]

Looking at that list, it seems clear that serious progress towards equality could be made if the duty were actually to do all of those things rather than merely give them due regard. The political climate seems unlikely to countenance such a radical approach, but it hardly seems unrealistic to call for the reinstatement in England of a list of specific duties like that in Scotland. There is even some indication that the Conservative government has more sympathy for such specific duties than did the coalition: Prime Minister David Cameron recently called for action to be taken under s 78 of the 2010 Act to require all employers (public and private) with 250 or more employees to publish information about their gender pay gap.[99] Although this is not technically an aspect of the positive duties scheme, it is in fact a specific positive duty relating to equal pay that was included in the Equality Act 2010 and then lay dormant up to now. Perhaps specific duties of this kind, which name and shame institutions and allow public, market and media pressure to be brought to bear, are the best hope for progress towards substantive equality.

97 Hepple, B, 'Enforcing Equality Law: Two Steps Forward, Two Steps Backwards for Reflexive Regulation' (2011) 40 ILJ 315–35.
98 Equality Act 2010 s 149.
99 Mason, R and Treanor, J, 'David Cameron to force companies to disclose gender pay gaps' The Guardian (14 July 2015), available at http://www.theguardian.com/society/2015/jul/14/david-cameron-to-force-companies-to-disclose-gender-pay-gaps.

Part II

Expression

Part II covers a number of aspects of expression including political expression, in the form of public protest, and pornographic expression. It also covers access to official information as an essential precursor to expression since, without such access, some expression will be curbed or cannot occur at all. This introduction considers the justifications underlying the legal protection offered to freedom of expression, their recognition in the Strasbourg and domestic jurisprudence and the implications of the justifications for the legal restrictions on expression. The chapters contained in Part II consider the restrictions domestic law places on expression – the traditional starting point for discussion of expression in the UK – but then they go on to consider the impact of the HRA on those restrictions. In so doing, it will take account of the discussion, in Chapter 2, of the freedom of expression guarantee under Art 10 of the European Convention on Human Rights, and of a number of the other aspects of the Strasbourg jurisprudence. The main focus of these chapters will be on the changes that are occurring in the protection for expression under the HRA as the Strasbourg jurisprudence permeates this area of law. This part is concerned with *expression*, since that is the term used in Art 10 – a wider term than speech: Art 10 protects expression, which could only very doubtfully be termed 'speech'. However, where the expression in question consists of speech, that term will be used.

In this Part, it will be found that the right to freedom of expression comes into conflict with the freedom to manifest racial hatred and with the right to a fair trial. It has also been viewed as conflicting with the right to freedom of religion. It is apparent from the Convention jurisprudence that, where two Convention rights come into conflict, some kind of balancing act between the two needs to be undertaken.[1] Although jurisprudence in this area is limited, it appears that the margin of appreciation tends to become particularly significant here, so that states have a fairly wide discretion in resolving the conflict.[2] Domestic courts therefore, have an appreciable degree of latitude in determining where to strike the balance between the two interests involved. Section 12 HRA,

---

1 *Otto-Preminger Institut v Austria*, Series A 295-A; (1994) 19 EHRR 34, para 55. The two Convention rights in conflict there were free speech itself and – so the Court found – the right to religious freedom, protected by Art 9.

2 See Chapter 10, pp 753–61. See in particular, *Otto-Preminger Institut v Austria*, Series A 295-A; (1994) 19 EHRR 34. The restriction on Art 10 entailed by the seizure of an allegedly blasphemous film was justified by reference to the Art 9 right to freedom of religious belief. The Court applied a wide margin

which, as Chapter 4 indicated, enjoins the courts to have 'particular regard' to Art 10 when making any order which might that infringe it, appears on its face to suggest a higher weighting for speech interests. Such imbalance is also prima facie suggested by the strength of the 'speech' jurisprudence at both the Strasbourg and domestic levels discussed above. In *Ex p Simms*,[3] Lord Steyn referred to free speech as 'the primary right . . . in a democracy' and some commentators take the view that Art 10 attracts an especially high level of protection at Strasbourg.[4]

However, save for admitting the distinction between those rights stated in absolute terms, such as Arts 3, 4 and 7 and those subject to generalised exceptions (8–11), Strasbourg has never sought to establish a hierarchy of Convention rights. Rather, where rights collide, it has advocated a careful examination of the competing claims of each in the light of all the circumstances of the case.[5] There is no indication that Parliament, in passing the HRA, intended to alter this position and create a serious imbalance between the two rights;[6] rather, it is evident that the sponsors of the amendment saw it merely as a domestic reflection of the Strasbourg approach.[7] Moreover, the un-balanced American approach is out of line with other jurisdictions and flows from factors peculiar to that jurisdiction, in particular the absolute nature of the First Amendment.[8] It is now clear that, despite the wording of s 12, the courts have rejected an approach under the HRA that gives Art 10 a higher status than the other qualified Convention rights.[9]

Free expression justifications

All countries that have a bill of rights protect freedom of expression because it is perceived as one of the most fundamental rights. But why should this particular freedom be viewed as so worthy of protection? Why, as Barendt puts it, should speech that offends the majority have any special immunity from government regulation 'while there would be no comparable inhibition in restraining conduct [such as public] love-making which has similar offensive characteristics?'.[10] Four main justifications for offering protection to free speech have been offered and will be considered here in turn. In each case, an indication will be given as to the kinds of expression the various justifications will support because all the theories will not be relevant to all forms of expression. Initially,

---

of appreciation, and simply said that 'the content of the film cannot be viewed as incapable of grounding' the conclusion of the national authorities that seizure was justified (para 56). Thus the test applied was reminiscent of the narrow *Wednesbury* standard of unreasonableness. See further Chapter 2, p 92. See also *Wingrove v UK* (1997) 24 EHRR 1.

3　[1999] 3 All ER 400, CA; [1999] 3 WLR 328, HL.

4　Leigh, I and Lustgarten, L, 'Making rights real: the courts, remedies, and the Human Rights Act' (1999) 58 CLJ 509, p 524 and fn 79.

5　See the views of Lord Steyn and Lord Cooke in *Reynolds v Times Newspapers* [1999] 4 All ER 609, pp 631 and 643.

6　An amendment providing that a court should 'normally' give precedence to Art 10 over Art 8 was rejected (HC Deb Vol 315 cols 542–43, 2 July 1998).

7　See, e.g., the speech of Jack Straw on cl 12: HC Deb Vol 315 cols 535–39, 2 July 1998.

8　See below, pp 289–90.

9　See Chapter 10, 753–61.

10　Barendt, E, *Freedom of Speech*, 1987, p 1. References will normally be to the 2nd edn, (2006) unless otherwise stated.

it should be noted that three of the justifications are inherently more contingent and therefore precarious than the first. These three justifications – the arguments for the opportunity to arrive at the truth through free discussion, for the necessity of free speech to enable meaningful participation in democracy and for individual self-fulfilment – all ultimately argue that speech is to be valued not for its own sake, but because it will lead to some other outcome we think desirable; thus, they may be characterised as teleological justifications. If, therefore, when considering a particular form of speech, a persuasive argument can be made out that allowing the speech is likely to achieve a result antithetical to the desired outcome, protection will no longer be justifiable. By contrast, as will be seen below, it is inherent in the first main justification for free speech – the argument for moral autonomy – that arguments about the likely effects of allowing the particular speech are not relevant to the question whether the justification applies – although clearly, such arguments may still be relevant in deciding whether the speech should nonetheless be abrogated.

The argument from moral autonomy

This argument was outlined in Chapter 1 as one of the most powerful justifications for human rights in general and so will only briefly be rehearsed here. Ultimately, whether the particular argument used is Rawls's hypothetical social contract[11] or Dworkin's basic postulate of the state's duty to treat its citizens with equal concern and respect,[12] this justification for free expression is centred around the liberal conviction that matters of moral choice must be left to the individual. In either case, the conclusion reached is that the state offends against human dignity,[13] or treats certain citizens with contempt if the coercive power of the law is used to enforce the moral convictions of some upon others. The argument perhaps has a more common and conspicuous application with regard to sexual autonomy and so is often disregarded in arguments about free speech.[14]

The justification is less contingent than the others, as mentioned above, because any restriction on what an individual is allowed to read, see or hear, clearly amounts to an interference with her right to judge such matters for herself. Thus, the argument consistently defends virtually all kinds of speech and other forms of expression,[15] whereas the arguments from truth and democracy[16] will tend to have a somewhat less comprehensive range of application. Since the argument also sets up freedom of speech as a strong 'trump' right,[17] or as part of the individual's claim to inviolability,[18] the right in both

---

11 See Chapter 1, p 16.
12 See Chapter 1, pp 9, 16–20.
13 Barendt makes the point, however, that unlimited speech may also assault human dignity (Barendt, E, *Freedom of Speech*, 1987, pp 16–17). This argument is considered in relation to pornography below: Chapter 7, pp 393–402.
14 Barendt, e.g., comments (*ibid*, p 16) that the 'general freedom to moral autonomy [is] perhaps without much relevance to free speech arguments'.
15 It also covers material which could only doubtfully be classified as speech, e.g., photographic pornography.
16 See below, pp 280–83.
17 Ronald Dworkin's phrase; see Chapter 1, p 16.
18 The idea is Rawls's; see Chapter 1, p 19.

cases overrides normal utilitarian arguments about the benefit or detriment to society of the particular form of speech under consideration.[19] By contrast, the justifications from democracy and truth both set out goals for society as a whole and, therefore, would seem reasonably to allow abrogation of speech in the interests of other public concerns which may be immediately and directly damaged by the exercise of speech. As Barendt puts it, in discussing the argument from truth: 'a government worried that inflammatory speech may provoke disorder is surely entitled to elevate immediate public order considerations over the long-term intellectual development of the man on the Clapham omnibus'.[20]

The argument from truth

The most famous exposition of this argument is to be found in JS Mill's *On Liberty*.[21] The basic thesis is that truth is most likely to emerge from free and uninhibited discussion and debate. It is worth noting that this is a proposition about a causal relationship between two phenomena – discussion and truth – which of course has never been conclusively verified. However, its general truth is taken as virtually axiomatic in the Western democracies and forms the basic assumption underpinning the whole approach of reasoned, sceptical debate that is the peculiar hallmark of Western civilisation. Nonetheless, the crude assumption that more free speech will always lead to more truth has been attacked by certain feminist writers, who consider that the free availability of pornography leads not to the revelation of truth, but to the creation of false and damaging images of women or, more controversially, that pornography actually 'constructs the [sexist] social reality of gender'[22] – a claim that will be examined in detail in Chapter 7.

It appears that Mill envisaged his argument as applicable mainly to the expression of opinion and debate, but it can equally well be used to support claims for freedom of information, since the possession of pertinent information about a subject will nearly always be a prerequisite to the formation of a well-worked-out opinion on the matter. However, prima facie, it may be thought that the theory does not immediately make it clear when we need to know the truth about a given subject. Thus, it could be argued that a delay in receiving certain information (owing, for example, to government restrictions) would not greatly matter, as long as the truth eventually emerged. In response to this, it may be argued that if truth is valued substantively – a position most would assent to[23] – then any period of time during which citizens are kept in ignorance of the truth or form erroneous opinions because of such ignorance, amounts to an evil, thus giving rise to a presumption against secrecy. If, alternatively or in addition, knowledge of the truth is valued because of its importance for political participation, then clearly it will be most important to know the information at the time that the issue it concerns is most likely to affect the political climate. This rationale would thus provide a strong

19 For a discussion of justifications allowing strong rights to be overridden, see Chapter 1, pp 17–19.
20 Barendt, E, *Freedom of Speech*, 1987, p 10.
21 Mill, JS, *On Liberty*, in Cowling, M (ed), *Selected Writings of John Stuart Mill*, Everyman, 1972.
22 MacKinnon, C, *Feminism Unmodified*, 1987, Harvard University Press, p 166.
23 Mill, as a utilitarian, would probably not see truth as inherently valuable, but rather as a very important means of ensuring the overall welfare of society.

argument against the propensity of UK governments to attempt to conceal political secrets until revelation would no longer have a damaging effect on their interests.[24]

Clearly, whether truth is valued instrumentally – for example, as essential to self-development – or as a good in itself, some kinds of truths must be regarded as more important than others.[25] Thus, in the context of a collision between free speech and privacy rights, the small intrinsic value of knowing the facts about (say) a film star's sexual life juxtaposed with the implausibility of the notion that such information would enable more effective political participation or individual growth, provides reasonable grounds for favouring the privacy interest in such a case. By contrast, revelations about corruption amongst prominent politicians will arguably not only have a more important part to play in the formation and development of individuals' general opinions, they will also play a vital role in enabling informed contribution to be made to the political process. Thus, a compelling argument for favouring free speech in this situation is readily made out. We will return to this argument in Chapter 10.

The argument from participation in a democracy

Barendt describes this theory as 'probably the most attractive of the free speech theories in modern Western democracies' and concludes that 'it has been the most influential theory in the development of 20th-century free speech law'.[26] The argument, which is associated primarily with the American writer Meiklejohn,[27] is simply that citizens cannot participate fully in a democracy unless they have a reasonable understanding of political issues; therefore, open debate on such matters is essential. In so far as democracy rests upon ideas both of participation *and* accountability, the argument from democracy may be seen to encompass also the function which a free press performs in exposing abuses of power,[28] thereby allowing for their remedy and also providing a deterrent effect for those contemplating such wrong-doing.[29] The influence of this argument can be seen in the fact that directly political speech has a special protected status in most Western democracies.

Such speech now has a legal guarantee in the UK under Art 10, taking into account the Strasbourg political speech jurisprudence. Pre-HRA, when the British judiciary considered the claims of free speech, they seemed in general to be particularly concerned to protect the free criticism of the political authorities. Thus, in the seminal House of Lords decision in *Derbyshire v Times Newspapers*,[30] Lord Keith, in holding that neither local nor central government could sustain an action in defamation, said: 'It is of the

---

24 As seen, e.g., in the so-called 'Thirty-Year Rule' now contained in the Public Records Act 1958, as amended. See below, Chapter 8, p 527.

25 It is outside the scope of this work to attempt a full-scale normative inquiry into the relative value of different truths. A commonsensical consensus approach is all that is employed in the text, where it is suggested only that the mere satisfaction of curiosity without more is of a relatively low value compared to the ending of a deception.

26 Barendt, E, *Freedom of Speech*, 1987, pp 20 and 23 respectively.

27 See, e.g., his 'The First Amendment is an absolute' (1961) Sup Ct Rev 245.

28 See Blasi, V, 'The checking value in First Amendment theory' (1977) Am B Found Res J 521.

29 See Greenwalt, K, 'Free speech justifications' (1989) 89 Columbia L Rev 119, p 143.

30 [1993] AC 534; [1993] 1 All ER 1011; [1992] 3 WLR 28, HL.

highest importance that a democratically elected governmental body should be open to uninhibited public criticism.' The fact that he based his decision on *this* justification for free speech and not on, for example, the individual right of journalists to express themselves freely, is evidence of judicial endorsement of the argument from democracy – and also, possibly, of their failure to give much consideration to other, rights-based justifications. The fact that the judiciary have mainly, or even only, this interest in mind when considering threats to free speech, helps to explain why they are so often prepared to allow speech to be overridden by other considerations. This is because this argument sees speech as a public interest and as justified instrumentally by reference to its beneficial effects on democracy, rather than seeing it as an individual right of inherent value. Therefore, clearly, it can render speech vulnerable to arguments that it should be overridden by competing public interests that are also claimed to be essential to the maintenance of democracy. Hence Margaret Thatcher's well-known justification for the media ban challenged unsuccessfully in the *Brind* case:[31] 'We do sometimes have to sacrifice a little of the freedom we cherish in order to defend ourselves from those whose aim is to destroy that freedom altogether.' Clearly, to a judge who sees the value of free speech only in terms of its contribution to the political process, an argument that allowing the speech in question will do more harm than good to the maintenance of democracy will always seem compelling. This is not to argue that this justification is fundamentally flawed – clearly its basic premise is correct and offers an important reason to protect speech – but rather that one should be wary of using it as the sole justification even for directly political speech.

There is, however, an argument that does see the justification as fundamentally flawed because it would appear to allow suppression of free speech by the democracy acting through its elected representatives. However, this objection may be answered by the argument that certain values, such as protection for minorities and fundamental freedoms generally, are implicit in any mature conception of a democracy.[32] Therefore, the term 'democracy' or the furtherance of democracy should not be narrowly defined to include only the decisions of the particular government in power, but should also encompass the general principles mentioned; by affording respect to such principles, democracy will ultimately be preserved. This argument would suggest that the justification would appear to have little direct relevance to sexually explicit forms of expression or blasphemous speech but, on the other hand, since freedom of expression is arguably one of the freedoms the suppression of which would undermine democracy, protection for these forms of speech can also be argued for by the justification. It should be borne in mind, however, that as this argument depends on a separate and somewhat controversial contention about the nature of democracy, it offers only an indirect defence of non-political speech.[33] Nevertheless, if the above contention is

---

31 *Secretary of State for the Home Dept ex p Brind* [1991] 1 AC 696; [1991] 1 All ER 720; [1991] 2 WLR 588, HL.

32 Such a view is in fact endorsed by a number of legal philosophers and civil libertarians, and amounts to the most satisfactory reply to the charge that an entrenched Bill of Rights is undemocratic. See Dworkin, *A Bill of Rights for Britain*, 1990; the view also clearly underpins his general political philosophy, see, e.g., 'Liberalism', in *A Matter of Principle*, 1985. See also Hart, HLA, *Law, Liberty and Morality*, 1963 and Lester, A, *Democracy and Individual Rights*, 1968.

33 Most commentators seem to assume that the argument from democracy has little, if any, application to pornographic material. See, e.g., Dworkin, A, 'Do we have a right to pornography?' *op cit*, fn 38, p 335. Similarly, the Williams Committee did not regard the argument as pertinent to their deliberations (*Report of the Committee on Obscenity and Film Censorship*, Cmnd 7772, 1979; see below, p 395).

accepted, one may then conclude that the argument from democracy is actually concerned to further two values: maintenance of the democracy and effective participation in it. The two values are distinct in that although effective as opposed to passive
or inert participation may help to secure maintenance of the democracy, nevertheless
some of its members, while wishing to see its continuance, might not wish to participate actively in it. Thus, political speech would contribute to the maintenance of both
values, while other forms of speech would contribute only to the first, confirming what
was suggested at the outset, namely that this justification argues for special protection
of political speech.

The argument from individual self-fulfilment

Finally, we may turn to the thesis that freedom of speech is necessary in order to enable
individual self-fulfilment. It is argued that individuals will not be able to develop morally and intellectually unless they are free to air views and ideas in free debate with
each other. However, as Barendt notes,[34] it may be objected that free speech should not
be singled out as especially necessary for individual fulfilment; the individual might
also claim that, for example, foreign travel or a certain kind of education was equally
necessary. On the other hand, freedom of speech represents a means of furthering
individual growth that it is possible to uphold as a 'negative freedom'; other methods of furthering individual freedom would require positive action on the part of the
government.

  This justification is clearly rights-based and, as such, in theory at least, is less vulnerable to competing societal claims; however, it does not value speech in itself, but rather,
instrumentally, as a means to individual growth. Therefore, in situations where it seems
that allowing free expression of the particular material will be likely to retard or hinder
the growth of others or of the 'speaker', the justification does not offer a strong defence
of speech.[35] Precisely this argument has been used by feminist commentators to justify
the censorship of pornography. Thus, MacKinnon asserts that, far from aiding in the
growth of anyone, 'Pornography strips and devastates women of credibility'[36] through
the images of women it constructs in its readers' minds. The thesis that forms the basis of
the UK law on obscenity – that certain kinds of pornography actually damage the moral
development of those who read it by depraving and corrupting them – similarly fastens
onto the argument that this kind of material achieves the opposite of the outcome which
allowing freedom of expression is designed to ensure.[37] The apparent vulnerability of
the argument from self-development when used to justify the protection of material

34 Barendt, E, *Freedom of Speech*, 1987, p 15.
35 Barendt argues (*ibid*, pp 16–17) that justifications for suppressing some forms of speech could be
    advanced on the basis that human dignity (the value promoted by allowing self-development) would
    thereby receive protection. He cites the finding of the German Constitutional Court that there was no
    right to publish a novel defaming a dead person as such publication might violate the 'dignity of man'
    guaranteed by Art 1 of the German Basic Law (*Mephisto* (1971) BVerfGE 173).
36 MacKinnon, C, *Feminism Unmodified*, 1987, p 193.
37 It should be noted first that pro-censorship feminists deny that their arguments have anything in com-
    mon with conservative objections to pornography, e.g., MacKinnon, *ibid*, p 175, and secondly that
    the feminist thesis on pornography is far more complex than this. It will be explored in more detail in
    Chapter 7.

which is arguably degrading[38] leads Barendt to suggest[39] that a sounder formulation of the theory is one that frames it in terms of the individual's right to moral autonomy. It is submitted that moral autonomy does provide the most persuasive defence of sexually explicit 'speech' and this argument will be developed when obscenity law is discussed. However, it will also be argued that autonomy is conceptually distinct from the notion of self-fulfilment and that nothing is to be gained by conflating the two concepts.

Implications for restrictions on expression

It is argued that the justifications considered would support the following propositions, which will be used as analytical tools to examine the soundness of the legal responses to expression considered in this Part, including those from Strasbourg. But the complex issues raised by these propositions cannot possibly be considered in sufficient depth here; full treatment can be found in books dealing specifically with theories underlying freedom of expression,[40] and it may be noted that the literature dealing with the domestic potential for importing free expression jurisprudence from other jurisdictions,[41] which has addressed many of the hard issues, is likely to become more extensive as one of the results of the inception of the HRA.

Content and form-based interferences

As a starting point, content-based restrictions should clearly be regarded with more suspicion than those based on *form*, since all of the free speech justifications potentially argue against such restrictions. Content-based restrictions, other than those constraining deliberate lies, prevent certain messages from ever entering the arena of debate and therefore run counter to the arguments from truth and self-fulfilment. Such restrictions prevent persons from knowing of, let alone evaluating, a particular message, thereby infringing their autonomy and, where the message is a political one, running counter to the argument from democracy. Thus, a regime committed to free speech would strongly condemn such restrictions. On this argument, a scholarly thesis arguing that the Holocaust caused far fewer deaths than is generally accepted would fall within the area of protected expression, while the handing out of leaflets and the putting up of posters by a Nazi group in a Jewish community designed to demonstrate precisely this point, might not.[42]

---

38 Dworkin also concludes that the argument from self-fulfilment fails to defend pornographic speech: 'Do we have a right to pornography?', in *A Matter of Principle* 1985; he founds his defence on moral autonomy and, like the present writer, clearly regards this concept as offering a separate head of justification.

39 Barendt, 1987, p 17.

40 See Schauer, F, *Free Speech: A Philosophical Enquiry*, 1982, CUP; Barendt, E, *Freedom of Speech*, 2nd edn, 2006, esp Chapter 1; Waluchow, WJ (ed), *Free Expression: Essays in Law and Philosophy*, 1994, Clarendon; Campbell, T and Sadurski, W (eds), *Rationales for Freedom of Communication*, 1994, Dartmouth.

41 A provocative and interesting forerunner of such books is Loveland, I (ed), *Importing the First Amendment, Freedom of Expression in Britain, Europe and the USA*, 1998, Hart. See also Fenwick, H and Phillipson, G, *Media Freedom under the Human Rights Act* (2006).

42 This example is, of course, reminiscent of the famous 'Nazis at Skokie' affair. A group of Nazis wished to demonstrate, wearing Nazi uniforms and displaying swastikas, in a predominantly Jewish community. They relied, successfully, on their First Amendment right to do so, in a case that divided civil libertarians: *Collin v Smith* (1978) 578 F 2d 1197, 7th Cir; (1978) 436 US 953; (1978) 439 US 916.

But the idea of seeking to ensure content neutrality (an inquiry into the validity of restrictions that completely ignores the *content* of expression) in an absolutist fashion immediately runs into some difficulties.[43] Two key problems are identified here. First, while the idea can be sustained in the example given above, it is clear that in others, the manner in which a message is conveyed may be as significant, or more significant, than the message itself.[44] The examples of symbolic protest, mime, music and art are only some of those that come to mind. The use of various techniques, such as imagery and symbolism, is not only significant, but indissociable from the message. Indeed, such techniques convey a message. In a crude sense, they are the vehicle by means of which the 'message' is conveyed, but they not only interact with it, but also convey a host of emotive and cognitive 'messages' themselves. Secondly, form-based restrictions cannot be fully divorced from content-based ones, since it is only in relation to certain contents that the issue of form is raised. Time, place and access (based on age) restrictions are less problematic, since the infringement of freedom of expression they represent may tend to be insignificant in relation to achieving the ultimate goals indicated by the free speech justifications.

Thus, while it is suggested that all four free speech justifications (depending on the message) would argue against content-based restrictions, they might all also be engaged by form-based restrictions. Moreover, when one examines the justifications themselves, it can be found that they will support restrictions on expression in the furtherance of non-expression values. The feminist argument in this respect is considered below. In relation to forms of hate speech, it can be argued that it is an invasion of moral autonomy and militates against self-fulfilment for someone to be *forced to witness* expression deeply offensive to her (either because it is so pervasive as to be unavoidable or because it is likely that she will encounter it unwittingly). *A fortiori* this is the case when the speech goes beyond offensiveness and becomes threatening.[45] Speech that is impliedly or expressly threatening or intimidatory (so-called 'fighting words') may well impair an individual's autonomy since it has such a direct impact on her in the free ordering of her life.

It is concluded, first, that while content-based restrictions should be viewed with great caution, an engagement in the nature of the content when considering restriction is necessary, especially in terms of the impact on identifiable individuals, defined by their group status. Secondly, the argument in favour of creating simplistic distinctions

---

43   See Feldman, D, 'Content neutrality', in Loveland, I (ed), *Importing the First Amendment, Freedom of Expression in Britain, Europe and the USA*, 1998, Chapter 8.

44   See *Cohen v California*, (1971) 403 US 15.

45   As in the case of attacks on religious faith or homophobic, racist or sexist expression targeted directly at specific individuals. Examples of offensive behaviour that might readily become threatening would include putting up pornographic posters of women in the workplace, sexist, homophobic or racist remarks directed at an employee, displaying an offensive symbol such as a swastika at work or targeting persons in their homes as part of a racist campaign and, e.g., putting leaflets through the door, painting racist graffiti on the house. Cf *RAV v City of St Paul, Minnesota* (1992) 112 S Ct 2538; 120 L Ed 2d 305 in which a group of racist youths burnt a homemade cross in the front yard of a black family. It was found in the Supreme Court that the Ordinance under which one of the youths was charged was overbroad and content-based: expressive conduct of this nature causing offence was protected speech under the First Amendment.

between content and form is unsustainable. The extent to which the form of the expression can be said to engage the free speech justifications has to be considered. Third, while time, place and access restrictions should be rigorously scrutinised on the basis of proportionality, they are prima facie less disturbing than content or form-based ones.

Market freedom and creative freedom

The second proposition is, contrary to the US 'marketplace' model,[46] that market freedom is far from consonant with creative freedom. As Barendt puts it, in relation to US thinking: 'A market-place which few can enter does nothing for the principle that debate on public issues should be uninhibited, robust and open.'[47] Promoting market freedom will tend to mean the dominance of the media by certain conglomerates.[48] It may, therefore, lead to homogenous expression that reflects unchallenged majority viewpoints. Thus, some intervention in the market, with the free speech justifications in mind, is warranted, with a view to furthering creative freedom. Such intervention would limit cross-media ownership – the concentration of ownership in different media sectors – and would seek to protect a public service element – as opposed to the reflection of purely commercial values – in, for example, the granting of licences to broadcast and in the monitoring of output. Such an element might include requirements to observe due impartiality, and to broadcast at peak times programmes reflecting minority interests, experimental and original drama, investigative documentaries ('must carry' requirements).[49] Toleration of such intervention is founded on the understanding that commercial television has a dual concern that will influence its output. It must satisfy the companies who use it to advertise their products that it can deliver a mass audience, which means that it must be able to provide programming that attracts and satisfies such an audience. Therefore, unlike books, music, art, or, to an extent, newspapers, a central concern is to satisfy the advertisers. Regulation is therefore warranted in order to prevent creative freedom from being outweighed by commercial concerns.

This is a matter that is, of course, especially pertinent in relation to media regulation, but the general proposition has implications going beyond current regulatory schemes[50] and, indeed, is relevant in relation to the HRA itself.[51] The proposition covers the use of libel laws by big business,[52] rights of access to the broadcast media,[53] interpretations of

---

46 See Schauer, F, 'The political incidence of the free speech principle' (1993) 64 US Colorado LR 935.
47 See 'The First Amendment and the media', in Loveland, I (ed), *Importing the First Amendment, Freedom of Expression in Britain, Europe and the USA*, 1998, Chapter 8, pp 43–44. The quotation is from *New York Times v Sullivan* (1964) 376 US 254, 270. Barendt goes on to attack the market place model on a number of further grounds; he argues that the pressures of advertisers will influence mass communication and, further, that when corporate interests determine the media agenda, and do not provide access to the means of communication for dissenters, certain ideas cannot enter the 'free' market.
48 See Feintuck, M, *Media Regulation, Public Interest and the Law*, 1999, Edinburgh University Press.
49 See Chapter 7, p 438, fn 219.
50 See Chapter 7, p 439.
51 See Chapter 4, p 211.
52 See Wilmo, P and Rodgers, W (eds), *Gatley on Libel and Slander*, 1998, para 2.19.
53 See Chapter 7, p 436.

contempt law,[54] access to publicity at election times, the suppression of protest (by, for example, environmental activists) in the corporate interest.[55]

Both these propositions suggest that the US freedom of expression model should be treated with caution, although this is not to say that it should not be referred to domestically, under the HRA, as providing an extensive and rich source of jurisprudence. Under the US model, all content-based restrictions on protected speech – speech protected under the First Amendment – are self-evidently unconstitutional, as indicated below.

The US model has been strongly influenced by the 'American's characteristically profound suspicion of government and the whole-hearted belief in the socially beneficial effects of unfettered economic freedom and individual endeavor . . . these traits have generated a model of the state which precludes government and courts from offering protection against significant forms of social and personal harm'.[56] The Strasbourg model, as this part will indicate, contrasts strongly with the American one in tolerating content-based restrictions that relate to the exceptions under Art 10(2).

Recognition of these justifications in Strasbourg and UK expression jurisprudence

The high regard in which freedom of expression, and particularly press freedom, is held by the Strasbourg institutions was indicated in Chapter 2. The Court has repeatedly asserted that freedom of expression 'constitutes one of the essential foundations of a democratic society',[57] and that it 'is applicable not only to "information" or "ideas" that are favourably received or regarded as inoffensive or as a matter of indifference, but also to those that "offend, shock or disturb"'.[58] Particular stress has been laid upon 'the pre-eminent role of the press in a state governed by the rule of law' which, 'in its vital role of "public watchdog"' has a duty 'to impart information and ideas on matters of public interest' which the public 'has a right to receive'.[59]

However, while the rhetorical attachment to free speech is always strong, it is a marked feature of the Strasbourg jurisprudence that clearly political speech, which may be seen as directly engaging the self-government rationale, receives a much more robust degree of protection than other types of expression. Barendt's contention that this is 'the most influential theory in the development of 20th century free speech law'[60] is supported by examination of the approach of UK and Strasbourg judges. As indicated above, the basic thesis is that citizens cannot participate fully in a democracy unless they have a reasonable understanding of political issues; therefore, open debate on such matters is necessary to ensure the proper working of a democracy; as Lord Steyn has put it: 'freedom of speech is the lifeblood of democracy'.[61]

54 See Chapter 6, pp 308–12.
55 See Chapter 9, p 597.
56 See Feldman, 'Content neutrality', in Loveland, I (ed), *Importing the First Amendment, Freedom of Expression in Britain, Europe and the USA*, 1998, Hart Chapter 8, p 140.
57 *Observer and Guardian v UK* A 216 (1991), para 59.
58 See, e.g., *Thorgeirson v Iceland* (1992) 14 EHRR 843, para 63.
59 *Castells v Spain* A 236 (1992), para 43.
60 Barendt, E, *Freedom of Speech* (1987), Clarendon, pp 20 and 23 respectively.
61 *R v Secretary of State for the Home Dept ex p Simms* [1999] 3 All ER 400, p 408.

Thus, the 'political' speech cases of *Sunday Times*,[62] *Jersild*,[63] *Lingens*[64] and *Thorgeirson*[65] all resulted in findings that Art 10 had been violated and all were marked by an intensive review of the restriction in question in which the margin of appreciation was narrowed almost to vanishing point.[66] By contrast, in cases involving artistic speech, supported by the values of autonomy and self-development rather than self-government, an exactly converse pattern emerges: applicants have tended to be unsuccessful and a deferential approach to the judgments of the national authorities as to its obscene or blasphemous nature has been adopted.[67]

A similar pattern may be discerned in the domestic jurisprudence: when speech supported by the arguments from self-development or autonomy rather than self-government is in question, decisions have tended to be cautious,[68] or downright draconian,[69] and accompanied by little or no recognition of these underlying values. The most lofty rhetorical assertions of the importance of free speech and the strongest determination to protect it have been evident in cases where journalistic material raises political issues, broadly defined.[70] In such cases, the courts have either overtly adopted the Strasbourg principles described above[71] or have strongly emphasised the high status freedom of speech holds in the common law, as 'a constitutional right', or 'higher legal order

---

62 *Sunday Times v UK* A 30 (1979). The case concerned a contempt of court action brought against the newspaper in respect of revelations it published concerning the dangers of the drug Thalidomide (for discussion, see Chapter 6, pp 313–14).

63 *Jersild v Denmark* (1994) 19 EHRR 1 concerned an application by a Danish journalist who had been convicted of an offence of racially offensive behaviour after preparing and broadcasting a programme about racism which included overtly racist speech by the subjects of the documentary.

64 *Lingens v Austria* (1986) 8 EHRR 103 concerned the defamation of a political figure.

65 *Thorgeirson v Iceland* (1992) 14 EHRR 843 concerned newspaper articles reporting allegations of brutality against the Reykjavik police.

66 See the discussion of the doctrine in Chapter 2, pp 95–98.

67 *Müller v Switzerland* (1991) 13 EHRR 212; *Gibson v UK*, Appl No 17634 (declared inadmissible by the Commission); *Handyside v UK*, A 24 (1976) (not a case involving artistic speech but where the issue was that of obscenity); *Otto-Preminger Institut v Austria* (1994) 19 EHRR 34; *Gay News v UK* (1982) 5 EHRR 123. In *Wingrove v UK* (1997) 24 EHRR 1, the Court remarked: 'Whereas there is little scope under Art 10(2) of the Convention for restrictions on political speech or on debate of questions of public . . . a wider margin of appreciation is generally available to the Contracting states when regulating freedom of expression in relation to matters liable to offend intimate personal convictions within the sphere of morals or, especially, religion' (para 58). These cases are discussed in Chapter 7, pp 407–08. See Harris, J, O'Boyle, M and Warbrick, C, *Law of the European Convention on Human Rights*, 1995, pp 397 and 414.

68 *Gibson* [1990] 2 QB 619. See Chapter 7, pp 471–72.

69 *Knuller v DPP* [1973] AC 435. In *Lemon* [1979] AC 617, the House of Lords held that the common law offence of blasphemy required no mental element, and that there was no defence of public interest. See further Chapter 7, p 410.

70 *Reynolds v Times Newspapers* [1999] 4 All ER 609; *Derbyshire CC v Times Newspapers* [1993] AC 534; *R v Secretary of State for the Home Dept ex p Simms* [1999] 3 WLR 328. However, deference to widely drafted primary legislation (*Secretary of State for Home Affairs ex p Brind* [1991] 1 AC 696) or governmental arguments from national security (*Attorney General v Guardian Newspapers (No 2)* [1990] 1 AC 109) has resulted in the ready upholding of restrictions on directly political speech.

71 See the approach of the Court of Appeal in *Derbyshire* [1993] AC 534 and in *Ex p Leech* [1994] QB 198, of the House of Lords in *Reynolds* [1999] 4 All ER 609, pp 621–22, *per* Lord Nicholls, pp 628 and esp 635, *per* Lord Steyn, p 643, *per* Lord Cooke and *Ex p Simms* [1999] 3 WLR 328, p 407, *per* Lord Steyn and pp 419–20, *per* Lord Hobhouse.

foundation'.[72] Earlier pronouncements to the effect that: 'The media . . . are an essential foundation of any democracy'[73] were emphatically reinforced by pronouncements in the House of Lords' decision in *Reynolds v Times Newspapers*,[74] which afforded an explicit recognition to their duty to inform the people on matters of legitimate public interest. Press freedom in relation to political expression has clearly been recognised as having a particularly high value in UK law and Convention jurisprudence.

The theory that freedom of speech is necessary for the discovery of truth[75] has been a strong influence in US jurisprudence,[76] but not historically at Strasbourg[77] or in the UK courts.[78] The argument from self-development – that the freedom to engage in the free expression and reception of ideas and opinions in various media is essential to human development[79] – has received some recognition at Strasbourg[80] and recently in the House of Lords.[81]

Free speech protection in practice[82]

In the US, the country with perhaps the greatest commitment to freedom of speech, the First Amendment to the Constitution provides: 'Congress shall make no law abridging the freedom of speech or of the press.' This stricture is not interpreted absolutely literally, but it does mean that US citizens can challenge a law on the sole ground that it interferes with freedom of expression. However, freedom of expression is not absolute

---

72 *Reynolds v Times Newspapers* [1999] 4 All ER 609, pp 628–29 (Lord Steyn). In *Ex p Simms* [1999] 3 WLR 328, p 411, Lord Steyn described the right as 'fundamental', as did Lord Hoffmann, p 412.

73 *Francome v MGN* [1984] 2 All ER 408, p 898, *per* Sir John Donaldson.

74 *Per* Lord Steyn [1999] 4 All ER 609, pp 633–34; Lord Nicholls: 'freedom to disseminate and receive information on political matters is essential to the proper functioning of the system of parliamentary democracy cherished in this country' (p 621).

75 See above, pp 280–81; see further Greenwalt, K, 'Free speech justifications' (1989) 89 Columbia L Rev 119, pp 130–41 generally.

76 See the famous *dicta* of Judge Learned Hand in *United States v Associated Press* 52 F Supp 362, p 372 (1943); and of Holmes J, dissenting but with the concurrence of Brandeis J, in *Abrams v United States* 250 US 616, p 630 (1919).

77 The repeated reference by the ECtHr to freedom of expression being one of the 'basic conditions for [society's] progress' (see, e.g., *Otto-Preminger Institut v Austria* (1994) 19 EHRR 34, para 49) could be seen as a reference to the justification.

78 But see *Secretary of State for the Home Department ex p Simms* [1999] 3 All ER 400, p 408, *per* Lord Steyn.

79 E.g., Emerson argues that the right to free expression is justified as the right of the individual to realise his character and potentialities through forming his own beliefs and opinions ('Towards a general theory of the First Amendment' (1963) 72 Yale LJ 877, pp 879–80); see also Redish, M, *Freedom of Expression*, 1984, pp 20–30 and K, 'Free speech justifications' (1989) 89 Columbia L Rev 119, pp 143–45.

80 One of the stock phrases of the European Court of Human Rights in relation the value of freedom of expression asserts that it is one of the 'essential foundations for the development of everyone' (e.g., *Otto-Preminger* (1995) 19 EHRR 34, para 49).

81 *Per* Lord Steyn in *Ex p Simms* [1999] 3 All ER 400, p 498.

82 For comment, see Marshall, G, 'Freedom of speech and assembly', in *Constitutional Theory*, 1971, OUP, p 154; Barendt, E, *Freedom of Speech*, 2nd edn, 2006, Clarendon; Gibbons, T, *Regulating the Media*, 1998, Sweet and Maxwell; Robertson, G and Nichol, L, *Media Law*, 1999, Penguin; Boyle, A, 'Freedom of expression as a public interest in English law' [1982] PL 574; Singh, 'The indirect regulation of speech' [1988] PL 212; Clayton, R and Tomlinson, H, *The Law of Human Rights*, 2006, Chapter 15; Lester (Lord) and Pannick, D (eds), *Human Rights Law and Practice*, 1st edn, 2000, Chapter 4, p 197.

in any jurisdiction; other interests can overcome it, including the protection of morals, of the reputation of others, the preservation of public order, national security and protecting the interest in a fair trial. In fact, freedom of expression comes into conflict with a greater variety of interests than any other liberty and is therefore in more danger of being curtailed. Most bills of rights list these interests as exceptions to the primary right of freedom of expression, as does Art 10 of the European Convention on Human Rights. This does not mean that the mere invocation of the other interest will lead to displacement of freedom of expression; it is necessary to show that there is a pressing social need to allow the other interest to prevail.[83]

Although, until the inception of the Human Rights Act, the UK had no Bill of Rights protecting freedom of expression, Art 10 of the European Convention on Human Rights was taken into account by the courts in construing ambiguous legislation on the basis, as Chapter 3 indicated, that as Parliament must have intended to comply with its treaty obligations, an interpretation should be adopted that would allow it to do so.[84] It has also, on occasion, been taken into account where there is ambiguity in the common law. Combined with the effects of certain very significant decisions against the UK at Strasbourg, Art 10 had a greater impact on UK law pre-HRA than its fellow article, Article 11. However, its impact has been variable. It has not had as much influence as might perhaps have been expected as far as the laws of obscenity and decency are concerned. As Chapter 9 explains, it has also had little effect on expression in the form of public protest. This part covers access to information which, as Chapter 8 indicates, is not covered by Art 10, although such access may be viewed as associated with expression.

Under s 3 of the HRA, the obligation to interpret legislation compatibly with Art 10, and the related Arts 9[85] and 11, is much stronger than it was in the pre-HRA era, while the courts and other public authorities, including the police, are bound by the Convention under s 6 to uphold freedom of expression. As Chapter 2 indicated, Art 10 provides a strong safeguard for freedom of expression in relation to competing interests, since it takes the primary right as its starting point. The content of speech will rarely exclude it from the protection of Art 10, although not all speech is included.[86] Article 10(2) demands that interferences with the primary right should be both necessary and proportionate to the legitimate aim pursued. But the interferences with expression, considered in the following chapters, have not all been subject to the same intensity of scrutiny at Strasbourg. The reasons why this is so will be considered in those chapters.

As the following chapters indicate, there are two methods of protecting the other competing interests mentioned: prior and subsequent restraints on freedom of expression. Prior restraints are generally seen as more pernicious and therefore countries with a bill of rights either outlaw them or keep them to a minimum. In the case of censorship, such restraints are viewed as particularly inimical to free speech, since they may operate outside the public domain and may therefore generate little or no publicity. Decisions

---

83 See Chapter 2, pp 98–101 for discussion of this point and p 336, below.
84 See further Chapter 3, pp 105–22.
85 See Chapter 2, p 95.
86 In *Jersild v Denmark* (1994) 19 EHRR 1 it was assumed that the actual racist utterances of racists in a broadcast were not protected. In *Janowskki v Poland* (1999) 5 BHRC 672 it was found that insults to civil servants acting in their public capacity were protected, although the interference was found to be justified.

will be taken by an administrative body, often with no possibility of challenge in the courts. On the other hand, subsequent restraints operate after publication of the article in question: the persons responsible may face civil or criminal liability. The trial may then generate publicity and the defendants may have an opportunity of demonstrating why they published the article in question. In other words, the case for allowing the speech in question is given a hearing.[87] However, the distinction between the two kinds of restraint may not be as stark as this implies. Subsequent restraints may have a chilling effect on publications; editors and others may well not wish to risk the possibility of incurring liability and may therefore themselves take the decision not to publish without reference to any outside body. In the case of prior restraints granted by the courts, usually injunctions, the case in favour of publication will normally be heard.

When one turns to consider UK law in this area, one confronts a mass of common law and statutory restrictions on freedom of expression and on expressive activities associated with it, such as marches or demonstrations. Traditionally, in order to determine how far freedom of expression was protected, it was necessary to consider the width of these restrictions in order to determine how much of an area of freedom was left within which expression could be exercised. Historically, in English law, there was no such thing as 'media freedom' as a constitutional or legal concept: as Dicey said, 'Freedom of discussion is in England little else than the right to write or say anything which a jury, consisting of twelve shopkeepers, think it expedient should be said or written.'[88] It was indeed crucial to the Diceyan paradigm that, in so far as press freedom was protected, it was a result of ordinary court judgments determining the rights of private citizens. In some areas of law affecting the media, where the media sought to make claims that could not be made by individual speakers, they were denied completely: perhaps the most notorious example is Lord Templeman's trenchant assertion at the beginning of his speech in a major case on protection of journalists' sources: 'This case is not about freedom of the press.'[89] More typically, under the traditional English view, freedom of the press was simply the absence of a prior system of censorship but, other than that, simply a negative liberty. As Lord Wilberforce observed in 1981: 'Freedom of the press imports, generally, freedom to publish without pre-censorship, subject always to the laws relating to libel, official secrets, sedition and other recognised inhibitions.'[90]

As the above passage suggests, 'the law of media freedom' consisted merely of a mechanical application of the law deriving from statute and common law precedents; and media freedom, like any other negative liberty, was simply what was left over after the scope of the restrictions had been determined. The HRA has altered that position in the sense that the media and citizens generally are able to rely on the Art 10 guarantee, against public authorities. Therefore, domestic freedom of expression should be determined by the scope of the Art 10 protection, bearing in mind the duty of national courts, discussed in Chapter 4, to disapply the margin of appreciation doctrine. The extent to which the judiciary are taking an activist or a minimalist approach to that doctrine in relation to expression is of particular significance, since Strasbourg has applied a review of very varying intensity in this context. The development of the domestic law, whether

---

87   See Barendt, E, 'Prior restraints on speech' [1985] PL 253.
88   Dicey, AV, *Introduction to the Study of the Law of the Constitution*, 10th edn, 1959, Chapter VI.
89   *British Steel Corp v Granada Television Ltd* [1981] AC 1096.
90   [1981] 1 All ER 417, 455.

by way of legislation or the common law, is still highly significant, since all of it is being tested more directly against Art 10, in Parliament or in the courts.

It will be found that the law in this area has developed in an incoherent fashion. A willingness to accept the values of freedom of expression,[91] rather than relying strongly on those that traditionally attracted protection, especially proprietorial rights, became apparent in the 1990s, as Chapter 3 indicated. But where expression came into conflict with those values that had traditionally gained acceptance, such as maintaining public order, such values remained in the ascendant. The lack of a consistent pattern was arguably due to the lack of a free expression clause against which the other interests had to be measured. The emphasis of these chapters has to be on the judges' concern to strike a balance between free expression and a variety of other interests in the pre-HRA era, and the impact of Art 10 on the stance adopted. A pervasive critical theme will be the exposure of the judges' readiness to allow freedom of expression to be restricted on uncertain or flimsy grounds. It will be found in certain contexts that some of the interests identified by judges as justifying such restrictions would not qualify as sufficient grounds for outweighing the right of free expression under the liberal conception of rights outlined in Chapter 1. In such contexts, the impact of Art 10 will, therefore, be of especial significance. In others, it will become apparent that domestic law already satisfies Art 10 requirements.

In considering UK law it will be argued that outside the public order or anti-terrorist context statutes in this area give, in general, greater protection to freedom of expression than does the common law and that during the 1980s and 1990s it came particularly under threat, partly, but not exclusively, through common law developments, although, as indicated above, there were also a number of recent important judgments favouring freedom of speech. A theme that runs through this part concerns the extent to which the common law has undermined statutory safeguards for freedom of speech. This is a matter of especial significance under the HRA, since inconsistent common law provisions are not protected under s 6(2) HRA when applying the guarantee under Art 10 to a public authority. As Chapter 4 explained, incompatible common law provisions do not enjoy the protection afforded to statutory ones, although their precise legal position in relation to the Convention is complex.[92]

Clearly, this is not to argue that no English statute governing freedom of expression has to be modified by interpretation under Art 10 relying on the Human Rights Act. In examining the statutory provisions considered in this part, it will become apparent that some of them, especially in the field of public protest, provide extremely wide powers intended to protect other interests. It must, however, be remembered that they were framed by a parliament that had no domestic legal brake upon its powers, although post-1951 the UK was bound by the Convention at the international level. At times, it has been prepared to frame laws that, if fully enforced, would severely damage freedom of expression. Post-2000, as Chapter 4 argues, new legislation affecting freedom of expression has almost invariably been accompanied by a statement of its compatibility with the Convention (the exception is the Communications Act 2003), but this does not

---

91 See the House of Lords' decisions in the *Derbyshire* case [1993] AC 534; [1993] 1 All ER 1011; [1992] 3 WLR 28 and in *Ex p Simms* [1999] QB 349, considered above in Chapter 3, p 112.

92 See pp 217–18.

mean that incompatibility will not be found. Further, the statement may be issued on the basis of an interpretation grounded in a minimal version of the Convention. It is suggested that this is true of parts of the Terrorism Acts 2000 and 2006, discussed further in Chapter 15, in relation to its effects on freedom of expression.

But pre- and post-Human Rights Act legislation affecting freedom of expression shares the same characteristic: the laws are not – in normal circumstances – fully enforced; if they were, the consequent clash between the media and the government would bring the law into further disrepute. Thus, although by examining the provisions of these statutes, an indication of the 'balance' Parliament had in mind may be gained, other more nebulous factors, including the influence of powerful media bodies, must also be taken into account. Such factors may not apply in relation to public protest, and one of the concerns of this Part is to reveal the different emphasis placed on expression arising as protest rather than as an aspect of media freedom.

But a key concern of this Part is to evaluate whether any change in this 'balance' is occurring under the Human Rights Act and to consider the extent to which any such a change reflects the theoretical justifications underpinning various aspects of freedom of expression. The extent to which such justifications are likely to play a part in determining the resolution of the conflict between expression and a number of societal and individual interests, under the Human Rights Act, will form a central theme.

Chapter 6

Restraining freedom of expression under the law of contempt

This chapter has been updated and revised for this edition by Paul Wragg, Associate Professor at the University of Leeds, UK.

I Introduction[1]

This chapter is essentially concerned with two interests that are frequently perceived as being in conflict – the administration of justice and media freedom. The protection of the administration of justice is a general aim that is not concerned solely with protecting the right of the individual to a fair trial, although it may have that effect. Domestically, the interest in the administration of justice has been protected by the law of contempt, although obviously the main responsibility for ensuring fairness in criminal trials or civil actions remains with the judge. A number of aspects of contempt law are discussed below, including its use in curbing pre-trial discussions and publicity in the media that might influence those involved in forthcoming proceedings; threats to justice in the long-term sense, and requirements to disclose journalistic sources. It is apparent that, prima facie, contempt law creates interferences with the guarantee of freedom of expression under Art 10. The interference may be justified where it has the legitimate aim of 'maintaining the authority and impartiality of the judiciary' under para 2. This phrase may be taken to cover the preservation of the integrity of the administration of justice, including the rights of litigants. Since contempt law has a role to play in preventing prejudice to proceedings or in deterring the media from causing such prejudice, it may be viewed as a means of protecting Art 6 rights,[2] although the main responsibility for providing such protection falls on the trial judge.[3] Viewed as exceptions to Art 10, such rights fall within the rubric 'the rights of others' in para 2, as well as that of 'maintaining the authority of the judiciary'. (Since court proceedings may bring an

---

1 Texts referred to in this chapter: Miller, CJ, *Contempt of Court*, 1999, OUP; Barendt, E, *Freedom of Speech*, 1st edn, 1987, 2nd edn, 2007, Clarendon, Chapter 8; Sufrin, B and Lowe, N, *The Law of Contempt*, 1996, Butterworths; Fenwick, H and Phillipson, G, *Media Freedom under the Human Rights Act*, 2006, OUP; Robertson, G, *Media Law*, 1999, Chapter 6; Arlidge, A and Smith, ATH, *Arlidge, Eady and Smith on Contempt*, 2nd edn, 1999, Sweet and Maxwell; Barendt, E and Hitchens, L, *Media Law: Cases and Materials*, 2000, Chapters 12, 13 and 14; Clayton, R and Tomlinson, H, *The Law of Human Rights*, 2nd edn, 2006, OUP, Chapter 15; Marshall, G, 'Press freedom and free speech theory' [1992] PL 40; Laws LJ, 'Problems in the law of contempt' (1990) CLP 99; Naylor, B [1994] CLJ 492; Laws LJ (2000) 116 LQR 157. For a historical overview, see: Fox, *The History of Contempt of Court*, 1927, Butterworths; Goodhart, AL, 'Newspapers and contempt of court in England' (1935) 48 Harv LR 885.
2 See Chapter 2, pp 57–64.
3 See the comments of Simon Brown LJ regarding the differing roles of the judge in contempt proceedings and at trial: *Attorney General v Birmingham Post and Mail Ltd* [1998] 4 All ER 49.

individual to the attention of the media, with the result that details of their personal lives are revealed, the guarantee of respect for private life under Art 8 may also be relevant; the implications of this possibility are discussed in Part III, Chapter 10.) Contempt law therefore comes into conflict with free expression, either on the basis of protecting general societal interests or other individual rights. Article 6 is not engaged where the threat is to the administration of justice in a general or long-term sense. Similarly, the use of contempt law to require the disclosure of sources would not normally engage Art 6, although it clearly does create an interference with the Art 10 guarantee, and moreover one which is viewed at Strasbourg as particularly serious, as indicated below.

But the notion that free speech and the administration of justice are likely to come into conflict should be examined further. This part began by arguing that one of the most influential justifications for free speech arises from the part it plays in furthering democratic values. Speech that, under strict scrutiny, undermines the fairness of a trial can be viewed as attacking such values rather than upholding them. Chapter 10 argues that the conflict between speech and privacy is more apparent than real since, as Emerson puts it, the rights are 'mutually supportive in that both are vital features of the basic system of individual rights'.[4] It is suggested that, to an extent, this may also be said of free speech and fair trials. In a democracy, free speech serves the ends of justice since the free debate of conceptions of justice may allow for the inclusion of a variety of views within the process of justice that will therefore enhance its moral authority.[5] Thus, if one of the justifications for speech is that it supports the fairness of trials by scrutinising justice, as an aspect of the 'open' justice principle, speech that, on careful scrutiny, creates unfairness may legitimately be restricted since it undermines that central justification. In other words, freedom of speech has a key role as an essential aspect of a fair system of justice, but speech that affects the impartiality of a hearing may undermine public confidence in the role of the courts and the administration of justice, and can therefore undermine its key role.

Further, it is a central tenet of a democracy that justice should not be arbitrary, and therefore the state has a duty to ensure that all have equal access to justice. As Chapter 1 indicated, rights are premised on the notion that the state has a duty to treat all its citizens with equal concern and respect. That notion underlies, it is argued, both free speech and fair trials. If the fair trial of an individual is arbitrarily affected by media coverage, since that individual is accused of a crime that has caught public attention, the state has failed to secure equal access to justice. Therefore, restrictions on such coverage may be justified on the basis that free speech that creates such an interference undermines an aspect of its own underlying rationale.

In many such instances, no sufficient competing aspect is available in order to found the argument that the restrictions are unjustified, since the speech in question may be trivial and sensationalist, motivated solely by profit-making concerns. The fact that newspaper coverage constitutes 'speech' should not be allowed to obscure the failure of some sensationalist coverage of certain cases to participate in almost all the

---

4 Emerson, C, 'The right to privacy and the freedom of the press' (1979) 14(2) Harvard Civil Rights-Civil Liberties L Rev 329, p 331.
5 See further Allan, TRS, 'Procedural fairness and the duty of respect' [1988] 18 OJLS 497, esp pp 507–10.

justifications for affording speech primacy over competing interests. Moreover, the guarantee under Art 10 is most strongly engaged, not only when those justifications, especially the argument from democracy, are at stake, but when the promulgator of the speech is also observing the duties and responsibilities that accompany the exercise of the freedom.[6] Such responsibilities include that of avoiding the invasion of the interests protected under para 2 in a manner that is unnecessary in a democratic society and that is motivated and determined merely by market considerations. Thus, it may be concluded that careful differentiation must be maintained between speech that conflicts with the underlying aims of both free speech and justice, and speech that furthers those aims.

But the argument regarding the harmony between the furtherance of the ends of both justice and speech may break down, it is suggested, where the dominant conception of justice is itself arguably flawed and an instance arises, related to a specific trial, that is especially illustrative of that flaw. In other words, it provides a strikingly paradigmatic example, which may not soon be repeated. For example, the percentage of convictions for rape is extremely low. In a rape trial, the fact that a defendant had a number of rape convictions, or had been acquitted of rape on numerous occasions, would not normally go before the jury. If a newspaper, which was campaigning for improvement in the conviction rate for rape, disclosed such facts pre-trial, as part of its campaign, and, in particular, as part of an argument that rape convictions should be disclosed to the jury, it might seek to justify its publication on the basis that it would influence debate as to conceptions of justice in such trials and might therefore serve the ends of both free speech and justice. The interest in the *efficacy* of speech as well as in its justifications in a formal sense could be relied on in an effort to outweigh the argument that the use of this particular trial in order to give bite to the campaign had undermined the principle of equal access to justice.

This example illustrates the difficulty of formulating a general principle of harmony between the interests involved. But, as a general proposition, subject to exceptions, it is argued that the idea of antinomy between free speech and fair trials is misconceived. If these underlying ideas are taken into account, they provide a means of analysing domestic and Convention rules for their legitimacy in terms of the harmony between the principles underlying free speech and the administration of justice. Where they fail to promote such harmony, reforms will be suggested. It will be argued that the Convention jurisprudence has gone somewhat further than domestic jurisprudence in recognising such harmony, bearing in mind the central aim of the Convention, which is to protect and promote democratic values. However, in certain instances, it will be suggested that the influence of the margin of appreciation doctrine has led to failures in this respect.

The central concern of this chapter is the impact, actual and potential, that the European Convention on Human Rights under the Human Rights Act is having and could have on aspects of domestic contempt law. It will indicate that the domestic development of the law of contempt was quite strongly influenced by the Strasbourg jurisprudence, pre-HRA. While the common law afforded supremacy to the administration of justice, Strasbourg aided in the creation of a shift in favour in freedom of expression. Nevertheless, despite the influence of the Convention, this chapter will contend that

6 Art 10, para 1.

domestic contempt law still fails to satisfy the demands of Art 10 in certain respects. It will also be argued that, as currently administered, it fails to protect the administration of justice and, in some respects, to meet the demands of Art 6. The response of UK contempt law to findings at Strasbourg and the judicial domestic interpretations of the Convention have not shown a sufficient appreciation, it will be argued, of its key underpinning values. In particular, the extent to which the apparent conflict between Arts 10 and 6 may be resolvable at the level of principle has largely gone unrecognised. These failings are revealed, it will be contended, by testing contempt law and practice more directly against Convention standards under the Human Rights Act.

2 Publications prejudicing proceedings: the strict liability rule

A central area of contempt law is that which is concerned with publications potentially interfering with the course of justice in civil or criminal proceedings. Media bodies may incur liability for contempt due to potentially prejudicial reporting of and discussion of, or relating to, pending proceedings. This form of contempt is therefore intended to limit the freedom of the media to report on or comment on issues arising from, or related to, the administration of justice. Such restriction answers to a genuine public interest in ensuring that justice is properly administered and is unaffected by bodies who are unlikely to judge the merits of a case fairly. If, for example, a large number of tabloids, in pursuit of a newsworthy story, take the view that a defendant is guilty, they may slant stories and pictures so that they seem to give that impression and such coverage may affect the jury. If so, the conviction will have been influenced by the partial views of a certain group of people who do not have all the evidence available to them and are influenced by concerns other than the concern to ensure fairness in decision making. If a trial seems to have been prejudiced by unfair reporting, a successful appeal may be brought on that basis,[7] but this method only creates a remedy for the defendant; it does not deter the media from such behaviour in future. No one would argue that this is a desirable method of preventing prejudice to the administration of justice, since it may allow the factually guilty to be acquitted or the innocent to be convicted.

In seeking to avoid such interferences with the course of justice while also affording protection to the freedom of the press, states have chosen to adopt either a *protective* or a *neutralising* model,[8] or a mixture of both. Under the protective model, the state seeks to protect court proceedings by deterring the media from the publication of potentially prejudicial material, while allowing non-prejudicial reporting of proceedings and of discussion relating to them. This model has traditionally been used in the UK. Under the neutralising model, the emphasis is placed on dealing with the potential effects of prejudicial material, by means of procedural devices aimed at ensuring the impartiality of the jury. The aim is to ensure that the potential effect of prejudicial publicity is neutralised. Such devices include the use of strong directions to the jury, jury challenges, changing the trial venue, stays, and sequestration of the jury. If neutralising measures fail, the

---

7 See the successful appeal on this basis in *Taylor* (1993) 98 Cr App R 361, CA (for discussion, see below, p 324).
8 See Cram, I [1998] EHRLR 742.

remedial measure of acquittal may be the last resort. Both models seek to ensure fair hearings, but the former seeks to do so by curbing media freedom to an extent, the latter by insulating the hearing from potentially prejudicial publications, while leaving media freedom largely intact.

It is argued below that, contrary to the view which some commentators have taken,[9] Strasbourg has on the whole adopted a protective or preventive rather than a neutralising approach, which explains why the Human Rights Act has not led to a radical change in the stance of UK law, in this context. Moreover, bearing in mind the arguments outlined above, regarding the underlying harmony of values between free speech and the fair administration of justice, it is argued that the preventive is, in general, to be preferred to the neutralising model since much speech which, under close scrutiny, creates prejudice to trials runs counter to its own underlying justifications, while at the same time the quality of justice may be affected by using neutralising measures.[10] It must be pointed out, however, that the preventive model may become unworkable owing to current technological changes, particularly the use of the internet and the proliferation of websites, a point that will be developed further below. Bearing these points in mind, the central argument will be that while radical change is unnecessary in this area of contempt law, certain reforms are necessary in order to meet, in full, the demands both of media freedom and the administration of justice, as recognised under the Convention, but interpreted domestically under the Human Rights Act.

The Strasbourg stance

Under Art 10, an interference with the guarantee of freedom of expression can be justified if it is prescribed by law, has a legitimate aim and is necessary in a democratic society. Proceedings against a media body for contempt in respect of its coverage of a forthcoming or ongoing action, or of issues impliedly or expressly linked to it, may be justified if they have the legitimate aims of protecting the 'rights of others' and/or of 'maintaining the authority and impartiality of the judiciary'. The 'rights of others' exception covers Art 6 rights. The 'authority' of the judiciary refers to the acceptance of the courts as the proper forums for the settlement of disputes.[11] The term 'impartiality' refers to the preservation of confidence in the courts by persons engaged in dispute settlement and the public in general.[12] This exception was apparently included in the Convention at the instigation of the UK precisely to cover contempt of court.[13] The other European signatories have no clearly comparable law, although laws regulating pre-trial publicity are common.

---

9 Mann, FA has written: 'In a potentially wide variety of cases the European Court may assume a revising function and impose continental standards or, perhaps one should say abuses, upon this country which, in the name of freedom of the press and discussion are likely to lower English usages by the substitution of trial by media for trial by courts', 'Contempt of Court in the House of Lords and the European Court of Human Rights' (1979) 95 LQR 348, p 352.

10 This point has been made by Chesterman (1997) 45 J Comp Law 109 and by Krause (1996) 76 Boston UL Rev 357. Clearly, devices such as delaying the trial may mean that defendants will spend longer in custody; the stress of victim-witnesses may be increased; memories of the relevant events may fade.

11 *Chorherr v Austria* (1994) 17 EHRR 358.

12 *Fey v Austria* (1994) 16 EHRR 387; *Worm v Austria* (1998) 25 EHRR 454, p 473.

13 See the Joint Dissenting Opinion in *Sunday Times v UK* (1979) 2 EHRR 245, p 285, para 2.

As indicated, this form of contempt law can be viewed as protecting the right to a fair trial, together with the societal interest in preserving the integrity of the administration of justice. It can be argued, therefore, that where this other 'strong' right is at stake, Strasbourg would accept that free speech must be more readily compromised, unless in the particular instance the speech would in fact further the ends of justice.[14] But resolving these matters under the Convention is not entirely straightforward owing to the particular approach it adopts, which is influenced by its own structural constraints. This approach is revealed by a consideration of the stance taken at Strasbourg to claims that Art 10 has been violated by prosecutions of journalists in respect of publications bearing upon legal proceedings in the line of authority stemming from *Sunday Times v UK*,[15] *Worm v Austria*[16] and *News Verlags v Austria*.[17]

Clashes between the administration of justice and media freedom

The *Sunday Times* case is discussed in full below. The state argued that the interference with freedom of expression could be justified since it served the legitimate aim of preserving the authority and impartiality of the judiciary. The stance adopted by the Court in finding a breach of Art 10 was explicable on the basis that the interest in protecting such authority or, at a more general level, the administration of justice, was very weak: little threat could be discerned since the litigation in question was dormant. Although, as an aspect of its application of the requirements of proportionality, the Court took the view that the strong free speech interest outweighed the slight impact on the administration of justice, a more satisfactory way of viewing the case is, it is argued, to say that the speech in question engaged strongly in the debate as to the proper ends of justice, but no countervailing considerations regarding equal access to justice or the creation of unfairness genuinely arose.

In contrast, in *Worm*, the interference with the freedom of speech guarantee had a link with the Art 6 guarantee. *Worm v Austria*[18] is now the leading authority on balancing expression and fair trial values. Unlike the *Sunday Times* case, it addressed a real clash between the two since in the circumstances the Art 6 guarantees were clearly engaged. The article in question created a high risk of prejudice: it was published during a criminal trial, clearly imputed guilt and made specific allegations against the defendant. In all these respects, therefore, it created a strong contrast with the article at issue in *Sunday Times*. Thus *Worm*, unlike *Sunday Times*, is properly characterised as a clashing rights case. A political periodical had published an article by Worm, a journalist, about the criminal trial for tax evasion of Hannes Androsch, a former minister of finance. The article, published while the trial was ongoing, stated that it had been known for a substantial period of time that Androsch was evading taxes and that it had been proved for some time, by the investigating judge, that Androsch was lying on this key point. In general, the article was highly critical of Androsch and clearly evinced a belief in his guilt. Worm was convicted and fined under s 23 of the Austrian Media Act, which

---

14   See the discussion as to when 'strong' individual rights may be infringed in Chapter 1, pp 17–19.
15   (1979) 2 EHRR 245.
16   (1997) 25 EHRR 557; (1998) 25 EHRR 454.
17   (2001) 31 EHRR 8.
18   (1998) 25 EHRR 454.

provides for the punishment of those who discuss 'subsequent to the indictment and before the judgment at first instance . . . the probable outcome of those proceedings or the value of evidence in a way capable of influencing the outcome'. There is no need to establish that the proceedings have in fact been influenced. The Vienna Court of Appeal considered that the article had a potential influence on the criminal proceedings since it had the capacity to affect at the least the two lay judges involved. It also found that Worm had intended to influence the proceedings.

The European Court of Human Rights accepted that Worm's conviction constituted an interference with the freedom of expression guarantee. The state argued that the prosecution had the legitimate aims of preserving the authority and impartiality of the judiciary and the 'rights of others.' The Court accepted that the conviction had a link with the Art 6(1) guarantee, although it did not pursue the question whether the article had created an interference with the rights of others by undermining the presumption of innocence which is guaranteed under Art 6(2). It found:

> In this regard, the Court has consistently held that the expression 'authority and impartiality of the judiciary' has to be understood 'within the meaning of the Convention'. For this purpose, account must be taken of the central position occupied in this context by Art 6 which reflects the fundamental principle of the rule of law. The phrase 'authority of the judiciary' includes, in particular, the notion that the courts are, and are accepted by the public at large as being, the proper forum for the settlement of legal disputes and for the determination of a person's guilt or innocence on a criminal charge; further, that the public at large have respect for and confidence in the courts' capacity to fulfil that function. 'Impartiality' normally denotes lack of prejudice or bias. However, the Court has repeatedly held that what is at stake in maintaining the impartiality of the judiciary is the confidence which the courts in a democratic society must inspire in the accused, as far as criminal proceedings are concerned, and also in the public at large . . . It follows that, in seeking to maintain the 'authority and impartiality of the judiciary', the contracting states are entitled to take account of considerations going – beyond the concrete case – to the protection of the fundamental role of courts in a democratic society.[19]

As to the question whether the interference was necessary in a democratic society, the Court found that although the limits of acceptable comment are wider as regards politicians than as regards a private individual, public figures are still entitled to the enjoyment of the guarantee of a fair trial set out in Art 6(1), which in criminal proceedings includes the right to an impartial tribunal. It went on:

> [T]his must be borne in mind by journalists when commenting on pending criminal proceedings since the limits of permissible comment may not extend to statements which are likely to prejudice, whether intentionally or not, the chances of a person receiving a fair trial or to undermine the confidence of the public in the role of the courts in the administration of criminal justice.[20]

19 *Ibid*, at para 40.
20 *Ibid*, at para 50.

The Court conceded a certain margin of appreciation to the state in relation to the particular choice made by the domestic authorities in relation to what was needed to protect the administration of justice, since – as it does not adopt the role of a domestic appellate court – it did not second guess the evidence. It accepted that there was no necessity to demonstrate that prejudice to the proceedings had actually arisen. It found that it was,

> in principle for the appellate court to evaluate the likelihood that at least the lay judges would read the article to ascertain the applicant's criminal intent in publishing it. It cannot be excluded that the public's becoming accustomed to the regular spectacle of pseudo-trials in the news media might in the long run have nefarious consequences for the acceptance of the courts as the proper forum for the determination of a person's guilt or innocence on a criminal charge.[21]

The sanction was found to be proportionate to the aim pursued since a fairly minor penalty only – a fine – was imposed and the publishing firm was ordered to be jointly and severally liable for its payment. Thus the proportionality analysis was based on means/end balancing[22] – the measures taken, it was found, did not go further than necessary to protect the right to a fair trial in the circumstances. No breach of Art 10 was therefore found.

This was an instance in which it could more readily be argued than in the *Sunday Times* case that the speech ran counter to the underlying speech-supporting rationales discussed above, in the sense that it was more likely to cause prejudice to the trial. The Court's approach rested on the possibility that the article had made it very difficult to ensure that the tribunal was impartial. It took the stance that the Art 10 guarantee could be justifiably infringed in order to protect Androsch's right to a fair trial under Art 6(1). But it also spoke of the general principles encapsulated under Art 6. The Court explicitly refused to look at the question whether the proceedings in question had actually been affected by the publication; it refused to consider whether the Austrian media law should have concerned itself with that issue. Therefore it explicitly denied that there was a need to show an actual interference with Art 6 rights (or at least a very strong probability that such an interference had occurred) before an interference with the Art 10 guarantee – in the context of political expression – could be justified. Thus, it seemed to adopt both a protective and a preventive approach, though laying more stress on the former. An obvious unfairness was potentially created by the article, but the Court also concentrated on the longer term harm that it might have created to the administration of justice in a broader sense. The state's case was obviously problematic in *Sunday Times* since the litigation in question was dormant. In contrast, in *Worm*, the state had acted to avert a genuine risk to the trial; the Court made it clear that Art 6 will take precedence over Art 10 where it can be said that there is a real likelihood of prejudice.

The stance adopted in *Worm* had been foreshadowed to an extent in the Commission's decisions in *C v UK*[23] and *BBC Scotland v UK*.[24] *C v UK* concerned a broadcast

---

21 *Ibid*, para 54.
22 See Chapter 4, p 242.
23 (1989) 61 DR 285.
24 (1998) 25 EHRR CD 179.

reproducing parts of the appeal in the *Birmingham Six* case. The intention of the broadcasters was that it should be shown before the final judgment in the appeal, but the Court of Appeal hearing the case granted an injunction preventing the broadcast of the programme until after the appeal had been heard. The Commission found no breach of Art 10 on the basis that there was a pressing social need to delay the programme; the portrayal of the hearing by actors would condition the response of the audience since the actors would be bound to communicate suggestions about the reliability of the witnesses they were portraying. Also the Commission accepted the view of the Court of Appeal that while the Courts' judgment would normally be unaffected, the appellants had the right to be assured that the Court had been unaffected by external matters.[25]

The application in *BBC Scotland v UK*[26] arose from the prohibition of a broadcast that featured allegations that prisoners moved to Barlinnie Prison after prison riots had been assaulted there by prison officers. The broadcast 'Beaten by the System' was an update on one previously broadcast on the same subject. An indictment had been served on three prison officers alleging that they had assaulted prisoners, about three weeks before the programme was to be broadcast. The Scottish High Court relied on its inherent equitable jurisdiction to issue an order prohibiting the broadcast until the completion of the trial of the officers, on the ground that the programme would create a risk of prejudice to the trial. The risk of prejudice arose, so the High Court found, since at least one of the jurors might have obtained from the programme the impression that the prison doctor interviewed, who was a witness for the prosecution, was a witness of considerable credit. The Court noted that the broadcast was not particularly urgent and that there was a more than minimal risk of prejudice. The applicants complained that the order of the High Court constituted a breach of Art 10.

The Commission accepted that the order constituted an interference with the freedom of expression guarantee. It went on to find that the order had the legitimate aim of protecting the right of the officers to a fair trial; therefore it was for the preservation of the authority and impartiality of the judiciary and for the protection of the 'rights of others'. In considering the question whether the order was necessary in a democratic society it might have been expected that the Commission would have subjected it to that 'most careful scrutiny' which prior restraints demand.[27] Instead the Commission largely adopted the High Court's assessment of the necessity and proportionality of the order. The Commission appeared to be assessing the reasonableness of the High Court's findings in balancing the free speech and fair trial interests, rather than considering the issues itself. In speaking of the 'balancing act' carried out by the High Court, the Commission clearly did not view itself as applying a principle of freedom of expression subject to exceptions to be narrowly construed. Thus the need for the interference was not subjected to a strict scrutiny. Had it been, it is possible that a breach of Art 10 might have been found, bearing in mind the uncertainty of the risk of prejudice and the probability that the programme would never be broadcast once it had been postponed.

The stance taken in this line of authority was confirmed in *News Verlags v Austria*.[28] At first sight *News Verlags* presents something of a contrast to *Worm v Austria, C v UK*

25 *Ibid*, p 294.
26 (1997) 25 EHRR CD 179.
27 *Observer and Guardian v UK* (1991) 14 EHRR 153, at para 60.
28 (2001) 31 EHRR 8; (2000) 9 BHRC 625.

and *BBC Scotland v UK* in terms of the intensity of the review, but ultimately the findings are consistent with the previous ones. The case concerned a somewhat weaker Art 10 claim; the 'rights of others' exception was invoked to justify the restriction on the speech in question, but the application succeeded. The case concerned the prosecution of the News Company for the publication of a photograph of a right-wing extremist, B, who was accused of sending letter bombs as part of a political campaign. The text accompanying the photograph accused him of being the perpetrator of the attacks. The applicant company complained that court decisions prohibiting it from publishing the photograph in the context of reports on the criminal proceedings against it, violated its right to freedom of expression. The aims pursued were to protect the rights of others and the authority of the judiciary. The Court noted that the 'rights of others' exception was relevant since, *inter alia,* the injunctions were intended to protect B against violations of the presumption of innocence, protected by Art 6(2).

The case turned on the proportionality of the interference with the legitimate aims pursued. The Court subjected this question to a detailed review, conceding only a narrow margin of appreciation to the state. It took into account the possible effect on the Art 6(2) rights of B. But it also took account of the facts that he had sought publicity as a Nazi activist and that the offences in question had a political background and were 'directed against the foundations of a democratic society'.[29] Reiterating the significance of the essential function of the press in a democratic society, the Court pointed out that the duty of the press to inform the public extends to reporting and commenting on court proceedings and noted the consonance of its discharge of such a duty with the requirement under Art 6(1) that hearings should be public. The injunctions restricted the choice of the newspaper as to its presentation of reports. The Court in particular took account of the fact that, although objection was taken only to the picture in conjunction with the adverse comments, the injunction created an absolute prohibition on publishing a picture of B with or without such comments. It may be argued that the intensity of the review undertaken in this instance was due partly to the special circumstances of the case, especially the fact that, as a right-wing extremist, B had himself sought publicity for his views in the past. But the key point was that the photograph alone was unlikely to cause prejudice to the proceedings and yet the effect of the injunction was to prohibit any publication of it, even if accompanying a fair and accurate factual report of the proceedings. The injunction, therefore, was manifestly overbroad since it caught harmless publications. Thus the proportionality analysis was again based on means/end balancing[30] – the measures taken, it was found, went further than needed to serve the end in question. The Court concluded on that basis that there was no reasonable relationship of proportionality between the interference and the aims pursued.

The injunction also affected the openness of the proceedings, since publication of such reports was found to be consonant with that aspect of Art 6(1). Although it might be argued that the publication of this particular photograph had little impact on open justice, the judgment may be said to protect both the substance and the form of reporting on court proceedings. Thus, the Court made explicit, in a partial sense, the consonance between Articles 10 and 6. That line of argument could have been taken further

---

29 *Ibid,* at paras 54 and 55.
30 See Chapter 4, p 242.

and the broader harmony between the aims of free speech and the protection for the administration of justice could have been more clearly articulated. *News Verlags* differs somewhat from the previous line of authority in terms of the intensity of the review that was undertaken, but does not represent a significant departure from it since the potential impact on the trial was thought to be very slight, whereas the effect on media freedom was viewed as quite significant. Moreover, the case concerned an obviously overbroad injunction.

Given the tendency of the Court to view its approach to the interests of freedom of expression and the administration of justice as 'the balancing of competing interests'[31] where a claim raising these issues arises under Art 10, it is arguable that the stance taken would have differed had the Austrian Court refused to grant the injunction and *B* had brought a claim to Strasbourg, arguing for a violation of Art 6(2). In *Ribemont v France*[32] an application brought on the basis of a violation of the Art 6(2) guarantee owing to the effect of publicity succeeded once the violation was found since, apart from provisions allowing for the exclusion of persons from a hearing in certain circumstances (see below), Art 6 is not qualified. The Court went on to find that the comments made about Ribemont went beyond merely providing information and had created a breach of Art 6(2):

> [S]ome of the highest-ranking officers in the French police referred to Mr Allenet de Ribemont, without any qualification or reservation, as one of the instigators of a murder and thus an accomplice in that murder. This was clearly a declaration of the applicant's guilt which, firstly, encouraged the public to believe him guilty and, secondly, prejudged the assessment of the facts by the competent judicial authority.[33]

Once the violation of Art 6(2) was found, the application succeeded since, apart from provisions allowing for the exclusion of persons from a hearing in certain circumstances, Art 6 is not qualified.

In contrast, in *Wloch v Poland*[34] an allegation that numerous newspaper comments shortly after the applicant's arrest had led to a violation of Art 6(2) was rejected on the basis that on the facts it was extremely unlikely that the comments could have affected the judges who were to preside over the trial. Long after the time of publication – a matter of about six years – the judges who would preside over the trial had still not been empanelled. It was clearly highly unlikely that the newspaper comments would be remembered with any clarity by the judges when they were eventually empanelled and even more unlikely that they would have any influence. Thus it was found that there was no evidence that the presumption of innocence had been violated and so this aspect of Wloch's application was dismissed as manifestly ill-founded. This decision is of little value in terms of supporting the argument that the British media have some leeway

---

31 Para 56, relying on the judgment in *Bladet Tromsø and Stensaas v Norway* (2000) 29 EHRR 125; (1999) 6 BHRC 599.

32 (1995) 20 EHRR 557. The Court found that Art 6(2) had been breached by a statement made by the French Minister of the Interior and senior police officers at a press conference in which they named the applicant as involved in a murder.

33 *Ibid*, at para 41.

34 March 2000, Information note No 16; for the other aspects of the application see (2002) 34 EHRR 9.

to comment on the guilt or innocence of a potential defendant, since it could only be utilised where there had been a very significant time lapse between publication and trial. A lapse of around six years would not normally occur in the UK.

Balance created between Art 6 and Art 10

As a preliminary comment on the above jurisprudence, it may be found that where a matter comes before the Court in the form of an Art 10 claim, the Court's reasoning follows the contours of that article, which require it to afford presumptive primacy to freedom of expression and to regard the administration of justice as an exception to that right. It is perhaps inevitable, then, that the two interests will be viewed, broadly, as competing. Where the same or similar issues arise, exceptionally, in the form of an Art 6 claim, it appears that there can be no balancing of competing interests,[35] except as regards the requirements of a public hearing in Art 6(1), since Art 6 is otherwise unqualified. The question is merely whether, on the facts, a breach of Art 6 could have arisen due to media comment – no question of justification arises. The choices thereby apparent, informing the moral framework of the Convention, indicate that in this context Art 6 takes precedence over Art 10. Therefore where an infringement of the guarantee under Art 6 might genuinely arise as a result of a publication, the Court is almost bound to find no breach of Art 10, despite the fact that when it is dealing with an Art 10 claim it has to treat an arguable violation of Art 6 as arising, technically, in the form of an exception under Art 10(2).

The Court's statement in *Worm* to the effect that 'the limits of permissible comment may not extend to statements that are likely to prejudice, whether intentionally or not, the chances of a person receiving a fair trial' bears out this finding. This comment suggests that speech (including political speech) which infringes the presumption of innocence, or is likely to infringe it, will readily be overridden by the fair trial guarantee. This is not because the speech is seen as of low value, but because the competing interest is so weighty.[36] In other words, the treatment of speech that invades another right protected by the Convention may tend to cut across the established categories of expression as 'political', 'artistic' and 'commercial'. This is especially the case where the expression affects one of the unqualified, or not materially qualified, rights. Even where the speech is within the category occupying the highest place in the hierarchy of speech, as in *Worm*, that factor does not appear to play a significant role in the stance taken – the value of the speech does not appear to be weighed up against the effect on the other Convention right.

One difficulty with the Court's approach is that it can allow interferences with freedom of expression even where the Art 6 rights of a particular defendant are only

---

35   See the discussion of the 'parallel analysis' in *Re S* [2003] 2 FCR 577, CA; [2004] UKHL 47; the decision is discussed in Chapter 10, pp 748–52.

36   To a lesser extent this is also the case in relation to privacy-invading speech and speech offensive to religious sensibilities – breaching Art 9. See *Otto-Preminger* (1994) 19 EHRR 34 in relation to speech that the Court has viewed as clashing with the Art 9 guarantee of freedom of religion. *Tammer v Estonia* (2003) 37 EHRR 43 and *N v Portugal* (Appl No 20683/92, 20 February 1995) both indicated that quite draconian penalties for invasion of privacy are compatible with Art 10. See further Chapter 10, p 696.

doubtfully threatened – as *BBC Scotland* indicates. A further difficulty is that the Court is also prepared to draw the line at allowing comments that 'are likely to . . . undermine the confidence of the public in the role of the courts in the administration of criminal justice'.[37] On the other hand, it avoided such a stance in the *Sunday Times* case. The exception – the 'authority of the judiciary' – is not linked to criminal proceedings alone and many of the comments made by the Court in *Worm* regarding the fear of undermining public confidence in such authority could have equal validity in relation to civil actions. It considered that one aspect of the mischief to be avoided was that of a threat to the administration of justice in a general sense. It justified such a stance by reference to the rule of law principle encapsulated in Art 6 regarding the need to maintain confidence in the courts. In other words, it sought to reconcile the stance taken under Art 10(2) with that taken in relation to Art 6, partly on the basis of infringing Art 10 in order to avoid a concrete harm in Art 6 terms, but *also* at a broader level of principle. The difference of approach may partly be explicable on the basis that the Court is particularly concerned with the protection of the administration of justice in criminal rather than *civil* proceedings. Clearly, where laypersons are concerned in the justice process – which is more likely to be the case in criminal proceedings[38] – the risk of unfairness due to the influence of publications may be higher. The fear of 'trial by newspaper' that exorcised the House of Lords in *Attorney General v Times* appeared to strike the Court as of especial significance in relation to criminal proceedings.

The Court's differences of approach to Art 10 claims in this context are therefore explicable by reference to the question whether the term 'the authority of the judiciary' can or cannot be viewed as covering interests that are quite closely linked to the concrete demands of Art 6 in that instance. The effect of the margin of appreciation doctrine is variable. Where the rhetoric of 'protection for the administration of justice' in a non-concrete sense is used in relation to a publication that in actuality relates closely to particular proceedings, especially criminal ones, and creates some risk to those proceedings, a margin of appreciation may be conceded in assessing the *degree* of risk. The *Sunday Times* case established that the interference with freedom of expression represented by curbing media freedom to comment on a forthcoming action or on issues linked to it must answer to a pressing social need.[39] Where, as in that instance, the interference is aimed – broadly – at the protection of the administration of justice, but has only a very indirect and uncertain justification in terms of protecting particular litigation, the review of the existence of such a need is likely to be intense. But where the interference appears to be fairly strongly linked to the preservation of Art 6 rights, since a particular trial is quite clearly affected, the margin of appreciation doctrine may not have a significant role, and the interference may be found to be justified, as in *Worm* and *BBC Scotland v UK*, since, where two rights are viewed as in conflict, the Court will prefer the (almost) unqualified right under Art 6. Free expression has a role in supporting confidence in the administration of justice; this is made explicit under the Art 6 guarantee of a public hearing and by the Court; but as the Court made plain in the cases

---

37   (1998) 25 EHRR 454, at para 50.
38   In the UK juries are used in certain civil proceedings, notably libel actions and in certain civil actions against the police: see Supreme Court Act 1981, s 69.
39   (1979) 2 EHRR 245, at para 62.

considered, speech that undermines that confidence may be fairly readily displaced by the competing administration of justice interest. Within the Strasbourg rhetoric, therefore, regarding competing interests, a recognition of the consonance between the values underlying them is evident.

Approaches to the domestic impact of the Convention under the Human Rights Act

A court, adjudicating on an action for contempt against a media organ is bound by all the Convention rights under s 6 HRA and in this context must ensure that Arts 10 and 6 – as particularly relevant – are satisfied. It must also interpret the provisions of the Contempt of Court Act 1981 compatibly with the Convention under s 3 if a potential incompatibility arises; the common law could potentially be modified in reliance on the courts' duty under s 6, although, as discussed below, significant change in the key common law contempt area is now unlikely. Section 2 HRA requires the courts to take the Convention jurisprudence into account in satisfying their duties under s 6 or s 3. But the discussion above has indicated that the impact of the Convention on this area of domestic contempt law is complex. It is not enough to argue merely that the Convention demands a shift towards freedom of expression, since such an argument fails to take account of the demands of Art 6 and the need to protect the administration of justice in a general sense.

In so far as, traditionally, domestic contempt law favoured the protection of the administration of justice over the protection of freedom of expression, it failed to strike a balance that is consistent with the Convention. The domestic inquiry pre-HRA always began by considering the law governing the interference with the negative liberty of expression. The domestic courts have traditionally been preoccupied with the administration of justice rather than with individual rights to free speech. This approach was modified in the pre-HRA era under the Contempt of Court Act 1981, which was a response to the finding at Strasbourg[40] that common law contempt had failed to afford sufficient weight to freedom of expression, as explained below. The approach adopted may now require further modification under the HRA, but the structure of domestic decision-making need not fully follow the Strasbourg model since Art 10 and, in some instances, Art 6 issues normally arise during a contempt action[41] rather than as aspects of an Art 10 claim. Art 6 issues may also be raised during a criminal trial or on appeal as part of an argument that the jury or others would be or had been affected by the publication of prejudicial journalistic material.

As argued above, although the overturning of a conviction or a stay of proceedings can be used as a remedy where there has been a violation of Art 6 rights due to media publicity, it would be more satisfactory to use preventive measures where the possibility of prejudice to proceedings genuinely arises. Strasbourg tends to favour such measures, as indicated, although where the connection between protecting the right to a fair trial and suppressing the speech in question is doubtful, it will subject them to an intense scrutiny. It will be argued that, at the present time, contempt law is not fulfilling this

---

40 In the *Sunday Times* case (1979) 2 EHRR 245 (see below, pp 312–14).
41 They might also arise in judicial review proceedings; this is discussed below in relation to *Taylor*, p 324.

preventive role, but that neutralising measures have not fully taken its place. Common law contempt afforded primacy to the interest in the administration of justice, but it is suggested that statutory contempt is not engaging fully with the core values underlying either free speech or the administration of justice. In particular, it will be argued that contempt law is failing to meet Art 6 demands that the relevant legislation, and executive decisions taken in relation to it, should be efficacious in protecting the right to a fair trial.[42] This failure is partly due to the height of the bar that must be surmounted if a contempt action is to be successful – this point is considered below. The failure also relates, it is argued, to the role of the Attorney General, who has the responsibility under s 7 of the Contempt of Court Act 1981 for initiating prosecutions against media bodies.[43] Theoretically, superior courts[44] can punish contempts on their own motion. This inherent power is preserved under s 7. In practice, the courts do not exercise this power in respect of publications subject to the strict liability rule (see below). A party to proceedings in a superior court could put, through counsel, the argument that a publication is prejudicial. The judge could then refer the matter to the Attorney General. This would not necessarily mean, however, that proceedings would be brought.[45]

The Attorney General can also seek an injunction to restrain a planned publication and, in this respect, can be viewed as having a limited vetting role.[46] He may also issue warnings to the media regarding coverage of cases which have attracted public attention.[47] The Attorney General is a member of the cabinet. Theoretically, he or she acts in two distinct capacities – as a member of the government and as an independent law officer. His role as law officer places him, theoretically, at a distance from the government. In practice, his impartiality may be questioned, owing to the conflict of interests inherent in his dual role. He may come under pressure to initiate prosecutions in cases in which the government itself has an interest. As Borrie and Lowe observe: 'in cases such as these the Attorney's role . . . does smack of partisanship'.[48] Conversely, it is possible that he may be reluctant to initiate proceedings when to do so would mean bringing the government – in effect – into conflict with powerful media proprietors. Clearly, there will be variable practice between the office-holders in these respects, but this inconsistency itself has a questionable effect on the quality of justice and the protection for media freedom. As certain of the decisions discussed below indicate, it cannot be said that when the massed tabloids act, effectively, in concert in their coverage of a trial-related story, they are immune from prosecutions. But it will be argued that a reluctance

---

42 Such demands are those indicated in *BBC Scotland v UK* (1998) 25 EHRR CD 179. See also *Worm v Austria* (1998) 25 EHRR 454 or *News Verlags* (2001) 31 EHRR 8, although the laws at issue in those instances were not contempt laws.

43 Section 7 provides: 'Proceedings for a contempt of court under the strict liability rule shall not be instituted except by or with the consent of the Attorney General or on the motion of a court having jurisdiction to deal with it.'

44 In England and Wales, the House of Lords, the Court of Appeal, the High Court of Justice, the Crown Court, the Restrictive Practices Court, the Employment Appeals Tribunal, the Courts-Martial Appeal Court.

45 See *R v Taylor and Taylor* (1993) 98 Cr App R 361 (discussed below, p 324).

46 This occurred in *Attorney General v Times Newspapers Ltd* [1974] AC 273 (see below, pp 313–14).

47 He issued such warnings in respect of the 'Yorkshire Ripper' case and in the case of Frederick and Rosemary West.

48 *The Law of Contempt*, 1996, p 485.

to prosecute a large number of media organs simultaneously, especially those with large circulations, is evident. The result is arguably that the tendency to prosecute those parts of the press which have the most central role in furthering the values underpinning political speech is not in proportion to their tendency to affect the fairness of trials.

The Attorney General is bound by s 6 HRA and, therefore, must ensure that both Arts 10 and 6 are satisfied. While it may be argued that contempt law does not directly provide a remedy where a publication has prejudiced a trial or may be about to do so, it has a link with Art 6, as indicated in the Strasbourg jurisprudence. Injunctions are infrequently granted,[49] but would be of value as a preventive measure. An injunction against one newspaper would prevent it from pursuing a story, while it would tend to deter others from running variations on the same story, since they might incur criminal liability for contempt. The use of injunctions could prevent the risk of prejudice arising from a wide-ranging and relentless coverage of issues relevant in a forthcoming trial. More generally, prosecutions for contempt, where Art 6 rights were violated, might have a future deterrent effect. In other words, the link between the use of contempt law and Art 6 should be given some weight in the current situation in which the judiciary understandably do not at present use neutralising measures, such as stays, extensively to combat possibly prejudicial publicity.[50]

As indicated above, once a contempt action is in being, the national court is not in the same position as Strasbourg since the part played by the margin of appreciation at Strasbourg should not be reflected in domestic decision making. Thus, where Arts 6 and 10 rights appear to be at stake, detailed and rigorous review could determine how far this is the case. The central concern should be the need to isolate the fundamental values at stake in terms of both free speech and fair trials and to tailor domestic law in order to protect them.

In a contempt action, the court is bound by the Convention rights under s 6 of the HRA and, where the statutory provisions were in question, could seek to ensure that it discharged that obligation by interpreting them compatibly with the relevant guarantees. It is suggested that the domestic court could examine the effect of finding liability in terms of both Arts 10 and 6. In so doing, it is argued, it would not only escape the structural constraints of the Strasbourg approach, but might more readily recognise the underlying harmony between the two articles.

In order to illustrate this approach, two instances will be considered taken from the cases discussed below. In the first example, based on the *Taylor* case,[51] it is assumed that all the tabloid newspapers have reported, in sensationalist and misleading terms, on a forthcoming trial that has happened to catch the public eye. They are prosecuted for contempt. (In fact, in *Taylor*, no prosecution was forthcoming, a factor that may have played a part in recent tabloid excesses.) Assuming that prima facie liability could be established under the 1981 Act, it must also be asked whether the creation of such

---

49 In *Attorney General v News Group Newspapers* [1987] 1 QB 1, an injunction would have been granted.
50 See the comments of Simon Brown LJ regarding the failure to use stays in certain instances in which prejudice to proceedings was found: *Attorney General v Birmingham Post and Mail Ltd* [1998] 4 All ER 49.
51 See below, p 345. For comment on the case and its implications within the Convention, see Borrie and Lowe, *The Law of Contempt*, 1996, Butterworths, pp 481–82.

liability would be unjustified under Art 10. The first question would be whether it would constitute an interference with the freedom of expression of the tabloids. Despite the lack of value of the speech, such an interference would be found, since Strasbourg rarely denies Art 10 protection to speech on the basis of its content. The interference would clearly be found to be prescribed by law – the 1981 Act. The legitimate aims in view would be the preservation of the authority and impartiality of the judiciary and of the rights of others. Those aims would probably be established, on the facts; they have been established in all the relevant claims considered at Strasbourg.

The key question would be whether the interference represented by the creation of liability would be necessary in a democratic society. In determining necessity, the proportionality of the potential interference would require careful scrutiny. This would be the point at which the domestic court would be expected to take a somewhat different stance from that taken by Strasbourg, in relation to the 'rights of others' exception, in that its scrutiny of this question should be much more intensive. Factors to be taken into account would include the extent to which the various newspapers had in fact misled readers and the ability of jurors to disregard the coverage, on strong directions from the judge. But the central importance of fair trials in a democratic society should also be considered, as should the lack of value of the speech. The question of proportionality can encompass such matters, as the decisions in *News Verlags* and *Sunday Times* demonstrated. On the facts, it is argued that a finding of liability against the newspapers under the 1981 Act would be justified under Art 10. The same result would be likely to arise if the liability was then considered from the Art 6 perspective since, on the facts, it could readily be found that the fairness of the trial had been affected and possibly that the presumption of innocence had also been undermined. The court would have discharged its duty under s 6 of the HRA. (Had it appeared that it would fail to do so if it found against the newspapers, it would then have had to examine the statutory provisions in detail for their compatibility with the Convention under s 3 of the HRA.) If, on the above facts, the Attorney General failed to bring a prosecution, it is argued that he would have failed to discharge that duty.

The opposing result would be reached, it is argued, in a case in which certain newspapers comment on a matter of grave public importance, relating to the possibility of abuse of power in part of the executive, where no criminal trial is affected. The comment may, however, affect the ability of the Attorney General to continue a breach of confidence action with a view to suppressing debate on the matter. Publications in other jurisdictions in fact render it extremely unlikely that the rights can be preserved in any event. This example is based on *Attorney General v Times Newspapers*,[52] which is discussed below. In this instance, the speech in question concerns a matter of great public significance while hardly affecting Art 6 rights. The interest in question, which might conceivably be viewed as falling within Art 6, concerns the preservation of the rights of one party to a civil action. (Strasbourg, however, did not view that right as engaging the 'rights of others' exception as a distinct exception when it considered the interference with freedom of expression created by the grant of an injunction on grounds of breach of confidence.[53]) The sanction of contempt of court would be, in this instance,

---

52 [1992] 1 AC 191; discussed below, p 345.
53 *Observer and Guardian v UK* (1991) 14 EHRR 153; discussed below, pp 518–23.

disproportionate to the aim of preserving the authority of the judiciary since it could not in fact be preserved by that means.[54] Thus, the action would fail, since the imposition of liability on the newspapers would be unjustified.

These two examples illustrate the harmony that exists between the values underlying Arts 6 and 10. They also, it is argued, indicate the proper approach to the infusion of Convention values into this area of contempt law. Essentially, it is an approach that seeks out and protects the core values at stake in relation to both media freedom and the administration of justice. In identifying the consonance that exists between such values it differentiates sharply between speech supported by the justifications from truth, democracy or self-fulfilment, and speech which is promulgated mainly to further the ends of media conglomerates. It seeks to preserve impartiality and fairness, especially in criminal proceedings, but demands a rigorous and careful scrutiny of the possibility that unfairness may arise.

Domestic provisions: the development of the common law pre-1981

This section discusses the background to the inception of the Contempt of Court Act 1981. The reasons for introducing the Act are key to understanding its provisions. Prior to the inception of the Act, this particular area of criminal contempt at common law curtailed the freedom of the media to discuss and report on issues arising from criminal or civil proceedings on the basis that those proceedings might suffer prejudice. However, it went further than was necessary to deal with very clear risks of interference with the administration of justice. The media was restricted in its reporting of issues relevant to civil or criminal proceedings which were, or were soon to be, in being. It is important to note that civil proceedings can also be prejudiced, even though usually no jury is involved, but obviously this danger may be less likely to arise. It is apparent that more weight was given to protecting the administration of justice rather than free speech, from the ease with which it was possible to satisfy the common law tests.

The elements of common law contempt pre-1981 consisted of the creation of a real risk of prejudice (the *actus reus*) and an intention to publish; it was therefore a crime of strict liability. The *actus reus* could be fulfilled if it were shown that the publication in question had created a risk that the proceedings in question might be prejudiced; it was irrelevant whether they actually had been. This distinction was clearly illustrated by *Thompson Newspapers Ltd ex p Attorney General.*[55] While the defendant was awaiting trial, the *Sunday Times* published his photograph and commented on his unsavoury background as a brothel keeper. This was held to amount to contempt. He was convicted and then appealed on the ground that the trial had been prejudiced by the article, but his appeal failed on the basis that jurors had not in actuality been so prejudiced. This case further illustrates the nature of the *actus reus*: it was not necessary to publish very damaging comments in order to create the risk in question.

At common law, there was a certain time before and a certain time after the action, known as the *sub judice* period, when there was a risk that any article published relevant

---

54 *Ibid.*
55 [1968] 1 All ER 268; [1968] 1 WLR 1.

to the action might be in contempt. The starting point of this period occurred when the proceedings were 'imminent' (*Savundranayagan and Walker*).[56] This test attracted much criticism because of its vagueness and width; it was obviously capable of applying a long time before the trial and it therefore had an inhibiting effect on the media out of proportion to its value. In particular, it gave rise to the restriction caused by so-called 'gagging writs'. A newspaper might be discussing corruption in a company. If a writ for libel was then issued – although there was no intention of proceeding with the case – the newspaper might find itself in contempt if it continued to discuss the issues. Thus, this method could be used to prevent further comment.

The need for reform that would, in particular, address the width of the imminence test was apparent and led to the setting up of the Phillimore Committee in 1974,[57] but it might not have come about without the influence of the European Court of Human Rights. The ruling that UK contempt law had breached Art 10 arose through the decision of the House of Lords in *Attorney General v Times Newspapers Ltd*.[58] The case concerned litigation arising out of the Thalidomide tragedy. The parents of the Thalidomide children wished to sue Distillers, the company that had manufactured the drug, because they believed that it was responsible for the terrible damage done to their unborn children. Distillers resisted the claims and entered into negotiation with the parents' solicitors. Thus, the litigation was dormant while the negotiations were taking place. Meanwhile, the *Sunday Times* wished to publish an article accusing Distillers of acting ungenerously towards the Thalidomide children. The article came close to saying that Distillers had been negligent, although it was balanced in that it did consider both sides.

The Attorney General obtained an injunction in the Divisional Court preventing publication of the article on the ground that it amounted to a contempt of court. The Court of Appeal then discharged the injunction in a ruling that weighed up the public interest in freedom of speech against the need to protect the administration of justice and found that the former value outweighed the latter: the article concerned a matter of great public interest and, since the litigation in question was dormant, it would probably be unaffected by it. The House of Lords then restored the injunction on the ground that the article dealt with the question of negligence and therefore prejudged the case pending before the court. It held that such prejudgment was particularly objectionable as coming close to 'trial by media' and thereby leading to an undermining of the administration of justice: a person might be adjudged negligent by parts of the media with none of the safeguards available in court. The confidence of the public in the courts might be undermined, thus creating a long-term detriment to the course of justice generally.

This ruling created a possible new test for the *actus reus* of contempt. Termed the 'prejudgment' test, it was wider than the test of real risk of prejudice, in that little risk to proceedings might be shown, but it might still be possible to assert that they had been prejudged. This test was heavily criticised by the Phillimore Committee; it had a

---

56 [1968] 3 All ER 439; [1968] 1 WLR 1761, CA.

57 See *Report of the Committee on Contempt of Court*, Cmnd 5794, 1974. For comment, see Dhavan, R, 'Contempt of court and the Phillimore Committee Report' (1976) 5 Anglo-Am L Rev 186–253.

58 [1974] AC 273; [1973] 3 All ER 54; [1973] 3 WLR 298, HL. For case notes, see Miller, CJ (1974) 37 MLR 96; O'Boyle, M (1974) 25 NILQ 57; Williams, DGT (1973) 32 CLJ 177 and Miller, CJ [1975] Crim LR 132.

potentially grave effect on freedom of speech because it was very difficult to draw the line between legitimate discussion in the media and prejudgment. Since it was easier to satisfy the prejudgment test than the old test for the *actus reus* of common law contempt, the Phillimore Committee considered that the *Sunday Times* ruling strengthened the case for reform. Meanwhile, the case was on its way to the European Court of Human Rights. The editor of the *Sunday Times* applied to the European Commission of Human Rights seeking a ruling that the imposition of the injunction breached Art 10 of the European Convention, and five years after the judgment of the House of Lords, the case came before the European Court of Human Rights (*Sunday Times* case).[59]

As indicated in the introduction to this part, the Art 10 guarantee of freedom of expression is subject to exceptions to be narrowly construed. The Court found that the injunction clearly infringed Art 10(1) and that this was not a trivial infringement; the free speech interest involved was very strong, because the matter was one of great public concern. However, the injunction fell within Art 10(2) because it had an aim permitted by one of the exceptions – maintenance of the authority of the judiciary.

The next question was whether the injunction was 'necessary in a democratic society' in order to achieve the aim in question: it was not enough merely to show that the injunction was covered by an exception. In order to make a determination on this point, the Court considered the meaning of the term 'necessary'. It ruled that this did not mean indispensable, but connoted something stronger than 'useful', 'reasonable' or 'desirable'. It implied the existence of a 'pressing social need'. Was there such a need? The Court employed the doctrine of proportionality in determining the existence of such a 'need' in the circumstances: it weighed up the strength of the free speech interest in considering whether the injunction was disproportionate to the aim of preserving the authority of the judiciary. It found that although courts are clearly the forums for settling disputes, this does not mean that there can be no newspaper discussion before a case. The article was couched in moderate terms and explored the issues in a balanced way. Moreover, the litigation in question was dormant and therefore unlikely to be affected by the article. Nevertheless, the injunction created an absolute prohibition on discussion of the issues forming the background to the case. Thus, on the one hand, there was a strong free speech interest; on the other, there was a weak threat to the authority of the judiciary. If the free speech interest had been weaker, it might have been more easily overcome. The Court, therefore, concluded that the interference did not correspond to a social need sufficiently pressing to outweigh the public interest in freedom of expression. In reaching its conclusion that a breach of Art 10 had therefore taken place,[60] the Court also adverted briefly to the value of the article in furthering the aim of preserving the authority of the judiciary since 'in bringing to light certain facts it might have served as a brake on speculative and unenlightened discussion'. In other words, the speech in question served the ends of justice in a general sense.

The UK government responded to this decision in the enactment of the Contempt of Court Act 1981, which was supposed to take account of the ruling of the European Court and was also influenced to an extent by the findings of the Phillimore Committee.[61]

---

59 Judgment of 26 April 1979, A 30; (1979) 2 EHRR 245. For case notes, see Mann, FA (1979) 95 LQR 348; Wong, W-WM (1984) 17 NY Univ JIL and Pol 35.
60 It may be noted that the Court was divided 11–9 in reaching this determination.
61 See *Report of the Committee on Contempt of Court*, Cmnd 5794, 1974; Green Paper, Cmnd 7145, 1978.

The Contempt of Court Act 1981

The 1981 Act was designed to introduce provisions based on a modification of the common law tests without bringing about radical change. It introduced various liberalising factors, but it was intended to maintain the stance of the ultimate supremacy of the administration of justice over freedom of speech, while moving the balance further towards freedom of speech.[62] In particular, it introduced stricter time limits, a more precise test for the *actus reus* and – in a departure from the common law rules – allowed some articles on matters of public interest to escape liability even though prejudice to proceedings was created.

These reforms brought about under the Act will be considered below, bearing the obligation of s 3 HRA in mind, in terms of their ability to satisfy the Convention, in particular Art 10, interpreted domestically. In any particular instance, the *current* Strasbourg standards should be taken into account in strictly scrutinising interferences with the Art 10 guarantee. It would not be sufficient to assume that such standards will be met on the basis that the 1981 Act was introduced in order to take account of the Strasbourg ruling in the *Sunday Times* case. In order to determine whether liability is created, the following steps must be taken under the Act. Possible modifications of the statutory tests under the HRA will be considered taking account of the Strasbourg standards discussed.

The publication falls within s 1 of the Act

Under s 1, conduct will be contempt if it interferes with the administration of justice in particular proceedings regardless of intent to do so. Thus, not all publications that deal with issues touching on the administration of justice will fall within the 1981 Act. The starting point under s 1 is to ask whether the publication touches upon particular legal proceedings. In other words, if the article appears to have a long-term effect on the course of justice generally, without affecting any particular proceedings, it would fall outside the Act and might be considered at common law. This point will be considered below. A publication can include blogs or social media postings, depending upon the nature of the privacy settings applied (if any). The key question for the court to resolve is whether the publication could be seen by 'a section of the public'. This may be satisfied if the publication could be disseminated by others, which may be possible using platforms like *Facebook*.

It is important to note that it is not necessary to show that the defendant intended to prejudice proceedings: the 'strict liability rule' under s 1 continues the position as it was at common law. After establishing that the publication might affect particular proceedings, a number of other tests must be satisfied if the strict liability rule is to be established. If the publication does affect particular proceedings, but one of these tests is unsatisfied, it might still be possible to consider it at common law. It should be noted that the proceedings must be 'court' proceedings. This test includes certain tribunals in the contempt jurisdiction.[63]

---

62 For comment on the 1981 Act, see Miller, CJ [1982] Crim LR 71; Lowe, NV [1982] PL 20; Smith, JC [1982] Crim LR 744; Zellich, GF [1982] PL 343; Redmond, M [1983] CLJ 9.

63 Section 19 provides that 'court' includes 'any tribunal or body exercising the judicial power of the state'. See further Borrie and Lowe, *op cit*, fn 1, pp 485–91.

The proceedings are 'active'

This test, which arises under s 2(3), is more clearly defined than the test at common law and therefore proceedings are 'active' (or *sub judice*) for shorter periods. Thus, the test is intended to have a liberalising effect. The starting and ending points for civil and criminal proceedings are defined in Sched 1. For criminal proceedings, the starting point (Sched 1, para 4(a)–(e)) is: the issue of a warrant for arrest, an arrest without warrant or the service of an indictment (or summons or an oral charge); the ending point is acquittal, sentence, any other verdict or discontinuance of the trial. The starting point for civil proceedings occurs when the case is set down for a hearing in the High Court or a date for the hearing is fixed (Sched 1, paras 12 and 13). This provision was clarified in *Attorney General v Hislop and Pressdram*:[64] it was found that s 2(3) was fulfilled because the proceedings in question (an action for defamation) had come into the 'warned' list at the time the articles in question were published. This starting point addresses the problem of gagging writs: the mere issuance of a writ would not mean that any further comment could give rise to an action for contempt because the issue of a writ is not the starting point. The end point of the active period for civil proceedings comes when the proceedings are disposed of, discontinued or withdrawn. The precision of these provisions, which allows the media to determine with reasonable certainty the point at which a risk of liability arises, means that they can be viewed as meeting the demands of Art 10.

Surprisingly, appellate proceedings are also covered by Sched 1. The starting point occurs when leave to appeal is applied for, by notice of appeal or application for review or other originating process; the end point occurs when the proceedings are disposed of or abandoned. Section 9 of the Criminal Appeal Act 1995 provides that a reference by the Criminal Cases Review Commission to the Court of Appeal is to be treated as an appeal under the Criminal Appeal Act 1968 for all purposes and, therefore, appellate proceedings become active when such a reference is made.

These provisions are less restrictive than the previous ones under the common law, which also covered the period during which notice to appeal could be given, but the key question is why appellate proceedings are covered at all. The Phillimore Committee recommended that most appellate proceedings should not be covered.[65] Given the principles at stake, discussed above, it is suggested that the ends of justice are unlikely to be served by seeking to stifle media comment that refers specifically to appeals, since the openness of the discussion supports confidence in the quality of justice that is unafraid of comment. The misinformed or biased nature of aspects of such discussion would not be expected to affect the judiciary, especially the senior judiciary. Therefore, no fear of arbitrariness due to prejudice should arise. As Lord Reid said in the *Sunday Times* case: 'It is scarcely possible to imagine a case when comment could influence judges in the Court of Appeal or noble and leaned Lords in this House.'[66] Nevertheless, Channel 4 was enjoined from broadcasting a re-enactment, in the form of a dramatic 'reconstruction', of the appeal of the Birmingham Six, until after the decision on the

---

64 [1991] 1 QB 514; [1991] 1 All ER 911; [1991] 2 WLR 219, CA.
65 Phillimore Committee Report, para 132.
66 *Attorney General v Times Newspapers*, [1974] AC 273; [1973] 3 All ER 54; [1973] 3 WLR 298, HL.

appeal had been taken.[67] This was a doubtful decision, since it was highly unlikely that the judges would have been influenced by the programme. The injunction was therefore obtained on the basis that the public's view of the judgment of the court might have been affected by it. This justification is flawed, since it does not appear to be covered by s 2(2) of the Act,[68] and also because the public's view of that judgment and of the Appeal Court generally would be more greatly influenced, it is suggested, by the impression given that a ban was necessary in order to prevent the programme from influencing the judges.

It is probable that prosecutions in respect of contempt of appellate courts will not be brought in future. In *Re Lonhro plc and Observer Ltd*,[69] the House of Lords relied on Art 10 in finding that since the possibility that a professional judge would be influenced by media coverage of a case is extremely remote, it would be extremely hard to establish a 'pressing social need', as required by Art 10, to suppress the speech in question. This stance has now been reinforced by the inception of the Human Rights Act.

The publication creates 'a substantial risk of serious prejudice or impediment to the course of justice in the proceedings in question' (s 2(2))

Introduction

The s 2(2) test can be viewed as taking a protective stance since it is intended to deter media bodies from publishing prejudicial material. Arguably, it goes further in terms of protecting the fairness of trials than neutralising or remedial measures (acquittals, abandonment of the proceedings) do. Section 2(2) can be said to punish media bodies that have created prejudice even where – from the point of view of the *trial* judge, as opposed to the judge in the contempt proceedings – a stay of proceedings or other measures are not viewed as necessary. Recent developments have helped clarify this point. In *Attorney General v MGN Ltd*,[70] the court was clear that it does not matter that proceedings may not be ongoing or, as in this case, that there are no proceedings at all. The test is predictive and, therefore, must be assessed from the point of publication. This case concerned the shocking treatment that Christopher Jefferies received when several newspapers published details of his arrest over the murder of his tenant, Joanna Yeates. In general, the reports were unflattering, portraying him as an eccentric pervert. The more extreme articles linked Jefferies to paedophile activity as well as another unsolved murder in the area. It did not matter, though, that Jefferies was later released without charge. The court held that the vilification of Jefferies amounted to a substantial risk of serious prejudice since the preparation of Jefferies' defence would have been seriously affected had he been prosecuted.[71]

67 *Re Channel 4 Television Co Ltd* (1988) *The Times*, 2 February; [1988] Crim LR 237.
68 Since it could not have been shown that a substantial risk of prejudice to the proceedings – the appeal – would arise. Section 2(2) does not refer to a substantial risk of prejudice to the course of justice in a general sense.
69 [1989] 2 All ER 1100, HL.
70 (2011) EWHC 2383 (Admin).
71 *Ibid*, [33]–[36].

Section 2(2) is an objective test; it is unconcerned with the question whether prejudice has actually been caused. The inclusion of a substantial risk of 'impediment' could be viewed as making it clear that UK law adheres more to a protective rather than a neutralising model in terms of seeking to ensure the fairness of trials. The more far-reaching neutralising measures, such as changing the venue of the trial or delaying it, would clearly tend to have an impeding effect on it. The distinction between prejudice and impediment was central to the decision in *Attorney General v Random House*.[72] Tugendhat J noted that the term 'prejudice' relates to the effect of publication on the jury (i.e., that they are prejudiced against the defendant) whereas 'impediment' relates to the criminal justice process in broader terms and, in this case, the necessity for the judge to issue an extreme warning to the jury to disregard the publication so as to ensure prejudice to the trial did not occur.[73] In other words, the fairness of the trial might be comprised if the instruction were not issued. Thus: 'there can be a contempt within s.2(2) by a publication provided only it requires some extreme direction to be given to the jury or creates at the very least a seriously arguable ground for an appeal on the basis of prejudice'.[74]

On the other hand, the use of lesser neutralising measures, such as warnings to the jury to disregard media coverage, are matters that may properly be taken into account when considering the risk in question. In *Attorney General v Times Newspapers*[75] it was found that jurors were able to ignore possibly prejudicial comment in newspapers. That case concerned a relatively trivial incident that happened to attract publicity because of the fame of one of the persons involved, a factor that jurors might be expected to appreciate, leading them to discount the press coverage. Recently, it has become more common for consideration to be afforded to the likelihood that the jury will be strongly directed to ignore prejudicial coverage of the trial.[76] Thus, responsibility is shifting to an extent from the media and is being placed upon judges and jurors. Perhaps, as indicated above, that shift of responsibility is not fully in accordance with the notion that the 'duties and responsibilities' of Art 10 are placed upon those exercising the right to freedom of expression it protects, that is the media.

Moreover, as Simon Brown LJ pointed out in *Attorney General v Birmingham Post and Mail*,[77] 's 2(2) postulates a lesser degree of prejudice than is required to make good an appeal against conviction. Similarly, it seems to me to postulate a lesser degree of prejudice than would justify an order for a stay.' He went on to conclude that where s 2(2) was satisfied, it would not follow that a conviction was imperilled or that a stay was required, but that the converse was not the case: 'I find it difficult to envisage a publication which has concerned the judge sufficiently to discharge the jury and yet is not properly to be regarded as a contempt.' Clearly, although this may be an accurate statement of the effect of s 2(2) where a particular publication creates a likelihood of prejudice to a criminal trial, the preventive or punitive effect can only occur if (a) the prejudicial effect is not the result of cumulative media coverage of issues relevant to or

72 [2009] EWHC 1727 (QB).
73 *Ibid*, [19]–[24].
74 *Ibid*, [24].
75 (1983) *The Times*, 12 February, DC. See also *Attorney General v MGN* [1997] 1 All ER 456.
76 See, e.g., *Attorney General v MGN* [1997] EMLR 284.
77 [1998] 4 All ER 49, pp 57, 59. See further *Mcleod* (2000) *The Times*, 20 December.

arising from a particular case, and (b) if contempt proceedings are actually brought. As the discussion below indicates, both these matters are problematic.

According to the Court of Appeal in *Attorney General v News Group Newspapers*,[78] both limbs of the test under s 2(2) must be satisfied: showing a slight risk of serious prejudice or a substantial risk of slight prejudice would not be sufficient. The question to be asked under the first limb could be broken down as follows: can it be argued that there is a substantial risk that a person involved in the case in question such as a juror would: (a) encounter the article; (b) remember it; and (c) be affected by it so that he or she could not put it out of his or her mind during the trial? Clearly, a person cannot be affected at all by something he or she has never encountered or has forgotten about. Thus, a number of factors may be identified that will be relevant to one or more of these questions. Having considered factors that are taken into account in determining whether a 'substantial risk' has arisen, the discussion will then consider the less problematic question of 'serious prejudice'.

Key factors

The circulation of a publication/viewing figures for a broadcast is a relevant factor in relation to the 'substantial risk' limb of the s 2(2) test.[79] This factor potentially has a greater impact on broadcasters than on newspapers, since the viewing figures for popular programmes tend to far exceed the circulation figures of individual newspapers: one broadcast will in general reach far more people than will one article. An exception arose in *Attorney General v BBC, Attorney General v Hat Trick Productions Ltd*.[80] During a programme on BBC2 in the irreverent, satirical series *Have I Got News for You*, remarks were made by celebrities that assumed that the Maxwell brothers were guilty of defrauding the *Daily Mirror* pensioners. The broadcast occurred six months before the trial of the Maxwells, but was viewed by an audience of several millions. An action for contempt was brought and it was found that despite the humorous context, the remarks assuming the guilt of the defendants might have been taken seriously by viewers and that therefore s 2(2) was satisfied.

Clearly, circulation figures cannot be calculated only on the basis of viewing or selling figures. The impact of newspapers depends on their readership, not just their circulation figures. Further, front-page, banner headlines may reach many more people in a

78 [1987] 1 QB 1; [1986] 2 All ER 833; [1986] 3 WLR 365, CA.
79 If a publication has a small circulation, this risk might be seen as too remote. This point was considered in *Attorney General v Hislop and Pressdram* [1991] 1 QB 514; [1991] 1 All ER 911; [1991] 2 WLR 219, CA which concerned the effect of an article in *Private Eye* written about Sonia Sutcliffe, wife of the Yorkshire Ripper. She began an action for defamation in respect of the article. Shortly before the hearing of the action, *Private Eye* published two further articles defamatory of Mrs Sutcliffe. The Attorney-General brought proceedings for contempt of court in respect of the second articles, and on appeal it was determined that as *Private Eye* had a large readership, many of whom might live in London, where the libel action was held, it could not be said that the risk of prejudice was insubstantial.
80 [1997] EMLR 76; *The Times*, 26 July 1996. See also *Attorney General v LWT* 3 All ER 116; *Attorney General v Jones and BBC* (1995) (unreported).

range of contexts. The existence of the internet clearly increases the circulation figures of both newspapers and broadcasts. All newspapers and some broadcasts have their own website on which material is archived. Internet users could access trial-related material on such websites, either by putting a key word into Google (or another search engine), or by choosing to search the website of a particular media organ in the expectation that some reporting would cover such material.[81]

The temporal proximity between the publication and the trial or civil action is the single most significant factor under s 2(2). However, the rapidly increasing popularity of the internet may be calling the current stance into question. The reliance on temporal proximity between publication and proceedings in relation to the 'substantial risk' limb of s 2(2) arguably favours the particular operational methods of the tabloid press. As Chapter 10 points out, the press are not restrained, as are broadcasters, by quite a strict statutory regime governing privacy and accuracy. The result is that tabloid newspapers are able to rely on sensationalist and frequently misleading reporting as a marketing tool. Such reporting is very unlikely to attract liability under the strict liability rule so long as it occurs some months or even weeks before the proceedings in question. It is very clear from decisions over the last ten years that the time at which coverage is most at risk is getting closer and closer to the time at which the proceedings occur. Prosecutions would probably no longer be brought where a time lag of the order of ten months between publication and proceedings had occurred. By 2007 it became possible to say that imputations of guilt in the active period probably would not incur liability unless they occurred contemporaneously with the trial.

In 1987 the ruling in *Attorney General v News Group Newspapers*[82] made it clear that the proximity of the article to the trial is highly relevant to the question of risk. The Court of Appeal held that a gap of ten months between the two could not create the substantial risk in question because the jury would be likely to have forgotten the article by the time the trial came on and even if it were faintly recollected at the time of the trial, it would be likely to have little impact. Similarly, in *Attorney General v Independent TV News and Others*[83] one of the factors founding the ruling that s 2(2) was not satisfied was the lapse of time before the trial; the risk that any juror who had seen the offending item would remember it was not seen as substantial. ITV News and certain newspapers had published the fact that a defendant in a forthcoming murder trial was a convicted IRA terrorist who had escaped from jail where he was serving a life sentence for murder. However, the trial was not expected to take place for nine months, there had only been one offending news item, and there had been limited circulation of only one edition of the offending newspaper items. In contrast, in *Attorney General v Hislop and Pressdram*,[84] a gap of three months between publication of the article and the trial of the libel action was not viewed as long enough to negate the risk. A publication during the trial is clearly most likely to create a risk.

In the late 1990s judges began to show a readiness to assume that somewhat smaller time lapses in months would still diminish the risk in question to the point where it could

---

81 See further, C Walker, 'Fundamental Rights, Fair Trials and the New Audio-Visual Sector' [1996] 59 MLR 517.
82 [1987] QB 1.
83 [1995] 2 All ER 370.
84 [1991] 1 QB 514; [1991] 1 All ER 911; [1991] 2 WLR 219, CA.

be viewed as negligible or minimal. In *Attorney General v Unger*[85] the article in question, discussed further below, was published about three-and-a-half months before the trial in a tabloid with a large circulation. It was found that its impact should be looked at at the time of publication and at the time of the trial – its residual impact on jurors should be taken into account. Over that period of time its impact would have faded; taking that 'fade factor' into account, it was determined that a substantial risk of prejudice did not arise. A similar stance was taken in *Attorney General v Unger*.[86] The respondent newspapers, the *Daily Mail* and *Manchester Evening News*, published newspaper articles, relating how the defendant, who was a home help, had been caught red-handed on video stealing money from a pensioner in her care. In other words, they imputed guilt. Simon Brown LJ found that articles of this nature which plainly prejudged guilt could influence jurors. But when he considered the 'crucial' matter of the residual impact of the publication on a notional juror at the time of trial, he attached great significance to the 'fade' factor, the effect of the lapse of time between publication and trial. Here the time lapse was of the order of nine months. He considered that this would greatly affect the recollections of the article by any juror who had happened to read it. He noted that this factor had been stressed in a number of the cases.[87] He considered that publications are most dangerously prejudicial when they are published contemporaneously with the trial, because then jurors read them with 'particular interest rather than merely as part of an everyday media diet', or when they disclose prejudicial material which is itself inadmissible in evidence, most obviously an accused's previous convictions. Neither of those two factors were present. But in *Attorney General v Newsgroup Newspapers*,[88] the *Sun* published a serious allegation regarding a defendant in a murder trial at the point at which the jury had retired to consider its verdict. The murder charge was dropped, and the *Sun* was prosecuted, convicted and fined for contempt.

The existence of the internet is highly relevant to temporal proximity. Trial-related material is often placed on a newspaper's website prior to or early in the active period – at the time when the reporting occurs of a high profile investigation or of an arrest. However, that material is likely to remain on the website, whereas the newspaper itself will be discarded by its readers very rapidly, often on the day that it is obtained. Thus the material may still be on the website and accessible as the trial date approaches. Jurors might decide deliberately to search newspapers' websites with a view to discovering more about the trial and, perhaps, the background of defendants. Where publicity is potentially prejudicial, but is subject to a significant fade factor, newspapers could ensure that such material is removed from the website's archives. However, if they fail to do so they clearly place themselves at risk of a prosecution for contempt even though there has been a significant time lapse between initial publication and trial. This factor, and the accessibility of the web-based material, should be taken into account when assessing the risk created by press material that has been published some time before the trial. It may be noted that where the internet service provider maintaining a website

---

85 [1997] 1 All ER 456.
86 *Attorney General v Unger* (1998) EMLR 280 at 319.
87 *Attorney General v NGN* [1987] QB 1; *ex p Telegraph plc* [1993] 1 WLR 980; *Attorney General v Independent TV News* [1995] 1 Cr App R 204.
88 16 April 1999 (unreported).

on which trial-related material is stored is not a domestic newspaper or broadcaster, but is a body outside the jurisdiction, it would not be possible to bring a prosecution even if highly prejudicial material was uploaded to an easily accessible website and maintained on it before and during the trial. It might be argued that the chance of a juror accessing the website could be viewed as remote, but the rapidly increasing use of the internet is undermining that argument.

On the face of it, the factor of proximity in time cannot be considered in isolation from other relevant ones: the celebrity status of defendants/plaintiffs; the subject matter of the publication; the language used. These three factors may make it more likely that a publication will be remembered even over a fairly substantial period of time. However, temporal proximity, combined with the effect of neutralising directions, is by far the most important factor. We now seem to have arrived at the point when it is almost possible to say that the active period runs de facto only from the start of the trial – from the point at which the jurors are empanelled, since from that point they are likely to take especial interest in articles relating to that particular trial. From that point judges view publications or broadcasts as no longer part of an ephemeral media diet (they have not yet, it seems, taken account of the fact that the use of the internet means that it is much less ephemeral than it used to be), but as of especial significance. In other words, even where other factors founding a 'substantial risk' are quite clearly present, unless material is disclosed that would be inadmissible in evidence, prejudicial publication/broadcasts, even very close to the trial, but not during it, may not reach the s 2(2) threshold.

This reliance on proximity means that where a high profile crime, such as the Soham murders in 2002 or the attempted terrorist bombings in London in July 2005,[89] occurs, the tabloids can report on the arrestees in lurid terms, as they did in both instances, in the knowledge that although the proceedings are 'active', there is likely to be quite a significant time lapse before the trial, and that therefore the risk of prejudice will probably be viewed as diminished to the point where it cannot be regarded as 'substantial'. Therefore newspapers that are – in contrast to broadcasters – already unrestrained in such reporting by a statutory regulatory scheme enjoining accuracy and impartiality on them, are likely to be equally unrestrained by the strict liability rule. In the instance of Soham the Attorney General did issue warnings to the tabloids reminding them of the rule, but no action was taken. Clearly, if the aim of s 2(2) is to protect the fairness of particular trials, it is inevitable that the proximity in time of a publication will be taken into account. But there may be instances, such as that of Soham, or of the terrorist incidents in 2003 and 2005, where the coverage is so extreme and so unremitting at the time of an arrest, that a fair trial, even months later, is likely to be prejudiced. The more recent rulings on temporal proximity suggest that the judges would not accept that s 2(2) was satisfied in such circumstances, especially when the findings from *Attorney General v MGN* regarding totality of coverage were also taken into account, since it would be difficult to ascribe responsibility for the creation of prejudice to any one newspaper. Once a substantial period of time had elapsed, it would be likely that a potential juror would merely remember an impression, rather than the specifics of the coverage of any one

89 See p 342, fn 174.

newspaper. But that impression – that the arrestees were guilty – might be deep-rooted and insidious.[90]

The totality of the news coverage is a relevant factor in the sense that where a large amount of arguably prejudicial publicity has occurred, it is difficult to isolate the contribution that one publication has made. Obtaining a conviction under the s 2(2) test, as currently interpreted, is especially difficult or impossible where a substantial risk of serious prejudice or impediment is created by the totality of the news coverage, rather than by the coverage of a particular article or broadcast. *Attorney General v MGN*[91] concerned the coverage of a case involving the notorious boyfriend of a soap opera actress, Gillian Taylforth, by five tabloid newspapers, which mentioned his previous criminal record and presented a misleading picture of the incident in question. It was found that none of the articles, considered separately, reached the required threshold under s 2(2). The judge, Schiemann LJ, said that where, in such an instance, the totality of the coverage had prejudiced the trial, it might be proper to stay the proceedings. This decision reveals a weakness in the use of the strict liability rule, since it means that the creation of serious prejudice to a trial by a large number of newspaper articles in combination cannot be addressed by means of contempt law where individual articles just fail to satisfy the strict test of s 2(2) as interpreted in *Attorney General v Guardian Newspapers*.[92] As discussed below, that decision significantly raised the s 2(2) bar. The use of a stay means that the coverage has had the effect of impeding the course of justice in the proceedings in question, but that the detriment thereby created cannot be laid at the doors of those responsible.

It is argued that the courts need to distinguish more clearly between 'threshold', 'generic' and prejudicial publicity.[93] 'Generic' publicity can be taken to indicate coverage that is not in itself prejudicial since it does not relate specifically enough to the trial. But it may have a general and all-pervasive effect in terms of painting 'the defendant with an incriminating brush'.[94] 'Threshold' publicity is merely coverage relating to someone involved in proceedings, making his or her name memorable. The existence of threshold or generic publicity tends to mean that prejudicial publicity has more impact.[95] Therefore such publicity is more, not less, likely to satisfy the s 2(2) test. On the other hand, where a number of newspapers publish material that does relate specifically to a case and that, combined, satisfies s 2(2), it may be difficult to show that any particular publication, alone, satisfies the test.

---

90 There would be the possibility of bringing an action for common law contempt in respect of such coverage, but editors would be able to show that due to the lapse of time they did not foresee the creation of a real risk of prejudice as a virtual certainty (oblique intent). So far, apart from cases relating to material covered by an injunction against another media body, it is only in cases in which a newspaper has a personal interest that a desire to prejudice proceedings (simple intent) has been shown: see discussion below pp 343–44, 346.

91 [1997] 1 All ER 456.

92 [1999] EMLR 904. See pp 326, 335 below.

93 See e.g., Doppelt, JC, 'Generic Prejudice: How Drug War Fervor Threatens the Right to a Fair Trial' (1991) 40 *American University Law Review* 821.

94 See Chesterman, M, Chan, J and Hampton, S, *Managing Prejudicial Publicity*, 2001, Justice Research Centre, Law and Justice Foundation of New South Wales, p 9.

95 *Ibid*, pp 111, 121, 122, 235.

Some of the prosecutions discussed above, and in particular that in *Attorney General v BBC, Attorney General v Hat Trick Productions Ltd*,[96] may be contrasted with the lack of action taken in respect of the facts of *R v Taylor*.[97] A large number of tabloid newspapers published a photograph that was taken of one of the defendants in a murder trial giving the husband of the victim a polite kiss on the cheek; it was distorted in such a way as to give the impression that it was a passionate mouth-to-mouth kiss and was captioned 'Cheats Kiss'. It was found that this was part of an 'unremitting, extensive, sensational, inaccurate and misleading press coverage' and had led to a real risk of prejudice to the trial. This determination was made on appeal in overturning the convictions of the two defendants. The Attorney General refused to bring an action against the newspapers for contempt, possibly because he considered that no individual publication would attract liability, and it was found that his decision not to act was non-reviewable.[98] The failure to act did not therefore have to be justified, but the uncertain nature of the s 2(2) test as applied to individual newspapers could be viewed as providing a degree of justification for it. On the other hand, the possibility cannot entirely be ruled out, as argued above, that government reluctance to take on a large number of press proprietors played a part in the decision.

In a number of the cases discussed below judges have taken account of the potential use of neutralising measures in assessing the risk of prejudice. They have stressed the ability of jurors to disregard media comment, especially when properly directed to do so. In taking the use of such 'neutralising' directions into account, they have also stressed the need for contempt law to use the same standards as those that would determine the need for a stay or the success of an appeal. The courts have, increasingly, emphasised the unlikelihood that jurors will be unaffected by prejudicial media comment. The probability that the lesser neutralising measure of warning the jury to disregard media coverage will be employed is increasingly taken into account when a court is considering the risk of prejudice, although two schools of thought can be discerned among the judiciary on this matter – broadly speaking, those of juror susceptibility and juror invulnerability.[99]

It was pointed out in *Attorney General v Times Newspapers*[100] that jurors are able to ignore possibly prejudicial comment in newspapers. That case concerned a relatively trivial incident that happened to attract publicity because of the fame of one of the persons involved, a factor that jurors might be expected to appreciate, leading them to discount the press coverage. Recently, it has become more common for consideration to be afforded to the likelihood that the jury will be strongly directed to ignore prejudicial coverage of the trial.[101] In *Attorney General v BBC*,[102] however, Staughton LJ said that

96 [1997] EMLR 76.

97 (1993) 98 Cr App R 361, CA.

98 *R v S-G, ex p Taylor*, *The Times*, 14 August 1995. For comment on the case see Stephens, M and Hill, P, 'The Role and Impact of Journalism', in Walker, C and Starmer, K (eds), *Miscarriages of Justice: A Review of Justice in Error*, 1997, Blackstone, 263, pp 264–67. For comment and the implications of the case within the European Convention on Human Rights, see Borrie and Lowe, *The Law of Contempt* (1996), pp 481–82.

99 See the National Heritage Committee Second Report (1997) *Press Activity Affecting Court Cases*, pp 33–34.

100 *The Times*, 12 February 1983.

101 See e.g., *Attorney General v MGN* [1997] EMLR 284.

102 1 December 1995 (unreported).

he did not have the confidence expressed by certain judges in 'the ability of jurors to disregard matters which they do remember but which they are not entitled to take into account'.

In contrast, in *Attorney General v Unger*[103] Simon Brown LJ found that the 'fade factor' should be coupled with the presumption that juries would decide cases solely according to the evidence put before them and the directions they were given. He considered that in the case before him, if the accused woman had elected jury trial and had been convicted, she could not have won an appeal on the basis of the published articles. A similar stance was taken in *Attorney General v Guardian Newspapers*.[104] The case concerned the trial of one Kelly for stealing body parts, apparently for artistic purposes; during the trial the *Observer* published an article suggesting in strong terms that Kelly had had no artistic purpose in stealing the parts, but was motivated merely by a morbid fascination with dead people. The writer linked Kelly's fascination to that experienced by a number of named serial killers. Since Kelly's honesty was a key issue in the trial, the article was very damaging to his case since in the jury's eyes it could have undermined his credibility. Both Collins and Sedley LJJ concluded that the article therefore created a risk of serious prejudice.

Sedley LJ wrestled with the question whether the risk should be described as substantial:

> In the end, and not without anxiety, I have concluded that it is simply not possible to be sure that the risk created by the publication was a substantial risk that a jury, properly directed to disregard its own sentiments and any media comment, would nevertheless have its own thoughts or value judgments reinforced by the article to a point where they influenced the verdict. As a first cross-check, I doubt whether an appeal would have been allowed had the jury which convicted Mr Kelly read the article. As a second cross-check, it seems to me that the threat from this article, published when it was, to the course of justice in Mr Kelly's trial was not sufficient to make either prior restraint or subsequent punishment a proportionate response in a society which, as a democracy, values and protects the freedom of the press.

In other words, some degree of serious prejudice had been caused, but it was accepted that the degree of risk was likely to be diminished by the use of such directions. Collins LJ also took into account the effect of judicial directions on the jury in terms of neutralising any prejudice created by the publication, although he differed from Sedley LJ in finding that once it could be assumed that 'serious prejudice' had arisen it would be difficult to be sure that it had been dispelled by the use of neutralising directions. However, Collins LJ felt that the issue was so finely balanced that he would not dissent from Sedley LJ's conclusion on this point. It was therefore found that the test of 'serious prejudice', but not that of 'substantial risk', was satisfied.

Sedley LJ's approach, which appears to be the dominant one, shifts the emphasis impliedly from the protective to the neutralising stance since it makes the assumption

103   (1998) EMLR 280 at 319.
104   [1999] EMLR 904.

that directions to the jury will be effective and can therefore properly undermine the need for protective measures. That approach also, to an extent, shifts the responsibility for the effect of prejudicial material from the media to judges and jurors. Arguably, that shift of responsibility is not fully in accordance with the Art 10 notion that the 'duties and responsibilities' it mentions in para 1 are placed upon those exercising the right to freedom of expression it protects – that is, the media. As pointed out in Chapter 7, Strasbourg has interpreted para 1, in general, to enhance media freedom rather than to limit it.[105] So any reliance on it in the sense suggested here would probably therefore have to be a development in the domestic Art 10 jurisprudence.[106]

There has been uncertainty as to the relationship between s 2(2) and the tests used to make good an appeal against conviction or to found a stay. Simon Brown LJ found in *Attorney General v Birmingham Post and Mail*:[107] 's 2(2) postulates a lesser degree of prejudice than is required to make good an appeal against conviction. Similarly, it seems to me to postulate a lesser degree of prejudice than would justify an order for a stay.' He went on to conclude that where s 2(2) was satisfied, it would not follow that a conviction was imperilled or that a stay was required, but that the converse was not the case:

> I find it difficult to envisage a publication which has concerned the judge sufficiently to discharge the jury and yet is not properly to be regarded as a contempt . . .
> In short, s 2(2) is designed to avoid (and where necessary punish) publications even if they merely risk prejudicing proceedings, whereas a stay will generally only be granted where it is recognised that any subsequent conviction would otherwise be imperilled, and a conviction will only be set aside . . . if it is actually unsafe.

However, Sedley LJ and Collins LJ in *Attorney General v Guardian Newspapers*[108] considered that the tests for contempt and for the risk of actual prejudice to a trial should be harmonised. Collins LJ said:

> It seems to me that the prejudice required by s 2(2), which must be serious, is not of a lesser degree than that required to make good an appeal against conviction. To establish contempt it needs only be shown that there was a substantial risk that serious prejudice, which must in my view mean such prejudice as would justify a stay or appeal against conviction, would result from the publication. That such prejudice does not in the event result is nothing to the point. Thus uniformity of approach is achieved by requiring that the prejudice within the meaning of s 2(2) must be such as would be likely to justify at least a stay.

105 *Cf* its use in *Otto-Preminger Institute v Austria* (1995) 19 EHRR 34.
106 See p 403. A notion of protection only for responsible journalism already appears to be impliedly occurring, as discussed in Chapter 10, pp 754–55, but not at present in reliance on the wording of Art 10(1).
107 [1999] 1 WLR 361, at 369H; [1998] 4 All ER 49, at 57, 59. See further *McLeod, The Times*, 20 December 2000.
108 [1999] EMLR 904.

These words were echoed by in *Attorney General v Unger*[109] by Simon Brown LJ in something of a departure from his previous stance:

> It seems to me important in these cases that the Courts do not speak with two voices, one used to dismiss criminal appeals with the Court roundly rejecting any suggestion that prejudice resulted from media publications, the other holding comparable publications to be in contempt, the Courts on these occasions expressing grave doubts as to the jury's ability to forget or put aside what they have heard or read . . . generally speaking it seems to me that unless a publication materially affects the course of trial in that kind of way, or requires directions from the court well beyond those ordinarily required and routinely given to juries to focus their attention on evidence called before them rather than whatever they may have heard or read outside court, or creates at the very least a seriously arguable ground for an appeal on the basis of prejudice, it is unlikely to be vulnerable to contempt proceedings under the strict liability rule.

Thus a growing perception among the judiciary can be discerned of a need to bring contempt law into line with criminal appeals, so that in Simon Brown LJ's words, the courts do not 'speak with two voices'. This stance, it is argued, encourages newspapers to publish prejudicial material in the hope that the risk it poses to proceedings is not substantial enough. The problem with this approach is that it detracts from the role of contempt law in protecting particular proceedings. It seems to assume that unless the resulting effect might approach one that had to be dealt with by a stay or an appeal, s 2(2) would not be satisfied. This stance undermines the role s 2(2) seemed to be intended to have – that of setting the threshold before that stage would be likely to be reached, thus protecting the criminal justice system. The fact that the judges are taking this stance is not surprising, given that the division of responsibility between contempt law and trial judge has always been problematic. But arguably it poses an unacceptable level of risk to the system.

Having established a substantial risk that jurors and others will be influenced by the article, it is then necessary to ask if the influence can be characterised as of a prejudicial nature or would be likely to impede the proceedings in question. A publication that was in some way relevant to a trial might be likely to create a substantial risk that it would influence persons involved in the trial, bearing the factors identified in mind, but without leading to prejudice to it. An article published in every national newspaper in the land on the day of the trial and discussing certain issues relevant to it in a striking and interesting, but fair and impartial, manner would have an influence, but not a prejudicial one. In considering whether it would be prejudicial, the two limbs of the test must be considered together: it must be shown that the language used, the facts disclosed or sentiments expressed would lead an objective observer to conclude that a substantial risk had been established that persons involved in the proceedings would be prejudiced, before going on to consider whether that effect could properly be described as serious.

Prejudice and its seriousness can be established in a number of ways: the article (or other publication) might be likely to have the effect of influencing relevant persons against or in favour of the defendant; it might be likely to affect either the outcome of the proceedings in question or their very existence – as where pressure is placed on one party to drop[110] proceedings. In *Re Lonhro plc*,[111] Lord Bridge said:

> [Pre-trial] it is easy to see how critical public discussion of the issues and criticism of the conduct of the parties, particularly if a party is held up to public obloquy, may impede or prejudice the course of the proceedings by influencing the conduct of witnesses or parties in relation to the proceedings. If [a jury is involved] the possibility of prejudice by advance publicity directed at an issue which the jury will have to decide is obvious.

It is assumed that laypersons are more likely to be affected by media coverage than professionals; as indicated above, it would be readily assumed that a judge would be unaffected.[112] Therefore, civil proceedings are less at risk of being prejudiced than criminal ones, except in those instances in which a jury is used.[113] But, as indicated, civil actions can be affected in other ways. Also, witnesses, especially lay witnesses, in both civil and criminal actions might be affected by media coverage. They might be deterred from coming forward[114] or they might be intimidated or influenced[115] by it.

As noted above, the proximity in time between the article and the proceedings can affect this limb of s 2(2), as can the extent to which it may be said that the trial concerns a person in the public eye. If the article is published some time before the trial, as in *Attorney General v News Group Newspapers*, its probable effect on the minds of jurors will be lessened because it may only exist there as a faint memory: any effect it has is unlikely to be of a seriously prejudicial nature. This might be the case even though the article would have been likely to have such an effect had it been fresh in their minds. In the *Hislop* case, however, the vitriolic nature of the article did suggest that it would be likely to have a seriously prejudicial effect. The serious allegations in question were held to blacken the plaintiff's character and might well have influenced the jurors against her. The fact that Peter Sutcliffe was well known also made it more likely that the article would have an impact. However, courts will not be quick to assume that jurors are incapable of ignoring prejudicial publications. In *Attorney General v Guardian Newspapers*[116] the publication of the fact that one unidentified defendant out of six in a Manchester trial was also awaiting trial elsewhere was not found to satisfy s 2(2), since it was thought that it would not cause a juror of ordinary good sense to be biased against the defendant.

---

110 See *Hislop and Pressdram* [1991] 1 QB 514; [1991] 1 All ER 911; [1991] 2 WLR 219, CA: this aspect of the case is discussed in relation to common law contempt, below, p 346.

111 [1990] AC 154, p 209B.

112 This is the general view expressed in the relevant jurisprudence in Britain and in other common law jurisdictions. e.g., Lord Salmon said in *Attorney General v BBC* [1981] AC 303, p 342: 'I am and always would be satisfied that no judge would be influenced by what may be said by the media.' Of course, it should be borne in mind that this stance is taken by the judges themselves.

113 In respect of defamation and in certain actions against the police.

114 See *Vine Products Ltd v Green* [1966] Ch 484, p 495.

115 See *Re Doncaster and Retford Co-operative Societies Agreement* [1960] LR 2 PC; *Hutchinson v Amalgamated Engineering Union, Re Daily Worker* (1932) *The Times*, 25 August.

116 [1992] 3 All ER 38, CA.

The test of 'impeding' proceedings is treated in a more specific fashion. It may be satisfied where the publication can be said to have led to the delay of the proceedings owing to the risk of prejudice.[117]

Use of s 2(2) in the post-HRA era

The post-HRA prosecutions have tended to occur in the more clear-cut cases. In two of them liability was not contested. In *Attorney General v BBC*[118] the BBC mistakenly released details about a complainant witness during a trial relating to charges of sexual abuse in an approved school, breaching his anonymity. The police had undertaken not to allow such details to be released and his anonymity was protected by s 1(1) of the Sexual Offences (Amendment) Act 1992. The witness was very distressed since his family had not known that he had – as he alleged – suffered sexual abuse. The BBC accepted that the publication of the details had satisfied the tests under s 2(2) and there-fore the only question was as to the penalty to be imposed. It was accepted that the publication of the details had resulted from negligence and that the journalist responsi-ble had had an exemplary record in relation to such matters. The penalty – a fine – was not excessive; it was imposed both on the BBC and on the journalist involved. The HRA was not mentioned during the case, although Art 10 would have been relevant to the heaviness of the fine[119] and to the decision to impose a separate penalty on the journalist.

Attorney General v MGN[120] concerned a somewhat similar instance in that liability was not disputed and the articles in question were apparently published in error. The articles, in the *Sunday Mirror*, concerned the trial of certain Premiership footballers for affray and causing grievous bodily harm with intent. The article revived allegations that the attack was racially motivated. The article was published at the time when the jury were considering their verdicts and, as the publishers recognised, its thrust was at vari-ance with the evidence as presented in the criminal trial. The publishers recognised that the judge had given a clear direction that there was no evidence of a racial motive. The second article concerned a co-accused, Duberry. He had been acquitted, but his credibil-ity and his evidence were still relevant in relation to the guilt or innocence of the four remaining defendants, in respect of whom verdicts had not been returned. Liability was not disputed but the court gave some consideration to the s 2(2) tests, finding that they were satisfied due to the timing of the article and the probability that the jurors might have been influenced for or against the four defendants. The trial had been abandoned as a result of the article and a retrial ordered. It was found that: ' "substantial" in that context connotes a risk which is more than remote and not merely minimal . . . and it has to be accepted that within the range of strict liability contempts, this case is towards the top end'. This indicates that a test akin to that of Lord Diplock in *Attorney General v English* is still influencing judges, particularly at first instance. Again the HRA was not mentioned and the fine imposed was high but not excessive.

---

117 See *Attorney General v BBC* (1992); *The Independent*, 3 January 1992.
118 [2001] EWHC Admin 1202.
119 See *Tolstoy Miloslavsky v UK* (1995) 20 EHRR 442.
120 [2002] EWHC 907.

A somewhat similar instance arose in *Attorney General v Express*.[121] The *Daily Star* published an article relating to the alleged gang rape of a 17-year-old girl at a London hotel by up to eight footballers on 27 September 2003. Between 30 September 2003 and 22 October 2003 the Attorney General and the Metropolitan Police had repeatedly issued advice and guidelines stating that identification was in issue and that suspects should not be identified by name or photograph or other likeness. There was a great deal of media interest, but the article in the *Daily Star* was unique in that it identified two potential defendants. The Attorney General contended that it was sufficient to establish a substantial risk that the course of justice would be prejudiced to show that there was a risk that the complainant did not know the identity of the footballers revealed in the *Daily Star*. It was found that at the point when the *Daily Star* published the article the complainant had not identified to the police either of the two footballers by name or by effective description. The Court found that the inference could be drawn therefore that the complainant did not know the identities of the accused at the time of the publication. Accordingly, the publication to millions in the *Daily Star* of items identifying the two individuals created a substantial risk that the course of justice would be seriously impeded or prejudiced. The HRA played no part in the judgment.

As noted above, the courts were required to consider the nature of the s 2(2) tests in *Attorney General v Random House* and *Attorney General v MGN Ltd*. In *AG v MGN Ltd*, though, the HRA dimension was less significant in determining the claim. The Art 10 claims would have been particularly weak in any event given that the claims about Jefferies were defamatory. In *Random House*, however, Tugendhat J was required to carefully balance the issues, having accepted that the publication raised matters of public interest about the conduct of the police. He concluded, however, that an injunction restraining publication was a proportionate response. The public interest in publication was outweighed by the serious impediment to justice that could be caused: 'if any of the accused is innocent, and is nevertheless convicted, the scale of the injustice involved would be difficult to exaggerate'.[122] Moreover, he also noted the extreme cost of retrial to the public purse. Although the Art 10 claims here were ultimately unsuccessful, the positive effect of the HRA is readily apparent: the judgment clearly shows the free speech arguments being taken seriously by the court.

Finally, it is worth considering the case of *Attorney General v Associated Newspapers Ltd*.[123] This decision shows the application of the strict liability rule to two online articles and highlights the significance of the judge's directions to jurors about use of the internet during the trial. By mistake, both publications contained images of the defendant holding a gun with the caption 'Drink-fuelled attack: Ryan Ward was seen boasting about the incident on CCTV'. The image was available for a matter of hours and published on the day that the trial began. The judge had issued the following warning to the jury about press coverage:

> I would imagine by the nature of this case, and you'll see there's obviously press interest in it there will be some reporting of this case. Again that's a matter the press

121   [2005] EMLR13.
122   *Random House, op cit*, [107].
123   [2011] EWHC 418 (Admin).

are free to report upon but you go on only the evidence you hear in this room, not the view other people may or may not have about it. . . . Please don't try and get information from outside this room about this case. Don't, for example, consult the Internet, if there is anything out there on it. I'm not saying for one moment there is but don't go there, don't try and get it from anywhere else. Again the reason for that is the evidence in this case is evidence that the defence know about and the prosecution know about. It's evidence that will evolve in this case in this room where all of us know what you're basing your decisions upon. If one person decides to go off and consult the Internet or something else about it, then we don't have any control over that and you may be taking into consideration matters which have no relevance whatsoever to the case.[124]

The newspapers claimed that the jury could only have viewed the images of Ward by disregarding the explicit instructions of the judge. The court, however, rejected this submission on the basis that the instruction could not be construed as a prohibition of reading newspapers. It concluded that there was a substantial risk that a juror could have encountered the picture ('jurors in the habit of reading a daily newspaper were likely to read about the case they were trying')[125] and that the impact of the photograph could result in serious prejudice ('the image of the accused brandishing the pistol and apparently doing so in a brazen manner could not have failed to create an adverse impression of a young man who enjoying demonstrating a propensity for violence').[126] Moreover, the court could not accept that a further direction from the judge to disregard anything they had seen could ameliorate matters: 'no juror, who saw it, could reasonably have been expected to put it out of his or her mind, however stringent the injunction to do so'.[127]

The threshold created by the s 2(2) test

The decisions on s 2(2) have not fully clarified its meaning, but it may be concluded quite firmly that the threshold to be reached under the test can now be viewed, more than 30 years after the inception of the 1981 Act, as quite a high one *in practice*. Therefore newspapers may risk publishing material concerning high-profile trials that they would not have published 35 years ago when the 1981 Act was introduced. A steady, if unacknowledged, raising of the bar denoted by the term 'substantial risk' can be discerned from the case law, which can largely be attributed to the influence of Art 10 of the European Convention, even before the HRA had come into force. It will be questioned below whether this raising of the bar is really in accord with Art 10 values, as some of the judges appear to assume.

Two years after the 1981 Act was introduced the bar was placed at a low level. In *Attorney General v English*[128] Lord Diplock interpreted 'substantial risk' as excluding a

---

124 *Ibid*, [4]–[5].
125 *Ibid*, [36].
126 *Ibid*, [41].
127 *Ibid*, [50].
128 [1983] 1 AC 116; [1982] 2 All ER 903.

'risk which is only remote',[129] a finding that still strongly influences the *formal* approach to s 2(2).[130] The finding that only remote risks would be excluded allowed the House of Lords to find that the reference in the article to the mercy-killing of handicapped babies might prejudice the jury in the trial of a consultant charged with the murder of a Down's syndrome baby. The article, published in the *Daily Mail* after the trial had begun, made no direct reference to him, but was written in support of a pro-life candidate, Mrs Carr, who was standing in a by-election. Mrs Carr had no arms; the article referred to this fact and continued: 'today the chances of such a baby surviving are very small – someone would surely recommend letting her die of starvation. Are babies who are not up to scratch to be destroyed before or after birth?' The Lords considered that jurors would be likely to take the comments to refer to the trial; therefore, the assertion that babies were often allowed to die if handicapped might influence them against the consultant. The timing of the article predisposed the court to find that s 2(2) was satisfied. Nevertheless, on any view the risk was quite low but could be viewed as more than remote. (Incidentally, the consultant was acquitted; therefore, the article presumably did not in fact influence the jurors against him.) The finding that only remote risks are excluded appears to lessen the impact of the term 'substantial', and it is hard to see that there is a difference between this test and the old common law 'real risk' one.

In *MGN Pension Trustees Ltd*[131] it was found that the term meant 'not insubstantial' or 'not minimal' rather than weighty. In *Attorney General v Independent TV News and Others*,[132] the same view was taken – the risk of prejudice was found to be too small to be termed substantial, although arguably it could have been viewed as more than minimal. The term 'substantial' has been afforded de facto greater weight in the instances discussed below,[133] effectively excluding fairly low but non-remote risks. *Attorney General v Guardian Newspapers*,[134] *Attorney General v Unger*[135] and *Attorney General v MGN*[136] marked the turning point in the approach. These cases were all decided around the time of the inception of the HRA but before it had come into force. The imminent reception of Art 10 into domestic law affected the judicial approach.

In *Attorney General v MGN*[137] an article creating the inference that a defendant in forthcoming proceedings was guilty was not found in itself to create a sufficiently

129 *Attorney General v English* [1983] 1 AC 116; [1982] 2 All ER 903; for comment, see Zellick G, 'Fair trial and free press' [1982] PL 343 (especially on the question of the degree of risk); Ward, A, 'A Substantial Change in the Law of Contempt?' (1983) 46 MLR 85; Redmond M, 'Of Black Sheep and too much Wool' [1983] 42 CLJ 9. It may be noted that aspects of *Attorney General v English* were the subject of an unsuccessful application to Strasbourg: *Times Newspapers Ltd and others v UK* (1983) 8 EHRR 45, p 54. Bearing in mind the comments in Chapter 2, p 33 as to the effect of the Commission on the Convention jurisprudence, especially in its older decisions, it is suggested that this finding of inadmissibility would be unlikely to be repeated today and that the decision is somewhat out of line with the generality of the jurisprudence relating to pre-trial publicity and the reporting of issues relating to litigation.

130 See Zellick G, *ibid*, on this point, p 344.

131 [1995] EMLR 99.

132 [1995] 2 All ER 370.

133 See in particular Lord Lane's comments in *Attorney General v Times Newspapers Ltd*, *The Times*, 12 February 1983.

134 [1999] EMLR 904.

135 *Attorney General v Unger* (1998) EMLR 280 at 319. The decision is discussed above at pp 342–43.

136 [1997] 1 All ER 456. The decision is discussed above at pp 344–45.

137 [1997] 1 All ER 456.

substantial risk of serious prejudice, despite the fact that that article in combination with others had led the trial judge to stay the proceedings. A straightforward imputation of guilt was made in *Attorney General v Unger*, but the time lapse led to the conclusion that the risk was not substantial enough. In *Attorney General v Guardian Newspapers* Sedley LJ in the Court of Appeal considered that he was placing a strong reliance on the Art 10(2) tests as interpreted in *Worm v Austria*[138] in finding that although a risk of serious prejudice arose, it was not certain that it could be viewed as a substantial one.

The previous rulings clearly do not give as much weight to the term 'substantial' as Sedley LJ did. The facts of *Guardian Newspapers*, discussed above, were in some respects far more compelling than those of *English* as far as s 2(2) was concerned. The *Observer* article at issue in *Guardian Newspapers* was centrally about the trial, whereas the comments in the *Daily Mail* article in *English* were only obliquely or inferentially linked to it; they were ambiguous and did not necessarily impute guilt. Both the articles at issue were published contemporaneously with the trial. Yet s 2(2) was found to be satisfied in *English*, whereas in *Guardian Newspapers* the opposing result was reached, indicating the incremental, stealthy raising of the bar that has occurred. The imminent inception of the Human Rights Act, encouraging the judiciary to afford a strong weight to the relevant Art 10 jurisprudence, appears to explain the difference. In *Worm*, which was relied on in *Guardian Newspapers*, the test used was that of 'likelihood' of risk; as discussed below, this appears to mean that the risk is more likely than not to materialise. This test denotes a higher threshold than does Lord Diplock's test in *English* of excluding only remote risks.

The only case to succeed under the strict liability rule in the late 1990s was *Attorney General v BBC and Hat Trick Productions Ltd*[139] where the words in question were spoken by celebrities during a popular television programme. Auld LJ said of them:

> The offending words are strikingly prejudicial and go to the heart of the case which the jury are to try, and . . . the offending publicity is great both because of its medium and repetition, and because both the speakers and the victims are already much in the public eye.

Taking account of the case law as a whole, it seems fair to conclude that although the courts continue in most instances to pay lip-service to Lord Diplock's *dictum* in *Attorney General v English*, they are not prepared to find that s 2(2) is satisfied on the basis of risks just above the 'minimal' threshold. And, clearly, a strict approach to s 2(2) seemed to be likely to prevail after the Human Rights Act came into force, on the basis that the judiciary in general were likely to accept that the *Guardian Newspapers* approach to the Strasbourg jurisprudence, and especially to *Worm v Austria*, was the correct one.

Following Simon Brown LJ's approach in *Unger* and Sedley LJ's in *Guardian Newspapers*, it seems to be clear that the s 2(2) bar is being raised. Clearly, this is a media-friendly approach. Whether it is protective of free speech values is more open to doubt. Collins LJ said, 'in applying s 2(2) due weight must be given to the protection of freedom of speech'. This assumes a complete convergence between the claims of the media

---

138 (1998) 25 EHRR 454.
139 [1997] EMLR 76; *The Times*, 26 July 1996.

and those of free speech, although it is questionable whether speech that undermines the presumption of innocence has a strong claim to protection, bearing in mind underlying free speech rationales.[140] This approach may also be under-protective of trials since it confuses the role of protective measures with that of neutralising ones. If the administration of justice is not protected from prejudicial comment on the ground that the courts should not 'speak with two voices' then the criminal justice system is potentially placed under strain. It may be exposed to prejudicial comment and have to take measures, such as stays, which may themselves cause impairment to trials,[141] in order to protect itself. If the less responsible sections of the media[142] perceive that they can cause prejudice just short of that sufficient to create a demand for a stay, then they will do so, and in pushing at that boundary they may overstep it. In particular they may do so where, amidst a mass of sensationalist, partial reporting, it is very difficult to ascribe responsibility to individual newspapers.

Reform of s 2(2) under the HRA in reliance on *Worm v Austria*?

The s 2(2) test appears at first glance to be in harmony with the Convention standards as indicated in *Worm v Austria*,[143] *News Verlags*[144] and *BBC Scotland v UK*.[145] But in requiring a substantial risk of serious prejudice, it could be said to set too high a threshold: publications merely creating a risk of serious prejudice will not be covered, although it is arguable that Art 6 demands that they should be. The discussion has sought to demonstrate that the strict liability rule, based on the protective approach, sets a high threshold, is unworkably imprecise and therefore ineffective in operation. As a result, in relation to high profile cases, it allows too much strain to be placed on the criminal justice system (and on individual defendants, witnesses and victims), which has to seek to combat the effects of prejudicial publicity by taking neutralising measures. It has been suggested that the adoption of such measures can create, in itself, unfairness in the system.[146] But at the same time, since the s 1 rule is capable of going beyond what is necessary to protect fair trials, freedom of expression can be unnecessarily curtailed. (And the very uncertainty of the rule can of course have a chilling effect.) This is especially apparent in relation to those decisions on proceedings, including civil actions, which are heard by a judge or judges, not by a jury or other layperson.

The inefficacy of s 2(2) considered here – in terms of protecting fair trials – could be addressed to an extent by adopting a change of interpretation under s 3(1) HRA. The s 2(2) test, on its face, differs from that accepted at Strasbourg as in harmony with the Convention standards indicated in *Worm v Austria*,[147] *News Verlags*[148] and *BBC Scotland*

---

140 See Part II, pp 278–84.
141 See Chapter 2, pp 57–64.
142 Generally, the tabloids in the lower and middle sectors of the market.
143 (1998) 25 EHRR 454.
144 (2001) 31 EHRR 8.
145 (1997) 25 EHRR CD 179.
146 See Corker, D and Levi, M, 'Pre-trial publicity and its Treatment in the English Courts' [1996] Crim LR 622. See also pp 328–29, above.
147 (1998) 25 EHRR 454.
148 (2001) 31 EHRR 8.

v UK.[149] In *Worm* Strasbourg set the limits of permissible comment at the point at which the material creates a likelihood of prejudice to the chances of a person receiving a fair trial.[150] This is, on its face, a test that is in one respect close to the old common law one in that it requires only that prejudice, as opposed to serious prejudice, should be caused. In this respect it is less strict than the terms used in s 2(2). However, the requirement of 'likelihood' appears to denote a stricter requirement in terms of risk than the term 'sub-stantial' in s 2(2). 'Likely' appears to mean 'more likely than not',[151] whereas substantial may be taken to mean 'not insubstantial' or not negligible. According to Lord Diplock, the term is cognate to the terms 'more than minimal' or not remote. The domestic courts, following the interpretation adopted by Lord Diplock in *Attorney General v English*, have, as discussed above, paid lip-service to this interpretation of the term 'substantial'.

Post-HRA, the test for the degree of risk could have relied on the test of likelihood from *Worm* under s 2 HRA. That test would have sounded the death knell for Lord Diplock's interpretation. An (unacknowledged) departure from Lord Diplock's inter-pretation has indeed occurred, but the interpretation of s 2(2) adopted in *Attorney General v Guardian*,[152] although influenced by *Worm*, created a higher threshold for the test than is denoted by the likelihood test. It appears then that the minimising interpretation adopted in *Attorney General v English* does not represent the current test, although the courts have not acknowledged that this is the case. The term 'serious prejudice' has not been afforded a minimising interpretation. Thus it is clear that there is a difference of emphasis between the domestic and the Strasbourg tests – at least in relation to the need for serious prejudice, and probably in relation to the need for a substantial risk, on the basis that that term as currently interpreted domestically still denotes, on the face of it, a lower risk than the term 'likelihood' does. Confusion is created since the courts, as discussed, are not relying in practice on establishing only a low level of risk.

This problem could be addressed if the domestic courts decided to rely on the *Worm* test to minimise the term 'serious' and to clarify the meaning of the term 'substantial' with a view to creating greater certainty as to the threshold to be reached under s 2(2). The need to show serious prejudice may go too far in protecting speech at the expense of fair trials under Art 6, even taking account of the use of neutralising measures. At the same time the high threshold that apparently needs to be reached under the term 'sub-stantial' following *Attorney General v Guardian* and *Attorney General v MGN* may also be overprotective of speech, although Lord Diplock's non-remote risks test was under-protective. It is suggested that the test of 'likelihood' from *Worm* should be used under ss 2 and 3 HRA and should be used to re-interpret the term 'substantial' in s 2(2) of the Act. So doing would only involve a minimal departure from Lord Diplock's test, since remote risks would still be excluded; it would merely mean that some non-remote risks were also excluded – which has been occurring in practice in any event since the late 1990s.

The result of this change would ultimately be that the strict liability rule could have more impact in curbing prejudicial comment and therefore on the fairness of trials since

---

149 (1998) 25 EHRR CD 179.
150 *Worm v Austria* (1998) 25 EHRR 454, at para 5.
151 See *Cream Holdings v Bannerjee* [2005] 1 AC 253; [2004] 3 WLR 918 which in a different context found that the term 'likely to succeed' meant 'more likely than not'. See Chapter 10, pp 784–85.
152 [1999] EMLR 904.

a greater deterrent effect could be created. It must be acknowledged that it could exacerbate the likelihood of interfering with freedom of expression unnecessarily since this is inevitable under the protective approach based on a test with a fairly low threshold. If the threshold was clarified in this way by interpretation under s 3 HRA, relying on s 2, the courts and Attorney General would then have leeway within the broader test to target only those publications which are genuinely likely to cause prejudice. For example, it would be possible and easier to target individual newspapers even where a number of papers had engaged in prejudicial reporting. Where, amid such reporting, one newspaper had given prominence to a single, highly telling, item of prejudicial information, it would clearly fall within s 2(2), even if it could be assumed that jurors would be told to disregard it. Instead of trying to disentangle the responsibility of individual newspapers from the collective impact of the reporting, the test should be: if one article by itself would have satisfied s 2(2), had there been no other prejudicial publications, liability should be established, taking all the circumstances into account, including the effect of generic and threshold reporting in raising the profile of the defendant and in focusing the public mind on the trial. It would be as legitimate to take account of the reporting as a whole in the manner suggested – considering generic reporting but not the cumulative effect of reporting – as it is to take account of the probability that neutralising measures, such as directions from the judges, would minimise the impact of the reporting. All such factors are part of the context within which the potentially prejudicial reporting should be judged.

The article amounts to 'a discussion in good faith of public affairs or other matters of general public interest' and 'the risk of impediment or prejudice to particular legal proceedings is merely incidental to the discussion' (s 5)

Introduction

Section 5 reflects the guarantee under Art 10. It affords a high value to political speech, broadly defined, and therefore reflects the value placed upon such speech at Strasbourg. If it appears that s 2(2) is fulfilled, it must next be established that s 5 does not apply. Section 5 does not, therefore, operate as a defence. If it did, it would not follow the contours of the inquiry to be conducted under Art 10. Section 5 conveys the message to the media that they can create a substantial risk of serious prejudice to a trial without incurring liability so long as they can also satisfy s 5, and they do not have the burden of proof in so doing. The existence of s 5 therefore offers further confirmation that the 1981 Act is partly based on the protective model since it accepts that a substantial risk of serious prejudice to a trial can be created but that no liability may arise. Section 5 is founded on the assumption that the prejudice would have to be dealt with by the adoption of neutralising measures in relation to trials, and it is only by taking that possibility into account that s 5 can be viewed as compatible with Art 6, as *Ribemont* and *Worm* make clear.

Interpretation of s 5

Attorney General v English[153] is the leading case on s 5 and is generally considered to provide a good example of the kind of case for which s 5 was framed. After the trial had

---

153　[1983] 1 AC 116; [1982] 2 All ER 903.

begun of a consultant who was charged with the murder of a Down's syndrome baby, an article was published in the *Daily Mail* which made no direct reference to him, but was written in support of a pro-life candidate, Mrs Carr, who was standing in a by-election. Mrs Carr had no arms; the article referred to this fact and continued: 'today the chances of such a baby surviving are very small – someone would surely recommend letting her die of starvation. Are babies who are not up to scratch to be destroyed before or after birth?' The trial judge referred the article to the Attorney General, who brought contempt proceedings against the *Daily Mail*. First, it was determined that the article did fulfil the test under s 2(2) on the basis that jurors would be likely to take the comments to refer to the trial; therefore, the assertion that babies were often allowed to die if handicapped might influence them against the consultant, Dr Arthur.

The burden then fell on the prosecution to show that s 5 did not apply. Lord Diplock adopted a two-stage approach in determining this issue. First, could the article be called a 'discussion'? The Divisional Court had held that a discussion must mean the general airing of views and debating of principles. However, Lord Diplock considered that the term 'discussion' could not be confined merely to abstract debate, but could include consideration of examples drawn from real life. Applying this test, he found that a discussion could include accusations without which the article would have been emasculated and would have lost its main point. Without the implied accusations, it would have become a contribution to a purely hypothetical issue. It was about Mrs Carr's election and also the general topic of mercy killing. The main point of her candidature was that killing of 'sub-standard' babies did happen and should be stopped; if it had not asserted that babies were allowed to die, she would have been depicted as tilting at imaginary windmills. Thus, the term 'discussion' could include implied accusations.

Second, was the risk of prejudice to Dr Arthur's trial merely an incidental consequence of expounding the main theme of the article? Lord Diplock held that in answering this, the Divisional Court had applied the wrong test in considering whether the article could have been written without including the offending words. Instead, the Court should have looked at the actual words written. The main theme of the article was Mrs Carr's election policy; Dr Arthur was not mentioned. Therefore, this article was the antithesis of the one considered in *Attorney General v Times Newspapers*,[154] which was concerned entirely with the actions of Distillers. Clearly, Dr Arthur's trial could be prejudiced by the article, but that prejudice could properly be described as incidental to its main theme.

Thus, s 5 applied; the article did not, therefore, fall within the strict liability rule. This ruling was generally seen as giving a liberal interpretation to s 5.[155] Had the narrow interpretation of the Divisional Court prevailed, it would have meant that all debate in the media on the topic of mercy killing would have been prevented for almost a year – the time during which the proceedings in *Arthur's* case were active from charge to acquittal. (It may be noted that Dr Arthur was acquitted; therefore, the article presumably did not influence the jurors against him. That fact, however, as pointed out above, would not have precluded a finding that there was a substantial risk of serious prejudice to his trial.) Lord Diplock's test under s 5 may be summed up as follows: looking at the

---

154 [1974] AC 273; [1973] 3 All ER 54; [1973] 3 WLR 298, HL.
155 See, e.g., Robertson, G, *Media Law*, 1999, Chapter 6, p 216.

actual words written (as opposed to considering what could have been omitted); was the article written in good faith and concerned with a question of general legitimate public interest that created an incidental risk of prejudice to a particular case? It seems that the discussion can be triggered off by the case itself; it need not have arisen prior to it.

This ruling gave an emphasis to freedom of speech that tended to bring the strict liability rule into harmony with Art 10 as interpreted by the European Court of Human Rights' ruling in the *Sunday Times* case. However, despite this broad interpretation of s 5, the media obviously does not have *carte blanche* to discuss issues arising from or relating to any particular case during the 'active' period.

The *Attorney General v English* ruling did not concern a direct reference to a particular case and therefore it was uncertain until the ruling in *Attorney General v Times Newspapers*[156] whether s 5 would cover such references. The *Sunday Times* and four other newspapers commented on the background of Michael Fagin, an intruder into the Queen's bedroom, at a time when he was about to stand trial. The comments of *The Mail on Sunday* about Fagin, which included the allegation that he had had a homosexual liaison with the royal bodyguard and that he was a 'rootless penniless neurotic', satisfied the s 2(2) test as it was thought that they would affect the jury's assessment of his honesty. However, they fell within s 5 as they were part of a discussion of the Queen's safety, which was a matter of general public concern. In contrast, the *Sunday Times'* allegation that Fagin had stabbed his stepson could not fall within s 5, as it was irrelevant to the question of the Queen's safety, but had nevertheless been considered in detail.

Attorney General v Random House further illustrates the limitations of the s 5 defence. It does not protect public interest expression *per se*, only that which is incidental to a prejudicial trial. In *Random House*, the Attorney General sought an injunction to prevent further sales of a book detailing a police operation into terrorism, known as Operation Overt. The book had sold in only small numbers at the time of the application. The Attorney General feared it would compromise the fairness of a trial involving three terror suspects who were arrested as part of Operation Overt. Although Tugendhat J accepted that the publication was of 'the greatest public interest',[157] it could not be said the publication was 'incidental': 'the impediment in the present case arises from the fact that the passages complained of discuss the very acts which led to the Trial'.[158] As noted above, the court conducted a very careful review, in which Art 10 and Art 6 rights were carefully balanced, but s 5 was of no assistance to this process. Instead, it was s 2(2) that was read in a manner compatible with the strong right to freedom of political expression under Art 10. Ultimately, this did not protect the publication because the restriction on sales for a short period (no more than eight weeks) did not outweigh the dire consequences that would befall the accused if the administration of justice was undermined and an innocent man was convicted (or public money wasted on a further retrial).

It must also be shown that the article was written in good faith. In *Attorney General v Hislop* the articles in question did not fall within s 5 because it could not be said that they were published in good faith: the finding – relevant to the question of contempt at

---

156 (1983) *The Times*, 12 February.
157 *Random House*, op cit, [89].
158 *Ibid*, [95].

common law – that the editor had intended to prejudice the relevant proceedings – was held to be incompatible with a finding of good faith under s 5.

It can be concluded that the term 'a discussion in good faith of public affairs or other matters of general public interest' has received quite a broad interpretation in the courts. However, this is less clearly the case in relation to the question whether the risk is 'merely incidental' to the discussion. In this respect s 5 clearly requires some fine lines to be drawn. Where a piece merely discusses a particular case and makes no attempt to address wider issues, s 5 will not apply (*Daily Express* case).[159] *Attorney General v TVS Television, Attorney General v HW Southey and Sons*[160] concerned a TVS programme entitled 'The New Rachman' which made allegations about certain landlords in the south of England, alleging that they were obtaining money by deceiving the DHSS. The programme focused on landlords in Reading and coincided with the charging of a Reading landlord with conspiring to defraud the DHSS. It was found that the focus on Reading landlords meant that the article could not be viewed as creating a merely incidental risk of prejudice. In *Attorney General v Guardian Newspapers*[161] the article in question dealt with the tendency of judges in fraud trials to impose reporting restrictions, and stated that the judge in a criminal trial in Manchester had banned all reporting of the trial under s 4(2) of the 1981 Act on the ground that it could influence a separate trial involving one of the defendants. When the judge's attention was drawn to the article, he discharged the jury. It was readily found that the effect on the trial, if any, should be viewed as 'merely incidental' to the wider discussion[162] since the inclusion of examples was no more than 'an incidental consequence of expounding the main theme of the article.'[163]

Reform of s 5?

These findings indicate that there can be a difficulty in more borderline cases in drawing lines between the creation of risks in an incidental and a non-incidental fashion. Since s 5 was adopted as a response to *The Sunday Times* case, as a measure intended to protect media freedom, it might be expected to be capable of creating a clear demarcation between two types of prejudicial publications – those consisting of inaccurate, misleading coverage of forthcoming proceedings and those that concern a general issue of public interest where the proceedings are used as an example – in a way that satisfies s 2(2). Section 5 does not fully succeed in creating such differentiation since, although reporting in the latter category would fall within s 5 as 'a discussion of public affairs', following the ruling in *English*, it might fail the 'incidental' test, as occurred in *Attorney General v TVS Television, Attorney General v HW Southey and Sons*. A clearer test is needed.

One possibility would be to re-interpret s 5 in reliance on ss 3 and 2 HRA and Art 10. Section 5 was intended to afford scope to the speech/harm balancing proportionality test under Art 10(2), as a response to *Sunday Times v UK*. But it fails to do so, since

159 (1981) *The Times*, 19 December.
160 *The Times*, 7 July 1989.
161 [1992] 3 All ER 38, CA.
162 It had already been found that s 2(2) was not satisfied.
163 [1992] 3 All ER 38, p 49.

it does not provide an effective means of weighing up the seriousness of the prejudice against the significance of the speech in question. In contrast to the previous common law position, it clearly does provide a means of affording value to political speech, broadly defined, and to that extent it reflects the value placed upon such speech at Strasbourg. However, it is not the equivalent of a proportionality test since it depends on problematic determinations as to the central focus of a publication, as opposed to its peripheral aspects. The courts are being asked to engage in literary as opposed to legal analysis. The 'incidental' test is not apt to encapsulate the notion of proportionality and it is hard to import that notion through interpretation of the term. It would, however, be possible to go some way in doing so, which could mean stretching the notion of 'incidental' under s 3(1) HRA where a publication would be viewed as of especial value at Strasbourg in terms of the justifications for free expression.[164] If, as discussed above, the threshold under s 2(2) was lowered in reliance on s 3(1), such a development would allow a counter-balancing value to be afforded to media freedom.

The problematic term 'incidental' can only be stretched so far, and if the courts were to seek to adopt a proportionality test within the terms of s 5, they would have to be prepared to depart from the literal meaning of the section and to read words into it.[165] A strong argument for so doing is that the parliamentary intention behind the introduction of the 1981 Act was to bring English law into compliance with the Convention. If the judges were prepared to accept that Parliament had partially failed to achieve its aim, then even reading words into the statute to achieve such compliance could be seen, not as *defeating* Parliament's intention, but as perfecting it. The new interpretation, moreover, does not go against a pervasive feature of the statute.[166] At the same time the reform proposed is largely a matter of interpretation rather than of implying into the statute an entirely new provision that was absent from it.[167] Moreover, the area in question – protecting the judicial process – is one that is clearly within the judicial domain in terms of constitutional competence and role.[168] Parliament is not otherwise addressing this issue – there are no plans at present to reform the 1981 Act.[169] No issues of resource allocation arise; thus there are positive reasons for activism in this context and none for deference.

---

164 See above, pp 287–89.

165 This might be possible: see *R v A* [2001] 2 Cr App R 21; [2002] 1 AC 45; for discussion see Chapter 4, p 174. Kavanagh's writings on s 3(1) have influenced this analysis. See in particular 'The elusive divide between interpretation and legislation under the HRA' (2004) 24(2) OJLS 259. A court could read in the words 'if the proportionality test under Art 10(2) is not satisfied, or' after the word 'if'.

166 *Cf R (on the application of Anderson) v Secretary of State for the Home Dept* [2003] 1 AC 837 in which the Secretary of State's role in sentencing was found to be incompatible with Art 6 since he could not be viewed as an independent and impartial tribunal. However, a declaration of incompatibility was made rather than seeking to use s 3(1) since the Secretary of State's role was such a fundamental feature of the statute as a whole – any other approach would have been against the grain of the statute.

167 As in the Court of Appeal in *Re S and Re W (Care Orders)* – as discussed in Chapter 4, pp 154–55 – the decision was overturned: it was made clear by the House of Lords [2002] 2 AC 291 that the Court of Appeal had gone too far under s 3.

168 In terms of both expertise and constitutional role the context is similar to those in *R v A* [2002] 1 AC 45 and in *R v Offen* [2001] 1 WLR 253; but not that in *Bellinger* [2003] 2 All ER 513 – where the court declined to read words into the statute in question under s 3 HRA. For discussion, see Chapter 4, pp 153–55.

169 *Cf Bellinger ibid*, where Parliament was about to address the situation at issue regarding the law relating to transsexuals.

The defence of 'ignorance' under s 3

A defendant charged with the s 1 offence can seek to use s 3 as a defence. Section 3 is a true defence, since the burden of proof lies on the defendant. The publisher or distributor will not be strictly liable if, having taken all reasonable care, he or she does not know and has no reason to suspect that the proceedings are active or that the publication contains the type of material likely to give rise to strict liability under s 2. It may be noted that since the common law (see below) does not depend on the use of the active test, liability could still arise outside the statute even where, within the statute, s 3 would have been applicable.

Conclusions: re-balancing the 1981 Act

It has been argued in this chapter that contempt law is failing as a means of protecting fair trials, but also that it is not sufficiently effective in protecting freedom of expression. A rarely enforced rule of a high but uncertain threshold such as that under s 2(2) inevitably tends to leave the ultimate responsibility for avoiding unfairness with trial judges. The current division of responsibility, almost inevitable under a largely protective model, between contempt law and trial judges, is deeply problematic. The current position may mean that freedom of expression is not fully protected since the media are uncertain at times whether or not a publication might infringe the imprecisely expressed rule under s 2(2). But at the same time the existence of the rule fails to provide protection for trials. Certain newspapers, especially the less responsible sections of the press, at times engage in reporting at the outer limits of what can be tolerated under s 2(2). They may do so in the knowledge that if a number of newspapers are involved, it may be hard to identify the responsibility of any particular one. Or they may merely take a risk, motivated by determination to maintain commercial advantage, on the basis that the uncertainty of the s 2(2) test (and of the common law test of real risk of prejudice), and the high threshold it appears to represent, make it difficult for a prosecution to succeed and quite probable, therefore, that it will not be undertaken.

The imprecision of the s 2(2) test is exacerbated precisely because the roles of contempt law and of the trial judge overlap. Judges in contempt cases must take account of the likelihood that neutralising measures will be or have been used. The use of such measures, including directions to the jury, make it hard to determine whether the risk in question at the time of publication still subsisted at the time of trial. Different judges take varying views as to the efficacy of such measures and the ability of the jury to disregard media comment. Thus contempt law is failing to delineate the boundary between the use of protective and of neutralising measures and therefore allowing too much pressure to be placed on the criminal justice system in high-profile cases. Possibly that boundary cannot be delineated effectively unless, as discussed below, a far more precise 'protective' test is adopted and preventive measures are used more extensively, accompanied by robust safeguards for media freedom. Most worryingly, parts of the media may rely, not merely on the uncertainty of s 2(2), but on some kind of complicity with the government in relation to their coverage, especially in terrorist cases. The uncertainty of s 2(2), and the high bar it appears to create in practice, clearly aid the Attorney General in justifying refusals to prosecute. As indicated above, such refusals probably do not in any event have to be justified in court.[170]

The reforms proposed could re-balance the statute by focussing it more closely on fair trial and free speech rights. Where prejudice has probably been caused and the speech in question consists of reportage with a misleading gloss,[171] s 5 could not be used, under the current interpretation of the section. But the speech might in any event escape liability since it would be probable that no prosecution would be brought for the reasons given above, founded partly on the unsatisfactory nature of s 2(2). The reform proposed under s 5 would not afford greater protection to such speech since its misleading quality would undermine its public interest value. Section 2(2), if interpreted more clearly, as discussed above, could provide an increased protection for fair trials; s 5 could only be viewed as providing a satisfactory countervailing protection for free speech if the courts were prepared to take this course. But the result might be – in something close to a reversal of the current situation – that near worthless and probably prejudicial speech would be caught by an enhanced s 2(2), while speech of the most value in Art 10 terms would be more likely to escape under the reformed s 5. Thus a re-balancing of the statute, based more firmly on both fair trial and free speech principles, could occur. This would accord more strongly with the speech/harm balancing test from *Sunday Times v UK*. Speech of value would be less likely to be caught but where there was a real possibility of harm to a trial, liability would be more likely to be established. This approach would echo the Strasbourg one as encapsulated in both *Sunday Times* and *Worm* more closely than is the case under the current position, but it would not replicate it. The problem would still remain that Art 10 values can overcome Art 6 ones under s 5 since the section allows speech to cause serious prejudice to a trial but escape liability due to its value. It is only possible to meet this argument by relying on the use of neutralising measures at trial, but for the reasons already discussed, this is not an entirely satisfactory position.

3 Intentionally prejudicing proceedings: common law contempt

Introduction

As explained above, the common law of contempt pre-1981 created an offence of strict liability. A residual and narrow area of common law contempt was preserved under the 1981 Act, based on a *mens rea* requirement. Section 6(c) of the 1981 Act preserves liability for contempt at common law if intention to prejudice the administration of justice can be shown. 'Prejudice [to] the administration of justice' clearly includes (and may solely denote – see below) prejudice to particular proceedings. Once the requirement of intent is satisfied, it is easier to establish contempt at common law rather than under the Act since it is only necessary to show 'a real risk of prejudice' and proceedings need only be imminent, not 'active'. Clearly, liability can be established at common law in instances when it might also be established under the 1981 Act, as occurred in the

---

170 See above fn 101 and p 324.
171 E.g., the *Sun* headline 'Got the Bastards!' in relation to the arrests of terrorist suspects in July 2005 referred to earlier, fn 92, above.

Hislop case, and also in instances when the Act will not apply because proceedings are inactive. Possibly, it might also be established where one of the statutory tests other than the 'active' requirement was not satisfied. These preliminary observations are developed below, taking Convention standards into account under the HRA. Section 3 HRA does not apply (except to s 6(c) itself) since intentional contempt arises at common law, but the court has a duty to ensure that that the common law is compatible with the Convention under s 6. It will be suggested, in particular, that the common law requirements should be subjected to a strict scrutiny in so far as they represent the possibility of circumventing a measure adopted specifically to meet Art 10 standards. A publication will fall within the area of liability preserved by s 6(c) if three elements are present – a specific intention to prejudice the administration of justice in *imminent* proceedings, and the creation of a real risk of prejudice to those proceedings.

Intention to prejudice the administration of justice

The test for intention to prejudice the administration of justice was established in *Attorney General v Times Newspaper*[172] and *Attorney General v News Group Newspapers plc.*[173] It was made clear that 'intention' connotes specific intent and therefore cannot include recklessness. The test may be summed up as follows: did the defendant either wish to prejudice proceedings or ('oblique' intent) foresee that such prejudice was a virtually inevitable consequence of publishing the material in question? Thus, it is not necessary to show a desire to prejudice proceedings or that where there was such a desire, that it was the sole desire. This test is based on the meaning of intent arising from rulings on the *mens rea* for murder: *Hancock and Shankland*,[174] *Nedrick*[175] and *Woollin*.[176]

A number of circumstances may allow the inference of intention to prejudice the proceedings to be drawn, although it is suggested that the relevance of the circumstances will depend on the form of intent – desire or oblique intent – which seems to be in question. In *Attorney General v News Group Newspapers plc*,[177] the newspaper's support for the prosecution in its columns and in funding a private prosecution allowed the inference to be made. A Dr B was questioned about an allegation of rape made against him by an eight-year-old girl, but eventually the county prosecuting solicitor decided that there was insufficient evidence to prosecute him. *The Sun* obtained the story and decided that it should offer the mother financial help in order to fund a private prosecution. It published various articles attacking Dr B: 'Rape Case Doc: Sun acts'; 'Beast must be named, says MP', etc. The Attorney General brought a prosecution against *The Sun* for contempt. The articles could not come within the strict liability rule because the proceedings in question – the private prosecution – were not active. The

---

172 [1992] 7 AC 191; [1991] 2 All ER 398; for a report of the Divisional Court proceedings, see *Re Attorney General v Observer and Guardian Newspapers Ltd* (1989) *The Times*, 9 May; for comment, see [1989] PL 477. For comment on the *mens rea* issue, see Laws (1990) 43 CLP 99, pp 105–10.
173 [1989] QB 110; [1988] 3 WLR 163; [1988] 2 All ER 906.
174 [1986] AC 455; [1986] 1 All ER 641; [1986] 3 WLR 1014.
175 [1986] 3 All ER 1; [1986] 1 WLR 1025.
176 [1999] 1 AC 82.
177 [1989] QB 110; [1988] 3 WLR 163; [1988] 2 All ER 906.

contempt alleged, therefore, arose at common law. It was found that intention could be established, either on the basis of a desire to prejudice the proceedings (presumably in order to vindicate the paper's stance) or because the editor must have foreseen that Dr B would almost certainly not receive a fair trial. The judgment would support either view, but probably favours the former: in his ruling, Watkins LJ said: 'they could only have printed articles of such a kind if they were campaigning for a conviction as they clearly were'. However, if he had the latter form of intent in mind, it may be said that although the newspaper had acted reprehensibly in using its power to attempt to influence a trial it had itself become involved in, it is arguable that intent should not have been so readily established. The fact that *The Sun* was personally involved was not, it is argued, relevant to oblique intent. The proceedings were clearly not going to occur for some time; therefore, although the defendants probably foresaw some risk of prejudice to them, it was not clear that such prejudice could be said to be a virtually inevitable consequence of publication. In fact, Dr B was acquitted; the jury were clearly able to put out of their minds any influence articles may have had.

The Sun case may be contrasted with *Attorney General v Sport Newspapers Ltd*[178] in which the test for intention was somewhat more strictly interpreted. One David Evans, who had previous convictions for rape, was suspected of abducting Anna Humphries. He was on the run when *The Sport* published his convictions; the proceedings were not therefore active, and so the case arose at common law. It did not appear that *The Sport* wished to prejudice proceedings. Was it foreseen as a virtual certainty that prejudice to Evans's trial would occur as a result of the publication? It was held that there was a risk of such prejudice of which the editor of *The Sport* was aware, but that such awareness of risk was not sufficient. Clearly, had the *mens rea* of common law contempt included recklessness, it would have been established. The requirement to prove intent was reaffirmed post-HRA in *Attorney General v Punch*, which is discussed below.

Imminence

At common law, the *sub judice* period began when proceedings could be said to be 'imminent' (*Savundranayagan*).[179] This test would of course be readily satisfied where proceedings were active. However, it may not always be necessary to establish imminence. In *Attorney General v News Group Newspapers plc*[180] it was held *obiter* that where it is established that the defendant intended to prejudice proceedings, it is not necessary to show that proceedings are imminent. In his judgment, Watkins LJ approved *obiter* of David Pannick's contention that 'no authority states that common law contempt cannot be committed where proceedings cannot be said to be imminent but where there is a specific intent to impede a fair trial, the occurrence of which is in contemplation'. It was found that even if the trial of Dr B was too far off to be said to be pending or imminent, the conduct of *The Sun* in publishing stories at the same time as assisting the mother in the private prosecution could still amount to contempt.

178 [1991] 1 WLR 1194.
179 [1968] 3 All ER 439; [1968] 1 WLR 1761, CA.
180 [1989] QB 110; [1988] 3 WLR 163; [1988] 2 All ER 906.

Bingham LJ concurred with this dilution of the imminence test in *Attorney General v Sport*,[181] although in the same case Hodgson J considered that proceedings must be 'pending'. He interpreted 'pending' as synonymous with 'active', an interpretation that would at one and the same time have curtailed the scope of common law contempt, but focused it more closely on the harm caused by deliberately creating prejudice to proceedings. This point, therefore, remains unresolved, leaving the media without a clear guide to the period during which publication of matter relevant to proceedings will be risky. If proceedings need not even be imminent, it appears that reporting of matters that may give rise to proceedings at some point in the future could be curbed, assuming that the other tests were satisfied. The test of 'imminence' is itself too wide and uncertain, but would be preferable to the uncertainty on this point which was exacerbated by *Attorney General v Sport*. It is uncertain what the alternative test contemplated by Bingham LJ could be. There cannot be an intention to prejudice something that cannot even be identified as a possibility. Thus the test at its least stringent must be that proceedings can be identified as a possibility before this head of common law contempt can be in question. At the same time it would only be possible to rely on this diluted imminence test in relation to instances of simple rather than oblique intent. Desired consequences can never be viewed as too remote, assuming that they in fact arise, but it would be almost impossible to show that a virtually certain consequence of prejudice had been foreseen in instances of a very lengthy time lag between publication and proceedings. Obviously, even in relation to simple intent the *actus reus* of a real risk of prejudice still has to be established, which would also be very difficult in relation to a lengthy time lag, except possibly in exceptional instances, such as that in *Attorney General v News Group Newspapers* itself, where the newspaper is personally involved. This development in common law contempt is therefore of little practical significance. It may have some slight curtailing impact on media freedom, but at the same time it is unlikely to protect the fairness of proceedings. The more uncertain the test becomes, the more, it is argued, common law contempt is divorced from a focus on such fairness.

In practice, unless a media body can be shown to have *desired* to prejudice proceedings through a publication, by creating bias in the minds of those involved such as jurors, it is almost impossible to show that such prejudice is a virtually certain consequence of publication if the proceedings are merely imminent but not active. *Virtual certainty* of such prejudice could normally only arise where publication occurred close to the action or during it. Therefore the 'imminence' test is only nominally of significance in most instances – it can be assumed that it may have become virtually otiose and that currently the strict liability rule will almost always be used rather than the common law in relation to the *Sun* type of case. The only reason for using the common law during the active period would be to seek a higher penalty where *mens rea* could be shown. But this could be done in any event if reforms to the 1981 Act abolished this form of common law contempt but allowed for higher penalties to be applied where the media body was shown to have *mens rea*. There would be an argument for including recklessness. Intentionally or recklessly creating a substantial risk of serious prejudice during the active period could become a new offence, creating an alternative to the strict liability rule, and attracting a higher sentence. The current common law rule has however a residual relevance in relation to other forms of creating prejudice to proceedings, as discussed below.

---

181 [1991] 1 WLR 1194.

A real risk of prejudice

Methods of fulfilling this test

It must be shown that the publication amounts to conduct which creates a real risk of prejudice to the administration of justice (*Thompson Newspapers*).[182] There are a number of different methods of fulfilling this test. In *Hislop and Pressdram*[183] it was found that the defendants, who were one party in an action for defamation, had interfered with the administration of justice because they had brought improper pressure to bear on the other party, Sonia Sutcliffe, by publishing material in *Private Eye* intended to deter her from pursuing the action. There was a substantial risk that the articles might have succeeded in their aim; had they done so, the course of justice in Mrs Sutcliffe's action would have been seriously prejudiced, since she would have been deterred from having her claim decided in a court. Counsel for *Private Eye* had argued that defamatory material that the defendant seeks to justify should not be restrained, because until it is clear that the alleged libel is untrue, it is not clear that any right has been infringed (*Bonnard v Perryman*).[184] This argument was rejected because the question of deterrence did not depend on the truth or falsity of the allegations. The possibility of justification was thus irrelevant. In this instance, it might also be noted that the relevant tests under the 1981 Act had been satisfied; therefore, it would seem that, *a fortiori*, common law contempt could be established, it having already been accepted that the articles had been published with the intention of putting pressure on Mrs Sutcliffe to discontinue the defamation action, thereby satisfying the *mens rea* requirement at common law. In *Attorney General v News Group Newspapers plc*[185] it was found that there was a risk of prejudice since jurors might have been influenced by the newspaper coverage which came close to imputing guilt to the defendant. This was however a doubtful finding due to the lapse of time between publication and trial. The almost dismissive treatment of the *actus reus* in that case came close to implying that the *Sun* was being punished for acting reprehensibly in seeking to prejudice the proceedings, rather than in relation to the risk it actually created.

The particular use of common law contempt in *Hislop* represents a clear and quite precisely defined area of liability targeted at a particular mischief. There is no division of responsibility between trial judge and contempt law: if contempt law did not fulfil this role, it could not be fulfilled at all, under the existing law. But the form of common law contempt based on creating bias in the minds of those involved in proceedings seems to be serving no useful purpose, since it overlaps with the use of the strict liability rule, and should be abolished. The imprecision and over-breadth of the tests for the *actus reus* sit uneasily with the demands of proportionality under Art 10. Since it is now hard to satisfy s 2(2) of the 1981 Act unless a publication occurs close to or during the trial, it is hard to imagine an instance in which it would be useful to invoke the test of imminence: if a publication was merely imminent as opposed to active it would not satisfy the 'real risk of prejudice' test under the more recent s 2(2) rulings on the creation of risk.[186]

---

182 [1968] 1 All ER 268; [1968] 1 WLR 1.
183 1991] 1 QB 514; [1991] 1 All ER 911; [1991] 2 WLR 219, CA.
184 [1891] 2 Ch 269, p 289.
185 [1989] QB 110.
186 See pp 322–23, 328 above.

A further very significant special form of common law contempt can arise if part of the media frustrates a court order (including orders made under s 4(2) of the 1981 Act)[187] against another part. Usually the order is made to restrain the publication of confidential material.[188] The three tests applicable are the same as those discussed above: proceedings must (probably) be imminent; specific intent to prejudice proceedings must be shown, and a real risk of prejudice must arise. But the last test has had to be interpreted in a very particular fashion in order to allow this particular form of contempt to arise.

Frustrating an injunction against another media body

This highly significant extension of common law contempt arose from one strand of the *Spycatcher* litigation. This case affirmed the principle that once an interlocutory injunction has been obtained restraining one organ of the media from publication of allegedly confidential material, the rest of the media may be in contempt if they publish that material, even if their intention in so doing is to bring alleged iniquity to public attention.

The principle laid down in the *Times* case was reconsidered in the HRA era by the House of Lords in *Attorney General v Punch*.[189] The case arose from the publication by *Punch* magazine of an article by David Shayler. Shayler had served as an officer with MI5 and when he left MI5 he took with him copies of confidential documents containing sensitive information relating to intelligence activities of MI5. According to the Attorney General, Mr Shayler then disclosed some of this material to a newspaper publisher, Associated Newspapers Ltd. Articles written by Mr Shayler, or based on information provided by him, were published in *The Mail on Sunday* and the *Evening Standard* in August 1997. The Attorney General then intervened and brought civil proceedings against Mr Shayler and Associated Newspapers. Hooper J granted an interlocutory injunction against Mr Shayler based on breach of confidence.[190] A similar order was made against Associated Newspapers. By this order, expressed to continue until the trial of the action, Mr Shayler was restrained from disclosing to any newspaper or anyone else,

> any information obtained by him in the course of or by virtue of his employment in and position as a member of the Security Service (whether presented as fact or fiction) which relates to or which may be construed as relating to the Security Service or its membership or activities or to security or intelligence activities generally.

Two provisos were attached to the order. First, the order did not apply to any information in respect of which the Attorney General stated in writing that the information was

---

187 Section 4(1) provides that a fair and accurate report of proceedings held in public published contemporaneously in good faith will not be a contempt. Section 4(2) of the 1981 Act provides that during any legal proceeding held in public, a judge may make an order postponing reporting of the proceedings if such action 'appears necessary for avoiding a substantial risk of prejudice to the administration of justice in those proceedings'. For discussion of s 4, see below, pp 353–58.

188 See, for discussion of breach of confidence in the context of state secrecy, Chapter 8, pp 518–23.

189 [2003] 1 AC 1046; [2003] 2 WLR 49; [2003] 1 All ER 289. For discussion of the case, see Smith, ATH 'Third Parties and the Reach of Injunctions' [2003] 62(2) CLJ 241.

190 On 4 September 1997.

not information the publication of which the Crown was seeking to restrain. Second, the order did not preclude repetition of the information disclosed in *The Mail on Sunday* on 24 August 1997. Neither Mr Shayler nor Associated Newspapers objected to the making of these orders.

Mr Shayler then began writing for *Punch* magazine; the editor, Mr Steen, was aware of the terms of the interlocutory non-disclosure orders made against Mr Shayler. The article which became the subject of the contempt proceedings dealt with the Bishopsgate bomb in 1993 and the death of WPC Yvonne Fletcher outside the Libyan Embassy in 1984. The Lords found that the purpose of the judge in making the order (that the administration of justice had been thwarted by the articles) was to preserve the confidentiality of the information specified in the order pending the trial so as to enable the court at trial to adjudicate effectively on the disputed issues of confidentiality arising in the action. It was to ensure that the court's decision on the claims in the proceedings should not be pre-empted by disclosure of any of the information specified in the order before the trial. The *actus reus* of contempt was satisfied by the thwarting of this purpose by destruction of the confidentiality of the material, through its publication in *Punch*, which it was the purpose of the injunction to preserve. Mr Steen had accepted that the publication of the offending magazine article had constituted the *actus reus* of contempt. Bearing in mind the purpose of the injunctions as already established, Lord Nicholls went on to find that the *mens rea* of common law contempt was also satisfied and so concluded that contempt of court was established. He said:

> The facts speak for themselves. Mr Steen . . . knew that the action against Mr Shayler raised confidentiality issues relating wholly or primarily to national security. He must, inevitably, have appreciated that by publishing the article he was doing precisely what the order was intended to prevent, namely, pre-empting the court's decision on these confidentiality. That is knowing interference with the administration of justice.[191]

Clearly, the finding of contempt represented an interference with freedom of expression as guaranteed by Art 10. However, Lord Nicholl's consideration of the impact of the HRA was brief and superficial. He noted, before coming to the argument as to the purpose of the injunction, that national security, one of the list of exceptions in Art 10(2), can justify a restraint on freedom of expression. He then went on to find, '[t]he rule of law requires that the decision on where this balance lies in any case should be made by the court as an independent and impartial tribunal established by law' and in the meantime the court must be able to prevent the information being disclosed. He went on to find that therefore:

> the law must be able to prescribe appropriate penalties where a person deliberately sets the injunction at nought. Without sanctions an injunction would be a paper tiger. Sanctions are necessary to maintain the rule of law; in the language of the Convention, to maintain the authority of the judiciary.

---

191 *Ibid*, at paras 51 and 52.

This analysis did not address the questions of necessity and proportionality; it implied that once a court had decided that material should be kept confidential before the trial of a permanent injunction and had imposed an interim injunction with that object in mind, it would *always* be justifiable to restrict freedom of expression by way of common law contempt in order to provide a sanction against publication of the material by third parties where publication would have a significant and adverse effect on the administration of justice in that trial. But the need to show such an effect does not necessarily satisfy the requirements of proportionality since the adverse effect would always be caused by publication of material covered by the injunction which was not already, or not to a significant extent, in the public domain. Further, in such circumstances the *mens rea* requirement would virtually always be satisfied since journalists would normally be aware that the material was covered by an injunction against another body or person.

Lord Hope gave brief consideration to the question of proportionality, but without citing any Strasbourg jurisprudence, although he came to the same conclusion as Lord Nicholl. He found that there can be no objection to an interim injunction against the publication of information on the ground of proportionality if three requirements are satisfied. He considered that the general principles from which the requirements are to be derived are well established and are indicated in three leading cases: *R (Daly) v Secretary of State for the Home Department*,[192] *R (Pretty) v Director of Public Prosecutions*,[193] and *R v Shayler*.[194] He found that in the context in question the requirements are: first, that there is a genuine dispute as to whether the information is confidential because its publication might be a threat to national security; second that there are reasonable grounds for thinking that publication of the information before trial would impede or interfere with the administration of justice and third, that the interference with the right of free speech is no greater than is necessary. Lord Hope concentrated on the third requirement and found that the requirements of proportionality were satisfied since the opening words of the interim injunction were qualified by the proviso allowing newspapers to apply to the Attorney General to publish innocuous material; the extent of the injunction remained subject to the further order of the court and that court itself would have to observe the principle of proportionality when it dealt with any application before the trial for the relaxation of the scope of the injunction.[195] He insisted that in each instance the analysis of proportionality should be fact-sensitive.

However, objection can be made to his findings on the basis that all interim injunctions would satisfy the second and third of these requirements and the first is open to the objection that it places a power of censorship in the hands, not only of a member of the executive but also in those of one party to the original and forthcoming actions, creating an appearance of bias. The Attorney General is the very person (or office) whose rights are being upheld by the threat of the invocation of the contempt of court jurisdiction. To determine whether liability under that jurisdiction can be justified as an interference with freedom of expression, partly by reference to his powers to allow publication, does not appear to provide an adequate safeguard for the media. This was far from the hard

192 [2001] 2 AC 532, at p 547A–B, *per* Lord Steyn.
193 [2001] 3 WLR 1598, at 1637A–B.
194 [2002] 2 WLR 754, at 783F–H, 786A–B.
195 *Attorney General v Punch* [2003] 1 AC 1046, at paras 114–120.

look at the proportionality that one would expect of a court which took its duty under s 6(1) HRA seriously. A further anomaly arises: the litigant who has obtained the interim injunction is thereby placed, in effect, in a more advantageous position than he or she will be in if the final injunction is obtained, since the *Spycatcher* doctrine has been found to cease to have effect once that injunction is granted.[196] In a sense, the litigant who has obtained the interim injunction obtains a very significant benefit, not enjoyed by the litigant who wins the final action, since the whole of the media will be deterred from publication of the confidential material during the period between the interim and the final injunction.

This form of common law contempt remains of very doubtful compatibility with Art 10, bearing in mind the emphasis placed upon the role of the media in *Goodwin v UK*[197] by the European Court of Human Rights. Although trivial or technical breaches of court orders made against other parties will not attract liability, the area of liability which remains creates a curb on media freedom which is out of accord with the crucial role of the press in a free society.[198] It is unlikely after *Attorney General v Punch* that reform can be expected in the domestic courts and therefore it can now only come from Strasbourg or Parliament. If a Strasbourg ruling eventually leads to abolition of this form of common law contempt, certain instances of the *Spycatcher* type could still fall within the statutory strict liability rule, if – which would rarely occur – the hearing of the permanent injunction had been set down at the time of publication. In such instances, however, s 5 would apply; therefore liability might be avoided, depending on a difficult application of the 'incidental' test where the information had public interest value.

For obvious reasons the political will to introduce reform to abolish this head of common law contempt is likely to be absent. From the government perspective the doctrine remains valuable as a means of creating secrecy that is in executive hands in terms of instigation – since in the *Punch* and *Spycatcher* category of case the initial temporary injunction will be sought by the Attorney General. Having obtained it on the basis of a test satisfied with relative ease, he need do nothing more to ensure that all the rest of the media are silenced on the matter at hand since criminal contempt at common law, after *Punch*, will do the job for him. If reform of this area of contempt eventually occurs as a result of a Strasbourg ruling, it will represent an indictment of the stance of a number of the senior judiciary in relation to a fundamental freedom in a democratic society. *Attorney General v Punch* is one of the most disappointing rulings there has been so far under the HRA: it represents a judicial acquiescence to the executive's predilection for secrecy, coupled with a determination to cling to anti-speech values reflected in common law doctrine even where they fly in the face of Convention principles.

Conclusions

This overview of this form of contempt, taking account also of the strict liability rule from the 1981 Act, gives rise, it is argued, to the conclusion that at present it is out of

---

196 *Jockey Club v Buffham* [2003] 2 WLR 178; [2003] EMLR 5.
197 *Goodwin v UK* (1996) 22 EHRR 123.
198 These issues are discussed further in Chapter 8, pp 518–23, in relation to the breach of confidence issue, the other strand of the *Spycatcher* litigation.

accord with Convention values and requirements in terms of both law and practice. Although, as discussed above, its jurisprudence in this context is open to criticism, certain thematic strands can be discerned. As *Worm*, *Ribemont*,[199] *News Verlags*[200] and *Sunday Times* indicate, Strasbourg seeks to protect fair trials where they appear to be genuinely threatened by media coverage. Where the threat is nebulous and the value of the speech in question is high, restraints on the media are not found to be justified. A comparison between the *Taylor*[201] and the *Spycatcher* or *Punch* cases[202] suggests that both statute and common law are insufficiently focused on the core Convention values at stake. In *Taylor*, the individual's right to a fair trial under Art 6 was genuinely threatened; at the same time, the speech in question was of virtually no value in Art 10 terms, since it was misleading. Yet no prosecution was forthcoming. In contrast, *Spycatcher* and *Punch* concerned political speech to which Strasbourg accords the highest value, while in both instances the Art 6 guarantee was only doubtfully engaged. A successful prosecution for contempt in *Taylor* on the basis that the trial in question had been severely affected by relentless and misleading publicity could almost certainly have justified under Art 10(2) as proportionate in terms of speech/harm balancing to the aim pursued – that of protecting the Art 6 rights of the defendants. The reverse is true, it is contended, of both *Spycatcher* and *Punch*.

A possible explanation for current practice in these and other similar instances is that where speech is directly critical of a part of the executive and therefore, impliedly, of government itself, the interests of the government in stifling it are most obviously engaged. Such an instance arose in both *Spycatcher* and *Punch*, arguably providing an example of the failure of Attorney Generals to ensure that an appearance of distance from the government was maintained. In contrast, as in *Taylor*, when the trial of an obscure personage, accused of a highly-publicised crime, is in question, there is little or no political advantage to be gained in seeking to prevent or punish interferences with it. But there may be quite severe political disadvantage in appearing to attack the massed ranks of the tabloids. As indicated above, it is not entirely possible to dismiss misgivings as to the ability of Attorney Generals to distance themselves fully from their political colleagues, who are likely to have such considerations in mind.

The problems created by the willingness of newspaper proprietors to damage the fairness of trials in pursuit of competitive advantage are likely to continue so long as they view contempt actions as improbable. Certain trials such as those of the Taylor sisters, of Harold Shipman in 2000, the trial in 2001 of the suspect charged with the murder of the television presenter Jill Dando, the arrest of the terrorist suspects in connection with the Ricin incident in 2003, the trial of Ian Huntley for the Soham murders in 2003 and the arrest of terrorist suspects in July 2005 tend to attract a misleading and sensationalist media coverage, which has, in the case of a number of newspapers, little connection with free speech values but is motivated merely by profit-making concerns. Obviously, horrifying incidents, especially terrorist ones, will be reported in extensive detail using untempered language, but the aim of some of the coverage appears to be to

---

199 (1995) 20 EHRR 557.
200 (2001) 31 EHRR 8.
201 [1993] 98 Cr App R 361. See pp 324–25 above.
202 See above pp 347–50.

come closest to expressing the baser instincts of readers, however prejudicial to a fair trial such expression might be. Assuming that in the very competitive media market, one newspaper is unlikely to forego the chance of attracting readers by its coverage of such cases, further intervention by Parliament appears to be essential if the criminal justice system and certain deeply unpopular defendants are not to bear the burden created by the demands of the media market.

The protective approach, as recognised under the 1981 Act and the common law, is not achieving its objective. At the same time, a shift towards the neutralising model has occurred in a piecemeal and incoherent fashion. The most extreme method of remedying the effects of prejudicial press coverage – acquittal – is used with some readiness despite its effect upon the administration of justice, while certain lesser measures, such as the use of a *voir dire* in order to determine jury knowledge of the case from the media,[203] or the delay of the trial, are shunned or rarely used. As argued above, such measures place burdens on the criminal justice system, while having, in many instances, no genuinely beneficial consequences in terms of freedom of speech. The question whether the use of such measures as a safeguard is warranted where contempt law is ineffective should be addressed as part of a general review of this area of law. In the meantime, it is suggested that judicial reliance on the Convention and especially on its underlying principles under the HRA could address certain of the deficiencies indicated above.

4 Prior restraints restricting reports of court proceedings

The general principle that justice should be openly administered is well established.[204] This principle is recognised in the Art 6 requirement that everyone is entitled to a 'fair and *public* hearing'. This Art 6 requirement is subject to a number of exceptions contained in para 1:

> the press and public may be excluded from all or part of the trial in the interests of morals, public order or national security in a democratic society, where the interests of juveniles or the protection of the private life of the parties so require or to the extent strictly necessary in the opinion of the court in special circumstances where publicity would prejudice the interests of justice.

In this respect, Articles 10 and 6 are not in conflict, since Art 10 may be said to require impliedly that restrictions on allowing journalists to attend hearings should be strictly scrutinised. Conflict is more likely to arise between the interest in open justice and the Art 8 guarantee of a right to respect for privacy. This issue is considered in Chapter 10.[205]

In general, in accordance with the open justice principle, courts are open to the public and therefore a fair and accurate factual report of the proceedings, in good faith, will not

---

203 In *Andrews (Tracey)* [1999] Crim LR 156, the Court of Appeal re-stated its view that juries should not be questioned regarding their knowledge of the case they are to judge upon.

204 See the comments to this effect and on the need to limit use of private hearings in *Preston* [1993] 4 All ER 638; 143 NLJ 1601.

205 See pp 716–19.

amount to a contempt. This is provided for under s 4(1) of the 1981 Act. The reverse is true of private sittings, a report of which will usually prima facie amount to a contempt. Section 4(1), therefore, creates an exception from strict liability in respect of proceedings held in public, so long as the other elements mentioned are present. Another way of putting this is to say that fair and accurate reports of proceedings would be unlikely to fall within s 2(2) in any event: s 4(1) merely makes this explicit, in statutory form. However, a number of exceptions to the principle of openness have been created to allow the withholding of information, either temporarily or indefinitely. For example, at common law, a judge can order prohibition of a publication in order to prevent, for example, the disclosure of the identity of a witness. The leading authority is *Attorney General v Leveller Magazine Ltd*[206] in which it was accepted that departure from the principle of openness would be warranted if necessary for the due administration of justice, and that therefore if a court made an order designed to protect the administration of justice, then it would be incumbent on those who knew of it not to do anything which might frustrate its object. All these exceptions must be considered for their compatibility with Art 10, since all clearly represent interferences with freedom of expression. In relation to reporting restrictions, as opposed to restrictions on those who may attend the hearing, a conflict between Articles 10 and 6 may arise where the restrictions are aimed at avoiding prejudice to the trial.

Postponing reporting of information to avoid a risk of prejudice

Section 4 provides:

(1) Subject to this section a person is not guilty of contempt of court under the strict liability rule in respect of a fair and accurate report of legal proceedings held in public, published contemporaneously and in good faith.

(2) In any such proceedings the court may, where it appears to be necessary for avoiding a substantial risk of prejudice to the administration of justice in those proceedings, or in any other proceedings pending or imminent, order that the publication of any report of the proceedings, or any part of the proceedings be postponed for such period as the court thinks necessary for that purpose.

(3) For the purposes of subsection (1) of this section . . . a report of proceedings shall be treated as published contemporaneously (a) in the case of a report of which publication is postponed pursuant to an order subsection (2) of this section, if published as soon as practicable after that order expires.

Thus s 4(1) contains an exception to the strict liability rule under s 1 of the Act. It may be noted that s 2(2) speaks of the creation of '*serious* prejudice', whereas s 4(2) speaks only of 'prejudice'. So in this respect s 4(2) creates a lower threshold than s 2(2). The effect of s 4(1) is that, even where the contemporaneous publication of a fair and accurate report of court proceedings creates a substantial risk that the course of justice will be seriously impeded or prejudiced (under s 2(2)), the publisher is not to be guilty of contempt of court under the strict liability rule. Clearly, it is highly unlikely in most

206 [1979] AC 440; [1979] 2 WLR 247, HL.

circumstances that such fair and accurate reporting could cause prejudice. However, this exception is intended to reassure newspaper editors in relation to trial-related reporting.

The freedom of the media to report proceedings is itself then limited, however, by the provision of s 4(2). Section 4(2) provides a discretion to be exercised during any legal proceeding held in public, allowing a judge to make an order postponing reporting of those proceedings, if such action 'appears necessary for avoiding a substantial risk of prejudice' to the proceedings or any other imminent proceedings, thus creating an exception to s 4(1).[207] In other words, despite the fairness and accuracy of such reporting – and its importance in relation to the open justice principle – there are special circumstances that mean that it should nevertheless be curbed. Section 4(2) is limited in one respect – it only covers reports *of* the proceedings, not reports of extraneous matters *relating to* the proceedings that could create the risk in question. They can be dealt with by way of subsequent sanctions, as discussed above. It is also important to note that reports of the proceedings can be postponed, not because they might affect the proceedings in question, but because *other* proceedings could be affected. Those other proceedings need only be 'imminent', not 'active',[208] and it is clear that the term 'imminent' denotes a longer and more imprecise period of time. Thus the period during which reporting is postponed can be very lengthy.

Lord Taylor CJ found in *R v Central Criminal Court ex parte Telegraph plc*[209] that s 4(2) contains two requirements for the making of an order. The first is that publication would create 'a substantial risk of prejudice to the administration of justice' and the second is that postponement of publication 'appears to be necessary for avoiding' that risk. He continued:

> It has been said that there is a third requirement, derived from the word "may" at the beginning of the sub-section, namely, that a court, in the exercise of its discretion, having regard to the competing public interests of ensuring a fair trial and of open justice, considers it appropriate to make an order.

In fact whether the element of discretion is to be regarded as part of the 'necessity' test or as a third requirement, the courts as a matter of practice have tended to merge the requirement of necessity and the exercise of discretion.[210] As regards the second element, it is important to note that the risk in question can concern 'any other proceedings pending or imminent'. This appears to mean that reports that would not satisfy the strict liability rule – since the other proceedings are merely imminent, not *active* – could nevertheless be the subject of a s 4(2) order. The term 'imminent' has been found to cover the possibility that those other proceedings might never in fact arise.[211] Orders under s 4(2) might typically involve the reporting of matters that the defence wished to argue should be ruled inadmissible.

---

207 For comment on s 4 of the 1981 Act, see Walker, C, Cram, I and Brogarth, D, 'The Reporting of Crown Court Proceedings and the Contempt of Court Act 1981' (1992) 55 MLR 647.
208 See above, at pp 344–45.
209 [1993] 1 WLR 980, p 984 D–G.
210 See *BBC, Petitioners* [2002] SLT 2.
211 See *R v Horsham Justices ex parte Farquharson and West Sussex County Times* [1982] QB 762, p 797 E. In *Galbraith v HM Advocate* [2001] SLT 465, p 468 J–K opinion was reserved on this matter.

Section 4(3) is not free from ambiguity, but appears to allow an order to be made relating to reports that would have been published – but for the s 4(2) order – some time after the proceedings in question had concluded.[212] A right of appeal against such orders in relation to trials on indictment was created by s 159 of the Criminal Justice Act 1988 (CJA) in order to take account of a challenge under Art 10 at Strasbourg.[213] The position of the media when a s 4(2) order is made in respect of reporting a summary trial is less clear. However, it was established in *R v Clerkenwell Metropolitan Stipendiary Magistrate, ex parte The Telegraph*[214] that in such circumstances, the media have a right to be heard and must be allowed to put forward the case for discharging the order. When the applicants, publishers of national newspapers, became aware of the existence of the order, they were granted a hearing before the magistrate at which they submitted that the court had power to hear representations from them as to why the order should be discharged. The magistrate held that the court had no power to hear from anyone but the parties to the proceedings. The applicants sought a declaration that the court did have the power to hear their representations, and it was determined, relying on *R v Horsham Justices ex parte Farquharson*,[215] that they had sufficient standing to apply for judicial review. It was found to be implicit in s 4(2) that a court contemplating use of the section should be able to hear representations from those who would be affected if an order was made. In determining whether the order should be maintained, it was found to be necessary to balance the interest in the need for a fair trial before an unprejudiced jury on the one hand and the requirements of open justice on the other. In performing this balancing exercise, the magistrate would need to hear representations from the press as being best qualified to represent the public interest in publicity.

A practice direction relating to the use of s 4(2) orders was issued by Lord Lane CJ on 6 December 1982:[216]

> a court may, where it appears necessary for avoiding a substantial risk of prejudice to the administration of justice in the proceedings before it or in any others pending or imminent, order that publication of any report of the proceedings or part thereof be postponed for such period as the court thinks necessary for that purpose. It is necessary to keep a permanent record of such orders for later reference. For this purpose all orders made under section 4(2) must be formulated in precise terms having regard to the decision of *Horsham Justices, ex parte Farquharson* . . . and orders under both sections must be committed to writing either by the judge personally or the clerk of the court under the judge's directions. An order must state (a) its precise scope, (b) the time at which it shall cease to have effect, if appropriate, and (c) the specific purpose of making the order. Courts will normally give notice to the press in some form that an order has been made . . . and court staff should be prepared to answer an inquiry about a specific case, but it is, and will remain, the responsibility of those reporting cases, and their editors, to ensure that no breach of any order occurs and the onus rests with them to make inquiry in any case of doubt.

212 See *Attorney General v Guardian Newspapers* [2001] EWCA Crim 1351 (see below pp 357–58).
213 *Hodgson, Woolf Productions and NUJ and Channel Four Television* (1987) 10 EHRR 503.
214 [1993] 2 All ER 183; *The Times*, 22 October 1992.
215 [1982] 2 All ER 269, [1982] QB 762, (1982) 76 Cr App R 87, CA.
216 [1982] 76 Cr App R 78.

The ruling of the Court of Appeal in *Horsham Magistrates ex parte Farquharson* was to the effect that such orders should be made sparingly; judges should be careful not to impose a ban on flimsy grounds where the connection between the matters in question and prejudice to the administration of justice was purely speculative. If other means of protecting the jury from possibly prejudicial reports of the trial were available, they should be used. Moreover, it must be ensured that the ban covers only the matters in question. This ruling was reinforced by the decision in *Central Independent Television plc*.[217] During a criminal trial, the jury had to stay overnight in a hotel and in order that they could watch television or listen to the radio, the judge made an order under s 4(2) postponing reporting of the proceedings for that night. The applicants, broadcasters, appealed against the order under s 159 CJA on the basis that there was no ground on which the judge could have concluded that there was a substantial risk of prejudice to the administration of justice. Further, they argued that the judge had incorrectly exercised his discretion under the sub-section and failed to take proper account of the public interest in freedom of expression and in the open administration of justice. The Court of Appeal found that it had not been necessary to make the order as there was little, if any, evidence of a risk to the administration of justice: the previous reporting of the case had not suggested that reporting on the day in question would be anything other than fair and accurate. Even had there been a substantial risk, it might have been possible to adopt alternative methods of insulating the jury from the media. Where such alternative methods were available, they should be used. Accordingly, the appeal was allowed.

The emphasis in this judgment on the need to restrict reporting only where clearly necessary is in accordance with Art 10 requirements: the convenience of the jury is not a sufficient reason for invoking the sub-section, since it would not fall within one of the legitimate aims of Art 10(2). Similarly, in *Ex parte The Telegraph plc*,[218] the Court of Appeal found that even where a substantial risk to proceedings might arise, this need not mean that an order must automatically be made. The court based this finding on the need to consider the two elements of s 4(2) separately; first, a substantial risk of prejudice to the administration of justice should be identified flowing from publication of matters relating to the trial, and, secondly, it should be asked whether it was necessary to make an order in order to avoid the risk. In making a determination as to the second limb, a judge should consider whether, in the light of the competing interest in open justice, the order should be made at all, and if so, with all or any of the restrictions sought. In the case in question, the order should not have been made, since the risk of prejudice was outweighed by the interest in open justice. In *MGN Pension Trustees Ltd v Bank of America National Trust and Saving Association*,[219] the Serious Fraud Office applied for an order postponing reporting of civil actions brought by trustees of the pension fund until after the criminal proceedings were concluded. Six newspapers opposed the application. The judge followed the steps indicated in *Ex parte The Telegraph* in determining that no order would be made.

---

217 [1991] 1 All ER 347.
218 [1993] 2 All ER 971.
219 [1995] EMLR 99.

These decisions suggests a concern on the part of the judiciary to prevent a ready use of s 4(2) orders, which would be prejudicial to the principle of open justice.[220] Incidentally, it is of some interest to note that this decision followed closely on that in *Attorney General v Guardian Newspapers (No 3)*,[221] which concerned an article written while a ban on reporting of a major fraud trial was in force, criticising the alleged propensity of judges in such trials to impose bans. It was held that the article created too remote a risk to constitute a contempt under the strict liability rule (see below), and Brooke J took the opportunity of re-emphasising the importance of the news media as the 'eyes and ears' of the general public. This approach was developed in *R v Beck ex parte Daily Telegraph*.[222] Beck, who had been a social worker in charge of children's homes, was charged with offences involving sexual abuse and, owing to the number of charges, the trial was split into three. At the first trial, a s 4(2) order was made, owing to the risk of prejudice to the subsequent two trials. On appeal, the Court of Appeal accepted that there was a substantial risk of prejudice, but went on to find that the public interest in the reporting of the trial outweighed the risk. In so finding, the Court emphasised the concern which the public must feel because of the particular facts of the case and the right of the public to be informed and to be able to ask questions about the opportunities created for those in public service to commit such offences.

The decisions discussed indicate that pre-HRA the domestic courts were already taking into account the demands of Arts 10 and 6 by reference to the principles underlying those two articles. The stance taken towards the role of journalists closely parallels that taken at Strasbourg, as indicated in Chapter 3.[223] A further practice direction, which also appears to be intended to ensure that the use of s 4(2) is Convention-compliant, was issued in 2002:

From 'Practice Direction (Criminal: consolidated)':[224]

3 Restrictions on reporting proceedings

. . .

3.2. When considering whether to make such an order [under s 4(2) or s 11] there is nothing which precludes the court from hearing a representative of the press. Indeed it is likely that the court will wish to do so. . . . [The Order continues in the same terms as the previous order.]

The important point is that this direction indicates that media representatives should be heard before the order is made, thus allowing them to challenge it in general and also to raise Art 10 points. However, even where the practice directions are followed, courts in making s 4(2) orders are under a duty due to s 6 HRA to ensure that the tests of necessity and proportionality under Art 10 are satisfied. This duty was not explicitly adverted to in the post-HRA decision in *Attorney General v Guardian Newspapers*[225] in which the reach of s 4(2) was widened and the tension between s 4(2) and s 2(2) was

---

220 See also *Saunders* (the Guinness trials) [1990] Crim LR 597; *Barlow Clowes Gilt Managers v Clowes, The Times*, 2 February 1990; *R v Sherwood ex p The Telegraph Group plc, The Times*, 12 June 2001.
221 [1992] 3 All ER 38.
222 [1993] 2 All ER 177.
223 See p 109.
224 [2002] 3 All ER 904, at pp 906–7.
225 [2001] EWCA Crim 1351.

exacerbated. The order in question in the case had been made in the criminal trial[226] of four Premiership footballers. During the trial the judge had given a direction that there was no evidence of a racial motive in the case. The jury retired to consider their verdicts and were eventually sent home for the weekend, still undecided.[227] That Sunday the *Sunday Mirror* published an interview with the father of the victim, which, in a double-page spread, with photographs, revived the allegations of racism.[228] The judge decided in consequence to discharge the jury. The *Sunday Mirror* article and the halting of the trial attracted a great deal of media publicity in a number of newspapers. The judge ordered that a retrial should take place and provisionally fixed the date for the retrial.

The judge had agreed to make an order under s 4(2) of the 1981 Act imposing stringent reporting restrictions. They covered any reference to material from the offending article and to racist motives in the case.[229] This order under s 4(2) was designed to obviate the possibility of prejudice to the future retrial. This order was the subject of the appeal by a number of newspapers under s 159 CJA. The main ground for the appeal was that the terms of the order were not limited to the publication of a report of the proceedings, or part of the proceedings, and therefore the order was made without jurisdiction. Without referring to the HRA, the Court of Appeal found that since the order concerned an article that had led to the halting of the trial: '[a]ny similar reporting or republication of [the *Sunday Mirror*] article or its contents, or discussion of the judge's reasons, after 10th April . . . would albeit indirectly, be a "report of part of the proceedings".' The order was able to cover reports intended to be published some time after the trial had been halted since it was found that such reporting could be treated as 'contemporaneous' due to the provision of s 4(3). It might have been expected, taking Art 10 into account, that a more media-friendly reading of s 4(3) – affording a more limited meaning to the term 'contemporaneous' – would have been adopted under s 3(1)HRA. However, this judgment exhibits the tendency, noted in other chapters of this book, to disregard the HRA even where a Convention article is clearly relevant.

Prohibiting reporting of information

Section 11 of the 1981 Act allows a court that has power to do so to make an order prohibiting publication of names or other matters if this appears necessary 'for the purpose

---

226 The order in question in the case had been made in the trial of four Premiership footballers, Woodgate, Bowyer, Clifford and Caverney, for offences of affray and causing grievous bodily harm with intent to Sarfraz Najeib. The case had of course attracted a considerable amount of publicity. See, for further discussion of the trial and the effect of the *Sunday Mirror* reporting, p 329, above.
227 On 4 April 2001.
228 It also included comments commending the evidence of a co-accused (who had by that time been acquitted) in suggesting that some of the remaining defendants, in relation to whom the jury were still considering their verdicts, were guilty.
229 The order was in the following terms: 1 There should be no further publication or broadcast of any matter contained within the headlines or the body of the article which appeared on pages 8 and 9 of the *Sunday Mirror* on 8 April 2001. 2 There should be no further reference in any publication or broadcast to the said article or headline, save for reference to the fact that this jury was discharged as a result of an article in the *Sunday Mirror*. 3 No publication or broadcast should make reference to racism or racist motivation in relation to the above proceedings. 4 For the avoidance of doubt, the above Order does not preclude publication or broadcast of any material relating to, or comment upon, the Macpherson Report, or issues of racism generally, provided that no reference in such publications or broadcasts is made to these proceedings.

for which it was so withheld'. Thus, s 11 does not itself confer such a power and therefore refers to other statutes[230] and to the imprecise common law powers. The leading authority is the House of Lords' decision in *Attorney General v Leveller Magazine Ltd*.[231] The majority found that if, in the course of regulating its own proceedings, a court makes an order designed to protect the due administration of justice, it is then incumbent on those who know of the ruling to do nothing which would frustrate the object of the ruling. At present, there are signs that a robust interpretation will be given to s 11 similar to that being taken to s 4(2): the fundamental importance of open justice will be outweighed only by a very clear detriment that answers to a general public interest flowing from publication of the matters in question – economic damage to the interests of the defendant will not suffice.[232] Nor will a concern to protect the 'comfort and feelings of the defendant'.[233] The courts may be prepared to make anonymity orders to protect the privacy of those involved in proceedings,[234] but only where the failure to afford anonymity would, under strict scrutiny, render the attainment of justice very doubtful.[235] Witnesses are placed in a somewhat different position. There is a clear public interest in encouraging witnesses to come forward and to cooperate in proceedings. Therefore, courts have shown a greater willingness to ensure the anonymity of witnesses.[236] If a court takes measures to protect the anonymity of witnesses such as sitting *in camera* or allowing the use of screens, there may be no need to make an express s 11 order.

Section 12(1) Administration of Justice Act 1960 adheres to the open justice principle in indicating that in general the reporting of private proceedings will not amount to a contempt in itself, before going on to specify the exceptional circumstances in which it will do so. It could therefore be said that in a sense the legal scheme relating to the first aspect of the open justice principle – that court hearings should be public – is more restrictive than that relating to the third – open reporting. Clearly, in practical terms, reporting of private hearings is often likely to be problematic, although those involved or witnesses may disclose matters to journalists, and so doing will not amount to a contempt so long as none of the exceptions under the 1960 Act apply.[237] Thus the mere fact that a hearing occurs in private does not automatically mean that reporting of the proceedings is restricted. Under s 12(1) of the 1960 Act it will only be a contempt to report on proceedings held in private where they relate to: wardship, adoption, guardianship, custody upbringing of or access to an infant; where they are brought under Part VII Mental Health Act 1983 or under any provision of the 1983 Act authorising an application or reference to be made to a mental health review tribunal or county court; where the court sits in private for reasons of national security; where the information relates to

---

230 A number of statutory provisions impose restrictions such as allowing certain persons concerned in a case to remain anonymous.

231 [1979] AC 440; [1979] 2 WLR 247, HL. For comment on s 11 of the 1981 Act, see Walker, C, Cram, I and Brogarth, D, 'The Reporting of Crown Court Proceedings and the Contempt of Court Act 1981' (1992) 55 MLR 647.

232 *R v Dover JJ ex p Dover DC and Wells* (1991) 156 JP 433; [1992] Crim LR 371.

233 *R v Evesham JJ ex p McDonagh* [1988] 1 QB 553, p 562.

234 See *H v Ministry of Defence* [1991] 2 QB 103 and *Criminal Injuries Compensation Board ex p A* [1992] COD 379.

235 *R v Westminster CC ex p Castelli and Tristan-Garcia* (1995) *The Times*, 14 August.

236 See *R v Watford Magistrates' Court ex p Lenman* [1993] Crim LR 388; *Taylor* [1994] TLR 484.

237 *Clibbery v Allan* [2001] FLR 819.

a secret process or invention at issue in the proceedings; where the court, acting within its powers, expressly prohibits the publication of all information relating to the proceedings or of information of the description which is published.

A report of information relating to all such proceedings is prima facie a contempt; it is not *automatically* a contempt since the section preserves all defences a person accused of contempt would normally have. Thus a conviction was not obtained where a newspaper editor published material relating to wardship proceedings without being aware of the connection.[238] It has been found that the press cannot report any aspect of wardship proceedings,[239] but this is not an absolute restriction: it has been found to cover 'statements of evidence, reports, accounts of interviews' and similar information.[240] The restrictions on reporting relating to children are largely intended to protect privacy, although the open justice principle may also be relevant.

The restrictions on the use of s 11 appear to render it compatible with Art 10. In *Atkinson Crook and the Independent v UK*[241] a journalist, Crook, had attempted to challenge a s 11 anonymity order: *Central Criminal Court ex parte Crook.*[242] When the challenge failed, Crook took the case to Strasbourg, arguing a breach of Art 10. In the circumstances of the trial it had been feared that matters disclosed in open proceedings might put the defendant's family at risk. The Commission found that the interest of the media in reporting arguments about the sentencing of a convicted defendant could be outweighed if, on reasonable grounds, the prosecution, the judge, and the defendant himself, wished to hear them in private.

Witnesses are placed in a somewhat different position. There is a clear public interest in encouraging witnesses to come forward and to cooperate in proceedings. Therefore, courts have shown a greater willingness to ensure the anonymity of witnesses.[243] And, clearly, if a court takes measures to protect the anonymity of witnesses, such as sitting in camera or allowing the use of screens, there may be no need to make an express s 11 order. Exceptionally, an injunction granted to protect the anonymity of a child may be extended, on grounds of the doctrine of confidence, once the child reaches 18. This was found in *Venables, Thompson v News Group Newspapers Ltd, Associated Newspapers Ltd, MGM Ltd.*[244] Although such a restraint relates to the administration of justice since it concerns an interference with the reporting of criminal justice matters, the object of the injunction is to protect privacy, not to protect a fair hearing, and therefore it is discussed in Chapter 10.[245]

A number of reporting restrictions are aimed at the protection of children. These reporting restrictions are discussed in Chapter 10[246] since they are mainly aimed at protecting privacy. However, it can also be argued that an aspect of the fair trial provision

---

238 *Re F (A Minor) (Publication of Information)* [1977] Fam 58.
239 See *Re X (A Minor) (Wardship: Injunction)* [1984] 1 WLR 1422 (the Mary Bell case).
240 *Re F (A Minor) (Publication of Information)* [1977] Fam 58, at 105.
241 (1990) 67 DR 244.
242 (1984) *The Times*, 8 November.
243 See *R v Watford Magistrates' Court, ex parte Lenman* [1993] Crim LR 388; *Taylor* [1994] TLR 484.
244 [2001] 1 All ER 908, Fam Div.
245 See pp 716–19.
246 See pp 717–19.

under Art 6(1) is to provide special protections for juveniles in the criminal justice system,[247] whether involved as witnesses or defendants. Under s 39 of the Children and Young Persons Act 1933 (CYPA), a court (apart from a Youth Court) could direct that details relating to a child, 'who was a witness or defendant, including his or her name', should not be reported and that 'no picture of the child should be broadcast or published'. The media could make representations to the judge, arguing that the demands of media freedom outweigh the possibility of harm to the child. Section 49 of the Act, as amended,[248] which relates to Youth Courts, now provides for an automatic ban on publishing certain identifying details relating to a juvenile offender, including his or her name and address, although the court can waive the ban. Under s 45 Crime (Sentences) Act 1997 (C(S)A), the court can lift reporting restrictions where it considers that a ban would be against the public interest.[249]

The s 39 restrictions were extended under s 44 of the Youth Justice and Criminal Evidence Act 1999, which now covers children involved in adult proceedings. The CYPA did not cover the period before proceedings begin. In contrast, the 1999 Act prohibits the publication once a criminal *investigation* has begun, of any matter relating to a person involved in an offence while he is under 18 that is likely to identify him. Thus, juveniles who are witnesses are also covered. Under s 44(4), the court can dispense with the restrictions if it is satisfied that it is in the public interest to do so. Thus, s 44 brings the restrictions relating to juveniles in adult proceedings into line with those under s 49 relating to youth proceedings, placing the onus on the court to find a good reason

---

247   See *Thompson and Venables v UK* (2000) 7 BHRC 659. It may be noted that r 5 of the Beijing Rules recommends that every juvenile justice system emphasise the well being of the juvenile and ensure that all reactions to such offenders are proportionate to the offence. The UN Convention on the Rights of the Child links fairness and privacy in relation to juveniles, Art 40(2)(b): every child has the right to the presumption of innocence, to informed promptly at the charges against him/her, to have the matter determined without delay by a competent and independent body, the right to silence, a right to an appeal, to understand the language used in proceedings and to have their privacy respected at each stage of the trial.

248   As amended by Sched 2 to the Youth Justice and Criminal Evidence Act 1999.

249   Section 45 provides:

   (1) After subsection (4) of section 49 of the 1933 Act (restrictions on reports of proceedings in which children or young persons are concerned) there shall be inserted the following subsections-

   (4A) If a court is satisfied that it is in the public interest to do so, it may, in relation to a child or young person who has been convicted of an offence, by order dispense to any specified extent with the requirements of this section in relation to any proceedings before it to which this section applies by virtue of subsection (2)(a) or (b) above, being proceedings relating to-
       (a) the prosecution or conviction of the offender for the offence;
       (b) the manner in which he, or his parent or guardian, should be dealt with in respect of the offence;
       (c) the enforcement, amendment, variation, revocation or discharge of any order made in respect of the offence;
       (d) where an attendance centre order is made in respect of the offence, the enforcement of any rules made under section 16(3) of the Criminal Justice Act 1982; or
       (e) where a secure training order is so made, the enforcement of any requirements imposed under section 3(7) of the Criminal Justice and Public Order Act 1994.

   (4B) A court shall not exercise its power under subsection (4A) above without-
       (a) affording the parties to the proceedings an opportunity to make representations; and
       (b) taking into account any representations which are duly made.

for lifting the restriction rather than having to find a good reason for imposing it. The discretion of the court is therefore more narrowly confined.[250] This is clearly an instance in which, as between the demands of press freedom and the interest in the protection of the privacy and reputation of juveniles, the latter interest has prevailed.[251]

A number of special restrictions also apply to the victims of certain sexual offences. Under s 4(1)(a) of the Sexual Offences (Amendment) Act 1976, once an allegation of rape was made it was an offence to publish or broadcast the name, address or photograph of the woman who was the alleged victim. Once a person was accused of rape, nothing could be published by the media which could identify the woman. These restrictions were extended under s 1(1) of the Sexual Offences (Amendment) Act 1992.[252] Section 1(1) covers a number of sexual offences as well as rape, and makes wider provision for anonymity: 'where an allegation has been made that an offence to which the Act applies has been committed against a person,[253] no matter relating to that person shall during that person's lifetime be included in any publication'. This restriction, unlike those considered above, is not subject to any exception. Therefore, in that respect, it affords less recognition to freedom of speech, although it does not prevent the reporting of the case or discussion of it once it is over, so long as details likely to identify the victim are not revealed.

Restrictions on the reporting of proceedings intended to preserve anonymity are likely to create conflict between Art 10, especially in relation to the interest in open justice, and the Art 8 guarantee of a right to respect for privacy. The main safeguard for media freedom is the possibility that the restrictions, apart from that of anonymity in relation to certain sexual offences, may be dispensed with in the public interest. In the HRA era, it would be expected that Art 10 jurisprudence would become an increasingly important influence upon the development of the public interest test. The granting of anonymity raises a number of Convention issues. From the perspective of Art 10, the imposition of anonymity clearly limits what can be reported about a case and may inhibit later reporting or discussion of any issues arising out of the case. However, such restrictions may be justifiable within the para 2 exceptions, which include 'for the rights of others'. The right to respect for privacy would therefore be covered, as would Art 6 rights. Therefore, the current emphasis on granting anonymity only on the basis that, otherwise, the administration of justice would suffer, is questionable. Courts are bound by Art 8; therefore witnesses, plaintiffs and defendants are able to argue in certain circumstances that anonymity should be granted even where such administration does not clearly demand it. If an order preserving anonymity is lifted it would appear that a breach of Art 6 would arise if the subject of the order had no means of challenging the lifting of the order, whether on the basis of the potential infringement of Art 8 that might arise or on the basis of his or her welfare within the criminal justice system. This argument was put in *R v Manchester Crown Court ex parte H and D*[254] in relation to the lifting of a s 39 CYPA order; the lifting of the order was challenged in the Divisional

---

250 See the discussion in *Lee* [1993] 1 WLR 103, pp 109–10.
251 See further Cram, I, *A Virtue Less Cloistered: Courts, Speech and Constitutions*, 2002, Hart, Chapter 4. See also Chapter 10, pp 717–18.
252 As amended by s 48 of the Youth Justice and Criminal Evidence Act 1999 and Sched 2.
253 Male victims are also covered, under the Criminal Justice and Public Order Act 1994, s 142.
254 [2000] 2 All ER 166.

Court, which found that it had jurisdiction to restore it under s 29(3) S(C)A. The Court however considered that clarifying legislation as to the scope of s 29(3) and s 159 CJA was required.

While Arts 6 and 10 may come into conflict in respect of anonymity granted to the defendant, they may have similar demands in respect of anonymity granted to witnesses. Allowing witnesses to give evidence behind screens or by means of a video link clearly raises Art 6 issues, as Strasbourg has accepted,[255] but it also raises Art 10 considerations. Again, argument could be raised under both articles to the effect that any measures affording anonymity to witnesses should be strictly scrutinised. But while arguments for anonymity might prevail under Art 10 since it is materially qualified, they would be less likely to do so under Art 6.

5 Protection of sources[256]

Introduction

The protection of sources is clearly vital to the role of journalists. As the Strasbourg Court put it in the seminal case of *Goodwin v UK*: 'Protection of journalistic sources is one of the basic conditions for press freedom.'[257] If sources do not believe that their identity will be protected, they will not normally contact journalists and, therefore, the most potent source of information, that of a person who is, in some sense, an 'insider', will be denied to them. If sources are afraid to come forward, the result will be that the public will not be informed on matters that are frequently of grave public interest, such as criminal activity, misconduct in public office or corruption in commercial organisations.

Thus, the use of and protection of sources serves a vital function in relation to the role of the media. In recognition of this, journalists view themselves as morally obliged to protect the identity of their sources, a principle that is recognised in cl 15 of the Press Complaints Commission Code.[258] Where the media exposes executive malpractice, it performs a vital constitutional role. In general, the speech generated, which relates to the matters mentioned, is of great value in a democracy and would be viewed as of the first importance within Art 10. Nevertheless, the protection it is afforded under UK law, is, it will be argued, inadequate.

Section 10 of the Contempt of Court Act

Section 10 of the 1981 Act states:

> No court may require a person to disclose, nor is any person guilty of contempt of court for refusing to disclose, the source of information contained in a publication for which he is responsible, unless it be established to the satisfaction of the court

---

255 See *Doorson v Netherlands* (1996) 22 EHRR 330.
256 For comment on s 10, see Allan, TRS 'Disclosure of Journalists' Sources, Civil Disobedience and the Rule of Law' [1991] CLJ 131; Miller, CJ 'The Contempt of Court Act 1981' CJ [1982] Crim LR 71.
257 (1996) 22 EHRR 123, at para 39.
258 For further comment on the Code, see Chapter 10, pp 711–12.

that disclosure is necessary in the interests of justice or national security or for the prevention of disorder or crime.

The exceptions regarding national security and the prevention of crime answer to the exceptions to Art 10. The term 'the interests of justice' is not repeated in para 2 of Art 10, although it may be covered to an extent by the term 'the preservation of the authority and impartiality of the judiciary' and, possibly, by the 'rights of others' exception. The key issue, therefore, is whether the interpretation of the term 'necessary' is compatible with the Strasbourg view of what is necessary in a democratic society in order to further those aims.

Section 10 does not provide any new power to require a journalist to disclose the identity of a source. As Lord Diplock put it in *Secretary of State for Defence v Guardian Newspapers*,[259] the leading case: 'Section 10 confers no powers upon a court additional to those powers, whether discretionary or not, which already existed at common law or under rules of court, to order disclosure of sources of information, its effect is restrictive only.' It was also determined in that case that s 10 will apply to the disclosure of information that might reveal the identity of the source. Thus, s 10 creates a presumption in favour of journalists who wish to protect their sources, which is, however, subject to four wide exceptions, the widest of which arises where the interests of justice require that disclosure should be made. It was found in *Secretary of State for Defence v Guardian Newspapers*[260] that disclosure of the identity of the source would only be ordered where this was necessary in order to identify him or her; if other means of identification were reasonably readily available, they should be used. On the other hand, this did not mean that all other means of inquiry which might reveal the identity of the source must be exhausted before disclosure would be ordered. The term 'necessary' was found in *Re an Inquiry under the Companies Security (Insider Dealing) Act 1985*[261] to mean something less than indispensable, but something more than useful. In *Guardian Newspapers* a civil servant, who considered that Parliament was being misled as regards the arrival of Cruise missiles in Britain, sent a photocopy of a memorandum regarding the timing to the *Guardian*, who published. The secretary of state wished to discover the identity of the civil servant and sought the return of the photocopy, since it would reveal the identity. The secretary of state, the plaintiff, claimed that the national security exception under s 10 applied on the basis that the fact of a secret document with restricted circulation relating to defence having come into the hands of a national newspaper was of great significance in relation to the maintenance of national security. The minority in the House of Lords were not convinced by this evidence, but the majority accepted it, Lord Bridge stating that any threat to national security ought to be eliminated by the speediest and most effective means possible. The identity of the source was duly discovered when the photocopy was returned and she was prosecuted. The majority, therefore, took the traditional stance of failing to afford a full scrutiny to imprecise claims of a threat to national security made by the executive. However, the House of Lords did suggest that more convincing evidence would be needed in future.

---

259 [1984] 3 All ER 601; [1985] AC 339, 347, HL.
260 [1985] AC 339.
261 [1988] 1 All ER 203.

The House of Lords clarified the nature of the balancing exercise to be carried out under s 10 in *X v Morgan Grampian Publishers*.[262] A confidential plan was stolen from the plaintiffs, a company named Tetra; information apparently from the plan was given by an unidentified source by phone to William Goodwin, a journalist. The plaintiffs applied for an order requiring Goodwin to disclose the source and sought discovery of his notes of the phone conversation in order to discover his or her identity. The House of Lords had to consider the application of s 10 to these facts. It found that when a journalist relies on s 10 in order to protect a source, it must be determined whether the applicant's right to take legal action against the source is outweighed by the journalist's interest in maintaining the promise of confidentiality made to him or her. The House of Lords took into account various factors in balancing these two considerations, including the threat to the plaintiffs' business and the complicity of the source in 'a gross breach of confidentiality'. Lord Bridge, with whom the other Law Lords unanimously agreed, found that the interest of the plaintiffs in identifying the source outweighed the interests of the journalist in protecting it. Goodwin refused to reveal the identity of the source and was fined £5,000 for refusing to obey the court's order.

The findings in the Lords were significant since they made it clear that a newspaper publishing information deriving from an employee of the plaintiff body in question would very frequently be ordered to disclose his or her identity, since the factors identified by Lord Bridge would almost always apply. In such instances there would almost always have been a breach of confidence (the judiciary are remarkably unwilling, in this context, to find that the public interest defence could have been made out)[263] and there would almost always be a threat, based on speculation, to the company. It would almost always be virtually impossible to rule that threat out, and the judiciary, as noted earlier, have not required any evidence to accept that the threat actually exists in any given instance: the mere fact that one disclosure has occurred is apparently sufficient. Clearly, an employee who has leaked information on one occasion might leak it again, but the likelihood of that occurring requires scrutiny, depending on the facts.

Thus, following the *Morgan Grampian* findings, the 'balancing' exercise appeared to be virtually a misnomer since once the factors identified were in the equation, it was unclear that they would ever be likely to be outweighed by the value of the information.[264] The term 'necessary' was being afforded very little weight: the key question was in reality whether the 'interests of justice' could be viewed as being at stake at all, and, as contended above, they inevitably would be. The Lords did find that very clear cases of exposing iniquity might mean that disclosure would not be ordered on the basis that the factors identified could be outweighed, but they made it clear that in most instances – outside such clear-cut cases – disclosure would be ordered. Lord Bridge mentioned the interest in protecting sources. However, when it came to conducting the balancing exercise, he considered that the public interest value of material would be a

---

262 [1991] AC 1; [1991] 2 All ER 1, HL.
263 See pp 377–78 below.
264 However, in *Chief Constable of Leicestershire v Gravelli* [1997] EMLR 543, DC, a case concerning revelations of malpractice in the police, it was found that in the circumstances of the case in question – disciplinary proceedings – it appeared that the interests of justice would not in fact be served by requiring the journalist to name her source. In other words, there could be no necessity to make such a demand when it was of viewed as of no, or virtually no, utility in the particular context that arose.

relevant factor, but he did *not* avert to the *general* and constant public interest in protecting sources in order to serve the interests of investigative journalism. That was the key error in the analysis. He did not set *that* factor against the need of the company to identify the untrustworthy employee. Since both interests would almost always be present in a source disclosure case they would always tend to need to be balanced against each other.

When Goodwin took his case to Strasbourg, it was made clear, it is argued, that the House of Lords had indeed failed to give proper weight to the term 'necessary' in s 10. Goodwin applied to the European Commission on Human Rights,[265] which gave its opinion that the order against Goodwin violated his right to freedom of expression under Art 10 of the Convention on Human Rights. When the case came before the Court it found that there was a vital public interest in protecting journalistic sources, since so doing was essential to the maintenance of a free press.[266] Thus, the margin of appreciation was circumscribed by that interest. It considered that limitations placed on the confidentiality of such sources would require the most careful scrutiny. Was the vital public interest in protecting sources outweighed by Tetra's interest in eliminating the threat of damage due to the dissemination of confidential material? The injunction was already effective in preventing the dissemination of such material and therefore the additional restriction on freedom of expression entailed by the disclosure order was not supported by sufficient reasons to satisfy the requirements of Art 10(2). Tetra's interest in disclosure, including its interest in unmasking a disloyal employee, was not outweighed by the public interest in the protection of journalistic sources. Taking these matters into account, it was found that the order was disproportionate to the purpose in question and therefore could not be said to be necessary. A breach of Art 10 was therefore established. The Court found:

> The court recalls that freedom of expression constitutes one of the essential foundations of a democratic society and that the safeguards to be afforded to the press are of particular importance. Protection of journalistic sources is one of the basic conditions for press freedom, as is reflected in the laws and the professional codes of conduct in a number of contracting states and is affirmed in several international instruments on journalistic freedoms. Without such protection, sources may be deterred from assisting the press in informing the public on matters of public interest. As a result the vital public watchdog role of the press may be undermined and the ability of the press to provide accurate and reliable information may be adversely affected. Having regard to the importance of the protection of journalistic sources for press freedom in a democratic society and the potentially chilling effect an order of source disclosure has on the exercise of that freedom, such a measure cannot be compatible with article 10 of the Convention unless it is justified by an overriding requirement in the public interest.[267]

Thus *Goodwin* made it clear that in *this* context the strictest form of scrutiny should be afforded to the application of the tests for proportionality. The Court insisted on looking

---

265 *Goodwin v UK* (1994) No 17488/90 Com Rep.
266 *Goodwin v UK* (1996) 22 EHRR 123. See also *Fressoz and Roire v France* (1999) 5 BHRC 654.
267 At para 39.

closely at the State's case regarding the degree of harm that Tetra had suffered, and took a view of it that differed significantly from that of the state. The interference was very severe, bearing in mind the significance for free expression of protection for journalistic sources. In coming to this conclusion the Court applied a strict test for scrutinising the balance between the two interests – had it conceded a wider margin of appreciation to the national authorities, it might have been satisfied that the balance struck between the two was not manifestly unreasonable. Thus the Court found that the proportionality test had not been met.

Despite the *Goodwin* decision, the government made no amendment to s 10. Subsequent court decisions do not provide reassurance that UK law protects journalistic sources to the extent envisaged in *Goodwin*. For example, in the immediate aftermath of *Goodwin*, the Court of Appeal, in *Camelot Group Ltd v Centaur Communications*,[268] allowed the 'necessary in the interests of justice' exception under s 10 a scope that was arguably as wide as that afforded to it in *X v Morgan Grampian*. The company, Camelot, runs the UK national lottery. An anonymous source sent Camelot's draft accounts to the newspaper, which published them. It appeared that Camelot was misleading the public regarding the dedication of the funds generated to charitable concerns. Camelot sought return of the documents in order to identify the source, and the newspaper relied on s 10.

Camelot had already obtained an injunction preventing any further dissemination of its accounts. Once the injunction had been obtained against Centaur, any other newspaper that published information covered by it would have risked liability for contempt of court as a result of the contempt ruling in the *Spycatcher* case, discussed in Chapter 8.[269] Therefore the disclosure order might have been viewed as disproportionate to the end in view. This was found to be the case in *Goodwin* in similar circumstances. The significance of the information itself might also have been taken into account in reaching this finding, since it concerned the accountability of a large and very profitable company, engaged, at least to an extent, in funding public and community services. On the *Goodwin* model the Court of Appeal could have balanced the weightiness of the expression interest against the degree of harm caused. In relation to the expression interest it could have taken account, not only of the significance of protecting sources, but also of the issues of public interest that are raised by the question of the proportion of lottery money that is diverted to community projects, and the like, and the proportion which is straightforward profit. There is clearly an important political dimension to Camelot's activities that might not arise to the same extent in respect of the activities of many private companies. In relation to the question of harm, it could have taken account of the effect of the injunction that was already in place.

Schiemann LJ, with whom the other judges concurred, concentrated, not on the public interest value of the information, but on the speculative harm to Camelot that might arise in future if the employee who had leaked the information, perpetrated further leaks:

> There is no threat now posed to the plaintiffs by further disclosure of the draft accounts. Such threat as there was has been dealt with by injunction or undertaking in relation to that material and the passage of time. There is however a continuing

---

268 [1998] EMLR 1; [1999] QB 124.
269 See p 518 *et seq.*

threat of damage of a type which did not feature significantly in the *Goodwin* case or in the *X v Morgan Grampian* case . . . Clearly there is unease and suspicion amongst the employees of the company which inhibits good working relationships. Clearly there is a risk that an employee who has proved untrustworthy in one regard may be untrustworthy in a different respect and reveal the name of, say, a public figure who has won a huge lottery prize.[270]

This speculative threat of damage was found to be sufficient to outweigh the interest in protecting sources. On the question of necessity the court found that the interests of Camelot in ensuring the loyalty of its employees and ex-employees should outweigh the public importance attached to the protection of sources. In the present instance, the Court considered that in any event, there was no public interest in protecting the source.[271] The Court of Appeal took the view that in reaching this finding it was applying the same test of necessity as was applied by the European Court of Human Rights in *Goodwin*.

Clearly, the term 'necessary in the interests of justice' used in s 10 leaves room for varying interpretations.[272] Nevertheless, the determinations as to necessity in *Camelot* and in *Goodwin* do not, it is contended, afford equal weight to the role of the media in informing the public. In asking whether the interference in question was proportionate to the legitimate aim pursued, the Strasbourg Court in *Goodwin* unpacked the 'harm' apparently caused, and applied a very high weight to the speech interest. In *Camelot* the court did not consider the question of proportionality as a distinct aspect of necessity and did not accord a high weight to source protection or look closely at the harm caused by the leak. Further, since the European Court of Human Rights allowed the domestic authorities a margin of appreciation (albeit highly circumscribed) in determining the issue of proportionality in *Goodwin*, one might have expected an even stricter view of the issue to be taken at the domestic level. It is argued that this threat did not provide a weighty enough basis for finding that the key *Goodwin* test for proportionality was satisfied, taking account of the strict scrutiny required.

Post-Human Rights Act jurisprudence

As cases arose under the HRA, bearing in mind the importance accorded at Strasbourg to the protection of sources under Art 10 as a vital part of the media's role, it was reasonable to expect at the least that the reasoning on the question of necessity would be affected by a determination to afford a stronger weight to the various media interests at stake[273] by applying the *Goodwin* test for proportionality under a strict form of scrutiny.

270 At p 138.
271 See e.g., p 139 of the judgment.
272 In two further cases, *Saunders v Punch Ltd* [1998] EMLR 1 and *John v Express Newspapers Ltd* [1998] 1 WLR 986, the courts arguably interpreted the word 'necessary' more narrowly than in *Camelot* so as to protect journalistic sources to a greater degree. Yet these cases did not concern employees of a company – someone who might potentially leak confidential information in the future – and consequently may be distinguished. In both cases it was highly unlikely a similar breach would happen again and so the courts were not being asked to consider the protection of a company from an untrustworthy employee, as in *Camelot* and *X v Morgan Grampion*.
273 See, for example, Feldman, D, in *Civil Liberties and Human Rights*, 2nd edn, 2002, p 856.

It appeared possible that an order to disclose the identity of a source would only be obtained in the most exceptional of circumstances and that Art 10 under the Human Rights Act would satisfy the role that had been assigned by some to s 10 of the 1981 Act, but which it had not fulfilled. The argument that *Goodwin* established a stricter standard than *Morgan Grampian* was put forward in *Camelot Group plc v Centaur Communications Ltd*[274] and rejected by Schiemann LJ; he held that the different result merely reflected the fact that different courts can reach different conclusions while applying the same legal principles to the same facts. However, Sedley LJ commented on this point in the post-HRA decision in *Interbrew SA v Financial Times Ltd*:[275] 'the decisions of the European Court of Human Rights demonstrate that the freedom of the press has in the past carried greater weight in Strasbourg that it has in the courts of this country'.

But it was already apparent that the strong established domestic traditions governing the approach of the courts ran counter to the Strasbourg jurisprudence. Therefore the possibility of departure from the jurisprudence, while appearing to adhere to it in a superficial or tokenistic fashion, became apparent. The key issue, therefore, in the post-HRA era was whether the interpretation of the term 'necessary' in s 10 would become fully consonant with the Strasbourg view of what is 'necessary in a democratic society' in order to further the aims in question.

In *Interbrew SA v Financial Times Ltd*[276] the claimant, the company Interbrew, maker of Stella Artois lager, was contemplating a possible takeover bid for another company, S. Interbrew's advisers prepared a presentation which they submitted to the company. Subsequently, an unidentified person obtained a copy of the presentation. The document referred to the intention of Interbrew to launch the bid. Most of the document was genuine, but whoever leaked it also doctored it to include a fabricated offer price and timetable. He or she then sent copies of the doctored version to various news media, including the defendants. The defendants then published articles about the takeover bid. The claimants applied for an order requiring the defendants to deliver up the copies of the presentation they had received so that there could be an attempt to identify the source. The defendants invoked s 10 of the Contempt of Court Act 1981, but the judge made the order sought. He took the view that the doctored leak had been perpetrated in order to affect S's share price. Since this would, on the face of it, be a criminal act, he considered that it would be in the public interest for Interbrew to be given the documents to try to trace the source. The defendants appealed.

The appeal therefore concerned the scope of the right of a newspaper to refuse to reveal its sources within the bounds of Art 10, applied under ss 3 and 6 HRA. The Court began by considering the effect of reading and applying s 10, so far as possible, compatibly with the Convention rights under s 3(1) HRA. Sedley LJ said, on the question of the meaning of the term 'interests of justice' in s 10 of the 1981 Act, that the Court of Appeal in *Ashworth*[277] (discussed below) had followed the line of authority now accepted as dominant, which attributes a broader meaning to the phrase 'the interests of

274 [1999] QB 124 (pp 367–68 above) at p 135.
275 [2002] EMLR 24 at para 97.
276 [2002] EMLR 24; [2002] EWCA Civ 274, CA.
277 [2001] 1 WLR 515 1 All ER 991, CA.

justice' in s 10 of the Contempt of Court Act 1981 than was initially given to it in *Secretary of State for Defence v Guardian Newspapers*,[278] where Lord Diplock had limited it to the technical interests of the administration of justice in court proceedings. He said: 'By common consent our approach is that of Lord Bridge in *X v Morgan-Grampian*:[279] the phrase is large enough to include the exercise of legal rights and self-protection from legal wrongs, whether or not by court action.' He further found that the term 'interests of justice' in s 10 means 'interests that are justiciable' and said that he could not envisage any such interest that would not fall within one or more of the catalogue of legitimate aims in Art 10(2).

The Court went on to consider whether the use of the disclosure order was necessary and proportionate to the aim in view – to protect the interests of justice, and one or more of the Art 10(2) aims. Sedley LJ went on to find that the term 'necessary' within s 10 must mean what is 'necessary in a democratic society' within Art 10(2). He found that this meant, 'to be necessary within what is now the meaning of section 10, disclosure must meet a pressing social need, must be the only practical way of doing so, must be accompanied by safeguards against abuse and must not be such as to destroy the essence of the primary right'. He also asked whether the importance of disclosure outweighed the public interest in protecting journalist's sources. He went on to find that it was clear that a democratic society accepts the need to protect press sources. Therefore it must be possible to identify a strong countervailing 'pressing social need' to set on the other side of the scale. The need was, he found, in terms of s 10, to enable Interbrew to restrain by court action any further breach of confidence by the source and possibly to recover damages for losses already sustained. In terms of Art 10(2) it was to protect the rights of Interbrew. No less invasive alternative had to be available – which appeared to be the case. So there were two significant interests on both sides of the scale. On the one hand, then, it was found that there was 'the legitimacy of Interbrew's intended resort to law'. On the other there was a constant public interest in the confidentiality of media sources.

The critical factor identified by the court in determining where the balance lay between the two interests was the source's evident purpose. Sedley LJ found that it was clearly a malevolent one. The public interest in protecting the source of such a leak was not, he considered, sufficient to withstand the countervailing public interest in letting Interbrew seek justice in the courts against the source. Therefore the order of disclosure was upheld, and the House of Lords refused leave to appeal[280] on the ground that the issues had been dealt with in the *Ashworth* case, below.

As will be contended in more detail below, this judgment did not fully apply the *Goodwin* speech/harm balancing test. It did not examine the two interests at stake in a sufficiently rigorous fashion. In particular it appeared to give less weight to the unvarying and strong interest in protecting sources than *Goodwin* did – in a fairly similar situation – although in *Goodwin* the source did not seem to be activated by malice. As part of the subsequent saga, lawyers for Interbrew immediately wrote to the organisations demanding that the document be handed over. Interbrew went on to ask the High Court to seize the *Guardian*'s assets for refusing to hand over a copy of the leaked document.

---

278   [1985] AC 339 at p 350.
279   [1999] 1 AC 1 at p 43.
280   On 11 July 2002.

However, after an outcry against the company in the media and in government, which might have affected its brand image, Interbrew withdrew its threat to seize the assets. It announced that it had abandoned its legal action against the *Guardian* and three other media organisations, the *Financial Times* and *The Times*, the *Independent* and Reuters, in the attempt to recover the leaked documents.[281]

Nevertheless, the newspapers complained to the ECtHR and were successful. In *Financial Times v UK*,[282] the ECtHR again found (as it had in *Goodwin*) that the UK courts had not attributed sufficient weight to the importance of preserving journalistic sources and had also attributed too much weight to the 'malevolent' intentions of the source. In particular, the Court stressed the general importance of the right: that any interference with the principle was capable of undermining the organs of the press and the security that sources felt in knowing their identity was safe from disclosure. More specifically, however, the ECtHR felt that the UK courts had been provided with compelling evidence of the source's malevolence and had, instead, relied too heavily on inference. It stated:

> While the Court considers that there may be circumstances in which the source's harmful purpose would in itself constitute a relevant and sufficient reason to make a disclosure order, the legal proceedings against the applicants did not allow X's purpose to be ascertained with the necessary degree of certainty. The Court would therefore not place significant weight on X's alleged purpose in the present case.[283]

The Court also thought it relevant that Interbrew had not sought to protect its legitimate interests by seeking an injunction to restrain the publication of commercially sensitive confidential information. Instead, they had taken the more extreme measure of identifying the source of the leak. Overall, therefore, the Court could not agree that Interbrew's interests sufficiently outweighed the strong Art 10 right to protect a source. This decision is further proof of the UK's inadequate approach.

Even in *Ashworth Hospital Authority v MGN Ltd*[284] where a somewhat stricter approach was taken to the interests of the media in protecting sources, the process of reasoning and the outcome were similar to those in *Interbrew*. The appeal concerned the right of a newspaper to refuse to reveal its sources. It arose from the publication of an article in the *Daily Mirror* which included extracts from the medical records of Ian Brady (one of the Moors murderers), a patient at Ashworth Security Hospital ('Ashworth'). He was, at the time of the publication, engaged on a hunger strike that had received a great deal of publicity.[285] In April 2000, Rougier J ordered the defendant, MGN Ltd, the publisher of the *Daily Mirror*, to make and serve upon the authority

---

281 On 26 July 2002.
282 [2010] EMLR 21.
283 *Ibid*, [66].
284 [2002] 1 WLR 2033; [2002] 4 All ER 193 HL; [2001] 1 WLR 515 1 All ER 991, CA.
285 On 2 February 2000, Ian Brady obtained permission to apply for judicial review, in order to challenge the continuing decision to force-feed him (see *R (Brady) v Ashworth Hospital Authority* [2000] Lloyd's Med R 355; (2001) 58 BMLR 173). Maurice Kay J ruled that force-feeding was lawful since it was reasonably administered as part of the medical treatment given for the mental disorder from which Ian Brady was suffering.

a witness statement aimed at identifying the source who had passed on the medical records.[286]

Following successive appeals, the case was heard by the House of Lords. MGN argued that the order should not have been granted, taking account of s 10 of the 1981 Act and Art 10. Although the court agreed that both s 10 and Art 10 have a common purpose in seeking to enhance the freedom of the press by protecting journalistic sources, they held that the duty to protect patient confidentiality was of a higher order and found for the trust. Giving the leading judgment, Lord Woolf found:

> The situation here is exceptional, as it was in *Financial Times Ltd v Interbrew SA* and as it has to be, if disclosure of sources is to be justified. The care of patients at Ashworth is fraught with difficulty and danger. The disclosure of the patients' records increases that difficulty and danger and to deter the same or similar wrongdoing in the future it was essential that the source should be identified and punished. This was what made the orders to disclose necessary and proportionate and justified. The fact that Ian Brady had himself disclosed his medical history did not detract from the need to prevent staff from revealing medical records of patients.

Lord Woolf also referred to the approach of the European Court to medical records in relation to Art 8 in *Z v Finland*.[287] The Court had found that:

> the protection of personal data, not least medical data, is of fundamental importance to a person's enjoyment of his or her right to respect for private and family life as guaranteed by Art 8 of the Convention. Respecting the confidentiality of health data is a vital principle in the legal systems of all the contracting parties to the Convention. The domestic law must therefore afford appropriate safeguards to prevent any such communication or disclosure of personal health data as may be inconsistent with the guarantees in Art 8 of the Convention.

In dismissing the appeal, Lord Woolf did not examine the question of proportionality in detail, but appeared to assume impliedly that since there was such a pressing need to protect medical records in the instant case, the measure in question was proportionate to the aim pursued. Thus he did not engage in a full application of the *Goodwin* proportionality tests under a strict level of scrutiny.

Some hope that the UK courts recognise the importance of protecting journalistic sources is offered by the Court of Appeal decision in *Mersey Care NHS Trust v Ackroyd (No 2)*.[288] This case concerned the aftermath of the House of Lords decision in *Ashworth Hospital Authority*. In that case, MGN had admitted that the information had come not

---

286 The statement, to be served within two working days, demanded of the publisher that it: (i) explain how it came to be in the possession or control of any medical records kept by the claimant in respect of Ian Brady whether that possession or control be of originals, copies or extracts; (ii) identify any employee of the claimant and the name of the person or persons (and any address, telephone and fax numbers known for such a person or persons) who were involved in the defendant acquiring possession or control of the said records.

287 (1998) 25 EHRR 371, [94] and [95].

288 [2008] EMLR 1.

from an employee but an intermediary. Compiling with the disclosure order, they identified the intermediary as Robin Ackroyd, an experienced freelance reporter with particular expertise on hospitals. Like MGN, Ackroyd refused to say who had given him the information. At first instance, Tugendhat J refused to compel Mr Ackroyd to disclose his source. In particular, he did not accept that it was necessary to do so. He took into account that the circumstances had changed radically since the time of the House of Lords decision. During that four-year period there had been no further disclosures, suggesting that the source had left the hospital. He also took account of Ackroyd's record as a responsible journalist and the absence of any apparent financial motive on the source's part to supply the medical information. The Court of Appeal dismissed the appeal. Agreeing with Tugendhat J's treatment of the competing issues, the court noted:

> the carrying out of that balance was essentially a matter for the judge, with whose conclusion this court. . .should not interfere unless persuaded that he erred in principle in carrying out the balancing exercise, or that he reached a conclusion that a reasonable judge could not have reached after having had regard to all relevant considerations.[289]

Whether this decision shows a preparedness to take the Art 10 claims more seriously in claims involving the protection of sources is debatable. Clearly, on any analysis, the circumstances had changed significantly over the four-year period since the House of Lords decision. Specifically, the concern of further leaks could be gauged more accurately. Presumably, though, the order would have been given had further leaks emerged, which is not necessarily compatible with the ECtHR decisions in *Goodwin* and *Financial Times*.

Flaws in the post-HRA judicial reasoning

As the ECtHR recognised in *Financial Times*, the domestic decisions clearly do not offer reassurance to sources who are uncertain whether to come forward. It could be argued that the source in the *Interbrew* case came forward for his or her own (arguably improper) motives and was hardly in the position of the source who is activated by conscience in seeking to reveal wrongdoing but is afraid of the repercussions. But potential sources are unlikely to understand the nuances of the decisions, but may merely receive the message that the protection for their anonymity is in jeopardy. It might appear in general that the courts are overzealously protecting the right of institutions or companies to bring actions against employees and others. Their tendency to envisage the potential harm that could be done to companies in clear and concrete terms remains very apparent, although they now also afford at least some degree of recognition to the interest in source protection. Although it is understandable that the courts would want to protect the right to bring an action where there is a legitimate grievance, the net result may be that companies are aided in seeking to maintain effective cover-ups.

In *Ashworth*, wrongdoing was not perceived as being revealed. It appears that unless it is revealed, freedom of expression may be at risk of being outweighed by varying public

289 *Ibid*, [80].

interests in disclosure of the identity of the source, *despite* the unvarying nature of the interest in protecting sources. The findings in *Ashworth* and in *Interbrew* stand in contrast to each other, to an extent. In *Ashworth*, now the leading decision, the importance of protecting sources was recognised in the test laid down for determining the 'necessity' of ordering disclosure. If the protection of sources is regarded as an inherent and constant public interest, the other party is forced into the position of seeking to establish very weighty reasons for displacing that interest. Thus the judgment of the court has to focus on the particulars of that other party's claim. This was a significant departure from *Interbrew*, since in that instance the focus of the decision was on the source's culpability rather than on identifying a clear public interest in disclosure of his or her identity. In *Ackroyd (No 2)* the test from *Ashworth* was applied, resulting in the finding that the need to preserve patient confidentiality could not represent an automatic justification for ordering disclosure: it would be necessary to consider the facts in any particular instance.

The House of Lords in *Ashworth* purported to do what the European Court did in *Goodwin*, but, it is argued, mis-weighed both the harm done to the privacy interest and the value of the speech. The Lords took the view that the protection of sources is in *itself* a highly significant public interest, regardless of the specifics of the case in question and the objective value of the information disclosed. That finding, relying on *Goodwin*, was clearly correct. But the point was not made clearly enough that the *converse* finding does not apply. In other words, where the information *is* of value in public interest terms it should weigh in the calculus as *another* weighty factor in favour of non-disclosure of the source, meaning that the other party would have to provide reasons of an exceptionally weighty nature pointing in the direction of disclosure. This point is of relevance to the key *Goodwin* proportionality test – weighing up the seriousness of the interference with speech against the importance of the aim that the plaintiff is seeking to pursue and the harm done to that interest. The seriousness can be judged in terms of its *extent* or its nature, or both. In this instance both aspects were at stake. In terms of *nature* the interference was serious for the reasons indicated: two weighty speech-based arguments went in favour of non-disclosure of the source's identity – the general interest in protecting sources, affirmed in *Goodwin*, and the public interest value of the information. In terms of extent, the interference was also serious since, unlike an injunction, which can be tailored to a particular situation, a source disclosure order is an all-or-nothing measure. The consequences for the source would have been very serious, and other sources at the hospital would have been deterred from coming forward. Thus it is arguable that, on strict scrutiny, this test would not have been found to be satisfied in *Ashworth*, meaning that the infringement of Art 10 would not have been viewed as justified.

This analysis is now, however, complicated where another Convention article – usually Art 8 – can be invoked as part of the justification for source disclosure. This was the case in *Ashworth*, as the House of Lords impliedly indicated in its references to *Z v Finland*. The term 'parallel analysis' was not used, but after the House of Lords' decisions in *Campbell*[290] and in *Re S*,[291] it is now clear that this is the proper means of weighing up two Convention articles against each other,[292] except in certain narrowly defined

---

290 [2004] 2 WLR 1232; see Chapter 10, pp 748–52 for further discussion of the decision.
291 [2005] 1 AC 593; [2004] UKHL 47. See Chapter 10, pp 748–52 for further discussion of the decision.
292 See Chapter 10, pp 748–61 for a full discussion of the use of the 'parallel analysis'.

(and anomalous) exceptional circumstances.[293] In fact, prior to *Ashworth*, it had already been found in *Douglas v Hello!*[294] that this was the proper method of proceeding where an apparent clash of rights arose. It might be thought at first sight that where another Convention right is engaged the standard of scrutiny from *Goodwin* is not applicable since *Goodwin* was not a clashing rights case, but a case in which an exception based on a societal concern had to be narrowly construed. At Strasbourg a wide margin of appreciation tends to be afforded in the case of clashing rights and therefore the standard of scrutiny is less strict.[295] However, as argued in Chapter 10, this is not and should not be the approach taken at the domestic level.[296] There are a number of reasons why the approaches at the domestic and the international levels inevitably differ. The most valuable precedent for future source disclosure cases involving a clash of rights is that of the House of Lords in *Campbell* in which, in a different context, but where Arts 8 and 10 were both engaged, a strict standard of scrutiny was adopted.[297] The precedent of *Von Hannover*[298] could also be taken into account, in which, unusually, Strasbourg did not concede a wide margin of appreciation in a case of a collision between Arts 8 and 10.

Had the parallel analysis been fully conducted in *Ashworth*, as arguably it should have been, it would have reached the stage of balancing the underlying values of both Arts 8 and 10 against each other. It would have been necessary to examine the restriction each article proposed to lay on the other and to ask which right would suffer the greater harm if the other prevailed. The question whether the invasion of Art 10 (via the source disclosure order) went further than necessary to protect the Art 8 right at stake should have been asked.

On the other side, the interference with the Art 8 rights of Brady as a patient was serious: the preservation of the confidentiality of medical records is itself recognised at Strasbourg as an unvarying and consistent public interest.[299] But in terms of *this particular context* the interference was of a less serious nature. The history of mismanagement at the hospital was not viewed as relevant in *Ashworth* for various reasons. In fact it was highly relevant in relation to the weightiness of the patient confidentiality claim *and* the claim for non-disclosure of the source. It was relevant to the former claim due to the particular context in question in which the key argument for preserving patient confidentiality was put forward. It could readily be argued that where patients themselves have deliberately breached their own confidentiality in order to serve a more pressing cause – to reveal the abuses suffered by patients at the hospital – that creates a particular focus from which to view the interest in preserving confidentiality. In the instance in question two patients, including Brady himself, had breached confidentiality with that end in view. In general, in terms of the experience of being in a secure hospital and in terms of treatment, patients are likely to view the interest in confidentiality as

---

293 See Chapter 10, pp 752–61 for further discussion. It is possible that eventually the courts may decide that there are no exceptional circumstances – there are merely instances in which the speech in question is especially valuable since it relates to the open justice principle.

294 [2001] QB 967. See Chapter 10, pp 757–59 for further discussion of the decision.

295 See Chapter 10, pp 725–29 for discussion.

296 See Chapter 10, pp 746–48 for discussion.

297 See Chapter 10, p 748 for discussion.

298 (2004) Appl No 59320/00, judgment of 24 June 2004; see in particular paras 63, 64, 65, 66.

299 See *Plon (Société) v France* No 58148/00.

outweighed by the interest in preventing the suffering and humiliation of patients due to maltreatment. In the hierarchy of interests relating to the hospital experience, the prevention of maltreatment – by exposing it – looms higher than the preservation of confidentiality.

It must be re-emphasised that this argument is being applied to the value of pre-serving patient confidentiality in a highly context-sensitive fashion, and on the basis, endorsed by *Goodwin*, of an intense scrutiny. It is undoubted that there is *general* value in enabling persons to be reassured that their medical records will remain confidential, and the Lords were clearly right to refer to that value. It has since been endorsed by the European Court of Human Rights in *Plon (Société) v France*[300] as an interest that can win out even when opposed by the countervailing interest in political speech. But while the Lords were right to place weight on the *general* value of preserving patient confidentiality, they failed to examine the very particular context in question which, it is argued, undermined that value as an individual right, or countered it. Thus, the general societal interest in preserving medical confidentiality remained of significance, but the interference with Brady's Art 8 right was of less significance than it would have been in a different context. The value of the parallel analysis and of concentration on the speech/harm balancing test from *Goodwin* is precisely that this method teases out the values genuinely at stake.

In the context of maltreatment, then, the preservation of patient confidentiality, gener-ally of very high importance, may be viewed as a near meaningless abstraction divorced from the idea of serving any worthwhile purpose. Indeed, it came close to being used in *Ashworth* in a perversion of its original purpose. Preservation of patient confidentiality is rooted in ideas about the intimacy of details of medical treatment – in itself linked to notions of humiliation and embarrassment. If that treatment itself directly causes humiliation – as was alleged in abundance in relation to Ashworth Hospital – then the underlying basis for maintaining confidentiality is undermined. Although it was true that the *Mirror* article in question did not directly concern mismanagement at Ash-worth, disclosure of the identity of the source was clearly likely to aid in the continuing attempt of the Ashworth management to cover up the failings there. Thus the ruling preserved patient confidentiality in a technical or formal sense without succeeding in examining the *real* value of that confidentiality in the circumstances. Lord Woolf relied on *Z v Finland* in relation to the value of confidentiality of medical records encapsu-lated in Art 8. But he failed to take account of other competing values underlying Art 8, including the preservation of dignity and privacy of patients in hospitals such as Ash-worth, or the general interest in the prevention of harm to patients, which would have pointed in the direction of protecting the source in order to aid in uncovering abuses of power in the hospital. However, there are precedents in a different context for weighing up such competing values.

In a series of cases the courts have recognised that the public interest in protect-ing patients, or potential patients, from harm outweighs the interest in maintaining the confidentiality of medical records.[301] In *Re A (Disclosure of Medical Records to the*

---

300 No 58148/00, 18 May 2004.

301 This has also been recognised legislatively: the Data Protection (Processing of Sensitive Personal Data) Order 2000, SI 2000/417, Sched para 2, allows disclosure for regulatory purposes if in the public interest.

GMC),[302] it was found that production of medical records could be justified on the ground of protecting persons from possible medical misconduct, even where the risk of such conduct is not established. Similarly, in *A Health Authority v X*,[303] at first instance, it was found that there was a public interest in the disclosure of health care records in order to aid in an investigation into a certain GP. Serious allegations had been made of misconduct and unsatisfactory standards of care, although these had not been substantiated. Further, in *Woolgar v Chief Constable of Sussex*[304] a patient in a nurse's care had died in suspicious circumstances. Disclosure of the medical records was authorised for disciplinary purposes to the United Kingdom Central Council for Nursing, Midwifery and Health Visiting on the basis of the general public interest of the proper regulation of the nursing profession in the interests of those receiving nursing care.

It was essential in *Ashworth* to identify the relevant Art 8 values at stake, under a strict level of scrutiny, in order to determine the seriousness of the interference, weighing it against the importance of the speech, without affording either value presumptive priority. In this instance, although interference with patient confidentiality had occurred, the more significant value at stake was that of the humiliation and indignity suffered by patients at the hospital, especially Brady. Publicity *aided* in addressing that matter and thus affected both aspects of the speech/privacy balancing analysis. The more significant privacy interest – the humiliation suffered by patients, which sought publicity – overcame, it is argued, the interest in confidentiality. Therefore the interference with the right to respect for private life – the disclosure of the notes to the newspaper – was proportionate to the legitimate aim pursued, that of preserving the Art 10 rights of the newspaper (under the Art 8(2) 'rights of others' exception). No breach of Art 8 occurred on this analysis.

In terms of the second half of the parallel analysis, conducted under Art 10(2), it is clear that under a strict scrutiny a very serious interference with speech rights occurred that was not justified by the aim pursued – the Art 8 rights of others. The discussion reveals that the unhappy history of the hospital was relevant to the claim for non-disclosure of the identity of the source in *Ashworth* on a basis other than that of the general interest in protecting sources: thus there was a *heightened* interest in non-disclosure. That interest arose in the context of a matter of grave public interest – a context that the House of Lords was aware of but chose not to place weight on. The fact that in the instance in question the revelations arguably did not add much of significance to discussions of the situation at Ashworth was not the end of the matter. Any order of disclosure was bound to have some broad stifling effect in a number of respects in relation to a matter of grave public interest. In other words, their Lordships should have looked beyond the specifics of the revelations in question, to that general effect in such a significant context. Had these factors been taken into account, and then weighed up in the calculus of proportionality, under the speech/harm balancing test, it is argued that the decision would have gone the other way since the doubly strong public interest on the side of non-disclosure would have outweighed the relatively weak public interest – in the particular context – of preserving patient confidentiality. The values enshrined in Art 3 could also have been taken into account in the balancing act since the disclosures were relevant to

302 [1998] 2 FLR 641, p 644.
303 [2001] 2 FLR 673, p 677.
304 [1999] 3 All ER 604 at p 615.

the use of degrading treatment.[305] Revelations leading to the uncovering of Art 3 treatment should surely be afforded a high value in speech terms.

Despite purporting to take account of Art 10, and in particular of the test of necessity, the House of Lords' decision fell into the trap, typical of British judicial reasoning, of assuming a narrow and technical basis, divorced from the realities of the context in question. Further, it may be argued that the source disclosure order went further than was needed to serve the end of preserving the value of confidentiality since an action for breach of confidence was available against the newspaper (although it might have failed on public interest grounds), and consequently the interference was disproportionate to the end pursued. Therefore it should have been found that a breach of Art 10, but not of Art 8, would occur if the source disclosure order was upheld.

Ackroyd (No 2) dealt more fully with the proportionality aspects of the instance before it, although the parallel analysis was not conducted. The decision focused on the lack of payment to the source and the chilling effect on other sources at the hospital if disclosure was ordered. If the interest in protecting sources is viewed as constant, those are significant factors in terms of *heightening* that interest. The unhappy history of mismanagement and abuse of power at the hospital was considered in relation to the nature of the interference, but it should have been taken into account both in relation to the preservation of confidentiality *and* in respect of the claim for non-disclosure of the source, as argued above. In other words, it potentially affected both sides of the speech/harm equation, diminishing the importance of the aim pursued (medical confidentiality) and enhancing the significance of the interference with freedom of expression. Following this argument, *Ackroyd (No 2)* reached the right result.

If the more complete version of the doctrine of proportionality argued for here – speech/harm balancing – had been applied to the facts of *Interbrew*, there is a strong argument that a breach of Art 10 would have been found. In *Interbrew* any weighing up of Arts 10 and 8 against each other would have had to concern the 'privacy' of a company. Although companies may have certain rights to private life and to protection for correspondence,[306] that argument has been accepted at Strasbourg only in relation to search and seizure of material from a company's premises.[307] It is unlikely that disclosure of information relating to a company could be viewed as ' "private" information'. Revelations as to share prices and the like are prima facie of a public character: Art 8 would be found to be unengaged or only peripherally engaged in such an instance. In *Interbrew* then it may be argued that the Art 10 claim did not have to be balanced by a

---

305 For example, Brady was quite seriously injured in the course of subjecting him to force-feeding, and a child was allowed unsupervised visits in the hospital and was subjected to sexual abuse on a number of occasions. Art 3 provides 'No-one shall be subjected to torture or inhuman or degrading treatment.'

306 See *R v Broadcasting Standards Commission ex p BBC* [2000] 3 WLR 1327 (concerning the privacy of the company Dixons).

307 In *Société Colas Est v France* (2002) Application No 37971/97 at para 41 the Court found: 'the time has come to hold that in certain circumstances the rights guaranteed by Art 8 of the Convention may be construed as including the right to respect for a company's registered office, branches or other business premises . . .'. However, the protection at present extends only to physical searches of the company's premises; it would not appear to cover information relating to it or held by it (although obviously the company personnel would have individual Art 8 rights to their own private information held in the company's files).

strong – or any – Art 8 claim. So the case was arguably correctly viewed as one in which Art 10 had presumptive priority, subject to exceptions to be narrowly construed.

Since another Convention right was not at stake, or barely at stake, the parallel analysis was not applicable and the interests of Interbrew were rightly viewed by Sedley LJ as protected only by Art 10(2) exceptions to be narrowly construed. The exception in question appeared to be that of 'the rights of others'. In this context, the case of *Chassagnou v France*[308] is of relevance. The Court said in that case that when dealing with 'rights of others' that are not themselves competing Convention rights, 'only indisputable imperatives can justify interference with enjoyment of a Convention right'. *Chassagnou* was not referred to in *Interbrew*, but it might be asked whether Interbrew's interest in bringing a legal action was an indisputable imperative. In any event, the public interest involved in requiring source disclosure was clearly less significant than that in *Ashworth* since an individual Convention right was not involved, and therefore the case for allowing it to outweigh the interest in protecting the confidentiality of media sources was less strong. Following *Goodwin*, that is a strong and unvarying interest; it would have had to be outweighed by a very compelling countervailing interest if it was to be overcome; on the facts that did not appear to be the case.

In *Interbrew*, Sedley LJ purported to use the *Goodwin* speech/harm balancing test, but when it came to weighing up the two interests against each other he allowed the apparently malevolent attitude of the source to undermine the interest in protecting sources, despite accepting at an earlier point in the judgment that that interest should be viewed as constant. If that interest had been viewed as constant it is argued that it would have outweighed the interest of Interbrew in resorting to law since source disclosure cases inevitably involve a desire to seek legal redress: thus there was no especially pressing need in this instance to aid Interbrew in seeking such redress. He said on this point: 'the relatively modest leak of which they are entitled to complain does not diminish the prospective seriousness for them of its repetition'.[309] This point could also have been made in *Goodwin*; it was highly speculative, and relied only on a possibility of future harm. It is suggested that this nebulous possibility of harm should not have been allowed to outweigh the constant interest in protecting sources. Had the *Goodwin* test been properly applied at this crucial point in the analysis, it is argued that a different outcome would have been reached.

The *Interbrew* decision is likely to deter those who have, prima facie, purer motives for leaking information – to expose malpractice in a powerful corporate player. Arguably, if the *Goodwin* speech/harm balancing test is applied, it is clear that the impact of such deterrence was not given sufficient weight when balanced against the interest of the company in the right to pursue an action for breach of confidence. Moreover, the other possible sanctions that could be brought to bear in relation to this (arguably successful) attempt to 'rig' the market by the Financial Services Authority (FSA) could have been taken into account and afforded greater weight in the reasoning on proportionality in relation to the 'least intrusive means' inquiry. In other words, in so far as wrong-doing had occurred, another means of redress was potentially available which was likely to deter many persons from seeking to promulgate financial misinformation. The interests of Interbrew were not therefore without protection due to the existence and powers of

---

308 (2000) 29 EHRR 615.
309 At para 54.

the FSA. Therefore, not only was the speech interest more weighty than the countervailing interest of Interbrew, but the interference represented by the source disclosure order went further than necessary to pursue the aim of protecting those interests.

The argument here is not only that an intense focus on the true values at stake in any particular instance is necessary in the proportionality analysis. It is also that judges should be wary of making unfounded assumptions about sources. Although, following *Ashworth*, the protection of sources has been accepted as a strong and unvarying interest, it appears that particular factors in a situation can strengthen the free speech claim under the *Goodwin* proportionality test. In *Ackroyd*, for example, they did so. But in *Interbrew* they were viewed as weakening it, and this appears now to be an illegitimate stance to take since it takes no account of the general deterrent effect on potential sources of source disclosure in a particular instance. This point may be made about a number of the cases discussed in this chapter; it is further enhanced since the matters that have sometimes tipped the balance in relation to the test of necessity often turned out to rest on judicial 'commonsense' and assumptions. Many of the pre- and post-HRA cases discussed rested on uncertain assumptions, which then turned out to be erroneous.[310] In *Ashworth* the assumption was made that the source was a dishonest employee motivated by greed. *Ackroyd v Mersey Care NHS Trust* showed that the sources were in fact motivated by the desire to expose malpractice at the hospital. The assumption is also often made that the source, if undetected, will continue to leak confidential information. But, as argued above, *Guardian Newspapers* indicated that this is not necessarily the case.

Seizure of journalistic material

This section moves on to look at the seizure of journalistic material in order to aid in criminal or terrorist investigations. Clearly, journalists will quite frequently possess material in the form of documents or film obtained as a result of pursuing a particular investigative story. The next section considers a selection of the key powers allowing for the seizure of journalistic material. In each case the information obtained might include material identifying sources. Even where that is not the case, seizure of such material affects press freedom, not only because it hampers the collection of information, but also because if journalists are viewed as likely to be forced to aid police investigative efforts, contacts and others may refuse to cooperate with them. Journalists might also be put at risk when, for example, trying to film or report on demonstrations, since those involved would be likely to be concerned about the use to which the material gathered could be put.

A partial 'shield' against seizure of journalistic material is provided in the key seizure power under the Police and Criminal Evidence Act (PACE) 1984. But despite the significance of the other powers, they contain no express protection for media freedom. No common law privilege against seizure of press material exists[311] and it appears, as discussed below, that where sources might be revealed by such seizure s 10 of the 1981

---

310 For example, as mentioned earlier, the assumption was made in *Guardian Newspapers* that the source was a senior Civil Servant, which turned out to be not to be the case.
311 See *Senior Holdsworth ex p Independent TV News* [1976] 1 QB 23.

Act nevertheless does not apply to any of the powers. However, some protection for press material could be imposed upon them since all these powers should of course be rendered compatible with Art 10, taking account of *Goodwin*, under s 3(1) HRA if at all possible. Following *Goodwin* some mechanism should be available within these powers to allow for the weighing up of the interest in protecting sources against the countervailing public interest in preventing crime or protecting national security that the power in question seeks to serve. Article 8 may also be applicable. As indicated above, Strasbourg has found that companies may have certain rights to private life and to protection for correspondence in the context of search and seizure of material from their premises.[312] A search and seizure of journalistic material could therefore engage both articles. Further, since all those involved in using the powers are public authorities (the police, the courts, civil servants), they should, under s 6 HRA, comply with Arts 10 and 8 in exercising them. The real possibilities of protecting the identity of sources where the varying powers are exercised are discussed below.

Search and seizure of journalistic material under the Police and Criminal Evidence Act 1984

The main search and seizure powers are provided in PACE, Part II.[313] The orders allowed for are intended to force journalists to disclose material where so doing is likely to assist in a criminal investigation, but certain restrictive conditions have to be met. Under s 9 PACE a search warrant cannot be issued in respect of journalistic material; a production order has to be sought under Sched 1, which can be challenged in an *inter partes* hearing before a circuit judge on the basis that the access conditions have not been met. This position is similar to that applying in the US, where such a hearing can be held, if necessary, and investigators cannot obtain the specified material by applying only for a search warrant.[314]

The protection is afforded to journalists against seizure of journalistic material by designating it as either excluded or special procedure material and then placing special conditions on obtaining access to it. Section 11 governs excluded material. Such material consists, *inter alia*, of documentary journalistic material[315] held in confidence[316] and can only be seized if the special restrictions under Sched 1 to PACE are satisfied. The provisions allow for production orders to be made by a judge only if there is reasonable

---

312   In *Société Colas Est v France* (2002) Application No 37971/97 at para 41 the Court found: 'the time has come to hold that in certain circumstances the rights guaranteed by Art 8 of the Convention may be construed as including the right to respect for a company's registered office, branches or other business premises . . .'.

313   For comment on these provisions see: Stone, R, *The Law of Entry, Search and Seizure*, 4th edn, 2005, OUP; Zander, M, *The Police and Criminal Evidence Act 1984*, 4th edn, 2003, Sweet and Maxwell; Feldman, D, *The Law Relating to Entry, Search and Seizure*, 1986, Butterworths; Stone, R, [1988] Crim LR 498.

314   94 Stat 1879 (1980).

315   Defined in s 13 as material created or acquired for the purposes of journalism – a circular definition that obviously is unhelpful in determining the limits of the privilege. It clearly covers material gathered for such purposes even if the material itself is not eventually published. See further Feldman, D, (2002) *ibid* on this point at 104–6.

316   Section 11(1)(c). Journalistic material is not afforded as much protection as legally privileged material, covered by s 10; no access to such material is allowed at all.

suspicion that the material is on the premises specified and that, but for s 9(2) PACE, it would have been possible and appropriate for a search warrant to have been issued.[317] Under s 14 non-confidential journalistic material is termed special procedure material and can only be seized if a serious arrestable offence has been committed and the material is on the premises and is likely to be of substantial value to the investigation. It must also be in the public interest to make the order, taking account of the benefit to the investigation and the circumstances under which it is held.[318] It is clearly of significance that the public interest requirement only applies to non-confidential journalistic material. It was intended as a safeguard but it has been subverted by judicial interpretation; pre-HRA it appeared that it would always be assumed to be served where the material would be of substantial benefit to the investigation or relevant in evidence.[319] However, this interpretation renders the inclusion of the public interest requirement otiose. This point is discussed further below.

Section 8(1) PACE covers general powers of search and seizure for material other than excluded material (s 8(1)(d)). The ruling in *Guildhall Magistrates' Court ex p Primlacks Holdings Co (Panama) Ltd*[320] made it clear that a magistrate must satisfy him or herself that there are reasonable grounds for believing that the items covered by the warrant do not include material subject to the special protection. The Criminal Justice and Police Act 2001 (CJP) s 50 extends the power of seizure very significantly. The further new power of seizure under s 50(2) allows the person in question to seize material that he has no power to seize but that is attached to an object he does have the power to seize, if it is not reasonably practicable to separate the two, and this includes the specially protected material.[321] Section 50 may serve to undermine the protection for journalistic certain material since where such material is part of other material and cannot practicably be separated, it can be seized.

Sections 50, 54 and 55 CJP taken together provide avenues to the seizure and use of journalistic material.[322] The provisions thus circumvent the limitations placed on the

---

317 Sched 1, para 3.
318 Sched 1, para 2.
319 See: *R v Bristol Crown Court ex p Bristol Press and Picture Agency Ltd* (1986) 85 Cr App R 190; *Chief Constable of Avon and Somerset Police v Bristol United Press*, *Independent*, 4 November 1986.
320 [1989] 2 WLR 841. The magistrates had issued search warrants authorising the search of two solicitors' firms. Judicial review of the magistrates' decision to issue a warrant was successfully sought; it was found that the magistrate had merely accepted the police officer's view that s 8(1)(d) was satisfied rather than independently considering the matter.
321 The further powers of seizure it provides in s 50 apply to police powers of search under PACE and also to powers of seizure arising under a range of other statutes and applicable to bodies other than police officers, as set out in Sched 1 of the CJP. This provision is significant since, *inter alia*, it allows police officers to remove items from premises even where they are not certain that – apart from s 50 – they have the power to do so. Thus a number of items can now be seized from media premises although no power of seizure – apart from that now arising under s 50 – in fact arises. It can also be seized where a police officer takes the view on reasonable grounds that it is something that he has the power to seize, although it turns out later that it falls within one of the special categories.
322 Special provisions are made under the 2001 Act for, *inter alia*, the return of excluded material. Under s 54 such material must be returned unless it falls within s 54(2). Section 57(3) provides that ss 53–56 do not authorise the retention of property where its retention would not be authorised apart from the provisions of Part 2 of the CJP. Under s 62 inextricably linked property cannot be examined or copied, but under sub-s (4) can be used to the extent that its use facilitates the use of property in which the inextricably linked property is comprised.

seizure of excluded material and, most importantly, mean that information contained in the material, identifying sources, will have been passed to the police even though the material is subsequently returned. It can be said that for the first time journalistic material has lost part of the protection it was accorded under PACE. These wide CJP powers are 'balanced' by the provisions of ss 52–61, which provide a number of safeguards.[323] Under s 60 a duty to secure the property arises which includes the obligation under s 61 to prevent, *inter alia*, copying of it. But despite these safeguards, it is unclear that the new powers, especially to seize and use journalistic material, are compatible with the requirements of the Convention under the HRA, as discussed below.

Production orders under the Terrorism Act 2000; requirements to provide information under the terrorism legislation

Schedule 7, para 3(5) of the Prevention of Terrorism (Temporary Provisions) Act 1989 provided for the production of material relating to terrorism if such production would be in the public interest. When inquiries relating to terrorist offences were made, Sched 7, para 3(5) allowed access to special procedure and excluded material. This provision was replaced by an equivalent provision under the Terrorism Act 2000, Sched 5. The judge only needs to be satisfied that there is a terrorist investigation in being, that the material would substantially assist it and that it is in the public interest that it should be produced. This procedure creates an exception to the PACE, Sched 1 special access conditions[324] and so can be viewed as undermining the PACE shield provisions. A police officer of the rank of superintendent or above can authorise a search if satisfied that immediate action is necessary since the case is one of great urgency.[325] It appears that once the first two requirements are satisfied, it will be rare to find that the third is not.[326]

It was assumed in *Director of Public Prosecutions v Channel Four Television Co Ltd*[327] that the existence of the Sched 7 provision meant that the making of an order precluded a defence under s 10 Contempt of Court Act. The potential danger of Sched 7 – now Sched 5 – in terms of media freedom was shown in that case. Channel 4 screened a programme in its Dispatches series called 'The Committee', which was based on the allegations of an anonymous source (Source A) that the RUC and Loyalist paramilitaries had colluded in the assassination of Republicans. The police successfully applied under Sched 7, para 3(5) for orders disclosing information that would probably uncover the identity of Source A. Channel 4 refused to comply with the orders on the ground that to do so would expose Source A to almost certain death and it was then committed for contempt of court. It attempted to rely on the public interest provision of Sched 7 in arguing that it was in the public interest for the identity of Source A to be protected,

---

323 Notice must be given to persons whose property has been seized under s 52, and under s 59 he or she can apply to the 'appropriate judicial authority' for the return of the whole or part of the seized property, on the ground that there was no power to seize, or that excluded material is not comprised in other property as provided for in ss 54 and 55.
324 This is also the case in respect of drug trafficking: see Drug Trafficking Act 1994, ss 55, 56.
325 Para 31.
326 See above fn 324.
327 [1993] 2 All ER 517.

but this was rejected on the following grounds. Channel 4 should not have given an unqualified assurance of protection to the source even though, had it not done so, the programme could probably not have been made, because so doing was likely to lead to flouting of the provisions of the Prevention of Terrorism (Temporary Provisions) Act 1989. Thus, giving such assurances could inevitably undermine the rule of law and therefore, it was held, help to achieve the very result that the terrorists in Northern Ireland were seeking to bring about. Channel 4 was therefore fined for non-compliance with the orders. In determining the amount of the fine, it was borne in mind that the defendants might not have appreciated the dangers of giving an unqualified assurance, but a warning was given that this consideration would be unlikely to influence courts in future cases of this nature. This ruling fails to accord sufficient weight to the public interest in the protection of journalistic sources in order to allow the media to fulfil its role of informing the public. The comment that the assurances given to Source A as a necessary precondition to publication of this material would undermine the rule of law, ignores the possibility that undermining of the rule of law might be most likely to flow from the behaviour alleged in the programme: it might appear that nothing would be more likely to undermine the rule of law than collusion between state security forces and terrorists. The decision not to impose a rolling fine on Channel 4 or make a seques-tration order may be welcomed in the interests of press freedom, but it is clear that such indulgence may be refused in future, thereby creating a significant curb on investigative journalism. Schedule 7, para 3(5), as interpreted in that instance, arguably breached Art 10. The power under the Terrorism Act 2000 affords primacy to national security without explicitly providing a defence for journalists.

This point was particularly apparent in the decision of *R (Miranda) v Secretary of State for the Home Department*.[328] The case concerned David Miranda, the partner of a journalist, who had obtained from Edward Snowden, the fugitive former NSA opera-tive, computer drives containing classified, encrypted data, some of which was UK related. Acting on intelligence that Miranda might have this classified information, the UK port authorities stopped him at Heathrow airport and seized the drives. This action was defended on the basis that Miranda was holding material severely damaging to UK national security interests, especially if published. Miranda sought judicial review of this decision and, in particular, asked whether the power conferred under the Terrorism Act 2000 was incompatible with Art 10. The High Court, though, was satisfied that there had been no such disproportionate interference on the facts. They noted that the case concerned 'two aspects of the public interest: press freedom itself on one hand, and on the other . . . national security'.[329] The court took into account the fact that the claim-ant was not a journalist and carrying journalistic material only in a very weak sense.[330] It was also held that Sched 7 did not offend Art 10 in a more general sense. The court found that the provisions contain four limitations to ensure compatibility with Art 10. First, that it requires there to be a reasoned basis for the interference, that is propor-tionate and made in good faith. Secondly, that the Act contains a sufficiently narrow meaning of the term terrorism in s 1(1)(b) and (c). Thirdly, that the provisions can only

328 [2014] EWHC 255 (Admin).
329 *Ibid*, [73].
330 *Ibid*, [72].

be exercised in limited circumstances, i.e. where the individual is in a port or border area and finally that they are limited in time to the period of nine hours detention. These safeguards were sufficient to ensure compatibility with Art 10.[331]

The current terrorism legislation, discussed fully in Chapter 15, provides a number of provisions criminalising failures to disclose information. They contain no journalistic shields at all, although they could clearly have an application to journalists. On their face, the obtaining of journalistic material is treated in precisely the same way as seizure of other material. Under s 19 Terrorism Act 2000 it is an offence to fail to report information to the police that comes to one's attention in the course of a trade, profession, business or employment and which might be of material assistance in preventing an act of terrorism or in arresting someone carrying out such an act.[332] Section 38B Anti-Terrorism Crime and Security Act 2001 broadens this provision immensely: it makes it an offence, subject to an un-explicated defence of reasonable excuse, for a person to fail to disclose to a police officer any information that he knows or believes *might* be of material assistance in preventing an act of terrorism or securing the apprehension or conviction of a person involved in such an act. A further wide range of people are potentially subject to criminal penalties under s 58(1) Terrorism Act 2000, the provision relating to the collection of information, which is based on s 16B Prevention of Terrorism (Temporary Provisions) Act 1989. Section 58(1) provides: 'A person commits an offence if (a) he collects or makes a record of information of a kind likely to be useful to a person committing or preparing an act of terrorism, or (b) he possesses a document or record containing information of that kind.' The offence lacks any requirement of *knowledge* regarding the nature of the information or any requirement that the person *intended* to use it in order to further the aims of terrorism, although a defence of 'reasonable excuse' is provided.

Powers under the Official Secrets Act 1989 s 8(4)

The Official Secrets Act 1989 s 8(4) makes it an offence for a person (this would normally be a journalist) to fail to comply with an official direction for the return or disposal of information that is the subject of s 5, and that is in their possession or control. Section 5, discussed in Chapter 8,[333] is headed 'information resulting from unauthorised disclosures or entrusted in confidence'. This is not a new category of information. Information will fall within s 5 if it falls within one or more of the previous categories (under ss 1, 2, 3, 4, discussed in Chapter 8) and it has been disclosed to the defendant by a Crown servant or falls within s 1 of the Official Secrets Act 1911. Section 5 is primarily aimed at journalists who receive information leaked to them by Crown servants, although it could of course cover anybody in that position.[334]

---

331 *Ibid*, [31] and [89].
332 Subsection (5) preserves an exemption in respect of legal advisers' privileged material.
333 See pp 503–04.
334 It is also aimed at the person to whom a document is entrusted by a Crown servant 'on terms requiring it to be held in confidence or in circumstances in which the Crown servant or government contractor could reasonably expect that it would be so held' (s 5(1)(ii)). The difference between entrusting and disclosing is significant in that, in the former instance, the document – but not the information it contains – will have been entrusted to the care of the person in question.

As s 5 is aimed at journalists and potentially represents an interference with their role in informing the public, it requires a very strict interpretation under s 3(1) HRA, in accordance with Art 10, bearing in mind the emphasis placed by Strasbourg on the importance of that role.[335] The fact that journalists were included at all in the net of criminal liability under s 5 has been greatly criticised on the basis that some recognition should be given to the important role of the press in informing the public about government policy and actions.[336] In arguing for a restrictive interpretation of ss 8(4) and 5 under s 3 of the HRA, a comparison could be drawn with the constitutional role of the press recognised in America by the *Pentagon Papers* case.[337]

Human Rights Act implications

Where journalistic material is seized, potentially revealing the identity of sources, Art 10 is engaged, as *Goodwin* made clear. The powers discussed, apart from the PACE power, make no express provision themselves for balancing the needs of criminal investigations against the requirements of Art 10. The powers must, however, be read and applied under the HRA compatibly with Art 10. If a source might be revealed by the exercise of the power, it would appear prima facie that s 10 of the Contempt of Court Act would apply. In *Secretary of State for Defence v Guardian Newspapers*,[338] it was found that, on its true construction, s 10 applied to all judicial proceedings irrespective of their nature, or the claim or cause of action in respect of which they had been brought.[339] However, the later decision in *Director of Public Prosecutions v Channel Four Television Co Ltd and Another* found otherwise, in relation to the Terrorism Act production power. Thus by analogy it might be argued, if the question of source disclosure arose, that s 10 does not apply to the other provisions, in PACE and the Official Secrets Act. One way out of this problem would be to argue that since there is ambiguity as to the question of the applicability of s 10 to all the powers discussed, it should be taken to apply, overruling the *Channel Four* case on that point. It is a pre-HRA case and therefore subject to over-ruling via s 3 HRA. The argument would be that s 10 should be read, in reliance on s 3(1), as applying to all provisions requiring the production of material, where that would lead to the disclosure of the identity of a source.

If this argument is not accepted in a suitable case, it could in any event be argued that Art 10 could be applied to the provisions via ss 6 and 3 HRA, and since s 10 has been rendered virtually synonymous with Art 10, as discussed in the main part of this chapter, source protection could be made available by that route. Clearly, the problem would be that these provisions do not make specific provision for source protection, so the courts would have to seek to read into them defences that do not exist. It could be argued at the least that it would be anomalous, given the protection offered to sources by both Art 10 and s 10, to consider ordering the seizure of journalistic material, revealing sources,

---

335 See, e.g., *Goodwin v UK* (1996) 22 EHRR 123.
336 See, e.g., Ewing, K and Gearty, C, *Freedom under Thatcher*, 1990, Chapter 6, pp 196–201.
337 *New York Times Co v US* (1971) 403 US 713. the Supreme Court determined that no restraining order on the press could be made in order to protect the role of journalism in relation to government scrutiny.
338 [1984] 3 All ER 601; [1985] AC 339, 347, HL.
339 At pp 349B–D, 356E–F, 362D–G, 368G–369A, 372A–C.

without taking account of the free expression implications as a specific and distinct exercise. So where the provisions offer any discretion to the court as to application or sentence, the factor of source protection should be influential via ss 3 and 6 HRA. That factor affected the sentence, as discussed, in the *Channel Four* case.

The special procedure under s 9 of and Sched 1 to PACE allow for production orders to be made only if the material is likely to be of *substantial* value to the investigation. That term could be used to limit the authorising of such orders where the identity of sources might be likely to be disclosed. A similar argument could be used in relation to the production power under the Terrorism Act 2000, Sched 5 since it can be invoked only if the material would substantially assist the investigation. Further, and more significantly, it must be in the public interest under PACE Sched 1, para 2 and under the Terrorism Act 2000 for the order to be made. That term would allow leeway to a court to impose an Art 10-based interpretation on the provisions, relying on s 3 HRA, Art 10 and *Goodwin*. The public interest could be read as requiring that the court should balance the needs of the investigation against the public interest in source protection. Indeed, Sched 1 para 2 lends itself to this interpretation since it requires the court to consider the benefit to the investigation *and* the circumstances under which the material was held.[340] In other words, a strong countervailing public interest would have to be shown in order to overcome the strong and constant interest in protecting sources. Admittedly, as *Miranda* shows, national security concerns will satisfy this requirement and the courts tend to be particularly deferential to the state where it is at stake. Yet *Miranda* is not necessarily a disappointing outcome from an Art 10 perspective. The difficulty in that case was the weakness of the freedom of expression claim. The fact of Miranda not being a journalist seems neither here nor there, but the court's view on the nature of the materials is significant. The materials being conveyed was the source information and had not been manipulated by the journalist, Miranda's partner. The public interest argument might, therefore, have been stronger if what was seized was a transcript of an interview between Snowden and a journalist. This does not mean that Miranda's claim would have succeeded necessarily but it would have made the balancing act more difficult for the judge. One proportionate method of interference in those circumstances would be to redact the most sensitive information. Although it is likely a court would still defer to the state on what counted as 'sensitive', in those circumstances, at least, permanent and total seizure could be viewed as disproportionate. Since this issue did not arise in *Miranda* it was not explored.

Additionally, where journalistic material was seized *without* revealing the identity of a source, Art 10 would still be applicable via ss 3 and 6 HRA, but the strong interest in protecting sources would not be engaged. It must be noted that it is not a prerequisite of the engagement of Art 10 that the seizure of the material would inevitably reveal the source; it is sufficient that it would be likely to do so.[341] The provisions under the

---

340 Sched 1, para 2.
341 In *Guardian Newspapers ibid*, Lord Bridge said (at p 372): 'Secondly, is it sufficient to attract the protection of the section that the order of the court in dispute *may*, although it will not necessarily, have the effect of disclosing a "source of information" to which the section applies? In agreement with Griffiths LJ and with all your Lordships I would answer both these questions in the affirmative for the reasons given in the judgment of Griffiths LJ [1984] Ch 156, and in the speeches of my noble and learned friends, Lord Diplock and Lord Roskill, with which I fully agree.'

terrorism legislation requiring provision of information are subject to defences of a reasonable excuse for failing to comply. That term would allow leeway to a court to impose an Art 10-based interpretation on the provisions, relying on s 3 HRA and Art 10. Once a journalist had put forward the excuse that the material had been collected for the purposes of journalism, this would enable a court to balance the value of the information in revealing terrorist activity against the public interest in protecting journalistic material in determining its reasonableness.

As mentioned above, companies can claim Art 8 rights to private life and to protection for correspondence where search and seizure of material from their premises has occurred.[342] Where a search and seizure of journalistic material takes place on the premises of a media organisation Art 10 as well as Art 8 is relevant. Even where a production order had been properly obtained, argument could be raised regarding the *effects* of the search, as *Ozgur Gundem v Turkey*[343] demonstrates. The Court found that the search operation at the newspaper's premises, which resulted in newspaper production being disrupted for two days, constituted a serious interference with the applicants' freedom of expression. It accepted that the operation was conducted according to a procedure 'prescribed by law' for the purpose of preventing crime and disorder within the meaning of the second paragraph of Art 10. It did not, however, find that a measure of such dimension was proportionate to this aim. No justification had been provided for the seizure of the newspaper's archives, documentation and library.

It has been argued that the judiciary have not provided sufficient protection for journalistic material.[344] Both Arts 8 and 10 could be relied upon in arguing that a production order under s 9 and Sched 1 PACE should not be issued on grounds of disproportionality. This occurred in *R v Central Criminal Court ex p Bright*.[345] Judicial review was sought of production orders under s 9 PACE. The orders concerned material relating to David Shayler, a former employee of MI5 who had made allegations about the involvement of MI6 in a plot to assassinate Colonel Gaddafi. The *Guardian* had published an e-mailed letter from Shayler; the *Observer* had published an article about his allegations; production orders were sought to obtain material from both newspapers regarding Shayler.

The court had to consider the principles to be applied. Judge LJ found that the judge personally must be satisfied that the statutory requirements have been established. The question to be asked was not whether the decision of the constable making the application was reasonable, nor whether it would be susceptible to judicial review on *Wednesbury* grounds. He found that this followed from the express wording of the statute: 'if . . . a circuit judge is satisfied that one . . . of the sets of access conditions is fulfilled' and considered that, '[t]he purpose of this provision is to interpose between the opinion of the police officer seeking the order and the consequences to the individual or organisation to whom the order is addressed, the safeguard of a judgment and decision of a circuit judge'.[346] Further, the material to be produced or disclosed could not be

---

342　See *Société Colas Est v France* (2002) Application No 37971/97 at para 41, fn 441 above.
343　(2001) 31 EHRR 49.
344　Costigan, R [1996] Crim LR 231.
345　[2001] 2 All ER 244.
346　At para 73 of the judgment.

merely general information which might be helpful to police inquiries, but relevant and admissible evidence. Once it was found that the relevant set of access conditions was fulfilled, it was made clear that the judge is empowered, but not bound, to make the order. The basis for refusing the order was found in the conditions stated to be relevant to the 'public interest' in para 2(c). It was found that this provision allows the judge to take account of matters not expressly referred to in the set of relevant access conditions including fundamental principles.

In adopting this approach the judge relied on *R v Bristol Crown Court ex p Bristol Press and Picture Agency Ltd*[347] in which Glidewell LJ noted with approval that the judge at the Crown court had rightly taken into account both 'the importance of the impartiality and independence of the press', and 'the importance of ensuring that members of the press can photograph and report what is going on without fear of their personal safety'. In the case of journalistic material the judge considered that the potential stifling of public debate could be taken into account. He did not consider that it was necessary to take account of Art 10 of the European Convention on the basis that the principles it encapsulates are: 'bred in the bone of the common law'.[348] Taking the public interest in freedom of expression into account, the judge decided that the orders must be quashed. The findings in that case were made just before the HRA came fully into force. The comments of Judge J as to the relationship between the ECHR jurisprudence and common law principle provide encouragement to argument that under the HRA such orders should not be made where the journalistic material is sought and there is a strong public interest in the material in question. The judge making the order would be bound by s 6 HRA and therefore he or she would have to take account of Strasbourg jurisprudence, unless it was clear that a result consistent with that required by Art 10 would be arrived at by following common law principles. Where the material revealed the identity of sources, that jurisprudence should be relied on since it provides the strongest statement of principle, as discussed above, regarding the significance of protecting sources.

Conclusions

Where s 10 of the 1981 Act applies, source protection has been enhanced in the UK post-HRA. But it is clear that where it does *not*, journalistic material that may reveal the identity of a source may be obtained under coercion in a range of circumstances, and that little leeway for Art 10 arguments has so far been made available. The duties of the courts under ss 6 and 3 HRA make this position no longer sustainable; where scope is available under the relevant provisions for speech/harm balancing, it must be explored, and in particular the 'public interest' provision under Sched 1, para 2 PACE requires reinterpretation.

The pre-HRA domestic decisions discussed above reveal that despite the introduction of s 10 the domestic courts were not affording the same weight to media freedom in examining the need for source disclosure as that afforded at Strasbourg, as revealed in the strong judgment in the *Goodwin* case. In particular, the 'interests of

---

347 (1987) 85 CAR 190.
348 At para 82 of the judgment.

justice' exception was being applied in a manner that afforded greater weight to the right of institutions to take legal action than to the principle of freedom of expression. This approach has now been modified by the decision in *Ashworth*, which did evince a determination to apply Art 10 under the HRA correctly, since it fully recognised the constant and unvarying interest in protecting sources. The findings in *Ashworth* demonstrate, however, that there is still a failure to engage fully with the Strasbourg reasoning process in respect of the doctrine of proportionality. The courts' approach to this journalistic privilege still appears to depend very much on the *nature* of the other interest at stake. The real *extent* to which it might be damaged still appears to be a largely subordinate consideration. If an employee of a company appears to be the source, that fact continues to have a very significant influence on the judicial response, while the stance taken under the national security exception presumably would not differ significantly from that taken in *Guardian Newspapers*.

The judges consider that the stance they are now taking is in accordance with the Strasbourg one. This chapter has argued that this is not the case – the judges have misapplied *Goodwin*. The ECtHR decision in *Financial Times* would seem to reinforce that conclusion. *Interbrew* suggests that they appear to prefer the means/end balancing proportionality test rather than the speech/harm balancing act. Where speech/harm balancing has occurred, as in *Ashworth*, the level of scrutiny adopted has not been strict enough. If that level of scrutiny was used, and use was made of the parallel analysis from *Campbell* where Art 8 is engaged, the analytical tools made available to the judiciary would allow for a more effective teasing out of the values at stake in any particular instance. The true value of confidentiality in the circumstances could be gauged. But on the other side of the coin, where sources appeared to be motivated by a desire to 'spin' or 'doctor' the information in question, the general interest in source protection would remain unvarying, but other speech arguments, based on the public interest value of the information, would be undermined since the speech rationale from truth would be lightly engaged at best.

In relation to the question of necessity a change has occurred. The difference, post-*Goodwin*, is that the Strasbourg Court has found that there is an unvarying interest in source protection. So there has to be a clear and strong interest to set on the other side *other than* the plaintiff's apparent desire to bring an action. The unvarying interest in protecting sources cannot be outweighed by the legitimacy of a resort to law alone since that would always be a factor. In *Interbrew* the other special feature was the malevolent purpose of the source; in *Ashworth* it was the interest in medical confidentiality. In both instances it is arguable that the courts did not examine the nature of that other factor closely since they were inclined towards the outcome achieved. There has been no post-HRA case yet where it would be difficult to identify a special factor *but* the source might perpetrate further leaks. *Camelot* arguably provided an example pre-HRA. How would the courts react in such an instance? In reality two interests would be opposed. First, there would be the interest of the company or institution in protecting its confidential information – something that the judges take very seriously. On the other side, there would be an imported notion, from *Goodwin*, of the need to protect sources – a matter that has not traditionally struck the judiciary as appealing. If a *Camelot* type of case arose post-*Ashworth* it would pose an interesting dilemma for the judges.

It may be asked *why* the British judiciary are traditionally disinclined to protect sources. First, it seems to be for the reason given earlier, that they can readily envisage the concrete harm done to a company by a leak, the 'ticking bomb argument', but the opposing interest strikes them as much more nebulous. Second, there appears to be a suspicion of s 10. It was introduced by a Labour government as a deliberate means of overturning a House of Lords' decision in the wake of a case with a controversial political dimension. The judges appear to view s 10 with some suspicion, partly because they may have expected the *government* to have been the main beneficiary of the protection s 10 offers – since leaking information is often associated with government activity.[349] No exception contained in s 10 would have covered leaked governmental information, unless there was a national security dimension, without the broad interpretation given to the interests of justice exception that would now cover it. Thus the courts have removed some of the protection government may have arrogated to itself for its own purposes.

It may be concluded that in the UK investigative journalism relying on sources has received some encouragement from legal developments and that post-HRA the judiciary have shown an enhanced determination to apply *Goodwin* to domestic decisions. But the protection for sources is still fairly precarious and is not embedded fully in the judicial consciousness as a common law principle to which they are strongly wedded.

---

349 In *Interbrew* fn 280 above, at para 7, Sedley LJ said: 'It should not be forgotten that in this country, then as now, the principal source of unattributable leaks to the media – in the form of off-the-record briefings – and therefore the principal beneficiary of a rule protecting the secrecy of sources, was government itself.'

Chapter 7

Offensive speech

This chapter has been updated and revised for this edition by Paul Wragg, Associate Professor at the University of Leeds, UK.

I Introduction[1]

> *Freedom of expression constitutes one of the essential foundations of a [democratic] society, one of the basic conditions for its progress and for the development of every man. Subject to paragraph 2 of Art 10, it is applicable not only to 'information' or 'ideas' that are favourably received or regarded as inoffensive, but also to those that offend, shock or disturb the state or any sector of the population. Such are the demands of that pluralism, tolerance and broadmindedness without which there is no democratic society.*
>
> *Handyside v UK (1976).*

This chapter in essence asks three questions. Where is the borderline in the twenty-first century between the images or words that can and cannot be published in the UK (including social media) on the ground of causing offence? How satisfactory is that borderline in free speech terms? Since the criminal law regulates expression on grounds of offence, how satisfactory is it that the important mediums of film and broadcasting are regulated beyond what the law allows?

1 Texts referred to below: Fenwick, H and Phillipson, G, *Media Freedom under the Human Rights Act*, 2006; Barendt, E, *Freedom of Speech*, 2nd edn, 2005 (1st edn will also be referred to); Feldman, D, *Civil Liberties in England and Wales*, 2002; Robertson, G and Nichol, D, *Media Law*, 1999; Bailey, S, and Taylor, N, *Civil Liberties and Human Rights Cases and Materials*, 6th edn, 2009; Carey, P, Coles, P and Armstrong, N, *Media Law*, 5th edn, 2010, Sweet and Maxwell; Hare, I, and Weinstein, J, *Extreme Speech and Democracy*, 2009, OUP; Gibbons, T, *Regulating the Media*, 1998; Dworkin, R, 'Do we have a right to pornography?', in *A Matter of Principle*, 1985; Itzen, C (ed), *Pornography: Women, Violence and Civil Liberties*, 1993, OUP; Feinberg, J, *The Moral Limits of the Criminal Law: Offense to Others*, 1985, OUP; MacKinnon, C, *Feminism Unmodified*, 1987; 'Feminism, Marxism, method and the state', in Bartlett and Kennedy (eds), *Feminist Legal Theory*, 1991, HarperCollins. See also Hare, I, 'Legislating Against Hate: the Legal Response to Bias Crimes' (1997) 17 OJLS 415; Weinstein, J, 'First Amendment challenges to hate crime legislation: where's the speech?' (1992) 11 Criminal Justice Ethics 6; Sumner, LW, *The Hateful And The Obscene: Studies in the Limits of Free Expression*, 2004, University of Toronto Press. Background: Marsh, J, *Word Crimes: Blasphemy, Culture, and Literature in Nineteenth-century England*, 1998, University of Chicago Press; O'Higgins, P, *Censorship in Britain*, 1972, Nelson; Robertson, G, *Obscenity*, 1979, Weidenfeld and Nicolson, and (with Nichol, D), *Media Law*, 1999, Chapter 3; MacMillan, PR, *Censorship and Public Morality*, 1983, Ashgate; Simpson, AWB, *Pornography and Politics: the Williams Committee in Retrospect*, 1983, Pergamon Press; Travis, A, *Bound and Gagged – A Secret History of Obscenity in Britain*, 2000, Profile Books.

This chapter covers a variety of forms of expression. Much of it is primarily visual and also falls outside the category of political expression. This may be said of most social media exchanges, some films, of music, opera, mime, plays, paintings, all of which are covered by aspects of the law and regulation considered below. But aspects of political expression are also covered, especially in a broadcasting context, while hate speech almost inevitably has a political message. Under the HRA 1998, the judiciary have found that[2] Strasbourg's hierarchical approach to the protection of expression reinforces their own pre-HRA view about freedom of speech (as discussed in Chapter 3),[3] although the value placed upon political speech at Strasbourg is arguably higher. However, if the justifications for freedom of expression considered in the introduction are taken into account, particularly those from truth and self-fulfilment, it is suggested that there is no convincing basis for relegating 'artistic' (or 'unimportant') expression to a lowly place in such a hierarchy, at the domestic level.

Restraints on explicit expression are found in a range of rules deriving from a number of common law doctrines, statutes, and the codes or guidelines of regulatory bodies. Some of the rules, based on concepts of obscenity, indecency or insult are far too subjective, imprecise and broad to be fully in harmony with the free speech justifications, either in theory or as found in Art 10 doctrine. The introduction to Part II is intended to provide a theoretical framework, based on the free speech justifications, within which to view the laws that are discussed below.

This chapter begins by examining the free speech justifications in their application to explicit speech. It moves on to examine the stance taken towards such speech at Strasbourg, and then proceeds to examine and evaluate the key substantive criminal offences relevant in this area, including offences relating to religious and racial sensibilities. Such offences form the backdrop to the following discussion of the regulatory regimes applicable to broadcasting and film. Finally, the legality of offensive expression on social media will be discussed. As will be seen, this has proven to be a particularly contentious issue in the past few years.

2 Law and pornography: theoretical considerations

The question as to how far sexually explicit speech deserves the same protection as other forms of expression and, if it does not, how far and for what reasons it should be suppressed, has, as Barendt notes, 'almost certainly elicited more academic commentary than any other [free speech] topic'.[4] As striking as the amount of writing on the subject is the failure by academics of different persuasions to reach a consensus view. Thus, for example, AWB Simpson, a former member of the Williams Committee appointed in 1977 to review obscenity law, recalls that the law certainly did not represent such a consensus: 'Before, during and after the Committee sat, the chorus of abuse against the law continued; virtually everyone claimed that it was unworkable.'[5] In a similar

---

2 See pp 287–89.
3 See pp 108–09.
4 Barendt, E, *Freedom of Speech*, 1987, 1st edn, p 245.
5 Simpson, AWB, *Pornography and Politics: the Williams Committee in Retrospect*, 1983, p 80.

vein, conservatives,[6] liberals[7] and feminists[8] have all attacked the Committee's findings and all for different reasons. In addition, even to speak of 'feminist' and 'liberal'
positions necessitates a conscious simplification, because these two opposing positions,
at first sight monolithic, are in fact riven by internal debate; in particular, the feminist
camp displays a conspicuous lack of unanimity.[9] Nevertheless, an attempt will be made,
in what follows, to outline briefly the 'core' of each stance and evaluate the strength of
their arguments, both against each other and directly on the subject of the permissibility
of censorship in this area.

The conservative position

The conservative position, which in the popular consciousness is probably most associated with Mary Whitehouse, a well-known activist strongly opposed to permissive society, finds its academic and somewhat more abstract exposition in Lord Devlin's work,
The Enforcement of Morals, 1965. In essence, Devlin's view is that since a shared set
of basic moral values is essential to society, it is as justified in protecting itself against
attacks on these values (such as that mounted by pornography) as it is in protecting
itself against any other phenomena which threaten its basic existence, such as violent
public disorder. On this thesis, moral corruption of the individual is to be prevented in
order to ensure the ultimate survival of society. By contrast, Whitehouse's concerns are
presumably more with damage to individuals *per se*, a position that, as argued below,
appears to reflect that taken by the case law in this area. Devlin's position, by contrast,
is clearly not compatible with most existing UK law:[10] it could neither support nor even
account for the existence of the public good defence in s 4 of the Obscene Publications
Act 1959,[11] or indeed any similar defence: it would appear somewhat absurd to argue
that material which threatened the very survival of society should be allowed to circulate freely on the grounds that it was somehow also in the public good.[12]

6 See, e.g., the comments of Mary Whitehouse in *The Sunday Times* that, as a result of the Committee's
   report, 'we are going from a quicksand into . . . a very, very mucky quagmire . . .', quoted in Simpson,
   ibid, p 44; he also quotes (p 45) a *Daily Telegraph* leader which criticised the 'some would say excessively liberal principle' it endorsed.

7 See, e.g., the detailed analysis in Dworkin, R, 'Do we have a right to pornography?', in *A Matter of
   Principle*, 1985, in which he broadly endorses the Committee's conclusions, but argues that these cannot
   be supported by the arguments they deployed.

8 The whole approach of the feminists is hostile to the broadly liberal stance adopted by the Committee;
   see, e.g., Brownmiller, S, *Against Our Will*, 1975, where it is asserted that all previous value systems,
   including the liberal tradition, have worked against the interests of women. For explicit criticism of the
   Committee by a more moderate feminist, see Eckersley, R, 'Whither the feminist campaign? An evaluation of feminist critiques of pornography', 15 Int J Soc of Law 149. Eckersley dismisses Williams as
   having 'simply fail[ed] to register the feminist objection' (p 174).

9 For comments on the divisions in the feminist critique of pornography see Eckersley, *ibid*. See also
   Lacey, N, 93 JLS 93.

10 It may however find reflection in some of the more obscure common law offences such as conspiracy
    to corrupt public morals and outraging public decency. The Lords, in *Knuller v DPP* [1973] AC 435;
    [1972] 3 WLR 143; (1972) 56 Cr App R 633, HL, a much criticised decision, arguably gave some sup-
    port to the Devlin thesis. For discussion of the decision, see below, pp 421–22.

11 For discussion of the defence, see below p 412 *et seq*.

12 Under the 1959 Act, the defence of public good only comes into play once it has been decided that the
    material is likely to deprave and corrupt: *Penguin Books* [1961] Crim LR 176 (the *Lady Chatterley's
    Lover* trial). See below, p 412.

Devlin's position also appears to have been placed in doubt on the theoretical level by Hart's incisive critique.[13] Briefly, Hart's objections are as follows: on the more favourable reading of Devlin's position, he is not assuming, but trying to establish the truth of the proposition that a shared set of moral standards (going on Devlin's account far beyond simple prohibitions on violence, theft, etc) is an essential attribute of society. If this is the case, argues Hart, Devlin fails to establish the proposition for the simple reason that he offers no empirical evidence to support it. This leads one, Hart continues, to the suspicion that Devlin actually *assumes* the truth of the proposition and thus builds his theory on a tautology: having defined society as a system of shared beliefs he then concludes, with perfect logic but some futility, that if those shared beliefs change radically or unanimity is lost, the society has disintegrated. Devlin's position, therefore does not strike one as particularly strong.

The liberal position

The liberal position on pornography is broadly united around general opposition to censorship in the absence of clear evidence of a concrete harm caused by its free availability.[14] However, unanimity does not exist as to the rationales for free speech most applicable to defending a liberty to read or view pornographic material. There is general agreement that Meiklejohn's argument from participation in democracy[15] is of little relevance; as Dworkin caustically remarks, 'No one is denied an equal voice in the political process . . . when he is forbidden to circulate photographs of genitals to the public at large.'[16]

A variant of Mill's argument from truth[17] was avowedly the free speech justification adopted by the Williams Committee convened in 1979 to report on obscenity; although they expressed some scepticism at Mill's perhaps rather naive conviction that in a *laissez faire* market of ideas, truth would always win out,[18] they endorsed the main thrust of his theory. Interference with the free flow of ideas and artistic endeavour was unacceptable since it amounted to ruling out in advance possible modes of human development, before it was known whether or not they would be desirable or necessary. Since they also reached the conclusion that 'no one has invented or in our opinion *could* invent, an instrument that would suppress only [worthless pornography] and could not be turned against something . . . of [possibly] a more creative kind',[19] they concluded that this risk of suppressing worthwhile creative art ruled out censorship of the written word. (They regarded standard photographic pornography as not expressing anything that could be regarded as an 'idea' and so as unprotected by the argument from truth.)

---

13 For a summary of Hart's critique, see 'Social solidarity and the enforcement of morality', in *Essays in Jurisprudence and Philosophy*, 1983.
14 See Feinberg, J, *The Moral Limits of the Criminal Law: Offense to Others*, 1985. For a brief discussion of the possible link between pornography and the commission of sexual offences, see below, p 468.
15 See above, pp 281–83 and fn 27, p 281.
16 Dworkin, R, *op cit*, fn 1, p 336.
17 See above, pp 280–81.
18 Report of the Committee on Obscenity and Film Censorship (Williams Committee), Cmnd 7772, 1979, para 5.20.
19 *Ibid*, para 5.24.

Ronald Dworkin has mounted a sustained attack on this rationale;[20] it rests, he contends, on the instrumental justification that allowing the free circulation of ideas is necessary to enable individuals to make intelligent and informed choices about how they want to lead their lives and then flourish in them. He finds that such an argument is unable to support its own conclusion against censorship; for, he urges, it must be accepted that allowing the free availability of pornography will 'sharply limit' the ability of some (perhaps the majority) to shape their cultural understanding of sexuality in a way they think best – a way in which sexuality has dignity and beauty. His argument appears to conclude that the justification from self-development does not argue conclusively against censorship, because of the plausible case that forbidding some pornography will for many people greatly assist in their self-development. Dworkin is surely correct when he concludes that not self-development, but the straightforward argument from *moral autonomy* amounts to the strongest case against censorship in this area. This argument simply points out that judging for an individual what will and will not be beneficial for him or her to read represents a clear invasion of the strong individual right to decide moral issues concerned with one's own life for oneself.[21] Such an invasion could therefore only be justified if a serious risk of substantial damage to the concrete well-being of society was shown.[22] Since the law does not posit such a risk, censorship is unacceptable. Whether this argument also provides a convincing answer to the radical feminist objections to free access to pornography will be considered below; this position must first be sketched out.

It should finally be noted that liberals are willing to support restrictions on the outlets and public display of pornography[23] on the grounds that such restrictions do not necessarily spring from contempt for those who read pornography, but may simply reflect the genuine and personal aesthetic preferences of those who would rather not have to suffer the continual and ugly spectacle of publicly displayed pornography.[24]

The pro-censorship feminist position

The views of feminist writers on the harms pornography does, on the justifications offered for allowing its free availability and on what, if anything, the law should do about it are many and varied.[25] However, the pro-censorship feminist position on the

---

20 Dworkin, R, *op cit*, fn 1.
21 See above, Chapter 1, pp 9, 16–20.
22 It is submitted that other possible justifications for abrogating speech (described in Chapter 1, pp 16–20) are not in most instances applicable here. But see below, p 468 for consideration of a possible link between pornography and sexual offences.
23 Such as, e.g., the recommendations of the Williams Committee; see their 'Summary of our proposals', above, fn 18.
24 See Dworkin, R, *op cit*, fn 1, pp 355–58, where he broadly endorses the Williams Committee's proposals.
25 For feminist writers who take a different stance on pornography from that broadly examined here, see any of the following: the chapters on pornography in Smart, *Feminism and the Power of Law*, 1989, Routledge, in which the author expresses distrust of using the law to control pornography; Rhode, *Justice and Gender*, 1989, Harvard University Press, in which the extent to which feminism has framed a puritanical ideology of sexuality and pornography is deplored: it is argued that women who find explicit depictions of, e.g., bondage or anonymous sex don't 'need more sexual shame, guilt and hypocrisy, this time served up as feminism'. See also Jackson, 'Catherine MacKinnon and feminist jurisprudence: a critical appraisal' (1992) JLS, pp 195–13 for a moderate critique, particularly of MacKinnon's views on the impossibility of non-coercive heterosexual activity in contemporary society.

possibility of legal control of pornography is generally equated with the views of Catherine MacKinnon and Andrea Dworkin, who framed an Indianapolis Ordinance giving rise to civil liability for trafficking in pornography or forcing it upon unwilling recipients; its constitutionality was successfully challenged on the grounds of incompatibility with the First Amendment.[26] The essence of this variant of feminist thought is that while pornography is regarded as causing harm to some individual women, by causing some individual men to perpetrate rape, battery and sexual abuse,[27] pornography causes a far more subtle and all-pervasive harm to all women. It is on the latter argument that the remainder of the discussion will concentrate.

In some of their more terse, dramatic statements, such as 'Pornography is violence against women',[28] and 'We define pornography as a practice of sex discrimination',[29] it sounds as if MacKinnon and A Dworkin regard the very existence of pornography as a concrete harm to women that goes far beyond mere offence and yet is not a physical harm. However, in the more precise explanations they offer, it seems clear that the harm is caused through the effect it has on men's view of women: 'Men treat women as who they see women as being. Pornography constructs who that is.' In other words, the argument does remain, as R Dworkin claims, 'a causal one'.[30] At this point, having posited a link between pornography and the way men treat women, the explanation draws in the more general radical feminist thesis that men have near total power over women and that consequently, 'the way men see women defines who women can be'.[31] Elsewhere, MacKinnon explains that this power is generated by the fact that men have managed to establish the total 'privileging' of their interests and perceptions and the concomitant complete subordination of women and then passed this off as reality or 'just the way things are'. MacKinnon calls the resulting illusion 'metaphysically nearly perfect'.[32] Several more moderate feminists have pointed out[33] that this view places feminism in the bizarre position of having to deny the possibility of its own existence because it entails assuming that all available modes of thought and perception are male, although masquerading as neutral. If this were true, it is hard to see how women could even come to realise that they were oppressed, let alone frame proposals for affirmative action to free themselves from male dominance. MacKinnon has indeed asserted

---

26 For the first instance decision, see *American Booksellers Assoc, etc v Hudnitt III, Mayor, City of Indianapolis* et al 598 F Supp 1316. For the (unsuccessful) appeal, see 771 F 2d 323.

27 See, e.g., MacKinnon, C, *Feminism Unmodified*, 1987, pp 184–91; 'Pornography as Sex Discrimination.' *Law and Inequality: A Journal of Theory and Practice* 38 (1986): 4; *In Harm's Way: The Pornography Civil Rights Hearings.* edited and introduced (with Andrea Dworkin), 'The Roar on the Other Side of Silence' (introduction), 1997; *Only Words*, 1993, Harvard University Press.

28 The basic thesis of Dworkin, A, *Pornography: Men Possessing Women*, 1979, The Women's Press, quoted in Simpson, *op cit*, fn 1, p 71.

29 MacKinnon, *op cit*, fn 1, p 175. The quotation given refers specifically to the Indianapolis ordinance, but equally summarises MacKinnon's analysis of pornography.

30 Dworkin, R, 'Liberty and pornography', *The New York Review of Books*, 15 August 1991, p 12.

31 MacKinnon, *op cit*, fn 1, p 172.

32 See 'Feminism, Marxism, method and the state', in Bartlett and Kennedy (eds), *Feminist Legal Theory*, 1991, HarperCollins, p 182, and 'Feminism, Marxism, Method and the State: An Agenda for Theory' *Signs: Journal of Women in Culture and Society*, 1983, University of Chicago Press, 515: 7.

33 See, e.g., Sandra Harding's introduction to MacKinnon's 'Feminism, Marxism, method and the state', in Harding, S, *Feminism and Methodology*, 1987, Indiana University Press.

that 'Feminism affirms women's point of view by . . . explaining its impossibility',[34] but since MacKinnon herself has in fact somehow managed to construct a substantive and highly influential feminist point of view – including the analysis of pornography under consideration – this reply is not fully convincing. It might be thought at this point that since acceptance of the radical feminist thesis on pornography is apparently only possible if one also accepts a metaphysical theory which seems both to deny its own existence and to involve acceptance of the most comprehensive conspiracy theory ever devised, the thesis can be summarily dismissed.

This, however, would be premature. The most significant feminist point with respect to pornography is the effect it is said to have on men's view of women and therefore on the way they treat them. One does not have to accept the general radical feminist thesis in order to give *some* consideration to the proposition that pornography, through the effect it has on men, oppresses women. Consequently, the discussion will now turn to considering whether the feminist thesis can still provide a justification for restrictions on the freedom to consume pornography even if the notion of total female subordination is rejected.

The oppression of women caused by pornography is claimed to manifest itself in the following three distinct ways. First, women are discriminated against, sexually harassed and physically assaulted in all walks of life; this constitutes a denial of their civil right to equality. Secondly, women are denied their positive liberty, their right to equal participation in the political process because of the image in men's minds constructed by pornography which 'strips and devastates women of credibility',[35] and consequently prevents women's contributions from being taken seriously. Finally, pornography 'silences' women – even their negative ability to speak is denied because they are not seen as fully human agents, but rather as dehumanised creatures who 'desperately want to be bound, battered, tortured, humiliated and killed'.[36] The argument that the state should, therefore, seek to ban pornography on the basis of furtherance of equality, just as it seeks to outlaw discrimination in employment, is developed in *Only Words*.[37]

Two points may be made in response to the above. First, this thesis attributes to men a uniformly passive and receptive attitude to all pornographic images.[38] Nowhere in a long essay on pornography[39] does MacKinnon appear to advert to the possibility that many men may completely reject the 'message' of violent misogynistic pornography,

---

34   Bartlett and Kennedy (eds), *Feminist Legal Theory*, 1991, p 181.

35   MacKinnon (1987), *op cit*, fn 1, p 193.

36   MacKinnon (1987), *op cit*, fn 1, p 172. *Cf* Andrea Dworkin's description of the view that rape law evinces of women as one in which rape is not really against a woman's will, 'because what she wants underneath is to have anything done to her that violates or humiliates or hurts her': *Pornography: Men Possessing Women*, 1979.

37   MacKinnon, C, *Only Words*, 1993. For criticism of the notion that banning pornography should be viewed as an aspect of the furtherance of equality, see Sadurski, 'On 'Seeing speech through an equality lens': a critique of egalitarian arguments for suppression of hate speech and pornography' (1996) 16(4) OJLS 713.

38   Andrea Dworkin attributes a similarly monolithic character to men; consider, e.g., the following description of the male sex: 'Terror issues forth from the male; illuminates his essential nature and his basic purpose' (*Pornography: Men Possessing Women*, 1979, p 74).

39   MacKinnon, 1987, Chapter 14.

even though some may be aroused by it. Her theory thus, in effect, amounts to a profound refusal to recognise the immense difference that men's backgrounds, education and life experiences will have on their responses,[40] and more generally, the enormous variety of human responses to any given phenomena which will be found even amongst those of similar backgrounds; ultimately, her theory denies (male) free will and with it men's individual voices.[41]

The second point is that if one leaves aside the extreme idea of the total control of men over women described above, it then becomes impossible to accept the immense influence that is attributed to the consumption of pornography. The idea, for example, that pornography silences women in all walks of life remains quite simply, 'strikingly implausible'[42] perhaps precisely *because* it is so eloquently expressed and it is hard to take seriously the notion that pornography denies women the right to participate in political life. One could only accept such arguments if one regarded women as defined completely by the images of pornography; as has been seen, that argument in turn could only have force if one first accepted that men's view of women is almost wholly constructed by pornography and then could agree to the assertion that men's view of women is all that women are. The impossibility of accepting such counterintuitive propositions means, it is submitted, that the radical feminist argument does not convincingly establish that the availability of pornography represents or causes actual infringements of the rights of women. In strict liberal theory, therefore, the argument from moral autonomy would, in the absence of competing individual rights, require that the choice as to which kinds of explicit literature to read and which to shun, remains properly with the individual. However, a number of comments may be made as to this finding. First, in contrast to many other types of speech, we have found that the only convincing argument for free speech in this area rests upon the interest in moral autonomy, unbolstered by other free speech justifications. Secondly, it seems self-evident that some invasions of autonomy – those that interfere with choices that go to the core of the individual's identity – must be more grave than invasions with respect to more peripheral areas. Interference with the individual's choice to view violent misogynistic pornographic films with no pretension to artistic expression is surely less of an infringement of his autonomy than, say, interfering with the right of the individual to have homosexual relations. If this argument is accepted, it follows that the autonomy interest here is comparatively weak.

These two points, taken together, would suggest that the total case for protecting inartistic violent pornography is not a particularly strong one. This case, such as it is, must then be balanced against the risk that there may possibly be a link between pornography and the commission of sexual offences. The argument as to this link is still ongoing and it is submitted that a proper evaluation of the evidence in this area falls within the ambit of the social sciences rather than a study of civil liberties. *Some* evidence has been

---

40 For criticism of this characteristic failing in MacKinnon's work generally, see Jackson, 'Catherine MacKinnon and feminist jurisprudence: a critical appraisal' (1992) JLS, pp 195–13.

41 An ironic point, since MacKinnon often talks of men 'silencing' women.

42 Dworkin, R, *op cit*, fn 1, p 14; Rhode also asks how, if women are silenced by pornography, a small group of feminists managed to mount a challenge to some of the most cherished principles of American constitutionalism and one of its most successful entertainment industries: Rhode, D, *Justice and Gender*, 1989, Harvard University Press.

produced of a link, although this evidence is disputed by other studies;[43] what is clear is that there may be said to be a chance of a risk that pornography contributes towards the motivation of sex offenders. It is submitted that until a consensus on the evidential question emerges, the law is entitled, given the relative weakness of the argument for protecting violent hardcore pornography, to take a pragmatic stance and allow narrow and selective censorship of at least sexual violence in films, subject to an artistic merits defence, rather than insist that pornography should be unrestricted until the hypothesised link with sex offences has been established beyond reasonable doubt. Further, the case for withdrawal of restrictions must also be balanced against the possibility that while a particular group of men may be influenced by pornography towards the commission of sexual offences, a further group may also be influenced by it towards psychologically damaging treatment of women falling short of any criminal offence. If the link discussed above were established, this further argument would come into play, since it would seem strange if pornography could have a highly significant influence on one group of men but none at all on any other. Thus, this point supports the pragmatic stance advocated above, although it falls well short of accepting the general pro-censorship feminist position.

A further, distinct argument concerns the harm that may be done to the *participants* in the making of hardcore pornographic films. This will depend on the nature of the pornographic industry in the particular jurisdiction. If such films portray a variety of actual sexual acts, including sadomasochistic ones, the participants may suffer psychological or even physical harm. This point is of especial pertinence to women since, typically, the female participants are subjected to sexual acts in which they are more victim than perpetrator. For example, a typical scenario might include one woman having sex with a large number of men and being 'roughed up' by them. In such circumstances, it is arguable that the woman's consent may be undermined owing to uncertainty as to what will occur, intimidation into accepting certain acts, such as anal sex, and, more generally, owing to the power disparity between the woman and the almost exclusively male directors of such films. The women participants are, typically, young and from economically deprived groups. If, for example, a woman is alone with a group of men in a house at which filming is taking place and has already been bullied and intimidated, the question whether she is continuing to give informed consent to a variety of sexual acts, which have been occurring for a period of time, begins to lose any reality.[44] If it

---

43 Evidence for a causal link is quoted in MacKinnon (1987), *op cit*, fn 1, pp 184–91, while R Dworkin, cites a recent UK study which finds against such a link: Cumberbatch, G and Howitt, D, *A Measure of Uncertainty – the Effects of the Mass Media*, 1989, University of Luton Press. The findings of this latter study were published in the *Daily Telegraph*, 23 December 1990. Eckersley discusses the issue (Eckersley, R, 'Whither the feminist campaign? An evaluation of feminist critiques of pornography', 15 Int J Soc of Law 149, pp 161–63). See also Itzen, C (ed), *Pornography: Women, Violence and Civil Liberties*, 1993, which puts forward a body of evidence supporting a causal link.

44 During the making of a documentary into the making of hard core pornographic films in Los Angeles, *Hard Core* (broadcast on Channel 4 on 7 April 2001), the director of the Channel 4 documentary intervened when it appeared that due to bullying and intimidation by the director of the pornographic film, the woman participant was no longer capable of giving informed consent. She had already been subjected to painful and humiliating acts to which it appeared probable that she had not given consent. In other words, consented-to acts had verged into actions going beyond the apparent boundaries of what she had consented to beforehand. Despite her distress occasioned by painful, forceful oral sex, the director wished to continue filming and she was told that she must next participate in a group orgy scene in which she would be the only woman. She appeared to acquiesce but, after the intervention, she, and the film crew, had to leave immediately. See further *The Times*, 9 April 2001, p 27.

was fairly clear that she was no longer giving such consent, it is hard to imagine that it would be possible, in practice, for her to seek the protection of the law, a fact of which she, and the film-makers, will be aware. The film-makers are under commercial pressures to push participants into accepting more extreme acts. If it appears from the nature of a film that participants may have been intimidated and subjected to actions verging on sexual abuse (owing to the circumstances, including the duration of one session), both feminists and liberals, on the arguments indicated, would unite in accepting regulation. On this argument, films depicting simulated sadomasochism or actual sexual acts would not necessarily be banned completely, but the conditions under which such filming could take place would be subject to rigorous controls, with the welfare of the participants in mind, and designed to be certain that full, informed consent had always been given. But where it was clear that such controls had not been in place, and that harm, such as psychological trauma, had occurred, censorship would clearly be warranted, except in exceptional cases owing to the strong artistic merits of the film. Where it could only be said that a risk of such harm was possible, it could be viewed as a further factor to be weighed in the balance, along with those identified above.

As a matter of interest, it is worth considering what the position would be if radical feminist scholars could somehow establish that pornography really did construct the social reality of women's identity. How would the feminist argument fare in competition with the liberal arguments for free speech? In the case of the three instrumental justifications, the arguments from democracy, truth and self-development,[45] the feminist thesis would be able to demonstrate how, in the case of pornography, each argues for restraint on speech. They would argue that free circulation of pornography hinders, even prevents women's participation in the democratic process; it assists not in finding the truth, but in constructing false and all-pervading images of women; it does *not* assist in the healthy development of those who take advantage of its free availability: rather they become rapists, abusers, misogynists.

The one liberal defence of free speech not *explicitly* addressed by the feminist argument is the argument from moral autonomy, which it was suggested above[46] provides the only arguable defence of the right to choose to read pornography. How would this argument fare if it was shown that the basic rights to equality, political participation and speech were in reality denied to all women by the consumption of pornography? Ronald Dworkin has considered this hypothetical position, in which he does not accept that pornography causes individual men to rape and assault women, but accepts the remainder of the feminist claims. One might consider that he would conclude that the massive infringements of women's strong individual rights and the concomitant loss of their moral autonomy would clearly override the comparatively minor invasions of men's free speech and autonomy represented by restrictions on pornography. Somewhat surprisingly, however, Dworkin argues that even if it were the case that the posited harms were actually visited upon all women by pornography, still this would provide no justification for restraining its free availability.[47] Such a view places the right to consume hardcore pornography over the rights of half the population to be treated with dignity and respect, to equal participation in democratic government and to free speech

---

45 See the Introduction to Part II, above, pp 283–84.
46 See pp 394–95.
47 Dworkin, R, *op cit*, fn 1, p 15.

itself. Such a conclusion represents, it is submitted, a complete betrayal of the premise on which Dworkin's whole theory of rights is based, namely the overriding duty of the state to treat all its citizens with equal concern and respect.

3 Legal responses to explicit expression

That the above conclusions on pornography are not in general accepted by states, is revealed by the fact that almost all bills or charters of rights, apart from the US Bill of Rights, contain an exception to the free speech clause which, *inter alia*, allows restraint on freedom of speech on the broad ground of protection of morality. The 'absolute' nature of the First Amendment, in contrast, has led the US courts to interpret the First Amendment so as to exclude obscene speech from the category of protected speech.[48] Section 14 of the New Zealand Bill of Rights protects freedom of expression, but the protection is subject to such 'reasonable limits prescribed by law as may be justified in a free and democratic society'. Such limits include the regulation of obscenity and pornography.[49] The justification borne in mind in interpreting such exceptions is the harm to be guarded against which seems to include three possibilities: the corruption of persons, particularly children as the more vulnerable; the shock or outrage caused by public displays of certain material and the commission of sex crimes.[50] The development of UK law has been based on the avoidance of the first two possibilities mentioned, although in relation to the visual media, the third has had some influence. On the ground of causing shock, the public display of certain publications can be regulated, while others viewed as having the potential to corrupt can be prohibited entirely, either by punishment of those responsible after publication or by being suppressed or censored before publication.

The type of restraint used tends to depend on the type of publication in question because it seems to be accepted that the harm that may be caused will vary from medium to medium. The print media are subject to a far more lax regime than the visual media. Printed matter, including magazines, newspapers and books, is not subject to censorship before publication, but punishment is available afterwards if indecent or corrupting material is published. Books are less likely to be punished than magazines because it is thought that something that has a visual impact is more likely to cause harm. Thus, films and broadcasts are censored because of their visual nature and are also subject to punishment. The theatre, however, is in an odd position; it has not been censored since 1968 despite its visual impact. Possibly, this may be due to the idea that theatre audiences are more sophisticated and less likely to be affected by what they have seen than cinema audiences. As indicated below, the internet is also in an anomalous position: although it may be viewed as broadly analogous to the visual media, it is not, and, under current proposals, will not be subject to the same regime.

---

48 See *Roth v US* (1957) 354 US 476; *Memoirs v Massachusetts* (1966) 383 US 413.
49 *Society for Promotion of Community Standards Inc v Waverley International (1988) Ltd* [1993] 2 NZLR 709.
50 These were the key notions of harm considered by the Williams Committee appointed in 1977 to review obscenity and indecency law (Williams Report, Cmnd 7772, 1979). Broadly, the Committee endorsed regulation of pornography with a view to preventing the second of the harms mentioned.

The Strasbourg stance

Article 10(1) specifically provides that the article 'shall not prevent states from requiring the licensing of broadcasting, television or cinema enterprises'. It is significant that this provision arises in the *first* paragraph of Art 10, thereby providing a limitation of the primary right that on its face is not subject to the test of para 2. However, a very restrictive approach to this sentence has been adopted. It has been found to mean that a licensing system is allowed for on grounds not restricted to those enumerated in para 2; the state may determine who is to have a licence to broadcast. But in general, other decisions of the regulatory bodies who normally grant licences and oversee broadcasting, etc, are not covered by the last sentence of para 1 and must be considered within para 2.[51] Thus, content requirements must be considered under para 2. The preservation of a state monopoly on broadcasting must also be considered within para 2.[52]

As discussed in Chapter 2, under Art 10(2), an interference with the guarantee of freedom of expression under Art 10 can be justified if it is prescribed by law, has a legitimate aim and is necessary in a democratic society. As the introduction to this part indicated, Strasbourg affords a very high value to freedom of expression and, in particular, views the scope for interference with political expression as very limited.[53] Even in respect of artistic expression, which appears to have a lower place in the hierarchy of expression,[54] the discussion below indicates that no decisions defending restrictions on the freedom of expression of adults can be found, except in respect of hardcore pornography, or where a risk to children is also present, or in the context of offending religious sensibilities.

As the introduction to Part II indicated, certain forms of expression that may be said to be of no value may fall outside the scope of Art 10(1) and it is arguable that, for example, material gratuitously offensive to religious sensibilities[55] or depictions of genitals in pornographic magazines intended merely for entertainment[56] may fall outside its scope. On the other hand, 'hardcore' pornography has been found by Strasbourg to fall within Art 10(1).[57] Given the breadth of para 2, it is unnecessary to seek to draw lines between artistic erotica and forms of pornography aimed at entertainment alone, even assuming that such line-drawing has any validity.[58] The jurisprudence under Art 10 in this context, as in others, concentrates on the para 2 tests. In other words, Strasbourg will focus on whether the reasons for interference are persuasive or not.

Interferences with explicit expression may be justified if they have the legitimate aim of providing for the protection of morals or – in certain circumstances – the 'rights of others'. The use of laws on obscenity, indecency or blasphemy against explicit expression or regulation of the media with a view to upholding 'standards of taste and decency' are matters that, potentially, could be addressed under the HRA, relying on Art

---

51 *Groppera Radio AG v Switzerland* (1990) 12 EHRR 321.
52 *Informationsverein Lentia v Austria* (1993) 17 EHRR 93.
53 See Chapter 2, pp 83–88.
54 See above, pp 287–89.
55 *Otto-Preminger Institut v Austria* (1994) 19 EHRR 34.
56 In *Groppera Radio AG v Switzerland* (1990) 12 EHRR 321, it was thought that mere entertainment might not fall within Art 10(1).
57 *Hoare v UK* [1997] EHRLR 678; *Vereinigung Bildender Kunstler v Austria* (2008) 47 EHRR 5.
58 See Kearns, P, 'Obscene and blasphemous libel: misunderstanding art' [2000] Crim LR 652.

10. Specific possibilities are considered below, at relevant points. Here, the Strasbourg stance on the application of Art 10 to explicit expression is considered.

The line of authority stemming from the *Handyside* case[59] suggests that although explicit expression, including some pornographic expression, is protected within Art 10(1), interference with it can be justified quite readily in certain circumstances. It is clear that the scope of the domestic margin of appreciation is not the same in respect of all the aims listed in Art 10(2). The protection of morals would appear to be viewed as requiring a wide margin owing to its subjective nature, in contrast with the protection of the authority of the judiciary, which is seen as a more objective notion.[60] The uncertainty of the notion of the protection of morals appears in the lack of a clearly discernible common European standard.

In the *Handyside* case, the European Court of Human Rights had to consider the test of 'deprave and corrupt'. A book called The *Little Red Schoolbook*, which contained chapters on masturbation, sexual intercourse and abortion, was prosecuted under the Obscene Publications Act 1959 (which is discussed below) on the basis that it appeared to encourage early sexual intercourse. The publishers applied for a ruling under Art 10 to the European Commission and the case was referred to the Court, which determined that the book fell within Art 10(1). In a famous passage, which strongly favours freedom of artistic or creative expression (the expression of information or ideas), it found:

> Freedom of expression constitutes one of the essential foundations of a democratic society, one of the basic conditions for its progress and for the development of every man. Subject to paragraph 2 of Article 10, it is applicable not only to information or ideas that are favourably received, or regarded as inoffensive but also to those that offend, shock or disturb the state or any sector of the population. Such are the demands of that pluralism, tolerance and broadmindedness without which there is no democratic society.[61]

However, as this passage indicates, the interference could be justified under para 2. The Court then considered the protection of morals provision under Art 10(2), in order to determine whether the interference with the expression was necessary in a democratic society. It suggested that the 'protection of morals' exception refers to the corruption of individuals rather than to an effect on the moral fabric of society.[62] The Court found that the requirements of morals vary from time to time and from place to place and that the domestic authorities were therefore best placed to judge what was needed. They must 'make the initial assessment of the reality of the pressing social need implied by the notion of necessity in this context'.[63] The judgment thus accepted that domestic authorities would be allowed a wide margin of appreciation in attempting to secure the freedoms guaranteed under the Convention in this area, although this was not to be taken as implying that an unlimited discretion was granted: the power of appreciation 'goes

---

59 Eur Ct HR, A 24; (1976) 1 EHRR 737.
60 See the judgment of the Eur Ct HR in the *Sunday Times* case (1979) 2 EHRR 245, discussed in Chapter 2, p 83.
61 *Ibid*, para 49. The 1959 Act is discussed below, pp 408–15.
62 *Ibid*, para 52.
63 *Ibid*, para 48.

hand in hand with a European supervision' that concerns the legislation in question – the Obscene Publications Act – and the decision applying it. The Court placed particular weight on the fact that the book was aimed at children between the ages of 12 and 18 and that it might encourage them 'to indulge in precocious activities harmful for them or even to commit certain criminal offences'.[64] Thus, the English judges were entitled to find that the book would have a 'pernicious effect on the morals' of the children who would read it. In finding that the tests under para 2 were satisfied, it was said that the fact that the book was circulating freely in the rest of Europe was not determinative of the issues, owing to the application of the margin of appreciation doctrine.

A similar stance was taken in *Müller v Switzerland*[65] in respect of a conviction arising from the exhibition of explicit paintings: the fact that the paintings had been exhibited in other parts of Switzerland and abroad did not mean that their suppression could not amount to a pressing social need. The Court took into account the fact that the paintings were exhibited to the public at large, without a warning as to their content, and that a young girl had seen them.

It is notable that the Court in *Handyside* based its justification for the protection of freedom of expression on the arguments from democracy and self-fulfilment rather than on those from truth or moral autonomy.[66] As indicated above, in the introduction to Part II, these justifications, as instrumental arguments, are open to attack in the way that the argument from moral autonomy is not. This stance of the Court is especially relevant in the context of explicit expression since the argument may provide, as indicated above, the sole justification. (It is not suggested that this was the case in *Handyside* itself; on the contrary, on the basis of the content of the book, three of the four justifications could have applied.) In the other contexts covered by Part II, all four justifications may be present. The Court's stance may have some bearing on the cautious nature of its jurisprudence in this area, although unlike the Supreme Court of Canada, it has not explicitly addressed this issue.[67]

These two decisions give a strong indication as to the stance taken by the Court in respect of Art 10, para 2, but may be viewed as turning on their special facts, particularly the fact that children might have been affected. The thinking behind the *Handyside* decision can find some parallels from the US[68] and Canada.[69] In the US, however, there has been a greater concentration on the question whether restrictions aimed at children might impinge also on the freedom of expression of adults and on the extent to which this should be tolerated,[70] a matter that was in issue in *Handyside*, although not afforded weight by the Court.

These decisions at Strasbourg do not determine the question of the consumption of explicit material solely or mainly by a willing adult audience – a matter that is especially

---

64 *Ibid*, para 52.
65 (1991) 13 EHRR 212. See Chapter 2, pp 83–88.
66 See the Introduction to Part II.
67 See *R v Butler* [1992] 1 SCR 452.
68 *Ginsberg v New York* 390 US 629 (1968).
69 *Irwin Toy Ltd v AG (Quebec)* [1989] 1 SCR 927 (broad limitation on broadcast advertising aimed at children).
70 *Reno v American Civil Liberties Union* (1997) 521 US 844.

pertinent in relation to films and videos, bearing their age classifications in mind. That question was considered in *Hoare v UK*,[71] which concerned the possession of 'hardcore' pornographic videos. The applicant had been convicted of possessing obscene material under s 2 of the Obscene Publications Act. The Commission found quite easily that the restriction on his freedom of expression had the legitimate aim of protecting morals and was not disproportionate to that aim. But the decision was largely based on the risk that children might view the videos since once they had left the applicant's possession he would not have been able to control their eventual audience. The Commission may have been influenced by the nature of the material: it had no artistic or political value and therefore the justifications underlying freedom of expression, referred to above, were not present, apart from the justification based on moral autonomy.

That decision is broadly in harmony with *Scherer v Switzerland*;[72] it was found that the conviction of the proprietor of a sex shop for showing obscene and explicit videos had breached Art 10, since access was restricted to adults and no one was likely to confront them unwittingly. *Scherer* demonstrates a preparedness, at Strasbourg level, to defend adult autonomy in relation to the consumption of explicit material, so long as control is retained over the ultimate consumer of the material. The difference between *Hoare* and *Scherer* related to the question of the restrictions on access to the material; in *Hoare* the penalty imposed was proportionate to the aim pursued since it was viewed as capable of protecting the 'rights of others' – the rights appeared to be those of minors to be protected from harmful material; in *Scherer* such rights could not be protected by the imposition of the penalty since they were not threatened by the showing of the videos.[73] Strasbourg is clearly content to restrict the expression rights of adults in order to protect children.

In *Otto-Preminger Institut v Austria*,[74] the Court considered the question of restrictions on freedom of expression in respect of a film where the expression was aimed at a willing adult audience. A warning had been given and therefore viewers knew what to expect. Nevertheless, owing to the shock caused to particular religious sensibilities in the local region, it was found, in a much criticised decision,[75] that the interference could be justified despite the fact that the measure had the effect of preventing the

---

71　[1997] EHRLR 678.

72　A 287 (1993) Com Rep (the case was discontinued in the Court owing to the death of the applicant).

73　In *Hoare* the Commission, having found that the material fell within Art 10(1), went on to find under Art 10(2): 'In the present case, the sole question which arises in the context of the relationship of proportionality between the interference with the applicant's right to freedom of expression and the aim pursued is the question of whether, given that the applicant only distributed his video cassettes to people who expressed a clear interest, it can be said that the penalty imposed was capable of protecting the "rights of others" (see, in this context, *Scherer v Switzerland*, Comm Report 14.1.93, Eur Court HR, Series A no 287, p 20, para 65). Where no adult is confronted unintentionally or against his will with filmed matter, there must be particularly compelling reasons to justify an interference (above-mentioned *Scherer* Report, p 20, para 65). The Commission considers that it cannot therefore be said with any degree of certainty that only the intended purchasers of the film would have access to it and not minors. To that extent the present case is different from the case of *Scherer*, where the only adults who saw the applicant's videos were those who had access to his shop (above-mentioned *Scherer* Report, p 19, para 62).'

74　(1994) 19 EHRR 34.

75　For an incisive critique, see Pannick, D, 'Religious feelings and the European Court' [1995] PL 7.

showing of the film across the whole country. That decision can be contrasted with the findings of the Commission in the same case that Art 10 had been violated.[76] In a more recent decision the Court found that a permanent injunction prohibiting pornographic art from being displayed violated Art 10.[77] The decision is not (necessarily) evidence of a softer approach to the issue but rather shows that interferences must be proportionate. The image, in this case, had featured a collage of doctored photographs, including one scene of two politicians 'ejaculating' over Mother Teresa. The injunction was granted following a complaint by one of the politicians involved yet, by this stage, the painting had been damaged (a protester had daubed red paint over it) and the politician no longer recognisable. As a result the permanent injunction was not justified.

Applying the Strasbourg jurisprudence under the Human Rights Act

The decisions in this line of authority confirm that where there is a chance that children might be affected or religious sensibilities offended, Strasbourg is particularly cautious. Even accepting the effect of the margin of appreciation doctrine, its stance is very significantly out of line with that taken under a number of national bills of rights at the end of the twentieth century and the beginning of the twenty-first. It is one of the weakest and most outdated areas of its jurisprudence, which entirely fails to follow up the principles established in *Handyside* in relation to Art 10(1). However, *Scherer* provides a basis of sorts from which to attack the current censorship of films for cinematic release in the UK since age restrictions are in place and are enforced. That decision and the jurisprudence in general provide, on its face, no basis for attacking the regulation and censorship of videos and broadcasting since there is a risk that children will encounter the material. In general the Strasbourg jurisprudence in this area does not set precise standards that could be followed effectively by regulators or by the courts; the standards may readily be referred to as 'soft-edged'. But clearly it can be argued that the Convention was never intended to set such standards since it provides a 'floor', not a 'ceiling', of rights.

Restrictions based on the idea of avoiding offence or maintaining certain standards of taste and decency tend to have a greater impact on 'artistic' rather than political expression – using the term 'artistic' very broadly. As indicated, the margin of appreciation doctrine has an especially significant impact on such expression due to the lack of consensus in Europe as to the proper extent of restrictions on it intended to prevent offence. So if the established Strasbourg hierarchy of expression is rigidly applied in relation to such restrictions they can be justified quite readily. However, if the justifications for freedom of expression considered are taken into account, particularly those from truth and self-fulfilment, it is suggested that there is no convincing basis for relegating 'artistic' expression to a lowly place in such a hierarchy. Possibly its place should be below that of political speech, but too sharp a distinction should not be drawn. Moreover, it is readily apparent that some forms of political speech are clearly less valuable than some forms of artistic speech. For example, a number of classic films that fall outside the category of political speech engage a number of the justificatory free speech arguments more strongly than do the more minor manifestations of political speech.

---

76 See also *Wingrove v UK* (1996) 24 EHRR 1; *Gay News v UK* (1982) 5 EHRR 123.
77 *Vereinigung Bildender Kunstler v Austria* (2008) 47 EHRR 5.

Generally, it may be said that UK courts tend to adopt a particularly dismissive approach to the protection of pornography under Art 10. In *Belfast City Council v Miss Behavin' Ltd*,[78] the House of Lords was asked to review a local council's refusal to grant a licence to a company intending to sell pornography. Amongst other things, the appellant claimed this was a breach of their Art 10 rights, to which Lord Hoffmann remarked that if the right is engaged at all, it must be,

> at a very low level. The right to vend pornography is not the most important right of free expression in a democratic society and the licensing system does not prohibit anyone from exercising it. It only prevents him from using unlicensed premises for that purpose.[79]

It cannot be said, therefore, that the HRA has had a liberalising effect on the protection of sexually explicit materials – and, arguably, not on offensive expression in general, as will be shown.

Statutory obscenity

Obscenity law operates as a subsequent restraint and is largely used in relation to books, magazines and other printed material, material posted on web-pages or videos;[80] theoretically it could also be used against broadcasts and films. The harm sought to be prevented is that of a corrupting effect on an individual. In other words, it is thought that an individual will undergo a change for the worse after encountering the material in question. The rationale of the law is thus overtly paternalistic. Of course, if all material which might appear capable of causing corruption were suppressed, a severe infringement of freedom of speech would occur. There are two key statutes that govern this area: s 63, Criminal Justice and Immigration Act 2008, and the Obscene Publications Act 1959.[81] Section 63 CJIA 2008 makes it an offence to possess images that are pornographic, extreme in nature (i.e. that are grossly offensive, disgusting or obscene) and portrays a prohibited act or acts (specified in s 63(7)) in an explicit and realistic way. The prohibited acts are where: a person's life is threatened; serious injury is or would be caused to the genitals, anus or breasts; sexual interference with a dead body occurs; intercourse or oral sex with an animal occurs; or, finally, any non-consensual penetration of the vagina, anus or mouth occurs.[82] The Obscene Publications Act, meanwhile, covers more than just images. It takes the stance that in preventing material which

---

78 [2007] UKHL 19.

79 *Ibid*, [16].

80 In *AG's Reference (No 5 of 1980)* [1980] 3 All ER 816, CA, it was found that a video constituted an "article" for the purposes of the 1959 Act.

81 The Obscene Publications Act 1959 does not apply in Scotland; the Civic Government (Scotland) Act 1982 makes it an offence to publish obscene material and prosecution is the responsibility of the Procurator Fiscal Service. Under the Scotland Act 1998, Scottish criminal law generally has been devolved and this includes the law on obscenity; however, the Video Recordings Act has been reserved to the UK Parliament. The Obscene Publications Act does not extend to Northern Ireland; nor do the relevant provisions of the Local Government (Miscellaneous Provisions) Act 1982.

82 McGlynn, C and Rackley, E, 'Striking a balance: arguments for the criminal regulation of extreme pornography' (2007) Crim LR 677.

may deprave and corrupt, a line must be drawn between erotic literature and the truly obscene on the basis that hardcore pornography does not deserve special protection.[83] This echoes the approach in the US, where this form of pornography is not defined as 'speech' because it is thought that the justification for the constitutional protection for freedom of speech does not apply.[84] In fact, oddly enough, pornography is more likely to be prohibited in the US than in the UK given that Art 10(1) is capable of applying to pornographic expression.[85]

The idea of preventing corruption had informed the common law long before the 1959 Act; it sprang from the ruling in *Hicklin*.[86] Determining whether material would 'deprave and corrupt' was problematic, especially as it was unclear to whom the test should be applied. Two cases in 1954 showed the uncertainty of the law. In *Martin Secker and Warburg*[87] it was determined that the test applied to persons who might encounter the material in question. But at the same time, in *Hutchinson*,[88] the Court held that the test should be applied to the most vulnerable person who might conceivably encounter the material and that the jury could therefore look at the effect it might have on a teenage girl. Moreover, the jury could find that something that could merely be termed 'shocking' could deprave and corrupt.

The 1959 Act was passed in an attempt to clear up some of this uncertainty, although it failed to lay down a test for the meaning of the term 'deprave and corrupt'. The *actus reus* of the offence involves the publication for gain (s 2(1)) or having for such publication (s 1(2) of the Obscene Publications Act 1964) an article that tends, taken as a whole (or where it comprises two or more distinct items, the effect of one of the items), to deprave and corrupt a significant proportion of those likely to see or hear it (s 1(1)). Although the Act refers to the corruption of 'persons', the Court of Appeal recently decided that the test can be satisfied even if it is only one other person that sees the publication.[89] This is a crime of strict liability: there is no need to show an intention to deprave and corrupt, merely an intention to publish. Once it is shown that an article is obscene within the meaning of the Act, it will be irrelevant, following the ruling of the Court of Appeal in *Calder and Boyars*,[90] that the defendant's motivation could be characterised as pure or noble. The Act does not cover live performances on stage, which fall within the similarly worded Theatres Act 1968.

'Deprave and corrupt'

This test could be applied to any material which might corrupt; it is clear from the ruling in *Calder (John) Publishing v Powell*[91] that it is not confined to descriptions or

---

83 See, for argument on this point, Dworkin, R, 'Is there a right to pornography?' (1981) 1 Ox JLS 177.
84 *Miller v California* (1973) 413 US 15. It should be noted that under the argument from moral autonomy, it is irrelevant whether the material concerned is classified as 'speech' or not.
85 E.g., *Miss Behavin' Ltd*, op cit.
86 (1868) 3 QB 360.
87 [1954] 2 All ER 683; [1954] 1 WLR 1138.
88 (1954), unreported. For an account of the proceedings, see St John Stevas, N, *Obscenity and the Law*, 1956, p 116.
89 *R v Smith* [2012] EWCA Crim 398.
90 [1969] 1 QB 151; [1968] 3 WLR 974; [1968] 3 All ER 644; (1968) 52 Cr App R 706.
91 [1965] 1 QB 159.

representations of sexual matters and it could therefore be applied to a disturbing book about drug-taking. This ruling was followed in *Skirving*,[92] which concerned a pamphlet on the means of taking cocaine in order to obtain maximum effect. In all instances, the test for obscenity should not be applied to the type of behaviour advocated or described in the article in question, but to the article itself. Thus, in *Skirving*, the question to be asked was not whether taking cocaine would deprave and corrupt, but whether the pamphlet itself would.

This test is hard to explain to a jury and uncertain of meaning, with the result that directions such as the following have been given: 'obscenity, members of the jury, is like an elephant; you can't define it, but you know it when you see it'.[93] However, it is clear from the ruling of the Court of Appeal in *Anderson*[94] that the effect in question must be more than mere shock. The trial judge had directed the jury that the test connoted that which was repulsive, loathsome or filthy. This explanation was clearly defective, since it would have merged the concepts of indecency and obscenity and it was rejected by the Court of Appeal on the basis that it would dilute the test for obscenity which, it was said, must connote the prospect of moral harm, not just shock. The conviction under the Act was therefore overturned because of the misdirection. The House of Lords in *Knuller v DPP*[95] considered the word 'corrupt' and found that it denoted a publication which produced 'real social evil' – going beyond immoral suggestions or persuasion.

This was quite a strict test, but it was qualified by the House of Lords in *DPP v Whyte*.[96] The owners of a bookshop which sold pornographic material were prosecuted. Most of the customers were old men who had encountered the material on previous occasions and this gave rise to two difficulties. First, the old men were unlikely to engage in anti-social sexual behaviour and therefore the meaning of 'corrupt' had to be modified if it was to extend to cover the effect on them of the material: it was found that it meant creating a depraved effect on the mind that need not actually issue forth in any particular sexual behaviour. Secondly, it was suggested that the old men were already corrupt and therefore would not be affected by the material. However, it was held that corruption did not connote a once-only process: persons could be 'recorrupted' and, on this basis, a conviction was obtained. (Interestingly, this finding suggests that there is a presumption that the 'deprave and corrupt' test is of universal application: no person or group of persons can be excluded in principle from its ambit. In this sense it differs from the test as put forward in *Hicklin*; that test applied only to those whose minds were open to immoral influences.) The test will not be satisfied if the material in question causes feelings of revulsion from the immorality portrayed. This theory, known as the 'aversion theory', derives from *Calder and Boyars*, which concerned *Last Exit from Brooklyn*; it was found that the horrific pictures it painted of homosexuality and drug taking in New York would be more likely to discourage than encourage such behaviour.[97]

92 [1985] QB 819.
93 Robertson, *Obscenity*, op cit, fn 1, p 45.
94 [1972] 1 QB 304.
95 [1973] AC 435; [1972] 3 WLR 143; (1972) 56 Cr App R 633, HL.
96 [1972] AC 849; [1972] 3 All ER 12, HL.
97 [1969] 1 QB 151; [1968] 3 WLR 974; [1968] 3 All ER 644; (1968) 52 Cr App R 706. For comment, see Robertson, *Obscenity*, 1979, pp 50–53.

The 'deprave and corrupt' test must be applied to those likely to see or hear the material in question and, therefore, the concept of relative obscenity is imported into the Act. In other words, the obscenity or otherwise of material cannot be determined merely by its consideration or analysis but, rather, will depend on the character of the consumer and, in this sense, the test presents a contrast with German obscenity law which absolutely prohibits hardcore pornography, although softcore material is quite freely available.[98] It was held in *DPP v Whyte*[99] that in order to make a determination as to the type of consumer in question, the Court could receive information as to the nature of the relevant area, the type of shop and the class of people frequenting it. The jury must consider the likely reader in order to determine whether the material would deprave and corrupt him or her rather than considering the most vulnerable conceivable reader. In *Penguin Books*,[100] which concerned the prosecution of publication of *Lady Chatterley's Lover*, the selling price of the book was taken into account and the fact that being in paperback, it would reach a mass audience.

The jury has to consider whether the article would be likely to deprave and corrupt a *significant proportion* of those likely to encounter it. It was determined in *Calder and Boyars*[101] that the jury must determine what is meant by a 'significant proportion' and this was approved in *DPP v Whyte*, Lord Cross explaining that 'a significant proportion of a class means a part which is not numerically negligible, but which may be much less than half'. This formulation was adopted in order to prevent sellers of pornographic material claiming that most of their customers would be unlikely to be corrupted by it. The effect of the article as a whole on persons likely to encounter it should be considered, not merely the effect of specific passages of a particularly explicit nature. However, in *Anderson*[102] it was made clear that where the article consists of a number of items, each item must be considered in isolation from the others. Thus, a magazine that is, on the whole, innocuous, but contains one obscene item, can be suppressed, although a novel could not be.

It may be reasonably straightforward to identify a group, of whom a significant proportion might encounter the material, but it is unclear how it can then be determined that they would be likely to experience depravity and corruption as a result. The ruling in *Anderson* was to the effect that in sexual obscenity cases and normally in other obscenity cases, the defence cannot call expert evidence as to the effect that an article may have on its likely audience. Thus, the view taken in *DPP v A and BC Chewing Gum Ltd*[103] that such evidence would be admissible may be regarded as arising only due to the very specific circumstances of that case. However, it was decided in *Skirving*[104] that in cases concerned with alleged depravity and corruption arising from factors other than the sexual nature of the material, expert evidence will, exceptionally, be admissible, although the evidence can only be as to the effects of the behaviour described in the material, not as to the likely effects of the material itself. Thus, generally, where

---

98 German Criminal Code, s 184(3).
99 [1972] AC 849; [1972] 3 All ER 12, HL.
100 [1961] Crim LR 176; see Rolph, CH, *The Trial of Lady Chatterley*, 1961, Andre Deutsch.
101 [1969] 1 QB 151.
102 [1972] 1 QB 304.
103 [1968] 1 QB 159.
104 [1985] QB 819.

the material deals with matters within their own experience, the jury will receive little help in applying the test. However, it seems clear that a jury will be able to take into account changing standards of morality (the 'contemporary standards' test from *Calder and Boyars*) in considering what will deprave and corrupt. Therefore, the concept of obscenity is, at least theoretically, able to keep up to date. The application of these tests at the present time was seen in the trial for obscenity of the book *Inside Linda Lovelace*,[105] which suggested that a prosecution brought against a book of any conceivable literary merit would be unlikely to succeed. Thus, in December 1991, the DPP refused to prosecute the Marquis de Sade's *Juliette*, even though it was concerned (fictionally) with the torture, rape and murder of women and children. But – aside from forfeiture proceedings, discussed below – the use of obscenity law is currently of great significance in relation to the internet; as discussed below the decision in *R v Perrin*[106] sought to adapt obscenity law to explicit web-based expression. Current proposals to introduce a new offence aimed at extreme pornography are also discussed below since they are aimed mainly at the internet, although they would also apply to other media, if implemented.[107]

The defence of public good

This defence, which arises under s 4 of the 1959 Act (as amended by s 53 of the Criminal Law Act 1977) and s 3 of the Theatres Act 1968, was intended to afford recognition to artistic merit. Thus it may be seen as a highly significant step in the direction of freedom of speech, acknowledging the force of a variant of the free speech argument from truth which was also used by the Williams Committee.[108] Under the 1959 Act, it is a defence to a finding that a publication is obscene if it can be shown that 'the publication of the article in question is justified as for the public good in that it is in the interests of science, literature, art, learning or of other objects of general concern'. Under the 1968 Act, the similarly worded defence that covers 'the interests of drama, opera, ballet or any other art or of literature or learning' is somewhat narrower as omitting the concluding general words. Under s 53(6) of the 1977 Act, this narrower defence applies to films. Expert evidence will be admissible to prove that one of these possibilities can be established and it may include considering other works.

It was determined in *Penguin Books* in respect of *Lady Chatterley's Lover* that the jury should adopt a two-stage approach, asking first whether the article in question is obscene and, if so, going on to consider whether the defendant has established the

---

105 For comment see (1976) NLJ 126. The prosecution failed.
106 [2002] EWCA Crim 747, CA. This case involved a French national based in the UK who was publishing from abroad (in the US). The appellant was convicted of publishing an obscene article and appealed. The obscene article in question was a web page on the internet. It depicted people covered in faeces, coprophilia or coprophagia, and men involved in fellatio. That web page was in the form of a trailer, a preview, available free of charge to anyone with access to the internet. Anyone wanting more of the type of material that it displayed could click on to a link marked 'subscription to our best filthy sites' and could gain access to a further web-page by providing credit card details. The preview web-page was accessed by an officer with the Obscene Publications Unit. To reach it a viewer would have to type in the name of the site, or conduct a search for material of the kind displayed.
107 See pp 483–84 below.
108 See above, p 282.

probability that its merits are so high as to outbalance its obscenity so that its publication is for the public good. The failure of the prosecution was seen as a turning point for literary freedom and the jury allowed it to be known that the second stage of the test afforded the basis on which the novel escaped suppression. In *DPP v Jordan*,[109] the House of Lords approved this two-stage approach and the balancing of obscenity against literary or other merit.

In *DPP v Jordan*, the attempt was made to widen the test. The main question was whether the articles in question – hardcore pornography – could be justified under s 4 as being of psychotherapeutic value for persons of deviant sexuality in that the material might help to relieve their sexual tensions by way of sexual fantasies. It was argued that such material might provide a safety valve for such persons, which would divert them from anti-social activities and that such benefit could fall within the words 'other objects of general concern' deriving from s 4. The House of Lords, however, held that these words must be construed *ejusdem generis* with the preceding words 'art, literature learning, science'. As these words were unrelated to sexual benefit, the general words that followed them could not be construed in the manner suggested. It was ruled that the jury must be satisfied that the matter in question made a contribution to a recognised field of culture or learning which could be assessed irrespective of the persons to whom it was distributed.

Although the test of public good has clearly afforded protection to freedom of expression in relation to publications of artistic merit, it has been criticised. It does not allow for consideration of the benefits of pornography and may be inapt as a means of considering 'new art at the cutting edge of art development'.[110] It requires a jury to embark on the very difficult task of weighing a predicted change for the worse in the minds of the group of persons likely to encounter the article, against literary or other merit. Thus, an effect or process must be imagined that, once established, must be measured against an intrinsic quality. Geoffrey Robertson has written: 'the balancing act is a logical nonsense [because it is not] logically possible to weigh such disparate concepts as "corruption" and "literary merit"'.[111] The test seems to create an almost complete paradox: it assumes that an individual can be corrupted, which suggests a stultifying effect on the mind and yet can also experience an elevating effect due to the merit of an article. However, such an interpretation of the test is open to two objections. First, a person could experience corruption in the sense that her moral standards might be lowered, but she might retain a sense of literary or artistic appreciation. Secondly – and this might seem the more satisfactory interpretation – the *message* of the article and its general artistic impact (through, for example, its influence on other works which followed it) might be for the public good although some individuals who encountered it were corrupted. Thus the term 'publication' in s 4 must mean publication to the public at large, not only to those who encounter the article if the test is to be workable.[112]

It should be noted that, as discussed below, the defence can be avoided by bringing a charge of indecency at common law; as *Gibson*[113] demonstrated, the merits of

---

109 [1977] AC 699.

110 Kearns, P, 'Obscene and blasphemous libel: misunderstanding art' [2000] Crim LR 652, p 654.

111 Robertson, *Obscenity, op cit*, fn 1, p 164.

112 The House of Lords in *Jordan* [1977] AC 699 appeared to take this view. See also Robertson, *ibid*, on the point (pp 168–69).

113 [1990] 2 QB 619; [1991] 1 All ER 439; [1990] 3 WLR 595, CA.

an obscene object may, paradoxically, prevent its suppression while the merits of less offensive objects may not.

Forfeiture proceedings

The vast majority of actions against allegedly obscene material take the form of forfeiture proceedings. Under s 3 of the 1959 Act, magazines and other material, such as videos, can be seized by the police if it is suspected on reasonable grounds that they are obscene and have been kept for gain. No conviction is obtained; if found to be obscene, the material is merely destroyed; no other punishment is imposed and therefore s 3 may operate at a low level of visibility. Seizure may mean that the safeguards provided by the Act can be bypassed: consideration is not given to the possible literary merits of such material because the public good defence is not taken into account in issuing the seizure warrant. The merits of an article can be taken into account in the forfeiture hearing in determining whether it out-balances its obscenity, but there is not much evidence that magistrates take a very rigorous approach to making such a determination. They do not need to read every item, but need only look at samples selected by the police[114] and seem, in any event, more ready than a jury to find that an item is obscene.[115] It seems, therefore, that the protection afforded by the 1959 Act to freedom of speech may depend more on the exercise of discretion by the police as to the enforcement of s 3 or on the tolerance of magistrates, rather than on the law itself. However, s 3 can be used only in respect of material which may be obscene rather than in relation to any form of pornography; it was held in *Darbo v DPP*[116] that a warrant issued under s 3 allowing officers to search for 'sexually explicit material' was bad on its face, as such articles would fall within a much wider category of articles than those that could be called obscene.

Statutory obscenity, the HRA and the protection of morals exception under Art 10(2)

Clearly, any prosecutions under the Act or forfeiture actions constitute interferences with the Art 10 guarantee of freedom of expression under the HRA, although subject to justification. In relation to any particular decision, the public authorities involved are bound by s 6 of the HRA to ensure that the tests under Art 10 are satisfied, while the provisions of the 1959 Act must be interpreted consistently with Art 10, if necessary, under s 3 HRA. As Chapter 4 indicated, s 12 HRA does not apply to criminal proceedings. Forfeiture proceedings have the hallmarks of criminal proceedings in certain respects, although a conviction is not obtained, and therefore they are probably outside the ambit of s 12.

---

114 *Crown Court at Snaresbrook ex p Metropolitan Police Comr* (1984) 148 JP 449.
115 Bailey and Taylor note (1st edn *op cit*, fn 1, p 328) that comment arose when forfeiture proceedings of an edition of the magazine *Men Only* coincided with the jury acquittal of the editors of *Nasty Tales* of the offence under s 2 ((1973) 127 JPN 82). Robertson argues (*Obscenity*, 1979, p 96) that as the hearing is before a tribunal which has already decided that the material is – at least prima facie – obscene, it is likely to have an appearance of unfairness. The Bench may be unlikely to be convinced that in effect, it was wrong in the first place in issuing the summons.
116 (1992) *The Times*, 4 July; [1992] Crim LR 56.

Given the wide margin of appreciation afforded to the domestic authorities in the relevant decisions, little guidance as to the requirements of Art 10 in this context is available, especially where the material is directed at a willing adult audience. The domestic judiciary are, therefore, theoretically free to take a different stance. The decisions considered above at Strasbourg on the 1959 Act indicate that the statutory regime relating to publication of an obscene article under s 2 is broadly in harmony with Art 10 of the European Convention. Nevertheless, a specific decision might not meet the proportionality requirements, when scrutinised either at domestic or Strasbourg level.

The UK forfeiture regime has not itself been tested at Strasbourg. The HRA requirements may be especially pertinent in relation to forfeiture: the magistrates conducting the proceedings are, of course, bound by Art 10 and therefore would be expected to approach the task with greater rigour. In particular, it is arguably necessary to examine each item, even where a large-scale seizure has occurred, rather than considering a sample of items only.[117] But since, in practice, a vast amount of material is condemned as obscene in legal actions for forfeiture, the practical difficulties facing magistrates make it possible, especially initially, that the impact of the HRA will be more theoretical than real. It seems probable that, in practice, magistrates will not examine each item and will give only cursory attention, if any, to considering the application of the somewhat elusive Strasbourg case law. However, if on occasion publishers seek to contest s 3 orders before a jury, the proportionality of the measures adopted may receive more attention. Moreover, it is arguable that Art 6 might be breached by the procedure since it could be said to lack impartiality, given that the same magistrate may sign the seizure order, and determine forfeiture.[118]

Statutory indecency

The concept of indecency, as opposed to obscenity, is contained in certain statutes and also exists at common law. The idea of prohibiting indecency is, essentially, to prevent *public displays* of offensive material or the possibility that such material will impinge in some way on the general public, or a part of it. Such prohibition is aimed at protecting persons from the shock or offence occasioned by encountering certain material, rather than at preventing moral deterioration. Therefore, except perhaps in a very broad sense, it may be said not to be aimed at the protection of morals and so might not fall within that exception to Art 10. The general lowering of moral standards or attacks on the moral fabric of society must occur – if it is assumed that it is likely to occur at all – through the medium of individual persons who are affected by encountering obscene material;[119] it would seem, therefore, that the 'moral fabric of society' would be unaffected by material which only serves to shock. However, it might be very broadly argued on a conservative view that indecent material might have a corrupting effect if it was repeatedly encountered because it might lead at each encounter to less outrage

---

117 It was found that such sampling was acceptable in *Snaresbrook Crown Court ex p Comr of the Metropolis* (1984) 79 Cr App R 184. For discussion, see Stone, R [1986] Crim LR 139.

118 See above, Bailey and Taylor (1st edn *op cit*, fn 1, p 328).

119 For criticism of the view that preventing the lowering of the moral tone of society justifies censorship, see the introduction to this chapter, pp 392–93.

as sensibilities became blunted. In any event, the European Court of Human Rights has found that material that was, arguably, merely shocking, fell within the protection of morals exception.[120]

If the material is not obscene and is either stored with a view to sale, or offered for sale, it will not attract liability, unless the provision of s 160 of the Criminal Justice Act 1988 apply (below). Indecency is easier to prove than obscenity because there is no defence of public good, there is no need to consider the whole article and there is no need to satisfy the difficult test of deprave and corrupt. Prosecuting authorities have taken note of these distinctions and have therefore tended at times to rely on the law against indecency where, arguably, the article in question could be said to be obscene.[121] It will be seen that the existence of these two strands of law has led to some anomalies.

Meaning of indecency

The test for indecency was discussed in *Knuller v DPP*;[122] it was determined by Lord Reid to be satisfied by material which creates outrage or utter disgust in 'ordinary decent-minded people'. This statement, coupled with the general tenor of Lord Reid's comments, suggested that the level of shock would have to be fairly high. In *GLC ex p Blackburn*,[123] Lord Denning approved the simple test of 'is this indecent?' since he considered that if jurors were asked the more complex question 'will it deprave and corrupt?' they would allow very offensive articles into circulation. However, Lord Bridge wondered whether asking whether something is shocking or disgusting could be a suitable test of criminality. Sir Robert Megarry has said that 'indecency' is too subjective and emotional a concept[124] to be workable as a legal test. It seems that the test is not confined to sexual material; Lord Reid in *Knuller* considered that 'indecency is not confined to sexual indecency'.[125] This is supported by the finding in *Gibson*[126] that the use of freeze-dried foetuses as earrings on a model of a head was indecent.

Uncertainty arises as to whether the term 'indecency' denotes a relative concept: a concept which, like that of relative obscenity, depends on its context or on the nature of the audience or recipient. According to the ruling of the Court of Appeal in *Straker*,[127] such considerations are irrelevant: indecency is an objective quality discoverable by examination in the same way that, for example, a substance might be discovered to be a certain chemical. However, *Wiggins v Field*[128] suggests otherwise; the ruling specifically demanded that the circumstances in which the alleged indecency occurred should be taken into account. A prosecution was brought in respect of a reading of Allen Ginsberg's poem 'America' on the basis of a charge of using indecent language

120 *Müller v Switzerland* (1988) 13 EHRR 212.
121 This trend is reflected in Lord Denning's comments in *GLC ex p Blackburn* [1976] 1 WLR 550, p 556.
122 [1973] AC 435, p 457; [1972] 3 WLR 143; (1972) 56 Cr App R 633.
123 [1976] 3 All ER 184.
124 *A Second Miscellany at Law*, 1973, p 316.
125 [1973] AC 435, p 458.
126 [1990] 2 QB 619; [1991] 1 All ER 439, CA.
127 [1965] Crim LR 239; this approach was affirmed by the Court of Appeal in *Stamford* [1972] 2 WLR 1055; [1972] 2 All ER 427.
128 [1968] Crim LR 50.

in contravention of a local bylaw. The Divisional Court held that if the context was considered – this was the work of a recognised poet, read without any intention of causing offence – the charge of indecency could not be supported. This stance was taken by the Court of Appeal in *AG ex rel McWhirter v IBA*;[129] it was agreed that the film in question 'taken as a whole' was not offensive, although a small percentage of it depicted indecent incidents. Thus it may be that the Straker ruling, to the effect that indecency may be treated as an objective concept, is confined to cases arising under the Post Office Act 1953, but the point cannot yet be regarded as settled. However, it is clear that the notion of indecency will vary from generation to generation and that the jury will be expected to apply current standards.[130]

The variety of specific statutory offences

The word 'indecent' is contained in a number of statutes and bylaws. Therefore, only specific areas are covered, but if no statute affects a particular area, the gap may be filled by the common law. Taking an indecent photograph or film of a person under the age of 18 is prohibited under s 1 of the Protection of Children Act 1978 (as amended by the Sexual Offences Act 2003), as is possessing it with a view to sale, showing it or distributing it. The only intention needed is the intention to take a photograph; whether the photograph is indecent depends on the view of the jury regarding recognised standards of propriety.[131] No artistic merits defence is available, although the distributor of the photographs, not the taker of them, can seek to show that he had a 'legitimate reason' for distributing or showing the photographs or for having them in his possession. Section 84 of the Criminal Justice and Public Order Act 1994 amended the 1978 Act to add 'pseudo-photographs' of children in order to cover digitally created photographs.[132] It also amended the Act so that the storage of data on computer disk or by other electronic means capable of conversion to a photograph is covered. Section 160 of the Criminal Justice Act 1988 created an additional offence of merely possessing the indecent picture of a child without a view to sale, display or distribution. The offence under either the 1978 or the 1988 Act can be committed merely by downloading an image onto a computer;[133] automatic storage of an image on a hard disk would not amount to making a photograph or pseudo-photograph.[134] Further, it has been found that possession requires knowledge.[135] In *Oliver, Hartrey and Baldwin*[136] the Court of Appeal found that pornographic images were to be categorised by the a number of levels of seriousness, beginning with images depicting erotic posing with no sexual activity.

---

129 [1973] QB 629.
130 *Shaw v DPP* [1962] AC 220, p 292. This approach was accepted in *Stamford* [1972] 2 WLR 1055; [1972] 2 All ER 427.
131 See *R v Graham-Kerr* (1988) 88 Cr App R 302: this offence is discussed further at pp 459–61 below in relation to films.
132 See further Manchester, C, 'Criminal Justice and Public Order Act 1994: obscenity, pornography and videos' [1995] Crim LR 123, pp 123–28.
133 *R v Bowden* [2000] 2 All ER 418.
134 *Atkins v DPP* [2000] 2 All ER 425.
135 *Ibid.*
136 [2003] Cr App R 28. See further below at p 460.

The breadth of these offences was illustrated when the Saatchi Gallery in London was threatened with prosecution in March 2001 for showing pictures of children playing naked on the beach, taken by their mother, a professional photographer, as what one commentator called 'a celebration of the wonderment and joie de vivre of her children'.[137] The prosecution did not materialise, apparently on the basis that no element of lewdness was present. Similarly, when the Mapplethorpe exhibition was shown at the Hayward Gallery in London in Autumn 1996, the gallery took legal advice owing to the sexually explicit nature of some of the exhibits. Prosecution under the 1959 and/ or under the 1978 Act appeared to be a possibility. It decided not to show three photographs, one of which was of a child.[138]

Offensive displays fall under the Indecent Displays (Control) Act 1981.[139] The Act provides, under s 1(1): 'If any indecent matter is publicly displayed the person making the display and any person causing or permitting the display to be made shall be guilty of an offence.' The Act provides in s 1(2) that 'Any matter which is displayed in or so as to be visible from any public place shall, for the purposes of this section, be deemed to be publicly displayed.' 'Public place' is then defined as 'any place to which the public have or are permitted to have access (whether on payment or otherwise) while that matter is displayed'.[140] There are various exceptions to the definition of 'public places': the Act does not apply to the theatre, cinema, broadcasting, museums, art galleries, local authority or Crown buildings (s 1(4)). Shops which display an adequate warning notice are exempted[141] as far as adults are concerned; thus, as will be seen below, art galleries are, anomalously, more constrained in their displays than sex shops, in that they will fall within the common law on indecency and will not be able to take advantage of this exception.

Mailing of obscene or indecent items is covered by s 85 of the Postal Services Act 2000;[142] sexual literature in luggage is covered by s 49 of the Customs and Excise Management Act 1979. In the 1970s, customs officials interpreted the term 'indecency' widely; in 1976, for example, they seized and destroyed 114,000 books and magazines and 4,000 films. It also appeared that the test was being used in an arbitrary and indiscriminate manner. For example, in 1985 books ordered by the bookshop 'Gay's the Word' were impounded, including books by Oscar Wilde and Gore Vidal. The trial was about to commence, but the proceedings were withdrawn because of the ruling of the European Court of Justice in *Conegate Ltd v Customs and Excise Comrs*.[143] It was held that under Art 36 of the Treaty of European Union[144] that Britain could not apply a more stringent test – indecency – to imported goods when the equivalent in terms of

---

137 See the *Guardian*, Report, 10 March 2001, p 9.
138 See further Warbrick, 'Federalism and free speech', in Loveland (ed), *Importing the First Amendment*, 1997, pp 177–79 and 190–92.
139 For discussion of the effect of the Act, see: (1982) Stat LR 31; (1981) 45 MLR 62; (1981) 132 NLJ 629.
140 Section 1(3).
141 Section 1(3)(b).
142 Formerly, the Post Office Act 1953, s 11.
143 [1987] QB 254; [1986] 2 All ER 688. Figures quoted by Robertson, *Obscenity*, 1979, p 193.
144 Formerly Art 30 of the Treaty of Rome.

domestically produced ones could circulate freely because they were not obscene. Thus, where obscenity or indecency existed as alternatives, the easier test should not be used to favour domestic goods since that would amount to arbitrary discrimination on trade between member states contrary to Art 36. Customs officers now apply this ruling but not just to EU imports, because it would be too impracticable to apply different tests to imports from different countries. This ruling has therefore resulted in a major relaxation of censorship. 'Hardcore' pornography is, however, still seized; this is justifiable under Art 36 because it would also be prohibited if disseminated internally under the Obscene Publications Act.

Anomalies have arisen from the dichotomy between the tests for indecency on the one hand and obscenity on the other in other contexts. In *Straker*,[145] obscenity charges which resulted in an acquittal were brought in respect of the sale of artistic nude studies. The defendant then sent the pictures by post to persons interested in photographic art and was prosecuted successfully under s 11 of the Post Office Act 1953. In other words, the mere fact that the articles happened to be transferred through the post meant that criminal liability could arise, although otherwise it could not have done so. The DPP has recognised the anomalies created by cases of this nature and therefore he indicated – in 1981 – that prosecutions under the Post Office Act would be confined to cases where the indecent material sent through the post was unsolicited.

Apart from statutes prohibiting the promulgation of indecent material in specific situations, the possibility also arises of using the Sexual Offences Act 1956 to prevent displays of indecency in stage plays and perhaps in the context of other live performances. A play, *The Romans in Britain*, which was staged in 1982 by the Royal National Theatre, included a depiction of the homosexual rape of a young druid priest by three Roman soldiers. Mary Whitehouse wanted to bring an action in respect of this scene, but the Attorney General refused permission as required under s 8 of the Theatres Act. Under s 2 of the Act, liability at common law could not arise in respect of a stage performance. Therefore, Mary Whitehouse invoked s 13 of the Sexual Offences Act 1956, which proscribes the procurement by one male of an act of gross indecency on another. This was arguably fulfilled by the procurement by the male director of the commission of an act of gross indecency by one actor on another. Had a female director been in charge, no prosecution would have been possible. It was determined on a preliminary ruling that prima facie liability might be established using this method.[146] At that point the prosecution was withdrawn; Mary Whitehouse had established the point in question and did not wish to take the risk that the prosecution would fail, as it might have done on various grounds. In particular, it was uncertain whether it could be shown that any indecency took place: it was unclear whether the actor's penis or thumb was shown in the scene. The significance of this possibility should not be over-emphasised; nevertheless, it clearly subverts the purpose of the Theatres Act, which should therefore be amended to prohibit liability arising under other statutes.

---

145 [1965] Crim LR 239; this approach was affirmed by the Court of Appeal in *Stamford* [1972] 2 WLR 1055; [1972] 2 All ER 427.
146 See *Bogdanov* (1982), unreported. See A Samuels 'Non-Crown Prosecutions: Prosecutions by non-police agencies and by private individuals' (1986) Crim LR 33.

Statutory indecency, the HRA and the protection of morals exception under Art 10(2)

Prosecutions under these provisions will normally constitute interferences with freedom of expression under the HRA. The public authorities involved are bound by s 6 of the HRA to ensure that the tests under Art 10 are satisfied, while the provisions of the various statutes must be interpreted consistently with Art 10 under s 3. As Chapter 2 indicated, state interference with the Art 10 guarantee must be in accordance with the law, under para 2, if it is to be justified. This requirement covers not only the existence of national law, but its quality. In *Kopp v Switzerland*[147] the Court clearly stated that the essential requirements of a national legal basis are those of accessibility and foreseeability. These requirements require precision so that, in this context, the citizen is sufficiently aware of the meaning of the term 'indecency'. It is suggested that, as currently interpreted, the term is so uncertain that there is at least room for argument that these statutory provisions do not meet the 'prescribed by law' requirement. In *Hashman and Harrup v UK*,[148] the Court found that the *contra bono mores* doctrine was too uncertain to meet this requirement, since it depended on a vague concept of anti-social behaviour. Arguably, the concept of indecency considered in *Knuller v DPP*,[149] which depends on considering whether material would disgust 'ordinary decent-minded people', is almost equally imprecise; as pointed out above, doubts have been expressed as to the suitability of such a concept as a basis for criminality.

It would, of course, be a bold domestic court that was prepared to find such a significant flaw in a large number of statutory provisions (and in respect of common law indecency, discussed below). The Commission has had the opportunity of making such a finding but has not done so,[150] and neither did the Court in *Muller*,[151] although this is not conclusive of the issue. It is much more likely that certain aspects of this statutory regime will be found to be disproportionate to the legitimate aim pursued, either in terms of the provisions themselves or in respect of decisions made under them. The Indecent Displays Act comports readily with the findings on adult autonomy from *Scherer* and *Hoare* since it impliedly does allow adults to choose to acquire explicit material, but does not allow it to be foisted upon an unwilling public, and makes special provision to protect children. However, it is suggested that the provisions of s 160 of the Criminal Justice Act 1988, affecting the downloading of pseudo-photographs of persons under 16 onto a computer, presumably from a website, might be viewed as disproportionate to the aim in view. The provisions criminalise a person merely for possessing a photograph, or its equivalent, which has been created without the involvement of a child. It is hard to view the use of the criminal law in this way as proportionate, since it is unclear that morals could be protected by this means. The breadth of the offences under the Protection of Children Act was indicated by the possibility of prosecution in respect of the Saatchi exhibition. Arguments regarding proportionality could be raised in a similar instance, especially regarding the lack of an artistic merits defence or a defence of

147 (1999) 27 EHRR 91, paras 70–71.
148 (2000) 8 BHRC 104. See Chapter 9, p 586.
149 [1973] AC 435, p 457; [1972] 3 WLR 143.
150 *Gibson v UK*, Application No 17634.
151 See p 405 above.

legitimate reason applicable to the creator of the photographs, so that the taking and distributing of photographs of children by paedophiles is not distinguished from the taking of them for artistic or scientific purposes.

Finally, the phenomena of 'revenge porn', in which intimate images of individuals are posted online, usually out of spite by former lovers, has recently been criminalised by ss 33–35 of the Criminal Justice and Courts Act 2015. This provision was enacted in response to the concern that the law was insufficient to protect those who had originally consented to the taking of the image at the time but objected after the end of the relationship. Section 33 makes it an offence to disclose private sexual photographs or firm if the disclosure is made without consent and with the intention of causing distress to the individual depicted. Defences are limited, such as disclosure in the public interest. Section 34 defines disclosure as giving or making available to another person. Section 35 defines private as something 'that is not of a kind ordinarily seen in public' and sexual as showing exposed genitals or pubic area or content that 'a reasonable person would consider to be sexual because of its nature'.

Common law offences of indecency and obscenity

Prosecutions for conspiracy to corrupt morals can be brought at common law, as can prosecutions for outraging public decency. Thus, common law indecency creates a much wider area of liability than is created under statute because the law is not confined to specific situations such as using the mail. In *Shaw v DPP*,[152] the House of Lords determined that the offence of conspiring to corrupt public morals existed on the basis that the law conferred a general discretion to punish immoral (not merely criminal) conduct which could injure the public. Thus, any subject-matter that could lead others astray – although not necessarily amounting to a criminal offence – could be the subject of a prosecution if two or more persons were involved. Lord Reid, in his dissenting judgment, argued that the decision offended against the principle that the criminal law should be certain; it would be very difficult to determine beforehand what a jury would consider to fall within the area of liability created. The DPP then used this form of liability in instances where the material in question appeared to fall outside the Obscene Publications Act or added a charge of conspiracy to corrupt public morals to a charge of obscenity as an alternative in case the obscenity charge failed. The decision in *Shaw* has been especially criticised on the basis that it left it unclear whether an agreement to commit adultery could amount to a criminal conspiracy.[153]

Despite such criticism, the House of Lords confirmed the existence of the offence of conspiring to corrupt public morals and also the existence of the substantive offence of outraging public decency and conspiring to commit it in *Knuller v DPP*,[154] which concerned publication of homosexual contact advertisements. The conviction on the latter count was, however, overturned because the trial judge had misdirected the jury as to the ingredients of the offence. The House of Lords ruled that the necessary 'public'

152 [1962] AC 220; [1961] 2 WLR 897, HL; for comment, see (1961) 24 MLR 626; (1964) 42 Canadian Bar Review 561.
153 See Robertson, *op cit*, fn 1, p 215.
154 [1973] AC 435; [1972] 3 WLR 143; (1972) 56 Cr App R 633, HL.

element would be present even if the indecency was not immediately visible, since it appeared on an inside page, so long as there was an express or implied invitation to penetrate on the cover and partake of the lewd contents; therefore there must be a reference on the cover to the contents. Furthermore, the contents must be so offensive that the sense of decency of the public would be outraged by seeing them. Whether or not a member of the public *would* be so outraged would be determined by reference to that section of the public likely to frequent the place where the publication in question was sold. In this respect, conspiracy to outrage public decency differs from conspiracy to corrupt public morals, which requires that the public at large must be considered. The motive in offering the article will be irrelevant, although it will be necessary to show that the defendant was aware both of the lewd nature of the material in question and that it was being placed on public sale.

Both these offences were preserved in s 5(3) of the Criminal Law Act 1977, and in *Gibson*[155] the Court of Appeal reaffirmed the ruling of the House of Lords in *Knuller* as to the ingredients of the offence of outraging public decency. The defendants were convicted of the offence after displaying in an art gallery a model of a human head with earrings made out of freeze-dried human foetuses of three to four months gestation. It may be noted that, at first instance, the jury was directed that they were entirely free to use their own standards in deciding whether the model was indecent. Argument on appeal centred on s 2(4) of the 1959 Act which provides that where a prosecution is brought in respect of an obscene article, it must be considered within the Act, not at common law, 'where it is of the essence of the offence that the matter is obscene'. 'Obscene' could denote something that disgusted the public or something that had a tendency to corrupt; if it carried the first meaning, the prosecution failed, as there was no suggestion that the exhibition of the earrings had a tendency to corrupt. Moreover, if the second, more restricted meaning were accepted, that would undermine the defence contained in s 4 of the Act which could be invoked if the material in question was, *inter alia*, of artistic worth. However, Lord Lane held that the words of s 1(1) were plain and clearly indicated that the restricted meaning of 'obscene' applied throughout the Act; he refused to depart from the normal canons of statutory construction.

If the defence argument on the meaning of obscene had been accepted, a greater number of publications would have fallen within the Obscene Publications Act and could have benefited from the s 4 defence, although this would also have meant extending the ambit of the Act, including the powers of seizure under s 3. As it is, the anomaly has been continued that the artistic merit of objects that more seriously breach normal moral standards – objects that may corrupt – can prevent their suppression while the merits of less offensive objects cannot. This anomaly could have been addressed not by extending the meaning of obscenity, but by introducing a defence of public good which would have applied to common law indecency. A further anomaly arises due to the exclusion from the Indecent Displays (Control) Act 1981 of art galleries, which, as noted above, are actually more restricted under common law. It was found in *Gibson* that the prosecution did not have to prove an intent to outrage public decency or recklessness as to the risk of such outrage; it was only necessary to prove that a defendant

---

155 [1990] 2 QB 619; [1991] 1 All ER 439; [1990] 3 WLR 595; for comment, see Childs [1991] PL 20–29.

had intentionally done an act that in fact outraged public decency; he could not escape liability merely because his own standards were so base that he could not appreciate that outrage might be caused. This requirement may be contrasted with the full *mens rea* required for conspiracy to corrupt public morals. In *Knuller*, the House of Lords found that the defendant must intend to corrupt morals.

In the HRA era, the opportunity may arise to consider whether the continued existence, unmodified, of these common law doctrines is justifiable, in the light of the statutory regimes with which they overlap. A court in the discharge of its duty under s 6 HRA could curtail these offences, by reference to Art 10. These two common law offences are each aimed at a distinct mischief. Conspiracy to corrupt public morals clearly stems from the same roots as the offence under the Obscene Publications Act, rather than forming a part of the laws against indecency. Its existence is therefore perhaps even less defensible than that of conspiracy to outrage public decency, since it covers an area of liability that cannot be distinguished from that covered by the 1959 Act and is therefore most likely to allow escape from the statutory safeguards. It can exist only on the basis that its *actus reus* is the agreement between the parties rather than the risk of corruption of morals, whereas common law indecency can be distinguished from the offence under the 1959 Act on the more substantial basis that it is concerned in essence with indecency rather than obscenity.

On the other hand, it may be argued that the protection of morals answers to a more weighty public interest than the prevention of shock or outrage, and this contention is reflected in Art 10, which contains an exception expressed in terms of the former interest, but not the latter. However, when the defendants in *Gibson* applied to the European Commission alleging a breach of Art 10,[156] the application was found inadmissible, suggesting either that in the particular circumstances, the conviction might have appeared to have the effect of protecting morals, as opposed to merely preventing outrage, or that the protection of morals exception may sometimes cover material which merely shocks. It must be said that, at present, the European Court has not always drawn a clear distinction between the two mischiefs: in *Müller v Switzerland*,[157] paintings found to offend morals under Swiss law fell within Art 10(2) as likely to 'grossly offend the sense of sexual propriety of persons of ordinary sensitivity'. This sounds like indecency rather than corruption, but the Court blurred the distinction between them in implying that the former would merge with the latter once a certain level of offensiveness was reached. That level may be reached, it is suggested, by speech that may best be termed 'very shocking'. The Court made it clear that speech that would merely be termed 'shocking' or 'disturbing' would not reach it. Thus, it seems that these common law offences may be viewed as having a legitimate aim under Art 10(2), although their curtailment is nevertheless warranted because of their uncertain ambit and the anomalies they create.

The capacity of the common law to respond to areas neglected by statute can be seen in *R v Hamilton*.[158] In this case, the Court of Appeal upheld the use of the outraging public decency offence to prosecute a man who had concealed a digital camera in

---

156 *Gibson v UK*, Appl No 17634.
157 (1991) 13 EHRR 212.
158 [2007] EWCACrim 2062.

a backpack and, without the knowledge of either those involved or the store where it occurred, had filmed up the skirts of female shoppers. The fact that others had not seen the defendant was irrelevant:

> the public element in the offence is satisfied if the act is done where persons are present and the nature of what is being done is capable of being seen; the principle is that the public are to be protected from lewd, obscene or disgusting acts which are of a nature that outrages public decency and which are capable of being seen in public.[159]

The question for the jury, therefore, was whether the acts were capable of being seen by members of the public, which in this case they clearly were.

4 Inciting hatred on racial, religious or sexual orientation grounds

As set out in the introduction to Part II, the liberal view, as exemplified by John Stuart Mill, is that citizens should be free to criticise the views held by others without fear of state punishment (such as imprisonment or fines) even though that criticism may shock, offend or disturb others unless serious consequences would follow, such as violence or social disorder. Intuitively, one might think UK law has long upheld this view; however, up until very recently, the common law offences of seditious libel and blasphemous libel made it an offence, in the case of the former, to invoke hatred or contempt toward the government and, in the latter, to insult Christianity. The offence of seditious libel, at one time, seemed to cover any attack on the institutions of the state, but in modern times, was interpreted to require an intention to incite to violence and the words used must have had a tendency to incite to violence.[160] Although prosecutions involving either form of libel were rare, the troubling case of *Whitehouse v Lemon*[161] demonstrated the chilling effect that these archaic measures could have. Here, Mary Whitehouse succeeded with a private prosecution against the publication of a poem in *Gay News*, which, amongst other things, ascribed homosexual practices with the apostles to Jesus and made explicit references to sodomy. The Court of Appeal, finding that the offence of blasphemous libel had been committed, held that the crime was of strict liability (and so intention or motive was irrelevant), that the likelihood of an deleterious effect upon the institution of Christianity sufficed, an actual impact need not be proved (i.e. it did not matter that the 'blasphemy' affected no one, only that it might) and that there could be no public interest defence to the prosecution (i.e. serious literature could be caught). In short, all that mattered was that the expression was an offensive treatment of matters sacred to Christians.

Unsurprisingly, this decision was a source of much criticism,[162] not least for its obvious potential to inhibits many, if not most, juxtapositions of sexuality with aspects of

---

159   *Ibid*, [39].
160   *Burns* [1886] 16 Cox CC 333; *Aldred* (1909) 22 Cox CC 1; *Caunt* (1947) unreported, but see case note 64 LQR 203; for comment see Barendt, *op cit*, fn 1 (1st edn), pp 152–60.
161   *Whitehouse v Lemon* [1979] AC 617.
162   See Robertson, *op cit*, fn 1, p 242; Law Commission Report, 1985.

the Anglican religion by writers and broadcasters. Even the courts seemed uncomfortable with the implications of this decision, and in two subsequent decisions refused to extend the crime (albeit on unconvincing grounds) to attacks on other religions[163] and interpreted the *actus reus* element of the crime generously such that, to be considered blasphemous libel, the expression must be not only offensive but so offensive as to '[undermine] society generally, by endangering the peace, depraving public morality, shaking the fabric of society or tending to be a cause of civil strife'.[164]

More recently, there has been a pronounced liberal shift in the law's treatment of speech that offends religious groups, influenced, in part, by the social and political developments of the past 15 years. Blasphemy and blasphemous libel were abolished on 8 July 2008 under s 79 of the Criminal Justice and Immigration Act 2008 and the abolition of seditious libel (along with the two other remaining forms of criminal libel: obscene and defamatory) followed soon after on 12 January 2010 under s 73 of the Coroners and Justice Act 2009. With these measures now removed there is now even greater freedom to attack religious dogma without fear of prosecution yet, as this chapter will discuss, considerably less scope to attack individuals or groups based on their religious beliefs, especially where violence or social disorder would follow.

Incitement to racial and religious hatred[165]

Hate speech: stirring up racial hatred

Domestic provisions

The offence of stirring up racial hatred was introduced under s 6 of the Race Relations Act 1965, in order to meet public order concerns and protect persons from the effects on others of provocative and inflammatory racist expression. The Public Order Act 1936 was amended in order to include this offence, but Part III (ss 17–23) of the Public Order Act 1986 extends its ambit. Section 18 provides that liability will arise if threatening, abusive or insulting words or behaviour are used or written material of that nature is displayed, intended by the defendant to stir up racial hatred or that make it likely that racial hatred will be stirred up against a racial group (not a religious group) in Great Britain.[166] Where intent is not shown, it is necessary to show that the accused realised

---

163 *Chief Metropolitan Magistrate ex p Choudhury* [1991] 1 QB 429.

164 *R (on the application of Green) v City of Westminster Magistrates' Court* [2007] EWHC 2785 (Admin), [16].

165 For discussion and literature referred to below, see: Hare, I and Weinstein, J *Extreme Speech and Democracy*, op cit; Hare, I, 'Crosses, Crescents and Sacred Cows: Criminalising Incitement to Religious Hatred' (2006) Autumn PL 2006, 521–38; Goodall, K, 'Incitement to Religious Hatred: All talk and no substance' [2007] 70(1) MLR 89–113; Hare, I, 'Legislating Against Hate: the Legal Response to Bias Crimes' (1997) 17 OJLS 415. For general discussion of this offence and its background, see: P Gordon, *Incitement to Racial Hatred*, 1982; J.N. Spencer 'Racial hatred, racial harassment and racial violence'(1997), 161(44) JP, 1012-1014; Weinstein, J, 'First Amendment challenges to hate crime legislation: where's the speech?' (1992) 11 Criminal Justice Ethics 6; Law Commission Report No 145, *Offences against Religion and Public Worship*, 1985. See Chapter 15, pp 1075–80 for discussion of the new offence of 'glorifying' terrorism.

166 'Racial group' is defined using the same terms as under the Race Relations Act. The result is that, e.g., hatred may be stirred up against Muslims – so long as the offence under the 1986 Act, s 5 (see Chapter 9, pp 663–70) is not committed – but not against Sikhs.

that the words used might be threatening, abusive or insulting.[167] Section 18(2) catches private or public meetings (unless held in a 'dwelling'). Section 19 makes it an offence to publish threatening, abusive or insulting material, either intended by the defendant to stir up racial hatred or which make it likely that racial hatred will be stirred up against a racial group. Section 21 extends the offence to the distributing, showing or playing of visual images or sounds. Section 20 makes it an offence to stir up racial hatred in the public performance of a play, but the likelihood that hatred will be stirred up must be judged by reference to 'all the circumstances' and 'in particular taking the performance as a whole'. Therefore, the context in which, for example, a character is racially abused must be considered: where the message of the play as a whole could not be viewed as one aimed at stirring up racial hatred, the offence will not be committed. Thus, plays that explore the theme of racism in society should escape liability.

Section 22 makes it an offence to use threatening, abusive or insulting visual images or sounds in a programme, intended by the defendant to stir up racial hatred, or that make it likely that racial hatred will be stirred up against a racial group. Section 164(2) of the Broadcasting Act 1990 amended s 22 so that it covers 'programme services', including cable programme services. The offence under s 22 can be committed by the programme producer, director, the television company and any person 'by whom the offending words or behaviour are used'. This is a broadly worded offence that encourages caution in producing programmes about the problem of racism, since it can be committed without any intent on the part of the producer or the company. Programmes can only be shown if it is made clear, editorially, that the message of racists is disapproved of. Section 23 of the 1986 Act places further obstacles in the way of those producing programmes about racism, particularly historical programmes. Section 23, as amended by s 164(4) of the Broadcasting Act 1990, creates an offence of possessing racially inflammatory (threatening, abusive or insulting) material with a view, in the case of written material, to publication or distribution and, in the case of a recording, to its being distributed, shown, played or included in a programme service, intended by the person possessing it to stir up racial hatred or that makes it likely, having regard to all the circumstances, that racial hatred will be stirred up. Television researchers must be sure that historical material will be placed in a context that makes it clear that its message is disapproved of.

These offences have a number of elements in common. None of them requires a need to show that disorder was caused, or that there was an intent to cause disorder, and there is no need to show that racial hatred is actually stirred up. It is not an essential ingredient to show that there was an intent to stir up racial hatred. It is sufficient to show that hatred *might* actually be stirred up. In that circumstance, s 18 imports an element of *mens rea*, but the other sections do not, a very significant difference.[168] The offence might be committed by broadcasting or using or promulgating words or material by the methods indicated above, threatening, abusive or insulting matter that, objectively

---

167 Section 18(5) governs the *mens rea* if it is not shown that the defendant intended to stir up racial hatred. He must intend the words, etc, to be or be aware that they might be, threatening, abusive or insulting. 'Awareness' as used in the 1986 Act seems to mean subjective recklessness.

168 *Ibid*. The other sections provide a defence – in effect, a reversed *mens rea*: the defendant could prove that he was not aware of the content of the recording/material/broadcast and had no reason to suspect that it was threatening, etc.

speaking, is incapable of stirring up racial hatred so long as the accused intended that it should do so. It may be noted that the s 18 offence is the only public order offence that may be committed by words alone unaccompanied by the need – as an essential ingredient – to show any likelihood that they would cause distress, since the offence could be committed by uttering words that were greeted with delight by those who heard them. But of most significance is the possibility that criminal liability can arise owing to the promulgation of material likely to stir up racial hatred unintentionally. These offences represent a restriction based on manner rather than content due to their specific requirements. Reasoned argument of a racist nature would not incur liability, since the racist words or material must be threatening, abusive or insulting. Further, the term 'hatred' is a strong one: merely causing offence or bringing into ridicule is not enough and nor is racial harassment. The difficulty of showing that race hatred would be likely to be stirred up or that the defendant intended to stir up race hatred was demonstrated when jurors cleared Nick Griffin of using words or behaviour intended to stir up racial hatred in 2006. He was accused of using words or behaviour intended to stir up racial hatred, and faced two alternative counts of using words or behaviour likely to stir up racial hatred. He was charged after making a speech to British National Party (BNP) supporters at a pub in Keighley, West Yorkshire, in January 2004. In it, he described Islam as a 'wicked, vicious faith' and said that Muslims were turning Britain into a 'multiracial hellhole'. The BNP's head of publicity, Mark Collett, was cleared of similar charges. He had referred to asylum seekers as 'cockroaches' and had told the Keighley gathering: 'Let's show these ethnics the door in 2004'. Nick Griffin told the jury that his speech was not an attack on Asians in general, but on Muslims. Mark Collett said that the speeches had only been intended to motivate BNP members to take part in 'legal and democratic' campaigning.[169] The speeches had been filmed by an undercover BBC reporter and were later broadcast as part of the documentary *The Secret Policeman*. The verdict caused a furore amongst anti-racist campaigners since, as a number of organisations stated, had the two been convicted that would not only have indicated the point at which racist speech would not be tolerated by the law, but also it would have indicated the law's intolerance of Islamophobia in British society.[170] The acquittals led to comments from cabinet members to the media about the possible need for a review of the race hatred law in Parliament.[171] The religious hatred offences that followed, discussed below, cover attacks on Muslims (as opposed to attacks on Asians generally) although it is unclear whether convictions would have occurred had they been deployed in the *Griffin* case since they are so narrowly drawn.

Since *Griffin*, the Court of Appeal has upheld a conviction against two men for possessing, publishing and distributing racially inflammatory material, which cast doubt on the existence of the holocaust and contained derogatory remarks about a number of racial groups.[172] Although the website hosting the material was located in California,

---

169 See the *Guardian*, 10 November 2006.
170 A spokesman for the Islamic Human Rights Commission said: 'I am very disappointed. I think this judgment is going to have very grave consequences indeed. It gives a very wrong message to the whole of society, both to the victims of his words and to those who are supporters of his racist and Islamophobic views and the promotion of them.' Sabby Dhalu, of Unite Against Fascism, commented in similar terms. (See the *Guardian* 10 November 2006.)
171 See the *Guardian*, 11 November 2006.
172 *R v Sheppard* [2010] EWCA Crim 65.

the convictions were upheld on the basis that the material was available to view and download in the UK (and other countries). The decision is significant in showing that the offence could be committed without actual proof that anybody had actually seen the material in question (here, the only evidence offered was that one police constable had seen the materials in the course of his duties).

Thus, the current race hatred offences are relatively narrowly conceived; although they cover political expression, they concentrate on the *manner* of the expression. Further, it is hard to conceive that the manner – the form of threats – could itself be defended by reference to the free speech justifications discussed in the Introduction to Part II. The terms 'abuse, insults' are significantly broader. Where the threat, etc, is thematically appropriate since it is placed within a context, such as a play or film touching on the theme or subject of racism, it would probably fall outside the area of liability, since all the circumstances must be taken into account. The breadth of the offences relating to broadcasting are particularly problematic, since, as suggested above, they are likely to deter the production of documentaries dealing with the subject of racism. This position has been exacerbated by the addition of offences of incitement to religious hatred as discussed below.

Hatred and Art 10 protection

Is the expression 'likely to stir up racial hatred' covered by Art 10(1)? In other words, would it be viewed as protected expression at all? In *Lehideux and Isornia v France*[173] it was found that if material is directed towards attacking the Convention's underlying values, it will be outside the protection of Art 10.[174] In that instance, the material supported a pro-Nazi policy. However, in *Kuhnen v FRG*,[175] Art 10 was found to cover the conviction of the applicant for advocating the reinstitution of the Nazi party, although the interference was justified under Art 10(2). Similarly, Art 10 applied in *Glimmerveen and Hagenbeeck v Netherlands*. The applicants had been convicted of possessing leaflets which incited racial discrimination. The interference was found to be justified under Art 10(2). In that instance, Art 17 was relied upon.[176] Where racist expression is concerned, reliance on Art 17, either in addition to Art 10(2) or alone, tends to produce the same result: the interference is found to be justified and the review is not intensive.[177]

Jersild[178] concerned an application by a Danish journalist who had been convicted of an offence of racially offensive speech after preparing and broadcasting a programme about racism that included overtly racist speech by the subjects of the documentary. A breach of Art 10 was found. The interference with expression was found to be disproportionate to the aim pursued – protecting the rights of others. The Court stressed that its finding was directed to the value of enabling the media to act as a public watchdog. The news value of the programme was a matter that could be best assessed by professional

---

173 (1998) 5 BHRC 540.
174 *Ibid*, p 558, para 53.
175 (1988) 56 DR 205.
176 (1979) 18 DR 187. See Chapter 2, p 101.
177 See *X v Germany* (1982) 29 DR 194; *T v Belgium* (1983) 34 DR 158; *H, W, P and K v Austria* (1989) 62 DR 216.
178 *Jersild v Denmark* (1994) 19 EHRR 1.

journalists. The Court also considered that the mode of presenting the broadcast should be determined by journalists. Had the racists who spoke on the programme applied to Strasbourg, their own convictions would have been found to be justified under Art 10(2), if indeed Art 10(1) would have been applicable, which is doubtful.

It seems to be clear that persons directly using threatening or abusive or insulting speech likely to stir up racial hatred would not obtain any benefit by invoking Art 10. But the position of those who aid in the dissemination of such speech, who do not have the purpose of stirring up racial hatred, is different. It is arguable that UK law does not draw a sufficiently clear distinction between the two groups. *Jersild* suggests that the restrictions on broadcasting in relation to racial hatred are open to challenge under the HRA since it would seem possible that if an equivalent situation arose in the UK, the presenter and producer of the programme could be convicted of the offence under s 22 of the 1986 Act. Possibly television researchers involved could also be convicted of the broader offence under s 23.

It is argued as a matter of principle that the prohibition of incitement to racial hatred under the Public Order Act creates an unacceptable infringement of freedom of speech since the offences as currently conceived go beyond the mischief that they are intended to prevent. There is an argument that some provision should be available to prevent some forms of racist speech owing to its special propensity to lead to disorder and that such protection should be extended to religious groups, but it is argued that the Public Order Act offences require reform to encompass a much more narrowly targeted area of liability. Such reform could be effected by narrowing them on the model now represented by the new offence of religious hatred. Possibly s 3 HRA could be relied upon, if necessary, to interpret the term 'circumstances' used in Part 3 of the 1986 Act narrowly. The term is used, as indicated above, in respect of material likely to stir up racial hatred rather than in respect of instances where the defendant intended to do so. No 'public good' defence is included in the 1986 Act. But consideration of the 'circumstances' could include consideration of the extent to which the broadcast or other material was for the public good in terms of its artistic or other merit. Since this is a strained interpretation, s 3 of the HRA might need to be relied upon, in order to achieve compatibility with the demands of Art 10 in respect of a particular provision, in particular ss 22 and 23 of the 1986 Act. Section 6 of the HRA could be relied upon, to find an application of the provision in question that would ensure compatibility with Art 10. For example, in 2007 competitors in the Channel 4 show *Big Brother* made allegedly racist remarks during the live show. If the presenter and producer of the programme were prosecuted under the s 22 offence of the 1986 Act *Jersild* would be relevant under s 2 HRA. It could be argued that s 22 should be narrowly construed in order to avoid bringing anyone other than the competitors themselves within the net of liability, on the grounds of proportionality.[179]

Incitement to religious hatred

The International Covenant on Civil and Political Rights, to which the UK is a signatory, requires contracting states to prohibit the advocacy of 'national, racial or *religious* hatred

179 A somewhat similar argument was used in *Percy v DPP* [2001] EWHC 1125 (Admin).

that constitutes incitement to discrimination, hostility or violence' (Art 20, emphasis added). In practical terms, it is fairly straightforward to amend ss 17–23 of Part III of the Public Order Act 1986 prohibiting incitement to racial hatred,[180] to include religious groups.[181] The first attempt to introduce an offence of inciting religious hatred was made by Lord Avebury's Bill in 2000, which was remitted to a committee for consideration; cl 38 the Anti-Terrorism, Crime and Security Bill 2001 provided for such amendation but was defeated by the Lords; the third attempt appeared in the Serious and Organised Crime Bill 2004; the provision was dropped in order to allow the Bill to go through Parliament in time for the 2005 general election. The Racial and Religious Hatred Act 2005 represents the successful conclusion of the fourth attempt to introduce the new offence.

The Act outlaws incitement to religious hatred. Under s 9B, amending Part 3 of the 1986 Act, a person who uses threatening words or behaviour, or displays threatening written material is guilty of an offence if he intends thereby to stir up religious hatred, and the subsequent sections apply this offence to the media. The Act leaves unchanged the five main ways in which the offence can be committed. These are:

- the use of words or behaviour or display of written material (s 18, Public Order Act 1986);
- publishing or distributing written material (s 19);
- the public performance of a play (s 20);
- distributing, showing or playing a recording (s 21); and
- broadcasting or including a programme in a programme service (s 22).

The version of the Bill that received royal assent included a number of Lords' amendments aimed at protecting freedom of expression. Ministers had urged MPs to reject the Lords' amendments and back instead a government compromise. On 1 February the government suffered two defeats over its attempts to overturn changes that the Lords had imposed on the Racial and Religious Hatred Bill.[182] The votes came after large numbers of persons protested against the bill outside Parliament. The Lords did some excellent work in free speech terms: they imposed an amendment ensuring that only 'threatening' words should be banned, not those that are only abusive or insulting. This was a very significant amendment since 'insulting' is clearly the most problematic term used in the 1986 Act, in free speech terms. They also ensured that the offence could only be committed intentionally. Under the 1986 Act, the offence can be committed

180 For discussion of racial hatred in the context of freedom of speech, see Hare, I, and Weinstein, J, *Extreme Speech and Democracy, op cit*; Robertson and Nichol, *op cit*, fn 1, Chapter 3, pp 129–32; Barendt, *op cit*, fn 1 (1st edn), pp 161–67 and generally Cotterell, R [1982] PL 378; Dickey [1968] Crim LR 489; Gordon, *Incitement to Racial Hatred*, 1982; Leopold, P [1977] PL 389; Wolffe [1987] PL 85. For the argument that the state should seek to ban racially motivated hate speech on the basis of furtherance of equality just as it seeks to outlaw discrimination in employment, see MacKinnon, *op cit*, fn 1. For criticism of the argument, see Sadurski, W, 'On 'Seeing speech through an equality lens': a critique of egalitarian arguments for suppression of hate speech and pornography' (1996) 16(4) OJLS 713.
181 The definition under the Race Relations Act of 'racial group' which will be used under the Public Order Act 1986 does not include religious groups; see *Mandla v Dowell Lee* [1983] 2 AC 548; [1983] 1 All ER 1062, HL. But discrimination on grounds of religion can be viewed as indirect racial discrimination.
182 In the first vote MPs voted by 288 votes to 278 to back the Lords amendments to the Bill. In the second vote, MPs voted by 283 votes to 282 to back the Lords.

either by means of specific intent – if the 'speaker' 'intends thereby to stir up racial hatred' *or* if, 'having regard to all the circumstances, racial hatred is likely to be stirred up thereby'.[183] This part of the Act, allowing for a conviction without intention to incite racial hatred, and indeed, in situations in which no racial hatred was in fact stirred up,[184] has been subject to criticism. The amendments introduced in the House of Lords[185] mean that it is harder to establish that the offence of incitement to religious hatred has been committed than it is to establish incitement to racial hatred since there is no alternative to proving that specific intent is present.

The Lords further imposed a saving clause for freedom of expression (now s 29J), specifying that:

> Nothing in this Part shall be read or given effect in a way which prohibits or restricts discussion, criticism or expressions of antipathy, dislike, ridicule, insult or abuse of particular religions or the beliefs or practices of their adherents, or of any other belief system or the beliefs or practices of its adherents, or proselytising or urging adherents of a different religion or belief system to cease practising their religion or belief system.

So satirising religion in films or plays or broadcasts by comedians cannot be an offence. The saving for free expression that is now s 29J makes it hard to imagine situations in which this offence could be used – since the saving is so broad. It could only be used where 'threatening' words were used intended to incite religious hatred, as opposed to being intended to express antipathy to religion. That leaves a very narrow area of liability. It is possible to imagine a situation in which a person was seeking, via such words, to arouse persons to hatred against e.g., Muslims, as opposed merely to expressing antipathy to Islamic beliefs, but the lines drawn are fine indeed.

However, the offences under the new Act could have been narrowed further. The new offences do not require a need to show that disorder was caused, or that there was an intent to cause disorder, and there is no need to show that religious hatred is actually stirred up, or even that in the circumstances it was likely to be stirred up. The offences might be committed by using or promulgating threatening words or material by the methods indicated above, which, objectively speaking, were incapable of stirring up religious hatred so long as the accused intended that they should do so. The various offences could be committed by uttering words or promulgating material that were greeted with delight by the audience. It may be pointed out that the cl 29B offence is noteworthy as a public order offence which may be committed by words alone unaccompanied by the need – as an essential ingredient – to show any likelihood that they would cause distress.

The fact that in all the media contexts mentioned offences of stirring up religious hatred can now also be committed, creates a serious inroad into freedom of expression. However, the impact of the provisions can be curbed. Prosecutions for the offences of stirring up racial or religious hatred can only be brought with the consent of the Attorney General, which has so far been sparingly given in respect of race hatred. Since the

---

183   Section 18 POA 1096; similar wording is used in all the other offences in ss 19–22.
184   Possible because the Act only requires that it be likely that hatred be stirred up, not that it actually was.
185   The measures referred to are those in the Bill as they were amended by the Lords on 15 October 2005.

Attorney General is a public authority under the HRA, he or she should give careful consideration to Art 10 before giving consent. If prosecutions are brought, the courts are in the same position. They need not, as argued above, give weight to Art 9, on the ground that protection for religious freedom does not include protection against attacks on religion. The term 'hatred' should be given full weight, while the term 'insulting' should, it is argued, be interpreted as meaning insulting to the reasonable, tolerant religious adherent rather than in relation to adherents of a particular sect (or group within a religion), which may be of an extreme nature.

Possibly s 3 HRA could be relied upon, if necessary, to narrow down relevant terms used in Part 3 of the 1986 Act, as amended by the 2005 Act. The 2005 Bill was accompanied by a statement of compatibility under s 19 of the HRA. But, as Chapter 2 argues, such a statement leaves the judges free to consider compatibility afresh. It may be argued that, rather than strive to ensure compatibility, a declaration of incompatibility should be made in order to mark the dangerous potential of the new provisions and to invite Parliament to think again. The view of the Joint Committee on Human Rights on the compatibility of the Bill as originally drafted with Art 10 was as follows:

> We accept the existence of a serious, albeit limited, problem of incitement to hatred on religious grounds. We consider that the measures proposed in the Bill are unlikely to give rise to any violation of the right to freedom of expression under Art 10 of the ECHR.[186]

The decision in *Norwood v UK*,[187] indicates that this view is correct. The applicant belonged to the BNP. The facts were as follows:

> Between November 2001 and 9 January 2002 he displayed in the window of his first-floor flat a large poster . . . supplied by the BNP, with a photograph of the Twin Towers in flame, the words 'Islam out of Britain – Protect the British People' and a symbol of a crescent and star in a prohibition sign.[188]

He was convicted in a magistrates court of the offence under s 5 of the Public Order Act of displaying 'any writing, sign or other visible representation which is threatening, abusive or insulting, within the hearing or sight of a person likely to be caused harassment, alarm or distress thereby'. He was moreover convicted of having committed the offence in religiously aggravated way. He unsuccessfully appealed his conviction to the High Court,[189] which found that the restriction upon his freedom of expression right represented by the offence was proportionate to the legitimate aim of protecting the rights of others, given also the fact that the speech arguably fell within Art 17 ECHR.[190] One of the applicant's arguments was that there was no evidence that any Muslim had

186   Eighth Report of the Joint Committee on Human Rights at [2.59].
187   (2005) 40 EHRR SE11.
188   *Ibid*, at [A].
189   *Norwood v DPP* (2003) WL21491815.
190   This provides: 'Nothing in [the] Convention may be interpreted as implying for any state, group or person any right to engage in any activity or perform any act aimed at the destruction of any of the rights and freedoms set forth herein or at their limitation to a greater extent than is provided for in the Convention.'; see Chapter 2 at p 101. For comment on Art 17 by the House of Lords see *DPP v Collins* [2006] UKHL 40.

in fact seen the poster. The Strasbourg Court, in a brief judgment, found the application inadmissible; in doing so it referred to Art 17:

> Such a general, vehement attack against a religious group, linking the group as a whole with a grave act of terrorism, is incompatible with the values proclaimed and guaranteed by the Convention, notably tolerance, social peace and nondiscrimination. The applicant's display of the poster in his window constituted an act within the meaning of Article 17, which did not, therefore, enjoy the protection of Articles 10 or 14.[191]

Given this judgment, it seems likely that prosecutions under the new law, provided they were used only in clear-cut cases, would be found to be compatible with Art 10. But ss 3 and 6 could possibly be relied upon in more doubtful cases, in which less grossly offensive statements were made than in *Norwood*. *Dehal v Crown Prosecution Service* provides an example of the application of the doctrine of proportionality under s 6 HRA in this type of context.[192] The appellant, a Sikh man, put up a notice at a Sikh temple that he had attended for many years. It was written in Punjabi and attacked the president of the temple and other members of the temple committee. Mr Dehal intended the notice to be read by those it was aimed at and other worshippers. He was convicted of the offence under the Public Order Act 1986, s 4A (1) (it is discussed in Chapter 9 and contains elements similar to those of s 5).[193] His appeal concerned in essence the relationship between Art 10 of the European Convention on Human Rights and the s 4A offence. The Court had to examine the following questions: was the prosecution of the appellant a proportionate response to his conduct and did Art 10 provide him with a defence, therefore making the interference with the appellant's freedom of expression unnecessary? In allowing the appeal, the Court determined that although all the elements of the offence were present, the prosecution had not presented enough evidence to establish that bringing a criminal prosecution was a proportionate response to the appellant's conduct.

The problem of defining religion, of course, still remains. The explanatory notes to the bill state:

> It includes, though this list is not definitive, those religions widely recognised in this country such as Christianity, Islam, Hinduism, Judaism, Buddhism, Sikhism, Rastafarianism, Baha'ism, Zoroastrianism and Jainism. Equally, branches or sects within a religion can be considered as religions or religious beliefs in their own right. The offences also cover hatred directed against a group of persons defined by reference to a lack of religious belief, such as Atheism and Humanism.[194]

Religion is also undefined in relation to discrimination on the grounds of religion and belief in the Employment Equality (Religion or Belief) Regulations 2003.[195] Further,

---

191 *Op cit.*
192 [2005] EWHC 2154.
193 See pp 599, 670.
194 Explanatory Notes to the Bill, at para 13, available: http://www.publications.parliament.uk/pa/ld200506/ ldbills/015/en/06015x –. htm.
195 Reg 2 (the interpretation section) offers no definition of 'religion' or 'belief'.

since such incitement represents a far narrower area of liability than blasphemy, the danger that a wide interpretation of 'religion' would lead to controversy when prosecutions in relation to claims from obscure groups were refused is accordingly less great. Furthermore, prosecutions in this area can only be brought with the consent of the DPP, so the possibility of frivolous prosecutions being brought is slight. The justification sometimes put forward for abrogating free speech in this area is that prohibiting the advocacy of racial hatred does not strike at the core value of free speech because neither individual self-fulfilment, nor the opportunity to arrive at the truth through free discussion, nor the chance to participate meaningfully in democracy[196] seem to be strongly threatened by such a prohibition.

However, the gap in the law that is filled by the new offences is either tiny or non-existent since a range of existing offences, most notably s 5 Public Order Act 1986, or incitement to criminal offences, would cover it in most circumstances.[197] The gap is prima facie only of significance when incitement to hatred, not to a criminal offence, occurs on grounds of religion, and such incitement would not be covered by the existing race hatred laws. But ss 5 and 4A of the 1986 Act would still be available. The obvious beneficiaries of the new law are therefore Muslims. The rationale for introducing the law was that the BNP and other groups were exploiting that gap by making pronouncements intended to stir up racial hatred, but hiding behind attacks on Islam. As Goodall argues, 'it is not difficult to decode . . . statements, from a BNP article called "The Islamic Menace" . . . as not simply anti-Muslim but racist, and [they] will be read so by BNP supporters'. The argument used by Nick Griffin in 2006 at his trial for incitement to racial hatred was that he was only inciting hatred against Islam – so the law may have some benefit in curbing Islamophobia stirred by BNP supporters, since the BNP is seeking to stay within the law, in order to seek to make itself electable.[198] But s 5 of the 1986 Act could have been used against Griffin.

The offences also represent an interference with the individual's moral autonomy, since it amounts to judging both for him and his possible audience what is and is not fit for them to hear.[199] The state is supposed to leave such judgments to the individual because to do otherwise would be to violate the individual's basic right to equal concern and respect.[200] But there is an arguable case for the offence: the interference with moral autonomy involved is necessary to avoid discrimination and there is an argument that the free speech interest involved is relatively weak; in addition, there are strong utilitarian arguments that such a measure would considerably ease racial tension since Muslims now have at least some protection. Nevertheless, it may be argued that the present situation, in which the advocacy of hatred against Muslims or Christians is allowed in a range of circumstances wider than those covered by the race hatred provisions, so that

196 See above, pp 281–83.
197 See on this point: Goodall, K, 'Incitement to Religious Hatred: All talk and no substance' [2007] 70(1) MLR 89–113; Hare, I, 'Legislating Against Hate: the Legal Response to Bias Crimes' (1997) 17 OJLS 415.
198 Goodall, K, 'Incitement to Religious Hatred: All talk and no substance' [2007] 70(1) MLR 89–113.
199 On this point see: Hare, I, 'Crosses, Crescents and Sacred Cows: Criminalising Incitement to Religious Hatred' (2006) Autumn PL 521–38.
200 See, e.g., Dworkin, R, 'Do we have a right to pornography?', in A Matter of Principle, 1985.

Sikhs and Jews enjoy a stronger (and dual) protection from hate speech,[201] still amounts to a denial of equal respect for Muslims.[202]

Prosecutions under the Act are rare. One of the few cases decided, although unreported, is *R v Bilal Ahmad*. Mr Ahmad was convicted for attempting to stir up hatred in an online posting in which he praised Roshanara Choudhry for stabbing her local MP during a constituency meeting. He also listed all other MPs who had voted in favour of the war in Iraq, provided instructions on how to make appointments with them and then provided a link to a supermarket website selling knives. Ahmad was found to have a considerable volume of other online activity, including threatening comments about Hindus posted in March 2009 in response to a newspaper article about Muslim girls being targeted for wearing the veil to college. Documents were also found on his computer either promoting terrorism or containing information likely to be of use to potential terrorists. He received an extended prison sentence of 17 years' imprisonment. Following his conviction, the CPS commented on the decision:

> People are entitled to express their views on the internet and elsewhere. The law seeks to protect the right of all to freedom of speech as is necessary in a democratic society. However, Bilal Ahmad crossed the line from expressing views which some might find unwelcome into serious criminal behaviour, going far beyond what the law allows.[203]

The prosecution for stirring up religious hatred was one of several against Ahmad, including soliciting murder and collecting material likely to be of use in committing terrorism.

Incitement to hatred based on sexual orientation

The offence of inciting hatred based on a person's sexual orientation was introduced by the Criminal Justice and Immigration Act 2008, which amended Part 3A of the Public Order Act 1986. The provision is analogous to that relating to inciting hatred on racial grounds and useful comparison can be made with cases involving that offence. There have been few decided cases so far. The first prosecution under the legislation was *R v Ali, Ahmed and Javed* in 2012. Only the sentencing remarks have been published.[204] These reveal that the convictions were due to the distribution of a threatening leaflet entitled 'Death Penalty?' which, amongst other things, claimed that the death sentence was the only way to erase the 'crime' of homosexuality from society. The three defendants were sentenced to prison terms of between 15 months and two years.

---

201 Muslims, unlike Sikhs and Jews, are not defined as a racial, as well as religious, group. See the definition from *Mandla v Dowell Lee* [1983] 2 AC 548; [1983] 1 All ER 1062, HL. But prejudice against Muslims can possibly be viewed as indirect racial discrimination; but that is not relevant in this context.

202 It might be argued from this that all measures prohibiting incitement to racial hatred should be repealed, but this is not a practicable possibility and would involve the UK in an even clearer breach of Art 20 of the ICCPR than is currently being committed by the lack of protection for Muslims.

203 http://www.cps.gov.uk/news/latest_news/cps_statement_on_bilal_ahmad/.

204 https://www.judiciary.gov.uk/wp-content/uploads/JCO/Documents/Judgments/sentencing-remarks-r-v-ali-javed-ahmed.pdf.

5 Regulating broadcasting

Introduction

This section considers the regulation of broadcasting[205] and concentrates on the regulatory regime that was put in place for broadcasting in 2003. Broadcasting is treated differently from the print media, which is subject only to the criminal law. The stricter system of controls seems to have been adopted in answer to the view that owing to their particular impact on audiences, broadcasting requires regulatory restraint, whereas it is now accepted that books and other printed material do not. Owing to such restraint, it is very unlikely that a broadcast could attract liability under the Obscene Publications Act;[206] nevertheless, it provides a further possibility of restraint and can also be used as a guide as to the standards censorship will observe. Thus, the regulatory regime in place means that broadcasting is censored beyond what the law demands. The impact of the HRA is complicated by the fact that a number of the media bodies involved are private bodies, while the administrative body is a public authority.

Historically, in the UK the scarcity of frequencies was thought to provide part of the rationale for broadcast regulation.[207] But it is not apparent that this rationale can support content-based curbs, although it might support rights of access to a scarce resource[208] of such significance in terms of the efficacy of expression. In any event, cable and satellite television have enormously increased the number of actual and potential channels. Digital technology is continuing to increase the number of channels available. There are far more channels available at present in the UK than there are individual newspaper titles. The high level of regulation to which broadcasting continues to be subject must now therefore be attributed mainly to its status as the most influential means of communication.[209] Since it comes into the home and since so much time is spent watching television, it has been viewed as having a unique impact on people and particularly on children who form a large part of the broadcast audience, especially at certain times of the day. Further, the potential for flouting viewer expectations by inadvertently causing offence when people tune in and out of programmes is thought to provide a cogent rationale for content regulation.[210] In other words, a viewer might be unexpectedly confronted by offensive broadcast material. That is the main reason usually advanced for providing a different and stricter regime for broadcasting as opposed to videos. But as this chapter will reveal, the UK regulatory regime has incrementally moved away from the *general* imposition of certain standards of 'taste and decency' on broadcasting, in favour of curbs premised mainly, although not solely, on protection for children. Thus it has focused more on the use of protective devices – such as the use of the watershed or

---

205 For a comprehensive treatment, see Gibbons, *Regulating the Media*, 1998.
206 The Obscene Publications Act, s 1 covers these media under s 1(2) since the Broadcasting Act 1990, s 162, has brought radio and television within its ambit.
207 See Briggs, A, *The History of Broadcasting*, Vols 1 and 2, 1961 and 1965, OUP; Barendt and Hitchens, *Media Law* 2000, Longman.
208 See the discussion of the US Supreme Court on this point in *Red Lion Broadcasting Co v FCC* (1969) 395 US 367.
209 See Barendt and Hitchens, 2000, pp 5–9.
210 See p 439 below.

of encryption[211] – as opposed to outright bans on the showing of explicit and offensive material. Nevertheless, broadcasting is still restrained to a greater extent than other media.

Adherence to a regulatory regime aimed at the avoidance of offence has been viewed as a part of a 'contract' for the privilege of coming directly into the home, which should be adhered to by responsible broadcasters. The Broadcasting Standards Commission made this point by referring in its code on standards to an implied contract between viewer and broadcaster about the terms of admission to the home.[212] Lord Hoffmann pointed out in *Pro-Life Alliance v BBC*[213] that a similar point was made by Stevens J giving the opinion of the US Supreme Court in *Federal Communications Commission v Pacifica Foundation*[214] in a case about the use of obscene language on sound radio:

> [T]he broadcast media have established a uniquely pervasive presence in the lives of all Americans. Patently offensive, indecent material presented over the airwaves confronts the citizen, not only in public, but also in the privacy of the home, where the individual's right to be left alone plainly outweighs the First Amendment rights of an intruder . . . Because the broadcast audience is constantly tuning in and out, prior warnings cannot completely protect the listener or viewer from unexpected program content. To say that one may avoid further offence by turning off the radio when he hears indecent language is like saying that the remedy for an assault is to run away after the first blow.

However, although these points may have been valid in 1978, they are clearly losing their cogency today, at least in relation to television, as it becomes more and more inter-active. Viewers usually tune in and out of programmes using a menu, which also provides them with consumer advice on programmes. 'Adult material' can be pin-protected or made available on pay-per-view channels only, decreasing the chance that children could access it and obviating the risk of coming across it inadvertently. Thus the chances of involuntary encounters with offensive material have diminished; the argument that children should be protected from material that they deliberately choose to view, continues to retain some cogency.[215] As the interactivity of television broadcasting and the provision of consumer information increases, while improvements occur in the use of security devices such as encoding, its position comes closer to that of the internet, which also comes into the home. Therefore there is a degree of tension in free speech terms between the lack of regulation for the internet and the high level of content-based regulation to which broadcasting is currently subject.

A very different rationale can be advanced to argue that regulation is necessary in order to preserve pluralism – in order to seek to ensure that a range of views, including a variety of political ones, are heard.[216] This can be achieved by imposing requirements

---

211 The broadcasting of adult material and '18'-rated films later in the evening. The provision of warnings and of consumer advice has also become much more prevalent. See pp 444–47 below.

212 Para 2 of the Code. The Code is discussed at p 447 below.

213 [2004] 1 AC 185; [2003] 2 All ER 977.

214 (1978) 438 US 726, 748–49.

215 See the 2005 research conducted by Ofcom on the efficacy of PIN protection systems, p 445, fn 248, below.

216 See Feintuck, M, *Media Regulation, Public Interest and the Law*, 1999.

to broadcast minority interest programmes, 'must carry' requirements,[217] or by imposing more general responsibilities that tend to support diversity, including impartiality
requirements.[218] The unregulated press are openly partisan in the UK, and right-wing and
anti-liberal views predominate.[219] Therefore a significant threat to free expression – in
terms of diversity – comes not from government, but from private corporate bodies. As
Barendt puts it, referring to the free speech rationale from truth:[220] 'it is . . . reasonable to
doubt whether any truth will emerge from an unregulated marketplace in which a handful of media corporations draw up the agenda of political and social discourse and carefully limit the access of individuals and groups which dissent from their programme'.[221]
Therefore this argument provides a rationale for broadcast regulation, even in the context
of a rapidly changing technological landscape, in so far as plurality and impartiality can
be ensured by this means. It does not, however, provide a necessary justification for
restraints based on offence-avoidance. Indeed, such restraints tend to run *counter* to the
enhancement of plurality and diversity since they may curb the more controversial forms
of broadcast speech, including that reflective of the practice of sexual minorities. The
regulatory regimes for broadcast regulation in the UK have tended at one and the same
time to impose curbs based on generally accepted standards of taste and decency, while
making some efforts in the direction of diversity. The contradiction between the two
goals appears to have gone unrecognised both by the legislation and by the regulators.

Content regulation on grounds of offence avoidance

Arguments based on pluralism and autonomy do not underpin the ethos of the current
broadcasting *content* regulatory regime, particularly the continued offensive material
restrictions, contained in the Communications Act 2003. Further, since the restrictions
apply to all forms of broadcasting, including political broadcasting, a matter discussed
further below, they militate against plurality since they may mean that minority forms of
expression are curbed. In terms of restrictions on grounds of offence avoidance, the UK
has traditionally operated one of the strictest regulatory regimes for broadcasting within

---

217 See Communications Act 2003 ss 296 and 309. Under s 296 C4C has obligations in relation to school
     programming. Under s 309 10% of the air time must be allocated to a range and diversity of independ-
     ent productions in digital services.

218 The due impartiality requirements are now contained in the Communications Act 2003, ss 319(c) and
     320; they are reflected in s 5 of Ofcom's Broadcasting Code which came into force in 2005. There
     are three key statutory requirements. First, under s 319(2)(c), news included in television and radio
     services must be presented with due impartiality. Second, under s 320(1)(a), the opinions of persons
     providing a programme service on matters of industrial or political controversy or current public policy
     must be excluded, and third, under s 320(1)(b), all programming should preserve due impartiality on
     those matters, although this last requirement can be satisfied in relation to 'a series of programmes
     taken as a whole'. The BBC's Charter (Cm 6925) was renewed with effect from 2007 until 2016; if a
     complaint relates to the accuracy and impartiality of a programme, the BBC remains finally responsible
     and this continued to be the case when the BBC Charter was renewed at the end of 2006, although
     under a new body – the BBC Trust.

219 Feintuck 1999, *ibid*, at 54–56; Gibbons, T, 'Freedom of the Press: ownership and editorial values'
     (1992) Summer PL 279. The *Telegraph*, the *Mail* and the *Sun* are the highest selling newspapers in their
     different sections of the market. Editorially, they tend towards the right and to anti-liberal views.

220 See Part II introduction, pp 280–81.

221 See *Importing the First Amendment* (1998) Loveland, I, (ed), Barendt, E, Chapter 3 at p 46.

Western Europe. The constraints created by the imposition of content-based responsibilities on broadcasters have inevitably meant that their creative freedom is curtailed. The government had the opportunity to overhaul the regime in 2000 when it was considering the changes to the regulatory regime that eventually came about under the Communications Act 2003,[222] but it drew back from seeking to bring about radical change. The traditional particularly strict regime in relation to matters of taste and decency was continued with some modification and presented in more detail under Part 3 of the 2003 Act. It is a regime that would clearly appear intolerable if applied to the print media. Broadcasting has also been subject to greater restraints than have videos, and such greater restraint continued under the post-2003 regime, although the regime itself is less restrictive and the current broadcast regulator, Ofcom, is taking a relatively liberal stance under its Broadcast Code. This special regime for broadcasting can only be justified by reference to the notion of intrusion into the home, discussed above. Proportionality issues must be considered when creating standards under the 2003 Act (s 3(3)(a)) and determining whether the duty to avoid offence and harm has been breached.[223] This is judged by context and by generally accepted standards; Ofcom has an express duty to abide by free expression principles in relation to that duty.[224] However, this of course adds nothing to the duty it is already under, as a public authority (s 6 HRA).

In making decisions as to offence-avoidance Ofcom is faced with choices on a spectrum of extreme liberality or extreme restraint. It can either deny all viewers the chance of watching explicit or disturbing material or it can operate a highly liberal regime, allowing broadcast audiences the freedom to view such material but expecting them to protect themselves from offence. It is clearly arguable that people have a responsibility to protect themselves from offensive material merely by accessing information via a remote control before tuning into a programme where such material might be present. As warnings, encoding, pin-protection and consumer advice become more effective, this argument becomes more compelling. The small burden placed on viewers in expecting them to take responsibility for their own viewing could readily be viewed as proportionate to the aim of allowing others autonomy in terms of choosing for themselves what they wish to see or hear. In other words, the small chance that someone might inadvertently view something they find offensive provides a doubtful justification for the infringement of autonomy involved in denying all viewers the chance to watch unexpurgated disturbing or sexually explicit material, within the limits created by the criminal law. This argument would apply in particular to the showing of films on television since they would already have been subject to the possibility of cuts to achieve a particular rating.

Regulation on grounds of avoiding offence under the Communications Act 2003

Public broadcasting was and – to an extent – still is governed by the Royal Charter of the BBC which partly comprises a licence agreement. The Broadcasting Act 1996 drew the BBC partly into the regulatory regime, as discussed below, and the 2003 Act

---

222 See the White Paper, *A New Future for Communications*, published 12 December 2000; www. communicationswhitepaper.gov.uk.
223 Sections 3(2)(e) and 319.
224 Section 3(3)(g).

takes that process somewhat further, but still leaves many regulatory matters to the BBC Charter and Agreement, which were renewed at the end of 2006.[225] Under the Charter and Agreement, the Board of Governors of the BBC has the responsibility for maintaining standards of taste and decency and of impartiality. The (1996) Charter and Agreement, amended in 2003, set out in more detail the obligations of the BBC as a public broadcaster operating by means of the licence fee, in particular its obligation to maintain independence. Although it is commercially funded, Channel 4 also has a public service remit governed by s 265 of the Communications Act 2003.

Section 325 of the 2003 Act covers observance of the Code in licensed TV services. It states that the s 319 standards for offence avoidance (see below) are observed in the service provision and a duty is imposed on Ofcom to establish procedures for handling and resolving complaints regarding adherence to the standards. Section 237 allows for the imposition of penalties, including financial penalties, for the contravention of licence conditions or of directions given by Ofcom. If Ofcom is satisfied that a licensee has contravened a provision of a licence or failed to comply with a direction from Ofcom, a penalty can be imposed.[226] Under its own penalty guidelines[227] Ofcom states that the amount of any penalty must be appropriate and proportionate to the contravention in respect of which it is imposed. It states that it must have regard to any representations made by the regulated body in breach, and accepts therefore that in setting the level of penalty, it will consider all relevant circumstances. In particular it states that it will take account of the seriousness of the contravention, precedents set by previous cases, and the need to ensure that the threat of penalties will act as a sufficient incentive to comply. The penalty will be higher where there are repeated contraventions by the same regulated body, where the contravention continues after the body becomes aware of it, or after it has been notified of it by Ofcom.

The Ofcom regime and the position of the BBC

Ofcom also affects public sector broadcasting.[228] This power, introduced under the current regime, represents a highly significant change from the previous regime. It undermines the BBC's independence and brings the BBC far more into conformity with independent television. But at the same time the current statutory regime represents a compromise between BBC editorial freedom and greater regulation by a government regulator[229] since the regime for the BBC has to operate within the parameters of its Charter and Agreement. Section 198 provides that Ofcom may impose financial penalties on the BBC within the powers conferred by the Charter and Agreement if it contravenes the provisions of Part 3 2003 Act or of its Charter and Agreement.[230] The Agreement was amended in 2003 in anticipation of the changes to be introduced

---

225 The Charter (Cmnd 6925) for the continuance of the BBC came into force in 2007 (previously Cmnd 8313); 2006 Agreement: Cmnd 6872.
226 This cannot exceed a fine of £250,000. See further fn 231.
227 From its website: www.Ofcom.org.uk/codes_guidelines/penalty.
228 Section 198(1): 'It shall be a function of OFCOM, to the extent that provision for them to do so is contained in- (a) the BBC Charter and Agreement, and (b) the provisions of this Act and of Part 5 of the 1996 Act, to regulate the provision of the BBC's services and the carrying on by the BBC of other activities for purposes connected with the provision of those services.'
229 See further First Report of Select Committee on Culture, Media and Sport (2004) A Public BBC HC 82-I.
230 Section 198 (2): 'For the purposes of the carrying out of that function OFCOM- (a) are to have such powers and duties as may be conferred on them by or under the BBC Charter and Agreement; and (b)

under the 2006 Agreement, the amendment coming into force in 2004. Clause 13 of the amended BBC Agreement allowed Ofcom to impose penalties, including financial ones, on the BBC[231] if it contravenes a 'relevant enforceable requirement'. A 'relevant enforceable requirement' includes the current Ofcom Broadcasting Code. Thus complaints about harm and offence may be addressed by the BBC, by Ofcom, or by both.

When the BBC's Charter was renewed at the end of 2006 this system changed, but not radically. Under the current Royal Charter[232] the government has created a new body called the BBC Trust to take on the oversight role previously discharged by the governors.[233] Thus the responsibility previously shared between Ofcom and the governors for ensuring offence-avoidance was from January 2007 shared between the BBC Trust and Ofcom. This is also true of complaints about fairness and privacy, as discussed in Chapter 10. But if a complaint relates to the accuracy and impartiality of a programme, the BBC will remain finally responsible.[234] So the BBC is now subject to a dual and overlapping system for complaints regarding offence. Under s 46 of the BBC's 2006 Agreement the Programme Content standards that must be observed are set by s 319 of the 2003 Act, which is discussed below.

Protection from offensive material under s 319 of the Communications Act

The key provision under the 2003 Act in terms of curbing the broadcasting of offensive material is s 319.[235] Section 319(1) of the 2003 Act requires Ofcom to set standards whereby the public is protected from offensive material.[236] The standards objectives for the Code are set out in s 319(2)[237] and include protection for children and a warning that

---

are entitled, to the extent that they are authorised to do so by the Secretary of State or under the terms of that Charter and Agreement, to act on his behalf in relation to that Charter and Agreement.' The maximum penalty that can be imposed is £250,000 (s 198(5)), although the 2003 Act also confers power on the Secretary of State to substitute a different sum (s 198(6)).

231 See Chapter 10, pp 710–11 for further discussion of the position of the BBC in relation to Ofcom.

232 The Green Paper that reviewed the BBC's Royal Charter stated that the government intended to create a new body called the BBC Trust (Review of BBC's Royal Charter *A strong BBC, independent of government*, published May 2005). The White Paper was published in 2006, and the Charter came into force in January 2007. It may be noted that parts of the Green Paper are to be treated as 'White', including the part on governance and accountability. See HL Paper 50-I, 15 March 2005 at para 47.

233 *Ibid*, at p 10, para 3.1.

234 For discussion see Fenwick and Phillipson, fn 1 above, Chapter 20.

235 See also s 3(2)(e), concerning the general duty of Ofcom to secure the application of standards to television and radio services, 'that provide adequate protection for members of the public from the inclusion of offensive and harmful material in such services'. That duty is then encapsulated in more detail in s 319.

236 (1) It shall be the duty of OFCOM to set, and from time to time to review and revise, such standards for the content of programmes to be included in television and radio services as appear to them best calculated to secure the standards objectives.

237 (2) The standards objectives are-

(a) that persons under the age of eighteen are protected;

(b) that material likely to encourage or to incite the commission of crime or to lead to disorder is not included in television and radio services . . .

responsibility must be exercised in relation to the content of religious programmes.[238] Persons under the age of 18 are specifically protected under s 319(2)(a).

The most general restriction is contained in s 319(2)(f), which provides that 'generally accepted standards are applied to the contents of television and radio services so as to provide adequate protection for members of the public from the inclusion in such services of offensive and harmful material'. The term 'generally accepted standards' can be assumed to refer to changing contemporary ideas of what is offensive material.

Section 319(4) gives further guidance as to the matters to be taken into account by Ofcom in securing the standards objectives;[239] they are particularly pertinent in relation to the objective of s 319(2)(f). Section 319(4) does not contain an exhaustive list of the matters that Ofcom must take into account in setting or revising the standards referred to, and, while minimum standards must be apparent under s 319(5)(a), which impliedly reflect the matters listed, Ofcom can take the listed matters into account to the extent that it deems them to be relevant to the securing of the standards objectives. Ofcom is warned not to be too interventionist since it must bear in mind the desirability of maintaining the independence of editorial control over programme content. At the same time it has to consider the extent to which harm or offence may be caused by the inclusion of certain forms of material in programmes.

A distinction is drawn in s 319(4) between material which could give offence in programmes generally, or where it is included in programmes of a particular description. Clearly, this is a crucial distinction: some forms of material may be viewed by Ofcom as too offensive or harmful to be broadcast at all, whereas in most instances the context is the determining factor. The issues most often encountered are likely to concern the suitability of showing particular forms of material before the watershed, or at what point after it, or in the context of a particular type of programme. Context clearly strongly influences audience expectations, and Ofcom is enjoined to take those expectations into account. In coming to such decisions as to contextual suitability, Ofcom must take into

---

(e) that the proper degree of responsibility is exercised with respect to the content of programmes which are religious programmes

(f) that generally accepted standards are applied to the contents of television and radio services so as to provide adequate protection for members of the public from the inclusion in such services of offensive and harmful material.

238 In relation to the statutory obligation regarding religious sensibilities, see Ofcom's ruling on the BBC's broadcast of *Jerry Springer – the Opera* in 2005, fn 251 below.

239 Section 319(4) provides: 'In setting or revising any standards under this section, OFCOM must have regard, in particular and to such extent as appears to them to be relevant to the securing of the standards objectives, to each of the following matters – the degree of harm or offence likely to be caused by the inclusion of any particular sort of material in programmes generally, or in programmes of a particular description; the likely size and composition of the potential audience for programmes included in television and radio services generally, or in television and radio services of a particular description; the likely expectation of the audience as to the nature of a programme's content and the extent to which the nature of a programme's content can be brought to the attention of potential members of the audience; the likelihood of persons who are unaware of the nature of a programme's content being unintentionally exposed, by their own actions, to that content; the desirability of securing that the content of services identifies when there is a change affecting the nature of a service that is being watched or listened to and, in particular, a change that is relevant to the application of the standards set under this section; and the desirability of maintaining the independence of editorial control over programme content.'

account the probable size and composition of the potential audience for particular radio and television programmes. But Ofcom also has to consider the nature of the audience for television and radio services generally. This appears to mean that Ofcom must look beyond the audience that might be attracted to, for example, a sexually explicit film shown late at night and take account of the expectations and wishes of the more general audience who might happen to tune in to it. Clearly, this provision might encourage Ofcom to take a more restrictive approach. The possibility that persons might be unintentionally exposed to the content of a programme, and the extent to which the nature of a programme's content can be brought to the attention of potential members of the audience, are specifically identified as relevant factors, but it is clearly implicit in this approach that even where a person could take steps to ascertain the content of a programme beforehand (i.e. outside the context of trailers or adverts which come upon the audience without warning), the programme makers must take their susceptibility to offence into account.

Section 319 has nothing to say about the responsibility of audience members to seek to avoid shock or offence by looking up the guidance given as to the nature of the programme beforehand or using interactive features to do so. The nod in the direction of editorial freedom in s 319(4)(f) does not amount to the far more comprehensive guidance that could have been given as to the showing of material at the boundaries of acceptability, such as material from films with an '18' rating which are towards the further end of the '18' classification band.[240] For example, specific guidance could have been given as to the conditions under which such material could be broadcast. The use of the term 'offensive' clearly implies that the material covered falls well outside the boundaries of criminal liability created by the common law, statutory indecency provisions, or the Obscene Publications Act 1959,[241] taking account of the 'public good' defence under s 4, which was discussed above. As discussed on p. 408 above, those provisions set variable but higher bars in terms of establishing the impact of the material in order to attract liability than is inherent in the term 'offensive'. Section 319 therefore indicates that there is a body of material that cannot be broadcast, although it lies well outside the boundaries created by the criminal law relating to explicit expression. At present, the statutory emphasis on the possibility that persons might view such material unawares appears to outweigh the emphasis on seeking to ensure that willing adult audiences can view such material. It is arguable that a full plurality of standards is not being maintained.

As indicated, it is extremely unlikely that a broadcast could fall foul of the Obscene Publications Act 1959. However, given the 'likely audience' test used in obscenity law, as discussed above, an argument could conceivably be made that the transmission of a film on television changes the analysis of that audience since individuals, including children or teenagers, switching between channels at random, could be confronted by explicit images without warning. Since obscenity is a relative concept, judged to its effect on a significant proportion of the likely audience, a televised film could be

---

240 The nature of the '18' rating is discussed below in relation to the current stance of the British Board of Film Classification (BBFC). See pp 456–65.

241 Under Broadcasting Act 1990 s 162 the 1959 Act is applied to broadcasting; s 162 was not repealed by the Communications Act 2003.

adjudged obscene where that would not be the case if it was made available only by hiring a DVD, since the publicity material on the DVD case, together with the age rating for the film, would give the individual some warning of its likely content. It would be even less likely that the same film could be viewed as obscene when shown in the cinema, since entrance to the cinema would be age-restricted; further, the advertisements for the film would provide a warning. Given therefore, that when a film is broadcast on television, there is the likelihood of a number of younger people stumbling upon it unawares, it is possible to conceive of a particular broadcast being deemed obscene, though the film itself obviously had not been – by the film regulator, the British Board of Film Classification (BBFC).[242] Since 'hardcore' pornography – film material rated R18 – is not broadcast on television under the current regulatory regime,[243] this is highly improbable but the possibility cannot be completely ruled out.

Ofcom's Broadcast Code[244]

Ofcom's Code places the emphasis on the avoidance of harm, rather than on the imprecise and subjective idea of avoidance of offence and the maintenance of standards of 'good taste'. It also places greater emphasis on the use of warnings rather than on restricting the broadcast of certain forms of material. Thus it assumes up to a point that the audience can exercise choice and protect itself from shock. It further assumes that people are entitled to view a wide and diverse range of programmes. The Code places particular emphasis on free expression principles and on editorial responsibility. There are, however, a number of prescriptive terms that are mandatory (rather than advisory or discretionary). In those instances, then, broadcasters clearly lay themselves open to the possibility of an adverse adjudication for breach of the Code if they do not follow the rules. However, the use of clear and precise rules, so long as their restraining effect is kept to a minimum, does obviate the potentially chilling effect of imprecision.

The Code is more firmly based on the principle of allowing for creative freedom. To this end, it creates a clear dividing line between provisions applicable to children and to adults. Section 1 of Ofcom's Code is headed 'Protecting the under-18s', while s 2 relates to protection from harmful or offensive material generally. It can be assumed therefore that s 2 relates mainly, although not exclusively, to adults. Ofcom's stance allows for a greater focus on the need for restrictions applicable largely to adult programming. The Code also lays greater emphasis on protecting persons from the inadvertent viewing of offensive material, not by barring it from broadcasts, but by requiring that it is accompanied by extensive warnings.

The Code places a strong emphasis on protecting children, not by restricting or banning the showing of explicit material completely, but by showing it at certain times, either after the watershed or by avoiding times when 'children are particularly likely to be listening'. Only 'material that might *seriously* impair the moral, mental or physical development of children (emphasis added)' must not be broadcast.[245] In other words, the

---

242 For the standards the BBFC currently uses in classifying films, see pp 456–65 below. Clearly, it would
      not classify a film that might be obscene within the meaning of the OPA 1959.
243 See p 446 below.
244 See s 324(1).
245 Section 1.1.

Code is focused on the avoidance of serious and specific harms to children (defined as those under 15). But under s 1.2 material that might merely *impair* their development in the ways specified *can* be shown so long as 'appropriate scheduling or technical devices' are used. The reference to scheduling means, following ss 1.3 and 1.4, that the material must be shown after the watershed and the probable number and age of the children present in the audience must be taken into account. If encoding is not used, 'a clear verbal warning' must be given prior to the programme. Encoding may provide an effective means of protecting children while allowing adults to view a range of material, including explicit or potentially disturbing material.

The use of the term 'seriously impair' creates, on its face, a standard that appears similar to that employed in the Obscene Publications Act 1959 with its use of the terms 'deprave and corrupt'. In fact the test under the OPA is not currently interpreted in this fashion,[246] but the apparent closeness of the boundaries between the two tests is of interest since, taking the previous regime into account, one would expect a broadcast regulatory body to impose standards lying well within the borders of the basic OPA test. In general, the emphasis of Ofcom's Code as regards children is on the use of various devices to protect them (the use of the watershed, detailed warnings, pin-protection and encoding of material), rather than on bans or on making cuts in the material. '18' rated films can be shown at any time while 'adult-sex' material can be shown between 2200 and 0530 so long as protections are in place to ensure that children cannot view the material.[247] A very clear distinction is drawn between pay-per-view and ordinary broadcasting, although 'R18' material still cannot be broadcast.[248] The convergence that appears to be occurring between video and pay per view broadcasting suggests that the current distinction between what can be shown on the two media may eventually disappear. In fact, ironically, it may now be less likely that children would view R18 material in pin-protected broadcasts than on video, once videos are brought into the home by adults.

Section 2 of the Code, focusing more on adult viewing, is aimed at ensuring that broadcasters provide 'adequate protection for viewers and listeners from the inclusion

---

246 See, e.g., Edwards, S, 'On the Contemporary Application of the Obscene Publications Act' (1998) Crim LR 843.

247 1.23 pay-per-view services may broadcast up to BBFC 18-rated films or their equivalent, at any time of day provided: there is a protection system pre 2100 and post 0530 (a mandatory PIN or other equivalent protection), that seeks satisfactorily to restrict access solely to those authorised to view when material other than BBFC U-rated or PG-rated or their equivalents is shown; information is provided about programme content that will assist adults to assess its suitability for children; there is a detailed billing system for subscribers which clearly itemises all viewing including viewing times and dates; and those security systems which are in place to protect children are clearly explained to all subscribers.1.24 Premium subscription services and pay per view/night services may broadcast 'adult-sex' material between 2200 and 0530 provided that in addition to other protections mentioned above: there is a mandatory PIN protected encryption system, or other equivalent protection, that seeks satisfactorily to restrict access solely to those authorised to view; and there are measures in place that ensure that the subscriber is an adult. 1.25 BBFC R18-rated films or their equivalent must not be broadcast.

248 In May 2005 Ofcom conducted a research study, *Research into the Effectiveness of PIN Protection Systems in the UK*. It found that a high percentage of children (about 50% of those in the relevant houses surveyed) knew that a PIN number was needed to access blocked channels and of those children about 50% knew of their parents' PIN number; of those just under half had used the number to access pay-per-view programmes without their parents' permission. Ofcom concluded that security methods in the current PIN environment are not likely to prevent children from accessing 'R18' material.

of harmful or offensive material', judged against 'generally accepted standards'. It is noticeable that the 'protection' to be provided in s 2 centres more on the provision of information, than on making cuts in the material. This is made clear in s 2.3. At the same time s 2.3 makes it clear that if the use of potentially offensive language and material, in particular, the inclusion of scenes of violence or sex, sexual violence, or scenes of humiliation, distress or the use of discriminatory treatment or language must be justified by the context, implying that otherwise they should not be broadcast or should be cut. The term 'context' refers, *inter alia*, to a number of the factors outlined in s 319(4)(a), (b), (c) and (d) of the Communications Act.[249] But s 2.3 also accepts that if information is included, presumably in the form of consumer advice and detailed warnings as to content, it can assist in preventing offence.

In relation to films, Ofcom's Code provides, in s 1.20: 'No version of a film or programme refused certification by the British Board of Film Classification (BBFC) may be broadcast.' Material rated 'R18' cannot be shown; '18' rated films can be shown after 9.00 pm, but even after that point they may be viewed as 'unsuitable' (s 1.21). As to suitability, Ofcom presumably takes the view that the provisions relating to the portrayal of sex and violence and the showing of disturbing material in general in s 1 regarding children and in s 2 cover the scheduling of films. But it is clear that Ofcom's Code is somewhat less prescriptive in this respect and leaves greater discretion to the broadcasters. But the BBFC standards are regarded as minimum ones; the mere fact that a film has an '18' certificate is not to be taken as implying that it is clearly proper to broadcast it.

It can be said that Ofcom's Code accords with the liberal free speech account of restrictions on broadcasting discussed above in so far as it concentrates on the avoidance of specific harms, and largely avoids the use of broad statements about ensuring the promotion of 'good taste and decency'. It strikes a balance between offence avoidance and the right of adult television audiences to receive a diverse range of broadcast expression, which differs somewhat from the balance struck under the superseded codes. The ability of people to take responsibility for protecting themselves from offence is more strongly emphasised. The restrictions placed on films shown on television appear to be more in line with those placed on videos, although it remains the case that 'hardcore' pornography cannot be broadcast. Since videos and the internet also come into the home this relaxation of the rules is readily defensible.

Ofcom's liberal approach is reflected in its treatment of complaints about the BBC screening of *Jerry Springer – the Opera*, a programme that satirised features of Christianity. In 2005 Ofcom cleared the BBC of flouting the BSC Code despite receiving 16,801 complaints.[250] Ofcom considered in particular the question of offence against

---

249 See above fn 239.

250 The BBC's Governors Programme Complaints Committee had also considered the complaints; it found: 'in all the circumstances, the outstanding artistic significance of the programme outweighed the offence which it caused to some viewers and so the broadcasting of the programme was justified'. Extracts from Ofcom's adjudication: Sections 26 and 27 – Respect and Dignity. The Code states that 'challenging and deliberately flouting the boundaries of taste in drama and comedy is a time-honoured tradition. Although these programmes have a special freedom, this does not give them unlimited licence to be cruel or to humiliate individuals or groups gratuitously'. Ofcom recognises that a great number of complainants felt that the *Opera* denigrated the Christian religion. The show was created as a caricature

religious sensibilities and balanced the possibility of offence against the need to protect freedom of expression. In coming to this finding, Ofcom took into account the significance of the work. This was a very important and telling decision, bearing in mind the subject-matter of the programme and the extremely large number of complaints.[251]

The public authority/private body distinction

Ofcom and the public sector broadcasters are susceptible to challenge under the Human Rights Act. Ofcom is probably a core public authority under s 6(1) HRA; it has clear governmental functions since it is a regulator set up by government. In any event, it is clearly a functional public authority as is reasonably clear from the discussion of the

---

of modern television. Importantly, in Ofcom's view the *Opera* did not gratuitously humiliate individuals or any groups and in particular the Christian community. Its target was television and fame. Conclusion: The programme did not contravene these sections of the Code. Sections 43–45 – Offences against Religious Sensibilities. The Code states that: 'Although religions should not be exempt from (the) critical scrutiny . . . particular care should be taken when referring to religion in entertainment.' Many complainants accused the BBC of committing the crime of blasphemy. However, criminal law is not a matter for Ofcom but for the courts. Ofcom is not required to determine whether the BBC committed blasphemy, but whether, in this case, the provisions of the Code had been contravened . . . Ofcom has sought to achieve the appropriate balance between, on the one hand the standards set in the Code (ex-BSC Code on Standards) and the need to apply those standards to give adequate protection from harmful and offensive material, and on the other hand the need, as appropriate, to guarantee freedom of expression. Freedom of expression is particularly important in the context of artistic works, beliefs, philosophy and argument . . . Their main concern arose from the depictions of figures at the heart of the complainants' religious beliefs. In considering offence against religious sensibilities, Ofcom took into account the clear context of the Opera. The fictional Jerry Springer lay dying in a delusional state. As he hallucinated, this character was asked to pitch Jesus against the Devil in his own confessional talk show. This 'dream' sequence was emphasised by the fact that the same actors, who played guests on his show in the first act, played the characters in the second act. What resulted was a cartoon, full of grotesque images, which challenged the audience's views about morality and the human condition. The production made clear that all the characters in the second act were the product of the fictional Springer's imagination: his concepts of Satan, God, Jesus and the others and modelled on the guests in his show . . . In light of this, Ofcom did not believe that the characters represented were, in the context of this piece, conveyed as faithful or accurate representations of religious figures, but were characterisations of the show's participants . . . It is not within Ofcom's remit to record a contravention of the Code on the basis that Christianity, as opposed to another faith, was the subject of *Jerry Springer: The Opera*. In considering freedom of expression, Ofcom recognises the UK's long-standing tradition of satirising political and religious figures and celebrities. Ofcom must consider each programme on its merits. No contravention was found. Ofcom broadcast bulletin 34, 9 May 2005. See Ofcom's website 10 May 2005. An application to seek judicial review of the BBC's decision to screen the film, by the Christian Institute and other groups was refused byCrane J, judgment dated 27 May 2005.

251 The stance it took in relation to *Jerry Springer* may be contrasted with its stance in relation to the timing of the broadcast of *Pulp Fiction* by the BBC Report: *Pulp Fiction BBC 2, 7 August 2004, 21:10* Nine viewers complained about the transmission of this film. The majority were concerned that its transmission shortly after the 21:00 watershed, when young people watch television, could encourage anti-social behaviour. Overall, viewers felt that the strong content, including graphic violence, seriously offensive swearing and scenes of drug abuse, made the film unsuitable at a time in the evening when young people and children were still part of the audience. It was found that such intense material is not normally expected so soon after the watershed and that the scheduling of this film at 21:10 was too early, given the strong, adult content from the start. The scheduling of this film was found to be in contravention of the Code. It may be noted that the case was appealed three times by the BBC. This decision was made by the Content Board following the BBC's third and final appeal.

meaning of 'public function' under s 6(3)(b) HRA in Chapter 4.[252] It can be viewed as a governmental body in being set up under a Royal Charter. Acceptance of its status as a functional public authority appeared to be implicit in the decision in the case of *Pro-Life Alliance*,[253] although, as discussed, the judges were reluctant to engage in argument as to the mechanisms of the HRA.

Assuming that the BBC is a functional public authority, there is then immense room for argument as to those functions it has that are 'public'. There is nothing inherently public about broadcasting, and if the BBC were to be viewed as acting publicly in relation to all aspects of programme-making, this would set up a clear anomaly in relation to the private broadcasters since they would be performing the same function but would not bound by the HRA. A distinction could be drawn between the BBC's function as a broadcaster and as a regulator, finding that it is providing a public function in the latter role but not the former. This would be a sensible line to draw, although it is not without its difficulties. This stance could be viewed as implicit in *Pro-Life*. This would mean that when the BBC regulates its *own* programmes it is performing a public function. Thus, decisions as to filming techniques and the making of programmes might not be viewed as 'public' while decisions to allow a programme to be broadcast taken at senior level would be. Decisions taken in relation to offence-avoidance could be viewed as public as so closely associated with the BBC's core role in providing programming for public consumption. Clearly, s 6 HRA inevitably creates difficult decisions and anomalies in relation to the public/private divide. The BBC provides an especially difficult example. But it must be noted for the purposes of this chapter that assuming it is a public authority in relation to decisions to broadcast, it is hard to imagine a situation in which a Convention right could be invoked against it in response to a positive decision to broadcast a programme that then caused offence. There is no Convention right not to be offended – the only possible candidate would be Art 9 in relation to offending against religious sensibilities.[254] The public/private function divide is far more significant in relation to invasion of privacy, discussed in Chapter 10.

Channel 4 may possibly have the status of a functional public authority since it has public service functions, but the independent broadcasting companies are almost certainly private bodies for HRA purposes. Thus the independent broadcasters cannot be challenged directly under the HRA. However, in any court action against Ofcom or the BBC concerning relevant sections of the 2003 Act, an interpretation of the provisions should of course be adopted, under s 3(1) HRA, which accords with the demands of Art 10. Any resultant modification of the Act by interpretation, or as a result of a declaration of incompatibility under s 4 HRA, would then affect the independent broadcasters. If s 319 itself were affected in this way the effect would be indirect, as a result of a change in Ofcom's stance. Also, as public authorities, Ofcom and the BBC must take the demands of Art 10 into account in coming to any decisions relating to content restrictions.

These issues came to a head in the litigation concerning a party political broadcast by the Pro-Life Alliance which the BBC refused to transmit in 2001 general election despite the group having sufficient parliamentary candidates to be eligible. Amongst

---

252 See pp 187–221.
253 [2003] 2 WLR 1403.
254 See *Otto-Preminger* (1994) 19 EHRR 34, discussed at p 487, above.

other things, the broadcast contained graphic images of an aborted foetus in a mutilated state. PLA complained that the decision was incompatible with their freedom of speech rights and did not fully account for the higher status of political expression. They sought judicial review on the grounds that the BBC had not properly applied the standards it was required to apply and, specifically, had not taken into account the election context. The House of Lords, reversing an earlier Court of Appeal decision in PLA's favour, determined that the BBC's refusal was justified under Art 10(2). Their Lordships concluded that the BBC had applied the correct standard and had reached a decision it was entitled to reach. Unfortunately, the House of Lords' judgment does nothing to mitigate the dangers of content-based regulatory schemes in free speech terms, discussed at the beginning of this chapter. In this instance all the free rationales were engaged in relation to Pro-Life itself as a speaker and in relation to the audience.

Lord Hoffmann's judgment is particularly problematic. He took the view that deference should be paid to the expertise of the regulator, as well as to Parliament. But it is argued that the notion of deferring to a regulator needs to be unpacked. Regulators have expertise as to matters of fact and can also give expert opinions. In this instance the regulator – the BBC – had expertise as to accepted standards of taste and decency in broadcasting and therefore as to audience expectations. Therefore it was entitled to take the stance that the Pro-Life video infringed those standards and it was reasonable for the Court to defer to those findings. But the regulator did not have expertise in *balancing* the concerns relating to taste and decency against free speech. That was a normative exercise for the court, basing itself on Strasbourg principles. It is precisely the role of the courts to conduct that balancing exercise under Art 10(2) between the right to freedom of expression and societal concerns. Lord Hoffmann fudged the issue – he elided the issue of deference on the basis of expert findings with the question of balancing those findings against free speech demands. Lord Hoffmann made much also of deference to Parliament, but Parliament had enacted not only s 6(1)(a) of the Broadcasting Act 1990 (which articulated the standard that the BBC applied: the old standard of 'taste and decency'), but also the HRA and had placed a responsibility on the judges to abide by the Convention rights, under s 6. Lord Hoffmann appeared almost to abrogate his responsibility as a judge to conduct the necessary balancing exercise. His motivation appeared to be a determination to avoid subjecting a regulator's decision to a real, systematic Strasbourg scrutiny.[255]

The *Pro-Life Alliance* decision with its strong emphasis on deference to the regulatory scheme and the regulator, gives little encouragement to the use of the HRA as a means of challenging restrictive decisions relating to broadcast material or the restrictions themselves. However, using a different approach, or on other, more compelling, facts a successful challenge remains a possibility. Overly restrictive decisions of public sector broadcasters and of Ofcom under the 'offensive material' provisions of s 319 of the 2003 Act and the current Code could theoretically be challenged by a programme-maker under s 7(1)(a) HRA, relying on Art 10. A challenge to Ofcom's use of its powers would normally have to occur after the event since Ofcom does not have censorship powers.

---

255 For further criticism of Lord Hoffmann's findings on deference in this instance, see Lord Steyn, 'Deference is a tangled web' (2005) PL 346–59.

There are some grounds for thinking that the inception of the Human Rights Act might have called the previous regime into question and that it might still do so as regards the current one. In this context the restraints on broadcast expression relate to offence-avoidance. Such restraints can be justified only where they meet the Art 10(2) tests.[256] In particular they have to be proportionate to the aims of protecting morality or the rights of others. On the face of it, one might not expect the restrictions on the basis of avoiding offence – essentially of a similar nature under the previous and the current regimes – to meet those tests since the term 'offence' is so broad and imprecise. However, as discussed above, the Convention jurisprudence interpreting Art 10(2) notoriously does not uphold freedom of expression very strongly where restrictions protecting children from offence in respect of non-political speech are concerned. Thus the possibility of mounting challenges to the decisions of regulators or broadcasters in court was always likely to be problematic since the regulatory regime tends to have its greatest impact on artistic rather than political speech. The message of political expression can frequently, although not invariably, be conveyed without the use of potentially offensive words or images. As discussed, a strong pronouncement was made in *Handyside*[257] to the effect that Art 10(1) covers speech that some might find offensive, but the Court went on to find that in the instance before it such speech (albeit of ideological significance) could justifiably be suppressed, and it reached this decision on the basis of conceding a wide margin of appreciation to the state since there is no uniform European conception of moral standards.[258] It can therefore readily be said in this context that the Art 10 standard is 'soft-edged': applied domestically, it very clearly leaves room for the adoption of either an activist or a minimalist approach, and *Pro-Life* adopted the latter approach. It might well support quite far-reaching restrictions on broadcasting owing to the possibility that children might be affected.

But, as discussed above, in the line of authority stemming from *Handyside*[259] a broad margin of appreciation was conceded to the state in finding against the applicant, especially where offensive 'artistic' speech was concerned – using that term loosely.[260] The pronouncement in *Handyside* to the effect that Art 10(1) covers offensive speech runs presumptively directly counter to the previous provision against such speech in broadcasting in s 6(1)(a) 1990 Act, aspects of the BBC's Agreement, s 108 1996 Act and now s 319 of the 2003 Act. As the domestic courts are not required to concede a margin of appreciation to the state, there is a case for expecting them to take a stricter stance in relation to restraints on broadcast speech. The use of the Convention jurisprudence on both political and, if afforded a creative interpretation, artistic expression,[261] has in principle the potential, applied domestically, to challenge accepted conceptions of offence-avoidance in broadcasting. This argument is reasonably strong in relation to restrictions on all forms of broadcasting on the ground of offence-avoidance, including soap operas, 'reality' TV programmes, and films. It is even stronger in relation to forms

---

256 Discussed in Chapter 2, pp 83–88.
257 See pp 404–05.
258 See p 404.
259 See pp 405–07.
260 As discussed, the effect of the doctrine should be irrelevant in the domestic courts since the margin of appreciation doctrine is an international one with no application domestically. See Chapter 2, pp 95–98.
261 See above, pp 407–08.

of political broadcasting, such as party political broadcasts, election broadcasts, news programmes and documentaries since the Strasbourg jurisprudence defends political expression in the media very strongly – as decisions such as that in *Jersild*,[262] discussed in Chapter 2, demonstrate. *Handyside*, as discussed above, concerned expression that could be viewed only as a very marginal form of political speech. Mainstream, 'core', political expression, even accompanied by explicit images, could in principle be treated as far more analogous with the expression in *Jersild*, which concerned the broadcast of a programme containing grossly racist language. If this argument were to be accepted, restraints based on offence-avoidance, particularly if applied to such speech, would be found to breach Art 10 as impermissibly over-broad.

Successful challenges to the current regulatory regime?

Nevertheless, successful HRA challenges to the current regime under the 2003 Act are conceivable, despite the *Pro-Life* decision. A claim could occur in relation to any form of broadcasting affected by the offence-avoidance Ofcom Code rules, but clearly it would be most likely to succeed in the context of political broadcasting. It is nevertheless important to point out that the following remarks could also apply to, for example, films of strong artistic merit if the relevant Art 10 jurisprudence was applied, but the effects of the margin of appreciation doctrine were disapplied,[263] when applied at the domestic level. Thus while the strongest impetus for change could come in the realm of political expression, it is not ruled out in relation to other forms.

A departure from the *Pro-Life Alliance* decision could come about if a case on a similar factual basis arose but the challenge was to the new statutory framework itself – specifically on s 319 – as requiring re-interpretation under s 3(1) HRA in order to achieve compatibility with the demands of Art 10. The decision in *Pro-Life Alliance* does not stand in the way of such a reinterpretation since the House of Lords deliberately considered only the application of the statutory provisions and not the provisions themselves.[264] The 2003 Act does not exempt PEBs from the s 319 requirements or the Ofcom Code, which applies to all forms of broadcasting. Thus, post-HRA Parliament did make the deliberate decision to continue to subject PEBs to the offence-avoidance requirements. Courts will inevitably consider that they should pay some deference to that decision, following *Pro-Life*. Nevertheless, the majority in the House of Lords left open the possibility that a challenge to the equivalent provisions under the previous regime might have succeeded. It may be noted that, as discussed above, the 2003 Act was *not* declared compatible with the Convention rights under s 19 HRA.[265] However, it can be assumed that the rest of the Act was viewed by Parliament as compatible with Art 10 and therefore it should be treated in the same way as any other Act of Parliament.[266]

262 (1994) 19 EHRR 1. See further Chapter 2, p 83.
263 As discussed above, a case can be made for arguing that comments of the Strasbourg Court support forms of artistic expression quite strongly. See pp 405–08.
264 If a challenge was mounted to the application of the rules themselves the outcome would probably be the same as in *Pro-Life* unless the decision to ban an election video was a far more marginal one.
265 As noted earlier, the lack of a declaration was due to the view taken that s 321(2) (the ban on political advertising) was incompatible with Art 10. This decision was based on the decision of the ECHR in *VGT v Switzerland* [2001] ECHR 408.
266 Indeed, it is argued that the lack of a statement of compatibility under s 19(1)(b) HRA has no effect on the ability of judges to seek to achieve compatibility under s 3(1) in relation to s 321(2)).

Section 3(1) HRA could be used to impose a different interpretation on s 319, reducing its impact quite dramatically in relation to PEBs or other forms of political broadcasting. As a result, where such forms were concerned, quite a radical modification of ss 1 and 2 of Ofcom's Code could be brought about by interpretation. The demands of offence-avoidance as a standards objective could be minimised in the context of political broadcasting. Such a modification may be possible since, although s 319 does cover PEBs, it is more nuanced and goes into more detail regarding context and audience expectations than s 6(1)(a) of the 1990 Act or s 108 of the 1996 Act did. Such matters were only taken into account previously by the ITC Programme Code and the BSC Standards Code. Section 319(4)(a)–(d) could be viewed as a gateway to allowing the radical re-interpretation suggested. For example, the term 'generally accepted standards' used in s 319(f) in relation to the protection of the public from 'offensive material' could be interpreted to mean that greater leeway should be accorded to PEBs since such standards can be assumed to accord particular weight to the nontramelling of political expression. The comments of the Court of Appeal in *Pro-Life* as to the greater public tolerance of controversial and explicit images in the context of serious political speech should be borne in mind. There is a case for limited deference to Parliament here since the re-interpretation argued for would not go against the grain of the statute or necessitate reading words into it, and the question of balancing the societal interest in maintaining standards of decency in broadcasting against the demands of free speech is very much one within the Courts' constitutional sphere under the HRA.[267]

Such a re-interpretation of s 319(f), and the resultant effect on ss 1 and 2 of the Code, could also affect other forms of political broadcasting. Such a result would in one sense enhance the freedom of broadcasters since it would widen choice as to what could be shown in documentaries, discussion programmes, etc. In relation to PEBs it would tend to remove some control from their hands in relation to their interpretation of their responsibilities and place it in the hands of the courts. Challenging and explicit images could be shown, if justified by context. A more effective representation of a plurality of views, including the views of minority groups, in broadcasting might occur.[268]

Conclusions

When the power of the owners of the television companies to influence the nature of broadcasting is compared with that of the media regulators or of the public service broadcasters, a human rights scheme in which the exercise of the powers of the latter, but not the former, can be challenged on free expression grounds looks fundamentally flawed. There is clearly a mismatch between the areas in which the HRA can intervene and the location of the main influences over the medium of most significance in terms of its cultural and opinion-forming impact. But the impact of the HRA on broadcasting has not been radical. This is in part because the regulatory regime already adheres to free expression principles in a reasonably comprehensive and advanced fashion.

267 See for discussion of the use of s 3, Chapter 4, pp 146–87.
268 As a further resort, there would also be the possibility of issuing a declaration of the incompatibility under s 4 HRA between Art 10 and s 319. Amendment in relation to PEBs might then come about in reliance on the s 10 procedure.

Nevertheless, this chapter has described quite significant restraints to avoid causing offence contained in Ofcom's Code and the 2003 Act. Currently broadcast material is subject both to special regulation in terms of a regime based on warnings, and use of the 'watershed', and *also* to restraint which in effect amounts to a form of censorship since the broadcasters must exercise self-censorship in order to adhere to the offence-avoidance aspects of Ofcom's Code. Despite its liberal outlook, the new Code is potentially quite restrictive in certain respects. Ofcom retains significant leeway in adopting a range of free expression standards.

This regime is not applied to any other medium and since, as discussed below, the BBFC appears to be operating a regime in respect of films and videos that has recently become much more liberal, the differences between the regimes for films and for broadcasting are becoming more marked. As technology advances, the range of channels widens and a wider range of information about programmes becomes more readily available to viewing audiences, these differences are arguably becoming less defensible. Although it might appear that Art 10 under the HRA could play a part in bringing about a greater liberalisation of the current offence-avoidance decency regime, it is probable, for the reasons discussed above, that its effect will continue to be marginal, especially after the *Pro-Life* decision. Regulation of UK broadcasting is in effect insulated from free speech principles applied by means of the HRA due to the excessive deference to the regulators enjoined upon the courts by *Pro-Life*.

6 Films and videos

Introduction[269]

This section considers the regulation of films and videos.[270] The regimes in place at present for each of these media differ from each other quite considerably. But they also contrast strongly with the regime in respect of books, newspapers, magazines and other printed matter. Broadcasting, films and videos are subject to regulatory schemes, which (as discussed) are wholly statute-based in the case of broadcasting and videos, and partly statute-based in respect of films. At present, there is no state regulation of the internet, apart from the application of the ordinary law. The new regulatory regime put in place for broadcasting in 2003 does not cover use of the internet.

The statutory regimes currently in place include elements of licensing, regulation by administrative bodies and censorship. The reasons behind treating broadcasting and films differently from the print media differ in a number of respects, but have a common historical basis. The stricter system of controls seems to have been adopted in answer to the view that owing to their particular impact on audiences, films, videos and broadcasting require a system of prior restraints, whereas it is now accepted that books and other printed material do not. These media are viewed as beneficial to the public in a number of respects, but are also seen as possible sources of harm. Owing to the availability of

---

269 Additional texts referred to below: Akdeniz, Y, Walker, C and Wall, D, (eds), *The Internet, Law and Society*, 2000, Longman; for background, see Hunnings, N, *Film Censors and the Law*, 1967, Allen and Unwin.

270 For a comprehensive treatment, see Gibbons, *Regulating the Media*, 1998.

censorship, it is very unlikely that a film or broadcast could attract liability under the Obscene Publications Act;[271] nevertheless, it provides a further possibility of restraint and can also be used as a guide as to the standards censorship will observe. Thus, the regulatory regimes in place mean that the visual media are censored beyond what the law demands. The impact of the HRA in these areas is variable and its effects are complicated by the fact that a number of the media bodies involved are private bodies, while the administrative 'watchdog' bodies are public authorities.

Regulation of films, videos and the internet differs sharply from the 'command and control' model of regulation provided by the Ofcom system. Regulation of films for cinematic release has some features in common with the self-regulation of the internet since it was originally entered into voluntarily by the film-makers themselves. However, the regulation of films is far less fragmentary and has achieved far greater recognition than the system for the internet. In relation to video, the film regulatory scheme does bear quite a strong resemblance to the Ofcom one. Generally, film regulation does not have a *full* statutory under-pinning, but is strongly associated with a number of statutes. As discussed below, a range of bodies set up by internet service providers, such as the Internet Watch Foundation, provide a self-censoring service for the internet. None of these bodies has a statutory underpinning or have so far received any statutory recognition. Nor can they be viewed as affecting the internet in a comprehensive fashion since, unlike the system for films, they do not apply controls at source but are consumer-driven. In other words, they rely on a voluntary engagement with their services by the public or by institutions, whereas films and videos are affected by regulation prior to release. The remit of the Advertising Standards Authority now not only covers broadcasting, but runs across all these different media; it is most significant in relation to the internet, so it will be discussed in the different contexts, below.

The British Board of Film Classification

Classification and censorship of films and video is undertaken by the British Board of Film Classification (BBFC), a self-censoring body set up by the film industry itself in 1912. It is an independent, non-governmental body which is funded by the fees it charges to those who submit films, videos, DVDs for classification. The video release of films has a firmer statutory under-pinning deriving from the Video Recordings Act 1984, and so the regulation of videos has a greater resemblance in that respect to the system for broadcasting.

The BBFC provides an interesting example of a body that does not possess statutory powers, in relation to the cinematic release of films, and yet whose decisions as to film classification are adhered to as though they had statutory force. It was originally set up in response to the Cinematograph Act 1909 (now Cinemas Act 1985), which allowed local authorities to grant licences in respect of the films to be shown in their particular area; the idea was that the film industry would achieve a uniformity of decision-making by local councils by providing authoritative guidance to them. So when the BBFC classifies films it does so, formally speaking, on behalf of the local authorities

---

271 The Obscene Publications Act, s 1 covers these media under s 1(2) since the Broadcasting Act 1990, s 162, has brought radio and television within its ambit.

who license cinemas under the Cinemas Act 1985. The idea behind this system, from the point of view of the film-makers and distributors, was that they would have a guide as to whether a film would be shown and as to where to make cuts in order to achieve a wider audience.

Statutory powers to control what is shown at cinemas still remain with local councils who may overrule any of the Board's decisions. Thus, films – not videos – can be classified on two levels: first, the BBFC may insist on cuts before issuing a certificate allowing the film to be screened or may refuse to issue a certificate at all. Second, the local authority may on occasion decide to depart from the BBFC classification or may refuse to allow a film to be shown despite the fact that it has received an '18' classification. Clearly, this is an anomalous system since it means that films are the only medium subject to censorship on a local level. But although the BBFC originates from an arbitrary and now outdated system, it performs a function that would otherwise be performed by a regulator such as Ofcom with statutory powers. The BBFC is not a creation of statute although, as discussed below, it does have statutory powers in relation to videos. Arguably, a regulator that has worked closely with the industry for a substantial period of time and which is not a governmental creation, or subject to government appointments, may be able to take a more effective, sensitive and nuanced stance in relation to classification and censorship than a government body, a point that is returned to below. However, at present, as the BBFC itself accepts, films and videos are still more likely to be subject to censorship in the UK. The reasons for this and the current pressure for change from a central focus of the discussion below. Below, the general classification and censorship system operated by the BBFC is considered, before turning to the differences between the way films are treated for cinematic release and for release on video.

The classification and censorship system

In relation to the theatrical release of films the BBFC operates within a broad statutory framework, but unlike Ofcom its decisions on classification are not driven by that statutory basis. This is also broadly true in relation to video, although the statutory basis in question is more prescriptive. The BBFC classifies and censors films and videos against the background of the relevant criminal law,[272] including the Obscene Publications Act 1959. Section 4(1)(a) Video Recordings Act 1984, as amended,[273] requires the BBFC to apply an additional test with regard to the classification of videos, that of suitability for viewing in the home. This requirement reflects the fact that, in the BBFC's words,

> unlike cinema films where age restrictions may be 'policed' by box office staff, videos in the home are more likely to be viewed by younger age groups and could be replayed many times with individual scenes taken out of context and repeated in slow motion or even frame by frame.[274]

272 The relevant criminal law is discussed above. Note also that the Cinematograph Films (Animals) Act 1937 makes it illegal to show any scene if animals were treated cruelly in the making of that scene.
273 Discussed below at p 465.
274 See the 2000 BBFC Response to the Home Office Consultation Paper on *the Regulation of R18 Videos* at para 2.1.

In relation to videos there is a right of appeal from the decisions of the BBFC to the Video Appeals Committee (VAC). No such right exists in relation to films.

The BBFC makes its decisions on the basis of published guidelines.[275] As it acknowledges, the application of the guidelines goes further in terms of creating restraints than the relevant law itself does. It states in the guidelines that it is complying with the requirements of the European Convention on Human Rights to make the classification criteria clear. It considers that it has fulfilled this duty by the publication of the guidelines and their availability on the BBFC website or directly from the Board. However, the mere fact that the guidelines can be readily accessed clearly does not mean that the criteria are sufficiently clear, and it is arguable that in a number of respects sufficient clarity has not been achieved. This is an especially significant matter since the BBFC is the only UK media regulator that operates by means of prior restraint: it can order cuts in films before they can be seen by the public. Adherence to the guidelines is intended to mean – and so far has meant – that the producers or distributors of a film are very unlikely to be prosecuted under the Obscene Publications Act 1959 (OPA) or other provisions imposing criminal liability in respect of explicit expression. Thus, as is the case in relation to broadcasting, it is probable that films do not fully explore the boundaries of the criminal law, but stop instead somewhere short of them.

Age restrictions

Films and videos are classified by age, creating a number of categories that restrict viewing. The age restrictions are more significant, for obvious reasons, in relation to films as opposed to videos. Clearly, children and teenagers under 15 or 18 may well be able to view videos privately that have the higher age rating; they are able to do so much more readily than in the cinema. This is a matter that the BBFC takes into account in its classification. There are seven classification categories. 'U' and 'Uc' films are open to anybody as, in effect, are 'PG' (parental guidance) classified films; these categories are advisory only. After that are '12'/'12A', '15' and '18' certificate films; '12A' is a new, recently introduced, category, which allows children under 12 to see '12'-rated films at their parents' discretion; it requires such children to be accompanied into the cinema by an adult. Children over 12 will be able to see the film unaccompanied, as previously. Thus the '12A' rating recognises that parents have a better understanding of the particular sensitivities of their individual children than a regulator can have. The introduction of the '12A' rating is a step in the direction of recognising the applicability of the free speech autonomy rationale to children as well as to adults.

The advice at the '18' rating is obviously crucial since it represents the outer limits of acceptability for mainstream films and sets the boundaries for most adult viewing. The '18' rating does not fully perform that function in relation to videos since the BBFC takes into account the possibility that people under 18 may see the film, although that is far from meaning that only material suitable for, say, 15-year-olds is promulgated. The majority of classifications issued by the BBFC are not 18; at the '18' classification cuts are usually minor. 'R [restricted viewing] 18' films are intended for viewing only on segregated premises. The 'R18' classification certificate was introduced by the BBFC

---

275   Available from the BBFC website: http://www.bbfc.co.uk.

following the introduction of the 1982 Local Government (Miscellaneous Provisions) Act which required the licensing of all cinema exhibitions operated for private gain, including those clubs that showed films containing more explicit sexual depictions than would be acceptable in the public adult – '18' – category. This classification is also used in the context of classifying sexually explicit video following the implementation of the Video Recordings Act 1984. There are strict controls on the sale of videos that are given an 'R18' classification. Under s 12 of the 1984 Act, such videos can only be sold in a licensed sex shop to adults aged 18 and over. They cannot be legally sold by mail order, supplied through ordinary video outlets or shown on television. Their supply other than in a licensed sex shop is a criminal offence.[276]

The issue of an 'R18' certificate means that the BBFC considers that the film or video would survive an OPA prosecution; it will refuse a certificate if a film is thought to be obscene within the meaning of the Act. Thus BBFC decisions as to the borderline between what can be shown in an 'R18' film and what would fall foul of the OPA are probably the best guide to the meaning and application of the problematic term 'obscenity' available in the UK. The BBFC may of course err on the side of caution: it may not wish to patrol very closely to that borderline, and the very uncertainty of the term 'obscenity' is likely to engender caution.

R v Video Appeals Committee of the BBFC ex p BBFC,[277] discussed further below, marked a very significant change in the use of the 'R18' certificate for videos. The decision resulted in the promulgation of new, more relaxed guidelines for 'R18' videos by the BBFC. The BBFC nevertheless takes the view that despite this relaxation the UK 'still probably has the strictest Guidelines of any European or Western nation'.[278] As film-makers outside the pornography industry obviously do not want to receive an 'R18' rating for their work, the vast majority of films aimed at adults must respect the BBFC guidelines in order to secure the UK adult market, as far as the UK cinema release of films is concerned. The BBFC states that it 'respects the right of adults to choose their own entertainment, within the law. It will therefore expect to intervene *only rarely* in relation to "18"-rated cinema films' (emphasis added).[279]

In coming to its decision, the BBFC will take the 'public good' defence under s 4(1A) of the 1959 Act, as amended, into account.[280] This defence is the more restricted defence under s 3 of the Theatres Act 1968; s 4(1A) provides that a film or soundtrack can be justified as being for the public good 'on the ground that it is in the interests of drama, opera, ballet or any other art or of literature or learning'. Therefore, the BBFC may grant a certificate on the grounds of artistic merit to a film which contains some obscene matter.

The '12A' to 'R18' classifications are mandatory, not recommendatory. In most of Europe and in the US the age classifications are intended to provide guidance to parents

---

276 The offence is subject to a fine of up to £5,000, six months' imprisonment, or both.
277 (2000) EMLR 850. The appeal to the VAC was brought by Sheptonhurst Ltd and Prime Time Promotions (Shifnal) Ltd and involved seven titles: *Horny Catbabe, Nympho Nurse Nancy, TV Sex, Office Tart, Carnival International Version (Trailer), Wet Nurses 2 Continental Version* and *Miss Nude International Continental Version*.
278 See the 2000 BBFC Response to the Home Office Consultation Paper on *the Regulation of R18 Videos* 28.7.00.
279 BBFC Guidelines, '18' ratings.
280 See above pp 412–14.

and to children, but children under the age in question can enter the cinema and view films in the 'older' category. For example, in the US the 'PG13' rating is roughly the equivalent of the '12A' rating in the UK; younger children in the US can view 'PG13'-rated films, but in the UK they can only view an equivalent rated film if accompanied by an adult. Thus in this respect the autonomy of children and teenagers is more fully acknowledged than it is in the UK. This restriction is not – in effect – applicable to videos and, as discussed further below, influences the BBFC in relation to determining the classification of videos and in deciding on cuts.

Most film distributors have no interest in achieving only a restricted publication for a film and are therefore prepared to make cuts to achieve a wider circulation. This is especially the case in relation to the '18' and 'R18' certificates. But profitability is also highly significant and determinative of pre-censorship: the system of control may be driven largely by commercial motives: studios may make relatively stringent cuts in order to ensure that, for example, a film receives a 'PG' or '15' certificate and so reaches a wider audience. The BBFC normally avoids having to impose cuts because film directors effectively pre-censor films in order to fall within a particular classification.

Explicit depictions of sex and violence in films and videos

The BBFC states in its guidelines that the acceptability of a particular theme at levels of classification is determined by 'the context and sensitivity of its presentation'. The guidelines state that the very problematic themes such as drug abuse or paedophilia are almost bound to be unacceptable below the '15' level of classification. Therefore it is accepted that in principle *any* theme could be viewed as acceptable if properly handled at '18' or even at '15'. But this must now be read subject to new restrictions, discussed below, on the depiction of teenage sexuality created by the inception of the Sexual Offences Act 2003. The guidelines state that the portrayal of human sexual activity is not permitted at 'U', 'Uc' or 'PG'; it may be implied in '12'-rated videos and in '12A' cinema works. Thereafter, 'progressively more graphic portrayal' may be included at the '15' and '18' classifications,[281] but the extent of the portrayal is context-dependent, and the emphasis given to 'responsible, loving and developing' relationships will be relevant. In taking this stance the BBFC lays itself open to the charge that it is engaging in ideological censorship – in other words, only an authorised view of sexuality is

---

281 At '12A'/'12': 'sexual activity may be implied. Sexual references may reflect the familiarity of most adolescents today with sex education through school'. At '15': 'sexual activity and nudity may be portrayed but without strong detail. The depiction of casual sex should be handled responsibly.' At '18': the Board may cut or reject the 'more explicit images' of sexual conduct unless, exceptionally, they are justified by context. The following are not acceptable, even at 'R18': 'any material which is in breach of the criminal law; material (including dialogue) likely to encourage an interest in abusive sexual activity (e.g., paedophilia, incest) which may include depictions involving adults role-playing as non-adults; the portrayal of any sexual activity, whether real or simulated, which involves lack of consent; the infliction of pain or physical harm, real or (in a sexual context) simulated. Some allowance may be made for mild consensual activity. Any sexual threats or humiliation which do not form part of a clearly consenting role-playing game are disallowed, as are the use of any form of physical restraint which prevents participants from withdrawing consent, for example, ball gags, penetration by any object likely to cause actual harm or associated with violence, activity which is degrading or dehumanising (examples include the portrayal of bestiality, necrophilia, defecation, urolagnia)'.

acceptable. Again, the effect of the 2003 Act is to create a further age-based constraint even within the depiction of such relationships. Certain forms of simulated consenting heterosexual or homosexual sexual behaviour can no longer be shown involving 16- or 17-year-old actors, or older actors portraying younger people. The 'R18' category is primarily reserved for explicit videos of consenting sex between adults. In contrast, nudity, providing there is 'no sexual context or sub-text', is stated to be acceptable at all classification levels. Films rarely depict actual as opposed to simulated, sexual acts, including intercourse. The film *9 Songs*, however, achieved an '18'-rating in 2004 for the cinematic release despite frequent and graphic portrayals of non-simulated sexual intercourse. Previously, *Ai No Corrida* was classified '18' in 1991, as were *Romance* (1999) and *Intimacy* (2001) – all three films contain images of non-simulated intercourse. No '18'-rated film has yet depicted actual homosexual intercourse (the term is used here to include oral sex as well as anal intercourse).

Significantly, the guidelines state that the standards set for *legal* heterosexual and homosexual behaviour are equal (emphasis added). The use of the term 'legal' is important: in the past there has been legal differentiation between homosexual and heterosexual behaviour. For example, the age of consent for heterosexual intercourse is 16, whereas until 1994 it was 21 for homosexual intercourse.[282] Now the two forms of behaviour are equal under the law. When the Sexual Offences Act 2003 came into force,[283] a range of forms of heterosexual and homosexual sexual behaviour were placed on an equal footing. These changes could potentially have some impact on depictions of homosexual behaviour on film, and some liberalisation in terms of what can be shown may occur, due indirectly to changes in the criminal law.

The 2003 Act also made a very important change in this context, which has further implications for the distribution of films and videos made prior to 2003. The change concerns the definition of a 'child' under the terms of the Protection of Children Act 1978 (PCA), discussed above in relation to offences of indecency.[284] Previously the PCA s 7(6) defined a 'child' as a person under 16 years of age and made illegal the manufacture, possession and distribution of indecent photographs of children under 16. Section 45(2) of the new Sexual Offences Act amended the PCA by raising the age of a 'child' for the purposes of this Act to 18. The effect of this is retrospective, applying to all such images, regardless of when they first came into circulation. The Act in effect bans from the screen all depictions of sexual activity involving someone under 18 that could fall within the term 'indecent'. It is uncertain whether older actors whose features have been digitally manipulated to make them appear to be under 18 could be used since this might amount to the use of a 'pseudo-image' of a child.[285] Section 51 of the 2003

---

282 Under the Sexual Offences Act 1967, s 1, the age of consent was 21; this was amended by the Criminal Justice and Public Order Act 1994 s 143 to 18. Until recently, when the Sexual Offences Act 2003 came into force, there were a number of legal differentiations between illegal heterosexual and homosexual acts/behaviour, apart from that stemming from the age of consent; the more restrictive laws applied to homosexual behaviour.

283 On 1 May 2004.

284 See pp 415–17.

285 Section 84 of the Criminal Justice and Public Order Act 1994 amended the 1978 Act to add 'pseudo-photographs' of children in order to cover digitally created photographs. This would of course depend on whether in the context the image would be seen as 'indecent'.

Act introduced a new offence of 'facilitating' child pornography. The new restraints are mainly aimed at internet pornography, but place film-makers exploring depictions of teenage sexuality in a very difficult position, and mean that 16- and 17-year-olds are constrained in relation to viewing people of the same age involved in sexual activity.

Sexual intercourse between over 16s is legal, and other forms of sexual activity short of intercourse were legal even before the age of consent was raised to 16, but although the acts themselves are legal, depictions of them may not be. It is anomalous, to say the least, that heterosexual or homosexual intercourse between 16-year-olds or with adults, is lawful, whereas depictions of forms of sexual activity involving 16- or 17-year-old actors, falling far short of intercourse, might not be. Clearly, depictions of some forms of sexual activity involving 16- and 17-year-old actors would not attract criminal liability, but the 2003 Act has created a number of grey areas in relation to such depictions which did not previously exist. The BBFC may find itself seeking to classify films that could fall foul of the PCA 1978.

Clearly, the key question is whether the depiction of the 'child' could be viewed as 'indecent'. Whether a photograph is indecent depends on the view of the jury regarding recognised standards of propriety.[286] In *Oliver, Hartrey and Baldwin*[287] the Court of Appeal found that pornographic images were to be categorised by the following levels of seriousness: (1) images depicting erotic posing with no sexual activity; (2) sexual activity between children, or solo masturbation by a child; (3) non-penetrative sexual activity between adults and children; (4) penetrative sexual activity between children and adults, and (5) sadism or bestiality. Thus level (1), covering a very wide range of images,[288] represents the 'lowest' level at which an image of a child could be termed 'indecent'. A number of films have depicted teenage actors, most frequently those aged between 16 and 18, in the situations described in (1)–(3).[289] The definition of indecency is obviously context-dependent. Where *Gillick*-competent child or teenage actors above the age of 13 engage in depictions of fairly restrained, non-nude, consensual heterosexual activity with each other it may perhaps be assumed that this would not violate recognised standards of propriety. Clearly, the older the teenager, the more this would be the case. The fact that a teenage actor of 17 had been made up or (perhaps) digitally altered to look,

---

286 *R v Graham-Kerr* (1988) 88 Cr App R 302. See further: Manchester, C, 'Criminal Justice and Public Order Act 1994: obscenity, pornography and videos' [1995] Crim LR 123, pp 123–28; Cram, I, 'Criminalising Child Pornography – a Canadian Study' [2002] 66 J Crim L 359.

287 [2003] Cr App R 28.

288 As discussed above (p 418), recent developments involving art galleries showing pictures of naked children have illustrated the breadth of the definition of indecency in this context. See further Warbrick, 'Federalism and free speech', in Loveland, I (ed), *Importing the First Amendment*, 1997, pp 177–79 and 190–92.

289 A number of examples could be given; in *The Ice Storm* a sequence depicted actors Elijah Wood and Christina Ricci 'dry-humping'; another scene depicted Christina Ricci and Adam Hann-Byrd half-naked and kissing in bed together. All three actors were very young teenagers at the time. Both scenes appear to fall within level (2) from *Oliver, Hartrey and Baldwin*. In *The Name of the Rose* Christian Slater, who was 17 at the time and depicting a teenager, had simulated sex with an adult woman. The film *Kids* depicted a number of teenagers engaging in sexual activity. In *Trainspotting* Kelly McDonald, 17 at the time, engaged in simulated intercourse with an adult male actor, Ewan McGregor. The key question, of course, would be whether such scenes in the context of acting, and taking account of the fact that the actors were teenagers and *Gillick*-competent, would violate accepted standards of propriety and so be viewed as 'indecent'.

say, 13 would also be taken into account in relation to a determination as to indecency. But the uncertainty of the definition of indecency hardly favours erotic creativity, and places film-makers and the BBFC in a difficult position. The Court of Appeal may have to revisit and clarify its definition of indecency under the PCA due to the effect of the 2003 Act. The retrospective effect of the current definition of a 'child' is also highly problematic since certain cinematic depictions of sexuality, using 16- or 17-year-old actors, would not have fallen foul of the constraints of the 1978 Act at the time.[290] In 2007 the film *Hounddog* was released in America and caused some controversy since it concerned the rape of a 12-year-old girl, played by an actress of that age, Dakota Fanning. The actress did not have to participate in the scene in a physical fashion since the rape sequence was created by a mélange of shots of her face or hand when alone in a studio – so it was suggested, not simulated. On its face, the scene would appear to fall well within the *Oliver* boundaries of indecency – at level 4. But presumably the context would mean that the images would not violate accepted standards of propriety.

Theoretically, homosexual acts (including simulated or actual intercourse) between 16- or 17-year-old actors or between such actors and an adult could be shown on screen. But if viewed as indecent such acts cannot be seen on screen regardless of the equalisation of the age of consent. This is now also true of heterosexual acts, and in this sense the effect of the 2003 Act was to 'level down' in terms of equalising cinematic depictions of sexuality involving teenagers or apparent (digitally manipulated images of adults or CGI) teenagers. But it is probable that homosexual acts might be more likely to be seen as indecent, and in this sense BBFC decisions might – in effect – indirectly discriminate against depictions of homosexuality. This point is pursued below in relation to the HRA.

This might also be true even outside the purview of the 1978 Act, where other criminal law provisions are or might be applicable, including the anomalous common law doctrine of outraging public decency.[291] Such other provisions create differentiation in the legal position, thereby creating difficulties affecting depictions of homosexual behaviour short of intercourse, and simulated sexual acts, even between actors on screen, since such acts might be more likely to be viewed as indecent. Therefore depictions of homosexual behaviour on films have been, and still are, subject to greater restriction.

---

290 The change might not be compatible with the demands of Art 7(1) in HRA, Sched 1. Art 7 provides: '(1) No one shall be held guilty of any criminal offence on account of any act or omission which did not constitute a criminal offence under national or international law at the time when it was committed. Nor shall a heavier penalty be imposed than the one that was applicable at the time the criminal offence was committed. (2) This Article shall not prejudice the trial and punishment of any person for any act or omission which, at the time when it was committed, was criminal according to the general principles of law recognised by civilised nations. Art 7 was found to have been breached in *Welch v UK* (1995) 20 EHRR 247. Before the trial of the applicant for drug offences, a new provision came into force under the Drug Trafficking Offences Act 1986, making provision for confiscation orders. This was imposed on the applicant, although the legislation was not in force at the time when he committed the offences in question. It clearly had retrospective effect and was found to constitute a 'penalty' within Art 7(1). The 2003 Act was not declared compatible with the Convention under HRA, s 19(1)(a), but only in respect of ss 319 and 321 (the ban on political advertising), so the government legal advice must have been to the effect that Art 7 had been complied with, probably on the basis that the exception under Art 7(2) applied. In any event compatibility remains a matter for the judiciary to determine.

291 See pp 421–24 above.

The classification system also addresses the degree and nature of violence depicted in films,[292] while accepting that violence is an inevitable aspect of entertainment at all ages, 'an element in many serious representations of the human condition'. But the guidelines advise against the portrayal of violence as 'a normal solution to problems' and against callousness to victims or the encouragement of aggression. The guidelines state that works which 'glorify or glamorise violence' will receive a more restrictive classification and may be cut. Sexual violence is of particular concern. The BBFC states that it has a strict policy on rape and sexual violence. Cuts may be made in material that associates sex with non-consensual restraint, pain or humiliation. If a portrayal eroticises or endorses sexual assault, the Board is likely to require cuts at any classification level. Cuts are more likely in video rather than film portrayals due to the possibility of repeat viewing of video scenes. The guidelines indicate that portrayals of the use of weapons easily accessible to young people will be restricted, and imitable combat techniques may be cut, as may imitable detail of criminal techniques. Works that promote or encourage or glamorise the use of illegal drugs will not in general receive even an '18' classification. Clear instructive detail as to drug use is only acceptable at the '18' classification 'if there are exceptional considerations of context'.

The guidelines highlight the use of expletives in films, a matter that is more problematic in relation to UK film audiences than it is in the rest of Europe. The BBFC finds that the degree of offence caused by the use of expletives varies according to age, background and beliefs; ethnicity may also be relevant. The context will also be significant. In the light of these variables it offers only general guidance rather than providing a comprehensive listing of unacceptable words. Specific terms are advised against at different classification levels only where there is a reasonable consensus of opinion.[293]

The 1984 Act does not make reference specifically to avoiding offence to religious sensibilities. In general videos are more restricted than films in respect of the depiction of sex and violence, but this does not appear to be the case in relation to filmic portrayals of religion. Under the BBFC guidelines for both films and videos:

> The acceptability of a theme depends significantly on its treatment, i.e. the context and sensitivity of its presentation. However, the most problematic themes (for example . . . incitement to racial hatred) are unlikely to be appropriate at the most junior levels of classification. Correspondingly, there is no reason in principle why most themes, however difficult, could not be satisfactorily handled at '18' or even '15'.

The BBFC had to update its guidelines to add the words 'or religious' to them after the word 'incitement' in the light of the introduction of the new offence of inciting to

---

292 At '12A'/'12': 'Violence must not dwell on detail. There should be no emphasis on injuries or blood. Sexual violence may only be implied or briefly indicated and without physical detail.' At '15': 'Violence may be strong but may not dwell on the infliction of pain, and of injuries. Scenes of sexual violence must be discreet and brief.' There should be no 'detailed portrayal of violent or dangerous acts which is likely to promote the activity'.

293 The Guidelines state, at '12'/'12A': 'The use of strong language (e.g., 'fuck') should be rare'. At '15': 'there may be frequent use of strong language; the strongest terms (e.g., 'cunt') are only rarely acceptable. Continued *aggressive* use of strong language and sexual abuse is unacceptable.' At '18' there are no constraints on language.

religious hatred, discussed above. The guidelines also state: 'Many people are offended, some of them deeply, by bad language, including the use of expletives with a religious or racial association.' Thus, the BBFC makes very little specific provision in relation to the portrayal of religion. However, it does state that it takes account of the criminal law, which includes the laws relating to blasphemy and religious hatred.

The theatrical release of films

This section looks at the different considerations that apply to the theatrical, as opposed to the video, release of films. The BBFC guidelines discussed are applied somewhat differently to films in relation to the cinematic and the video release. Since cinema films are viewed by an adult, willing audience who has access to information about the nature of the film, it might have been expected that '18'-rated films would fall just outside the boundaries of criminal liability as determined by the Obscene Publications Act, as amended, and common law offences. There is a greater risk in relation to videos that children might view adult films. The difficulty with the availability of the 'R18' classification in relation to the cinematic release is that it may mean that the BBFC are not exploring the boundaries of the legal definition of obscenity in adult films in general, those that receive the '18' classification. The 'R18'-classification may, in effect, drive a wedge between such films and the outer limits of acceptability under the criminal law.

Consideration of recent decisions by the BBFC suggests that there is some basis for these concerns. However, at the 'PG' to '15' levels the BBFC has shown a willingness in some instances to place films within a non-restrictive category, even where they fall at the outer limits of that category. For example, the BBFC took a creative approach in 2001 to the classification of *The Lord of the Rings – the Fellowship of the Ring*. The Board found that the battle violence and fantasy horror in the film were a matter for concern since children under the age of eight might be frightened or disturbed. However, it decided to give the film a 'PG' rating, on the basis that the film's distributor had agreed that all advertising and publicity for the film would carry the consumer advice that the film contained scenes that might not be suitable for children under eight years of age. Most films do not carry such advice, over and beyond the classification rating; the only other films to carry consumer advice on all publicity and advertising were *Jurassic Park* and *The Lost World – Jurassic Park*, both of which were rated 'PG'.[294] The BBFC was presented with greater difficulties in relation to the film *Spiderman*. It was aimed at a young audience by the film-makers, and Hollywood had marketed it with that audience in mind. But the BBFC considered it 'possibly the most violent film . . . aimed at a young audience that the BBFC has classified'. Therefore the Board considered that it was clearly unsuitable for a 'PG' rating since very young children would then be able to view the film. Classifying it as '12', the BBFC found that the film '[carries] . . . a clear message that the use of violence is the normal and appropriate response when challenged'.[295] The '12A' rating was not available at the time.

At the '18' level the BBFC has to deal with the even more problematic issue of censorship of material aimed at adults, as opposed to the issues raised by restrictive age

294 See BBFC press release, 22 November 2001.
295 See BBFC press release, 13 June 2002.

classifications. In 2002 the BBFC decided to classify the French film *Irreversible* as '18' uncut for the cinema release. The film centres around a graphically depicted rape and its consequences. The Board found, in line with its current classification guidelines and having taken advice from a clinical forensic psychiatrist, that the depiction of the rape did not eroticise or appear to endorse sexual violence. The Board considered that the rape scene was a harrowing and vivid portrayal of the brutality of rape which was not designed to titillate.[296] In contrast, in the same year the BBFC passed the French-language cinema film, *The Pornographer*, as '18' but required a cut to a graphic unsimulated sex scene in which a woman was seen with semen on her face following oral sex.[297] This cut was in line with the BBFC's Guidelines at '18', which state that the Board may cut or reject 'the more explicit images of sexual activity – unless they can be exceptionally justified by context'. The Board did not find that the context justified the scene. As mentioned above, the film *9 Songs* obtained an '18' rating in 2004 for the cinematic release, although it depicted actual as opposed to simulated sexual intercourse. The Board decided that the film's sensitive exploration of the relationship between the two people provided sufficient contextual justification. The consumer advice provided a warning of the content.

The emphasis on context as providing a justification for portrayals of sexual activity or violence is questionable since it depends on value judgments made by the Board members as to 'acceptable' contexts. Films are a very significant medium for the exploration of controversial themes and such themes may depend on the use of images from outside the boundaries of those contexts. There is a case for arguing that the 'R18' classification should be abolished for the theatrical release of films and that mainstream films should therefore be able to explore the boundaries created by the criminal law more vigorously and closely. If a film viewed only by adults is to be cut, the starting-point should be the demands of the criminal law. Clear justification based on the avoidance of specific harms, as opposed merely to offence-avoidance, should be available for cuts made reaching beyond those demands. The possibility of more extensive use of detailed consumer guidance should be pursued in order to avoid the causing of offence.

The second level of classification is operated, as discussed above, by local authorities under the Cinemas Act 1985, which continues the old power arising under the Cinematograph Act 1909. The local authority will usually follow the Board's advice; authorities are reluctant to devote resources to viewing films and will tend to rely on the BBFC's judgment.[298] But authorities may, on occasion, choose not to grant a licence to a film regardless of its decision. Films which have been licensed but which nevertheless have been banned in some areas include *A Clockwork Orange*, *The Life of Brian*, *The Last Temptation of Christ* and *Crash*. Conversely, local authorities may come under pressure to change the classification of a film in order to make it less restrictive. Two local authorities downgraded *Spiderman* to a 'PG' rating for that reason, since some parents had been disappointed by the '12' rating.[299] There is no requirement of consistency between authorities and thus discrepancies have arisen between different local authority

---

296 See BBFC press release, 21 October 2002.
297 See BBFC press release, 2 April 2002.
298 See Holbrook (1973) 123 NLJ 701.
299 See BBFC press release, 13 June 2002.

areas. It is notable that the cinema is the only art form subject to moral judgment on a local level and clearly it may be asked why it should be so singled out. This dual system of censorship was criticised unavailingly over 35 years ago by the Williams Committee in 1979,[300] partly on the ground of the anomalies caused by having two overlapping levels of restraint and partly due to the inconsistency between local authorities. It considered that a unified system should be adopted. In particular, it criticised a system which allowed adult films to be censored beyond the requirements of the OPA.

Statutory regulation of video

The Video Recordings Act 1984 was introduced after a campaign about the dangers posed by 'video nasties' to children. The campaign, by the *Daily Mail* and a group called the Festival of Light managed to convince Parliament that legislation was necessary in order to address the problem.[301] Under the Video Recordings Act 1984, the BBFC was established as the authority charged with classifying videos for viewing in the home.[302] It currently classifies videos, DVDs and some digital works under the 1984 Act. Videos[303] are classified and therefore censored in almost the same way as films, and under s 9 of the 1984 Act, it is an offence to supply a video without a classification certificate, unless it is exempt on grounds of its concern with education, sport, music or religion. Under s 2(2) the exemption will not apply if the video portrays human sexual activity or gross violence or is designed to stimulate or encourage this. Section 4 of the 1984 Act requires that the BBFC should have 'special regard to the likelihood of videoworks being viewed in the home'. Thus, makers of videos may find that videos are censored well beyond the requirements of the OPA.

The regime in respect of videos was made potentially more restrictive in 1994. Fears that children might be more likely to commit violence after watching violent videos[304] led the government to include a number of provisions in the Criminal Justice and Public Order Bill 1994, which was then before the Commons. Under s 90 of the Criminal Justice and Public Order Act 1994, inserting s 4A into the 1984 Act, the BBFC must have 'special regard' to harm which may be caused to 'potential viewers or through their behaviour to society' by the manner in which the film deals with criminal behaviour, illegal drugs, violent behaviour or incidents, horrific incidents or behaviour or human sexual activity. These criteria are non-exhaustive. The BBFC can consider any other relevant factor. 'Potential viewers' include children, but it is not necessary to show that children had in fact viewed the video. The kind of harm envisaged, to a child or to society, is not specified and nor is the degree of seriousness envisaged although the use of the word 'may' implies that there must be some likelihood of harm. Section 4A does not prescribe the Board's response once it has taken the above

300 See Williams Committee on Obscenity and Film Censorship, which conducted a review of the area, Cmnd 7772, 1979.
301 See Petley, J, *Screen*, Vol 25 No 2, p 68.
302 After the introduction of the Video Recordings Act 1984, the President and Vice-Presidents of the Board were designated by the Home Secretary under s 4(1) as the authority responsible for applying the statutory classification system for videoworks set out in the Act.
303 When the term 'videowork' or 'video' is used it will be used to cover video material presented on DVDs and digital games.
304 See further, Home Affairs Committee, *Video Violence and Young Offenders*, Fourth Report (1994) HC 514.

factors 'into account'.[305] Section 89 of the 1994 Act also amended s 2(2) in respect of the scope of the exemptions mentioned above. These exemptions will not apply if a video 'depicts techniques likely to be useful in the commission of offences' or 'criminal activity likely to any significant extent to stimulate or encourage the commission of offences'. It is not necessary to show that the video is designed to stimulate or encourage the activity mentioned above, but only that it is likely to do so. If the BBFC considers that a particular work is unacceptable for viewing, it can, and does, refuse to issue a classification certificate altogether. This has the effect of banning the vide concerned since under the 1984 Act, ss 9–11 it is a criminal offence to supply, offer or possess for supply an unclassified video. It is also an offence to supply a video in breach of the classification certificate issued by the BBFC.[306]

A right of appeal from the decisions of the BBFC to the Video Appeals Committee (VAC), which operates as a tribunal, was created under the provisions of s 4(3) of the 1984 Act.[307] No other party has the right of appeal under the Act. The Home Secretary has sought to intervene in this classification and appeals scheme, with the result that in the 1990s the BBFC and the VAC came into conflict in respect of a number of explicit videos that depicted actual, rather than simulated, sexual scenes. The Board relaxed their guidelines in 1997 and classified a number of videos containing more explicit material than had been classified before, including scenes of actual penetration and oral sex. The Home Secretary was apparently concerned that this action would create a potential conflict with the enforcement policies of both Customs and Excise and the police who may seize material of similar explicitness for forfeiture proceedings via magistrates' courts under the Customs Consolidation Act 1876 and the Obscene Publications Act 1959 respectively. He instructed the Board to rescind their policy change. The Board set up an enforcement sub-group, which was established to consider the issue of consistency of standards between the Board and the prosecuting authorities.[308]

In 1998 the Board refused to classify an explicit sex video, *Makin' Whoopee*, to which they had given, but subsequently withdrawn, an interim classification certificate under their revised guidelines. The publishers appealed to the VAC who found in their favour, rejecting arguments that the video might be obscene within the meaning of the 1959 Obscene Publications Act. The Board classified the video in the 'R18' category but did not accept that the judgment, which was limited to the issue of obscenity, set

---

305 See on this issue, Manchester, C, 'Criminal Justice and Public Order Act 1994: obscenity, pornography and videos' (1995) Crim LR 123, pp 129–30.

306 It may be noted that it is a defence under the Video Recordings Act 1993 to a charge of any offence under the 1984 Act to prove that the offence was due to the act or default of another person or that the accused took all reasonable precautions to avoid the commission of the offence 'by any person under his control'.

307 Under s 4(3) of the 1984 Act the Home Secretary must be satisfied that the designated authority (in practice this meant the principal officers at the BBFC) have adequate arrangements for appeals against classification determinations which producers or distributors feel are too restrictive. This may be because the video works in question have been given too high a classification or because they have been refused a classification altogether. The 1984 Act itself is silent as to the nature of the appeals body but the BBFC itself set up the VAC. The BBFC was responsible for the mechanics of recruitment and appointment of its members.

308 See BBFC Response to the Home Office Consultation Paper on *The Regulation of R18 Videos*, paras 2.3 and 1.4.

a precedent for consideration of similar videos.[309] A further seven videos were subsequently refused classification certificates and the Board then faced appeals against their decisions in respect of the videos. The VAC found in favour of the appellants and the Board subsequently sought leave to apply for judicial review of the VAC's judgement: *R v Video Appeals Committee of the BBFC ex p BBFC*.[310] The Board was unsuccessful on the basis that the VAC had taken all the relevant factors into account, including any risk to children. It was thought that since the videos were to be sold in adult sex shops, the risk that they would come into the hands of children and the risk that they would cause harm to them was very slight. In the proceedings, Hooper J concluded: 'I have no doubt that the conclusion "that the risk of [the videos in question] being viewed by and causing harm to children or young persons is, on present evidence, insignificant" is one that a reasonable decision maker could reach ...'. He found that the VAC had acted reasonably in reaching the decision they did on the basis of the arguments put before them, and dismissed the Board's application. In other words, it could not be said that this was a decision that no reasonable regulator could have come to – the familiar low threshold. Thus the judgment was based on the *Wednesbury* unreasonableness standard only, not on Art 10 demands, and indicated quite a high degree of deference, common in this context, to the expert decision-maker – the VAC.[311] It was *consistent* with the view that the access of adults to explicit material should not be prevented on the basis that there was an unquantifiable risk of harm to children if it happened to come into their hands. However, it would be overstating the matter to find that the judgment laid down a statement of principle of this nature.

The then Labour Home Secretary, Jack Straw, attacked the decision of the VAC, and the Home Office published a consultation paper indicating that new legislation on the VAC and the use of the 'R18' classification might be necessary.[312] The possibility that the VAC could be newly set up under statute, with government-appointed officers, was raised.[313] In response the BBFC did not accept the government's criticisms of the VAC, but recommended that its jurisdiction should be confined to deciding whether the Board, as the designated authority under the Video Recordings Act, had been 'fair, consistent and legally correct in the application of its published policy and Guidelines'.[314] It may be noted that the VAC has not always been so bold: it did not reverse the decision of the BBFC in relation to the video *Visions of Ecstasy*, on the basis that it was possibly blasphemous. This decision turned, however, on the problematic nature of the law of blasphemy.[315]

The decision in *R v Video Appeals Committee of the BBFC ex p BBFC* highlighted one of the problems inherent in the 1984 Act, a flaw that became especially apparent in relation to 'R18'-rated videos, under the more relaxed guidelines. Section 4A of the Act operates on the assumption that children may be harmed if they view sexually explicit

---

309 *Ibid.*
310 (2000) EMLR 850.
311 See further Chapter 4, pp 218–47 on deference in this context.
312 Home Office Consultation Paper on *The Regulation of R18 Videos* 28 July 2000; see also the *Guardian*, 17 May 2000.
313 Home Office Consultation Paper on *The Regulation of R18 Videos*, paras 3.16–3.21.
314 BBFC Response to the Home Office Consultation Paper on *The Regulation of R18 Videos*.
315 See pp 424–25.

or very violent videos. However, there is no firm evidence that this is the case in relation to explicit depictions of sexuality,[316] as the government itself accepts,[317] and therefore it is very difficult to establish that harm is likely. Also, the connection between violence on film and violent behaviour in children has not been firmly established. It appears to be possible that there is a greater likelihood, not that children may perpetrate violence as an immediate reaction to exposure to violent films, but that they may be de-sensitised to violence in a long-term sense if they watch a great deal of it.[318] However, psychologists disagree as to the creation of this effect and there is no clear consensus among them as to the general proposition that watching violent films harms children.[319]

Likelihood of harm should arguably be established on the balance of probabilities,[320] and on the basis of the current research it is unclear that it can be. If a greater risk of harm could be established it would at the least support the continuance of the restrictions on the sale of 'R18' videos. There are clearly two separate issues – that of the likelihood of harm and that of the likelihood that children might view the video. The small chance that they might do so in respect of videos with the 'R18' classification due to the restrictions on sale makes it difficult to give effect to s 4A in relation to such videos, as the High Court accepted in *R v Video Appeals Committee of the BBFC ex p BBFC*. It could also be argued that it is difficult to give legal effect to s 4A, even in relation to videos classified '15' or '18', since although there is a higher probability that children may view them, it is even harder to establish that they might be harmed if they do. Possibly s 4A has become legally ineffectual. Therefore it is unclear that there is a sound legal basis for creating distinctions between videos and films in terms of cuts at those classification levels.

316   BBFC News Release, 26 October 2000, *Abused children most at risk from pornography*: 'The BBFC commissioned the research in response to the Video Appeals Committee's ruling that the Board had failed to provide sufficient evidence of harm to children from viewing pornography in an appeal to the VAC by two porn distributors in 1999. The research was focused on finding out whether pornography by itself harmed children . . . The majority of those interviewed [child psychologists] believed that viewing pornography would be harmful to any child, and that they should be protected from it. They were, however, able to quote very little in the way of evidence to support this belief, either from their own case loads or those of their colleagues. Some felt that viewing pornography depicting consensual sex would *not* be harmful to children who were well cared for and not being harmed in other ways. Determining the harm pornography does is not easy because it is difficult to disentangle it from other features of a child's situation, especially as the majority of children who are exposed to pornography are usually being harmed in other ways. Several of the experts argued that pornography was less regulated and more readily available in Europe and the USA. Yet they were not aware of any evidence that a higher proportion of children in those countries needed professional help because seeing pornography had upset them. Nor were related outcomes like teenage pregnancies or marital breakdowns higher in countries where pornography circulated more freely . . . Robin Duval, Director of the BBFC, said: " . . . this research shows that there is in fact little clear evidence to support the natural view that 'accidental' viewing will have seriously harmful effects. It is reasonable to assume that a sample of 38 leading professionals would have been able to cite more anecdotal evidence from their case loads if harm to children, outside abusive or negligent situations, were significant or common".'
317   Home Office Consultation Paper on *The Regulation of R18 Videos*, para 1: 'There is little conclusive evidence of harmful effects'.
318   See further, Home Affairs Committee, *Video Violence and Young Offenders*, Fourth Report (1994) HC 514.
319   See M Barker and J Petley *Ill Effects: The Media Violence Debate* (London: Routledge, 1997).
320   See further above, pp 399–400 on this point.

The 1984 Act places the BBFC in the position of official censors and in that role their work has in the past been criticised as over-strict and arbitrary.[321] Taking account of s 4 of the 1984 Act, the BBFC uses cuts and restrictive classification more stringently with videos than with films partly because of the greater possibility that younger children will view them, despite the age classification, and also because – as it states – certain techniques, such as the use of weapons or of drugs, can be watched repeatedly 'until the lesson is learned'. The possibility of repeat viewings may also, in the Board's view, be a matter of concern in relation to sexually explicit and violent scenes. So the age classifications may be used more restrictively in relation to videos and cuts are more likely to be made to videos before being rated '18'. For example, after taking specialist advice, the BBFC required a cut of one minute 28 seconds to the video version of *A Ma Soeur!*, a film about the rape of a young girl, to achieve an '18' rating. The Board had previously passed the film version '18' uncut, but took the advice of a leading consultant clinical psychologist who considered that the rape scene was similar to material that paedophiles use to groom their victims.[322] This was perceived as more of a problem in relation to the video, as opposed to the cinematic, release due to the possibility that the scene in question could be played repeatedly and in a private context.

The impact and influence of the Human Rights Act

The stance of the BBFC is obviously influenced by the composition of the Board. Its effect on film-makers has been criticised as militating against creativity. It has been suggested that a cosy relationship has developed with film-makers that is insufficiently challenging – the acceptable boundaries are not fully explored in the name of artistic integrity and creative freedom.[323] Although there has been liberalisation, it is still arguable that commercial judgments rather than artistic considerations tend to dominate. The most pressing consideration for distributors is to find the widest possible audience, which may mean instituting cuts in order to obtain a '15' or '12A' certificate. The fact that the classifications are mandatory is also relevant, since distribution in the UK is therefore more restricted by age restraints than in countries in which it is recommendatory. Children under the age in question are still part of the targeted market in such countries. The relationship between 'artistic' and 'commercial' considerations is, clearly, a complex one. There is clear commercial mileage in obtaining the widest possible release of a film by way of the 'PG' certificate. But there may also be commercial advantage in producing sexually explicit and controversial films. In both instances, in a very competitive market where backers and distributors are unwilling to take commercial risks, directors and producers may be forced to institute cuts for the UK release of a film where clearly they would prefer to release it uncut. The BBFC accepts that its application of its guidelines leads to a more restrictive censorship and classification of films in the UK than in almost all of Europe or the US.

It seems possible that the inception of the HRA could have some impact on this situation, although ultimately by far the most significant matter is the stance of the BBFC.

---

321 See Hunnings, N, 'Video censorship' [1985] PL 214; Robertson, G, *Freedom, the Individual and the Law*, 7th edn, 1993, Penguin, pp 263–72.
322 See BBFC press release, 25 June 2002.
323 See Robertson and Nichol, *op cit*, fn 1, p 593.

For example, a film-maker whose film was refused a classification without certain cuts, could refuse to institute the cuts and seek to challenge the decision of the BBFC or, in the case of a video, that of the VAC, if it upheld the BBFC's decision. The VAC is a body set up under statute with a public function in the sense of hearing appeals regarding the classification of material to be promulgated to the public; it is also subject to judicial review. It is therefore almost certainly a functional public authority under s 6 HRA. The BBFC has a public function that is also statutory in respect of providing classification certificates for videos. Its function in relation to films is not statutory, but can clearly be termed public. Had it not undertaken the classification of films, the government would have been likely to set up a statutory body.[324] It is suggested therefore that it too is also almost certainly a functional public authority under s 6.[325] If this is correct, private bodies or persons could bring an action against either body under s 7(1)(a) of the HRA, or by way of judicial review, relying on Art 10. In such an action, a court would have to give effect to s 12(4) HRA.[326]

Assuming that the VAC and BBFC are public authorities and so bound by the Convention rights under s 6, they should also ensure that their decisions do not breach Art 10, or any other relevant Article. For example, a film-maker whose film portraying actual homosexual intercourse or other explicit homosexual activity did not receive a certificate, could put forward the argument that Art 10 read with Art 14 (the freedom from discrimination article)[327] should affect the interpretation, under s 3 HRA of the term 'indecency' in the PCA (if one of the actors was 17) or 'obscene' in the OPA. The argument would be that the same standards should be applied as would be applied to films showing explicit heterosexual activity. Importantly, as a public authority, the VAC cannot be confined to considering only whether the BBFC's decisions are 'fair, consistent and legally correct'; it also has to consider whether its own decisions on appeals might breach Art 10. It can of course be argued that 'legally correct' includes consideration of the BBFC's own duty under s 6(1) HRA not to breach Art 10 in its decisions, and therefore the VAC must decide whether the BBFC has acted compatibly with the

---

324 See Chapter 4, pp 189–98, on functional public authorities.

325 The BBFC takes the view that because of its public functions in respect of the statutory classification of videoworks, it is a 'public authority' under the HRA. In taking this view it has not distinguished between its function in relation to videos and that in relation to films. Clearly, it would be anomalous if such a distinction was drawn given the similarity of the two functions. (See the 2000 BBFC Response to the Home Office Consultation Paper on *The Regulation of R18 Videos* at para 1.16.) See also Chapter 4, pp 199–202.

326 See further Chapter 4, pp 189–202, on the provisions of s 12(4).

327 Art 14 provides: 'The enjoyment of the rights and freedoms set forth in this Convention shall be secured without discrimination on any ground such as sex, race, colour, language, religion, political or other opinion, national or social origin, association with a national minority, property, birth or other status.' Thus, Art 14 does not provide a general right to freedom from discrimination, only that the rights and freedoms of the Convention must be secured without discrimination. In the context under discussion Art 14 could be employed in order to argue that the right under Art 10 should be secured without discrimination on grounds of sexual orientation. This ground of discrimination is clearly covered by Art 14 (*Salgueiro da Silva Mouta v Portugal*, judgment of 21 December 1999); the question that would arise in this context would be whether differentiation between film-makers' output on the grounds of the *nature* of the output would be covered.

demands of Art 10. Nevertheless, the VAC has a duty in relation to Art 10 under the HRA distinct from that of the BBFC itself. The 1984 Act, as amended, must be interpreted compatibly with the Convention rights under s 3(1) HRA. Given that a number of its terms are very open-ended, there is room for a range of interpretations.

However, in the case of a sexually explicit or violent film, the problem would be, as indicated above, that the Strasbourg jurisprudence appears to support quite far-reaching restrictions. It might be argued that where the risk of children viewing the cinema release of a film is very slight due to the use of age restrictions, *and* the question of offending religious sensibilities does not arise, the jurisprudence could be viewed as supporting the availability of even very explicit films.[328] This contention would be based on the unavailability of the margin of appreciation doctrine at the domestic level, and also derives from the principles underlying the jurisprudence, which, as indicated above, relate to the familiar free speech justifications, including that of self-fulfilment.[329]

But it must be acknowledged that this argument is not situated firmly in the Strasbourg jurisprudence at present. It rests mainly on one decision of the Commission – that of *Scherer*.[330] The decisions of the Court, in particular those of *Handyside*[331] and *Otto-Preminger*,[332] lend it only speculative support. The Court may have found it easier, in those decisions, to rest its argument on risks to children or to religious sensibilities, rather than enter the extremely difficult debate as to the proper limits of adult autonomy in relation to controversial, offensive and explicit speech. The argument that decisions at Strasbourg heavily influenced by the margin of appreciation doctrine should be applied domestically 'stripped' of its effects, is an appealing and compelling one that has been canvassed elsewhere in this book.[333] But the judges have shown little receptivity to it under the HRA so far.[334]

If a suitable case in this context arose domestically – which in itself is unlikely – a judge who wanted to impose a liberalising interpretation on the domestic law would have to have a *pre-existing* determination to take a liberal stance in relation to the PCA 1978 or the OPA 1959. If so, he or she would be able to find some, admittedly meagre, support in the jurisprudence for that stance. But equally the opposing, conservative stance could be taken and could find support in the jurisprudence, particularly from *Gibson v UK*.[335] The OPA itself clearly takes an overtly paternalistic stance since it assumes that judgments can be made and imposed on others as to what might deprave and corrupt them. The HRA could be viewed as legitimising this existing position since the Strasbourg jurisprudence, especially the decisions of the Court on explicit expression,

---

328 See p 406, above.
329 See above, pp 283–84.
330 A 287 (1993). See, for discussion, pp 406–08.
331 (1976) 1 EHRR 737. See, for discussion, p 404.
332 (1994) 19 EHRR 34.
333 See Chapter 4, pp 218–47.
334 For example, in *R v Perrin* [2002] EWCA Crim 747, a recent case on the OPA 1959 (discussed at pp 584–85 below) in relation to the internet, *Handyside* and other relevant Strasbourg decisions were fully considered. The Court noted that the margin of appreciation doctrine was relevant in them, especially *Handyside*. But it did not appear to appreciate that by applying *Handyside* without seeking to disregard as far as possible the parts of the decision affected by the doctrine, it was in effect allowing the doctrine to have an impact on domestic law.
335 For discussion of the domestic case, see Childs, M, 'Outraging Public Decency' (1991) PL 20.

is itself paternalistic. Recent case law on the OPA and PCA in the context of internet pornography indicates that the courts are taking the latter stance. On the other hand, in this context, courts are likely to defer to the expertise of the regulators,[336] rather than rely on the Strasbourg jurisprudence, however it could be interpreted. So if the BBFC adopts a liberal stance – and it appears, increasingly, to be doing so[337] – the courts are unlikely to interfere with its decisions.

On the assumption that the relevant Strasbourg freedom of expression jurisprudence lends a degree of support to adult autonomy in this context, it can be argued that there is fairly limited scope under Art 10(2) for interferences with the freedom of expression of film-makers in respect of the theatrical release of films targeted at adults. It would be expected that they would be afforded an '18' certificate and appropriate warnings should be posted at cinemas and on the internet so that an unwitting viewer would not be offended. Art 10 might be viewed as underpinning the policy of awarding 'R18' certificates to films not viewed as obscene since there is virtually no chance of children viewing them due to the restrictions.

Taking account of *Scherer*[338] and *Hoare*,[339] different considerations might appear to apply to *videos*, owing to the possibility that, despite the restrictions on sale they might be viewed by children in the home, but this argument should be considered carefully, in terms of its impact on adults. The effect of the margin of appreciation doctrine on those decisions should be taken into account, following the argument discussed above.[340] The question of the harm that might be caused should also be considered, bearing in mind the lack of evidence mentioned above regarding a connection between behaviour seen on film and actual behaviour. The mere invocation of the possibility that children might view a video might not appear to be enough to satisfy the demands of proportionality, although it was found to be enough in *Hoare*. Theoretically, a domestic court could take a harder look at those demands than the Commission did in *Hoare*, since the margin of appreciation doctrine would be inapplicable. In practice, as discussed, the court would probably defer to the BBFC or VAC decision as in *R v Video Appeals Committee of the BBFC ex p BBFC*; possibly the HRA would add little in this context to the reasonableness standard applied in that instance although a nod in the direction of proportionality would be expected. In respect of videos, the small chance that children might view a video with an 'R18' certificate (bearing in mind the controls on buying such videos), and the unquantifiability of the risk that a child might be harmed by it, could be taken to mean that refusing to classify a video at 'R18', even where it is not obscene, would be disproportionate, under Art 10(2), to the aim pursued. Guidance on this matter might also usefully be sought from other jurisdictions,[341] since it is not a matter that Strasbourg has inquired into in any depth.

---

336 This is strongly indicated by the House of Lords' decision in *Pro-Life Alliance v BBC* [2004] 1 AC 185; [2003] 2 All ER 977 (for discussion, see p 437) and by the *R v Video Appeals Committee of the BBFC ex p BBFC* decision [2000] EMLR 850.
337 See pp 458–63 above.
338 A 287 (1993) Com Rep.
339 [1997] EHRLR 678.
340 See above, p 404.
341 (1994) 19 EHRR 34.

The stance taken by Strasbourg in relation to films likely to offend religious sensibilities was indicated in the leading decision, *Otto-Preminger*,[342] discussed above.[343] The film in question was not likely to be viewed by children, but was found to be offensive to religious sensibilities. The seizure and forfeiture of the film was not found to breach Art 10. Further guidance derives from the decision of the Court of Human Rights in *Wingrove v UK*.[344] It concerned a decision of the BBFC, upheld by the VAC, to refuse a certificate to the short, explicit film, *Visions of Ecstasy*. The Court found that the decision to refuse a certificate was within the national authorities' margin of appreciation. But the film, which was to be promulgated as a short video, was viewed as offensive to religious sensibilities and as quite likely to come to the attention of children, since it could be viewed in the home.[345] No breach of Art 10 was found.

Conclusions

The view of the Williams Committee on Obscenity and Film Censorship, which conducted a review of the area in 1979,[346] was that the censorship of films should continue. The Committee considered that in the light of some psychiatric evidence to the effect that violent films might induce violent behaviour, a policy based on caution was justified.[347] The point has often been made, however, that the evidence that films have a very different impact from books or magazines is not strong: the difference in treatment may be due to historical reasons: new forms of expression take time to gain the acceptance accorded to traditional mediums and are viewed with some suspicion.[348] Many of the BBFC guidelines are aimed at preventing specific forms of harm which might come about as a result of the viewing of films. Clearly, the causal relationship between the viewing and the harm in many instances may be debatable, but the BBFC does have the prevention of particular harms – over and above the causing of offence – in mind. For example, rejecting or cutting the depiction of imitable combat techniques in films aimed at children is defensible on that basis. Glamorisation of images of sexual violence, including rape, may have some effect on the incidence of male aggression towards women, or other men. However, the avoidance of specific harms cannot be said to be the sole aim of cutting explicit sexual images in films aimed at adults, where they are not linked to non-consensual acts or violence. If such images are not obscene, although, admittedly, as pointed out above, that concept creates its own grave difficulties of interpretation, the basis for cutting them is unclear.

Although the BBFC clearly has in mind the invasion of adult autonomy created by imposing constraints on films beyond those demanded by the criminal law, it continues to accept that such constraints are necessary, even though they create a stricter

---

342 See pp 405–07.
343 (1996) 24 EHRR 1. The question of the validity of taking the stance adopted in *Wingrove* and *Otto-Preminger* is considered above, at pp 406–7.
344 See paras 61 and 63 of the judgment.
345 Cmnd 7772, 1979. See Simpson, AWB, *Pornography and Politics: The Williams Committee in Retrospect*, 1983, pp 35–37.
346 See Simpson, AWB, *ibid*, p 37.
347 See e.g., Barendt, *Freedom of Speech, op cit*, fn 1, 1st edn, p 125.
348 See Fenwick, H and Phillipson, G, (2006), *op cit*, fn 1 at Chapter 9, pp 450–62.

censorship regime in the UK than in the rest of Europe. Such constraints are partly based on necessarily subjective interpretations of the contextual validation of explicit images. In taking its particular stance towards the censorship and classification of films the BBFC appears to an extent to be bowing to government pressure, as the story behind *R v Video Appeals Committee of the BBFC ex p BBFC* reveals. The possibility of mounting successful challenges to restrictive BBFC decisions in reliance on Art 10, as discussed above, remains open and would provide a counter to the paternalistic stance sometimes taken by the government.

But it is not suggested that the only consideration that should inform BBFC decisions is that of moral autonomy. In dealing with the portrayal of sexuality the BBFC is in a position to shift the focus from traditional concerns as to offence and the undermining of traditional moral values, to the protection of what may be termed 'constitutional morality'.[349] Indeed there are some signs in the stance it takes to the classification of films portraying sexual violence that it is already beginning to do so. In other words, on the model provided by the Supreme Court of Canada which reconceptualised the concern of obscenity law as focused on the protection of foundational values such as equality and dignity,[350] the BBFC could increasingly bring such factors into its deliberations into the portrayal of sexual activity in film.

7 The internet[351]

Introduction

The question of the regulation of the internet is immensely complex.[352] The issues raised can only be touched on here, but one of the most significant concerns its regulation in the converged environment, which is considered below. The most obvious problem is that the internet provides a complex global communications network that cannot be fully subject to regulation applied within the boundaries of one state. The application of criminal and civil law to the internet is also challenging.

The internet is already a highly significant medium in terms of the provision of both information and entertainment. Its current and future significance as a medium cannot be over-stated – it is probably overtaking broadcasting as the culturally supreme medium. Its role in providing information has been recognised for some time; its role in relation to entertainment has perhaps been less emphasised. Many websites seek to provide both information and entertainment by the provision of video clips, photographs, narrative. The association between the use of the internet and the other media considered here is very strong; for example, a number of websites, official and unofficial, are dedicated to a range of films and broadcasts and show trailers, advertisements and clips.

---

349 See *R v Butler* [1992] 1 SCR 452. See also Harel, A, 'Bigotry, Pornography and the First Amendment' 65 (1992) S Cal L Rev 1887, 1897.

350 See generally: Barendt, E, *Freedom of Speech*, 2nd edn, 2005, Chapter 13; Akdeniz, Y, Walker, C and Wall, D (eds), *The Internet, Law and Society*, 2000; Graham, G, *The Internet: A Philosophical Inquiry*, 1999, Routledge.

351 For detailed treatment, see Akdeniz, Y, Walker, C and Wall, D (eds), *The Internet, Law and Society*, 2000.

352 See Barendt (2005), *op cit*, fn 1, at p 451.

But the internet is also a strongly *participatory* medium, especially social media like Twitter and Facebook;[353] it not only enables ideas to be expressed by individuals, it also affords – more significantly – efficacy to such expression in terms of audience access.[354] Social media has taken on a new and important role as a platform for the mass expression and exchange of ideas, globally. Individuals in general are largely excluded from mainstream discourse in the media. Journalists may claim to speak for them, and also their views find a very limited opportunity for expression in 'letters' pages or audience-participation broadcasts, but such expression hardly overcomes the dominance of the media by professionals, meaning that it is unrepresentative, especially of the views of women and minority groups, since journalism in general, and the higher positions in the media hierarchy, still tend to be a white male domain. In this sense the internet can be compared to public protest since protest also provides a means of affording efficacy to the speech of individuals, and particularly of minority or excluded groups.[355] The German Supreme Court, in the *Brokdorf* case, viewed participation in protest as a form of 'active engagement in the life of the community'.[356] But the internet provides opportunities for the mass exchange of ideas that far transcend the role of protest since it allows for such engagement with the global community, providing a means of exchanging views across national boundaries that has never existed before with such efficacy. Further, such ideas include, but are not confined to, the political arena. As Barendt notes:

> The Net certainly affords much more equal opportunities for communication than the traditional press and broadcasting media, where the entry costs are high and which are in practice for the most part available only to professional journalists and to the political and social elite.[357]

It may be said therefore that it engages with the broadly based speech justifications, engaging values of autonomy[358] and self-development.[359]

There might appear then to be a strong case for viewing regulation of the internet with suspicion in free speech terms. The US Supreme Court has found that it should not be equated with broadcasting in relation to regulation, but, impliedly, with the print media.[360] The argument that the choice that can be exercised over encountering

---

353 According to a major research study published in April 2005 (*UK Children Go Online*, Sonia Livingstone and Magdalena Bober, April 2005: www.children-go-online.net), 75% of 9–19-year-olds surveyed had accessed the internet from a computer at home. The *Guardian* reported in October 2005 that one third of UK teenagers had their own website or live journal.

354 See: Chapter 9, pp 562–64; Barnum, DG, 'The Constitutional Status of Public Protest Activity in Britain and the US' [1977] PL 310; Barendt, *op cit*, at pp 9, 14–15; Williams, D, *Keeping the Peace: the Police and Public Order* 1967, Hutchinson, pp 10 and 130–31; see also Sherr, *Freedom of Protest, Public Order and the Law* 1989, Blackwell, at pp 10–12.

355 69 Bverfge 315, 343–47 (1985).

356 See Barendt, E, *Freedom of Speech*, 2nd edn, 2005, Chapter 13, p 452.

357 See generally, Dworkin, R, 'Do We Have a Right to Pornography?' Chapter 17, in *A Matter of Principle*, 1985; Scanlon, T, 'A Theory of Freedom of Expression' (1972) 1 Phil & Pub Aff. 216.

358 See generally, Emerson, C, 'Towards a General Theory of the First Amendment' (1963) 72 Yale LJ 877, at pp 879–80; Redish, M, *Freedom of Expression*, 1984, Lexis, pp 20–30 and Greenwalt, K, (1989) 89 Columbia Law Review 119, at pp 143–45.

359 *Reno v ACLU* 521 US 844. For further discussion of this point, see Barendt (2005), Chapter 13, p 455.

360 For discussion, see above, pp 283–84.

online expression differentiates it from broadcasting is reasonably persuasive, although as argued above, it is becoming increasingly possible to exercise greater choice over broadcast expression as it becomes more interactive. In other words, it is becoming less of an intruder into the home and more of a deliberately invited visitor. Thus there is an argument for relaxing the regulation of broadcasting – which Ofcom appears to accept – but not for extending that model of regulation to the internet.

But the strength of the internet – its ready accessibility and susceptibility to choice – can also be viewed as its weakness. Its use by groups excluded from the mainstream media is not necessarily benign. For example, a range of racial hatred offences can be committed by broadcasters, film-makers or playwrights under the Public Order Act 1986 ss 20, 21, 22 and 23. As discussed above, Part 3 of the 1986 Act was amended to include religious hatred under the Racial and Religious Hatred Act 2005. The Public Order Act offences have not been specifically amended to apply to the internet, although s 21 probably covers it, but in any event the general difficulty of prosecuting ISPs, discussed below, would apply. Hate speech can be available from websites that would not appear in UK newspapers and could not appear in broadcasting due to Ofcom's regulation, and it can also be much more rapidly disseminated throughout the world. The ready dissemination of hate speech (and possibly of extreme depictions of sexual violence) arguably cannot be supported by the free speech argument from self-fulfilment.[361] Thus, as Barendt puts it:

> it is surely wise at least to retain those controls on Internet speech which are justifiable in the case of speech disseminated by other means. The mere facts that the Internet is easy and cheap for most people to use, and that they enjoy equal access as speakers and receivers on it, does not constitute an argument for a bonfire of controls.[362]

The discussion below of law and regulation of the internet is not therefore premised on the desirability of a complete relaxation of control over the internet.

This concern as to the 'weakness' of the internet particularly exorcises the authorities in relation to the availability of pornography and the protection of children. This is the case at EU level and in relation to the UK government, as discussed below. As a UK government consultation paper put it in 2005:

> [The Internet is a] spectacular communications development . . . transforming our lives, offering unparalleled opportunities to communicate, to discover and to learn. Alongside these benefits, the Internet also brings challenges for, amongst other things, the regulation of potentially illegal pornographic material which is readily accessible . . . In pre-Internet days, individuals who wished to view this kind of material would need to seek it out, bring it into their home or have it delivered in physical form as magazines, videos, photographs etc, risking discovery and embarrassment at every stage. Now they are able to access it from their computers at home . . . .[363]

361　See Barendt, *Freedom of Speech*, 2nd edn, 2005, Chapter 13, p 454.
362　*Consultation Paper on The Possession of Extreme Pornographic Material*: Home Office 30.8.05 – URL: news.bbc.co.uk/1 shared/bsp/hi/pdfs/30 08 05 porn doc.pdf.
363　Published 12 December 2000: www.communicationswhitepaper.gov.uk.

Concern about the use of the internet is not confined to the availability of extreme or child pornography. It expresses itself in the UK partly through prompting developments in the criminal law, but also in supporting other initiatives aimed at regulation. Below, issues relating to UK law and regulation of the internet are considered, followed by consideration of the current efforts at regulation and the application of the current and proposed criminal law, taking account of free speech arguments.

Regulation of the internet

Internet advertising is regulated in the UK by the Advertising Standards Authority (ASA), but otherwise the internet is not at present regulated in accordance with any of the models considered above. In the white paper, *A New Future for Communications*,[364] the government did not propose a means of drawing the internet within the Ofcom regime in relation to the regulation of programme services on the internet, or otherwise. Visual images available on a service provided by the internet prima facie fall within the definition, in the 2003 Act, of a 'licensable programme service', but such services also appear to fall within the exception provided for 'two-way' services, depending on the interpretation given to that exception. It is clearly intended to cover internet services. However, even on the very doubtful assumption that it could do, Ofcom, like the ITC,[365] has not sought so far to apply its powers to the internet. There would be severe practical difficulties in doing so, although it could in relation to broadcast material placed on websites by licensed broadcast services already under its purview. The result is that material is shown on various websites that clearly could not be shown in a broadcast.[366]

The internet provides a complex global communications network that cannot be fully subject to regulation applied within the boundaries of one state. The government has recognized the problems of seeking to applying regulation on the Ofcom model to the internet.[367] It has been contended that: 'By creating a seamless global-economic zone, borderless and unregulatable, the internet calls into question the very idea of a nation-state.'[368] But in considering controls over the internet, as over the other media considered here, it is necessary to distinguish between the application of the ordinary law and the use of a general regulatory regime monitored and policed by a regulatory body. In relation to the use of the law, a range of views have been expressed. It has been argued that the internet is not inherently unregulatable, even at the national level, on the ground that 'the Internet creates new contexts for old problems rather than new problems *per se*'.[369] Robin Duval, President of the BBFC from 1999 to 2004, has also argued that the internet can be regulated, pointing out that corporations have successfully brought actions against ISPs on commercial grounds.[370] This is also the stance of the EU Commission,

364 See the ITC website: http://www.itc.co.uk.
365 For example, Channel 4 has shown material on its website that has been excluded from films broadcast on television. See e.g., *Guardian* Unlimited Special Report 27 April 2004.
366 See *Regulating Communications: The Way Ahead* June 1999, www.dti.gov.uk/convergence-statement. htm at para 3.20.
367 Barlow, JP, 'Thinking locally, acting globally' (1996) Cyber-Rights Electronic List 15 January.
368 Akdeniz, Y, Walker, C and Wall, D (eds), *The Internet, Law and Society*, 2000, Chapter 1, p 17.
369 See RSA lecture 21 February 2001, available from the BBFC website, www.bbfc.co.uk.
370 *Consultation Paper on The Possession of Extreme Pornographic Material*, Home Office 30.8.05 – URL: news.bbc.co.uk/1 shared/bsp/hi/pdfs/30 08 05 porn doc.pdf.

which is discussed further below. But as the UK government pointed out in a consultation paper,[371] the general application of the criminal law in one jurisdiction to ISPs based abroad faces almost insuperable problems, as discussed below. The solutions being canvassed at present include reaching international agreements, particularly on the availability of pornography, and adapting or developing offences aimed at consumers and only indirectly at ISPs.

The availability of explicit and pornographic material on the internet has prompted significant changes in EU audio-visual policy. The Council Recommendation concerning the protection of minors and human dignity[372] was the first legal instrument at EU level that was concerned with the content of material on the internet. The European Parliament and the Council had already taken measures in 1999 with a view to protecting minors from harmful material on the internet.[373] But in 2002 the Commission found that the development of the internet was continuing to create difficulties in relation to the policy of protecting children.[374] It noted that the volume of material on the internet is immense in comparison to broadcasting and also that in traditional broadcasting (analogue or digital) it is not difficult to identify the individual broadcaster, while it may be impossible to identify the source of content on the internet. At the same time access to harmful and illegal content is very easy and may even be unintentional. As a result the Commission proceeded in 2004 to propose an additional Recommendation[375] which calls on the member states, the industry and other interested parties to:

> take steps to enhance the protection of minors and human dignity in the . . . Internet sector . . . Illegal, harmful and undesirable content and conduct on the Internet continues to be a concern for law-makers, industry and parents. There will be new challenges both in quantitative (more 'illegal' content) and qualitative terms (new platforms, new products). . . . [states should take] into account the ever-increasing processing power and storage capacity of computers . . . .[376]

371 24 September 1998 98/560/EC, OJ L 270, 7 October 1998, p 48.
372 In order to promote a safer internet, the European Parliament and the Council adopted on 25 January 1999 a multi-annual Community Action plan on promoting safer use of the internet by combating illegal and harmful content on global networks Decision No 276/1999/EC, OJ L33, 6/2/1999 p 1 (the 'Safer Internet Action Plan'). On 16 June 2003, the European Parliament and the Council adopted a two-year extension to the Safer Internet Action Plan Decision No 1151/2003/EC amending Decision No 276/1999/EC, OJ L 162, 1 July 2003, p 1.
373 In accordance with section III of the Recommendation, para 4. The implementation of the Recommendation was evaluated for the first time in 2000, and the first report was published in 2001: Evaluation Report to the Council and the European Parliament on the application of Council Recommendation of 24 September 1998 on protection of minors and human dignity COM(2001) 106 final, 27 February 2001. Parliament adopted a resolution on the report on 11 April 2002: C5–0191/2001–2001/2087(COS), in which it called on the Commission to draw up a further report preferably before 31 December 2002. This was produced in 2003: Second Evaluation Report From The Commission to the Council and the European Parliament on the application of Council Recommendation of 24 September 1998 concerning the protection of minors and human dignity, Brussels, 12 December 2003, COM(2003) 776 final.
374 *Proposal for a recommendation of the European Parliament and Council on the protection of minors and human dignity and the right to reply in relation to the competitiveness of the European audiovisual and information services industry*, COM(2004) 341 final 2004/0117 (COD) 30.4.04, press release 04/598.
375 Para 2 of the proposal for a recommendation.
376 Fn 373 above, Introduction.

The original and the proposed Recommendations favour the development of co-regulatory and self-regulatory mechanisms for the internet rather than regulation based on the imposition of an external regulatory regime via legislation. Such approaches, especially the co-regulatory one, are viewed by the Commission as more likely to be 'flexible, adaptable and effective . . . with regard to the protection of minors'.[377] At present the approach in the UK is largely self- rather than co-regulatory. At the same time it may be said that self-regulation is giving way to an extent to co-regulation at present since a loose cooperative framework covering public authorities, the industry and the other interested parties, including consumers, is becoming apparent, as indicated below.

So in accordance with the EU stance, which is reflected in current government policy as indicated below, Ofcom is likely to continue to take the approach that the ITC took – that it will support and contribute to the voluntary regulation of the internet in relation to television programme material and advertisements on websites.[378] It will be argued below, however, that current policy may not result in the creation of the level of protection for minors envisaged in the proposed 2004 Recommendation. A more overt and formal movement towards co-regulation may be necessary.

The remit of the Advertising Standards Authority covers standards of taste and decency in internet advertising. But the ASA does not seek to apply the British Code of Advertising, Sales Promotion and Direct Marketing (the CAP Code) to all internet advertising. It only applies it to online advertisements in 'paid for' space, such as banner and pop-up advertisements;[379] advertisements in commercial e-mails and sales promotions wherever they appear online (including in organisation's websites or in e-mails). It does not apply the CAP Code, which includes requirements of offence-avoidance and 'decency' in advertising,[380] to organisations' claims on their own websites. This is mainly because it would be almost impossible to apply sanctions effectively for breach of the Code in such advertising. When the ASA and CAP apply sanctions against companies that do not cooperate with their requests, they usually rely on third parties, such as the owners of newspapers, magazines and poster sites, to enforce decisions by refusing to accept advertising by the company in question. As the ASA acknowledges on its

---

377 See further: Ballard, T, 'Main Developments in Broadcasting Law' Yearbook of Copyright and Media Law, 2001–2, 329 at pp 334–35; Ballard, T, 'Survey of the Main Developments in the Field of Broadcasting Law in 1999' Yearbook of Copyright and Media Law, 2000, p 367 at pp 373–74.

378 In relation to these forms of internet advertising, the ASA states: 'There are a number of different online advertising formats (or Interactive Marketing Units (IMUs) as they are sometimes called) that are available to marketers. Banner advertisements are probably the best known, but other forms of IMUs include interstitials, superstitials, buttons, pop-ups, skyscapers, floating ads, advertorials and text links. A banner is an advertisement found on a website page. Banners appear on a rotating basis in windows, usually at the top, bottom or side of web pages, and are used by marketers to make consumers aware of their products and services and to drive consumers directly to a particular website.'

379 The Code states: 'Decency (i.e. avoiding serious or widespread offence) 5.1 Marketing communications should contain nothing that is likely to cause serious or widespread offence. Particular care should be taken to avoid causing offence on the grounds of race, religion, sex, sexual orientation or disability. Compliance with the Code will be judged on the context, medium, audience, product and prevailing standards of decency. 5.2 Marketing communications may be distasteful without necessarily conflicting with 5.1 above. Marketers are urged to consider public sensitivities before using potentially offensive material. 5.3 The fact that a particular product is offensive to some people is not sufficient grounds for objecting to a marketing communication for it.'

380 See asa.org.uk.

website: 'the direct relationship between the internet user and the organisation bypasses any middleman and makes the medium almost impossible to regulate effectively'.[381] The ASA also views the relationships between consumers who visit an organisation's own website as direct rather than involuntary: 'the information is therefore "pulled to" rather than "pushed at" them unlike traditional forms of advertising'. In relation to the forms of online advertising that it does seek to regulate, it appears to have a very high compliance rate.[382] It reacts to consumer complaints, if upheld, by contacting the organisations in question and requesting changes to internet adverts.[383] The advertisers appear to perceive commercial advantage in complying with the CAP Code – on the 'tit-for-tat' principle. If one advertiser defaults by refusing to comply, others are also likely to do so, thus damaging the level playing field for marketers within each sector. Also the ASA could seek to apply sanctions against that company's advertising in other media sectors where middle-men can be utilised.

Thus the ASA has informal, commercial sanctions that can be brought to bear in relation to online advertising. They are aimed more at misleading adverts rather than at offensive ones. A general UK internet regulator would not have such sanctions at its command. Nor could it have the licensing power that Ofcom possesses or the classification power of the BBFC since ISPs may well be based outside the jurisdiction. The internet is clearly not as susceptible to control on the basis of offence-avoidance as the other visual media are. In relation to explicit and pornographic speech in films and photographs on websites, the internet has the potential in a sense to undermine the regulatory regimes applied to the other media, precisely because no regulatory body stands between it and the criminal law, creating a regulated 'no-go' area beyond the requirements of the law. In other words, there is no one regulator monitoring explicit internet material via a code with sanctions attached – a code that would, on the Ofcom model, impose standards for offence-avoidance going beyond those demanded by the relevant criminal law. This is not an argument for seeking to impose regulation on that model on the internet, even assuming that that could be done. The argument is that the availability of legal, explicit material on the internet that at present could not be broadcast, places Ofcom's regulation under pressure.

Since there is no regulatory regime on the broadcasting model, material posted on the internet is more likely to come directly into conflict with the criminal law in relation to explicit expression. The internet is subject to the criminal law just as the other media considered here are, although the law has required adaptation in order to bring websites within its ambit. Procedurally and substantively speaking, there are problems

---

381 See *Compliance Report: Internet banner and pop-up adverts Survey* (2002), available from the ASA website: asa.org.uk.

382 The ASA upheld its first complaint against a banner advertisement in May 2000. The advertisement, by an internet service provider, appeared on a financial web page and a complaint was upheld on the ground that the advertiser did not make it sufficiently clear that the banner was an advertisement, not editorial content. Since that time, complaints against a further six banner advertisements have been upheld by the ASA.

383 *Reno v ACLU* 521 US 844. For further information on the struggle between the American Civil liberties Union (ACLU) and official attempts to curb expression on the internet, see the ACLU site: www.aclu. org/issues/cyber/hmcl.html, 2000. The CDA made it a crime, punishable by up to two years in jail and/ or a $250,000 fine, for anyone to engage in speech that is 'indecent' or 'patently offensive' on computer networks, if the speech can be viewed by a minor. The ACLU argued that the censorship provisions are unconstitutional because they would criminalize expression that is protected by the First Amendment and because the terms 'indecency' and 'patently offensive' are unconstitutionally overbroad and imprecise. See Vick, D [1998] 61 MLR 414 on the Supreme Court decision.

in securing convictions in respect of web-based material that do not arise in relation to broadcasts or films. The use of the criminal law to strike directly at the consumer of pornography rather than at the supplier immediately engages speech-based autonomy arguments balanced against weaker countervailing justifications, as discussed below.

Applying criminal law to web-based material

The US has sought to suppress and restrict sexually explicit expression on the internet; initially by means of the Communications Decency Act 1996; but its main provisions were struck down as unconstitutional on the basis of over-breadth.[384] In so doing, the Supreme Court found, following a number of precedents relating to other media, that if restraints aimed at protecting children also affect adults disproportionately, they may not be used as the means of denying children access to sexually explicit material. In other words, traditional free speech principles were applied to the internet. So a more narrowly targeted provision in terms of cyber-censorship was needed, if it was to survive challenges. The 1996 Act was followed by the more narrowly drafted Child Online Protection Act 1998.

In contrast, no statute with special application has so far been introduced in the UK. Instead, amendments have been made to existing statutes creating criminal liability in relation to explicit expression in order to apply them to web-based material. The situation is similar in Australia where the Broadcasting Services Amendment (Online Services) Act 1999 (Cth) drew the internet within the generally applicable prior restrictions on sexually explicit expression.[385] As discussed above, explicit web-based material can be considered within the Obscene Publications Act 1959, as amended (OPA). Section 168 of the Criminal Justice and Public Order Act 1994 added the transmission of electronically stored data to the Obscene Publication Act's definition of 'publication'. Creating a link from a UK-based web-page to another in another jurisdiction on which obscene material is posted arguably amounts to 'publication'.[386] In *Graham Waddon*,[387] the defendant was convicted of the offence under s 2(1) of the 1959 Act on the basis that he had maintained a website in the USA onto which he had uploaded obscene material from the UK. Thus the fact that the material was placed on a US-based website did not prevent the defendant from being charged and convicted of the s 2(1) offence in England.

But in general there are, in practice, particular problems in applying the Obscene Publications Act (and its equivalent in Scotland – the Civil Government (Scotland) Act 1982) to web-based material. For example, the definition of obscenity is a relative one, dependent on the susceptibilities of those who are likely to encounter the material.[388]

---

384 For discussion and criticism of the Act, see Chen, P 6(1) UNSWLJ.

385 See Akdeniz, Y, 'To link or not to link?' (1997) 11(2) *International Review of Law, Computers and Technology* 281.

386 See pp 470–72 above.

387 (1999) Southwark Crown Court, 30 June; appeal dismissed 6 April 2000.

388 [2002] EWCA Crim 747, CA. This case involved a French national based in the UK who was publishing from abroad (in the US). The appellant was convicted of publishing an obscene article and appealed. The obscene article in question was a webpage on the internet. It depicted people covered in faeces, coprophilia or coprophagia, and men involved in fellatio. That webpage was in the form of a trailer, a preview, available free of charge to any one with access to the internet. Any one wanting more of the type of material which it displayed could click on to a link marked 'subscription to our best filthy sites' and could gain access to a further webpage by providing credit card details. The preview webpage was accessed by an officer with the Obscene Publications Unit. To reach it a viewer would have to type in the name of the site, or conduct a search for material of the kind displayed.

Web-based erotic and pornographic material, including material from '18'- or 'R18'-rated films, is available on a range of websites to any user who possesses a computer of the correct specification, although a credit card would often have to be used to gain access to it. Children can therefore gain access to such material and images, and the question of the obscenity of the material might therefore have to be determined by reference to that likely audience, depending on the circumstances, including the nature of the website and the likelihood that children would be able to access it. It would be harder to establish the extent of the likelihood that children might access the information than it is to make the same calculation in relation to print material, although probably it would be as hard as it is in relation to videos. But videos are of course regulated by the BBFC and it is an offence in itself to publish an unclassified video, without reference to its obscenity or indecency. Further, the BBFC has already taken the decision to continue to censor video films beyond the demands of the criminal law, thereby obviating the possibility of a prosecution under the 1959 Act, a decision that is, in effect, as discussed above, a compromise between defending adult autonomy and risking the promulgation of pornography to children. Since the internet is not subject to the policing of an equivalent regulator, this problem is more significant in that context.

Although the thrust of UK policy in relation to web-based pornography is against individual consumers under the OPA, where the manager of the ISP happens to be in this jurisdiction successful prosecution can occur. At least one successful prosecution has been brought against a web-page provider – R v Perrin.[389] In that judgment a number of findings were made that were intended to adapt obscenity law so as to catch web-based pornography, addressing some of the issues discussed above. The defence argued that the only relevant publication of the web page was to the police officer who had downloaded it, and therefore it was wrong to test obscenity by reference to others who might have gained access to the preview page, and it was very unlikely that it would be visited by accident. However, the Court of Appeal accepted that there was publication whenever anyone accessed the preview page. No evidence that children would be likely to access it or had accessed it was put forward, but the Court appeared to assume that this was a possibility and that therefore the obscenity of the material could be judged against that likely audience. The lack of interest in the evidence in relation to children could be viewed as creating an appearance of departure from the basic principle of relative obscenity. The Court also rejected the suggestion that a prosecution should only be brought against a publisher where the prosecutor could show that the major steps in relation to publication were taken within the jurisdiction of the court. The possibility that the main steps towards publication might have occurred in another jurisdiction with less restrictive laws (the US) was not accepted as relevant. In relation to Art 10 the Court found: 'In the result we are satisfied that the statutory provision relied upon does fall within the scope of Art 10:2. For a legitimate purpose the offence was prescribed

---

389   This was pointed out on behalf of the defence in R v Perrin [2002] EWCA Crim 747, CA, referring to 'the world wide accessibility of the Internet' and the opinion of the United States Court of Appeal was relied on to the effect that (Third Circuit) in ACLU v Reno (No 3) [2000] 217 F 3d 162 at 168–69 any court or jury asked to consider whether there has been publication by a defendant of a webpage which is obscene should be instructed to consider first where the major steps in relation to publication took place, and only to convict if satisfied that those steps took place within the jurisdiction of the court. As discussed, this argument was not accepted by the Court of Appeal.

by law. Parliament was entitled to conclude that the prescription was necessary in a democratic society.' In other words, the Court refused to look beyond the balance that Parliament had struck in amending the OPA in 1994 order to include the internet. This was a highly restrictive interpretation of Art 10 since the Court refused to accept that it itself had a responsibility, under s 6 HRA, to examine the application of the law, taking the requirements of proportionality into account, in the instant case.

In general the gravest problem facing the UK authorities is the practical one of seeking to bring prosecutions against ISPs operating abroad. Clearly, jurisdictions differ greatly as to the speech that they criminalise. This potentially places both the national authorities and the internet service providers in a difficult, almost impossible, position. If national laws *could* be enforced against ISPs regardless of jurisdiction, they would be forced to limit the provision of material on websites very severely since they would have to obey the most draconian and restrictive of the speech laws available.[390]

As Barendt points out:

> Website operators and other senders may have no idea who picks up their messages and which jurisdiction they live in, so the law imposes a great burden of them if they can be prosecuted whenever, say, a sexually explicit communication is accessed by a child, or extremist speech is accessed by anyone living in a country with strict hate speech laws.[391]

On the other hand, the national authorities are placed in an impossible position since they may well be unable to enforce sanctions against ISPs who are in another jurisdiction that is unlikely to aid in the enforcement of stricter national laws than it itself recognises. Such countries would be likely to have little interest in prosecuting. Publishers might take the main steps towards internet publication in countries with the most relaxed laws. According to the UK government, very little potentially illegal pornographic material found on the internet originates from within the UK.[392] It appears probable that the lack of UK-hosted material is the result of the deterrent effect of the OPA and the Civil Government (Scotland) Act 1982.

Thus the UK is a more restrictive jurisdiction that the government views as in an especially difficult position in terms of holding the line against internet material hosted on websites outside the jurisdiction. The UK is addressing these problems, as discussed below, partly by enforcing laws against explicit expression against the ultimate consumer rather than against the ISP, and partly through voluntary regulation of the internet. In relation to extreme adult pornography, the government stated in its *Consultation Paper on The Possession of Extreme Pornographic Material*:[393] 'the global nature of the internet means that it is very difficult to prosecute those responsible for publication who are mostly operating from abroad' (the introduction of offences for 'extreme pornographic' material are discussed above). In its consultation paper the government noted that it is already illegal to publish such material under the Obscene Publications

---

390 See Barendt, *Freedom of Speech*, 2nd edn, 2005, Chapter 13, p 452.
391 It notes in its 2005 Consultation paper (fn 537 below) that the Internet Watch Foundation (IWF) received no reports of UK-hosted material in 2003 or 2004.
392 Home Office 30 August 2005 – URL: news.bbc.co.uk/1 shared/bsp/hi/pdfs/30 08 05 porn doc.pdf.
393 [2000] 2 All ER 418.

Act 1959 and, in Scotland, under the Civic Government (Scotland) Act 1982. However, it pointed out that the global nature of the internet means that it is very difficult to prosecute those responsible for publication who tend to operate from abroad. Yet as the paper also states: 'We believe the material which is under consideration would be abhorrent to most people and has no place in our society. Our intention in proposing a possession offence is to try to break the demand/supply cycle.' The similar child pornography offence under the Protection of Children Act (PCA) 1978, s 1 requires possession for gain. However, as far as the internet is concerned, possession has been criminalised since downloading child pornography from the internet is covered by the PCA; it has been found to constitute the 'making' of a photograph or pseudo-photograph.[394]

The experience in the US indicates that forms of self-regulation of the internet provide a more sensitive, nuanced and, arguably, more effective form of restraint than creating broad criminal sanctions relating to explicit material on websites. However, the restraints on the internet described above indicate that the situation in the UK is a confused and anomalous one. The criminal law has been applied in an arguably over-inclusive fashion. An imprecise and archaic law – the Obscene Publications Act – has been afforded a very broad interpretation in *R v Perrin*[395] that applies it to a relatively new medium. The same could be said of the interpretation of the PCA in *R v Bowden*.[396] The OPA creates restrictions in the UK that are not duplicated in a number of other jurisdictions; if the new possession offence is introduced, that position will be exacerbated. At the same time public authorities, such as libraries and schools, are drifting into a situation similar to that appertaining in the US, whereby rating and filtering systems are used to block access to a number of websites, without full inquiry into the over-inclusiveness of such systems or the value judgments underlying them. The decision so far of the UK government not to follow the dubious US example in seeking to introduce general legislation to protect children in this context is a readily defensible one, but the lack of government intervention or – it appears – of recognition of the potential problems could lead to an overly restrictive stance. The analogy of book-burning has been used quite frequently[397] to describe the scenario that might arise in the UK, whereby cyber-censorship creates the same effect, but in a hidden fashion, in relation to controversial and explicit expression in cyberspace.

8 Social media

The idea that Art 10 protects expression that shocks, offends or disturbs has proven to be enigmatic, for whilst the principle is mentioned frequently by the European Court of Human Rights remarkably few decisions have upheld it with anything like the fervour with which it is expressed in *Handyside*. Consequently, identifying the significance and effect

---

394 [2002] EWCA Crim 747, CA.
395 [2000] 2 All ER 418.
396 See the ACLU Report www.aclu.org/issues/cyber/burning.html, 1997.
397 See, e.g., Wildhaber, L, 'The Right to Offend, Shock or Disturb? Aspects of Freedom of Expression Under the European Convention on Human Rights' (2001) *Irish Jurist* 17; Khan, A, 'A 'Right Not to be Offended' under Art 10(2) ECHR? Concerns in the Construction of the 'Rights of Others' [2012] EHRLR 191.

of the principle has become a matter of some debate.[398] Indeed, the dissenting judges in the Strasbourg case of *IA v Turkey* (a case concerning blasphemy) expressed frustration at the flimsy protection afforded by the principle: 'We consider that these words should not become an incantatory or ritual phrase but should be taken seriously and should inspire the solutions reached by our Court'.[399] Similar comments can be made about the domestic jurisprudence. For example, in *Redmond-Bate v DPP*, Sedley LJ stated:

> Free speech includes not only the inoffensive but the irritating, the contentious, the eccentric, the heretical, the unwelcome and the provocative provided it does not tend to provoke violence. Freedom only to speak inoffensively is not worth having.[400]

Yet in the later case of *Connolly v DPP*, the prosecution of a woman for sending images of aborted foetuses to her local pharmacy in the hope they would stop selling the 'morning after' pill was found to be a justifiable interference with her right to freedom of political expression. In doing so, the court stopped far short of the standard adopted in *Redmond-Bate* (that only the provocation of violence justifies interference). Amongst other things, the court thought the offensiveness of the expression was not outweighed by its contribution to public interest debate: 'even if the three pharmacies were persuaded to stop selling the pill, it is difficult to see what contribution this would make to any public debate about abortion generally and how that would increase the likelihood that abortion would be prohibited'.[401]

Admittedly, the protection to be afforded to offensive expression is contentious. As Barendt asks, why should the law single out expression for special treatment when other forms of offensive behaviour, like public love-making, are readily regulated by the state?[402] Before considering the law in this area it is worth considering the potential justifications to the question since they should inform discussion on whether the law does, or does not, satisfy free speech principle. Of course, there is no undisputed answer to this question. It is a knotty problem for which a variety of solutions might be offered, some more persuasive than others.

In justifying special protection for offensive expression, it might seem helpful to distinguish ostensibly 'important' expression, like political expression, from ostensibly 'unimportant' or 'worthless' expression, like gossiping, name-calling or other forms of everyday conversational speech. Indeed, a former president of the European Court of Human Rights has suggested that this distinction animates the intended meaning of the 'right' to offend; that it is no more than a 'guarantee' of speaker 'participation in the democratic process through public debate of questions of general concern. The strength of the protection offered will depend on the extent to which the expression can be linked to the direct functioning of democratic society.'[403]

398   *IA v Turkey* (2007) 45 EHRR 30, OI-1.
399   (1999) 7 BHRC 375, [20].
400   [2007] EWHC 237 (Admin), [32].
401   Barendt, E, *Freedom of Speech*, 1987, p 1.
402   Wildhaber, op cit.
403   'Azhar Ahmed, a tasteless Facebook update, and more evidence of Britain's terrifying new censorship', *The Independent*, 9 October 2012.

Yet although this might seem like an intuitively appealing solution, some pause for thought is required to consider its full implications. In particular, we should ask: who is qualified to determine what counts as 'important' expression? Can a judge – and, more importantly, should a judge – make decisions about the apparent societal importance of particular instances of expression? Consider these two examples:

> People gassin about the deaths of soldiers! What about the innocent familys who have been brutally killed. The women who have been raped. The children who have been sliced up..! Your enemy's were the Taliban not innocent harmless familys. All soldiers should DIE & go to HELL! THE LOWLIFE F*****N SCUM! gotta problem go cry at your soliders grave & wish him hell because that where he is going' [sic];[404]

> How we can possibly be giving a billion pounds a month when we're in this sort of debt to bongo bongo land is completely beyond me.[405]

These examples are not hypotheticals: the author of the first, 19-year-old Azhar Ahmed, was given a community service order of 240 hours over two years and a £300 fine;[406] the author of the second, UKIP MEP Godfrey Bloom, was publicly ridiculed for his remarks but refused to apologise: he claimed it was 'absurd' anyone would find them racist.[407] Both express a political view, of sorts, and both are clearly offensive: should it matter, for the purposes of determining legal sanctions, that one was made by an ordinary member of the public and the other by a politician? Is one or both worthless to democratic decision-making because of the level of offensiveness? More to the point, is a judge capable of saying how valuable a contribution these instances of political expression make to democratic participation? In some instances the answer may be clear cut but not in others. Giving judges this kind of powerful is problematic.

John Stuart Mill perceived this sort of problem clearly when he argued that state interferences based on the apparent inherent worth of the expression are 'assumptions of infallibility' since others may find the expression worthwhile regardless of its inherent defects. This argument animates the defences of free speech found not only in Mill's argument from truth but also other classic arguments relating to autonomy and self-fulfilment. These three arguments are united in the claim that determinations about protection should be based on the consequences of expression and not its quality.

The inexorable rise of Web 2.0, in which internet usage has transformed from static engagement with website pages to a more immersive experience, has generated new problems for the law to deal with. It is no exaggeration to say that mass engagement with social media has become so ubiquitous, and in such a short space of time, that it has taken the law by surprise. The House of Lords Select Committee on Communications heard evidence that the police have been 'inundated' by complaints about offensive

404 http://www.bbc.co.uk/news/uk-england-leeds-19883828.
405 Ukip MEP Godfrey Bloom criticises aid to 'bongo bongo land', *The Guardian*, 7 August 2013.
406 *The Guardian*, 7 August 2013.
407 House of Lords Select Committee on Communications, 1st Report of Session, 'Social Media and Criminal Offences', 29 July 2014, p 21, [76].

online expression.[408] Since there are no legislative measures directed specifically towards offensive expression encountered through platforms like Twitter, Facebook, Pinterest, LinkedIn, etc, the courts and prosecution services have been left to apply laws created with no contemplation of social media when victims of offensive expression have complained to the police. This imaginative approach has had disastrous consequences, with laws being applied with too much vigour and too little rigour, as most graphically demonstrated by the high profile case of *Chambers v DPP*.[409] Here, an individual called Paul Chambers, frustrated by the possibility that Doncaster airport's closure (due to adverse weather conditions) might affect his impending travel plans, was prosecuted for tweeting that he would blow up an airport if it did not 'get [its] shit together'. Although intended to be light-hearted (and certainly not to be taken seriously), the Crown Court reasoned differently and agreed with the Crown Prosecution Service's conclusion that the message was menacing and could have alarmed those who came upon it.

Thankfully, when the Crown Court referred the case to the High Court on points of law, common sense prevailed, Mr Chambers was exonerated and the High Court took the opportunity to remind itself that:

> satirical, or iconoclastic, or rude comment, the expression of unpopular or unfashionable opinion about serious or trivial matters, banter or humour, even if distasteful to some or painful to those subjected to it should and no doubt will continue at their customary level, quite undiminished [by the law].[410]

Yet this does not mean that the law protects offensive expression disseminated through social media on all occasions. It must be recalled that social media posts are of a different character to everyday speech: mass audiences can be reached, of a magnitude previously only available to traditional forms of media, and expression is easily accessible and preserved for long periods of time due to search engines. These qualities combined ratchet up the impact of social media expression over normal speech: the damage can be much more immediate and long-lasting. In short, online speech is *not* comparable to the spoken word and possibly not the printed word either given its greater 'searchability'. One commentator recently reported that there were 2,347 investigations into social media postings in 2010 and 2,490 in 2011, equivalent to about 50 per week across the UK.[411] Moreover, although subjective reactions (and sometimes over-reactions, as in the case of Paul Chambers) will occur, the distinctly unpleasant phenomena of social media 'trolling' illustrates that there are often compelling reasons why offensive messages seem deserving of penalty. Defending such odious behaviour on freedom of expression grounds is rarely appealing.

In its report on social media offences,[412] the House of Lords Select Committee on Communications, applying its own definitions, grouped problematic social media expression into four distinct categories: 'cyberbullying', 'trolling', 'virtual mobbing'

---

408 At pp 405–07.
409 *Chambers v DPP* [2012] EWHC 2157 (Admin).
410 *Ibid*, [28].
411 Scaife, L, 'The DPP and social media: a new approach coming out of the Woods?' (2013) 18(1) *Communications Law* 5, 6.
412 http://www.publications.parliament.uk/pa/ld201415/ldselect/ldcomuni/37/37.pdf.

and 'revenge porn'. The first three are largely variants on a theme in which, for categories (1) and (2), an individual attacks a particular person (cyberbullying) or a particular discussion (trolling) or a group engages in the same behaviour (virtual mobbing). A range of motivations might account for this behaviour, including hatred, malice, anger or even boredom. The final category is more distinctive and intended to capture circumstances where (typically) following a relationship break-up a person posts online explicit images of their former lover (consent having been obtained for such images at the time of capture). Although these distinctions are helpful they do not delineate all the possible connotations of what counts as 'offensive' expression. Arguably, such delineation is not possible because what is being described is not the expression or even the underlying behaviour but the *reaction* to it, which, as noted, may range from the reasonable to the idiosyncratic. For the purposes of discussion, the term 'offensive expression' refers to that which upsets audiences without amounting to a threat of violence, harassment (see discussion in Chapter 9), pornographic expression or racial/religious intolerance (these last two categories are discussed below). With these observations in mind, the purpose of this section is to map out, to the extent it is possible to do so, the limits of protection for online offensive expression by examining, in turn, the legislative provisions that have been applied to such expression.

Section 127(1)(a) Communications Act 2003 states that it is an offence to send 'by means of a public electronic communications network a message or other matter that is grossly offensive or of an indecent, obscene or menacing character'. As the High Court reminds us in *Chambers v DPP*, this provision has a lineage traceable to s 10(2)(a) of the Post Office (Amendment Act) 1935, which protected telephone operators from any sort of indecent, offensive or menacing messages.[413] A remarkably similar provision is to be found at s 1 Malicious Communications Act 1988, which states that any person sending a 'letter, electronic communication or article of any description' conveying a threat, false information or which is indecent or grossly offensive will commit an offence if the perpetrator intends to cause distress or anxiety to the recipient (or audience). Aside from the additional requirement of intention and greater applicability in the latter, clearly there is a considerable degree of overlap between these two complementary offences. Both are currently summary only, which must be prosecuted within six months of the act, and for which the maximum penalty is imprisonment for six months (although the government is currently considering whether to make them triable either way and to increase the sanctions that can be imposed).

Both offences rely upon the court deciding what 'offensive' and 'grossly offensive' means and applying the term in a manner that is consistent with the right to freedom of expression which, as noted, purportedly includes a right to express oneself offensively. In *DPP v Collins*,[414] the House of Lords found that 'the test is whether a message is couched in terms liable to cause gross offence to those to whom it relates', noting that the standard 'grossly offensive' should be judged 'by the application of reasonably enlightened, but not perfectionist, contemporary standards to the particular message sent in its particular context'.[415] Following the decision in *Chambers*, the Director of

---

413 *Chambers v DPP* [2012] EWHC 2157 (Admin), [27].
414 [2006] UKHL 40.
415 *Ibid*, [9].

Public Prosecutions produced some helpful guidance intended to assist the Crown Prosecution Service on this issue.[416] In it, prosecutors are reminded of the great 'potential for a chilling effect on free speech' if either s 1 MCA 1988 or s 127 CA 2003 are utilised too readily and, therefore, are urged to 'exercise considerable caution' before commencing such prosecutions. They are further advised that there is a 'high evidential threshold' to meet: 'in many cases a prosecution is unlikely to be required in the public interest'. As an indicative list, the DPP advises that prosecutions should not be met if a) the suspect has expressed genuine remorse; b) swift and effective action has been taken by the suspect and/or others for example, service providers, to remove the communication in question or otherwise block access to it; c) the communication was not intended for a wide audience, nor was that the obvious consequence of sending the communication; particularly where the intended audience did not include the victim or target of the communication in question; or d) the content of the communication did not obviously go beyond what could conceivably be tolerable or acceptable in an open and diverse society which upholds and respects freedom of expression. In summary, the guidance confirms that only *serious* incidents should be taken to court. Whether this guidance would have prevented Paul Chambers from being prosecuted may be doubted because, of course, the CPS concluded that Chambers' tweet *was* serious.

There remains a problem, though, in criminalising expression that is not coercive (such as advocating violence) but is nevertheless deeply unpleasant. An officious approach to offensive social media speech, particularly that which has an obvious political dimension, is most likely to have a disproportionate impact on the speech of young people and curb their tenacity to engage in robust political discussion. Young people are most likely to use social media and it is a truism of the Twitter and Facebook age that wild, shocking and exaggerated statements are more likely to be heard than staid and reasonable observations. Consider the two examples given above concerning Azhar Ahmed and Godfrey Bloom. Is it right that an ordinary member of the public should be prosecuted in circumstances where a politician is not? Similarly, consider these examples of journalists speaking outrageously. Richard Littlejohn once described Gordon Brown as a 'cowardly, bullying, dysfunctional, undemocratic self-obsessive' with an 'unnerving kiddiefiddler grin'.[417] Katie Hopkins, meanwhile, described migrants as 'cockroaches' and 'a plague of feral humans':

> Show me pictures of coffins, show me bodies floating in water, play violins and show me skinny people looking sad. I still don't care. Because in the next minute you'll show me pictures of aggressive young men at Calais, spreading like norovirus on a cruise ship.[418]

The dehumanisation of migrants is particularly troubling. Whereas Ahmed's statement may be considered an insensitive attempt to convey a political message – and even Bloom's might fall within that category if a generous outlook is applied – Hopkins' expression is far more disturbing in its disregard for the sanctity of human life. Yet

---

416 http://www.cps.gov.uk/news/latest_news/dpp_publishes_final_guidelines_for_prosecutions_involving_social_media_communications/.

417 *Daily Mail*, 7 January 2008.

418 http://www.sunnation.co.uk/hopkins-rescue-boats-use-gunships-to-stop-illegal-migrants/.

Hopkins was not prosecuted for this article. It is hard to justify the prosecution of ordinary people offending others through ill-judged comments when professional journalists are not.

Of course, it is not only political expression that is affected. The problem, as Rowbottom recognises, is that social media is often treated as an alternative for everyday conversation. Yet whilst things said in the company of friends and in familiar surroundings will be quickly forgotten, things said on the internet are near-enough permanent and could be read by anyone. Plainly, tone and context are not always conveyed in electronic messages, particularly when read by strangers. What might be acceptable in a discussion with friends may not be when published to the world at large. Thus Rowbottom argues 'casual and amateur' speech (as opposed to speech by trained journalists, etc) should be held to a lower standard, taking account of the fact that such speech is more akin to everyday conversation.[419] Although his argument is persuasive, it does not entirely address the bystander issues that arise when those who discover the speech are deeply offended by it. For example, in 2012, 19-year-old Matthew Woods was jailed for 12 weeks for offence caused by his publicly available 'jokes' on his Facebook page about two missing children, April Jones and Madeline McCann.[420] That same year, Daniel Thomas, a semi-professional footballer, was arrested for posting a homophobic message on Twitter about Olympians Tom Daley and Peter Waterfield.[421] Later that year, the police arrested Neil Swinburne, who had established a Facebook page celebrating the individual who shot dead two female police officers in Manchester.[422] There is little doubt that such expression is distasteful and troubling; however the state must be careful that it is not seen to prosecute people simply because they hold opinions that others find shocking. Whereas Rowbottom argues that tolerance should be exercised because such speech may have been expressed hastily and with little or no consideration for the consequences, it may also be said that even if such consequences were intended, the state must be careful that it is not regulating (or seen to be regulating) the way that individuals think. Whereas the state is entitled to pursue liberal policies where it has the support of the majority to do so, this does not mean it is entitled to persecute those who do not hold liberal ideals. Of course, it should be remembered that this is the position simply in relation to state intervention. It is apparent that where social media expression causes offence the speaker may find that there are social consequences. Beyond audience members expressing their intense disapproval, there has been a noticeable rise in employers dismissing employees for expression they dislike. Whether employment law offers sufficient protection for such expression is beyond the ambit of this book.[423]

The best justification (indeed, arguably, the only defensible one) for interfering with offensive expression is where the consequences of the expression are so harmful that they demand state intervention. This may be because the expression incites violence in others or is directed toward an individual and causes them to apprehend physical harm

---

419 Rowbottom, J, 'To rant, vent and converse: protecting low level digital speech' (2012) *CLJ* 355.

420 *R v Woods*, unreported, 1 November 2012, Preston Crown Court.

421 See discussion in McGoldrick, D, 'The Limits of Freedom of Expression on Facebook and Social Networking Sites: A UK Perspective' (2013) 13(1) *Human Rights Law Review* 125, 132–33.

422 See McGoldrick, *ibid.*

423 Though see Wragg, P, 'Free Speech Rights at Work: Resolving the Differences between Practice and Liberal Principle' (2015) 44(1) *Industrial Law Journal* 1.

or causes them psychological injury or emotional distress. For occasions like this the police might use s 4A of the Public Order Act 1986. The offence stipulates that harassment, alarm or distress must have been caused to a person, and intentionally so. There is no requirement, however, that the words must be within hearing or sight of a person likely to be caused harassment, alarm or distress. Section 4A can apply to the internet, as existing in a form of public space, although this has not yet been fully established. In *S v DPP* the district judge stated that 'any person who posts material on the Internet puts that material within the public ambit'.[424] However, a prosecution under s 4A will not be deemed consistent with Art 10 under s 6 of the HRA unless the demands of proportionality under Art 10(2) are satisfied (e.g., the prosecution was necessary to protect public order).[425] In *S v DPP*, the defendant was convicted under s 4A after posting a photograph of a laboratory worker on a website with the caption 'C'mon I'd love to eat you! We're the Covance Cannibals.' In *R v Stacey*,[426] the defendant was convicted of a racially aggravated s 4A offence, upheld on appeal, after sending abusive messages on Twitter when Bolton Wanderers midfielder Fabrice Muamba collapsed during an early evening FA Cup tie against Tottenham Hotspur on 17 March. Stacey tweeted: 'LOL. F*** Muamba. He's dead!!!' (the tweet did not use asterisks) when the footballer collapsed on the field. When the tweet attracted criticism he replied with a series of racist and personally abusive posts. He was sentenced to 56 days in prison.[427]

In *R v Sorley and Nimmo*,[428] Isabella Sorley was jailed for 12 weeks and co-defendant John Nimmo for eight weeks for subjecting Caroline Criado-Perez to a period of intense bullying through Twitter. Criado-Perez had incurred their wroth for her part in championing a female figure to appear on a Bank of England note. The judge said: it was 'hard to imagine more extreme threats' and the harm threatened against Criado-Perez 'must have been intended to be very high'. Nimmo also targeted his abuse at Stella Creasy, the Labour MP for Walthamstow, with the message: 'The things I cud do to u [smiley face]' and: 'Dumb blond bitch'. The judge said the effect of the abuse on Criado-Perez had been 'life-changing'. She described 'panic and fear and horror', he said. He added that the abuse had also had a substantial impact on Creasy, who had had a panic button installed in her home. The judge said of the abusive tweets:

> The fact that they were anonymous heightened the fear. The victims had no way of knowing how dangerous the people making the threats were, whether they had just come out of prison, or how to recognise and avoid them if they came across them in public.

Clearly, these messages were of a different type to the messages prosecuted under s 127 CA and s 1 MCA. They were not merely offensive but threatening.

---

424 [2008] EWHC 438 (Admin).
425 *Dehal v CPS* [2005] EWHC 2154 (Admin), although the correctness of that decision is open to question.
426 28.3.12 (unreported) http://blog.cps.gov.uk/2012/03/liamstaceys-conviction-for-tweet-about-fabrice-muamba.html.
427 Note: the evidence did not suggest that the tweets in reply were from persons present at the match in question.
428 (2014) reported – *The Guardian* 24 January 2014.

In conclusion, and as the DPP's guidance makes clear, all instances of offensive expression must be dealt with on their specific facts. Those conveying a credible threat of violence, or other forms of proscribed behaviour (such as breaching a court order), should be treated differently from those that do not. Where the offence generates moral disapproval or outrage, the police should be slow to intervene (and the CPS slower to prosecute). They should take into account the impact of the expression on others and seriously consider whether it would be in the public interest to prosecute. In doing so they should remember the values of tolerance and pluralism.

9 Conclusions

Despite the well-established principle that Art 10 applies equally to expression that 'shocks, offends or disturbs', the protection afforded to offensive expression is highly questionable. The UK position in respect of restraints on freedom of speech in the name of the protection of morality does not appear to breach Art 10. The exuberance with which offensive social media expression has been prosecuted is cause for alarm, particularly to the extent it may have a chilling effect on the willingness of young people to engage in tenacious political debate. The DPP's insistence that merely offensive speech (as opposed to that which is threatening, for example) offers some promise that prosecutions may not arise, but that is not an end to the problem if a culture of intolerance for offensive political expression is now culturally embedded. That said, the UK's decision to abolish blasphemy and similar forms of outdated measures is a welcome development. The shift toward examining harmful effects and, specifically, protecting individuals from hostility (through the Racial and Religious Hatred Act 2006 and Criminal Justice and Immigration Act 2008) offers little threat to freedom of expression. Indeed, there is arguably more that might be done to protect other minority groups from hatred, particularly trans people not covered by the CJI Act 2008.

It is, though, not only the state that regulates offensive expression. The most significant decisions about what it is acceptable for people to see or hear are often taken by media regulators, not by courts. The discussion demonstrated that regulation is subject to rapid change, which to an extent reflects the rapidly changing technological environment in the visual as opposed to the print sector. But it is suggested that regulation has not kept pace with such technological change and, in particular, with the impact of the internet and with developments in Western broadcasting. Developments in broadcasting and in internet access have led to a globalisation of outlook in the current younger generation – an expectation that standards relating to explicit expression in the more progressive Western countries will be broadly in harmony with each other, while strongly differing standards will not be apparent across the different audiovisual sectors. The discussion reveals that such expectations are not being met, while justifications for maintaining anomalous differences between the sectors or for taking a specifically UK-based stance on offence-avoidance have not been forthcoming. At present, it will be suggested, the government is tending to avoid the difficult questions that harmonisation in both respects would create, in particular the question of the anomaly of non-regulation of the internet alongside regulation of broadcasting by Ofcom. The judiciary continues to prefer to defer to the decisions of regulators rather than accepting that it has a duty under the HRA to call them to account in terms of maintaining free expression standards.

The position of the visual media is particularly difficult in relation to such forms of expression. From a liberal standpoint, cuts in film or broadcast material on the basis of avoiding offence may be condemned as an infringement of autonomy, especially where they go beyond what is demanded by the criminal law.[429] There is general opposition to such censorship in other mediums in the absence of clear evidence of the concrete harm caused by the material.[430] However, explicit images conveyed in the print as opposed to the visual media may not only have less impact on people, but the encounter with them may represent more of a genuine choice. Liberals are willing to support restrictions on the outlets and public display of explicit material[431] on the ground that such restrictions do not necessarily spring from contempt for those who wish to view such material, but may simply reflect the genuine and personal aesthetic preferences of those who would rather not be confronted unexpectedly with offensive images.[432] The position of the broadcast media, film, the internet is more problematic since adults can normally protect themselves from offence. Following the liberal argument from autonomy, the provision of information and advice in order to warn persons of the content of particular films or broadcasts is clearly acceptable. Provision of such information, far from infringing personal autonomy, upholds it. But cuts or outright bans of visual material aimed at adult audiences, beyond the requirements of the criminal law, represent a failure to respect the right of adults to choose their own diverse forms of entertainment, within the law.

429 See Schauer, F, Free Speech: A Philosophical Enquiry, 1982, Chapters 5 and 6; Feldman, D, Civil Liberties and Human Rights, 2nd edn, 2002, 13.2; Tucker, DFB, Law, Liberalism and Free Speech, 1985, 11–56; Barendt, E, Freedom of Speech, 2nd edn, 2005, Chapter 1; see also above, pp 301–02.

430 See Feinberg, J, The Moral Limits of the Criminal Law: Offense to Others, 1985. For a brief discussion of the possible link between pornography and the commission of sexual offences, see above, pp 399–400.

431 Such as, e.g., the recommendations of the Williams Committee (Report of the Committee on Obscenity and Film Censorship Cmnd 7772, 1979); see their 'Summary of our proposals'.

432 See Dworkin, R, 'Do we have a right to Pornography?', in A Matter of Principle (1985) pp 355–58, where he broadly endorses the Williams Committee's proposals.

Chapter 8

Official secrecy; access to state information

This chapter has been updated and revised for this edition by Paul Wragg, Associate Professor at the University of Leeds, UK.

I Introduction[1]

This chapter is concerned with restraints upon access to information created directly or indirectly by the law governing the release of sensitive government information, of 'official secrets'. It also considers the corollary – the positive rights to access to information held by public authorities now granted by the Freedom of Information Act 2000 (FoI), which came into force on 1 January 2005. This Act is not, strictly speaking, an aspect of the law of freedom of expression; since it gives positive rights to information, it does not, strictly, affect media free expression: it does not place restraints upon what the media may publish; rather it assists media bodies in their attempts to extract information from public authorities.[2] This is the stance taken at Strasbourg: Art 10 does not, as discussed below, offer rights of access to information. The Act is of concern in free expression terms in that it is very likely that journalists, along with opposition politicians and campaigners, as well as concerned individuals, will make particular use of it, in order to obtain information. This chapter offers a brief treatment, taking account of developments since the Act came into force, because the Act is relevant to the overall position of the media as it seeks to hold government to account. For example, the law on disclosure of journalistic sources is difficult to assess without some knowledge of the means by which information about bodies such as hospitals, the police, and local authorities may be freely obtainable.

In contrast, the law on official secrecy has some direct application in free expression terms: there are indeed particular provisions of the Official Secrets Act that are aimed

---

1 General reading, see: Birkinshaw, P, *Freedom of Information: The Law, the Practice and the Ideal*, 4th edn, 2010; Vincent, D, *The Culture of Secrecy, Britain 1832–1998*, 1998, OUP; Feldman, D, *Civil Liberties and Human Rights in England and Wales*, 2nd edn, 2002, Chapter 14; Bailey, SH, and Taylor N, *Bailey, Harris and Jones: Civil Liberties: Cases and Materials*, 6th edn, 2009, Chapter 12; Baxter, JD, *State Security, Privacy and Information*, 1990, Macmillan; Shetreet, S (ed), *Free Speech and National Security*, 1991, Dordrecht; Gill, P, *Policing Politics: Security, Intelligence and the Liberal Democratic State*, 1994, Frank Cass; Lustgarten, L and Leigh, I, *In From the Cold: National Security and Parliamentary Democracy*, 1994, Clarendon; Whitty, N, Murphy, T and Livingstone, S, *Civil Liberties Law*, 2001, Chapter 7.

2 See for example Austin, R, 'Freedom of information: – a Sheep in Wolf's Clothing?', in Jowell, J and Oliver, D, *The Changing Constitution*, 5th edn, 2004, OUP; similarly, Birkinshaw, P, 'Regulating information' in 8th edn, 2015, OUP.

3 See below at pp 502–05.

specifically at journalists,[3] while the restrictions the Act lays upon, for example, members of the security services, directly affects their ability to tell their stories through the media, as in the notorious David Shayler affair,[4] considered in detail below.

The overall concern of this chapter is with the degree to which a proper balance has been and is currently being struck between the interest of the individual in acquiring information and the interest of the state and public authorities in withholding it. Clearly, there are genuine public interests, including that of protecting national security, in keeping some information out of the public domain; the question is whether other interests that do not correspond with and may even be opposed to the interests of the public are also at work. Initially, it may be said that in the UK, the area of control over government information is one in which the state's supposed interest in keeping information secret has in general prevailed very readily over the individual interest in question. It has often been said that the UK is more obsessed with keeping government information secret than any other Western democracy.[5] It is clearly advantageous for the party in power to be able to control the flow of information in order to prevent public scrutiny of certain official decisions and in order to be able to release information selectively at convenient moments. The UK government has available a number of methods of keeping official information secret, including the deterrent effect of criminal sanctions under the Official Secrets Act 1989, the Civil Service Conduct Code,[6] around 80 statutory provisions engendering secrecy in various areas and the civil action for breach of confidence. The situation of the civil servant in the UK who believes that disclosure as to a certain state of affairs is necessary in order to serve the public interest may therefore be contrasted with the situation of his or her counterpart in the US, where he or she would receive protection from detrimental action flowing from whistle-blowing[7] under the Civil Service Reform Act 1978. A weak form of a public interest defence might have been adopted under proposals in the then government's white paper on freedom of information, published in July 1993.[8] It was proposed that the disclosure of information would not be penalised if the information was not 'genuinely confidential'. But when the Labour government introduced the Public Interest Disclosure Act 1998, Crown servants involved in security and intelligence activities, or those whose 'whistle-blowing' breaches the 1989 Act, were expressly excluded from its ambit, leaving them unprotected from employment detriment.

The UK has traditionally resisted freedom of information legislation and, until 1989, criminalised the unauthorised disclosure of any official information at all, however trivial, under s 2 of the Official Secrets Act 1911, thereby creating a climate of secrecy in the civil service that greatly hampered the efforts of those who wished to obtain and publish

---

4 For an overall look at the implications of that episode, see Best, K, 'The Control of Official Information: Implications of the Shayler Affair' (2000) 5(6) *Journal of Civil Liberties* 18.

5 E.g., Robertson, G, *Freedom, the Individual and the Law*, 1989, pp 129–31.

6 See Drewry, G and Butcher, T, *The Civil Service Today*, 1991, Blackwell. It should be pointed out that the Civil Service Code, which came into force on 1 January 1996, contains a partial 'whistle-blowing' provision in paras 11–12.

7 For discussion of the situation of UK and US civil servants and developments in the area, see Cripps, Y, 'Disclosure in the public interest: the predicament of the public sector employee' [1983] PL 600; Zellick, 'Whistle-blowing in US law' [1987] PL 311–13; Starke (1989) 63 ALJ 592–94.

8 *Open Government*, 1993, HMSO.

9 Vincent, *The Culture of Secrecy, Britain 1832–1998*, 1998, p 321.

information about the workings of government. The Freedom of Information Act 2000 (FoI) signalled a break with the traditional culture of secrecy: 'the principle that communication was the privilege of the state rather than of the citizen was at last . . . reversed'.[9]

2 Official secrets

The Official Secrets Act 1989[10]

Whilst the Act allows disclosure of some official information, although an official who makes such disclosure may, of course, face an action for breach of confidence as well as disciplinary proceedings,[11] but it makes no provision for allowing the release of any official documents into the public domain. Thus, claims made, for example, by Douglas Hurd (the then Home Secretary) that it is 'a great liberalising measure' clearly rest on other aspects of the Act. Aspects which are usually viewed as liberalising features include the categorisation of information covered which makes relevant the *substance* of the information, the introduction of tests for harm, the *mens rea* requirement of ss 5 and 6, the defences available and decriminalisation of the receiver of information. In all these respects, the Act differs from its much stricter predecessor (of 1911), but the nature of the changes led commentators to question whether they would bring about any real liberalisation.[12] Other aspects of the Act have also attracted criticism: it applies to persons other than Crown servants, including journalists; it contains no defences of public interest or of prior disclosure and no general requirement to prove *mens rea*. Thus, what is omitted from its provisions, including the failure to provide any right of access to information falling outside the protected categories, is arguably as significant as what is included. The Human Rights Act has not yet tempered the effects of the Official Secrets Act 1989. There is obviously a tension between the two statutes, since the one binds public authorities – which includes government departments – under s 6 to observe the Convention rights, including the right to freedom of expression, while the other creates criminal liability for disclosure of information whether or not the disclosure is in the public interest. Further, the 1989 Act must be interpreted under s 3 of the HRA so as to render it compatible with the Convention rights. The tension between the two was explored in the preliminary hearing in the *Shayler*[13] case (discussed below) in which it was argued unsuccessfully that s 1 of the 1989 Act is incompatible with Art 10. Below, the possible effects of Art 10 on the Official Secrets Act are indicated.

Criminal liability for disclosing information

The general prohibition on disclosing information under the Official Secrets Act 1911 was replaced by the more specific prohibitions under the Official Secrets Act 1989.

---

10 For comment on the 1989 Act see Palmer, S, 'The Government proposals for reforming s 2 of the Official Secrets Act 1911' [1988] PL 523; Hanbury, W, 'Illiberal reform of s 2' (1989) 133 Sol Jo 587; Palmer, S, 'Tightening secrecy law' [1990] PL 243; Griffith, J, 'The Official Secrets Act 1989' (1989) 16 JLS 273; Feldman, D, *Civil Liberties and Human Rights*, 1st edn, 1993, Chapter 14.3.
11 see Ministry of Defence v Griffin [2008] EWHC 1542 (QB).
12 E.g., Ewing and Gearty, *Freedom under Thatcher* (1989), at 200.
13 Preparatory hearing: (2001) *The Times*, 10 October, 98(40) LSG 40; CA.
14 Section 1(9).

Sections 1–4 of the 1989 Act (excepting the provisions of s 1(1)), which also determine the categorisation of the information, all concern unauthorised disclosures by any present or former Crown servant or government contractor of information which has been acquired in the course of his or her employment. If a civil servant happens to acquire by other means information falling within one of the categories that he or she then disclosed, the provisions of s 5 apply. Section 7 (below) governs the meaning of 'authorisation', while ss 5 and 6 apply when *any* person – not only a Crown servant – discloses information falling within the protected categories.

Security and intelligence information is covered by s 1. The category covers 'the work of or in support of, the security and intelligence services' and includes 'references to information held or transmitted by those services or by persons in support of . . . those services'.[14] It is, therefore, a wide category and is not confined only to work done by members of the security and intelligence services. Section 1(1) is intended to prevent members or former members of the security services (and any person notified that he is subject to the provisions of the sub-section) disclosing anything at all relating or appearing to relate to[15] the operation of those services. All such members thus come under a lifelong duty to keep silent even though their information might reveal a serious abuse of power in the security services or some operational weakness. There is no need to show that any harm will or may flow from the disclosure, and so all information, however trivial, is covered. On its face, this blanket ban raises one of the most serious prima facie incompatibilities with Art 10. It is therefore worth examining briefly the government arguments for such a ban. Essentially, four main reasons are put forward.[16]

First, it is argued that disclosures by agents or former agents carry particular credibility; however this is presumably only relevant if the disclosure is in fact harmful. If the disclosure itself is anodyne, then its extra authority makes no difference. This therefore does not provide an argument for a blanket ban.

Second, it is said that such disclosures reduce confidence of the public in the security services' ability and loyalty. This is (a) speculative and (b) not very convincing. If non-harmful revelations were made, it is unlikely that they would affect the publics' view. Moreover, it begs the question why the public should have an exaggeratedly positive view of the ability of the security services. Why is it especially important that the public at large have a positive view of the abilities of the security services, any more than, say, the armed forces or the cabinet?

Third, it is said that disclosures by agents or former agents ought to be criminal because of the special duty of secrecy that the members of the security service accept. This is a circular argument: that special duty of secrecy is imposed by the law – of the Official Secrets Act, and the law of confidence. This cannot be an argument for determining what the law should in fact be.

Fourth, it is said that because governments do not traditionally comment on assertions about the security services, a false report made by a former agent could be as damaging as a true one, because it would go un-denied. Against this, it may be said that

---

15 Under s 1(2), misinformation falls within the information covered by s 1(1) as it includes 'making any statement which purports to be a disclosure of such information or which is intended to be taken as being such a disclosure'.

16 They are summarised in the White Paper, *op cit*, fn 27 at para 40.

17 See Best, *op cit* fn 4, at 20.

governments could simply make an exception to this general rule when a former agent is involved. Moreover, this argument again posits only a possible harm, that might come about in particular cases, not an invariable one. In fact, the government did deny aspects of the claims made by former agent David Shayler: in particular his assertion that the SIS had planned for the assassination of Colonel Gadaffi was vigorously rebutted.[17]

A further point to be noted about s 1(1) is that there is no defence that the material released was already in the public domain. This runs clearly counter to the finding both in *Attorney General v Guardian Newspapers Ltd (No 2)*[18] and in *Observer and Guardian v UK*[19] that the maintenance of a ban on the publication of information when it has entered the public domain is contrary to both common law and Art 10.[20]

Similar in nature to the blanket prohibition in s 1(1), and therefore considered here, is s 4(3), which covers information obtained by the use of intercept and security service warrants.[21] There is no harm test under this category. Thus, in so far as it covers the work of the security services, it creates a wide exception to the general need to show harm under s 1(3) when a Crown servant who is not a member of the security services makes a disclosure about the work of those services.

The government's defence of this blanket ban is as follows: '*no* information obtained by means of interception can be disclosed without assisting terrorism or crime, damaging national security or seriously breaching the privacy of private citizens'.[22] This is simply implausible. As for the privacy point, the *nature* of the information gained through phone tapping (e.g., details of a large drug transaction) may barely engage private life, although the mode of interception does, and there may be very strong public interest arguments on the other side sufficient to make the interference with private life proportionate. The fact that privacy is in question does not begin to justify a blanket ban on disclosure: to have such a ban does not allow for a balancing between Arts 10 and 8 but simply creates an abrogation of one at the expense of the other. It is not clear that the first part of the statement can be taken seriously: whether any damage would be caused by such revelations would plainly depend upon what was disclosed, and what information revealed thereby about the techniques of the security services.

The white paper also addressed the argument that there should be a general public interest to which all the offences in the Act would be subject. It first of all deliberately mis-characterises this argument – that there should be a defence of making revelations that were in the public interest, judged objectively – as being an argument that a defendant's good *motivation* should be a defence. The white paper correctly states that the

18 [1990] 1 AC 109.
19 (1991) 14 EHRR 153; for comment see Leigh, I, '*Spycatcher* in Strasbourg' [1992] PL 200–8.
20 As was argued in the *Shayler* case: see fn 37 below.
21 This applies to (a) any information obtained by reason of the interception of any communication in obedience to a warrant issued under s 2 of the Regulation of Investigatory Powers Act 2000, any information relating to the obtaining of information by reason of any such interception and any document or other article which is or has been used or held for use in or has been obtained by reason of any such interception; and (b) any information obtained by reason of action authorised by a warrant issued under s 3 of the Security Service Act 1989, any information relating to the obtaining of information by reason of any such action and any document or other article which is or has been used or held for use in or has been obtained by reason of any such action.
22 The White Paper, *op cit*, fn 27 at para 53.
23 *Ibid*, at paras 59–60.

general rule is that motive is not relevant and that there are good grounds for sticking to this general rule.[23] This is true, but simply irrelevant: the argument about the public interest test does not revolve around motivation. The white paper adds to this:

> the proposals in this White Paper are designed to concentrate the protection of the criminal law on information which demonstrably requires its protection in the public interest. It cannot be acceptable that a person can lawfully disclose information which he knows may, for example, lead to loss of life simply because he conceives that he has a general reason of a public character for doing so.[24]

This is extraordinarily poor reasoning. The first sentence is simply question-begging: by including a blanket ban on all disclosures by members and former members of the security services, it clearly covers information that is *not* required to be protected in the public interest. The example given is simply a gross exaggeration. No one is arguing for a defence for those who release information risking life; second, the wording 'because *he* conceives' implies that what is being argued for is a subjective test, rather than, of course, the actual objective public interest that is being proposed.

A more general, final concern about the white paper is that it nowhere mentions Art 10 ECHR. As Lord Hope commented in *Shayler*, this 'leaves one with the uneasy feeling that . . . the problems which it raises were overlooked'.[25] The point is returned to below.

Section 1(3), which criminalises disclosure of information relating to the security services by a former or present *Crown servant* as opposed to a member of the security services, does include a test for harm under s 1(4) which provides that:

> a disclosure is damaging if:
>
> (a) it causes damage to the work of or any part of, the security and intelligence services; or
> (b) it is of information or a document or other article which is such that its unauthorised disclosure would be likely to cause such damage or which falls within a class or description of information, documents or articles the unauthorised disclosure of which would be likely to have that effect.

Taken at its lowest level, it is clear that this test may be very readily satisfied: it is not necessary to show that disclosure of the actual document in question has caused harm or would be likely to cause harm, merely that it belongs to a class of documents, disclosure of which would be likely to have that effect. Disclosure of a document containing insignificant information and incapable itself of causing the harm described under s 1(4)(a) can, therefore, be criminalised, suggesting that the importation of a harm test for Crown servants as opposed to members of the security services may not inevitably in practice create a very significant distinction between them. However, at the next level,

24 *Ibid*, at para 60.
25 [2003] 1 AC 247, at para 41.
26 [1990] 1 AC 812; [1989] 2 All ER 852, HL; for criticism of the ruling, see Walker [1990] PL 354.

harm must be likely to flow from disclosure of a specific document where, owing to its unique nature, it cannot be said to be one of a class of documents.

In such an instance, the ruling of the House of Lords in *Lord Advocate v Scotsman Publications Ltd*[26] suggests that the test for harm may be quite restrictively interpreted: it will be necessary to show quite a strong likelihood that harm will arise and the nature of the harm must be specified. The ruling was given in the context of civil proceedings for breach of confidence, but the House of Lords decided the case on the basis of the principles under the 1989 Act even though it was not then in force. The ruling concerned publication by a journalist of material relating to the work of the intelligence services. Thus, the test for harm had to be interpreted, according to s 5, in accordance with the test under s 1(3) as though the disclosure had been by a Crown servant. The Crown conceded that the information in question was innocuous, but argued that harm would be done because the publication would undermine confidence in the security services. The House of Lords, noting that there had already been a degree of prior publication, rejected this argument as unable alone to satisfy the test for harm. The case therefore gives some indication as to the interpretation the harm tests may receive. This ruling affords some protection for journalistic expression concerning the intelligence services which, under the HRA, would be in accordance with the high value Strasbourg has placed on expression critical of the workings of the state and state agents.[27]

Even taken at its highest level, the harm test is potentially very wide because of its open-textured wording. It states, in effect, that a disclosure of information in this category is damaging if it causes damage to the area of government operation covered by the category. No clue is given as to what is meant by 'damage'; in many cases it would, therefore, be impossible for a Crown servant to determine beforehand whether or not a particular disclosure would be criminal. The only safe approach would be non-disclosure of almost all relevant information; the position of Crown servants under the 1989 Act in relation to information in this category is therefore only with some difficulty to be distinguished from that under the 1911 Act. However, the fact that there is a test for harm at all under s 1(3), however weak, affirms a distinction of perhaps symbolic importance between two groups of Crown servants because the first step in determining whether a disclosure may be criminalised is taken by reference to the *status* of the person making the disclosure rather than by the nature of the information, suggesting that s 1(1) is aimed at underpinning a culture of secrecy in the security services rather than at ensuring that no damaging disclosure is likely to be made.

Section 2 covers information relating to defence.[28] What is meant by 'defence' is set out in s 2(4):

(a) the size, shape, organisation, logistics, order of battle, deployment, operations, state of readiness and training of the armed forces of the Crown;

(b) the weapons, stores or other equipment of those forces and the invention, development, production and operation of such equipment and research relating to it;

---

27 See generally *Stankovic v Chief Constable of the Ministry of Defence* [2007] EWHC 2608 (QB).
28 See *Thorgeirson v Iceland* (1992) 14 EHRR 843; *The Observer* and the *Guardian v UK* (1991) 14 EHRR 153.

(c) defence policy and strategy and military planning and intelligence;

(d) plans and measures for the maintenance of essential supplies and services that are or would be needed in time of war.

It must be shown that the disclosure in question is or would be likely to be damaging as defined under s 2(2):

(a) it damages the capability of, or of any part of, the armed forces of the Crown to carry out their tasks or leads to loss of life or injury to members of those forces or serious damage to the equipment or installations of those forces; or

(b) otherwise than as mentioned in para (a) above, it endangers the interests of the United Kingdom abroad, seriously obstructs the promotion or protection by the United Kingdom of those interests or endangers the safety of British citizens abroad; or

(c) it is of information or of a document or article which is such that its unauthorised disclosure would be likely to have any of those effects.

The first part of this test under (a), which is fairly specific and deals with quite serious harm, may be contrasted with (b), which is much wider. The opening words of (b) may mean that although the *subject* of the harm may fall within (a), the level of harm can be considered within (b) since it does not fall within terms denoting harm used in (a). This could occur where, for example, there had been *damage* as opposed to 'serious damage' to installations abroad. Clearly, this interpretation would allow the harm test to be satisfied in a wider range of situations. On this interpretation, as far as disclosures concerning UK armed forces operating *abroad* are concerned, it would seem that (b) renders (a) largely redundant, so that (a) would tend to play a role only where the disclosure concerned operations within the UK. It may be noted that parts of this test are mere verbiage; it would be hard to draw a significant distinction between 'endangering' and 'seriously obstructing' the interests of the UK abroad. In fact, the overlapping of the harm tests within the categories and across the categories is a feature of this statute; the reasons why this may be so are considered below.

Information relating to international relations falls within s 3(1)(a). This category covers disclosure of 'any information, document or other article relating to international relations'. Clarification of this provision is undertaken by s 3(5), which creates a test to be used in order to determine whether information falls within it. First, it must concern the relations between states, between international organisations or between an international organisation and a state; second, it is said that this includes matter which is capable of affecting the relation between the UK and another state or between the UK and an international organisation. The harm test arises under s 3(2) and is identical to that arising under s 2(2)(b) and (c).

Section 3(1)(b) refers to confidential information emanating from other states or international organisations. This category covers 'any confidential information, document or other article which was obtained from a state other than the United Kingdom or an international organisation'. Clearly, the substance of this information might differ from that covered under s 3(1)(a), although some documents might fall within both categories. Under s 3(6), the information will be confidential if it is expressed to be so treated due to the terms under which it was obtained or if the circumstances in which it was obtained impute an obligation of confidence. The harm test under this category contained in s 3(3) is somewhat curious: the mere fact that the information is confidential or its nature or contents 'may' be sufficient to establish the likelihood that its disclosure would cause harm within the terms of s 3(2)(b) (which uses the terms of s 2(2)(b)). In other words, once the information is identified as falling within this category, a fiction is created that harm may automatically flow from its disclosure. This implies that there are circumstances (such as a particularly strong quality of confidentiality?) in which the only ingredient which the prosecution *must* prove is that the information falls within the category.

Given that s 3(3) uses the word 'may', thereby introducing uncertainty into the section, there is greater leeway for imposing a Convention-friendly interpretation on it. If the word 'may' is interpreted strictly, the circumstances in which it would be unnecessary to show harm would be greatly curtailed. It could then be argued that since harm or its likelihood must be shown, the harm test itself must be interpreted compatibly with Art 10. It would have to be shown that the interference in question answered to a pressing social need.[29] Depending on the circumstances, it could be argued that if, ultimately, the 'interests of the UK abroad' would be benefited by the disclosure, or on balance little affected, no pressing social need to interfere with the expression in question could be shown.

Section 4 is headed 'crime and special investigation powers'. Section 4(2) covers any information the disclosure of which:

> (a) . . . results in the commission of an offence; or facilitates an escape from legal custody or the doing of any other act prejudicial to the safekeeping of persons in legal custody; or impedes the prevention or detection of offences or the apprehension or prosecution of suspected offenders; or
> (b) which is such that its unauthorised disclosure would be likely to have any of those effects.

'Legal custody' includes detention in pursuance of any enactment or any instrument made under an enactment (s 4(6)). In contrast to s 3(3), in which the test for harm may be satisfied once the information is identified as falling within the category, in s 4(2), once the test for harm has been satisfied, the information will necessarily be so identified. As with s 2, parts of this test could have been omitted, such as 'facilitates an escape', which would have been covered by the succeeding general words.

Section 5 is headed, 'information resulting from unauthorised disclosures or entrusted in confidence'. This is not a new category. Information will fall within s 5 if it falls within one or more of the previous categories and it has been disclosed to the defendant by a Crown servant or falls within s 1 of the Official Secrets Act 1911. Section 5 is primarily aimed at journalists who receive information leaked to them by Crown servants, although it could of course cover anybody in that position. It is also aimed at the person to whom a document is entrusted by a Crown servant 'on terms requiring it to be held in confidence or in circumstances in which the Crown servant or government contractor could reasonably expect that it would be so held'.[30] The difference between entrusting

---

29 *Sunday Times v UK* (1979) 2 EHRR 737.
30 Section 5(1)(ii)).

and disclosing is significant in that, in the former instance, the document – but not the information it contains – will have been entrusted to the care of the person in question.[31]

These provisions are presumably aimed mainly at the journalist or other non-Crown servant who receives the information from another journalist who received it from the civil servant in question. However, this does not apply where the information has been entrusted to the defendant, but has never been disclosed to him or her; in that case, it must come directly from the civil servant, not from another person who had it entrusted to him or her.[32] The disclosure of the information or document by the person into whose possession it has come must not already be an offence under any of the six categories.

Since s 5 is aimed at journalists and potentially represents an interference with their role of informing the public, it requires a very strict interpretation under s 3 of the HRA, in accordance with Art 10, bearing in mind the emphasis placed by Strasbourg on the importance of that role.[33] In contrast to disclosure of information by a Crown servant under ss 1–4, s 5 does import a requirement of *mens rea* under s 5(2) which, as far as information falling within ss 1, 2 and 3 is concerned, consists of three elements. The defendant must disclose the information knowing or having reasonable cause to believe that it falls within one or more of the categories, that it has come into his possession as mentioned in sub-s (1) above and that it will be damaging (s 5(3)(b)). As far as informa-tion falling within s 4 and probably s 3(1)(b) is concerned, only the first two of these elements will be relevant. Under s 5(6), only the first of these elements need be proved if the information came into the defendant's possession as a result of a contravention of s 1 of the Official Secrets Act 1911. Thus, as far as disclosure of such information is concerned, the *mens rea* requirement will be fulfilled even though the defendant believed that the disclosure would not be damaging and intended that it should not be. Indeed, since the *mens rea* includes an objective element, it may be satisfied under all the categories where the defendant did not in fact possess the belief in question, but had reasonable cause to possess it.

The requirement of *mens rea*, although not as strict as may at first appear, represents the only means of differentiating between journalists and Crown servants. The test for damage will be determined as it would be if the information was disclosed by a Crown servant in contravention of ss 1(3), 2(1) or 3(1) above. A court could afford recognition to the significance of the journalistic role, as required by Art 10, by placing a strong emphasis on the *mens rea* requirement. Where a journalist appeared to be acting in the public interest in making the disclosure, it would be possible for a court to interpret the *mens rea* requirement as disproved on the basis that it would be impossible to show that the defendant knew or should have known that the disclosure was damaging to the interest in question if on one view (even if mistaken) it could be seen as beneficial to it, and that was the view that the journalist took.

Section 4 is not mentioned, because the information will not be capable of fall-ing within s 4(1) unless the harm test is satisfied. As already mentioned, there is no harm test under s 4(3). Thus, an interesting anomaly arises: if, for example, information

---

31 If the Crown servant has disclosed or entrusted it to another who discloses it to the defendant, this will suffice (s 5(1)(a)(i) and (iii)).
32 Section 5(1)(b)(ii)).
33 See, e.g., *Goodwin v UK* (1996) 22 EHRR 123.

relating to the work of MI5 is disclosed to a journalist by a security service agent, a distinction is drawn between disclosure by the agent and by the journalist: in general, it will not be assumed in the case of the latter that the disclosure will cause harm, but if the information relates to (say) telephone tapping, no such distinction is drawn. If the journalist is then charged with an offence falling within s 5 due to the disclosure of information under s 4(3), both he or she and the agent will be in an equally disadvantageous position as far as the harm test is concerned. The apparent recognition of journalistic duty effected by importing the harm test under s 1(3) into the situation where a security service member discloses information to a journalist, may therefore be circumvented where such information also falls within s 4(3).

Another apparent improvement that might tend to affect journalists more than others is the decriminalisation of the receiver of information. If he or she refrains from publishing it, no liability will be incurred. Of course, this improvement might be said to be more theoretical than real in that it was perhaps unlikely that the mere receiver would be prosecuted under the 1911 Act even though that possibility did exist. The fact that journalists were included at all in the net of criminal liability under s 5 has been greatly criticised on the basis that some recognition should be given to the important role of the press in informing the public about government policy and actions.[34] In arguing for a restrictive interpretation of s 5 under s 3 of the HRA, a comparison could be drawn with the constitutional role of the press recognised in the US by the *Pentagon Papers* case:[35] the Supreme Court determined that no restraining order on the press could be made so that the press would remain free to censure the government.

Section 6 covers the unauthorised publication abroad of information that falls into one of the other substantive categories apart from crime and special investigation powers. It covers the disclosure to a UK citizen of information that has been received in confidence from the UK by another state or international organisation. Typically, the section might cover a leak of such information to a foreign journalist who then passed it on to a UK journalist. However, liability will not be incurred if the state or organisation (or a member of the organisation) authorises the disclosure of the information to the public (s 6(3)). Again, since this section is aimed at journalists, a requirement of *mens rea* is imported: it must be shown under s 6(2) that the defendant made 'a damaging disclosure of [the information] knowing or having reasonable cause to believe that it is such as is mentioned in sub-s (1) above and that its disclosure would be damaging'. However, it is important to note that under s 6(4), the test for harm under this section is to be determined 'as it would be in relation to a disclosure of the information, document or article in question by a Crown servant in contravention of s 1(3), 2(1) and 3(1) above'. Thus, although it appears that two tests must be satisfied in order to fulfil the *mens rea* requirement, the tests may in fact be conflated as far as s 3(1)(b) is concerned because proof that the defendant knew that the information fell within the relevant category may satisfy the requirement that he or she knew that the disclosure would be damaging. The requirement that *mens rea* be established is not, therefore, as favourable to the defendant as it appears to be because – as noted in respect of s 5 – it may be satisfied even where the defendant believes that no damage will result. Once again,

---

34 See, e.g., Ewing and Gearty, *op cit*, fn 12, at 196–201.
35 *New York Times Co v US* (1971) 403 US 713.

aside from this particular instance, this applies in all the categories due to the objective element in the *mens rea* arising from the words 'reasonable cause to believe'.

The requirement that the information, document or article is communicated in confidence will be satisfied as under s 3 if it is communicated in 'circumstances in which the person communicating it could reasonably expect that it would be so held' (s 6(5)). In other words, it need not be expressly designated 'confidential'.

A disclosure will not lead to liability under the Act if it is authorised and so it is necessary to determine whether or not authorisation has taken place. The meaning of 'authorised disclosures' is determined by s 7. A disclosure will be authorised if it is made in accordance with the official duty of the Crown servant or a person in whose case a notification for the purposes of s 1(1) is in force. As far as a government contractor is concerned, a disclosure will be authorised if made 'in accordance with an official authorisation' or 'for the purposes of the functions by virtue of which he is a government contractor and without contravening an official restriction'. A disclosure made by any other person will be authorised if it is made to a Crown servant for the purposes of his functions as such; or in accordance with an official authorisation.

Defences; disproving mens rea – a reversed burden

The defence available to Crown servants arises in each of the different categories and reads:

> it is a defence to prove that at the time of the alleged offence he did not know and had no reasonable cause to believe that the information, document or article in question was such as is mentioned (in the relevant subsection) or that its disclosure would be damaging within the meaning of that subsection.

Belief in authorisation will also provide a defence under s 7. Thus, the Act appears to provide three defences for Crown servants: first, that the defendant did not know and had no reasonable cause to believe that the information fell into the category in question; secondly, that he or she did not know and had no reasonable cause to believe that the information would cause harm, and thirdly, that he or she believed that he had lawful authorisation to make the disclosure *and* had no reasonable cause to believe otherwise. However, very significantly, in *R v Keogh*[36] it was found that the imposition of reverse legal burdens is incompatible with the demands of Art 6(2), so they should be read down under s 3 HRA to an evidential burden only. So it is a defence for a defendant to prove lack of knowledge in the different categories if he adduces evidence sufficient to raise an issue with respect to it; the court or jury should then assume that the defence is satisfied, unless the prosecution proved beyond reasonable doubt that it is not.

The first two defences may be conflated in certain categories, largely because the second defence is intimately tied up with the harm tests and therefore, like them, operates on a number of levels. Where the harm test operates at its lowest level, only the first defence is available. Thus, a person falling under ss 1(1) or 4(3) has no opportunity at all of arguing that, for example, the triviality of the information or the fact that it was

---

36 [2007] All ER (D) 105 (Mar).

already in the public domain had given rise to an expectation that its disclosure would cause no harm at all. At the next level, under s 3(1)(b), because the test for harm may be satisfied merely by showing that the information falls within the sub-section, the second defence could be viewed as more apparent than real and could therefore be categorised along with the defence under s 1 as non-existent. However, following the argument regarding the interpretation of the harm test under this section above, this defence could be afforded some substance, under s 3 of the HRA. Under s 1(3), the second defence is extremely circumscribed. It would not necessarily avail the defendant to prove that for various reasons, it was believed on reasonable grounds before the disclosure took place that it would not cause harm. So long as the prosecution could prove a likelihood that harm would be caused from disclosure of documents falling into the same class, the harm test under the section would be satisfied and the defendant would be forced to prove that he or she had no reasonable cause to believe that disclosure of documents of that class would cause harm – a more difficult task than showing this in relation to the particular disclosure in question.

Generally, under all the other categories the harm test allows for argument under both the first and second defences, assuming that they are expressed disjunctively. However, under s 4(4), the second defence alone applies to information falling within the category under s 4(2)(a), while the first alone applies to information likely to have those effects under s 4(2)(b). This is anomalous, as it means that the disclosure of information that had had the effect of preventing an arrest could be met by the defence that it was not expected to have that effect, while information which had not yet had such an effect, but might have in future, would not necessarily be susceptible to such a defence. So long as the disclosure of the document was in fact likely to have the effect mentioned, it would be irrelevant that the defendant, while appreciating that it might in general have such effects, considered that they would not arise in the particular instance. Thus, a broader defence would be available in respect of the more significant disclosure, but not in respect of the less significant. This effect arises because, under s 4(2), the first defence is contained in the second owing to the use of the harm test as the means of identifying the information falling within the section.

Thus, it is clear that the Act is even less generous towards the defendant in terms of the defences it makes available than it appears to be at first glance. Moreover, it is important to note that, although it is a general principle of criminal law that a defendant need have only an honest belief in the existence of facts that give rise to a defence, under the Act a defendant must have an honest and reasonable belief in such facts. However, as indicated, s 3 of the HRA could be used to broaden the defences in certain respects.

The Act contains no explicit public interest defence and it follows from the nature of the harm tests that one cannot be implied into it; on the face of it, any good flowing from disclosure of the information in question cannot be considered, merely any harm that might be caused. Thus, while it may be accepted that the Act at least allows argument as to a defendant's state of knowledge (albeit of very limited scope in certain instances) in making a disclosure to be led before a jury, it does not allow for argument as to the good intentions of the persons concerned, who may believe with reason that no other effective means of exposing iniquity exists. In particular, the information may concern corruption at such a high level that internal methods of addressing the problem would be ineffective. Clearly, good intentions are normally irrelevant in criminal trials: not many would argue that a robber should be able to adduce evidence that he intended to use the proceeds of his robbery to help the poor. However, it is arguable that an exception to this rule should be made in respect of the Official Secrets Act. A statute aimed specifically at those best placed to know of corruption or malpractice in government should, in a democracy, allow such a defence. The fact that it does not argues strongly against the likelihood that it will have a liberalising impact. However, s 3 of the HRA could be used creatively, as indicated, to seek to introduce such a defence – in effect – through the back door.

The Shayler *litigation*

Whether or not such a use of the HRA is possible in respect of categories of information covered by a harm test, it appears that it is not possible in respect of s 1(1) and s 4(1). David Shayler, a former member of MI6, was charged with an offence under s 1(1) and s 4(1) in respect of his allegations that MI6 had been involved in a plot to assassinate Colonel Gadaffi; further allegations exposed, Shayler claimed, serious illegality on the part of MI6, and were necessary to avert threats to life and limb and to personal property.[37] A preliminary hearing was held regarding the effect of the Human Rights Act on s 1(1). It was argued that since s 1(1) and s 4(1) are of an absolute nature, they are incompatible with Art 10 of the Convention, under the Human Rights Act, owing to the requirement that interference with expression should be proportionate to the legitimate aim pursued. In other words it was not possible, using s 3 of the HRA to harmonise these provisions of the 1989 Act with the requirements of the Convention would not be possible, since the two were plainly incompatible. Therefore a declaration of incompatibility should be granted, under s 4 of the Act. This argument was rejected in *Shayler*;[38] Moses J at first instance found that there was no need to rely on s 3 HRA since no incompatibility between Art 10 and s 1(1) arose.[39] He reached the conclusion that s 3 could be ignored in reliance on the finding of the Lord Chief Justice in *Donoghue v Poplar Housing and Regeneration Community Assoc Ltd and the Secretary of State for the Environment*;[40] he said that 'unless legislation would otherwise be in breach of the Convention s 3 can be ignored; so courts should always first ascertain whether, absent s 3, there would be any breach of the Convention'.[41] The conclusion that ss 1(1) and 4(1) were not in breach of Art 10 was reached on the basis that Mr Shayler did have an avenue by which he could seek to make the disclosures in question. There were various persons to whom the disclosure could be made, including those identified in s 12. Further, significantly, under s 7(3) of the 1989 Act a disclosure can be made to others if authorised; those empowered to afford authorisation are identified in s 12. Shayler could have sought authorisation to make his disclosures from those identified under s 21 or from those prescribed as persons who can give authorisations. Such persons or bodies now include the tribunal established

---

37 *R v Shayler* [2003] 1 AC 247.
38 (2001) 28 September, CA.
39 Para 78 of the transcript.
40 [2001] 3 WLR 183.
41 *Ibid*, para 75.

under the Regulation of Investigatory Powers Act 2000 s 65[42] and a minister of the Crown. Such persons could have authorised disclosure to other persons *not* identified in s 12 or prescribed.

Also, Moses J found, a refusal of authorisation would be subject, the Crown accepted in the instant case, to judicial review. The refusal to grant authority would have to comply with Art 10 due to s 6 HRA; if it did not, the court in the judicial review proceedings would be expected to say so.[43] Moses J went on to say:

> It is not correct . . . to say that a restriction [under s 1(12) and 4(1)] is imposed irrespective of the public interest in disclosure. If there is a public interest it is . . . not unreasonable to expect at least one of the very large number of persons identified [by reference to s 12 and to the bodies prescribed] to recognise the public interest and to act upon it.[44]

He went on to call the suggestion that all those so identified would not authorise the disclosure in such circumstances farfetched. But he thought that even if that possibility might arise,

> it is a step too far to say that the proportionality of this legislation must be judged in the light of the possibility that the courts themselves [in judicial review proceedings in respect of a refusal of authorisation] would countenance suppression of a disclosure which they considered necessary to avert injury to life, limb or serious damage to property even before October 2000.

Therefore he found that no absolute ban on disclosure was imposed.

The Court of Appeal agreed that the interference with freedom of expression was in proportion to the legitimate aim pursued – that of protecting national security on the basis that the members of the security services, and those who pass information to them, must be able to be sure that the information will remain secret. The Court of Appeal also agreed that for the reasons given the absence of a 'public interest' defence in the 1989 Act does not breach the Convention. Moses J had stated that had he found otherwise he would have considered the use of s 3 of the HRA, but would have rejected the possibility put forward on behalf of Shayler, of inserting the word 'lawful' into s 1(9) so that s 1(1) would only cover the *lawful* work of the secret services. He also rejected the similar argument in respect of s 4. In so finding he again relied on *Donoghue v Poplar Housing and Regeneration Community Association Ltd and the Secretary of State for the Environment*[45] in which Lord Woolf said that s 3 does not entitle the court to legislate.[46] This decision means that s 3 need not be used in relation to s 1(1) and

---

42 The old tribunals set up under s 7 of the Interception of Communications Act, s 5 of the Security Services Act 1989 and s 9 of the Intelligence Services Act 1994 were prescribed for this purpose under the Official Secrets Act 1989 (Prescription) Order 1990, SI 1990/200, as amended by SI 1993/847. That prescription now applies to the single tribunal.

43 Paras 25 and 26 of the Transcript.

44 *Ibid*, para 54.

45 See fn 41.

46 *Ibid*, paras 75 and 76.

s 4(1) and it is probable that the same arguments would apply if, in respect of disclosure of information falling within other categories, the defence sought to introduce a public interest defence.

The House of Lords' judgment in the case contains some encouraging signs, in terms of the influence of Art 10 ECHR upon the judgment, but is ultimately open to the same criticisms as the earlier judgments. Essentially, the House found that the OSA 1989 did need to be read compatibly with the requirements of proportionality under Art 10, but that the method of seeking permission to reveal information provided in the Act rendered the relevant provisions proportionate. The encouraging point that was stressed by their Lordships, especially Lord Hope, was that, upon any judicial review of a refusal to authorise release of information, a full Art 10 analysis would apply and be used. However, as argued below, this is likely to be a moot point. Looking at the decision more closely, the problem with it appears to lie, not in the assessment of what Strasbourg case law on Art 10 demands, but upon the conclusions drawn from that case law as applied to the OSA. Thus Lord Bingham states:

> The acid test is whether, in all the circumstances, the interference with the individual's Convention right prescribed by national law is greater than is required to meet the legitimate object which the state seeks to achieve.[47]

It was accepted generally that a truly blanket ban could not, by its nature, be proportionate. Lord Bingham conceded that such a ban 'permitting of no exception' would be inconsistent with 'the rigorous and particular scrutiny required to give effect to article 10(2)'.[48] Differences of approach were apparent between Lords Bingham and Hutton on the one hand, who were quite readily convinced of the compatibility of the challenged provisions with Art 10, and the analysis of Lord Hope, which was both more sceptical on this point and gave more detailed consideration to the Strasbourg requirements. Thus, Lord Bingham did not consider the proportionality test in any detail, or give much consideration to the type of expression in issue. Indeed, his lordship appeared to assume that once it was shown that the ban was not technically a blanket one, proportionality was automatically satisfied.

There was no detailed examination as to whether such routes were likely to prove effective – indeed, his lordship's view on this matter appeared positively naïve – a point returned to below. Lord Hutton found that in the absence of any attempt by the applicant to lay his case before the authorities under the relevant provisions of the Act,[49] there was no evidence to show that these procedures would have been ineffective. This essentially turns the proportionality exercise on its head. Under Art 10(2) the state has the burden of showing that the restrictions placed upon the right in question are justifiable; Lord Hutton's approach essentially asks the applicant to prove that the state's alternative means of protecting expression are *in*effective, rather than requiring the state, by adducing 'relevant and sufficient reasons',[50] to show their effectiveness.

---

47   *Ibid*, at para 26.
48   *Ibid*, at p 275.
49   Under s 7(3)(a) or (b).
50   The standard often referred to under Art 10: see *Sunday Times v UK* (1979) 2 EHRR 245.

In contrast, Lord Hope did look at proportionality closely: identifying the second and third parts of the proportionality test from the *Daly* case, he said:

> The problem is that, if they are to be compatible with the Convention right, the nature of the restrictions [placed upon the right] must be sensitive to the facts of each case if they are to satisfy the second and third requirements of proportionality. The restrictions must be rational, fair and not arbitrary, and they must impair the fundamental right no more than is necessary. As I see it, the scheme of the Act is vulnerable to criticism on the ground that it lacks the necessary degree of sensitivity.[51]

But he then examined the fact that the authorisation system would be subject to judicial review, which would provide the necessary safeguard. Lord Hope did address the point that technically it would be impossible for an agent or former agent to bring judicial review, since the disclosure by him to his lawyer for the purposes of preparing the case of the information he wished to disclose would itself breach s 1 OSA. Therefore an implied right to legal advice was read into the scheme – a right, that is, to disclose the substance of the information covered by s 1(1) to a legal adviser, in order to prepare for a judicial review to challenge the refusal of the authoriser to give permission to disclose. As Lord Hope said:

> I think that it follows that he has an implied right to legal assistance of his own choosing, especially if his dispute is with the state. Access to legal advice is one of the fundamental rights enjoyed by every citizen under the common law.[52]

Having granted this point, Lord Hope went on to hold that where permission to reveal information was sought and refused, the appropriate test on judicial review challenging that refusal would be as follows:

> (1) What, with respect to that information, was the justification for the interference with the Convention right? (2) If the justification was that this was in the interests of national security, was there a pressing social need for that information not to be disclosed? And (3) if there was such a need, was the interference with the Convention right which was involved in withholding authorisation for the disclosure of that information no more than was necessary. This structured approach to judicial control of the question whether official authorisation should or should not be given will enable the court to give proper weight to the public interest considerations in favour of disclosure, while taking into account at the same time the informed view of the primary decision maker. By adopting this approach the court will be giving effect to its duty under [s 6(1) HRA] to act in a way that is compatible with the Convention rights . . . .[53]

Essentially therefore the broad choice is between a legislative scheme in which the applicant makes disclosure and the court judges directly whether the disclosure should

---

51 *Ibid*, at paras 69–70. The case referred to is *R (on the application of Daly) v SSHD* [2001] 2 AC 532.
52 *Ibid*, at para 73.
53 *Ibid*, at para 79.

be permitted (whether under the OSA or under the breach of confidence doctrine) and the actual scheme of the Act, which rests on 'judicial review of decisions taken before-hand by administrators'[54] as to whether disclosure should be permitted. The first choice of course would require an Act that, *unlike* the OSA, subjects all the offences to a 'harm' test. Lord Hope came down in favour of the second system (judicial review) on the basis of a number of factors. First, the would-be discloser may not be in a position to appre-ciate all the harm that his disclosures might do; second, gathering evidence of harm to bring a criminal prosecution could do more damage than the original disclosure.[55] This argument was constantly floated but no examples given; moreover, this argument ignores the point that, on judicial review, the government would have to put forward evidence of harm to justify its prior refusal to authorise disclosure. Therefore this argu-ment, although possibly true, does not help us to choose between the two choices of system, since it applies equally to each. Finally, Lord Hope makes the point that a suc-cessful prosecution would not in fact remedy the harm done by the original disclosure.[56]

The basic problem with the reliance placed by all the judges who heard this case upon the internal complaint route and judicial review is that the means they viewed as available to members or former members of the security services to expose iniquity are so unlikely to be used. It seems, to say the least, highly improbable that such a member would risk the employment detriment that might be likely to arise, especially if he then proceeded to seek judicial review of the decision. It would appear that it would place him in an impossible position in relation to colleagues and superiors. Of course, simply making the disclosure directly and then being prosecuted for it would also risk such detriment, even if the person was acquitted. However, the obvious route in such circum-stances would be to make the disclosure anonymously. Former members of the services would not be subject to the same constraints in terms of employment detriment, but might be deterred from using this route for the simple reason that they would probably view it as inefficacious. Lord Bingham cannot but sound naïve when he says:

> If . . . the document or information revealed matters which, however, scandalous or embarrassing, would not damage any security or intelligence interest or impede the effective discharge by the service of its very important public functions, [a] deci-sion [in favour of disclosure] might be appropriate.[57]

To date, there is no report of any such member availing themselves of this route, although persons other than Shayler have made or sought to make disclosures to the public at large, as this chapter reveals. Moreover, one point that Lord Hope and the oth-ers wholly fail to recognise is that requiring a person wishing to speak to the media to take legal action *before* he can do so (judicial review of the refusal to allow disclosure) is to place a very weighty fetter upon his freedom of expression. Effectively, such a system reverses the principle under Art 10(2) that the state must justify interference with freedom of expression. It places upon the would-be speaker the burden of forcing

54 *Ibid*, at para 83.
55 *Ibid*, at para 84.
56 *Ibid*, at para 85.
57 *Ibid*, at para 30.

the state, through legal action, to allow him to speak. One would not normally think of human rights as being those that cannot be exercised without prior legal action. Moreover, one of the most important principles recognised at Strasbourg is that rights must be real, not tokenistic or illusory. It is argued that the right to freedom of expression – one of the central rights of the Convention – is rendered illusory by ss 1(1) and 4(1) of the OSA in relation to allegedly unlawful activities of the security services – a matter of great significance in a democracy.

One of the specific arguments heavily relied upon by their lordships was one previously cited by the courts. Lord Hutton cited *dicta* of Lord Nicholls in *Attorney General v Blake*:[58]

> It is of paramount importance that members of the service should have complete confidence in all their dealings with each other, and that those recruited as informers should have the like confidence. Undermining the willingness of prospective informers to cooperate with the services, or undermining the morale and trust between members of the services when engaged on secret and dangerous operations, would jeopardise the effectiveness of the service. An absolute rule against disclosure, visible to all, makes good sense.

The obvious rejoinder to this argument, that members of the service and others must be able to trust each other to keep information secret, is that such trust would surely be expected to extend only to information which did not reveal illegality. Otherwise the policy of ss 1(1) and 4(1) of the OSA seems to be to promote criminal conspiracies among members of the services or between members and informants to conceal information revealing unlawful activities. Moreover, whilst it is common sense to believe that the willingness of informants to give information to the security services would be undermined if they feared that their identities might be later unmasked, this argument *cannot* support a blanket ban on *any* disclosures by members or former members of the services. It is highly doubtful that those considering giving information to the services are aware of the precise legal position under the OSA: a simple guarantee by the agent cultivating the source that their identity would always be kept secret would suffice.

As noted above, the impact of the OSA in terms of freedom of expression is further exacerbated since no general defence of prior publication is provided; the only means of putting forward such argument would arise in one of the categories in which it was necessary to prove the likelihood that harm would flow from the disclosure; the prosecution might find it hard to establish such a likelihood where there had been a great deal of prior publication because no further harm could be caused. Obviously, once again, this will depend on the level at which the harm test operates. Where it operates at its lowest level, prior publication would be irrelevant. Thus, where a member of the security services repeated information falling within s 1 which had been published all over the world and in the UK, a conviction could still be obtained. This position is out of accord with Art 10: in such an instance, the imposition of criminal liability would be unable to preserve national security and therefore, it would be disproportionate to the aim of so doing.

---

58 [2001] 1 AC 268, 287.

If such publication had occurred, but the information fell within s 1(3), the test for harm might be satisfied on the basis that although no further harm could be caused by disclosure of the particular document, it nevertheless belonged to a class of documents the disclosure of which was likely to cause harm. However, where harm flowing from publication of a specific document is relied on, *Lord Advocate v Scotsman Publications Ltd* suggests that a degree of prior publication may tend to defeat the argument that further publication can still cause harm. However, this suggestion must be treated with care, since the ruling was not given under the 1989 Act and the link between the Act and the civil law of confidence may not form part of its *ratio*.[59] It should also be noted that s 6 provides that information that has already been leaked abroad can still cause harm if disclosed in the UK. The only exception to this arises under s 6(3), which provides that no liability will arise if the disclosure was authorised by the state or international organisation in question.

Conclusions

The claim that the Act is an improvement on its predecessor rests partly on the substance or significance of the information it covers. Such substance is made relevant first by the use of categorisation; impliedly, trivial information relating to cups of tea or colours of carpets in government buildings is not covered (except in security services buildings) and, second, because even where information *does* fall within the category in question, its disclosure will not incur liability unless harm will or may flow from it. Thus, on the face of it, liability will not be incurred merely because the information disclosed covers a topic of significance such as defence. In other words, it does not seem to be assumed that because there is a public interest in keeping information of the particular type secret, it inevitably relates to any particular piece of information. However, in relation to many disclosures it is, in fact, misleading to speak of using a second method to narrow down further the amount of information covered because, as noted above, establishing that the information falls within the category in question is in fact (or may be; no guidance is given as to when this will be the case) synonymous with establishing that harm will occur in a number of instances.

Clearly, if only to avoid bringing the criminal law into disrepute, 'harm tests' that allow the substance of the information to be taken into account are to be preferred to the width of s 2 of the 1911 Act. However, although the 1989 Act embodies and emphasises the notion of a test for harm in its reiteration of the term 'damaging', it is not necessary to show that harm has *actually occurred*. Bearing this important point in mind, it can be seen that the test for harm actually operates on four different levels:

(a) The lowest level arises in two categories, s 1(1) and s 4(3), where there is no explicit test for harm at all – impliedly, a disclosure is of its very nature harmful.
(b) In one category, s 3(1)(b), the test for harm is more apparent than real in that it may be identical to the test determining whether the information falls within the category at all.

---

59 [1990] 1 AC 812; [1989] 2 All ER 852, HL. Only Lord Templeman clearly adverted to such a link.

(c) In s 1(3), there is a harm test, but the harm need not flow from or be likely to flow from disclosure of the specific document in question.

(d) In three categories, ss 2, 3 and 4, there is a harm test, but it is only necessary to prove that harm would be *likely* to occur due to the disclosure in question, whether it has occurred or not.

Even at the highest level, where it is necessary to show that the actual document in question would be likely to cause harm, the task of doing so is made easy due to the width of the tests themselves. Under s 2(2), for example, a disclosure of information relating to defence will be damaging if it is likely to seriously obstruct the interests of the UK abroad. Thus, the harm tests may be said to be concerned less with preventing damaging disclosures than with creating the *impression* that liability is confined to such disclosures.

These tests for harm are not made any more stringent in instances where a non-Crown servant – usually a journalist – discloses information since, under s 5, if anyone discloses information that falls into one of the categories covered, the test for harm will be determined by reference to that category. The journalist who publishes information and the Crown servant who discloses it to him or her are treated differently in terms of the test for harm only where the latter is a member of the security services disclosing information relating to those services.

One of the objections to the old s 2 of the 1911 Act was the failure to include a requirement to prove *mens rea*. The 1989 Act includes such a requirement only as regards the leaking of information by non-Crown servants; in all other instances, it creates a 'reversed *mens rea*': the defence can attempt to prove that the defendant did not know (or have reasonable cause to know) of the nature of the information or that its disclosure would be damaging. However, under ss 5 and 6 the prosecution must prove *mens rea*, which includes a requirement to show that the disclosure was made in the knowledge that it would be damaging. This is a step in the right direction and a clear improvement on the 1911 Act; nevertheless, the burden of proof on the prosecution is very easy to discharge where the low level harm tests of ss 1(3) and 3(1)(b) apply once it was shown that the defendant knew that the information fell within the category in question.

Under s 3 of the HRA it is strongly arguable that the Act needs to afford greater recognition to the important constitutional role of the journalist in order to bring it into line with the recognition afforded to that role at Strasbourg under Art 10. But unless s 3 is used creatively in order to create such recognition, a journalist who repeated allegations made by a future Peter Wright as to corruption or treachery in MI5 could be convicted if it could be shown, first, that he or she knew that the information related to the security services and, secondly, that disclosure of that *type* of information would be *likely* to cause damage to the work of the security services, regardless of whether the particular allegations would cause such damage. In the case of a journalist who repeated allegations made by a future Cathy Massiter, it would only be necessary to show that the allegations related to telephone tapping and that the journalist knew that they did. Clearly, this would be a burden that would be readily discharged.

It may be argued – bearing in mind the scarcity of prosecutions under the 1911 Act – that the Official Secrets Acts were put in place mainly in order to create a deterrent effect and as a centrepiece in the general legal scheme engendering government secrecy, rather than with a view to their invocation. The 1989 Act may be effective as a means of creating greater government credibility in relation to official secrecy than its predecessor. It allows the claim of liberalisation to be made and gives the impression that the anomalies in existence under the 1911 Act have been dealt with. It appears complex and wide ranging partly due to overlapping between and within the categories and, therefore, is likely to have a chilling effect because civil servants and others will not be certain as to the information covered except in very clear cut cases. It may, therefore, be proving more effective than the 1911 Act in deterring the press from publishing the revelations of a future Peter Wright in respect of the workings of the security services. Thus, it may rarely need to be invoked and, in fact, may have much greater symbolic than practical value.

In considering the impact of the Act, it must be borne in mind that many other criminal sanctions for the unauthorised disclosure of information exist and some of these clearly overlap with its provisions. Sections 1 and 4(3) work in conjunction with the provisions of the Security Services Act 1989 to prevent almost all scrutiny of the operation of the security services. Even where a member of the public has a grievance concerning the operation of the services it will probably not be possible to use a court action as a means of bringing such operations to the notice of the public: under s 5 of the Security Services Act, complaint can only be made to a tribunal and, under s 5(4), the decisions of the tribunal are not questionable in any court of law. In a similar manner s 4(3) of the Official Secrets Act, which prevents disclosure of information about telephone tapping, works in tandem with the Regulation of Investigatory Powers Act 2000. Under the 2000 Act, complaints can be made only to a tribunal whose decisions are not published, with no possibility of scrutiny by a court. Moreover, around 80 other statutory provisions provide sanctions to enforce secrecy on civil servants in the particular areas they cover. For example, s 11 of the Atomic Energy Act 1946 makes it an offence to communicate to an unauthorised person information relating to atomic energy plant. Further, s 1 of the Official Secrets Act 1911 is still available to punish spies. Thus, it is arguable that s 2 of the 1911 Act could merely have been repealed without being replaced.

A number of the provisions of the 1989 Act look increasingly anomalous in the Human Rights Act era. Although repeal of the Act is unlikely, the pressure to amend s 1(1), as the most pernicious section – in terms of its impact on state accountability – may eventually become irresistible, although the decision in *Shayler* now makes it clear that it will not come from the judiciary.

Prosecutions under the Act are rare, and, where they attempt to punish a member of the security services for revealing illegality or abuse of power by the security services, are likely to expose the government to a huge amount of negative publicity, particularly if the matter to which the revelation relates is a sensitive one. The Katharine Gunn affair in 2003 illustrated these points powerfully. Ms Gunn was an employee at GCHQ, the government's listening installation. She discovered, through correspondence that crossed her desk, that the UK government had been requested by the US government to give assistance in spying on the diplomats of states who were temporary members of the UN Security Council, at UN headquarters in New York, in order to gain information making it easier to convince such states to vote for the US–UK resolution in favour of military action. Such action would plainly have violated the Vienna Convention on diplomatic relations[60] and Gunn disclosed the request to the *Observer* newspaper, which, not surprisingly, splashed the story on its front cover on 2 March 2003. Gunn was arrested and a prosecution commenced for breach of s 1(1) of the OSA. However, the prosecution was abandoned in February 2004, when it emerged that the CPS would offer no evidence.[61] Gunn had stated her intention to plead a defence of necessity – the revelation of illegal conduct by the security services, and the avoidance of an illegal war, and thus the saving of lives; specifically, she had intimated that her lawyers would seek disclosure, as part of her defence, of the Attorney General's advice on the legality or otherwise of the Iraq war, before its inception, a matter of enormous political sensitivity to the government. The case not only illustrated the undesirability from a government's point of view of using the Act against a seemingly honest and concerned whistleblower, but raised questions as to the real independence of the decision to drop the prosecution, given the intense embarrassment the case looked likely to cause the government. The indefensible nature of s 1(1), leaving Gunn no ability to raise a public interest defence, even in an instance of such enormous public importance, was once more vividly illustrated.

3 Breach of confidence

Introduction[62]

Breach of confidence is a civil remedy affording protection against the disclosure or use of information that is not generally known and that has been entrusted in circumstances imposing an obligation not to disclose it without authorisation from the person who originally imparted it. This area of law developed as a means of protecting secret information belonging to individuals and organisations.[63] However, it can also be used by the government to prevent disclosure of sensitive information and is, in that sense, a back-up to the other measures available, including the Official Secrets Act 1989.[64] It is clear that governments are prepared to use actions for breach of confidence against civil servants and others in instances falling outside the protected categories – or within them. In some respects, breach of confidence actions may be more valuable than the criminal sanction provided by the 1989 Act. Their use may attract less publicity than a criminal trial, no jury will be involved and they offer the possibility of quickly obtaining an interim injunction. The latter possibility is very valuable because, in many instances, the other party (usually a newspaper) will not pursue the case to a trial of the permanent injunction since the secret will probably be stale news by that time. However, where the

---

60 As well, seemingly, as the 1946 General Convention, Art 2(3), which provides the premises of the UN shall be immune from any form of search or interference.

61 See the statement by Harriet Harman QC to the House of Commons: HC Deb, col 427 (26 February 2004).

62 General reading: Gurry, F, *Breach of Confidence*, (OUP, 2nd edn, 2012), Clarendon; Bailey and Taylor, *op cit*, fn 1; Robertson, G and Nichol, AGL, *Media Law*, 5th edn, 2007, Sweet & Maxwell; Wacks, R, *Personal Information*, 1989, Clarendon, Chapter 3; Feldman, *op cit*, fn 1 at 648–68; the general development of the doctrine is discussed in Chapter 10 at p 719 *et seq*.

63 See Chapter 10, at p 720.

64 For comment on its role in this respect see Bryan, MW, 'The Crossman Diaries: developments in the law of breach of confidence' (1976) 92 LQR 180; Williams, DGT, 'The Crossman Diaries' (1976) CLJ 1; Lowe and Willmore, 'Secrets, media and the law' (1985) 48 MLR 592.

government, as opposed to a private individual, is concerned, the courts will not merely accept that it is in the public interest that the information should be kept confidential. It will also have to be shown that the public interest in keeping the information confidential due to the harm its disclosure would cause is not outweighed by the public interest in disclosure.

Thus, in *AG v Jonathan Cape*,[65] when the Attorney General invoked the law of confidence to try to stop publication of Richard Crossman's memoirs on the ground that they concerned cabinet discussions, the Lord Chief Justice accepted that such public secrets could be restrained, but only on the basis that the balance of the public interest came down in favour of suppression. As the discussions had taken place ten years previously, it was not possible to show that harm would flow from their disclosure; the public interest in publication therefore prevailed.

The nature of the public interest defence – the interest in disclosure – was clarified in *Lion Laboratories v Evans and Express Newspapers*.[66] The Court of Appeal held that the defence extended beyond situations in which there had been serious wrongdoing by the plaintiff. Even where the plaintiff was blameless, publication would be excusable where it was possible to show a serious and legitimate interest in the revelation. Thus, the *Daily Express* was allowed to publish information extracted from the manufacturer of the intoximeter (a method of conducting breathalyser tests) even though it did not reveal iniquity on the part of the manufacturer. It did, however, reveal a matter of genuine public interest: that wrongful convictions might have been obtained in drink driving cases owing to possible deficiencies of the intoximeter.

Just as the Official Secrets Act creates a direct interference with political speech, the doctrine of confidence as employed by the government can do so too. Therefore, the use of the doctrine in such instances requires careful scrutiny, with Art 10 in mind. Since this is a common law doctrine, s 3 will not apply. But the courts have a duty under s 6 of the HRA to develop the doctrine compatibly with Art 10. Thus a court, as itself a public authority under s 6, is obliged to give effect to Art 10, among other provisions of the Convention, when considering the application of this doctrine. In so doing, the courts arguably have nearly as much leeway as they do under s 3 of the HRA, and it must be remembered that no provision was included in the HRA allowing the common law to override the Convention rights. Since, in an action between the individual and the state, the vexed issue of horizontal effect does not arise,[67] this matter can be regarded as settled, since the state as employer is also presumably a public authority under s 6. Section 12(4) is also applicable where interference with the right to freedom of expression is in issue, as it inevitably will be in this context. Section 12(4) requires the Court to have particular regard to the right to freedom of expression under Art 10. Thus, s 12(4) provides added weight to the argument that in the instance in which the state seeks to suppress the expression of an individual using this doctrine, the court must consider the pressing social need to do so and the requirements of proportionality very carefully, interpreting those requirements strictly. In considering Art 10, the court should, under s 12(4)(a), take into account the extent to which the material is or is about to become

---

65 [1976] QB 752.
66 [1985] QB 526; [1984] 2 All ER 417, CA.
67 See *Commissioner of Police of the Metropolis v Times Newspapers Ltd* [2011] EWHC 2705 (QB).

available to the public and the public interest in publication.[68] These two matters are central in breach of confidence actions. They imply that the state's task in obtaining an injunction where a small amount of prior publication has taken place – or is about to – has been made harder.

In breach of confidence actions the state, as indicated below, typically seeks an interim injunction and then, if it has obtained it, may proceed to the trial of the permanent injunction. However, s 12(3) of the HRA provides that prior restraint on expression should not be granted except where the court considers that the claimant is 'likely' to establish at trial that publication should not be allowed, which the House of Lords has found will generally mean 'more likely than not'.[69] Moreover, *ex parte* injunctions cannot be granted under s 12(2) unless there are compelling reasons why the respondent should not be notified or the applicant has taken all reasonable steps to notify the respondent. All these requirements under the HRA must now be taken into account in applying the doctrine of confidence. The result is likely to be that the doctrine will undergo quite a radical change from the interpretation afforded to it in the *Spycatcher* litigation, which is considered below.

The Spycatcher *litigation*

The leading case in this area is the House of Lords' decision in *AG v Guardian Newspapers Ltd (No 2)*,[70] which confirmed that the *Lion Laboratories Ltd v Evans* approach to the public interest defence is the correct one and also clarified certain other aspects of this area of the law. In 1985, the Attorney General commenced proceedings in New South Wales[71] in an attempt (which was ultimately unsuccessful)[72] to restrain publication of *Spycatcher* by Peter Wright. The book included allegations of illegal activity engaged in by MI5. In the UK on 22 and 23 June 1986, the *Guardian* and *The Observer* published reports of the forthcoming hearing which included some *Spycatcher* material and on 27 June the Attorney General obtained temporary *ex parte* injunctions preventing them from further disclosure of such material. *Inter partes* injunctions were granted against the newspapers on 11 July 1986. On 12 July 1987, *The Sunday Times* began publishing extracts from *Spycatcher* and the Attorney General obtained an injunction restraining publication on 16 July.

On 14 July 1987, the book was published in the US, and many copies were brought into the UK. On 30 July 1987, the House of Lords decided[73] (relying on *American Cyanamid Co v Ethicon Ltd*)[74] to continue the injunctions against the newspapers on the basis that the Attorney General still had an arguable case for permanent injunctions. In making this decision, the House of Lords was obviously influenced by the fact that publication of the information was an irreversible step. This is the usual approach at

---

68 See Chapter 4, pp 211–18.

69 See Chapter 10 at pp 784–85.

70 [1990] 1 AC 109; [1990] 3 WLR 776; [1988] 3 All ER 545, HL.

71 [1987] 8 NSWLR 341.

72 HC of Australia (1988) 165 CLR 30; for comment see Mann, FA (1988) 104 LQR 497; Turnbull, M (1989) 105 LQR 382.

73 *AG v Guardian Newspapers Ltd* [1987] 3 All ER 316; for comment, see Lee, S (1987) 103 LQR 506.

74 [1975] AC 396; [1975] 1 All ER 504, HL.

the interim stage: the court considers the balance of convenience between the two parties and will tend to come down on the side of the plaintiff because of the irrevocable
nature of publication. However, since an interim injunction represents a prior restraint
and is often the most crucial and, indeed, sometimes the *only* stage in the whole action,
it may be argued that a presumption in favour of freedom of expression should be more
readily allowed to tip the balance in favour of the defendant. This may especially be
argued where publication from other sources has already occurred which will be likely
to increase, and where the public interest in the information is very strong.

It is arguable that the House of Lords should have been able in July 1986 to break
through the argument that once the confidentiality claim was set up, the only possible
course was to transfix matters as at that point. The argument could have been broken
through in the following way: the public interest in limiting the use of prior restraints
could have been weighed against the interest in ensuring that everyone who sets up a
legal claim has a right to have it heard free from interference. A prior restraint might be
allowed even in respect of a matter of great public concern if the interest it protected
was clearly made out, it did not go beyond what was needed to provide such protection
and it was foreseeable that the restraint would achieve its objective. If it seemed probable that the restraint would not achieve its objective, it would cause an erosion of freedom of speech to no purpose. In the instant case, although the first of these conditions
may have been satisfied, the other two, it is submitted, were not; the restraint should
not, therefore, have been granted. Such reasoning would bring the law of confidence
closer to adopting the principles used in defamation cases as regards the grant of interim
injunctions.[75] When cases of this nature recur under the HRA, such reasoning would be
taken into account under s 12(4) and s 6; since relying on either section the demands
of Art 10 must be met, so an injunction should not be granted where it is probable that
it will not be able to serve the legitimate aim in question, owing to the probability that
further publication abroad, or on the internet, will occur.

The judgment of the House of Lords did nothing to curb the use of 'gagging injunctions' in actions for breach of confidence where there had not been prior publication of
the material. In any such action, even where the claim was of little merit, and the public
interest in publication strong, it was possible to argue that its subject matter should be
preserved intact until the merits of the claim could be considered. Even in an instance
where the plaintiff (the state) then decided to drop the action before that point, publication of the material in question could be prevented for some substantial period of time.
The House of Lords' decision was found to be in breach of Art 10 of the European Convention on Human Rights, as discussed below, but on the ground of prior publication,
rather than public interest in the material.

In the trial of the permanent injunctions, *AG v Guardian (No 2)*,[76] the Crown argued
that confidential information disclosed to third parties does not thereby lose its confidential character if the third parties know that the disclosure has been made in breach of
a duty of confidence. A further reason for maintaining confidentiality in the particular

---

75 See *Bonnard v Perryman* [1891] 2 Ch 269; *Herbage v The Times Newspapers and Others* (1981) *The
    Times*, 1 May.
76 [1990] 1 AC 109; [1990] 3 WLR 776; [1988] 3 All ER 545, HL; in the Court of Appeal [1990] 1 AC 109;
    [1988] 3 All ER 545, p 594.

instance was that the unauthorised disclosure of the information was thought likely to damage the trust which members of MI5 have in each other and might encourage others to follow suit. These factors, it was argued, established the public interest in keeping the information confidential.

On the other hand, it was argued on behalf of the newspapers that some of the information in *Spycatcher*, if true, disclosed that members of MI5 in their operations in England had committed serious breaches of domestic law in, for example, bugging foreign embassies or effecting unlawful entry into private premises. Most seriously, the book included the allegations that members of MI5 attempted to destabilise the administration of Mr Harold Wilson and that the Director General or Deputy Director General of MI5 was a spy. The defendants contended that the duty of non-disclosure to which newspapers coming into the unauthorised possession of confidential state secrets may be subject, does not extend to allegations of serious iniquity of this character.

It was determined at first instance and in the Court of Appeal that whether or not the newspapers would have had a duty to refrain from publishing *Spycatcher* material in June 1986 before its publication elsewhere, any such duty had now lapsed. The mere making of allegations of iniquity was insufficient, of itself, to justify overriding the duty of confidentiality, but the articles in question published in June 1986 had not contained information going beyond what the public was reasonably entitled to know and in so far as they went beyond what had been previously published, no detriment to national security had been shown that could outweigh the public interest in free speech, given the publication of *Spycatcher* that had already taken place. Thus, balancing the public interest in freedom of speech and the right to receive information against the countervailing interest of the Crown in national security, continuation of the injunctions was not necessary. The injunctions, however, continued until the House of Lords rejected the Attorney General's claim (*AG v Guardian Newspapers Ltd (No 2)*)[77] on the basis that the interest in maintaining confidentiality was outweighed by the public interest in knowing of the allegations in *Spycatcher*. It was further determined that an injunction to restrain future publication of matters connected with the operations of the security services would amount to a comprehensive ban on publication and would undermine the operation of determining the balance of public interest in deciding whether such publication was to be prevented; accordingly, an injunction to prevent future publication that had not yet been threatened was not granted.

It appears likely that the permanent injunctions would have been granted but for the massive publication of *Spycatcher* abroad. That factor seems to have tipped the balance in favour of the newspapers. It is arguable that the operation of the public interest defence in this instance came too close to allowing for judicial value judgments rather than application of a clear legal rule. Without a bill of rights to protect freedom of speech, the Law Lords, it is suggested, showed a tendency to be swayed by

---

77 [1990] 1 AC 109; [1990] 3 WLR 776; [1988] 3 All ER 545, p 638; for comment, see Williams (1989) 48 CLJ 1; Cripps, Y, 'Breach of copyright and confidence: the *Spycatcher* effect' [1989] PL 13; Barendt, E, '*Spycatcher* and freedom of speech' [1989] PL 204; Michael, J, 'Spycatcher's end?' (1989) 52 MLR 389; Narain, BJ (1988) 39 NILQ 73 and (1987) 137 NLJ 723 and 724; Burnett, D and Thomas, R (1989) 16 JLS 210; Jones, G, 'Breach of confidence – after *Spycatcher*' (1989) 42 CLP 49; Kingsford-Smith, D and Oliver, D (eds), *Economical With the Truth*, 1990, ESC, chapters by Pannick and Austin; Ewing and Gearty, *op cit*, fn 28 at 152–69; Turnbull, M, *The Spycatcher Trial*, 1988; Bailey and Taylor, *op cit*, fn 1.

establishment arguments. The judgment also made it clear that once the information has become available from other sources, even though the plaintiff played no part in its dissemination and indeed tried to prevent it, an injunction would be unlikely to be granted. This principle was affirmed in *Lord Advocate v Scotsman Publications Ltd*,[78] which concerned the publication of extracts from *Inside Intelligence* by Antony Cavendish. The interlocutory injunction sought by the Crown was refused by the House of Lords on the ground that there had been a small amount of prior publication and the possible damage to national security was very nebulous. The decision suggests that the degree of prior publication may be weighed against the significance of the disclosures in question: if less innocuous material had been in issue, an injunction might have been granted.

The Observer and the *Guardian* applied to the European Commission on Human Rights claiming, *inter alia*, that the grant of the temporary injunctions had breached Art 10 of the Convention, which guarantees freedom of expression. Having given its opinion that the temporary injunctions constituted such a breach, the Commission referred the case to the court. In *Observer and Guardian v UK*,[79] the Court found that the injunctions clearly constituted an interference with the newspapers' freedom of expression; the question was whether the interference fell within one of the exceptions provided for by para 2 of Art 10. The injunctions fell within two of the para 2 exceptions: maintaining the authority of the judiciary and protecting national security. However, those exceptions could be invoked only if the injunctions were necessary in a democratic society in the sense that they corresponded to a pressing social need and were proportionate to the aims pursued.

The Court considered these questions with regard first to the period from 11 July 1986 to 30 July 1987. The injunctions had the aim of preventing publication of material that, according to evidence presented by the Attorney General, might have created a risk of detriment to MI5. The nature of the risk was uncertain as the exact contents of the book were not known at that time because it was still only available in manuscript form. Further, they ensured the preservation of the Attorney General's right to be granted a permanent injunction; if *Spycatcher* material had been published before that claim could be heard, the subject matter of the action would have been damaged or destroyed. In the court's view, these factors established the existence of a pressing social need. Were the actual restraints imposed proportionate to these aims? The injunctions did not prevent the papers pursuing a campaign for an inquiry into the operation of the security services and, though preventing publication for a long time – over a year – the material in question could not be classified as urgent news. Thus, it was found that the interference complained of was proportionate to the ends in view.

The court then considered the period from 30 July 1987 to 30 October 1988, after publication of *Spycatcher* had taken place in the US. That event changed the situation: in the court's view, the aim of the injunctions was no longer to keep secret information secret; it was to attempt to preserve the reputation of MI5 and to deter others who might be tempted to follow Peter Wright's example. It was uncertain whether the injunctions could achieve those aims and it was not clear that the newspapers who had not been concerned with the publication of *Spycatcher* should be enjoined as an example to others.

---

78 [1990] 1 AC 812; [1989] 2 All ER 852, CA.
79 (1991) 14 EHRR 153; for comment see Leigh, I, '*Spycatcher* in Strasbourg' [1992] PL 200–8.

Further, after 30 July it was not possible to maintain the Attorney General's rights as a litigant because the substance of his claim had already been destroyed; had permanent injunctions been obtained against the newspapers, that would not have preserved the confidentiality of the material in question. Thus, the injunctions could no longer be said to be necessary either to protect national security or to maintain the authority of the judiciary. Maintenance of the injunctions after publication of the book in the US therefore constituted a violation of Art 10.

This was a cautious judgment. It suggests that had the book been published in the US after the House of Lords' decision to uphold the temporary injunctions, no breach of Art 10 would have occurred, despite the fact that publication of extracts from the book had already occurred in the US[80] and the UK. The Court seems to have been readily persuaded by the Attorney General's argument that a widely framed injunction was needed in July 1986, but it is arguable that it was wider than it needed to be to prevent a risk to national security. It could have required the newspapers to refrain from publishing Wright material which had not been previously published by others until (if) the action to prevent publication of the book was lost. Such wording would have taken care of any national security interest; therefore, wording going beyond that was disproportionate to that aim.

Thus, although the newspapers 'won', the judgment is unlikely to have a significant liberalising influence on the principles governing the grant of temporary injunctions on the grounds of breach of confidence. The minority judges in the court set themselves against the narrow view that the authority of the judiciary is best preserved by allowing a claim of confidentiality set up in the face of a strong competing public interest to found an infringement of freedom of speech for over a year. Judge Morenilla argued that prior restraint should be imposed in such circumstances only where disclosure would result in immediate, serious and irreparable damage to the public interest.[81] It might be said that such a test would impair the authority of the judiciary in the sense that the rights of litigants would not be sufficiently protected. However, following the judgment of the Lords, the test at the interlocutory stage allowed a case based on a weak argument to prevail on the basis that the court could not weigh the evidence at that stage and therefore had to grant an injunction in order to preserve confidentiality until the case could be fully looked into. As noted above, this stance can mean that the other party does not pursue the case to the permanent stage and, therefore, freedom of speech is suppressed on very flimsy grounds. Thus, a greater burden to show the well-founded nature of the claim of danger to the public interest – even if not as heavy as that under the test proposed by Judge Morenilla – should be placed on the plaintiff, and such a burden would be, it is argued, more in accord with the duties of the court under ss 6 and 12 of the HRA.

The result of the ruling in the European Court of Human Rights appears to be that where there has been an enormous amount of prior publication, an interim injunction should not be granted, but that it can be when there is at least some evidence of a threat to national security posed by publication coupled with a lesser degree of prior

---

80 The *Washington Post* published certain extracts in the US on 3 May 1987.
81 He relied on the ruling to this effect of the US Supreme Court in *Nebraska Press Association v Stuart* (1976) 427 US 539.

publication. It meant that the action for breach of confidence was still of great value as part of the legal scheme bolstering government secrecy.

The position, however, has now been affected by the decision of the House of Lords in *Cream Holdings Ltd v Banerjee*.[82] This decision gives the definitive interpretation of the meaning of s 12(3) HRA, which provides, *inter alia*, that no relief affecting the Convention right to freedom of expression 'is to be granted so as to restrain publication before trial unless the court is satisfied that the applicant is likely to establish that publication should not be allowed'. It is discussed in detail in Chapter 10 and it is not proposed to repeat that discussion here. The key point is that the effect of the decision of the House of Lords, in nearly all cases – absent the claim of immediate and serious danger to life, limb, or presumably national security – is that the party seeking the injunction, that is the government in these kinds of cases, must show not only an arguable case, as previously, but that it is 'more likely than not' that they will succeed at final trial.[83] This approach, assuming it is applied consistently to *Spycatcher*-type cases, should make it significantly harder for future governments to obtain gagging injunctions against the media. The post-HRA decision discussed below, although made before *Cream Holdings*, was taken under s 12(3) and appears to confirm this.

Case law subsequent to Spycatcher and conclusions

The decision in *AG v Times*[84] suggests that Art 10 is having a greater impact in breach of confidence actions than it had at Strasbourg. Tomlinson, a former MI6 officer, wrote a book, *The Big Breach*, about his experiences in MI6[85] which *The Sunday Times* intended to serialise. There had been a small amount of publication of the material in Russia. The Attorney General sought an injunction to restrain publication. The key issue concerned the degree of prior publication required before it could be said that the material had lost its quality of confidentiality. The Attorney General proposed the formula: 'publication has come to the widespread attention of the public at large.'[86] This formula would have meant that injunctions could be obtained even after a high degree of prior publication and therefore it was unacceptable to *The Sunday Times*. However, the two parties agreed on a formula: that the material had already been published in any other newspaper, magazine or other publication whether within or outside the jurisdiction of the court, to such an extent that the information is in the public domain (other than in a case where the only such publication was made by or caused by the defendants). The Attorney General, however, contended that the defendants had to demonstrate that this was the case, which meant that they had to obtain clearance from the Attorney General before publishing.

In arguing against this contention at first instance, the newspaper invoked Art 10 and also relied on s 12(3) and (4) of the HRA.[87] It was argued that the restriction proposed

82 [2004] 3 WLR 918. For comment see Smith ATH, [2005] 64(1) CLJ 4.
83 See further Chapter 10 at pp 784–85.
84 [2001] EMLR 19.
85 Tomlinson was charged with an offence under the Official Secrets Act, s 1, pleaded guilty and was imprisoned for six months.
86 *Ibid*, para 2.
87 For discussion of s 12(4) HRA, see Chapter 10, pp 778–84.

by the Attorney General would be disproportionate to the aim pursued and therefore could not be justified in a democratic society. The decision in *Bladet-Tromsø v Norway*[88] was referred to, in which the Court said that it is incumbent on the media 'to impart information and ideas concerning matters of public interest. Not only does the press have the task of imparting such information and ideas, the public has the right to receive them.'[89] Taking these arguments into account, it was found at first instance that the Attorney General had to demonstrate why there was a public interest in restricting publication. No injunction was granted since it was found that he had not done so. On appeal, the same stance was taken. It was found that the requirement to seek clearance should not be imposed: the editor had to form his own judgment as to whether the material could be said to be already in the public domain. That position was, the Court found, most consonant with the requirements of Art 10 and s 12.

This decision suggests that, bearing in mind the requirements of the HRA, an injunction is unlikely to be granted where a small amount of prior publication has already taken place. It does not, however, decide the question of publication where no prior publication has taken place, but the material is of public interest (which could clearly have been said of the Wright material). Following *Bladet-Tromsø v Norway* it is suggested that an injunction should not be granted where such material is likely, imminently, to come into the public domain, a position consistent with the demands of s 12(4), which refers to such a likelihood. Even where this cannot be said to be the case, it would be consonant with the requirements of Art 10 and s 12 to refuse to grant an injunction on the basis of the duty of newspapers to report on such material. The burden would be placed on the state to seek to establish that a countervailing pressing social need was present and that the injunction did not go further than necessary in order to serve the end in view.[90]

4 Defence advisory notices[91]

The government and the media may avoid the head-on confrontation that occurred in the *Spycatcher* litigation by means of a curious institution known until 1992 as the 'D' (Defence) notice system. This system, which effectively means that the media censor themselves in respect of publication of official information, can obviate the need to seek injunctions to prevent publication. The 'D' Notice Committee was set up with the object of letting the press know which information could be printed and at what point: it was intended that if sensitive political information was covered by a 'D' notice, an editor would decide against printing it. The system is entirely voluntary and in theory the fact that a 'D' notice has not been issued does not mean that a prosecution under the Official Secrets Act 1989 is precluded, although in practice it is very unlikely. Further, guidance obtained from the secretary to the committee does not amount to a straightforward

---

88   (1999) 6 BHRC 599.
89   *Ibid*, at para 62.
90   The manner in which the law of common law contempt may allow for the imposition of widespread restrictions upon the media on the back of an initial breach of confidence injunction is considered in detail in Chapter 6 at p 343 *et seq*.
91   On the system generally, see Jaconelli, J, 'The 'D' Notice system' [1982] PL 39; Fairley, D 'D notices, official secrets and the law' (1990) 10(3) OJLS, 430–440.

'clearance'. Press representatives sit on the committee as well as civil servants and officers of the armed forces.

The value and purpose of the system was called into question due to the injunction obtained against the BBC in respect of *My Country Right or Wrong*, a programme that concerned issues raised by the *Spycatcher* litigation; the BBC consulted the 'D' Notice Committee before broadcasting and were told that the programme did not affect national security. However, the Attorney General then obtained an injunction preventing transmission on the ground of breach of confidence, thereby disregarding the 'D' Notice Committee.

Some criticism has been levelled at the system: in the Third Report from the Defence Committee,[92] the 'D' notice system was examined and it was concluded that it was failing to fulfil its role. It was found that major newspapers did not consult their 'D' notices to see what was covered by them and that the wording of 'D' notices was so wide as to render them meaningless. The system conveyed an appearance of censorship which had provoked strong criticism. It was determined that the machinery for the administration of 'D' notices and the 'D' notices themselves needed revision. The review that followed this reduced the number of notices and confined them to specific areas. The system was reviewed again in 1992 (*The Defence Advisory Notices: A Review of the D Notice System*, MOD Open Government Document No 93/06) leading to a reduction in the number of notices to six. They were renamed 'Defence Advisory Notices' to reflect their voluntary nature.

A more recent review, in March 2015, concluded that although there was widespread support for the system it suffered from several weaknesses. These included a lack of strategic direction from the committee overseeing its operation, 'patchy' engagement by government departments as well as weak accountability. It recommendations that these be addressed, including through structural changes to the committee itself.[93]

5 Freedom of information: general principles

Principles of freedom of information and Art 10 ECHR

The citizen's 'right to know' is recognised in most democracies including the US, Canada, Australia, New Zealand, Denmark, Sweden, Holland, Norway, Greece and France. In such countries, the general principle of freedom of information is subject to exceptions where information falls into specific categories. In terms of principle, and in particular, as seen through the lens of Art 10 ECHR, an assertion of a right to access to information can be distinguished from an assertion of a free speech right,[94] although the two are clearly linked. This distinction receives support from the wording of Art 10 itself, which speaks in terms of the freedom to 'receive and impart information', thus appearing to exclude from its provisions the right to demand information from the unwilling speaker. Moreover, the phrase 'without interference from public authorities' does not suggest that governments should come under any duty to act in order to ensure that information is received.

92 http://www.dnotice.org.uk/.
93 (1979–80) HC 773, 640 i–v, *The 'D' Notice System*.
94 *Leander v Sweden* (1987) A 116; *Guerra v Italy* (1998) 26 EHRR 357, esp. at para 53.

There are at least three reasons why access to information is often treated as a distinct interest by commentators and constitutional courts. First, freedom of information can be justified by reference to values that go beyond those underlying freedom of speech. It is generally accepted that the quality of decision-making will improve if access to official information allows citizens to scrutinise the workings of the government and public authorities generally. Moreover, the accountability of the government to the public is increased, since pressure can more readily be brought to bear on the government regarding the effects of its policies and citizens are able to make a more informed choice at election times, in accordance with the argument from democracy.

Second, information may be sought even though it is not intended that it should be communicated to others. It is not clear that the free speech justifications considered in the introduction to Part II would apply to such a situation, and therefore it would tend to be considered purely as an access to information or privacy issue. Indeed, in such instances, the seeker of information might well be asserting a right not merely to gain access to the information, but also to have its confidential quality maintained. Access rights under the Data Protection Act 1998[95] often take account of both interests, and therefore may be said to be opposed to free speech interests. Thus, it is clear that many demands for access to information are not based on an assertion of free speech interests. Rights of access to information overlap with certain privacy interests since they may cover many situations in which a person might wish to receive information, apart from that of the individual who wishes to obtain and publicise government information. However, freedom of information is most readily associated with the demand for the receipt of information with a view to placing it in the public domain.

Third, information intended to be placed in the public domain may be sought when there is no speaker willing to disclose it, or where the body that 'owns' the information is unwilling that it should be disclosed. Whether such communication of confidential information should be regarded as 'speech' or not,[96] it is clearly a necessary precondition for the production of speech and therefore can be treated as deserving of the same protection as 'speech' in that the result will be that the public will be informed and debate on issues of public interest will not be stifled. The argument that such dissemination of information will render the government more readily accountable is strongly related to the justification for free speech discussed in the introduction to Part II,[97] which argues that it is indispensable to democracy, since it enables informed participation by the citizenry.

However, freedom of speech guarantees, including Art 10, do not tend to encompass the imposition of positive obligations and, therefore, in general, are violated when a willing speaker is prevented from speaking rather than in the situation where information deriving ultimately from an unwilling speaker – usually the government – is

---

95 For discussion, see Chapter 10 at pp 772–73 *et seq.*
96 The European Court of Human Rights takes the view that it should not. In the *Gaskin* case (1990) 12 EHRR 36 it viewed a demand for access to information which the body holding it did not wish to disclose as giving rise only to an Art 8 issue, not an Art 10 issue. The US Supreme Court has held that the First Amendment does not impose an affirmative duty on government to make information not in the public domain available to journalists (417 US 817). For discussion of this issue generally, see Barendt, *Freedom of Speech* (2005), at 108 *et seq.* But see Chapter 2, p 85, n 377.
97 See pp 281–83.

sought, entailing the assertion of a positive right. Thus, a distinction should be drawn between gaining access to the information and then placing it in the public domain – the second situation giving rise to a free speech interest. However, these issues have tended to arise together within the legal scheme in the UK, which has traditionally protected a 'closed' system of government; it is therefore convenient to consider both within the same chapter.

As these remarks indicate, Art 10 of the ECHR cannot be expected to have much impact on access to information, in the sense of using Art 10 to create an access right. This is why the FoI Act is so important. However, the basic values underlying Art 10, in particular the argument from democracy,[98] are also an important means of interpreting the provisions of the Act.

Probably the most important value associated with freedom of information is the need for the citizen to understand as fully as possible the working of government, in order to render it accountable. The following discussion therefore places a strong emphasis on the choices that were made as to the release of information relating to public authorities – not only to central government – in the FoI Act.

The Public Records Acts

The UK Public Records Act 1958, as amended by the Public Records Act 1967, provides that public records will not be transferred to the Public Records Office (which is part of the National Archives) in order to be made available for inspection until the expiration of what used to be 30 years. Since 2013, this period has been reducing by a factor of one per year so that by 2022 the standard period will 20 years. Longer periods can be prescribed for 'sensitive information'. Such information will include personal details about persons who are still living and papers affecting the security of the state. Some such information can be withheld for 100 years or for ever, and there is no means of challenging such decisions. For example, at the end of 1987, a great deal of information about the Windscale fire in 1957 was disclosed, although some items are still held back. Robertson argues that information is withheld to prevent embarrassment to bodies such as the police or civil servants rather than to descendants of persons mentioned in it; and in support of this he cites examples such as police reports on the NCCL (1935–41), flogging of vagrants (1919), and decisions against prosecuting James Joyce's *Ulysses* (1924) as instances of material that in January 1989 was listed as closed for a century.[99]

However, a somewhat less restrictive approach to the release of archives became apparent in 1994. In 1992–93, a review was conducted of methods of ensuring further openness in government and its results were published in a white paper entitled *Open Government* (Cm 2290).[100] The white paper, as well as proposing the Code of Practice on Access to Government Information already discussed, promised that there would be a reduction in the number of public records withheld from release beyond the standard period. A review group established by Lord Mackay in 1992 suggested that records

---

98 For discussion of the Court's 'privileging' of political speech, see Part II introduction, pp 287–89.

99 See Robertson, G and Nicol, A *Media Law*, op cit.

100 The White Paper proposals in relation to public records are considered by Birkinshaw, P, 'I only ask for information – the White Paper on open government' [1993] PL 557.

should only be closed for more than the standard period where their disclosure would cause harm to defence, national security, international relations and economic interests of the UK; information supplied in confidence; personal information which would cause substantial distress if disclosed. Under s 3(4) of the 1958 Act, records may still be retained within departments for 'administrative' reasons or for any other special reason.

The FoI, Part VI and Sched 8 amends the 1958 Act. Part VI amends the exemptions of Part II of the 1958 Act in respect of historical records, with a view to enhancing the ease of access to them. Section 63(1) of the FoI Act reduces the number of exemptions that apply to such records. This is done in three tranches. First, exemptions are removed after the standard period in respect of a number of categories of information, including information prejudicial to the economic interests of the UK, information obtained with a view to prosecution, court records, information prejudicial to public affairs and commercial interests. Second, one exemption is removed after 60 years – in respect of information concerning the conferring of honours. Third, a large number of exemptions under s 31 relating to various investigations and the maintenance of law and order are removed after 100 years. These modest provisions are to be welcomed, as easing the task of historians, but their limited nature should be questioned; especially, it must be asked why any absolute exemptions, in particular those relating to intelligence information, remain.[101]

6 The Freedom of Information Act 2000

Introduction

The FoI Act has been in force since 2005 and a body of principles has developed steadily, through decisions and revised guidance from the Commissioner, to provide a fairly detailed picture of how the Act works in practice. It has proven to be an extremely effective tool for investigative journalism. Most notably, persistence by journalists Jon Ungoed-Thomas and Heather Brooke ensured details of MPs expenses were obtained under a freedom of information request.[102] Once it was eventually obtained, this information revealed a pattern of abuse by MPs, leading to prosecutions for false accounting, in some cases, and reform of the expenses system. More recently, a journalist obtained partial disclosure of correspondence between Prince Charles and various government departments.[103] The Supreme Court held that the Attorney General could not exercise his discretion to withhold this information, in its entirety, from public disclosure.[104] This is a momentous decision that illustrates the power of the Act – an Act that was, until recently, relatively alien to the UK. Previously, the UK had nothing more substantial than a code of practice concerning access to government information ('the Code'). As might be expected, the Code was weak as a means of achieving genuine freedom of information; a position illustrated best by the Matrix Churchill affair and subsequent

---

101 *Cf* the provision in respect of intelligence information held in the Public Record Office of Northern Ireland is no longer subject to an absolute exemption due to s 64(2) FoI Act.

102 *Corporate Officer of the House of Commons v The Information Commissioner* [2008] EWHC 1084 (Admin).

103 *R (Evans) v Attorney General (Campaign for Freedom of Information intervening)* [2015] UKSC 21.

104 Lord Wilson and Lord Hughes dissenting.

Scott inquiry,[105] which revealed a distinct lack of 'openness' in government. The Labour government of 1997, which introduced the Act, provided a white paper proposing an FoI regime that would have had a more radical impact[106] than what was implemented.[107]

Fundamentals of FoI and the 2000 Act[108]

Rodney Austin identifies a number of common features of FoI regimes, which, together, indicate in essence how FoI legislation differs from the approach taken by the UK up until the 2000 Act.[109] As indicated above, the historical approach of the UK has been to make no comprehensive statutory provision for disclosure of official information, except under the very limited provisions of the Public Records Act 1958; the starting point instead was the criminalisation of disclosure in certain categories under the Official Secrets Acts and by virtue of numerous other statutory provisions. By contrast, the essence of FoI regimes, identified by Austin, are: the creation of public rights of access to official information; placing the determination and enforcement of those rights in the hands of 'an authority independent of government', whether the courts or an information commissioner; the extension of the basic right to information to cover 'all official information other than that specified to be exempt'.[110] The assumption lying behind FoI legislation is that the release of information is something which is desirable in general terms, the burden lying upon government to justify refusal to release in particular cases.

The Act may be said partially to share the bases of FoI legislation identified above; as will be explained below, it will give UK citizens, for the first time, a statutory right to official information, which extends to all such information except that which the Act defines as exempt. In terms of enforcement, there is a mixed picture: as will also appear below, the right to information given by the Act is enforceable by an independent Information Commissioner (the Information Commissioner's Office), who, in the final resort, can enforce her orders through invoking the courts' power to punish for contempt of court. However, the Commissioner's power to force government to disclose information will not apply to some of the information that may be released under the Act: her disclosure orders can in some cases be quashed by ministerial veto. This continues to be a major concern about the Act. The second is the great number and width of the exemptions it contains and the fact that many of these amount to 'class

105 Birkinshaw, P, 'Freedom of Information' (1997) 50 *Parliamentary Affairs* 166; Tomkins, A, *The Constitution after Scott: Government Unwrapped*, 1998, Clarendon, Chapter 3, at 124–26.

106 See Birkinshaw, P, 'An "All singin' and all dancin'" affair: New Labour's proposals for FoI' (1998) PL 176.

107 See Birkinshaw, P and Parry, N, 'Every trick in the book: the Freedom of Information Bill 1999' (1999) 4 EHRLR 373.

108 It should be noted that environmental information is covered separately by the Environment Information Regulations, which also came into force on 1 January 2005 and which cover 'information about pollution, energy, noise and radiation . . . GMOs, air and water borne disease agents, food contamination, planning, road building and transport schemes'. The basic scheme of the Regulations is that of the 2000 Act, but 'The exemptions are fewer, all are subject to a public interest test and there is no upper cost limit for requests.' See 'Freedom of Information for Journalists' – CFOI website.

109 'Freedom of information: a Sheep in Wolf's Clothing?', in Jowell, J and Oliver, D (eds), *The Changing Constitution*, 5th edn, 2004, p 362.

110 *Ibid.*

exemptions' where, in order to refuse release of the information, it is not necessary to satisfy a 'harm test', that is, show that release of the particular information requested would prejudice a particular interest, but merely that the information falls into a specified class and is, for that reason alone, exempt.

The scope of the Act

The Act covers 'public authorities'. Section 3 sets out the various ways in which a body can be a public authority. Instead of using the method adopted in the HRA, which, similarly, covers only 'public authorities' and which defines them by means of a very broad and general, non-exhaustive definition, the FoI Act takes the different route of listing a number of public authorities in Sched 1. The list is divided into two halves. First, Parts I–V list those bodies that are clearly public authorities; under s 6 of the HRA they would be standard public authorities.[111] Second, Parts VI–VII list those bodies that are only public authorities so long as they continue to meet the conditions set out in s 4(2) and (3) – that they have been set up by government and their members appointed by central government. Such bodies would probably also be viewed as standard public authorities under the HRA. But the list is not exhaustive, since s 4(1) gives the Secretary of State the power to add bodies to the list in Parts VI–VII if they meet the conditions set out in s 4(2) and (3), by order. Further, s 5 provides the Secretary of State with a power to designate a body as a public authority even though it is not listed in Sched 1, and does not meet the conditions set out in s 4(2) and (3), but that appears to him to be exercising public functions. These bodies would probably be viewed as functional public authorities under s 6 of the HRA.[112] One of the first designated bodies using this process was UCAS (in November 2011). In March 2015, Network Rail was added to the list. Under s 3(1)(b), a publicly owned company as defined in s 6 is automatically a public body; no formal designation is needed. Section 6[113] defines such bodies as those wholly owned by the Crown and/or the wider public sector.

Some public authorities are covered only in respect of certain information they hold, in which case the Act only applies to that class of information (s 7(1)). As the House of Lords confirmed in *BBC v Sugar*,[114] this includes hybrid authorities, like the BBC. Such authorities have a mixture of public and other functions. Its FoI obligations are limited to its public functions, i.e. the BBC has no obligation to disclose information relating to journalism, art or literature. Rather disturbingly, under s 7(3), the Secretary of State can amend Sched 1 so that a particular public authority becomes one that is subject only to such limited coverage by the Act – in effect potentially drastically limiting the range of information that can be sought from that authority.

It is suggested that although the FoI follows the model of the HRA in differentiating between public authorities as indicated, and between private and public bodies, Sched 1 read with ss 3–6 does *not* provide an exhaustive list of those bodies that are public authorities for the purposes of s 6 of the HRA, although these provisions provide a

---

111 See Chapter 4 at pp 189–98.
112 As amended by s 103, Protection of Freedoms Act 2012.
113 [2009] UKHL 9.
114 See Chapter 4 at pp 189–98.

useful guide. The security and intelligence services, which are presumably standard public authorities under s 6 of the HRA, are omitted from Sched 1 and therefore they are completely excluded from the Act. They meet the conditions set out in s 4(2) and (3), but are – it is readily apparent – unlikely to be added to Sched 1, Parts VI–VII. The difference of approach between the two statutes is defensible; there may be cogent reasons why a body, such as the security service, should not provide information (although a *complete* exclusion is hard to defend), although it would be expected to observe the Convention rights in its operations.

Thus, the Act covers, in Sched 1, all government departments, the House of Commons, the House of Lords, quangos, the NHS, administrative functions of courts and tribunals, police authorities and chief officers of police, the armed forces, local authorities, local public bodies, schools and other public educational institutions, public service broadcasters. Under s 5, private organisations may be designated as public authorities in so far as they carry out statutory functions, as may the privatised utilities and private bodies working on contracted-out functions. The coverage of the Act is therefore far greater than under the Code and it is notable that some private sector bodies may be covered, although the government made it clear in debate on the bill that a distinction between private and public bodies in terms of their obligations under the FoI Act should be strictly maintained and that s 5 should be used only to designate bodies discharging public functions.[115] The FoI is clearly *not* to be extended into the realm of business. The Act has been praised for the very wide range of bodies which it covers; in comparison with FoI regimes abroad, the coverage is very generous. But it should be noted that in fact, its coverage of private bodies discharging public functions is subject to the exercise of a discretion by the Secretary of State.

The basic rights granted by the Act

The Act begins with an apparently broad and generous statement of the rights it confers. The Act grants two basic rights. Section 1(1) states:

Any person making a request for information to a public authority is entitled –

  (a) to be informed in writing by the public authority whether it holds information of the description specified in the request [this is referred to in the Act as 'the duty to confirm or deny']; and
  (b) if that is the case, to have that information communicated to him.

It may be noted that the right conferred under s 1(1)(b) can cover original documents as well as 'information',[116] and in this respect the Act is clearly an improvement on the code.

Both these fundamental rights are subject to the numerous exemptions that the Act contains. In other words, broadly, where an authority is exempt from providing information

---

115 HC Standing Committee B, 11 January 2000, col 67.
116 Section 84 defines information broadly to cover information 'recorded in any form', and in relation to matters covered by s 51(8) this includes unrecorded information.

under the Act, it is also entitled to refuse even to state whether it holds the information or not, although in some cases it may only do this where stating whether it holds the information would have the effect of causing the prejudice that the exemption in question is designed to prevent. Such cases will be considered below.

Exemptions under the Act

Under the white paper, certain public bodies were to be completely excluded from the Act. One was Parliament, on the ground that, as stated in the white paper, its deliberations are already open and on the public record. The security services, including GCHQ, were also excluded on the ground that they would not be able to carry out their duties effectively if subject to the legislation. Thus, the security services were to be subject to a blanket agency exemption. Apart from these exemptions, there were no exempt categories of information at all held by bodies which are subject to the Act. But seven specified interests were indicated in the white paper, which took the place of the exemptions under the code. The test for disclosure was based on an assessment of the harm that disclosure might cause and the need to safeguard the public interest. The test was: will this disclosure cause *substantial* harm to one of these interests? The first of these interests covered national security, defence and international relations. Obviously, this interest covered a very wide range of information. A further five interests were: law enforcement, personal privacy, commercial confidentiality, the safety of the individual, the public and the environment, and information supplied in confidence. Finally, there was an interest termed 'the integrity of decision-making and policy advice processes in government'. In this category, a different test was used: it was not necessary to show that disclosure of the information would cause substantial harm; a test of simple harm only was used. The reason for placing this information in a special category was, in the words of the white paper: 'now more than ever, government needs space and time in which to assess arguments and conduct its own debates with a degree of privacy . . . [decision making in government] can be damaged by random and premature disclosure of its deliberations under Freedom of Information legislation'. This exemption was possibly the most controversial, since it meant that the full background to a decision could remain undisclosed, tending to restrict debate and challenge to it.

Thus, the exemptions under the white paper were relatively narrow and were subject to quite a strict harm test. They may be sharply contrasted with those that emerged under the Act, which include a number of 'class'-based exemptions. Nevertheless, the exceptions under the Act are, on the whole, less wide ranging than those under the Code, taking into account the limitations of the PCA's remit. In certain respects, however, the Code was, on its face, more generous, as indicated at various points below. In particular, the total exemption under s 21 did not appear in the Code in as broad a form,[117] and the exemption under s 35 is broader than the equivalent exemption was under the Code – in para 2.

The exemptions under the Act rely on the key distinction between 'class-' and 'harm-based' exemptions mentioned above. The harm-based exemptions under the Act are similar to those indicated in the white paper: they require the public authority to show

117 https://ico.org.uk/media/for-organisations/documents/1214/the_prejudice_test.pdf.

that the release of the information requested would, or would be likely to, cause prejudice to the interest specified in the exemption. However, it should be noted that even in
relation to the 'harm-based' exemptions, the test used has been substantially watered
down from that proposed in the white paper. That document, as noted above, had used a
'substantial harm' test; the Act itself refers simply to 'prejudice' – a test that is evidently
easier to satisfy.

The Commissioner's guidance on this test applies the approach taken from the Information Tribunal in *Hogan v Information Commissioner*:[118] the prejudice claimed must
be 'real, actual or of substance' and there must be a 'causal link' between the disclosure
and prejudice claimed. The guidance is clear that 'trivial or insignificant' consequences
are insufficient to amount to a prejudice. They also note, though, that neither is the level
of prejudice required to be 'particularly severe or unavoidable.' They suggest that the
exemption is not necessarily engaged if the prejudice can be mitigated.

A number of exemptions are in any event class-based, meaning that in order to refuse
the request, the authority only has to show that the information falls into the class of
information covered by the exemption, not that its release would cause or be likely
to cause harm or prejudice. It may be noted that the class exemptions can be further
divided into two groups: those that are content-based, in the sense that no access to the
information under the FoI or any other interest is available; and others, that relate not to
the content of the information, but to the process of acquiring it. These distinctions are
made clear below, in the first group of exemptions considered.

The Act complicates matters further by providing that, in relation to some, but not
all, of the class exemptions, and almost all the 'harm exemptions', the authority, having decided that the information is prima facie exempt (either because the information
falls into the requisite class exemption, or because the relevant harm test is satisfied, as
the case may be), must still then go on to consider whether it should be released under
the public interest test set out in s 2. This requires the authority to release the information unless 'in all the circumstances of the case, the public interest in maintaining the
exemption outweighs the public interest in disclosing the information'. It should be
noted that this provision was amended in the Lords so as to require release unless the
interest in maintaining secrecy '*outweighs*' the interest in disclosure. This was thought
to provide greater protection for freedom of information, since it must be demonstrated
that the need for secrecy is the more compelling interest in the particular case.

The strengthening of the public interest test that took place in the Lords led some
Liberal Democrat peers to claim that its application to class exemptions in effect transformed them into 'harm-'based exemptions. However, it should be noted that the Campaign for Freedom of Information (CFOI) emphatically rejected this view, on cogent
grounds. While the application of a public interest test to the class exemptions does provide for the opportunity to balance the interest in disclosure against that in secrecy, the
test is not the same as it would be if considering a harm test. As the CFOI notes, where
information falls into a class exemption, and an authority objects to disclosure even
under the public interest test, it will be able not only to argue that the specific disclosure
would have harmful effects, but also that the public interest would be harmed by any
disclosure from within the relevant class of documents, regardless of the consequences

---

118 Para 8 of the Code refers to information obtainable under existing statutory rights.

of releasing the actual information in question.[119] By contrast, under a prejudice test, the authority must be able first to identify that harm would be caused by releasing the *specific information* requested, and then go on to show that that specific harm outweighs the public interest in disclosure.

In the result, the exemptions under the Act can actually be broken down into four different categories, starting with the most absolute exemptions and moving to the least. It is helpful to consider them in the order suggested by this categorisation, because the Act does not set out the exemptions in any systematic way, but rather randomly, so that class exemptions are mixed in with 'harm-based' exemptions, and 'absolute exemptions' with both. It should be noted that the following categorisation relates to categories of exemptions not necessarily to categories of information, although the two may be synonymous. The four suggested categories are as follows, and are described in order of their illiberality.

(a) 'Total' exemptions: that is class exemptions to which the public interest test in s 2 *does not apply*. Thus, the public authority concerned only has to show that information sought falls into the exempt class, not that its disclosure would cause any harm or prejudice; and, there is no duty to consider whether the public interest in maintaining the exemption outweighs the public interest in disclosing the information.

(b) Class exemptions to which the s 2 public interest test does apply. This is self-explanatory.

(c) Harm-based exemptions to which the s 2 public interest test does not apply. In these exemptions, the authority has to show that the release of the particular information concerned would cause or be likely to cause the relevant prejudice, but then need not go on to consider whether this prejudice outweighs the public interest in disclosure: once prejudice is established, that is the end of the matter.

(d) Harm-based exemptions to which the s 2 public interest test *does* apply. These are the exemptions under which it is hardest for the public authority concerned to resist the release of information. To do so, it must first demonstrate prejudice or likely prejudice from the release of the particular information request and then, even if prejudice is shown, go on to consider whether the public interest in forestalling that prejudice outweighs the public interest in disclosing the information under s 2.

These categories are important, not only in terms of the substantive legal tests that must be satisfied before information may be withheld: they also have crucial practical consequences in terms of time limits and enforcement. As explained below, the 20-day deadline for releasing information does not apply to information released only on public interest grounds. More importantly, the Commissioner's decision to order release on such grounds can, in relation to information held by certain governmental bodies, be vetoed by ministers (a matter discussed further below).

As to what 'the public interest' in the Act means, the Commissioner has again given guidance.[120] This states that 'the public interest can cover a wide range of values and principles relating to the public good, or what is in the best interests of society'. It

---

119   https://ico.org.uk/media/for-organisations/documents/1183/the_public_interest_test.pdf.
120   *Ibid*, [9].

further states that, when applying the public interest test to a request for disclosure, 'the public authority must decide whether the public interest is better served by maintaining the exemption' or by disclosure. It expands on this rather bald statement to say:

> Thus, for example, there is a public interest in transparency and accountability, to promote public understanding and to safeguard democratic processes. There is a public interest in good decision-making by public bodies, in upholding standards of integrity, in ensuring justice and fair treatment for all, in securing the best use of public resources and in ensuring fair commercial competition in a mixed economy.[121]

Further, it is also noted that:

> However, these examples of the public interest do not in themselves automatically mean that information should be disclosed or withheld. For example, an informed and involved public helps to promote good decision making by public bodies, but those bodies may also need space and time in which to fully consider their policy options, to enable them to reach an impartial and appropriate decision, away from public interference. Revealing information about wrongdoing may help the course of justice, but investigations into wrongdoing may need confidentiality to be effective. This suggests that in each case, the public interest test involves identifying the appropriate public interests and assessing the extent to which they are served by disclosure or by maintaining an exemption . . . The public interest is not necessarily the same as what interests the public. The fact that a topic is discussed in the media does not automatically mean that there is a public interest in disclosing the information that has been requested about it.

This should be self-evident, but it is worth stating. Reassuringly, the Commissioner recognises that 'there will always be a general public interest in transparency'.[122] The Guidance goes on to enumerate, non-exhaustively some of the specific public-interest arguments in favour of disclosure generally:

- furthering the understanding of and participation in the public debate of issues of the day. This factor would come into play if disclosure would allow a more informed debate of issues under consideration by the government or a local authority;
- promoting accountability and transparency by public authorities for decisions taken by them. Placing an obligation on authorities and officials to provide reasoned explanations for decisions made will improve the quality of decisions and administration;
- promoting accountability and transparency in the spending of public money. The public interest is likely to be served, for instance in the context of private sector delivery of public services, if the disclosure of information ensures greater competition and better value for money that is public. Disclosure of information as to gifts

---

121 *Ibid.*
122 Freedom of Information Bill, House of Lords Third Reading, 21 November 2000 briefing notes, p 10.

and expenses may also assure the public of the personal probity of elected leaders and officials;

*   allowing individuals and companies to understand decisions made by public authorities affecting their lives and, in some cases, assisting individuals in challenging those decisions;
*   bringing to light information affecting public health and public safety. The prompt disclosure of information by scientific and other experts may contribute not only to the prevention of accidents or outbreaks of disease but may also increase public confidence in official scientific advice.[123]

This is an encouraging statement of general principles. In particular, bearing in mind the sweeping exemptions relating to health and safety matters that might lead to an investigation, the last point made above is of great interest, as is the general weight placed upon the desirability of transparent decision-making and accountability.

We now turn to enumerating and commenting upon the numerous exemptions the Act contains, classifying them in accordance with the scheme outlined above.

Class exemptions not subject to the public interest test

First, there are the total exemptions – class exemptions that are not subject to the public interest test. Most of these exemptions are fairly self-explanatory; therefore, explanation is given where necessary. Section 21 covers information that is reasonably accessible to the applicant from other sources. It should be noted that this exemption applies even if the applicant would have to pay a higher fee than that provided by the Act to obtain the information (s 21(2)(a)) so long as the information can still be viewed as reasonably accessible. If the fee is excessive, this may no longer be the case. But, in order to be reasonably accessible, the information must be provided *as of right*. The duty to confirm or deny *does* apply, so an applicant would at least have to be told whether the authority to which he applied was holding the information. This is not an exemption in the usual sense of the word – as applied to freedom of information schemes – since it is not content-based and does not deprive the applicant of access to the information in general; it merely prevents her from obtaining it under the Act itself.

Section 23(1) covers information supplied by or which relates to the intelligence and security services, GCHQ, the special forces and the various tribunals to which complaints may be made about their activities and about phone tapping. It should be noted that, as indicated above, the bodies mentioned in this exemption are not themselves covered by the Act at all. This exemption therefore applies to information which is held by *another public authority*, but which has been supplied by one of these bodies. Since it is a class exemption, it could apply to information that had no conceivable security implications, such as evidence of a massive overspend on MI5 or MI6's headquarters. The duty to confirm or deny does not apply to information in this category where complying with it would itself involve disclosure of information covered by this exemption. Bearing in mind the complete exclusion of the security and intelligence services from the Act, the use of this exemption unaccompanied by a harm test, and not subject to the

---

123   Section 44.

public interest test, is likely to mean that sensitive matters of great political significance remain undisclosed, even if their disclosure would ultimately benefit those services or national security.

Section 32 covers information *which is only held* by virtue of being contained in a document or record served on a public authority in proceedings or made by a court or tribunal or party in any proceedings or contained in a document lodged with or created by a person conducting an inquiry or arbitration, for the purposes of the inquiry or arbitration. The duty to confirm or deny does not apply. Section 34 covers information where exemption from s 1(1)(b) is required for the purpose of avoiding an infringement of the privileges of either House of Parliament. The duty to confirm or deny does not apply to information in this category where compliance with it would entail a breach of parliamentary privilege.

The exemption under s 40(1) is a complex one, but essentially it covers two classes of data. The first is information which the inquirer would be able to obtain under the Data Protection Act (DPA) 1998 because it is personal information which relates to himself; the second covers personal information which relates to *others*, the disclosure of which would contravene one or more of the data protection principles or the right under the Act to prevent processing likely to cause damage or distress. The first part of this exemption is designed to ensure that the FoI Act does not give rights that overlap with those granted by the DPA; the second, to ensure that the FoI Act does not give rights that contravene the DPA.

There are a number of further total exemptions. Vexatious requests (s 14) and unduly costly requests (those where compliance would cost more than a reasonable amount, to be specified (s 12)), are exempt, but the duty to confirm or deny applies. Information the disclosure of which would contravene any other Act of Parliament (for example, the Official Secrets Act 1989), or would be incompatible with any EU obligation, or constitute a contempt of court, is exempt[124] and the duty to confirm or deny does not apply to the extent that compliance with it would itself amount to a contravention of any of these provisions. This exemption ensures that the FoI Act cannot be seen impliedly to repeal the numerous provisions that criminalise the release of information, but rather preserves them all.

Information the disclosure of which would be an actionable breach of confidence (s 41) is exempt and the duty to confirm or deny does not apply if compliance with it would itself amount to a breach of confidence. This exemption requires some comment. While it is expressed as an absolute exemption, with no need to show that prejudice would be caused by release of the information, and no requirement to consider the public interest in disclosure, in fact the doctrine of confidence may contain the first of these requirements (that is, a need to show detriment – there are conflicting *dicta* on the matter)[125] and certainly contains the second – a need to consider any countervailing public interest in disclosure. This is clearly recognised by the relevant guidance.[126] The CFOI expressed concern at the time of the passage of the Act that while there is clearly some need to protect genuine confidences, governments could seek to protect all information supplied

---

124 See Chapter 10, p 720.
125 *Ibid.*
126 https://ico.org.uk/media/for-organisations/documents/1193/confidentialinformation_v4.pdf.

by third parties simply by agreeing with the third party at the time of the communication of the information that it would be treated in confidence. The information would then become confidential, provided that it was not already in the public domain, and subject to the public interest test and, possibly, to the need to show detriment. This potential problem – of 'contracting out' of the obligations under the Act – is recognised by the Commissioner. The guidance warns public authorities that they should 'carefully consider' the compatibility of confidentiality clauses, agreed with non-public authority contractors, with the demands of the Act.[127] Both public authority and contractor should be under no illusions that such clauses are automatically exempt from disclosure. Moreover, in *Bluck v Information Commissioner*, the Tribunal explicitly recognised the promotion of freedom of expression under Art 10 ECHR as a sufficient reason to override confidentiality.[128]

Class exemptions subject to the public interest test

The second category covers class exemptions subject to the public interest test. It will be recalled in relation to these exemptions that, in practice, while the Commissioner will always have the last word on whether the information falls into the class in question, he or she will not always be able to enforce a finding that it should nevertheless be released on public interest grounds if the information is held by certain governmental bodies, since the ministerial veto may be used.

It is most convenient to quote the Act itself for the first of these exemptions. Under s 30(1):

> Information held by a public authority is exempt information if it has at any time been held by the authority for the purposes of –
>
>   (a) any investigation which the public authority has a duty to conduct with a view to it being ascertained –
>
>   (i) whether a person should be charged with an offence, or
>   (ii) whether a person charged with an offence is guilty of it,
>
>   (b) any investigation which is conducted by the authority and in the circumstances may lead to a decision by the authority to institute criminal proceedings which the authority has power to conduct, or
>   (c) any criminal proceedings which the authority has power to conduct.

This exemption, together with that contained in s 35, is one of the most widely criticised provisions in the Act. It is a sweeping exemption, covering all information, whenever obtained, which relates to investigations that may lead to criminal proceedings. It represents a specific rejection of the recommendation of the MacPherson Report[129] that there should be no class exemption for information relating to police investigations. It

---

127 https://ico.org.uk/media/for-organisations/documents/1183/the_public_interest_test.pdf.
128 *Ibid*, 21.
129 The *MacPherson Report on the Stephen Lawrence Inquiry*, Cm 4262, 1999, proposed that all such matters should be covered by the FoI Act, subject only to a substantial harm test.

overlaps with the law enforcement of s 31, which does include a harm test. The exclusion of police operational matters and decisions echoes the approach under s 4 of the Official Secrets Act, but unlike s 4, no harm test is included. There are certain aspects of information relating to investigations, which would appear to require disclosure in order to be in accord with the principle of openness enshrined in the Act. For example, a citizen might suspect that his or her telephone had been tapped without authorisation or that he or she had been unlawfully placed under surveillance by other means. Under the Act, no satisfactory method of discovering information relating to such a possibility will exist. It is therefore unfortunate that telephone tapping and electronic surveillance were not subjected to a 'substantial harm' or even a 'simple harm test'.

This exemption extends beyond protecting the police and the CPS. Other bodies will also be protected: it will cover all information obtained by safety agencies investigating accidents. Thus, it will cover bodies such as the Health and Safety Executive, the Railway Inspectorate, Nuclear Installations Inspectorate, Civil Aviation Authority, Marine and Coastguard Agency, environmental health officers, trading standards officers and the Drinking Water Inspectorate. It will cover routine inspections as well as specific investigations, since both can lead to criminal prosecution. Thus, anything from an inspection of a section of railway track by the Railway Inspectorate, to a check upon hygiene in a restaurant by the Health and Safety Executive could be covered. The duty to confirm or deny does not apply (s 30(3)). As the CFOI commented:

> Reports into accidents involving dangerous cars, train crashes, unsafe domestic appliances, air disasters, chemical fires or nuclear incidents will go into a permanently secret filing cabinet. The same goes for reports into risks faced by workers or the public from industrial hazards. The results of safety inspections of the railways, nuclear plants and dangerous factories would be permanently exempt. This is the information that most people assume FoI legislation exists to provide.[130]

It is particularly hard to understand the need for such a sweeping class exemption when s 31 specifically exempts information which could prejudice the prevention or detection of crime, or legal proceedings brought by a public authority arising from various forms of investigation. That exemption will ensure that no information is released which could damage law enforcement and crime detection, while we have noted above that information that could amount to a contempt of court is also exempted. The CFOI noted the views of a former director general of the Health and Safety Executive, who had publicly denied the HSE required such sweeping protection.[131] It should be noted that, where it has been decided that the information falls into the protected class, the authority must then go on to consider whether it should be released under the public interest test. Since most of the information above will not be held by a government department (see below), the Commissioner will be able to order disclosure if he or she thinks the information should be released under this provision, with no possibility of

---

130 Freedom of Information Bill, House of Lords Committee Stage, 19 October 2000, briefing, notes. Under the Act as passed, information under this exemption would not go into a *permanently* sealed filing cabinet': after 20 years it would become a historical record; the s 30 exemption would no longer apply.

131 *Ibid.*

a ministerial veto. The Commissioner's own views on this exemption are therefore of particular importance.[132] One point the Commissioner makes in the relevant published guidance relates to timing and is of considerable importance: 'As a general rule there will always be a strong public interest in maintaining the section 30 exemption whilst an investigation is ongoing' and, similarly:

> Where a criminal offence is unsolved there is always the possibility that the investigation could be reopened . . . Where there is a real possibility that a case could be reopened there will still be a public interest in not prejudicing any future investigations into the matter. Therefore, the age of the information is relevant, though not critical, to the application of the public interest test.[133]

The picture changes once the case is concluded:

> Once a case has been closed because there is no evidence that an offence has been committed, there is no longer any realistic prospect of solving the case, or any proceedings have concluded, the public interest in maintaining the exemption may wane. However, this will depend on the actual information in question. Revealing the identity of confidential sources, even in relation to investigations from many years ago, could still deter people from providing information in the future.[134]

Assuming it is applied thoroughly, this approach lays to rest some of the more negative views as to the effect of this exemption, such as those of the CFOI, quoted above. The exemption can be seen as one designed to provide time-limited protection for sensitive on-going investigations, rather than the very sweeping one that it first appears to be. This is particularly reassuring for the purposes of revisiting a potentially unjustified conviction, as the tribunal recognised in *Guardian Newspapers Ltd v Information Commissioner*.[135]

This can also be seen in an early decision by the Commissioner, made under s 31 rather than s 30 (but, since the two categories cover such similar ground, it is relevant). The facts are scarcely dramatic:[136] an individual requested from Bridgend County Borough Council 'A copy of the last hygiene inspection report of the Heronston Hotel'; the council refused the request,[137] arguing that to reveal it would prejudice the exercise of its function of 'ascertaining whether circumstances which would justify regulatory action in pursuance of any enactment exist or may arise'.[138] The enactment in question was the Food Safety Act 1990. The council's argument was that:

> the release of inspection reports would undermine the way it carries out food hygiene inspections. It promotes an informal approach to the inspection of premises, where

132 See generally Freedom of Information Act Awareness Guidance No 16.
133 https://ico.org.uk/for-organisations/guide-to-data-protection/exemptions/.
134 https://ico.org.uk/media/for-organisations/documents/1205/investigations-and-proceedings-foi-section-30.pdf.
135 *Guardian Newspapers Ltd v Information Commissioner* (EA/2006/0011 & 0013, 8 January 2007).
136 Decision Notice dated 9 December 2005; ref: FS50073296.
137 Citing s 31(1)(g).
138 A function listed in s 31(2)(c).

advice and practical assistance is given to businesses . . . If information was publicly available, businesses would no longer be willing to have open discussions with inspectors. The Council would then be forced to adopt a formal inspection regime without the ability to protect the public by what it believes to be more effective means. This, it argues, would be prejudicial to the purpose at section 31(2)(c) of the Act.

The Commissioner rejected the Council's view. Significantly, this was done without reliance on the public interest test: it was decided that the exemption itself was not fulfilled. This was because the Commissioner took the view that 'that the release of this information would bring greater clarity to, and reinforce public confidence in, the inspection system'.[139] It was also found that whilst release of the information might, as the Council argued, prejudice its informal inspections system, it would not affect the specific duties the Council had under the Food Safety Act, because it would still be obliged to carry out inspections and, if necessary, 'pursue formal regulatory action'. These points indicate a robust upholding of transparency as a good in itself and a sceptical attitude to the arguments of public authorities against it. More strikingly still, whilst the Commissioner did not formally have to consider the argument based on the public interest, since the exemption was not found to apply, it was noted 'that there is an overwhelming public interest in the disclosure of this category of information'. This is a significant statement, and indicates that robust policing by the Commissioner, who will not in this area be subject to the Ministerial veto, may lay to rest some of the fears generated by s 30, as to the transmission of information to the public about issues affecting health and safety.

The other major class exemption in this category, under s 35, has been just as criticised. It amounts to a sweeping exemption for virtually all information relating to the formation of government policy. Under s 35(1):

Information held by a government department or by the National Assembly for Wales is exempt information if it relates to –

(a) the formulation or development of government policy,
(b) Ministerial communications,
(c) the provision of advice by any of the Law Officers or any request for the provision of such advice, or
(d) the operation of any Ministerial private office.

The duty to confirm or deny does not apply.

This exemption is presumably intended to prevent government from having to decide policy in a goldfish bowl – to protect the freeness and frankness of civil service advice and of internal debate within government – but, once again, it appears to go far beyond what would sensibly be required to achieve this aim. Section 36 contains a harm-based exemption that covers almost exactly the same ground: it exempts government

139 Statement of Reasons, *op cit.*

information that would, or would be likely to, inhibit (a) the free and frank provision of advice, or (b) the free and frank exchange of views for the purposes of deliberation, or (c) would otherwise prejudice, or would be likely otherwise to prejudice, the effective conduct of public affairs. Since this covers all information whose release might cause damage to the working of government – and is framed in very broad terms – it appears to be unnecessary to have a sweeping class exemption covering the same ground. Moreover, this exemption is not restricted to civil service advice; it covers also the background information used in preparing policy, including the underlying facts and their analysis. As the CFOI commented:

> There would be no right to know about purely descriptive reports of existing practice, research reports, evidence on health hazards, assumptions about wage or inflation levels used in calculating costs, studies of overseas practice, consultants' findings or supporting data showing whether official assertions are realistic or not.[140]

The sole, and very limited exception to this exemption appears in s 35(2); it applies only 'once a decision as to government policy has been taken', and covers 'any statistical information used to provide an informed background to the taking of the decision'. This was a concession made by the government fairly late in the Bill's passage through Parliament and it is very limited. First, unlike most other FoI regimes, by excluding only statistical information from the exemption, it allows the *analysis* of facts to be withheld. Second, it only applies once a decision has been taken. Thus, where the government gave consideration to introducing a new policy but then shelved the matter without a decision, statistics used during the consideration process would, bizarrely, remain exempt. However, the tribunal's interpretation of the Act allows for a broad reading of the phrase 'statistical information'. In *DWP v Information Commissioner*,[141] it was decided that the term extended beyond purely factual information in a numerical format to include any further mathematical or scientific analysis of those figures. It did not, however, extend to any other form of analysis or discussion of it. The Commissioner guidance on this is clear that to qualify as 'statistical' the information must be 'derived from some recorded or repeatable methodology and qualified by some explicit or implicit measures of quality, integrity and relevance'.[142]

The Act is much more restrictive in this respect than the previous voluntary Code of Practice on Access to Government Information. The latter required both facts and the analysis of facts underlying policy decisions, including scientific analysis and expert appraisal, to be made available, once decisions were announced. Material relating to policy formation could only be withheld under a harm test – if disclosure would 'harm the frankness and candour of internal discussion'. The white paper preceding the bill proposed that there should be no class exemption for material in this area, but rather that, as under the code, a harm test would have to be satisfied to prevent disclosure.

---

140 https://ico.org.uk/media/for-organisations/documents/1200/government-policy-foi-section-35-guid ance.pdf.
141 EA/2006/0040, 5 March 2007.
142 https://ico.org.uk/media/for-organisations/documents/1200/government-policy-foi-section-35-guid ance.pdf, 40.

However, the exemptions, although class-based, are subject to the public interest test. Information can only be withheld if the public interest in doing so outweighs the public interest in disclosure. The Commissioner's view is that public interest arguments against must focus on the 'potential damage to policymaking from the content of the specific information and timing of the request'.[143]

It will be immediately seen that this approach means that the Commissioner is in effect requiring prejudice to be shown. This requirement at least ameliorates some of the negative effects of the s 35 exemption. The Commissioner has issued guidance on common public interest arguments and how they measure in the balancing test. Those likely to carry 'significant weight' are where the principle of collective ministerial responsibility would be undermined or, of a similar nature, that the government's 'safe space' in which to make decisions would be threatened. This argument relates to internal discussions and captures the idea that governments need room to 'develop ideas, debate live issues, and reach decisions away from external interference and distraction'.[144] This reasoning was accepted by the tribunal in *Department for Business, Enterprise and Regulatory Reform v Information Commissioner*.[145] It has also been accepted that a related argument, that disclosure may have a 'chilling effect' on future discussions, also carries some weight in most claims,[146] although will not 'automatically carry significant weight'. The Commissioner is more sceptical about the view that disclosure will cause less information to be officially recorded in future. His firm view is that this cannot carry much weight because 'departments are expected to keep adequate records for their own purposes'. This view is also shared by the tribunal.[147] Similarly, the claim that civil servants (individually or collectively) would be affected in their work by disclosure is also likely to carry minimal weight. The Commissioner's view is that 'officials should not be easily deterred from doing their job'.[148]

As for the public interest in disclosure, the Commissioner's guidance repeats its general position on the public interest test: 'there will always be some public interest in disclosure of this type of information to promote government transparency and accountability, to increase public awareness, and to enable public participation in the democratic process'.[149] Furthermore, it adds that 'even if the information would not in fact add much to public understanding, disclosing the full picture will always carry some weight as it will remove any suspicion of "spin"'.[150] Even more positively, it reminds public authorities they 'should also consider whether disclosure could actually encourage better quality advice and more robust, well considered and defendable decision making in future'.[151]

Two things are noteworthy about this guidance: first, the whole thrust shows the *effect* of release is most significant: as mentioned, this comes very close to re-working

---

143 *Ibid.*
144 *Ibid.*
145 EA/2007/0072, 29 April 2008.
146 *Friends of the Earth v Information Commissioner* [2008] EWHC 638, [38].
147 *Guardian Newspapers Ltd v Information Commissioner* (EA/2006/0011 & 0013, 8 January 2007).
148 https://ico.org.uk/media/for-organisations/documents/1200/government-policy-foi-section-35-guidance.pdf.
149 *Ibid.*
150 *Ibid.*
151 *Ibid.*

the exemption into one based on harm or prejudice. Second, the guidance adverts to reasons why disclosure may actually *improve* the quality of advice and of policy deliberation. This runs directly against the notion of a class-based exemption, which of course is a legislative *presumption* that release will be harmful: by instructing public authorities, and being prepared itself to consider reasons why release may in fact be beneficial, this presumptive quality of the exemption is radically undermined.

The guidance on the application of the public interest test to this exemption is also positive. It emphasises two distinct interests in disclosure in this area – participation and accountability. These are powerful statements of principle in favour of disclosure. In terms of accountability, the guidance specifically recognises the role of FoI legislation in counterbalancing government control over the release of information by 'spin doctors', seeking to put the most favourable gloss upon it: release of information under the Act would, it asserts. It also sets out further situations in which there will generally be a strong public interest in disclosure:

> For example, these could include transparency in relation to the influence of lobbyists, accountability for spending a large amount of public money, the fact that a proposal has a significant impact on the public, a reasonable suspicion of wrongdoing or flaws in the decision making process, or a potential conflict of interest.[152]

It should however be recalled that, because, by definition, it will generally be information held by a government department, if the Commissioner orders disclosure on public interest grounds, the ministerial veto allows the decision to be overridden (see below).

Information intended for future publication where it is reasonable that it should be withheld until that future date is exempt (s 22), and the duty to confirm or deny does not apply to the extent that complying with it would itself entail disclosing such information. The problem with the class exemption under s 22 is its imprecision: it does not specify a period within which the information has to be intended for publication for this exemption to apply. The government repeatedly rejected amendments that would have provided that this exemption could only be relied upon if a date for publication within a short, specified period had already been fixed.

There are a number of further class exemptions. Information subject to legal privilege (s 42) is exempt. The duty to confirm or deny does not apply if compliance with it would itself breach legal privilege. Trade secrets (s 43(1)) are exempt, but the duty does apply. 'Communications with Her Majesty, with other members of the Royal Family or with the Royal Household' are exempt, as is information relating to 'the conferring by the Crown of any honour or dignity' (s 37), and the duty to confirm or deny does not apply. It is unclear why it is necessary to bestow a class exemption relating to the royal household and honours and dignities, although this follows the practice under the previous voluntary code. A separate class exemption covers information obtained for the purposes of conducting criminal proceedings and a very wide variety of investigations (specified in s 31(2)) carried out under statute or the prerogative, and which relate to the obtaining of information from confidential sources.

---

152 https://ico.org.uk/media/for-organisations/documents/1200/government-policy-foi-section-35-guidance.pdf.

Harm-based exemptions not subject to the public interest test

This third category of exemptions has only one member. There is a general, harm-based exemption under s 36 for information the disclosure of which would be likely to prejudice the effective conduct of public affairs or inhibit free and frank discussion and advice. This exemption is subject to the general public interest test with one exception: for a reason that is not readily apparent; where the information in question is held by the Commons or Lords, the public interest test cannot be considered.

Harm-based exemptions that are subject to the public interest test

As harm-based exemptions, these are in one respect the least controversial aspect of the Act. But it should be noted that the Act departed from one of the most liberal and widely praised aspects of the white paper, namely, the requirement that, in order to make out such exemptions, the authority concerned would have to demonstrate 'substantial' harm. This has been changed to a test of simple prejudice, although government spokespersons attempted to deny that the change would make any difference in practice. In each case, the duty to confirm or deny does not apply if, or to the extent that, compliance with it would itself cause the prejudice that the exemption seeks to prevent.

These exemptions cover information the disclosure of which would prejudice or would be likely to prejudice: defence and the armed forces (s 26); international relations (s 27); the economy (s 29); the mental or physical health or safety of any individual (s 38); auditing functions of other public authorities (s 33); the prevention, detection of crime, legal proceedings brought by a public authority arising from an investigation conducted for any of the purposes specified in s 31(2) (above) and carried out under statute or prerogative; collection of tax; immigration controls; good order in prisons; the exercise by any public authority of its functions for any of the purposes specified in s 31(2) (above); relations between administrations in the UK (for example, between the government and the Scottish Executive) (s 28). These exemptions are relatively straightforward, although they go beyond the information covered by the Official Secrets Act.

A number of these exemptions are more contentious. Section 24 covers information the disclosure of which would prejudice or would be likely to prejudice national security. The use of the national security exemption, albeit accompanied by the harm test, may mean that sensitive matters of great political significance remain undisclosed. In particular, the breadth and uncertainty of the term 'national security' may allow matters which fall only doubtfully within it to remain secret. Had the Act been in place at the time of the change in policy regarding arms sales to Iraq, the subject of the Scott Report, it is likely that information relating to it would not have been disclosed since it could have fallen within the exception clauses. The whole subject of arms sales will probably fall within the national security exception and possibly within other exceptions as well.[153]

---

153 Freedom of Information Bill, House of Lords Committee Stage, 19 October 2000 briefing notes, p 1.

Under s 43, information the disclosure of which would prejudice or would be likely to prejudice the commercial interests of any person (including the public authority holding it) is exempt. The CFOI commented that under this exemption, the prejudice referred to could be caused by consumers refusing to buy a dangerous product. Thus they noted that the fact that a company had sold dangerous products, or behaved in some other improper manner, could be suppressed if disclosure would lead customers to buy alternative products or shareholders to sell their shares.[154] This is clearly correct; however, in the case of unsafe products, the public interest test would surely require disclosure. The Commissioner has indeed said specifically that:

> There would be strong public interest arguments in allowing access to information which would help protect the public from unsafe products or unscrupulous practices even though this might involve revealing a trade secret or other information whose disclosure might harm the commercial interests of a company.[155]

Section 36 covers information which, in the reasonable opinion of a qualified person, would prejudice or be likely to prejudice collective Ministerial responsibility, or which would be likely to inhibit the free and frank provision of advice, or the free and frank exchange of views for the purposes of deliberation, or would otherwise prejudice, or would be likely otherwise to prejudice, the effective conduct of public affairs. Two main criticisms of this exemption can be made. First, the test is not a wholly objective one, but is dependent upon 'the reasonable opinion of a qualified person'. The intention behind this provision is apparently to allow a person representing the department or body in question to make the primary determination of prejudice, with the Commissioner only being able to take issue with such a finding if it is irrational in the *Wednesbury* sense. The second main objection to this section is the 'catch-all' provision covering information the release of which could 'prejudice the effective conduct of public affairs', a phrase that is so vague and broad that it could mean almost anything.

Expiry of certain exemptions

As indicated above, the Act, through amendments to the Public Records Act, provides that some of the exemptions will cease to apply after a certain number of years, although these limitations are hardly generous. The following exemptions will cease to apply at all after the standard period (which will be 20 years from 2022, see above) (s 63(1)): s 28 (inter-UK relations); s 30(1) (information obtained during an investigation); s 32 (documents generated in litigation); s 33 (audit functions); s 35 (information relating to internal government discussion and advice); s 36 (information which could prejudice effective conduct of public affairs); s 37(1)(a) (communications with royal household); s 42 (legal professional privilege) and s 43 (trade secrets and information which could

---

154 See further the Minutes of Evidence before the Public Service Committee HC 313–1 of 1995–96 QQ 66 *et seq.*
155 https://ico.org.uk/media/for-organisations/documents/1178/awareness_guidance_5_v3_07_03_08.pdf, 8.

damage commercial interests). The exemptions under s 21 (information accessible by other means) and s 22 (information intended for future publication) will cease to apply after the standard period where the relevant document is held in a public record office (s 64(1)). Still less generously, information relating to the bestowing of honours and dignities (s 37(1)(b)) only ceases to be exempt after 60 years, while we will have to wait 100 years before the expiry of the exemption for information falling within s 31, that is information that might prejudice law enforcement, the administration of justice, etc.

Additionally, one of the absolute exemptions – information provided by the security, intelligence, etc services (s 23(1)) – *will cease to be absolute* after the standard period, i.e. disclosure must be considered once the standard period has expired.

Applying for information and time limits

Requests for information must be in writing (s 8) and, under s 9, a small fee may be charged. Information requested must generally be supplied within 20 days of the request (s 10(1)). However, there is an important exception to this: where an authority finds that information is prima facie exempt, either because it falls within a class exemption, or the requisite prejudice is thought to be present, but then goes on to consider whether the information should nevertheless be released under the public interest test, it does not have to make a decision within the normal 20-day deadline. Instead, it must release the information only within an unspecified 'reasonable period'.

Clearly, there are practical problems in using the Act. The citizen may have difficulty in obtaining the document he or she requires. He or she may not be able to frame the request for information specifically enough in order to obtain the particular documents needed. The request may be met with the response that several hundred documents are available touching on the matter in question; the citizen may lack the expert knowledge needed to identify the particular document required. If so, under s 1(3), the authority arguably need not comply with the request and can continue to postpone its compliance until and if the requester succeeds in formulating the request more specifically. Section 1(3) does not allow the authority to postpone the request until it has had a chance to obtain further information, enabling it to deal with the request. However, the duty to provide advice and assistance so far as reasonable, provided for in s 16 of the Act,[156] would apply to an instance in which the authority was itself able to identify the requisite documents and did not genuinely require further information to do so. It would then come under a duty to assist the applicant in choosing the relevant documents. The code of practice published by the Department for Constitutional Affairs[157] deals with the s 16 duty. In relation to the instant point, it states:

> 8   Authorities should, as far as reasonably practicable, provide assistance to the applicant to enable him or her to describe more clearly the information requested.

156 (1) It shall be the duty of a public authority to provide advice and assistance, so far as it would be reasonable to expect the authority to do so, to persons who propose to make, or have made, requests for
information to it.
157 Under s 45 of the Act. The Code is available at www.justice.gov.uk/downloads/information-access-
rights/foi/foi-section45-code-of-practice.pdf.

10   Appropriate assistance in this instance might include:

- providing an outline of the different kinds of information which might meet the terms of the request;
- providing access to detailed catalogues and indexes, where these are available, to help the applicant ascertain the nature and extent of the information held by the authority;
- providing a general response to the request setting out options for further information which could be provided on request.[158]

This is a helpful clarification that authorities cannot rely upon the applicant's ignorance as to the documents available, without seeking to provide a reasonable level of assistance in identifying the relevant documents. A 2011 memorandum from the Ministry of Justice to the Justice Select Committee reported positively on the timeliness of FoI responses. It found that 86% of central government and 88% of local government responses were within the 20-day period, or a permitted extension.[159] It noted that performances had improved as knowledge of the Act increased, but found that in complex cases meeting the deadline was usually challenging. The picture was bleaker, though, where the public interest test had to be applied. Since the Act says no more than that a 'reasonable' amount of time should be taken, the provision is hard to regulate. Nevertheless, it noted that in 2010 375 requests involving the public interest test took between 40 and 100 working days to resolve, with 4% lasting more than 100 working days. This, they noted, was an area of concern, although they provided no solution to the problem.[160]

The enforcement mechanism

The basic mechanism

The enforcement review mechanism under the Act is far stronger than the mechanism established under the Code. The internal review of a decision to withhold information, established under the Code, was formalised under the Act and the role of the Ombudsman was taken over by that of the Information Commissioner. The Commissioner's powers are also much more extensive than those of the Ombudsman. As indicated below, she has the power to order disclosure of the information and can report a failure to disclose information to the courts who can treat it in the same way as contempt of court. Under the white paper, it was to be a criminal offence to destroy, alter or withhold records relevant to an investigation of the Information Commissioner. It was also to become a criminal offence to shred documents requested by outsiders, including the media and the public. However, the two offences are omitted from the Act. No civil liability is incurred if a public authority does not comply with any duty imposed by the Act (s 56).

The rights granted under the Act are enforceable by the Commissioner. Importantly, he has security of tenure, being dismissible only by the Crown following an address by both Houses of Parliament. An appeal lies from decisions of the Commissioner to the

158 *Ibid.*
159 https://www.gov.uk/government/uploads/system/uploads/attachment_data/file/217339/post-legislative-assessment-of-the-foi-act.pdf.
160 *Ibid*, [135]–[142].

Information Tribunal, which is made up of experienced lawyers and 'persons to represent the interests' of those seeking information and of public authorities (Sched 2, Part II).

Under s 50: 'Any person (in this section referred to as "the complainant") may apply to the Commissioner for a decision whether, in any specified respect, a request for information made by the complainant to a public authority has been dealt with in accordance with [the Act].' The Commissioner must then make a decision unless the application has been made with 'undue delay', is frivolous or vexatious or the complainant has not exhausted any complaints procedure provided by the public authority (s 50(1)). If the Commissioner decides that the authority concerned has failed to communicate information or confirm or deny when required to do so by the Act, he must serve a 'decision notice' on the authority stating what it must do to satisfy the Act. He may also serve 'information notices' upon authorities, requiring the authority concerned to provide him with information about a particular application or its compliance with the Act generally.

The Commissioner may ultimately force a recalcitrant authority to act by serving upon it an enforcement notice, which (s 52(1)) 'requir[es] the authority to take, within such time as may be specified in the notice, such steps as may be so specified for complying with those requirements'. If a public authority fails to comply with a decision, enforcement or information notice, the Commissioner can certify the failure in writing to the High Court, which, the Act provides (s 52(2)):

> may inquire into the matter and, after hearing any witness who may be produced against or on behalf of the public authority, and after hearing any statement that may be offered in defence, deal with the authority as if it had committed a contempt of court.

In other words, the Commissioner's decisions can, in the final analysis, be enforced just as can orders of the court. These powers are buttressed by powers of entry, search and seizure to gain evidence of a failure by the authority to carry out its obligations under the Act, or comply with a notice issued by the Commissioner (detailed in Sched 3).

The MOJ reported in 2011 that between 23 and 35 information notices had been issued per year since 2007 and enforcement notices rarely issued at all.[161] Of concern, though, is the time taken for the Commissioner to process complaints. In November 2005, this was a serious issue. After only 11 months of being operational, there was a backlog of over 1,300 cases, with some being unallocated to an investigating officer for a period exceeding six months. Although this situation has improved, it has not been removed entirely. The MOJ reported that the proportion of cases aged 90 days or more was at 36% in 2010.[162] This delay is of particular concern to the media, given that news stories usually have a temporary shelf life. Where a response is made to a public authority for documents that would reveal some embarrassing failure or scandal, and media interest in the matter is temporarily intense, the authority may well be tempted just to refuse the request, in the knowledge that even if the Commissioner will almost certainly overturn its decision, by the time that is done, media interest in the story will have died down, and the interest generated by the eventual release of the documents will be minimal.

161 https://www.gov.uk/government/uploads/system/uploads/attachment_data/file/217339/post-legislative-assessment-of-the-foi-act.pdf, [150].
162 https://www.gov.uk/government/uploads/system/uploads/attachment_data/file/217339/post-legislative-assessment-of-the-foi-act.pdf, [153].

Appeals

The Commissioner's decisions are themselves subject to appeal to the tribunal, and this power of appeal is exercisable upon the broadest possible grounds. The Act provides that either party may appeal to the tribunal against a decision notice, and a public authority may appeal against an enforcement or information notice (s 57(2) and (3)), either on the basis that the notice is 'not in accordance with the law', or 'to the extent that the notice involved an exercise of discretion by the Commissioner, that he ought to have exercised his discretion differently' (s 58(1)). The tribunal is also empowered to review 'any finding of fact on which the notice in question was based' and, as well as being empowered to quash decisions of the Commissioner, may 'substitute such other notice as could have been served by the Commissioner'. There is a further appeal from the tribunal to the High Court, but on a 'point of law' only (s 59).

The ministerial veto of the Commissioner's decisions

The ministerial veto is another highly controversial aspect of the Act, albeit some of the potential controversy has been resolved by the decision in *Evans*, as will be discussed shortly. For the veto to be exercisable, two conditions must be satisfied under s 53(1). First, the notice that the veto will operate to quash must have been served on a government department, 'any public authority designated for the purposes of this section by an order made by the Secretary of State.' Second, the notice must order the release of information which is prima facie exempt but which the Commissioner has decided should nevertheless be released under the public interest test in s 2. (By prima facie exempt, it will be recalled, is meant information that either falls into a class exemption or, where prejudice is required to render it exempt, the Commissioner has adjudged the prejudice to be present.)

The veto is exercised by means of a certificate signed by the minister concerned, stating that he has 'on reasonable grounds formed the opinion that, in respect of the request or requests concerned, there was no failure' to comply with the Act. The decision must be made at a relatively senior level. For a UK government department or any other public authority, the person responsible is a cabinet minister. The reasons for the veto must be given to the complainant (s 56), unless doing so would reveal exempt information (s 57), and the certificate must be laid before Parliament. So far, the veto has been used rarely.[163] However, as the Campaign for FOI has pointed out, a worrying precedent exists in that the government has on several occasions refused to comply with rulings by the Ombudsman (PCA) under the previous Code of Practice on Access to Information. [164] Examples include: refusals to comply fully with a recommendation by the PCA as to the release information on ministerial gifts; preventing the PCA from seeing papers of cabinet committees which were dealing with the Human Rights Act; and the issuance of a certificate blocking disclosure of information about ministerial conflicts of interest on the grounds that it would be contrary to the public interest. These precedents are far from encouraging.

---

163 See discussion in Carter, E, 'A Prince, a journalist, some letters and a veto' (2015) FOI 6.
164 For the full report Parliamentary Ombudsperson Investigation Report, HC 951 (2002–2003).

R (Evans) v Attorney General[165] offers some reassurance about the limits of the veto. It concerned a request, in 2005, by Mr Evans, a journalist at the *Guardian*, for disclosure of communications passing between HRH The Prince of Wales and different government departments. The departments refused to disclose the information (having eventually admitted they had them), claiming they were exempt under ss 37, 40 and/or 41. Mr Evans complained to the Information Commissioner who upheld the refusal. Following Mr Evans's complaint, the matter was dealt with by the Upper Tribunal, which concluded in September 2012 that the information should be disclosed. On 16 October 2012, however, the AG intervened, issuing a s 53(2) certificate to the effect that he believed there were reasonable grounds to refuse such disclosure. In particular, the AG concluded that the Prince of Wales should be able to speak with ministers about departmental matters in order to fulfill his royal duties to advise and warn government about its actions and that such discussions should remain confidential. He concluded that the public interest in disclosure was far outweighed by the public interest against it. The Supreme Court held that the AG was not entitled to issue the certificate in the manner he did.

The case raises an particularly significant constitutional principle – though the facts are slightly less important since royal correspondence is now subject to an absolute exemption and has been since 2010. It reaffirms that s 53 cannot be used by the executive to override judicial decisions simply for expediency:

> where, as here, a court has conducted a full open hearing into the question of whether, in the light of certain facts and competing arguments, the public interest favours disclosure of certain information and has concluded for reasons given in a judgment that it does, section 53 cannot be invoked effectively to overrule that judgment merely because a member of the executive, considering the same facts and arguments, takes a different view.[166]

Thus, the public interest considerations included the strong constitutional principle that the executive should not usurp its position. Lord Neuberger, agreeing with the Court of Appeal on the point, found that, to be valid, the veto could be exercised only if new grounds or facts arose that had been unavailable to the Tribunal or if there was a demonstrable flaw in the tribunal's reasoning.[167] Whilst this offers some comfort that the use of s 53 is safeguarded by judicial oversight, it still relies upon a determined claimant to pursue matters that far.

Publication schemes

Under ss 19 and 20, public authorities must adopt 'publication schemes' relating to the publication of information by that authority, that is, schemes by which information is made generally available to the public, without a specific request having to be made. This is a significant aspect of the Act, since more citizens will thereby gain access to a wider range of information. The difficulty and expense of making a request will be

---

165 *R (on the application of Evans) v Attorney General* [2015] UKSC 21.
166 Evans, op cit, 59. See also 52, 58, 86, 88–91, 115.
167 *Ibid*, [71]–[78].

avoided. The scheme can be devised by the authority or, under s 20, a model scheme devised by the Information Commissioner can be used. If a tailor-made scheme is used, it must be approved by the Commissioner (s 19(1)(a)). Therefore, authorities are likely to use the model schemes, thereby avoiding the need to submit the scheme for approval. Consistency between authorities is probably desirable as promoting transparency and thereby enhancing access to information. For early indications as to the schemes prepared by central government departments, see a report by the CFOI.[168]

Conclusions

Despite its weaknesses, this is a constitutional development whose significance can hardly be over-stated. The FoI Act, enforceable by the Information Commissioner, will be a clear improvement on the code introduced by the Major government. Rodney Austin described the draft bill as 'a denial of democracy'.[169] It is suggested that the improvements made to the bill during its passage through Parliament, while still leaving it a far weaker and more illiberal measure than the scheme proposed by the widely praised white paper that preceded it, render this view no longer accurate. In particular, the public interest test has been strengthened, and applies to most of the exemptions in the Act, including, crucially, the key class exemptions relating to investigations and to the formation of government policy; however, as the CFOI points out, it is misleading to view this as converting class exemptions into 'harm-based' ones, since the very existence of a class exemption is based upon a presumption, built into the Act, that such information is, as a class, of a type which generally should not be released. Nevertheless, although it is still too early to tell, the attitude of the Information Commissioner as expressed in the published guidance indicates that, in reality, evidence of individual damage that would be done by publication will be required where a public authority seeks to resist the argument that publication should take place on public interest grounds.[170]

The Act does represent a turning point in British democracy in, for the first time in its history, removing the decision to release many classes of information from government and placing it in the hands of an independent agency, the Information Commissioner, and in giving a statutory 'right' to information, enforceable if necessary through the courts, to citizens. However, as seen, the Act fences this basic right around with so many restrictions that, depending upon its interpretation, much information of any conceivable interest could still be withheld. That said, it is promising that central and local government response times have improved. This shows the Act is being taken seriously. It is also promising that the Commissioner is equally serious about the Act as a means of ensuring the government is transparent and accountable. What remains vital, though, is that the use of ministerial veto is kept to a minimum. Reliance on determined litigants to challenge veto usage in the courts is an insufficient safeguard.

---

168 'Central Government Publication Schemes: Good Practice' http://www.cfoi.org.uk/pdf/ps_report. pdf.
169 Austin, R, 'Freedom of information: a Sheep in Wolf's Clothing?', in Jowell, J and Oliver, D (eds), *The Changing Constitution*, 5th edn, 2004, at 237.
170 See above at 542–43.

Chapter 9

Freedom of protest and assembly

This chapter has been updated and revised for this edition by Michael Hamilton, Senior Lecturer in Public Protest Law, University of East Anglia, UK.

I Introduction[1]

Within the UK, three very different legal frameworks exist to protect (or arguably, primarily to regulate) the right to protest and the freedom of peaceful assembly. The statutory framework in England and Wales differs significantly from the law in Scotland[2] and in Northern Ireland.[3] However, while the regional institutions, their statutory

---

1 For texts referred to below and further reading, see: Mead, D, *The New Law of Peaceful Protest: Rights and Regulation in the Human Rights Act Era*, 2010; Wainwright, T, Morris, A, Craig, K and Greenhall, O, *The Protest Handbook*, 2012; Thornton, P, Brander, R, Thomas, R, Rhodes, D, Schwartz, M, and Rees, E, *The Law of Public Order and Protest*, 2010; OSCE-ODIHR – Venice Commission *Guidelines on Freedom of Peaceful Assembly*, 2nd edn, 2010 (3rd edn forthcoming); Barendt, E, 'Freedom of Assembly', chapter 9 in Beatson, J and Cripps, Y (eds), *Freedom of Expression and Freedom of Information: Essays in honour of Sir David Williams* (2000) pp 161–176; Harris, DJ, O'Boyle, M, Bates, EP, and Buckley, CM, *Harris, O'Boyle and Warbrick: Law of the European Convention on Human Rights*, 3rd edn, 2014, Chapter 15, pp 710–723; Elliot, M and Thomas, R, *Public Law*, 2nd edn, 2014, Chapter 20, pp 782–811; Ormerod, D and Laird, K, *Smith and Hogan's Criminal Law*, 14th edn, 2015, Chapter 32, pp 1227–1265; Ewing, KD, *Bonfire of the Liberties: New Labour, Human Rights and the Rule of Law*, 2010, Chapter 4, pp 96–135; Feldman, D, *Civil Liberties and Human Rights in England and Wales*, 2nd edn, 2002, Chapter 18, pp 1008–1085; Fenwick, H and Phillipson, G, 'Public protest, the Human Rights Act and judicial responses to political expression' (2000) *PL* 627–50. For further background, see: Williams, DGT, *Keeping the Peace*, 1967; Townshend, C, *Making the Peace: Public Order and Public Security in Modern Britain*, 1993; Waddington, PAJ, *Liberty and Order: Public Order Policing in a Capital City*, 1994; Sherr, A, *Freedom of Protest, Public Order and the Law*, 1989; Ewing, KD and Gearty, CA, *The Struggle for Civil Liberties*, 1999; Ewing, KD and Gearty, CA, *Freedom under Thatcher*, 1990, Chapter 4. For a comparative study (including the UK, France, Germany and the US), see Salát, O, *The Right to Freedom of Assembly*, Hart: 2015. For useful discussion of freedom of assembly in the United States, see: Zick, T, *Speech Out of Doors: Preserving First Amendment Liberties in Public Places*, 2008; Abu El-Haj, T, 'The Neglected Right of Assembly' 56 *UCLA Law Rev* 543–589 (2009); Abu El-Haj, T, 'All Assemble: Order and Disorder in Law, Politics and Culture' 16 *U. Pa J Const L* 949 (2014); Inazu, J, *Liberty's Refuge: The Forgotten Freedom of Assembly*, 2012; Krotoszynski, R, *Reclaiming the Petition Clause: Seditious Libel, 'Offensive Protest', and the Right to Petition the Government for a Redress of Grievances*, 2012; Bhagwat, A, 'Associational Speech' 120 *Yale LJ* 978 (2011).

2 See, for example, Part V of the Civic Government (Scotland) Act, 1982 as amended by the Police, Public Order and Criminal Justice (Scotland) Act 2006 in light of recommendations by the 'Review of Marches and Parades in Scotland' (2005) by Sir John Orr.

3 See the Public Order (NI) Order 1987 and the Public Processions (NI) Act 1998, as amended; Hamilton, M 'Processions, Protests and Other Meetings', in Dickson, B and Gormally, B, *Human Rights in Northern Ireland*, 2015, Hart, 179–206. The Stormont House Agreement (23 December 2014) noted that powers governing parades and related protests should, in principle, be devolved to the NI Assembly.

powers and the relevant offences might differ, the police, courts and public authorities throughout the UK share the same obligations under the Human Rights Act 1998 (HRA). The extent to which these HRA obligations have (or have not) reshaped the protection of public protest in England and Wales is the focus of this chapter – noting, in particular, the Coalition government's May 2010 commitment to 'restore rights to non-violent protest'.[4]

According to Sedley LJ, the HRA marked a historic, 'constitutional shift'[5] towards the recognition and protection of Convention rights. Individuals, are today able to claim their rights under Arts 10 and 11 ECHR – respectively, the right to freedom of expression, and the right to peacefully assemble – and public authorities, including the police, have positive obligations to protect and facilitate the exercise of these rights. While 'qualified' rights may be circumscribed, any limitations must be compatible with specified Convention exceptions. However, there has been an incremental extension of regulatory power – a creeping criminalisation, and indeed terrorisation,[6] of forms of protest and dissent. Accompanying such criminalisation, there has also been a worrying trend towards the use of sanctions based on the civil standard of proof against protesters. Indeed, the common law doctrine of breach of the peace effectively overshadows all the statutory changes of the last 30 years. Breathtakingly broad, bewilderingly imprecise in scope, it provides the police with such wide powers to use against protesters as to render the statutory powers almost redundant.

That these statutory and common law incursions into the right of peaceful assembly have coincided with the period in which the HRA has been in force is an intriguing – and worrying – contradiction. It will be argued that the 'constitutional shift' vaunted by Sedley LJ has not been realised in practice. In fact, it is tempting to conclude, as Keith Ewing has argued, that this is an area where the HRA 'appears to be sleeping'[7] and its contribution 'to the right of peaceful assembly has been little more than a mirage'.[8] In the words of David Mead, the right of protest under the HRA 'is the dog that didn't bark.'[9] In contrast to judicial preferencing of 'orthodox'[10] and 'predictable'[11] forms of demonstration, this chapter argues that there ought to be a thumb on the scale in favour of what might be regarded as transgressive and disruptive protest[12]

---

4 *The Coalition: Our Programme for Government*, p 11.
5 Sedley LJ in *Redmond-Bate v Director of Public Prosecutions* (1999) 163 JP 789, 795; cited by Lord Bingham in *R (on the application of Laporte) (FC) v Chief Constable of Gloucestershire* [2006] UKHL 55, para 34.
6 See, for example, A/HRC/23/39/Add.1, *Report of the Special Rapporteur on the rights to freedom of peaceful assembly and of association, Maina Kiai, Addendum: Mission to the United Kingdom of Great Britain and Northern Ireland* (17 June 2013), para 35 (critiquing the police categorization of Occupy London as a terrorist group). Anti-terrorism law and policy are considered more fully in Chapter 15, but see the discussion of s 1 Terrorism Act at p 597, and of the 'PREVENT' strategy and Part 5 of the Counter-Terrorism and Security Act 2015 at pp 1117 and 1120–21 below.
7 Ewing, K D, 2010, *op cit*, fn 1, p 97.
8 *Ibid*, p 135.
9 Mead, D, *op cit*, fn 1, p 393.
10 *Hall and Others v Mayor of London (On Behalf of the Greater London Authority)* [2010] EWCA Civ 817 (16 July 2010), para 48 per Lord Neuberger MR.
11 *Minio-Paluello v Commissioner of Police of the Metropolis* [2011] EWHC 3411 (QB), para 47 per Eder J.
12 See, for example, Abu El-Haj, T, *op cit*, fn 1 (2014). See also, Bailey, D J, 'Resistance is futile? The impact of disruptive protest in the "silver age of permanent austerity"', *Socio-Economic Review* (2014) 1–34.

if the protection of these Convention rights is to be 'practical and effective' (rather than 'theoretical or illusory').[13]

2 Protest policing[14]

It is often claimed that 'the increasing unpredictability of protests' poses particular challenges for the police.[15] Equally, though, police practices and priorities – especially in the face of budgetary constraints[16] – pose grave challenges for the right to protest. A willingness to recognise the challenges facing the police must therefore be matched by a recognition of the essential nature and value of public protest (see further, 'Underlying justifications' below).

The police role should be oriented towards enabling demonstrations to take place in accordance with the preferences of the organiser. Yet, in too many cases, the police appear to construe their obligations more in terms of 'managing' and 'controlling' rather than 'facilitating' protest.[17] In addition, while judges have occasionally questioned police assessments of risk,[18] the courts have traditionally been exceedingly deferential to the police as the 'primary definers'[19] of public order. Courts have long been reluctant to find police decisions unlawful.[20] Recent examples of judicial deference to operational policing decisions can be seen in the *Austin* case regarding the containment of protesters, and in the weak scrutiny afforded to the deployment by the Metropolitan police of

---

13 See, for example, *Airey v Ireland*, Appl No 6289/73, 9 October 1979, para 24.

14 For a useful (US focused) critique of protest policing strategies (especially, 'command and control' public order policing in the context of large political demonstrations), see Vitale, A, 'From Negotiated Management to Command and Control: How the New York Police Department Polices Protest' 15(3) *Policing and Society* 283–304 (2005). See also, Noakes, JA, Klocke, BV and Gillham, PF, 'Whose Streets? Police and Protester Struggles over Space in Washington, DC, 29–30 September 2001', 15(3) *Policing and Society* 235–254 (2005).

15 See, for example, JCHR, *Facilitating Peaceful Protest: Tenth Report of Session 2010–11* (HL Paper 123; HC 684: 25 March 2011) p 5, para 4.

16 See, for example, *Wright v Commissioner of Police for the Metropolis* [2013] EWHC 2739 (QB), paras 60 and 62 where Jay J, stated that the police were 'undoubtedly entitled to have in mind an issue such as the level of police resources'.

17 See, for example, the description of the detailed operational policing plan put in place by the chief constable of Gloucestershire in the case of *Laporte* [2006] UKHL 55, para 8 (discussed further below at pp 645–48). See also the language used by Garnham J in *R (Barda) v Mayor of London on behalf of the GLA* [2015] EWHC 3584 (Admin), para 1.

18 See, for example, *R (on the application of Laporte) (FC) v Chief Constable of Gloucestershire* [2006] UKHL 55, especially para 55 (per Lord Bingham), para 90 (per Lord Rodger), and para 106 (per Lord Carswell). See also the Court of Appeal judgment in *Wood v Commissioner of Police for the Metropolis* [2009] EWCA Civ 414 per Dyson LJ and Lord Collins. Compare too the High Court's preparedness to question the evidence underlying police decision-making in *R (Moos and McClure) v Commissioner of Police of the Metropolis* [2011] EWHC 957, paras 56–64, with the avowedly more deferential approach of the Court of Appeal [2012] EWCA Civ 12, paras 69–76.

19 To borrow a phrase used by Stuart Hall to describe how criminal justice institutions (especially the police and judiciary) have become regarded as the 'primary definers' of 'crime'. Hall, S et al, *Policing the Crisis: Mugging the State and Law and Order*, 2nd edn, (2013) 71–72.

20 See, e.g., *Chief Constable of Sussex ex p International Ferry Traders Ltd* [1999] 1 All ER 129. See also the CND's unsuccessful challenge to the use of the banning power under s 13 POA in *Kent v Metropolitan Police Commissioner, The Times*, 15 May 1981. See also, *Secretary of State for the Home Department ex p Northumbria Police Authority* [1989] QB 26; [1988] 2 WLR 590; [1988] 1 All ER 556 CA.

'Anti Demonstration patrols' during the royal wedding.[21] In these examples, amongst others, the 'preventive turn' described by leading criminologists[22] can clearly be recognised in the present day regulation of protest in the UK.

As Andrew Ashworth has noted, 'any new statute . . . is soon surrounded and enveloped by working practices which push and pull, this way and that'.[23] The statutory provisions and common law powers are therefore only one factor contributing to the real extent of the rights to protest and assemble – a key factor continues to be the working practice of the police.[24] This may be especially so given the increasing reliance on liaison-based protest policing,[25] a development that owes much to developments in crowd psychology (and efforts to develop non-escalatory police interventions).[26] On the one hand, police willingness to liaise with protesters might be viewed positively – as preferable to more intrusive or forceful interventions.[27] However, concerns have been raised about the extent to which police efforts to liaise with protesters both draw upon, and feed into, police intelligence gathering.[28] Moreover, as PAJ Waddington has previously documented, there are risks for protesters in entering into informal negotiations with the police. Such negotiations may be used by the authorities primarily for the purposes of regulation and control – '[b]y "winning over" the organiser, the police achieve much more extensive control over the conduct of the march than the law alone would allow.'[29] If public assemblies are valuable partly because they have the potential to challenge the

21 See the testimony of PC Hemmings in *Hicks and Others v Commissioner of the Police of the Metropolis* [2012] EWHC 1947 (Admin), para 42. See also para 40 (reference in PC Portlock's notebook to foot patrols 'to detect and prevent Anti-Demonstrations against the Royal Wedding').

22 McCulloch, J and Wilson, D, *Pre-crime: Pre-emption, precaution and the future* (Routledge: 2015); Also, Lucia Zedner, 'Pre-Crime and Post-Criminology?' 11(2) *Theoretical Criminology* 261 (2007); Jude McCulloch and Sharon Pickering, 'Pre-crime and counter-terrorism: imagining future crime in the "war on terror" ', *Brit J Criminol.* 628 (2009).

23 Ashworth, A 'Criminal Justice and the Criminal Process' 28 *B J Criminology* (1988) 111, 112.

24 See generally, Waddington, PAJ, *Liberty and Order: Public Order Policing in a Capital City*, 1994.

25 HMIC, *Adapting to Protest: Nurturing the British Model* (November 2009), especially, chapter 3, 'Communication', 73–82 and chapter 4, 'Crowd Dynamics and Public Order Policing', 85–90. See also, *The Barton Moss Environmental Protest: A report by the Police and Crime Commissioner's Independent Panel on the Policing of Protests and Demonstrations October 2014*: www.gmpcc.org.uk/wp-content/uploads/2014/10/ProtestPanel-FrackingReport-Oct-2014.pdf, p 20, recommendations 3 and 5 (and for critical commentary, see Netpol, *Manchester protest panel report 'a significant missed opportunity'*, 27 October 2014: https://netpol.org/2014/10/27/gmpcc-protest-panel-report/).

26 See, Stott, C, Scothern, M and Gorringe, H, 'Advances in Liaison Based Public Order Policing in England: Human Rights and Negotiating the Management of Protest?' *Policing* (2013) 1–15, and references therein.

27 See, for example, *Frumkin v Russia*, Appl No 74568/12, 5 January 2016, paras 126–130 concerning the obligation of the authorities to communicate with the assembly leaders. Here, the Russian authorities failed both to establish a 'reliable channel of communication with the organisers before the assembly' and to respond to 'real-time developments in a constructive manner.'

28 See, for example, 'Sussex police criticized for harassment during protester liaison', *The Guardian*, 4 September 2012.

29 Waddington, PAJ, *op cit*, fn 1, p 101. See also, Gorringe, H, Rosie, M, Waddington, D and Kominou, M, 'Facilitating Ineffective Protest? The Policing of the 2009 Edinburgh NATO Protests' 22(2) *Policing and Society* (June 2012), 115–132; Gorringe, Hugo and Rosie, Michael, 'It's a long way to Auchterarder! 'Negotiated management' and mismanagement in the policing of G8 protests', 59(2) *British Journal of Sociology* 187 (2008). As Gorringe and Rosie argue (pp 200–01): '[n]egotiated management' proves a misnomer when asymmetries of power preclude meaningful interaction, or when 'negotiated' solutions

status quo, they cannot become so routinised that the only assemblies to occur are those that are negotiated with, and deemed acceptable by, the very authorities against which protest might legitimately be directed.[30]

Two further aspects of policing practice in the UK deserve preliminary consideration – respectively, (1) the use of force and police weaponry and (2) surveillance of protesters.

The use of force and police weaponry

The potential for forceful tactics to exacerbate public order situations has been recognised since Lord Scarman's report into the Brixton disorders in 1981.[31] More recently, the IPCC initiated a research project (albeit not limited to protest policing) examining the use of force by police, and the factors that might properly be taken into account in determining whether any force used was 'reasonable' (or excessive) under s 3 of the Criminal Law Act 1967.[32] Recent years have seen the unlawful killing of Ian Tomlinson during the G20 protests in London,[33] and (by way of illustration) forceful tactics have been used against pro-Palestinian demonstrators outside the Israeli embassy in London in January 2009[34] and student protesters (including Alfie Meadows and Jody McIntyre) in November–December 2010. Concerns have also been substantiated in relation to the lack of appropriate public order training and failure to wear visible ID numbers during the G20 protests in 2009.[35]

There are multiple Strasbourg authorities that emphasise that any force used must be necessary and proportionate.[36] Nonetheless, the conditions under which particular

---

are underpinned by the threat of escalated force.' See further, 'Imposing conditions on processions and assemblies' at p 608 below.

30 Relatedly, there have been cases in which police have sought to develop a written 'Memorandum of Understanding' with protesters. For two examples of such MOUs (drafted by Bedfordshire Police and South Yorkshire Police respectively), see, Netpol, 'More evidence of huge police pressure on organisers of protest marches' 8 July 2015, available at: https://netpol.org/2015/07/08/police-pressure-protest-organisers/.

31 *The Brixton Disorders*, Cmnd 8427, 1981.

32 This states that: 'A person may use such force as is reasonable in the circumstances in the prevention of crime, or in effecting or assisting the lawful arrest of offenders or suspected offenders or of persons unlawfully at large' (also discussed below in relation to the criminalisation of trespass under s 68 CJPOA, below at pp 631–37). See further, IPCC Report on the Use of Force, available at: https://www.ipcc.gov.uk/page/use-of-force.

33 The officer who pushed Mr Tomlinson was ultimately acquitted of manslaughter but dismissed for gross misconduct.

34 *Minio-Paluello v Commissioner of Police of the Metropolis* [2011] EWHC 3411 (QB), awarding damages of £14,303 for assault of a protester by a police officer who used a degree of force, deemed neither reasonable nor proportionate.

35 See HMIC, *Adapting to Protest* (2009); Home Affairs Committee, *Policing of the G20 Protests* (HC 418: 2009), chapter 5, and Home Affairs Committee, *Policing of the G20 Protests: Government Response to the Report on the Policing of the G20 Protests* (HC 201: 2010). See also, Gordon, J, 'A developing human rights culture in the UK? Case studies of policing' *EHRLR* (2010) 609–20.

36 See, for example, the cases of *Abdullah Yaşa v Turkey* Appl No 50275/08 (16 July 2013); *İzci v Turkey*, Appl No 42606/05 (23 July 2013); *Cestaro v Italy*, Appl No 6884/11 (7 April 2015, available only in French or Italian). See also, A/HRC/26/36 *Report of the Special Rapporteur on extrajudicial, summary or arbitrary executions, Christof Heyns* to the UN Human Rights Council, 1 April 2014; Amnesty International, *Use of Force: Guidelines for Implementation of the UN Basic Principles on the Use of Force and Firearms by Law Enforcement Officials* (August 2015).

weapons and tactics may be relied upon by UK police officers are not defined in any statute.[37] The 2003 Home Office Code of Practice on Police use of Firearms and Less Lethal Weapons places the responsibility to determine 'what types of weapons need to be available within their forces' on chief police officers who, in consultation with their police authorities, are also 'responsible for the acquisition of weapons requiring special authorisation for use in their force areas'.[38] Ultimately, however, local police authorities, have no powers to prevent chief constables from purchasing public order equipment from the central store maintained by the Home Secretary,[39] since this store is maintained under a prerogative power to do all that is 'reasonably necessary to preserve the peace of the realm'.[40] CS spray has been used on several occasions against demonstrators,[41] and tasers – although apparently subject to a 'self-imposed ban . . . in public protest situations'[42] – have also been used against individual protesters.[43] Proposals to re-introduce water cannon in England and Wales were rejected by the Home Secretary in July 2015.[44]

Surveillance of protesters

Any analysis of the protection afforded to freedom of assembly in the UK must also take account of the pervasive surveillance of protesters, both overt and covert. As recognised by Lady Hale in 2015 in her concurring opinion in *R (Catt) v Commissioner of Police of the Metropolis*, such surveillance can potentially exert a significant chilling effect on the exercise of the right to protest.[45]

Police surveillance during demonstrations generally takes the form of the deployment of forward intelligence teams (FITs)[46] and specifically tasked evidence gathering

---

37 See instead, the (non-binding) Association of Chief Police Officers (ACPO)/National Police Improvement Agency (NPIA) manual of guidance on 'Keeping the Peace'. ACPO was replaced in April 2015 by the National Police Chiefs' Council (NPCC): http://www.npcc.police.uk.

38 At para 3.2.6(a) and para 4.1.1. Despite consultations on the Code of Practice in 2009, no revised Code has yet been issued.

39 *Report of HM Chief Inspector for Constabulary for 1981*, 1981–82, HC 463.

40 *Secretary of State for the Home Dept ex p Northumbria Police Authority* [1989] QB 26; [1988] 2 WLR 590; [1988] 1 All ER 556, CA.

41 See, for example, 'CS spray used on UK Uncut protest', *BBC News*, 30 January 2011; 'Police use CS spray on Brixton gentrification protesters', *BBC News*, 25 April 2015.

42 Home Affairs Committee, *Policing of the G20 Protests* (HC 418: 2009), p 24, para 75. See also, Home Affairs Committee, *Police Use of Tasers* (HC 646, Session 2010–12) Evidence of Assistant Chief Constable Simon Chesterman, 7 December 2010: EV9, Q78-Q80 and EV10, Q91-Q93.

43 For example, by West Midlands police at a protest at Warwick University in December 2014. See, 'Police use CS spray and Taser at Warwick University protest', Channel 4 News, 4 December 2014. At the time of writing, an IPCC investigation into allegations of 'inappropriate force' was ongoing.

44 See Home Secretary's oral statement on water cannon (15 July 2015): http://www.parliament.uk/business/news/2015/july/statement-on-water-cannon-15-july-2015/.

45 *R (on the application of Catt) v Commissioner of Police of the Metropolis and another* [2015] UKSC 9, para 51 per Lady Hale. The UN Special Rapporteur on the Rights to Freedom of Peaceful Assembly and of Association, Maina Kiai, noted reports that 'student protests held in November 2012 were smaller than expected by organizers due to the students' fear of being targeted.' A/HRC/23/39/Add.1, fn 6 above, para 32.

46 FITs are regarded by the police as a tactical response requiring no specific authority. See further: https://www.whatdotheyknow.com/request/forward_intelligence_teams.

(EG) teams.[47] Undercover police officers are also sometimes deployed during demonstrations, but the police generally 'neither confirm nor deny' any such deployment on the basis of safety concerns for the undercover officers involved.[48] Furthermore, in recent years there have been alarming revelations about the infiltration of protest groups by undercover police officers (who, in several cases, developed intimate relationships with the activists about whom they were gathering intelligence).[49] Such practices are deeply troubling, and met with strongly worded criticism from the UN Special Rapporteur on Freedom of Peaceful Assembly, Maina Kiai, following his country visit to the UK.[50] In November 2015, the Met apologised unreservedly to the women concerned, paying substantial, undisclosed sums by way of compensation.[51]

The police also routinely and systematically collect and retain data about demonstrators.[52] While the privacy concerns to which such surveillance and its uses might give rise are discussed in detail in Chapter 11, it is worth noting here that in *R (Catt) v Commissioner of Police of the Metropolis*,[53] the Supreme Court upheld as proportionate the police retention of the personal details of a peaceful demonstrator on the 'Domestic Extremism Database'. The case concerned a challenge to the retention by police of data about a 91-year-old peace campaigner, John Catt, who had taken part in demonstrations organised by Smash EDO, had twice been arrested for obstructing the highway, but had never himself been convicted of any offence. The information retained in Mr Catt's case were incidental references to his presence at demonstrations in information reports about those events, and in the 'nominal records' retained in relation to others.[54] Only Lord Toulson in the Supreme Court agreed with the Court of Appeal that the retention of Mr Catt's data was disproportionate (the Court of Appeal judgment had previously been welcomed by the UN Special Rapporteur on the Rights to Freedom of Peaceful

---

47 See generally, *Wood v Commissioner of Police for the Metropolis* [2009] EWCA Civ 414 (21 May 2009), on appeal from [2008] EWHC Admin 1105. McCombe J, in the Administrative Court, set out the police policy in relation to the taking, processing and retention of photographs (paras 5–9).

48 See, for example, JCHR, *Facilitating Peaceful Protest: Tenth Report of Session 2010–11* (HL Paper 123; HC 684: 25 March 2011), at EV 25, Q 106, Evidence of Lynne Owens (Assistant Commissioner, Metropolitan Police) and Bob Broadhurst (Head of Public Order, Metropolitan Police).

49 In March 2015, the Home Secretary established an inquiry (under the Inquiries Act 2005, and chaired by Lord Justice Pitchford) to examine undercover policing and the operation of the Metropolitan Police's Special Demonstration Squad (SDS). See further https://www.ucpi.org.uk/. See also: Taylor, S, *Investigation into links between Special Demonstration Squad and Home Office* (January 2015). Relevant cases include: *DIL and others v Commissioner of Police of the Metropolis* [2014] EWHC 2184 (QB); *AKJ and others v Commissioner of Police for the Metropolis and others* [2013] EWHC 32 (QB); *R v Barkshire and Others* [2011] EWCA Crim 1885. See also: Home Affairs Committee, Thirteenth Report: *Undercover Policing: Interim Report* (26 February 2013); HMIC, *A review of national police units which provide intelligence on criminality associated with protest* (January 2012); Regulation of Investigatory Powers (Directed Surveillance and Covert Human Intelligence Sources) Order 2010, SI 2010/521 (as amended); Evans, R and Lewis, P, *Undercover: The True Story of Britain's Secret Police*, 2013. See separately, Lubbers, E, *Secret Manoeuvres in the Dark: Corporate and Police Spying on Activists*, 2012 describing widespread infiltration of social movements and protest groups *by corporations*.

50 See A/HRC/23/39/Add.1, fn 6 above, paras 24–28.

51 'Police apologise to women who had relationships with undercover officers', *The Guardian*, 20 November 2015.

52 See *R (Catt) v Commissioner of Police of the Metropolis* [2015] UKSC 9, para 20.

53 *Ibid.*

54 *Ibid*, para 51 per Lady Hale, and para 60 per Lord Toulson.

Assembly and of Association, Maina Kiai).[55] Lord Toulson emphasised that, 'in modern society the state has very extensive powers of keeping records on its citizens. If a citizen's activities are lawful, they should be free from the state keeping a record of them unless, and then only for as long as, such a record really needs to be kept in the public interest.'[56]

One fundamental question raised in *Catt* was whether protesters in public places might ever conceivably have 'a reasonable expectation of privacy'. As discussed in Chapters 10 and 11, this has hitherto been the threshold test used to determine whether Art 8 is engaged.[57] While the proposition that an individual might reasonably expect a degree of privacy during a public protest – an event seeking to attract public attention – might seem far-fetched, it is less so when one considers (a) the multi-faceted nature of personal autonomy protected by Art 8 (including a person's 'physical and psychological integrity' which might itself be contingent on the age, or other relevant characteristic, of the individual concerned);[58] (b) the multiple ways in which such autonomy might be interfered with, and the extent of any such intrusions (from overt photography to the covert deployment of undercover officers, and from the processing and storage of data to its possible disclosure to third parties); (c) the differential purposes that the police might be pursuing (from investigating a specific criminal offence to profiling individual protesters in case they might become involved in future disorder), and (d) the need also to recognise the value of anonymity to public protest.[59]

Lord Sumption in *Catt* recognised that 'there may be some matters about which there is a reasonable expectation of privacy, notwithstanding that they occur in public and are patent to all the world'.[60] Lady Hale similarly noted that Art 8 was engaged 'even though, in the case of Mr Catt, the information collected related to his activities in public'.[61] Lord Sumption added, however, that 'mere observation [by the police] . . . save perhaps in extreme circumstances' could not engage Art 8.[62] Previously, Laws LJ in *R (Wood) v Commissioner of Police for the Metropolis*[63] had emphasised that 'the bare act of taking the pictures, by whoever done, is not of itself capable of engaging Art 8(1) unless there are aggravating circumstances'.[64] The situations he had in mind involved intimidation or harassment, whereupon the taking of the photograph or 'snapping of the shutter' might not only engage, but grossly violate, Art 8 (irrespective of how the photographs were used).[65]

---

55 Dyson MR and Moore-Bick and McCombe LJJ in the Court of Appeal ([2013] EWCA Civ 192) held that the retention of Mr Catt's data was disproportionate to the legitimate purpose of policing the community (since it had no value for policing purposes). See also, A/HRC/23/39/Add.1, fn 6 above, para 31.
56 *Catt* [2015] UKSC 9, para 69 per Lord Toulson.
57 See, *Campbell v MGN* [2004] UKHL 22; *Von Hannover v Germany* (2005) 40 EHRR 1, para 51.
58 See, for example, *Wood* [2009] EWCA Civ 414, paras 19–22 per Laws LJ.
59 It might be asked, for example, whether the wearing of a mask during a demonstration should have any bearing on whether a protester had a reasonable expectation of privacy.
60 *Catt*, para 4.
61 *Ibid*, para 47.
62 *Ibid*, para 4.
63 [2009] EWCA Civ 414, [2010] 1 WLR 123.
64 *Ibid*, para 36.
65 *Ibid*, para 34.

In *Wood*, an employee of the Campaign Against Arms Trade (CAAT) successfully challenged the taking and retention by police of photographs of him in April 2005, after he had attended the AGM of a company involved in the organisation of industry trade fairs, including those relating to the arms industry, and had been seen briefly in the company of a 'known trouble maker'. The police argued that the retention of his photograph was justified because they feared he might attend and commit an offence at an arms fair several months later, in September 2005.[66] While his image was not placed on any police database,[67] all three judges (Laws and Dyson LJJ and Lord Collins) agreed that Art 8 was engaged. Laws LJ noted 'that the touchstone for Art 8(1)'s engagement is whether the claimant enjoys on the facts a "reasonable expectation of privacy"'.[68] Emphasising that the taking of photographs by the police is qualitatively different from the taking of photographs by, for example, journalists.[69] While Laws LJ then concluded (in the minority) that 'the retention of the images was proportionate to the legitimate aim of the exercise',[70] both Dyson LJ and Lord Collins held that the retention of the photographs could *not* be justified under Art 8(2).[71] It is undoubtedly true, as Lord Collins concluded, 'that the last word has yet to be said on the implications for civil liberties of the taking and retention of images in the modern surveillance society'.[72]

In conclusion, to gauge the level of protection currently afforded to the right to peacefully assemble in the UK, these two aspects of protest policing – the use of force and the routine surveillance of demonstrators – must be considered alongside other trends inimical to the protection and facilitation of public protest. These include recent attempts in England and Wales to charge protesters for the costs of traffic management, a move that would seriously erode the effective enjoyment of the right to protest, rendering it contingent on the financial wherewithal of groups wishing to assemble.[73]

---

66 See also, *Kinloch v HM Advocate* [2012] UKSC 62, [2013] 2 AC 93, paras 19–21 per Lord Hope.
67 *Wood* [2009] EWCA Civ 414, para 46.
68 *Wood*, para 22 per Laws LJ.
69 *Wood*, paras 45–6 per Laws LJ. Note separately, *University of Oxford and Others v Broughton and Others* [2006] EWHC 1233 (QB), para 32, in which Holland J set aside the terms of an earlier injunction that had restricted anti-vivisection protesters from using photographic equipment within an exclusion zone, in part because both the police and pro-vivisectionists had unrestricted use of cameras.
70 *Wood*, para 60 per Laws LJ.
71 *Ibid*, see especially paras 85–86 per Dyson LJ.
72 *Ibid*, para 100 per Lord Collins. See especially the split Supreme Court judgment in *JR38* [2015] UKSC 42 in which Lord Kerr (in the minority, with Lord Wilson agreeing) sought to depart from the Art 8 threshold test of a 'reasonable expectation of privacy'. This case concerned 'Operation Exposure' in which police in Northern Ireland released to the press photographs of a 14-year-old, alleged to have been involved in rioting, with a view to identifying him.
73 'Charging protest groups "outrageous" says MP', *BBC News*, 9 February 2015; '*The Guardian* View on the Right to March: Protest must be Beyond Price', *The Guardian*, 10 February 2015; Hanna Noyce, 'Art 11 and the Met's "pay to protest" proposal' (UK Human Rights Blog, 8 March 2015). Of parallel concern, in Scotland, s 63(8)(b) Civic Government (Scotland) Act 1982 now requires local authorities to take into consideration 'the extent to which containment of risks arising from the procession would (whether by itself or in combination with any other circumstances) place an excessive burden on the police' when deciding whether to prohibit or impose conditions on a procession. Scottish councils may also seek to recover costs incurred by the holding of processions. The UN Special Rapporteur was highly critical of this practice, and emphasised that 'financial charges should not be levied for the provision of public services during an assembly.' A/HRC/23/39/Add.1, fn 6 above, para 81. The response of the UK government provided little reassurance, arguing instead that the 'costs are appropriate, legitimate and

On occasion too, the scope of regulatory powers has been enlarged because the bodies charged with implementing the law have either overlooked or failed to pay sufficiently close attention to critical nuances in the statutory scheme.[74] Before examining the legal framework in England and Wales in greater depth, it is necessary first to consider why it is that freedom of assembly is important and, second, to overview the parameters of the right to freedom of peaceful assembly laid down in the jurisprudence of the European Court of Human Rights. The following two sections address these issues in turn.

3 Underlying justifications

The right to protest may be regarded as having value for several different – and sometimes complementary – reasons. As such, its protection may of itself be said to be in the public interest. Its exercise, however, can impact on other, sometimes competing, public interests. These include the maintenance of order, the preservation of property, freedom of movement, and respect for personal autonomy – all of which, to some degree, are also fundamental to a vibrant and functioning democracy.[75] A tension thus exists between the protection of the freedoms of protest and assembly, and the legitimate interest of the state in maintaining order and protecting other rights and freedoms.

In seeking to delineate the parameters of freedom of protest and assembly, it is vital to have an appreciation of the values underpinning these rights. The following section therefore briefly examines the core rationales for the protection of protest and assembly. While these may often overlap with the philosophical arguments underlying rights protection more generally (as discussed in Chapter 1), and with the justifications for freedom of speech (as explored in the Introduction to Part II), some arguments may be especially (or perhaps uniquely) salient to the protection of protest and assembly.

It has long been accepted 'that the freedom of peaceful assembly covers not only static meetings, but also public processions'.[76] Different interests and rationales will inevitably come into play depending on the manner and form of the particular protest or assembly concerned.[77] It has been argued, for example, that the relative permanence of a protest camp is of symbolic importance as a 'constant reminder to those in power'.[78]

---

proportionate' and do not have 'the effect of unduly restricting the exercise of peaceful assembly'. See, *Mission to the United Kingdom of Great Britain and Northern Ireland: comments by the State on the report of the Special Rapporteur*, A/HRC/23/39/Add.3, 28 May 2013, para 31.

74 See, for example, the purported 'conditions' for anyone seeking to exhibit a placard or banner in Parliament Square Garden, discussed under 'Demonstrations in the vicinity of Parliament' at fn 506 below. In a similar vein, see the guidance leaflet, 'Police Advice on Protest', issued by police in Northern Ireland before the G8 meeting in Enniskillen in June 2013. This stated: 'You should not conceal your identity by covering your face.' However, contrary to the leaflet, the law (Art 23A, Public Order (NI) Order 1987, as inserted by s 95 Anti-terrorism, Crime and Security Act 2001) does permit a person to conceal their identity by covering their face. What it prohibits is someone from covering their face *to* conceal their identity. The PSNI 'Police Advice on Protest' is available at: https://twitter.com/PSNIG8/status/346910696656748544.

75 See Bailey, SH and Taylor, N, *Bailey, Harris & Jones: Civil Liberties Cases, Materials & Commentary*, 6th edn, p 275.

76 E.g., *Christians Against Racism and Fascism (CARAF) v UK* (1980), Appl No 8440/78, (1980) 21 DR 138, 148, para 4.

77 For example, *R (Singh) v Chief Constable of West Midlands Police* [2006] EWCA Civ 1118, para 54.

78 *R (on the application of Gallastegui) v Westminster City Council and Others* [2013] EWCA Civ 28, para 13.

Furthermore, not all assemblies are acts of protest (an assembly may, for example, be of a celebratory, ceremonial or commemorative nature) and not all protests take the form of an assembly (a lone human rights campaigner, standing in a symbolically significant location reading out the names of those killed by drone strikes, is not relying on group impact to make the point).

Public assembly and protest occurs in various forms, admittedly overlapping, ranging from the peaceful expression of a message or views to rioting and extreme violence (though since the latter categorically falls outside the protection of Art 11, serious public order offences are not covered in this chapter). These different forms may be categorised as follows: (1) peaceful persuasion,[79] (2) offensive or insulting persuasion,[80] (3) intimidation,[81] (4) symbolic or persuasive physical obstruction or interference,[82] (5) actual physical obstruction or interference,[83] (6) forceful physical obstruction,[84] and (7) violence.[85] The last three categories (and, on occasion, also the third and fourth categories) may loosely be regarded as forms of 'direct action'.[86] Unlike the first two categories, the last three categories cannot be termed 'speech', but may be viewed as forms of expression and as having, to varying degrees, the same role as political speech. Some forms of non-violent action may well be combined with attempts at verbal persuasion, but may also be intended in themselves to bring about the object in question (or at least to obstruct the efforts of others to realise alternative goals). Examples include industrial and labour picketing, protests by hunt or fishing saboteurs who physically obstruct the activity in question, and anti-roads campaigners who lie down in front of earth-moving machinery. Such symbolic acts of protest may be primarily expression-based: the assembly element may not be significant. Thus, in some instances the 'assembly' element is dominant; in others, it is almost absent.

Importantly, the rights of expression and assembly are separable and it would be a mistake to view 'assembly' as merely a sub-category of 'expression'. The right to gather and to come together in public is also valuable for entirely non-expressive reasons – perhaps, in particular, the associational bonds which may be established and networks consolidated.[87] Indeed, given the variation in forms of assembly, possibly involving amorphous or avowedly leaderless (or 'leaderful') groups,[88] or global organisations with

---

79 E.g., offering innocuous leaflets or chanting inoffensive slogans.
80 E.g., carrying racist banners, displaying pictures of dead foetuses.
81 E.g., shouting and gesturing at individuals crossing picket lines.
82 E.g., lying passively in front of earth moving machinery, conducting a vigil.
83 E.g., blowing horns during a hunt or chaining oneself to a tree.
84 E.g., resisting official attempts to remove members of a sit-in.
85 E.g., attacking counter-demonstrators or police officers.
86 It is noteworthy that an ACPO guidance document, 'Policing linked to Onshore Oil and Gas Operations' (2011) included (p 8) a diagram on 'The Structure of Protest' which distinguished between four different types of action: (1) 'passive support/opposition', (2) 'protest' ('peaceful assembly and civil disobedience'); (3) 'activism' (worryingly conflated with 'Criminality (Criminal Damage)'; and (4) 'Extremism' ('Serious Criminality (Arson, Burglary, Conspiracy'). Available at: http://library.college.police.uk/docs/Onshore-Oil-and-Gas-Operations-2015.pdf.
87 See especially, Bhagwat, A, 'Assembly Resurrected' 91 *Tex L Rev* 351–373, 364 (2012); Bhagwat, A, 'Liberty's Refuge, or the Refuge of Scoundrels?: The Limits of the Right of Assembly,' 89 *Wash UL Rev* 1381, 1383–84 (2012).
88 Though, for a critique of 'horizontalism', see Gerbaudo, P, *Tweets and the Streets: Social Media and Contemporary Activism*, 2012.

autonomous local branches,[89] it can be argued that there is also a fluid and evanescent boundary between the rights of assembly and association,[90] depending in part on the formality and permanence of organisational form and structure (or lack thereof).

These qualifications aside, the rights to assemble and protest are underpinned by the four interests classically regarded as being foundational to freedom of expression – (a) furthering the search for truth, (b) participation in democracy, (c) upholding norms of tolerance, and (d) the exercise of (individual or group) autonomy. While each of these rationales for protecting freedom of assembly are discussed only briefly below, it is always worth considering the degree to which judges attach weight to these factors when deciding whether to uphold or restrict the right to protest in light of other competing interests (such as the free movement of city traffic, or the aesthetics of renowned landmarks such as St Paul's Cathedral in London).[91] As laudable as such other goals might seem, they can quickly hollow out the substantive protection of the right to protest if the value of the latter is not properly articulated and considered.

Truth

Arguments from 'truth' emphasise that protest should be valued because it enables individuals to communicate with one another, and to bring a specific message to a particular audience.[92] Through increased exposure to different points of view, as John Stuart Mill famously argued, individuals will thereby reach a better understanding of 'the truth'.[93] Truth-based rationales are potentially wider than democracy-based rationales, since even an assembly that promotes anti-democratic views might contribute to a sharper appreciation of particular truths. Such rationales thus stand to insulate even unpopular messages from state interference, helping to ensure 'freedom for the thought that we hate'.[94] One example of such reasoning was seen in the High Court's refusal to issue an injunction to prohibit the leaders of 'Britain First' (a far-right party) from entering the town of Luton. Emphasising the need 'not to inhibit ... the freedom to demonstrate and the freedom to organize politically', Knowles J noted that 'it is sometimes through

---

89 Consider, for example, the relationship between the global campaign organisation 'Greenpeace International' (GPI) and its national or regional organisations (NROs), such as Greenpeace UK. In *Cairn Energy PLC v Greenpeace International and Others* [2013] CSOH 50, a Scottish court refused to issue an interdict (the Scottish equivalent of an injunction) against GPI following a protest action carried out by Greenpeace UK activists: Lord Glennie (at para 23) held that: 'the fact that GPI may have given advance publicity to the proposed action, or later rejoiced in what it regarded as its success' does not mean 'that it can be regarded as having taken part in it.'

90 The right to freedom of association is also protected under Art 11 ECHR.

91 In *R (on the application of Gallastegui) v Westminster City Council and Others* [2013] EWCA Civ 28, Dyson MR (at para 31) rejected the assertion that the aim of Part 3 of the Police Reform and Social Responsibility Act 2011 was 'no more than the protection of aesthetic values or the aesthetic sensibilities of others'.

92 Consider, for example, the argument made by an animal rights protester that the use of amplified sound is a right under Art 10 'so people can hear what is being protested about and can form their own opinions based on the facts we present' – see *Bayer Cropscience Ltd and Another v Stop Huntingdon Animal Cruelty ('SHAC')* [2009] EWHC 3289 (QB), para 31.

93 Mill, JS, *On Liberty*, 1972.

94 This phrase was coined by Justice Oliver Wendell Holmes in his dissent in *US v Schwimmer* (1929) 279 US 644 at 655.

allowing views to be heard, that error in views can be exposed'.[95] Similarly, Paul Wragg has observed that the silencing of controversial protests under s 5 POA (in cases like *Abdul v DPP* – see p 667 below) 'wholly neglects the value of conflicting views so vital to Mill's theory'.[96] Indeed, Wragg further suggests that the argument from truth might favour the protection of long-term protest encampments (in cases like *Hall* and *Samede*) despite the inconveniences that these may cause for others.[97] That said, truth-based rationales may have limited relevance to certain types of assembly – particularly, those in which the message expressed does not significantly rub against alternative viewpoints, or that are more associational than expressive.

Democracy

A further line of argument values protest instrumentally on the basis that it enables democratic participation[98] or otherwise promotes democratic goals. Such arguments are closely related to the notion that protest and assembly can function as a democratic 'safety valve' – an outlet for frustrations and grievances that neither periodic elections nor other formal channels of democratic participation are capable of channelling. Public protest provides a means of democratic participation outside election periods. As such, protest is one way in which ordinary citizens can bring matters to the attention of others, including members of parliament. Citizens will thereby be able to signal their response to government proposals and encourage changes in policy. As the Strasbourg Court has stated, 'one of the aims of freedom of assembly is to secure a forum for public debate and the open expression of protest'.[99] On this argument, the acceptance of the freedom to protest poses no threat to the established authorities, but rather underpins the democratic process. In particular, protesters could be viewed as exercising, through the protest, a choice as to their mode of participation in political activity. As Eric Barendt has argued, 'put most radically', the right of assembly is valuable for active citizens who 'are unwilling to participate in conventional party politics' – it serves precisely to challenge 'the exclusivity of conventional modes of civic activity'.[100] This choice, particularly in the case of some minority groups, may not be a real one, in the sense that they may have long been excluded from mainstream politics. Its exercise may also be bolstered, therefore, by arguments in favour of equality of democratic participation.[101] As Barnum argues: 'the *public* forum may be the *only* forum available to many

---

95 *Chief Constable of the Bedfordshire Police v Golding and Fransen* [2015] EWHC 187 (QB) para 37.

96 Wragg, P, 'Mill's dead dogma: the value of truth to free speech jurisprudence' (2013) PL 363, 376–77, noting that 'dislike, disapproval or offence should never be considered good reasons to interfere with expression if Mill's theory is to be observed'.

97 *Ibid*, p 378, citing *Mayor of London v Hall* [2010] EWCA Civ 817 and *City of London v Samede* [2012] EWCA Civ 160 at [48]. These cases are discussed at p 682 below.

98 See Meiklejohn, A, 'The First Amendment is an absolute' (1961) *Sup Ct Rev* 245. See further, Cram, I, 'Coercing Communities or Promoting Civilised Discourse? Funeral Protests and Comparative Hate Speech Jurisprudence' 12(3) *HRLR* 455, 466–467, contrasting Meiklejohn's 'circumscribed' focus on the participation of *electors* in political debate with the more far-reaching emphasis of Robert Post and Jim Weinstein on the inclusive participation of autonomous individuals in public discourse.

99 *Nosov and others v Russia*, Appl Nos. 9117/04 and 10441/04, 20 February 2014, para 55.

100 Barendt, E, *op cit*, fn 1, p 168.

101 See, for example, Gross LJ in *Abdul and Others v DPP* [2011] EWHC 247 (Admin), para 49.

groups or points of view'.[102] Similarly, in the words of Bevan: '[public protest] assists the "unknowns", those who do not have the capability or resources to exercise expression through the conventional media'.[103] Thus, public protest can act both as a means of access to the media and as a substitute for fair media exposure, and restrictions on protest may deter people from participating in open political debate at all.[104]

While democracy-based rationales are to some degree implicit in both the text and interpretation of the ECHR – restrictions on Arts 10 and 11 can only be imposed if they are 'necessary in a *democratic* society'[105] and political speech has traditionally been highly prized by the European Court of Human Rights[106] – there are at least three reasons why democracy-related rationales might also be regarded as somewhat suspect, in the sense of not conferring sufficiently strong protection on the right to protest. First of all, close attention must be paid to the precise conception of 'democracy' being pursued – the regulation of protest and assembly should never be hostage to majoritarian considerations. This is not a spurious risk – 'majority' opposition to an assembly (by residents in a given locality, for example) can too easily masquerade as seemingly legitimate 'public order' or 'disruption' based justifications for the imposition of protest restrictions. However, as Steven Greer has argued in relation to freedom of expression, 'there can be no legitimate consideration of the demographic characteristics of a particular locality' since doing so 'makes the right to freedom of expression contingent upon the will of a majority, a utilitarian consideration at variance with the rights-privileging character of the Convention.'[107] Instead, as the Strasbourg Court has often been at pains to emphasise, the conception of democracy being protected must not be of the purely majoritarian ilk, but one characterised by pluralism, tolerance and broadmindedness – a vibrant democracy which does not impose one vision of the good life on its citizens but accommodates the public expression of various political visions.[108]

102 Barnum, DG, 'The constitutional status of public protest activity in Britain and the US' (1977) PL 310, p 327. See also Williams, *op cit*, fn 1, p 10.
103 Bevan, VT, 'Protest and public disorder' (1979) PL 163, p 187.
104 See, for example, *Mammadov v Azerbaijan*, App No 60259/11, judgment of 15 October 2015, para 67.
105 Indeed, the Strasbourg Court has emphasised that: '[d]emocracy . . . appears to be the only political model contemplated by the Convention and, accordingly, the only one compatible with it.' *United Communist Party of Turkey and Others* v *Turkey*, Appl No 133/1996/752/951, 30 January 1998, para 45.
106 See, for example, *Castells v Spain* A 236 (1992), paras 42, 46; *Goodwin v UK* (1996) 22 EHRR 123.
107 Greer, S, *The European Convention on Human Rights: Achievements, Problems and Prospects*, 2006, CUP at 269 (critiquing the Strasbourg judgment of *Otto-Preminger-Institut v Austria*, Appl No 1347-/87, 20 September 1994). Greer also notes that 'if the scope of the right to freedom of expression depends upon the tolerance threshold of those criticized it becomes progressively more limited the less tolerant they are'. More recently, in *SAS v France* Appl No 43835/11, 1 July 2014, the European Court of Human Rights upheld the French 'Burqa ban', holding that the authorities were entitled to consider 'the requirements of living together' and that this consideration could properly be regarded as falling within 'the protection of the rights and freedoms of others' limb of Arts 8(2) and 9(2) (see para 117). Ostensibly, ensuring that communities are cohesive and able to 'live together' is a worthy goal. However, as highlighted by the dissenting opinion of Judges Nussberger and Jäderblom (para 5), 'living together' is a 'far-fetched and vague' concept. Furthermore, given its amenability to broad interpretation, it potentially invites precisely the kind of demography-based considerations, critiqued by Greer, in *Otto-Preminger-Institut*.
108 See, for example, *Handyside v UK* (1976) 1 EHRR 737; *Stankov and the United Macedonian Organisation, Ilinden v Bulgaria*, Appl Nos 29221/95 and 29225/95, 2 October 2001, para 97, emphasising

A second reason that democracy-based rationales may under-protect the right to freedom of assembly is that protest is often not directed at the state and so may not touch upon matters of public interest (as traditionally conceived). It is argued, however, that protest against privately owned interests (for example, multinational companies or a grouse shoot on a private estate) should never attract lower level protection on this basis alone. In one case involving the actions of animal-rights protesters, the judge erred close to suggesting that the non-public nature of the intended addressee (here, a pharmaceutical company and its employees) might properly temper the weight attached to Arts 10 and 11.[109] Sweeney J stated:

> The assembly and procession is not a political or public interest demonstration (as normally understood) aimed, for example, at politicians in Whitehall, but rather a protest aimed at a number of citizens in Horsham who are employed in work which the law requires to be carried out, and . . . my approach to the protestors' Art 10 and 11 rights should be in that light.[110]

A third reason for treating democracy-related rationales with a modicum of caution is that they sometimes import an 'alternative channels' argument, shrinking the protection afforded to one 'channel' of participation or communication (such as public protest) because others (such as untrammeled access to social media) exist. The danger with this argument is not only that it may disadvantage certain *forms* of assembly and protest,[111] but that it could potentially relegate assembly altogether as being merely one of many possible modes of participation and communication.[112] As such, democracy-based rationales that do not adequately recognise the qualitative differences between alternative modes of democratic participation can serve to sideline protest and, with it, the many other (perhaps associational) benefits that might accrue from the facilitation of gatherings in public places.

---

the importance of not restricting assemblies or expression 'however shocking and unacceptable certain views or words used may appear to the authorities, and however illegitimate the demands made may be'.

109 Though ultimately, Sweeney J rejected key aspects of the company's application for the imposition of harsher protest restrictions.

110 *Novartis Pharmaceuticals UK Ltd and Grantham v Stop Huntingdon Animal* Cruelty (SHAC) [2009] EWHC 2716 (QB), para 50(xii). *Cf West Sussex County Council v Persons Unknown* [2013] EWHC 4024 (QB), para 4, per Seymour J; *Taranenko v Russia*, Appl No 19554/05, 15 May 2014, para 77.

111 In *Hubbard v Pitt* [1976] QB 142 (discussed below at p 680), for example, Forbes J noted that the protesters were 'free at some other place and by legitimate means, to bring their dislike ... before the public'. Klug, Starmer and Weir described this approach as being 'simply wrong'. See, *The Three Pillars of Liberty*, 1996, p 193. Such reasoning has also been applied in order to uphold restrictions on protest encampments in Parliament Square Garden: see, *Tabernacle v Secretary of State for Defence* [2009] EWCA Civ 23, para 19 per Laws LJ, and *R (Barda) v Mayor of London on behalf of the GLA* [2015] EWHC 3584 (Admin), para 122; and to uphold the proportionality of Part 3 of the Police Reform and Social Responsibility Act 2011: see, *R (on the application of Gallastegui) v Westminster City Council and Others* [2013] EWCA Civ 28, para 41 per Dyson MR (for discussion, see further below, 'Demonstrations in the vicinity of Parliament' at pp 622–26).

112 In this regard, the European Court of Human Rights has noted that, 'access to alternative media is key to the proportionality of a restriction on access to other potentially useful media'. See, *Animal Defenders International v UK*, Appl No 48876/08, 22 April 2013 at para 124, recalling *Appleby and Others v UK*, Appl no 44306/98, 6 May 2003, at para 48. Such logic was evident in early freedom of assembly decisions heard by the Commission (such as *Rai, Allmond and 'Negotiate Now' v UK*, Appl No 25522/94, 6 April 1995).

At face value, the argument from democracy most clearly supports peaceful assemblies or marches that use speech in some form to persuade others, including the authorities, to a particular point of view. In a mature democracy, it might therefore be expected that the extent to which a protest was persuasive rather than simply obstructive would tend to determine the extent of its constitutional protection. But even the peaceful/non-peaceful distinction cannot provide a bright-line rule in terms of potential democratic gains – obstructive protest often also leads incidentally to publicity for the cause and so can also be viewed as a form of persuasive expression.[113] Moreover, even purely obstructive protest without any expressive component could be valued for its associational benefits and, arguably, also for enabling a form of political participation.

In this light, it is of concern that judges have often shown a preference for established democratic channels and an intolerance of direct action protest.[114] Examples are manifest in the 'aggravated trespass' cases under s 68 of the CJPOA 1994 (discussed further below). In a GM crops destruction case, for example, Mummery LJ held that protesters (at least, protesters contemplating illegality such as trespass) must first seek to articulate their claims through established public channels: trespass can never be justified 'if there exists a public authority responsible for the protection of the relevant interests of the public' (here, the Department of the Environment) whose assistance has not been enlisted.[115] Similarly, in *Jones and others*, a case in which anti-war protesters broke into RAF Fairford and Marchwood Military Port with a view to damaging military equipment so as to prevent (in their view) the commission of war crimes, Lord Hoffmann (*obiter*) stated that: 'The law will not tolerate vigilantes. If this citizen cannot get the courts to order the law enforcement authorities to act . . . then he must use democratic methods to persuade the government or legislature to intervene.'[116] In such cases some may regard the democratic process as having been circumvented rather than underpinned. On a more critical view, however, judicial arguments from democracy may sometimes ultimately do more to entrench rather than to challenge (in Barendt's words) 'the exclusivity of conventional modes of civic activity'.[117]

Tolerance

The third rationale for protecting freedom of protest and assembly relates to the value of 'tolerance'. The Strasbourg Court has repeatedly emphasised that public authorities must

---

113 Such protest will be viewed as an expression of opinion according to the findings of the European Court of Human Rights in *Steel v UK* (1999) 28 EHRR 603 and *Hashman and Harrup v UK* (1999) 30 EHRR 241. The protests at issue in those decisions might be viewed as having both persuasive and destructive elements.

114 One might here contrast Professor Howard Zinn's famous aphorism that: 'Protest beyond the law is not a departure from democracy; it is absolutely essential to it.'

115 *Monsanto Plc v Tilly and Ors* [1999] EWCA Civ 3044 (25 November 1999).

116 [2006] UKHL 16, para 83 (discussed further below at p 635). See, in a similar vein, *SOAS v Persons Unknown* [2010] EWHC 3977 (Ch), a case involving the occupation of part of a university building by student protesters, emphasizing (at paras 6 and 18) that 'negotiations should be with elected representatives of the SOAS student community, namely the Student Union'. Judges have also expressed a certain level of distain at the co-option of the *judicial* process by protest groups. See, *City of London v Samede and Others* [2012] EWCA Civ 160, para 63; *R (on the application of Bancoult) v Secretary of State for Foreign and Commonwealth Affairs* [2008] UKHL 61, para 53 per Lord Hoffman; *Monsanto, ibid*, para 26, per Stuart-Smith LJ.

117 Barendt, E, *op cit*, fn 1, p 168.

'show a certain degree of tolerance towards peaceful gatherings' which present no danger to public order except for a minor, inevitable level of disturbance.[118] It is also often said that toleration of public protest is a hallmark of a democratic, free society. Indeed, the argument from tolerance avoids some of the pitfalls of the other consequentialist rationales considered thus far – tolerance stands as a deontological principle which does not measure the value of assembly in terms of its contribution to the attainment of some higher goal (such as truth or democracy). As David Richards highlights in relation to freedom of expression: '[w]e value . . . speech intrinsically, certainly not because it always advances democratically determined policies and aims.'[119] Richards, in turn, bases his argument for toleration on the right to freedom of conscience, which, he says, 'enables persons, on terms of equal respect, to be the sovereign moral critics of values, including political values like the legitimacy of government'.[120] This deontological strength, however, is also arguably the greatest weakness of the argument from tolerance. If it is conceded that there are limits to what should be tolerated, it is not at all obvious how such limits ought to be drawn in the absence of any external benchmark or measure. In this sense, it might be said that the argument from tolerance is ultimately tautologous – tolerance as a rationale for justifying the protection of protest encompasses only those forms of assembly which we are prepared to tolerate and excludes those which we are not.[121] At a minimum, however, tolerance based rationales do at least emphasise that the right to protest (which inevitably entails some level of disruption) should not easily be trumped by arguments favouring either convenience or civility. Furthermore, requiring a level of tolerance for protest should not be confused with 'mere tolerance' on the part of the state. The HRA requires more of public authorities than a mere tolerance of public protest or a recognition of freedom of assembly that can be readily abrogated – it also requires the authorities to fulfil certain positive obligations (see, 'Protest and assembly under the ECHR' below).

Autonomy

Finally, arguments relating to individual and group autonomy[122] may provide a fourth justification for the protection of protest and assembly. To emphasise the autonomy-enhancing role of the right to assemble is usually also to imply a suspicion or distrust of government. As John Inazu argues, '[a]ssemblies function in our democratic structure to challenge and limit the reach of the state', offering 'a check against majoritarian standards and the attempt of government to control dissent'.[123] As such, the rights of protest and assembly should extend protection to groups with radically different conceptions of political life.[124] The question of whether *individual* and/or *group* autonomy

---

118 See, for example, *Bukta v Hungary*, Appl No 25691/04, para 37, citing *Oya Ataman v Turkey*, no 74552/01, 5 December 2006, paras 41–42.

119 Richards, D, *Free Speech and the Politics of Identity*, 1999, p 20.

120 *Ibid*, p 25.

121 Hamilton, M, 'Freedom of Assembly, Consequential Harms and the Rule of Law: Liberty Limiting Principles in the Context of Transition' 27(1) *OJLS* (2007) 75, 87.

122 On the centrality of 'group autonomy' to a theory of freedom of assembly, see Inazu, J, *Liberty's Refuge: The Forgotten Freedom of Assembly* (Yale University Press: 2012).

123 *Ibid*, p 151.

124 *Ibid*, pp 105–6. See also, Baker, CE, *Human Liberty and Freedom of Speech* (1989), 134: 'the constitutional right of assembly ought to protect activities that are *unreasonable* from the perspective of the existing order'.

is at stake will largely depend on the particular circumstances of each case.[125] Indeed, the freedoms of assembly and association are closely intertwined – in the words of Judge Harlan in the US Supreme Court in 1958: 'Effective advocacy of both public and private points of view, particularly controversial ones, is undeniably enhanced by group association.'[126]

Clearly, autonomy-based arguments may pull in different directions from those relating to democracy, truth or tolerance. The question then becomes, why should autonomy have priority over and above other values?[127] Even more fundamentally, however, different autonomy-based arguments may also exist in direct tension with one another: As Simon Lee has argued, '[a]t some times free speakers can help us become more autonomous ... At other times, when we are weak, autonomy is better served by building up self-confidence than by undermining self-respect.'[128] Contrasting views about how best to protect autonomy (and the appropriate role of law in doing so) underlie many of the debates about the regulation of 'hate speech'.[129] These same issues come to the fore in debates about the regulation of assemblies where the intended audience seeks protection from the message being communicated by – or, indeed, from the very presence of – an assembled group. Examples might include pro-life protests outside abortion clinics,[130] prolonged demonstrations by animal rights protesters in the vicinity of research laboratories,[131] protestant/unionist/loyalist parades in Northern Ireland through areas where the residents are predominantly catholic/nationalist/republican,[132] and rallies and marches by far-right groupings (such as the EDL or 'Britain First') in

---

125 While a 'protest' can be carried by a lone individual, the notion of an assembly necessarily entails a coming together of more than one person. See also Bhagwat, fn 87 above.

126 *NAACP v Alabama* (1958) 357 US 449, p 460. Carl Stychin, for example, has described parading as a performative spectacle in the acting out of national and group identities. Stychin, C, 'Celebration and Consolidation: National Rituals and the Legal Construction of American Identities', 18 OJLS 265 at 284 fn 129 (1998).

127 See Raz, J, 'Autonomy, Toleration, and the Harm Principle', in Ruth Gavison (ed), *Issues in Contemporary Legal Philosophy: The Influence of HLA Hart* (1987) 313 at 332–33. As David Feldman has argued, 'one person's dignity must give way to somebody else's autonomy or security'; Feldman, D, 'Human Dignity as a Legal Value: Part 2' (2000) *Public Law* 61–76, 76.

128 Lee, S, *The Cost of Free Speech* (1990) p 130. Relatedly, as noted at pp 283–84, autonomy and self-fulfilment are conceptually distinct.

129 Contrast, for example, the views of Ronald Dworkin (see, for example, Dworkin, R, 'Foreword', in Hare, I and Weinstein, J (eds), *Extreme Speech and Democracy*, 2009) with those of Jeremy Waldron (see, for example, the 2009 Holmes Lectures, Harvard Law School: Lecture 2 'What does a well-ordered society look like?).

130 The regulation of such protests continues to be a highly controversial issue in the US. See, most recently, the Supreme Court judgment in *McCullen v Coakley* 573 U.S. __ (2014). The introduction of protest buffer zones in the vicinity of abortion clinics has also been proposed in the UK – see, Luciana Berger MP (then Shadow Minister for Public Health), 'Abortion protests: Can't we all just agree harassment of women is wrong?' *The Telegraph* (10 December 2014); Holly Watt, 'Abortion clinics should get "buffer zones", says Yvette Cooper', *The Telegraph* (8 December 2014).

131 See, *Oxford University v Broughton and Others* [2004] EWHC 2543 (QB), para 81, suggesting (in a case concerning the imposition of exclusion zones for animal rights protesters in the vicinity of the construction of a research laboratory) 'an equal right not to listen' in the sense that there is 'no right to coerce an unwilling citizen to receive . . . opinions'.

132 See, for example, *Re Pelan* [1998] NIJB 260; *Re Farrell* [1999] NICA 7; *Re Tweed* [2000] NICA 24; [2001] NIJB 165–171; *Re Pelan* [2001] NICA 35; *Re McRoberts* (11 July 2003, unreported); *Re KA's Application for Judicial Review* [2014] NIQB 108. See further, the determinations of the Northern

towns with ethnically diverse populations,[133] or protests in the immediate vicinity of residential properties.[134]

One legal doctrine which might be thought to provide some level of protection in cases where autonomy is perceived to be threatened by demonstrators is that of the 'captive audience': 'A captive audience exists where listeners are either unable to avoid exposure to speech or avoidance entails a significant burden.'[135] While the doctrine is a creature of US First Amendment jurisprudence and has rarely been raised in UK protest cases, it has occasionally arisen. For example, it was relied upon to justify the imposition of an exclusion zone on an anti-fur trade protest outside 'Harrods' in London:

> [P]ersons using the café are entitled to enjoy their food and drink in peace[136] . . . it is a balancing act between the legitimate right of the defendants to make their protest heard and the avoiding of any possibility of noise and nuisance to those who might essentially be a captive audience to the loudhailing if they are in the café and, therefore, essentially immobile and unable to move away from it.[137]

One might question whether autonomy (rather than, for example, the commercial interests of Harrods, or the mere annoyance experienced by those in the café) was really the value being protected by these restrictions, but a deeper level objection against the captive audience doctrine can also be raised – one that strikes again at the question of how best to promote autonomy-related aspirations. As Crocker argues, 'the very idea of protecting a "captive audience" presumes that an audience is not actively engaged in the exchange of ideas, but is passively receptive to whatever the given social structure presents'.[138]

Ireland Parades Commission (www.paradescommission.org), and for discussion, Hamilton, *op cit*, fn 121.

133 E.g., far-right groups (such as the EDL or Britain First) have been restricted from marching in areas of community tension (by conditions imposed under ss 12–14 of the 1986 Act). In May 2015, for example, Rotherham Council sought the consent of the Home Secretary to prohibit marches in Rotherham under s 13 of the Public Order Act.

134 In *Wife and Children of Omar Othman v English National Resistance and others* [2013] EWHC 1421 (QB), Silber J granted an anti-harassment order under s 3 Protection from Harassment Act 1997 against far-right demonstrators who had protested outside the house of Omar Othman (otherwise known as Abu Qatada) making his wife and children 'prisoners in their own house' (para 30). Particular weight was given to the rights of children – here, under Art 8 ECHR (paras 48–50). See also, *Novartis Pharmaceuticals UK Ltd and Another v Stop Huntingdon Animal Cruelty* ('SHAC') [2009] EWHC 2716 (QB), para 31, Sweeney J relying on *Connolly v DPP* [2007] EWHC 237 (Admin) (see fn 275 below), and para 50(vii)), noting that 'the employees of [Novartis] have significant Art 8 rights'. See also the discussion at p 680 below of *Hubbard v Pitt* [1976] QB 142, and the offence of 'Harassment etc. of a person in his home' and related powers under ss 42 and 42A of the Criminal Justice and Police Act 2001, and s 2(1)(b) and (2) of the Anti-Social Behaviour, Crime and Policing Act 2014.

135 Lee, W, 'The Unwilling Listener: Hill v. Colrado's Chilling Effect on Unorthodox Speech' 35 *UC Davis L Rev* 387 at 404 (2001–2002).

136 *Harrods Ltd v McNally and Others* [2011] EWHC 4096 (QB), para 22. Subsequently, see also [2013] EWHC 1479 (QB).

137 *Ibid*, [2011] para 24. Even 'people waiting' were regarded as comprising 'an equally captive audience' (para 25).

138 Crocker, TP, 'Displacing Dissent: The Role of "Place" in First Amendment Jurisprudence' 75 *Fordham Law Review* 2587, 2633 (2007).

In conclusion, it can be seen that several justifications – dovetailing with the rationales often relied upon to protect free speech – underpin freedom of assembly and public protest. But it is also clear that these justifications are not equally present in relation to all assemblies or all forms of what may loosely be termed protest. Furthermore, each rationale offers a somewhat imperfect justification for protecting the rights to protest and assemble – and most importantly, the arguments from both democracy and autonomy also yield arguments that might be used against protesters in order to justify restrictions. The double-edged nature of some of these rationales will be evident in the following section that overviews the case law of the European Court of Human Rights in relation to protest and assembly.

4 Protest and assembly under the ECHR

The now expansive Art 11 jurisprudence of the European Court of Human Rights lays down a number of important guiding principles which should serve to structure the discretion of the police and inform judicial interpretation of the right to protest in the UK. There is also now a wealth of 'soft law' guidance relating to freedom of assembly that could be taken into consideration by domestic courts.[139] This section overviews (a) the scope of the Art 11 right (considering its overlap with Art 10 and the extent to which different forms of protest and assembly, including direct action protest, are protected under the ECHR; (b) the state's obligations (both negative and positive) in relation the right of assembly, considering also the impact of the 'margin of appreciation' doctrine; (c) notification and authorisation requirements for assembly organisers; and (d) justifications for imposing restrictions on protest and assembly.

The scope of the Art 11 right

The Strasbourg Court has on the whole followed an inclusive approach to the scope of Art 11(1). A foundational principle, repeated in a number of cases, is that 'the right to freedom of peaceful assembly . . . is a fundamental right in a democratic society, and, like the right to freedom of expression, is one of the foundations of such a society . . .'.[140] In addition, Art 11 protects only *peaceful* assembly. It does not therefore cover a demonstration where the organisers and participants have violent intentions.[141] Peaceful intentions should generally be presumed, and any argument to the contrary must be fully supported with relevant and convincing evidence.[142] In this regard, the court has emphasised that '[t]he burden of proving the violent intentions of the organiser of a

139 Examples include the OSCE-ODIHR – Venice Commission *Guidelines on Freedom of Peaceful Assembly*, 2nd edn, 2010 (3rd edn forthcoming); the Reports of the UN Special Rapporteur on the Rights to Freedom of Peaceful Assembly and of Association; and the *Protest Principles* developed by 'Art 19'.

140 *Rassemblement Jurassien v Switzerland* (1980) 17 DR 93, p 119.

141 For example, *Stankov and the United Macedonian Organisation (UMO) Ilinden v Bulgaria*, Appl Nos 29221/95 and 29225/95, 2 October 2001, para 77; *Galstyan v Armenia*, Appl No 26986/03, 15 November 2007, para 101; *Karpyuk and Others v Ukraine*, Appl Nos 30582/04 and 32152/4, 6 October 2015, para 190.

142 See, for example, *Makhmudov v Russia*, Appl No 35082/04, 26 July 2007, para 68; *Pekaslan v Turkey*, Appl Nos 4572/06 and 5684/06, 20 March 2012, para 61.

demonstration lies with the authorities'.[143] Furthermore, the right to counter-demonstrate – to protest against another demonstration – does not mean that counter-protesters may block the assembly rights of others: '[i]n a democracy the right to counter-demonstrate cannot extend to inhibiting the exercise of the right to demonstrate.'[144] Indeed, counter-protesters who deliberately seek to prevent others from exercising their right to assemble (by engaging in an activity 'aimed at the destruction of' the Convention rights of others) might themselves be precluded from relying on Art 11, under the prohibition of abuse of rights in Art 17 ECHR.[145]

In *Ezelin v France*[146] the Court made an emphatic and foundational statement of basic principle:[147] 'The Court considers . . . that the freedom to take part in a peaceful assembly . . . is of such importance that it cannot be restricted in any way . . . so long as the person concerned does not himself commit any reprehensible act on such an occasion.'[148] While it is not entirely clear what exactly the term 'reprehensible' encompasses, the Court has clarified that unlawful and seriously obstructive protest may be viewed as 'reprehensible' even if it remains peaceful.[149] On its face, the *Ezelin* judgment would prohibit the application of civil or criminal sanctions to peaceful protesters. The applicant, an advocate, took part in a demonstration against the judicial system generally and against particular judges, involving the daubing of slogans attacking the judiciary on court walls, and eventual violence. Ezelin did not himself take part in any illegal acts, but did not disassociate himself from the march, even when it became violent. He was disciplined by the Bar Association and eventually given a formal reprimand, which did not impair his ability to practise. No fine was imposed. The French government's argument was that, '[b]y not disavowing the unruly incidents that had occurred during the demonstration, the applicant had ipso facto approved them [and that] it was essential for judicial institutions to react to behaviour which, on the part of an "officer of the court" . . . seriously impaired the authority of the judiciary and respect or court decisions'.[150] The argument was rejected and Art 11 was found to have been violated.

Against the backdrop of *Ezelin*, and in order to limit the possibility of authorities relying on incidental violence as a pretext for imposing restrictions on peaceful

---

143 *Christian Democratic People's Party v Moldova (No 2)* Appl No 25196/04, 2 February 2010, para 23.

144 *Plattform 'Ärzte für das Leben' v Austria*, Appl No 10126/82, 21 June 1988, para 32. It is noteworthy that in *R (English Defence League) v Commissioner of Police of the Metropolis* [2013] EWHC 3890 (Admin), para 30, King J described this as being 'a far too formulaic and simplistic approach'.

145 See further, *Norwood v UK* Appl No 23131/03, 16 November 2004, below at p 666.

146 Appl No 11800/85, 26 April 1991.

147 Note that within the Convention system, there is no difference in weight between *'obiter'* comments' and those which, in common law terms, form part of the 'ratio' of the case: see Harris, DJ, O'Boyle, M, Bates, EP, and Buckley, CM, *Harris, O'Boyle and Warbrick: Law of the European Convention on Human Rights*, 2nd edn, 2009, p 17.

148 Appl No 11800/85, 26 April 1991, para 53. The Court has since repeatedly emphasised that this *dicta* – precluding restrictions in the absence of 'reprehensible behaviour' – includes subjection to a sanction, 'even one at the lower end of the scale of disciplinary penalties'. See, for example, *Taranenko v Russia*, Appl No 19554/05, 15 May 2014, para 88.

149 See, *Kudrevičius and Others v Lithuania*, Appl No 37553/05, 15 October 2015 (GC); though *cf Taranenko v Russia*, Appl No 19554/05, 15 May 2014, para 92: 'the domestic courts did not establish whether the applicant had personally participated in causing that damage or had committed any other reprehensible act.'

150 *Ibid*, para 49.

demonstrators, the Court has also emphasized that 'an individual does not cease to enjoy the right to peaceful assembly as a result of sporadic violence or other punishable acts committed by others in the course of the demonstration, if the individual in question remains peaceful in his or her own intentions or behaviour'.[151] Furthermore:

> [T]he possibility of violent counter-demonstrations, or the possibility of extremists with violent intentions, not members of the organising association, joining the demonstration cannot as such take away that right. Even if there is a real risk of a public procession resulting in disorder by developments outside the control of those organising it, such procession does not for this reason alone fall outside the scope of Article 11(1).[152]

The Court has emphasised that 'the right to freedom of assembly covers both private meetings and meetings on public thoroughfares, as well as static meetings and public processions'.[153] It is worth noting, however, that the 'right to protest' *qua* 'protest' is not expressly recognised in either regional or international human rights treaties. This does not mean that no such right exists, but rather, that the right to protest is protected in international human rights law through an amalgam (or a 'cluster' or 'bundle') of cognate rights – primarily, the rights of expression and assembly, and also the rights to freedom of association and to participate in the conduct of public affairs.[154]

The ECHR is to be read as a whole, and the interpretation of any individual article must be in harmony with the overall logic of the Convention. Thus, where issues under both Art 10 and Art 11 rights are raised, the European Court has considered the substantive issues primarily under the right deemed most relevant to the facts (the *lex specialis*), drawing on relevant jurisprudence relating to the other right (the *lex generalis*) where this is helpful.[155] Following this approach, the court has, for example, found 'a violation of Art 10 read in the light of Article 11'.[156] The court has also emphasised that 'notwithstanding its autonomous role and particular sphere of application, Article 11 must also be considered in the light of Article 10, where the aim of the exercise of freedom of

151 *Ziliberberg v Moldova*, Appl No 61821/00, 4 May 2004 (admissibility), para 2. This was relied upon, for example, by Lord Bingham in *Laporte* so as to limit the application of powers to prevent a breach of the peace to peaceful demonstrators – see below at pp 645–48.

152 *Christians against Racism and Fascism (CARAF) v UK*, Appl No 8440/78, Commission decision of 16 July 1980, 21 DR 138, 148.

153 *Kuznetsov v Russia*, Appl No 10877/04, 23 October 2008, para 35; *Christians against Racism and Fascism (CARAF) v UK*, Appl No 8440/78, Commission decision of 16 July 1980, 21 DR 138, 148. Also, *Huseynov v Azerbaijan*, Appl No 59135/09, 7 May 2015, para 91. In the latter case, the dispersal (without legal basis) of a gathering held in a privately owned café was held to be a violation of the right to freedom of peaceful assembly (paras 89–102).

154 See, Report of the UN High Commissioner for Human Rights, A/HRC/25/32, OHCHR Report on the Seminar on 'Effective Measures and Best Practices to Ensure the Promotion and Protection of Human Rights in the Context of Peaceful Protests' (2 December 2013). See also, Wilton Park, Conference Report, 'Peaceful protest: a cornerstone of democracy. How to address the challenges?' (26–28 January 2012, WP1154).

155 For example, *Kudrevičius and Others v Lithuania*, Appl No 375553/05, 15 October 2015 (GC), para 85.

156 See, for example, *Fáber v Hungary*, Appl No 40721/08, 24 July 2012 at para 59; *Taranenko v Russia*, Appl No 19554/05, 15 May 2014, paras 69 and 97.

assembly is the expression of personal opinions'.[157] One consequence of this approach is that the high threshold for interfering with the right to freedom of speech – which affords protection to the expression of ideas which 'offend, shock or disturb'[158] – also extends to freedom of assembly.[159] Furthermore, the high degree of protection afforded by the Strasbourg Court to *political* expression[160] suggests that *political* demonstrations might attract stronger protection than, for example, commercial or non-political events.[161]

Some forms of protest, such as handing out leaflets or expressing an opinion through direct action – where the 'assembly' element of the protest may be insignificant – may be considered only within Art 10. For example, in *Kandzhov v Bulgaria*,[162] in spite of the Pleven mayor's refusal to grant permission, the applicant set up two stands in the city to obtain signatures on a petition calling for the resignation of the then minister of justice. When asked by the police to remove them, he argued that the law did not require permission for such actions. He was then arrested and prosecuted for publicly insulting the minister of justice and for 'aggravated hooliganism'. The Strasbourg Court found a violation of Art 10,[163] emphasising that the applicant was exercising his right to freedom of expression, and that his actions were entirely peaceful, did not obstruct any passers-by, and were unlikely to provoke others to violence.[164] Similarly, in *Tatár and Fábar v Hungary*[165] the Court found a violation of Art 10 because the Hungarian authorities had fined two protesters for purportedly abusing the right of assembly when they hung items of dirty clothing on a rope outside the Parliament building in Budapest (with the aim of symbolically hanging out the nation's dirty laundry). The Court refused to accept that this 'political performance' was, in fact, an assembly and therefore rejected the government's assertion that the two individuals ought to have complied with the law governing assemblies (specifically, the advance notification requirement).

The Court has also emphasised, in *Women on Waves v Portugal*, that the right to freedom of expression includes 'the choice of the form in which ideas were conveyed, without unreasonable interference by the authorities, particularly in the case of symbolic

---

157 *Kudrevičius and Others v Lithuania*, Appl No 37553/05, 15 October 2015 (GC), para 86.

158 *Handyside v UK* (1976) 1 EHRR 737, para 49.

159 The Court has also repeatedly asserted that freedom of expression 'constitutes one of the essential foundations of a democratic society', that exceptions to it 'must be narrowly interpreted and the necessity for any restrictions ... convincingly established'. *Observer and Guardian v UK*, Appl No 13585/88, 26 November 1991, para 59.

160 One of the leading works on the Convention examines the Court's differential approach to four categories of expression (political expression, civil expression, artistic expression and commercial expression) – see, Harris, DJ, O'Boyle, M, Bates, EP, and Buckley, CM, *Harris, O'Boyle and Warbrick: Law of the European Convention on Human Rights*, 2009, pp 455–465.

161 See, for example, *Primov and Others v Russia*, Appl No 17391/06, 12 June 2014, para 135. In *Friend and Others v UK*, Appl Nos 16072/06 and 27809/08, 24 November 2009 (admissibility), the Court however emphasized that it would 'be an unacceptably narrow interpretation of [Art 11] to confine it only to that kind of assembly, just as it would be too narrow an interpretation of Art 10 to restrict it to expressions of opinion of a political character.' See also the discussion of 'recreational' assemblies in fn 172 and fn 339 below.

162 Appl No 68294/01, 6 November 2008.

163 *Ibid*, para 70.

164 *Ibid*, para 73.

165 Appl Nos 26005/08 and 26160/08, 12 June 2012.

protest activities'.[166] Here, the applicants (a group of Dutch activists) had chartered a ship and were seeking to promote the decriminalisation of abortion and reproductive rights more generally. A Chamber of the Strasbourg Court found unanimously that the Portuguese ministerial order which prohibited them from entering Portuguese territorial waters was in violation of Art 10. The Court has made similar averments in relation to Article 11. In another case against Hungary – *Sáska v Hungary*[167] – the applicants had applied to hold a demonstration in Kossuth Square (directly in front of the Hungarian Parliament building in Budapest), commemorating the 1956 Hungarian uprising and the events of 2006. The police proposed that the demonstration be held in a secluded part of the square, but the applicant refused this suggestion, arguing that another demonstration two days earlier had not been forbidden. The court found a violation of Art 11, stating that: 'the right to freedom of assembly includes the right to choose the time, place and modalities of the assembly, within the limits established in paragraph 2 of Article 11'.[168]

Protest on private and quasi-public land

Both the OSCE/ODIHR–Venice Commission *Guidelines on Freedom of Peaceful Assembly*, and the UN Special Rapporteur on the Rights to Freedom of Assembly and of Association have emphasised that protests and assemblies should be able to be held within 'sight and sound' of their target audience.[169] If the right of assembly is to be effective, this principle becomes all the more important in view of the increasing privatisation of public space.[170]

When the issue of exclusion of persons from a quasi-public place, a shopping mall, was raised before the Commission, it declared the application inadmissible on the basis that Art 11 was not applicable because the applicants were gathering there for a purely social purpose.[171] Clearly, a different outcome might have been achieved had Art 11

---

166 *Women on Waves and Others v Portugal*, Appl No 31276/05, Press release issued by the Registrar, 3 February 2009.

167 Appl No 58050/08, 27 November 2012.

168 *Ibid*, para 21. This aligns with a number of UK judicial statements recognizing the essential importance of an assembly's 'manner and form' – see, *R (Barda) v Mayor of London on behalf of the GLA* [2015] EWHC 3584 (Admin), paras 87–89 for a summary of relevant authorities. In *Barda*, however, it is notable that the 'manner and form' argument only had purchase in relation to the question of whether or not there had been an interference with the claimant's rights (see para 92), and that it clearly carried much less weight when considering the proportionality of that interference (para 101). Garnham J also noted (paras 90–91) that this 'caselaw is certainly not authority for the proposition that a protester's choice of place and form must always be respected' – 'a protest does not acquire that status simply by declaring it to be so'.

169 OSCE/ODIHR and Venice Commission, *Guidelines on Freedom of Peaceful Assembly*, paras 99 and 101; Annual Reports of the UN Special Rapporteur on the Rights to Freedom of Assembly and of Association, A-HRC-20–27 (21 May 2012), para 40 and A/HRC/23/39 (24 April 2013), para 60.

170 Although as Evelyn Ruppert notes, to decry the privatization of public space perpetuates 'the myth that public space was at one time open to all citizens and activities'. As such, she argues for a conception of public space as 'constituted not by ownership but by a regime made up of regulatory practices': Ruppert, ES, 'Rights to Public Space: Regulatory Reconfigurations of Liberty' 27(3) *Urban Geography* 271–292 (2006) at 273.

171 *Anderson v UK*, Appl No 33689/96, 27 October 1997 (admissibility), an application which followed from *CIN Properties Ltd v Rawlins* [1995] 2 EGLR 130.

been engaged – and this would now be a more likely prospect in light of the Court's subsequent rulings that assemblies of a social character *are* protected by Art 11.[172] However, the premium placed on property rights in *Appleby v UK*[173] does not afford encouragement to this proposition. The applicants were stopped from setting up a stand and distributing leaflets in a privately owned shopping centre. The Court said that while freedom of expression is an important right, it is not unlimited. Regard, it was found, must also be had to the property rights of the owner of the shopping centre under Article 1 of Protocol No 1. The Court found that Art 10 does not bestow any 'freedom of forum' for the exercise of that right. While 'private meetings' (thus encompassing meetings on private property) fall within the scope of Art 11, neither Arts 10 or 11 have been interpreted to confer rights of *access* to privately owned property. The only concession made by the Court is where the bar on access to property has the effect of preventing *any* effective exercise of freedom of expression or where it can be said that the essence of the right has been destroyed. In such circumstances, a positive obligation could arise for the state to protect the enjoyment of the Convention rights by regulating property rights.[174] But in this particular case, the restriction on the applicants' ability to communicate their views was limited only to certain areas. They were able to campaign in the old town centre and to employ other alternative means of making their protest. The Court therefore found no breach of Art 10 and stated that as the same issues arose under Art 11 it did not require separate consideration.

Direct action

While Strasbourg freedom of assembly jurisprudence has significantly expanded, relatively few cases deal with direct action protest. The case of *G v FRG*[175] concerned a sit-in that had blocked the road to a US army barracks in a protest against nuclear weapons.[176] The protest was primarily symbolic, rather than obstructive, since the demonstrators blocked the road for only 12 minutes in every hour. The applicant ignored an order to leave the road, was arrested and convicted of the offence of coercion by force or threats.[177] It was found that 'the applicant's conviction . . . interfered with his [Art

---

172 In *Friend and Others v UK*, Appl Nos 16072/06 and 27809/08, 24 November 2009 (admissibility), the Court acknowledged (para 50) that Art 11 'may extend to the protection of an assembly of an essentially social character'. See also, *Huseynov v Azerbaijan*, Appl No 59135/09, 7 May 2015, para 91. This supersedes the Commission's earlier holding in *Anderson*.

173 Appl No 44306/98, 6 May 2003; see, for discussion Morgan, J [2003] *J Civ Lib* 98–112; Mead, *op cit*, fn 1, pp 132–136.

174 *Ibid*, para 48. More recently, Judge Pinto de Albuquerque, drawing on the US public forum doctrine, urged his fellow judges in Strasbourg to distinguish between traditional public forums, limited public forums and non-public forums (see his dissenting opinion in *Mouvement Raëlien Suisse v Switzerland* [GC], Appl No 16354/06, 13 July 2012). Such a taxonomy transcends strict questions of ownership, arguably affording greater protection to assemblies on privately-owned land so long as it can be regarded as a public forum. See also his concurring opinion in *Krupko and Others v Russia*, no. 26587/07, 26 June 2014, para 8.

175 Appl No 13079/87, (1989) 21 DR 138.

176 The protest was intended to mark the third anniversary of the NATO Twin-Track Agreement (NATO Doppelbeschluß).

177 Under the German Criminal Code, s 240.

11] rights'.[178] However, the interference was again quite readily found to be justified. The Commission considered that the applicant's conviction for having participated in the sit-in could be viewed as necessary in a democratic society for the prevention of disorder and crime since the blocking of a public road had caused more obstruction than would normally arise from the exercise of the right of peaceful assembly. The application was dismissed as manifestly ill-founded – a fate that has befallen several other direct action cases.[179]

Art 11 also extends to less traditional forms of assembly. For example, in *Friedl v Austria*[180] the European Commission on Human Rights suggested that Art 11 could potentially encompass protracted encampments. Ultimately, however, the Commission found it unnecessary to resolve this question, holding instead that the dispersal of the gathering, after a week, was necessary for the prevention of disorder.[181] More recently, in *Barraco v France*, a drive-slow protest by lorry drivers on a French motorway was regarded as at least falling within the scope of Art 11, and in *Nosov and Others v Russia*[182] the Court impliedly accepted that a tent encampment in a city centre location – for which the organisers had not indicated an end date – also fell within the scope of Art 11(1).[183] As with *Friedl*, however, no violation of Art 11 was found in either *Barraco* or *Nosov*. In both cases, the Court held that the authorities had shown the requisite degree of tolerance before intervening, thereby enabling the protesters to express their position and to draw their concerns to the attention of the public.[184]

Prima facie therefore, most forms of assembly (including encampments and occupations) and all forms of protest that express an opinion (including 'direct action' involving physical obstruction) will fall within the scope of Art 10(1) and/or Art 11(1). In *Steel and Others v UK*, for example, protesters who were physically impeding grouse shooters and road builders were found to be engaging in 'expression' within the meaning of Art 10.[185] This finding was reiterated in *Taranenko v Russia*,[186] where Art 10

---

178 The Court accepted that 'the applicant and the other demonstrators had not been actively violent in the course of the sit-in concerned'.

179 See, *Drieman v Norway*, Appl No 33678/96, 4 May 2000 (concerning a protest at sea by Greenpeace activists against a whaling ship – 'the particular method of action used by the applicants amounted to a form of coercion forcing the whalers to abandon their lawful activity'); *Nicol and Selvanayagam v UK*, Appl No 32213/96, 11 January 2001 (the arrest and detention of protesters who, with the declared intention of 'sabotaging' a fishing competition, persistently obstructed the fishermen was not disproportionate).

180 Appl No 15225/89, 30 November 1992 (admissibility).

181 The application was found to be manifestly ill-founded.

182 Appl Nos 9117/04 and 10441/04, 20 February 2014.

183 Appl No 31684/05, 5 March 2009.

184 See, *Nosov v Russia*, Appl Nos 9117/04 and 10441/04, 20 February 2014, paras 59–60.

185 (1999) 28 EHRR 603, para 92: 'It is true that the protests took the form of physically impeding the activities of which the applicants disapproved, but the Court considers nonetheless that they constituted expressions of opinion with the meaning of Art 10.' Indeed, the interferences with the Art 10 rights of the the third, fourth and fifth applicants in *Steel, Lush, Needham, Polden and Cole v UK* (who had together been holding a banner and giving out leaflets outside a 'Fighter Helicopter' conference in London) were found to be disproportionate to the aim of preventing disorder.

186 Appl No 19554/05, judgment of 15 May 2014, para 70. See also, *Hashman v UK* (2000) 8 BHRC 104; (1999) 30 EHRR 241. See, however, *Kudrevičius and Others v Lithuania*, Appl No 37553/05, 15 October 2015 (GC) in which an unlawful and obstructive assembly was deemed to be 'reprehensible' in *Ezelin* terms (*cf* the earlier Chamber judgment of 26 November 2013).

was found to be engaged by the occupation of a room in the Presidential Administration building by approximately 40 anti-Putin protesters (some of whom were members of the National Bolsheviks party). The protesters were prosecuted under the Criminal Code for attempted violent overthrow of the state and intentional destruction of others' property. They were remanded in custody for almost a year, and received a suspended sentence of three years' imprisonment. Crucially, the European Court found that the protesters' conduct 'did not amount to violence',[187] and while their arrest and removal from the building was justified by the demands of the protection of public order,[188] the severity of the penalty distinguished their case from that of *Steel v UK*. On this basis, the court found a violation of Art 10, noting that the 'unusually severe sanction . . . must have had a chilling effect on the applicant and other persons taking part in protest actions'.[189]

The fact that the reach of Arts 10(1) and 11(1) may extend to certain forms of direct action, does not however mean that the Court has recognised a right to engage in disruptive direct action protest (where the level of disruption exceeds that which might inevitably be associated with a public gathering). The Grand Chamber of the European Court of Human Rights delivered a much more regressive judgment in *Kudrevičius and Others v Lithuania*.[190] The Grand Chamber found that, in charging a group of protesting farmers with taking part in a 'riot', the Lithuanian authorities had not violated their right to freedom of peaceful assembly. The farmers had peacefully blocked several main roads over a period of two days to protest against falling milk purchase prices and the inadequacy of agricultural subsidies. They did so in breach of both permit conditions and police instructions, and caused considerable disruption to others. The inappropriacy of the 'riot' charge was critical to an initial finding of a violation of Article 11 by a Chamber of the Court: this charge was disproportionate, the Chamber had ruled, because 'the applicants gave evidence of their flexibility and readiness to cooperate with the other road users' and 'the element of violence was clearly absent'. The Chamber judgment did not imply that there was an implied right to obstruct traffic – rather, only that any penalties must be proportionate. However, the Grand Chamber subsequently held that causing such serious disruption could be regarded as a 'reprehensible act' (in the language of *Ezelin*, see above), and that prosecuting the farmers for inciting a riot was within the Lithuanian authorities' margin of appreciation. At one level, this judgment is not entirely surprising (the Court has held that obstructive and unlawful protest can properly be dispersed after the protesters have been able to make their views known for a sufficient period of time).[191] What is worrying, however, is the willingness

---

187 Para 93.

188 Para 79.

189 *Taranenko*, paras 94–95. A useful overview of the Court's case law relating to the proportionality of the sentences imposed on protesters is contained in paras 80–89 (though discussion of all these cases is beyond the scope of this chapter). See also, *Karpyuk and Others v Ukraine*, Appl Nos 30582/04 and 32152/4, 6 October 2015, paras 227–238.

190 Appl No 37553/05, 15 October 2015. In contrast to the earlier Chamber judgment of 26 November 2013 (finding a violation of Art 11).

191 See, *Bukta v Hungary*, Appl No 25691/04, 17 July 2007; *Éva Molnár v Hungary* Appl No 10346/05, 7 October 2008. Indeed, it is not generally the role of the Strasbourg Court to reinterpret the domestic courts' characterisation of the facts – though see fn 195 below.

of the Grand Chamber to countenance the domestic authorities' conflation of peaceful but obstructive protest with 'riot'.

The state's obligations and the margin of appreciation

Once Art 10(1) or Art 11(1) is engaged, certain obligations are triggered on the part of the state. In one foundational case concerning the policing operation mounted to protect pro-life demonstrators from pro-choice counter-demonstrators, the Court emphatically stated that:

> [g]enuine, effective freedom of peaceful assembly cannot . . . be reduced to a mere duty on the part of the State not to interfere: a purely negative conception would not be compatible with the object and purpose of Article 11 [ECHR] . . . Article 11 sometimes requires positive measures to be taken, even in the sphere of relations between individuals, if need be.[192]

Article 11 may thus impose certain positive duties on the state to ensure that an assembly or protest can occur even though it is likely to provoke others to violence.

Recognising the practical difficulties facing the police in such circumstances, however, the Strasbourg Court also noted that, in discharging their obligations to enable lawful demonstrations, states 'cannot guarantee this absolutely and they have a wide discretion in the choice of the means to be used . . . [T]he obligation they enter under Article 11 . . . is an obligation as to measures to be taken and not as to results to be achieved.'[193] Furthermore, when reading Strasbourg cases, it must always be remembered that responsibility for securing the enjoyment of Convention rights lies primarily with state parties,[194] and that the regional court is subsidiary to national courts. It is thus generally unwilling to substitute its opinion for any findings of fact made by a domestic court.[195] The margin of appreciation – which gives effect to the principle of subsidiarity – operates as a brake on the Strasbourg Court and the degree to which it will intervene. Given too the renewed emphasis on the doctrine of subsidiarity in Protocol 15 ECHR (albeit not yet in force), it may be that a wide margin of appreciation will more frequently be afforded to states in protest cases.[196]

---

192 See, for example, *Plattform 'Ärzte für das Leben' v Austria*, Appl No 10126/82, 21 June 1988, para 32; *Promo Lex and Others v Moldova* Appl No 42757/09, 24 February 2015, para 22 (distinguished on its facts, at para 24, from *Plattform 'Ärzte für das Leben'*). See also *Frumkin v Russia*, Appl No 74568/12, 5 January 2016, paras 96, 126–130.

193 *Plattform 'Ärzte für das Leben'*, para 34.

194 Art 1 ECHR.

195 Though see, for example, the concurring opinion of Judge Pinto de Albuquerque in *Navalnyy and Yashin v Russia*, Appl No 76204/11, 4 December 2014, arguing that the Strasbourg Court should re-examine the factual findings in circumstances where 'grave procedural shortcomings' tainted the domestic proceedings (here, in relation to the 'legally flawed' classification by police of those arrested after a demonstration as participants in an unlawful spontaneous march). His opinion resonates with the argument in the section on 'Protest Policing' above, that courts may sometimes too uncritically accept the police narrative.

196 See, for example, the Grand Chamber judgment in *Kudrevičius and Others v Lithuania*, Appl No 37553/05, GC, 15 October 2015, paras 156 and 175.

In support of this view, the margin of appreciation was highly significant in several early protest cases heard by the Commission.[197] Of particular note are the cases of *Pendragon*[198] and *Chappell*,[199] both challenges to blanket bans on assemblies at and around Stonehenge.[200] In each case, the bans prevented druids from holding bona fide religious ceremonies, which had been held for over 80 years, during the summer solstice period. Since such bans were prior restraints on protest, and since their effect was to criminalise those engaged in purely peaceful gatherings, it might have been expected that they would have been subjected to that 'most careful scrutiny' that prior restraints in other contexts demand.[201] The Commission, however, exhibited a clear unwillingness to examine the proportionality of the bans to the purported risks with any rigour.

It is difficult to reliably predict how the margin of appreciation might influence the court's reasoning – sometimes a wide margin is construed narrowly,[202] and sometimes a narrow margin is construed widely.[203] Sometimes too there is disagreement within the Court about the role, or proper application, of the doctrine.[204] For example, in one of the key judgments of the Court finding a violation of the freedom of assembly guarantee of Art 11, *Ezelin v France*,[205] two of the partly dissenting judges considered that the interference in question fell within that margin,[206] although the majority found that the state had exceeded it. Sometimes too, the breadth of the margin granted to a state is contingent on perceived political sensitivities (which may increase the margin afforded to the national authorities).[207] In *Rai, Allmond and 'Negotiate Now' v UK*, for example, the Commission had to consider a ban on public demonstrations relating to Northern Ireland in Trafalgar Square. The Commission granted the UK a wide margin, noting that, '[i]n the circumstances of Northern Ireland, where sensitive and complex issues arise as to the causes of the conflict and any possible solutions, the Government can be considered in its general policy of banning demonstrations concerning the subject to be pursuing the aim of preventing disorder and protecting the rights and freedoms

---

197 See, for example, *Christians Against Racism and Fascism v UK* (1980) 21 DR 138; *Rassemblement Jurassien v Switzerland* Appl No 8191/78 (1980); *Pendragon v UK* Appl No 31416/96 (1998); *Chappell v UK* Appl No 12587/86 (1987); 17 DR 93; *Rai, Allmond and 'Negotiate Now v UK'* 81-A D and R 146 (1995).

198 Appl No 31416/96 (1998).

199 Appl No 12587/86 (1987).

200 In *Chappell*, these were made under the National Heritage Act 1983, and the Ancient Monuments and Archaeological Areas Act 1979, in *Pendragon*, under s 14A Public Order Act 1986.

201 *Observer and Guardian v UK* (1991) 14 EHRR 153, para 60.

202 For example, *Fáber v Hungary*, Appl No 40721/08, 24 July 2012, paras 39, 42 and 47 (violation of Art 11).

203 For example, *Vona v Hungary*, Appl No 35943/10, 9 July 2013, para 69 (No violation of Art 11 in relation to restrictions on freedom of association).

204 See, for example, the Joint dissenting opinion of Judges Ziemele, Sajó, Vučinić and De Gaetano in *Animal Defenders International v UK*, Appl No 48876/08, 22 April 2013, para 10; *Vo v France*, Appl No 53924/00, 8 July 2004, para 82 (controversially applying the margin of appreciation to the determination of the very scope of the right to life under Art 2); and *Cossey v UK* A 184 (1990), para 3.6.5, per Judge Martens.

205 A 202-A (1991).

206 Judges Ryssdal and Pettiti, pp 26 and 28–30. See also, the dissenting opinion of Judge Keller, and the concurring opinion of Judge Pinto de Albuquerque, in *Fáber v Hungary*.

207 *Sejdić and Finci v Bosnia and Herzegovina*, Appl Nos 27996/06 and 34836/06, 22 December 2009, partially dissenting opinion of Judge Mijović (joined by Judge Hajiyev).

of others'.[208] More recently, in *Vona v Hungary*, the Court held that the disbanding of the Hungarian far-right Magyar Garda (a highly draconian sanction when compared with the less intrusive option of prohibiting the association's most egregious activities – namely the intimidatory marches that it held in towns with large Roma communities) fell within Hungary's permitted margin of appreciation.[209]

Conversely though, in *Stankov and the United Macedonian Organisation (ILINDEN) v Bulgaria*, the Court – in finding a violation of Art 11 – did not accept the Bulgarian government's assertion that restrictions on a separatist group's commemorative events were necessary '[i]n the context of the difficult transition from totalitarian regimes to democracy, and due to the attendant economic and political crisis, tensions between cohabiting communities, where they existed in the region, were particularly explosive'.[210] Similarly, in *Schwabe and MG v Germany* the court stressed that police officers must always respond in a proportionate manner, even in highly tense situations where violence is anticipated.[211] Importantly too, the Court has been prepared to grant only a narrow margin to states when scrutinising *preventive* restrictions on protest,[212] when interferences have concerned the rights of those who have faced persistent discrimination or who are most at risk,[213] and when the state authorities were well-placed to put in place adequate protections.[214]

In the case of *Karaahmed v Bulgaria*,[215] a protest was organised in May 2011 in Sofia by a far-right party (Ataka) against the call to prayer being broadcast through a mosque's loudspeakers. The protest was notified to the authorities and took place outside the mosque during Friday prayers. As those attending the mosque began to spread prayer rugs on the pavement in front of the mosque, protesters played Bulgarian nationalist songs from car-mounted loudspeakers, shouted insults and then started throwing missiles (including eggs and stones) at worshippers. The Court found a violation of Art 9 on the basis that the police had failed to protect the worshippers and their right to exercise their religious beliefs. In this case, the focus was ultimately less on the particular balance achieved between Arts 9 and 11 (see further p 590 below), and more

208 Appl No 25522/94, decision of 6 April 1995.
209 *Vona v Hungary* Appl No 35943/10, judgment of 9 July 2013; *cf* the finding of a violation of Art 11 in *Association Rhino and Others v Switzerland*, Appl No 48848/07, 11 October 2011, on the basis that dissolution was a disproportionate interference – notwithstanding the illegal tactics (occupations) used by the campaign group. Note, in particular, the separate concurring opinions of Judge Pinto de Albuquerque in both cases (arguing that dissolution is 'appropriate only where the primary goal of the association is illegal').
210 Appl Nos 29221/95 and 29225/95, 2 October 2001, para 73.
211 Appl Nos 8080/08 and 8577/08, 1 December 2011.
212 In *Fáber v Hungary*, Appl No 40721/08, 24 July 2012, para 44, for example, the Court held that: '[i]n the exercise of the State's margin of appreciation . . . [e]xperience with past disorders is less relevant where the situation, as in the present case, allows the authorities to take preventive measures . . .'.
213 The Court has held that where individuals are members of groups that have faced societal stigmatisation, a state's margin of appreciation 'should be substantially narrower and it must have very weighty reasons for the restrictions in question'. See the (non-protest) cases of: *Alajos Kiss v Hungary*, Appl No 38832/06, 20 May 2010; *MSS v Belgium and Greece*, Appl No 30696/09, 21 January 2011; *Kiyutin v Russia*, Appl No 2700/10, 10 March 2011. See also, *Vejdeland and Others v Sweden*, Appl No 1813/07, 9 February, 2012, paras. 54–55.
214 *Karaahmed v Bulgaria*, Appl No 30587/13, 24 February 2015, para 105.
215 *Ibid*, para 95.

on the wholesale failure of the authorities to give any prior consideration to how these competing rights might be fairly balanced.[216] As such, the authorities failed to satisfy their positive obligations under Art 9 (especially since it was clear that the demonstration was calculated to provoke violence).[217]

The case of *PF and EF v UK*[218] raised a similar argument to that in *Karaahmed*: it was argued that the police in Northern Ireland (the PSNI), by not taking action to disperse a long-running and violent protest,[219] had failed in their positive obligation to uphold the Art 3 right to freedom from ill-treatment of the applicants (a mother and daughter who passed the protest on a daily basis on their way to school in north Belfast). However, in contrast to the Bulgarian police in *Karaahmed*, the PSNI had at least given thought to the risks (and did provide some level of protection to the school children by way of a cordon). Consequently, the application to Strasbourg was declared inadmissible. The Strasbourg Court has repeatedly specified that, in assessing the risks before banning an event, 'the authorities must produce concrete estimates of the potential scale of disturbance in order to evaluate the resources necessary for neutralising the threat of violent clashes'.[220]

Notification requirements

Notwithstanding the positive obligations triggered by Arts 10 and 11, many forms of assembly – for example, small demonstrations and those that do not interfere in any significant way with the rights of others – do not need to be subjected to regulation at all. In this regard, it is apt to recall one of the joint dissenting opinions in the broadcasting case of *Animal Defenders International v UK*: '[t]here is a risk that by developing the notion of positive obligations to protect the rights under Articles 8 to11, and especially in the context of Articles 9 to 11, one can lose sight of the fundamental negative obligation of the State to abstain from interfering.'[221] Given this negative obligation, many forms of assembly ought to be able to take place without any form of regulation. As the court recognised in *Tatár and Fáber v Hungary*, assembly notification requirements should certainly not be expanded to cover other (non-assembly) types of protest.[222]

---

216 *Ibid*, para 101.

217 *Ibid*, Para 102.

218 Appl No 28326/09 admissibility, 23 November 2010. For the preceding House of Lords judgment, see *Re E (a child) (AP) (Appellant) (Northern Ireland)* [2008] UKHL 66.

219 The protesters' behaviour included: '. . . throwing bricks, rubbish, balloons filled with urine and dog excrement, firecrackers and, on one occasion, an explosive device at those making the journey to and from the school; shouting death threats, sectarian abuse and obscenities of a sexual nature; displaying explicit pornographic material; accusing priests on the school's Board of Governors of being paedophiles; spitting at the children and their parents; wearing masks; and using whistles, sirens, horns and other instruments to create an intimidating atmosphere.' *PF and EF v UK*, Appl No 28326/09, admissibility decision of 23 November 2010, para 15.

220 See, for example, *Fáber v Hungary*, Appl No 40721/08, 24 July 2012, para 40; *Alekseyev v Russia*, Appl Nos 4916/07, 25924/08 and 14599/09, 21 October 2010, para 75; *Barankevich v Russia*, Appl No 1051/03, 26 July 2007, para 33.

221 *Animal Defenders International v UK*, Appl No 48876/08, 23 April 2013. Joint Dissenting Opinion of Judges Ziemele, Sájo, Kalaydjieva, Vučinić and De Gaetano, para 12.

222 See *Tatár and Fáber v Hungary*, Appl Nos 26005/08 and 26160/08, 12 June 2012.

Still, the Strasbourg Court has held that 'subjection to an authorisation procedure does not normally encroach upon the essence of the right. Such a procedure is in keeping with the requirements of Art 11(1), if only in order that the authorities may be in a position to ensure the peaceful nature of a meeting, and accordingly does not as such constitute interference with the exercise of the right . . .'.[223] The Court has further emphasized 'that since States have the right to require authorisation, they must be able to apply sanctions to those who participate in demonstrations that do not comply with the requirement'[224] and to hold otherwise 'would render illusory the power of the State to require authorisation'.[225] It was on this basis that, in 2009, the Strasbourg Court declared inadmissible the case of *Rai and Evans v UK*.[226] The applicants had been prosecuted for organising and participating in an unauthorised demonstration in a 'designated area' close to Downing Street. At their protest, they read out the names of Iraqi citizens and British soldiers killed in the Iraq conflict. They had not sought the requisite authorisation (under the now repealed provisions of the Serious Organised Crime and Police Act, 2005), though the police had been orally informed in advance. Milan Rai was fined £350 plus £150 in costs, and Maya Evans was given a conditional discharge of 12 months and required to contribute £100 in costs. The domestic courts (and Strasbourg) held that the pre-authorisation procedure could not be regarded as a 'blanket ban', accepting police evidence that had they applied for authorisation under the statutory procedure, 'it was unlikely that conditions would have been imposed given the nature of the demonstration the applicants proposed'.[227]

The European Court's stance in relation to notification (that it is not normally an interference with the right to assemble) has the unfortunate effect of insulating such procedural requirements from any form of scrutiny whatsoever – if they are not regarded as an interference, then no assessment of their necessity or proportionality need be made.[228] This is a vital point – bureaucratic procedures, perhaps involving extensive prior liaison between assembly organisers and the police or local authorities, potentially exert a powerful chilling effect on the practical enjoyment of the right[229] (one

---

223 *Ziliberberg v Moldova*, Appl No 61821/00, admissibility decision of 4 May 2004.

224 *Ibid.*

225 *Ibid.*

226 *Rai and Evans v UK*, Appl Nos 26258/07 and 26255/07, admissibility decision of 17 November 2009. See also, *Primov and Others v Russia*, Appl No 17391/06, 12 June 2014, paras 117–118: 'Organisers of public gatherings should respect the rules governing that process by complying with the regulations in force', though the enforcement of such rules 'cannot become an end in itself', and (para 122): 'the "duty of notification" is not an aim in itself.'

227 See also (in relation to blanket bans), *R (on the application of Gallastegui) v Westminster City Council and Others* [2013] EWCA Civ 28, paras 43–44 (discussed under 'Demonstrations in the vicinity of Parliament' below, pp 622–26).

228 As David Mead has argued, '[c]onstruing the need to obtain an authorisation as an interference would be a more favourable approach . . .' Mead, *op cit*, fn 1, pp 79–80. Both the UN Special Rapporteur, and the OSCE-ODIHR and Venice Commission, have argued that, 'notification should be subject to a proportionality assessment . . .' A/HRC/20/27, Report of the Special Rapporteur on the rights to freedom of peaceful assembly and of association, Maina Kiai to the UN Human Rights Council, 21 May 2012, para 28.

229 See, for example, Waddington, PAJ, *Liberty and Order*, 1994, especially chapter 4, 'Negotiating protest: policing by consent?' and chapter 8, 'Institutionalizing dissent'. For further references in relation to liaison policing, see also fn 25–30 above.

which should be enjoyed as far as possible without any form of interference from the state). While the Strasbourg Court has qualified its approach, emphasising that mandatory notification procedures should 'not represent a hidden obstacle to the freedom of peaceful assembly',[230] there are no cases as yet in which the Court has found the procedural obligations imposed on an assembly organiser to constitute such an obstacle. In contrast, the UN Special Rapporteur on the Rights to Freedom of Assembly and of Association has emphasised that even informal requirements that assembly organisers negotiate the time and place of the assembly with the authorities are tantamount to an interference and thus 'would need to pass the strict test of necessity and proportionality, as defined in article 21 of the Covenant'.[231]

In contrast to its indifferent approach to notification requirements, the Strasbourg Court has been more attentive to the issue of spontaneous demonstrations, holding that state authorities should ultimately afford greater weight to the 'peacefulness' of a demonstration than to its strict lawfulness.[232] As such, the court has emphasized that:

> in special circumstances when an immediate response, in the form of a demonstration, to a political event might be justified, a decision to disband the ensuing, peaceful assembly solely because of the absence of the requisite prior notice, without any illegal conduct by the participants, amounts to a disproportionate restriction on freedom of peaceful assembly.[233]

The 'special circumstances' in which the right to hold a spontaneous assembly might 'override' the obligation to give prior notification are 'if an immediate response to a current event is warranted in the form of a demonstration' – especially 'if a delay would have rendered that response obsolete'.[234] Given that many assemblies will be 'time specific',[235] the Court's recognition of the need sometimes to exempt spontaneous assemblies from the strictures of a statutory notification regime is vital to ensure that the enjoyment of the right to freedom of peaceful assembly is 'practical and effective'.

Justifying interferences with protest and assembly

Owing to the likelihood that most forms of protest will fall within Art 10 and/or Art 11 (see above), scrutiny by the Council of Europe institutions has tended to focus on the familiar formula discussed in Chapter 2: in order to be justified, state interference with Arts 10 and 11 guarantees must be non-discriminatory, prescribed by law, pursue

---

230 See, for example, *Berladir v Russia*, Appl No 34202/06, 10 July 2012, para 39.
231 *Report of the Special Rapporteur on the rights to freedom of peaceful assembly and of association, Maina Kiai* A/HRC/23/39 (24 April 2013) at para 56, and more generally regarding notification procedures, paras 52–58. See also, UN Special Rapporteur, *Freedom of Assembly: Best Practices Fact Sheet* (5 November 2014).
232 *Karaahmed v Bulgaria*, Appl No 30587/13, 24 February 2015, para 98: 'where the authorities have not been properly notified of a public event but there is no danger or disturbance to public order from that event, those participating in it do not automatically lose the protection of the Convention'.
233 *Bukta v Hungary*, Appl No 25691/04, 17 July 2007, para 36.
234 *Éva Molnár v Hungary*, Appl No 10346/05, 7 October 2008, para 38.
235 See, for example, *Zeleni Balkani v Bulgaria*, Appl No 63778/00, 12 July 2007, para 40.

a legitimate aim, and be necessary in a democratic society. This section examines each of these requirements in turn.

Rights must of course also be applied in a non-discriminatory fashion, and the provisions against non-discrimination arising under Art 14 and Protocol 12 (the latter has not yet been ratified by the UK) are potentially significant in relation to protests. Non-discriminatory facilitation entails equal treatment for like-assemblies, and in particular, that assemblies with unpopular (perhaps minority) participants or messages do not face more onerous and restrictive forms of regulation. In several Strasbourg cases relating to the failure to protect and facilitate pride parades in central and eastern Europe, the Court has found a violation of Art 14 in conjunction with Art 11.[236]

The requirement that any restrictions be 'prescribed by law' has almost always been found to be satisfied. The Commission introduced a significant qualification to the requirement: 'The level of precision required depends to a considerable degree on the content of the instrument, the field it is designed to cover, and the number and status of those to whom it is addressed.'[237] In *Rai, Allmond and 'Negotiate Now'*,[238] for example, the Commission found that the power to ban – contained in secondary legislation[239] – was sufficiently prescribed by law: 'It is compatible with the requirements of foreseeability that terms which are on their face general and unlimited are explained by executive or administrative statements, since it is the provision of sufficiently precise guidance to individuals . . . rather than the source of that guidance which is of relevance.'

Nonetheless, there have been a number of protest-related judgments of the Court – two directly concerning the UK – in which the 'prescribed by law' requirement was not satisfied. In *Hashman and Harrup v UK*, having found that blowing a horn with the intention of disrupting a hunt was a form of expression within Art 10, the Court went on to find that the UK's interference was not 'prescribed by law': the domestic law – the *contra bono mores* (contrary to a good way of life) power arising under the Justices of the Peace Act 1361 – was found to be insufficiently precise.[240] Perhaps the most notable finding of the Court in this regard was in the case of *Gillan and Quinton v UK*. In this case, the (now repealed) stop and search power under s 44 Terrorism Act 2000 – which did not require a police officer to have reasonable suspicion that an offence was being committed – was found to lack sufficient precision or safeguards to be 'prescribed by law'. The Strasbourg Court emphasised that 'there is a clear risk of arbitrariness in the grant of such a broad discretion to the police officer' and furthermore, 'a risk that such a

---

236 *Bączkowski and Others v Poland*, Appl 1543/06, 3 May 2007; *Alekseyev v Russia*, Appl Nos 4916/07, 25924/08 and 14599/09, 21 October 2010; *Identoba v Georgia*, Appl No 73235/12, 12 May 2015. At the time of writing, a judgment in the case of *Đorđević and Others v Serbia*, Appl Nos 5591/10, 17802/12, 23138/13, 25474/14 was awaited.

237 See, for example, *Chorherr v Austria*, Appl No 13308/87, 25 August 1993, para 25.

238 Appl No 25522/94, decision of 6 April 1995.

239 The power in question arose from the Trafalgar Square Regulations 1952, SI 1952/776, para 3, made under the Parks Regulation (Amendment) Act 1926. The Act allowed the Secretary of State to 'make any regulations considered necessary ... for the preservation of order ...' in the parks.

240 *Hashman and Harrup v UK*, Appl No 25594/94, 25 November 1999, paras 36–41. See also, *Mkrtchyan v Armenia*, Appl No 6562/03, 11 January 2007, paras 39–43; and *Vyerentsov v Ukraine*, Appl No 20372/11, 11 April 2013, paras 51–55.

widely framed power could be misused against demonstrators and protestors in breach of Art 10 and/or 11 of the Convention.'[241]

Strasbourg's main concern in scrutinising restrictions on assemblies has been with the 'necessary in a democratic society' requirement in Art 11(2). The requirement that restrictions only be imposed if they are in pursuit of one or more of the 'legitimate aims' listed in para 2 ('in the interests of national security ... public safety ... for the prevention of disorder or crime ... for the protection of the ... rights of others') will normally be readily satisfied; as Harris, O'Boyle and Warbrick point out, the grounds for interference are so wide that 'the state can usually make a plausible case that it did have a good reason for interfering with the right'.[242]

The Court has long accepted that any assembly in a public place will inevitably cause some level of disruption (often of traffic) and that such disruption, of itself, is not sufficient to justify interference with an assembly (let alone its dispersal). The case of *Patyi and Others v Hungary*[243] usefully illustrates how the response of state authorities to protest can too easily follow what Nicholas Blomley has termed 'traffic logic':[244]

> Traffic logic serves to reconstitute public space in important ways. Public space is not a site for citizenship, but a transport corridor. Legal battles, often reliant on claims to rights, are reframed as collisions between forms of traffic. Speech and expression, for example, become reconstituted as blockage and flow. Collective actions are suspect: individual movement is valorized.[245]

In *Patyi*, the Hungarian police refused to permit several short silent protests of no more than 20 people in front of the prime minister's private residence, arguing first that 'the pavement was not wide enough to secure the necessary space for the demonstrators and other pedestrians at the same time', and then (drawing upon 'expert opinion' of the Department of Traffic Administration) stating that traffic would be especially heavy because it was All Saints' Day when many people would be visiting cemeteries, and because it was December, many people would be leaving for the ski resorts around Budapest via the street in question.[246] The Strasbourg Court rejected these traffic-based arguments,[247] and found a violation of Art 11.

Moreover, 'where demonstrators do not engage in acts of violence it is important for the public authorities to show a certain degree of tolerance towards peaceful gatherings if the freedom of assembly guaranteed by Article 11 ECHR is not to be deprived of all

---

241 Appl No 4158/05, 12 January 2010, paras 76–87. See also, Cormac Mac Amhlaigh, 'Revisiting the rule of law under the ECHR: *Gillan and Quinton v United Kingdom*', *Edinburgh Law Review* 477 (2010).

242 *Law of the European Convention on Human Rights*, 2009, p 348. Occasionally, the Strasbourg Court has questioned the particular aims relied upon by the state. See, for example, the freedom of association case of *Association Rhino and Others v Switzerland*, Appl No 48848/07, judgment of 11 October 2011, paras 60–64.

243 Appl No 5529/05, 7 October 2008.

244 Blomley, N, 'Civil Rights Meet Civil Engineering: Urban Public Space and Traffic Logic' 22(2) *Canadian Journal of Law and Society* (2007) 55–72.

245 *Ibid*, p 64.

246 *Patyi and Others v Hungary*, Appl No 5529/05, 7 October 2008, paras 13–15.

247 *Ibid*, para 40.

substance.'[248] Indeed, in *Fáber v Hungary*[249] the court elucidated a new threshold of 'intimidation', emphasising that there must be close evaluation of the particular context when deciding whether or not this threshold had been met. Drawing on its previous judgment in the 'Red Star' case of *Vajnai v Hungary*,[250] the Court stated that: 'it is only by a careful examination of the *context* in which offending expressions appear that one can draw a meaningful distinction between shocking and offensive expression which is protected . . . and that which forfeits its right to tolerance in a democratic society'. In *Fáber*, the Court had to determine whether the display of a provocative 'historical' flag (the Árpád-striped flag associated with the fascist 1944/45 Arrow Cross regime in Hungary) by a silent lone demonstrator, near a demonstration by the Hungarian Socialist party, and at the site on the bank of the Danube where large numbers of Jewish people had been killed during the Arrow Cross regime, constituted a 'reprehensible act' (in the language of *Ezelin*). While the flag was viewed as offensive, shocking, and even 'fascist', the European Court held that its 'mere display' was not capable of disturbing public order as it was 'neither intimidating, nor capable of inciting to violence by instilling a deep-seated and irrational hatred against identifiable persons'. Finding that the prosecution of the individual protester for disobeying police instructions to remove the flag violated his Art 10 right (read in the light of Art 11), the Court stated: 'Ill feelings or even outrage, in the absence of intimidation, cannot represent a pressing social need for the purposes of Art 10(2), especially in view of the fact that the flag in question has never been outlawed.' Nonetheless, the Court also acknowledged that restrictions might legitimately be imposed on demonstrations 'to be held on a specific day of remembrance – which are offensive to the memory of the victims of totalitarianism who perished at a given site.'[251] The Court stated:

> The need to protect the rights to honour of the murdered and the piety rights of their relatives may necessitate an interference with the right to freedom of expression, and it might be legitimate when the particular place and time of the otherwise protected expression unequivocally changes the meaning of a certain display.[252]

One might critique the *Fáber* judgment by questioning the application of this very test to its own facts – in other words, it might be asked: in what location, if not on the banks of the Danube, would the meaning of an Arrow Cross flag be unequivocally changed so as to give rise to a pressing social need capable of justifying its restriction? Nonetheless, *Fáber* supplements the Court's well-established position on the scope of Art 10 (that it protects the expression of ideas 'that offend, shock or disturb. . .') and emphasises that a high threshold ('intimidation') must be overcome before restrictions on symbolic displays can be justified. In doing so, the judgment arguably nudges the European jurisprudence closer to the level of protection afforded to provocative speech in the US.[253]

---

248 For example, *Ashughyan v Armenia*, Appl No 33268/03, 17 July 2008, para 90; *Balcik v Turkey*, Appl No 25/02, 29 November 2007, para 52; *Oya Ataman v Turkey*, Appl No 74552/01, 5 December 2006, paras 38–42.
249 Appl No 40721/08, 24 July 2012.
250 Appl No 33629/06, 8 July 2008.
251 *Ibid*, para 58.
252 *Ibid.*
253 It is notable that the judgment (para 18) draws on US 'cross-burning' case of *Virginia v Black*, 538 US 343 (2003).

The question of for how long peaceful but disruptive assemblies ought to be tolerated is no doubt one that state authorities would like to be answered definitively. But such decisions must inevitably be made on the facts of each particular case. While the Strasbourg Court has consistently been critical of blanket restrictions on assemblies (i.e. those that prohibit all assemblies in certain places or at certain times),[254] it has accepted that restrictions, including dispersal as a last resort, may sometimes be necessary and proportionate. Thus, in *Nosov v Russia*,[255] the court stated that: 'after a certain lapse of time long enough for the participants to attain their objectives, the dispersal of an unlawful assembly may be considered to be justified in the interests of public order and the protection of the rights of others in order, for example, to prevent the deterioration of sanitary conditions or to stop the disruption of traffic caused by the assembly'.[256] In this case, the Court judged the applicants' two-month long unlawful encampment to have 'lasted sufficiently long for them to express their position of protest and to draw the attention of the public to their concerns'. Similarly, in *Barraco v France* (a case involving a go-slow protest by a lorries on a busy motorway), the Strasbourg Court observed that the complete blockage of motorway traffic, several times, had gone beyond the disruption inherent in any demonstration and that the three demonstrators had been arrested only after a number of warnings about stopping vehicles on the motorway had been given.[257] And in *Cisse v France*,[258] the Court unanimously found there to have been no violation of Art 11 after police cleared a church that had been peacefully occupied for two months by a group of over 200 illegal immigrants.[259]

The rights and freedoms of others that might conceivably be affected by a protest include rights under Art 8 (respect for private life, the home or family)[260] and Art 1 of Protocol 1 (peaceful enjoyment of possessions) – particularly if protesters enter onto privately owned property.[261] It could also be argued that those who engage in group

---

254 See, *Fáber v Hungary*, Appl No 40721/08, 24 July 2012, para 37; *Stankov and the United Macedonian Organisation, Ilinden v Bulgaria*, Appl Nos 29221/95 and 29225/95, 2 October 2001, para 97: 'Sweeping measures of a preventive nature to suppress freedom of assembly and expression other than in cases of incitement to violence or rejection of democratic principles . . . do a disservice to democracy and often even endanger it.' In *Mammadov v Azerbaijan*, Appl No 60259/11, 15 October 2015, para 50, the court further recognized that: 'A prior ban can have a chilling effect on the persons who intend to participate in a rally and that amounts to interference, even if the rally subsequently proceeds without hindrance on the part of the authorities.'

255 Appl Nos 9117/04 and 10441/04, 20 February 2014.

256 *Ibid*, paras 58–60.

257 *Barraco v France*, Appl No 31684/05, 5 March 2009. For similar reasons, no violation of Art 11 was found in *Éva Molnár v Hungary*, Appl No 10346/05, 7 October 2008 – the demonstrators had been able to exercise, for several hours, their right to peaceful assembly.

258 Appl No 51346/99, 9 April 2002, especially paras 47–54 (consideration of 'necessary in a democratic society').

259 The Court also emphasised that the 'fact that the applicant was an illegal immigrant' was itself 'insufficient to justify a breach of her right to freedom of assembly' (*ibid*, para 50).

260 See, for example, *Oxford University v Broughton and Others* [2004] EWHC 2543 (QB), para 80; *Wife and Children of Omar Othman v English National Resistance and others* [2013] EWHC 1421 (QB) paras 48–50 (see also text accompanying fn 134 above).

261 It was partly on this basis, for example, that the UK Court of Appeal upheld the decision of police to disperse a group of Sikh protesters who sought to disrupt a theatre performance (see *R (Singh) v Chief Constable of West Midlands Police* [2006] EWCA Civ 1118, paras 75 and 95. The court placed emphasis on the right to freedom of expression of the play's author, producers and other members of the public who wished to see the play.

activities (such as hunting, shooting or fishing) which might be the target of protest action are themselves enjoying Art 11 freedoms, which should therefore be considered alongside the Arts 10 and 11 rights of the protesters.[262] In certain circumstances, those most closely and directly affected by a protest might also find that their Art 3 right to freedom from inhuman or degrading treatment is engaged. The 'Holy Cross' school case of *PF and EF v UK* (discussed above) is significant in this regard because it was the first case in which it was acknowledged (by both the House of Lords and then the Strasbourg Court) that the actions of protesters could constitute inhuman and degrading treatment within the scope of Art 3[263] with the attendant positive obligation for the police to protect others from such treatment. While the application in *PF and EF* was deemed inadmissible (given that the policing response was found to be reasonable), a violation of Art 3, in conjunction with Art 14, was later found in a case concerning the failure of the police to protect an LGBT march in Tbilisi to mark the International Day Against Homophobia on 17 May 2012.[264] In assessing whether the minimum threshold level of severity under Art 3 had been met, the Court highlighted how verbal and, in this case, homophobic abuse had created a situation of intense fear and anxiety.[265]

Sometimes, those who assemble do so for religious reasons, and so they might themselves seek to rely on their Art 9 right to freedom of religion in addition to their rights under Arts 10 and 11.[266] However, there might also potentially be a conflict between the exercise of one group's Art 11 right and another individual's Art 9 right.[267] Such a conflict has been raised in two Strasbourg cases (though successfully only in one). Finding a violation of Art 11 in *Öllinger v Austria* (in relation to the banning of a counter-demonstration against a 'commemorative' wreath-laying by former members of the SS, both of which were to be held in the Salzburg municipal cemetery), the European Court refused to accept the Austrian authorities' argument that the ban was necessary to protect the Art 9 rights of those visiting the cemetery on All Saints' Day to commemorate the dead.[268] The Court noted that the counter-demonstration (which was to be small, and without banners or chanting) was 'to express an opinion on an issue of public interest',[269] and was not directed against cemetery-goers' beliefs. Moreover, the court noted that an alternative policing strategy (short of a prohibition) could have allowed the two events to proceed. The court thus (properly) set a high threshold for the engagement of Art 9 – 'the responsibility of the state may be engaged where religious beliefs are opposed or denied in a manner that inhibits those who hold such beliefs from exercising their freedom to hold or express them'.[270]

In *Karaahmed v Bulgaria*,[271] finding a violation of Art 9 ECHR on account of the failure of the authorities to take adequate steps to prevent violent clashes between

---

262   See fn 172 above.
263   *PF and EF v UK*, Appl No 28326/09, 23 November 2010 (admissibility), para 38.
264   *Identoba v Georgia* Appl No 73235/12, 12 May 2015.
265   *Ibid*, paras 68–71.
266   See, for example, *Barankevich v Russia*, Appl No 1051/03, 26 July 2007. See also the Concurring Opinion of Judge Pinto de Albuquerque in *Krupko and Others v Russia*, Appl No 26587/07, 26 June 2014.
267   In the UK, see *City of London v Samede and Others* [2012] EWHC 34 (QB) para 15 (upheld, in [2012] EWCA Civ 160).
268   Appl No 76900/01, 29 June 2006.
269   *Ibid*, para 44.
270   *Ibid*, para 39.
271   Appl No 30587/13, 24 February 2015, para 95.

demonstrators and worshippers in front of a mosque in Sofia during Friday prayers, the Strasbourg Court importantly elaborated on the nature of the balancing exercise when two such conflicting rights are engaged:

> The Convention does not establish any a priori hierarchy between these rights: as a matter of principle, they deserve equal respect. They must therefore be balanced against each other in a manner which recognises the importance of these rights in a society based on pluralism, tolerance and broad-mindedness. Three further principles follow from this: First, it is incumbent upon the State to ensure that – insofar as is reasonably possible – both sets of rights are protected . . . Second, to do so, the State must ensure that a legal framework is put in place to safeguard those rights from third parties and to take effective measures to ensure that they are respected in practice . . . Third, as is always the case when a Contracting State seeks to protect two values guaranteed by the Convention which may come into conflict with each other . . . the Court's task is to verify whether the authorities struck a fair balance between those two values . . . In doing so, the Court should not act with the benefit of hindsight. Nor should it simply substitute its view for that of the national authorities who, in any given case, are much better placed to assess where the appropriate balance lay and how best to achieve that balance. This is particularly true when it is the police who must in practice strike that balance.[272]

While at one level, this final point appears to afford significant deference to the police, it also emphasises that, in the context of public protest, it is incumbent on the police to make an assessment both of the appropriate balance between competing rights, and of the methods suited to achieving that balance. Indeed, this could be argued to endorse 'process-based' decision-making on the part of the police (rather than the 'result-oriented approach' approved by the House of Lords in *R (Begum) v Governors of Denbigh High School*).[273] In any case, the twin questions of *who* assesses the impact of an assembly on the rights of freedoms of others, and *how* they undertake any balancing exercise, are of vital importance to the effective protection of the rights to assemble and to protest.

This is especially so given the potential complexity of such assessments. The phrase, 'rights and freedoms of others' in Art 11(2) is not limited only to Convention rights. As explained in Chapter 6, in *Chassagnou v France*,[274] the Strasbourg Court noted that 'where restrictions are imposed on a right or freedom guaranteed by the Convention

---

272 Paras 92–96.
273 *R (Begum) v Denbigh High School* [2006] UKHL 15 (though contrast the different opinions of the Law Lords in *Miss Behavin' Ltd v Belfast City Council* [2007] UKHL 19). Under a 'result-oriented approach' the primary decision-maker – here, the police – would not be required to undertake a formulaic proportionality analysis ('with textbooks on human rights law at their elbows') – *Begum*, para 68. Instead, it would be left to the courts – inevitably, retrospectively – to undertake parallel scrutiny of the different rights engaged to ensure that the correct balance had been struck. See, for example, *Hall and Others v Mayor of London (On Behalf of the Greater London Authority)* [2010] EWCA Civ 817 (16 July 2010) [2011] 1 WLR 504, para 43, per Lord Neuberger MR; *City of London v Samede and Others* [2012] EWHC 34 (QB), para 99, per Lindblom J. For critique, see Mead, D, 'Outcomes aren't all: defending process-based review of public authority decisions under the Human Rights Act' (2012) PL 61.
274 (2000) 29 EHRR 615.

in order to protect "rights and freedoms" not, as such, enunciated therein . . . only indisputable imperatives can justify interference with enjoyment of a Convention right.'[275] The obvious question here is whether an 'indisputable imperative' could potentially encompass interests which would not otherwise be protected in domestic law. If so, the 'rights and freedoms of others' limb of Art 11(2) could be interpreted in ways which undermine the essence of the Art 11(1) right, with 'indisputable imperatives' providing a shield against the myriad 'annoyances' that a demonstration might cause.[276]

Conclusions

Setting aside the early Commission decisions that granted an exceedingly wide margin to states, the Court's more recent interpretation of the limiting paragraphs in Arts 10 and 11 has generally afforded strong protection to the right to assemble. The Strasbourg Court will not tolerate the arrest and detention of purely peaceful protesters, even if the protest degenerates into violence, so long as the protesters in question have not themselves committed 'reprehensible acts'.[277] Indeed, apart from intentionally violent or intimidatory protest,[278] most forms of protest and assembly will fall within the scope of Arts 10 and 11. The finding of the Court that direct action protest, such as physical obstruction, falls within the scope of Art 10[279] is of great significance, as are the findings that protesters engaged in 'sit-ins',[280] occupations,[281] encampments,[282] road-blocking[283] and deliberately disruptive protest[284] are also likely to benefit (to some degree) from the protection of Arts 10 and 11.

275 See further, *Connolly v Director of Public Prosecutions* [2007] EWHC 237 (Admin) at paras 23–25 per Dyson LJ: 'The protection of the right not to be insulted by racist remarks was a legitimate aim within art 10(2). It was a "right of others" which, by implication, must have been considered to be an "indisputable imperative" (to use the language of *Chassagnou*)'; *Re Tweed's Application for Judicial Review (No 5)* [2009] NICA 13; *R (on the application of Boots Management Services Ltd) v Central Arbitration Committee and another* [2014] All ER (D) 148, para 30.

276 See also fn 107 above, and the discussion of *Harrods Ltd and Others v McNally and Others* [2011] EWHC 4096 (QB) in relation to autonomy based rationales at p 571 above. See also Mead, D, *op cit*, fn 1, p 201. See too the courts' reasoning for upholding prosecutions under s 5 POA in the cases of *Abdul and Others v DPP* [2011] EWHC 247 (Admin) and *CPS v Haque and Choudhury*, 7 March 2011, unreported (see p 668 below).

277 *Ezelin v France*, Appl No 11800/85, 26 April 1991.

278 *Fáber v Hungary*, Appl No 40721/08, 24 July 2012.

279 *Steel and Others v UK* (1999) 28 EHRR 603.

280 *Taranenko v Russia*, Appl No 19554/05, 15 May 2014.

281 *Cisse v France*, Appl No 51346/99, 9 April 2002, paras 34–40. See also *Kuznetsov* v Russia, Appl No 10877/04, 23 January 2008, para 44 concerning a small and short (less than one hour) picket blocking a passage way at the entrance to a court building during which the protesters complied with the requests of the authorities. In *City of London Corporation v Samede and others*, the UK Court of Appeal distinguished *Kuznetsov* from the Occupy protest in London – see [2012] EWCA Civ 160, para 43. See also *Hall and Others v Mayor of London (on behalf of the GLA)* [2010] EWCA Civ 817, para 37 (see 'Demonstrations within the vicinity of Parliament' at pp 622–26 below).

282 *Nosov and Others v Russia*, Appl Nos 9117/04 and 10441/04, 20 February 2014; *Ludwig Friedl v Austria*, Appl No 15225/89, decision of 30 November 1992.

283 *G v FRG* Appl No 13079/87, 6 March 1989; but note, *Kudrevičius and Others v Lithuania*, [GC] Appl No 37553/05, 15 October 2015 (in contrast to the earlier Chamber judgment in the same case of 26 November 2013).

284 *Barraco v France*, Appl No 31684/05, 5 March 2009.

Holding that an event is protected under these Convention rights both triggers the state's positive obligations to protect and facilitate the assembly (subject to any legitimate restrictions),[285] and also ensures that any restrictions will be scrutinised to ensure that they are 'prescribed by law' and 'necessary in a democratic society' for one or more of the 'legitimate aims'. That said, the failure of the court even to classify notification schemes as a de facto interference with Art 11 unduly shields such procedures – and the informal 'negotiations' between protesters and police which commonly accompany them – from scrutiny. Ultimately, the Strasbourg jurisprudence permits state authorities to take proportionate measures against protesters – including dispersal as a last resort – if the authorities have 'displayed the requisite tolerance' and protesters 'have been able to exercise their Art 10 and 11 rights for a reasonable duration'.[286]

5 The domestic application of Arts 10 and 11 under the HRA

The expanding volume of Strasbourg's freedom of assembly jurisprudence (as overviewed in the preceding section) serves to demarcate the contours of the rights of assembly and protest, and the limited circumstances in which restrictions can be justified. This case law must be taken into account by domestic courts under s 2 HRA. Indeed, the HRA entailed a fundamental shift in the methodology adopted by domestic courts. Rather than focusing primarily upon the limitations upon otherwise lawful conduct, the starting point for any judicial analysis in the UK must be a positive recognition of the right to peaceful assembly, which can be restricted only if it is necessary and proportionate to do so.

Grounding a challenge under the HRA

Protesters may be able to challenge restrictions imposed upon them by seeking to judicially review the relevant decisions of the police or other public authorities under s 7(1)(a) HRA. In order to do so, they must themselves have been 'victims' – or be likely to become victims in the future – within the meaning of s 7(7). Protesters are also able to argue that a public authority has acted incompatibly with their Convention rights in any civil or criminal proceedings in which they are a party (under s 7(1)(b) of the HRA).[287] In such proceedings, it must be shown that a public authority has acted in a way that is incompatible with a Convention right – in other words, that it has breached its duty under s 6 HRA. The most likely argument to be made is that the imposition of the particular restrictions (whether these be prior restrictions or penalties imposed after an assembly, and whether they have a statutory or a common law footing) were disproportionate to the aims pursued. If less intrusive measures were available which would still achieve the end in view, it can be argued that these should have been imposed instead. Depending on the facts, it might also be possible that the restrictions imposed were discriminatory.

---

285 *Plattform 'Ärzte für das Leben' v Austria*, Appl No 10126/82, 21 June 1988.
286 *Éva Molnár v Hungary*, Appl No 10346/05, 7 October 2008.
287 For further discussion of possible arguments that might be raised (using s 7(1)(a) as a 'sword' or s 7(1)(b) as a 'shield'), see Mead, *op cit*, fn 1, pp 50–52.

There might also be scope to argue that the statutory or common law provisions were not sufficiently 'prescribed by law' so as to satisfy this requirement of the Convention rights.[288] It may also be possible to argue that the aims pursued by the authorities did not fall within the 'legitimate aims' prescribed in Arts 10(2) and 11(2) – although, as discussed above, the permitted aims under the Convention are themselves broadly framed (including, for example, 'the prevention of disorder'), open to expansive interpretation (such as 'the protection of the rights and freedoms of others'),[289] and generally not closely interrogated by the Strasbourg Court.

In regulating the rights of protesters, if the owner of the land is a public authority (for example, a local council), they are bound by s 6 HRA not to act incompatibly with a protester's Convention rights. Thus, in judicial review proceedings, it might be argued that the restriction (such as an injunction or possession order) was not one that a reasonable public body could have imposed or that it was disproportionate. The position would be the same if the owner was acting as a hybrid authority, as might be the case, for example, with university campuses.[290] In contrast, however, where the owner of the land is a private individual or corporation, no s 6 duty would operate directly. Instead, the courts themselves are bound by s 6 to apply the law compatibly with the rights of protesters – thus affording protection under the Convention indirectly, through the horizontal effect of the HRA.[291] In this way, arguments based on Arts 10 and 11 can still be relied on, for example, by way of a defence in possession proceedings. On occasion, the right to a fair hearing under Art 6 ECHR might also be raised.[292]

As explained in Chapter 4, under s 3 HRA, primary and secondary legislation (including the panoply of statutory powers enacted both pre- and post- HRA that enable the regulation of public protest) must be read and given effect in a way which is compatible with Convention rights 'in so far as it is possible'. Such an argument has particular currency where the broad wording of a statute would otherwise allow the imposition of incompatible restrictions. The question of what is required in order to achieve compatibility is of course open to interpretation, and will depend on the court's approach to the relevant Strasbourg jurisprudence. Two alternative approaches in this regard – described here (and see also Chapter 4 above) as 'minimalism' and 'activism' – are of particular significance in the context of protest and assembly.

Minimalism versus activism

While acknowledging that judicial reasoning cannot always be neatly pigeonholed, the difference between these two approaches hinges upon the attitude of domestic courts, under their s 2 HRA obligation to take into account any relevant Strasbourg jurisprudence,

---

288 See, *Gillan and Quinton v UK*, Appl No 4158/05, 12 January 2010, discussed above.
289 See *SAS v France*, Appl No 43835/11, 1 July 2014 at fn 107 above.
290 For example, Mead, *op cit*, fn 1 at pp 48–9, discusses universities as a 'functional authority with a mix of public and private functions' under the principles of *YL v Birmingham City Council* [2007] UKHL 27 and *R (Weaver) v London and Quadrant Housing Trust* [2009] EWCA Civ 587). Another example of a hybrid authority might be the 'Olympic Delivery Authority' – see *Olympic Delivery Authority v Persons Unknown* [2012] EWHC 1012 (Ch). For comment, see Mead, D, 'The Continuing Mystery of "Publicness" Within Section 6 of the HRA' UK Const L Blog (17th October 2013), available at http://ukconstitutionallaw.org.
291 For example, *Sun Street Property Limited v Persons Unknown* [2011] EWHC 3432 (Ch), para 28.
292 *R (on the application of Gallastegui) v Westminster City Council* [2013] EWCA Civ 28 paras 51–59 (though *cf Re Duffy* UKHL 4 (2008), para 31, per Lord Rodger).

subject to the margin of appreciation doctrine. As commentators have agreed[293] and as the House of Lords has stressed,[294] the margin of appreciation should not in itself be applied by domestic courts since it is a distinctively international law doctrine. Furthermore, given the often vague grounds for imposing restrictions on assemblies (such as in ss 12–14 Public Order Act 1986, discussed below), and the sheer breadth of statutory powers available (many of which were not intended to be used to regulate demonstrators), courts should be slow to conclude that Parliament, in legislating on a matter, has itself already achieved the requisite balancing of rights necessary for HRA compliance.[295] To do so would be to institute an 'indigenous' version of the margin of appreciation.[296] This is especially so where the legislation confers wide discretionary powers, or indeed, presumptively concludes that certain locations (such as Parliament Square Garden) are 'wholly unsuited' for certain forms of protest. Such statutory proscription should not be rendered immune from proportionality analysis just because Parliament has spoken – Parliament's seal should not be able to future-proof bans on protest activity.[297]

Under a minimalist approach, the courts, while pronouncing the margin of appreciation doctrine inapplicable, would not take the further step of recognising and making due allowance for its influence on the Strasbourg cases in which it was applied. Thus, judges would rely simplistically and solely on the *outcomes* of these decisions – some of which may be adverse to the applicants – without acknowledging the margin of appreciation's influence on those outcomes (and Strasbourg's general refusal to second-guess the judgment of the domestic decision-maker). Judges would thus be taking the European Court's case law into account, but would be failing to disentangle the margin of appreciation aspects from it. In doing so, they would be importing the effects of 'light-touch' Strasbourg review – and therefore a 'soft-edged' proportionality standard, likely to catch only grossly unreasonable decisions – into domestic decision-making. This, in turn, would likely encourage the continuance of a deferential approach to the decisions of police officers and other bodies, either on democratic grounds,[298] or on the well-established and familiar basis that the issue is one of expertise and on-the-spot discretionary decision making that should be interfered with only in cases of manifest injustice.[299]

---

293 See Laws, J (Sir), 'The limitations of human rights' (1999) PL 254, p 258; Feldman, D, 'The Human Rights Act and constitutional principles' (1999) 19(2) LS 165, p 192; Pannick, D, 'Principles of interpretation of Convention rights under the Human Rights Act and the discretionary area of judgment' (1998) PL 545; Hunt, M, Singh, R and Demetriou, M, 'Is there a role for the 'margin of appreciation' in national law after the Human Rights Act?' (1999) 1 EHRLR 15, especially p 17.

294 *R v DPP ex p Kebilene and Others* [1999] 3 WLR 972, p 1043. See further Chapter 4, pp 231–34.

295 Remarks from Lord Bingham in *Laporte* [2006] (discussed below) might suggest that when judges confront statutory provisions that have a relatively limited impact on Convention rights – either because they regulate the enjoyment of the right rather than removing it, or because they may only be invoked in relatively narrow circumstances – they should assume that the task of satisfying the demands of proportionality has already been undertaken satisfactorily by Parliament. See similarly, *R (on the application of Keep Streets Live Campaign Ltd) v Camden London Borough Council* [2014] LGR 286, para 94 per Patterson J.

296 See, for example, Craig, P, 'The courts, the Human Rights Act and judicial review' (2001) *LQR* 592.

297 See further, *Wilson v First County Trust*, 2003 UKHL 40; *Padfield v Minister of Agriculture, Fisheries and Food* [1968] 1 All ER 694; [1968] AC 997; *R (on the application of Gallastegui) v Westminster City Council and Others* [2013] EWCA Civ 28.

298 I.e., on the basis of Parliament's decision to enact the relevant legislation in the first place.

299 See also Fenwick, H, *Civil Rights: New Labour, Freedom and the Human Rights Act*, 2000, pp 138–39, and Ewing and Gearty, *op cit*, fn 1, pp 91–93.

Of course, the task of disentangling the margin of appreciation aspects may be far from straightforward. It might mean giving consideration to the likely outcome of the case at Strasbourg had the doctrine been disregarded. However, the doctrine often has the effect, not of influencing a particular part of the judgment in a clear way, but rather simply of rendering the whole assessment quite rudimentary. Thus, stripping away the effects of the doctrine might mean having to treat certain Strasbourg judgments as non-determinative of the points raised at the domestic level. As this suggests, an activist approach implies that the courts would make a real attempt to 'strip away' or 'disapply' the effects of the margin of appreciation doctrine in applying Strasbourg jurisprudence. UK judges would regard themselves as required to go *beyond* the minimal standards applied in the Strasbourg jurisprudence.[300] Thus, they may eventually apply a more rigorous approach to proportionality than has Strasbourg, being attuned to the values underlying these Convention rights in the attempt to more fully flesh out the case-led Strasbourg jurisprudence. A domestic protest jurisprudence – a common law ceiling founded on a Strasbourg floor – would thus come into existence.

The potential merits of an activist approach are heightened if one contemplates the possibility of future HRA repeal, or indeed, if 'subsidiarity' obtains notably greater traction as a structural principle in human rights litigation (a development presaged by Protocol 15 ECHR).[301] Increased emphasis on subsidiarity would underscore the recognition that domestic courts can look simply to the general principles developed by Strasbourg for guidance.[302] Even before the HRA was fully in force, Sedley LJ remarked that 'the common law should seek compatibility with the values of the Convention'.[303] More recently, Lord Reed has explained, noting that 'the guarantees set out in the substantive articles of the Convention . . . are mostly expressed at a very high level of generality', these must 'be fulfilled at national level through a substantial body of much more specific domestic law'.[304] Furthermore, since the prospects of an activist approach might appear to be even greater where there is no 'clear and constant' Strasbourg authority (whether because Strasbourg is silent on a particular topic,[305] or where there are inconsistencies in the development of the jurisprudence),[306] an activist approach would also enhance the prospects of a progressive dialogic interaction between Strasbourg and the higher national courts.[307]

---

300 Judge Martens, 'Opinion: incorporating the Convention: the role of the judiciary' (1998) 1 *EHRLR* 3.

301 See generally, Dickson, B, 'Repeal the HRA and Rely on the Common Law', in Ziegler, K, Wicks, E and Hodson, L (eds), *The UK and European Human rights: A Strained relationship?*, 2015, Hart, pp 115–134.

302 As the House of Lords stressed: 'in the national courts also the Convention should be seen as an expression of fundamental principles rather than as a set of mere rules' (*R v DPP ex p Kebilene* [1999] 3 WLR 972 per Lord Hope).

303 *Redmond-Bate v DPP* (1999) *The Times*, 28 July; [1999] All ER (D) 864.

304 *R (Osborne) v Parole Board* [2013] UKSC 61, para 55 per Lord Reed JSC (cited in *Hicks and Others v Commissioner of the Police of the Metropolis* [2014] EWCA Civ 3, paras 74–76).

305 For example, *JR38* [2015] UKSC 42, per Clarke LJ at paras 110–113, citing *Kinloch v HM Advocate* [2012] UKSC 62, [2013] 2 AC 93, para 20.

306 *Hicks and Others v Commissioner of the Police of the Metropolis* [2014] EWCA Civ 3, from para 34 (considering the ramifications of *Ostendorf v Germany*, Appl No 15598/08, 7 March 2013), and especially paras 68–81.

307 See *R (Chester) v Secretary of State for Justice* [2013] 3 WLR 1076, para 27 per Mance LJ. See also, Fenwick, H, 'Prisoners' Voting Rights, Subsidiarity, and Protocols 15 and 16: Re-creating Dialogue with the Strasbourg Court?' *UK Const L Blog* (26 November 2013) (available at http://ukconstitution-allaw.org).

6 Protest and assembly: the legal framework in England and Wales[308]

Introduction

The main statutory framework governing protest in England and Wales (the Public Order Act – POA) was put in place in 1986, and amended in 1994 by the Criminal Justice and Public Order Act (CJPOA).[309] The legal regime relies on the use of both prior and subsequent restraints. Prior restraint on assemblies may mean that an assembly cannot take place at all or that it can take place only under certain conditions. Subsequent restraints, usually arrests and prosecutions for public order offences, may be used after the assembly has occurred. The over-broad provisions introduced in 1986 have been extended incrementally in a range of statutes, several of which, on their face, are not concerned with freedom of assembly or public protest at all but generally at keeping the peace or preventing 'anti-social behaviour'.[310] These statutes are also supplemented by a large number of wide-ranging and sometimes archaic powers that spring partly from the common law and partly from the royal prerogative.[311] In combination, they severely affect the freedoms of protest and of assembly, and, it will be argued, there continues to be a creeping criminalisation, and even terrorisation, of many forms of dissent.

Anti-terror legislation potentially narrows the scope for protest activity. Most fundamentally, the statutory definition of 'terrorism' in s 1 TA[312] expressly covers threats of serious disruption or damage to, for example, computer installations or public utilities. Moreover, the definition also encompasses damage to property, violence or a serious risk to safety that can be described as 'ideologically, politically, or religiously motivated'. Such dangers may commonly arise in the context of demonstrations and other forms of public protest, including industrial disputes and 'direct action' by, for example, animal rights or environmental activists.[313] Some forms of 'direct action', such as the destruction of genetically modified crops, may be intended both to disrupt and to draw attention to a cause. And forms of protest that go beyond mere persuasion may actually substantively influence public opinion, providing *in fact* a more effective means of communicating with others (since they are most likely to attract media attention). Many forms of 'direct action' may thus be viewed as expressive and as having, to varying

---

308 For contemporaneous discussion and criticism of the Public Order Act 1986, see: Bonner, D and Stone, R, 'The Public Order Act 1986: steps in the wrong direction?' (1987) PL 202; Card, R, *Public Order: the New Law*, 1987; Smith, ATH, 'The Public Order Act 1986 Part I' [1987] Crim LR 156; For contemporaneous discussion and criticism of the Criminal Justice and Public Order Act 1994, see Allen, MJ and Cooper, S, 'Howard's way: a farewell to freedom?' (1995) 58(3) MLR 364.

309 Historically, the UK had no formal constitutional or statutory provision providing rights to protest and assemble. The activities of the followers of Oswald Mosley underpinned the enactment of the Public Order Act 1936. For an excellent account of this period, see Ewing and Gearty, *op cit*, fn 1, 1999.

310 Examples include the Protection from Harassment Act 1997; Part 3 (ss 141–149) of the Police Reform and Social Responsibility Act 2011; and the Anti-Social Behaviour, Crime and Policing Act 2014.

311 For discussion of the various offences, see Mead, *op cit*, fn 1; Wainwright, T, Morris, A, Craig, K and Greenhall, O, *op cit*, fn 1; Thornton, P, Brander, R, Thomas, R, Rhodes, D, Schwartz, M, and Rees, E, *op cit*, fn 1. Ormerod, D, and Laird, K, *op cit*, fn 1.

312 Discussed in Chapter 15. For contrary statement of statutory intent, See, *Legislation Against Terrorism: A Consultation Paper*, Cm 4178, 1998, para 3.18.

313 See also Mead, D, *op cit*, fn 1, pp 239–40.

extents, a role and value comparable to 'pure' political speech.[314] Terrorism and protest are the antithesis of each other – terrorism is about intimidating people and undermining the democratic process whereas protest is part of that process, about persuasion and changing minds in a manner that may be reflected at the ballot box. However, s 1 TA blurs this distinction and potentially allows protest-based activities to be re-designated as terrorist. To label such action 'terrorist' is not only to devalue that term, but to take a stance towards particular forms of protest more characteristic of a totalitarian state than of a democracy. Furthermore, the breadth of the definition of 'terrorism' is even more problematic when viewed in light of the Terrorism Act 2006. Section 21 of the 2006 Act widened the grounds for proscribing organisations by including those that promote or encourage terrorism through 'the unlawful "glorification" of the commission or preparation (whether in the past, in the future or generally) of acts of terrorism'. Under the TA 2006, 'glorification' includes any form of praise or celebration,[315] and the glorification is unlawful if there are persons who may become aware of it (i.e. they need not have actually become aware of it).[316]

Counter-terrorism law and policy may also dangerously encroach upon freedom of assembly, and freedom of speech more generally, on university campuses. Under s 26(1) of the Counter-Terrorism and Security Act 2015, universities have a statutory duty to 'have due regard to the need to prevent people from being drawn into terrorism'. Section 31(2) of the 2015 Act requires that universities have particular regard to the duty to ensure freedom of speech, as well as to 'the importance of academic freedom', when carrying out its s 26 duty.[317] However, the guidance issued by the government states:

> [W]hen deciding whether or not to host a particular speaker, institutions should consider carefully whether the views being expressed, or likely to be expressed, constitute extremist views that risk drawing people into terrorism or are shared by terrorist groups. In these circumstances the event should not be allowed to proceed except where institutions are entirely convinced that such a risk can be fully mitigated without cancellation of the event. . . . Where institutions are in any doubt that the risk cannot be fully mitigated they should exercise caution and not allow the event to proceed.[318]

By placing the duty at the level of full mitigation of risk (rather than merely reducing it in part), the guidance will likely lead university authorities to adopt highly risk averse and precautionary attitudes to controversial speakers and events. Indeed, the overlapping

314 Such action is likely to be tortious or criminal but defendants can raise Arts 10 and 11 arguments in defence.
315 Section 20(2) TA 2006.
316 See further, for example, *Faraz v R* [2012] EWCA Crim 2820; *R v Gul* [2013] UKSC 64.
317 Similar considerations apply to the Secretary of State (by s 31(4)) if exercising the power to give directions to a university under s 30 (if the secretary of state believes that the s 26 duty has not been satisfactorily discharged).
318 'Prevent duty guidance: for Higher Education institutions in England and Wales' (revised, September 2015), p 4, para 8. See also, Universities UK, 'External speakers in higher education institutions' (2013).

obligations to protect freedom of speech by virtue of s 6 HRA, s 43 Education (No 2) Act 1986[319] and s 31(2) of the 2015 Act may not have sufficient bite in the face of security and safety concerns when raised by university authorities.[320]

The following sections outline the legal framework (and key cases) relating to private meetings, protest on quasi-public land, processions and assemblies in public places, and the wide range of further powers (both common law and statutory) that have been used to regulate public protest.

Private meetings

This chapter is primarily concerned with the legal regulation of marches and assemblies in public places. However, as has been noted, the right to assemble under Art 11 also includes assemblies inside buildings.[321] The statutory provisions governing marches and assemblies (ss 11–14A of Part II of the Public Order Act 1986) do not cover meetings on private premises.[322] The public order provisions of ss 4, 4A and 5[323] – which concern the causing of fear or provocation of violence and the causing of harassment, alarm or distress – do, however, apply to 'private places'. However, if the place in question is a 'dwelling' (a term that is undefined), the words or behaviour must affect a person outside that dwelling.[324] A more narrow right to enter premises (which might be applicable in respect of some meetings) arises under s 17(1)(c) of the Police and Criminal Evidence Act 1984. Under this provision, a police officer has the right to enter and search premises with a view to arresting a person for the offence arising under s 1 of the Public Order Act 1936 of wearing a uniform in connection with a political object.

Provisions aimed at violent disorder – ss 1, 2, 3 of the 1986 Act – apply equally to private and public places, without any qualification regarding dwellings. Thus, a meeting during which violence might be threatened to persons present[90] would give police officers the right to enter if they had reasonable suspicion that such could be the case. If it was thought that one of the serious public order offences under ss 1, 2 or 3 of the 1986 Act was occurring or about to occur, the police could also arrest under the general arrest power of s 24 of the Police and Criminal Evidence Act 1984. The counter-terrorism measures (discussed in Chapter 15) could also be used in respect of private meetings.

Section 17(6) of the Police and Criminal Evidence Act 1984 also preserves the power of the police to enter premises to prevent a breach of the peace.[325] The primary case in this

319   For discussion of this provision see Barendt, E, *Freedom of Speech*, 1st edn, 1987, pp 321–22; Barendt, E, 'Freedom of speech in the universities' (1987) PL 344.

320   See, for example, *R (on the application of Ben-Dor) v Vice Chancellor University of Southampton* [2015] EWHC 2206 (Admin). See http://www.southampton.ac.uk/israelpalestinelaw/index.page.

321   See, for example, *Huseynov v Azerbaijan*, Appl No 59135/09, 7 May 2015.

322   Indeed, since s 14 of the 1986 Act uses the term 'assembly' rather than 'meeting', in contrast to Art 2 of the Public Order (NI) Order 1987, the 1986 Act does not define 'meeting' (or 'public meeting' or 'open-air public meeting').

323   See, 'Low-level disorder: sections 5, 4A and 4 of the Public Order Act 1986' at p 663 below.

324   See the second paragraphs of ss 4, 4A and 5 POA 1986.

325   In the words of Neill LJ in *McLeod v Commissioner of Police of the Metropolis* [1994] 4 All ER 553 'as a form of preventive justice', not restricted 'to particular classes of premises such as those where public meetings are held.'

regard is *Thomas v Sawkins*,[326] in which a meeting was held in a hall to protest against the provisions of the Incitement to Disaffection Bill which was then before Parliament. The police entered the meeting, and its leader, who considered that they were trespassing, removed one of the officers (who resisted the ejectment). In response, the leader brought a private prosecution in which he sought to show that the officers were trespassers and that he therefore had a right to eject them (and indeed, that their resistance amounted to assault and battery). The court found that the officers had not been trespassing. Although the meeting had not constituted or given rise to a breach of the peace, the officers had reasonably apprehended a breach because seditious speeches and incitement to violence might have occurred. The police had therefore been entitled to enter the premises. This decision has been much criticised.[327] Nevertheless, it does not hand the police *carte blanche* to enter private meetings; it should mean that the police can enter a meeting only if there is a clear possibility that an imminent breach of the peace may occur.

Protest on quasi-public land[328]

An increasingly important dimension of public protest law concerns the regulation of protest on quasi-public land – in general terms, land that is privately owned, but ordinarily dedicated to public use.[329] Protests on 'quasi-public' land engage a much wider range of regulatory powers than do purely private meetings, and yet they may not benefit from the same safeguards (and positive obligations) as protests on public land. Prima facie, assemblies on privately owned land (whether ordinarily accessible to the public or not) will always be trespassory, and therefore could attract liability under ss 68, 69 or 61 of the CJPOA (see further below). Protesters may also be liable for the torts of trespass or nuisance, or be made subject to possession orders,[330] often supported by prohibitory injunctions (see further pp 680–81 below). Indeed, the nature of the place may also determine whether or not policing costs are met from the public purse.[331]

---

326 [1935] 2 KB 249. For further discussion, see Mead, *op cit*, fn 1, pp 322–325.
327 See Goodhart, AL [1936–38] CLJ 22.
328 For perspectives from social and critical geography, and also for comparison with the US, see Staeheli, LA and Mitchell, D, *The People's Property: Power, Politics and the Public*, 2008, Routledge, especially chapter 4 (pp 73–93), 'Publicly Private: Regulating Space and Creating Community in Syracuse's Carousel Center'.
329 For discussion of the meaning of 'quasi-public' land, see Gray, K and Gray, S, 'Civil Rights, Civil Wrongs and Quasi-Public Space' [1999] EHRLR 46, especially fn 65; Mead, *op cit*, fn 1 pp 129–132; See also, Rowbottom, J, 'Property and Participation: A Right of Access for Expressive Activities' (2005) EHRLR 186; Mead, D, 'A Chill through the Back Door? The Privatised Regulation of Peaceful Protest' (2013) PL 100; and Mead, D, 'Expert Commentary: the right to protest, police discretion and access to land', in Elliot, M and Thomas, R, *Public Law*, 2nd edn, 2014, pp 809–810.
330 See, for example, *Warwick University v De Graaf and others* [1975] 3 All ER 284; *University of Essex v Djemal and others* [1980] 1 WLR 1301 (Buckley LJ holding that it was not necessary to limit a possession order only to the particular part of the university property of which students were then in actual adverse possession and that the university's right to possession of its campus was indivisible), cited approvingly by the Supreme Court in *Secretary of State for Environment Food and Rural Affairs v Meier and Others* [2009] UKSC 11 (a case concerning a travellers' camp on Forestry Commission land).
331 Note the 'pay to protest' proposals discussed in the text accompanying fn 73 above, and the cases in which football clubs and music festivals have contested charges for 'special police services' (under s 25 Police Act 1996). See, e.g., *Leeds United Football Club v Chief Constable of West Yorkshire* (2012) EWHC 2113 (QB); *Reading Festival Limited v West Yorkshire Police Authority* EWCA Civ 524 (3 May 2006). See also, Stephen Weatherill, 'Buying Special Police Services' (1988: Spring) PL 106–127.

The definitional boundaries of 'quasi-public' land, however, are notoriously difficult to draw – privately owned places may be 'public', and publicly owned places may not be accessible to the public all of the time. For example, privately owned places have been held to fall within the statutory definition of '*public* place': in a case concerning the power to issue dispersal orders against groups engaging in anti-social behaviour, May LJ remarked that the definition of 'public place' in s 36(b) of the Anti-social Behaviour Act 2003[332] would 'it seems, include cinemas, restaurants, coffee bars and public houses'.[333] Conversely, places within publicly-owned buildings – such as town halls and local council meeting rooms – are neither fully nor permanently open to the public, but yet the public are granted limited access at particular times or for particular purposes.[334]

Indeed, ostensibly fully 'public' land may be regarded as quasi-public because the purposes for which it may be used have been circumscribed. For example, statutes may ascribe particular functions to certain places: s 46(2)(c) of the Forestry Act 1967 provides that Forestry Commissioners may make byelaws 'for regulating the reasonable use of the land by the public *for the purposes of exercise and recreation*' (emphasis added).[335] In a similar vein, in *Mayor and Burgesses of the London Borough of Islington v Jones, Melluish and Persons Unknown*,[336] Hickinbottom J held that the Open Spaces Act 1906 was 'intended to ensure that certain identified land in public ownership is kept as open space, for use of the public to walk and sit, and otherwise recreate' and for no other purposes. As such, the 'Occupy Finsbury Square' protest was judged to be preventing the local authority from administering the Square 'to allow . . . the enjoyment thereof by the public as an open space'.[337] Whilst seemingly preserving a civic or public façade, quasi-public land thus commonly excludes unruly or undesirable uses (vagrancy, busking, revelry, protest and dissent etc.) and is instead reserved for narrowly beneficent purposes (consumption, movement, recreation, education, debate etc.). Indeed, the presumption that public protest either does not, or cannot, also serve such bona fide functions promotes an essentialized view of protest[338] and undervalues the associational and recreational aspects of gathering together in public.[339]

---

332 This provision (now repealed) extended to 'any place to which at the material time the public or any section of the public has access, on payment or otherwise, as of right or by virtue of express or implied permission', and is identical to the definition of 'public place' in its successor, s 74(1) Anti-social, Crime and Behaviour Act 2014, and in s 16(b) POA 1986.

333 See, *R (W and PW) v Commissioner of Police for the Metropolis and Another* EWCA Civ 458 (11 May 2006).

334 See further the discussion of *Laporte v Commissioner of the Police of the Metropolis* [2014] EWHC 3574 (QB) below. See also, for example, s 100A of the Local Government Act 1972 which concerns admission to council meetings.

335 Even more emphatically, the Department for Environment, Food and Rural Affairs issued a (non-binding) 'Information Note' relating to the term 'open-air recreation' in the Countryside and Rights of Way Act 2000, stated that: 'Examples of activities which we consider are not forms of open-air recreation are political rallies, filming activities and professional dog walking. The right of access cannot in our view be relied on to undertake such activities . . .'. Cited in Mead, *op cit*, fn 1, at p 137.

336 [2012] EWHC 1537 (QB), para 16.

337 *Ibid*, paras 13 and 66.

338 See similarly the point made by Fitzpatrick and Taylor that the 'disruption to community' criterion in ss 12–14 POA serves to construct 'marches' as being somehow opposed to 'community' and communal life, rather than themselves being regarded as intrinsically 'communal'. Fitzpatrick, P and Taylor, N, 'Trespassers might be prosecuted: the European Convention and restrictions on the right to assemble' [1998] EHRLR 292, p 298. See also text accompanying fn 403 below.

339 As David Mead has argued, protest may be 'an activity that is enjoyed, that feeds the soul, that is creative and/or is a fillip from the humdrum of work and routine' (Mead, *op cit*, fn 1, p 137). See also his

Notwithstanding these definitional hurdles, the concept of 'quasi-public' space can be regarded as including shopping centres, transport hubs, the grounds and forecourts of town halls or civic centres, monuments and their surrounding land, rights of way across private land, parks or land owned by the Forestry Commission, and university campuses. One specific example (illustrating how quasi-public space may arise in central, symbolically significant, and previously public, locations) is Paternoster Square near St Paul's Cathedral in London – a site now owned by 'Paternoster Square Management Limited', and the desired location of the 'Occupy LSX' protest in October–November 2011.[340] As such, the privatisation of public land has the potential to significantly diminish the 'civic space' in which protest can physically be held.[341]

The preceding paragraphs have sought to explain *why* the regulation of protest in quasi-public spaces deserves close attention. It is important to examine *how* such legal regulation occurs – especially in terms of the application of the Human Rights Act. As noted above,[342] the HRA will still afford some protection (indirectly) where land is privately owned (and its owner is not thus bound directly by the s 6 obligation). The fundamental problem with any HRA based argument in this regard, however, is that the Strasbourg Court has been reluctant to concede that the rights of protesters might, in certain circumstances, outweigh the rights of property owners (under Art 1 of Protocol 1 ECHR, P1–1) to peacefully enjoy their property, ultimately through its vacant possession. As the discussion of the *Appleby* case (in which individuals were banned from collecting signatures in a privately owned shopping centre) makes clear, Art 11 ECHR has not yet been interpreted to guarantee a 'freedom of forum'.[343] Only exceptionally (where the very essence of the Art 11 right would otherwise be destroyed) might the state have an obligation to interfere with rights of private property ownership in order to compel owners to make their land available to those seeking to assemble.[344] As such, it is largely immaterial whether the owner of the land is a public authority, hybrid authority, or private corporation:[345] *Appleby* has been relied upon by UK judges in several protest cases to defeat any suggestion that the rights in Arts 10 or 11 might prevail over the rights of a landowner.

One such case concerned the Occupy protest encampment in London in 2011 (mentioned above). The Court of Appeal acknowledged that, in one respect, the case of the

---

example of the 'all-night drinkathon' on the London tube – a protest, 'as well, of course, as a revelling party' (p 152). The European Court of Human Rights has acknowledged that Art 11 covers assemblies 'of an essentially social character' – see, *Friend and Others v UK*, Appl Nos 16072/06 and 27809/08, 24 November 2009 (admissibility), para 50; *Huseynov v Azerbaijan*, Appl No 59135/09, 7 May 2015, para 91. See above fn 161 and fn 172. See also James, M and Pearson, G, 'Public Order and the rebalancing of football fans' rights: legal problems with pre-emptive policing strategies and banning orders', PL (2015: July) 458, 468–69.

340   See further, http://www.paternostersquare.info/history.aspx. See also, *City of London Corporation v Samede and others* [2012] EWCA Civ 160, on appeal from [2012] EWHC 34 (QB).

341   See also, Finchett-Maddock, L, 'Responding to the Private Regulation of Dissent: Climate Change Action, Popular Justice and the Right to Protest' (2013) 25(2) *Journal of Environmental Law* 293–304.

342   See, 'Grounding a challenge under the HRA', p 593.

343   See pp 576–77 above.

344   See, for example, *Sun Street Property Limited v Persons Unknown* [2011] EWHC 3432 (Ch), para 32 per Roth J (applying *Appleby* to dismiss a challenge by protesters of an injunction and related possession order concerning their occupation of a commercial property owned by UBS banking group).

345   See, for example, *SOAS v Persons Unknown* [2010] EWHC 3977 (Ch), para 27 per Henderson J.

Occupy protesters was stronger than that of the applicants in *Appleby*, since part of the land involved was publicly owned (by the City of London).[346] However, the case of the Occupy protesters was also regarded as being weaker than that of the *Appleby* defendants since the latter had not sought in any way to possess or occupy the shopping centre (but rather only to gather signatures for a petition), and moreover, had not – again, unlike the Occupy camp – significantly interfered with the enjoyment of other peoples' rights.[347] Lord Neuberger thus held:

> while the protesters' Art 10 and 11 rights are undoubtedly engaged, it is very difficult to see how they could ever prevail against the will of the landowner, when they are continuously occupying public land, breaching not just the property owner's rights and certain statutory provisions, but significantly interfering with the public and convention rights of others.[348]

Similarly, in a case involving the occupation by students at the School of Oriental and African Studies (SOAS) of part of a university building, Henderson J emphasised that 'the SOAS Campus is private land'[349] and relied on *Appleby* to hold that: 'Art 10 does not give any general freedom to exercise the relevant rights upon private land'.[350] Furthermore, '[t]he proposition that Art 10 requires the law to override the property rights of SOAS in its own buildings is, in my view, unarguable and offers no prospects of success at trial' and 'for the same reasons, it would be equally fanciful to suppose that the Article 11 right to freedom of peaceful assembly required the court to override the property rights of SOAS in its own premises'.[351]

Protesters seeking to assemble on private or quasi-public property thus have a weak Convention argument, and only a decisively 'activist' approach by UK judges would be capable of redressing the timidity of Strasbourg in this sphere. Such an 'activist' approach was attempted by Sir Alan Ward in the case of *Malik v Fassenfelt*, but his opinion was obiter, and indeed, in marked contrast with the views of the other two members of the Court of Appeal, Toulson and Lloyd LLJ.[352] The case concerned the

---

346 *City of London Corporation v Samede and others* [2012] EWCA Civ 160, para 45. Arguably, this concession might pave the way for UK judges to bring forward a modest advance on *Appleby*, in cases involving non-possessory protest on quasi-public (publicly-owned) land.

347 Also distinguishing *Samede*, on its facts, from the successful judicial review of byelaws brought by a member of the Aldermaston Women's Peace Camp (which had hitherto taken place during the second weekend of every month for 23 years) – see *Tabernacle v Secretary of State for Defence* [2009] EWCA Civ 23, especially the recognition by Laws LJ (para 43) that 'Rights worth having are unruly things. Demonstrations and protests are liable to be a nuisance. They are liable to be inconvenient and tiresome, or at least perceived as such by others who are out of sympathy with them.'

348 *City of London v Samede and others* [2012] EWCA Civ 160, para 49 (see also, paras 26, 28, and 42). See also *West Sussex County Council v Persons Unknown, O'Donnell, Sherborne and Lucas* [2013] EWHC 4024 (QB), para 30.

349 *SOAS v Persons Unknown* [2010] EWHC 3977 (Ch), para 5. See also, *University of Sussex v Persons Unknown and others* [2013] EWHC 862 (Ch), para 47 per Sales J; *University of Birmingham v Persons Unknown* [2015] EWHC 544 (Ch).

350 *Ibid*, para 21.

351 *Ibid*, para 25. See also *Cairn Energy PLC v Greenpeace International and Others* [2013] CSOH 50, para 30 per Lord Glennie.

352 [2013] EWCA Civ 798.

eviction of 'Grow Heathrow' campaigners who had occupied (and cleaned up) a privately-owned area of land, earmarked for potential development as a third runway at Heathrow airport. In the Court of Appeal, the protesters sought to challenge the granting of an order of immediate possession against them, arguing that the court's obligation to prevent a disproportionate interference with their right to a home under Art 8 ECHR[353] meant that they should be allowed a reasonable period to vacate the land (they suggested this should be a number of months). Sir Alan Ward held that ownership should not oust proportionality considerations in relation to eviction.[354] This approach – whilst still according significant weight to ownership as a factor in determining proportionality – implies that it should not be regarded as an absolute and automatic bar to the protection of other competing Convention rights, such as those under Arts 10 and 11. As noted, however, Sir Alan Ward's approach was not adopted by the majority of the Court of Appeal. Indeed, a subsequent attempt to rely on his opinion by anti-fracking protesters in Barton Moss, Manchester (challenging the possession order made against them) was rejected.[355]

The previous cases have concerned protest on privately-owned but publicly-accessible land. An example of quasi-public land that is publicly-owned but not fully accessible is the case of *Laporte & Anor v The Commissioner of Police of the Metropolis*[356] in which the common law power of exclusion (referred to in s 100A of the Local Government Act 1972)[357] was invoked against protesters who sought entry to a public meeting of Haringey London Borough Council in February 2011. Notwithstanding the fact that parts of the civic centre building could be regarded as quasi-public spaces to which the public ordinarily had access, Turner J held that this 'did not, however, confer upon protesters an irrevocable right to remain within the building . . . regardless of the occurrence of disorderly conduct or other misbehaviour threatening to disrupt the meeting'.[358] Citing *Appleby*, he concluded that 'Art 10 does not bestow any freedom of forum for the exercise of such a right which gives rise to the automatic creation of rights of entry to all publicly owned property'.[359] Similar considerations would presumably apply to protesters inside a court building,[360] while additional security considerations would apply to protests within prisons.[361]

As can be seen, the traditional stance of the UK judiciary is thus to favour property rights when they conflict with rights of protest. In general, judges tend to uphold

---

353 Since they had been on the land since March 2010 and thus established a 'sufficient and continuous link with a specific place'.
354 See especially, paras 26–28 and 39. Sir Alan also held that courts do have jurisdiction to extend time for possession, even when no 'exceptional hardship' (under s 89 of the Housing Act 1980) would result.
355 *Manchester Ship Canal Developments v Persons Unknown*, 2014 EWHC 645 CH, para 43.
356 [2014] EWHC 3574 (QB) (31 October 2014).
357 This section relates to admission to council meetings, and empowers councils to exclude the public from meetings if confidential, or otherwise exempted information under Sched 12A of the 1972 Act, would be disclosed.
358 Para 42.
359 *Laporte v Commissioner of the Police of the Metropolis* [2014] EWHC 3574 (QB) (31 October 2014) paras 43–44, and 125–128.
360 Section 52 of the Courts Act 2003 empowers a court security officer to exclude or remove a person from a court building for the purposes of enabling court business to be carried on without interference or delay, maintaining order or securing the safety of any person in the building).
361 See, *Alleyne and another v Secretary of State for Justice* [2012] EWHC 1232 (Admin), paras 13 and 15.

proprietorial rights in an abstract fashion, regardless of any real harm that may occur due to their infringement.[362] Against this backdrop, Tom Watson MP sought to introduce a novel provision into the Public Order Act, through the Protection of Freedoms Bill, on 'Freedom of protest on quasi-public land'.[363] The provision emphasised that the right to hold 'a procession, assembly, or individual stand' could not be excluded by the owner or occupier of the land, and proposed a six-day advance notice requirement to the land owners or occupiers for any such event. In turn, the provision would have conferred a power on the owner/occupier to impose reasonable conditions upon the holding of the event, or to give reasonable directions as to its holding. It also suggested the creation of a process whereby the chief police officer could impose reasonable conditions if, on application, an organiser believed the conditions or directions imposed by the owner/occupier to be unreasonable, or if the owners/occupiers (plural) fail to agree amongst themselves as to the suitable conditions. There would also have been a power for senior police officers to impose conditions in the circumstances specified in the existing s 12(1) Public Order Act. Although this provision was not enacted – and it elicited strong opposition from consumer groups such as the British Retail Consortium and British Council of Shopping Centres[364] – it demonstrated an innovative approach to the issues thrown up by protest on quasi-public land: whilst still affording significant powers to property owners and occupiers, it would at least have provided an entry point for Arts 10 and 11, and the corresponding principle that protest should be permitted 'within sight and sound' of its target audience.

Advance notice of public processions

Section 11 of the Public Order Act 1986 provides that the organiser of a march (but not a static assembly)[365] must give advance notice of it to the police in the relevant police area[366] six clear days before the date when it is intended to be held.[367] From the perspective of the authorities, advance notification of upcoming processions may be highly desirable for a number of reasons. These interests include the co-ordination of traffic (though when taken to excess, this too easily translates into the 'traffic-logic' critiqued by Nicholas Blomley);[368] mitigating the risk of scheduling conflicts (perhaps with other

---

362 See on this point Gray and Gray, *op cit*, fn 329.

363 See, http://www.publications.parliament.uk/pa/bills/cbill/2010-2011/0146/amend/pbc1461705a.2205-2209.html.

364 See Christian Metcalfe, 'Quasi-public spaces and protest – Tom Watson MP proposals', *Estates Gazette*, 21 June 2011.

365 The Metropolitan police website nonetheless contains the following strongly worded proviso: 'There is no legal requirement to notify police that you wish to hold a static protest. However, it is very important that you do let the police know if you wish to do this and provide us with the following details: Organiser name, phone number and address; Anticipated numbers of participants; Event location; Reason for event; Start time; Finish time; Any advance publicity you are aware of; Details of any stewards.' See, http://content.met.police.uk/Article/Organising-a-protest-march-or-static-demonstration/1400002380711/1400002380711.

366 Section 11(4).

367 Section 11(5) and (6). In Northern Ireland, the Public Processions (Electronic Communication of Notices) (NI) Order 2015 provides for notification to be submitted electronically.

368 See above, fn 244.

marches or demonstrations); protecting public safety (of both march participants and non-participants); and providing efficient and/or effective policing in satisfaction of the state's positive obligations.[369]

Of course, organisers of a sizeable march may also wish to involve the police in the planning process, as they might need traffic to be stopped or redirected. However, given the state's negative obligation not to interfere with the freedom to assemble (and given too the argument raised earlier in this chapter that a notification requirement should itself be regarded as an interference with Art 11, one that is subjected to proportionality analysis), the need for a national provision of this nature is questionable.[370] This is especially so when one considers that there have been examples of the police forewarning the targets of upcoming protests that an assembly is going to take place.[371] While prosecutions under s 11 have rarely been brought, the fact that the notice requirement has not been fully adhered to may influence the police response to a procession, and may predispose a judge, if a case comes to court, to take a stance that is more sympathetic to the police action.[372]

The notice requirement does not apply under s 11(1) if it was not reasonably practicable to give 'any' advance notice. This provision was intended to exempt spontaneous demonstrations from the notice requirement, but is defective as an exemption because of the use of the word 'any'.[373] Strictly interpreted, this word suggests that a telephone call made five minutes before a march begins would fulfil the requirement, thereby exempting very few marches indeed. In most circumstances, even though a march sets off suddenly, it might well be reasonably practicable to make such a telephone call. However, it can be argued that the word 'any' should not be interpreted so strictly as to exclude spontaneous processions where only a few minutes are available to give

---

369 In one US case, the district judge held that permit-based regulation was justified in order to avoid 'resource-depleting guessing games.' *Five Borough Bicycle Club v City of New York*, 684 F Supp 2d 423, 437 (SDNY 2010) per Kaplan J.

370 For a persuasive argument against mandatory parade permits in the US (where a permitting process is widely regarded as being constitutionally valid), see Baker, CE 'Mandatory Parade Permits', Chapter 7 in *Human Liberty and Freedom of Speech*, 138–160.

371 Although not in relation to a notified *procession*, see, for example, the memorandum of understanding between Sussex Police and Cuadrilla Ltd regarding arrangements for the exploratory drilling near Balcombe. This document states that: 'Sussex Police will ensure that where appropriate they . . . [i]nform Cuadrilla, of known planned protest activity at the site.' Available at: https://netpol.org/wp-content/uploads/2014/07/Sussex-Police-MOU.doc.

372 For example, the High Court judgment in *Austin and Saxby v Commissioner of Police of the Metropolis* [2005] EWHC 480 (QB) – discussed more fully under 'Action to prevent an imminent breach of the peace' at p 653 below – refers to the deliberate decision of protesters to take part in an 'unlawful' assembly (see, for example, the police logs cited in paras 271, 299 and 570). The assumption appeared to be that it was unlawful partly because the notice requirement had not been fully complied with (the notification submitted that the march would start at 4pm, whereas in fact it began at 2pm). While the failure to comply with the notification requirement could only give rise to liability on the part of the organisers under s 11(7), not the participants, this aspect of *Austin* indicates that s 11 is of significance in terms of how the police view and control protest (even if it is unlikely that a breach of s 11 itself would lead to a prosecution).

373 In the Divisional Court in *Kay v MPS*, Sedley LJ argued that the exemption dealt only 'with the practicalities of timing, not with the feasibility of giving the required details' ([2006] EWHC 1536 (Admin) at para 14) – a position with which Carswell LJ in the House of Lords agreed ([2008] UKHL 69 at para 58).

notice, because to do so would defeat the intention behind the provision. If read in combination with the requirement to give notice by hand or in writing six days in advance, it should be interpreted (under s 3 HRA) to mean 'any written notice'.[374] As noted previously, there is now categorical Strasbourg jurisprudence that the peacefulness of an assembly should be accorded higher priority than its strict legality – so even the absence of 'any' notification should not of itself justify intervention against participants in a peaceful demonstration, less still their immediate dispersal. Following *Bukta v Hungary* (see p 585 above) any intervention by the authorities due to a mere lack of notification must demonstrate a high level of tolerance for peaceful assemblies.[375] This, however, does not preclude prosecution for failing to comply with the s 11 requirement.[376]

Advance notice under s 11 must be given if the procession is intended 'to demonstrate support or opposition to the views or actions of any person or body of persons, to publicise a cause or campaign or to mark or commemorate an event'. This provision was included in order to exempt innocuous crocodiles of children from the requirement. The notice must specify the date, time and proposed route of the procession and give the name and address of the person proposing to organise it. Under s 11(7), the organisers may be guilty of an offence if the notice requirement has not been satisfied or if the march deviates from the date, time or route specified. If it does, an organiser may have a defence under s 11(8) or (9) that he or she either had no reason to suspect that it had occurred or that it arose due to circumstances outside his or her control. It is noteworthy that a failure to comply with the notification requirement gives rise only to individual liability of the organisers – participants cannot be prosecuted for taking part in an unnotified procession (in contrast to s 13(8) which criminalises taking part in a procession known to be prohibited).

Processions 'commonly or customarily held' are also expressly exempted from the notification requirement,[377] but the meaning of 'commonly or customarily held' is far from clear. In a case concerning a 'Critical Mass' bicycle ride in London, *Kay v Metropolitan Police Commissioner*,[378] the House of Lords held that a procession 'commonly or customarily held' did not necessarily mean that it had a fixed route. Lord Phillips argued that the bicycle ride possessed sufficient common features to render it 'commonly or customarily held'.[379] These features included: being comprised of cyclists, starting at 6pm on the last Friday of every month from the same place, participants having a common intention, the procession being both recognised and publicised as 'Critical Mass', and the very element of spontaneity that would, at first glance, exclude it from the class of 'commonly or customarily held' processions – the fact that its route

374 See too, *Re CE's Application for Judicial Review* [2015] NIQB 55, para 18.
375 See also *Nosov and others v Russia*, Appl Nos 9117/04 and 10441/04 (20 February, 2014) para 57.
376 This point was confirmed by *Rai and Evans v UK* Appl Nos 26258/07 and 26255/07, decision of 17 November 2009, albeit concerning the different authorisation procedure under the now repealed provisions of the Serious Organised Crime and Police Act 2005, citing *Ziliberberg v Moldova*, Appl No 61821/00, admissibility decision of 4 May 2004. See also *Primov and Others v Russia*, Appl No 17391/06, 12 June 2014, para 117.
377 Section 11(2). Funeral processions are also covered by this exemption.
378 [2008] UKHL 69.
379 *Ibid*, para 16.

was determined on a follow-my-leader basis.[380] In addition, since notification need only be given if a procession is 'intended' to achieve one or more of the specific goals listed in s 11(1), the requirement would not apply to a procession that is purely – or perhaps even primarily – to facilitate transit.[381]

Even more fundamentally, in the absence of a notification, it may be difficult to ascertain who the organizer is, or if indeed there is an organizer at all.[382] In this regard, it is notable that the 1986 Act does not define the term 'organiser' but rather simply presumes the existence of one.[383] As such, it is at least arguable that the notice requirement is simply not applicable to a procession or protest meeting that has no immediately apparent organiser.[384] However, if, for example, an individual circulates a message about an upcoming procession via social media, it should certainly not be assumed that they are an organiser on that basis alone.[385] Given the statements of their lordships to the effect that Parliament did not intend the notification requirement to introduce prohibitory regulation of non-conventional events by the back door,[386] an argument could be made that s 11 should be interpreted in such a way as to recognise the preferred organisational form (or lack thereof) of the group seeking to assemble.

Such arguments notwithstanding, once notice is correctly given, the march can take place, although conditions may be imposed on it (as considered in the following section).

Imposing conditions on processions and assemblies

In another case concerning a 'Critical Mass' bicycle ride, *Powlesland v Director of Public Prosecutions*,[387] the court rejected an argument that the police had no power to impose conditions on a procession simply because its route had not been formally

---

380　It seems unlikely, however, that such a common element of spontaneity would of itself (i.e. without at least several of the other shared characteristics also being present) be sufficient to meet the common/customary threshold.

381　Mead, D, p 175.

382　Though see Paulo Gerbaudo's critique of 'horizontalism', fn 88 above.

383　In this regard, *Flockhart v Robinson* [1950] 2 KB 498 could be regarded as authority for the proposition that a person who indicated the route to be followed should be designated an organiser as well as the person who planned the route (thereby potentially including stewards as well as other leaders of the assembly or march within the term 'organiser').

384　Lord Brown (*obiter*, but rather convincingly) argued that the Critical Mass bicycle ride should not be viewed as a 'procession' falling within s 11 at all since it was 'inherently disorganised' (paras 67–68) and that only organised processions fell within the scope of the POA. See Lord Phillips, similarly, at para 22. Such a conclusion was resisted by Lord Rodger (para 37) who thought that such an approach 'would risk significantly curtailing the scope of' ss 12 or 13. Neither Baroness Hale (paras 52–53) nor Lord Carswell (paras 57 and 62) thought it necessary to resolve these more fundamental questions about the scope of s 11.

385　Such assessments are not uncommon. By way of comparison, see the case law relating to 'representative orders' (noting the type of evidence relied upon to demonstrate an individual's connections with a particular group). For example, *Astrazeneca UK Ltd v Aran Mathai and Others* [2014] EWHC 2774 (QB), paras 10–29; *Harlan Laboratories UK Ltd v Stop Huntingdon Animal Cruelty (SHAC)* [2012] EWHC 3408 (QB), paras 13–18 and 37–43. See also fn 89 above (*Cairn Energy PLC v Greenpeace International and Others* [2013] CSOH 50).

386　See, for example, para 24, per Lord Phillips; para 42, per Lord Rodger; and para 48, per Baroness Hale.

387　EWHC 3846 (2013).

notified.[388] The Court emphasised that the purpose of s 12 of the Public Order Act 1986 was 'to enable an advance precautionary direction to be given for processions which are proposed, notified or not.' The court stated that:

> [t]here is no purpose in excluding unnotified processions from the scope of the power to give an advance precautionary direction . . . The power to give directions is to be used, not just when the organisers of a procession have been cooperative enough to tell the police in advance of their intentions as to a specific route, but and perhaps more importantly when they have not done so. It would be an absurd interpretation if a direction, aimed at preventing serious disruption, could not be given unless the police knew as a matter of objectively provable fact that the procession would follow a specific route . . . despite disruptive organisers masking their intentions.[389]

The advent of liaison policing (and deployment of police liaison officers at protests) means that organisers of static assemblies will likely be encouraged to enter into dialogue with the police – even in the absence of a notification requirement.[390] Such dialogue – if not genuinely voluntary and consensual – could exert a significant chilling effect on the right of assembly. Since the very terms of 'negotiated management' are usually set by the police,[391] organisers may feel pressure to make concessions about, for example, the timing, duration or route of a procession, thereby potentially undercutting the protection afforded by Art 11. It also potentially plays into a larger narrative of good (willing to engage) and bad (refusing to engage) protesters, a narrative that the Home Affairs Committee appeared to champion in its review of the policing of the G20 protests (recommending that non-communicative protest groups simply 'put ideological concerns to one side and instead do everything they can to aid communications both before and during the protests').[392] This view – which stands to negate the oppositional *value* of protest[393] – has underpinned the willingness of courts to uphold protest restrictions in a number of cases (even in relation to static assemblies for which there is no

---

388 Note the related point made by Hallett LJ in *R (Singh) v Chief Constable of West Midlands Police* [2006] EWCA Civ 1118, paras 81–83, and 97, regarding the use of the dispersal power, against participants in an unnotified procession, under (then) s 30 Anti-social Behaviour Act 2003 (now, s 35 Anti-social Behaviour, Crime and Policing Act 2014) – see the text accompanying fn 789 below.

389 EWHC 3846 (2013), para 27.

390 Note, for example, the advice on notification for organisers of static assemblies on the Metropolitan Police website (see fn 365 above).

391 Gorringe, H and Rosie, M, 'It's a long way to Auchterarder! 'Negotiated management' and mismanagement in the policing of G8 protests' 59(2) *British Journal of Sociology* 187 at 197.

392 Home Affairs Committee, *Policing of the G20 Protests* (HC 418: 2009), p 12, paras 33–34.

393 Lucy Grace Barber has noted that: 'The conventionality, familiarity, and predictability of marches have encouraged journalists to treat marches as unremarkable events, to pay less attention to their political demands, and to give them minimal coverage.' Barber, LG, *Marching on Washington: The Forging of an American Political Tradition* (2002), p 225. This reality might, in turn, support an argument in favour of extending protection, within a democracy, to more 'dramatic' forms of protest action (including direct action). A version of this argument (albeit in relation to Art 10 rather than Art 11) was unsuccessfully advanced by the applicants in *Peta Deutschland v Germany*, Appl No 43481/09, 8 November 2012, para 31.

statutory notification requirement).[394] Informal dialogue between the police and protest organisers may thus potentially transform what ought to be a negative freedom (one that is enjoyed without regulation), into an emaciated right, negotiated away in 'the shadow of the law'.[395] Unfortunately, though, this is an area where there is little presently to be gained from Strasbourg jurisprudence.[396] As argued previously, the notification process in its entirety should be regarded as a prima facie interference with Art 11, which must pass proportionality analysis.[397]

The s 12 power (processions)

Section 12 of the 1986 Act reproduced in part the power under s 3 of the Public Order Act 1936 that allowed the chief officer of police to impose conditions on a procession if he or she apprehended serious public disorder.[398] However, the power to impose conditions under s 12 may be exercised in one of four situations (or 'triggers') – namely, where a senior officer reasonably believes that (1) serious public disorder, (2) serious damage to property, or (3) serious disruption to the life of the community, may result, or (4) where the purpose of the persons organising it is the intimidation of others with a view to compelling them not to do an act they have a right to do, or to do an act they have a right not to do. This is a much wider range of situations than the old power. In making a determination as to the existence of one of these 'triggers', the senior police officer in question should 'have regard to the time or place at which and the circumstances in which, any public procession is being held or is intended to be held and to its route or proposed route'.

The third 'trigger' – 'serious disruption to the community' – has attracted particular criticism from commentators for its imprecision and for decisively lowering the level and nature of risk that must be shown before conditions can be imposed.[399] The white paper that preceded the 1986 Act suggested that this provision would enable the police 'to limit traffic congestion, or to prevent a bridge from being blocked, or to reduce the severe disruption sometimes suffered by pedestrians, business and

---

394 For example, in *Howarth v MPC* [2011] EWHC 2818 (QB), para 33 per McCombe J. In *R (Barda) v Mayor of London on behalf of the GLA* [2015] EWHC 3584 (Admin), Garnham J (paras 108 and 114) emphasised that their failure either to obtain authorisation, or to engage with the GLA prior to April 2015, while not negating their Arts 10 and 11 rights, was 'relevant in judging the proportionality of the state's response'.

395 Mnookin, R and Kornhauser, L, 'Bargaining in the Shadow of the Law: The Case of Divorce' 88 *Yale LJ* 950 (1978–1979). See also Mead, *op cit*, fn 1, p 45 (citing Reiner, R, 'Policing the Police', in Maguire, M, Morgan, R and Reiner, R, *The Oxford Handbook of Criminology*, 2nd edn, 1997, p 1002).

396 See, for example, the disappointing judgment in *Berladir v Russia* Appl No 34202/06, 10 July 2012 in which the Court failed to assess the proportionality of what was, in fact, a highly onerous notification process containing a 'reconciliation' procedure, effectively imposing a 'good faith' obligation on assembly organizers to 'agree' to limitations. *Frumkin v Russia*, Appl No 74568/12, 5 January 2016 focuses instead on the obligation of the *authorities* to put in place adequate channels of communication.

397 See further the authorization procedure for protests in the vicinity of Parliament at pp 624–25 below.

398 If the march is already assembling, the conditions may be imposed by the senior police officer present at the scene who may be a constable; if the conditions are being considered some time before this point, the Chief Officer of Police must determine them.

399 See, e.g., Bonner and Stone, *op cit*, fn 1, p 308; Ewing and Gearty, *op cit*, fn 1, p 121.

commerce'.[400] The examples cited were of 'marches being held through shopping centres on Saturdays, or through city centres in the rush hour'.[401] Professor D.G.T. Williams notes that a government minister stated that he hoped the criterion would seldom be used.[402]

It has been argued that this vague and ambiguous phrase 'would appear to subsume, and indeed go beyond, the criteria for restricting public protest laid down in Article 11(2)'[403] of the Convention, especially since marches inevitably give rise to some inconvenience and disruption.[404] Indeed, 'disruption' under the POA could be caused by the size of the group or the particular circumstances applicable: it is not necessary for the group to be disorderly (or non-peaceful). As such, Williams suggested that the addition of the criterion reflected a policy shift away from the 'democratic' or 'safety valve' view of the right to demonstrate and towards a 'disruption' view.[405] In a similar vein, Bonner and Stone warned of 'the dangers that lie in the vague line between serious disruption and a measure of inconvenience'.[406] Indeed, it has been said that '[t]he Act threatens to permit only those demonstrations that are so convenient that they become invisible.'[407] Notwithstanding the judgment in *Police v Reid*[408] (where it was determined that the 'triggers' should be strictly interpreted, and the words used should not be diluted) the provision leaves significant scope for interpretation – even to the extent that it may be said to render the other two 'triggers' redundant. For example, in the case of London, it is unclear whether the term 'the community' could be applied to Oxford Street or central London or the whole Metropolitan area.[409] The more narrowly 'the community' is defined, the more readily a given march could be said to cause serious disruption. Serious obstruction of traffic might arguably amount to some disruption of the life of a small area that might be said to constitute a 'community'. Indeed, since the imposition of conditions may serve to reduce the size of the necessary police deployment at an assembly and the related costs of the policing operation,[410] it may encourage the police to interpret 'community' or 'disruption' in the manner most likely to bring the 'trigger' into being.

Furthermore, under s 12 (and ss 14 and 14A discussed below) those engaging in protest – that could be seen as an 'intrinsically communal' activity – 'are constructed by [it] as being inherently in opposition to the exercise of the day-to-day rights of members

---

400 Cmnd. 9510, para 4.22.
401 *Ibid.*
402 Williams, DGT, 'Processions, Assemblies and the Freedom of the Individual' *Criminal Law Review* (1987), 167–179, p 173 citing HL Deb, Vol 480, col 13, 6 October 1986.
403 Fitzpatrick, and Taylor, *op cit*, fn 338, p 297.
404 Probably, it could cover the prevention of disorder (as opposed to 'serious disorder', the first 'trigger') and the protection of 'the rights and freedoms of others', an aim which has itself received a broad and imprecise interpretation at Strasbourg. See above, pp 591–92.
405 Williams, DGT (1987), *op cit*, fn 1, p 168, also noting that this might be argued to reflect changes in society since 1936 (including the increase in the number of demonstrations held and the commensurate increase in the level of disorder at, and the cost of policing, such events).
406 'The Public Order Act 1986: steps in the wrong direction?' (1987) PL 202, p 226.
407 Ewing and Gearty, *Freedom under Thatcher*, 1990, p 121.
408 [1987] Crim LR 702.
409 Ewing and Gearty, *Freedom under Thatcher*, 1990, p 121.
410 See, for example, fn 16 above (citing *Wright v Commissioner of Police for the Metropolis* [2013] EWHC 2739 (QB), paras 60 and 62).

of the community within which the assembly takes place'.[411] In this light, a compelling argument can be made that this aspect of the 1986 Act is in opposition to one of the most basic values underlying the Convention – that the key characteristics of a 'democratic society', the values of which are the touchstone by which the legality of restrictions on individual rights must be determined, are 'pluralism, tolerance and broadminded-ness'.[412] A UK court might properly reject such a 'monolithic'[413] conception of 'com-munity', having regard instead to the Strasbourg Court's dicta in *Barankevich v Russia*, that 'the role of the authorities . . . is not to remove the cause of tension by eliminating pluralism, but to ensure that the competing groups tolerate each other.'[414]

The fourth 'trigger', arising under s 12(1)(b), consists of an evaluation of the pur-pose of the assembly rather than an apprehension that a particular state of affairs may arise. The senior police officer must reasonably believe that the purpose of the assembly is 'the intimidation of others with a view to compelling them not to do an act they have a right to do or to do an act they have a right not to do'. This requires a police officer to make a political judgment as to the purpose of the group in question because it must be determined whether the purpose is coercive or merely persuasive. Asking police officers to make such a judgment clearly lays them open to claims of partiality in instances where they are perceived as out of sympathy with the aims of the group in question.[415] It should be noted that the fourth 'trigger' requires a reason-able belief in the presence of two elements – intimidation and coercion. Therefore, a far-right march through an ethnically diverse area would probably fall outside its terms since the element of coercion may be absent. Such a march might, in any case, fall within the terms of the third 'trigger' (see below). On the other hand, a march might be coercive without being intimidatory. In *Reid*,[416] the defendants shouted and raised their arms; it was determined that such behaviour might cause discomfort, but not intimidation, and that the two concepts could not be equated. In this regard, the courts should also be guided by the Strasbourg Court's rulings in *Fáber v Hungary*[417] (where neither intimidation nor coercion were deemed to be present) and *Vona v Hun-gary*[418] (in which the elements of intimidation and coercion were both present), noting in particular the importance of a fact-based and contextual analysis of this 'intimida-tion' threshold.

---

411 Fitzpatrick and Taylor, *op cit*, fn 338, p 298. They further point out that protests, such as that at New-bury, attracted both support and opposition from the local communities: 'thus ... the intra-community factions could be simultaneously causing each other "serious disruption".' See also: Gray and Gray, 'Civil rights, civil wrongs and quasi-public places' [1999] EHRLR 46, p 51. Also, the 'essentialized view of protest' discussed at p 601 above in relation to 'Protest on quasi-public land'.

412 *Handyside v UK* (1976) 1 EHRR 737, para 49; *Bączkowski and Others v Poland*, Appl No 1543/06, 3 May 2007, paras 62–4; *Barankevich v Russia*, Appl No 10519/03, 26 July 2007, para 30. *Identoba v Georgia*, Appl No 73235/12, 12 May 2015, paras 93–4. Such an argument is strengthened further if one considers early interpretation of the parallel criterion in the Public Order (NI) Order 1987 (see, *Re Murphy* (CA) 11/7/91 (LEXIS transcript) per Hutton LCJ).

413 Fitzpatrick and Taylor, *op cit*, fn 338, p 298.

414 *Barankevich v Russia*, Appl No 10519/03, 26 July 2007, para 30.

415 See, for example, Majeed, A, *Policing, Protest and Conflict: A Report into the Policing of the London Gaza Demonstrations in 2008–2009* (Islamic Human Rights Commission: 2010), p 24.

416 [1987] Crim LR 702.

417 Appl No 40721/08, 24 July 2012.

418 Appl No 35943/10, 9 July 2013.

If one of the four 'triggers' is thought to be present, the conditions that can be imposed under s 12 are very wide (in contrast to those that can be imposed on static assemblies): any condition may be imposed that appears 'necessary' to the senior police officer in order to prevent the envisaged mischief occurring. They may include changes to the route of the procession or a prohibition on it entering a particular public place. Obviously, however, they are not completely unlimited; if the condition imposed bears no relationship to the mischief it was intended to avert, it may be open to challenge. Feldman argues that '[c]onditions which are so demanding that they amount in effect to a ban are an improper use of the power and so are unlawful on ordinary public law principles.'[419] This wide discretion is also of course subject to the proportionality requirement of Arts 10 and 11, para 2 – and such a requirement should be read into the term 'necessary' in s 12(1) POA under s 3 HRA. The duty of the police under s 6 HRA also means that they must seek to ensure that conditions are not imposed that go beyond the legitimate aim pursued.[420]

One question that might conceivably arise in relation to s 12 concerns the precise time at which a person ceased to take part in a restricted procession, so as to be no longer bound by police conditions. In the case of *Jukes and another v Director or Public Prosecutions*,[421] two individuals participating in a student-led procession in London against education cuts (upon which route conditions had been imposed) planned to leave that march to join an anti-capitalist 'Occupy' protest in Trafalgar Square. Even though they were arrested an hour after they left the original march, they were still found guilty of breaching the route conditions imposed on the march because at the time they crossed the police cordon they had been advised by the police to remain within the confines of the march, and *at that time* were regarded as still taking part in the procession.

The key cases (involving both s 12 and s 14) – *R (Brehony) v Chief Constable of Greater Manchester*[422] and *R (on the application of the English Defence League) v*

---

419 Feldman, D, *Civil Liberties and Human Rights in England and Wales*, 2nd edn, 2002, at p 1063.

420 Tugendhat J, in *Austin and Saxby v Commissioner of Police of the Metropolis* [2005] EWHC 480, found that both ss 12 and 14 allow for the imposition of extremely broad and restrictive conditions. As David Mead notes, these were 'very surprising conclusions'. It was held, for example, that s 12 gives a power to bring a procession that is in progress to an end. The judge sought to distinguish between a ban (which would be impermissible under s 12) and a ban on the continuance of a march that had, to some extent, already taken place. It was also found that s 12 included a power to detain persons who are part of a protest if that was necessary in order to achieve the objectives of preventing disorder or disruption of the life of the community. Since the Court of Appeal (and later, the House of Lords) disposed of the challenge in *Austin* on other grounds, it was deemed unnecessary to resolve these questions regarding the scope of conditions under ss 12 and 14. As Mead argues (*op cit*, fn 1, p 189), '[t]hat is regrettable as authoritative rejection of all these holdings is needed lest they resurface.' See also, *In the Matter of an Application by JM for Judicial Review* [2014] NIQB 102, 8 August 2014, para 26.

421 [2013] EWHC 195 (Admin), CO/8237/2012. There are some parallels here with the Strasbourg case of *Navalnyy and Yashin v Russia*, Appl No 76204/11, 4 December 2014. This concerned a group of individuals who were arrested some time after they had left a demonstration, with the police stating that they believed they were taking part in an unauthorised and spontaneous public march. See also, *Broadwith v DPP* (2000) All ER (D) 225; [2000] Crim LR 924 DC (discussed in Mead, *op cit*, fn 1, pp 190–192).

422 [2005] EWHC 640.

Commissioner of Police of the Metropolis[423] – do not suggest that the courts are eager to take a restrictive approach to the use of these powers in reliance on Arts 10 and 11 (and both are discussed below under 'Sections 12 and 14 in practice').

The s 14 power (assemblies)

Section 14 of the 1986 Act allows the police to impose conditions on assemblies (remembering, of course, that unlike processions, there is no legal obligation to notify assemblies to the police).[424] It was introduced in the 1986 Act as an entirely new power. Conditions may be imposed only if one of four 'triggers' under s 14(1) – identical to those arising under s 12 – is present. However, once it is clear that one of the 'triggers' is present, the conditions that may be imposed are much more limited than those that may be imposed on marches. They are confined to such 'directions . . . as to the place at which the assembly may be (or continue to be) held, its maximum duration or the maximum number of persons who may constitute it' as appear to the senior police officer 'necessary to prevent the disorder, damage, disruption or intimidation'.[425] In *DPP v Jones*[426] conditions as to the movement of the assembly had been imposed, but were found to be ultra vires on the basis that they could only have been imposed on a march under s 12. In *Austin and Saxby v Commissioner of Police of the Metropolis*,[427] the judge concluded that a direction under s 14, that some or all members of an assembly disperse, can include a direction that they disperse by a specified route, and that they stay in a specified place for as long as is necessary for the dispersal to be effected. It is suggested that this was a very doubtful extension of the law. Had Parliament wished to allow for the imposition of a broad range of conditions in s 14, as in s 12, the two sections could have been framed in the same terms. It was also found, somewhat less controversially, that a direction under s 14 may bring an existing assembly to an end. Tugendhat J said that this would be allowable since the section refers to 'the circumstances in which any public assembly is being held . . .' and authorises a direction imposing the 'maximum duration'.[428]

It must be clear that the conditions were communicated to the participants in an assembly. In this regard, concerns have on several occasions been raised about police use of s 14. One such instance concerned the policing of the G20 'Climate Camp' protest in April 2009,[429] where criticisms focused on whether (and if so how) the decision to disperse protesters under s 14 had been communicated: 'To the protesters being dispersed it seemed as if the police, without warning had begun to use force

---

423 [2013] EWHC 3890 (Admin).
424 Under s 16, as amended by the Anti-Social Behaviour Act 2003, an assembly consists of two or more people in a public place; a public place is defined as one which is wholly or partly open to the air. Section 16 defines a public procession as one in a place to which the public have access. No further guidance is given. Presumably the procession must be moving and will become an assembly if it stops and if it consists of two or more people, in which case different rules will apply (though note also fn 365 above).
425 Section 14(1).
426 [2002] EWHC 110.
427 [2005] EWHC 480.
428 For criticism, see fn 420 above.
429 See, *McClure and Moos v Commissioner of the Police of the Metropolis* [2012] EWCA Civ 12.

to clear a peaceful protest.'[430] Such concerns are not new. In *Brickley and Kitson v Police*,[431] for example, the convictions of anti-apartheid demonstrators for failing to abide by a condition were quashed on the basis that it was unclear whether the condition (relayed by the police using a megaphone) had actually been communicated to them.

The defences available if there is a failure to comply with the conditions are identical to those under s 12, as is the power of arrest arising under s 14(7). In this regard, Gabrielle Moore has noted that the summary nature of the offence means that defendants are frequently unrepresented and 'may enter guilty pleas due to the absence of legal advice when the conditions imposed may have been unlawful'.[432]

Sections 12 and 14 in practice

A member of a march or assembly will incur liability under s 12(5) or s 14(5) if he or she knowingly fails to comply with a condition. An organiser[433] will incur liability under s 12(4) or s 14(4) if he or she knowingly fails to comply with the conditions imposed, although he or she will have a defence if it can be shown that the failure arose from circumstances beyond his or her control. Thus, the *organiser* must actually breach the condition in question; he or she would not incur liability merely because some members of the march or assembly did so. Therefore, where a march contains an unruly element which deliberately breaches conditions imposed, the persons involved will incur liability, but the organiser should properly escape it.[434] An organiser may also incur liability if he or she incites another knowingly to breach a condition that has been imposed (ss 12(6) and 14(6)). According to the Court of Appeal in *Hendrickson and Tichner*,[435] incitement requires an element of persuasion or encouragement. Moreover, following *Krause*,[436] the solicitation must actually come to the notice of the person intended to act on it. Therefore, merely assuming the position of leader of a march or assembly which is in breach of a condition would not seem to be sufficient of itself to amount to incitement. However, express or implied encouragement to bring about or continue a breach, such as leading the group in a certain forbidden direction, would amount to incitement if the leader was aware of the breach of the condition.

430 Home Affairs Committee, *Policing of the G20 Protests* (HC 418: 29 June 2009), p 11, paras 27 and 63. Available at: http://www.publications.parliament.uk/pa/cm200809/cmselect/cmhaff/418/418.pdf See also, Home Affairs Committee, *Policing of the G20 Protests: Government Response to the Report on the Policing of the G20 Protests* (HC 201: 2010) p 10, para 25. Available at: http://www.publications.parliament.uk/pa/cm200910/cmselect/cmhaff/201/201.pdf.

431 *Legal Action*, July 1988, p 21 (Knightsbridge Crown Court).

432 See, Moore, G, 'Policing Protest' 175 *Criminal Law and Justice Weekly* (8 January 2011), also noting a trend in the incorrect application of s 14 'to prevent people from protesting'.

433 Note the discussion above (text accompanying fn 382–386) in relation to s 11 POA and the absence of any statutory definition of 'organiser', and the 'Critical Mass' case of *Kay v Metropolitan Police Commissioner* [2008] UKHL 69.

434 This is in line with the principles (discussed above) enunciated in *Ezelin v France*, Appl No 11800/85, 26 April 1991, and in *Ziliberberg v Moldova*, Appl No 61821/00, 4 May 2004 (admissibility). See also, OSCE-ODIHR – Venice Commission *Guidelines on Freedom of Peaceful Assembly*, 2nd edn, 2010, para 197.

435 [1977] Crim LR 356.

436 (1902) 18 TLR 238.

The courts have made little attempt to curb the use of ss 12 and 14 against protesters. In the 'Climate Camp' case of *Moos and McClure v Commissioner of the Police of the Metropolis* (discussed further below in relation to 'containment' and 'breach of the peace'), the applicants were critical of 'the overzealous use'[437] of s 14, which had been invoked by the police 'Bronze Commander' against different groups of demonstrators at different times of the day.[438] In the High Court, Sweeney J noted that the use of s 14 to aid termination of the demonstration was 'fully justified' since the protest 'had lasted the best part of 12 hours – quite long enough to take full advantage of rights under Articles 10 and 11 of the Convention'.[439] In *R (Brehony) v Chief Constable of Greater Manchester*[440] a very light-touch approach was taken to the demands of proportionality in the circumstances. A regular demonstration had occurred outside a branch of Marks and Spencer, protesting about the firm's support for the government of Israel; a counter-demonstration had also occurred, supporting the government. The chief constable issued a notice under s 14 requiring the demonstration to move to a different location due to the disruption it would be likely to cause to shoppers over the Christmas period when the number of shoppers was likely to treble in number. The demonstrators sought judicial review of this decision; the judge refused the application on the basis that, in Arts 10 and 11 terms, the restraint was proportionate to the aim, of maintaining public order, pursued. This decision confirms that 'serious disruption to the life of the community' can mean mere anticipated inconvenience to shoppers. The decision indicates that ss 12 and 14 provide the police with extremely wide powers to interfere with demonstrations and marches, despite the inception of the HRA.

In another case,[441] the English Defence League (EDL) sought to judicially review both route and place restrictions (imposed under s 12 and s 14 respectively) on their proposed march and assembly in September 2013 in the London borough of Tower Hamlets (reported, in the judgment, to be 'home to the largest Muslim population in the country').[442] A number of counter-demonstrations had been notified, and these were also subject to s 12 and s 14 restrictions. The EDL stated that the desired end-point of their march – where a number of speeches were to be delivered – was 'the only location at which those speeches will have any meaning'.[443] The EDL also pointed to the wide range of less intrusive powers that the police might instead have relied upon.[444] In contrast, the borough (represented in the case as an interested party) sought to argue that to allow the march to proceed without any restriction would allow the participants 'to seek intentionally to intimidate those who would be witnessing it in the local

---

437 [2011] EWHC 957, para 38.
438 [2011] EWHC 957, paras 22 and 28; [2012] EWCA Civ 12, para 27.
439 *Moos and McClure v Commissioner of Police of the Metropolis* [2011] EWHC 957, para 63.
440 [2005] EWHC 640.
441 *R (on the application of the English Defence League) v Commissioner of Police of the* Metropolis [2013] EWHC 3890 (Admin). See, Parpworth, N, 'Processions or Public Disorder?' (2014) 178 *JPN* 178–180.
442 Para 10.
443 Para 11.
444 Including (para 7) the power of arrest for actual or anticipated breach of the peace, and powers to authorize stop and search under s 60 Criminal Justice and Public Order Act 1994. The EDL's arguments were rejected.

community, with the resulting risk of serious public disorder.'[445] While King J considered this to be a 'powerful case', the 'intimidation' ground was not the sole trigger relied upon by the Police Commissioner – indeed, the police arguments in favour of imposing conditions addressed all four triggers: to 'reduce the risk of serious public disorder, serious damage to property, serious damage to the life of the community and the threat of intimidation'.[446] While noting the 'important principles' deriving, *inter alia*, from Lord Bingham's judgment in *Laporte v Chief Constable of Gloucestershire*,[447] the judge noted the wide discretion afforded to state authorities in terms of the 'means to be used' in seeking to enable lawful demonstrations to proceed peacefully.[448] He concluded that no case had been made that, in imposing either set of conditions, the Metropolitan Police Commissioner had acted unlawfully, outside his powers, irrationally, unreasonably or disproportionately.

Imposing banning orders on marches – s 13

As indicated above, the 1986 Act for the first time gave the police the power to impose very wide ranging conditions[449] if they were thought necessary for the prevention of serious public disorder, serious damage to property or (the least grave trigger condition) 'serious disruption to the life of the community'.[450] It also provided, as did its predecessor,[451] for the possibility of an outright ban on public processions,[452] but only if the chief constable reasonably believed that his powers to impose conditions on processions under s 12 would be inadequate to prevent 'serious public disorder'.

The power under s 13(1) of the 1986 Act is exercised as follows: 'If, at any time, the chief officer of police reasonably believes that, because of particular circumstances existing in any district or part of a district, the powers under s 12 will not be sufficient to prevent the holding of public processions in that district or part from resulting in serious public disorder, he shall apply to the council of the district for an order prohibiting for a period not exceeding three months the holding of all public processions (or of any class of public procession specified in the application) in the district or part concerned'. In response, the council may make the order as requested or modify it with the approval of the secretary of state. It should be noted that once the chief officer of police has come to the conclusion in question he or she *must*, not *may*, apply for a banning order. This power is exercised in respect of London by the Commissioner of Police for the City of London or the Commissioner of Police of the Metropolis. A member of the march or a

---

445 Para 31.
446 Para 28, citing para 4 of Police Commander Terry's witness statement. Ultimately, it appears (see para 31) that greatest reliance was placed by the police on the 'serious public disorder' criterion.
447 [2006] UKHL 55, para 37, discussed below at pp 645–48.
448 At para 6, citing *Plattform 'Ärzte für das Leben' v Austria*, Appl No 10126/82, 21 June 1988, para 34.
449 Directions may be given as to the number of persons who may attend an assembly, its duration and location.
450 These conditions were considerably broader than the single one of anticipated 'serious public disorder' which alone could trigger the power to impose conditions upon processions under the Public Order Act 1936, s 3.
451 Under s 3 of the Public Order Act 1936.
452 Section 13.

person who organises it knowing of the ban will commit an offence under s 13(7) and (8) and can be arrested under s 13(10).

Assuming that a power was needed to ban marches expected to be violent, this power is nevertheless open to criticism in that once a banning order is imposed, it prevents all marches in the area it covers for its duration. Thus, a projected march likely to be of an entirely peaceful character could be caught by a ban aimed at a violent march. The only judicial review case involving a challenge to the decision of a chief constable to seek a ban on processions was brought by the Campaign for Nuclear Disarmament (CND) after it had had to cancel a number of its marches – *Kent v Metropolitan Police Commissioner*.[453] The court held that an order quashing a ban could be made only if there were no reasons for imposing it at all. In the eyes of the court, the Commissioner had considered the relevant matters and, further, the CND had a remedy under s 9(3) (now s 13(5) of the 1986 Act) as they could apply to have the order relaxed. This judgment, however, is an example of the most attenuated form of *Wednesbury* review, the courts affording the Commissioner a very wide margin of discretion.[454]

It is arguable that the 1986 Act should have limited the banning power to the particular marches giving rise to fear of serious public disorder (and such calls for reform have more recently surfaced),[455] but this possibility was rejected by the government on the ground that it could be subverted by organisers of marches who might attempt to march under another name. It would therefore, it was thought, have placed too great a burden on the police, who would have had to determine whether or not this had occurred. However, in this regard, it might be argued that too great a weight was given to the possible administrative burden placed on the police and too little to the need to uphold freedom of assembly.

In light of Strasbourg jurisprudence, there is a strong case to be made that the s 13 power, because it enables the imposition of a blanket ban, would be in breach of Arts 10 and 11. While in *Christians Against Racism and Fascism v UK*,[456] the applicants' argument that a ban on processions[457] infringed Art 11 was rejected by the Commission as manifestly ill-founded, this is an elderly decision of the Commission, strongly affected by the margin of appreciation doctrine and superseded by more recent judgments of the Court.[458] The domestic judiciary would be free to scrutinise the extent of the risk and the proportionality of a ban, having regard to the question of whether a particular march affected by the ban was likely in itself to give rise to disorder. A court confronted with such a ban could take the view that the geographical or temporal scope of the ban had been greater than was needed to obviate the risk of serious disorder, or that the 'class of processions' prohibited had been defined too widely to be compatible with Art 11.

---

453 (1981) *The Times*, 15 May.

454 See especially, Ackner LJ at p 6. See also Mead *op cit*, fn 1, pp 170–1, and pp 204–5, and Channing, I, *The Police and the Expansion of Public Order Law in Britain, 1829–2014*, 2015, Routledge, pp 94–5.

455 For example, 'Call for new powers to ban EDL demonstrations', *Bradford Telegraph and Argus*, 15 October 2013.

456 Appl No 8440/78, 16 July 1980 (admissibility).

457 The ban, imposed, here, under s 3(3) of the Public Order Act 1936 prohibited 'all public processions other than those of a religious, educational, festive or ceremonial character customarily held within the Metropolitan Police District.'

458 See, fn 254 above (citing *Fáber*, para 37 and *Stankov*, para 97).

A court willing to examine the evidence relied upon by the police could also find that the ban need not have been imposed at all since the imposition of conditions under s 12 would have been sufficient.

This power was being used with increased frequency up to the mid-1980s: there were 11 banning orders in the period 1970–80 and 75 in the period 1981–84[459] (39 in 1981, 13 in 1982, nine in 1983 and 11 in 1984). Interestingly, however, as Waddington has noted, there were few bans of marches in London following the passage of the 1986 Act.[460] Between 2005 and 2012, there were 12 proscriptions under s 13 Public Order Act 1986. All but two of these (which related to marches by anti-capitalist and anti-globalisation groups in Derby and Sheffield in 2005) concerned the far right (either the National Front or English Defence League (EDL)). Two of these (in Luton in 2006 and 2009) were for the maximum permissible three-month period, five were for periods of one month/30 days, and the remaining five were for periods between two days and two weeks. The others were for two weeks.[461] The power may have been used sparingly because police officers preferred to police a march known about for some time, drawing on the array of alternative powers available,[462] as opposed to an assembly formed hastily in response to a ban or a hostile, unpredictable and disorganised march. However, the power to ban and to impose conditions gives the police bargaining power when negotiating with marchers and also enables them to adopt a policy of strategic under-enforcement as part of the price of avoiding trouble when a march occurs.[463] The availability of the power may also lead a court to look more favourably upon lesser restrictions imposed under s 12.[464]

Imposing banning orders on assemblies – s 14a

Prior to the Public Order Act 1986, there was no statutory power at all to place prior restraints, still less a ban, upon assemblies as opposed to marches. The police therefore dealt with outbreaks of disorder at such assemblies using their powers to arrest for breach of the peace and for specific common law[465] and statutory public order offences.[466] When s 13 of the 1986 Act was passed, no parallel power to ban assemblies was

459 White Paper, (1985) Cmnd 9510, para 4.7.
460 Waddington, PAJ, *op cit*, fn 1, pp 58–61.
461 Freedom of Information request submitted by Iain Channing to the Home Office (Ref: 31049). Available at: https://www.gov.uk/government/publications/applications-for-a-banning-order-under-section-13-of-the-public-order-act-1986. See also, Channing, I, *The Police and the Expansion of Public Order Law in Britain, 1829–2014*, 2015, Routledge, pp 99–101. Mead, *op cit*, fn 1, p 183 records that under the s 13 power, '[a]cross England and Wales, in the period 2004–08, only eight public processions were banned . . .'.
462 See, for example, reliance by Essex police on s 60 CJPOA 1994: 'Essex police granted extra stop and search powers for EDL rally', *The Telegraph*, 26 September 2015.
463 See also, Parpworth, N, 'Processions or Public Disorder?' (2014) 178 JPN 178, at 180. Note, too, the case of *R (Laporte) v Chief Constable of Gloucestershire* [2006] UKHL 55 (discussed below at pp 645–48) in which the chief constable decided not to invoke s 13 to seek an order prohibiting all processions in the Fairford area.
464 See (arguably), for example, *R (on the application of the English Defence League) v Commissioner of Police of the Metropolis* [2013] EWHC 3890 (Admin), para 24.
465 Namely the old common law offences of riot, rout, unlawful assembly and affray.
466 E.g., Public Order Act 1936, s 5 (as amended): using threatening or abusive words or behaviour likely to cause, or with intent to provoke, a breach of the peace.

included – apparently, the then Thatcher government considered that it would represent too serious an inroad upon freedom of speech.[467]

Only eight years later, however, the power to ban assemblies was introduced in the CJPOA 1994 by inserting s 14A into the 1986 Act.[468] Although the power is only to ban assemblies taking place on private land, the widespread 'privatisation' of previously common land (discussed above at p 576) means that there is in fact little land on which demonstrations may take place without the landowner's consent which are non-trespassory.[469] The introduction of a banning power, deemed unnecessary and too draconian less than 10 years previously and not even requested by the police,[470] itself represented a decisive movement towards authoritarianism. The Act compounded this trend by basing the power to ban not, as in the case of processions, upon the most grave risk (a belief that serious public disorder would otherwise occur), but the least and most ill-defined criterion: anticipation of 'serious disruption to the life of the community'. In this respect, it is a much wider power than that arising under s 13. Records show that 'in the period 2004–2008, there were 13 bans on assemblies under section 14A'.[471]

Section 14A(1) provides that a chief officer of police may apply for a banning order[472] if he reasonably believes (a) that an assembly is likely to be trespassory and (b) may result in serious disruption to the life of the community or 'significant' damage to certain types of buildings and structures, in particular, historical monuments. The requirement of trespass is made out where the chief constable believes that an assembly is intended to be held on land (a) to which the public has no right of access and is likely to be held without the permission of the occupier of the land or (b) on land to which the public has only a limited right of access and the assembly is likely to exceed the limits of any permission of the landowner or the public's right of access. If an order is made, it will subsist for four days, operate within a radius of five miles around the area in question, and prohibit any trespassory assembly held within its temporal and geographical scope.[473]

Just as s 13 catches peaceful processions, the provisions of s 14A mean that assemblies that are not likely *in themselves* to cause the prohibited harm under s 14A(1) or s 14A(4) may nevertheless be banned once the ban is in place. Section 14A is backed up by s 14C (inserted into the 1986 Act by s 71 of the 1994 Act). Section 14C provides a very broad power to stop persons within a radius of five miles from the assembly if a police officer reasonably believes that they were on their way to it and that it is subject to a s 14A order. If the direction is not complied with and if the person to whom it has been given is aware of it, he or she may be arrested and may be subject to a fine if convicted. Thus, this power operates before any offence has been committed and hands the police a very wide discretion.[474]

---

467 'Meetings and assemblies are a more important means of exercising freedom of speech than are marches' *Review of Public Order Law*, Cmnd 9510, 1985, pp 31–32.
468 Under s 70.
469 See further below, pp 630–40.
470 See Marston, J and Tain, P, *Public Order Offences*, 1996, p 124.
471 Mead, *op cit*, fn 1, p 183.
472 Orders are granted by the local authority, with the approval of the secretary of state.
473 Section 14A(5).
474 See further below, p 638.

The case of *Jones and Lloyd v DPP*[475] – decided before the HRA came into force – concerned an assembly near Stonehenge at a time when an order under s 14A was in force. The order prohibited the holding of trespassory assemblies within a four-mile radius of Stonehenge and covered the period from 29 May to 1 June 1995. While the ban was still in force, a protest was held against it, in the form of an assembly on a road within the four-mile radius covered by the ban. It was found as a fact at trial that the assembly was non-obstructive, orderly and wholly peaceful.[476] Nevertheless, the protesters were asked by the police to move on; some did, but others refused and were arrested and charged with the offence under s 14A.

Following their conviction, the defendants successfully appealed to Salisbury Crown Court which held that the group was reasonably using the highway. This led the DPP to appeal the point by way of case stated to the Divisional Court. The main issue to be determined was whether the assembly was 'trespassory', so as to fall within the s 14A order. The question, therefore, was whether the category of legitimate purposes for which the public might lawfully use the highway included peaceful, non-obstructive assembly. The Divisional Court, disagreeing with the Crown Court on the point, found that it did not.[477] The Divisional Court found that the highway was to be used for passing and repassing only and that assembling on it was outside the purpose for which the implied licence to use it was granted.[478] The Divisional Court reinstated the convictions, and the defendants – assisted by Liberty – appealed to the House of Lords, which, by a three to two majority, upheld the defendants' appeal and quashed their convictions.

Those law lords in the majority (Lord Irvine, Lord Clyde and Lord Hutton) delivered substantial and quite different speeches and it is a matter of some difficulty to identify the *ratio*. Despite the advent of the HRA, their lordships declined the opportunity to move beyond the traditional limited judicial perspective adopted in protest cases and to consider instead the political expression dimension of public protest. The key finding in common was that since *the particular assembly in question* had been found by the tribunal of fact to be a reasonable use of the highway, it was therefore not trespassory and so not caught by the s 14A order.[479] The conduct of the protesters, according to the

---

475 [1999] UKHL 5.

476 See p 15 of the Crown Court's judgment, cited at [1999] 2 WLR 625, p 627, *per* Lord Irvine.

477 [1999] UKHL 5. For the Crown Court's reasoning on the point, see the speech of Lord Hutton ([1999] 2 WLR 625, p 657).

478 In so finding, the court relied on *Hickman v Maisey* [1900] 1 QB 752, CA. This decision concerned the defendant's use of the highway in order to gain information by looking over the plaintiff's land. The defendant was on the highway watching the plaintiff's land. It was found that the plaintiff owned the sub-soil under the highway and that the defendant was entitled to make ordinary and reasonable use of it. Such watching was held not to be reasonable; the defendant had gone outside the accepted use and therefore had trespassed.

479 See, subsequently, *Westminster City Council v Hall* (2002) EWHC 2073, in which Gray J, applying *Jones*, held the obstruction caused by the defendant's placards (for a period of 15 months) was reasonable since no pedestrian had ever actually been obstructed, and the police had not thought it necessary to intervene. Similarly, in *Scott v Mid-South Essex Justices* [2004] EWHC 1001, the High Court – also applying *Jones* – upheld a magistrates' court finding that the nightly parking of a burger and kebab trailer amounted to a reasonable use of the highway. Goldring J noted that the magistrate had been 'heavily influenced by the absence of traffic in this industrial estate at the time of the obstruction; the absence of any obstruction in fact; [and] the ease with which the public could pass and repass along this highway'.

majority, thus had the classic character of an English negative liberty: since it was not unlawful, it was permitted, and the police had 'no right' to remove the protesters. This was the basis of the judgment, not any finding that the protesters had a positive right to peacefully protest, which the police were under a corresponding duty to respect and facilitate.[480] Even more remarkably, not one of their lordships was prepared to find that assemblies on the highway that were both peaceful and non-obstructive were invariably lawful.[481] It was common ground between all their lordships that no use could be lawful which impeded the primary rite of passage.

The decision in *Jones* – still regarded as an accurate exposition of the common law[482] – makes it clear that peaceful non-obstructive assemblies are not inevitably non-trespassory and therefore they can fall foul of s 14A, if a ban is in place. Thus, those assemblies recognised at Strasbourg as most worthy of protection can yet attract liability under the statutory framework created by the 1986 Act. This position is clearly in tension – and is arguably incompatible – with Arts 10 and 11.

Demonstrations in the vicinity of Parliament

In an ostensibly forthright statement underscoring the importance of the right to protest in the vicinity of Parliament, Lord Neuberger MR noted that:

> The right to express views publicly, particularly on the important issues about which the defendants feel so strongly, and the right of the defendants to assemble for the purpose of expressing and discussing those views, extends to the manner in which the defendants wish to express their views and to the location where they wish to express and exchange their views. If it were otherwise, these fundamental human rights would be at risk of emasculation. Accordingly, the defendants' desire to express their views in Parliament Square . . . and to do so . . . on the basis of relatively long term occupation with tents and placards, are all, in my opinion, within the scope of articles 10 and 11.[483]

Recognition of the importance of the right to protest in Parliament Square, however, has not prevented significant restrictions from being imposed on demonstrations held near the seat of democracy in the UK (and in *Hall* a possession order was granted in the terms sought by the mayor). An additional statutory regime exists in relation to the 'controlled area' of Parliament Square under Part 3 of the Police Reform and Social Responsibility Act 2011 (PRSRA).

The PRSRA was enacted because of the perceived ineffectiveness of existing civil law remedies (chiefly, the possibility of the council obtaining an injunction under s 130(5) Highways Act 1980 and/or initiating possession proceedings) to prevent

---

480　Lord Hutton did appear to assert this ([1999] 2 WLR 625, p 660), but his conclusion (p 666), upholds only the narrow and precarious liberty formulated by Lords Irvine and Clyde.

481　See Lord Irvine, [1999] 2 WLR 625, pp 632–33; Lord Clyde, *ibid*, p 655; and Lord Hutton, *ibid*, p 666.

482　*Minio-Paluello v Commissioner of the Police of the Metropolis* [2011] EWHC 3411 (QB), para 4(c).

483　*Hall and Others v Mayor of London (On Behalf of the Greater London Authority)* [2010] EWCA Civ 817 (16 July 2010), para 37.

long-term camp protests in Parliament Square Garden.[484] Section 143 confers on a constable or an 'authorised officer' (which can be any person authorised by the Greater London Authority or Westminster City Council as appropriate)[485] a power to direct a person (or two or more persons together)[486] to cease doing a 'prohibited activity' where they have reasonable grounds for believing that a person is doing, or is about to do, such an activity. So-called 'prohibited activities' include, within the controlled area, 'operating any amplified noise equipment',[487] erecting 'any tent, or ... any other structure that is designed, or adapted, (solely or mainly) for the purpose of facilitating sleeping or staying in a place for any period', and placing or using any 'sleeping equipment', defined as 'any sleeping bag, mattress or other similar item designed, or adapted, (solely or mainly) for the purpose of facilitating sleeping in a place'.[488] Home Office guidance on the application of the PRSRA states that this may include 'cardboard boxes and wooden boxes, which are also being used to store camping equipment or food supplies'.[489] However, in one case, a s 143 direction was issued on the basis that the tarpaulin on which a number of Occupy protesters were sitting (and which had been forcibly seized by police) was a structure adapted for the purposes of sleeping or staying in a place for any period. The charges, for refusing to comply with the direction, were later dropped by the CPS after a district judge ruled that the tarpaulin could not be classed as a structure for facilitating sleeping or as sleeping equipment.[490]

A direction need not be in writing and can be given orally,[491] and can 'include a direction that the person does not start doing that activity again after having ceased it' within a period of 90 days.[492] Furthermore, a court may impose on any person convicted of a s 143 offence whatever conditions it considers appropriate (potentially without time limits) in order to prevent that person from engaging in any prohibited activity in the controlled area.[493] In contrast to existing civil law powers, the PRSRA provides an

---

484 For historical background and a useful overview, see, Reid, K, 'Letting Down the Drawbridge: Restoration of the Right to Protest at Parliament' (2013) 3(1) *Law, Crime and History* 16–51. See also, *R (Gallastegui) v Westminster City Council and Others* [2013] EWCA Civ 28 paras 4–12.

485 Section 148. These may, for example, be GLA 'Heritage Wardens' (a service which is contracted out to a private security company – presently, Accent On Security (AOS); and previously, Chubb Security Personnel Ltd).

486 Section 144(6)(b).

487 Though under s 144(4)–(5), a direction not to operate sound equipment can only be given if it appears to the officer that the sound produced will, or is likely to, be heard by persons in the vicinity of Parliament Square.

488 Section 143(2) and (7).

489 See, Home Office, *Police Reform and Social Responsibility Act 2011 (as amended by the Antisocial Behaviour Crime and Policing Act 2014): Guidance Relating to Parliament Square and the Area Surrounding the Palace of Westminster* (2014), p 6.

490 See, 'Occupy Democracy Cases Dismissed in court', 21 July 2015, http://occupydemocracy.org.uk/2015/07/21/occupy-democracy-cases-dismissed-in-court/; Perraudin, F, 'Occupy protesters forced to hand over pizza boxes and tarpaulin', *The Guardian*, 24 October 2014, http://www.theguardian.com/world/2014/oct/24/occupy-protesters-forced-to-hand-over-pizza-boxes-and-tarpaulin. Also, *R (Barda) v Mayor of London on behalf of the GLA* [2015] EWHC 3584 (Admin), paras 23–34, and (in summary) paras 57–59, explaining how these protests led the GLA to use both high level, and later low-level, fencing to restrict access to the grassed area of PSG.

491 Section 144(6)(a).

492 Section 144(1)–(3).

493 Section 146.

immediate power of seizure (using reasonable force if necessary) of prohibited items,[494] and makes it a criminal offence (subject to a 'reasonable excuse' defence) to fail to comply with a direction that has been issued.[495] A direction can be varied or withdrawn by the person who gave it.[496] The PRSRA also enabled local authorities in England and Wales to introduce new powers of seizure regarding camping and sound amplification equipment (and a number of councils have since amended their byelaws accordingly).[497]

Crucially, however, and notwithstanding the fact that the legislation itself uses the term 'prohibited activity', the activities listed are not actually prohibited unless and until a direction is given.[498] The human rights compatibility of ss 143–145 of the 2011 Act was unsuccessfully challenged by a peace campaigner, Maria Gallastegui, who, for six years previously, had maintained a 24-hour camp protest in Parliament Square, authorised under the previous SOCPA framework.[499] She was given a direction to cease her protest under s 143 of the 2011 Act, and sought a declaration of incompatibility under s 4 HRA, arguing that s 143 and s 145 of the 2011 Act were incompatible with Arts 10 and 11 because (*inter alia*) they imposed a blanket – and hence disproportionate – ban with no element of discretion as to their implementation. In this regard, it is note-worthy that the explanatory notes to the PRSRA expressly state: 'In terms of the pro-hibition on tents and sleeping bags, the Government does not consider that this is a disproportionate interference with Art 10 and 11 rights.' Dyson MR held that s 143 did not constitute a blanket ban – even though 'Parliament must have intended that the discretion not to exercise the power should be exercised only in exceptional circum-stances'.[500] As such, he held that the 2011 Act contains a power, not a duty, to issue a prohibitory direction. This ruling has important implications for the way in which the term 'prohibited activity' should be understood when it is used in the Parliament Square byelaws and the corresponding application forms for organising a demonstration or displaying a placard or banner (as discussed below).

In addition to the PRSRA,[501] and despite the repeal of the authorisation requirement for assemblies within a 1 kilometre radius of Parliament (under ss 132–133 Serious Organised Crime and Police Act 2005),[502] an authorisation requirement – one that is in

---

494 Section 145. See also *Galastegui* [2013] EWCA Civ 28, para 8.
495 Section 143(8).
496 Section 144(6)(c).
497 Section 150 PRSRA, 2011, inserting s 237ZA into the Local Government Act 1972.
498 See, *R (on the application of Gallastegui) v Westminster City Council and Others* [2013] EWCA Civ 28, para 19.
499 For brief discussion, see Davies, K, 'Thou doth protest too much' *New Law Journal* (17 January 2014), pp 14–15.
500 *Galastegui* [2013] EWCA Civ 28, paras 22, 43–44.
501 *Ibid*, para 112.
502 The Serious and Organised Crime Act 2005 ss 132–38 (and related Serious Organised Crime and Police Act 2005 (Designated Area) Order 2005, SI 2005/1537) restricted the right to demonstrate within an exclusion zone of up to one kilometre from any point in Parliament Square. Demonstrators had to apply to the Commissioner of the Metropolitan Police for an authorisation for the protest six days in advance, or if this was not reasonably practicable, no less than 24 hours in advance. It was argued in (*R (Haw) v Secretary of State for the Home Department* [2006] EWCA Civ 352) that the provisions could not be applied retrospectively against a protest begun by Brian Haw in 2001, but the Court of Appeal found that Parliament clearly intended to regulate all demonstrations within the designated area, when-ever they began. On this basis, existing demonstrations were deemed to start on the date of the Act's

some ways more onerous than the SOCPA scheme – remains for assemblies in both Parliament Square Garden and Trafalgar Square under the applicable byelaws.[503] Indeed, serious questions arise in relation to the scope (and *vires*) of the mayor's powers to 'manage' and 'control' protest in Parliament Square Garden.[504] The byelaw requires that the mayor's written permission be obtained for certain activities (including, to 'organise or take part in any assembly, display, performance, representation, parade, procession, review or theatrical event'). In *Hall*, Lord Neuberger MR held that '[t]he Byelaws themselves cannot be said to fall foul of articles 10 and 11: they envisage demonstrations, speeches, camping, placards and the like being permitted subject to the Mayor's consent'.[505] However, subsequent litigation calls this conclusion into question. The byelaw states that permission 'will not be given in respect of any matter defined as a "prohibited activity" under s 143 of Part 3 of the Police Reform and Social Responsibility Act 2011'. This latter provision, however, appears to negate the distinction in *Gallastegui* (which, of course, was heard after the Byelaws were made) that s 143 is a discretionary power, rather than a duty. In other words, to categorically refuse permission under the byelaw for all activities described as 'prohibited' under the PRSRA (but which, according to the Court of Appeal in *Gallastegui*, may actually take place until the discretionary power to issue a direction under s 143 has been exercised) calls into question the proportionality, and indeed compatibility, of what might be regarded as a blanket prohibition in the byelaw (notwithstanding *Gallastegui's* contrary holding).[506]

The judicial review brought by George Barda, a member of 'Occupy Democracy', unsuccessfully sought to challenge the proportionality of the GLA decision to erect and maintain fencing on and around Parliament Square Garden after 21 October 2014, thereby interfering with a series of planned 'Occupy' demonstrations between

---

commencement. It is debatable whether this decision is in accord with Art 7 ECHR. Brian Haw was arrested and his site dismantled under these powers. It is noteworthy that the Strasbourg Court later also rejected as inadmissible an application challenging the SOCPA authorisation requirement (*Rai and Evans v UK*, Appl Nos 26258/07 and 26255/07, decision of 17 November 2009, admissibility).

503 Section 5(l)(j) Parliament Square Garden Byelaws, 2012 and s 5(1)(o), Trafalgar Square Byelaws, 2012, enacted under ss 383–385, Greater London Authority Act 1999. Available at: https://www.london.gov.uk/sites/default/files/parliament_square_gardens_byelaws.pdf and https://www.london.gov.uk/sites/default/files/trafalgar_square_byelaws.pdf respectively. Similar byelaws may be made by District Councils in other parts of England and Wales (under section 235 *Local Government Act* 1972) for the 'good rule and government' of the district and the 'prevention and suppression of nuisances'. Under s 9 of the Byelaws, '[W]here an authorised person has reasonable ground for belief that a person has contravened any one or more of the Byelaws, that person shall give on demand his name and address to that authorised person.'

504 See *Hall and Others v Mayor of London (on behalf of the GLA)* [2010] EWCA Civ 817, paras 21–33, confirming the mayor's right to claim possession of Parliament Square Garden under ss 384 and 385, Greater London Authority Act 1999.

505 *Hall and Others v Mayor of London (On Behalf of the Greater London Authority)* [2010] EWCA Civ 817 (16 July 2010), para 39.

506 In like fashion, the Greater London Authority's (GLA's) application forms for holding public meetings, demonstrations and rallies in Parliament Square Garden and Trafalgar Square, and for displaying a placard or banner, are deeply problematic. Overlooking the 'power' versus 'duty' distinction made in *Gallastegui*, they too categorically state that: 'You must not use . . . anything else prohibited by the Police Reform and Social Responsibility Act . . .'. Nor is it at all clear that the numerous additional terms and conditions specified in the forms would be regarded as being either 'prescribed by law' or 'necessary in a democratic society'. The forms are available at: https://www.london.gov.uk/about-us/venue-hire/book-parliament-square-garden.

October 2014 and March 2015 (for which authorisation had not been sought). Garnham J acknowledged that 'when the fencing was at its most extensive, it effectively sealed off PSG from the Claimant and his colleagues'[507] and that the fences thus constituted a real interference with their rights.[508] However, he noted that 'they were able to continue' their events on the pavements around the square or on the wider pavement area in front of the Supreme Court building,[509] and ultimately found the use of different kinds of fencing, at different times, to be a 'measured and graduated approach adopted by GLA to the threats of periodic occupation of PSG'.[510]

7 Public nuisance, obstruction of the highway and the criminalisation of trespass

In order to assemble or demonstrate, protesters require access to land. Moreover, in order to create an impact, persons normally assemble in large groups. If they are on the highway, they are very likely to cause some obstruction to free passage and therefore may fall foul of the offence of obstructing the highway. Further, the tendency for public spaces to be privatised has been reinforced by the direction of UK law. Not only are there virtually no positive rights of access to forums for the holding of meetings,[511] but under the provisions discussed below, a 'creeping criminalisation of trespass'[512] has occurred, denying protesters access to private or quasi-public land on pain of the risk of arrest and conviction, not merely of incurring tortious liability. There are now a number of circumstances in which a person who merely walks onto land may incur criminal liability. A central issue, therefore, is the impact of the HRA on the creation of such liability, and on the offence of obstructing the highway when used against assemblies.

Public nuisance

The statutory offences also bear similarities with the common law doctrine of public nuisance, which has occasionally been used against public protest. This common law offence will arise if something occurs which inflicts damage, injury or inconvenience on all members of a class who come within the sphere or neighbourhood of its operation.[513] Liability for committing a public nuisance may arise by blocking the highway; however, according to *Clarke (No 2)*,[514] the disruption caused must amount to an unreasonable use of the highway in order to found such liability. Thus, once obstruction has been shown, the question of reasonableness arises. As the courts have reiterated, 'a determination of

---

507 *R (Barda) v Mayor of London on behalf of the GLA* [2015] EWHC 3584 (Admin), para 61.
508 Para 91.
509 Para 61.
510 Para 123.
511 See the Representation of the People Act 1983, ss 95 and 96 (providing a right for Parliamentary candidates to hold meetings at election times) and the Education (No 2) Act 1986, s 43 (providing that university and college authorities must secure freedom of speech for persons, including visiting speakers, within their establishments), discussed above (text accompanying fn 319–320).
512 See Wasik and Taylor, *The Criminal Justice and Public Order Act 1994*, 1995, Blackstone, p 81.
513 See *Halsbury's Laws of England*, 4th edn, Vol 34, para 305. For discussion of the offence, see Spencer, JR [1989] CLJ 55.
514 [1964] 2 QB 315; [1963] 3 All ER 884, CA.

nuisance is contextual. Liability for nuisance is kept under control by the principle of a reasonable user. Reasonableness is to be judged objectively. . ..'[515] It would appear from *News Group Newspapers Ltd v SOGAT*[516] that to cause minor disruption for a legitimate purpose such as a march does not constitute an unreasonable use of the highway and will not therefore amount to a nuisance (see further, 'Injunctions' below).

Obstructing the highway

Section 137 of the Highways Act 1980 provides that a person will be guilty of an offence if he 'without lawful authority or excuse in any way wilfully obstructs the free passage of the highway'. The fact that a protest was not actually occurring on a highway would provide one such excuse. For example, three anti-fracking protesters at Barton Moss in Salford were given an absolute discharge (following their conviction for obstructing a police officer in the execution of her duty, under s 89(2) Police Act 1996) because they believed, correctly as it turned out, that they were not committing the offence of obstructing a highway since they were in fact on a private road, not a public highway (and as such, genuinely believed that they were not required to comply with police instructions based upon s 137 Highways Act).[517]

To attract liability, the obstruction caused must be more than trifling (*de minimis*), but in *Nagy v Weston*,[518] Lord Parker CJ held that '[a]ny occupation of part of a road, thus interfering with people having the use of the whole of the road, is an obstruction.' In this case it was held that a 'reasonable use' of the highway will constitute a lawful excuse, and that reasonableness must be judged on the particular facts, taking into account 'all the circumstances, including the length of time the obstruction continues, the place where it occurs, the purpose for which it is done, and . . . whether it does in fact cause an actual obstruction as opposed to a potential obstruction.'[519] The obstruction caused by a hot dog van in this case was held to be an unreasonable use.

---

515 *R (on the application of Keep Streets Live Campaign Ltd) v Camden London Borough Council* [2014] LGR 286 at paras 71–72, citing *Sturges v Bridgman* (1879) 11 Ch D 852 at 865, per Thesiger LJ and *Coventry v Lawrence* [2014] UKSC 13 at [4], [2014] 2 WLR 433 at [4], per Lord Neuberger.

516 [1986] ICR 716; [1986] IRLR 337.

517 This was notwithstanding the fact that the police subsequently sought to rely on s 68 CJPOA rather than s 137 Highways Act (Treacy LJ and Edis J accepting that 'it was not necessary for the officer to have had the correct offence in mind at the time the direction to move was given' and that it was sufficient for the officer to have taken steps which reasonably appeared to her to be necessary to prevent crime). See, *McCann v CPS* [2015] EWHC 2461 (Admin). Relatedly, however, the Court of Appeal judgment in *Austin and Saxby* [2007] EWCA Civ 989 (in which none of the police officers present on May Day 2001 had claimed at the time to be acting under the powers in ss 12 and 14 POA, but later sought to do so). Giving judgment for the court (and rejecting Tugendhat J's contrary assertion in the High Court – see, [2005] EWHC 480 (QB), para 98), Sir Anthony Clarke MR stated (at paras 82–83): 'It does seem to us that, whatever the strict position as a matter of law, the police should consider their statutory powers in a case of this kind and decide whether or not to exercise them. If they decide to exercise them, it is at least desirable to make it clear that they are doing so, especially since (for example) sections 12(4) and (5) and 14(4) and (5) contain penal sanctions for knowing failure to comply with directions given under them.'

518 [1966] 2 QB 561; [1965] 1 WLR 280.

519 *Ibid*. See also, *Minio-Paluello v Commissioner of the Police of the Metropolis* [2011] EWHC 3411 (QB), paras 39–40, where an argument relating to reasonable use of the highway was advanced (*obiter*)

The issue of 'reasonable use' was also raised in *Hirst and Agu v Chief Constable of West Yorkshire*,[520] in which it was noted that courts should have regard to the freedom to demonstrate when assessing whether a particular use was reasonable. Here, a group of animal rights supporters who held an anti-fur demonstration in a busy street, displaying banners and handing out leaflets, were acquitted of the obstruction charge on appeal. The crucial issue was whether peaceful protest on the highway constituted a reasonable use, thus amounting to a 'lawful excuse'. Glidewell LJ pointed out that, logically: 'for there to be a lawful excuse ... the activity in which the person causing the obstruction is engaged must itself be inherently lawful. If it is not, the question whether it is reasonable does not arise.'[521] The Court found that the activities of the protesters here were lawful, and that peaceful assembly was a reasonable use and thus constituted a lawful excuse.[522]

The *Hirst and Agu* judgment was highly influential in a subsequent case involving a protracted protest in Parliament Square. In October 2002, Westminster City Council applied (under s 130(5) of the 1980 Act) for an injunction to prevent Brian Haw from continuing his protest, which began in June 2001, and which the council argued was obstructing the pavement beside Parliament Square. Declining to issue the injunction sought by the council, Gray J noted that 'the factors which come into play when judging reasonableness include the length of time for which the obstruction continues, the place where it occurs, its purpose and whether actual obstruction occurs'.[523] While emphasising that Art 10 was not a 'trump card entitling any political protestor to circumvent regulations relating to planning and the use of highways', the right conferred by Art 10 'is a significant consideration when assessing the reasonableness of any obstruction to which the protest gives rise'.[524] As such, taking into account the requirement in s 12(4) HRA to 'pay particular attention to the right of freedom of expression', Gray J held that the obstruction caused by Brian Haw's protest was not unreasonable.

In an earlier judgment however (one not cited at all in *Westminster City Council v Haw*) doubt was cast on the notion that there is a right to demonstrate on the highway (which could constitute a reasonable use).[525] In *Birch v DPP*,[526] the defendant was arrested under s 137 for lying down in the road in front of a vehicle destined for the premises of a chemical wastage plant, SARP UK. The defendant alleged that the company

---

on behalf of a Pro-Palestinian protester based on Lord Denning's dissenting opinion in *Hubbard v Pitt* [1975] 3 All ER 1 (see further below at p 680).

520 (1987) 85 Cr App R 143. For comment, see Bailey, S, 'Wilfully obstructing the freedom to protest?' (1987) PL 495.

521 *Ibid*, p 151.

522 In an earlier case – *Arrowsmith v Jenkins* [1963] 2 QB 561; [1963] 2 All ER 210 – minor obstruction of traffic led to liability under s 121 Highways Act 1959. Here, the organiser of a pacifist meeting was convicted when a street was completely blocked for five minutes and partly blocked for 15 minutes, notwithstanding that she cooperated with the police in unblocking it. The issue here centred on the 'wilfulness' of the defendant's conduct, Lord Parker CJ holding that '[i]f anybody by an exercise of free will does something which causes an obstruction, then I think that an offence is committed.'

523 *Westminster City Council v Haw* [2002] EWHC 2073 (QB), para 20.

524 *Ibid*, para 24.

525 See also *Jones and Lloyd v DPP* [1999] UKHL 5, discussed above at pp 621–22.

526 [2000] Crim LR 301.

was engaging in unsafe and illegal practices, putting residents in the area at risk.[527] Both this vehicle and other (public) vehicles were obstructed. On appeal against his conviction he unsuccessfully argued that the activity of lying down in the road was a reasonable one, giving rise to a defence of 'lawful authority or excuse' under the Highways Act 1980.[528] The court dismissed this argument by distinguishing *Hirst and Agu*, noting that the question there was about whether handing out leaflets – an entirely lawful activity, thus providing lawful excuse. In the present case, in contrast, the court found that deliberately lying down in the road so as to obstruct the highway was not a lawful activity; the appellant's actions gave rise to trespass, public nuisance and private nuisance, so they were not within any category of lawful excuse.[529]

The decision in *Birch* makes it more difficult to defend any action as part of a protest or demonstration that is deliberately obstructive.[530] However *Birch* is not fully in accordance with the values of Arts 10 and 11 since it suggests that *any* peaceful protest or demonstration that is obstructive cannot rely on the 'lawful authority or excuse' part of the s 137 defence. As the *Haw* case underscores, a further possible argument (interpreting s 137 in light of s 3 HRA) is that the defence should apply to (otherwise) lawful obstructive activities that are also reasonable. On this basis, a peaceful, albeit obstructive, assembly would normally amount to a reasonable use of the highway, but where the obstruction created a risk to safety or impinged disproportionately on the right of others to free movement, due to its length, it might then no longer be viewed as reasonable.

The question of the reasonableness of an obstruction thus provides a key entry point for Arts 10 and 11 arguments – in particular, (a) a focus on whether the demonstrators had themselves committed any 'reprehensible' act;[531] (b) the recognition that 'any demonstration in a public place inevitably causes a certain level of disruption to ordinary life, including disruption of traffic' which ought to be tolerated to a certain degree;[532] and (c) the principle that demonstrators should be able to exercise their right to peaceful assembly for a duration sufficient for them 'to express their position of protest and to draw the attention of the public to their concerns'.[533] While it is certainly true that prosecution for obstruction of the highway may, depending on the circumstances, be justified if it is necessary to protect the 'rights and freedoms of others',[534] any prosecution under

527 On 30 May 1988 SARP leaked a cloud of nitric-dioxide gas over the village of Killamarsh in north Derbyshire and surrounding areas.

528 As used in the cases of *Hirst and Agu v Chief Constable of West Yorkshire* and *Nagy v Weston*.

529 This, however, is somewhat circular since blocking the highway is only 'patently unlawful' under the Highways Act 1980 itself. Aside from the Act (and the actions for nuisance and trespass), lying in the road is no more unlawful than handing out leaflets; it is arguably circular to find that it is the Act itself that prevents you from raising a defence under it.

530 The second argument relied upon (again, unsuccessfully) was that the activity was undertaken in order to prevent crime, in accordance with s 3 of the Criminal Law Act 1967.

531 *Ezelin v France*, Appl No 11800/85, 26 April 1991. Though see also the Strasbourg Court's Grand Chamber judgment in *Kudrevičius and Others v Lithuania* (2015) Appl No 37553/05, 15 October 2015[GC] (*cf* the earlier Chamber judgment of 26 November 2013), discussed at p 579 above.

532 See especially, *Patyi and Others v Hungary*, Appl No 5529/05, 7 October 2008, discussed at p 587 above.

533 See text accompanying fn 255–57 above.

534 Art 11(2) ECHR. Even though the right of free passage on the highway is not a Convention right, it would likely be regarded as an 'indisputable imperative' and so would qualify as a legitimate aim (see *Chassagnou v France* (2000) 29 EHRR 615 – see text accompanying fn 274–75 above).

s 137 would have to survive proportionality analysis. In this regard, it is imperative that the authorities neither over-emphasise nor rely exclusively upon purported traffic hazards as the basis for imposing liability on peaceful protesters under the Highways Act. Moreover, it might be argued that the use of a *criminal* charge against peaceful protesters who had merely caused some obstruction cannot be defended on proportionality grounds.

Criminalising trespass

The Criminal Justice and Public Order Act 1994 introduced a number of trespass provisions in response to the activities of hunt saboteurs, ravers and the travelling community. This led to a distortion of this area of the criminal law, to the detriment of freedom of protest. As such, Wasik and Taylor, for example, noted fears that the criminalisation of various forms of trespass in the 1994 Act would 'provide an inappropriate disincentive to group protest'.[535] The following sections examine the operation of these different trespass offences.

The statutory scheme: mass trespass

Simple trespass – walking onto someone's land without permission or refusing to leave when asked to do so – has never been a *crime* under UK law. However, s 61 CJPOA 1994[536] empowers a senior police officer, under certain conditions, to direct two or more people who are trespassing on land[537] to leave. The exercise of the s 61 power involves the application of a two-limb test. First, a senior police officer must reasonably believe that two or more persons are trespassing[538] with the common purpose of residing there for some period of time,[539] and that the occupier has taken reasonable steps to ask them to leave. Second, the senior officer must also reasonably believe that

---

535 *The Criminal Justice and Public Order Act 1994*, 1995, p 81.

536 As Stanley Burnton J noted, the s 61 provision appears 'to be aimed at Gypsies and Travellers: persons with an unconventional nomadic life-style, living in caravans or trailers, moving from time to time in their vehicles from place to place, and sometimes encamping on open land without the permission of the landowner.' *R (Fuller and Others) v Dorset Police and Another* [2001] EWHC Admin 1039 (12 December, 2001), para 1. Section 61 repealed, but closely resembles, s 39 Public Order Act 1986 (though the changes it introduced effectively widened the s 39 offence). For comment, see, Mead, *op cit*, fn 1, pp 162–167; Smith, ATH, *Offences Against Public Order*, 1987, paras 14–18; Card, R, *Public Order: The New Law*, 1987, pp 146–48; Vincent-Jones (1986) 13 JLS 343; *Stonehenge* (1986) NCCL; Ewing and Gearty, *op cit*, fn 1, 1990, pp 125–28.

537 In contrast to ss 68 and 69 of the 1994 Act (as amended, and as discussed below), the definition of 'land' in s 61 does *not* include buildings (except for those expressly specified in the s 61(9)(a)). See, *DPP v Chivers* [2010] EWHC 1814 (Admin) (23 June 2010).

538 The old s 39 Public Order Act offence had required that the persons actually came onto the land as trespassers. Under s 61, if they were not originally trespassers (for example, if the landowner or occupier had initially permitted their presence), the police officer must have a reasonable belief that the other conditions in s 61(1) (either damage caused or threats made, or the presence of 6 or more vehicles) were satisfied after the point at which they became trespassers, before being able to direct them to leave.

539 The term 'residing' is undefined in the Act. As David Mead suggests, it therefore lacks the clarity and certainty to be 'prescribed by law'. See further, Mead, D, *op cit*, fn 1, p 164.

they have brought six or more vehicles onto the land with them[540] or, alternatively, that one or more of the trespassers has threatened or abused the occupier or his agents or family or damaged (in any way) either the land itself or property on the land.[541] Section 61 creates a criminal offence for failing to leave as soon as is reasonably practicable thereafter, or for entering the land again as a trespasser within three months (punishable by up to three months' imprisonment and a £2,500 fine). It is a defence for someone to show either that they were not trespassing, or that they had a reasonable excuse for not leaving as soon practicable,[542] or for re-entering as a trespasser within the three-month window.[543]

Aggravated trespass – the intention and conduct elements of the s 68 offence

The CJPOA 1994 also created the offence of aggravated trespass under s 68, which was initially aimed at groups such as hunt saboteurs or motorway protesters.[544] In its original manifestation s 68 created a two-stage test; first, it had to be shown that the defendant trespassed on land in the open air[545] and, second, in relation to 'lawful activity' that persons are engaging in or are about to engage in, that he did there anything intended by him to have the effect of either intimidating those persons so as to deter them from the activity or of obstructing or disrupting that activity.[546] No defence is provided (though protesters may of course dispute the different elements of the offence – see the discussion of *Tilly v DPP, R v Jones (Margaret)* and *Richardson v DPP* under the 'The unlawful activity "defence"' below). Crucially, it is not necessary to show that the activity was actually affected. Moreover, while (on the face of the statute) if persons engaging in a lawful activity are in fact impeded by a protest, but the protesters did not intend to impede or intimidate (intending instead, for example, to engage in a purely symbolic protest), it would appear that s 68 does not apply – reckless, negligent or accidental intimidation or obstruction would not be enough. However, the structure of s 68(1) effectively collapses the distinction between the conduct element and the *mens rea* of the offence, and courts have readily inferred the missing intention from the protesters' conduct – or even from the very fact of the protest itself.[547]

---

540 The old threshold in the s 39 offence was 12 vehicles.
541 David Mead (*op cit*, fn 1, p 164) argues that s 3 HRA could be used here to import a more than *de minimis* interpretation of 'damage' – noting, in particular, the *Ezelin* standard of 'reprehensible behaviour'.
542 In cases involving travellers, a reasonable excuse might be established if no alternative pitch site has been offered by the relevant council. See, *R (on the application of O'Brien) v Bristol City Council* [2014] EWHC 2423 (Admin) para 69. In similar terms, it would conceivably remain open to a protester to argue a reasonable excuse defence if no alternative venue had been made available so as to facilitate the *effective* enjoyment of their rights to freedom of assembly and/or expression (within sight and sound of their intended audience).
543 Section 61(6).
544 See HC Deb col 29, 11 January 1994. By virtue of s 172(10), the section applies throughout the UK.
545 The 'open air' qualification has now been deleted, see below.
546 Section 69(1)(a).
547 See, for example, *Bauer and Others v DPP* [2013] EWHC 634 (Admin), discussed further below, in which Moses LJ (and the district judge before him) appear to infer an intention to intimidate primarily from the mere presence of protesters *en masse*.

While limited in its application (in that it does not apply to demonstrations on a met-alled highway),[548] the section was significantly widened by an amendment introduced through s 57 Anti-Social Behaviour Act 2003 which deleted the reference in s 68 to 'the open air'. The offence now encompasses trespass (and by extension, trespassory protest actions) within buildings.[549] Indeed, a number of troubling s 68 (and the related s 69) judgments have had the effect of widening the area of liability created still further.

One such example is the ruling of Laws LJ in *DPP v Barnard and Others*.[550] *Barnard* concerned the prosecution of protesters against open-cast mining who came onto land at an open-cast site. The magistrate found that three elements were required to establish the offence of aggravated trespass: namely, (1) trespass, (2) an intention to disrupt a lawful activity and (3) an act done towards that end. Based on the informa-tions originally submitted against protesters, the magistrate found that the allegation that the respondents 'unlawfully entered on land' alleged no more than that they had trespassed, and therefore was not capable of amounting to the aggravating act. The magistrate refused an application by the prosecution to amend the informations against them to allege the act of 'unlawfully occupying the site in company with numerous other people' on the ground that it still would not have disclosed an offence, as occu-pation of the site was the act of trespass, and not an additional act aggravating that trespass. Reference to the number of people was no more than an indication that some were trespassing. Laws LJ found that the magistrate was clearly correct in finding the original information to be defective. Proof was required of trespassing on land in the open air and of doing a distinct and overt act other than the act of trespassing that was intended to have the effects specified under paras (a)–(c) of s 68(1). Unlawful occupa-tion could equate to no more than the original trespass, but crucially, there might, he found, be circumstances where it could constitute the second act, other than trespass, required under the offence.[551]

This concession by Laws LJ in *Barnard* was cemented by the High Court in *Bauer and Others v DPP* – a case in which the human rights organisation, 'Liberty', inter-vened.[552] This case concerned the occupation by approximately 130 'UK Uncut' protesters of the 'Fortnum & Mason' shop in Piccadilly in March 2011 for approxi-mately two and a half hours.[553] The High Court upheld the district judge's finding that the holding of a demonstration could itself constitute the additional aggravating act (over and above 'mere occupation'), so as to make out the charge under s 68.

---

548 Although it does include public paths such as bridleways. See also *McCann v CPS* [2015] EWHC 2461 (Admin), discussed above at fn 517.

549 This was confirmed in an appeal by way of case stated by Kingsnorth protesters in *DPP v Chivers* [2010] EWHC 1814 (Admin) (23 June 2010).

550 Before Laws LJ and Potts J (judgment of 15 October 1999); *The Times*, 9 November 1999.

551 However, a bare allegation of occupation was insufficient. It had to be supported by particulars of what the defendant was actually doing, and the occupation had to be distinct from the original trespass. The proposed amendment would, he found, have disclosed an offence under s 68(1) of the 1994 Act, but it would not have been appropriate to allow the amendments. The appeal was dismissed accordingly.

552 [2013] EWHC 634 (Admin). See para 37 of the judgment for discussion of Liberty's intervention.

553 For background, see also, Malik, S, 'Fortnum and Mason protest: CPS drops charges against 109 UK Uncut activists' *The Guardian*, 18 July 2011.

Noting that *Barnard* was concerned only with pleading,[554] Moses LJ held that an occupation 'in force' or by 'mass invasion'[555] could justify a demonstration being regarded as 'a further act distinct from the initial trespass'.[556] It is suggested, however, that to treat a 'mass demonstration' as being an aggravating factor in a criminal charge is deeply troubling, and shows scant regard for the value of protest. The apparent willingness of the courts to entertain the notion that mere presence on land *per se* might constitute 'doing there anything' intended to be intimidatory, obstructive or disruptive under s 68(1) effectively removes the need to prove one of its constituent elements.[557]

In addition, a crucial element of the s 68 offence is an intention to intimidate, obstruct or disrupt. Based on (1) the 'chaotic scene', (2) the 'confined space', (3) the 'sheer mass of protesters' who remained in the store, (4) the duration of the protest, and (5) the protesters' actions (some were masked, several shouted or screamed at high volume using megaphones, and bagpipes were even played), the Court of Appeal concluded that 'the District Judge was entitled to infer that anyone who chose to remain in the store after it was closed . . . as part of the demonstration, had an intention to intimidate'. It is remarkable that, on these facts and without particularlised evidence in relation to the behaviour of each person charged,[558] the court chose to ground the prosecution in 'intimidation' (since inferring an intention either to obstruct or to disrupt would still have been sufficient to establish the offence). In doing so, Moses LJ undercut any meaningful distinction between 'disrupting', 'obstructing' and 'intimidating', notwithstanding his avowed desire not to diminish the force of the word 'intimidate'.[559] The judgment in *Bauer* also makes the distinction between simple (tortious) and aggravated (criminal) trespass much more difficult to discern (especially for protest participants themselves), potentially raising the question of whether the offence is adequately 'prescribed by law.' and compatible with the ECHR.

554 As such, *Barnard* 'is not authority of the proposition that "mere occupation of land" cannot be a further act distinct from the act of trespass' – see paras 16–17, also citing *Peppersharp v DPP* [2012] EWHC 474 (Admin) to which Moses LJ returns at paras 35–36. *Peppersharp* concerned the prosecution as an accessory of a protester found inside the building – Millbank Tower – some time after the initial fear-causing damage to the building had been caused. Moses LJ argued that Gross LJ was wrong in *Peppersharp* to prosecute the protester as an accessory, since it was precisely his continued presence in the building which constituted the conduct element of the s 68 offence.

555 Terms that appear both to fall short of actual or imminent violence, and to be deliberately preferred over other formulations, such as '*by* force'.

556 Para 16.

557 In *Bauer*, Moses LJ concluded that: '. . . each one of these appellants was guilty of aggravated trespass *by virtue of their presence* within Fortnum and Mason over a period of nearly two and half hours as part of the demonstration . . .' (para 41, emphasis added). See similarly, Lord Bingham (*obiter*) in *DPP v Capon*, fn 583 below.

558 Paras 26–28 (emphasising that each individual was guilty of the s 68 offence as a principal, not merely as an accessory).

559 Moses LJ in the High Court did not accept the district judge's view that 'to intimidate' could helpfully be regarded as meaning 'to cow' (paras 23–25), recognising that 'intimidation' connotes 'in its Latin root, the notion of putting someone in fear' and is more serious than either intentional obstruction or intentional disruption (para 22). However, in accepting the district judge's conflation of 'intimidation' with an intention to take control of the store (para 20), little space is left for any notion of obstruction or disruption falling short of intimidation.

The 'no persons' and the 'unlawful activity' defences

As noted above, s 68 does not expressly provide for a defence. However, those charged under the provision may certainly contest the prosecution's case. The first argument that might be raised is that no persons were actually engaging in, or about to engage in lawful activities, on the land in question. This was the argument advanced in *Tilly v DPP* (discussed below). A second line of 'defence' might be that the activities of the persons deemed to have been intimidated, or the activities that the protest sought to obstruct or disrupt, were not 'lawful activities' for the purposes of s 68 (see the cases of *Bayer*, *Jones* and *Richardson* also discussed below). As Thornton et al state, '[s]ince it is for the prosecution to prove each of these elements to the criminal standard, they are not strictly speaking defences, but rather the defendant putting the prosecution to proof of every necessary element.'[560]

In *Tilly v DPP*[561] the defendant was charged on two occasions with aggravated trespass. The case involved the damaging of genetically modified crops, where the farmer was not present at the time. It was argued on behalf of the defendant that aggravated trespass could not be established since no one was engaging in a lawful activity at the time in question. The question that was asked on appeal was whether the element of 'engaging in a lawful activity' in s 68(1) required the physical presence of a person engaged in such activity. It was found, significantly, that a person cannot be convicted of aggravated trespass if no one is physically engaged in lawful activity on the land at the time of the disruption: aggravated trespass was designed to deal with situations where people were intimidated or prevented from carrying out activity as they wished. It therefore followed that it could not be applied to situations where there was no one actually present. *Tilly* is thus of significance in relation to a number of forms of direct action protest, occurring before the lawful activity – the subject of the protest – gets underway, such as disabling traps or 'pre-beating' a hunt, in order to rid an area of foxes before the hunt arrives.[562]

The situation in *DPP v Bayer*[563] differed from that in *Tilly* since, in the former, disruption to a lawful activity had clearly occurred. The defendants went on to private land that was being drilled with genetically modified (GM) maize. The crop had been granted a marketing consent and could be grown legally anywhere in the UK. The defendants attached themselves to tractors engaged in the drilling process, thereby disrupting that activity. They were charged with aggravated trespass contrary to s 68(1) and (3) of the Criminal Justice and Public Order Act 1994. At trial the defendants submitted that their actions were justified to protect damage to the environment since GM crops could cause damage to surrounding property. The district judge dismissed the charges, finding that the defendants' actions were reasonable in the circumstances and came within the common law private defence of property. The question for the opinion of the High Court on

---

560 *The Law of Public Order and Protest*, 2010, p 196, para 5.63.

561 (2001) *The Times* 27 November.

562 Lord Hughes JSC suggests in Richardson that the use of the word 'may' in the s 68(2) definition of 'lawful activity' was 'because the section has to apply to activity by the occupant which has not yet commenced.' *Richardson and another v DPP* [2014] UKSC 8 at para 29 (appealing the s 68 aspect of *Nero and another v DPP*, [2012] EWHC 1238 (Admin)).

563 [2003] EWHC 2567 (Admin).

appeal was whether the finding that the actions of all four defendants was reasonable in the defence of property was a finding properly open to the district judge, judging the issue of reasonableness objectively. The appeal was allowed. It was found that where the common law private defence of property was raised the court had first to ask itself whether the defendants were contending that they had used reasonable force in order to defend property from actual or imminent damage, which constituted or would constitute an unlawful or criminal act. If the answer to that was 'no' then the defence was not available. If the answer was 'yes' then the court had to go on to consider the facts as the defendants honestly believed them to be and then had to determine objectively whether the force that had been used was reasonable in all the circumstances. In the instant case, it was found that it was clear that the defendants were well aware that there was nothing unlawful about the drilling of GM maize on the land, whether or not the seed might be transferred by one means or another to the neighbouring land. They had acted as they had because they considered that the seed represented a danger to neighbouring property, not to prevent an activity that was unlawful or criminal. It followed that the district judge should have directed himself as a matter of law that the private defence of property was not available to the defendants on the facts. These findings were unsurprising.

In *R v Jones*; *R v Milling*; *R v Olditch*; *R v Pritchard*; *R v Richards*; *Ayliffe v Director of Public Prosecutions*; *Swain v Director of Public Prosecutions*,[564] the argument again centred on the 'lawful activity' that was being disrupted, the argument being that it was not lawful. The appellants had all been charged with or convicted of aggravated trespass or criminal damage arising out of their separate, independent actions taken at military bases by way of protest against the war in Iraq. It was claimed on their behalf that they were entitled to rely upon s 3 of the Criminal Law Act 1967,[565] on the basis that they were using reasonable force to prevent the commission of a crime, or that their acts of disruption were not aggravated trespass because the activities of the Crown at the military bases were not lawful within the meaning of s 68(2) of the Criminal Justice and Public Order Act 1994, since they were being carried out in pursuance of a crime of aggression under customary international law. The questions certified were whether the crime of aggression was capable of being a 'crime' within the meaning of s 3 of the 1967 Act and, if so, whether the issue was justiciable in a criminal trial, and whether the crime of aggression was capable of being an 'offence' within s 68(2) of the 1994 Act and, if so, whether the issue was justiciable in a criminal trial. The House of Lords found that it was very unlikely that Parliament had understood 'crime' in s 3 as covering crimes recognised in customary international law but not assimilated into domestic law by any statute or judicial decision. Therefore, 'crime' in s 3 did not cover a crime established in customary international law, such as the crime of aggression.[566] The House concluded that the crime of aggression was neither capable of being a 'crime' within the meaning of s 3 of the Criminal Law Act 1967, nor an 'offence' within s 68(2) of the Criminal Justice and Public Order Act 1994. Therefore, individuals facing charges for criminal damage and aggravated trespass arising out of their actions in protesting

564 [2006] UKHL 16. For the previous decisions in the cases, see: [2004] EWCA Crim 1981; [2005] QB 529 and [2005] EWHC 684; [2005] 3 WLR 628.
565 See above, fn 32.
566 *R (Rottman) v Commissioner of Police for the Metropolis* (2002) UKHL 20 was applied.

against the war in Iraq could not argue that they were using reasonable force to prevent the commission of a crime, or that the activities of the Crown at the military bases were unlawful. The appeals were therefore dismissed.

An even more limiting conclusion was reached by the Supreme Court in *Richardson v DPP*. On 2 October 2010, protesters entered an 'Ahava' shop, in Covent Garden, which sold cosmetic products, manufactured in an Israeli settlement on the West Bank but labelled as being manufactured in Israel rather than the Occupied Palestinian Territories. The protesters peacefully locked their arms together through a concrete tube, and refused to leave the store. They were convicted of the s 68 offence, and sought to argue in their defence that the manufacturing and trading activities of Ahava were not 'lawful activities' for the purposes of s 68(1). The Supreme Court had to decide what specific 'activities' were relevant to the protesters' argument that Ahava was engaging in 'unlawful activity' and that s 68 was therefore inapplicable. The primary allegation was that Ahava was complicit in the commission of war crimes (under the International Criminal Court Act 2001) by enabling the transfer of Israeli citizens to its factory in the OPT. Relatedly, the protesters also pointed to money laundering (by virtue of benefiting from the proceeds of these war crimes), and false or misleading product labelling (which indicated that the products were made in Israel rather than the OPT). The Supreme Court accepted that 'person' 'plainly included a company',[567] and that, as previous cases had emphasised, in order to benefit from this 'defence', protesters must identify a specific offence and provide evidence of such unlawful activity.[568] Following *Jones*, it was also reiterated that s 68 is 'concerned only with a criminal offence against the law of England and Wales'.[569] The Supreme Court, however, refused to find any of these activities relevant to the proper construction of 'lawful activity' in s 68, finding instead that this phrase should be limited to acts or events that are 'integral' to the activities at the premises in question.[570] This, in their Lordships' view, meant only the activity of retail selling in the shop.

This purported distinction between core or integral activities on the one hand, and collateral, extraneous, supplemental, antecedent or remote activities on the other, will no doubt be the focus of future litigation. What is core and what is collateral reaches the very essence of the message being conveyed by the protesters. In *Richardson*, the Supreme Court wholly inverted the protesters' perception of what is core (the transfer of Israeli civilians to the OPT) and what is collateral (the activity of selling beauty products in the London shop). In doing so, the 'larger evil' was written out, and the judgment inscribed a limiting narrative that speaks only of the most anodyne activity (selling) and those most incidentally affected (shop-floor employees). Moreover, the judgment

---

567 [2014] UKSC 8, para 8. See also *Nero and another v DPP* [2012] EWHC 1238 (Admin) (from which *Richardson* appealed to the Supreme Court in relation to the Divisional Court's s 68 finding) per Laws LJ at para 13: 'The term "person" where it appears in statute includes a body corporate unless the contrary intention appears . . .Though terms such as "obstruct" and "disrupt" apply naturally to the activities of individuals, there may be cases where an activity is properly categorised as that of a company.'

568 See Lord Hughes in *Richardson* at para 9, citing *Ayliffe v DPP* [2006] QB 227. This is a reasonable requirement so as to eliminate the equivalent of protest-led 'fishing expeditions' that could otherwise compel judicial examination of the legality of all activities carried on by the company concerned, or indeed, by its parent company and subsidiaries.

569 *Ibid.*

570 Para 24.

in *Richardson* effectively nullifies the unlawful activity defence implied by s 68. This has serious implications for demonstrators whose only 'practical and effective' avenue of protest may be to target the high street branch of a large multinational, or their trading partners.[571] Even more worrying is the conclusion reached by Lord Hughes that any reference to the rights of free expression was misplaced because s 68 'is not concerned with the rights of the trespasser, whether protester or otherwise' and that '[p]ut shortly, Art 10 does not confer a licence to trespass on other people's property in order to give voice to one's views'.[572] These statements seek to draw a bright-line, proprietary threshold for Arts 10 and 11 – one that is at odds with Strasbourg's emphasis on facilitating peaceful protest for a certain period of time, even if it is disruptive and happens to be unlawful for other reasons.[573]

An 'activist' re-interpretation of ss 68 and 69 under s 3(1) of the HRA would not presumptively exclude trespassory protest from the ambit of Arts 10 and 11. Furthermore, *Bauer*, which classified the mass presence of demonstrators as an aggravating act in itself (giving rise to significant uncertainty about when trespass *simpliciter* might attract criminal liability under s 68) would also have to be reconsidered and, it is suggested, overruled.

Directions under s 69

Far-reaching provisions in s 69 underpin s 68. Section 69(1)(a) provides that if the senior officer present at the scene reasonably believes that a person is committing, has committed or intends to commit the offence under s 68, or (b) that two or more persons are trespassing and have the common purpose of intimidating persons so as to deter them from engaging in a lawful activity or of obstructing or disrupting that activity, he can direct any or all of those persons to leave the land. Under s 69(3), if the person in question, knowing that the s 69 direction has been given that applies to him, fails to leave the land as soon as practicable[574] or re-enters it as a trespasser within three months,[575] he commits an imprisonable offence. It is a defence for the person to show that he or she was not trespassing on the land[576] or that he or she had a reasonable excuse[577] for failing to leave the land or for returning as a trespasser. Notably, it has been held that s 68 (not s 69) should be relied upon in circumstances where protesters would be physically unable to leave the land 'as soon as practicable' (however construed) – perhaps, because they

---

571 Lord Hughes JSC stated (at para 17): 'Even if that company could have been aiding and abetting [the transfer of Israeli civilians into the OPT], that cannot amount to an offence by the separate retailing company, *whatever* the corporate links between the two companies.'

572 Para 3.

573 See, for example, the discussion of *Ezelin v France* and *Bukta v Hungary* above. They also stand in flat contradiction to the approach of Laws LJ in the Divisional Court: 'The charge of aggravated trespass constitutes an interference with the right [of peaceful protest], indeed an interference with this right of free expression guaranteed by art 10 ECHR. Accordingly, its purported legal justification . . . ought at the least be strictly construed. This serves to emphasise . . . the need for the prosecution strictly to prove the legality of the activity.' See *Nero and another v DPP* [2012] EWHC 1238 Admin, para 19.

574 Section 69(3)(a).

575 Section 69(3)(b).

576 Section 69(4)(a).

577 Section 69(4)(b).

had used 'lock-on' (or similar) techniques, linking their arms together through pipes. On this basis, Laws LJ held that the use of s 69 in *Nero and another v DPP* was unjust and unreasonable.[578]

It may be noted that s 69 is the equivalent of s 14C of the Public Order Act 1986, which allows a constable to stop a person whom he reasonably believes is on her way to an assembly in an area to which a s 14A order applies, and to direct her not to proceed in that direction. The power can only be used within the area to which the order applies. Failure to comply is an offence and renders the person liable to arrest. The similarities between s 14C and s 69 mean that much of the discussion below would apply also to s 14C.

Although s 68 may not lead to the criminalisation of persons who simply walk on to land as trespassers, s 69 has the potential to do so, depending on the interpretation given by the courts to the 'reasonable excuse' defence. For example, where a person is in receipt of the direction under s 69, even though it was erroneously given (since in fact, although she was trespassing, she did not have the purpose of committing the s 68 offence), she may still commit an offence if thereafter she re-enters the land in question during the specified time. The fact that on the second occasion she was merely walking peacefully on to land in order to engage in a non-obstructive public protest would be irrelevant unless she could also produce an excuse that could be termed reasonable. Whether the erroneousness of the senior police officer's original 'reasonable belief' would amount to a reasonable excuse is left unclear.

Capon v DPP[579] made it clear that the offence under s 69 could be committed even though the offence under s 68 was not established. The defendants were videoing the digging out of a fox when they were threatened with arrest under s 68 by a police officer if they did not leave and were asked whether they were leaving the land. This exchange and question was found to be sufficient, in the circumstances, to constitute the direction necessary under s 69.[580] Their intention in undertaking the videoing was not found to be to disrupt, intimidate or interfere with the activity in question. Despite the fact that the protesters had been peaceful and non-obstructive throughout,[581] and it was very doubtful whether the officer had directed his mind towards all the elements of the offence, including the *mens rea*,[582] it was found that there was sufficient evidence. It was further found that there was no defence of 'reasonable excuse' in the circumstances,[583] even

---

578   The magistrate's fear that this 'could open the doors to trespassers taking ever more extreme steps to frustrate the powers of the police under section 69', and the similar argument advanced by the prosecution, that protesters should not be 'allowed to obtain an advantage by reason of a state of affairs caused by their own wrongdoing' were rebutted by Laws LJ who held that this was 'to confuse s 68 with s 69' and that s 68 was the only appropriate charge. See, *Nero and another v DPP* [2012] EWHC 1238 (Admin), paras 34–39.

579   Case CO/3496/97 Judgment of 4 March 1998 LEXIS; considered: Mead [1998] Crim LR 870.

580   In this regard, it might be argued that if a direction can be given in the imprecise form of a question, that it is too imprecise to satisfy the test denoted by the term 'prescribed by law' under Arts 10 and 11 – assuming that the activity in question could be viewed as constituting the expression of an opinion so as to engage those articles.

581   In the exchange with the officer, one said, 'I have no intention of disrupting [the hunt] ...'; another, 'We're here quite peacefully ... simply videoing what is going on' (Mead [1998] Crim LR 870, p 871).

582   As Mead notes, *ibid*, p 875.

583   'The fact that the appellants were not ... committing an offence under s 68 plainly ... does not provide a reasonable excuse for not leaving the land. So to hold would emasculate the obvious intention of the section' (*per* Lord Bingham, Case CO/3496/97 (1998), transcript).

though the protesters were still in the process of trying to find out what offence they were being arrested for[584] when they were, in fact, arrested, and genuinely believed that no direction under s 69(1) had been made against them.

The judgment consisted of a fairly orthodox exercise in statutory interpretation, coupled with a generous approach to the reasonableness of the officer's belief.[585] Since criminalisation of what will often, in Convention terms, be an act of political expression,[586] rests primarily upon the state of belief of a single officer, perhaps formed in a few moments, a court with any appreciation of the enormous discretion that this statute affords the police to interfere with political protest would have been expected to conclude both that it should construe the statute as strictly as possibly against the executive, and, further, that it should scrutinise the actions of the police officer, especially the clarity of his instructions,[587] and the findings of the trial court with particularly anxious care. Further or alternatively, the court could have found that where the defendants were in fact engaged in peaceful protest, they could plead 'reasonable excuse'; the very broad phrasing of that defence provides the most obvious means by which to import human rights values into s 69. The court, unfortunately, showed no awareness of any of these factors, engaging instead in a purely mechanistic interpretation of the law; indeed, there was no (explicit) *normativity* in its approach at all.

The interpretation of s 69 in *Capon* is problematic when viewed through an 'activist' lens.[588] As *Capon* made clear, s 69 allows peaceful protesters to be arrested even though in fact there was no obstruction, intimidation or disruption of others and no risk of disorder, as long as a police officer reasonably believed that such factors were present. This belief is supposed to be 'reasonable',[589] but as *Capon* vividly demonstrates, the inhibiting effect of this requirement in practice can all but disappear due to the courts' marked disinclination to take issue with the judgments of police officers on the spot. Therefore, it may be argued, depending on the particular circumstances, that certain s 69 'bans' may be unjustifiable under para 2 of Arts 10 and 11, bearing in mind the extent of the discretion to interfere with peaceful protest which this section vests in the police without any independent check, and the extent of the interference – in effect, a complete ban on entering the land in question, potentially lasting for three months. Since s 69 can operate as a prior restraint, Art 10 would demand that any direction given should be strictly scrutinised.

584   The first protester said, immediately before he was arrested, 'I'm not prepared to leave the land because I don't believe I'm committing any offence'; the second, 'I don't understand' (Mead [1998] Crim LR 870, p 871).

585   In particular, as Mead points out, no inquiry was made as to whether he had directed his mind towards all the elements of the offence, including the *mens rea* (*ibid*, pp 874–75).

586   The ECHR had not delivered judgment in *Steel* at this point (judgment was delivered on 23 September 1998) and *Capon* was decided on 4 March 1998; however, the decision of the Commission, which made a like finding as to the applicability of Art 10, was delivered on 9 April 1997.

587   As Mead remarks: '. . . it must be very difficult to "know" within section 69(3) that a direction has been given if the police are permitted such wide and uncertain language as this'. See, Mead, D, 'Will Peaceful protesters be foxed by the Divisional Court decision in *Capon v DPP*' [1998] Crim LR 870, p 872; Mead, *op cit*, fn 1, pp 262–63.

588   See above, p 596.

589   Section 69(1).

Peaceful protesters – like the two defendants in *Capon* – have clearly committed no 'reprehensible' acts, as *Ezelin* requires (though the more recent Grand Chamber judgment in *Kudrevičius* reopens the question of what might properly constitute 'reprehensible' behaviour). One possible response, therefore, would be to reinterpret s 69 under s 3(1) of the HRA so as to allow for a lawful direction to be given only where in fact one of the above elements is actually present. Reasonable belief would have to be taken to mean reasonable and true belief.[590] While such a reading renders s 69 largely otiose (since s 68 would cover such a situation) it is again, a 'possible' reading under s 3(1) HRA. A further, more likely, possibility would be to find by reference to Arts 10 and 11 that the erroneousness of the senior police officer's original 'reasonable belief' should amount to a reasonable excuse.[591] It would also be possible to find that purely peaceful protesters have a 'reasonable excuse' for not obeying a s 69 direction under s 69(4)(b). Moreover, under this view, courts could surely find that the Convention requires officers to use the clearest possible words when ordering persons to leave the land, precisely what the court failed to do in *Capon*.

It is suggested that these decisions reveal a judicial approach that, far from engaging with the thorny issues raised by the direct action form of protest, show a continuance of traditional, formalist reasoning, coupled with marked executive-friendly tendencies: a willingness to widen the scope of already widely drafted offences and a reluctance to interfere with the exercise of broad police discretion. Such tendencies proceed directly from the evident lack of judicial recognition (or indeed, express exclusion or redefinition)[592] of the issues of principle at stake and the values underpinning the right to protest.

8 Breach of the peace, binding over and bail conditions

Any court of record having criminal jurisdiction has a power at common law to bind over persons to keep the peace.[593] Under the Justices of the Peace Act 1361, there was also a power – the *contra bonos mores* (contrary to a good way of life) power – to bind over persons to be of good behaviour.[594] The latter power allowed for the binding over of persons whose behaviour was deemed by a bench of magistrates to be anti-social although not necessarily unlawful. This vague and broad power conferred a very wide discretion on magistrates to determine standards of good behaviour, and unsurprisingly, was criticised for being a grave breach of rule of law standards.[595] It was also critiqued by the European Court of Human Rights for being 'imprecise' and offering 'little guidance'

---

590 It should be noted that s 69 raises an issue distinct from that of arresting under s 68(4) on the basis of reasonable suspicion of committing the offence under s 68. Since s 68(4) requires reasonable suspicion as to the commission of an offence, it is in principle compatible with Art 5 under the exception of para (1)(c).

591 See, similarly, *McCann v CPS* [2015] EWHC 2461 (Admin).

592 See, for example, Lord Hughes in *Richardson v DPP* [2014] UKSC 8, para 3.

593 See the Justices of the Peace Act 1968, s 1(7).

594 See *R v Sandbach ex parte Williams* [1935] 2 KB 192: as described in *Hashman and Harrup v UK*, Appl No 25594, 25 November 1999, para 14. See too, *R v Buxton and Others* [2010] EWCA Crim 2923, para 24, noting that this power could not be used to exclude persons from particular places.

595 Williams, G, 'Preventive justice and the rule of law' (1953) 16 MLR 417. See also Hewitt, P, *The Abuse of Power*, 1984, p 125.

in the case of *Steel v United Kingdom*.[596] Then, in the case of *Hashman and Harrup v UK*[597] (where, unlike the *Steel* case, the binding-over order imposed had purely prospective effect and did not coincide with a finding that there had been a breach of the peace),[598] the Court found that the power was too vague and unpredictable in its operation to satisfy the 'prescribed by law' requirement under Arts 10 and 11.[486] A practice direction, now consolidated in the Criminal Procedure Rules 2014,[599] was subsequently issued in order to take account of the *Steel* and *Hashman* judgments.[600] The practice direction emphasises that:

Before imposing a binding over order, the court must be satisfied so that it is sure that a breach of the peace involving violence, or an imminent threat of violence, has occurred or that there is a real risk of violence in the future. Such violence may be perpetrated by the individual who will be subject to the order or by a third party as a natural consequence of the individual's conduct.[601]

Furthermore, rather than binding an individual over 'to be of good behaviour', courts should instead detail in a written order the specific conduct or activity from which the individual should refrain. Any such order 'should not generally exceed 12 months',[602] and courts should give the individual who would be subject to the order an opportunity to make representations regarding the making of the order and its terms.[603] The court should also take into consideration the individual's financial circumstances before deciding on the amount of any recognisance.[604] If a person refuses a binding over order, he or she can be imprisoned for up to six months.[605]

---

596 (1999) 28 EHRR 603, [1998] Crim LR 893, in which the Court noted (at para 76) that: 'the orders were expressed in rather vague and general terms; the expression "to be of good behaviour" was particularly imprecise and offered little guidance to the person bound over as to the type of conduct which would amount to a breach of the order.'

597 (2000) 8 BHRC 104; (1999) 30 EHRR 241. For the admissibility proceedings, see *Hashman and Harrup v UK* (1996) 22 EHRR CD 184. The case concerned the behaviour of hunt saboteurs. One of the applicants had blown a horn with the intention of disrupting a hunt. There was no threat of violence, and blowing a horn was not unlawful. However, on the basis that he would likely have repeated these actions, he was bound over to be of good behavior, and this order was upheld on appeal. This, in turn, led to the application to Strasbourg.

598 (2000) 30 EHRR 241, [2000] Crim LR 185.

599 The 2014 Practice Direction came into force on 6 October 2014, and can be found at: https://www.gov. uk/government/publications/criminal-procedure-rules-2014-and-criminal-practice-directions. Binding over orders and conditional discharges are contained in Division VII (Sentencing) J. It applies to orders made under the court's common law powers, under the Justices of the Peace Act 1361, s 1(7) of the Justices of the Peace Act 1968, and s 115 of the Magistrates' Courts Act 1980. See also the CPS Guidance on the binding over power: http://www.cps.gov.uk/legal/a_to_c/binding_over_orders/.

600 This was to the satisfaction of the Council of Europe's Committee of Ministers in its supervision of the execution of Strasbourg judgments. See Resolution CM/ResDH(2011)1801, Execution of the judgment of the European Court of Human Rights, *Hashman and Harrup against the United Kingdom*.

601 Para J.2.

602 Para J.4 of the Practice Direction. So this would presumably militate against the two year order imposed on the anti-fishing protesters in *Nicol and Selvanayagam v UK*, Appl No 32213/96, 11 January 2001, and held to be proportionate.

603 Para J.5.

604 Para J.11.

605 In *Nicol and Selvanayagam v UK*, Appl No 32213/96, 11 January 2001, for example, the applicants were imprisoned for 21 days for refusing to comply with the binding over order.

These powers are of great significance in relation to direct action, demonstrations and public protest generally due to the wide discretion they confer upon police and magistrates. The notion of maintaining the Queen's peace has been said to express the idea that 'people should be free to act as they choose so long as they do not cause violence'.[606] This simple concept appears to be unobjectionable in civil libertarian terms, since it would not allow interference with the freedom to protest peacefully. However, it will be argued below that this idea no longer expresses the central value underlying the doctrine of breach of the peace. In many respects, it has been replaced by a notion of freedom of action so long as serious inconvenience is not caused. Since the breach of the peace doctrine has the potential to curb all forms of protest it has come into domestic conflict with Arts 10 and 11 of the Convention. Moreover, while its breadth was somewhat narrowed by the seminal House of Lords' decision in *Laporte* in 2006, it still retains the capacity to undermine the statutory schemes discussed. As such, this doctrine provides the most significant power for use against protesters discussed in this chapter. Protests involving protesters with a history of causing disorder, and protests including a few individuals who are disorderly or who may become so, are potentially subject under this doctrine to an array of restraints, including the ending of the demonstration or detention for several hours with or without arrest.

Breach of the peace

Introduction

Lord Bingham in the case of *Laporte* (discussed below) summarised the breach of the peace doctrine as follows:

> Every constable, and also every citizen, enjoys the power and is subject to a duty to seek to prevent, by arrest or other action short of arrest, any breach of the peace occurring in his presence, or any breach of the peace which (having occurred) is likely to be renewed, or any breach of the peace which is about to occur.[607]

If a police officer suspects that a breach of the peace is likely to be committed – for example, a march is expected to be disorderly – a person or persons can be arrested without a warrant under common law powers to prevent a breach of the peace.[608] They can also be bound over to keep the peace, in other words not to continue the behaviour thought likely to lead to the breach of the peace. Thus, a protest or march could be prevented from occurring. If the person refuses the binding over order, he or she can be imprisoned. This nebulous common law power overlaps with a number of the powers

---

606 Feldman, *Civil Liberties and Human Rights in England and Wales*, 1st edn, 1993, p 787.
607 *R (on the application of Laporte) v Chief Constable of Gloucestershire* [2006] UKHL 55, paras 29–30, citing *Albert v Lavin* [1982] AC 546 and the nineteenth century Irish case of *Humphries v Connor*, (1864) 17 ICLR 1, 8–9.
608 For comment, see Smith, ATH, 'Breaching the peace and disturbing the quiet' (1982) PL 212; Williams, *op cit*, fn 1. It should be noted that breach of the peace, though arrestable, is not a criminal offence.

arising under the 1986 and 1994 Acts, but is in general more useful to the police since its definition is so broad.[609] This means that it can readily be used in ways that undermine attempts in the statutory provisions to carve out more clearly defined areas of liability, and can apply in situations where statutory powers might be inapplicable.[610] Given also the reluctance of the courts to question the judgment of a police officer on the ground, this is a wide power indeed.

Furthermore, in protest situations, the common law power is often used in conjunction with statutory powers under both the Criminal Justice and Public Order Act 1994 (CJPOA) and the Police Reform and Social Responsibility Act 2011 (PRSRA). Authorisations under s 60 CJPOA can be issued in anticipation of serious violence, and empower a police officer to stop and search individuals in the specified locality, whether or not there are grounds for suspecting the individual(s) of carrying weapons. In addition, s 60AA contains powers (again, only exercisable if an authorisation is in place) to require the removal of, and/or to seize, any item which an officer reasonably believes a person is wearing 'wholly or mainly for the purpose of concealing his identity'.[611] Section 50 PRSRA empowers a police officer to require a person to give his name and address if the officer has reason to believe that the person has been behaving in an anti-social manner.[612] Routine reliance on these powers against protesters risks conflating peaceful protest with both violence and anti-social behaviour.

The leading breach of the peace case is *R v Howell*,[613] in which it was determined that a breach of the peace will arise if 'harm is actually done or is likely to be done to a person or in his presence to his property or a person is in fear of being so harmed through an assault, an affray, a riot, unlawful assembly or other disturbance'.[614] The *Howell* definition is extremely wide – albeit not as wide as some other definitions that have been suggested.[615] The reference to harm 'likely to be done' means that threatening words that do not in themselves amount to a breach of the peace, might lead a police

---

609 The 1986 Act itself provides (s 40(2)) that nothing in it 'affects the common law powers ... to deal with or prevent a breach of the peace'.

610 For example, in *Wright v Commissioner of Police for the Metropolis* [2013] EWHC 2739 (QB), paras 48, 53 and 68, Jay J held that the common law containment power could lawfully be used even if s 14 POA could not be invoked.

611 See fn 74 above for an example of the misinterpretation of the scope of the equivalent power in Northern Ireland.

612 'Anti-social behaviour' is as defined in s 2 of the Anti-social Behaviour, Crime and Policing Act 2014. In the absence of such statutory authority (and unless being arrested for an offence) refusal to disclose one's name and address is lawful. See *Laporte* [2006] UKHL 55, para 55 per Lord Bingham ('her refusal to give her name . . . however irritating to the police was entirely lawful'). See also, *Mengesha v Commissioner of Police of the Metropolis* [2013] EWHC 1695 (Admin), paras 12–13 (per Moses LJ). Though note also s 9 of the Parliament Square Garden Byelaws, 2012 and Trafalgar Square Byelaws 2012 (see above fn 503).

613 [1981] 3 All ER 383.

614 *Ibid*, 389.

615 See, for example, Lord Denning's much broader definition of the offence in *Chief Constable for Devon and Cornwall ex p Central Electricity Generating Board* [1982] QB 458. In *Percy v DPP* [1995] 3 All ER 124, DC, the *Howell* definition was preferred and Lord Denning's definition was rejected as erroneous. See further, Mead, *op cit*, fn 1, p 320; Thornton, P, et al, *op cit*, fn 1, p 161 at para 4.63, and p 256 at para 6.129.

officer to reasonably apprehend a breach. Indeed, there is no requirement that the 'fear' of harm itself be reasonable.[616] Furthermore, the 'harm' done or 'other disturbance' are not confined to violence or threats of violence – or even, to behaviour that is unlawful under civil or criminal law.[617]

At least two related issues are worthy of further consideration. First, what degree of imminence is required before the police can justifiably intervene? In other words, at what point could it be said that a breach of the peace was too distant to justify police intervention, including arrest? Second, if a breach can be said to be imminent, what action can the police legitimately take to prevent its occurrence, and against whom can such action be taken? These two issues are addressed in turn below. It is noteworthy – in relation to the second question – that the actions taken by the police may potentially also engage the rights to liberty (Art 5 ECHR) and freedom of movement (Art 2 of Protocol 4, ECHR, and Art 12 ICCPR).[618] As such, the question of whether these rights in any way limit or constrain the possibility of police intervention by way of 'containment' (sometimes known as 'kettling') will also be examined.

The imminence test

A number of authorities establish that the duty to arrest for breach of the peace arises only when the police officer apprehends that a breach of the peace is 'imminent' (*O'Kelly v Harvey*;[619] *Foulkes v Chief Constable of the Merseyside Police*)[620] or is 'about to take place' or is 'about to be committed' (*Albert v Lavin*)[621] or will take place 'in the immediate future' (*R v Howell*).[622] The officer's apprehension 'must relate to the near future' (*McLeod v Commissioner of Police of the Metropolis*).[623] If the officer reasonably apprehends that a breach of the peace is likely to occur in the near future, there is a duty to take reasonable steps to prevent it.

This power, in conjunction with the offence of obstruction of an officer in the execution of his duty, was used extensively during the miners' strike.[624] It was made clear then that an arrest could occur well before the point is reached at which a breach of the peace is apprehended. The most notorious instance of its use occurred in *Moss v McLachlan*.[625] A group of striking miners in a convoy of cars were stopped by the police a few miles away from a number of collieries and prevented from travelling on to pits a few miles away where non-striking miners were working. The police officers had reason

---

616 See Mead, *op cit*, fn 1, p 320, citing: Stone, R, 'Breach of the Peace: the case for abolition' [2001] 2 Web Journal of Current Legal Studies.
617 For example, in *Minio-Paluello v Commissioner of Police of the Metropolis* [2011] EWHC 3411 (QB), paras 46–7 per Eder J).
618 Art 2 of Protocol 4 has not yet been ratified by the UK, but the UK has ratified the ICCPR.
619 (1883) 14 LR Ir 105, 109.
620 [1998] 3 All ER 705, 711b–c.
621 [1982] AC 546.
622 [1982] QB 416, 426, also: 'where there is reasonable apprehension of imminent danger of a breach of the peace'.
623 [1994] 4 All ER 553, 560F.
624 March 1984 to March 1985.
625 [1985] IRLR 76 at 78–79, paras 22–23. The case attracted widespread criticism; see, Mead, *op cit*, fn 1, pp 341–2; Ewing and Gearty, *op cit*, fn 1, pp 111–12; Newbold (1985) PL 30.

to believe that violent clashes would break out, not at the motorway exit where their cordon was positioned, but at the pits. The police told them that they feared a breach of the peace if the miners reached the pits and that they would arrest the miners for obstruction if they tried to continue. After some time, a group of miners tried to push past the police, and were arrested and convicted of obstruction of a police officer in the course of his duty. Their appeal on the ground that the officers had not been acting in the course of their duty was dismissed. It was said that there was no need to show that individual miners would cause a breach of the peace, nor even to specify at which pit disorder was expected.

The court in *Moss* cited with approval Lord Parker CJ's *dicta* in *Piddington v Bates*[626] that the police must anticipate 'a real, not a remote, possibility of breach', seeming to prefer this test over the 'immediate future test' advanced in *R v Howell*.[627] On the former test, therefore, a reasonable belief that there was a real risk that a breach would occur in close proximity to the point of arrest (the pits were between two and four miles away) was all that was necessary.[628] In assessing whether a real risk existed, news about disorder at previous pickets could be taken into account; in other words, there did not appear to be a requirement that there was anything about these particular miners to suggest they might cause a breach of the peace.[629] Thus, a number of individuals were lawfully denied their freedom of both movement and assembly apparently on no more substantial grounds than that other striking miners had caused trouble in the past. When later Strasbourg jurisprudence is considered, this finding is plainly at odds with the ruling in *Ezelin* (even allowing for the subsequent judgment in *Kudrevičius*) that an individual should not face restrictions unless they themselves have acted 'reprehensibly'.[630]

In the subsequent House of Lords judgment in *Laporte v Chief Constable of Gloucestershire Police*,[631] Lord Bingham described the 'real possibility' or 'real risk' test in *Piddington* as 'aberrant'.[632] In *Laporte*, a group calling themselves Gloucestershire Weapons Inspectors, in conjunction with other anti-war groups, had organised a protest in March 2003 at RAF Fairford (which was being used as a base for hostile operations

---

626 [1961] 1 WLR.
627 [1981] 3 All ER 383; [1982] QB 416, 426. It should, however, be noted that in *Moss*, the Court did conclude that, on the facts, 'a breach of the peace was not only a real possibility, but also, because of the proximity of the pits and the availability of cars, *imminent, immediate* and not remote' (emphasis added).
628 A case in Kent in which striking miners were held up over 200 miles away from their destination suggested that this requirement of close proximity might become otiose: *Foy v Chief Constable of Kent* (20 March 1984) unreported. As Mead notes (op cit, fn 1, p 342, fn 160), under the HRA, and following *Laporte*, this decision 'is no longer sustainable, if ever it was before'. Similarly, Thornton, P, et al, *op cit*, fn 1, p 162, para 4.64, fn 91.
629 The miners apparently gave a hostile reception to passing NCB coaches but this, it appears, occurred after the police had stopped them and informed them that they could not proceed. It does not appear, therefore, that it could have formed part of the basis for the police decision that a breach of the peace was to be expected.
630 See also, *Ziliberberg v Moldova*, discussed above at p 574. *Ezelin* and *Ziliberberg* informed their Lordships reasoning in *Laporte* [2006] UKHL 55 – see Lord Bingham (para 36); Lord Rodger (paras 82 and 85); and Lord Mance (paras 144 and 149).
631 [2006] UKHL 55, on appeal from *R (on the application of Laporte) v Chief Constable of Gloucestershire* [2004] EWCA Civ 1639.
632 *Ibid*, paras 47 and 51 (per Lord Bingham).

in Iraq) to demonstrate against the policy and conduct of the UK and US governments in Iraq. Since part of the protest involved a procession, the Gloucestershire Weapons Inspectors had provided the chief constable with written notification as required by s 11 of the 1986 Act. There was to be a rally at the main gate of the base, with several speakers and an estimated 1,000–5,000 attendees. The claimant was a peace protester who sought to join the RAF Fairford protest.

The chief constable considered that the protesters would likely include hardline activists intent on violence and entry to the base. Various demonstrations had occurred in the past, and on one occasion an otherwise peaceful protest was attended by a hardcore anarchist group known as the Wombles (White Overalls Movement Building Libertarian Effective Struggles), resulting in serious disorder. It appeared from websites advertising the Fairford protest that members of the Wombles might travel to the event along with other protesters on coaches from London. The chief constable's plan for the demonstration had been to allow it take place peacefully and to minimise the risk of serious public disorder. Among the preparatory steps taken by police was the issuance of a direction under s 12 of the 1986 Act, prescribing (in accordance with the notification) the time, place of assembly and procession route, and drawing attention to the criminal offence of failing to comply with the conditions laid down. A statutory stop and search authorisation under s 60 of the Criminal Justice and Public Order Act 1994 was issued.[633] It applied to an area around Fairford, and was extended on the following day. An authorisation under s 60AA of the 1994 Act, giving power to require the removal of disguises, was also issued. Police officers were mustered in large numbers, supported by anti-climbing teams, patrols on both sides of the perimeter fence, dog teams, a member of the Metropolitan Police Public Order Intelligence Unit (to recognise those known to be 'extreme' protestors), a facial recognition team, forward intelligence teams,[634] three police support units ('PSUs') and helicopters. It was the largest ever policing operation undertaken by the Gloucestershire Constabulary.

On the day in question, the claimant joined a group of about 120 passengers who boarded three coaches at Euston bound for Fairford. Eight members of the Wombles were also on the coaches. The three coaches were stopped by the police at Lechlade near Fairford. The police searched the coaches and found a few items that could possibly have been used in a non-peaceful protest, such as face masks, spray paint, two pairs of scissors and a safety flare, home-made shields. All these articles were seized. Many of the passengers were apparently not questioned about their intentions or affiliations. After the search the coaches and passengers were directed by the officer in charge to be escorted by the police back to London. The officer took the view that had the coaches been permitted to continue to RAF Fairford the protesters on the coaches would have been arrested upon arrival at RAF Fairford, as a breach of the peace would then have been 'imminent'. He stated that he had concluded that he had a choice of either allowing the coaches to proceed and managing a breach of the peace at RAF Fairford, arresting the occupants of the coaches in order to prevent a breach of the peace, or turning the coaches around and escorting them back away from the area in order to avert a breach of the peace. Officers stood by the doors as the coaches moved off, holding them shut to prevent passengers

---

633 See Chapter 12, p 851.
634 See the explanation of 'forward intelligence teams' above at fn 46.

from disembarking, as some had tried to do on learning that they were to be returned to London. The coaches were driven to the motorway, where police motorcycle outriders prevented them from stopping on the hard shoulder or turning off to motorway services, even to allow passengers to relieve themselves.[635]

The claimant issued an application for judicial review, seeking to challenge the actions of the chief constable in (1) preventing her travelling to the demonstration in Fairford, and forcing her to leave the area, and (2) forcibly returning her to London, keeping her on the coach and preventing her from leaving it until she had reached London. At first instance her first complaint was rejected but her second was upheld.[636] In upholding the claimant's second claim, May LJ concluded that the claimant had been detained on the coach back to London and that such detention could not be held to be covered by Art 5(1)(b) or (c) of the Convention. The Court of Appeal (Lords Woolf CJ, Clarke and Rix LJJ) upheld the Divisional Court's decision.[637] The claimant, however, appealed to the House of Lords against the rejection of her first complaint, and the chief constable cross-appealed against the upholding of her second complaint. The Lords unanimously concluded that the actions of the police, in turning away the coach and then detaining the passengers on the return journey to London, were unlawful since they exceeded the common law power to take steps to prevent a breach of the peace. Lord Bingham framed this excess in the language of the Convention, stating that the police response was neither prescribed by law nor proportionate.[638]

Focusing on the 'prescribed by law' limb of the argument, counsel for the police had relied on *Moss v McLachlan*[639] in support of an argument that, for police intervention short of arrest, it is not necessary to show that the breach of the peace was so imminent as to justify an arrest. On this approach, '[t]he imminence or immediacy of the threat to the peace determines what action is reasonable',[640] and so a police officer would have had the power – and duty – to take action short of arrest (such as stopping cars or directing protesters away from a protest) at an earlier stage than that at which he would have the power and duty to arrest persons on the grounds of breach of the peace. The House of Lords, however, rejected this argument and accepted that there is nothing in domestic authority to support the proposition that action short of arrest may be taken when a breach of the peace is not so imminent as would be necessary to justify an arrest.[641] Significantly, Lord Bingham took this view partly on the basis that the common law doctrine would otherwise undermine Parliament's intention in enacting 1986 Act.[642]

---

635 Footage of the policing operation is contained in the 'shockumentary' film, *Taking Liberties* directed by Chris Atkins (Revolver Entertainment: 2007).

636 The case came before the Queen's Bench Divisional Court (May LJ and Harrison J) [2004] EWHC 253 (Admin), [2004] 2 All ER 874.

637 [2004] EWCA Civ 1639; [2005] QB 678.

638 [2006] UKHL 55, paras 45, 55 and 56.

639 [1985] IRLR 76 (discussed above).

640 *Ibid*, at p 79, para 24. Similarly, in the New Zealand case of *Minto v Police* [1987] 1 NZLR 374, 377, Cooke P said that 'the degree of immediacy is plainly highly relevant to the reasonableness or otherwise of the action taken by the police officer'.

641 See *Laporte*, [2006] UKHL 55, paras 114–115 (per Lord Brown), emphasising that 'prior restraint (pre-emptive action) needs the fullest justification'. David Mead thus describes *Laporte* as establishing a 'uniform test of imminence' (*op cit*, fn 1, pp 338, 340).

642 *Laporte*, at para 46.

However, while *Laporte* was widely acclaimed, its subsequent application suggests that the qualifications to the imminence test conceded by two of their lordships in the judgment have had at least as much traction as the more positive aspects of the case. Lord Rodger conceded that there was no need for a police officer 'to wait until an opposing group hoves into sight before taking action', as that would 'turn every intervention into an exercise of crisis management'.[643] Lord Carswell added that while the imminence of a breach of the peace 'is an essential condition which should not be diluted, . . . it can be properly applied with a degree of flexibility which recognises the relevance of the circumstances of the case' and where 'events are building up inexorably to a breach of the peace it may be possible to regard it as imminent at an earlier stage temporally than in the case of other more spontaneous breaches'.[644]

Perhaps unsurprisingly therefore, in two high profile cases – one concerning the containment of G20 'Climate Camp' protesters in London on 1 April 2009 and the other concerning preventive arrests of protesters on the day of the royal wedding on 29 April 2011 – the courts upheld the police action and confirmed that 'imminence is not an inflexible concept but depends on the circumstances'.[645] In the Climate Camp case – *R (Moos and McClure) v Commissioner of the Police of the Metropolis* – the Court of Appeal further emphasised that the Court must assess only the reasonableness of the police apprehension of imminence (rather than forming its own view on the question of imminence).[646] It is however the royal wedding case that is most troubling.

The lockdown policing operation put in place for the wedding of Prince William and Kate Middleton was described in detail in the testimony of several police officers in *R (Hicks, 'M', Pearce and Middleton) v Commissioner of Police of the Metropolis*.[647] On the strength of police intelligence that anti-monarchist protesters might seek to disrupt the wedding, the police issued authorisations for stops and searches under s 60 CJPOA and s 60AA CJPOA. Some protesters were also searched under s 1 PACE for items that might be used to commit criminal damage. The operation involved the

643 [2006] UKHL 55, para 69.
644 Para 102. Lord Mance's view (at para 141) is somewhat equivocal. He expressly rejected 'the suggestion that imminence is a flexible concept', emphasising that 'the threshold for preventive action is neither a broad test of reasonableness nor flexible'. However, it seems that he was using the word 'flexibile' merely to describe the 'flexibility' of the 'sliding-scale' *Moss dicta*, i.e. that 'different degrees of [imminence] may justify different forms of preventive action' (and so he was not rejecting Lord Carswell's suggestion that the notion of 'imminence' itself could be applied flexibly). This reading is borne out by Lord Mance's further statement that 'imminence' does not fall 'to be judged in absolute and purely temporal terms, according to some measure of minutes. What is imminent has to be judged in the context under consideration, and the absence of any further opportunity to take preventive action may thus have relevance'.
645 *R (Moos and McClure) v Commissioner of Police of the Metropolis* [2012] EWCA Civ 12, paras 32–36 (approving the Divisional Court's summary of *Laporte*). Similarly, *R (Hicks, 'M', Pearce and Middleton) v Commissioner of Police of the Metropolis* [2012] EWHC 1947 (Admin), para 133.
646 [2012] EWCA Civ 12, para 69. It is notable that the Court of Appeal approved the approach of Sedley LJ in the pre-HRA case of *Redmond-Bate v DPP* (1999) 163 JP 789. The Court of Appeal judgment was subsequently cited approvingly in *Hicks* [2012] EWHC 1947 (Admin), para 160.
647 [2012] EWHC 1947 (Admin). The Pearce and Middleton claims related to searches of a squat and a protest camp respectively, both of which the police claimed were housing individuals suspected of intending to commit criminal acts against the Royal Wedding, some of whom may have been involved in disorder during the TUC march a month earlier on 26 March. See, paras 28, 85 and 103.

deployment of 'anti demonstration patrols'[648] and briefings that emphasised that the police response would be 'pre-emptive, if necessary' and would show 'zero tolerance of potential disorder'.[649]

Several cadres of protesters were arrested at different locations on the morning of the wedding. These included Brian Hicks who had sought to participate in the 'Not the Royal Wedding' street party in Red Lion Square, but who, having been recognised as an anarchist protester from previous demonstrations, was stopped en route by a plain clothed police officer. He was searched under s 1 PACE, arrested to prevent a breach of the peace, then taken to a police station, strip-searched, and detained until the wedding had finished. The nine so-called 'Charing Cross claimants' arrived at Charing Cross station at around 10.30am intending to attend a republican protest in Trafalgar Square, but on realising this to be impossible, also decided to go to the 'Not the Royal Wedding' party in Red Lion Square.[650] On their way, they were stopped and searched under s 60 CJPOA by British Transport Police, then were arrested to prevent a breach of the peace by Tactical Support Group officers, and taken to a police station where they were held until the wedding had finished at 3.30pm. The four 'Starbucks claimants' had the intention of taking part in a 'zombie picnic' organised by Queer Resistance. They were searched under s 60 CJPOA shortly after exiting a branch of Starbucks, and were then arrested to prevent a breach of the peace (on the basis that they had expressed anti-royalist views and possessed placards, a loudhailer and climbing helmet).[651] 'The second zombie claimant' known as 'JMC' had gone to the 'zombie picnic', but on realising that that the event was not taking place, decided, together with a friend, to go home.[652] They covered their faces momentarily to avoid being photographed, but shortly thereafter were stopped by police officers who searched them under s 60 and questioned why they had masked their faces. On being found to be in possession of a leaflet for the 'zombie picnic', they too were arrested and detained until approximately 3pm. Finally, 'M' was a 16-year-old who was stopped and searched under s 1 PACE after he was seen 'carrying a megaphone and walking with purpose'.[653] The search of his rucksack unearthed two large marker pens and he was arrested under s 3 Criminal Damage Act 1971. The police officer, in explaining why it was not considered appropriate simply to confiscate the pens, stated (seemingly without irony) that: 'Without the arrest, the offence would not be prevented because . . . "M" could simply purchase new marker pens and carry out what I thought was his intention to scrawl graffiti slogans. The shops were open for him to buy new pens.'[654]

In each instance, the High Court held that the police had reasonably apprehended a breach of the peace to be imminent, and that the arrests were necessary and proportionate.[655]

---

648 *Ibid*, para 42, extract from notebook of PC Hemmings.
649 *Ibid*, para 51, witness statement of PC Morris.
650 *Ibid*, paras 54–71.
651 *Ibid*, para 170. The police also had information that protesters dressed as zombies were intending to throw maggots as confetti as the wedding procession left Westminster Abbey – see para 38(10).
652 *Ibid*, paras 46–53.
653 *Ibid*, paras 76 and 79.
654 *Ibid*, para 79.
655 *Ibid*, paras 171–172: the Court concluded that any suggestion that the police could have used less coercive measures (such as a 'request to desist') was 'wholly unrealistic'.

Richards LJ and Openshaw J also rejected the suggestion that the police had 'operated a policy, or practice . . . of equating intention to protest with intention to cause unlawful disruption' or that they had adopted an impermissibly low threshold of tolerance for public protest.[656] The Court further dismissed out of hand the claimants' Art 11 arguments, stating that Art 11 could legitimately be restricted if peaceful assembly might provoke others to violence.[657] This conclusion rests on the highly dubious proposition that the hordes of flag-waving royal wedding well-wishers would likely have responded with violence at the first sign of any anti-wedding agitation (see further, 'Provoking a breach of the peace' below). Moreover, the court held that the Strasbourg judgment in *Plattform 'Ärzte für das Leben' v Austria*[658] did *not* mean that the police were obligated to protect the anti-monarchist protesters from the violent actions of others in such a situation. Rather, 'the likelihood that protest may lead to violence against the protesters themselves can be an entirely legitimate ground for police intervention against the protesters under the domestic law of breach of the peace'.[659] This interpretation of the power both embeds a 'heckler's veto' in the common law framework and upends the core principle established in *Plattform Ärzte* that peaceful demonstrators, in the absence of relevant and sufficient evidence of non-peaceful intentions, should be protected from violence by others.

In summary therefore, given the latter-day emphasis on the flexibility of the 'imminence test', and Lord Carswell's suggestion that tension, in the context of protests, may build up 'inexorably', the *Laporte* judgment has presented less of a brake on the police reflex to 'control' and 'manage' (rather than to 'facilitate') public protest than may first have been thought. This was most starkly demonstrated in the royal wedding case of *Hicks*.[660] As such, the positive elements of *Laporte* – namely, the decisive rejection of the *Moss* 'sliding-scale' *dicta* that action short of arrest can be taken if a breach of the peace is not imminent, and the finding, on the particular facts, that a breach of the peace was not imminent and so the police action was therefore both premature and indiscriminate – should not be over-stated. While the judgment took ss 2 and 6 HRA seriously by analysing the Strasbourg jurisprudence and subjecting the facts to close scrutiny under the doctrine of proportionality, the concessions pertaining to the imminence test ultimately mean that the police still retain extraordinarily wide powers to interfere with the actions of protesters. As Maurice Kay LJ has subsequently noted, the power to prevent a breach of the peace remains 'unapologetically, a preventative power'.[661]

Provoking a breach of the peace

Cases such as *Moss v McLachlan* concerned the use of preventive powers against those who could be viewed as likely to breach the peace at some future point. The courts have

656 *Ibid*, paras 142–155.
657 *Ibid*, paras 120–127, quoting Sedley LJ in *Redmond-Bate v Director of Public Prosecutions* [2000] HRLR 249, para 20: 'Free speech includes not only the inoffensive but the irritating, the contentious, the eccentric, the heretical, the unwelcome and the provocative *provided it does not tend to provoke violence*'.
658 Appl No 10126/82, 21 June 1988.
659 [2012] EWHC 1947 (Admin), para 123, based on the findings of the Strasbourg Court in *McLeod v UK* (1998) 27 EHRR 493, 23 September 1998, para 42 and *Steel v UK* (1999) 28 EHRR 603, 23 September 1998 (para 55), that the concept of breach of the peace, as defined in *Howell*, met the 'prescribed by law' test.
660 [2012] EWHC 1947 (Admin), paras 128–139, and in the Court of Appeal, [2014] EWCA Civ 3, para 26.
661 *Hicks and Others v Commissioner of the Police of the Metropolis* [2014] EWCA Civ 3, para 27.

taken an equally broad view of conduct that might provoke others to breach the peace. *Beatty v Gillbanks*[662] established the important principle that persons acting lawfully could not be held responsible for the actions of those who were thereby induced to act unlawfully. However, in *Duncan v Jones*,[663] a speaker wishing to address a public meeting opposite a training centre for the unemployed, was told to move away to a different street because the police apprehended that her speech might cause a breach of the peace. A year previously there had been some restlessness among the unemployed following a speech by the same speaker. She refused to move away from the centre and was arrested for obstructing a police officer in the course of his duty. On appeal, it was found that the police had been acting in the course of their duty because they had reasonably apprehended a breach of the peace.

The case therefore clearly undermined the *Beatty v Gillbanks* principle in that the freedom of the speaker was infringed, not because of her conduct, but because of police fears about the possible response of the audience. In the later case of *Jordan v Burgoyne*,[664] it was found that a public speaker could be guilty of breach of the peace if he spoke words which were likely to cause disorder amongst the particular audience present, even where the audience had come with the express intention of causing trouble. In *Wise v Dunning*[665] it was found that a breach of the peace would arise if there is an act of the defendant 'the natural consequence of which, if the act be not unlawful in itself would be to produce an unlawful act by other persons'.[666]

In *Percy v DPP*,[667] Collins J ruled: 'The conduct in question does not in itself have to be disorderly or a breach of the criminal law. It is sufficient if its natural consequence would, if persisted in, be to provoke others to violence.'[668] Similarly, in *Morpeth Ward JJ ex p Ward*,[669] which concerned the behaviour of protesters against pheasant shooting, Brooke J stated: 'provocative disorderly behaviour which is likely to have the natural consequence of causing violence, even if only to the persons of the provokers, is capable of being conduct likely to cause a breach of the peace'.[670] Thus, the reasonableness of the shooters' response or potential behaviour was not called into question. The court did not lay down a test to determine the point at which a violent reaction to provoking behaviour might be regarded as an unnatural consequence of such behaviour. It focused simply on the question of whether the natural consequence of the behaviour in question was to provoke violence, thus leaving open the possibility that an extreme reaction from those provoked, although probably unreasonable, might be termed natural.

---

662 (1882) 9 QBD 308.

663 [1936] 1 KB 218; for comment, see Daintith, T (1966) PL 248.

664 [1963] 2 QB 744; [1963] 2 All ER 225, DC. It should be noted that the case was concerned with breach of the peace under the Public Order Act 1936, s 5.

665 [1902] 1 KB 167. See also *Duncan v Jones* [1936] 1 KB 218.

666 An extremely wide interpretation of this possibility was accepted in *Holmes v Bournemouth Crown Court* (1993) unreported, 6 October 1993, DC; cited in Bailey, Harris & Jones, *op cit*, fn 1, p 256. Here, an anti-smoking campaigner who held up a placard and shouted anti-smoking slogans, but in no way threatened violence, was arrested on the ground that if he stayed in his position – outside the designated lobbying area at a Conservative party conference – a breach of the peace might arise. The finding that in arresting him, the officer had acted in the execution of his duty, was upheld on appeal. See also, *Kelly v Chief Constable of Hampshire* (1993) *The Independent*, 25 March.

667 [1995] 3 All ER 124, DC.

668 *Ibid*, p 131.

669 (1992) 95 Cr App R 215.

670 *Ibid*, p 221.

This very wide finding received a more restrictive interpretation in *Nicol v DPP*,[671] which concerned the behaviour of anti-fishing protesters. During an angling competition the protesters blew horns, threw twigs into the water and attempted verbally to dissuade the anglers from fishing. This provoked the anglers so that they were on the verge of using force to remove the protesters. The protesters were arrested for breach of the peace. It was found that they were guilty of conduct whereby a breach of the peace was likely to be caused since their conduct, although lawful, was unreasonable and was likely to provoke the anglers to violence. Thus, the reasonableness of the behaviour of those provoked was considered. Simon Brown LJ found that a natural consequence of lawful conduct could be violence in another only where the defendant rather than the other person could be said to be acting unreasonably, and, further, that, unless the anglers' rights had been infringed, it would not be reasonable for them to react violently. It was assumed that their rights had been infringed,[672] and that as between the two groups the behaviour of the fishing protesters was clearly unreasonable. The need to show that a potentially violent reaction would be reasonable (or that the conduct of those being arrested was unreasonable because it materially interfered with the rights of others) was a welcome narrowing of the 'natural consequence' test, one not present in *Wise v Dunning*.

Sedley LJ sought to simplify the tests from *Nicol* further in *Redmond-Bate v DPP*,[673] a case decided in the period just before the HRA was fully in force. Ms Redmond-Bate and other women, a group of fundamentalist Christians, were preaching forcefully on the steps of Westminster Cathedral. A large crowd gathered, who were angered by their preaching. Fearing a breach of the peace, a police officer asked the women to desist; when they refused, he arrested them. The Divisional Court found that in the circumstances, two questions should be asked of the action of the police officer. First, was it reasonable to believe that a breach of the peace was about to be caused? Secondly, where was the threat coming from? The Divisional Court found, in answer to both the questions posed, that there were no sufficient grounds on which to determine that a breach of the peace was about to be caused or, moreover, on which to determine that the threat was coming from Ms Redmond-Bate, bearing in mind the tolerance one would expect to be extended to offensive speech. Sedley LJ said: 'Free speech includes not only the inoffensive, but the irritating, the contentious, the eccentric, the heretical, the unwelcome and the provocative providing it does not tend to provoke violence. Freedom only to speak inoffensively is not worth having.'[674] He went on to find that the Crown Court had correctly directed itself that 'violence is not a natural consequence of what a person does unless it clearly interferes with the rights or liberties of others so as to make a violent reaction not wholly unreasonable'[675] and he emphasised that the court should make its own independent judgment of the reasonableness of the police officer's belief.

Redmond-Bate still leaves significant uncertainty as to the status of provocative speech. The test of reasonableness is no more precise in its application than Simon

671 (1996) 1 J Civ Lib 75. See further, *Nicol v UK* Appl No 32213/96, 11 January 2001 (admissibility).
672 The rights referred to were left unclear. While there is, of course, no express 'right to fish', see fn 161, fn 172 and fn 339 above.
673 (1999) *The Times*, 28 July; [1999] All ER (D) 864.
674 Transcript, para 12.
675 Transcript, para 16.

Brown LJ's *dicta* in *Nicol* and leaves open a considerable margin of judgment – with a corresponding chilling effect on protest – in terms of deciding when a violent response to a provocative protest is *wholly* unreasonable.[676] The judiciary may well be disinclined to find that the behaviour of groups espousing minority, 'alternative' viewpoints, such as hunt saboteurs or anti-monarchist protesters, while lawful, were also reasonable (see further, 'A case for reform?' below).

Action to prevent an imminent breach of the peace

The rejection by the House of Lords in *Laporte* of the sliding-scale approach advocated by Skinner J in *Moss*[677] means that a breach of the peace must be imminent before the police may intervene under this doctrine, either by arrest or action short of arrest. Nevertheless, as the previous section also demonstrated, while *Laporte* was in some ways a high watermark for the protection of freedom of assembly, it is equally an authority that permits preventive interventions, so long as they are proportionate and a police officer reasonably believes a breach of the peace to be imminent (this test being flexibly applied). As such, it appears that preventive policing tactics, including arrest (*Hicks*)[678] and action short of arrest such as 'containment' or 'kettling' – (*Austin*;[679] *Castle*;[680] *Moos and McClure*;[681] *Mengesha*;[682] and *Wright*[683]) are readily available to the police in such circumstances. In this light, it is notable that Maina Kiai – the UN Special Rapporteur on the Rights to Freedom of Peaceful Assembly and of Association – following his official mission to the UK, pointed to the chilling effect that 'kettling' may have, describing this tactic as 'intrinsically detrimental to the exercise of the right to freedom of peaceful assembly, due to its indiscriminate and disproportionate nature'.[684]

Given too that s 14(1) of the Public Order Act 1986 allows the police to impose only a fairly limited range of directions on a static assembly (these may relate only to its place, maximum duration, or maximum number of participants),[685] the statutory scheme

---

676   See further, *Bibby v Chief Constable of Essex* [2000] All ER (D) 487.

677   [1985] IRLR 76, 79, para 24, whereby '[t]he imminence or immediacy of the threat to the peace determines what action is reasonable.'

678   *Hicks and Others v Commissioner of the Police of the Metropolis* [2014] EWCA Civ 3; on appeal (regarding Art 5 only) from [2012] EWHC 1947 (Admin).

679   *Austin and Saxby v Commissioner of the Police of the Metropolis* [2009] UKHL 5; and the subsequent Strasbourg Grand Chamber judgment: *Austin and Others v UK*, Appl Nos 39692/09, 40713/09 and 41008/09, 15 March 2012.

680   *R (Castle and Others) v Commissioner of the Police for the Metropolis* [2011] EWHC 2317.

681   *R (Moos and McClure) v Commissioner of the Police of the Metropolis* [2012] EWCA Civ 12, on appeal from [2011] EWHC 957 (Admin).

682   *Mengesha v Commissioner of the Police of the Metropolis* [2013] EWHC 1695 (Admin).

683   *Wright v Commissioner of Police for the Metropolis* [2013] EWHC 2739 (QB), see above fn 610.

684   A/HRC/23/39/Add.1, fn 6 above, paras 36–8. See also, JCHR, Demonstrating Respect for Rights? Follow-up, HL Paper 141, HC 522 (28 July 2009), para 28; Home Affairs Committee, Policing of the G20 Protests: Eighth Report of Session 2008–09, HC 418 (29 June 2009), paras 44–46.

685   Though, see fn 420 above, noting Tugendhat J's conclusion in the High Court in *Austin and Saxby* that a s 14 dispersal order may include a direction to 'stay in a specified place for as long as is necessary for the dispersal to be effected . . .' [2005] EWHC 480 (QB) para 95. As noted earlier in this chapter, no such limitations exist under s 12(1) in relation to the conditions that may be imposed on public processions.

is likely to be regarded by the police as something of a straitjacket when compared to the flexibility offered by the breach of the peace power. Furthermore, since the *Howell* definition of the breach of the peace doctrine (on which *Laporte* rests) requires merely that *some* harm be done to a person (or, in his presence, to his property), the common law power is also likely to be regarded as preferable to the statutory powers in ss 12 and 14 POA for which there is a higher threshold (i.e. *serious* public disorder, damage to property, or disruption to the life of the community).[686] It is therefore vital to consider whether there are any limits on the actions that the police may legitimately take under this broad common law power.

What, for example, if a large group of mostly peaceful protesters appears to the police to include some unruly, or aggressive, or potentially aggressive, elements? Given especially the ruling of the European Court of Human Rights in *Ezelin v France*, that an individual should not face restrictions unless they themselves have acted 'reprehensibly',[687] need the police attempt to differentiate innocent parties from those who may be about to commit a breach of the peace? In *Laporte*, Lord Rodger conceded that a police officer could stop a coachload of protesters from proceeding towards a protest, even if it included protesters who were 'entirely peaceful' provided 'there was no other way of preventing an imminent breach of the peace'.[688] The case law further indicates that, in such situations, temporary containment (perhaps for several hours) of peaceful protesters or even bystanders will not constitute a deprivation of liberty under Art 5 ECHR. That said, the police are duty bound to consider the best interests of children and other vulnerable individuals who may be caught up in any such containment,[689] and cannot use containment for ulterior purposes (such as requiring disclosure of the identities of those contained as a condition for their release).[690]

---

686 Mead, *op cit*, fn 1, p 348.

687 See also, *Ziliberberg v Moldova* – both discussed above at pp 573–74. These cases informed their Lordships reasoning in *Laporte* [2006] UKHL 55 – see Lord Bingham (para 36); Lord Rodger (paras 82 and 85); and Lord Mance (paras 144 and 149).

688 [2006] UKHL 55, para 84. See similarly, Sir Anthony Clarke MR's later summary of the effect of *Laporte* in relation to third parties in the Court of Appeal in *Austin v Commissioner of the Police of the Metropolis* [2008] EWCA Civ 989, para 35(iii) and (iv). Also too, Sweeney J in the Divisional Court in *Moos and McClure*, [2011] EWHC 957 (Admin), para 12, approved by the Master of the Rolls in the Court of Appeal, [2012] EWCA Civ 12, paras 36 and 39; and *Mengesha v Commissioner of Police of the Metropolis* [2013] EWHC 1695, para 12.

689 In *R (Castle and Others) v Commissioner of the Police for the Metropolis* [2011] EWHC 2317, the three claimants were 16 years old or under, and had joined a London demonstration against tuition fees on 24 November 2010. They were caught within a police containment for between 6 and 7½ hours. The court held that the delayed release of the claimants was justified because of violence taking place outside the containment (paras 31, 69) and – based on evidence that a number of protesters were carrying weapons – in order to carry out s 60 CJPOA searches and make related arrests (para 70). The court held that the duty imposed on the police under s 11 Children Act 2004 to promote and safeguard the welfare of children had been fulfilled (paras 64, 70 and 73), especially because the police had made efforts, in accordance with their stated policy (para 41) 'to allow vulnerable or distressed persons or those inadvertently caught up in the police containment to exit', which the court regarded had been applied by the police to include children (paras 65 and 67). Permission to appeal was refused in July 2012.

690 *Mengesha v Commissioner of the Police of the Metropolis* [2013] EWHC 1695 (Admin), para 12 (holding that containment must be for the sole purpose of preventing an imminent breach of the peace, and therefore, that '[i]t was not lawful for the police to maintain a containment for the purposes of

The leading case is *Austin and Saxby v Commissioner of Police of the Metropolis*. This concerned a political demonstration against capitalism and globalisation that was organised in the heart of the West End of London on May Day 2001.[691] Publicity material had given the police reason to believe that it would begin at 4 pm, but in fact it started two hours earlier. About 3,000 people had gathered in Oxford Circus and thousands more in the surrounding streets. The protest was made up of disparate groups, some of whom, according to police intelligence, had been involved in violent acts during protests in the past. The first claimant, Austin, took part in the demonstration and made political speeches using a megaphone. The second claimant, Saxby, had come to London on business and had inadvertently become caught up in the crowd. The police faced a difficult public order situation, and stated that they had been taken by surprise by the timing of the demonstration; in order to prevent a breakdown of law and order, they detained thousands of demonstrators for about seven hours by forming a cordon around them. The cordon was absolute, in that persons were completely trapped in the area for the whole seven-hour period in cold and uncomfortable conditions and without recourse to any facilities. The police planned to release the crowd slowly, but this was hindered, according to the police evidence, by some outbreaks of disorder or violence either from the trapped group or from persons outside the cordon. It was considered unsafe to release the groups en masse but a few individuals were released because, for example, they were suffering panic attacks. The claimants asked to be released but were refused on the ground that some protesters were threatening a breach of the peace. The claimants had not created a threat; nor had they provoked others. They remained peaceable throughout the period. The claimants brought a claim for damages, alleging false imprisonment and also deprivation of liberty, contrary to Art 5, ECHR, raising the claim under s 7 HRA.

The case raised for the first time the important question of whether the police strategy of containment constituted a deprivation of liberty such as to engage Art 5 ECHR. As Chapter 2 has shown, the Art 5 right entails an apparently straightforward two-stage test: First, is there an interference constituting a 'deprivation of liberty' (the ambit or threshold question)? In this regard, the distinction between a deprivation of, and mere restriction upon, liberty is one of degree or intensity and not one of nature or

---

obtaining identification, whether by questioning or by filming'). See also, *Donat and Fassnacht-Albers v Germany*, Appl Nos 6315/09 and 12134/09, 11 February 2014, paras 51–53. In this case, however, and in contrast to *Mengesha*, the anti-nuclear protesters were under a statutory obligation to disclose their identity to the police, and so any deprivation of liberty that resulted from the containment (though the Strasbourg Court left open the question of whether there had been such a deprivation) would thus have been justified under Art 5(1)(b) – 'in order to secure the fulfilment of any an obligation prescribed by law.'

691 For further discussion of the Grand Chamber ruling of the European Court of Human Rights, see Mead, D, '(Case Comment) Kettling comes to the boil before the Strasbourg Court: is it a deprivation of liberty to contain protesters en masse?' 71(3) CLJ (2012) 472–75; Oreb, N, '(Case Comment) The Legality of "Kettling" After *Austin*' 76(4) MLR (2013) 735–42; Hamilton, M, 'Austin and Others v UK: Grand Chamber Judgment on "Kettling"' (ECHR Blogspot, 23 March 2012). For discussion of the domestic court proceedings, see: Mead, D, *op cit*, fn 1, pp 349–56; Fenwick, H, 'Marginalising human rights: breach of the peace, "kettling", the Human Rights Act and public protest' (2009) PL 737–65; Feldman, D, '(Case Comment) Containment, Deprivation of Liberty and Breach of the Peace' 68(2) CLJ (2009) 243–245; Smith, ATH, '(Case Comment) May Day, May Day – Policing Protest' (2008) CLJ 10–12.

substance.[692] Second, if this threshold is met and Art 5 is engaged, is the deprivation justified under one of the six categories in subparagraphs (a)–(f), and 'in accordance with a procedure prescribed by law'?

Tugendhat J in the High Court found that the measure effected a close confinement and was thus a deprivation of liberty under Art 5(1). However, he ruled that this interference was justified under Art 5(1)(c) since it had been imposed with the conditional purpose of arresting those whom it would be lawful and practicable to arrest and bring before a judge. This reasoning problematically implied that the police suspected each individual protester (amongst a crowd of thousands) of being about to breach the peace. The Court of Appeal overturned the High Court ruling and its invocation of Art 5(1)(c), but found instead that no deprivation of liberty under Art 5(1) had occurred (and thus no further justification was needed). The House of Lords agreed with this conclusion, as did the Grand Chamber of the European Court of Human Rights three years later.

The threshold Art 5(1) question – in the absence of any bright-line rule – has repeatedly been stated in the following terms:

> In order to determine whether someone has been "deprived of his liberty" within the meaning of Art 5, the starting point must be his concrete situation and account must be taken of a whole range of criteria such as the type, duration, effects and manner of implementation of the measure in question.

However, both the House of Lords[693] and the Grand Chamber in Strasbourg[694] noted that the application of this test was more complicated in *Austin* because the containment of demonstrators was a 'non-paradigm' interference with individual liberty (the paradigm case being detention 'in prison, in the custody of a gaoler').[695] As such, Lord Hope in the House of Lords stated: 'Account must be taken of a whole range of factors, including the specific situation of the individual and the context in which the restriction

---

692 *Engel and Others v the Netherlands*, Appl Nos 5100/71, 5101/71, 5102/71, 5354/72 and 5370/72, 8 June 1976, para 59; *Guzzardi v Italy* judgment of November 6, 1980, Series A no.39, para 92; *Ashingdane v UK* (1985) 7 EHRR 528, para 41. See also Chapter 2, p 51 for brief discussion of the concept of deprivation of liberty. In *Austin*, the Strasbourg Court (para 55) did not want to interpret Art 5 'in such a way as to incorporate the requirements of Protocol No 4 in respect of States which have not ratified it', the UK being one of only four Council of Europe member states not yet to have ratified Protocol 4. However, the UK has ratified the ICCPR, Art 12 of which affords protection to freedom of movement in similar terms.

693 [2009] UKHL 5, especially Lord Neuberger at paras 56 and 63 (noting, at para 52, that the paradigm case is 'being in prison, in the custody of a gaoler').

694 *Austin and Others v UK*, Appl Nos 39692/09, 40713/09 and 41008/09, 15 March 2012, para 59.

695 [2009] UKHL 5, para 52 per Lord Neuberger citing Lord Hoffmann in *JJ* [2008] 1 AC 385, para 36 (though for a critique, see Mead, *op cit*, fn 1, p 353). Similarly, *Donat and Fassnacht-Albers v Germany*, Appl Nos 6315/09 and 12134/09, 11 February 2014, para 46. While violations of Art 5 have previously been found in protest cases, these cases have also involved more typical detention scenarios. See, for example, *Steel and Others v UK*, Appl No 67/1997/851/1058, 23 September 1998; *Schwabe and MG v Germany*, Appl Nos 8080/08 and 8577/08, 1 December 2011. *Schwabe* concerned the arrest and detention of two demonstrators for five and a half days in anticipation of the G8 summit protests in Rostock, June 2007. The Strasbourg Court emphasised that such preventive detention, where there is no evidence of an intention to commit specific and imminent unlawful acts, constitutes a violation of Art 5(1) irrespective of the significant challenges of guaranteeing security at the G8 summit.

of liberty occurs.'[696] The addition of 'context' to the traditional threshold test is critical since it enabled Lord Hope to take a 'pragmatic approach' and to consider the purported 'purpose' of the police intervention when seeking to determine whether or not Art 5 was engaged.[697] The court thereby reached the conclusion that there had been no deprivation of liberty because the policing operation had been resorted to in good faith, was not arbitrary, and was 'undertaken in the interests of the community'.

This addition of 'context' to the list of threshold considerations seriously strains the textual integrity of Art 5 itself. Unlike the limiting clauses in Art 11 or Art 2 of Protocol 4, there is no 'exception' under Art 5(1) for security measures or public order considerations (or corresponding questions of proportionality). As such, no other purposes (however well-intentioned) or extraneous factors (such as public order) should be able to justify what has already been decided, under the threshold test, to be a deprivation of liberty. The admission of 'contextual' factors in *Austin* serves to introduce a de facto public order exception to Art 5(1).[698] In doing so, it also arguably opens the door to a host of other police-oriented considerations (for example, limited police resources), as being relevant to the question of whether or not a deprivation of liberty has in fact occurred. The judgment clearly undervalues the Arts 10 and 11 rights of demonstrators – and indeed, *these* 'contextual' factors were largely overlooked by the courts.[699]

The Strasbourg Court largely accepted Lord Hope's reasoning in the House of Lords. Despite first suggesting that 'the coercive nature of the containment . . . its duration, and its effect on the applicants, in terms of physical discomfort and inability to leave . . . point towards a deprivation of liberty',[700] the Court then highlighted the size of the crowd, the 'volatile and dangerous conditions', and the purported lack of any alternative policing measure capable of averting serious injury or damage, in order to support the domestic court's conclusion that 'kettling' was indeed 'the least intrusive and most effective means to be applied'.[701]

The Strasbourg Court's judgment can be further criticised because it asserted that it was 'unable to identify a moment when the measure changed from what was, at most, a restriction on freedom of movement, to a deprivation of liberty'.[702] While the principle of subsidiarity inevitably limits the degree of specificity that might be expected from the European Court of Human Rights, and while the issue of the duration should not

---

696 [2009] UKHL 5, para 21.

697 *Ibid*, paras 22 and 26–34. See also, para 60 per Lord Neuberger, and contrast Lord Walker's initial hesitancy regarding the relevancy of 'purpose' (para 43) with his later framing of what he regarded to be the essential (and clearly, purpose-based) question: 'what were the police doing at Oxford Circus on 1 May 2001? What were they about?' (para 47).

698 It is noteworthy that such a provision was deliberately omitted during the drafting of the Convention in 1950. The Travaux Préparatoires reveal that an early draft of Art 5 stated: 'No person shall be deprived of his liberty . . . save by legal procedure in the case of: (a) the lawful detention of a person after a conviction *or as a security measure* involving deprivation of liberty' (emphasis added).

699 The lack of weight attached to Arts 10 and 11 is further demonstrated by the analogies drawn by the domestic courts between 'kettled' protesters and measures taken to separate rival football crowds and measures hemming in motorists in the aftermath of a traffic accident. See respectively: [2005] EWHC 480 (QB), paras 594–5; [2007] EWCA Civ 989, paras 91 and 102; [2009] UKHL 5, paras 23 and 58; Appl Nos 39692/09, 40713/09 and 41008/09, paras 43 and 59. See further the commentaries cited in fn 691 above.

700 *Austin and Others v UK*, para 64.

701 *Ibid*, para 66.

702 *Ibid*, para 67.

necessarily be dispositive in itself,[703] the Court should not be able to abdicate its responsibility to assess when a mere restriction has become a deprivation.[704]

Deprivation of liberty to prevent a breach of the peace

Unlike either *Austin* or *Moos and McClure* (where the 'kettling' of protesters was found not to be a deprivation of liberty), in both *Nicol* and *Hicks*, the arrest and detention of protesters did clearly constitute a deprivation of liberty (in the paradigm sense). In such circumstances, the question for the court will usually be whether this deprivation is capable of justification under Art 5(1)(c) – though Art 5(1)(b) may also be arguable.[705] These provisions permit deprivations of liberty in the following circumstances:

> (b) the lawful arrest or detention of a person for noncompliance with the lawful order of a court or in order to secure the fulfilment of any obligation prescribed by law;

> (c) the lawful arrest or detention of a person effected for the purpose of bringing him before the competent legal authority on reasonable suspicion of having committed an offence or when it is reasonably considered necessary to prevent his committing an offence or fleeing after having done so . . .

In *Nicol* (the anti-fishing protesters were initially arrested and detained for three and a half hours to allow for 'a period of calming and to determine method of processing'. Similarly in *Hicks*, (which the Court of Appeal regarded as being factually akin to *Nicol*),[706] the different groups of protesters were arrested and detained for approximately five hours until the royal wedding had finished. In Strasbourg admissibility proceedings in *Nicol*,[707] the UK government argued that the arrest and detention was 'with the purpose of bringing [them] before the competent legal authority' so as to satisfy Art 5(1) (c), or, in the alternative, 'to secure the fulfilment of any obligation prescribed by law' in accordance with Art 5(1)(b). Drawing upon its earlier holding in *Steel v UK* (where it was confirmed that breaching the peace could be regarded as a criminal offence for Convention purposes and was sufficiently well defined as to meet the requirements of lawfulness), the Court held that this detention was justified under Art 5(1)(c).

The Court of Appeal in *Hicks* noted that Art 5(1)(c) gave rise to two questions, both of which it answered in the affirmative: First, were the arrests 'reasonably considered

---

703 See further, *Huseynov v Azerbaijan*, Appl No 59135/09, 7 May 2015, para 82.

704 See similarly, the joint dissenting opinion of Judges Tulkens, Spielmann and Garlicki, para 12, noting that '[i]n a situation of uncertainty, the presumption is normally in favour of respect for individual rights.'

705 See further Chapter 12. For a case where the containment of protesters was regarded as justifiable under Art 5(1)(b), see *Donat and Fassnacht-Albers v Germany*, Appl Nos 6315/09 and 12134/09, 11 February 2014. See also Ostendorf paras 92–103. The Court of Appeal in *Hicks* [2014] EWCA Civ 3, paras 89–95, also considered Art 5(1)(b) in light of *Ostendorf v Germany* Appl No 15598/08, 7 March 2013 – noting (at paras 93–4) that to answer this point, there would need to have been a factual determination of whether each appellant had been made aware of 'the specific act which he or she was to refrain from committing and that the person showed himself or herself not to be willing to refrain from so doing.' Since the Court of Appeal recognized that this test 'might not produce the same results in relation to all appellants' (para 94) it preferred to confine its conclusions to Art 5(1)(c). Note that, at the time of writing, the Supreme Court's judgment in Hicks is pending.

706 [2014] EWCA Civ 3, para 55.

707 *Nicol and Selvanayagam v UK*, Appl No 32213/96, 11 January 2001.

necessary to prevent [the appellants from] committing an offence'? Secondly, 'at the outset of the deprivation of liberty, were the relevant police officers effecting the arrests for the purpose of bringing the persons in question before the competent legal authority *when it was considered reasonably necessary* in order to prevent them from committing an offence'?[708] The court concluded that 'the appellants were arrested and detained "for the purpose of bringing [them] before the competent legal authority", *if that were to become necessary, so as to prolong detention on a lawful basis*'.[709] In framing the two questions and in reaching this conclusion, the court declined to follow two cases (*Ječius v Lithuania*[710] and *Ostendorf v Germany*[711]) – having closely analysed the case law concerning s 2 HRA[712] – which they regarded as having departed from the 'clear and constant' jurisprudence of the Strasbourg Court.[713] These judgments had suggested that arrest and detention could only be permitted under Art 5(1)(c) 'in conjunction with criminal proceedings' – in other words, that Art 5(1)(c) could be invoked only in relation to *pre-trial* detention where there was, from the outset, an intention to bring the detainee before a court *on suspicion of his having committed a criminal offence*. The court in *Hicks* also drew support from a statement of the Strasbourg Court in *Austin*, that 'Art 5 cannot be interpreted in such a way as to make it impractical for the police to fulfil their duties of monitoring order and protecting the public, provided they comply with the principle of Art 5 which is to protect the individual from arbitrariness.'[714]

While this strand of the court's decision undoubtedly holds the door open to preventive detention of protesters, the court in *Hicks* did enter one important corrective to a line of reasoning in earlier judgments. It criticised both the Strasbourg Court's admissibility decision in *Nicol* and the High Court's ruling in *Hicks* because they departed from the holding in the seminal internment case of *Lawless v Ireland (No 3)*[715] that 'even if the detention is to prevent the applicants from committing an offence, it must still be for the purpose for bringing the detainee before the competent legal authority'.[716] The High Court in *Hicks* had suggested that *Lawless* should be disregarded in favour of an interpretation of Art 5(1)(c) that disaggregated the two grounds for detention contained therein so as to hold that detention 'to prevent his committing an offence' (unlike detention 'on reasonable suspicion of having committed an offence') would not be qualified by the words 'for the purpose of bringing them before the competent legal authority'.[717]

---

708 [2014] EWCA Civ 3, para 82 (emphasis added).

709 *Ibid*, para 86 (emphasis added), relying also on both *Brogan v UK*, Appl Nos 11209/84, 11234/84, 11266/84, and 11386/85, 29 November 1988; (1989) 11 EHRR 117 as authority that for Art 5(1)(c) purposes there need not be a charge either at the outset or when the detainee is brought before the competent judicial authority, and *Williamson v Chief Constable of West Midlands Police* [2004] 1 WLR 14, as authority for the common law presumption that a person must be brought before a magistrate as soon as possible once they have been arrested on the reasonable belief that a breach of the peace is imminent.

710 Appl No 34578/97, 31 July 2000.

711 Appl No 15598/08, 7 March 2013, in particular, paras 68, 82 and 85.

712 *Hicks*, [2014] EWCA Civ 3, paras 69–81. *Ostendorf* is are discussed further in Chapter 4, pp 160–61. At the time of writing, the Supreme Court judgment in *Hicks* (heard on 28–29 June 2016) is awaited.

713 *Hicks*, [2014] EWCA Civ 3, para 68. Both *Lawless v Ireland (No 3)*, Appl No 332/57, 1 July 1961 and *Brogan v UK*, Appl Nos 11209/84, 11234/84, 11266/84, and 11386/85, 29 November 1988.

714 *Austin v United Kingdom* (2012) 55 EHRR 14, para 56.

715 Appl No 332/57, 1 July 1961.

716 [2014] para 57.

717 [2012] EWHC 1947 (Admin), paras 183–4, drawing on *Steel v UK*.

The Court of Appeal described *Nicol* as being 'not an entirely satisfactory decision' and ruled that the High Court 'was not justified in marginalising *Lawless* on this point,'[718] and that detention for preventive purposes must also be for the purpose of bringing an individual before the competent legal authority. To this extent, the Court of Appeal ruling in *Hicks* may be welcomed as a reaffirmation of the *Lawless* interpretation of Art 5(1)(c).

Bail conditions

Binding over to keep the peace may form part of a bail condition, but bail conditions may be more specific than this. A person charged with any offence may be bailed as long as they promise to fulfil certain conditions.[719] This aspect of criminal procedure can readily be used by the police against protesters or demonstrators; they can be charged with a low level public order offence or bound over to keep the peace, thus allowing the imposition of conditions that may prevent participation in future protest. If the conditions are broken, the bailee can be imprisoned. The Bail Act 1976 requires that applications for bail should be individually assessed in order to determine whether conditions should be imposed, thereby reflecting concern that the bailing procedure should not result in any further deprivation of liberty than is necessary. Despite this, during the miners' strike there was evidence that conditions were being routinely imposed without regard to the threat posed by the individual applicant. The Divisional Court, however, found that such practices were lawful (Mansfield JJ *ex p Sharkey*).[720] More recently, there have been cases in which bail conditions have been imposed prohibiting an individual from future participation in protest activity[721] or from entering onto private land for the purpose of demonstration activity.[722]

A case for reform?

Austin confirmed that the police have a wide range of powers to use against even entirely peaceful protesters if just a few protesters are – or may be – disorderly. The police could have employed ss 12 and 14 of the 1986 Act against the protest beforehand, but chose not to. The common law powers are thus so broad that the use of the statutory scheme under the 1986 or 1994 Acts becomes almost irrelevant. Indeed, the flexible application of the 'imminence' test suggested by Lord Rodger and Lord Carswell in *Laporte* has underpinned judicial scrutiny of preventive police action against protesters in subsequent cases such as *Moos and McClure*[723] and *Hicks*.[724] In addition, both the minimalist

---

718 [2014] EWCA Civ 3, para 67.
719 See Feldman, *op cit*, fn 1, 1st edn, pp 835–42.
720 [1985] QB 613.
721 For example, BBC News, 'Woodburn Forest: Leading environmentalist arrested at oil drill site' 13 June 2016 http://www.bbc.co.uk/news/uk-northern-ireland-36519174. See further, Wainwright, T, Morris, A, Craig, K and Greenhall, O, *The Protest Handbook*, 2012, pp 74–78, paras 2.16–2.37, especially p 76, paras 2.24–2.26. See also, Thornton et al, *The Law of Public Order and Protest*, 2010, pp 304–318, paras 7.109–7.165, especially p 308, para 7.127. See also, A/HRC/23/39/Add.1, fn 6 above, paras 45–46.
722 See, for example, *Edo Technology Ltd and Anor v Campaign To Smash Edo and Ors* [2006] EWHC 598 (QB), para 28(a).
723 [2012] EWCA Civ 12, paras 34–35.
724 [2012] EWHC 1947 (Admin), paras 131–133.

approach to the protective obligation established in *Plattform 'Ärzte für das Leben' v Austria*,[725] and the addition of 'context' to the threshold considerations for Art 5(1), will inevitably further erode the level of protection afforded to the right to peacefully assemble.

These are significant and deeply worrying judgments for public protest. The police can use this common law doctrine against protesters in order to: arrest them; detain them for several hours without arresting them; or to stop an assembly or march or divert it or to disperse most or all of it. The power to do all this arises if some members of the group have been involved in disorder in the past, or if intelligence suggests that this is the case, or if some members are disorderly, or appear likely to become disorderly. While the Court in *Austin* did not wholly exclude the possibility that 'the use of containment and crowd control techniques could, in particular circumstances, give rise to an unjustified deprivation of liberty in breach of Art 5(1)',[726] the ruling – as the dissenting judges recognised – sends 'a bad message to police authorities'.[727]

In addition, Richards LJ and Openshaw J in *Hicks*, noted that the claimants fell within the category of 'people whose acts are lawful and peaceful in themselves but are likely to provoke others into committing a breach of the peace'.[728] It is therefore both remarkable and troubling that, not only did the Strasbourg Art 11 jurisprudence seem to have very limited purchase against the preventive strategies deployed by the police,[729] neither too did the *Nicol* and *Redmond-Bate* qualifications to the 'natural consequence' test regarding provoking a breach of the peace.[730] Since it also drew upon the flexible approach to 'imminence' conceded in *Laporte* by Lord Rodger and Lord Carswell,[731] the *Hicks* case epitomises all that is problematic about the breach of the peace doctrine. Neither the Convention right to peacefully assemble nor the purported constitutional shift brought about by the Human Rights Act proved capable of challenging the rationale underlying the policing operation that 'any display of anti-wedding sentiment in the faces of [the] supportive crowd could lead to breaches of the peace'.[732]

In this light, and given the baseline protection extended by the European Court of Human Rights to the expression of ideas which 'offend, shock or disturb',[733] there is a case for replacing the test put forward by Sedley LJ in *Redmond-Bate* with a presumption that it is normally unreasonable to be provoked to violence, or the threat of

---

725 Appl No 10126/82, 21 June 1988.
726 *Austin and Others v UK*, para 60.
727 Joint dissenting opinion of Judges Tulkens, Spielmann and Garlicki, para 7.
728 [2012] EWHC 1947 (Admin) paras 135–137. This was the second category of cases identified by Lord Carswell in *Laporte*, paras 94–99.
729 See *Hicks* [2012] EWHC 1947 (Admin), paras 120–127. In outlining the contours of the legal framework relating to freedom of expression and assembly, Richards LJ and Openshaw J considered four Strasbourg authorities – *Plattform 'Ärzte für das Leben' v Austria*, Appl No 10126/82, 21 June 1988; *Steel and Others v United Kingdom*, Appl No 67/1997/851/1058, 23 September 1998, (1999) 28 EHRR 603; *Öllinger v Austria*, Appl No 76900/01, 29 June 2006, (2008) 46 EHRR 38; and *Aldemir v Turkey*, Appl Nos 32124/02, 32126/02, 32129/02, 32132/02, 32133/02, 32137/02 and 32138/02, 18 December 2007. There was no mention of *Ezelin v France*.
730 *Hicks* [2012] EWHC 1947 (Admin), paras 136, 164 and 169.
731 See, *Hicks* [2012] EWHC 1947 (Admin), paras 132–134. See also fn 644 above regarding Lord Mance's more equivocal opinion in *Laporte*.
732 [2012] EWHC 1947 (Admin) paras 51, 55, 60 (sub-para 11) and 170.
733 *Handyside v UK* (1976) 1 EHRR 737, para 49.

it, by speech or peaceful assembly. Indeed, it is suggested that it might only ever be reasonable to be provoked to violence where a provocative protest is itself deemed to meet the threshold of criminality – for example under ss 4, 4A or 5 of the Public Order Act 1986. On this basis, most – if not all – of the *Hicks* protesters would have been deserving of protection, and their actions might have been distinguished from – for sake of illustration – the protesters in *CPS v Haque and Choudhury*[734] (a case involving a poppy-burning protest on Remembrance Sunday, discussed below in relation to s 5 POA).[735] Indeed, there is merit in the argument that even these statutory offences under the POA do not establish a high enough threshold (they are not, for example, confined to instances of extreme provocation). A peaceful protest that angers others should not be subjected to preventive restrictions under the auspices of the breach of the peace doctrine unless there is demonstrable evidence that the protesters themselves do not have peaceful intentions. More radically, it is suggested that the common law powers being claimed under the breach of the peace doctrine should be abolished.[736] In this way, the powers that may potentially be used against protesters would at least be subject to democratic scrutiny through the legislative process. In view of the cases discussed, only such bold and far-reaching reform may be sufficient to ensure that the right to freedom of peaceful assembly is indeed 'practical and effective' rather than 'theoretical or illusory'.

9 Low-level disorder, harassment and anti-social behaviour

The criminalisation of low level forms of disorder, including anti-social behaviour, allowing for curbs to be placed on protests has been a feature of public order law. The process was begun under s 5 of the Public Order Act 1986, continued under s 154 of the CJPOA 1994,[737] and was taken further under the Protection from Harassment Act 1997, ss 42 and 42A of the Criminal Justice and Police Act 2001,[738] and most recently, the Anti-Social Behaviour, Crime and Policing Act 2014. These provisions target similar forms of anti-social behaviour which had previously been viewed as too trivial or too imprecise to attract criminal or, in most instances, civil liability.

All are aimed at behaviour causing harassment, alarm or distress or, under the 1997 Act, amounting to harassment, and all are targeted at particular social problems, largely unrelated to public protest. While s 42 of the 2001 Act was aimed at direct action protest (in particular, the actions of protesters against the use of animals in experiments at Huntingdon Life Sciences), s 5 of the 1986 Act was aimed at the perceived problem of disturbance from football hooligans or late night rowdies, and the 1997 Act at

---

734 7 March 2011, unreported.
735 A further comparison might, for example, be made between the *Hicks* protesters and the Wimbledon protester in *Brutus v Cozens* [1973] AC 854, whose prosecution under s 4 POA 1936 was overturned (discussed below at p 665).
736 See also, Fenwick, H, 'Marginalising human rights: breach of the peace, "kettling", the Human Rights Act and public protest' (2009) PL 737–65, at 757–62.
737 Which inserted s 4A into the 1986 Act.
738 Section 42 was amended, and s 42A inserted, by ss 126–127 of the Serious Organised Crime and Police Act 2005.

the problem of so-called 'stalkers'. Indeed, in the immediate pre-HRA period, Eady J found, in a decision concerning animal rights' activists, that the Protection from Harassment Act 'was ... not intended by Parliament to be used to clamp down on ... the rights of political protest and public demonstration which are so much a part of our democratic tradition'.[739]

Low-level disorder: sections 5, 4a and 4 of the Public Order Act 1986

Section 5 of the 1986 Act has been the most problematic provision because it catches a wide range of relatively trivial behaviour.[740] As originally enacted, the provision criminalised the use of 'threatening, abusive or insulting words or behaviour or disorderly behaviour' or the display of 'any writing, sign or other visible representation which is threatening, abusive or insulting' that takes place within the 'hearing or sight of a person likely to be caused harassment, alarm or distress thereby'.[741] In October 2011, however, the Home Office launched a consultation on police powers relating to face coverings, curfews, and the relevance of the word 'insulting' in s 5 of the 1986 Act.[742] The government, in its response, emphasised the unacceptability of 'swearing at police officers' and 'burning poppy wreaths on Remembrance Day' but nonetheless indicated its intention to remove the word 'insulting' from s 5.[743] This was subsequently achieved by s 57 of the Crime and Courts Act 2013 (though it is notable that the word 'insulting' survives in several other statutory provisions – in particular, ss 4 and 4A of the 1986 Act, and also the power to power to remove trespassers in s 61 Criminal Justice and Public Order Act 1994).

Even with the removal of 'insulting', s 5 remains the lowest level public order offence contained in the 1986 Act. Far from being confined to restraining rowdy hooligans, s 5 has been used against political speech. In the so-called *Madame M* case, four students were prosecuted for putting up a satirical poster depicting Margaret Thatcher as a 'sadistic dominatrix';[744] the students were acquitted, but the fact that such a case could even be brought in a rights-based democracy is highly disturbing.[745] As one commentator noted when the Act was passed: 'In the context of pickets shouting or gesturing at

---

739 *Huntingdon Life Sciences Ltd and Another v Curtin and Others* (1997) *The Times*, 11 December; (1998) 3(1) J Civ Lib 37. The Joint Committee on Human Rights has subsequently also expressed concern that this Act is being used in this way. See JCHR *Demonstrating respect for rights? A human rights approach to policing protest* (2009), para 99.

740 For background to s 5, see Law Commission Report No 123, *Offences Relating to Public Order*, 1983.

741 See comment on s 5 in (1987) PL 202. It should be noted that in *Brutus v Cozens* [1973] AC 854; [1972] 2 All ER 1297; [1972] 3 WLR 521; (1973) Cr App R 538, HL, Lord Reid said that the previous Public Order Act 1936, s 5 was 'not designed to penalise the expressions of opinion that happen to be disagreeable, distasteful or even offensive, annoying or distressing'.

742 Home Office, 'Consultation on Police Powers to Promote and Maintain Public Order'(October 2011). For background, see, Strickland, P and Douse, D, ' "Insulting words or behaviour": Section 5 of the Public Order Act 1986' (House of Commons Research Briefing, SN/HA/5760, 15 January 2013). Available at: http://researchbriefings.files.parliament.uk/documents/SN05760/SN05760.pdf.

743 Home Office, 'Police powers to promote and maintain public order Section 5 of the Public Order Act 1986: Summary of consultation responses and Government response' (January 2013).

744 Thornton, P, *Decade of Decline: Civil Liberties in the Thatcher Years*, 1990, p 37.

745 See also, for example, *DPP v Fidler* [1992] 1 WLR 91; *DPP v Clarke* [1992] Crim LR 60.

those crossing their picket lines, the elements of this offence will usually be established without difficulty.'[746]

The offences under ss 5, 4A and 4 of the 1986 Act can be charged as racially or religiously aggravated (as provided by ss 28 and 31 of the Crime and Disorder Act 1998, amended by s 39 of the Anti-terrorism, Crime and Security Act 2001), and these aggravated offences carry higher maximum penalties. According to ss 28(1)(b) and 31(1)(c) of the 1998 Act, an offence under s 5 of the 1986 Act is 'racially or religiously aggravated' if it is 'motivated (wholly or partly) by hostility towards members of a racial or religious group based on their membership of that group'. Section 18 POA also covers incitement to racial hatred if expressed in threatening or abusive or insulting terms, and the Racial and Religious Hatred Act 2006 added Part 3A to the Public Order Act, to cover incitement to religious hatred expressed in threatening terms. Part 3A was subsequently further extended – by the Criminal Justice and Immigration Act 2008 – to capture hatred on grounds of sexual orientation.[747] Since these offences are applied in the context of a range of media, they are considered in greater detail in Chapter 7.[748] Due to their breadth, however, these provisions also have potential application to most forms of protest.

The offences under ss 5 and 4A of the 1986 Act, as amended, require establishment of a minimal and imprecise *actus reus*. The word 'likely' imports an objective test into the section: it is necessary to show that a person was present at the scene, but not that he or she actually experienced the feelings in question, although it must be shown that in all the circumstances, he or she would be likely to experience such feelings. In so showing, it is not necessary to call the person in question as a witness. In *Swanston v DPP*,[749] it was found that if a bystander gives evidence to the effect that the 'victim' perceived the threatening, abusive or insulting words, then the court can draw the inference that they were so perceived. There is no need to aim the words or behaviour at a specific individual, so long as an individual can be identified and the inference can be drawn that he or she would have perceived the words or behaviour in question. It was further determined in *DPP v Orum*[750] that a police officer may be the person caused harassment, alarm or distress, but in such instances Glidewell LJ thought it might be held that a police officer would be less likely to experience such feelings than an ordinary person. These two decisions enhance the ease with which this offence may be deployed, as does *DPP v Fidler*,[751] in which it was found that a person whose own behaviour would not satisfy the requirements of s 5 may be guilty of aiding and abetting this offence if he or she is part of a crowd who are committing it. The term 'distress' is used in both ss 5 and 4 and so will be interpreted in the same way (although under s 4 it is necessary to establish that the person concerned actually suffered distress). In the Divisional Court

---

746 Williams, *op cit*, fn 1.
747 See, 'Derby men jailed for giving out gay death call leaflets', BBC News, 10 February 2012.
748 See pp 425–35. See also: Geddis, A, 'Free Speech Martyrs or Unreasonable Threats to Social Peace? – "Insulting" Expression and Section 5 of the Public Order Act 1986' (2004) *Public Law* 853; Newman, C, 'Divisional Court: Public Order Act 1986, s 4A: Proportionality and Freedom of Expression' (2006) 70 *Journal of Criminal Law* 191.
749 (1997) *The Times*, 23 January.
750 [1988] 3 All ER 449.
751 [1992] 1 WLR 91.

ruling in *R v DPP*[752] on s 4, it was found that an insult to a police officer, from a 12-year-old boy (he called the officer, who was arresting his sister at the time, a 'wanker') had not caused distress. The evidence did not establish that the police officer had suffered 'any real emotional disturbance'. Thus the harm caused, or likely to be caused, must be real emotional disturbance. Nonetheless, in *Chambers v DPP*[753], the Court of Appeal held that for behaviour to constitute harassment, feelings of insecurity did not need to be evoked – an individual did not need to fear for their personal safety (and so the peaceful blocking of the line of sight of a land surveyor's theodolite to protest against the construction of the M11 link road was, in this case, found to be disorderly and to have caused harassment).[754]

It remains to be seen how the amended s 5 – and the higher threshold of 'threatening or abusive' – will differ in practice from the lower bar of 'insulting'. In *Brutus v Cozens*,[755] a case involving the prosecution of an anti-apartheid demonstrator who disrupted a Wimbledon tennis match with a South African player (albeit brought under the predecessor to s 4), it was held that whether words used were insulting, etc, is a question of fact for the magistrates. The terms used must be given their ordinary meaning.[756] In this case, some of the crowd were provoked to violence, but the conduct of the demonstrator could not be described as insulting and his conviction was therefore overturned. However, what constitutes 'insulting' was held not to be a purely subjective test and therefore the mere fact that a recipient found them so was not sufficient.[757] The test appears to be whether a reasonable person sharing the characteristics of the persons at whom the words in question are directed would find them insulting. Following *Ambrose*,[758] rude or offensive words or behaviour are not necessarily insulting, while mere swearing may not fall within the meaning of 'abusive'. However, threatening gestures such as waving a fist might suffice. In one case concerning the renowned 'naked rambler', *Gough v DPP*,[759] the judge ruled that:

> 'insulting' meant disrespectful or scornfully abusive, 'threatening' was behaviour that was hostile, had a deliberately frightening quality or manner or which caused someone to feel vulnerable or at risk. 'Abusive' meant extremely offensive and insulting and 'disorderly behaviour' was behaviour that involved or contributed to a breakdown of peaceful and law abiding behaviour.[760]

However, when the case came before Sir Brian Leveson and Openshaw J, by way of case stated, Sir Brian Leveson found that it was unnecessary to decide whether the

---

752 [2006] All ER (D) 250.
753 [1995] Crim LR 896.
754 *Ibid*, per Keene J.
755 [1973] AC 854; [1972] All ER 1297; [1972] 3 WLR 521; (1973) 57 Cr App R 538, HL.
756 *Ibid.*
757 *Ibid.*
758 (1973) 57 Cr App R 538.
759 [2013] EWHC 3267 (Admin). Subsequently (though concerning earlier prosecutions in Scotland), see also *Gough v UK*, Appl No 49327/11, 28 October 2014, para 176 'Art 10 does not go so far as to enable individuals, even those sincerely convinced of the virtue of their own beliefs, to repeatedly impose their antisocial conduct on other, unwilling members of society.'
760 *Ibid*, para 10.

judge had correctly found the appellant's conduct to be threatening, abusive or insulting: 'the district judge was clearly entitled to conclude that, by walking through a town centre entirely naked, he was violating public order or, in the language of the case contributing "to a breakdown of peaceful and law-abiding behaviour as evidenced by the reactions of the public": he was thus disorderly.'[761] Since it was also found that Gough knew that many members of the public would both be alarmed and distressed by sight of his naked body, the s 5 offence was made out. Referring to the judgment in *Gough*, CPS guidance implies that 'insulting' and 'abusive' will, more often than not, overlap:

> prosecutors will need to carefully consider whether behaviour taking place on or after 1 February 2014 amounts to the commission of the section 5 offence. In the majority of cases, prosecutors are likely to find that behaviour that can be described as insulting can also be described as abusive.[762]

This suggests that the impact of the removal of 'insulting' by the Crime and Courts Act 2013 may be more symbolic than real. Thus, while the 2013 Act remedies a glaring anomaly in the face of the Strasbourg Art 10 jurisprudence – the criminalisation of merely 'insulting' speech that is deemed likely to cause harassment, alarm or distress – it may ultimately make little difference in practice to the reliance upon s 5 by police officers and prosecutors.

At the higher end of the spectrum of behaviour caught by s 5, including where the speech in question is offensive on racial or religious grounds, Art 10 may not be engaged at all since, depending on the gravity of the attack. Article 17 of the Convention may apply. This provides:

> Nothing in [the] Convention may be interpreted as implying for any state, group or person any right to engage in any activity or perform any act aimed at the destruction of any of the rights and freedoms set forth herein or at their limitation to a greater extent than is provided for in the Convention.

The decision in *Norwood v UK*[763] applied this Art 17 ouster. The applicant, who belonged to the BNP, displayed in the window of his first-floor flat a large poster, supplied by the BNP, with a photograph of the Twin Towers in flame, and the words 'Islam out of Britain – Protect the British People' and a symbol of a crescent and star in a prohibition sign.[764] He was convicted in a magistrates' court of the offence under s 5 of displaying 'any writing, sign or other visible representation which is threatening, abusive or insulting, within the hearing or sight of a person likely to be caused harassment, alarm or distress thereby'. He was convicted of having committed the offence in religiously aggravated

761 *Ibid*, para 15.
762 CPS, 'Public Order Offences incorporating the Charging Standard', available at: http://www.cps.gov.uk/legal/p_to_r/public_order_offences. See also, College of Policing, 'Guidance on the Amendment to Sections 5(1) and 6(4) of the Public Order Act 1986' (December 2013). Available at: http://library.college.police.uk/docs/APPREF/Guidance-amendment-public-order-2013.pdf.
763 Appl No 23131/03, 16 November 2004 (admissibility). For discussion, see Turenne, S, 'The compatibility of criminal liability with freedom of expression', Crim LR (2007) 866–881.
764 *Ibid.*

way. He unsuccessfully appealed his conviction to the High Court;[765] one of the applicant's arguments was that there was no evidence that any Muslim had in fact seen the poster. The High Court rejected this argument on the basis that s 5 does not require that a person should actually experience distress, and found that the restriction upon his freedom of expression right represented by the offence was proportionate to the legitimate aim of protecting the rights of others, given also the fact that the speech arguably fell within Art 17 ECHR.[766] The Strasbourg Court found his application inadmissible; referring to Art 17, the Court found that an attack of this nature against a religious group, linking them to a grave act of terrorism, was not compatible with the values proclaimed and guaranteed by the Convention, notably 'tolerance, social peace and non-discrimination'. The applicant's display of the poster in his window constituted an act within the meaning of Art 17 and therefore it did not enjoy the protection of Arts 10 or 14.

In *Abdul and Others v DPP*,[767] the Divisional Court (hearing the matter by way of case stated) upheld the magistrate's s 5 convictions in relation to protesters demonstrating against a military homecoming parade in Luton in 2009 at which slogans such as 'British soldiers murderers'; 'Baby killers'; 'Rapists all of you' had been shouted and displayed on banners. The magistrate had been of the view that the actions of the defendants 'crossed the threshold of legitimate protest'.[768] As such, while Art 10(2) protects the rights of people to hold and express a different viewpoint, it does not confer a right to abuse and insult soldiers gratuitously.[769] She further argued – to some extent, mirroring the Art 17 reasoning in *Norwood* – that 'the method they chose to convey an otherwise legitimate belief . . . was so unreasonable and disproportionately expressed so as to deprive them of the protection of article 10'.[770] The Divisional Court broadly agreed: Gross LJ stated that it must be recognised that legitimate protest can be offensive at least to some – and on occasions must be, if it is to have impact',[771] but that 'context is of the first importance' and 'what the Appellants shouted was potentially defamatory and undoubtedly inflammatory'.[772] Similarly, Davis J explained the s 5 prosecution on the basis that 'these were not just generalised statements of views, vigorously expressed, on the morality of the war but were personally abusive and potentially defamatory of those soldiers'.[773]

In Art 10 terms, the magistrate in *Abdul* emphasised not only the legitimate aim of preserving public order, but also pointed to the need to protect the rights and freedoms of others – specifically, that 'citizens of Luton are entitled to demonstrate their support for the troops without experiencing insults and abuse. Their freedom of expression must be protected.'[774] A similar emphasis on the protection of the rights of others arose

---

765 *Norwood v DPP* [2003] EWHC 1564.
766 See further Chapter 4, p 143; Chapter 7, p 428, and pp 432–33; Chapter 15, p 1038, p 1051 and p 1123.
767 [2011] EWHC 247 (Admin).
768 [2011] EWHC 247 (Admin), para 30 – a view with which Gross LJ (para 50(i)) and Davis J (para 60) in the Divisional Court agreed.
769 *Ibid.*
770 *Ibid*, para 30.
771 *Ibid*, para 49(i). See also fn 101 above in relation his acknowledgment of the importance of protecting the expression of minority views.
772 Para 50(i).
773 *Ibid*, para 61.
774 See pp 591–92 above discussing the Strasbourg Court's holding in *Chassagnou v France* and the preceding discussion at pp 590–91 regarding parallel scrutiny of conflicting rights in *Karaahmed v Bulgaria*.

in *CPS v Haque and Choudhury*.[775] In this case, a small group of protesters (members of a group called 'Muslims Against Crusaders', MAC) had gathered near the route of a 'March for Heroes' on Remembrance Day 2010, had chanted 'British soldiers burn in hell' through the two-minute silence, and then burned two large orange plastic poppies. As in *Abdul*, the magistrate in *Haque and Choudhury* considered the implications of Art 10 and recognised that 'shocking and offending people is sometimes a necessary part of effective protest.'[776] He concluded, however, that the conviction of the protesters under s 5 was proportionate in order to protect the rights and freedoms of others – which, in his view, included 'the right to express publicly support, sympathy and remembrance for the armed forces'.

While the prosecutions in these cases might be regarded as striking an appropriate balance between competing rights (given the gratuitous nature of the insults and the particular context in which the events occurred)[777] and may even be considered as deserving of prosecution under s 4A,[778] they also illustrate the potential dangers of an unduly elastic interpretation of the legitimate aim of protecting the rights and freedoms of others. Indeed, the circumstances in which Art 10 would be deemed inapplicable because (under Art 17) the words used were 'aimed at the destruction of' Convention rights and freedoms' must be narrowly construed so that notions of 'illegitimate' or 'unreasonable' protest do not begin to encroach on the protection afforded by the right to peacefully assemble (see further, 'Defences', and *Hammond v DPP* discussed below).

The *mens rea* requirements of the s 5 offence offers some degree of protection to free expression. Under s 6(4), it must be established that the defendant intended his words, etc, to be threatening, or abusive or was aware that they might be. Again, it remains to be seen whether the removal of the word 'insulting' from s 6(4) will noticeably raise the *mens rea* threshold regarding the s 5 offence. Arguably, for example, the magistrate's finding in *CPS v Haque and Choudhury*,[779] that 'it was the intention of this protest to shock and offend' and it was 'a calculated and deliberate insult' may no longer be sufficient in light of the need to show that the individual intended his words or behaviour to be either 'threatening or abusive' (though this particular case – as College of Policing guidance suggests – could instead have been prosecuted under s 4A).[780]

---

775 7 March 2011, unreported.

776 Transcript, p 5.

777 See further the discussion of *Fáber v Hungary*, Appl No 40721/08, 24 July 2012 at p 558 above. In the royal wedding case of *Hicks*, the police tactical plan developed by the police similarly noted '. . . this event is one of celebration and solemnity. The tipping point for harassment alarm or distress may be lower in this environment than it would be in other [sic], for example outside a football match or in a town centre at closing time' (para 19).

778 See fn 780 below.

779 7 March 2011, unreported.

780 College of Policing, 'Guidance on the Amendment to Sections 5(1) and 6(4) of the Public Order Act 1986' (December 2013), para 4.3.5: 'More serious, planned and malicious incidents of insulting behaviour, e.g., the burning of poppy wreaths on Remembrance Sunday (see *CPS v Haque and Choudhury* . . .), could still constitute an offence under section 4A.' Available at: http://library.college.police.uk/docs/APPREF/Guidance-amendment-public-order-2013.pdf.

In *DPP v Clarke*[781] it was further found that to establish liability, it is insufficient to show only that the defendant intended or was aware that he might cause harassment, alarm or distress; it must also be shown that he intended his conduct to be threatening or abusive (or, at that time, 'insulting'), or was aware that it might be. Both mental states have to be established independently. Thus, showing that the defendant was aware that he might cause distress was not found to be equivalent to showing that he was aware that his speech or behaviour might be threatening or abusive. Applying this subjective test, the magistrates acquitted the defendants and this decision was upheld on appeal. It was found that anti-abortion protesters had not realised that their behaviour in shouting anti-abortion slogans, displaying plastic models of foetuses and pictures of dead foetuses would be threatening, abusive or (again, prior to the 2013 amendment) insulting. This decision allows those who believe fervently in their cause, and therefore fail to appreciate that their protest may be threatening or abusive to others, to escape liability. It thereby curbs the ability of s 5 to interfere with Art 10 and Art 11 rights. Persons participating in forceful demonstrations may sometimes be able to show that behaviour that could be termed disorderly and which might be capable of causing harassment to others, was intended only to make a point and that it had not been realised that others might find it threatening or abusive. Once a particular group of protesters has been prosecuted, however, and it has been found, as in *Clarke*, that others found their protest threatening or abusive, the subjective element of the *mens rea* will be in future readily made out, even if the instant prosecution fails. The burden imposed by the subjective test for intention or awareness is to be welcomed, since it means that an offence that strikes directly at freedom of expression and can only doubtfully be justified is harder to make out.

Section 154 of the CJPOA 1994 inserted s 4A into the 1986 Act, thereby providing a new and wide area of liability that to some extent overlapped with s 5. Section 4A of the 1986 Act criminalises threatening, abusive, insulting words or behaviour or disorderly behaviour that causes a person harassment, alarm or distress thereby. Thus, the *actus reus* under s 4A is the same as that under the old (pre-2013) s 5, with the proviso that the harm in question must actually be caused as opposed to being likely to be caused. As noted above, the Divisional Court ruling in *R v DPP*[782] will apply – the harm caused will have to amount to real emotional distress. The *mens rea*, however, differs somewhat from that under s 5, since the defendant must intend the person in question to suffer harassment, alarm or distress. Section 4A provides another possible level of liability with the result that using offensive words is now imprisonable, without any requirement (as under s 4, below) to show that violence was intended or likely to be caused. Like s 5, its use against protesters or demonstrators can come into conflict with Art 10 due to the protection Art 10 affords to forceful or offensive forms of speech.[783]

Section 4 of the Act covers somewhat more serious behaviour than s 5. It is couched in the same terms (the use of threatening, abusive or insulting words or behaviour)

---

781 [1992] Crim LR 60.
782 [2006] All ER (D) 250.
783 See Newman, C (2006) 'Divisional Court: Public Order Act 1986, s 4A: Proportionality and Freedom of Expression' 70 *Journal of Criminal Law* 191.

except for the omission of 'disorderly behaviour', but instead of showing that a person present was likely to be caused harassment, etc, it is necessary to show '[1] intent to cause that person to believe that immediate unlawful violence will be used against him or another by any person or [2] to provoke the immediate use of unlawful violence by that person or another or [3] whereby that person is likely to believe that such violence will be used or [4] it is likely that such violence will be provoked'. Whether or not the speaker knows that such persons will hear the words is immaterial.[784] One or more of these four possibilities must be present. The behaviour in question must be specifically directed towards another person. If the defendant does not directly approach the person being threatened, he or she might be unlikely to apprehend immediate violence. However, there might remain the possibility that the defendant intended his or her words to provoke others to violence against the victim. Under s 6(3), it must also be established that the defendant intended his words, etc, to be threatening, abusive or insulting or was aware that they might be. It was found in *Horseferry Road Metropolitan Stipendiary Magistrate ex p Siadatan*[785] – a case arising from the publication and distribution of *The Satanic Verses* by Salman Rushdie – that 'violence' in s 4 must mean immediate and unlawful violence.[786] Section 4 is also subject to a defence of reasonableness, providing a further entry point for Art 10 considerations.

Anti-social behaviour – directions to disperse and public space protection orders

Under the guise of 'streamlining' the powers previously available to tackle anti-social behaviour (under both the Crime and Disorder Act 1998 and the Anti-Social Behaviour Act 2003), the Anti-Social Behaviour, Crime and Policing Act 2014, which came into force on 23 March 2015, wholly revised the powers that can be used (and injunctions obtained) in relation to 'anti-social behaviour'. The power to grant injunctions under Part I of the 2014 Act is discussed under 'Injunctions' below.

Part 3 contains a power for a senior police officer to authorise (in writing) the use by police constables of dispersal powers against anyone causing, or considered likely to cause, harassment, alarm or distress, and who either is, or is considered likely to be, taking part in crime or disorder. The s 35 dispersal power effectively replaces s 30 of the 2003 Act,[787] and failure to comply with a direction to disperse without reasonable excuse can result in imprisonment for up to three months, or a fine of up to £2,500. While s 35 powers cannot be used against anyone who is peacefully picketing or taking part in a notified public procession,[788] it seems likely that they may be used against both non-peaceful protesters and anyone taking part in an unnotified procession for which prior notification was required.[789]

---

784 *Jordan v Burgoyne* [1963] 2 QB 744; [1963] 2 All ER 225.
785 [1991] 1 QB 260; [1991] 1 All ER 324; [1990] 3 WLR 1006.
786 Confirmed in *Winn v DPP* (1992) 142 NLJ 527.
787 Though the dispersal power under s 35 of the 2014 Act can be used against individuals whereas the old s 30 dispersal power could be used only against groups or two or more persons.
788 Section 36(4).
789 *R (Singh) v Chief Constable of West Midlands Police* [2006] EWCA Civ 1118, paras 81–83, and 97 per Hallett LJ.

Furthermore, the reasons relied upon by a police officer in issuing a dispersal order need not correspond with the reasons provided by the senior officer when granting the prior authorisation to use the s 35 dispersal powers.[790] In *R (Singh) v Chief Constable of West Midlands Police*, two entirely unrelated authorisations were in place – one to deal with skateboarders, and another to tackle anti-social behaviour by 'seasonal revellers' in the run up to Christmas – and the possibility of the use of the power against protesters had not been contemplated.[791] Nonetheless, the dispersal (under these authorisations) of Sikh protesters who sought to disrupt a theatre performance that they considered to be grossly offensive was upheld by the Court of Appeal.[792]

Part 4 of the Act provides for 'public space protection orders' (PSPOs), which local councils may impose for a period of up to three years (extendable), following consultations with the chief police officer and local policing body. PSPOs can prohibit, or require specified things from, anyone carrying on (or likely to carry on), activities 'in a public place' which have had, or are likely to have, 'a detrimental effect on the quality of life of those in the locality' and where any such effect 'will be, or is likely to be, of a persistent or continuing nature . . . or . . . such as to make the activities unreasonable'. The breadth of these powers, potentially enabling the imposition of blanket bans on any activity deemed to meet the exceedingly vague threshold ('detrimental effect on the quality of life') has already been demonstrated by councils that have sought to ban buskers, street entertainers and 'street speakers'.[793] Indeed, before issuing a PSPO that restricts a public right of way over a highway, in addition to the 'detrimental effect' criteria already noted, a local authority need only consider – under s 64 – its likely effect on the occupiers of premises adjoining or adjacent to the highway, other persons in the locality and (if the highway constitutes a through route) the availability of a reasonably convenient alternative route. The statute does emphasise[794] that particular regard must be had to the rights of freedom of expression and freedom of assembly set out in Arts 10 and 11 – but this obligation merely to 'have regard' to these rights gives next to no guidance in relation to the weight that should properly be afforded to them (and no corresponding qualification is attached to Part I of the Act regarding the issuing of injunctions, see further below).

Harassment

Section 42 of the Criminal Justice and Police Act 2001, as amended by the Serious Organised Crime and Police Act 2005, allows a constable to give any direction to persons, including a direction to leave the scene where they are outside or in the vicinity of a dwelling (either alone or together with others), if the constable reasonably believes (a) that they are seeking to persuade a person living at the dwelling not to do something

---

790 Section 34 of the 2014 Act.

791 [2006] EWCA Civ 1118, paras 22–24, and 102–106.

792 See also the discussion of the 'rights and freedoms of others' limb of Art 11(2) at fn 261 above.

793 For example, Birmingham City Council, 'Public Spaces Protection Order Consultation: Noise from Buskers, Street Entertainers and Street Speakers in the City Centre' (June 2015).

794 In s 34(3) regarding the issuance of an authorization to use s 35 dispersal powers, s 36(5) regarding an officer's power to give a direction under s 35, and s 72(1) regarding the council's power to issue a PSPO.

that he/she has a right to do or to do something she/he is not under any obligation to do, and (b) that the presence of the persons is likely to cause harassment, alarm or distress to the person living at the residence. A direction can be given so as to make it an offence to return to the vicinity for a specified period, which can be for up to three months. Section 42A makes it an offence to harass a person in his or her home in like terms if a reasonable person would think that the presence of the person(s) was likely to amount to the harassment of, or to cause alarm or distress to, anyone in the dwelling or another dwelling in the vicinity. Disobedience of a s 42 direction is an arrestable offence, and the maximum penalty, as for the s 42A offence, is 51 weeks' imprisonment and a fine of £2,500.

Sections 42 and 42A clearly draw on the ingredients of ss 5 and 4 of the 1986 Act, although there are also significant differences. There are also similarities with the offences under s 14C of the 1986 Act and s 69 of the 1994 Act. Section 42 of the 2001 Act is problematic in the sense that it strikes directly at peaceful protest – protest that need not be abusive, etc, but is aimed only at persuading. The protesters need have no intention of causing harassment, alarm or distress so long as a constable reasonably believes that the target of the protest might experience those feelings. In catching peaceful protest, this offence comes directly into conflict with Arts 10 and 11. While s 42 could also be viewed as protecting Art 8 rights of residents in a dwelling, a court would be expected to consider the extent to which those rights could be said to be engaged and the proportionality of the police response, in using s 42 as opposed to a lesser measure.[795]

Sections 42 and 42A of the 2001 Act contain offences with a minimal *actus reus*, as is apparent when they are compared with the requirements of s 5 of the 1986 Act or ss 69 and 68 of the 1994 Act. The requirement that the words or conduct should be abusive, etc, in s 5 is missing; the requirements of ss 69 or 68 that the persons in question should be trespassing and must do something intended to be obstructive or intimidatory or disruptive are also absent. But s 42 is similar to s 69, and a number of the other recent offences discussed in this chapter, in that it conflates the exercise of police powers with the substantive offence (under s 42A). The key limiting requirement is that the persons must be outside or in the vicinity of a dwelling, although the term 'the vicinity' is open to quite a wide interpretation. The need for the introduction of this offence must be questioned, bearing in mind that s 5 or s 4A could be used against intimidation by protesters gathered outside the home of the person targeted. The offence of harassment under the 1997 Act would also be available, as might the offence under s 2(1)(b) and (2) of the Anti-Social Behaviour, Crime and Policing Act 2014.

Section 1 of the Protection from Harassment Act 1997 is available to cover harassment in a broader[796] sense than its use in either s 5 of the Public Order Act 1986[797] or in s 1 (now repealed) of the Crime and Disorder Act 1998.[798] It 'defines' harassment as a

---

795 See fn 134 above (regarding the Art 8 considerations in *Wife and Children of Omar Othman v English National Resistance and others* [2013] EWHC 1421 (QB)), and the discussion of parallel scrutiny of competing rights following *Karaahmed v Bulgaria* Appl No 30587/13, 24 February 2015, para 95, at pp 590–91 above.

796 See, *Heathrow Airport Ltd and Another v Garman and Others* [2007] EWHC 1957 (QB), para 99(c).

797 See *Chambers v DPP*, at p 665 above.

798 See *R v Jones and Others* [2006] EWCA (Crim) 2942, at fn 836 below. See too, *Dowson and Others v Chief Constable of Northumbria Police* [2010] EWHC 2612 (QB) para 142(6), per Simon J: 'A line is to be drawn between conduct which is unattractive and unreasonable, and conduct which has been

course of conduct which a reasonable person would consider amounted to harassment of another where the harasser knows or ought to know that this will be its effect. The Serious Organised Crime and Police Act 2005 added s 1(1A) which prohibits knowingly harassing two or more persons to persuade a third person to act or refrain from acting in a particular way – the purpose of this amendment being 'to prohibit the harassment of employees or members of their families or others in order to put pressure on a third party'.[799]

A key feature of the 1997 Act is the hybrid nature of the harassment provisions in allowing for criminal sanctions, including imprisonment, on the civil standard of proof for breach of an order or injunction. Indeed, criminal proceedings relating to the same course of conduct, but under s 2, may also be affected once an injunction has been obtained – this was the case in *DPP v Moseley, Woodling and Selvanayagam*.[800] One of the defendants, Ms Selvanayagam, had been served with an *ex parte* interim injunction under s 3 of the 1997 Act (see further 'Injunctions' below), which she was seeking to challenge. After she had been served with the injunction, she and the other two defendants continued to demonstrate peacefully against the fur trade, at a fur farm. They were arrested and charged with the offence under s 2 of the 1997 Act. All of them relied on the defence that the conduct was reasonable in the circumstances under s 1(3)(c), and this defence was accepted by the magistrate. He further found that the injunction was obtained only on the basis of affidavit evidence and could not as a matter of law preclude the finding of reasonableness. Therefore, he acquitted all three. On appeal, however, the High Court found that pursuit of a course of harassment in breach of an injunction would preclude establishing the defence of reasonableness and that the magistrate had not been entitled to go behind the terms of the injunction. The other two respondents were not named in the injunction and there was no basis for considering that they were acting in concert with Ms Selvanayagam. Therefore, they were not precluded from putting forward the defence of reasonableness. Accordingly, Ms Selvanayagam was convicted under s 2.

The most striking aspect of this case is the acceptance that a central issue in a criminal trial can be predetermined in civil proceedings, particularly uncontested *ex parte* proceedings, in which the only evidence is 'on the papers'. There is no reason why a breach of a s 3 injunction (see 'Injunctions' below) should also be determinative of separate criminal proceedings. This matter clearly raises Art 6 issues:[801] it comes close to obtaining a conviction 'on the papers' since, if an injunction has been previously obtained, the burden on the prosecution will be considerably eased.

In addition to the provisions in ss 1 and 2 of the 1997 Act, it has also been held that there may be circumstances (where evidence exists of actual harassment, or of

described in various ways: "torment" of the victim, "of an order which would sustain criminal liability' – cited approvingly by Lang J DBE in *Harlan Laboratories UK Ltd and Another v Stop Huntingdon Animal Cruelty ('SHAC')* [2012] EWHC 3408 (QB) paras 27–28, and paras 49 – explaining that the conduct of the protestors was 'oppressive' and had 'gone far beyond legitimate peaceful protest.'

799 *Astellas Pharma v Stop Huntingdon Animal Cruelty ('SHAC')* [2011] EWCA Civ 752, para 7 per Moore-Bick LJ.

800 Judgment of 9 June 1999; reported [1999] J Civ Lib 390.

801 See, for example, *Unterpinger v Austria* (1991) 13 EHRR 175; *Van Mechelen v Netherlands* (1998) 25 EHRR 647; *Kostovski v Netherlands* (1989) 12 EHRR 434; *Delta v France* (1993) 16 EHRR 574; *Doorson v Netherlands* (1996) 22 EHRR 330.

a perceived danger that puts anybody in fear of violence) in which the granting of a restraining order against protesters under s 5 of the 1997 Act would be appropriate (including to protect a company). In *R v Buxton and Others*,[802] Calvert-Smith J – with some hesitation – decided not to grant a restraining order against a number of environmental protesters (because of the limited evidence presented) who had chained themselves to a railway line as part of their protest against open-cast coal-mining. However, he noted that a s 5 restraining order may well be an appropriate remedy – one that would potentially exert a powerful deterrent effect, and which would also obviate the need to go to another court to seek a civil injunction to ban protesters from further disruptive actions.[803]

Defences

With the exception of the Anti-social Behaviour, Crime and Policing Act 2014, the statutory offences discussed in this section all provide defences of reasonableness (though none are defined or specifically aimed at protecting expression).[804] The defence of reasonableness assumes special significance in relation to the provisions of the 1997 Act, since in contrast to those under the 1986 Act, there is either no need to establish *mens rea* or its establishment is likely to have little inhibitory effect.[805]

Demonstrators shouting at passers-by to support their cause, whose behaviour could readily be termed threatening or disorderly, etc, and likely to cause one of the passers-by harassment, distress or alarm,[806] will have a defence under s 5(3)(c) of the 1986 Act if they can show that their behaviour was reasonable. The Act gives no guidance as to the meaning of the term, but it was determined in *DPP v Clarke*[807] that the defence is to be judged objectively, and it will therefore depend on what a bench of magistrates considers reasonable. In that case, the behaviour of the protesters outside an abortion clinic was not found to be reasonable. The use of pictures and models of aborted foetuses appeared to contribute to this conclusion. This decision would clearly also apply to charges under s 4A (and, where appropriate, to the interpretation of s 1(3)(c) of the 1997 Act as well),[808] but obviously does not give much guidance to protesters seeking to determine beforehand the limits or meaning of 'reasonable' protest. An 'activist' interpretation of this defence – one that prioritises conformity with Arts 10 and 11 – would have to adopt a wide interpretation of the term 'reasonable' in order to align with the general values underlying freedom of assembly articulated earlier in this chapter.

---

802 [2010] EWCA Crim 2923, para 26.

803 *Ibid*, para 23.

804 Under s 5(3)(c) and s 4A(3)(b) of the 1986 Act and s 1(3) of the 1997 Act. It may be noted that under the 1997 Act, the 'defence' operates as partially reversed *actus reus*, in the sense that if the defence is proved (the burden of so doing is on the defendant), then harassment is not established.

805 Thus, the decision in *Clarke*, below, will not be readily applicable under the 1997 Act.

806 It is not necessary to prove that anyone actually experienced harassment, merely that this was likely.

807 Above, text accompanying fn 781.

808 See, for example, *Cheshire West and Chester Council and Others v Pickthall* [2015] EWHC 2141 (QB), paras 39–49 in relation to defence that the course of conduct was pursued for 'the purpose of preventing and detecting crime'.

The decisions in *Norwood*,[809] *Abdul*,[810] and *Haque and Choudhury*[811] suggest that the defence of reasonableness under s 5 of the 1986 Act could at least provide one entry-point for the consideration of proportionality under Arts 10 and 11. Similarly, in *Hammond*:[812] here, the appellant took a placard with the words 'Stop Immorality', 'Stop Homosexuality', 'Stop Lesbianism', and 'Jesus is Lord' to the centre of Bournemouth and began preaching. This attracted a large group of people who were provoked by the preaching and who physically attacked the appellant. He was requested by two police officers to stop preaching. Upon refusing to comply with this request the appellant was arrested and subsequently charged and convicted of a s 5 offence. It was found that the interference with the appellant's right to freedom of expression under s 5 was a proportionate response in view of the fact that his behaviour went beyond legitimate protest, was provoking violence and disorder and interfered with the rights of others. In those circumstances it was found that the appellant's conduct was not reasonable. The conclusion on appeal was that the lower court had embarked upon the necessary exercise and had reached a decision that was open for them to take, namely, that the defendant's conduct was not reasonable in the particular circumstances.[813] It was accepted that Art 10 considerations apply to the evaluation of a reasonableness defence.[814] Thus, although Art 10 was taken into account on appeal, it was again found that the conviction was proportionate to the harm sought to be averted.

Aside from rebutting the defence of reasonableness, the prosecution may also have to demonstrate – where Art 10 or 11 is engaged – that bringing a prosecution under s 4 or 5 is a proportionate response to the conduct in question. This was established in *Dehal v Crown Prosecution Service*.[815] The appellant, a Sikh man, had put up a notice at a Sikh temple that he had attended for many years. It was written in Punjabi and attacked the president of the temple and other members of the temple committee. Mr Dehal intended the notice to be read by those it was aimed at and other worshippers. He was convicted of the offence under the Public Order Act 1986, s 4A(1).[816] His appeal concerned in essence the relationship between Art 10 of the European Convention on Human Rights and the s 4A offence. The Court had to examine the following questions: was the prosecution of the appellant a proportionate response to his conduct and did Art 10 provide him with a defence, therefore making the interference with the appellant's freedom of expression unnecessary? In allowing the appeal, the Court determined that although all the elements of the offence were present, the prosecution had not presented enough evidence to establish that bringing a criminal prosecution was a proportionate response to the appellant's conduct.

Injunctions against protesters

Notwithstanding the web of overlapping powers which enable state authorities to regulate public protest, the actions of demonstrators may also be curbed at the behest of

---

809 [2003] EWHC 1564.
810 [2011] EWHC 247 (Admin).
811 7 March 2011, unreported.
812 [2004] EWHC 69.
813 At para 33.
814 At para 22.
815 [2005] EWHC 2154.
816 The case is also discussed in Chapter 7; see p 433.

private persons (including corporate entities) who seek injunctions to prevent some actual or apprehended harm. The harms apprehended may have a statutory foundation (such as 'harassment', 'anti-social behaviour', or obstruction of the highway)[817] in which case the relevant statute sets out the particular requirements for applying for injunctive relief. Alternatively, they may instead be tortious harms (such as 'trespass' or 'nuisance')[818] with a common law footing. Those seeking injunctive relief will often advance parallel arguments in favour of injunctions on both statutory and common law grounds. Indeed, reliance on these remedies is commonplace – particularly by companies against whom protracted protest campaigns have been waged. The terms of injunctions can significantly limit the right to protest, they are usually far-reaching in terms of their scope (commonly being issued against 'persons unknown'),[819] and are sometimes reliant on evidence (such as hearsay or police intelligence) that would not be admissible in criminal proceedings.[820] Moreover, injunction orders are often used in aid of the criminal law (it would seem to copper-fasten and facilitate the enforcement of already existing offences).[821]

Injunctions are future-facing, and impose blanket prohibitions that operate as prior restraints on freedom of assembly. This, however, is not conclusive of their compatibility with the Convention since Strasbourg has accepted that the use of prior restraints may be justified in certain circumstances.[822] Furthermore, even when the rights of expression and assembly are taken into account, their scope may be given a narrow interpretation that ultimately offers little in the way of protection to certain forms of protest (such as disruptive and/or protracted assembly).[823]

Injunctions under the Protection from Harassment Act 1997

Section 3 of the 1997 Act allows for an injunction to be obtained to prevent an actual or apprehended breach of s 1(1) of the Act, and injunctions under s 3A can be granted to

---

817　See respectively, ss 3 and 3A Prevention from Harassment Act 1997, ss 1 and 3 Anti-social Behaviour, Crime and Policing Act 2014, and s 130 Highways Act 1980.

818　Relevant torts may also extend to economic torts such as inducing breach of contract or causing loss by unlawful means. For discussion, see Mead, D, 'A chill through the back door? The privatised regulation of peaceful protest' (2013: Jan) PL 100–118, at 108–9.

819　In *Astrazeneca UK Ltd v Aran Mathai and Others* [2014] EWHC 2774 (QB), the definition of 'protesters' bound by the injunction included not only members of SHAC or those acting in its name, but also extended to any 'supporter' of SHAC who was acting to expose experimentation on live animals by Huntingdon Life Sciences. By way of contrast, in *Harlan Laboratories UK Ltd and Another v Stop Huntingdon Animal Cruelty ('SHAC')* [2012] EWHC 3408 (QB), para 11, Swift J refused to expand the protective scope of an anti-harassment Order to include the 'clients' of the corporate claimant.

820　For a non-protest example, see *Birmingham City Council v Shafi and Anor* [2008] EWCA Civ 1186 (30 October 2008), paras 7, 16 regarding the admissibility of police intelligence.

821　For example, *Hall and Others v Mayor of London* [2010] EWCA Civ 817 paras 52–57; *Mayor and Burgesses of the London Borough of Islington v Jones, Melluish and Persons Unknown* [2012] EWHC 1537 (QB) at 66; *Heathrow Airport Ltd and Another v Garman and Others* [2007] EWHC 1957 (QB) paras 105–6; *Novartis Pharmaceuticals UK Ltd and Another v Stop Huntingdon Animal Cruelty ('SHAC')* [2009] EWHC 2716 (QB), para 4.

822　See, e.g., the decision of the Commission in *Christians Against Racism and Fascism v UK*, Appl No 8440/78 (1980) 21 DR 138.

823　*West Sussex County Council v Persons Unknown, O'Donnell, Sherborne and Lucas* [2013] EWHC 4024 (QB), para 30. See also, for example, text accompanying fn 110 above.

prevent an actual or apprehended breach of s 1(1A) (as discussed above).[824] These injunctions can be sought at the instigation of the 'victim' in *ex parte* proceedings, merely on his or her affidavit. Furthermore, while s 7(5) of the Act provides that '[r]eferences to a person, in the context of the harassment of a person, are references to a person who is an individual',[825] it has since been clarified that ' "person" in section 1(1A)(c) is not limited to individuals and may be a body corporate. Thus a company may apply for an injunction pursuant to section 3A where the company falls within section 1(A)(c).'[826] Breach of an injunction granted under either s 3 or 3A is an offence (s 3(6)) punishable by up to five years' imprisonment (s 3(9)).

The scope of ss 3 and 3A injunctions – including their hybrid nature (i.e. allowing for criminal sanctions for breach of an injunction granted on the civil standard of proof) – clearly has the potential to allow for significant interferences with Arts 10 and 11 guarantees. Equally, though, a few cases demonstrate that heightened judicial scrutiny – what might be regarded as an activist approach to s 3 applications – can limit the breadth of the injunctive relief sought. In *Huntingdon Life Sciences Ltd and Another v Curtin and Others*,[827] the company (HLS) obtained an *ex parte* injunction against six groups under s 3 of the Act, which prohibited conduct amounting to harassment within the terms of the Act, or entering HLS research sites. HLS was engaged in animal experimentation and was the subject of a campaign by a number of animal rights' organisations. One of the defendants, the British Union of Anti-Vivisectionists (BUAV), a peaceful campaigning group, applied to have the injunction varied so that it was not covered. Eady J found, in the *inter partes* proceedings, that the plaintiff had not provided sufficient evidence to support the claim that the defendants should be covered by the injunction. He also considered it unfortunate that the provisions of the Act were couched in such wide terms that they could appear to cover 'the rights of political protest and public demonstration which are so much a part of our democratic tradition'. This judgment clearly recognised, as the legislators did not, the general need to seek to delineate forms of anti-social behaviour sufficiently clearly so as to avoid infringing the rights in question.

Similarly, in *Novartis Pharmaceuticals UK Ltd and Another v Stop Huntingdon Animal Cruelty ('SHAC')*,[828] the claimants sought to extend the terms of an existing injunction against SHAC protesters in order to prohibit them from, amongst other

---

824 See, for example, *Hall v Newchurch Guinea Pigs* [2005] EWHC 372 (QB); *EDO MBM Technology Ltd v Campaign to Smash EDO and Others* [2005] EWHC 837 (QB); *Wife and Children of Omar Othman v English National Resistance and others* [2013] EWHC 1421 (QB). See also the multiple (and related) injunctions obtained against 'Stop Huntingdon Animal Cruelty' ('SHAC').

825 In *Heathrow Airport Ltd and Another v Garman and Others* [2007] EWHC 1957 (QB), paras 82 and 101, Swift J cited the fact that Heathrow Airport Ltd was a body corporate as one reason (amongst others) for not granting the injunction sought under s 3 of the 1997 Act. In *Oxford University v Broughton* [2004] EWHC 2543 (QB) para 47, Grigson J similarly thought it unlikely (though he declined to decide) that the 1997 Act could be invoked to protect corporations (citing *DPP v Dziurznski* [2002] EWHC 1380).

826 *Smithkline Beecham Plc and Others v Avery and Ors (Representing Stop Huntingdon Animal Cruelty ('SHAC')* [2009] EWHC 1488 (QB) para 43, per Jack J. Applied in *AGC Chemicals Europe Ltd v Stop Huntingdon Animal Cruelty ('SHAC')* [2010] EWHC 3674 (QB); *Harlan Laboratories UK Ltd and Another v Stop Huntingdon Animal Cruelty ('SHAC')* [2012] EWHC 3408 (QB) para 9.

827 (1998) 3(1) J Civ Lib 37.

828 [2009] EWHC 2716 (QB).

things, wearing Halloween or 'blood splattered clothing or costumes', and from displaying any banner, sign or placard alleging that the claimants murder, torture or abuse animals.[829] Sweeney J refused to grant the extension, observing that 'the implementation of such a blanket prohibition . . . is likely . . . to cause considerable practical problems for the Police, risk the raising of tensions, and interfere with the rights of those who simply wish to wear inoffensive masks'.[830] While a more robust affirmation of the illegitimacy of content-based regulation[831] would have been preferable to this more pragmatic reasoning (based on the challenges of enforcement), this is nonetheless a welcome judgment. As noted, however, it also clearly illustrates the severity of protest restrictions that corporations have sought under s 3, and the imperative of close scrutiny when granting interim injunctions to constrain public protest.

In this regard, it is noteworthy that in *University of Oxford v Broughton*[832] Grigson J held that the test under s 12(3) HRA must be applied where an interlocutory injunction would encroach on an individual's Convention rights.[833] Section 12(3) HRA is most obviously oriented towards injunctions against the press, providing that: 'no such relief is to be granted so as to restrain publication before trial unless the Court is satisfied that the applicant is likely to establish that publication should not be allowed', but its invocation in relation to prior restraints on protest is indeed preferable to the less stringent test in *American Cyanamid Co v Ethicon Ltd (No. 1)*[834] – simply, whether or not there is a serious question to be tried – which previously governed all applications for interlocutory injunctions. While s 12(3) HRA – and also s 12 (4), which provides that 'the court must have particular regard to the importance of the convention right to freedom of expression' – could conceivably tip the scales against the granting of a restrictive order in a protest case, the potential gains of s 12 are likely to be defeated in cases where the Art 11 right is itself interpreted narrowly, and where the nature of a particular protest is regarded as falling outwith its scope (as, for example, in relation to protracted or indefinite encampments on public land).[835]

Injunctions under the Anti-social Behaviour, Crime and Policing Act 2014

Replacing the old scheme of anti-social behaviour orders,[836] Part 1 of the 2014 Act empowers a court to grant an injunction if satisfied that the respondent has engaged in,

---

829　*Ibid*, para 6.

830　*Ibid*, para 51(ii).

831　See, for example, *Primov and Others v Russia*, Appl No 17391/06, 12 June 2014, para 135.

832　[2004] EWHC 2543 (QB) paras 32–33.

833　Citing *Cream Holdings Limited and others v Banerjee and others* [2004] UKHL 44; [2005] 1 AC 253 (a case involving breach of confidentiality). See too, *Wife and Children of Omar Othman v English National Resistance and others* [2013] EWHC 1421 (QB), paras 41–50.

834　[1975] AC 396; [1975] 2 WLR 316; [1975] 1 All ER 504.

835　See, for example, *West Sussex County Council v Persons Unknown, O'Donnell, Sherborne and Lucas* [2013] EWHC 4024 (QB), para 30.

836　Under the Crime and Disorder Act 1998. For an example of an ASBO being used against protesters, see: *R v Avery and Others* [2009] EWCA Crim 2670; *Cf R v Jones and Others* [2006] EWCA (Crim) 2942 in which the imposition of an ASBO on demonstrators who had disrupted the Docklands Light Railway in connection with their protest against an arms fair was held to be disproportionate.

or threatens to engage in, anti-social behaviour,[837] and if the court regards it as just and convenient to grant the injunction.[838] Private individuals or entities that are the subject of protest may (indirectly) instigate proceedings,[839] and the procedure to be followed (under s 6 of the 2014 Act) allows the grant of *ex parte* interim injunctions (though these should only be made in exceptional or urgent circumstances).[840] A power of arrest may be specified for any breach of the injunction if the anti-social behaviour includes threatened violence or harm to other persons.[841]

In one case, four separate year-long injunctions were granted against the leader and deputy leader of the far-right party, 'Britain First', after it proposed to hold a procession through the centre of Luton. The injunctions (to which powers of arrest were attached) included prohibitions on the respondents from entering any mosque within England and Wales and from carrying or displaying a banner in the notified procession with the words 'No More Mosques' (or words to that effect). The evidence relied upon to support these injunctions included previous 'mosque invasions' carried out by 'Britain First',[842] and the fact that the march date was within the month of Ramadan and coincided with a community event called 'Luton in Harmony'.[843] The court did, however, reject the chief constable's application for an injunction forbidding the respondents from entering 'the town of Luton and its surrounding area' altogether.

While the police must apply to the High Court or county court for such injunctions, it is clear that they could be used against protesters, perhaps especially in relation to sustained protests over a period of weeks or months in localities where some regard them as a nuisance or annoyance. Given the duration of the injunctions (no maximum length is specified in the legislation, except where the injunction is granted against persons under the age of 18, in which case it cannot be for longer than 12 months), they could effectively impose de facto blanket bans on protest activity. Furthermore, there is nothing in Part I the 2014 Act (in contrast to the later sections dealing with dispersal powers and PSPOs) to emphasise the need to have regard to the rights of freedom of expression and freedom of assembly.

---

837 Section 2 of the 2014 Act defines 'anti-social behaviour' in Part I of the Act to mean: '(a) conduct that has caused, or is likely to cause, harassment, alarm or distress to any person, (b) conduct capable of causing nuisance or annoyance to a person in relation to that person's occupation of residential premises, or (c) conduct capable of causing housing-related nuisance or annoyance to any person'. In *R v Jones and Others* [2006] EWCA (Crim) 2942, para 45, Moses LJ distinguished between 'activity likely to cause harassment, alarm or distress, and activity which merely causes frustration, disappointment, anger, or annoyance' noting that the latter was 'plainly not what the Crime and Disorder Act 1998 is aimed at. It is aimed at actions likely to cause what might be globally described as "fear for one's own safety".' It is certainly arguable that the same qualification should apply to the interpretation of 'harassment' under s 2(1)(a) of the 2014 Act.

838 The wording of this second criterion is identical to s 37(1) of the Supreme Courts Act 1981, discussed under 'Common law injunctions' below.

839 The application for an injunction under s 1 of the 2014 Act may only be made by the bodies listed in s 5(1) – which includes the police, local authorities and housing authorities – but may be triggered by allegations made to these authorities.

840 Anti-Social Behaviour, Crime and Policing Act 2014, Explanatory Notes, para 124.

841 Section 4 of the 2014 Act.

842 *Ibid*, para 22.

843 *Chief Constable of Bedfordshire Police v Paul Golding and Jayda Fransen* [2015] EWHC 1875 (QB).

Common law injunctions

In addition to the statutory injunctions discussed above, the High Court is empowered grant an injunction (interlocutory or final) 'in all cases in which it appears to the Court to be just and convenient to do so' under s 37(1) of the Supreme Courts Act 1981. Such injunctions are most commonly granted against protesters to prevent the torts of nuisance or trespass (and may also be granted in conjunction with a possession order where protesters have occupied land or premises). An interim injunction may be obtained very quickly in a hearing in which the other party is not represented. Even if a permanent injunction is not eventually granted, the aim of the demonstration may well have been destroyed by that time. As such, swift action is necessary to apply to a court to set aside or vary an order.[844]

In assessing the likelihood of future tortious conduct in relation to (primarily, direct action) protest, the courts have emphasised that the criteria are neither fixed nor invariable: 'the greater the . . . inconvenience that may be caused by the apprehended injury, if it occurs, the more readily will the court intervene despite uncertainties and deficiencies of proof.'[845] On this basis, common law injunctions may be more readily obtainable than those under the Protection from Harassment or Anti-social Behaviour, Crime and Policing Acts. In *Heathrow Airport Ltd and Another v Garman and Others*, for example, Swift J declined to grant an injunction under the 1997 Act (because of the weak evidential basis for the apprehended breach of s 1(1)),[846] but was readily satisfied that 'the balance of convenience clearly lies in favour' of granting injunctive relief based on trespass, nuisance and/or the Airport byelaws.[847]

Perhaps the best-known protest case involving the granting of an injunction on public nuisance grounds is *Hubbard v Pitt*.[848] The defendants mounted a demonstration outside an estate agents in order to protest at what was seen as the ousting of working class tenants in order to make way for higher income buyers, thereby effecting a change in the character of the area. The plaintiffs sought an injunction to prevent the protest on various grounds, including that of nuisance. At first instance, it was held that a stationary meeting would not constitute a reasonable use of the highway and the grant of the interim injunction was upheld by the Court of Appeal. It is difficult – if not impossible – to reconcile the Court's judgment in *Hubbard* (on the unlawfulness of picketing) with Strasbourg jurisprudence regarding the right to freedom of peaceful assembly – and Lord Denning dissented on this point, arguing that the right to demonstrate is so closely analogous to freedom of speech that it should be protected.[849] Furthermore, the judgment in *Hubbard* relied on the old threshold test in *American Cyanamid*[850] (whether there is a

---

844 For example, *Sunstreet Properties v Persons Unknown* [2011] EWHC 3432 (Ch).

845 Spry, *Principles of Equitable Remedies*, 7th edn, p 46, cited approvingly in *Astrazeneca UK Ltd v Aran Mathai and Others* [2014] EWHC 2774 (QB), para 7; *Smithkline Beecham Plc and Ors v Avery and Ors (Representing Stop Huntingdon Cruelty ('Shac')* [2009] EWHC 1488 (QB) para 62.

846 [2007] EWHC 1957 (QB), para 99.

847 *Ibid*, paras 107–116.

848 [1976] QB 142.

849 For further discussion, see Mead, *op cit*, fn 1, pp 394–7.

850 *American Cyanamid Co v Ethicon Ltd (No 1)* [1975] AC 396; [1975] 2 WLR 316; [1975] 1 All ER 504.

serious question to be tried) that was expressly disfavoured by Grigson J in *University of Oxford v Broughton*[851] in cases where Convention rights were engaged (see above).

While common law injunctions resemble those available under s 3 and s 3A of the 1997 Act, because they are based on the common law, s 3 of the HRA does not apply. Furthermore, s 6 HRA does not apply directly unless the party seeking the injunction is a public authority or a private body discharging a public function. In *Hubbard*, those seeking the injunctions would not have fallen within either of those categories. But, as Chapter 4 indicated, s 6 has implications even for private parties.[852] Thus, the Strasbourg protest jurisprudence should be taken into account when considering the grant of an injunction in similar circumstances (and proportionality considerations should inform the 'just and convenient' test under s 37(1) of the Supreme Courts Act 1981).

10 Conclusions

This chapter has sought to demonstrate that certain narrow assumptions about protest and public space often underlie the legal regulation of freedom of assembly in the UK. These include the essentialised view that assemblies are invariably political and non-recreational, that they are (or ought to be) temporary by definition, and that they tend atavistically towards disorder. Moreover, it has been too readily assumed that streets are primarily for the passage of pedestrian and vehicular traffic, that other locations may properly have dedicated functions (such as recreation or education) to the exclusion of protest activity, and that property rights should automatically trump protest rights. It is commonly also taken for granted that the police have a monopoly upon public order expertise, and that the police role is primarily one of 'management' and 'control' (rather than 'facilitation').

Highly significant developments in Strasbourg case law relating to Arts 10 and 11 ECHR over the past 15 years have begun to challenge some of these assumptions. The European Court of Human Rights has found that the activities of protesters engaged in 'sit-ins' (*Taranenko*), occupations (*Cisse*; *Kuznetsov*), encampments (*Nosov*), and deliberately disruptive protest (*Steel*; *Barraco*) fell within the protective scope of Arts 10(1) and 11(1). The Court has also emphasised that the facilitation of the Art 11 right entails certain positive obligations on the part of the State (*Plattform 'Ärzte für das Leben'*; *Frumkin*), that the rights of those with peaceful intentions should be protected even if others are disorderly or violent (*Ezelin*; *Ziliberberg*), that sweeping blanket restrictions are inherently problematic (*Stankov*), and that both spontaneous assemblies (*Bukta*; *Molnár*) and peaceful provocative displays short of intimidation (*Fáber*) should be protected. The Court has also now acknowledged that Art 11 covers assemblies 'of an essentially social character' (*Friend*; *Huseynov*), and emphasised the importance of tolerance in a pluralist society (*Barankevich*).

Nonetheless, the Strasbourg jurisprudence is not uniformly positive. There has been a continued failure to consider notification requirements as an 'interference' with Art 11,

---

851 [2004] EWHC 2543 (QB) paras 32–33, citing *Cream Holdings Limited and others v Banerjee and others* [2004] UKHL 44; [2005] 1 AC 253 (a case involving breach of confidentiality). It is not entirely clear on what basis the initial injunction Grigson J thought it unlikely that the 1997 Act could be used to protect corporations (though in subsequent related litigation, the injunctions are indeed).

852 See pp 211–218.

and thus to subject these sometimes onerous requirements to proportionality analysis (*Berladir*). Moreover, two Grand Chamber judgments – *Kudrevičius* and *Austin* – are particularly concerning. In the former, the Court relied heavily on the margin of appreciation doctrine to uphold the conviction for 'riot' of Lithuanian farmers who held a peaceful but obstructive protest. In the latter, the Court's reasoning (aligned with that of the House of Lords) allowed the context and purpose of a policing operation to be factored into the assessment of whether the 'containment' of protesters constituted a 'deprivation' of liberty (thereby effectively importing a public order exception into Art 5). Both of these judgments are likely to erode the core protections that the Convention ought to afford domestically.

When it comes to the domestic implementation of international human rights standards relating to freedom of assembly, the state's positive obligations should not be interpreted in ways that might undermine its negative obligation not to interfere with essential freedoms. The chapter highlighted two related factors likely to shape the approach of the domestic courts to public protest (and thus to determine whether this approach should be characterised in terms of minimalism or activism): first, their attitude towards the margin of appreciation doctrine (noting Protocol 15 ECHR) and, second, their preparedness to recognise, and give appropriate weight to, the fundamental values (truth, democracy, tolerance and autonomy) underlying the rights of assembly and expression – even allowing for the fact that these values may sometimes pull in different directions.

How far, then, have the expectations of the HRA been realised in terms of the right to protest? This chapter has on the whole painted a dismal picture. The 'constitutional shift' heralded by Sedley LJ in *Redmond-Bate* (and which Lord Bingham also clearly signalled in *Laporte*) has, if anything, been more whimper than bang. There have been some progressive judicial pronouncements – for example, Laws LJ's recognition in *Tabernacle* that '[r]ights worth having are unruly things' (in turn, finding that the 2007 Aldermaston byelaws violated the appellant's Art 10 and 11 rights). Ostensibly too, Lord Neuberger's acknowledgment in *Hall* – that 'these fundamental human rights would be at risk of emasculation' if they did not extend protection to the manner of, and location in which, protest sought to be exercised – provides strong affirmation of the right to protest. Yet, in both *Hall* (and similarly, in *Samede* regarding the 'Occupy' camp at St Paul's Cathedral) the injunctions and possession orders sought by the mayor were broadly upheld or granted in the terms sought. Protest in the vicinity of Parliament continues to be significantly curtailed (*Gallastegui*; *Barda*; the PRSRA and relevant byelaws). Indeed, the subsequent application of *Laporte* has tended to emphasise Lord Rodger's and Lord Carswell's pragmatic view of 'imminence' and thus to confirm a preventive role for the police (e.g., *Moos and McClure*).

Such examples support the view that judicial recognition of the value of protest has largely been tokenistic, and that lip service continues to be paid to questions of proportionality. The chapter has noted a preference for 'orthodox' and 'predictable' forms of demonstration; attempts to charge protesters for the costs of traffic management; the routine surveillance of demonstrators by police (*Catt*); rolling long-term injunctions imposed on demonstrators and 'persons unknown' at the behest of private actors (often multinational corporations); extensive reliance on the breach of peace doctrine against protesters in ways that have marginalised the statutory framework (the low points being *Austin* and *Hicks*); and statutory provisions that are themselves excessively broad (such as the banning powers under s 13 and s 14A POA), and that have been incrementally extended – such as those relating to aggravated trespass under s 68 CJPOA (*Bauer*; *Richardson*). Indeed, attention must also be paid to the informal regulation of protest 'in the shadow the law' (both through liaison policing and the ways in which the relevant authorities might, in practice, expand upon their statutory powers).

Against this backdrop, it is patently clear that greater recognition of the communicative and associational value of protest and assembly in the UK is required. The right to protest too readily loses out to norms of convenience and civility. It is unsurprising that Maina Kiai, the UN Special Rapporteur on the Rights to Freedom of Peaceful Assembly and of Association, concluded his UK mission in 2013 by stating that 'the focus of the legal framework on freedom of peaceful assembly is overall more on ensuring public order, rather than on a human rights-based approach to facilitating peaceful assemblies'.[853]

---

853 A/HRC/23/39/Add.1, fn 6 above, para 17.

Part III

The protection of privacy[1]

The right to respect for privacy is now accepted as part of the domestic law of a number of countries[2] and of international human rights instruments.[3] However, the limits of the right are still unclear and a generally accepted definition of privacy has not emerged. As Raymond Wacks has observed, 'the voluminous [theoretical] literature on the subject has failed to produce a lucid or consistent meaning of [the] concept'.[4] It may be said, therefore, that privacy has become a complex and very broad concept due to the variety of claims or interests which have been thought to fall within it.[5] The European Court of Human Rights has accommodated many disparate issues within the concept of privacy arising under Art 8 of the European Convention on Human Rights: they range from the rights of homosexuals[6] to the right to receive information about oneself.[7] The scope of Art 8 continues to widen.

---

1 Texts referred to in this Part and further reading: Warby QC, M, Moreham, N, and Christie, I, (eds), *The Law of Privacy and the Media*, 2nd edn, 2011, OUP; Mckay, S, *Covert Policing: Law and Practice*, 2015, OUP; Kenyon, A, (ed), *Comparative Defamation and Privacy Law*, 2016, CUP; Fenwick, H and Phillipson, G, *Media Freedom under the Human Rights Act*, 2006, Chapters 13–17; Witzleb et al, *Emerging Challenges in Privacy Law*, 2014, CUP; Wacks, R, *The Protection of Privacy*, 1980, Sweet and Maxwell; Westin, AF, *Privacy and Freedom*, 1970, The Bodley Head; Wacks, R (ed), *Privacy*, 1993, New York University Press; Tugendhat and Christie, *The Law of Privacy and the Media*, 2002, OUP; Feldman, D, *Civil Liberties and Human Rights in England and Wales*, 2nd edn, 2002, Part 3; Markesinis, B (ed), *Protecting Privacy*, 1999, OUP; Birks, R (ed), *Privacy and Loyalty*, 1997, Clarendon; Clayton and Tomlinson, *The Law of Human Rights* (2009), OUP, Chapter 12; Whitty, N, Murphy, T and Livingstone, S, *Civil Liberties Law: the Human Rights Era* (2001) Chapter 6; Fenwick, H and Phillipson, G, 'Breach of confidence as a privacy remedy in the Human Rights era (2000) 63 (5) MLR 660; Seipp, D, 'English judicial recognition of the right to privacy' (1983) 3 OJLS 325.

2 For example, the US Privacy Act 1974 and the tort or torts of invasion of privacy, the Canadian Personal Information Protection and Electronic Documents Act 2000, Art 9 of the French Civil Code; German courts can protect privacy under s 823(1) of the Civil Code and a right to privacy arises under the German Basic Law Art 10 (albeit limited to posts and telecommunications).

3 It appears in the European Convention on Human Rights, Art 8 and the International Covenant on Civil and Political Rights, Art 17.

4 'Introduction', in Wacks, *op cit*, fn 1, p xi.

5 See Wacks, *op cit*, fn 1, Chapter 1, pp 10–21.

6 See e.g., *Dudgeon v UK* (1982) 4 EHRR 149; *Oliari v Italy* application no. 18766/11 and 36030/11 21 July 2015.

7 *Gaskin v UK* (1990) 12 EHRR 36.

The Strasbourg Court has not attempted to provide an exhaustive definition of privacy,[8] but various definitions have been put forward by theorists which tend to be very broad: it has been termed 'a circle around every individual human being which no government . . . ought to be permitted to overstep' and 'some space in human existence thus entrenched around and sacred from authoritative intrusion'.[9] Feldman has found that the desire for a private area in life derives its justification from personal autonomy, which is linked to the idea of 'defensible space', and from the 'idea of utility' – the idea that 'people operate more effectively and happily when they are allowed to make their own arrangements about domestic and business matters without interference from the state'.[10] Such phrases suggest that some aspects of an individual's life, which can be identified as private aspects, are of particular value and therefore warrant special protection from state intrusion. At an intuitive level, the notion that boundaries can and should be placed around such aspects of an individual's life, preventing such intrusion and thereby protecting personal autonomy, seems to be accepted as the fundamental basis of the idea of privacy[11] and underlies decisions under Art 8.[12] However, as recognised at Strasbourg, the guarantee under Art 8 goes further than simply requiring that the individual should have an area of privacy that the state should respect – in two ways. As indicated below, the right also encompasses positive obligations on the part of the state authorities. It also places obligations on private bodies, which can include positive obligations.[13] In *X and Y v Netherlands*[14] the Court stated: 'these [Art 8] obligations may require the adoption of measures even in the sphere of relations between individuals'.

Protection for private life generally is referenced in a number of chapters in this book, including Chapter 12 on police powers; the two chapters in this part specifically concern protection for personal information as an aspect of respect for private life. The disparate obligations thereby created are reflected in the different concerns of the two chapters in Part III. Chapter 11 considers state surveillance; it covers a selected range of intrusions of state agents into private life to gather information via forms of surveillance, and considers the safeguards available to the individual. Chapter 10 covers the protection of personal information from non-consensual use by the media on the basis that press and broadcasting bodies have very significant opportunities and often the intention of invading privacy in the interests of freedom of expression, but also of commercial advantage.[15] It will be argued that in each of these contexts the Human Rights Act (HRA), which has imported the Strasbourg conceptions of privacy into domestic law, has been and is of great significance. The statutes that have a central impact in this context, in particular the Regulation of Investigatory Powers Act 2000, have to be applied by those afforded powers under them compatibly with the

8   See further Chapter 2, p 66 *et seq.*
9   Mill, JS, *Principles of Political Economy*, 1970, Penguin, p 306.
10 See Feldman, D, *Civil Liberties and Human Rights in England and Wales*, 1st edn, 1993, pp 353–54.
11 See Seipp, *op cit*, fn 1, at p 333.
12 See, e.g., *Leander v Sweden* (1987) 9 EHRR 433; *McVeigh, O'Neill and Evans v United Kingdom* (1981) 45 EHRR 71.
13 See Chapter 2, pp 67–68.
14 (1985) 8 EHRR 235.
15 See Lord Justice Leveson, *An Inquiry into the Culture, Practices and Ethics of the Press: Report* (HC 780, 2012); discussed in Chapter 10 pp 702–03.

Convention rights under s 6 HRA. Most importantly, s 6 HRA and Art 8 ECHR have provided the impetus for the development of further protection for private information by effecting a transformation of the doctrine of confidence into the tort of misuse of private information.

Theoretical considerations

Privacy can be associated with a range of underlying values. The key values are, it is argued, informational autonomy (control over private information), self-fulfilment, dignity, substantive autonomy.[16] As will be discussed below, these values are often strongly associated with each other. It has often been argued that privacy is associated with self-fulfilment in the sense that protection for the private life of the individual tends to provide the best conditions under which he or she may flourish.[17] In other words, self-fulfilment may be fostered if the individual is able to enjoy the benefits most obviously associated with the private: the dropping of the public mask, the communion of intimates, and the expression of the deepest emotions.

If it is accepted that a key value underlying differing conceptions of privacy is that of personal autonomy,[18] it is necessary to draw a distinction between what may be termed 'substantive' and 'informational' autonomy. The former denotes the individual's interest in being able to make certain substantive choices about personal life for him- or herself, such as the choice to engage in certain sexual practices, or follow certain lifestyles without state interference or coercion.[19] Privacy derives its value partly from its close association with personal autonomy, in the sense that freedom from interference by the authorities will foster the conditions under which autonomy can be exercised. Thus, some authoritative invasions of privacy may be said to lead to interference with individual autonomy.

The term 'informational autonomy', on the other hand, the central concern of the following chapters refers to the individual's interest in controlling the flow of personal information about herself, the interest referred to by the German Supreme Court as 'informational self-determination'[20] or, as Beardsely has put it, the right to 'selective disclosure'.[21] In accordance with the views of a number of writers, it is contended that this interest is one of the primary concerns of the law in this area.[22] The ability to exercise control in this manner also affords some protection to other

---

16 See further Feldman, D, 'Secrecy, dignity or autonomy? Views of privacy as a civil liberty' (1994) 47(2) CLP 42.

17 See Feldman, *op cit*, fn 1, p 512.

18 See Wacks, *op cit*, fn 1, pp 10–21; Westin, *op cit*, fn 1, p 7; Miller, A, *Assault on Privacy*, 1971, University of Michigan Press, p 40.

19 See further Chapter 2, pp 71–79, Chapter 10, p 720.

20 BGH, 19 December 1995, BGHZ 131, pp 322–46.

21 'Privacy: autonomy and selective disclosure', in Pennock and Chapman (eds) *Nomos XIII: Privacy*, 1971, Atherton, p 56.

22 Ruth Gavison's definition of privacy – 'a limitation of others' access to an individual' – has three aspects: information; attention; physical access ('Privacy and the limits of law' (1980) 89(3) Yale LF 421); see also Gross's similar definition: 'The concept of privacy' (1967) 42 NYULR 34, p 36.

values, as Feldman[23] has pointed out: 'If people are able to release [private] information with impunity, it might have the effect of illegitimately constraining a person's choices as to his or her private behaviour, interfering in a major way with his or her autonomy.'[24] In other words, control over information thus indirectly protects substantive autonomy. Personal dignity, which must be diminished when information relating to intimate aspects of a person's life is widely published, giving rise to feelings of violation, shame and embarrassment, is also afforded a measure of protection. Informational control also protects what Feldman identifies as the value in forming and maintaining spheres of social interaction and intimacy – for example, work colleagues, friends, family, lovers – which may be seen as essential to human flourishing.[25] It is clear that the intimacy that such relationships entail is predicated upon an ability of the individual to ensure that information that may be circulated within one sphere is not, without her knowledge or consent, transferred to another sphere or the outside world. A privacy law gives legal force to that ability.

Since considerations of this nature involve an implied contrast between the public and the private, it may be helpful at this point to consider the division between the two spheres in order to come closer to examining what may be encompassed by the notion of privacy. A variety of referents may be used. The public includes state activity, aspects of the world of work, the pursuit of public interests, while the private includes the home, the family, the expression of sexuality and of the deepest feelings and emotions. Postulating such a division need not obscure the fact that these spheres are not entirely distinct, but may interact; the distinction is not, it is argued, dependent on physical space.[26]

The success of claims that respect for informational autonomy has not been accorded may be affected in legal terms, as the following chapters explain, by the nature of the obligations sought to be imposed on public authorities or private bodies, and by their potential effect on competing interests. 'Control over private or personal life' is treated under Art 8 ECHR as covering areas as disparate as allowing persons to communicate with each other via social media free from state interference[27] and enabling an individual to enjoy his or her private life free from the attentions of reporters. On the one hand, the individual's privacy may be invaded due to state surveillance, while on the other the citizen is seeking a legal remedy to prevent an invasion of privacy. Thus both negative and positive obligations are placed on the state. In the latter instance the state comes under a positive obligation to ensure that a legal remedy is available to the citizen to use against the press.

In the former case, the right to respect for private life must compete with the countervailing societal interests in the prevention of terrorism and crime, while in the latter

---

23 Feldman, D, 'Secrecy, dignity or autonomy? Views of privacy as a civil liberty' (1994) 47(2) CLP 42, p 54.

24 *Ibid*, p 51. Chapters 10 and 11 deal with 'informational privacy'; for the attempt to bring both informational and substantive autonomy under one definition: see Parent, W 'A new definition of privacy for the law' (1932) 2 Law and Philosophy 305, at pp 309 and 316 and Wacks, *op cit*, fn 1, esp p 79.

25 *Ibid*, pp 51–69. As Fried notes, privacy is essential for 'respect, love, friendship and trust' – 'without it they are simply inconceivable' 'Privacy' (1968) 77 Yale LJ 477, p 483.

26 See Paton-Simpson, E, 'Privacy and the Reasonable Paranoid: the Protection of Privacy in Public Places' (2000) 50 University of Toronto Law Journal 305.

27 See Chapter 2, pp 71–79.

case it must compete with another individual right – freedom of expression. If the state were to monitor data relating to use of social media, the state authorities would be using coercive powers to invade citizens' informational privacy in order to serve the ends of preventing crime or terrorism. If effective safeguards were not in place, as discussed in Chapter 11, the power would be open to abuse and the guarantee of respect for private life would be violated. If so the state would clearly be failing in its duty to treat its citizens' private life with respect; to prevent this, under the liberal analysis of rights discussed in Chapter 1, the state would have to accept that societal claims based on detecting and preventing certain harmful activities had to be demonstrated to a certain standard. In contrast, the state, in failing to control the activities of the reporter is erring on the side of free expression as it collides with the interest of the individual in securing her privacy. In this case, two individual rights are at stake. In the case of public figures claiming privacy rights against the press, the argument that views free speech as essential in order to ensure meaningful participation in a democracy may have particular strength, depending on the specific nature of the free speech claim.[28] This would be the case in relation to public figures where the information gained was clearly related to their fitness to carry out their public functions.[29] In the case of a purely private figure, or of private facts unrelated to the public function of public figures, freedom of expression would also compete with the claim of privacy. However, two of the important justifications for free speech – the arguments from truth and from political participation – would be largely irrelevant so that the strength of the free expression claim would be appreciably diminished.

It may be concluded that privacy is in a difficult position in so far as its ability to overcome other individual rights is concerned – *if* the values underpinning that other right are genuinely at stake. However, as Chapter 10 argues, the strength of both claims have to be weighed up when an apparent conflict arises.[30]

Domestic protection for privacy

Traditionally, UK law recognised no general right to respect for privacy, although there was some evidence, as will be seen, that the judges considered this to be an evil which required a remedy.[31] It has been argued that various areas of tort or equity, such as trespass, breach of confidence, copyright and defamation are instances of a general right to privacy,[32] but it is reasonably clear from judicial pronouncements pre-HRA that these areas and others were treated as covering specific and distinct interests which only incidentally offered protection to privacy[33] – despite the fact that the term 'privacy'

---

28 The role of the press as the 'public watchdog' was stressed in, for example, *K v News Group*, [2011] EWCA Civ 439, at [13]. See Fenwick, H and Phillipson, G, *Media Freedom under the Human Rights Act*, 2006, OUP at pp 683–688 and 792–794.

29 See Markesenis, B and Nolte, N, 'Some Comparative Reflections on the Right of Privacy of Public Figures in Public Places', in Birks, R (ed), *Privacy and Loyalty*, 1997, Oxford, pp 118 *et seq*.

30 See p 747 *et seq*.

31 Seipp, D, 'English judicial recognition of the right to privacy' (1983) 3 OJLS 325.

32 See Warren and Brandeis, 'The right to privacy' (1890) 4 Harv L Rev 193.

33 See the comments of Glidewell LJ in *Kaye v Robertson* [1991] FSR 62, CA: 'It is well known that in English law there is no right to privacy . . . in the absence of such a right the plaintiff's advisers have sought to base their claim on other well-established rights of action'.

was used in a number of rulings.[34] In such instances, it could usually be found that a recognised interest such as property actually formed the basis of the ruling. Thus, prior to the inception of the HRA, UK law offered only a piecemeal protection to privacy and therefore a number of privacy interests were largely unprotected. In so far as the protection for privacy broadened in the years immediately prior to the inception of the HRA, the initiative came not from the courts or the government, but from Europe – either from European Union Directives[35] or from decisions under the European Convention on Human Rights.[36]

When Art 8 ECHR was received into domestic law under the HRA, UK citizens acquired, for the first time, a guarantee of respect for their private life. Under ss 6 and 7(1)(a) of the HRA the right is directly enforceable against public authorities, such as the police or security services, as discussed in Chapter 11, and the need to ensure compliance with Art 8 has led to further development of the statutory basis for surveillance. But Art 8 was not directly enforceable against private bodies, including the press, as discussed in Chapter 10. But it has been found that citizens can sue the media relying on an existing cause of action, breach of confidence, relying on the court itself as a public authority under s 6 HRA, and to its obligations under s 12, to develop the action into a tort of misuse of private information by reference to Art 8.[37] The balancing act between Arts 8 and 10 that has been developed within the context of that action is explored in Chapter 10.

---

34 E.g., *Prince Albert v Strange* (1848) 2 De Gex & Sm 652; *Clowser v Chaplin* (1981) 72 Cr App R 342.
35 See the section on Data Protection, Chapter 10, p 763 *et seq.*
36 For decisions relating to state surveillance against the UK, see Chapter 11, p 821 *et seq.*
37 See Chapter 4, p 211 *et seq.*

Chapter 10

Private information and media freedom

This chapter has been updated and revised for this edition by Daniel Fenwick, Lecturer in Law at the University of Northumbria, UK, in conjunction with Helen Fenwick.

I Introduction[1]

The creation of a tort of invasion of privacy aimed at the protection of personal information against media intrusion filled one of the most serious lacunae in English law. Described by the Law Commission as 'a glaring inadequacy',[2] and condemned by the Court of Appeal,[3] *dicta* in a pre-Human Rights Act 1998 (HRA) decision of the House of Lords[4] remarked upon 'the continuing, widespread concern at the apparent failure of the law' in this area.[5] That failure was remedied under this largely HRA-driven legal development although, as this chapter will argue, recent developments in 2012–15 have undermined the efficacy of the tort in practice to an extent. It must also be borne in mind that, as the House of Lords stated in *Wainwright v Home Office*,[6] there is no general, comprehensive tort of invasion of privacy, reaching far beyond protection for private information.[7]

---

1 Texts and articles that will be referred to in this chapter: Wragg, P, 'The legitimacy of Press Regulation' [2015] PL 290; Cappuccio, A, 'The private nature of information: a light keeping the courts from straying into the "privacy" penumbra' [2014] IPQ 159; Wacks, R, *Privacy and Media Freedom*, 2013, OUP; Wragg, P 'The Benefits of Privacy-Invading Expression' (2013) 64(2) NILQ 187; Tugendhat and Christie, *The Law of Privacy and the Media*, 2nd edn, 2011, OUP; Harris, D, O'Boyle, M, Bates, E, and Buckley, C *Law of the European Convention on Human Rights*, 2009, OUP; Fenwick, H and Phillipson, G, *Media Freedom under the Human Rights Act*, 2006; Tugendhat and Christie, *The Law of Privacy and the Media* 2002, OUP; Wacks, R, *Privacy and Press Freedom*, 1996, Blackstone; Markesinis, B (ed), *Protecting Privacy*, 1999, OUP; Phillipson, G, 'Transforming breach of confidence? Towards a common law right of privacy under the Human Rights Act' (2003) 66(5) MLR 726; Tambini, D and Heyward, C (eds), *Ruled by Recluses? Privacy, Journalism and the Media after the Human Rights Act*, 2002, Institute for Public Policy Research; Wright, J, 'How private is my private life?', in Betten, L (ed), *the Human Rights Act 1998: What it Means*, 1999, Brill; Harris, D, O'Boyle, Warbrick, C *Law of the European Convention on Human Rights*, 1995, OUP. This chapter draws in places upon Fenwick, H and Phillipson, G, 'The Doctrine of Confidence as a Privacy Remedy in the Human Rights Act Era' [2000] 63 (5) MLR 660.
2 Law Commission 'Breach of Confidence' Report No 110, Cmnd 8388, 1981, para 5.5. The Commission was referring specifically to the fact that 'the confidentiality of information improperly obtained . . . may be unprotected'.
3 *Kaye v Robertson* [1991] FSR 62, CA.
4 *R v Khan* [1997] AC 558.
5 *Ibid, per* Lord Nicholls.
6 [2004] 2 AC 406 paras 28–35.
7 See Chapter 2, pp 70–79 for the areas covered by Art 8 ECHR.

The developments discussed below are driving forward a respect for the privacy of personal information still not fully evident in the publishing of a number of media bodies, especially the tabloid press. The misuse of private information by private individuals in other contexts, such as in relation to 'cyberbullying'[8] or 'revenge porn',[9] is considered elsewhere in this book.[10] The acquisition and use of personal information by state agents, with the purpose of preventing or detecting crime or protecting national security, is considered in Chapter 11. While Chapter 11 considers the laws relating to interception of communications and surveillance aimed at the regulation of investigative techniques by state agents, it must be remembered that they can also be used against intrusive methods employed by the media to gather information.[11]

The tort of misuse of personal information could of course be used against the broadcast media or against a private individual who discloses personal information non-consensually, but the press is by far the worst offender in terms of acquiring and publishing personal information. This chapter gives approval to the development of the tort but in doing so the implications for press freedom must not be over-looked. Thus the operation of the tort must be balanced by protection for speech, so as to allow the publication of matters of genuine public interest, although they should not be confused with the exercise of media commercial freedom. At the same time the serious harm caused by press invasion of privacy must be emphasised. Warren and Brandeis' verdict in the nineteenth century, 'The Press is overstepping in every direction the obvious bounds of propriety and decency . . . [inflicting] through invasions of privacy . . . mental pain and distress far greater than could be inflicted by mere bodily injury',[12] is still alarmingly true today, over 100 years later. Anyone familiar with the output of our print media will be wearily aware of its penchant for publishing what one journalist has described as 'toe-curlingly intimate details' about the sex lives not only of celebrities, but of 'quite obscure people'.[13] Further, the tendency to publish trivial details about the personal lives of well-known figures also affects their children who, even as babies, may become the subject of press intrusion using techniques to obtain photographs that may be dangerous.[14]

---

8   Protection from Harassment Act 1997, ss 2, 2A, 4; the Communications Act 2003, s 127.
9   Criminal Justice and Courts Act 2015, ss 33–35; the Communications Act 2003, s 127; Malicious Communications Act 1988, s 1.
10 See Chapter 7, p 484 *et seq*.
11 Interception of voice messages is an offence under s 1(1) of the Regulation of Investigatory Powers Act 2000. An example of successful prosecution is Clive Goodman, the royal editor of the *News of the World*, who pleaded guilty in November 2006 to plotting to intercept private phone messages involving the royal family. Glenn Mulcaire also admitted the same charge. Mulcaire further admitted five charges of unlawfully intercepting voicemail messages left by a number of people, including publicist Max Clifford and Elle Macpherson: *R v Stanford (Clifford)* [2006] EWCA Crim 258.
12 'The right to privacy' (1890) IV(5) Harvard L Rev 193, p 196.
13 Marr, A, *The Independent*, 25 April 1996. In a conference speech, the editor of the *Guardian*, Alan Rusbridger, listed a string of recent examples in which newspapers had published intimate details about the personal lives of celebrities, in some cases surreptitiously obtained, with either no or the flimsiest of 'public interest' justifications (Human Rights, Privacy and the Media, organised by the Constitution Unit, and the Centre for Communication and Information Law, UCL, 8 January 1999).
14 See press reports 14 August 2015 as to the warning from the Palace to the press via a letter from their communications secretary Jason Knauf to respect the privacy of the Duke of Cambridge's children – George, two, and Charlotte, three months. The royal couple said that there had been an 'increasing

Intrusive prurience or the commodifying of the private lives of celebrities or their children is not the only complaint: Victim Support has detailed a large number of case histories in which ordinary victims of crime and their families had had their suffering markedly exacerbated by intrusive and insensitive publications in local and national newspapers describing their plight in quite needless detail, causing in some cases diagnosable psychiatric harm, making others feel forced to move from the area where the crime had been committed, and causing all intense emotional distress.[15] In contrast to the position in virtually every Western democracy, such injuries had until fairly recently no remedy in a privacy law in this country, and a toothless Press Complaints Commission (now abolished) could only request the offending newspaper to print its adjudication on the matter.[16] However, it must be remembered that ordinary people caught up in newsworthy events, such as dramatic crimes, whose privacy is then hurtfully invaded by the press, are unlikely to have the resources to take powerful newspaper companies to court, something of which the newspapers themselves are well aware. It could be said that the HRA-driven development of a privacy law has merely advantaged already powerful figures – millionaire celebrities, although it would be hard to make that argument about their young children. But the value of a privacy law could relate to creating changes in press culture and influencing press working practices. It is frequently remarked of countries that have a privacy law, such as France and Germany, that their media does not exhibit the 'gutter' quality associated with the UK tabloid press.[17] In our cut-throat media market, the tendency of debased and lurid 'news' coverage in one newspaper to drive down the standards in another is very marked. Within this pervasive 'gutter' culture, which will influence the choices of readers, a newspaper that is unwilling to debase its standards may not survive, detracting from the diversity of opinion one would expect of a free press.

While the notion of respect for individual privacy could be said to be a clear underlying common law value,[18] it failed pre-HRA to find full expression in law, perhaps because intermittent governmental interest in the latter half of the twentieth century in statutory protection for privacy distracted the courts with the chimera of possible

---

number of incidents of paparazzi harassment' in recent months 'and the tactics being used are increasingly dangerous'. See also e.g., p 736 below.

15 See Fourth Report of the National Heritage Select Committee on Privacy and Media Intrusion Minutes of Evidence, Appendix 24 HC 294-II (1993).

16 See below, p 701 *et seq* for discussion of the role of the Press Complaints Commission (now replaced by the Independent Press Standards Organisation).

17 As Markesinis remarks, 'the possible extra-marital affairs of German politicians and businessmen hold little or no appeal for most readers of German newspapers.' (Markesinis, *op cit*, fn 1.) See also: Seaton, J 'Public, Private and the Media' (2003) *Political Quarterly* 174.

18 See *dicta* of Laws J in *Hellewell v Chief Constable of Derbyshire* [1995] 1 WLR 804, p 807; *Francome v Mirror Group Newspapers* [1984] 1 WLR 892, in which the Court of Appeal recognised (in effect) a right to privacy in telephone conversations; *Stephens v Avery* [1988] Ch 449; *dicta* of Lord Keith in *AG v Guardian Newspapers (No 2)* [1990] 1 AC 109, p 255, 'The right to personal privacy is clearly one which the law [of confidence] should seek to protect'. In the decision in *Dept of Health ex p Source Informatics Ltd* [2001] 2 WLR 953; (2000) *The Times*, 21 January, Simon Brown LJ stated clearly that in cases involving personal information, 'The concern of the law [of confidence] is to protect the confider's personal privacy'. In *R v Khan* [1997] AC 558, Lords Browne-Wilkinson, Slynn and Nicholls left open the question whether English law already recognised a right to privacy.

legislative action.[19] Quite clearly, however, no government in the past grasped this net-tle, out of a fear of press hostility.[20]

The HRA, however, introduced Art 8 of the European Convention on Human Rights into UK law, providing for a right to respect for private life.[21] Most public authorities and a number of private bodies engage in the processing of personal information. They are therefore subject to the provisions of the Data Protection Act (DPA) 1998, discussed below,[22] and any other relevant statute creating reporting restrictions to protect privacy, and such statutes must be interpreted compatibly with the Convention rights under s 3 of the HRA, whether or not both parties concerned are private bodies.[23] So under the HRA, if a *statute* concerning privacy is applicable in a given situation, the issue of indi-rect horizontal effect (discussed in Chapter 4)[24] is not significant. In ensuring that such statutes are interpreted compatibly with the Convention, it is clear that Art 8 is of par-ticular relevance. In determining whether information is to count as private, Art 8 must now be viewed as the source of interpretation under ss 3 and 2 HRA. That is clearly the case in respect of all statutory provisions that mention or could relate to personal infor-mation, including the DPA 1998. By virtue of ss 2 and 6 of the HRA, it is also the case in relation to the common law. Article 8 is not *directly* justiciable against the press or other private bodies; its reception into UK law under the HRA nevertheless provided an impetus for the notion of respect for privacy finally to find expression through the com-mon law, as this chapter explains. This chapter will concentrate on the development of a common law privacy remedy and the implications of this development for privacy for freedom of expression will be considered. The developments discussed below, under the Communications Act 2003 and the DPA, were influenced by Art 8, but the work in developing the privacy rights was done initially by Parliament and then by the regulator in both cases – the Data Protection Registrar and Ofcom (the broadcast regulator). The difficult area, and the one that has seen the most dynamic and dramatic development,

---

19 The Younger Committee, *Report of the Committee on Privacy* (Cmnd 5012, 1972), Calcutt Committee on Privacy and Related Matters, hereafter *The Calcutt Report* (Cmnd 1102, 1990), Review of Press Self Regulation (Cm 2135), Fourth Report of the National Heritage Select Committee in 1993, HC 294-II (1993), all proposed the introduction of statutory measures to protect privacy, as did the Lord Chancel-lor's Green Paper of the same year (CHAN J060915NJ.7/93).

20 Such fear was clearly evident during the passage of the HRA itself. In response to the press outcry over the possibility that the Act would create a right to privacy, the government introduced a specific amend-ment in favour of press freedom (HRA, s 12, discussed below), and repeatedly and explicitly sought to reassure the press during the Bill's debate. As Lord Ackner put it, the Lord Chancellor devoted 'a very large part of his [second reading] speech . . . to trying to pour oil on ruffled waters.' (HL Deb col 473, 18 November 1997). In fact, bearing in mind the effect of s 12(4)(b), discussed below, the government may have deceived the press as to the impact that s 12 was actually likely to have. For an example of blanket hostility from the press' representative body – the Newspaper Society – to the possible development of any privacy law in the UK, see Rasaiah, 'Current legislation, privacy and the media in the UK' (1998) 3(5) Communications Law 183.

21 As Chapter 2 explained, p 66 *et seq*, Art 8 of the Convention provides a person with a right to respect for four different rights: 'his private and family life, his home and his correspondence'. Para 2 then specifies a number of grounds permitting interference by 'a public authority' with this right.

22 Unless they are excluded from its ambit: see pp 768–70.

23 Due to the effect of HRA, s 3(1) which, in covering all statutes, also covers those which create a number of rights binding private bodies.

24 See p 211 *et seq*.

was the transformation of the doctrine of confidence by the judges into a privacy law, under the impetus of the HRA.

The chapter begins by examining basic principles of protection for private information under the HRA and Art 8 ECHR (section 2). It then considers protection for privacy under media regulation (section 3); it moves on to look at selected specific reporting restrictions under statute and, in relation to children, under the ECHR jurisdiction of the court (section 4). The main part of this chapter examines in section 5 the transformation of the doctrine of confidence into a privacy tort. The chapter then moves on to consider the overlapping and further protection for personal information offered by the DPA in section 6. Remedies for privacy invasion are considered in the penultimate section.

2 Strasbourg jurisprudence on protection for personal information: basic principles

As Chapter 2 explained, Art 8(1) provides a 'right to respect for private and family life, the home and correspondence' which is qualified under para (2).[25] There is a substantial Strasbourg jurisprudence on the data protection obligations of public authorities. It is clear that the actions of such bodies in the gathering, storing and use of information relating to private or family life, including photographs,[26] engages Art 8.[27] Certain categories of material, such as those relating to health[28] or sexual orientation or activity[29] are regarded as 'particularly sensitive or intimate',[30] requiring especially compelling grounds to justify interference. As Chapter 11 will discuss, surreptitious methods of obtaining information, such as telephone tapping, are seen potentially as particularly serious breaches of Art 8 at Strasbourg.[31] The collection of personal information by *private* bodies, including, in particular, the press, sometimes using surreptitious means, and its publication, is in reality only one, often highly objectionable, manifestation of data collection and processing.

The simple transposition of Convention obligations upon public authorities onto private agents cannot be assumed in all instances covered by Art 8. But the Court found over 30 years ago[32] that Art 8 obligations may require the adoption of measures even in the sphere of relations between individuals. Strasbourg originally approached the notion of an obligation to intervene between private parties with a caution related to the significance which the margin of appreciation doctrine has had in this context. The essence of the doctrine,[33] as Chapter 2 explained, is that in assessing compliance with

---

25 See further Chapter 2, pp 68–69.

26 *Murray and Others v United Kingdom* (1994) 19 EHRR 193 (photographing of a person at a police station without her consent was found to be a prima facie violation of Art 8).

27 See, e.g., *Leander v Sweden* (1987) 9 EHRR 433; *McVeigh, O'Neill and Evans v United Kingdom* (1981) 45 EHRR 71.

28 *Z v Finland* (1998) 25 EHRR 371.

29 *Lustig-Prean v United Kingdom* (1999) 29 EHRR 548.

30 Feldman, D, 'Information and privacy'; conference paper, Cambridge Centre for Public Law, Freedom of Expression and Freedom of Information, 19–20 February 2000.

31 *Kopp v Switzerland* [1998] HRCD 6 (356), para 72.

32 *X and Y v Netherlands* (1985) 8 EHRR 235.

33 For discussion, see Chapter 2, p 95 *et seq*; see also Fenwick, H, 'The right to protest, the Human Rights Act and the margin of appreciation' (1999) 62(4) MLR 491, pp 497–500.

the Convention, the Court will afford states a certain latitude, principally in deciding what kinds of interferences with Convention rights are necessary. Three principal factors influence Strasbourg in conceding a particularly wide margin of appreciation: first, where a complainant seeks to lay a positive obligation on the state; second, where the harm complained of flows from the action of a private party, rather than the state itself, so that the so-called 'horizontal effect' of the Convention is in issue; third, where there is a potential conflict with another Convention right. Clearly, these factors may arise independently of each other. Or they may, as in the context under discussion, arise contiguously, thereby demanding that an especially wide margin should be allowed. In a number of the earlier private life decisions all three were present,[34] which may explain the somewhat unsatisfactory and misleading nature of some of those judgments.

Prior to the decision in *Von Hannover*, discussed below, Strasbourg had been prepared to extend the notion of private space beyond obvious places such as the home; as Harris, O'Boyle and Warbrick put it: 'it is not enough just for the individual to be himself: he must be able to a substantial degree to keep to himself what he is and what he does . . . the idea of private space need not be confined to those areas where the person has some exclusive rights of occupancy'.[35] In this respect, the Strasbourg approach had been developing for some time in a direction that went beyond the pre-HRA UK common law approach. When the case of *Von Hannover v Germany*[36] was decided, making it clear that Art 8 *does* require that there should be a remedy for invasions of privacy by private parties, it was already apparent that this was the course that Strasbourg was preparing to take.[37] A significant decision pre-dating *Von Hannover*, and arguably highly indicative of the Court's eventual stance in that case, was *Peck v United Kingdom*.[38] *Peck* was a case about the obligations of public authorities, but it made it clear that media intrusion into privacy can lead to a breach of Art 8. The applicant had been captured on council CCTV cameras, wandering through the street carrying a knife, immediately after he had attempted to commit suicide by cutting his wrists. This footage was passed by the local authority on to a news broadcast and a popular television programme, *Crime Beat*, both of which showed extracts from the CCTV footage, from which the applicant was recognisable, to an audience of hundreds of thousands.

The Court said that the relevant moment was viewed to an extent that far exceeded any exposure to a passer-by or to security observation and to a degree surpassing that which the applicant could possibly have foreseen. Therefore the Court found that the disclosure by the council of the relevant footage constituted a serious interference with the applicant's right to respect for his private life.[39] In terms of the proportionality of the interference, the Court accepted that the state has a strong interest in detecting and preventing crime and that the CCTV system plays an important role in furthering that interest. But the Court noted that the council had other options available to it to allow it

---

34   All three were present in: *Winer v UK* (1986) 48 DR 154; *Spencer (Earl) v UK* (1998) 25 EHRR CD 105 and *N v Portugal* Appl No 20683/92, 20 February 1995; however, the third was influential only in *Winer*.
35   Harris, O'Boyle and Warbrick, *op cit*, fn 1, p 309.
36   (2005) 40 EHRR 1; [2004] EMLR 21 – for a summary and comment, see (2004) 5 EHRLR p 593.
37   See further: *Stjerna v Finland*, Series A no 299-B, p 61, judgment of 25 November 1994, para 38; *Verliere v Switzerland* (dec), Appl No 41953/98, ECHR 2001-VII; (1999) *Barclay v UK* Appl No 35712/97.
38   (2003) 36 EHRR 41. For comment, see Welch, J (2003) EHRLR (Privacy Special) 141.
39   At paras 62 and 63.

to achieve the same objectives. It could have identified the applicant through inquiries with the police and thereby obtained his consent prior to disclosure. Alternatively, the council could have masked the relevant images itself, thereby concealing his identity. It was concluded that the disclosure constituted a disproportionate interference with his private life and therefore had created a violation of Art 8 of the Convention. The Court also found – as discussed further below – that the applicant had no effective remedy in relation to the violation of his right to respect for his private life. Therefore the Court also found a breach of Article 13.

Von Hannover v Germany[40] finally made it clear that had the filming of Peck been undertaken by a private media body which had then published the images, a breach of Art 8 would have arisen if Peck had been unable to obtain a domestic remedy. *Von Hannover* made it clear that Art 8 rights are applicable in the private sphere and there is a positive obligation on the state to provide a remedy in national law for privacy-invasion by private media bodies. The case represented the culmination of a long legal fight by Princess Caroline of Monaco in the German courts to stop pictures of herself and her children, obtained by paparazzi without consent, appearing in various newspapers and magazines across Europe. The pictures were of the princess engaged in various everyday acts: shopping, horse-riding, at a beach club, or a restaurant. The German courts had afforded her a privacy remedy in relation to the more intrusive photographs she had complained of. The approach taken was that one may still be entitled to respect for privacy in semi-public places if, as the German Supreme court put it, it is clear by reference to 'objective criteria' that one wishes to 'left alone' so that one can, 'relying on the fact of seclusion, act in a way that [one] would not have done . . . in public'.[41] The Strasbourg Court found, unanimously, that the failure of the German courts to provide her with a remedy in relation to a number of the unconsented-to paparazzi pictures amounted to a breach of Art 8:

> The Court reiterates that although the object of Art 8 is essentially that of protecting the individual against arbitrary interference by the public authorities, [but] there may be positive obligations inherent in an effective respect for private or family life. These obligations may involve the adoption of measures designed to secure respect for private life even in the sphere of the relations of individuals between themselves.[42]

The Court found in relation to the specific facts of the case:

> In the present case there is no doubt that the publication by various German magazines of photos of the applicant in her daily life either on her own or with other people falls within the scope of her private life.[43]

This finding suggests that the Court equated the idea of 'daily life' with that of 'private life'. This was made clear in the following passage: 'the photos of the applicant in the

---

40 (2005) 40 EHRR 1.
41 BGH, 19 December 1995 BGHZ 131, pp 322–46.
42 *Op cit* at para 57.
43 *Ibid*, at para 53.

various German magazines show her in scenes from her daily life, thus engaged in activities of a purely private nature such as practising sport, out walking, leaving a restaurant or on holiday.[44] These findings are also discussed below.[45]

In other words, although the photographs were taken in places that could be viewed as 'public' in the sense of open or semi-open to the public, the activities captured on film acquired a private quality since they self-evidently related to everyday life activities with no 'public life' dimension. The princess was obviously not acting in her public capacity at the times in question – as when taking part in a ceremonious occasion. She was not engaging in activity of a more borderline private/public nature such as, for example, visiting war graves or paying homage to local monuments or dignitaries while visiting a city informally. The Court stated that it had previously 'had regard to whether the photographs related to private or public matters'. It had also found that there is 'a zone of interaction of a person with others, even in a public context, which may fall within the scope of 'private life'.[46] These findings could be taken to suggest that the *place* in which activities occur is of secondary importance to the *nature* of the activities. In other words, while activities occurring in obviously private places such as the home are normally – not always – to be viewed as private activities by virtue of that fact, the converse is not the case.

It would not appear to comport readily with the values Art 8 is seeking to protect to impose an obligation on celebrities to confine activities such as dining to private places in order to avoid paparazzi attention. This may be inferred from the finding at Strasbourg that Art 8 is 'primarily intended to ensure the development, without outside interference, of the personality of each individual in his relations with other human beings'.[47] The question of affording a remedy now turns on a changing cultural understanding of privacy and not on a simplistic distinction between places, based on physicality. Persons in the princess's position will constantly attract attention purely by virtue of their position, so there are strong reasons for differentiating between the positions of celebrities and non-celebrities under Art 8 in order to recognise the risk to which the one is exposed while the other is not. In common parlance, being photographed and followed while engaging in daily life activities is an invasion of privacy. So is being photographed when engaging in an activity of great personal significance in public. It is not evident, it is argued, that the unwelcome feelings generated in each instance – of outrage, humiliation, resentment of intrusion and so on – are conceptually distinct from each other.

The trend in the Strasbourg jurisprudence has been incrementally to discard the simplistic public/private space dichotomy in favour of focusing on the public/private nature of activities, and that is still, broadly speaking, the case in the post-*Von Hannover* decisions discussed below.[48] If the activity is one that could readily occur in a public or a private place, and it is one which is self-evidently within the daily life sphere as opposed to the formal one, the case for Art 8 engagement that the Court clearly accepted

44   *Ibid*, para 61.
45   See p 735.
46   *Op cit* at para 50. The findings referred to are from the previous decisions in *PG and JH v United Kingdom*, Appl No 44787/98, judgment of 4 September 2001, at para 56, and *Peck v United Kingdom* (2003) 36 EHRR 41, at para 57.
47   *Botta v Italy* (1998) 26 EHRR 241, at para 33.
48   See p 735 *et seq*.

in *Von Hannover* is a strong one. To fail to recognise this is to fail to understand the harm caused to personal everyday life choices if they must be made under threat of surveillance. The Court took account of the reality of celebrity life in which constant surveillance by paparazzi amounts to harassment and even persecution:

> [The princess] alleged that as soon as she left her house she was constantly hounded by paparazzi who followed her every daily movement, be it crossing the road, fetching her children from school, doing her shopping, out walking, practising sport or going on holiday . . . The context in which these photos were taken – without the applicant's knowledge or consent – and the harassment endured by many public figures in their daily lives *cannot be fully disregarded.*[49]

But the concluding words of this statement make it clear that the Court is *not* basing its judgment mainly on the element of harassment that was present, although that element was taken into account. The judgment makes it clear that every-day activities of a personal nature can find Art 8 protection from press intrusion regardless of the place in which they occur and without the need to demonstrate that an especially intimate act was occurring. It was indicated in *Sciacca v Italy*[50] that there is no need for press harassment in order to bring reporting of daily life details within the scope of Art 8; the Strasbourg Court applied *Von Hannover* to a case that was not one of press harassment, and cited the jurisprudence of *Von Hannover* in general terms.[51]

This approach adopts quite an expansive understanding of the notion of 'private life' that has not been fully adopted domestically, as discussed below. However, the Strasbourg Court and the domestic courts, discussed in section 5 below, have developed a means of balancing Arts 8 and 10 against each other which, it will be argued, has led to an undermining of that expansive approach in relation to celebrities since it has recently been found, contrary to this first *Von Hannover* decision, that they have a reduced expectation of privacy.[52] Section 5 references the above jurisprudence but focuses especially on the more recent Strasbourg jurisprudence that has influenced recent developments in the tort of misuse of private information.

3 Broadcasting regulation and press self-regulation

Introduction

Successive governments have considered that the press should regulate itself as regards protection of privacy rather than seeking to impose reliance on a statute-based regulatory model – the Ofcom model. Self-discipline has been preferred to such a model in order to preserve press freedom. In contrast, as Chapter 7 indicated, broadcasting privacy regulation has a statutory basis and the broadcast regulator, Ofcom, is government-appointed.

---

49 *Von Hannover v Germany* (2005) 40 EHRR 1 at para 44, para 68 (emphasis added).
50 (2006) 43 EHRR 20, at paras 27 and 29 of the judgment.
51 It should be noted however that the facts of *Sciacca* differed from those of *Von Hannover* in a number of respects and the breach of Art 8 was found on the basis that the interference was not in accordance with the law.
52 See p 727 *et seq* below.

The model used for broadcasting diverges in a number of respects from the previous and current press self-regulatory schemes.

Certain especially sensitive information is covered by these regulatory models, but is also the subject of specific reporting restrictions, discussed in section 4 below. In some instances, these were adopted once it was clear that self-regulation could not be trusted to ensure that some newspapers would behave responsibly.[53] The media are also subject to the DPA 1998 in respect of their processing of personal information, although, as explained below, the Act does not provide a full protection against intrusion on privacy by the media.

As discussed below, the Press Complaints Commission (PCC), replaced by a similar regime under the Independent Press Standards Organisation (IPSO) in 2014, and Ofcom (previously the Broadcasting Standards Commission (BSC)) have powers to adjudicate upon violation of their respective privacy codes. Their adjudications will be published by offending newspapers or broadcasters; IPSO and Ofcom can also fine offenders; this arguably constitutes some degree of 'respect' for private life.[54] The requirement to broadcast Ofcom adjudications is statutory in the case of the independent broadcasters; it arises under its agreement in the case of the BBC. Thus the Ofcom regime, which has powerful sanctions at its command, as detailed further in Chapter 7,[55] tends to deter broadcasters from breaching Art 8, although it does not provide an effective remedy for breaches of Art 8 since it cannot provide compensation to victims of broadcast privacy violation. But the press has been subject to no similar constraints under the PCC; it remains to be seen, as discussed below, whether self-regulation by IPSO will lead to further restraint on press invasion of privacy.

When the European Commission on Human Rights considered the PCC in *Spencer (Earl) v UK*,[56] it made no suggestion that its activities could satisfy the requirement of respect for private life. Rather, it pointedly remarked: 'the PCC has no legal power to prevent publication of material, to enforce its rulings or to grant any legal remedy against the newspaper in favour of the victim'. Thus, it was reasonably clear that reliance on the PCC alone was inconsistent with the Convention principle that rights should be 'practical and effective', not 'theoretical or illusory'.[57] *Peck v UK*[58] made it clear that media self-regulation cannot be considered an adequate way of protecting the guarantees under Art 8. In relation to the relevant regulation of the broadcast media, which are subject to a much tougher regulatory regime on privacy matters than the press, the Court found, as regards the provision of a remedy for breach of Art 8:

> The Court finds that the lack of legal power of the Commissions to award damages to the applicant means that those bodies could not provide an effective remedy to

---

53   The law regarding the anonymity of rape complaints was prompted by public outrage in 1986 after the *Sun* published a picture of a rape victim without her consent in the 'Ealing vicarage' rape case taken as she was leaving church. The Press Council adjudication one year later censured the *Sun* for its unwarranted invasion of privacy: Press Council 'The Press and the People' 34th Annual Report, 1987, p 241.
54   See further Wright, *op cit*, fn 1, pp 137–38.
55   See p 439 *et seq*.
56   (1998) 25 EHRR CD 105.
57   *Airey v Ireland* (1979) 2 EHRR 305, p 314.
58   (2003) 36 EHRR 41.

him. It notes that the ITC's power to impose a fine on the relevant television company does not amount to an award of damages to the applicant.[59]

Thus, *a fortiori*, the PCC and now IPSO systems cannot be viewed as providing an effective remedy in ECHR terms. The Ofcom regime, although it is more effective, does not appear to satisfy the demands of Art 8 either: no damages for the complainant are available and the sanctions only operate post-broadcast. This question is considered further below. So it is apparent that self-regulation of the press is not sufficient to protect privacy under the ECHR, but nor is broadcast regulation, although it is more effective. Thus there is an obvious tension between press self-regulation, broadcasting regulation and the demands of Art 8 of the Convention, introduced into UK law by the HRA.

Further protection for privacy via civil liability, reflecting the demands of the HRA, has been relied on to obtain an effective remedy in ECHR terms, as discussed in section 5.[60] The self-regulatory regime for the press described below, therefore, has to an extent become increasingly marginalised by actions relying on common law privacy liability under the impetus of the HRA. The broadcasting regime is also influenced by the HRA, but less radically.

Press self-regulation

The Press Council

The Press Council was created in 1953 with a view to allowing the press to regulate itself. It issued guidelines on privacy and adjudicated on complaints. It could censure a newspaper and require its adjudication to be published. In practice, however, a number of deficiencies became apparent: the Council did not issue clear enough guidelines, its decisions were seen as inconsistent and in any event ineffective: it had no power to fine or to award an injunction.[61] Moreover, it was seen as too lenient towards the press; it would not interfere if the disclosure in question could be said to be in the public interest, and what was meant by the public interest was uncertain. These problems led eventually to the formation of the Committee on Privacy and Related Matters chaired by Sir David Calcutt (hereafter 'Calcutt 1') in 1990[62] which considered a number of measures, some relevant to actual publication and some to the means of gathering information. The Committee decided that improved self-regulation should be given one final chance and recommended the creation of the Press Complaints Commission, which was set up in 1991 to police a code of practice for the press.

The Press Complaints Commission

The Press Complaints Commission agreed a code of practice in 1990, which the newspapers accepted. The PCC Code was given added status in 2000 since it, and the Ofcom Broadcasting Code discussed below, are recognised in s 12(4)(b) of the HRA and in s

---

59 *Op cit* at para 109.
60 See p 719 *et seq* below.
61 See further Levy, HP, The *Press Council History, Procedure and Cases*, 1967, Macmillan.
62 'Report of the Committee on Privacy and Related Matters', Cm 1102, 1990 (Calcutt Report); for comment see Munro, C, 'Press freedom – how the beast was tamed' (1991) 54 MLR 104.

32(3)of the DPA.[63] Section 12(4)(b) requires that when a court is considering a grant of relief that could affect the exercise of Art 10 rights it should, *inter alia*, have regard to 'any relevant privacy code'. In this sense the HRA affords the code (the PCC Code now policed by IPSO) statutory recognition. The Commission could, until it was disbanded in 2014, receive and pronounce on complaints of violation of the code and could demand an apology for inaccuracy, or that there should be an opportunity for reply.[64]

After self-regulation by the Press Complaints Commission in accordance with the revised code of practice had been in place for a year, Sir David Calcutt (hereafter 'Calcutt 2') reviewed its success[65] and determined that the Press Complaints Commission 'does not hold the balance fairly between the press and the individual . . . it is in essence a body set up by the industry, dominated by the industry'. Similar findings as to the PCC were made by the Leveson Report.[66] The Leveson Inquiry, set up in 2011, was prompted by public revulsion about the hacking of the mobile phone of a murdered teenager, Milly Dowler. The PCC's response to this scandal was entirely defective. In a report, now withdrawn, it repeatedly excused the conduct of the *News of the World*.[67] After the *Guardian* raised allegations (subsequently confirmed) of phone hacking by the *News of the World*, including allegations that the paper had misled the PCC, the PCC were quick to dismiss such suggestions and were critical of the 'dramatic billing' of the *Guardian* articles.[68]

The Leveson report focused on 'the culture, practices and ethics of the press' in the context of the latter's relationship with the public, the police and politicians. In particular it considered press regulation under the PCC, finding it deficient in various respects. The Leveson Inquiry produced proposals for a regulatory solution to the problem of press invasion of privacy, intended to replace the system under the Press Complaints Commission.[69] Leveson did not propose that legislation should establish a body to regulate the press, finding that it should be up to the press to come forward with their own body to meet the criteria laid down.[70] But in order to police press self-regulation more effectively, Leveson LJ proposed in his report that the new press self-regulator should receive official recognition in the form of the creation of a press recognition panel.[71]

63 The Secretary of State has power to designate the Code by order for the purposes of the sub-section, under s 32(3)(b).

64 In 2013 the PCC issued rulings, or brokered agreed resolutions, in respect of 2050 cases; 43.5% of complaints related to privacy issues (cll 3–9 & 11); see 'PCC 2013 Complaint Statistics' (http://www.pcc.org.uk).

65 'Review of Press Self-regulation', Cm 2135, Dept National Heritage, Jan 1993.

66 Note 70 below.

67 9 November 2009 (on 6 July 2011 the PCC withdrew this report). See e.g., 'Did the PCC fail when it came to phone hacking?' Media Standards Trust, December 2011; see at http://mediastandardstrust.org/.

68 At paras 13.2–13.5 of the withdrawn 2009 report (see e.g., Oliver, L, 'PCC finds no evidence of further phone hacking at News Group,' 9 November 2009; https://www.journalism.co.uk/).

69 Leveson Enquiry Draft Criteria for a Regulatory Solution 1. (a) – (d) 12 June 2011; see at www.leveson-inquiry.org.uk.

70 Lord Justice Leveson, *An Inquiry into the Culture, Practices and Ethics of the Press: Report*, HC 780, 2012, Vol 4, Pt K, Ch 7, para 4.1.

71 *Ibid*, para 6.23.

As a result of the Leveson Report the Press Recognition Panel was created.[72] The Panel, set up by the Royal Charter on Self-regulation of the Press, differs in the scope of its powers from a statutory body, such as Ofcom, which has extensive legal powers, for example, to withdraw broadcasting licenses; the recognition body has no such special legal powers, although it does have the power to recognise an independent press regulator as an 'approved regulator' for the purpose of ss 34(2),40(2) Crime and Courts Act 2013, which radically alters the nature of remedies available against publishers of news-related material in various court proceedings (s 34(1),s 40(1)); the remedies and costs regime under the Act is discussed further below.[73]

The recognition criteria that provide the basis for approval of the regulator follow the Leveson proposals. Schedule 3 of the Royal Charter on Self-regulation of the Press 2013 sets out the substantive requirements, which include independent appointment of the board, and chair, by an appointment panel with no more than one member who is a current serving editor. The appointment of the board of the self-regulatory body should be carried out in accordance with various criteria that are designed to ensure the board's independence and industry-relevant expertise (Sched 3 para 5):

a) be nominated by a process which is fair and open; b) comprise a majority of people who are independent of the press; c) include a sufficient number of people with experience of the industry (throughout the United Kingdom) who may include former editors and senior or academic journalists; d) not include any serving editor . . . .

The code adopted, while remaining the responsibility of the regulator, must meet various criteria (Sched 3, para 8):

The Code must take into account. . .the rights of individuals. Specifically, it must cover standards of:

a) conduct, especially in relation to the treatment of other people in the process of obtaining material;
b) appropriate respect for privacy where there is no sufficient public interest justification for breach . . . .

The charter emphasises that the self-regulatory body should provide guidance on the interpretation of the public interest that would justify what would otherwise amount to a breach of the code.

In response to Leveson, the PCC was disbanded in 2014, but sections of the press established the Independent Press Standards Organisation (IPSO), which is currently hearing privacy complaints. But IPSO does not satisfy the Leveson principles, and will not apply for recognition by the Press Recognition Panel, since it considers that the panel oversight represents an unacceptable encroachment on press freedom. The Independent Monitor of the Press (IMPRESS) has also been established, but without general acceptance from the press, and indeed as in effect a Leveson-compliant potential rival to IPSO. In contrast to IPSO, IMPRESS is clearly an attempt at self-regulation that

72 See at http://pressrecognitionpanel.org.uk/.
73 See pp 776–77.

meets the Leveson principles; however, at present it lacks the support of any publishers, who have broadly rejected it in favour of IPSO.[74] IMPRESS has applied to the Press Recognition Panel to become an approved regulator.

IPSO closely resembles the PCC; it has largely the same composition, relies on the PCC Code, and retains the support of publishers who were previously members of the PCC, although it has greater power to impose sanctions for breaches of the code (see below). As discussed below, it is clear that the model of self-regulation under IPSO fails to meet the recognition criteria in the charter and the Leveson proposals, and it does not accept the validity of the Royal Charter or the Press Recognition Panel. Thus in so far as the Leveson Inquiry revealed that gross invasions of privacy by the press were occurring, including phone-hacking, its attempt to curb such invasions in future has so far failed. Leveson appears to represent yet another failed attempt to curb the excesses of the British press. However, although the press in general obviously prefer IPSO's self-regulation, they may find themselves faced with enhanced awards of compensation and costs in privacy cases if IMPRESS becomes an approved regulator in 2016, as seems probable. Thus, pressure may be placed on the press to sign up to IMPRESS, something to which most newspapers are strongly opposed. Failure to join an approved regulator is expected to have, from 2016 onwards, potentially serious financial implications for the press due to the enhanced remedies and awards of costs available under the Crime and Courts Act 2013, discussed below.

IPSO Code Provisions

Clause 3(i) of the PCC Code, now being policed by IPSO, incorporates part of the wording of Art 8(1) ECHR into the code; it provides: 'Everyone is entitled to respect for his or her private or family life, home, health and correspondence', and that publications intruding into private life without consent must be justified. When cl 3 was amended in 2004 it added 'respect for his or her . . . correspondence, including digital communications'. The code makes special mention of hospitals and similar institutions in cl 8 and requires that the press must identify themselves and obtain permission before entering non-public areas of such institutions. Intrusion into grief and shock must be done with sympathy and discretion under cl 5.

Children receive special protection under cl 6: they must not be interviewed or photographed on subjects involving the welfare of the child or any other child in the absence of or without the consent of a parent or other adult who is responsible for the children. Children must not be approached or photographed at school without the permission of the school authorities.[75] In 1999, Tony Blair complained to the PCC regarding a news story about his daughter, Kathryn.[76] The complaint was upheld. It was in fact the first complaint to be made under cl 6 regarding the privacy of the children of public figures at school. The PCC said: 'if every story about the PM's children which relates to their

---

74 The basis upon which the Press Recognition Panel will determine whether IMPRESS meets the recognition criteria is as yet unclear. See for discussion e.g., Wragg, P 'The legitimacy of Press Regulation' [2015] PL 290.

75 See e.g., Press Complaints Report (1999). Complaint upheld: 17 July 1999.

76 *Ibid.*

education is to be justified on the basis that he has made statements about education, then the Code provides no protection for his children or others in a similar position.' But the PCC also said that the press should be free to report on matters relating to children of public figures if such stories revealed hypocrisy or had an impact on policy. It said further that the child should only be identified if that child alone had to be the centre of the story.

IPSO has also recently upheld complaints concerning children. In *A woman v Chester*,[77] a newspaper published a court report about the complainant's partner's conviction for charges relating to an incident in which the child's safety had been placed at risk. The article included details from which the child could be identified, in particular the name of the complainant's partner, his partial address, and his relationship to the child concerned.[78] These details were contrary to a reporting restriction imposed by the court that was intended to shield the child from publicity (see below). IPSO found that while newspapers had a right to report matters heard in open court, the existence of a reporting restriction must be taken into account. It found 'that the complainant's child had a reasonable expectation that this material – which related to a distressing incident that raised significant safety concerns – would not be published to the wider public'.[79] IPSO recently upheld a complaint under cl 3 in relation to pixelated photos of children which were nevertheless identifiable in the community in which the children's families were resident.[80]

However, IPSO, like the PCC, has faced criticism for failing to have a role in relation to flagrant breaches of cl 3(i) in relation to children.[81] In July 2014, Conservative MP Dr Sarah Wollaston complained to the PCC about the publication of an article by the *Sun* newspaper concerning her son.[82] The story, which featured on the front page, described the child, who has a serious medical condition, as having a mark of the 'devil' on his torso. IPSO, which took over the complaint from the PCC, also failed to act, because the paper arrived at a private settlement with Dr Wollaston, who subsequently withdrew her complaint. As the campaign group Hacked Off observed at the time, this result is problematic if IPSO is to act to set press standards.[83] IPSO did publish a resolution statement on its website, but this omitted reference to the code and lauded the private settlement; furthermore, while the *Sun* did publish an apology it was not on the front page, was short and lacked genuine contrition (describing the paper as 'proud of our record of standing up for children').

Clause 3(ii) of the IPSO Code provides that it is 'unacceptable to take photographs of individuals in private places without their consent'. 'Private places' are stated to be public or private ones 'where there is a reasonable expectation of privacy'. The taking of photographs in private places, persistent phoning, questioning, photographing or pursuit of individuals after being asked to desist, or failing to leave private property after

---

77   (ISPO 01431–14) 02/01/2015.
78   *Ibid*, paras 2 and 3.
79   *Ibid*, para 8.
80   *A woman v Lancashire Evening Post* (IPSO, 00256–15), 7 April 2015.
81   See 'IPSO falls at first hurdle' HackedOff, 23 March 2015; see at https://ipsowatch.com.
82   *Ibid*.
83   *Ibid*.

being asked to do so (cl 4(ii)), harassment (cl 4(i)), and the use of listening devices or phone interception (cl 10), are also all proscribed.

IPSO has largely continued the PCC's lenient approach to the publication of photographs. An example is provided by the decision of *Dalton v The Times Literary Supplement*[84] in which photos of the complainant's daughter receiving her GCSE results, which had been published in a national newspaper (with consent) at the time, had been stored and reused two years later without consent in an article concerning sexism. IPSO found that consent for republication of photographs taken in a public place was unnecessary and that only where republication would gratuitously embarrass or humiliate an individual could the republication of such photos constitute a breach of cl 3.[85]

Further provisions of the code reflect certain of the statutory reporting restrictions mentioned below, but go further than they do. Under cl 7, the press must not, even where the law does not prohibit it, identify children under 16 who are involved in cases concerning sexual offences, whether as victims or witnesses. Equally, cl 11 provides that the press must not identify victims of sexual assault unless they are free to do so by law and there is 'adequate justification'.

But, very importantly, all the clauses of the code mentioned here that relate to intrusion into private life, except cls 5 and 11, are subject to exceptions in the public interest; this is defined non-exhaustively as including 'detecting or exposing crime or serious impropriety' (previously 'serious anti-social conduct'), 'protecting public health or safety or preventing the public being misled by some statement or action of an individual or organisation'. The code also states that 'There is a public interest in freedom of expression itself.' The code requires that 'Whenever the public interest is invoked, the Regulator will require editors to demonstrate fully how the public interest was served.' So obviously it is IPSO's interpretation of the 'public interest' in policing the code that is crucial, since a range of invasions of privacy by the press can occur without breaching the code if that somewhat imprecise test is deemed to be satisfied.

A very significant decision concerning the public interest elements of the code concerned a 'sting' by journalist Alex Wickham on Conservative MP and then Minister for Civil Society, Brooks Newmark.[86] The sting involved setting up a fake Twitter account of a female Conservative party activist, which proceeded to tweet compliments to various Conservative MPs, including Mr Newmark.[87] Mr Newmark responded to these tweets and engaged in personal contact with the fake account. Following an exchange of several pictures using WhatsApp the journalist suggested that they 'take it to the next level' after which the journalist sent Mr Newmark an explicit picture of a woman and, in return, Mr Newmark sent the journalist an explicit picture of himself.[88] IPSO agreed that the paper had provided evidence that it had complied with cl 10, since there was credible information to suggest that a number of women had been approached on social media by members of Parliament, including Mr Newmark, based on information from

---

84   (IPSO 01390–14).
85   *Ibid*, para 6.
86   *Issues arising from an article in the Sunday Mirror on 28 September 2014* (IPSO Ruling).
87   *Ibid*, para 1.
88   *Ibid*, para 4.

a confidential source.[89] IPSO considered the separate question of whether publication was in the public interest. IPSO found that:

> a Government Minister who had made public his commitment to promoting a positive role for women in politics and was subject to a duty to uphold the highest standards in public life had engaged in an exchange of messages of a sexual nature with a woman he believed to be a junior party activist. IPSO is satisfied that both the investigation and publication were in the public interest.[90]

This significance of this decision is attested to by the fact that, very unusually, IPSO proceeded *without* a complaint – a decision that was unsuccessfully challenged by the *Mirror*.[91] The infringement of Mr Newmark's privacy was serious but the public interest arguments were strong (if the *Sunday Mirror*'s account is accepted) given that the incident had some relation to an MP's public life. The result of this decision is generally accepted as a reasonable interpretation of the concept of 'public interest'.

Interpretation of the privacy provisions of the Code

It remains to be seen, after it has been in operation for a significant period, whether IPSO will be as generous towards the press in its interpretations of the code as was the PCC. The PCC's interpretation of the very significant privacy clause, cl 3, suggested that the non-consensual publication of specific identifying personal information, including addresses, was not necessarily a breach of the code unless the person in question might thereby be put at risk from stalkers,[92] or if such a person was 'potentially vulnerable'.[93] Clause 3, covering unconsented-to photographs refers to places where there is a 'reasonable expectation of privacy', so the interpretation of that term is clearly a significant matter. Since IPSO is probably a public authority under s 6 HRA,[94] it is suggested that it should adopt the post-*Von Hannover* Strasbourg interpretation of a 'reasonable expectation of privacy', thus extending it well beyond obviously private places or places accessible to the public, but semiprivate, such as restaurants. *Von Hannover*, as discussed above,[95] obviously takes an approach that renders privacy no longer dependent on location. As argued above, public/private distinctions based on location are too simplistic, so the reasonable expectation of privacy should not depend on whether the photographs were taken in a public place.[96]

The PCC appeared to accept a fairly expansive interpretation of a 'reasonable expectation of privacy', but not one that was clearly in full harmony with *Von Hannover* as

---

89 *Ibid*, para 15.
90 *Ibid*, para 36.
91 *Ibid*, para 6.
92 Complaint by a well-known entertainer, complaint dated 16 July 2000.
93 Complaint of Mrs Renate John, adjudication, 2000.
94 See Chapter 4, p 199 *et seq* and p 715, below.
95 See pp 697–99.
96 The code of practice defines 'private places [as] public or private property where there is a reasonable expectation of privacy'.

it was not made fully clear that people have such an expectation in the street.[97] It has also found that publication of pictures of children in crowds on public occasions, such as sporting events, do not amount to breaches of the code.[98] As indicated, IPSO's interpretation of the public interest test in the code is also of crucial significance. In making a determination, IPSO will take into account – as did the PCC – the extent to which the material is already in the public domain, and the specific issues of public interest that are raised.[99]

Sanctions

The press regulator's board adjudicates upon complaints received, making a public finding as to whether the code was violated, and requesting newspapers to publish its adjudication – a request invariably complied with, to date. The code preamble states that any publication criticised by the regulator must publish the adjudication 'in full and with due prominence'. Editors and publishers are required by the preamble to ensure that the code is observed. The terms of the code are incorporated into the conditions of employment of many members of the staff of newspapers, although not all. No fund has been set up in order to compensate members of the public whose privacy has been invaded.

A significant difference between the PCC and IPSO is that the regulator's board has the power to award fines, although it still cannot award compensatory damages nor prevent publication of offending items. The current regulator's board has the power to fine a publisher up to 1% of its UK annual turnover (up to £1,000,000), but only following a standards investigation that establishes that the editor had committed systemic breaches of the Editors' Code.[100]

Conclusions

It is suggested that various fundamental problems are still apparent in respect of protecting privacy via IPSO's self-regulation of the press. IPSO's policing of the code is still likely to err on the side of generosity towards the newspapers.[101] Despite the code, or due to its press-friendly interpretation by the PCC, editors have previously been prepared to

---

97 Adjudication on 28 April 2006, as regards Mark Kisby. The article was a feature on millionaire 'lottery lout' Michael Carroll and included a picture of him withdrawing £15,000 from his local bank. The complainant was the cashier at the branch and was included in the picture. The complaint was upheld because the cashier was in a publicly accessible building; it was not made clear that it would have been upheld if the two were in the street.

98 In an adjudication issued 23 June 2006 as regards such a picture the PCC stated that it would not normally consider that a photograph of a child in a crowd at an FA Cup tie – a public event at which there would be many photographers and television cameras, as well as tens of thousands of people – was intrusive or involved the child's welfare.

99 See PCC, Report No 43 (1998), paras 3.0–3.2.

100 IPSO Financial Sanctions Guidance, para 2.1; IPSO Regulations, para 40 (see at https://www.ipso. co.uk).

101 See *Guardian* article 8 September 2015 '*Ipso denounced as "sham body" controlled by member newspapers'*: 'The Independent Press Standards Organisation is facing renewed attacks from campaigners who have labelled it a "sham body" which is "controlled by the newspapers" it regulates.' See further as to the PCC Tambini, D and Heyward, C, 'Regulating the trade in secrets: policy options', in Tambini and Heyward (2002) *op cit*, fn 1. See also Rozenberg, J, *Privacy and the Press*, 2004, OUP.

publish pictures of individuals in obviously private places (such as holiday villas), often taken with a long-range lens, without consent, even when it is virtually impossible to argue that a public interest in publication exists. The PCC adopted a very press-friendly stance towards paparazzi pictures of well-known figures taken in public, if secluded, places.[102] A pre-*Von Hannover* example of such flouting of the code occurred in the case of *Holden (Amanda) v The Star*.[103] Holden, the star of a sitcom, was holidaying in a private villa in Italy when, without her consent, agency reporters took photographs of her sunbathing topless. One of the photographs was published in the *Star*. She obtained an *ex parte* injunction on grounds of breach of confidence, as interpreted in *Douglas and Others v Hello!*[104] preventing further publication of the photographs. Although the case was clearly covered by cl 3(ii) of the PCC's code of practice, she did not make a complaint, preferring – for obvious reasons – to go straight to the courts to obtain the injunction. She claimed damages in respect of the publication, which did occur.[105] A number of more recent examples are given below in section 5 in which celebrities disregarded the PCC route, and this is likely to continue to occur under IPSO.[106] The *Holden* case indicates that the code alone was not proving a sufficient deterrent to newspapers which, for obvious commercial reasons, were prepared to invade privacy.

As mentioned, IPSO cannot prevent publication of material obtained even in gross breach of the code. Absent radical changes to its powers, which would have to be agreed to by the industry, it is clear that it cannot be regarded as providing an effective remedy under Art 13 ECHR for violations of privacy under Art 8. This does not mean that it has no role now that effective remedies have been developed under the impetus of the HRA. It continues to provide an alternative to using the law for those who cannot or do not wish to incur legal costs. It continues, in conjunction with the National Union of Journalist's Code, to set benchmarking ethical standards for the profession. It also provides a means of appeasing and satisfying complainants, which may be less stressful and more speedy than court action. But taking the right to private life seriously obviously requires that the IPSO Code and its sanctions have a genuine impact in deterring the press from invading privacy except where a genuine public interest arises. However, the damages and costs regime, discussed in Section 7 below, under the Crime and Courts Act 2013, may eventually lead to ensuring greater respect for privacy via a press self-regulatory regime.

Broadcasting and privacy

Introduction

The regime governing broadcasting regulation was described in Chapter 7. In relation to privacy it is (anomalously) much tougher than the one just described under IPSO. It is set up under statute and the broadcast regulator has a number of relatively strong sanctions at its command. Ofcom took over the role of the broadcast regulator under the Communications Act 2003. However, it is still necessary to consider the previous

---

102 See e.g., the Anna Ford decision: *R (Ford) v Press Complaints Commission* [2001] EWHC Admin 683.
103 Unreported; see the *Guardian*, 2 July 2001; (2001) *The Observer*, 15 July.
104 [2001] 2 WLR 992.
105 See *The Observer*, 15 July 2001.
106 See p 735 *et seq* below.

Broadcasting Act 1996, and the fairness and privacy code published under s 107 of that Act, now revised and policed by Ofcom.

The Ofcom privacy regime

The model of regulation adopted is described in Chapter 7 regarding the control of potentially offensive or harmful material in broadcasting. Court sanctions are not provided under the regulatory regime; persons aggrieved by privacy-invading broadcasting can complain to the regulator, Ofcom, which can provide redress, if it finds that the code on privacy that it polices has been breached. Ofcom's remedies do not, however, extend to the provision of injunctions or damages.

Ofcom took over the previous duties of the Broadcasting Standards Commission (BSC)[107] to draw up, revise, and hear complaints under the fairness and privacy code issued under s 107 of the Broadcasting Act 1996. It also took over the powers under s 119 of that Act to force broadcasters to carry apologies and statements of findings following complaints. The meagre case law relating to the interpretation of its predecessors, probably still a reliable guide to the interpretation of the current code,[108] is considered below.

The 2003 Act opened the way for the BBC to be able, for the first time, to be fined by an independent regulator – Ofcom. Section 198 of the 2003 Act gives power to Ofcom to regulate the BBC in so far as that is provided for in the BBC's agreement with the government.[109] In other words, it created the possibility of regulation by Ofcom on privacy matters. The amendments subsequently made in December 2003 to the BBC agreement inserted, for the first time, the requirement to observe the fairness and privacy code drawn up under the Broadcasting Act 1996. Previously, the BBC agreement had no provisions relating to invasion of privacy. Section 198(3) of the 2003 Act allows for the imposition of penalties upon the BBC for breach of provisions in its agreement and charter.[110] The 2007 agreement provides for the imposition by Ofcom upon the BBC of financial penalties for breach of various enforceable requirements,[111] which includes

---

107   Schedule 1, para 14 of the 2003 Act provides:
　　　The following functions of the Broadcasting Standards Commission under Part 5 of the 1996 Act are transferred to OFCOM –
　　　(a) the Commission's function of drawing up and from time to time revising a code of practice under
　　　　　section 107 of that Act (codes of practice relation to fairness and privacy); and
　　　(b) their functions in relation to fairness complaints under that Part.
108   The most recent version of which took effect on 9 May 2016.
109   The BBC's current charter and agreement came into force in 2007 and will expire 31st December 2016; 'Broadcasting: Copy of Royal Charter for the continuance of the British Broadcasting Corporation' Cm 6925, October 2006, Secretary of State for Culture, Media and Sport.
110   Section 198(3) provides:
　　　The BBC must pay OFCOM such penalties in respect of contraventions by the BBC of provision made by or under
　　　(a) this Part, or
　　　(b) the BBC Charter and Agreement, as are imposed by OFCOM in exercise of powers conferred on
　　　　　them by that Charter and Agreement.
111   Clause 94 provides:
　　　1 If OFCOM are satisfied that the Corporation has contravened a relevant enforceable requirement, they may serve on the Corporation a notice requiring it to pay them, within a specified period, a specified penalty.

the fairness code in para 45.[112] Moreover, cl 93 provides that if Ofcom is satisfied that the BBC has breached an enforceable requirement, it may require the BBC to carry a correction or statement of Ofcom's findings upon its adjudication on any complaint.

The independent broadcasters are regulated by Ofcom under the 2003 Act directly. Section 326 provides that they too are bound by the fairness and privacy code; they may be directed by Ofcom to carry statements of findings and corrections;[113] they can be fined for breaches of the code, and, in extreme cases, licences may theoretically be revoked.[114] These provisions are bolstered by s 3(2) of the 2003 Act under which Ofcom has the duty of ensuring the application of standards that provide adequate protection to members of the public and all other persons from what the Act calls 'unwarranted infringements of privacy', balanced of course against freedom of expression. Thus the BBC is now in the same position as the other broadcasters in relation to standards of privacy protection, correcting the anomalous position that existed previously.

Ofcom's privacy code

Ofcom's rules on privacy, taken over from the BSC Code, are part of its current Broadcasting Code, discussed in Chapter 7.[115] Ofcom's Code, like the IPSO Code, goes beyond what the law demands in a number of respects; it is binding in the sense that Ofcom can apply sanctions if it is breached. This code is similar to that of IPSO, but in certain respects, it is more extensive and offers greater guidance on the operation of the overriding public interest test. Under cl 8.1 the creation of an infringement of privacy by making and broadcasting programmes can only occur if 'warranted'. Under the public interest test, an infringement of privacy can be justified (warranted) on a number of grounds. They include: revealing or detecting crime or disreputable behaviour, protecting public health or safety, exposing misleading claims made by individuals or organisations or disclosing significant incompetence in public office (cl 8.1).

The privacy of persons suffering grief or distress must in particular be respected, under cl 8.16, but footage of accidents etc can be broadcast without consent if 'warranted'. Such persons should be approached with sensitivity, and they should not be put under pressure to provide interviews unless this is warranted. Clauses 8.13–8.15 provide that surreptitious filming, the use of hidden microphones etc must be justified by an overriding public interest. Clause 8.1 of Ofcom's Code accords with the approach in *Von Hannover*:[116]

> Legitimate expectations of privacy will vary according to the place and nature of the information, activity or condition in question, the extent to which it is in the public domain (if at all) and whether the individual concerned is already in the

---

2 The amount of the penalty that may be imposed on any occasion under this clause shall not exceed the maximum specified for the time being in subsection 198(5) of the Communications At 2003 [that is, £250,000].

112 By virtue of cl 95(1)(a).
113 Under s 236.
114 Under s 238.
115 See p 444.
116 *Von Hannover v Germany* (2005) 40 EHRR 1.

public eye. There may be circumstances where people can reasonably expect privacy even in a public place. Some activities and conditions may be of such a private nature that filming or recording, even in a public place, could involve an infringement of privacy. People under investigation or in the public eye, and their immediate family and friends, retain the right to a private life, although private behaviour can raise issues of legitimate public interest.

Thus the code impliedly adopts a nuanced approach to public domain issues. But under cl 8.11 filming of people in the news can occur in public places without prior warning. Clause 8.11 does not state that this can occur only if 'warranted'. In other words, it does not, on its face, demand that broadcasters perform a balancing act between Arts 8 and 10 in relation to such filming. In light of *Von Hannover*, and the developing UK privacy jurisprudence discussed below, it is argued that cl 8.11 requires amendment.

Children receive special protection under cl 8.20–8.22. If under 16 they must not be interviewed without the consent of a parent or other adult who is responsible for them. If consent is refused a decision to go ahead must be justified by an overriding public interest. Under cl 2.6 of the ITC Code children could not be interviewed regarding private, family matters. This requirement was not subject to the public interest test. But under cl 8.22 such interviewing can be warranted The code makes special mention of agency operations in cl 8.8 (such as police investigations) and requires that the broadcasters should obtain consent to film unless it is warranted to proceed without consent. Clause 8.8 also covers filming in institutions, such as hospitals, and requires that the broadcasters must obtain consent to transmit material when persons are shown in sensitive situations, such as in psychiatric hospitals, unless exceptions can be made in the public interest. Broadcasters can record phone calls if they identify themselves (cl 8.12); door-stepping can occur on private property if there is an overriding public interest (cl 8.11). Clause 8.10 provides: 'Broadcasters should ensure that the re-use of material, i.e. use of material originally filmed or recorded for one purpose and then used in a programme for another purpose or used in a later or different programme, does not create an unwarranted infringement of privacy.'

The relationship between the ECHR and media regulation

In debates on the Human Rights Bill, a great deal of concern was voiced in Parliament about the possibility, as regards the PCC, that it would be deemed a public authority for the purposes of the HRA. It was thought that it would be subject to judicial review for violation of the Convention in its rulings and therefore in some way in a position to threaten press freedom.[117] Although it appears that it was subject to the Convention,[118] and this appears to be the case as regards IPSO,[119] that route was unlikely to be explored: it would be likely to provide, even if proceedings succeeded, a merely paper remedy. If a finding was made that IPSO had violated the Convention rights, for example by

---

117 See Hansard, HL col 784, 24 November 1997.
118 See *R (on the application of Ford) v PCC* [2002] EMLR 5.
119 See *PCC ex p Stewart-Brady* (1997) 9 Admin LR 274; *R (on the application of Ford) v PCC* [2002] EMLR 5.

finding that someone's privacy had not been invaded when, in the court's view on judicial review, Art 8 required a contrary conclusion,[120] the very most that the court could do would be to quash the finding of IPSO by a quashing order (formerly *certiorari*) and require it to reconsider the case by a mandatory order (formerly *mandamus*). Damages could conceivably be awarded against it also under s 8 HRA, but that is very unlikely.

Clearly, the statutory powers affecting Ofcom must all be interpreted compatibly with the Convention under s 3 HRA. Thus, in so far as the concept of privacy at Strasbourg in this context has undergone a change post-*Von Hannover*, the duties placed upon Ofcom under the statute should be interpreted relying on ss 3 and 2 HRA to reflect that change. The Convention rights of course also have a direct impact on Ofcom via s 6 HRA. The BSC and ITC were subject to judicial review,[121] as is Ofcom.[122] As Chapter 7 indicated, it is clear that Ofcom is a functional public authority under s 6 HRA and it is probably a core authority.[123] The duties of Ofcom under s 6 HRA can be viewed as additional and complementary to those it has under the 2003 Act and the Broadcasting Act 1996. If these bodies fail to uphold complaints relating to invasion of privacy, proceedings can be brought against them under s 7(1)(a) HRA. In any such proceedings, a court now has to satisfy s 12(4)(b) HRA, which means that the privacy codes of these bodies are admissible in evidence and can be considered.[124] By this means, Ofcom's Code has acquired, it is suggested, a quasi-legal status. It already has such a status since it was set up under statute, but its status can be viewed as enhanced under s 12 HRA. It may be noted that the BSC Code was taken into account in any event in the pre-HRA ruling in *Broadcasting Standards Commission ex p BBC*.[125]

But the private media bodies – the newspapers and non-public service broadcasters – are not bound by the Convention rights under s 6. So if they invade privacy the aggrieved individual has three options. He or she could use the complaints mechanisms represented by Ofcom or IPSO. If a successful adjudication occurs the individual would not receive damages, but would have the satisfaction of an acknowledgement that a breach had occurred. He or she might be appeased and would not have had to incur the cost, risk and publicity of a court action. Clearly, a court action seeking to uphold privacy runs the risk of drawing attention to the subject-matter of the original complaint. Most members of the public are not in a position to take newspapers/broadcasters to court. So the benefits of these non-court-based methods of obtaining redress for privacy invasion should not be overlooked.

If the complaint was not upheld he or she could seek review of the Ofcom or IPSO decision, relying on Art 8 and s 7(1)(a) HRA, as discussed above. Finally, he or she could bring an action relying on breach of confidence/privacy, possibly coupled with

---

120 Anna Ford, a BBC journalist, applied to the High Court for judicial review of the PCC's decision to reject her claim that the *Daily Mail* breached her right to privacy by publishing pictures of her on holiday with her partner (*R (Ford) v Press Complaints Commission* [2001] EWHC Admin 683). The PCC's decision was vindicated.

121 The bodies they replaced were so subject and this was found to be the case in respect of the BSC: see *R v BCC ex p Owen* [1985] QB 1153; *R v BSC ex p BBC* [2000] 3 WLR 1327; *R v IBA ex p Whitehouse* (1985) *The Times*, 4 April.

122 See the *Pro-Life Alliance* case, discussed Chapter 7, pp 448–52.

123 See Chapter 7, p 447 *et seq*; Chapter 4, p 199 *et seq*.

124 See e.g., *BKM ltd v BBC* [2009] EWHC 3151 [20].

125 [2000] 3 WLR 1327.

action under the DPA 1998. But the position would be different if the broadcast body itself was a public authority for HRA purposes. The BBC as a body with a public service remit, is probably a functional public authority.[126] If this is the case, under s 6 HRA, these bodies are bound to comply with the Convention rights in exercising their public functions. The question then would be whether decisions as to filming are part of that function. Assuming that they are, an effective remedy would potentially be available under s 8 HRA.

But since private broadcasters are not public authorities the only 'remedies' they are subject to are those available through the courts. However, an action brought directly against Ofcom under s 7(1)(a) on grounds of failing to use sanctions in respect of an invasion of privacy in breach of its privacy code could lead to a mandatory order requiring it to use the sanctions it has available, including, ultimately, withdrawal of its licence, against the broadcaster concerned. Nevertheless, that would still not provide an effective remedy for breach of Art 8, following the *Peck* ruling discussed above, since Ofcom cannot award damages to complainants. The effective remedy for breach of Art 8 rights is provided in most circumstances by the action for breach of confidence/privacy discussed below. The Data Protection Act 1998 could also be invoked, as will be discussed, in order to provide such a remedy in certain circumstances against data-processing by broadcasters.

Deference to the regulators

If an aggrieved individual brought an action directly against IPSO, the BBC or against Ofcom in respect of an invasion of privacy, relying on s 7(1)(a) HRA and Art 8, the chances of success would be low. The courts take a markedly deferential approach to reviewing decisions of the regulators, being reluctant to interfere in the exercise of its expert judgment unless Ofcom has made a plain error of law, or abused its discretion. This stance has also been taken in respect of the BBC. In *R v Broadcasting Complaints Commission ex p Granada Television Ltd*,[127] an application for judicial review of the then Commission's finding under a privacy code, Balcombe LJ found:

> [Decisions related to] the concept of an infringement of privacy, are best left to a specialist body, such as the BCC, whose members have experience of broadcasting . . . Unless on no interpretation of the word 'privacy' could the findings of the BCC be justified . . . there is no basis for the grant of judicial review . . . Whether in such a case there is an unwarranted infringement of privacy is a matter of fact and degree and as such for the decision of the BCC with which the court cannot interfere.[128]

126 This seemed to be assumed in the *Pro-Life Alliance* case, as discussed in Chapter 7, pp 448–52. The BBC is a public authority (with certain qualifications) for the purposes of the Freedom of Information Act 2000 (see also *BBC v Sugar (No 2)* [2012] UKSC 4). There is a possible difficulty with this proposition which may need to be addressed by the courts. Arguably, the BBC (and Channel 4) may also, exceptionally, be viewed as both public authorities and victims for HRA purposes. For example, in *BKM v BBC* [2009] EWHC 3151 (Ch) (an application for injunction against the BBC filming in a care home on the basis of the residents' reasonable expectation of privacy) it was found that the BBC 'has its own [Convention] rights' i.e. Art 10 (*ibid*, [17]).
127 [1995] EMLR 163.
128 *Ibid*, at p 167–68.

R v BSC ex p BBC[129] concerned an application by the BBC for judicial review of the BSC's findings that the privacy of a company, in this case Dixon's, had been invaded by secret recording in one of its stores by the BBC. Lord Woolf observed:

> So long as the approach which [the Regulators] adopt is one to which, in their statutory context, the words 'infringement of privacy' are capable of applying then the courts should not interfere. It is only if an approach to 'infringement of privacy' by [them] goes beyond the area of tolerance that the courts can intervene . . . having regard to the role the legislation gives to [them], the answer to the scope of their remit is that it is something for [them] to determine not the courts . . . This is not an area on which the courts are well equipped to adjudicate.[130]

In the post-HRA *Anna Ford* case,[131] which concerned an application for judicial review of the decision of the PCC on a complaint under its own privacy code, the judge found:

> English courts will continue to defer to the views of bodies like the [Press Complaints] Commission even after the HRA came into force. In summary, the type of balancing operation conducted by a specialist body such as the Commission is still regarded as a field of activity to which the courts *should and will* defer. The Commission is a body whose membership and expertise makes it much better equipped than the courts to resolve the difficult exercise of balancing the conflicting rights of Ms Ford and Mr Scott to privacy and of the newspapers to publish.[132]

The decision of the House of Lords in *R (on the application of Pro-Life Alliance) v BBC*,[133] discussed in detail in Chapter 7, gives very strong endorsement to the notion that a high degree of deference should be paid to media regulators and to media bodies due to their special expertise.[134] In that instance the BBC was acting in effect in its regulatory role in deciding whether the film in question offended too greatly against taste and decency to be broadcast in its original form. *Pro-Life* indicates impliedly that the courts do not regard it as their task to decide what the outcome of a privacy complaint should have been. They view their role as merely demanding that they review the decisions of the regulators, or media bodies, affording them a very broad area of discretion, even where the Convention rights are in issue. They take this stance, as Chapter 7 pointed out, partly on the basis that the primary determination as to the requirements of privacy has been entrusted to the regulators by Parliament, not the courts, but perhaps mainly on the ground of institutional competence – on the basis that the courts are not well equipped to adjudicate in this context due to lack of the special expertise possessed by the media bodies in question. It might appear that the HRA should have affected this

129 [2000] 3 WLR 1327, p 1332.
130 *Ibid*, at p 1332.
131 *R (on the application of Ford) v Press Complaints Commission* [2002] EMLR 5.
132 *Ibid*, at paras 28, 29.
133 [2003] 2 WLR 1403.
134 In this case to the BBC Governors, in deciding not to broadcast a PEB submitted to the BBC by the Pro-Life Alliance party. See Chapter 7, pp 437–38.

stance radically since under s 6, the courts must ensure that Convention standards are adhered to. But this was not the stance that was adopted in *Pro-Life*.

It can however be argued that *Pro-Life* concerned a matter that the courts are arguably not well equipped to inquire into – the acceptability to television audiences of disturbing material in election broadcasts. But the courts are, clearly, well equipped to consider the proper means of balancing conflicting legal rights. As discussed below, they have shown themselves readily capable of performing the balancing act between Arts 8 and 10 of the Convention in the context of breach of confidence/privacy claims and of the inherent jurisdiction of the court to protect children.

R (Gaunt) v OFCOM,[135] which concerned the compatibility of Ofcom rules on offence and Art 10, took a stance which differed to an extent from that taken in *Prolife*; the Court of Appeal found that the assessment of whether the Convention right was infringed is 'ultimately one for the court', although the court should give 'due regard' to the judgment of Ofcom as the statutory regulator.[136] That decision was again related to matters of offensiveness in broadcasting, not privacy. But it is argued that if a privacy claim, as opposed to a claim relating to offensive broadcast material, is considered at the highest level under the HRA, the court might be prepared to take a stance that differed from that taken in *Pro-Life*. The degree of deference shown to the media body in that instance might, and should, be repudiated.

In the *Campbell* case discussed below, the House of Lords showed no inclination to defer to the newspaper's expertise in determining how far it had balanced public interest and privacy factors in taking the decision to publish the photos of Naomi Campbell. Instead, the Lords engaged in a rigorous scrutiny of that decision. It is hard to see why the mechanism by which the claimants get into court (breach of confidence or s 7(1)(a) HRA) should affect this stance. It is also difficult to see why greater deference should be paid to a broadcaster as opposed to a newspaper editor. Possibly there is an argument that Ofcom has greater expertise than a media body in this matter, but it would be hard to argue that it would have the experience or authority of a court in dealing with the quintessentially legal problem of the balancing act between Arts 8 and 10 based on proportionality.

4 Selected reporting restrictions

Victims of sexual offences

A number of special restrictions on reporting apply to the victims of certain sexual offences. Under s 4(1)(a) of the Sexual Offences (Amendment) Act 1976, once an allegation of rape was made it was an offence, punishable by a fine, to publish or broadcast the name, address or photograph of the woman or man who was the alleged victim. Once a person was accused of rape, nothing could be published by the media that could identify the woman or man. These restrictions were extended under s 1(1) of the Sexual Offences (Amendment) Act 1992 as amended by s 48 of the Youth Justice and Criminal Evidence Act 1999 and Sched 2. Section 1(1) covers a number of sexual offences as

---

135 [2011] EWCA Civ 692.
136 *Ibid*, [47].

well as rape, and provides: 'where an allegation has been made that an offence to which the Act applies has been committed against a person,[137] no matter relating to that person shall during that person's lifetime be included in any publication'. So it is a specific offence to publish a picture of the alleged victim, or his or her name and address, once an allegation of a rape offence has been made. Once a person has been charged with a rape offence, no material likely to lead members of the public to identify an individual as the complainant in relation to the offence may be published.[138] A publisher whose conduct falls within this offence would have a defence if a victim had given his or her consent to such a disclosure (Sexual Offences (Amendment) Act 1976 s 1(5A)).

The courts have powers to direct restrictions to be removed; this may be done on the narrow ground of encouraging witnesses to come forward,[139] or on the broader ground that a refusal to lift the restrictions 'would impose a substantial and unreasonable restriction upon the reporting of proceedings at the trial and it is in the public interest to remove or relax the restriction'. This clearly allows a judge to undertake a broad balancing act between the privacy rights of the victim – and the policy of encouraging victims to bring cases to trial, given that rapes are notoriously under-prosecuted – and the media interest in reporting on trials, including, specifically the open justice principle.

Selected reporting restrictions relating to children

Juveniles involved in criminal proceedings

Under s 39 of the Children and Young Persons Act (CYPA) 1933, a court (apart from a youth court) could direct that details relating to a child, who was a witness or defendant, including his or her name, should not be reported and that no picture of the child should be broadcast or published. The media could make representations to the judge, arguing that the demands of media freedom outweigh the possibility of harm to the child. In relation to any proceedings in any court the court may make an order under s 39 of the 1933 Act prohibiting publication of particulars calculated to lead to the identification of any child concerned in the proceedings. Section 39 orders are especially problematic for journalists since they frequently provide insufficient guidance as to what can safely be published.[140]

Section 49 of the CYPA, as amended,[141] which relates to youth courts, places restrictions on the identification of children or young persons convicted in the youth court.[142]

---

137 Male rape victims are also covered under the CJPOA 1994, s 142, as are offences of incitement, attempt, conspiracy.
138 Section 4(1)(b).
139 Upon the application of the person accused of rape; the defendant must additionally show that his defence is likely to be substantially prejudiced without such a direction.
140 See *Briffett v DPP; Bradshaw v DPP* [2001] EWHC 841 (Admin) and commentary: Dodd, M 'Children, the press – and a missed opportunity' [2002] 14(1) CFLQ 103–8.
141 As amended by Sched 2 to the Youth Justice and Criminal Evidence Act 1999.
142 Under the Crime Sentences 1997 s 45, which inserted s 49(4)(A) into the 1933 Act. The Youth Justice and Criminal Evidence Act 1999 s 44 creates an earlier starting point for the imposition of anonymity: protection against disclosure of identity for suspects, victims, witnesses now begins at the point of commencement of the criminal investigation. The Anti-Social Behaviour Act 2003 amended the Crime and Disorder Act 1998 s 1 to provide that s 49 does not apply to proceedings for orders under the 2003 Act, but that s 39 does apply.

Section 49 provides for an automatic ban on publishing certain identifying details relating to a juvenile offender, including his or her name and address, although the court can waive the ban. Under the Crime (Sentences) Act 1997, the court can lift reporting restrictions where it considers that a ban would be against the public interest.

The s 39 restrictions were extended under s 44 of the Youth Justice and Criminal Evidence Act 1999, which covers children involved in adult proceedings. The 1933 Act did not cover the period before proceedings begin. The 1999 Act prohibits the publication once a criminal investigation has begun, of any matter relating to a person involved in an offence while he is under 18 which is likely to identify him. Thus, juveniles who are witnesses are also covered. Under s 44(4), the court can dispense with the restrictions if it is satisfied that it is in the public interest to do so. Thus, s 44 brings the restrictions relating to juveniles in adult proceedings into line with those under s 49 relating to youth proceedings, placing the onus on the court to find a good reason for lifting the restriction rather than having to find a good reason for imposing it. The discretion of the court is therefore more narrowly confined.[143] This is clearly an instance in which, as between the demands of press freedom and the interest in the protection of the privacy and reputation of juveniles, the latter interest has prevailed.

The 'ECHR jurisdiction' of the court

Where specific statutory restrictions do not apply, the High Court may nevertheless grant an injunction restraining reporting that might reveal a child's[144] identity or other matters relating to a child as an aspect of its inherent jurisdiction to protect minors.[145] After the decision in *Re X (A Minor) (Wardship: Jurisdiction)*[146] (the Mary Bell case), it can be seen that there was an increasing recourse to the court's asserted power to grant injunctions to restrain the publication of information about its wards or other children. The invention of this jurisdiction was described by Hoffmann LJ in *R v Central Independent Television*[147] in the following terms: 'the courts have, without any statutory or ... other previous authority, assumed a power to create by injunction what is in effect a right of privacy for children'.

After the House of Lords decision in *Re S (A Child)*[148] the term 'inherent jurisdiction' was replaced by the term 'the Convention jurisdiction'. In *Re S* the House of Lords

---

143 See the discussion in *R v Lee* [1993] 1 WLR 103, pp 109–10.
144 It should also be noted that the jurisdiction of the High Court to protect juveniles caught up in the criminal justice system extends to cover vulnerable adults with mental health problems, in *Re A Local Authority* [2003] EWHC 2746 at paras 66 and 86–97.
145 In *Re M and N (Minors) (Wardship: Publication of Information)* [1990] Fam 211 Butler-Sloss LJ found: 'The power of the courts to impose restrictions upon publication for the protection of children is derived from the inherent jurisdiction of the High Court exercising the powers of the Crown as *parens patriae*. It is not restricted to wardship.' She relied on Lord Donaldson of Lymington MR who said in *Re C (A Minor) (Wardship: Medical Treatment) (No 2)* [1990] Fam 39, 46 that wardship 'is the machinery for its exercise' (*Re M and N*, op cit, at 223).
146 [1975] Fam 47.
147 [1994] Fam 192, 204.
148 *Re S (a child)* [2004] UKHL 47; [2005] 1 AC 593. CA decision: [2003] 2 FCR 577; (2003) 147 SJLB 873. See also *Harris v Harris* [2001] 2 FLR 895 in which, while there was no detailed consideration of the balancing exercise between Art 10 (and 11) on the one hand and Art 8 on the other, Munby J

had to adjudicate on an appeal against an order made by Hedley J in the Family Division of the High Court.[149] The appeal raised a short but difficult point: 'can or should the court [under the inherent jurisdiction] restrain the publication of the identity of a defendant and her victim in a murder trial to protect the privacy of her son who is the subject of care proceedings?' The murder victim was S's brother and there was psychiatric evidence to the effect that S, as an already vulnerable child, would suffer greater trauma and be at greater risk of later mental illness if he was subjected to bullying and harassment at school once the identity of his mother became known. The House of Lords determined that it was no longer necessary to show that the inherent jurisdiction applied. Lord Steyn said: 'The foundation of the jurisdiction to restrain publicity in a case such as the present is now *derived from convention rights under the ECHR*' (emphasis added).[150] In other words, the jurisdiction was not the 'vehicle' allowing for the balancing exercise between free expression and privacy to occur – the Convention rights themselves provided the vehicle. Having come to that determination the Lords found that the Art 10 interest in open reporting of criminal trials, since such reporting was of particular significance, outweighed the Art 8 privacy interest of the child. That decision is also discussed in section 5 below, which considers the balancing exercise between Arts 8 and 10 in relation to liability for disclosing personal information under the tort of misuse of private information.

The courts must in general balance the privacy interest of a child against the interest in speech, without giving either presumptive priority.[151] Briefly, the factors of relevance to the privacy interest include the impact of newspaper coverage especially on young or particularly vulnerable children and whether the children were themselves victims of or witnesses to the crimes being tried.[152] Factors of relevance to the speech interest include the nature of the crime, the relevance of reporting upon the child's identity to the coverage of the case and the outcome of the case itself.[153]

5 Liability for disclosing personal information under the tort of misuse of private information

Introduction

This section will set out to demonstrate that far more protection from privacy-invading journalism is available in UK law now than ever before. It is no longer possible for the press to treat privacy merely as a commodity that can be used to sell newspapers without facing the possibility that liability may arise. Protection for personal information is now available under the tort of misuse of private information, developed under the impetus of s 6 HRA and Art 8 ECHR. But along with enhanced protection for privacy, it is necessary to seek to ensure that media freedom is preserved, in the sense that speech of genuine public

---

accepted (at para 384) that the approach adopted by Sedley LJ in *Douglas v Hello!* [2001] QB 967 should be followed in which Art 10 was *not* given presumptive priority.
149 19 February 2003.
150 *Op cit* at para 23.
151 *Re S (a child)* [2004] UKHL 47. See below.
152 *R v Winchester Crown Court ex parte B (A Minor)* [1999] 1 WLR 788.
153 *Ibid*; see also *Z v News Group Newspapers* [2013] EWHC 1371.

interest is not suppressed. Since two Convention rights are involved – Arts 8 and 10 – it is now necessary to find a way of striking a fair balance between them. In order to do so, the extent to which the value of preserving informational autonomy and dignity is at stake in any particular claim for protection of private life must be pinpointed, as must any countervailing free expression value – the issue to which this section now turns in considering how far free speech values are genuinely likely to be at stake in privacy claims.

Free speech theories and privacy

The theory that freedom of speech is necessary for the discovery of truth, discussed in the introduction to Part II,[154] has been a strong influence in US jurisprudence[155] but not historically at Strasbourg[156] or in the UK courts.[157] It has been persuasively argued that this rationale has little application to the paradigm privacy case, in which intimate facts about an individual are revealed. Barendt has contended that 'Mill's argument . . . applies more strongly to assertions of opinion . . . than to . . . propositions of fact'.[158] The argument is that since privacy actions attempt to prevent the publication of private facts only, and not general expressions of opinion, they will pose little threat to that free and unhindered public debate about matters of importance that Mill's argument seeks to protect. Much intrusive journalism merely communicates a set of probably trivial facts about a given figure and it is very hard to maintain plausibly that the simple acquisition of such factual information has any inherent truth value. However, that is not the case in relation to some investigative journalism. For example, the revelation of the paedophile tendencies of a right-wing evangelist leading a campaign against homosexual rights would contribute to various strands of public debate.

Similarly, the justification for speech that may be referred to as the argument from autonomy[159] arguably has minimal application in this area, and indeed the values it espouses actually point to a reasonable degree of privacy protection. The basic thesis is that matters of substantive moral choice must be left to the individual as an autonomous, rational agent (subject, of course, to his duty to respect the basic rights of others); therefore, the state offends against human dignity, or treats certain citizens with contempt, if the coercive powers of the law are used to enforce the moral convictions of some upon others by, say, banning certain kinds of pornography or extreme political discourse.[160] It is immediately apparent that much privacy-invading speech,

154   See pp 277–78. The most famous exposition of the 'truth' argument is to be found in Mill's *On Liberty*, in Cowling (ed), *Selected Writings of John Stuart Mill*, 1968, p 121.

155   See the famous *dicta* of Judge Learned Hand in *United States v Associated Press* (1943) 52 F Supp 362, p 372; and of Holmes J, dissenting but with the concurrence of Brandeis J, in *Abrams v United States* (1919) 250 US 616, p 630.

156   The repeated reference by the ECtHR to freedom of expression being one of the 'basic conditions for [society's] progress' (see, e.g., *Otto-Preminger Institut v Austria* (1994) 19 EHRR 34, para 49) could be seen as a reference to the justification.

157   But see *R v Secretary of State for the Home Department ex p Simms* [1999] 3 All ER 400, p 408, *per* Lord Steyn.

158   Barendt, E, *Freedom of Speech*, 1st edn, 1985, p 191.

159   The argument has been most influentially put by writers in the tradition of deontological liberalism. See Chapter 1, p 23 *eq seq*.

160   The particular concern of Thomas Scanlon's influential approach set out in 'A theory of freedom of expression' (1972) 1 Phil & Pub Aff 216.

by both directly assaulting informational autonomy and indirectly threatening the individual's freedom of choice,[161] far from being bolstered by the autonomy rationale, is in direct conflict with it. The state, in restricting what one citizen may be told about the private life of another, is not acting out of a paternalistic desire to impose a set of moral values thereby, but rather to assure an equal freedom to all to live by their own values.

The argument from self-development – that the freedom to engage in the free expression and reception of ideas and opinions in various media is essential to human development[162] – has received some recognition at Strasbourg[163] and in the House of Lords.[164] As with the argument from autonomy, it is immediately apparent that this justification, since it seeks to facilitate human flourishing, far from inevitably opposing the right to privacy, must support it to some extent since, as argued above,[165] a reasonable degree of privacy is a requirement, not a threat, to individual self-development, particularly the human capacity to form intimate relationships, without which the capacity for individual growth would be severely curtailed.

Moreover, as Barendt has argued,[166] it is implausible to view most newspaper reporters as freely serving their own human need for self-development. The focus must therefore be on the readers of such material. Joseph Raz has proposed a theory of freedom of expression that, he argues, provides a reader-based justification for expression and is concerned not with 'serious' public debate, but with the type of speech that is 'often overlooked' or seen as 'trivial'.[167] He points out that much public expression in the media portrays and expresses aspects of forms of different lifestyles[168] that, he argues, 'validate the styles of life portrayed'. Conversely, he considers that censorship is not only an 'insult' to the persons leading the lifestyle censored – a point that sounds very like Dworkin's argument for freedom of expression based on equal respect for citizens[169] – but it also, in a more instrumental vein, denies those living the lifestyle the opportunity for reassurance, the sense that they are not alone in their lifestyles and its problems, and also the chance for the public to learn about the widest possible range of lifestyles, thus maximising their freedom of choice.[170]

Raz considers that his argument does not in general justify revelations about particular individuals, but may do so in relation to 'individuals who have become symbols of

161 See p 687 et seq.
162 See the Introduction to Part II, pp 277–78. Emerson, C, for example, argues that the right to free expression is justified as the right of the individual to realise his character and potentialities through forming his own beliefs and opinions: 'Towards a general theory of the First Amendment' (1963) 72 Yale LJ 877, pp 879–80; see also Redish, M, *Freedom of Expression*, 1984, Lexis, pp 20–30.
163 One of the stock phrases of the European Court of Human Rights in relation the value of freedom of expression asserts that it is one of the 'essential foundations for the development of everyone' (e.g., *Otto-Preminger Institut v Austria* (1994) 19 EHRR 34, para 49).
164 *Per* Lord Steyn in *R v Secretary of State for the Home Department ex p Simms* [2000] 2 AC 115, p 498.
165 See p 687 et seq.
166 Barendt and Hitchens, *Media Law, Cases and Materials*, 2000, Pearson, p 68; he concedes that such arguments may have some applicability to the writers of 'fringe or underground journals'.
167 Raz, J, 'Free expression and personal identification' (1991) 11(3) OJLS 303, p 310.
168 *Ibid*: 'Views and opinions, activities, emotions etc, expressed or portrayed are an aspect of a wider net of opinions, sensibilities, habits of action or dressing, attitudes etc which taken together form a distinctive style of form of life.'
169 Dworkin, R, *A Matter of Principle* 1985, HUP, esp pp 272–74.
170 Raz, J, 'Free expression and personal identification' (1991) 11(3) OJLS 303, p 312.

certain cultures, or ideologies, or . . . styles of life'.[171] It is clear, however, that if speech that invades the privacy of such individuals is restricted, the 'message' sent by the state thereby, far from suggesting condemnation or contempt for the lifestyle revealed, in fact displays *respect* for the ability of the individual to decide for himself whether he wishes to share his life decisions with the public at large. Moreover, the reassuring knowledge that control of such information rests with the individual will surely further the core aim of the self-fulfilment justification – the ability of persons to make free choices to experience and experiment with the widest possible range of lifestyles and activities. Conversely, the inability of the individual to exercise such control would, as argued above, amount to a significant 'chilling effect' upon the willingness of individuals to make controversial choices about their personal lives. The self-development justification for freedom of expression therefore tends to support a reasonable degree of protection for informational autonomy.

As the introduction to Part II explained, the 'self-governance' or argument from democracy is viewed as 'the most influential theory in the development of 20th century free speech law',[172] an assertion supported by examination of the approach of UK and Strasbourg judges, discussed in that introduction. Its basic thesis is that citizens cannot participate fully in a democracy unless they have a reasonable understanding of political issues; therefore, open debate on such matters is necessary to ensure the proper working of a democracy;[173] as Lord Steyn has put it, 'freedom of speech is the lifeblood of democracy'.[174] In so far as democracy rests upon ideas both of participation and accountability, the argument from democracy may be seen to encompass also the function that a free press performs in exposing abuses of power,[175] thereby allowing for their remedy and also providing a deterrent effect for those contemplating such wrong-doing.[176]

As has been indicated previously, it is a marked feature of the Strasbourg jurisprudence that clearly political speech receives a much more robust degree of protection than other types of expression.[177] Thus, the 'political' speech cases discussed in this book[178] all resulted in findings that Art 10 had been violated and all were marked by an intensive review of the restriction in question. In contrast, in cases involving artistic speech, supported by the values of autonomy and self-development rather than self-government, an exactly converse pattern emerges: applicants have tended to be unsuccessful and a deferential approach to the judgments of the national authorities as to its obscene or blasphemous nature has been adopted.[179] As indicated in Part II, a similar

---

171　*Ibid*, p 316.
172　See p 277 *et seq*.
173　See Meiklejohn, A, 'The First Amendment is an absolute' (1961) Sup Ct Rev 245 and *Political Freedom*, 1960, Harper & Brothers, esp pp 115–24.
174　*R v Secretary of State for the Home Department ex p Simms* [2000] 2 AC 115, p 408.
175　See Blasi, V: 'The checking value in First Amendment theory' (1977) Am B Found Res J 521.
176　See Greenwalt, K, 'Free speech justifications' (1989) 89 Columb L Rev 119, p 143.
177　See Part II, pp 287–89 above.
178　See, e.g., *Jersild v Denmark* (1994) 19 EHRR 1; *Lingens v Austria* (1986) 8 EHRR 103, see Pt II p 281 *et seq*.
179　See Part II, p 288; see also *Müller v Switzerland* (1991) 13 EHRR 212; *Gibson v UK*, Appl No 17634 (declared inadmissible by Commission); *Handyside v UK*, A 24 (1976) (not a case involving artistic speech but where the issue was obscenity); *Otto-Preminger Institut v Austria* (1994) 19 EHRR 34; *Gay News v UK*

pattern may be discerned in the domestic jurisprudence: the most lofty rhetorical assertions of the importance of free speech and the strongest determination to protect it
have been evident in cases where journalistic material raises political issues, broadly
defined.[180] In such cases, the courts have either overtly adopted the Strasbourg principles described above[181] or have strongly emphasised the high status freedom of speech
holds in the common law, as 'a constitutional right'.[182] Media freedom in relation to
political expression has clearly been recognised as having a particularly high value in
UK law and Convention jurisprudence. In contrast, when speech supported by the arguments from self-development or autonomy rather than self-government is in question,
decisions have tended to be far more cautious.[183]

Two points emerge from this discussion. Where speech is supported mainly by arguments from autonomy, truth and self-development, there will in general be little or no
justification at the level of principle for allowing it to override privacy; indeed, the
discussion above reveals the truth of Emerson's remark that, far from being invariably
in conflict, the twin rights to freedom of speech and to privacy 'are mutually supportive, in that both are vital features of the basic system of individual rights'.[184] In more
practical terms, the type of speech which, as we have seen, receives the highest level of
protection, namely political speech, is by its nature most unlikely to conflict with the
right to privacy. In many cases it will not raise privacy issues, as where it consists of the
discussion of political ideas, institutions, and policies. Where political speech does concern individuals, as where it reveals abuse of state power, the conflict is more likely to
be with reputation than privacy.[185] Conversely, the paradigm cases of journalistic invasions of privacy that, by definition, involve the personal, not the public–political affairs
of its subject, usually involve celebrities rather than public servants, and are driven by
purely commercial considerations. Such publications simply do not engage core Art 10
values such as the furtherance of a democratic society. Thus, it will only be in a fairly
narrow category of cases that any real conflict will arise – those where the publication in

---

(1982) 5 EHRR 123. In *Wingrove v UK* (1997) 24 EHRR 1, the Court remarked: 'Whereas there is little
scope under Art 10(2) of the Convention for restrictions on political speech or on debate of questions of
public . . . a wider margin of appreciation is generally available to the Contracting states when regulating
freedom of expression in relation to matters liable to offend intimate personal convictions within the sphere
of morals or, especially, religion' (para 58). See Harris, O'Boyle and Warbrick, *op cit*, fn 1, pp 397 and 414.

180 *Reynolds v Times Newspapers*; *Derbyshire CC v Times Newspapers* [1993] AC 534; *R v Secretary of
State for the Home Department ex p Simms* [2000] 2 AC 115. However, deference to widely drafted
primary legislation (*Secretary of State for Home Affairs ex p Brind* [1991] 1 AC 696) or governmental
arguments from national security (*AG v Guardian Newspapers* [1987] 1 WLR 1248) has resulted in the
ready upholding of restrictions on directly political speech.

181 See the approach of the Court of Appeal in *Derbyshire* (*ibid*) and in *Ex p Leech* [1994] QB 198, of the
House of Lords in *Reynolds* (*ibid*, pp 621–22), *per* Lord Nicholls, pp 628 and esp 635, *per* Lord Steyn,
p 643, *per* Lord Cooke and *Ex p Simms*, p 407 *per* Lord Steyn and pp 419–20 *per* Lord Hobhouse.

182 *Reynolds v Times Newspapers*, pp 628–29 (Lord Steyn). In *Ex p Simms* (*ibid*, p 11), Lord Steyn
described the right as 'fundamental', as did Lord Hoffmann (*ibid*, p 412).

183 *R v Gibson* [1990] 2 QB 619; *Knuller v DPP* [1973] AC 435; *R v Lemon* [1979] AC 617.

184 Emerson, T, 'The right of privacy and the freedom of the press' (1979) 14(2) Harvard Civil Rights –
Civil Liberties L Rev 329, p 331.

185 As in the case of *Reynolds v Times Newspapers* [1993] AC 534, in which the former Irish Taoiseach
sued newspapers which published reports accusing him of lying to the Irish Dail; see also, e.g., *Lingens
v Austria* (1986) 8 EHRR 103 and *Thorgeirson v Iceland* (1992) 14 EHRR 843.

question relates to the personal life of a particular public figure,[186] and there is a serious argument that it serves a valuable purpose in revealing a matter relevant to that person's fitness for office, or in furthering public knowledge or debate about matters of serious public concern.

Lack of a remedy for privacy invasion

Historically the UK has not sought to strike a balance between media freedom and protection of privacy since no general liability for journalistic invasion of privacy existed, pre-HRA. Thus there was a gap in the law, and so a failure to protect informational autonomy, which was illustrated by the ruling in *Kaye v Robertson and Another.*[187] Mr Kaye, a well-known actor, was involved in a car accident and suffered severe head injuries. While he was lying in hospital two journalists from the *Sunday Sport*, acting on Mr Robertson's orders, got into his room, photographed him and interviewed him. Owing to his injuries, he did not object to their presence and shortly after the incident had no recollection of it. The resultant article gave the impression that Mr Kaye had consented to the interview. His advisers sought and obtained an injunction restraining the defendants from publishing the photographs and the interview. On appeal by the defendants the Court of Appeal ruled that the plaintiff's claim could not be based on a right to privacy as such a right is unknown to English law. His true grievance lay in the 'monstrous invasion of privacy' which he had suffered but he would have to look to other rights of action in order to obtain a remedy, namely libel and malicious falsehood. The basis of the defamation claim was that the article's implication that Mr Kaye had consented to a first 'exclusive' interview for a 'lurid and sensational' newspaper such as the *Sunday Sport* would lower him in the esteem of right-thinking people. The Court of Appeal held that this claim might well succeed, but that as such a conclusion was not inevitable it could not warrant grant of an interim injunction, basing this ruling on *Herbage v Times Newspapers and Others.*[188]

The court then considered malicious falsehood. First, it had to be shown that the defendant had published about the plaintiff words that were false. Their lordships considered that any reasonable jury would find that the implication contained in the words of the article was false. As the case was, on that basis, clear cut, an interim injunction could in principle be granted. Secondly, it had to be shown that the words were published maliciously. Malice would be inferred if it was proved that the words were calculated to produce damage and that the defendant knew them to be false. The reporters clearly realised that Mr Kaye was unable to give them any informed consent. Any subsequent publication of the falsehood would therefore be malicious. Thirdly, damage must have followed as a direct result of the publication of the falsehood. The words had produced damage in that they had diminished the value of Mr Kaye's right to sell the story of his accident at some later date. That ground of action was therefore made out.

---

186 See the conclusions of the Calcutt Report on this point (*op cit*, fn 19, at paras 12.24–12.29).
187 [1991] FSR 62; for comment, see Prescott, P, '*Kaye v Robertson*: a reply' (1991) 54 MLR 451; Bedingfield, D, 'Privacy or publicity: the enduring confusion surrounding the American tort of invasion of privacy' (1992) 55 MLR 111; Markesinis, BS, 'The Calcutt Report must not be forgotten' (1992) 55 MLR 118.
188 (1981) *The Times*, 1 May.

Therefore, an injunction restraining the defendants until trial from publishing anything that suggested that the plaintiff had given an informed consent to the interview or the taking of the photographs was substituted for the original order. However, this was a limited injunction that allowed publication of the story with certain of the photographs, provided that it was not claimed that the plaintiff had given consent. Thus, it seemed that no effective remedy was available for the plaintiff. Legatt LJ concluded his ruling by saying: 'We do not need a First Amendment to preserve the freedom of the Press, but the abuse of that freedom can be ensured only by the enforcement of a right to privacy.'[189] *Kaye* was a very telling decision: it is possible that had breach of confidence (see below) been argued in that instance it could have succeeded; but the case highlighted the need for the judges to develop a privacy remedy, if Parliament continued to refuse to do so. Breach of confidence was not argued in *Kaye* because at the time it was not readily apparent that it covered situations in which there was no prior confidential relationship.

Background to the tort of misuse of private information

The following discussion traces the creation for the first time in UK law of common law liability for invasion of privacy by the unauthorised disclosure of personal information – a liability that would now clearly cover the situation that arose in *Kaye*. Of all the areas of law covered by this book, this one has undergone the most dramatic transformation under the impetus of the HRA. The discussion documents the incremental transformation of the doctrine of confidence into a privacy remedy in the HRA era.[190]

The common law doctrine of breach of confidence

Traditionally, the common law doctrine of breach of confidence protected some confidential communications,[191] and the breadth of the doctrine had for some time supported the view that it could provide a general means of protecting personal information, although this area of law had developed largely as a means of protecting commercial secrets.

The House of Lords in *AG v Guardian Newspapers (No 2)*[192] found that the ruling in *Coco v AN Clark (Engineers) Ltd*[193] conveniently summarised the three traditionally accepted key elements of the law of confidence: 'First the information itself . . . must have the necessary quality of confidence about it. Secondly, that information must have been imparted in circumstances importing an obligation of confidence. Thirdly, there must be an unauthorised use of that information to the detriment of the party communicating it.' Even if these elements were made out, publication of the information was still possible if the defence of public interest applied.

189 *Kaye v Robertson* [1991] FSR 62, p 104.
190 This section draws on selected parts of Fenwick, H and Phillipson, G, 'The Doctrine of Confidence as a Privacy Remedy in the Human Rights Act Era' [2000] 63(5) MLR 660.
191 See generally Gurry, F, *Breach of Confidence*, 1991; Jones, G, 'Restitution of Benefits Obtained in Breach of Another's Confidence' (1970) 86 LQR 463.
192 [1990] 1 AC 109.
193 [1969] RPC 41, p 47.

To satisfy the requirements of the first element, information must, it seemed, not be in the public domain and must not be trivial. The third element, unauthorised use of information, was fairly self-explanatory; as to detriment, it appeared from the cases either that unwanted revelation of private facts *per se* might constitute detriment for the purposes of the law of confidence,[194] or, alternatively, that establishing detriment might not always be necessary.[195] However, it was in relation to the second element – the circumstances in which the courts would find an obligation of confidence to have been imposed – that the most radical development occurred. Under the traditional model of confidence, one important ingredient had to be satisfied for such an obligation to arise. This was that, at least in cases involving personal, as opposed to commercial information, there had to be some identifiable pre-existing intimate or necessarily confidential relationship between confider and confidant, such as a professional relationship of trust,[196] or marriage,[197] from which the obligation of confidence could be inferred, in the absence of an express agreement on the matter.

The discarding of the test of showing an obligation to keep the information confidential was the single most important step in the transformation of the doctrine of confidence into a privacy remedy. This development occurred as follows. First, pre-HRA, the traditional categories of relationship imposing obligations of confidence were broadened, and it was recognised that the relationship between the parties was not the determining factor. The key factor appeared to be that the receiver of the information was bound by conscience not to disclose it. The focus on conscience transmuted into a different test: it began to be recognised even pre-HRA, that the obligation could be imposed whenever a reasonable man would recognise that the information was confidential.[198] Thus the need for some kind of prior bond of trust between the parties began to disappear.

In a number of pre-HRA cases, including *Francome v Mirror Group Newspapers*,[199] *Shelley Films*,[200] *Creation Records*,[201] and *Hellewell*,[202] no prior relationship of

---

194 *AG v Guardian Newspapers (No 2)* [1990] 1 AC 109, p 265, *per* Lord Keith.

195 Lord Goff explicitly left the point open (*ibid*, pp 281–82), while Lord Griffiths (*ibid*, p 270) thought that it was required. The remainder of the House did not address the point. In *X v Y* ([1988] 2 All ER 650, pp 651 and 657) it was held *per curiam* that actual or possible detriment to the plaintiff was 'not a necessary precondition to injunctive relief' ([1988] 2 All ER 650, pp 651 and 657). In *R v Department of Health, ex parte Source Informatics* [2000] 2 WLR 953, the Court of Appeal did not attempt to resolve the matter, but appeared to favour Lord Keith's view.

196 See, e.g., *W v Egdell* [1990] Ch 359 (doctor-patient); *X v Y* (*op cit*); *AG v Guardian Newspapers (No 2)* [1990] 1 AC 109 (both employer-employee).

197 As in *Duchess of Argyll v Duke of Argyll* [1967] 1 Ch 302.

198 For further discussion see: Phillipson, G, 'Transforming breach of confidence? Towards a common law right of privacy under the Human Rights Act' (2003) 66(5) MLR 726 and 'Judicial Reasoning in Breach of Confidence Cases under the Human Rights Act: not taking privacy seriously? [2003] EHRLR 53.

199 [1984] 1 WLR 892. The information concerned (that the plaintiff, a well-known jockey, had breached various rules of racing) was obtained by means of tapping the plaintiff's telephone; the tapes so made were sold to the press.

200 *Shelley Films v Rex Features Limited* [1994] EMLR 134. An injunction was granted to prevent the use of a photograph taken surreptitiously on the film set of Frankenstein.

201 *Creation Records Ltd v News Group Newspapers Ltd* [1997] EMLR 444; an injunction was granted against a newspaper to prevent it from publishing a photograph of a new album cover designed for the group Oasis which had been taken surreptitiously on the set where the album cover was being shot.

202 *Hellewell v Chief Constable of Derbyshire* [1995] 1 WLR 804. The 'information' here was a mug-shot of the plaintiff taken by the police which was later passed by them to local shopkeepers to aid the prevention of shoplifting.

confidentiality was present. As a result of the successful actions in *Shelley Films*,[203] *Creation Records*[204] and *HRH Princess of Wales*[205] (all involving surreptitiously taken photographs), *Francome*,[206] (where information was obtained by a newspaper using a telephone tap) and *Lam v Koo and Chiu*[207] (involving the surreptitious obtaining of a document), any requirement for a communication between plaintiff and defendant disappeared, a development also supported by *dicta* of Lord Goff in *AG v Guardian Newspapers (No 2)*.[208] This was possible because the requirement of an 'implied agreement' of confidentiality was radically re-interpreted: the approach of the courts was to imply the agreement of confidentiality into the dealings between the parties, not on the basis of any mutual agreement on the matter, but instead on the basis that the reasonable man in the position of the defendant would have assumed such an obligation.[209] The central interest served by protecting confidences ceased to be enforcing promise-keeping, or preserving certain kinds of relationships; rather, it became simply that of preventing private or personal information entering the public domain without the plaintiff's consent. The action, therefore, while still termed 'breach of confidence',[210] was moving closer, even pre-HRA, to becoming a privacy tort.[211]

Due to the courts' own duty under s 6 HRA, these developments were consolidated under the impetus of the HRA, but in general the courts considered initially in the very early post-HRA years, that they were dealing with an extension of the doctrine of confidence. Finally, the notion of imposing an obligation of confidence was discarded entirely: the only requirement was that the information was private in Art 8 terms; if that was the case the other party came under a duty not to disclose it. In other words,

---

203 [1994] EMLR 134. The case was discussed extensively in the case of *Spencer v UK* (1998) 25 EHRR CD 105.

204 *Creation Records Ltd v News Group Newspapers Ltd* [1997] EMLR 444.

205 *HRH Princess of Wales v MGN Newspapers Limited and Others* (1993) Transcript, Association of Official Shorthandwriters Ltd, 8 November 1993. Photographs of the plaintiff exercising in a private gymnasium taken by a hidden camera were sold to and published by a tabloid newspaper.

206 [1984] 1 WLR 892.

207 [1992] Civil Transcript No 116, CA (a Hong Kong case): a medical researcher accidentally or surreptitiously obtained a confidential research document produced by the plaintiff.

208 *AG v Guardian Newspapers (No 2)* [1990] 1 AC 109; [1990] 3 WLR 776. Lord Goff considered *obiter* that confidentiality would be imposed in instances where, e.g., 'an obviously confidential document is wafted by an electric fan out of the window into a crowded street, or when an obviously confidential document . . . is dropped in a public place and is then picked up by a passer-by' (*ibid*, p 281).

209 Thus, in *Creation Records v NGN* [1997] EMLR 444, Lloyd J reasoned: 'the circumstances were such that any reasonable man in the shoes of [the photographer] would have realised on reasonable grounds that he was obtaining the information, that is to say the view of the scene, in confidence'.

210 As Laws J remarked in *Hellewell v Chief Constable of Derbyshire* [1995] 1 WLR 804: 'In such a case the law would protect what might reasonably be called a right of privacy, although the name accorded to the cause of action would be breach of confidence'.

211 Confidence does, however have one limitation in such a guise: it cannot directly cover cases where there is intrusion but no information is gained or where information is gathered but never used (the Protection from Harassment Act 1997 might apply in cases of persistent intrusion). However, a reporter could be prevented by the terms of an injunction from passing any information gained on to anyone else in a newspaper, and presumably from processing and storing the information in the newspaper's archives (activities which might also engage the Data Protection Act 1998 (see below, pp 764–65). Moreover, the availability of a remedy in confidence against the publication of private information obtained by, e.g., a bugging device, might give rise to a perception that such use was pointless if lawful publication of the material gained was not possible; it might thus come to have a 'chilling effect' upon this form of intrusion.

the action in question became that of breach of privacy (that term is used as short-hand for liability for misuse of private information). In identifying these stages of development, it must be borne in mind that the traditional relationships imposing an obligation of confidence, such as master/servant or patient/doctor, are still relevant: they can figure as weighty factors tipping the balance in favour of privacy at the stage of balancing the speech and privacy interests.[212]

Perhaps the most important concern relating to the development of confidence as a remedy for invasion of privacy was the fear that the action would pose an unacceptable risk to media freedom. The main insurance against this possibility pre-HRA rested with the public interest defence, whereby disclosure of admittedly private or confidential information was permitted if this would serve the public interest.[213] Traditionally, confidential information would not be protected if the public interest served by disclosing the information in question outweighed the interest in preserving confidentiality. There were two key developments in the defence in the pre-HRA era. First, while originally only allowing disclosure if it would reveal wrongdoing on the part of the plaintiff,[214] the strength of the public interest in question rather than the individual wrongdoing of the plaintiff became the determining factor.[215] Secondly, where disclosure was said to be in the public interest because it exposed particular criminal or anti-social behaviour, or revealed some specific risk to public health, it was clear that this would not always justify disclosing the matter in the press.[216] The public interest defence provided a means of reconciling the demands of speech and confidence. Under the impetus of the HRA, this balancing exercise has become, as indicated below, more sophisticated since it is now largely undertaken as a balancing act between Arts 8 and 10 with their associated jurisprudence.

The 'indirect horizontal effect' of Art 8 under the Human Rights Act

There is now a statutory tort of invasion of privacy, under the HRA, but it is applicable *only* against public authorities, relying on Art 8 and s 6 HRA. So where a body processing personal information (which includes its publication) is *also* a public authority it can be sued directly under s 7(1)(a) of the HRA in respect of breaches of Art 8 – thus creating a statutory tort of invasion of privacy. But most media bodies are private

---

212 See below p 754.
213 While originally only allowing disclosure if it would reveal wrongdoing on the part of the plaintiff (*Gartside v Outram* (1856) 26 LJ Ch 113, p 114 and in relation to copyright, *Glyn v Weston Feature Film* Co [1916] 1 Ch 261) the strength of the public interest in question rather than the individual wrongdoing of the plaintiff is now the determining factor: see *AG v Guardian Newspapers (No 2)* [1990] 1 AC 109, p 282, *per* Lord Goff, and p 268, per Lord Griffiths.
214 *Gartside v Outram* (1856) 26 LJ Ch 113, p 114 and in relation to copyright, *Glyn v Weston Feature Film Co* [1916] 1 Ch 261.
215 See *Fraser v Evans* [1969] 1 QB 349; *Schering Chemicals v Falkman* [1981] 2 WLR 848, esp p 869; *X v Y* [1988] 2 All ER 648 and *AG v Jonathan Cape* [1976] 1 QB 752; *Lion Laboratories v Evans and Express Newspapers* [1984] 1 QB 530, *W v Egdell* [1990] Ch 359; and *Hellewell (op cit)*; *AG v Guardian Newspapers (No 2)* [1990] 1 AC 109.
216 See *Francome v MGM* [1984] 1 WLR 892; *Initial Services Ltd v Putterill* [1968] 1 QB 396, pp 405–6, *per* Lord Denning; *AG v Guardian Newspapers (No 2)* [1990] 1 AC 109, p 269, per Lord Griffiths, p 282, per Lord Goff.

companies, not public authorities, and it now seems clear that there is no possibility under the HRA of suing *private* bodies for breach of Art 8 ECHR directly under s 7(1) (a), principally because, as Chapter 4 explained, s 6 HRA makes the Convention rights binding only upon 'public authorities'. However, since the courts, as 'public authorities'[217] themselves have a duty not to act incompatibly with the Convention rights, this creates a role for the rights even in litigation between private parties, thus giving rise to 'indirect horizontal effect'. This does not require the courts to create new causes of action in such litigation;[218] rather, the s 6(1) duty to act compatibly with the Convention rights can bite upon their adjudication of existing common law actions. This was confirmed by the House of Lords in *Wainwright v Home Office*.[219] The effect is 'horizontal' as it is between two private parties – often a celebrity and a newspaper. It is 'indirect' because one of the two private parties cannot directly sue the other relying on ss 6 and 7 HRA, but must rely on an existing cause of action; once in court the court itself since it *is* a public authority must abide by the ECHR in adjudicating on the action.

As Chapter 4 indicates, the courts accepted in the early HRA years – in the context of privacy, but not, so far, in other contexts – that the common law doctrine of confidence must be developed compatibly with the rights. Further, s 2(1) HRA requires the domestic judiciary to take any relevant Strasbourg jurisprudence into account.[220] Since they are not bound by the case law, the courts could depart from it when so minded. However, as Chapter 4 pointed out, the courts tend to follow Strasbourg jurisprudence where it is of a settled nature. Lord Nicholls said in *Campbell*:

> The values embodied in articles 8 and 10 are as much applicable in disputes between individuals or between an individual and a non-governmental body such as a newspaper as they are in disputes between individuals and a public authority.[221]

In *Douglas (No 3)*,[222] Lord Phillips considered that the House of Lords had accepted the doctrine of indirect horizontal effect in *Campbell v MGN*[223] and in *Re S (a child)*.[224] Lord Phillips summarised Lady Hale's comments on the matter:

> Baroness Hale said that the Human Rights Act did not create any new cause of action between private persons . . . But where there is a cause of action the court, as a public authority, must act compatibly with both parties' Convention rights.[225]

217 Section 6(3)(a).
218 See Chapter 4, p 211 *et seq*.
219 [2004] 2 AC 406 [34].
220 See Chapter 4, p 157 *et seq*.
221 [2004] 2 WLR 1232 at paras 17 and 18. (*Von Hannover v Germany* (2005) 40 EHRR 1, affirmed that the Convention does have this effect.)
222 [2005] EWCA 595.
223 [2004] 2 WLR 1232.
224 [2005] 1 AC 593.
225 *Op cit* [52].

In *HRH Prince of Wales v Associated Newspapers Ltd*[226] Lord Phillips in the Court of Appeal said:

> The English court has recognised that it should also, in so far as possible, develop the common law in such a way as to give effect to Convention rights. In this way horizontal effect is given to the Convention.[227]

The caveat contained in the words 'so far as possible' may indicate that the courts were holding back from accepting the absolute duty to give effect to the rights within the common law in the sense that it might be impossible to give effect to the rights where they conflicted with clear common law rules. But Buxton LJ in the Court of Appeal in *Mckennitt v Ash*[228] summed up the post-*Campbell* position without any such caveat:

> the court, as a public authority, is required not to act in a way which is incompat-ible with a Convention right. The court is able to achieve this by absorbing the rights which articles 8 and 10 protect into the long-established action for breach of confidence. This involves giving a new strength and breadth to the action so that it accommodates the requirements of those articles.[229]

The word 'accommodate' suggests that the action in question should reflect the Convention rights, even if the Convention requirements *do* conflict with established common law rules. The course that has been taken in this context, by the incremental steps described below, was not one that required difficult decisions to be made at each stage. The favoured common law mode of reasoning, resembling the creeping in of the tide rather than the breaching of a dam, lent itself very readily to this new context. But despite Buxton LJ's comments, the expansive version of private life accepted in the first *Von Hannover* case, above, has *not* been fully accepted domestically.

Remaining relevance of the doctrine of confidence

It must be remembered, not only that the privacy action has grown out of the confidence doctrine, but that the confidence doctrine is still relevant in non-privacy cases – and may also be pleaded *within them* as an alternative possibility. The fact that a traditional confidence claim would have succeeded is no longer an essential element of the tort, but, as discussed below, it will weigh in the balance in favour of the privacy claim when it is balanced against the competing speech interest. Confidence is also relevant in commercial cases, which are not the concern of this book, and in state cases, in which the government asserts a breach of confidence claim in respect of a leak or other use of government information, as in the well-known *Spycatcher* case, discussed in Chapter 8.[230]

---

226 [2006] EWCA Civ 1776.
227 *Ibid*, [25].
228 [2006] EWCA Civ 1714.
229 *Ibid*, [10].
230 See p 518 *et seq*.

The tort of misuse of private information: a reasonable expectation of privacy rather than an obligation of confidence

The role of s 6 HRA in infusing Art 8 into the doctrine of confidence was apparent in the significant early post-HRA decision of the Court of Appeal in *Douglas and Others v Hello! Ltd.*[231] The magazine *OK!* secured an agreement with two celebrities, Michael Douglas and Catherine Zeta-Jones, before their wedding under which it agreed to pay a very large sum of money to them in respect of rights to publish exclusive photographs of the wedding and an article about it. The couple trusted *OK!* to project only the images they wanted projected to the public. *Hello!* clearly knew that exclusive rights were to be granted for coverage of the wedding, and that it had not secured them. However, the security operation at the wedding failed to prevent some unauthorised photos from being taken and *Hello!* obtained them. The couple were informed after the wedding that copies of *Hello!* were already in the UK with a photo of the wedding on the front cover and that they would be distributed very shortly. They rapidly obtained an *ex parte* injunction restraining publication.

The Court of Appeal had to decide whether an injunction restraining the publication should be continued in force until trial, thereby effectively 'killing' that issue of *Hello!*. The key issues were (a) the applicability of the law of confidence; (b) the relevance of the HRA 1998. The Court noted that the doctrine of confidence originally arose from the exercise of the equitable jurisdiction to restrain freedom of speech in circumstances in which it would be unconscionable to publish private material. It said that it was clearly established that where information was accepted on the basis that it would be kept secret, the recipient's conscience would be bound by that confidence, and it would be unconscionable for him to break his duty of confidence by publishing the information to others.[232]

Sedley LJ found that the law of confidence had developed to the point at which it could provide a right to privacy, in so far as a privacy right could be viewed as covering matters which are distinct from those that confidence has come to be viewed as capable of covering. He accepted that it might have reached that point even independently of the HRA. In particular, he found that it is arguable that confidence does not cover surreptitious takings of personal information by someone whose conscience cannot be said to be bound to maintain confidence – a 'stranger' – and that such takings are more readily covered by a right to privacy, albeit originating from confidence. His point appeared to be that although such takings could be covered by confidence, as indicated above,[233] the

---

231 [2001] 2 WLR 992. See for discussion Moreham, N [2001] 64(5) MLR 767–74; Elliott, M [2001] CLJ 231–33.

232 *Stephens v Avery* [1988] Ch 449, p 456. The court noted that in *Argyll v Argyll* [1967] Ch 302, 329f–330b it was said: 'It . . . seems to me that the policy of the law, so far from indicating that communication between husband and wife should be excluded from protection against breaches of confidence given by the court in accordance with *Prince Albert v Strange* ((1848) 2 De Gex & Sm 652; on appeal 1 Mac & G 25), strongly favours its inclusion'. The court also relied on *Michael Barrymore v News Group Newspapers Ltd* [1997] FSR 600; Jacob J had followed those principles in a case in which a newspaper sought to publish information concerning an intimate homosexual relationship.

233 See *Francome v MGM* [1984] 1 WLR 892 and *dicta* in *AG v Guardian Newspaper (No 2)* [1990] 1 AC 109, p 281, discussed above.

notion of an implied obligation to maintain confidence might be viewed as artificial, depending on the circumstances.

However, if the photos in the instant case had been taken by a 'stranger', the cause of action in his view could arguably be termed a right to privacy, and the HRA aided that conclusion. Thus, the HRA gave a force to the above argument – that confidence had developed in such a way as to provide a right to privacy – which it might not otherwise have had. Sedley LJ made this clear: 'we have reached a point at which it can be said with confidence that the law recognises and will appropriately protect a right of personal privacy'. He based this finding in part on the coming into force of the HRA since it required the courts – as public authorities under s 6 HRA – to give effect to the right to respect for private and family life set out in Art 8 of the European Convention on Human Rights. He said that the jurisprudence of the Court and the common law:

> now run in a single channel because, by virtue of s 2 and s 6 of the Act, the courts of this country must not only take into account jurisprudence of both the Commission and the European Court of Human Rights which points to a positive institutional obligation to respect privacy; they must themselves act compatibly with that and the other Convention rights. This, for reasons I now turn to, arguably gives the final impetus to the recognition of a right of privacy in English law.[234]

His key point in relation to a possible difference between confidence and privacy was:

> The law no longer needs to construct an artificial relationship of confidentiality between intruder and victim: it can recognise privacy itself as a legal principle drawn from the fundamental value of personal autonomy.[235]

Clearly, in an action between private parties – as in the instant case – it could not be said that the defendant magazine was bound by the Convention since it was not a public authority under s 6 of the HRA. Sedley LJ found that the Court, as itself a public authority under s 6, was obliged to give some effect to Art 8, among other provisions of the Convention. Its duty, he said, appears to allow it to 'take the step from confidentiality to privacy'.[236]

The court concluded that the claimants had an arguable case that they had suffered a breach of their privacy; this claim was based on the law of confidence, interpreted compatibly with Art 8. Although the court was unanimous in reaching this conclusion, Sedley LJ differed from the other two judges in differentiating between confidence and privacy in respect of surreptitious takings of information.

The following decisions make more explicit the shift from confidence to privacy post-HRA. In *A v B plc* the Court of Appeal dealt with the vexed issue of the requirement of an obligation of confidentiality very straightforwardly as follows:

> The need for the existence of a confidential relationship should not give rise to problems as to the law . . . A duty of confidence will arise whenever the party

234 [2001] 2 WLR 992 [111].
235 *Ibid*, [126].
236 *Ibid*, [129].

subject to the duty is in a situation where he either knows or ought to know that the other person can reasonably expect his privacy to be protected.[237]

The seminal case of *Campbell*[238] in the House of Lords was the turning point in the final transformation of confidence into privacy. Naomi Campbell complained in an action both in breach of confidence and under the Data Protection Act 1998 after the *Mirror* newspaper had published details of her treatment for drug addiction with Narcotics Anonymous, including surreptitiously-taken photographs of her leaving the clinic and hugging other clients. Importantly, this photo made the location of the NA centre that Campbell had been attending clearly identical to anyone familiar with the area.[239] In the trial the information in question was divided into five classes as follows:

(1) the fact of Miss Campbell's drug addiction;
(2) the fact that she was receiving treatment;
(3) the fact that she was receiving treatment at Narcotics Anonymous;
(4) the details of the treatment – how long she had been attending meetings, how often she went, how she was treated within the sessions themselves, the extent of her commitment, and the nature of her entrance on the specific occasion; and
(5) the visual portrayal [through photographs] of her leaving a specific meeting with other addicts and being hugged before such a meeting by other members of the group receiving treatment.[240]

The applicant had conceded that the *Mirror* was entitled to publish the information in categories (1) and (2) – the vital fact that Campbell was a drug addict and was receiving treatment for her addiction;[241] the dispute therefore centred on the question whether publishing the further details and the photographs (categories (3)–(5)) could attract liability.

It was clear that most of the 'information' in the case – the fact of, and details of the treatment – were provided to the *Mirror* by another patient at Narcotics Anonymous or one of Campbell's staff, sources who would have been caught by the obligation of confidence even under the traditional doctrine of confidence.[242] But the photographs had clearly been covertly taken. A majority of the House of Lords found liability in confidence in respect of the publication of surreptitiously-taken photographs of the model outside Narcotics Anonymous, in the street. There were clearly no circumstances that could impose an obligation of confidentiality in the traditional sense. There was obviously no pre-existing relationship between Campbell and the photographer. Clearly,

---

237 [2002] 3 WLR 542, at 551B.
238 [2004] 2 WLR 1232.
239 As Lord Nicholls found: *ibid*, at [5].
240 *Ibid*, at [23].
241 This was because it was accepted that the press was entitled to expose the falsity of Campbell's previous public statements that she did not take drugs and was not a drug addict.
242 On the basis of an express or implied promise of confidentiality (with a fellow patient) or relationship of trust and confidence (with clinic staff).

there had been no express or implied promise by the photographer of confidentiality. The duty to refrain from disclosing the information arose purely from the private nature of the information itself, whereas in *Douglas* there were warning signs forbidding photography that could be viewed as indicating to the reasonable person that the information was to remain confidential. As Lord Nicholls put it: 'This cause of action has now firmly shaken off the limiting constraint of the need for an initial confidential relationship.'[243]

Lord Hope said: 'If the information is obviously private, the situation will be one where the person to whom it relates can reasonably expect his privacy to be respected.'[244] He further said that the only element required to give rise to the reasonable expectation of privacy is the fact that the information is obviously private. So all that is needed is that there is private information which the defendant publishes without consent, or seeks to publish. With the decision in *Campbell* the action therefore became one for breach of privacy. The 2005 Court of Appeal judgment in *Douglas v Hello! Ltd*,[245] strongly re-affirmed this development, and was prepared to discard the terminology of confidence in favour of that of privacy.

Buxton LJ in *Mckennitt v Ash*[246] referred to 'the rechristening of the tort as misuse of private information' which had occurred in *Campbell*.[247] The case concerned the publication in 2005 of a book *Travels with Loreena Mckennitt: My Life as a Friend*. The book was written by the defendant, Niema Ash, who was formerly a friend of Ms Mckennitt, a well-known folk star with a global reputation. She had often travelled and socialised with Ms Mckennitt and she entertained her while she was in England. Ms Mckennitt claimed that a substantial part of the book revealed personal and private detail about her which she was entitled to keep private. Ms Mckennitt had always very carefully guarded her personal privacy but she accepted that she had occasionally released some personal information that she felt comfortable with, and in respect of which she was able to control the boundaries herself.[248] The information sought to be restrained contained in the book included: Ms Mckennitt's personal and sexual relationships; her personal feelings, in particular, in relation to her deceased fiancé and the circumstances of his death; matters relating to her health and diet; matters relating to her emotional vulnerability, and as to the specifics of the interior of her home. Buxton LJ found that all of it was obtained within a pre-existing relationship of confidence, in the traditional sense. He found that not only would a reasonable man standing in Ms Ash's shoes have realised that the information was confidential, but that Ms Ash herself clearly realised that it was, from comments that she had made in the book.

---

243 *Campbell v MGN Ltd* [2004] 2 AC 457 at [13]–[14]. Part of the argument on *Campbell* draws on that of my co-author, Gavin Phillipson, in *Media Freedom under the Human Rights Act* (2006) at pp 738–39
244 *Ibid*, [96].
245 [2005] EWCA Civ 595. This is the decision of the Court of Appeal on the appeal from the decision to award damages at final trial made by Lindsay J: [2003] 3 All ER 996 (*Douglas II*), the Court of Appeal having in 2001 declined to grant an injunction in the case: [2001] QB 967.
246 [2006] EWCA Civ 1714.
247 *Ibid*, [8]. Lord Nicholls of Birkenhead had used this term in *Campbell* [2004] 2 AC 457 at [14].
248 *Op cit*, [6].

Against that background he found that the information in relation to which relief was sought could be accounted private information – the key question – because, he noted, relying on *Von Hannover v Germany*:

> private life, in the Court's view, includes a person's physical and psychological integrity; the guarantee afforded by Art 8 of the Convention is primarily intended to ensure the development, without outside interference, of the personality of each individual in his relations with other human beings. There is therefore a zone of interaction of a person with others, even in a public context, which may fall within the scope of private life. . .publication of photos of the applicant in her daily life either on her own or with other people falls within the scope of her private life.[249]

The defendant had sought to suggest that the ECtHR went no further in *Von Hannover* than to hold that the princess's privacy had been invaded by a campaign of media intrusion into her life, and otherwise the taking and publication of the photographs would not have been in itself an invasion of privacy. Buxton LJ rejected that contention, on the basis that the findings in *Von Hannover* were not confined to an instance of a campaign of media intrusion. It was concluded on that basis that the information in question was covered by Art 8. Although *Von Hannover* was taken into account, it was clear that the information was of a more personal nature than the information about the princess. But the references to *Von Hannover* indicated that the Court of Appeal would probably have been prepared to find that less intimate information was also covered. The key question was whether Art 8 was engaged, as determined by reference to *Von Hannover*.[250]

In *Mckennitt* and in *Campbell* it can be seen that the need to demonstrate that an obligation of confidentiality had been imposed was entirely discarded. Both judgments clearly accepted that the step from confidence to privacy had been taken, and that the determination as to whether the information should be accounted private, relying on Art 8, had become the only necessary step in deciding that relief could be afforded, subject to the speech/privacy balancing act. Lord Nicholls of Birkenhead in *Campbell v MGN Ltd* found:[251] 'Essentially the touchstone of private life is whether in respect of the disclosed facts the person in question had a reasonable expectation of privacy.' The acceptance that a key element of confidence could and should be discarded in favour of relying on Art 8 is indicative of an acceptance in this context of a near-absolute duty to develop the common law by reference to the Convention rights, under the s 6 HRA doctrine of indirect horizontal effect.

What is 'private' information under recent decisions?

What 'information' is now protected under the privacy tort? Private information covers all sorts of obviously private activities such as medical treatment (*Campbell*);[252]

---

249 At para 38.
250 See pp 697–98.
251 *Campbell v MGN Ltd* [2004] 2 AC 457 [21].
252 *Campbell v MGN Ltd* [2004] 2 WLR 1232.

it also covers private functions such as weddings (*Douglas*),[253] and, according to *Von Hannover*,[254] but not domestically, daily life activities that happen to be carried out in public. In terms of privacy-invasion, photographs are viewed as representing a very effective way of conveying minute details, including facial expressions, in a way that cannot be replicated by reporting. So photographs appear to represent a particularly pernicious form of privacy invasion. The fact that photographs have been taken may give weight to the argument that the invasion of privacy at stake should be accounted serious enough to allow prima facie for the grant of relief. The Art 8 jurisprudence should be taken into account in order to determine whether information should be viewed as private or not,[255] but in the more recent decisions the domestic courts have developed a set of criteria to determine whether or not information should be deemed 'private'.

It was found in *David Murray v Big Picture Ltd*[256] that targeting children for photographs when engaging in everyday activities may be covered as 'private' information by the tort of misuse of private information. JK Rowling's children had been photographed in public without consent; she argued that she and her child found it distressing to be pursued by the media in this way.[257] The agency's defence was that the English courts had refused to recognise the right of an individual not to be photographed in a public place, except when special factors such as harassment, distress to a child or disclosure of confidential information was involved.[258] The Court of Appeal found that it was at least arguable that her child had a reasonable expectation of privacy.[259] The fact that he was a child was found to be of particular significance.[260]

> The Court found that there could be circumstances in which there will be no reasonable expectation of privacy, even after *Von Hannover*.[261] But the Court did not think that a clear distinction could be drawn between a child (or an adult) engaged in family and sporting activities and something as simple as a walk down a street or a visit to the grocers to buy the milk. It was thought that the distinction could be contemplated on the basis that the first type of activity would be clearly part of a person's private recreation time intended to be enjoyed in the company of family and friends and that, on the test deployed in *Von Hannover*, publicity afforded to such activities is intrusive and can adversely affect the exercise of such social activities. The Court considered that in certain circumstances the second, more anodyne, type of everyday activity could fall within the scope of 'private' information.[262] It found that a reasonable expectation of privacy could arise, taking account of all the

---

253 *Douglas and Others v Hello!* [2001] 2 WLR 992.
254 *Von Hannover v Germany* (2005) 40 EHRR 1.
255 See further Warby, M, Moreham, NA and Christie, I (eds), *The Law of Privacy and the Media*, 2nd edn, 2011, OUP; Moreham, NA 'Beyond information: physical privacy in English law' (2014) 73(2) CLJ 350; Hughes, K 'A Behavioural Understanding of Privacy and its Implications for Privacy Law' (2012) 75 MLR 806.
256 *David Murray v Big Picture ltd* [2008] HRLR 33.
257 [2007] EWHC 1908 (Ch) and [2008] EWCA Civ 446 [13].
258 *Ibid*, [11].
259 *David Murray v Big Picture ltd* [2008] HRLR 33 [45].
260 *Ibid*.
261 *Ibid*, [55]. *Von Hannover v Germany* (2005) 40 EHRR 1.
262 *David Murray v Big Picture ltd* [2008] HRLR 33 [45].

circumstances of the case, including 'the attributes of the claimant, the nature of the activity in which the claimant was engaged, the place at which it was happening, the nature and purpose of the intrusion, the absence of consent and whether it was known or could be inferred, the effect on the claimant and the circumstances in which and the purposes for which the information came into the hands of the publisher'.[263]

Murray was significant since the Court of Appeal brought domestic law on privacy much closer to accepting the *Von Hannover* 'everyday life' principle, although only in relation to a *child*. In contrast, *Max Mosley v News Group Newspapers Ltd*[264] dealt with a far more typical situation, since the newspaper in question disclosed intimate facts concerning Mosley's sexual life. In 2008, the *News of the World* published a series of articles revealing that Max Mosley, president of Formula One, had engaged in group sex sessions, of a mildly sado-masochistic nature, with five prostitutes, in private, residential property. The information had been obtained from one of the prostitutes hired to take part in the sessions, who had also used a hidden camera to make a video recording of the sexual activity. The *News of the World* reported on Mosley under the heading 'F1 boss has sick Nazi orgy with 5 hookers' with an inside double-page spread story referring to 'a depraved Nazi-style orgy in a torture dungeon';[265] it contained explicit detail of the sexual activity, as well as numerous still photographs.[266] Similar information and video footage was posted on the defendant's website.[267] Mosley served legal proceedings on the *News of the World* alleging breach of privacy and claiming unlimited damages. The claim was specifically for breach of confidence and/or the unauthorised disclosure of personal information said to infringe the claimant's rights to respect for his private life as protected by Art 8 ECHR.[268] The information was found to be obviously private; it was therefore found that the newspaper had committed a breach of confidence as well as a violation of the Art 8 rights of all those involved in the relevant sexual acts, and considered that publication could only be justified if it was in the public interest, discussed below.

Terry v Persons Unknown[269] concerned Terry's (John Terry was a member of the England football team) extra-marital relationship with Vanessa Perroncel, the long-term girlfriend of Wayne Bridge, a fellow England defender. The claimant sought to renew an interim injunction to prevent information known to a number of people via word of mouth being printed to the world at large.[270] The court found that Terry would not be likely to establish that there had been a breach of a duty of confidence owed to him as there was insufficient evidence as to what he and the other person had each told to whom and in what circumstances.[271]

263 *Ibid*, [56].
264 [2008] EWHC 1777 (QB).
265 *Ibid*, [26].
266 *Ibid*, [27].
267 *Ibid*, [28].
268 *Ibid*, [3].
269 [2010] EWHC 119 (QB).
270 *Ibid*, [15].
271 *Ibid*, [52].

But in relation to misuse of private information he was found to be on somewhat stronger ground. The court found that at a trial of a claim for such misuse a claimant must first establish that he has a reasonable expectation of privacy in relation to the information of which disclosure is threatened.[272] That would arise if 'a reasonable person of ordinary sensibilities would [have such an expectation] if he or she was placed in the same position as the claimant and faced the same publicity' in all the circumstances.[273] These included:

> the attributes of the claimant, the nature of the activity in which the claimant was engaged, the place at which it was happening, the nature and purpose of the intrusion, the absence of consent and whether it was known or could be inferred, the effect on the claimant and the circumstances in which and the purposes for which the information came into the hands of the publisher . . . Photographs attract special protection because they can be much more intrusive and informative than words.[274]

It was found that there could be a reasonable expectation of privacy. The next step in the case concerned the balancing act between Art 8 and Art 10, considered below.

Very similar finding were made in *Ferdinand v MGN Ltd.*[275] Ferdinand brought the claim for misuse of private information over an April 2010 *Sunday Mirror* article in which interior designer Carly Storey gave her account of their 13-year relationship in return for £16,000. The article included a photograph and text messages. It was found that the information in the article was in principle protected by Art 8 since sexual behaviour in private was found to be part of the core aspect of individual autonomy which Art 8 protects, and that the texts were examples of 'correspondence' and so, again, in principle, were subject to protection.

The situation that arose in *Weller v Associated Newspapers Ltd*[276] strongly differed from those in *Terry* and *Ferdinand*. The claimants were the children of Paul Weller, a well-known musician and former member of The Jam and Style Council. Photographs had been taken of them in the street and at a cafe while they were out on a shopping trip with him in Santa Monica, California.[277] The defendant newspaper publisher published the photographs on *Mail Online* for one day before removing them from the internet. The claimants' faces were not pixellated. They brought proceedings against the defendant for damages and an injunction for misuse of private information and for compensation under s 13 of the Data Protection Act 1998 (DPA).[278]

The relevant attributes of the claimants identified were the images of each of their faces.[279] The place in question was a public place on the street, and partly in a café which was visible from the street and partly situated on the street. The Editors' Code recognises that private activities can take place in a public place. The *Mail Online* knew

272 *Ibid*, [55].
273 *Ibid.*
274 *Ibid.*
275 [2011] EWHC 2454.
276 [2014] EWHC 1163.
277 *Ibid*, [2].
278 *Ibid*, [4].
279 *Ibid.*

that the photographs had been taken without consent because of the wording of the accompanying caption.[280] The publication of the photographs distinguished the claimants from their peers and had a strong effect on the claimants in terms of causing distress.[281] On that basis it was found that there was a reasonable expectation of privacy.[282] The photographs were found to be different in nature from crowd shots of the street showing unknown children.[283]

When the activity engaged in is *public* in nature, such as an appearance – for example, at an awards ceremony to receive an award – at a public event or the performance by a public figure of a civic role, then there is clearly no question that there can be a 'reasonable expectation of privacy'. This point was made in *Von Hannover*.[284] However, in relation to 'public figures' there is a possibility that normally private acts, such as an affair, could be of relevance to the public function that they perform. That point would be expected to be raised in relation to speech/privacy balancing, but it has also been raised in relation to reducing or denying that a person has a reasonable expectation of privacy.

As discussed above, in *Von Hannover* it was established that a public figure cannot be deemed to *lose* their reasonable expectation of privacy for all purposes, but that has not been found domestically to mean that there is no distinction between such persons and individuals without a public profile. An example of this is the case of *Trimingham v Associated Newspapers*,[285] which concerned an affair between the politician Chris Huhne and his press officer Ms Trimingham. Ms Trimingham did not challenge publication of the fact of the affair, but objected to the nature and breadth of the news coverage against her, which attacked her reputation and discussed her sexuality and previous relationships.[286] It was found that Ms Trimingham had no reasonable expectation of privacy regarding information concerning even a previous relationship, *despite* the fact that it was found to be unrelated to the scandal.[287] Tugendhat J found that:

> If these statements had stood alone and there had been no scandal with Mr Huhne, for example if they had appeared in a short diary piece, I would have accepted that Ms Trimingham had a reasonable expectation of privacy, and that there was little to be said by way of defence. . . In the actual circumstances I conclude that the addition of these statements is not sufficiently serious to justify a finding that the Defendant has misused Ms Trimingham's private information.[288]

Typically, only personal information that is related to a public role would lack a reasonable expectation of privacy; however, the weight of the general public role associated with being a press officer and engaging in an affair with such a high profile politician was found to have, in effect, qualitatively reduced Ms Trimingham's reasonable

---

280 *Ibid*, [125].
281 *Ibid*, [162]–[168].
282 *Ibid*, [170].
283 *Ibid*, [171].
284 *Von Hannover v Germany* (2005) 40 EHRR 1 para 51.
285 [2012] EWHC 1296 (QB).
286 *Ibid*, [291].
287 *Ibid*, [305].
288 *Ibid*, [305].

expectation of privacy. This finding is in striking contrast to the findings in *Tammer v Estonia*[289] in which it was found that under Art 8 the publication of personal information of public figures that is unrelated to their public status should not be deemed to be in the public interest.[290] Tugendhat J's finding is obviously highly objectionable in terms of valuing informational autonomy; the issue of public status and relevance of the information to a public role should have been considered in relation to the balance between Arts 10 and 8, discussed below.[291]

Conclusions as to 'reasonable expectation of privacy'

The domestic courts, despite finding (in *Mckennitt*) that the privacy action should be structured by reliance on the Art 8 ECHR jurisprudence, have not gone all the way down the *Von Hannover* path – to accepting that images of daily life (as opposed to a person's 'public' life) are covered as 'private' information in relation to *adults*. No liability in a *Von Hannover* situation (where the information was acquired in a public place and was prima facie anodyne) has yet been imposed in the UK courts, except in respect of children.[292] Instead, the domestic courts have found that the information in question will be deemed private when a reasonable person of ordinary sensibilities *in the same position as the claimant* would have had a reasonable expectation of privacy in all the circumstances. These have been found to include (see *Weller* for a structured application): the attributes of the claimant, the nature of the activity in which the claimant was engaged, the place at which it was happening, the nature and purpose of the intrusion, the absence of consent, the effect on the claimant and the circumstances in which the information was acquired and the purposes for which the information came into the hands of the publisher. The result is that in the domestic courts information appears now to need to pass a threshold test of seriousness before it can be accounted 'private', especially where some form of link to a public role can be discerned as in the very press-friendly decision in *Trimingham*. The fact that information about daily life activities may be deemed private where it concerns a child may indicate that such information will of its nature be deemed to pass such a threshold.

Taking account of *Von Hannover* it can be concluded that the UK courts adopted, in the early years of the HRA, an increasingly strong line in relation to privacy complaints. At Strasbourg and domestically it is possible to say that from around 2004 to 2008 a clear shift occurred in more fully recognising a right to privacy to be exercised against the media. That shift was reaffirmed between 2008–15 to an extent, but the tendency has been to move away from the *Von Hannover* notion of a readily accepted expectation of privacy in relation to well-known figures. That tendency has also been, as discussed below, accompanied by a more ready acceptance of dubious free speech arguments put forward by newspapers.

---

289 (2003) 37 EHRR 43.
290 *Ibid,* para 68.
291 See also *Ruusunen v Finland,* Appl no, 73579/10, judgment of 14 January 2014. In *Ruusunen*, the ECtHR emphasised that publication of details concerning an extra-marital relationship between a woman and the Norwegian Prime Minister was justifiable (para 47) despite upholding an injunction was justified under A10(2).
292 *Murray v Express Newspapers Plc* [2008] EWCA Civ 446 at [24], [36], [52]; *Weller v Associated Newspapers Ltd High Court* [2014] EWHC 1163.

Information in the public domain

Information could be protected by the doctrine of confidence if it retained a quality of confidentiality. But, clearly, information is not confidential if it is already in the public domain. As discussed, it is now only necessary to ask whether the information qualifies as private information. However, information will be neither confidential nor private if it is already in the public domain. So the discussion begins by considering the point at which information can be said to have lost its quality of confidentiality or, now, of privacy. It will be found that privacy values, such as seeking to prevent humiliation, distress, indignity, and to preserve informational autonomy, have come to dominate the public domain inquiry to a very significant extent.

Section 12(4) HRA confirms that, when considering when to grant an injunction, the court must 'have regard to the extent to which the information has become, or is about to become, available to the public'. Information could be viewed as public, as opposed to private, either because it is already known to many people, so it has lost its private quality, or – it was thought pre-HRA and in the early HRA years – because it was made available in a public place on the basis that it would then be known to anyone who happened to be present.

Making a determination that information has lost its private quality because it is known to a number of people has often been problematic. In the US prior publicity generally negatives liability.[293] In contrast, the English doctrine of confidence and s 12(4)(a)(i) of the HRA have adopted a more nuanced approach, whereby the existence of prior publicity is a relevant but not conclusive factor. Thus, in the leading pre-HRA decision, *AG v Guardian Newspapers Ltd (No 2)*,[294] Lord Keith argued that whether information is in the public domain will often be a matter of degree and therefore prior disclosure to a limited group of people might not rob the information of its confidentiality, an approach which received general support in the case.[295]

It is now clear that information can remain 'private' or confidential even though it is known to a number of persons. In *Mills v News Groups Newspapers*,[296] which concerned the threatened publication of the applicant's address in the *Sun*, the judge said: 'The fact that information may be known to a limited number of members of the public does not of itself prevent it having and retaining the character of confidentiality, or even that it has previously been very widely available.'[297] Similarly, in *Campbell*, there was no suggestion that the limited number of people who knew the details of the model's attendance at Narcotics Anonymous had robbed the information of its confidential quality.

---

293 See, e.g., *Sidis* 113 F 2d 806 (2d Cir 1940) and *Forsher v Bugliosi* 26 Cal 3d 792, 608 P 2d 716, 163 Cal Rptr 628 (1980); *cf* the earlier decision in *Melvin v Reid* 112 Cal App 283 (1931). See also, the decision in *Ann-Margret v High Society Magazine Inc* (1980) 498 F Supp 401 in which a well-known actress was denied relief in respect of the publication of a nude photograph of her.

294 [1990] 1 AC 109.

295 *Ibid*, p 260. His Lordship was referring specifically to the possibility of publication abroad – *Spycatcher* had been published in the United States – but the principle is of general application. Sir John Donaldson in the Court of Appeal took the same approach, remarking that 'it is a matter of degree' (*ibid*, p 177), as did Scott J (*ibid*, p 149). See also *AG v Guardian Newspapers* [1987] 1 WLR 1248 (the first *Spycatcher* case).

296 [2001] EMLR 41.

297 *Ibid*, at para 25.

Similarly, in *Blair v Associated Newspapers*,[298] in which Cherie Blair was granted a series of injunctions against various parties to prevent the publication of details of her domestic arrangements, provided by a former nanny, the fact that one print-run of the *Mail on Sunday* carrying the offending article had already been distributed was held not to have robbed the information of its confidential quality. That was a significant decision since thousands of people would have read the article. In principle, it is argued, it was correct since the mere fact that a newspaper manages to put out one print run before the plaintiff can obtain an interim injunction should not preclude the grant of relief on the basis that the defendant should not be able to profit from his own wrongdoing. In *Mckennitt v Ash* Eady J said at first instance: 'it does not necessarily follow that because personal information has been revealed impermissibly to one set of newspapers, or to readers within one jurisdiction, that there can be no further intrusion upon a claimant's privacy by further revelations'.[299] Thus, the judges are strongly adhering to a key principle of informational autonomy – that persons constantly choose the forums and the persons to whom they disclose some personal information: the fact that it is disclosed in a particular setting to a particular group – as in *Mckennitt* in respect of some of the information – does not mean that the individual condones its mass dissemination.

This approach is clearly to be preferred to the more absolutist US stance. While the latter has the advantage of making it relatively easy to predict in advance what can be disclosed with impunity, it relies, as Paton-Simpson has persuasively argued, on a simplistic and misleading attitude whereby privacy is treated as an all-or-nothing concept, rather than as a matter of degree.[300] Attention in privacy cases now focuses on the value of the speech (see below), not on a mechanistic application of a public domain test – a test that fails to focus on the key issue: the distress caused by the disclosure of the information.

A second public domain matter is that it used to be the case pre-HRA that confidence would in general not cover instances where the information was initially obtained through observation in a public place. However, the decision in *HRH Princess of Wales v MGN Newspapers Ltd and Others*[301] casts some doubt on this contention, since the information in question was obtained in a gymnasium attended by other club members and therefore, clearly, it had been disseminated to an extent, albeit in a manner limited enough to prevent it from being viewed as in the public domain. An interim injunction to protect the information was nevertheless granted. Thus, at the time it appeared to be clear that information obtained by means of observation in similar semi-public places, such as restaurants, might be found to retain the necessary quality of confidence.

It became much clearer post-HRA that the courts were prepared to view information already partly in the public domain as worthy of protection on the ground that it could still be viewed as private.[302] *Campbell* made it clear that the gathering of information in a public location did not mean that it was robbed of its confidentiality. *Von Hannover* confirmed that that is clearly the position adopted at Strasbourg. Baroness Hale in

298 Case no HQ0001236.
299 [2005] EWHC 3003 (QB) [81].
300 See Paton-Simpson, E, 'Private circles and public squares: invasion of privacy by the publication of "private facts"' (1998) 61 MLR 318.
301 Transcript, Association of Official Shorthandwriters Limited, 8 November 1993.
302 See *Mills v News Group Newspapers* [2001] EMLR 41, above p 741 on this point.

Campbell qualified her finding on the public domain point by demanding that where a private/daily life activity takes place in public, it must have an *added* privacy element in order to overcome the argument that the material was in the public domain since the activity occurred in a public location. She said: 'The activity photographed must be private.'[303] *Von Hannover*, as discussed above, did *not* demand this added privacy element. But Lord Hope did not demand that the activity captured by photographers should be of an especially significant nature in terms of privacy; he said: 'But these were not just pictures of a street scene where she happened to be when the photographs were taken. They were taken deliberately, in secret and with a view to their publication in conjunction with the article.'[304] Those *dicta* comport quite readily with the findings of the Strasbourg Court, but Baroness Hale's view appears to have prevailed, as discussed above.

What is the guiding principle to be derived from these findings on the public domain issue, including those in *Peck* and *Von Hannover*? It is suggested that it is simply that of recognising the value of allowing persons control over the mass dissemination of private information, taking private information to mean information relating to a person's personal, as opposed to public, life.[305] Obviously there will be circumstances where mass dissemination of the information has already occurred to the point where the information cannot be viewed as private. But the courts appear to be reluctant, as the *Blair* case indicated, to accept that a person has *lost control* of their private information, unless prior mass publicity forces them to that conclusion. In taking this stance it is clear that the judges have shown recognition of the underlying values of dignity and autonomy at stake.

So it is reasonable to conclude that the law is now seeking to protect the ability of the individual to control the mass dissemination of private information. The fact that the information is already known to some or that it was obtained in an inherently uncontrolled environment, such as the street, are not the key factors. Private life activities ranging from the everyday (walking with a friend in the street), to the intensely intimate (attempting suicide), can occur in public. Private *facts* – such as a revelation that a person, thought to be straight, is in a gay relationship, or that a person is having an affair – can be revealed in public locations. The *location* of the activities has already been discarded as non-determinative and, as indicated, it plays only a residual role in UK privacy cases in the sense that private facts relating to an adult public figure revealed in a public place appear to need some added seriousness in comparison with such facts revealed in a private place. The role of 'public domain' as a limiting factor in terms of location has diminished but not disappeared in privacy claims, although arguably it can still play an important part in confidentiality ones. The first public domain issue is still of significance where the plaintiff, not the defendant, deliberately placed the information in the public domain by revealing it to reporters or others.[306]

---

303   *Campbell v MGN Ltd* [2004] 2 AC [154].
304   *Ibid*, at [123].
305   See e.g., Hughes, K, 'Photographs in Public Places and Privacy' (2009) 1(2) Journal of Media Law 159.
306   It can also be argued that in a number of circumstances a person has impliedly consented to the placement of the information in the public domain; this is true of reporting of public occasions such as sporting events or ceremonies where the person in question is taking part in a public sense in the event. The position of spectators is not so clear-cut. See the comments of the Major government in *Privacy*

A note on 'public domain' in state confidentiality cases[307]

It may be noted that *state* confidentiality claims appear to be moving in a direction entirely opposed to that indicated in *Campbell* and in *Von Hannover*. In other words, a *contrary* development is apparent, it is suggested, in relation to *government* assertions of a breach of confidence. As Chapter 8 indicated, *AG v Times*, the Tomlinson case,[308] suggested that a tendency to find that information is already in the public domain, even where it has been disseminated only to a small group of persons, is apparent.[309] If it can eventually be said that the interpretation of 'public domain' differs depending on whether the plaintiff is the government or a private individual, this would accord with the requirements of Strasbourg jurisprudence as recognised under s 2 HRA since, in the former instance, the strong individual right under Art 8 is not also at stake.

Section 12(4)(a)(i) HRA requires a court to 'have particular regard' to 'the extent to which the material has, or is about to become available to the public' when considering the grant of relief which, if granted, might affect the exercise of the Art 10 right (s 12(1)). If the development indicated becomes a settled one, this would mean that the courts had accepted that differing approaches should be taken to the interpretation of s 12(4)(a)(i) of the HRA, depending on whether Art 8 was or was not at stake. The requirement to take into account the extent to which the material is *about to* become available could have the effect of widening the public domain test in a manner reconcilable with the spirit of *AG v Times* (Tomlinson case), but not with *Von Hannover* or *Campbell*. So since s 12(4) should be interpreted compatibly with Art 8 under s 3 HRA, a differentiated use of the public domain argument in privacy cases and in state ones under the doctrine of confidence, is justified.

The so-called doctrine of 'waiver'

It can be argued that a plaintiff has 'waived' his or her right to respect for private life due to seeking publicity on the potentially private matter in question. In the pre-HRA case of *Woodward v Hutchins*,[310] intimate facts about Tom Jones and another pop star were revealed to the *Daily Mirror* by a former agent who had been their confidante. The plaintiffs sought an injunction on the ground of breach of confidence. There had been a confidential relationship and they claimed that the agent should not be able to take unfair advantage of that confidentiality. The Court of Appeal refused to uphold the claim on the basis that the plaintiffs had sought to publicise themselves in order to present a certain favourable 'image' and therefore could not complain if the truth were later revealed. The public interest in knowing the truth about the plaintiffs seemed to rest on a refusal to use the law to protect their attempt to mislead the public.

---

and *Media Intrusion: The Government's Response*, Cm 2918, para 3.14 and the rejoinder by Bingham LJ (writing extra-judicially) 'Should There Be a Law to Protect Personal Rights to Privacy' (1996) 5 EHRLR 450. Under the US tort, the test for consent is whether the complained of publicity differed 'materially . . . in kind or extent' from the informational material in relation to which consent was actually given, Prosser, D, 'Privacy' (1960) 48 Calif L Rev 383, p 420.

307 These cases are briefly discussed in Chapter 8, pp 523–34.

308 See Chapter 8, p 523.

309 See pp 523–24.

310 [1977] 1 WLR 760, CA.

In *Campbell*, however, it was made clear that there is no *general* defence of waiver as in *Woodward*. The applicant herself had conceded that *the Mirror* was entitled to publish the fact that she was a drug addict and was receiving treatment for her addiction; it was accepted that the press was entitled to expose the falsity of her previous public statements that she did not take drugs and was not a drug addict. As Phillipson puts it, 'This, however, was on the basis that there was a public interest in preventing the public from being misled,[311] *not* on any notion that that publicity-seeking *in itself* destroys an individual's reasonable expectation of privacy.'[312] Campbell's general statements that she was not a drug addict did not defeat, it was found, her expectation of privacy in relation to the *details* of her treatment for drug addiction. Lord Hoffmann found, '[Campbell] is a public figure who has had a long and symbiotic relationship with the media. A person may attract or even seek publicity about some aspects of his or her life without creating any public interest in the publication of personal information about other matters.'[313] None of their lordships accepted that Campbell's publicity-seeking in the past would destroy protection for her private life.

However, certain post-HRA cases indicate a judicial acceptance of a position whereby a claimant's reasonable expectation of privacy as regards his personal information is subject to a 'zonal waiver' – a partial waiver, albeit not a blanket waiver as in *Woodward*. In *A v B*[314] the claimant sought an injunction against an article written by the claimant rock singer's former wife, which he believed would contain disclosures about the effects of drugs on him and his drug rehabilitation at Narcotics Anonymous. He had himself admitted to the press on previous occasions his own use of drugs. The judge found as regards the 'waiver' argument that it was critical to the claim that the claimant has a reasonable expectation of privacy as regards personal information that he has not conducted himself in a way that evinces a desire to publicise personal information in a similar category to the information that he claims is private.[315] The judge found that where a claimant had decided to 'lift the veil' on his personal affairs:

> the court's characterisation of what is truly in the public domain will not be tied specifically to the details revealed in the past *but rather focus upon the general area or zone of the claimant's personal life (e.g., drug addiction) which he has chosen to expose*. (emphasis added)[316]

The idea of a 'zonal waiver' in *A v B* is clearly in tension with the idea of informational autonomy, since it imposes on the plaintiff an intention to place one's information in the

---

311 See, e.g., [2004] 2 AC 457 per Lord Nicholls at [24]: 'where a public figure chooses to present a false image and make untrue pronouncements about his or her life, the press will normally be entitled to put the record straight.' This approach was endorsed by Lord Hoffmann at [58] and Lord Hope at [82].

312 *Media Freedom under the Human Rights Act, op cit* fn 1, at p 776. For a now out-dated view, see the remarks of Lord Wakeham, former chair of the Press Complaints Commission, to the effect that the former Princess of Wales had made herself 'fair game' for public analysis of her private life by discussing it herself on television (*The Times*, 2 May 1996). A similar argument was also put forward in *Mills v News Group Newspapers* [2001] EMLR 41, by the *Sun*.

313 [2004] 2 WLR 1232 at [57].

314 *A v B* [2005] EWHC 1651 (QB).

315 *Ibid*, [21].

316 *Ibid*, [28].

public domain, not only in relation to one revelation, but in relation to future ones in the same 'zone' of activity. The doctrine has subsequently received judicial criticism,[317] but has been confirmed in *Murray v Express Newspapers Plc*,[318] and has received a degree of support in recent Strasbourg case law.[319] *Axel Springer v Germany*,[320] discussed further below, concerned a media company that had been prevented from reporting the arrest and conviction of an actor for a drug offence. The German courts had upheld the issuance of an injunction to prevent the publication of this information on the basis of the actor's right to the protection of his 'personality rights'.[321] The ECtHR accepted that this injunction amounted to a disproportionate interference with the media company's Art 10(1) right.[322] The Court's reasoning is relevant to the reasonable expectation of privacy under Art 8(1). The Court confirmed that 'the conduct of the person concerned prior to publication of the report or the fact that the photo and the related information have already appeared in an earlier publication are. . . factors to be taken into consideration', but emphasised that 'the mere fact of having cooperated with the press on previous occasions' could not deprive a claimant of his reasonable expectation of privacy.[323] The Court found that the actor 'had. . . revealed details about his private life in a number of interviews . . . he had therefore actively sought the limelight'[324] and therefore his reasonable expectation of privacy was accordingly reduced.

The 'zonal waiver' approach arguably influenced the decision of *AAA v Associated Newspapers*.[325] In *AAA* the child claimant sought damages and an injunction against a newspaper in relation to a publication discussing her paternity. In particular, the newspaper sought to publish speculations that her father, an elected politician, had engaged in extra-marital sex with her mother. (The public interest element of this claim is examined below; the current discussion is limited to the judicial finding regarding the reduction in the claimant's reasonable expectation of privacy.) It was found that the publication of an interview with the mother in another magazine that had contained references to the claimant's father had reduced the daughter's reasonable expectation of privacy, despite it also including an explicit reference to the mother's refusal to discuss her daughter's paternity. The mother's agreement to proceed with the interview in the knowledge that there would be discussion of the father was found to be indicative of an

---

317   *HRH Prince of Wales v Associated Newspapers Ltd* [2006] EWHC 522 (Ch) 'I dissent from the view that, by speaking out publicly both in speeches and in published articles on issues which in the widest sense are political, the claimant has somehow forfeited any reasonable expectation of privacy in respect of such matters when committed to a handwritten journal not intended by the claimant to be open to public scrutiny' (at [115]). See also *Mckennitt v Ash* [2005] EWHC 3003 (QB) 'there is . . . a significant difference between choosing to reveal aspects of private life with which one feels comfortable and yielding up to public scrutiny every detail of personal life' ([79]).

318   [2008] EWCA Civ 446: 'It should be noted that if the parents of a child courted publicity by procuring the publication of photographs of the child in order to promote their own interests, the position would or might be quite different from a case like this, where the parents have taken care to keep their children out of the public gaze'.

319   See e.g., *Axel Springer v Germany* (2012) 55 EHRR 6.

320   *Ibid.*

321   Paras 18 and 42.

322   Paras 110–111.

323   Para 92.

324   Para 101.

325   [2013] EWCA Civ 554.

'ambivalent' desire to keep her daughter's paternity private, which was insufficient to create a reasonable expectation of privacy about that information.[326]

The High Court judge's assessment, confirmed by the Court of Appeal, was that the mother's behaviour was indicative of a 'wish to inform certain individuals, if not of the father's identity, then at least to point them in a certain direction'.[327] The judge found that the mother wished to correct a perception that the daughter's conception was a 'drunken mistake' and the speculation she thus engendered prevented her claiming a reasonable expectation of privacy on behalf of her daughter in relation to the specific information of her daughter's paternity.[328]

To conclude on 'waiver' – it is clear that as a general 'defence' to privacy claims it has been marginalised, although *Woodward* has not been expressly over-ruled.[329] A person who has placed details of her private life in the public domain by giving interviews to magazines on a specific matter may find that that defeats her expectation of privacy, because the matter is not accounted private (possibly even if some details as to the matter in question were not previously disclosed). Or if a person has misled the public that may provide a public interest argument that the record should be set straight. In *Campbell* the claimant's denial of her drug addiction meant that the fact that she was receiving drug treatment lost protection on the basis that there was a public interest in knowing the truth that defeated her expectation of privacy. Thus the defence of waiver appears to have been partly swallowed up by the balancing act between speech and privacy that is discussed below. However, the influence of 'waiver' can be discerned in various post-HRA cases, especially *A v B*.[330] The idea of 'zonal waiver' is perhaps now best interpreted – as it was in *Axel Springer* and *AAA* – as a particularly persuasive factor weighing against the finding that a claimant who has courted publicity regarding an area of his personal life should have a reasonable expectation of privacy regarding personal information pertaining to that area.

Balancing speech and privacy claims under the HRA

The statutory scheme of the HRA, the Convention rights and the relevant privacy codes – now the IPSO (formerly PCC) code – provide the ground rules for determining when material should be published despite the invasion of privacy that will occur. Under the HRA, it was thought originally, as *Venables*[331] and *Mills*[332] indicated, that the balancing act would occur by reference to s 12(4) HRA that appears to accord priority to Art 10.[333] The House of Lords in *Campbell*[334] gave far more extensive guidance on

---

326 *Ibid*, [32], [34].
327 [2012] EWHC 2103 (QB) [28].
328 *Ibid*, [27].
329 Brooke LJ in *Douglas v Hello!* dismissed the argument that the couple's admitted previous courting of publicity precluded protection for their privacy; he said that he 'did not obtain any assistance' by citation of *Woodward v Hutchins*': [2001] QB 967, 995.
330 *A v B* [2005] EWHC 1651.
331 [2001] 1 All ER 908.
332 [2001] EMLR 41.
333 As pointed out in *Campbell v MGN Ltd* [2004] UKHL 22 [138] this is consistent with Resolution 1165 (1998) of the Parliamentary Assembly of the Council of Europe, para 10, which affirms the equal value of the two rights.
334 *Campbell v MGN Ltd* [2004] UKHL 22.

the balancing act and made it clear that Arts 8 and 10 must be treated equally despite s 12(4). The balancing act is affected by the importation of the Strasbourg concepts of necessity and proportionality as applied under Arts 10 and 8 ECHR, scheduled in the HRA. The second paragraphs of Arts 8 and 10 under the HRA provide the principal mechanism by which to seek to create a balanced resolution of the two rights of privacy and speech. The IPSO privacy code provisions may be relevant in terms of the weight to be placed on either side of the equation. Public interest factors may go to the value to be placed on the speech.

Development of the 'parallel analysis'

The House of Lords in the seminal decision of *Campbell v MGN* set out the domestic approach to balancing Arts 8 and 10 in privacy cases.[335] The House of Lords adopted the approach taken in the Court of Appeal decision of *Re S*.[336] Lady Hale in *Re S* found that it was not merely necessary to consider Art 8 as an exception to Art 10 under Art 10(2); it was also necessary to consider Art 10 as an exception to Art 8, under Art 8(2). Thus, the Court must first ask whether Art 10 is engaged in a privacy case against the press. The standard Convention tests should then be followed, under Art 10(2), asking whether the interference with the Art 10 guarantee proposed by the plaintiff would be necessary in a democratic society and proportionate to the legitimate aim of protecting private life, as a 'right of others'. The Court should then consider the issue from the opposing perspective under Art 8, with the rights reversed in position, so that the speech interest is treated as an exception to the primary right to respect for privacy under Art 8. The same inquiries as to necessity and proportionality should then be made from this opposing perspective, again under the rights of others exception which also appears in Art 8(2). Lord Steyn, in *Re S*, a speech with which the other members of the House concurred, deduced a number of principles from the decision of the House in *Campbell v MGN*:

> First, neither article has as such precedence over the other. Secondly, where the values under the two articles are in conflict, an intense focus on the comparative importance of the specific rights being claimed in the individual case is necessary. Thirdly, the justifications for interfering with or restricting each right must be taken into account. Finally, the proportionality test must be applied to each.[337]

This process may be termed the 'parallel analysis'.[338] The method of resolving conflicts between Arts 8 and 10 is well established in Strasbourg case law. An illustration of this is provided by the case of *Tammer v Estonia*.[339] In *Tammer v Estonia* the journalist applicant had been subject to a criminal penalty in respect of the publication of a

---

335   *Re S (a child)* [2005] 1 AC 593.
336   *Re S (a child)* [2003] 2 FCR 577, subsequently reaffirmed by the House of Lords [2005] 1 AC 593.
337   *Ibid*, [17].
338   Tomlinson, H, and Rogers, H, coined the term 'parallel analysis': 'Privacy and Expression: Convention Rights and Interim Injunctions' [2003] EHRLR 37, 50.
339   *Tammer v Estonia* (2003) 37 EHRR 43.

hard-hitting interview relating to a former political aide, alleging that she had broken up the prime minister's marriage by having an affair with him and had deserted her own children. His application under Art 10 failed before the Court, which found that the remarks in question related to the former aide's private life; the restriction upon the journalist's Art 10 rights, taking into account the lightness of the penalty imposed, was therefore a necessary and proportionate response to the need to uphold the privacy of the aide.[340]

Similarly in *Peck v United Kingdom*[341] the Court found a breach of Art 8 rights even where significant restrictions on Art 10 rights were thereby created. As mentioned above, the case concerned CCTV footage of an attempted suicide in the street, which was then shown on national television. The applicant was identifiable from the footage and the broadcasting of it was found to create a breach of Art 8. The decision is of significance, not only because it allowed for the suppression of freedom of expression on a matter of some significant public interest, but also because it demonstrates that freedom of expression can be curbed even where the speech suppressed is already partly in the public domain.

In *Campbell*, as part of the 'parallel analysis' of proportionality, the poverty of the speech claim was made clear. Lord Nicholls found: 'The need to be free to disseminate information regarding Miss Campbell's drug addiction is of a lower order than the need for freedom to disseminate information on some other subjects such as political information.'[342] Lady Hale similarly held: 'there are undoubtedly different types of speech' and that some of those 'are more deserving of protection in a democratic society than others'; speech would be valuable where it included:

> revealing information about public figures, especially those in elective office, which would otherwise be private but is relevant to their participation in public life. Intellectual and educational speech and expression are also important in a democracy, not least because they enable the development of individuals' potential to play a full part in society and in our democratic life. Artistic speech and expression is important for similar reasons, in fostering both individual originality and creativity and the free-thinking and dynamic society we so much value.[343]

Lord Hope found:

> But it should also be recognised that the right of the public to receive information about the details of her treatment was of a much lower order than the undoubted right to know that she was misleading the public when she said that she did not take drugs. In *Dudgeon v United Kingdom* (1981) 4 EHRR 149, para 52 the European Court said that the more intimate the aspects of private life which are being interfered with, the more serious must be the reasons for doing so before the interference can be legitimate. Clayton and Tomlinson, *The Law of Human Rights* (2000), para 15.162, point out that the court has distinguished three kinds of expression:

---

340 *Ibid*, paras 69–70.
341 *Peck v United Kingdom* (2003) 36 EHRR 41. See above pp 696–97.
342 *Campbell v MGN* [2004] 2 WLR 1232 [29]; for further discussion of *Campbell*, see above pp 733–34.
343 *Ibid*, [148].

political expression, artistic expression and commercial expression, and that it consistently attaches great importance to political expression and applies rather less rigorous principles to expression which is artistic and commercial. According to the court's well-established case law, freedom of expression constitutes one of the essential foundations of a democratic society and one of the basic conditions for its progress and the self-fulfilment of each individual: *Tammer v Estonia* (2001) 37 EHRR 857, para 59. But there were no political or democratic values at stake here, nor has any pressing social need been identified.[344]

He concluded that a person's right to privacy can be limited by 'the public's interest in knowing about certain traits of her personality and certain aspects of her private life'.[345] But he found that in order to deprive Miss Campbell of her right to privacy it would not be enough to argue 'that she is a celebrity and that her private life is newsworthy'.

> Treating the complained-of details merely as background was to undervalue the importance that was to be attached to the need, if Miss Campbell was to be protected, to keep these details private. And it is hard to see that there was any compelling need for the public to know the name of the organisation that she was attending for the therapy, or for the other details of it to be set out.[346]

Therefore he found that in relation to the details complained of, including the picture taken of Ms Campbell outside the NA clinic, other than the fact of receiving drug treatment, a remedy should be granted, a conclusion with which the Lords in the majority agreed.

In *Von Hannover v Germany*,[347] which was decided shortly after *Campbell*, the Strasbourg Court addressed an Art 8 claim in respect of journalism that invaded the applicant's privacy. As indicated above, journalists had followed Princess Caroline, photographing and recording trivial details of her personal life, such as dining with her children or shopping. The Strasbourg Court found as regards the public interest dimension:

> the publication of the photos and articles in question, of which the sole purpose was to satisfy the curiosity of a particular readership regarding the details of the applicant's private life, cannot be deemed to contribute to any debate of general interest to society despite the applicant being known to the public.[348]

The Court further found:

> a fundamental distinction needs to be made between reporting facts – even controversial ones – capable of contributing to a debate in a democratic society, relating to politicians in the exercise of their functions, for example, and reporting details

---

344 *Campbell v MGN Ltd* [2004] 2 AC 457 at [117].
345 He relied on L'Heureux-Dubé and Bastarache JJ in the Supreme Court of Canada recognised in *Aubry v Les Editions Vice-Versa Inc* [1998] 1 SCR 591, paras 57–58.
346 *Campbell v MGN Ltd* [2004] 2 AC 457 [120].
347 *Von Hannover v Germany* (2005) 40 EHRR 1; see in particular paras 63, 64, 65, 66, 76.
348 *Ibid*, para 65.

of the private life of an individual who, moreover, as in this case, does not exercise official functions. While in the former case the press exercises its vital role of 'watchdog' in a democracy by contributing to 'impart[ing] information and ideas on matters of public interest . . . it does not do so in the latter case . . . The situation here does not come within the sphere of any political or public debate because the published photos and accompanying commentaries relate exclusively to details of the applicant's private life.[349]

Since the photographs and publications 'made no contribution' – due to their banal and anodyne nature – to a debate of general interest, the interest in press freedom under Art 10 had to give way, it was found, to the princess's privacy interests. Thus, the Court found that the reporting of the private life of a public figure is not an aspect of the media's watchdog role, except in special circumstances where aspects of his or her private life relate to political or public debate. In *Campbell* the details related exclusively to the applicant's private life and in those circumstances, it was determined, freedom of expression had to be narrowly interpreted. That narrow interpretation appeared to mean impliedly that while the reporting was viewed as constituting expression, interferences with it would almost inevitably be justified due to its nature. The Court did appear to accept that Art 10 was engaged, but it made it clear that the type of speech in question would always, as a general rule, tend to be afforded a very low weight.[350] Material consisting merely of photographs showing daily life activities of celebrities accompanied by no reporting attempting to create links to wider issues is the staple fare of many magazines and newspapers. So the possible public interest value of such photographs should not be exaggerated. Further, it must be borne in mind that consented-to photographs of celebrities are readily available. Any desires of the audience to see their lifestyles ratified, or to observe social trends embodied in the lives of celebrities, already have a ready outlet.

In the House of Lords in *Re S*,[351] – deciding upon a very different application of the balancing act in *Campbell* and *Von Hannover* – Lord Steyn, giving the leading judgment, found, as indicated above, that the interest in open reporting of the criminal process outweighed the privacy interest of the child in question. He relied on making a finding as to the strong general rule allowing for the reporting of criminal trials, and allowed the Art 10 argument therefore to prevail over the Art 8 interest at stake. But in *Re S* the private and family life claim was very strong in terms of both informational and substantive autonomy. The revelation of the mother's identity was likely to affect S's ability to recover from the impact on him of his brother's death and mother's trial for the murder, and therefore it was especially crucial that her identity should not be revealed in the immediate aftermath of his brother's death. S was a victim in a very real sense of the alleged offence: he lost his mother (who was later imprisoned for the murder of his brother) and his brother and his high risk of psychiatric harm was likely to be enhanced, according to expert evidence, depending on the level of publicity.[352] The suffering he was likely to undergo as a result of the publicity in terms of bullying and teasing was thought likely to have such an impact on him, in terms of exacerbating

---

349 *Von Hannover v Germany* (2005) 40 EHRR 1 at paras 63, 64.
350 See further *Media Freedom under the Human Rights Act, op cit* fn 1, at p 695.
351 [2004] UKHL 47.
352 See *Re S* [2003] EWCA Civ 963 [39] (CA) per Hale LJ.

the inevitable psychiatric harm he would suffer, that the precarious placement with his father was thought to be likely to break down. So very intimate relationships were at stake in extremely compelling circumstances. A range of Art 8 values were very strongly engaged. Nevertheless, Lord Steyn gave the privacy claim a very cursory treatment, dismissing it in two paragraphs of his speech.

In contrast to the privacy claim in *Re S*, the speech claim was weak; Lord Steyn was obviously right to identify the interest in open justice as a very significant matter in terms of speech values, but wrong, it is argued, to proceed to the assumption that knowledge of S's identity was necessary in order to serve that interest. The speech interest engaged in publishing photographs of the mother with the dead boy and revealing the mother's name was minimal: discussion of the circumstances surrounding the murder could have occurred in the press on a basis of anonymity, at least during the mother's trial. The mother's name would clearly mean nothing to the vast majority of the readers of the newspapers in question. Thus the public interest could have been served, since the case raised certain wider issues, while still protecting S. This judgment suggests that the courts are more comfortable with free speech than with privacy claims: as discussed above, free speech values have traditionally had far more hold on the common law than privacy values have. Although the parallel analysis was formally conducted in *Re S*, it is suggested that it was undertaken in a tokenistic fashion – no real effort was made to subject the true value of the speech claim to scrutiny; conversely, the privacy claim was accorded insufficient weight. Thus, although the Lords in *Re S* endorsed *Campbell*, there seemed to be no recognition of the fact that the decision gave the impression of departing in spirit from the fundamental approach of *Campbell*, that of presumptive equality of Arts 10 and 8.

Factors affecting the balancing Act

It is possible to identify a range of factors that will weigh strongly in the balance on one side or the other at the second stage of the proportionality enquiry.[353] Clearly, that inquiry will be highly fact-sensitive. As *Campbell* made clear, the speech claim will be weakened if the speech fails to partake in the justificatory speech rationales discussed above; that is particularly the case where the speech does not relate to a civic function (including involvement in the legal process, such as arrest).[354] The decision in *Von Hannover* identified a category of speech – 'infotainment' – that will in most circumstances be overridden by privacy interests since it is devoid of the speech value indicated by those rationales.[355] The speech at issue in *Von Hannover* was not illustrative of social trends; it had no wider purpose than to entertain; it was aimed at an audience motivated purely by curiosity. The photograph at issue in *Campbell* was also of very little

---

353 For further discussion of such factors see *Media Freedom Under the Human Rights Act, op cit*, fn 1 at Chapters 15 and 16.

354 Above, p 733. See also Recommendation Rec(2003)13 of the Committee of Ministers, Appendix, Principle 1.

355 See also *Mosley v UK* [2011] ECHR 774 para 114; *Rocknroll v News Group Newspapers Ltd* [2013] EWHC 24; *K v News Group Newspapers Ltd* [2011] EWCA Civ 439 [33]–[39]. It may be noted that the Supreme Court has found this category of speech is covered by the First Amendment in the US: 'There is no doubt that entertainment, as well as news, enjoys First Amendment protection': *Zaccchini v Sciprrs-Howard Broad Co*, 433 US 562, 578 (1978).

value in speech terms, as Lord Hoffmann pointed out. Conversely, the speech claim will be strengthened if one of the speech-based rationales is present, even if it cannot be viewed as political expression. If the interest in open justice is at stake that will tend to strengthen it very strongly (as the House of Lords found in *Re S*), but it will not inevitably overcome the privacy claim. Where speech of public interest value is in issue, taking account *inter alia* of the public interest factors discussed above,[356] it would have a higher value than the speech at issue in *Von Hannover*.

The privacy claim will be strengthened if sensitive personal data as designated by the DPA 1998 is at stake (see below). If a case concerns a child that will also strengthen the claim. If intrusive methods such as phone hacking are used to obtain the information, particularly those that could potentially attract criminal sanctions,[357] that will weigh in the balance in favour of privacy. In assessing the gravity of the invasion of privacy involved, further considerations might be of relevance. It could be asked whether the events reported happened in a very intimate setting (for example, the plaintiff's home) or in a more 'public' environment, such as a restaurant, a beach, or the street. On the other hand, if selective disclosure of personal information appears to be part of a deliberate, systematic attempt to manipulate the media by giving a false impression of the claimant's life to the public on a matter of some importance that might arguably weaken the privacy claim,[358] although great caution must be used in deploying this argument since selective disclosure of certain personal matters is entirely in accord with informational autonomy; the mere fact that a person is a celebrity does not mean that they are under a duty to reveal intimate details of their sex life. The fact that the public is in ignorance as to certain aspects of it should be irrelevant.

If breaches of the IPSO Code have occurred, including breaches relating to the use of clandestine devices and subterfuge, it is suggested that that is a matter a court can properly take into account in terms of strengthening the privacy claim, under s 12(4) HRA. The *Mills* case in particular made it clear that the code provides a guide to the weight to be accorded to privacy factors.[359] If traditional duties of confidence are involved, including in particular contractual duties, that will also add strongly to the privacy claim (as in *HRH Prince of Wales v Associated Newspapers Ltd*).[360] The *form* in which the information is recorded (e.g., in a diary or on a personal mobile phone), or the form in which it is captured by the defendant may also be relevant in enhancing the privacy claim. The fact that other Convention rights are also implicated may strengthen the privacy claim. If the values underlying other rights could be viewed as engaged, as in *Re S*, in respect of Art 6(1), that might strengthen either claim.

Recent approaches to the 'parallel analysis'

This section considers a number of significant recent cases in which the parallel analysis was conducted in order to resolve the clash between speech and privacy in each

---

356 See p 728.
357 See p 692, fn 11 above, which refers to the conviction of Goodman, editor of the *News of the World*, in relation to phone-tapping.
358 See Tugendhat and Christie on this point (2002), *op cit*, fn 1 at p 344.
359 *Mills v News Group Newspapers Ltd* [2001] EMLR 41.
360 [2006] EWCA Civ 1776; see also the first instance judgment per Blackburne J [2006] EWHC 522 (Ch).

instance. In *HRH Prince of Wales v Associated Newspapers Ltd*[361] the Court of Appeal had to consider a claim for breach of privacy and confidence brought by the prince against the *Mail on Sunday*, which had published details from his private diary. The diary in question was one of eight given to the paper by Sarah Goodall, a secretary in his private office from 1988 to 2000. The journals were handwritten accounts that Charles made following foreign visits over the past 30 years and that he circulated 'in confidence' to between 50 and 75 people, including politicians, actors, journalists and other people in the media. The employment contracts of each of those in Prince Charles' service provided that any information in relation to him that was acquired during the course of his or her employment was subject to an undertaking of confidence and was not to be disclosed to any unauthorised person.

Prince Charles alleged that the publication of the extracts from the journal interfered with his right to respect for his private life and his correspondence under Art 8 of the Convention, so that it constituted in a breach of privacy. The *Mail on Sunday* denied this but alleged, in the alternative, that any interference with this right was justified under Art 8(2) as necessary to protect the rights of the newspaper and the public under Art 10. Prince Charles had accepted that the relief that he claimed amounted to a restriction on the newspaper's right of freedom of expression under Art 10, but he alleged that this restriction was justified under Art 10(2) as necessary to protect his right to privacy, his copyright and to prevent the disclosure of information received in confidence.

The Court of Appeal found that the action concerned a claim for breach of privacy but that all the elements of a claim for breach of confidence under the old law were evident since the information was disclosed in breach of a 'well-recognised relationship of confidence, that which exists between master and servant'.[362] So a weighty element affecting the balance was the importance in a democratic society of upholding duties of confidence between individuals. It was argued on the other hand on behalf of the newspaper that Prince Charles, as heir to the throne, was a public figure who had controversially courted public attention and used the media to publicise views, particularly in relation to the Chinese, of a similar kind to those expressed in the journal, so he could have no reasonable expectation that the journal would remain confidential.[363] The first instance judge had found, and the Court of Appeal agreed, that this factor did not go to the question of whether the content of the journal was confidential, but rather to the question whether that confidentiality would have to give way when weighed against the rights of freedom of expression enjoyed by the newspaper and its readers.

The Court found that in general the Strasbourg Court views with disfavour attempts to suppress publication of information that is of genuine public interest and noted that where it relates to a matter of major public concern, even medical confidentiality may not prevail.[364] The Court noted that where no breach of a confidential relationship is involved, the balance will be between Art 8 and Art 10 rights and will usually involve weighing the nature and consequences of the breach of privacy against the public interest, if any, in the disclosure of private information. But the Court found that position

---

361 *HRH Prince of Wales v Associated Newspapers Ltd* [2006] EWCA Civ 1776.
362 *Ibid*, at [28].
363 *Ibid*, [45].
364 The Court relied on *Editions Plon v France* (2006) 42 EHRR 36.

would be different where the disclosure related, as it did in the instant case, to 'information received in confidence'. It found:

> the test to be applied when considering whether it is necessary to restrict freedom of expression in order to prevent disclosure of information received in confidence is not simply whether the information is a matter of public interest but whether, in all the circumstances, it is in the public interest that the duty of confidence should be breached. The claimant is as much entitled to enjoy confidentiality for his private thoughts as an aspect of his own 'human autonomy and dignity' as is any other.[365]

The newspaper identified a number of matters of public interest revealed by the diary: (1) the nature of lobbying to which Prince Charles subjected this country's elected leaders; (2) the political conduct of the heir to the throne; (3) the conduct of Prince Charles in failing to attend the 1999 Chinese banquet; (4) Prince Charles' public statements about his non- attendance at that banquet. He had termed Chinese officials 'waxworks'. However, the first instance judge concluded that the contribution that the journal or the articles in the newspaper made to providing information on any of those matters was minimal, and the Court of Appeal took the same view. The Court concluded that the first instance judge had been correct to hold that Prince Charles had an unanswerable claim for breach of privacy. When the breach of a confidential relationship was added into the balance, the Court found that his case was overwhelming. This case was of interest in that matters of some public interest were revealed – matters of much greater interest than those revealed by the reporting in *Von Hannover*, but the Court had little difficulty in finding that the privacy and confidentiality interest outweighed them.

Arguably, this case followed a pattern rather similar to that taken in the Lords in *Re S*, in the sense that one of the claims was dealt with in a somewhat cursory fashion, while still paying lip service to the balancing act. The speech claim was dismissed with rapidity, after a fairly cursory examination of its weight. If the future monarch exhibits tendencies that could be viewed as non-diplomatic in relation to Chinese officials, that is a matter of public interest that the public have a right to know about. Thus, the speech claim required far more thorough consideration than it received. The strength of the privacy claim, the morally reprehensible methods used to obtain the information, and the public interest in protecting the prince's ability to protect his record of his confidential thoughts, seemed to obscure the competing strengths of the speech claim.

The Court of Appeal took a similar approach to the public interest argument advanced under Art 10 in *K v News Group Newspapers*[366] but in this instance it was weaker. The case concerned K, a married man working in the entertainment industry who began a sexual relationship with a colleague. Subsequently the relationship became known to other colleagues and to K's wife and K ended his extra-marital relationship. Information concerning the affair was then leaked to a newspaper, and K, having been alerted to this fact, sought an injunction against publication. He argued that the publication would cause his family distress, particularly his children whom, he argued, would be bullied in school. The Court found that the benefits to be achieved by publication in the interests

---

365   *HRH Prince of Wales v Associated Newspapers Ltd* [2006] EWCA Civ 1776 [68].
366   [2011] EWCA Civ 439.

of free speech were wholly outweighed by the harm that would be done through the interference with the rights of privacy of all those affected.[367] Ward LJ emphasised that there was a distinction between the public interest and matters the public are interested in, and that satisfaction of the 'public prurience' was not a sufficient justification for interfering with the private rights of those involved.[368]

A contrasting example of a weak privacy interest and relatively much stronger speech interested is provided by *Hutcheson v NGN*.[369] In that case the newspaper sought to publish information about an individual who had been dismissed from employment with the Gordon Ramsay Group for financial misconduct. An anonymous tip-off to the newspaper related the financial misconduct (which concerned diversion of company funds) to the claimant's second family, whose existence he had sought to keep secret from the general public and the company. Hutcheson's privacy claim related to this second family. It was found that the public interest in exposing the financial misconduct outweighed Hutcheson's reasonable expectation of privacy, given that the family's existence had already been exposed and the importance of the public interest in question.

In relation to Art 8 it was found that while there was a *possible* argument that a reasonable expectation of privacy as regards the existence of the second family, given that the family would be subject to press intrusion if publication went forward, it was weak since it concerned the bare fact of a family relationship which was readily able to be established from publicly available information.[370] As regards Art 10 it was found that the reference to the family relationship was justifiably linked to the public interest, given that the second family was among the private purposes towards which Hutcheson was accused of diverting company funds.[371] Furthermore, Hutcheson had argued publicly about the financial misconduct.[372] Gross LJ appealed to an argument similar to the truth-based justification for freedom of speech discussed above:

> there is a public interest in NGN being free to publish the fact of Mr Hutcheson' second family to authenticate the allegation of diversion of corporate funds for private purposes. In doing so, NGN is obviously subject to the law of defamation, should the allegation turn out to be unfounded.[373]

Therefore an arguable privacy claim was readily outweighed by a strong public interest that was clearly linked to the information the claimant had sought to keep private;

---

367 *Ibid*, [13]–[14], [17]–[20] and [22].
368 *Ibid*, [23]–[24].
369 [2011] EWCA Civ 808.
370 *Ibid*, [26], [47].
371 *Ibid*, [46]. The judge found that: 'The judge must . . . balance the claim to privacy with the equally fundamental art.10 right to freedom of expression, in the public interest and including the freedom to criticise.' This language has been subject to criticism on the basis of its vagueness. As Phillipson argues, the idea of a "right to criticise" *prima facie* provides a general licence to reveal virtually any private behaviour in order to be able to criticise it, provided only that the behaviour either might generally be considered improper or even. . . that some people *reasonably consider* that it *ought* to be regarded as improper' (emphasis in original). 'Press freedom, the public interest and privacy' in Andrew Kenyon (ed), *Comparative Defamation and Privacy Law*, 2016, CUP, at p 159.
372 *Op cit*, [45].
373 *Ibid*, [46].

no injunction was awarded.[374] The case of *BKM v BBC*[375] concerned a similarly strong public interest and weak privacy interest. Briefly, BKM sought an injunction to prevent the BBC filming in a care home, despite the fact that the BBC had offered to avoid recording the characteristics or other personal information of residents; in particular, the BBC assured residents that they would be non-identifiable in any footage.[376] The judge found that BKM retained a reasonable interest in privacy as regards the bare fact of filming in the care home, but that – on balance – it was of limited weight.[377] As regards the speech interest, it was found that there was a strong public interest in reporting potential mismanagement of the care home.[378] On that basis the application for an injunction was rejected.[379]

Recent cases on the speech/privacy balance, however, which have tended towards favouring newspapers, are not – it will be contended – characterised by strong speech claims opposing weak privacy ones. This is the result of a recently developed approach at Strasbourg that has been increasingly deferential towards press interests. The approach taken to speech/privacy balancing in *Von Hannover v Germany (No 2)*[380] differed significantly from the approach taken in the first *Von Hannover* case. Relying on the Court's judgment in the first applicant's case, the applicants subsequently brought several sets of proceedings in the civil courts seeking an injunction against any further publication of photos that had appeared in German magazines. The Court first found that the concept of private life would extend to covering personal information including photos, even where that person is a public figure.

In relation to the next step – the balancing act – the Court found that where the balancing exercise has been undertaken by the national authorities in conformity with the criteria laid down in the Court's case law, the Court would require strong reasons to substitute its view for that of the domestic court. It then considered a number of criteria relating to the balancing test. They included the nature of the public interest involved. The Court did not criticise the approach of the German Court which found that the subject in question – the illness affecting Prince Rainier III – qualified as an event of contemporary society on which the magazines were entitled to report. It further found that the accompanying photo – which had a slight bearing on that subject – was inoffensive.[381] However, the same could have been said of the photos in the first *Von Hannover* case,[382] which nevertheless were found to have virtually no speech value.[383] The Court concluded that the German Court had remained within the state's margin of appreciation in carrying out the balancing act, and the Strasbourg Court did not therefore determine that it should depart from the national court's approach.

---

374 *Ibid*, [48].
375 [2009] EWHC 3151.
376 *Ibid*, [10].
377 *Ibid*, [33].
378 *Ibid*, [35].
379 *Ibid*, [40].
380 (2012) 55 EHRR 15 (Grand Chamber).
381 *Ibid*, para 123..
382 *Von Hannover v Germany* (2005) 40 EHRR 1.
383 *Ibid*, para 65.

This decision clearly gave some encouragement to the taking of photos of well-known figures without consent engaged in every-day life activities if the photo could be deemed innocuous and in some way linked to an article relating to an event of some significance in society. The case of *Axel Springer v Germany*[384] led to a similar outcome in which however the Court did depart from the stance taken in the domestic courts as to the balancing act. The case concerned publications relating to the arrest and conviction of a well-known television actor for possession of drugs. The domestic courts held that the actor's right to protect his privacy prevailed over the public's interest in being informed, granting an injunction against the newspaper.

The newspaper claimed a violation of its right to freedom of expression under Art 10 ECHR. The Grand Chamber considered a range of factors in considering the balancing act between Arts 10 and 8.[385] It considered in particular: the contribution made by the article to a debate of general interest; the actor's prior conduct in relation to the media; the circumstances and method of obtaining the information; how well known the actor was; the content and consequences of the publications. In terms of proportionality it considered the severity of the interference. It found that there was a degree of public interest in the information, that the actor was well known and had actively sought previous publicity. The publication of the article, it was found, had not had serious consequences for the actor in terms of invasion of privacy, and while the injunction did not represent a severe sanction, it might have had a chilling effect on the press. Thus the Grand Chamber held that the grounds advanced by the Government was not sufficient to establish that the interference with Art 10 was 'necessary in a democratic society' to protect the actor's right to respect for his private life. There was, therefore, a violation of Art 10. Again, this decision took into account factors, such as that the actor had previously sought publicity, which were very doubtfully linked to the claimed speech value of the publications. The acceptance of the relevance of that factor is likely to give encouragement to the so-called 'zonal waiver' factor considered above.

Phillipson points out that the Strasbourg Court in both *Von Hannover (No 2)* and *Axel Springer* has started to fully embrace the notion that 'public figures' have a reduced expectation of privacy, and, importantly, has expanded the notion of 'public figure' to encompass those who are simply well known to the public.[386] This trend is reflected in a number of cases concerning footballers, discussed below, whose public status has provided the basis for allowing the publication of details of intimate details of their lives on the basis of flimsy free speech justifications.[387] Phillipson finds this trend objectionable since it fails to answer specific questions as to the justification for invading privacy in the specific circumstances.

384   (2012) 55 EHRR 6.
385   *Ibid*, paras 89–95.
386   See Phillipson, G, 'Press freedom, the public interest and privacy' in Andrew Kenyon (ed), *Comparative Defamation and Privacy Law*, 2016, CUP at p 161.
387   See also *Spelman v Express Newspapers* [2012] EWHC 355; *McClaren v News Group Newspapers* [2012] EWHC 2466.

The domestic case of *AAA v Associated Newspapers*,[388] the facts of which were considered above, raised more difficult issues than *Von Hannover (No 2)* in the sense that the private facts at issue related to the public life of a public figure, but had a degree of genuine public interest. In *AAA* the public interest was arguably stronger in relation to the politician in question, but the privacy claim also related to a child. In relation to the balancing act between Arts 10 and 8, it was found that the judge had not clarified what she meant by adverting to the 'recklessness' of the politician in fathering two children as a result of affairs as fully as she might have done, but that it was clear that she had had in mind that the daughter was alleged to have been the second child conceived as a result of the father's extra-marital affairs.[389] It was found that the judge was entitled to hold that that was of itself reckless behaviour. It was found that the balancing exercise between Arts 8 and 10 conducted by the first instance judge was to be treated as analogous to the exercise of a discretion and that an appellate court should not intervene unless the judge had erred in law. It was noted that in sensitive privacy cases, particularly where there were cogent public interest arguments in play, there was a difficult judgment to be made in balancing those competing rights. It was determined that the first instance judge had been best placed to undertake the balancing exercise since she had had the advantage of hearing witnesses and assessing them, and there could be no criticism of the way she conducted that exercise.[390] It was therefore found that the judge's refusal to grant an injunction could not be criticised.

However, in finding that privacy should be overcome by free expression, it is suggested that the impact on the child was not given enough weight. In that respect *AAA* may be contrasted with *Weller*,[391] discussed above in relation to 'reasonable expectation of privacy' which also concerned children, but in *Weller* it was hard if not impossible to identify any public interest value of the information. In turning to the balancing act in *Weller*, it was accepted that there is no 'threshold of seriousness' to be overcome in relation to finding that Art 10 is engaged, due to the importance of freedom of expression.[392] In considering the balance between the two rights the issues of proportionality were approached as in *Re S*[393] and *Von Hannover v Germany (No 2)*.[394] Section 12(4) HRA and the (then) PCC Code were also considered. The criteria from *Von Hannover (No 2)* were applied in turn. The publication of the photographs, it was found, did not contribute to a current debate of general interest. Also the pictures of the children with their father (Weller) had not previously been published. As regards the circumstances in which the photos were taken, it was found that it was clear at the time that the taking of the photos was not consented to. It was found that the balance came down in favour of finding that the Art 8 rights overrode the Art 10 rights engaged.

This outcome was unsurprising given that the case concerned children, and it was impossible to put forward a plausible argument that the photos answered to a public interest. However, the case showed a willingness to accept dubious free speech

---

388 [2013] EWCA Civ 554.
389 *Ibid*, [43].
390 See *ibid*, [8], [9], [38]–[45].
391 *Weller v Associated Newspapers Ltd High Court* [2014] EWHC 1163.
392 See *ibid*, [49]–[50].
393 [2005] 1 AC 593.
394 (2012) 55 EHRR 15.

arguments that might well prevail in a case in which it could be argued that the figure in question had previously sought publicity and if it could be argued that he/she could be deemed to be a 'role model'. The stance taken suggests that a willingness to allow Art 10 to prevail over Art 8, despite paying lip service to the equality of the two rights, is apparent in these instances, bolstered by *Von Hannover (No 2)*, the IPSO Code and s 12(4) HRA.

The trend of the Strasbourg Court towards a position in which it favours very flimsy or non-existent free expression arguments when balancing Arts 8 and 10 in privacy cases was confirmed in the third *Von Hannover* case.[395] In *Von Hannover v Germany (No 3)*[396] a German magazine had published an article about a trend among celebrities of renting out their holiday homes and it described the von Hannover family villa. The article was accompanied by a photograph of Princess Caroline and her husband on holiday, taken without consent or knowledge. Princess Caroline ultimately failed to obtain an injunction in the domestic courts against any further publication of the photograph, and brought the case to Strasbourg. The Court found that the German courts had given due consideration to the criteria for the balancing exercise that were set out in *Von Hannover v Germany (No 2)* and *Axel Springer AG v Germany*. So, taking account of the margin of appreciation enjoyed by the national courts in undertaking such a balancing exercise, it was found that Germany had not failed to comply with its positive obligations under Art 8. The Court considered the criteria the national court had taken into account. In considering the public interest value of the photograph – its contribution to a debate of public interest – the Court appeared to accept that although there was no link between the photo and article, and the photo itself made no contribution to any potential debate about celebrities renting out holiday homes, the photo made some sort of contribution to a general interest debate, a conclusion that is very hard to understand.[397]

The Court reaffirmed the point made in *Von Hannover v Germany (No 2)* to the effect that the applicant and her husband must be regarded as public figures, and so were unable to claim the same protection for their private life as ordinary private individuals. In other words, this point applied in the UK context would mean that public figures automatically had a reduced expectation of privacy and therefore the privacy of a figure deemed to be well known would have difficulty in overcoming a free expression claim, even if very weak, as in this instance, of a newspaper. This third *Von Hannover* case demonstrates a clear departure from the first one, which clearly found that celebrity gossip makes no contribution to the role of the press in a democracy and that in such instances the free expression claim will usually be overcome by the privacy one.

The situation now reached appears to be that privacy claims in 'celebrity gossip' cases may well lose out partly because the celebrity in question, as a person the public is

395 See also *Lillo-Stenberg v Norway*, Appl No 13258/09, judgment of 16 January 2014 in which the ECtHR found that the publication of photographs concerning a wedding between a popular musician and actress came within the idea of 'general interest,' since a wedding 'cannot itself relate exclusively to details of a person's private life' (para 37). On this basis and with regard to the 'margin of appreciation' accorded to Norway it was found that the publication did not unjustifiably interfere with the applicants' Art 8 right (paras 44–45).

396 Appl No 8772/10, judgment of 19 September 2013 (in French and German only).

397 *Von Hannover v Germany* ECHR 264 (2013), press release 19 September 2013, p 3.

interested in, will inevitably have a weak privacy claim purely by virtue of that status, and the inquiry into the public interest value of the expression in question has become a virtually empty one; the privacy claim will only be likely to prevail if intrusive or intimate details are published. This third *Von Hannover* case has gone even further down the path of accepting spurious public interest arguments than the second one, since in the second one there was a weak connection between the objected-to photo and the accompanying article. In this instance even that connection was not required. It is argued that free expression has not been advantaged by this latest decision since the free expression justifications would not have supported the publication of the photo.[398]

Despite the influence of the two recent *Von Hannover* cases and *Axel Springer*, in certain very recent instances a refusal of *domestic* judges to accept dubious public interest arguments under Art 10 is arguably apparent. In *CHS v DNH*[399] a well-known woman brought an action to prevent details of her affair from being divulged when her partner discovered she had been adulterous by reading her diary. The argument based on her privacy interest was to the effect that the potential damage that could be done, both to the claimant, as a public figure of trust, and to Mr Y, as a public figure who is married to someone else, was enormous.[400] The judge also found that the motivation for the threatened publication was malicious.[401] In an unreported case based on somewhat similar facts a well-known sportsman obtained a temporary injunction preventing the *Sun* newspaper publishing a story about a sexual relationship he had with a female celebrity before his marriage.[402] The order was made by Elisabeth Laing J, who explained her reasons for granting the injunction. She said that publication would 'no doubt cause embarrassment to the man and his current wife'.[403] She said:

> It is not for me to moralise about such conduct. But I do express a suitably diffident doubt whether this conduct was socially harmful . . . no-one was corrupted or coerced. The conduct had no ramifications beyond the three people who were affected by it. It did not affect society in any way.[404]

In other words, the judge was unable to discern a genuine public interest in the publication of the information. Her remarks stand in contrast to those expressing the notion that there could be a public interest in discussions of adultery in the *Terry*[405] case, above. The problem with the idea put forward in that case is that it gives no weight to the real motivation of the newspaper in exposing an affair – to make a profit, and fails to explain why allowing specific persons to be named could be necessary to further the debate in question.

---

398 For a contrary view see Wragg, P, 'The Benefits of Privacy-Invading Expression' (2013) 64(2) NILQ 187.
399 See *the Independent* 22 May 2015.
400 [2015] EWHC 1214.
401 *Ibid*, [12].
402 See Press Association Report 'Sportsman Wins Injunction Over 'Previous Sexual Relationship With Celebrity,' *Huffington Post*, 6 August 2015; http://www.huffingtonpost.co.uk.
403 *Ibid.*
404 *Ibid.*
405 *Terry v Persons Unknown* [2010] EWHC 119.

Conclusions

The current tort of misuse of private information covers liability for publishing personal information outside reliance on s 7(1)(a) of the HRA. In other words, it covers a remedy for invasion of privacy that can be utilised against private *and* public bodies, although, as the discussion has shown, its invocation as a means of curbing press intrusion onto privacy has represented by far its most significant role.[406] Any law protecting a person from unwanted publication of personal information must inevitably become 'a legal porcupine, which bristles with difficulties',[407] but in the decade since *Campbell* English law has seen the development of a pragmatic and yet, it is argued, principled approach based on the reasonable expectation of privacy. In particular, it is strongly contended that the perception of conflict between speech and privacy is often exaggerated and simplistic, and indeed that an examination of the values underlying each reveals them to be in many respects mutually supportive, rather than invariably antagonistic.

Where the press uses claims based on free speech values to hide the fact that it is in reality merely seeking commercial gain by selling details of private lives of well-known figures, court scrutiny in the course of a privacy action may be able to reveal the reality of the situation. In other instances, both claims should be probed with a view to considering how crucial it is to the speech value of a publication that a person's identity or other details are revealed. But, despite very recent developments, it is argued that the courts continue to be more comfortable with free speech than with privacy claims. That is probably one of the most significant points emerging from this chapter. The Strasbourg Court and domestic courts are also tending in recent decisions to downgrade the privacy claims of public figures, and accepting a notion of their reduced expectations of privacy.

As discussed above, the common law accorded a very high value to free speech, elevating it, pre-HRA, to the status of a common law right. In *ex parte Simms*[408] Lord Steyn referred to free speech as 'the *primary* right . . . in a democracy' (emphasis added). In contrast, the judges pre-HRA failed to create a common law tort of invasion of private life or of the non-consensual use of personal information.[409] Despite the apparent acceptance post-HRA that speech and privacy claims are to be treated equally, it is suggested the strong common law tradition of free speech in fact influenced a number of the decisions discussed, including the decision in *Re S*, to the detriment of the more nebulous demands of privacy – demands that appear to have less of a hold on the judicial imagination. Where the judiciary perceive a clash between common law and Convention values, their tendency, despite the inception of the HRA, still appears to be to give preference to the former. In any event, recent decisions at Strasbourg, in particular *Von Hannover (No 3)*, are also failing to probe the true strength of the speech claim. As Phillipson has argued

---

406   See the comments in *Mckennitt v Ash* [2006] EWCA Civ 1714.
407   The phrase is borrowed from *dicta* in an administrative law case: *Inner London Education Authority ex p Westminster CC* [1986] 1 WLR 28.
408   [1999] 3 WLR 328, HL.
409   See *Kaye v Robertson* [1991] FCR 62. See also Fenwick, H, and Phillipson, G, *Confidence and Privacy: A Re-examination* [1996] 55(3) CLJ 447. The article traces the somewhat uncertain steps that the judges were taking towards the creation of such a tort by utilising the action for breach of confidence.

'what Strasbourg has done, by accepting . . . a broad and undefined notion of the public interest, is to rob that notion of any coherent boundaries it might once have had'.[410]

Clearly, Art 8 ECHR's primary role has been to protect the citizen's privacy against the arbitrary and oppressive use of state power – the main concern of the subsequent chapter. But the ability of large media corporations to invade privacy is equal to, or even arguably surpasses, that of the state, as the state does not possess the power *in itself* to create widespread dissemination of private information. Therefore provision of protection for the citizen against the mass media is equally necessary. However, the recent approach at Strasbourg, and to an extent domestically, has strayed dangerously close to one that is tolerant of extensive media intrusion into privacy based on flimsy free speech arguments, unrelated to classic free speech values. In other words, press commercial freedom to exploit privacy, rather than freedom of expression, is becoming the dominant concern.

6 The Data Protection Act 1998

Introduction

Until 1998, there was no statute in the UK equivalent to the US Privacy Act 1974, which enables persons to obtain access to information held on them in paper-based and electronic state files. In the UK, certain categories of information covered by the Official Secrets Act 1989 could not be disclosed, but if personal information fell outside those categories there was still no general right of access to it. No full general statutory rights of access to stored personal information in electronic or manual files, or control over the processing of such information, were created until the Data Protection Act 1998 (DPA) was passed. The electronic storage and processing of information obviously presents a particular threat to privacy because, for example, personal information gathered for a purpose acceptable to its subject may be transferred to another data bank without the subject's knowledge or consent. It may also be linked up with other information, thus creating what may be a distorted picture.

The Data Protection Act 1998 was passed in response to the European Data Protection Directive on the protection of individuals with regard to the processing of personal data and the free movement of such data.[411] The aim of the directive was to ensure that the same level of data protection was established in all member states in order to facilitate the transfer of personal data across national boundaries within the European Union. The DPA 1998[412] creates a comprehensive protection for personal information. The following discussion is not intended as a comprehensive guide to the 1998 Act, something that

---

410 See Phillipson, G, 'Press freedom, the public interest and privacy' forthcoming in Andrew Kenyon (ed), *Comparative Defamation and Privacy Law*, 2016, CUP at p 154.

411 Directive 95/46/EC of the European Parliament and of the Council of 24 October 1995 (1995) OJ L281/31, mainly Art 6. Recital 10 reads: 'Whereas the object of the national laws on the processing of personal data is to protect fundamental rights and freedoms, notably the right to privacy, which is recognised both in Art 8 of the European Convention for the Protection of Human Rights and Fundamental Freedoms and in the general principles of Community law.'

412 Certain sections came into force on the date of the passing of the statute – 16 June 1998. Most of the provisions came into force in 1999. As indicated below, certain provisions came into force after the first transitional period, ending on 24 October 2001; further provisions came into force after the end of the second transitional period, ending on 24 October 2007. Transitional provisions under Sched 14 provide

would be out of place in a book of this nature. Instead, it will focus on certain specific privacy issues, and especially on their relationship with media freedom of expression.[413]

Definitions under the Data Protection Act 1998[414]

Section 1(1) defines data as information processed by equipment operating automatically or recorded with the intention that it should be processed by means of such equipment or recorded as part of a relevant filing system or which forms part of an accessible record. The most significant part of this definition refers to data recorded as part of 'a relevant filing system'. Such a system is defined in s 1(1) as any set of information relating to individuals that is structured by reference to individuals or by reference to criteria relating to individuals 'in such a way that specific information relating to individuals is readily accessible'. This definition is clearly imprecise, but it seems that most, if not all, structured filing systems relating to paper-based materials containing personal information will be covered. Thus 'data' is caught by the Act either if it is held on any electronic storage system, typically a computer, or if it forms part of a filing system.[415]

The Act protects against the wrongful processing of 'personal data'. 'Personal data' means 'data which relate to a living individual who can be identified (a) either from those data', or (b) 'from those data and other information which is in the possession of, or is likely to come into the possession of, the data controller'. Any data relating to a living person is termed 'personal data'.[416] Personal data covers expressions of opinions about an individual, but now also covers indications of intentions in relation to that individual. This would include, for example, the intentions of a personnel manager regarding the promotion or demotion of an employee. Photographs of an individual clearly fall within the Act. The Court of Appeal's decision in *Durant v Financial Services Authority*[417] narrowed the prima facie meaning of these terms to an extent. It was held that the interpretation of personal data should be guided by the principle of respect for privacy. It means: 'information that affects his privacy, whether in his personal or family life, business or professional capacity'. Thus it was held that, to be personal, data about an individual must go beyond:

> the recording of the putative data subject's involvement in a matter or an event that
> has no personal connotations . . . The information should have the putative data

---

for the transition from the regime of the 1984 Act to that of the 1998 Act while transitional relief from the full rigour of the Act is provided in Sched 8. Schedule 16 repeals the whole of the 1984 Act.

413 See for further discussion e.g., Tugendhat and Christie, *The Law of Privacy and the Media*, 2nd edn, 2011, OUP, Chapter 6.

414 For a basic guide, see Carey, P, *The Data Protection Act 1998*, 1998, Blackstone; for early discussion of the impact of the Act on the media, see Tugendhat, M, 'The Data Protection Act 1998 and the Media' [2000] YBMCL 115; Rasaiah, S and Newell, D, 'Data protection and press freedom' [1997–98] 3 YMEL 209.

415 Under s 1(1) DPA: 'data' means information which –
    (a) is being processed by means of equipment operating automatically in response to instructions given for that purpose,
    (b) is recorded with the intention that it should be processed by means of such equipment,
    (c) is recorded as part of a relevant filing system or with the intention that it should form part of a relevant filing system . . .

416 The definition of 'personal data' is found in s 1(1) of the Act.

417 [2003] EWCA Civ 1746; [2004] FSR 28.

subject as its focus rather than some other person with whom he may have been involved or some transaction or event in which he may have figured or have had an interest.[418]

Especially intimate private information is classified as 'sensitive personal data'; this covers a person's sexual life, along with matters such as a person's religious and political opinions, and his or her physical and mental health (s 2). It also includes some other, more wide-ranging categories of information, including information relating the racial or ethnic origin of the data subject, his or her political opinions, membership of a trade union and information relating to the commission by the individual of any offence and any proceedings relating to that offence.[419]

Under the law of confidence, as discussed above, it used to be the case that once it could be determined that information was in the public domain, through, for example, previous media attention or other participation in a public process, such as a trial, an individual was no longer able to protect it through legal action. That is accorded some confirmation by s 12(4)(a)(i) HRA, discussed above. However, as discussed, the courts are reluctant, under the current privacy liability, to find that information is unprotected as already in the public domain. The public domain issue is addressed only in a very limited fashion by the DPA, in Sched 3, para 5, which provides that one of the conditions for the processing of sensitive personal data is that the data subject has deliberately placed the information in the public domain. That stance is not far from the one the courts have reached under the privacy doctrine in relation to the notion of a zonal waiver.

The data principles

The data principles, contained in Sched 1 of the Act, form its central core. The rest of the Act elaborates on the system for ensuring that these principles are adhered to. Subject to the exemptions, *all* personal data must be processed in accordance with the data protection principles. The principles set out a number of fundamental privacy rights that encapsulate the value of informational autonomy. They accept that personal information must be stored and used by others, but surround such use by safeguards intended to preserve informational autonomy so far as possible, consistent with such acceptance.

Part II of Sched 1 deals with interpretation of the principles and makes the following provision in relation to the first principle:

> 1 (1) In determining for the purposes of the first principle whether personal data are processed fairly, regard is to be had to the method by which they are obtained, including in particular whether any person from whom they are obtained is deceived or misled as to the purpose or purposes for which they are to be processed.

The most important of the principles is data principle 1, which states that personal data must be processed fairly and lawfully and shall only be processed if at least one of

---

418 *Ibid*, [28].
419 Under s 2, the definition includes: '(g) the commission or alleged commission by him of any offence, or (h) any proceedings for any offence committed or alleged to have been committed by him, the disposal of such proceedings or the sentence of any court in such proceedings.'

the conditions in Sched 2 is met. The conditions include the requirement that the data subject has given consent to the processing, or it is necessary for the administration of justice or for the exercise of statutory functions, of functions of a minister or government department or for the exercise of other functions of a public nature exercised in the public interest, or for the purposes of legitimate interests pursued by the controller or a third party, except where the processing is unwarranted by reason of prejudice to the legitimate rights or freedoms of the subject. Thus, in the case of all data, one of the conditions in Sched 2 must be met while in the case of sensitive personal data, one of the conditions in Sched 3 must also be met.

Thus the processing of 'sensitive personal data' attracts a higher level of safeguards than personal data under data principle 1(b) (Sched 1), as elucidated by Sched 3. The conditions include the requirement that the data subject has given her explicit consent to the processing, or the information has deliberately been made public by the subject, or it is necessary for medical purposes, or for the administration of justice, or for the exercise of statutory functions, of functions of a minister or government department, or for the purposes of legitimate interests pursued by certain non-profit-making bodies.

Data principle 2 provides that the data may be obtained only for one or more specified purposes and shall not be processed in any manner incompatible with that purpose. Under data principles 4 and 5, data must be accurate and, where necessary, kept up to date; when it is kept for a specific purpose, it must not be kept for longer than is necessary for that purpose. Also, data must be processed in accordance with the rights of data subjects under data principle 6, and under data principle 7 it must be adequately protected; appropriate security measures must be taken.

A number of subject exemptions, however, allow certain activities to be exempted from a number of the new provisions. The data principles and most of the key provisions of the Act do not apply where the exemption is required for the purpose of safeguarding national security. Thus, the security and intelligence services are exempt. Data related to the prevention and detection of crime are exempt from the first data principle and the subject access provisions in s 7. As indicated below, there is a special exemption for journalistic purposes; where the media exemption operates, the media will be exempt from a number of the provisions, including all the data principles, except the seventh.

Obligations of data controllers

Any person using a computerised system in order to store data relating to people is designated the 'data controller' (s 1(1)), while the person who is the subject of the data remains the 'data subject'. However, the processing of personal data no longer requires the performance of operations by reference to a data subject (s 1(1)). Under s 17, the data controller must register with the Data Protection Registrar, now renamed the Data Protection Commissioner. The data controller must notify the holding of data to the Commissioner under s 17(1), who will then make an entry in the register maintained under s 19 unless, under s 17(3), processing is unlikely to prejudice the rights or freedoms of data subjects or unless, under s 23(1), the data controller has an approved in-house supervision scheme. However, the Act requires compliance with the data principles and therefore such compliance is not dependent on the registration of the data holder.

Section 7 provides that if the data controller is asked by the data subject in writing whether personal data is being processed by or on behalf of the data controller, that information must be given within 40 days. If such data is being processed, the data subject is entitled to a description of the data, of the purposes for which it is being processed and of the recipients to whom it may be disclosed. Also, the data subject is entitled to have the data communicated to her and any information available to the controller as to the source of the data, in a form that is capable of being understood. Under Sched 1, Part II in relation to the fourth principle it is provided that if the data is found to be inaccurate, the data subject can notify the controller of the fact, which should then be indicated in the data. If it is so indicated, the fourth principle is not contravened. If a court is satisfied on the application of a data subject that personal data of which the applicant is the subject is inaccurate the court under s 14 can make an order erasing, blocking, destroying or rectifying the data.

Under s 10, the data subject has a right, enforceable by court order, to prevent the processing of data likely to cause substantial damage or distress, if that damage or distress is or would be unwarranted.

Impact of the DPA on the media

The media are regarded as data controllers under the DPA 1998.[420] The Act covers the 'processing' of data, which is defined extremely widely; of particular significance for the media is the fact that the definition covers both the obtaining and the publishing of data.[421] The 'data' controller – the person who has responsibilities under the Act – is the person[422] who controls the manner in which and the purposes for which the data is processed. In relation to newspapers, this will generally be the editor or editorial board. In so far as the DPA offers remedies that can affect media freedom, s 12 HRA is relevant, whether the body against which relief is sought is a private body or a public authority under the HRA.[423]

Conditions

A key question in relation to the first data protection principle is, as indicated above, that of consent, since data cannot be processed unless one of the conditions in Sched 2, in relation to all personal data, or Sched 3, in relation to sensitive personal data, is met. The obvious condition that would apply in relation to journalism would be that consent had

---

420 See further Rasiah and Newell, 'Data protection and press freedom' [1997–98] 3 YMEL 209.
421 'Processing', in relation to information or data, means obtaining, recording or holding the information or data or carrying out any operation or set of operations on the information or data, including-
     (a) organisation, adaptation or alteration of the information or data,
     (b) retrieval, consultation or use of the information or data,
     (c) disclosure of the information or data by transmission, dissemination or otherwise making available, or
     (d) alignment, combination, blocking, erasure or destruction of the information or data; 'using' or 'disclosing', in relation to personal data, includes using or disclosing the information contained in the data.
422 Either alone or in company with others.
423 Since s 12 is not limited in its application to public authorities.

been obtained, since in most circumstances it is unlikely that one of the other conditions could be met. But consent by the data subject would rarely be present in a privacy case. Schedule 3 refers to explicit consent. Thus, in relation to non-sensitive personal data, implied consent is sufficient. In relation to sensitive data, it is sufficient if the information has deliberately been made public by the subject. The Act does not explain what is meant by consent. The proper approach to the question of consent under the DPA is to align it with that discussed above under the privacy doctrine. It should be asked therefore whether the plaintiff has in fact robbed the information disclosed of its private quality through prior, voluntary publicity of the information in question or related information. It is essential that this test is applied in a nuanced fashion, basing it on the core privacy value of informational autonomy.[424] The notion of 'consent', then, should be used only where there is an arguable claim of actual consent to the publication in question, express in respect of sensitive personal data or implied in respect of personal data.

The only other condition that could be fulfilled by a media body to escape liability under the Act would be that the processing is necessary for the purposes of legitimate interests pursued by the data controller, or by the third party or parties to whom the data are disclosed, except where the processing is unwarranted in any particular case by reason of prejudice to the rights and freedoms or legitimate interests of the data subject. While this provision is imprecise, it would appear, in the context of press publication, to require the Court to examine, in the light of Arts 8 and 10, whether it was 'necessary' to publish the complained of data for the purposes of exercising the Art 10 right to freedom of expression. Thus, it might be relied upon by the press generally to argue that the data had been gathered and published in order to carry out the press's legitimate role as watchdog.[425] However it will not assist a newspaper that had obtained information surreptitiously, as will often be the case in privacy cases, and that therefore cannot claim to have obtained it 'fairly'.

Media exemptions

The Act gives the media quite generous conditional exemptions from many of its provisions, and, importantly, protection from the possibility of interim injunctions to restrain publication. Where data is processed for the 'special purpose' of journalism[426] under s 32(1) and (2), the key protective provisions (including data principles 1 and 2 and s 10) do not apply at all if the processing is undertaken with a view to publication, the data controller reasonably believes that, having regard to the special importance of the public interest in freedom of expression, publication is in the public interest, and compliance with the protective principles is incompatible with journalistic activity.[427] In considering the belief of the data controller that publication is in the public interest, regard may be had under s 32(3) to his compliance with any relevant code of practice that has been designated by the secretary of state for the purposes of the sub-section. Journalists are not exempt from data principle 7, which in essence requires that care

---

424   Prosser suggests that consent is only impliedly given 'if the plaintiff has industriously sought publicity of the same kind' Prosser, D, 'Privacy' (1960) 48 Calif L Rev 383, p 396, pp 420–21.

425   This was not, however, accepted in *Campbell v MGN* [2002] EWCA Civ 1373.

426   Section 3(a).

427   For further discussion, see Carey, P, *The Data Protection Act 1998*, 1998, pp 196–98.

must be taken of the personal data, but this provision alone does not provide a significant protection for privacy.

Although the Act gives an individual the right to apply to the Court for an order that a journalist, as a data controller, cease processing information about him which is causing or is likely to cause substantial, unwarranted distress (s 10), the mere claim that the processing is for the purposes of journalism with a view to publication stays the proceedings and the case is referred to the Data Commissioner for a determination on the point (s 32(4)). Thus, interim injunctions to prevent unfair processing by the press – a critical remedy in privacy cases – are not available. Even if a journalist was found to have breached the Act due to a failure to take such care, no interim injunction could be granted – under s 32. Where the exemption applies, it may be said then that the DPA 1998 probably has only a marginal impact on non-consensual media use of personal information. The remedies under the Act, discussed below, for breach of the data protection principles include a right to compensation[428] and a right to prevent processing likely to cause damage or distress.[429] However, there is a specific exemption designed to benefit the media in s 32 of the Act. In essence, it both prevents the media from being subject to interim injunctions preventing the publication of personal data[430] and allows them to be exempted from the data protection principles[431] if the media body in question was acting for journalistic purposes and the data controller reasonably believed publication to be in the public interest and that he could not comply with the provisions of the Act, given the journalistic purposes he was carrying out. This provision has been held, controversially, to apply both before and after publication,[432] so that it provides a comprehensive media defence.

The right under s 10 to demand that the data controller ceases processing and the right if they do not to seek a remedy in court is unlikely, in any event, to bite against the media since the data subject must first notify the data controller to require that she cease processing, and the controller has 21 days to reply stating the action she intends to take. In the case of the media it seems probable that if publication of the personal data is intended, the media body in question would publish it, if possible, within the 21-day period.

However, these protections for the media do have limits. If data is being processed for the special purposes without a view to publication – which could be the case if it has already been published – the exemption does not apply. Equally, it does not apply to unpublished personal information if no reasonable belief could be demonstrated that publication of the information would be in the public interest. Clearly, there would also be cases where it was uncertain whether that belief could be demonstrated. Thus, the requirements of the Act have a practical impact on journalists in certain circumstances.

---

428 Section 13: it applies either where the individual suffers damage as a result of unlawful processing under the Act or suffers distress and the processing is done for the purposes of (*inter alia*) journalism.

429 Under s 10.

430 See s 32(4)–(5), under which the Court must stay any proceedings under the DPA relating to the publication of hitherto unpublished material, including proceedings under section 10(4) (obtaining an order preventing processing – i.e. an injunction) *if* the data is being processed for journalistic purposes with a view to publishing it.

431 Except for Principle 7, which, however, merely provides that the data controller shall take appropriate measures against accidental loss of or damage to data or unauthorised processing of it.

432 See the finding of the Court of Appeal in *Campbell v Mirror Group Newspapers Ltd* [2002] EWCA Civ 1373 at [129]–[31].

Thus the DPA gives the public broad rights against the publication of sensitive personal data without consent by the media, and against the publication of any unfairly obtained personal data, subject however to a broad defence of public interest. Phillipson has observed that the DPA may provide one of the few ways that English law can provide a remedy for the publication of photographs of daily life activities that might not attract the protection of the law of confidence/privacy,[433] although it now appears that such activities are covered in relation to children, as *Murray* and *Weller* established.

The DPA has not, however, proved popular with litigants asserting privacy rights against the press, probably largely because interim injunctions cannot be obtained under it against the media. It was pleaded in *Campbell*,[434] discussed above, but it was virtually ignored in the House of Lords findings. The case confirmed the application of the Act to the media. At first instance it was found:

> Under s 1(1), the claimant was termed a 'data subject', the information, including the details and photographs, that the claimant was receiving therapy at Narcotics Anonymous was 'personal data', the defendant was the 'data controller', the obtaining, preparation and publication of the claimant's personal data was 'processing'.[435]

These findings were not questioned on appeal; the Court of Appeal in fact specifically confirmed that the publication of hard copies of newspaper does fall within the definition of processing of data.[436] In relation to the media, it was found in *Campbell* at first instance, that the obtaining of information by surreptitious photography was unfair, and that if information is obtained in breach of confidence, it will not be obtained 'lawfully'.[437] *Campbell* demonstrated that the position of the media in relation to sensitive personal data, is particularly difficult. Under Sched 3, the media body has to show that the data subject has given 'explicit consent' to the processing or the data was deliberately 'made public' by the subject. Otherwise the media body must bring itself within the conditions set out in the Data Protection (Processing of Sensitive Personal Data) Order 2000, which essentially requires a very weighty 'public interest defence' involving the revelation of criminality, dishonesty, malpractice or mismanagement.[438] It would

---

433 *Media Freedom under the Human Rights Act, op cit* fn 1, at 767–68. See also above at pp 742–43, for Baroness Hale's comments on the point in *Campbell*.
434 *Campbell v Mirror Group Newspapers Ltd* [2002] EMLR 30 (QB); [2002] EWCA Civ 1373 (CA); *Campbell v MGN Ltd* [2004] 2 AC 457 (HL).
435 [2002] EMLR 30 [85].
436 [2002] EWCA Civ 1373 [107].
437 [2002] EMLR 30 [108]–[110].
438 The only circumstances which could normally apply to journalism under Sched 3 are:
    3(1) the disclosure of personal data –
        (a) is in the substantial public interest;
        (b) is in connection with –
            (i) the commission by any person of any unlawful act (whether alleged or established),
            (ii) dishonesty, malpractice, or other seriously improper conduct by, or the unfitness or incompetence of, any person (whether alleged or established), or
            (iii) mismanagement in the administration of, or failures in services provided by, any body or association (whether alleged or established);
        (c) is for the special purposes [of, *inter alia*, journalism] as defined in section 3 of the Act; and
        (d) is made with a view to the publication of those data by any person and the data controller reasonably believes that such publication would be in the public interest.

clearly be very difficult to make out such a defence in a normal case concerning the revelation of private facts; it was not made out in *Campbell*.[439] It is clear from *Campbell* that the DPA claim will normally stand or fall with the privacy claim.

It is concluded, therefore, that the 1998 Act does have an impact on the media[440] since, except in a narrow range of instances, they are not exempt from the requirement to obtain consent where one or more of the conditions set out in s 32 do not apply. Although, from the point of view of protecting privacy, it may be argued that this is a welcome development, it may be suggested that the Act does not properly hold the balance between Arts 10 and 8. If so, since s 3 HRA applies, the courts have to consider the scope within the Act for creating a fairer balance in accordance with the demands of both those articles. For example, s 10 speaks of unwarranted disclosures, a terminology that creates leeway for arguments based on Art 10. Although publication or processing in the public interest is not a general defence under the Act there is, as indicated, scope for interpreting what is meant by the public interest in s 32 in order to create such a balance, a matter that is considered further above.[441] Once the stage of considering the balancing act between Arts 8 and 10 is reached, it should be conducted as for a privacy claim.

Enforcement of the DPA

The enforcement mechanisms allow for the enforcement of privacy rights against a range of bodies, including private ones, thus affording greater respect for Art 8 rights than is afforded under the HRA, since under it only public authorities are directly bound. The Act creates a number of offences in relation to data processing and the Act's requirements. In particular, it is a criminal offence for an unregistered person or body to store personal data under s 21(1).

Under s 13(1), compensation can be awarded if damage has resulted from the contravention by a data controller of any of the requirements of the Act, including the requirement to rectify, destroy, block or erase inaccurate data. However, by s 13(3) it is a defence for the controller to prove that he had taken such care as is reasonable in the circumstances to comply with the requirement. The compensatory damages awarded under the DPA in media cases have tended to be nominal.[442] However, the recent case of *Vidall v Google*[443] found that the requirement to show both distress *and* 'damage' by s 13(2) was contrary to Directive 95/46.[444] Section 13(2) was therefore disapplied and thus compensatory damages are now recoverable for distress.[445] This development could affect awards in media cases.

---

439 As the Court of Appeal confirmed: [2002] EWCA Civ 1373 [88]–[89].
440 See, for further discussion of the impact of the Act on the media, Foster, S 'Press photographs: protecting the privacy of celebrities and their children' (2014) 19(3) Comms L 86; Erdos, D 'Data protection and the right to reputation: filling the "gaps" after the Defamation Act 2013' (2014) 73(3) CLJ 536.
441 See p 747 *et seq.*
442 See e.g., *Douglas v Hello! (No 6)* [2005] 4 All ER 128.
443 [2015] EWCA Civ 311.
444 Directive 95/46/EC of the European Parliament and of the Council of 24 October 1995 on the protection of individuals with regard to the processing of personal data and on the free movement of such data, Official Journal L 28, 23/11/1995 pp 31–50.
445 *Vidall v Google* [2015] EWCA Civ 311 [70]–[79].

The rights granted under the Act are largely enforceable by the Data Protection Commissioner. The Commissioner has security of tenure, being dismissible only by the Crown following an address by both Houses of Parliament. Under s 47, a failure to comply with a ruling of the Commissioner is a criminal offence. But the Commissioner can only make such a ruling after serving an enforcement notice under s 40 and such a notice may only be served if one or more of the data principles has been breached. The enforcement mechanism under the 1998 Act is based on the serving of notices on data controllers. If a person thinks that data of which she is the subject is being processed in contravention of the Act she can apply to the Commissioner for an assessment as to whether this is the case (s 42). The Commissioner can serve an information notice under s 43 on a data controller requiring the controller to furnish information to her within certain time limits.

Where the Commissioner is satisfied that a controller is contravening the Act, she may ultimately force the controller to act by serving upon it an enforcement notice, which (under s 40(1)) requires the controller to take, within such time as may be specified in the notice, such steps as may be specified for complying with the requirements of the Act. The notice may either ask the controller to rectify, block, erase or destroy any inaccurate data or data containing an expression of opinion or take steps to check the accuracy of the data. If a controller fails to comply with an enforcement or information notice, it will commit a criminal offence.

Under s 48, an appeal lies from decisions of the Commissioner to the tribunal which is made up of experienced lawyers and 'persons to represent the interests' of data subjects under (s 6(6)). This power of appeal is exercisable upon the broadest possible grounds. The Act provides that any person may appeal to the tribunal against an enforcement or information notice (s 48) either on the basis that the notice is not in accordance with the law, or that the Commissioner ought to have exercised her discretion (if any) differently' (s 49). The tribunal is also empowered to substitute such other notice as could have been served by the Commissioner. There is a further appeal from the tribunal to the High Court, but on a 'point of law' only (s 49(6)). In practice, this will probably be interpreted so as to allow review of the tribunal's decisions, not just for error of law, but also on the other accepted heads of judicial review.

Thus, the Commissioner's decisions can, in the final analysis, be enforced, just as can orders of the Court. These powers are buttressed by powers of entry, search and seizure to gain evidence of a failure by the authority to carry out its obligations under the Act or of the commission of a criminal offence under the Act (detailed in Sched 9).

Relationship between the HRA and DPA

The DPA 1998 is precisely aimed, *inter alia*, at the preservation of informational autonomy in a very broad sense, going beyond the obligations created by the HRA, under Art 8, which, as discussed, is *directly* applicable only to public authorities. The 1998 Act is of immense significance as a privacy measure that reaches fully into the private sphere. In so far as they are reflected in the DPA, the rights under Art 8 also bind private as well as public bodies.

The Data Protection Commissioner and tribunal operating under s 6 of the DPA 1998 are public authorities and therefore they are directly bound, under s 6 of the HRA, by the Convention rights. Both bodies are consequently subject to judicial review for violation of the Convention in their rulings. Because under s 47 a failure to comply with a ruling of the Commissioner is a criminal offence, a significant possibility of enforcing Art 8 rights might appear to arise.

The exemptions under the Act are broad; where they apply to bodies that are public authorities under s 6 of the HRA, Art 8 can be relied upon to seek to prevent the unfair processing of data where an infringement of its guarantee had occurred or appeared likely to occur. It should be noted that Art 8 clearly views the processing of personal data as prima facie falling within para 1.[446]

7 Remedies for privacy invasion

Introduction

The privacy measures considered in this chapter offer a variety of remedies. Ofcom and IPSO have a number of internal remedies at their command, and since Ofcom (and probably IPSO) it is a public authority under s 6 HRA, it must act in accordance with Arts 10 and 8 in applying them. Various criminal offences arise under the DPA 1998, while reporting restrictions can be enforced in contempt proceedings. Compensation is available under s 13 of the DPA in respect of unfair processing by data control-lers. However, as indicated above, it appears that interim injunctions are not obtainable under s 32 DPA unless the claimant is seeking to prevent re-publication of the material. If the doctrine of confidence/privacy is relied on, a number of civil remedies are avail-able, and those remedies are also available under s 8 HRA where an action is brought directly for invasion of privacy under Art 8 under s 7(1)(a) of the HRA against a media body that is a public authority.[447]

Where an action is brought directly against a media body, either under the doctrine of confidence/privacy or, in the case of the BBC or Channel 4 under the HRA, the claimant would normally be seeking an injunction. In the case of Ofcom, the order sought by the claimant under s 8 HRA could be a declaration or a mandatory order, since he or she would be asking Ofcom to use its powers, discussed above, which include either to pun-ish a broadcaster or to prevent a future broadcast. The discussion below revolves mainly round the privacy cases brought under the privacy/confidence action and the impact on them of s 12(3) HRA.

Damages and costs

Damages are available, in addition to, or in substitution for, injunctive relief,[448] and regardless of whether or not the court could also have ordered injunctive relief in the

---

446 In *MS v Sweden* (1997) 3 BHRC 348, the applicant complained that disclosure of her medical records in respect of a compensation claim infringed Art 8. The Court found that state information relating to an individual's sexual life may merit protection, a decision clearly in harmony with the approach under the DPA.

447 See further Chapter 4, p 207 *et seq.*

448 Under Lord Cairns' Act; see Wacks, *op cit*, fn 1, pp 149, 151. Damages were awarded in the decisions in *Douglas II* (2003) EWCA Civ 139 (affirmed in *Douglas (No 3)* [2005] EWCA Civ 595) and in *Campbell v MGN* [2004] 2 WLR 1232.

particular circumstances.[449] Until *Campbell* there was no authority for the award of damages for emotional distress, but precedents exist in other areas of law.[450] It is now established that damages for emotional distress may be awarded in 'private fact' cases. In *Campbell* damages were assessed at a little over £14,000, including £1,000 for aggravated damages, in respect of the 'trashing' of Campbell's character in articles published after she commenced her action against the *Mirror*.

The Court of Appeal in *Douglas (No 3)* said as to damages in confidence/privacy cases:

> The sum [of damages awarded] is also small in the sense that it could not represent any real deterrent to a newspaper or magazine, with a large circulation, contemplating the publication of photographs which infringed an individual's privacy. Accordingly, particularly in the light of the state of competition in the newspaper and magazine industry, the refusal of an interlocutory injunction in a case such as this represents a strong potential disincentive to respect for aspects of private life, which the Convention intends should be respected.[451]

In *Douglas* the High Court and the Court of Appeal accepted that there had been a breach of the couple's privacy by virtue of the publication of the unauthorised photographs, and awarded around £14,000 damages. The Court of Appeal in *Douglas (No 3)*[452] found that this interference with an exclusive contract gave no cause of action to *OK!* – the original beneficiaries of it. It therefore overturned the award of £1m damages to *OK!* (the figure reflected the amount paid by rival company *Hello!* to the celebrity couple for exclusive coverage of their wedding). The Court of Appeal referred to the damages awarded to the Douglases as 'a very modest sum in the context of this litigation'.[453] The £1m award was restored by the House of Lords; the case is illustrative of the limited benefit of the remedy awarded under the *privacy* aspect of the applicants' claim since the £1m damages did not relate to that claim.

449   Provided the court has jurisdiction to grant an injunction: see *Hooper v Rogers* [1975] 1 Ch 43, p 48, per Russell LJ. See also *Race Relations Board v Applin* [1973] 1 QB 815 and the views of Capper, D 'Damages for breach of the equitable duty of confidence' (1994) 14 LS 313 and Gurry, F, *Breach of Confidence* 1984, Chapter 23. See Wacks, *op cit*, fn 1, p 151, fn 46; *cf* the views of Megarry VC in *Malone v Comr of Police for the Metropolis (No 2)* [1979] 1 Ch 344.

450   Examples include contract (*Jarvis v Swans Tours Ltd* [1973] 1 QB 233), copyright and under the Equality Act 2010, which gives the courts power to award damages on the same basis as in tort actions and which under s 119(4) allows courts to award damages for injury to feelings alone. Space precludes full discussion of the point, but it was until *Campbell* an area free of authority; however, to decide that as a blanket rule, such damages could never be available, by leaving the plaintiff potentially remediless, would be clearly have been out of line with the Convention notion of effective protection for rights; Strasbourg has recognised the need to compensate for 'moral damage', including emotional distress (see Van Dijk and Van Hoof, *Theory and Practice of the European Convention on Human Rights*, 1998, pp 179–82).

451   *Douglas (No 3)* [2005] EWCA Civ 595 [225]–[257].

452   *Douglas II* (2003) EWCA Civ 139 was affirmed in *Douglas (No 3)* [2005] EWCA Civ 595. HL decision: [2007] UKHL 21.

453   *Ibid*, at [110].

The limited utility of damages in privacy litigation was also raised in the *Mosley*[454] case, which is considered above. Briefly, this case, as mentioned above, concerned the *News of the World's* lengthy and extremely explicit coverage of the applicant's group sex, quasi-sado-masochistic sexual activities, which were falsely represented by the paper as having Nazi undertones. Mosley claimed unlimited damages for breach of confidence and/or the unauthorised disclosure of personal information contrary to Art 8. Mosley claimed that the level of damages should reflect the fact that the newspaper had deliberately given him no advance warning of the publication of the story so as to deprive him of an opportunity to obtain an interim injunction in order to prevent publication. In the course of the proceedings before the High Court, the court heard evidence from the editor of the *News of the World*. As to the reasons for providing no advance warning to the applicant of the imminent publication of the story, it was made clear that the failure to do so was based on the fear that an interim injunction would be awarded (see further below).

The judge found that a claim for compensatory damages could reflect an element of aggravation. The principles governing such a finding for infringement of privacy were detailed as follows:

(1) compensatory damages could include an element of aggravation;
(2) the purpose of damages addressed the specific public policy factors in play when there had been a breach of confidence including personal dignity, autonomy and integrity;
(3) as well as providing for distress, hurt feelings and loss of dignity there was an element for vindication to mark the infringement of the right, and nominal damages would not serve this purpose;
(4) the award must be proportionate and not open to the criticisms of arbitrariness, to which end there had to be a readily identifiable scale, and therefore it would be legitimate to pay some attention to the current levels of personal injury awards;
(5) it was legitimate to take into account the effect on the claimant of the defendant's advancing its case on public interest; on the other hand the extent to which the claimant's own conduct had contributed to the nature and scale of the distress might be a relevant factor on causation.[455]

In the circumstances he found that it was appropriate to award the claimant a sum of £60,000. Eady J recognised that the sum awarded would not constitute adequate redress, noting:

I have already emphasised that injury to reputation is not a directly relevant factor, but it is also to be remembered that libel damages can achieve one objective that is impossible in privacy cases. Whereas reputation can be vindicated by an award of damages, in the sense that the claimant can be restored to the esteem in which he was previously held, that is not possible where embarrassing personal information

---

454 *Max Mosley v News Group Newspapers Limited* [2008] EWHC 1777 (QB).
455 *Ibid*, [230]–[231].

has been released for general publication. As the media are well aware, once privacy has been infringed, the damage is done and the embarrassment is only augmented by pursuing a court action. . . .

Notwithstanding all this, it has to be accepted that an infringement of privacy cannot ever be effectively compensated by a monetary award. Judges cannot achieve what is, in the nature of things, impossible. That unpalatable fact cannot be mitigated by simply adding a few noughts to the number first thought of . . . At the same time, the figure selected should not be such that it could be interpreted as minimising the scale of the wrong done or the damage it has caused.[456]

The judge noted that the applicant was hardly exaggerating when he said that his life was ruined. The judge did not however make the unprecedented award of punitive – rather than compensatory – damages that had been sought by Mr Mosley. Section 39 of the Crime and Courts Act 2013 has confirmed that a 'relevant publisher' cannot be subject to punitive aggravated damages in privacy litigation.

Clearly, these generally meagre awards of damages provide little financial disincentive to journalists inclined to invade privacy in pursuit of profit-making photographs and stories. In the exceptional circumstances of phone hacking, which involved extremely prolonged privacy invasions, far higher awards have been made, including one payment of £260,000 (to Sadie Frost).[457] The court found that damages in privacy cases should compensate not merely for distress but also, where appropriate, for the loss of privacy or autonomy arising out of the infringement. A parallel was drawn between privacy invasion and harassment and set forth the following criteria to determine the level of compensation:

(a) the disclosure of certain types of private information was more significant than others; (b) information about mental and physical health and significant private financial matters attracted a higher degree of privacy, and therefore compensation; (c) information about social meetings attracted a lower degree of privacy and compensation; (d) information about matters internal to a relationship would be treated as private, and disclosures which disrupted a relationship or were likely to adversely affect a couple's attempts to repair it were likely to be treated as a serious infringement deserving substantial compensation; (e) the appropriate compensation would depend on the nature of the information, its significance as private information, and the effect on the victim of its disclosure; (f) the effect of repeated intrusions by publication could be cumulative; (g) in relation to distress, the "egg-shell skull" principle applied, so that a thinner-skinned individual might be caused more upset, and therefore receive more compensation, than a thicker-skinned individual who was the subject of the same intrusion.[458]

It is not clear at present how or if these principles would be applied in cases other than phone hacking but, where very serious invasion of privacy had occurred, such an approach could result in greater awards of damages in privacy cases.

456 *Ibid.*
457 *Gulati v MGN* [2015] EWHC 1482 [701].
458 *Ibid,* [229]–[230].

Another possibility for meaningful compensation for privacy invasion is created by the Crime and Courts Act 2013. Linked to the Leveson framework of an approved press regulator discussed above, was the creation of enhanced financial penalties in privacy litigation for relevant publishers who were not members of such a regulator. By s 34 of the 2013 Act exemplary damages will be available in such proceedings unless the publisher is a member of an approved regulator (s 34(2)). They could be awarded if s 34(2) applied and if it was deemed appropriate to do so in all the circumstances of the case under s 34(4). In considering all the circumstances the court will take into account the availability of membership of such a regulator.[459] This provision came into force on 3 November 2015 (one year after the creation of the Press Recognition Panel). Exemplary damages would be awarded where (s 34(6)):

> (a) the defendant's conduct has shown a deliberate or reckless disregard of an outrageous nature for the claimant's rights, (b) the conduct is such that the court should punish the defendant for it, and (c) other remedies would not be adequate to punish that conduct.

The terms used in s 34(6)(a) create a high bar for the award of exemplary damages, and therefore are likely to satisfy Art 10(2). Clearly, s 34 was designed to create an incentive to join an approved regulator. If IMPRESS obtains approval from the Recognition Panel, a newspaper in a privacy claim could find that exemplary damages were awarded against it if it had failed to join IMPRESS.

However, damages are not the primary disincentive – the cost of litigation far exceeds even aggravated damages. In the *Mosley* case, as well as the damages, the newspaper faced an additional bill of around £850,000 after the judge ordered it to pay Mr Mosley's legal fees, estimated at £450,000, in addition to its own costs of £400,000. In the *Campbell* litigation the reliance of the claimant on a conditional fee arrangement for her appeal to the House of Lords was itself challenged and appealed to the House of Lords on the basis that the exorbitant litigation costs (in excess of £1m) were contrary to Art 10. The challenge was unsuccessful domestically,[460] but succeeded at Strasbourg (*Mirror Group Newspapers Ltd v United Kingdom*).[461] However, in that case the scheme for conditional fee arrangements was challenged for its arbitrariness and unfairness[462] rather than for the principle that a publisher should bear the costs of litigation that has determined it is responsible for infringing another's privacy.[463]

Following the Leveson recommendations, the Crime and Courts Act 2013 radically alters awards of costs against publishers who are not members of an approved regulator. By s 41(3) a court *must* award costs against a publisher involved in privacy litigation,

---

459   Under s 35 the court must take account of the following –
    (a) whether membership of an approved regulator was available to the defendant at the material time;
    (b) if such membership was available, the reasons for the defendant not being a member.
460   *Campbell v MGN Ltd (Costs)* [2005] UKHL 61.
461   (2011) 53 EHRR 5.
462   *Ibid*, [192], [194], [197]–[198], [206]–[210], [217]–[220].
463   The issue litigated in *MGN v UK* was addressed by the Legal Aid, Sentencing and Punishment of Offenders Act 2012 s 44(2) which amended s 58 of the Courts and Legal Services Act 1990 s 58(4A), (4B) so that the maximum costs payable under such an agreement are tied to a percentage of the damages awarded.

which could be a member of an approved regulator but is not, *regardless of whether it is successful* unless 'it is just and equitable in all the circumstances of the case to make a different award of costs or make no award of costs' (s 40(3)(b)). It is possible that s 40 could be challenged as incompatible with Art 10 after *MGN v UK*.[464] However, such a challenge is unlikely to be successful since subsequent case law has distinguished *MGN v UK* to its specific context, and it is clear that the Supreme Court has adopted a deferential stance to legislation imposing enhanced costs on certain categories of litigant.[465] The s40 provision, whose financial implications should not be understated, will only come into force once a regulator has been approved by the Press Recognition Panel (s 40(6)), which may shortly occur. As discussed above, the Conservative government has indicated that IPSO can continue to operate without oversight,[466] despite its inability to satisfy 'approved regulator' status. But nevertheless, this costs regime could lead to pressure being brought to bear on publishers who do not join an approved regulator.

Interim injunctions

Clearly, the most important issue both for privacy and for media freedom is the question of the basis on which the courts will grant an interim injunction to restrain publication. The main flaw of the Data Protection Act, as indicated, as a statutory privacy remedy, is its bar on interim injunctions against the press. From the plaintiff's perspective, obtaining an injunction is vital in privacy cases, far more so than in defamation. This is because the damage done to reputation by initial publication can be subsequently restored by a public finding that the allegation was false. By contrast, if private information is made public, the law can compensate for this harm at final trial by awarding damages, but it cannot in any way cure the invasion of privacy: it cannot erase the information revealed from people's memories. From the defendant's perspective, on the other hand, if the story is topical, even an interim injunction might kill it off completely. Thus, as Robertson and Nichol put it: 'In breach of confidence . . . the critical stage is usually the application for an interim injunction . . . If the publisher is able to publish . . . the action will often evaporate . . . If the story is injuncted the publisher will often lose interest.'[467] Similarly, Leigh and Lustgarten comment: 'the interim stage is the critical one . . . [it is] effectively the disposition of the matter'.[468] However, while all privacy is lost if the story is published, the speech claim could be served by a limited injunction designed to protect identity – it might, depending on the circumstances, still be possible to publish the story itself. This point is returned to below.

Prior to the inception of the HRA it was only necessary for the plaintiff to make out an arguable case for confidentiality[469] in order to obtain an injunction; the courts then sought to maintain the *status quo*, on the basis that if the story was published, the material

464 (2011) 53 EHRR 5.
465 *Lawrence v Coventry* [2015] 1 WLR 3485.
466 See e.g., 'Maria Miller "happy" with current situation where most publishers back IPSO regulator, press freedom mission told' *Press Gazette*, 21 January 2014; http://www.pressgazette.co.uk.
467 *Media Law*, 2nd edn, 1992, Penguin, p 190.
468 Leigh, I and Lustgarten, L, 'Making rights real: the courts, remedies, and the Human Rights Act' (1999) 58 CLJ 509, p 533 (referring to the granting of interim injunctions generally); and see also p 551.
469 E.g., *HRH Prince of Wales v Associated Newspapers Ltd* [2006] EWCA Civ 1776; *Shelley Films v Rex Features Limited* [1994] EMLR 134; *Francome v MGM* [1984] 1 WLR 892.

would lose its confidential character, and there would be nothing to have a final trial about.[470] However, this consideration could be outweighed by the defence of public interest at the interlocutory stage. The view of Lord Denning in *Woodward v Hutchins*,[471] that the mere fact that defendants intends to plead public interest at final trial should preclude interim relief, did not find wide support; instead, it appeared that, whilst a plea of public interest could defeat a claim for such relief, the defence had to be supported by evidence and have a credible chance of success at final trial.[472] Since the judges had the confidential information in question before them at that stage, they were able to find quite readily that the defence was made out (as Laws J did in *Hellewell*) or will probably succeed (as in *Lion Laboratories*) or that it did not justify publication at large (as in *Francome*). Since, as suggested above, the paradigmatic privacy claim often involves speech of little or no value in public interest terms,[473] it is fairly easy, at least in some instances, to determine that the publication in question raises no serious speech or public interest issue.

However, that test was thought to be potentially unfavourable to the media because, in balancing the rights of the two parties, courts took the view that while the plaintiff's right to confidentiality would be wholly defeated by publication, the press could always still publish the story if they won at trial; they were thus inclined toward protecting the more fragile right of the plaintiff.[474]

The HRA addressed this issue directly. In this context, s 12 is of interest in respect of injunctions or other orders granted under its own powers, contained in s 8,[475] and at common law, where freedom of expression is affected. It will be recalled from Chapter 4 that s 12 applies (*per* sub-s (1)): 'if a court is considering whether to grant any relief which, if granted, might affect the exercise of the Convention right to freedom of expression';[476] it provides (*per* sub-s (3)) that: 'no such relief is to be granted so as to

---

470 See *AG v Guardian Newspapers (No 2)* [1990] 1 AC 109. Thus in *Francome v MGM* [1984] 1 WLR 892, p 900, Fox LJ said: 'Unless Mr Francome is given protection until the trial, I think that a trial might be largely worthless from his point of view even though he succeeded.' Similarly, in *Lion Laboratories ltd v Evans* [1984] 1 QB 530, p 551, Griffiths LJ said: 'there will usually be a powerful case for maintaining the status quo by the grant of an interlocutory injunction to restrain publication until trial of the action'.

471 [1977] 1 WLR 760 (CA).

472 See *Lion Laboratories ltd v Evans* [1984] 1 QB 530, pp 538 and 553, *per* Stephenson LJ (explicitly rejecting Lord Denning's approach in *Woodward*); *ibid*, p 548 *per* O'Connor LJ and p 553 *per* Griffiths LJ; similarly in *Hellewell*, where the public interest argument prevented the award of an injunction.

473 E.g., Alan Rusbridger, the editor of the *Guardian*, in a conference speech, listed a string of examples in which newspapers had published intimate details about the personal lives of celebrities, in some cases surreptitiously obtained, with either no or the flimsiest of 'public interest' justifications; he instanced a story in the *News of the World* in January 1999, in which a lap dancer gave full details of a recent sexual encounter with the singer Tom Jones ('Human Rights, Privacy and the Media', organised by the Constitution Unit, and the Centre for Communication and Information Law, UCL, 8 January 1999).

474 This generally followed under the 'balance of convenience' test (*American Cyanamid Co v Ethicon* [1975] AC 396). See *AG v Guardian Newspapers* [1987] 1 WLR 1248, which concerned an application for an interim injunction to restrain publication of confidential information (extracts from *Spycatcher*). Lord Brandon remarked (*ibid*, p 1292): 'the choice lies between one course [allowing publication] which may result in permanent and irrevocable damage to the cause of [the plaintiff] and another course which can only result in temporary and in no way irrevocable damage to the cause of the newspapers . . . it seems to me clear that the second . . . course should . . . be preferred . . .'; see also the similar reasoning of Lord Ackner, *ibid*, p 1305.

475 See Chapter 4, p 207 *et seq*.

476 See pp 184–85.

restrain publication before trial unless the court is satisfied that the applicant is likely to establish that publication should not be allowed'. Section 12(4) specifically instructs the courts that when they are dealing with, *inter alia*, journalistic material, they should consider the extent to which 'it is, or would be, in the public interest for the material to be published' and thus remove any lingering doubts as to whether the court should consider the strength of the public interest defence at the interim stage. Sub-section (3), in allowing the court to grant injunctions only where it believes that the plaintiff will succeed at trial, requires the court to undertake a substantial balancing test at the interim stage; it also makes it clear that the burden is on the plaintiff to show that the privacy interest would probably succeed at trial.[477]

Undertaking this evaluation at the interim stage is not proving to be an especially difficult task, as the findings in *Douglas*,[478] *Venables*[479] and *Mills*[480] suggested. The courts obviously have to take account of Art 10 jurisprudence on interim injunctions since s 12 instructs them to have 'particular regard' to Art 10. The leading Strasbourg case on prior restraints is *Observer and Guardian v UK*,[481] in which the Court considered the compatibility with Art 10 of interim injunctions preventing those newspapers from publishing *Spycatcher* material. The Court laid down the basic principle that:

> while Art 10 does not in terms prohibit the imposition of prior restraints on publication . . . the dangers inherent in [them] are such that they call for the most careful scrutiny on the part of the Court . . . news is a perishable commodity and delay of its publication, even for a short period, may well deprive it of all its value and interest.[482]

While the court's actual decision in the case seemed to suggest that the need to preserve the plaintiff's rights would in itself point strongly towards the imposition of an interim injunction,[483] the relatively cautious approach adopted may have been influenced by the fact that the very sensitive issue of national security was at stake. It is suggested that the domestic judiciary should look rather to the general principle laid down in the case

477   Sub-section (2) provides some procedural protection against interim injunctions. It provides:
    If the person against whom the application for relief is made ('the respondent') is neither present nor represented, no such relief is to be granted unless the court is satisfied –
    (a) that the applicant has taken all practicable steps to notify the respondent; or
    (b) that there are compelling reasons why the respondent should not be notified.
    This clearly limits the circumstances in which *ex parte* injunctions against publication can be granted.
478   [2001] 2 WLR 992.
479   [2001] 1 All ER 908, Fam Div.
480   [2001] EMLR 41.
481   (1991) 14 EHRR 153; for comment see Leigh, I, '*Spycatcher* in Strasbourg' [1992] PL 200.
482   *Ibid*, [60].
483   It was found that the initial injunctions, which prevented publication for over a year, had the aim of maintaining the Attorney General's ability to bring a case claiming permanent injunction, a case which would have been destroyed if *Spycatcher* material had been published before that claim could be heard. This factor was found to establish the existence of a pressing social need justifying the restriction of Art 10. The finding that the continuation of the injunctions after the book had been published in the US could not be justified was based simply on the fact that such publication had destroyed the confidentiality of the material, making it impossible to maintain the Attorney General's rights as a litigant. See Chapter 8, pp 522–23.

that the granting of interim injunctions is a particularly significant prima facie infringement of Art 10, given the perishable qualities of news. This factor would then have to be
weighed against the strength of the privacy claim, in the manner suggested earlier and,
in accordance with s 12, a court should award the interim injunction only if it considers
that the privacy argument is the stronger one.

In *Douglas* the Court of Appeal had to consider whether the injunction against *Hello!*
should be continued. Section 12(3) HRA provides that prior restraint on expression
should not be granted except where the court considers that the claimant is 'likely' to
establish at trial that publication should not be allowed. Under s 3 HRA the court has a
duty to construe all legislation, which must include the HRA itself, compatibly with the
Convention rights 'so far as it is possible to do so'. Therefore, clearly, both sub-sections
must be read in such a way as to ensure that all the rights are given full weight; s 12(3)
must not accord more weight to Art 10 than to the other rights. The outcome, in any particular instance, would be determined, the Court found, principally by considerations of
proportionality. Sedley LJ said that the Court has to:

> look ahead to the ultimate stage and to be satisfied that the scales are likely to
> come down in the applicant's favour. That does not conflict with the Conven-
> tion, since it is merely requiring the Court to apply its mind to how one right is
> to be balanced, on the merits against another right, without building in additional
> weight on one side.[484]

Taking into account the fact that the claimants had in a sense already 'sold' their privacy,
Sedley LJ found that their rights to privacy were outweighed by the right of publication
and considered that they should be left to a claim for damages at the trial of the action.

But the Court also had to consider the effects of leaving the claimants to a damages
claim. In *American Cyanamid Company v Ethicon Ltd*[485] it was found that a judge must
weigh the respective risks that injustice may result from his deciding one way or the
other at the interim stage. If an injunction is refused, but the claimant does succeed in
establishing his legal right at the trial that he sought to protect by means of the injunction, he might in the meantime suffer harm that could not adequately be compensated
for by an award of money. On the other hand, there was the risk that if the injunction
was granted, but the claimant failed at the trial, the defendant in the meantime might
have suffered harm that was also non-compensable. This weighing up is sometimes
termed 'the balance of convenience'. Brooke LJ found that the balance of convenience appeared to favour leaving *OK!* to assert its legal rights at the trial of what he said
was 'essentially a commercial dispute between two magazine enterprises'. Therefore,
although the Court found that the claim might succeed at trial and result in an award of
compensation, it also found that the injunction should be discharged. Thus, *Hello!* could
publish the issue which contained the wedding photographs.

In *Venables*[486] the Court was satisfied that there was a real and serious risk to the
rights of the claimants under Arts 2 and 3, and it was found that, in principle, jurisdiction

484 [2001] 2 WLR 992 at 1008.
485 [1975] AC 396.
486 *Venables v News Group Newspapers Ltd* [2001] 2 WLR 1038.

to grant the injunctions to protect the claimants was present. The Court went on to assess the strength of the evidence relating to those risks; finding that a real risk existed and that the protection represented by the injunctions was proportionate to the need for confidentiality, the injunctions were granted. The injunctions were intended to last for their whole lives, although the existence of the internet makes their efficacy in practice somewhat doubtful.

The leading case on the interpretation of s 12(3) is now *Cream Holdings Ltd and Others v Banerjee and Others*.[487] Banerjee was a senior accountant for Cream Holdings. She was dismissed and took with her copies of documents that appeared to show illegal and improper financial activities by the company, which she then passed to the *Echo* newspaper. The *Echo* published articles allegedly showing corruption involving a director of Cream and a council official. Cream sought injunctions to prevent further publication. The Court had to consider the proper test to be applied in deciding whether to grant such an injunction, taking account of the terms of s 12(3) HRA. The old test, as indicated above, was that the applicant, as a threshold test, had to show that he or she had a 'real prospect of success' at final trial. If so, the court would consider where the 'balance of convenience' lay[488] between the case for granting an injunction and that of leaving the applicant to his or her remedy in damages. So the Court had to consider the modification of that test under the HRA. Lord Nicholls noted that press concerns under the old 'balance of convenience' test, which were discussed above, lay behind the enactment of s 12(3). The leading speech was delivered by Lord Nicholls, with whom all their lordships agreed. His lordship said:

> the effect of section 12(3) is that the court is not to make an interim restraint order unless satisfied that the applicant's prospects of success at the trial are sufficiently favourable to justify such an order being made in the particular circumstances of the case. As to what degree of likelihood makes the prospects of success 'sufficiently favourable', the general approach should be that courts will be exceedingly slow to make interim restraint orders where the applicant has not satisfied the court he will probably ('more likely than not') succeed at the trial. In general, that should be the threshold an applicant must cross before the court embarks on exercising its discretion, duly taking into account the relevant jurisprudence on article 10 and any countervailing Convention rights. But there will be cases where it is necessary for a court to depart from this general approach and a lesser degree of likelihood will suffice.[489]

Lord Nicholls said that he had in mind, as instances in which a lesser degree of likelihood would suffice, two categories of case. As to the first, he clearly had the *Venables* situation in mind, where the claimant would be placed in immediate danger if the injunction was not granted. It is contended that he was right to take that stance since arguably the courts' duty under s 6 HRA would not be satisfied if an injunction was not granted in such circumstances, since the court is bound to observe Arts 2 and 3.[490]

---

487 [2004] 3 WLR 918. For comment, see Smith, ATH 'Freedom of the Press and Prior Restraint' [2005] 64(1) CLJ 4.
488 *American Cyanamid Co v Ethicon Ltd* [1975] AC 396.
489 *Cream Holdings Ltd v Banerjee, op cit*, [22].
490 *Ibid*, [19].

Lord Nicholls further had in mind the less contentious instance in which an injunction of short duration (days or hours) is required in order to give a judge time to consider the case properly:

> an application [may be] made to the court for an interlocutory injunction to restrain publication of allegedly confidential or private information until trial. The judge needs an opportunity to read and consider the evidence and submissions of both parties. Until then the judge will often not be in a position to decide whether on balance of probability the applicant will succeed in obtaining a permanent injunction at the trial.[491]

Thus, it is now clear that an injunction will normally be awarded only if the judge considers it more likely than not that the applicant will succeed at final trial. If the scales appear to be evenly balanced between the parties, injunctive relief will be refused.

A further problem is that the grant of an injunction may become pointless. In *Max Mosley v News Group Newspapers Ltd*[492] the information in question was known to so many people, partly because part of it had been posted on the newspaper's website, that an injunction was deemed inappropriate since it would have been unable to prevent dissemination of the information. *Terry v Persons Unknown*[493] (also known as *LNS v Persons Unknown*) raised the question whether a celebrity, who suspects that any one of a number of newspapers might publish private information, can prevent publication via an injunction aimed at the world at large.[494] Obviously if the celebrity has to wait until the information has been published that might mean that privacy liability would become a merely empty remedy.[495] It was found, as indicated above, that since no newspaper was able to put forward arguments in respect of free expression, liability did not arise. Clearly that meant that the task of obtaining an injunction at an early stage, well before publication – in contrast to the situation in *Mosley* – was rendered more difficult.

An injunction may take the form of a 'super-injunction'; the term refers to a legal gagging order that not only prevents the media from reporting the details of a story, but also forbids mention of the existence of the injunction itself – since knowledge that an injunction has been obtained by a particular celebrity obviously arouses curiosity as to what it covers. However, the use of super-injunctions has not overall been successful: people, including journalists, have taken to online forums and social networking websites to 'expose' the celebrities involved, as the internet is much harder to regulate than traditional media outlets. Several celebrities alleged to be those subject to super-injunctions have been named on Twitter and Wikipedia. Identification by tens of thousands of Twitter users of the footballer Ryan Giggs as the holder of a super-injunction occurred, in defiance of a High Court ruling.[496] Ryan Giggs was one of several celebrity super-

---

491 *Ibid*, at [17]–[18].
492 [2008] EWHC 1777.
493 [2010] EMLR 16.
494 *Ibid*, [2].
495 Busuttil, G, and McCafferty, P 'Interim Injunctions and the Overlap between Privacy and Libel' (2010) 2(1) *Journal of Media Law*, 1 at p 10.
496 *Ryan Joseph Giggs v News Group Newspapers* [2012] EWHC 431 (QB), [27].

injunction holders to be widely identified on Twitter but could not be named by other media until an MP used parliamentary privilege to break the gagging order.

The courts may consider that there is a case for an injunction, but not a 'super-injunction', which has a greater impact on media freedom. Thus in *Ntuli v Donald*[497] Donald had obtained a super injunction that maintained his own anonymity, and restrained an anonymised defendant from doing specified but unpublishable things. The defendant was also restrained from publishing the fact that the injunction had been obtained. The Court found that the injunction would be maintained but the order for anonymisation of the parties and for non-disclosure of the injunction would be discharged as not in the interests of open justice and unnecessary to maintain the claimant's Art 8 right.

Are the remedies satisfactory?

It is argued that the stance taken as to the grant of injunctions as the most effective remedy does not necessarily comport readily with the establishment of the presumptive equality of Arts 8 and 10. Once privacy has been breached, it cannot be reinstated, while the speech claim could be served at a later date, or could be served by a limited injunction concealing identity. In other words, there are nuanced methods of answering to the speech claim but not the privacy claim. The findings in *Bannerjee*, it is argued, elevate the speech claim over the privacy one in a manner which is not fully in accordance with the Strasbourg clashing rights jurisprudence. Since s 12(3) must be interpreted compatibly with the Convention rights under s 3 HRA, and the Convention jurisprudence must be taken into account under s 2, it is arguable that if a suitable case arises, the test from *Bannerjee* should be re-visited in future by the Supreme Court.

Ironically, the pre-HRA test gave a more equal weight to the two competing claims. The idea that newspapers would lose interest if the reporting was enjoined arose in a climate in which free speech had primacy and newspaper editors considered that their working practices should remain unfettered, confusing this idea quite frequently with free speech claims. Such confusion is also evident in a number of post-HRA decisions. But in the changed privacy-valuing culture that is now fairly well established, the idea of maintaining relatively unfettered media working practices needs to be revisited: now that the press have to face the grant of interim injunctions quite frequently, they have had to modify their working practices accordingly. The need to show that it is more likely than not that the privacy claim would succeed at final trial can distort, it is argued, the parallel analysis, encouraging a judge, worryingly, to overstate a weak or unclear speech claim, in the face of a strong competing privacy interest, in order to avoid the grant of an injunction.

Further, a judge will not award an injunction if it would represent an impotent remedy because the information has already reached so many people; in particular that may occur when it is accessible via a website or on social media. That point is distinguishable from the point about public domain made above – information may still attract a reasonable expectation of privacy even if it is partially in the public domain. But given that a newspaper is not under a duty to give prior notification to a potential plaintiff that

497 [2010] EWCA 1276.

it is about to publish privacy-invading material,[498] and that it may well be difficult to obtain an interim injunction based merely on the rumour that publication of such material is about to occur (*Terry*), it may be concluded that the remedy of an injunction may not always be available when it is most needed.

Thus at present it may be concluded that the remedies available are not satisfactory: no compensation is available via regulatory bodies; the level of damages awarded is usually much too low to create a deterrent effect; injunctions against the press are not available under the DPA, and in relation to the tort are sometimes not awarded due to circumstances outside the control of the plaintiff. The use of damages and costs as sticks under the Crime and Courts Act 2013 to encourage the press to join an approved regulator could mean that the press tendency to invade privacy diminishes, either to avoid the sanctions available for failing to do so and/or simply to avoid joining such a regulator in the first place.

8 Conclusions

So what can finally be said as to the current state of legal protection for privacy in the UK? As far as private actors are concerned, the main focus of this chapter, the position has changed dramatically in the post-HRA years. A more comprehensive but complex and piecemeal protection against invasion of privacy can now be identified. It has a number of strands. First, misuse of private information can now give rise to civil liability and has shaken itself free of the constraints previously imposed by the doctrine of confidence. Second, if a public authority breaches Art 8, ss 7 and 8 HRA can be relied on to obtain a remedy against it. Obviously tortious liability could also be relied upon as an alternative against a public authority. Thirdly, children and vulnerable adults can rely on the ECHR jurisdiction of the Court in seeking reporting restrictions. So it is apparent that although a quite comprehensive protection from invasion of privacy is now available, gaps and anomalies are still evident.

Nevertheless, the existence of the tortious privacy liability, together with the provisions of the DPA, indicate that the available comprehensive domestic protection against invasion of privacy by gathering and publishing private information is almost as extensive as the protection provided by Art 8 at Strasbourg. In terms of rapidity of development, it outstripped the Strasbourg protection at certain stages. The protection provided by the developments under the HRA, together with that available under the various privacy statutes (including those discussed in the next chapter), is fairly comprehensive.

However, there are a range of flaws in the protection. Apart from the doubts expressed above as to the *Bannerjee* decision, it must also be pointed out that an appellate court has yet to deal with the *Von Hannover* situation in which snatched paparazzi photographs of daily life activities of an adult taken in the street or in public places, such as beaches, are published. The tone of the relevant decisions, despite *Mckennitt*, suggests that the courts are not prepared to grant relief in the *Von Hannover* situation, but instead

---

498 See e.g., *Mosley v UK* [2011] 53 EHRR 30, para 132 [132] in which the ECtHR found that the absence of a requirement in UK law that publishers notify individuals whose private information they plan to publish does not breach Art 8. See also on the right of notification generally in EU law and under the ECHR: DeHert, D and Boehm, F 'The right of notification after surveillance is over: ready for recognition?' (2012) *Digital Enlightenment Yearbook* 19.

have developed tests intended to find that the invasion of privacy can be viewed as *serious*. The seriousness of the invasion of privacy can be evaluated on the basis of a range of factors, as this chapter has indicated and not *merely* on the basis of the nature of the location. On the other hand, while the privacy claim has to meet a test of seriousness, that is not the case in respect of the speech claim. The recent tendency, as discussed above, has been to downgrade the privacy claim.

The ECHR jurisdiction, the tort of misuse of private information and the liability of public authorities for breaches of Art 8 are essentially the same cause of action since all are based on Art 8 and s 6 HRA. Something close to a strong but not absolute duty to bring the common law into line with the Convention rights has clearly been accepted in the transformation of confidence into privacy – the change that has been brought about to the doctrine of breach of confidence is dramatic. Legitimisation of the judicial enterprise in creating the privacy liability was found in the HRA: its introduction of the Convention into UK law allowed the courts to draw upon the general principles expressed in the Strasbourg privacy jurisprudence.[499] The achievement of the judges, especially in the early post-HRA years, documented in this chapter is impressive; they have shown, it is argued, moral courage in imposing privacy values on a press culture that pre-HRA resembled the impoverished US one in many respects.[500] The principal objection to the development of privacy rights has always been the perceived threat to media freedom. This chapter has argued that that fear is largely misplaced, especially in light of decisions such as that in *Von Hannover (No 3)* or *Trimingham*, and indeed that the right to free speech and to protection for privacy are 'mutually supportive',[501] because, as the German Supreme Court has put it, both are 'essential aspects of the liberal democratic order'.[502]

The introduction of legal protection for privacy may to an extent be encouraging a movement away from the prurient scandal that has often infested so much of the print media, and therefore, far from threatening free speech in the press, could enhance it. On the other hand, over a decade since *Campbell* was decided, the evidence that press willingness to intrude on privacy has diminished is not apparent, although it may be said that there is a greater press awareness, especially post-Leveson, of the acceptable boundaries of intrusion, broad as they still appear to be. As factors limiting the circumstances in which privacy claims can be raised at all, such as 'public domain' and the defence of waiver, are diminishing in importance, so the focus of attention has become – even more clearly – the nature of the speech claim. As discussed, it is at that point that a failure to apply free speech principles has occurred, especially in more recent cases, which have relied instead on imprecise and dubious justifications largely or wholly unrelated to those principles. The notion, unsupported by the principle of informational autonomy, that 'public figures' have a reduced expectation of privacy, so the speech

---

499 A comparison may be drawn with Canada; see: Craig, JDR, 'Invasion of Privacy and Charter Values: The Common-Law Tort Awakens' (1997) 42 McGill LJ 355.

500 See further Anderson, D, 'The Failure of American Privacy Law', in Markesenis, B, (ed), *Protecting Privacy op cit*, fn 1.

501 Emerson, C, 'The right of privacy and the freedom of the press' (1979) 14(2) Harvard Civil Rights–Civil Liberties Law Review 329. See also Kenyon, A and Richardson, M (eds), *New Dimensions in Privacy Law*, 2007, CUP, Chapters 7 and 8.

502 BGH 19 December 1995 BGHZ 131, 322–46.

claim can readily win out regardless of those justifications, is insidiously creeping in to both the domestic and the Strasbourg privacy jurisprudence. The scope of the concept of privacy was clearly being diminished in the two most recent *Von Hannover* cases, in *Axel Springer*, and in domestic decisions such as *AAA* and *Trimingham*, while the scope of media freedom to publish commercially advantageous photos has been broadened. That tendency, together with the failure so far to implement the Leveson Report in terms of regulation, suggests that the value accorded to privacy is losing out to media claims – under the banner of free speech – that they should be able to enjoy that freedom.

Chapter 11

State surveillance

This chapter has been updated and revised
for this edition by Daniel Fenwick, Lecturer in Law
at the University of Northumbria, UK.

1 Introduction[1]

In recent years the security services and police have invaded privacy with increasing frequency as the technology allowing them to do so has become more advanced, and as those involved in criminal behaviour or terrorism use increasingly sophisticated techniques of communication. The documents leaked by the whistleblower Edward Snowden concerning the extent of surveillance carried out by GCHQ[2] revealed a massive extension of the state capacity to gather information about the online activities of individuals. The justification given for such an extension is primarily the need to address new forms of electronic communications used by criminals, especially terrorists, to organise their operations.[3] However, the scale of GCHQ's surveillance activities appears to go far beyond this justification, and, despite official reassurances,[4] there is now a widespread concern that current surveillance powers, particularly those relating to the interception of communications, are too broad and institutions conducting surveillance lack accountability.[5]

The concerns with the adequacy of safeguards against abuses of state surveillance powers are clearly relevant to the ECHR Art 8 right to respect for private life, which is currently enforceable domestically under the Human Rights Act (HRA). Under the requirements of Art 8, safeguards have to include a clear remedy for the citizen who has been the subject of unauthorised surveillance or other intrusion, and should create strict

---

1 For texts referred to below and further discussion see: Mckay, S, *Covert Policing: Law and Practice*, 2015, OUP; Murphy, M, 'A shift in the approach of the European Court of Human Rights in Surveillance cases: a rejuvenation of necessity' [2014] EHRLR 507; Glover, P, 'Legal uncertainty surrounding the acquisition by UK intelligence-gathering bodies of communications content intercepted outside the UK' (2014) 18(1) Edin LR 114; Fenwick, H, Phillipson, G, and Masterman, R, (eds), *Judicial Reasoning under the Human Rights Act*, 2011, CUP; Starmer, K, Strange, M, and Whitaker, W, *Criminal Justice, Police Powers and Human Rights*, 2001, Blackstone; Taylor, N, 'State Surveillance and the Right to Privacy' 1(1) Surveillance & Society 84; Etzioni, A, *The Limits of Privacy*, 1999, Basic Books Inc.; Fenwick, H, *Civil Rights: New Labour, Freedom and the Human Rights Act*, 2000, Pearson.
2 See 'Edward Snowden's surveillance revelations explained' *the Guardian*, 1 November 2011 (see at http://www.theguardian.com.
3 See Intelligence and Security Committee 'Privacy and Security: A Modern and Transparent Legal Framework', HC 1075, 12 March 2015, para 51.
4 See e.g., *ibid*, para 59F.
5 See e.g., Privacy International 'ISC report exonerates GCHQ for mass surveillance program' 12 March 2015 (see at https://www.privacyinternational.org).

Convention-compliant controls over the power to effect such intrusion or issue authorisation for it. The latter safeguard is particularly crucial since the citizen may not even be aware that intrusion is taking place. This is particularly true of telephone tapping and the use of surveillance devices.

In 2015 the Intelligence and Security Committee found that legal developments had failed to keep pace with technological ones, emphasising the need for legal powers addressing emergent platforms, such as social media and recommending legal reform of surveillance powers.[6] The new Conservative government included such reform within the Queens Speech, in which it was announced that a new Investigatory Powers Bill 2015–16 would reform and consolidate the law in this area. The details of the Bill have thus far not been announced, but it is likely that the new Bill will seek to extend surveillance powers rather than enhance accountability, in line with the recommendations of the 2015 report. These recommendations have been strongly criticised by civil liberties groups on the basis that they would, if adopted, undermine the right to private life.[7]

The common law has always given a high priority to preventing interference with personal property[8] and therefore, prior to the inception of the HRA, privacy received some incidental protection, but tortious remedies are indirectly limited.[9] Under the common law, when an invasion of privacy did not fall within narrow areas of tortious liability,[10] it did not require lawful authority. Therefore the common law has had little or no role in defining either legal powers or accountability mechanisms relevant to state surveillance. Thus, under the common law, police search and seizure of property required legal authority (discussed in Chapter 12), but the interception of communications and much state surveillance had no comprehensive legal basis. State surveillance is currently placed on a statutory basis which largely determines the balance to be struck between the need for state surveillance to prevent organised crime and to counter terrorism, and the protection of individual privacy.

However, the creation of a legal basis for state invasion of privacy does not, of course, necessarily mean that the requirements of Art 8 have been met. The changes to the tribunal system that occurred under the Regulation of Investigatory Powers Act 2000 represented a step in the direction of greater accountability, but, it will be contended below,

---

6 Intelligence and Security Committee 'Privacy and Security: A Modern and Transparent Legal Framework', HC 1075, 12 March 2015, p 2.

7 See e.g., Liberty '"Undemocratic, unnecessary and – in the long run – intolerable:" government reviewer condemns snooping laws' 11 June 2015; see at https://www.liberty-human-rights.org.uk.

8 See *McLorie v Oxford* [1982] 1 QB 1290.

9 Remedies for intrusion on property are found in the torts of trespass and nuisance, while seizure of goods is also prima facie tortious.

10 The tort of trespass was potentially relevant, as shown by the finding in *Hickman v Maisey* [1900] 1 QB 752, CA in which the defendant, who was on the highway, was watching the plaintiff's land and it was found that this constituted unreasonable use and amounted to trespass. However, in *Bernstein v Skyviews and General Ltd* [1978] QB 479 the defendants flew over the plaintiff's land in an aircraft in order to take photographs of it and it was found that the plaintiff lacked a right in trespass to prevent such intrusion. The approach in the latter case was confirmed by the House of Lords in *Hunter v Canary Wharf* [1997] AC 655, pp 691G–692B in which it was confirmed that the tort is essentially concerned with injury to land.

ministerial responsibility, parliamentary oversight and the complaints and checking mechanisms of the relevant commissioners create only a limited and flawed control of the agencies. The HRA has aided in providing some of the impetus for such change, but its direct impact on the agencies, in terms of ensuring protection for privacy, has been limited, for the reasons discussed below.

The influence of the ECHR upon the development of surveillance law is addressed first, before the range of surveillance powers relied on by the security and intelligence services is considered.[11] The chapter primarily concerns interception of communications and covert surveillance, not the retention of data.[12] The main mechanisms of accountability are also considered; these include parliamentary oversight, independent oversight by the surveillance commissioners and the role of the single tribunal. The role of the ECHR and HRA in is analysed in detail. Finally, the potential nature and implications of the changes to be introduced in the Investigatory Powers Bill 2015–16 are examined.

2 The ECHR, HRA and state surveillance

The ECHR rights, particularly Art 8, represents a set of principles against which the statutory framework governing surveillance can be tested. The security agencies, relevant ministers and oversight bodies (apart from the Intelligence and Security Committee)[13] as public authorities are currently bound by the rights under s 6 of the HRA. Although, formally, this is the legal position, the means whereby the Convention rights can be enabled to have a real rather than a theoretical impact on the agencies are highly circumscribed. They are discussed below, but although possible methods of bringing the HRA to bear on the agencies in court are considered, it is contended that the main impact of the HRA in this context is an educative and cultural one: it provides the openness the Intelligence and Security Committee has favoured with a clearer basis, and it may have had some, incremental impact on the work of the oversight bodies, in terms of the attitude they bring to their work. Most significantly, the HRA may have helped to provide the impetus for the further evolution of the oversight.

ECHR requirements

The Art 8(1) guarantees of respect for private life, the home and correspondence are clearly of most relevance to the activities of the agencies. The introduction to Part III argued for a broad view of what constitutes invasion of privacy, based as a core value on the notion of control of personal information.[14] An interference with property nor-

---

11 The provisions considered in this chapter are immensely extensive, complex and detailed, so in a book of this breadth and comprehensiveness, only a selective overview can be undertaken.

12 See Mckay, S, *Covert Policing: Law and Practice*, 2015, OUP, Chaps 4 and 7 for discussion of data acquisition and disclosure relevant to state surveillance powers and the legal framework governing covert human intelligence sources.

13 Parliament itself is not a public body under s 6 and nor is a person exercising a function in connection with proceedings in Parliament (s 6(3)(b)). It is probable that the Committee is not a public authority under this definition.

14 See pp 685–86.

mally creates an interference with one or more of the guarantees.[15] That would include planting a 'bug' on the premises in question.[16] Less obvious invasions can also engage Art 8. In *Harman and Hewitt v UK*,[17] the European Commission of Human Rights found that secret surveillance by MI5 of two former NCCL officers, Patricia Hewitt and Harriet Harman, had infringed Art 8(1), although they had not been subjected to direct intrusion. The intrusion was termed 'indirect' since information about them obtained from the telephone or mail intercepts of others had been recorded.

The use made of personal information, including disclosure to others, can also engage Art 8(1). In *MS v Sweden*,[18] the applicant complained that the use of medical records in respect of a compensation claim had infringed Art 8. The Court found that the disclosure did constitute an interference with the respect for private life, although it was found to be justified under Art 8(2).[19] The finding in *Hilton v UK*[20] implied that the compiling and use of personal files by the Security Services can fall within Art 8, although they also raised questions regarding the onus placed on applicants to establish that they were likely to have been the victims of surveillance – in that instance of positive vetting for civil service posts. *Esbester v UK*[21] confirmed that a security check based on personal information could fall within Art 8. It may be concluded that many, if not almost all, activities of the agencies in obtaining, collecting, using and disclosing personal information tend to engage Art 8(1).

Once Art 8(1) is engaged, the question is whether the interference can be justified under para 2. To be justified, state interference with the Art 8 guarantee must first be in accordance with the law. As indicated in Chapter 2, when interpreting the 'prescribed by law' requirement in Art 8(2), Strasbourg has asked first whether the interference has some basis in domestic law, and secondly whether it is of the right 'quality'.[22] In the state surveillance cases of *Huvig v France*[23] and *Kruslin v France*[24] the Court said that the requirement of quality means that the law 'should be accessible to the person concerned, who must moreover be able to foresee its consequences for him, and compatible with the rule of law'. The application in *Harman and Hewitt v UK*[25] was declared admissible since the activities of MI5 in placing the applicants under surveillance were not in accordance with the law. No sufficient basis in law existed at the time, and the successful application led to the passing of the Security Services Act 1989.

Any residual activities undertaken by the security and intelligence services which at present are not covered by the provisions of the Security Services Act 1989, Intelligence Services Act 1994 and Regulation of Investigatory Powers Act 2000 may not be in accordance with the law, assuming that the primary right under Art 8(1) is engaged.

---

15 See Chapter 12, pp 872–73.
16 See below, p 822.
17 (1992) 14 EHRR 657.
18 (1999) 28 EHRR 313.
19 On the grounds of being necessary in a democratic society to further the economic wellbeing of the state.
20 (1981) 3 EHRR 104.
21 (1993) 18 EHRR CD 72. See also *Harman v UK* Appl No 20317/92 (1993) unreported.
22 See also *Sunday Times v UK* A 30, para 49 (1979) and *Hashman v UK* (1999) 30 EHRR 241, discussed in Chapter 7, p 420.
23 (1990) 12 EHRR 528, para 26.
24 (1990) 12 EHRR 547, para 27.
25 (1992) 14 EHRR 657.

Assuming that an interference is 'in accordance with the law', under the 1989, 1994 or 2000 statutes, it must also, under Art 8(2), have a legitimate aim, be necessary in a democratic society and be applied in a non-discriminatory fashion (Art 14).[26] In cases of invasion of privacy by the state, Strasbourg's main concerns have been with the requirements of 'in accordance with the law' and 'necessary in a democratic society'. In this context, the 'legitimate aim' requirement has always been found to be satisfied. This is unsurprising since the grounds available for interference under Art 8(2) are so broad. They are: the interests of national security, public safety or the economic well-being of the country, the prevention of disorder or crime, the protection of health or morals, the protection of the rights or freedom of others. The provision against non-discrimination under Art 14 has not been so far a significant issue in the state-invasion of privacy jurisprudence. But possibly Art 14 arguments could be raised domestically in conjunction with Art 8 ones on the basis that certain racial or religious groups were being singled out as the target for surveillance in relation to suspected terrorist activity. The question would then be one of proportionality.[27] The Court has interpreted 'necessary in a democratic society' as meaning: 'an interference corresponds to a pressing social need and, in particular, that it is proportionate to the legitimate aim pursued'.[28] As explained in Chapter 2, the doctrine of proportionality is strongly linked to the principle of the margin of appreciation. The width of the margin conceded appears to depend partly on the aim of the interference in question and partly on its necessity. In relation to the aim of national security, the Court has allowed a very wide margin to the state.

The case of *Kennedy v UK*,[29] considered in detail below, concerned an allegation of telephone tapping by the British security services and involved detailed consideration of the compatibility of powers granted to the security services under the Regulation of Investigatory Powers Act 2000 (RIPA) with Art 8. The Court found that the safeguards created by RIPA were sufficient to meet the requirements of Art 8. The reasons for these finding, and possible remaining areas of incompatibility, are discussed below.

Using the HRA in practice

Clearly, there have always been, theoretically, methods of seeking to curb surveillance powers when they impinge on individual citizens. Prosecution of agents of the intelligence and security services is, however, highly unlikely, since no means of referring an investigation to the police is provided in the statutes; further, any risk of revealing secrets would probably be avoided simply by taking a decision not to prosecute. It would also be difficult to acquire evidence due to the provisions against providing evidence to complainants. Actions for trespass to property or other tortious liability could be brought against agents, although the secrecy of operations makes this very unlikely. Any such action brought in the post-HRA era has to accord with the Convention. The HRA extended the theoretical protection available for the citizen since, under ss 6, 7 and 8, it creates civil liability where activities are carried out that were not previously unlawful, but which breach the Convention guarantees. However, consideration

---

26 See Chapter 2.
27 See Chapter 2, p 93 *et seq*.
28 *Olsson v Sweden* A 130 (1988), para 67.
29 (2011) 52 EHRR 4.

of the compatibility of interception of communications with Art 8 in court proceedings is almost entirely precluded by s 17 of the RIPA (Part I) which renders material deriving from intercepts inadmissible in court proceedings.[30] This is not the case as regards surveillance operations (such as observation or placing bugging devices) which is governed by Part II RIPA and the Police Act 1997.

Section 18(1) RIPA provides that s 17(1) does not apply in proceedings before the tribunal, for an offence under the RIPA, s 1 of the 1985 Act, s 4(3)(a) of the Official Secrets Act, and a number of other provisions relating to the secrecy of interceptions. Sections 17 and 18 are most relevant to criminal proceedings, but other proceedings are also affected.

Significantly, there is no equivalent in the Police Act or Part II of the RIPA to s 17 in Part I of the RIPA. Clearly, any such provision would be counterproductive in prosecution terms. But that does mean, depending on the extent of disclosure to the defence, that a defendant may become aware at some point during criminal proceedings that a surveillance operation has occurred, and therefore will be able to take any avenues of redress that may be open, including raising Convention arguments in the trial itself.[31] The general issue of exclusion of evidence and of disclosure is discussed further in Chapter 13.[32] Although arguments may be raised in court that Art 8 has been breached in conducting surveillance, it is not the case that such evidence must be excluded on that basis.[33] Therefore use of this avenue as a means of encouraging the police to respect the Art 8 guarantees has been at present almost entirely closed off.

The primary method for raising Art 8 in domestic proceedings is the single tribunal. The tribunal has a duty under s 6 HRA to comply with the Convention in adjudicating on complaints, and the Commissioner has such a duty in overseeing not only warrants, but also the discharge of the duties of the Home Secretary and the agencies under the RIPA (see below). The route to judicial review of the decisions of the single tribunal is barred by the ouster clause contained in s 67(8) of the RIPA;[34] s 65(2), which provides that the jurisdiction of the tribunal is to be 'the only appropriate tribunal' for the purposes of s 7(1)(a) of the HRA, also stands in the way of review.

3 Surveillance powers

Introduction

Surveillance powers clearly present a profound threat to the core value of privacy identified in the introduction to Part III, informational autonomy. As the Supreme Court of Canada has said: 'one can scarcely imagine a state activity more dangerous to individual

---

30 As regards interception of communications, action in the ordinary courts at the citizen's instigation is almost entirely ruled out.

31 See e.g., *R v Khan* [1996] 3 All ER 289; *AG's Reference (No 3 of 1999)* [2001] 2 WLR 56; *R v Sang* [1980] AC 402; [1979] 2 All ER 1222, HL; *R v Allsopp* [2005] EWCA Crim 703.

32 Page 963 *et seq.*

33 *R v SL* [2001] EWCA Crim 1829; *R v Khan* [1996] 3 All ER 289.

34 Replacing s 7(8) of the 1985 Act and replacing s 91(10) of the 1997 Act in so far as complaints are concerned, and creating an ouster clause in relation to complaints regarding surveillance by a range of other public authorities.

privacy than electronic surveillance'.[35] The approach, which succeeds in preserving respect for democracy and for the value of individual privacy, as a hallmark of democracy, while affording respect to state interests, is one that is increasingly reflected in the jurisprudence of the European Court of Human Rights, even taking into account the wide margin of appreciation conceded in this particular area.[36]

As regards interception of communications, telephonic interception was possible for much of the twentieth century, but its incidence and the interception facilities have recently increased.[37] In other words, its value in terms of combating crime and terrorism has long been recognised. But legal recognition of the harm interception causes, in terms of creating invasions of privacy, has lagged behind. Prior to 1985, there was no requirement to follow a particular legal procedure when authorising the tapping of telephones or the interception of mail. The tapping of telephones was neither a civil wrong[38] nor a criminal offence.

The Interception of Communications Act 1985 was introduced as a direct result of the ruling in the European Court of Human Rights in *Malone v UK*[39] that the existing British warrant procedure violated the Art 8 guarantee of privacy. The Court held that UK domestic law did not regulate the circumstances in which telephone tapping could be carried out sufficiently clearly or provide any remedy against abuse of the power. This meant that it did not meet the requirement of being 'in accordance with the law' under Art 8(2). The decision therefore required the UK government to introduce legislation to regulate the circumstances in which the power to tap could be used.

Thus, the driving force behind the response of the UK Government in the Interception of Communications Act 1985 was the need to provide a statutory basis for interception. Nevertheless, it was an incomplete reform. Despite its misleading name, the 1985 Act only covered certain limited means of intercepting communications. It did not cover interception by means of listening devices or all forms of telephone tapping. It covered the interception of only one means of telephonic communication – communication via the public telecommunications system. This covered telephone, fax, telex and any other data transmission on the system, such as e-mail.[40] Given the immense increase in the use of mobile phones,[41] pagers, cordless phones, the potential for e-mail transmission outside the telecommunications system, and the growth of internal telephone systems over recent years, the Act became increasingly marginalised. Marginalisation was likely to increase since e-mails were being sent more frequently via mobile phones, using satellites.[42] It therefore became apparent that the statutory basis for interception provided by the 1985 Act was inadequate and would probably be shown to be so in reliance on the HRA.[43] The then Labour government responded by introducing a far more comprehensive basis under the Regulation of Investigatory Powers Act 2000, Part I.

---

35 *R v Duarte* (1990) 65 DLR (4th) 240.
36 See, e.g., the pronouncements of the Court in *Klass v FRG* (1978) 2 EHRR 214.
37 See e.g., 'Report of the Interception of Communications Commissioner' HC 1113, SG /2015/28, para 7.6.
38 *Malone v MPC (No 2)* [1979] Ch 344.
39 (1984) 7 EHRR 14; for comment, see Lloyd, I 'The Interception of Communications Act 1985' (1986) 49 MLR 86.
40 Prior to the inception of the RIPA 2000, the government maintained that some use of email was covered by the 1985 Act where public telephone lines were used.
41 Mobile-to-mobile communication fell outside the 1985 Act.
42 Possibly without use of a server.
43 See the Consultation Paper 'Interception of Communications in the UK' (1999) Cm 4368.

The use of bugging devices as a form of surveillance by the police was placed on a statutory basis in the Police Act 1997. Following the lead of the Interception of Communications Act 1985, it gives an impression of covering the use of surveillance devices by the police, while in fact leaving many areas of their use outside its statutory framework. The incorporation of Art 8 into domestic law under the HRA was the driving force for reform. The unsatisfactory nature of the arrangements was pointed out in 1998 by *Justice* in a report[44] that argued for integration of surveillance techniques with interception, in one comprehensive statute. The Regulation of Investigatory Powers Act provides that comprehensive basis in Part II.

Overlapping with the 1997 Act, most of which it does not repeal, Part II of the RIPA covers a wide range of surveillance techniques and public institutions, including the police. It places the use of surveillance by the security and intelligence services on a clearer statutory basis, overlapping with the Intelligence Services Act 1994. By providing a comprehensive statutory basis that coincided (roughly) with the coming fully into force of the HRA, Part II sought to avoid domestic legal challenges to state surveillance based on the failures of the UK's surveillance to respect the Art 8 rights previously identified by Strasbourg.[45] The forms of surveillance covered by Part II of the RIPA also engage Art 8,[46] and the same arguments raised in interception of communications cases could have been raised in the domestic courts under the HRA,[47] particularly in respect of forms of so-called 'directed' surveillance (see below) if Part II of the RIPA had not been introduced.

But it is questionable whether RIPA is any more adequate at the level of principle than the previous scheme. It is clearly not as vulnerable to challenges under the Convention at Strasbourg or under the HRA. Nevertheless, its compatibility with the Convention remains in doubt, as discussed below. The *Justice* Report (1998) influenced its introduction, but while the first of their key recommendations – that there should be an integrated, comprehensive statutory basis for surveillance – has largely been met in relation to intercepted material, it is questionable whether that is true of the second – using a 'coherent set of principles as required by Art 8' to underpin the scheme.[48] The latter conclusion is supported by the Independent Reviewer of Terrorism Legislation, David Anderson, who has recently criticised the operation of RIPA and proposed a number of further safeguards to achieve compliance with Art 8.[49]

Interception of communications

The Regulation of Investigatory Powers Act 2000, Part I

The intention of the Labour government was to bring all forms of interception within the Regulation of Investigatory Powers Act 2000 (RIPA), Part I so that the Interception

---

44 *Under Surveillance: Covert Policing and Human Rights Standards*, 1998.
45 *Malone v UK* (1984) 7 EHRR 14; *Halford v UK* [1997] IRLR 471; *Khan v UK* (2000) 8 BHRC 310.
46 See below p 822.
47 Under s 7(1)(a) or (b).
48 *Under Surveillance: Covert Policing and Human Rights Standards*, 1998, Recommendation 1, p 107.
49 Anderson, D 'A question of trust: report of the investigatory powers review'. June 2015; see at https://terrorismlegislationreviewer.independent.gov.uk.

of Communications Act 1985 would be superseded and could be repealed.[50] Under s 2(1) of the RIPA, the term 'public telecommunications system' used in s 2(1) of the 1985 Act, covers any system 'which exists (whether wholly or partly in the UK or elsewhere) for the purpose of facilitating the transmission of communications by any means involving the use of electrical or electro-magnetic energy'. This includes all such systems which provide or offer a telecommunications service to the public or part of it. This definition covers all the forms of communication, including e-mail, mentioned above, provided by any private company.[51] Section 2(1) of the RIPA also covers private telecommunications systems – most obviously those confined to a particular company or body – although its coverage of private systems is limited to those which are attached to the public system directly or indirectly.[52] Its wording appears to be wide enough to cover most forms of telecommunication currently available, apart from entirely self-standing private systems,[53] although its inception obviously predates new forms of public electronic communications, such as social media. Ironically, the point was made in parliamentary debate that 'the Bill does not recognise the changing technologies'.[54]

Issuance of warrants

Under s 5(3) RIPA, a warrant may be issued if necessary '(a) in the interests of national security'; '(b) for the purpose of preventing or detecting serious crime';[55] or '(c) for the purpose of safeguarding the economic well-being of the UK'. In relation to the third ground, the information must relate, under s 5(5), to 'the acts or intentions of persons outside the British Isles'. These grounds are significantly wider than those under the old Home Office guidelines previously relied upon in order to authorise warrants. The last ground falls under sub-para (d): 'in circumstances appearing to the Secretary of state to be equivalent to those in which he would issue a warrant by virtue of paragraph (b), for the purpose of giving effect to the provisions of any international mutual assistance agreement'. Its purpose is to require satellite operators based in the UK to provide technical assistance to another member state. The discussion below reveals that the safeguards relating to warrants issued on this ground are significantly weaker than those relating to the other three. This is an instance in which the EU's 'Third Pillar' policies relating to law and order and national security have allowed decisions to be taken on matters that may infringe human rights, possibly to the extent of breaching the ECHR. Such decisions are taken within a framework where the EU's democratic deficit is most prominent.[56]

Section 5(2) of RIPA, however, contains a stronger proportionality requirement than that which was contained in s 2(3) of the Interception of Communications Act 1985,

---

50 Part I repealed key sections of the 1985 Act: ss 1–10, s 11(2)–(5), Sched 1.
51 These would include, e.g., BT, Orange, Vodafone. It would also cover other providers of e-mail systems such as Yahoo or Google.
52 Its coverage of private systems is a direct response to *Halford v UK* [1997] IRLR 471.
53 Such as intranet systems not connected to any public system.
54 HC Deb col 806, 6 March 2000.
55 Defined in s 81(3).
56 Snell, J, '"European constitutional settlement", an ever closer union, and the Treaty of Lisbon: democracy or relevance?' (2008) 33(5) EL Rev 619. See also *Enhancing Parliamentary Scrutiny of the Third Pillar*, Select Committee of the European Communities, HL Session 1997–98, 31 July 1997.

which it replaced. The Secretary of State 'shall not' issue an interception warrant unless s/he believes that the conduct it authorises 'is proportionate to what is sought to be achieved'. This includes asking, under s 5(4), whether the information that it is thought necessary to obtain under the warrant could reasonably be obtained by other means. This question also had to be asked under s 2(3). But s 5(2) implies that further matters should be considered. For example, where the information *cannot* reasonably be obtained by other means, the proportionality of the particular interception warrant with its objective could still be considered. This might involve considering its contents and duration, which must be disclosed pursuant to s 8. Clearly, s 5(2) was introduced in an effort to meet the proportionality requirement under Art 8(2), discussed further below. Under s 7(1) of RIPA, the warrants must be personally signed by the Secretary of State or, under s 7(2) in urgent cases or cases under the fourth ground, by 'a senior official' with express authorisation from the Secretary of State. A 'senior official' is defined in s 81(1) as 'a member of the Senior Civil Service' and under s 81(7) the Secretary of State 'may by order make . . . amendments [to] the definition of "senior official"'.

This procedure is based on the model previously provided by the Interception of Communications Act 1985 in that it allows for administrative oversight, but maintains executive authorisation of interception; it may therefore be contrasted with the scheme in the US, where prior judicial authorisation is required,[57] and with that in Denmark where authorisation is by an investigating magistrate.[58] A commissioner is appointed under s 57(8) of RIPA. The commissioner has a role in overseeing the issuance of warrants, but this is a general review role, which occurs after the event. The possibility of replacing an executive with a judicial mechanism was entirely rejected by the then Labour government. In debate on the bill, it received support only from the Liberal Democrats.[59] Judicial involvement only at the complaint stage (discussed below) is of limited significance as a safeguard since many persons will have no means of knowing that tapping is occurring. Nevertheless, prior judicial involvement in authorising warrants cannot be said at present to be a requirement of Art 8.[60]

Under s 4(5) and (6) of the 1985 Act, the warrants were issued for an initial period of two months and could be renewed for one month in the case of the police and for six months in the case of the security and intelligence services. Under s 9(6) of the 2000 Act, warrants are issued for an initial period of three months if by the secretary of state and can be renewed for six months if he states his belief that the grounds under s 5(3)(a) or (c) apply. If the other grounds apply, the renewal period is three months. If signed by a senior official, they can be issued initially for five working days but renewed for three months. In the case of all warrants, particularly those issued in respect of the prevention or detection of serious crime, to the police, these are significant increases. The period in respect of the serious crime ground may be compared with that in Denmark, which is four weeks, renewable.[61]

As was the case under the 1985 Act, there is no overall limit on renewals and so some warrants are very long standing. The number of interception warrants issued is increasing. The commissioners' reports only cover the warrants authorised by the Home Office

57 *Berger v NY* (1967) 388 US 41.
58 Code of Criminal Procedure, Art 126m.
59 HC Deb col 8076, March 2000.
60 *Kennedy v UK* (2011) 52 EHRR 4.
61 Code of Criminal Procedure, Art 126m.

and Scottish Office. These figures show that at the end of 1989, 315 warrants were in force and 522 were issued during the year.[62] By 2003, 2,525 warrants were issued by the Home Office.[63] In 2014, 2,795 warrants were issued.[64]

Section 8(1) of RIPA suggests that the warrants should be precise; they must specify a person or an address. However, a 'person' can equal 'any organisation and any association or combination of persons'.[65] Once a warrant is obtained, all communications to or from the property or 'person' specified must be intercepted, if that is what is required in order to give effect to the warrant.[66] Failure to comply with the warrant is an offence under s 11(7) carrying a maximum sentence of two years. Under s 11(4), telephone tapping and mail interceptions are conducted by Post Office or 'public telecommunications employees' or by persons controlling or partly controlling private systems wholly or partly in the UK.[67]

Under s 6(2), the request for the warrant may be made by a number of persons from a non-exhaustive list. They include: the Director General of the Security Service, the Chief of MI6, the Director of GCHQ, the Director General of the National Criminal Intelligence Service, the Commissioner of Police of the Metropolis; the Chief Constable of the RUC, chief constables in Scotland,[68] the Commissioners of Customs and Excise; the Chief of Defence; the relevant person for the purposes of any international mutual assistance agreement. The bill originally provided: 'or any such other person as the Secretary of State may by order designate'. The government was eventually persuaded to omit the last provision. A number of other such powers are, however, scattered throughout the Act, meaning that this statute, comprehensive as it is, leaves open a great deal of leeway for significant and more covert extension. On second reading of the bill in the Commons this list was criticised on two grounds. The Conservative opposition considered that the list was not extensive enough and that, in particular, the Benefits Agency of the DSS[69] and HMRC[70] should be added to it. The Liberal Democrats, supported by Tom King, chair of the Intelligence and Security Committee, argued that primary legislation, not a statutory instrument, should be used in order to add bodies to the list.[71]

Lawful interception without a warrant

Sections 3 and 4 of RIPA allow for lawful interception without a warrant. Section 3(2) covers instances where it is reasonably believed that both parties to the communication

---

62 Report of the Commissioner for 1989, Cm 1063, p 2. Similar figures are available for other years; see reports for 1986, Cm 108 and for 1987, Cm 351.
63 'Report of the Interception of Communications Commissioner', HC 883, SE/2004/133.
64 'Report of the Information Commissioner', March 2015, HC 1113, SG/2015/28.
65 RIPA 2000, s 78(1) which, with the addition of an 'association', reproduces s 10(1) of the 1985 Act.
66 Section 11(4).
67 Bearing in mind the range of companies which are affected and the difficulty of complying, especially in relation to the internet, a provision regarding practicality was necessary. Section 11(5) recognises that there may be circumstances under which it is not reasonably practicable to comply with the duty to implement the warrant. The prosecution must prove that it was practicable.
68 'Of any police force maintained under or by virtue of section 1 of the Police (Scotland) Act 1967.'
69 HC Deb cols 778 and 831, 6 March 2000.
70 HC Deb col 821, 6 March 2000.
71 HC Deb cols 768 and 831, 6 March 2000.

have consented to the interception.[72] In such circumstances, the interception must also be authorised within Part II, s 26. This provision effects a compromise in relation to so called 'participant monitoring' (where one party is aware of the interception). It has been pointed out by the Canadian constitutional court[73] that the consent of one party does not affect the infringement of privacy suffered by the other. But s 3(2) does not demand that 'participant monitoring' should be subject to the controls necessary for other interceptions; it is subject only to the lesser controls for 'directed' surveillance, discussed below. Section 4 covers persons whose communications are intercepted who are believed to be outside the UK, instances where the Secretary of State has made regulations covering the interception for business[74] purposes (s 4(2)), and instances in psychiatric hospitals or prisons (within the relevant applicable statutes).

Use and retention of the intercepted material

Section 15 provides safeguards regarding the retention and use of the intercepted material. They are intended to limit the persons who can see the material and to ensure that it is destroyed once it is no longer necessary to retain it for the authorised purposes. However, the Act does not state how these objectives are to be achieved; it is left to the Secretary of State to put arrangements into place to secure them. Further, s 15 does not apply to material obtained without warrant, under ss 3 or 4. Since personal criminal intelligence information obtained from interceptions and then stored and processed electronically is not subject to the stronger controls under the data protection regime of the Data Protection Act 1998,[75] it is clear that the controls created under s 15 are potentially crucial in protecting this aspect of privacy.

Further guidance on the safeguards in s 15 is provided by the current code of practice *Interception of Communications* (2016). Dissemination of surveillance material is limited to the minimum that is necessary for the authorised purpose in s 15(4) on a need to know basis and only to those within the agency who have the required level of security clearance (para 7.3). Copying of the information, including summarised versions of it, is limited to that necessary for the authorised purpose (para 7.6) as is storage (para 7.7). The destruction of such information is of particular significance; the Code reads (para 7.8):

> Intercepted material, and all copies, extracts and summaries which can be identified as the product of an interception, must be securely destroyed as soon as it is no longer needed for any of the authorised purposes. If such material is retained, it should be reviewed at appropriate intervals to confirm that the justification for its retention is still valid under section 15(3) of the Act.

The retention of data from bulk surveillance was questioned in the ISC's 2014 special report, in which concerns were raised about 'the length of time that GCHQ store

---

72   This provision is clearly more protective of privacy than its counterpart under the 1985 Act, s 1(2), which relied on the consent of one party only.
73   *R v Duarte* [1990] 53 CCC (3d) 1.
74   'Business' includes government departments.
75   The DPA 1998 contains various exceptions applicable to such data e.g., ss 28,29.

information obtained from bulk interception . . . and the security of GCHQ's data stores'.[76] The committee found as regards the second concern that various efforts had been made to reduce such 'information risk' – in particular by enhanced tracking of those accessing the information network. As regards the first concern the committee found that the RIPA-based legal framework under s 15 sufficiently limited access to bulk surveillance data.[77] The tribunal went on to confirm the Commission's stance;[78] however, as discussed below, it also subsequently found that GCHQ's policies, particularly as regards retention and destruction of data, had not been followed in the case of two complainants.[79]

Unauthorised interceptions

Section 1 of the Interception of Communications Act 1985 dealt with unauthorised interceptions and made it a criminal offence to intercept a postal communication or telecommunication intentionally without authorisation. It did not cover taps outside the public telecommunications system. So, for example, no criminal or even civil wrong was committed by the chief constable of Merseyside when a tap on the internal police phone system was used against Alison Halford in order to seek to discredit her and undermine her sex discrimination claim against the police service.[80] The RIPA, which under s 1 reproduced the old s 1 offence with extensions, also covers interception of private systems, unless they are entirely freestanding. However, it is subject to an exception under s 1(6) which might have been applicable in the *Halford* case.[81] Section 1(6) provides that conduct is excluded from criminal liability if the interceptor 'is a person with a right to control the operation or the use of the system; or he has the express or implied consent of the [person intercepted]'. Section 1(3) creates civil liability in relation to unauthorised interception of a private, not a public system.

Covert surveillance and property interference

The Police Act 1997, Part III

The House of Lords in *Khan*,[82] confronted with evidence obtained by police bugging involving trespass, recommended legislation, taking into account the fact that the regime governing the use of bugging devices was not on a statutory basis and therefore might not comply with the 'in accordance with the law' requirement under Art 8.[83]

---

76 Intelligence and Security Committee 'Privacy and Security: A Modern and Transparent Legal Framework,' HC 1075, 12 March 2015, para 119.
77 *Ibid*, paras 123–126.
78 *Liberty & Others v the Security Service, SIS, GCHQ* (2015) IPT/13/77/H.
79 *Liberty & Others v the Security Service, SIS, GCHQ* [2015] UKIPTrib 13_77-H_2.
80 See *Halford v UK* (1997) 24 EHRR 523.
81 *Ibid*.
82 [1996] 3 WLR 162.
83 See the comments of Lord Nolan [1996] 3 WLR 162, p 175 and Lord Slynn, p 166. See also the Home Affairs Select Committee 3rd Report for 1994–5, Organised Crime HC 18–1, which recommended a statutory basis. It may be noted that *Khan v UK* (1999) 27 EHRR CD 58 was declared admissible at Strasbourg, and the application was successful (2000) 31 EHRR 1016 since at the time there was no sufficient basis in law for the interference with Art 8.

Their recommendation was one of the factors behind the passing of the Police Act 1997, which therefore represents another instance in which powers posing a grave threat to privacy and other individual rights were governed only by administrative guidelines until it became apparent that such a course could not be justified under the ECHR.

The authorisation procedure

The Police Act, Part III placed police use of bugging and other surveillance devices on a statutory basis, with certain changes. It only covers the installation of devices which could have attracted liability under trespass, criminal damage or unlawful interference with wireless telegraphy, under the Wireless Telegraphy Acts 1949 and 1967. Therefore, it does not cover 'stand off' devices. Also, it does not cover devices installed with the consent of the person able to give permission in respect of the premises in question.[84] The use of surveillance devices in a range of circumstances therefore falls outside it, as do a range of techniques, in particular the use of informants.[85] Such matters continued to be governed by the guidelines until Part II of the RIPA (see below) came into force.

Part III of the Police Act is largely modelled on the Interception of Communications Act 1985 and therefore contains certain similar objectionable features. The basis for allowing the use of bugging is very broad. An authorisation may be issued if the action is expected to be of substantial value in the prevention and detection of serious crime and that the taking of the action is proportionate to what the action seeks to achieve (s 93(2)). Serious crime is defined under s 93(4) to include crimes of violence, those involving substantial financial gain, and those involving a large number of people in pursuit of a common purpose.[86] The current code of practice, however, adopted under s 71 of RIPA, emphasises that the bugging powers must only be used in cases of serious crime such as drug trafficking.[87]

Under s 93(5), an authorisation to interfere with property may be issued by the chief officer of police or, if that is not practicable, by an officer of the rank of assistant chief constable of the force in question (s 94), if s 93(2) applies. The authorisation will be given in writing, except in cases of emergency, when it may be given orally by the chief officer in person (s 95(1)). A written authorisation will last for three months, an oral one for 72 hours. Both forms may be renewed in writing for a further three months. The commissioners appointed under s 91(1) must be notified of authorisations as soon as they are made (s 96), but this does not prevent the police acting on the authorisation. There is no administrative check under the 1997 Act, and no minister is involved in the bugging authorisations. Apart from authorisations falling within s 97, no other independent prior check is available, although the Chief Surveillance Commissioner has an oversight role. However, subsequent independent checks are clearly not as effective as prior ones. Again, these arrangements may be compared with those in Denmark,

---

84 Under the guidelines and the code of practice then in force, *Intrusive Surveillance*. One example would be the placing of listening devices in a police station: see *Bailey and Smith* [1993] Crim LR 861; *Musqud Ali* [1966] QB 668.

85 See *H* [1987] Crim LR 47 and *Jelen and Katz* [1990] 90 Cr App R 456. The use of a wired informant may require permission under the HO Circular; Part II of the RIPA – provisions covering covert human sources – now applies.

86 Or the crime is one for which a person of 21 or over with no previous convictions could reasonably be expected to receive a prison sentence of three or more years.

87 *Covert Surveillance and Property Interference* 2014, para 7.10.

where authorisation of the use of listening devices, wherever placed, and including 'participant monitoring', must be by an investigating magistrate.[88] Furthermore, prior approval of authorisation is not required in all instances. Under s 97(2), such approval by a commissioner is required where the specified property is believed to be a dwelling, hotel bedroom or office premises. It is also needed where the authorising officer believes that information of a more sensitive nature may be acquired – matters subject to legal privilege; confidential personal information; confidential journalistic material.

The code of practice issued under s 71 RIPA, *Covert Surveillance and property interference* (2014) provides that where the action authorised is likely to result in 'any person acquiring knowledge of matters subject to legal privilege, confidential personal information or confidential journalistic material', prior authorisation is required. Under s 98, 'matters subject to legal privilege' include communications between a professional legal advisor and his or her client connected with the giving of legal advice or relating to legal proceedings. Once approval for an authorisation has been given, allowing, for example, for a solicitor's office to be bugged, all conversations between solicitors and clients would be recorded. Under s 99, 'confidential personal information' includes information relating to a person's physical or mental health or to spiritual counselling.

A key weakness in the authorisation procedure is that under s 97(3), even where s 97 applies, no approval is needed if the authorising officer 'believes that the case is one of urgency'. No requirement that the belief should be based on reasonable grounds is included. Paragraphs 6.6–6.8 of the current RIPA Code state that the urgency provision should not be used routinely and that the reason for the urgency must be explained to the Commissioner.

The Regulation of Investigatory Powers Act, Part II[89]

Part II of RIPA 2000 covers surveillance activities of immense potential to infringe privacy that previously had no – or only a narrow – basis in law. For the first time, a comprehensive statutory basis was created for the expanding use of covert surveillance. The growth in proactive intelligence-led policing (targeting suspects using covert surveillance rather than investigating a crime after it has happened), and the proliferation of various forms of surveillance devices, provided part of the impetus for reform.[90] Unlike Part III of the Police Act 1997 or s 5 of the Intelligence Services Act 1994 with which it overlaps,[91] Part II of RIPA covers a very wide range of

---

88 Art 126(1) and Code of Criminal Procedure.

89 It may be noted that under s 46, there are restrictions on Part II authorisations extending to Scotland.

90 The use of covert surveillance together with other targeting methods, including the use of informers, has expanded rapidly and is seen as immensely useful by the police: see, e.g., Mckay, S, *Covert Policing: Law and Practice*, 2015, OUP.

91 Under the Police Act 1997, Part III, s 92: 'No entry on or interference with property or with wireless telegraphy shall be unlawful if it is authorised by an authorisation having effect under this Part.' Thus, forms of directed surveillance involving an actual interference with property – on non-residential premises – were covered by the Police Act 1997, Part III. Under the 1994 Act, s 5, the Home Secretary, on an application from a member of the Intelligence Service, can issue a warrant authorising the 'taking of any such action as is specified in the warrant in respect of any property so specified or in respect of wireless telegraphy so specified'.

public authorities. It also covers a much wider range of circumstances. Prior to the introduction of Part II, invasions of privacy by means of covert surveillance falling outside the narrow scope of the 1997 or 1994 provisions were occurring, not on the basis of a legal power, but on the basis that the state is in the same position as the individual citizen in being free to do that which the law does not forbid. Since there was no legal right to privacy – in a broad, general sense – no legal power to invade it was needed.[92]

The pre-existing statutory provisions were mainly (although not exclusively) aimed at the form of surveillance termed 'intrusive' by Part II. Most significantly, a warrant or authorisation was required where there was a physical invasion of property by the police or security and intelligence services. So a wide area of surveillance fell outside those statutes, and the need to cover this particular form of surveillance – in anticipation of the effects of the HRA – provided the immediate impetus for the introduction of Part II. Under the HRA it is clearly necessary for surveillance to be placed on a statutory basis even where previously it would not have attracted any form of liability, if it would amount to an invasion of privacy under Art 8 of the European Convention on Human Rights, since para 2 provides that an interference with individual privacy must be 'in accordance with the law'. The key aim of Part II is therefore to meet a central requirement under the Convention – that of legality. The RIPA Code of Practice *Covert surveillance and Property Interference*,[93] makes this clear:

> Part II of the 2000 Act provides a statutory framework under which covert surveillance activity can be authorised and conducted compatibly with Art 8. Where covert surveillance would be likely to result in the obtaining of any *private information* about a person, no interference with Art 8 rights occurs and an *authorisation* under the 2000 Act is therefore not appropriate.[94]

It is clear that Part II has gone some way towards achieving this aim in the sense that it has provided a much more comprehensive statutory underpinning for covert surveillance than the pre-existing one. A basis in national law has been created which purports to meet the requirements of legality under the Convention. The Code provides:

> The 2000 Act, 1997 Act and 1994 Act stipulate that the person granting an *authorisation* or *warrant* for directed surveillance, or interference with property, must believe that the activities to be authorised are necessary on one or more statutory ground. If the activities are deemed necessary on one or more of the statutory grounds, the person granting the *authorisation* or *warrant* must also believe that they are proportionate to what is sought to be achieved by carrying them out. This involves balancing the seriousness of the intrusion into the privacy of the subject of the operation (or any other person who may be affected) against the need for the activity in investigative and operational terms.[95]

---

92 See above, pp 689–90; clearly, certain aspects of privacy received protection in the pre-HRA era, especially under the doctrine of trespass.
93 2014, The Home Office.
94 Para 1.14.
95 Paras 3.3–3.4.

Below, it will be considered whether it has succeeded in meeting those requirements and whether the further Convention requirements of necessity and proportionality have also been met. In order to do so, the provisions governing so called 'intrusive' and 'directed' surveillance will be examined with a view to contending that when the two regimes are contrasted, certain inadequacies of the latter, in Convention terms, are revealed.

Intrusive surveillance

Under s 26(3) of the RIPA, 'intrusive' surveillance occurs when a surveillance device is used or an individual undertaking surveillance is actually present on residential premises, or in a private vehicle, or it is carried out by such a device in relation to such premises or vehicle without being present on the premises or vehicle. Following *Re C*,[96] the Regulation of Investigatory Powers (Extension of Authorisation Provisions: Legal Consultations) Order 2010 was passed, which has the effect of rendering as 'intrusive surveillance' any surveillance operation concerning communications that are the subject of legal privilege.

'Residential' is defined in s 48(1) of the RIPA as premises used as living accommodation, while 'premises' includes movable structures and land. The definition expressly excludes common areas of residential premises and clearly does not cover office premises (s 48(7)(b)). Thus, covert surveillance of office premises falls within the term 'directed', rather than intrusive, surveillance. Section 26(3), read with s 48(7), creates confusion, since it covers all forms of covert surveillance taking place in relation to residential premises. Some forms of such surveillance can be treated as directed surveillance, as indicated below, and it is in relation to residential premises that an area of uncertainty is created as to the category into which surveillance falls.

Under s 32(3) of the RIPA authorisation of intrusive surveillance is on the grounds of 'the interests of national security, for the purpose of preventing or detecting serious crime or of preventing disorder, in the interests of the economic well-being of the UK'. 'Serious crime' is defined in s 81(3)[97] in substantially the same terms as in s 93(4) of the Police Act 1997. Proportionality requirements are introduced under s 32(2): the authorising person must be satisfied that the action to be taken is proportionate to what is hoped to be achieved by carrying it out. Authorisations for such surveillance are granted by the Home Secretary under s 41 or, for police or customs officers, by senior authorising officers, who are the highest-ranking police officers in Britain (see s 32(6)). There is also provision for the grant of authorisations in a case of urgency by persons of almost equally high rank, other than the senior authorising officer.[98]

96 In *Re C* [2009] UKHL 15 it was found that the refusal of the police to issue an assurance that a prisoner's interviews and consultations with his lawyer would not be bugged amounted to a disproportionate interference with his Art 8 rights.

97 Section 81(2) provides that such crime satisfies the tests of sub-s (3)(a) or (b). Under s 81(3), those tests are (a) that the offence is one for which a person of twenty one (eighteen in relation to England and Wales) with no previous convictions could reasonably expect a sentence of three years' imprisonment or more, or (b) that the conduct involves the use of violence, results in substantial financial gain, or is conduct by a large number of persons in pursuit of a common purpose.

98 Under s 34(4), such persons are of a rank almost as high as such officers. In the case of police forces, this means a person holding the rank of assistant chief constable or, in the case of the Metropolitan or City of London forces, of commander.

The provisions for urgent and non-urgent authorisations under ss 33, 34, 35 and 36 mirror those under the Police Act, Part III in that, under s 35, notice must be given to a 'surveillance commissioner' and, under s 36, the authorisation will not take effect until it has been approved, except where it is urgent and the grounds for urgency are set out in the notice, in which case the authorisation will take effect from the time of its grant. Under s 38, senior authorising officers can appeal to the Chief Surveillance Commissioner against decisions of ordinary surveillance commissioners. The commissioners have responsibility for the destruction of material obtained by surveillance, under s 37, but there is no requirement that material no longer needed for proceedings and no longer subject to an authorisation *must* be destroyed.

Under s 43, authorisations can be granted or renewed urgently orally by senior authorising officers or in writing by persons authorised to act on their behalf in urgent cases. If, under s 43(3)(a), an authorisation is granted or renewed by a person entitled to act only in urgent cases, or was renewed by such a person or orally, it ceases to take effect after 72 hours. Section 42 provides special rules for the intelligence services which overlap with those of s 5 of the Intelligence Services Act 1994. Under s 42, the security and intelligence services can undertake intrusive surveillance on grant of a warrant. The grounds are those under s 32(3). As far as intrusive surveillance is concerned, the function of the services in support of the prevention or detection of serious crime is excluded where the application is by a member of GCHQ or the SIS (under s 42(3)). Under s 44(3), a warrant authorising intrusive surveillance issued by a senior official, and not renewed under the hand of the secretary of state, 'shall cease to have effect at the end of the second working day' after its issue. In the case of other such warrants, that point will be at the end of the period of six months from the day of issue or renewal.

This authorisation regime follows the model adopted for telephone tapping under the Interception of Communications Act 1985 and continued with minor modifications under Part I of RIPA. That regime has been subjected to criticism on the basis that the mechanisms for creating executive accountability were so weak,[99] but it has been found to meet Strasbourg requirements, as discussed below.[100] The regime for intrusive surveillance provides for independent checks and for the possibility that an authorisation will not be able to take effect if it does not satisfy the requirements, including those of proportionality. Clearly, the standard of scrutiny may be variable, but the very fact that an authorisation will be checked independently may tend to foster rigour in preparing the papers.

Directed surveillance

Under s 26(2) of RIPA, all covert surveillance is directed surveillance if it is not intrusive and it is undertaken 'otherwise than by way of an immediate response to events or circumstances, the nature of which is such that it would not be practicable for an authorisation to be sought', and for the purposes of 'a specific investigation or . . . operation', and 'in such a manner as is likely to result in the obtaining of private information about

---

99 See: Lloyd, I 'The Interception of Communications Act 1985' (1986) 49 MLR 86; Leigh, I 'A tapper's charter?' [1986] PL 8.

100 p 821 *et seq.*

a person', even if he is not identified in relation to the investigation. If the device or person is not on the premises or in the vehicle, the surveillance is 'directed', not 'intrusive' unless 'the device is such that it consistently provides information of the same quality and detail as might be expected to be obtained from a device actually present on the premises or in the vehicle' (s 26(5)). The Code of Practice on Covert Surveillance made under s 71 of the RIPA seeks to draw a distinction between general law enforcement functions carried out covertly as an immediate response, and the systematic targeting of an individual (para 2.2); only the latter may amount to directed surveillance. Anomalously enough, the term 'directed surveillance' also covers an interception of communications in the course of its transmission that is consented to by the sender or recipient and in respect of which there is no interception warrant (s 26(4)(b) and s 48(4)).

To illustrate the distinction between directed and intrusive surveillance, the former would occur where a 'bugging' device is placed in the hallway of a block of flats that provides information of a lesser quality than would be obtained if the device was inside one of the flats. Intrusive surveillance would occur, for example, when a 'bugging' device is placed in a car parked near a private house that normally provides information of the same quality as would be obtained if the device was inside the house. These examples make it clear that very fine lines may be drawn between the two forms of surveillance, although, as indicated below, the two regimes differ sharply. Moreover, the distinction between directed surveillance and 'general law enforcement' functions, such as observing persons entering or leaving a house, turns on the question whether or not the observation can be viewed as an immediate response – another instance in which fine lines may be drawn. If observation of a house occurs over a period of time, it can be argued that an invasion of privacy is occurring that can no longer be viewed as an immediate response. In such an instance an authorisation should be sought. It could also be argued that such surveillance requires a more specific statutory underpinning.[101]

Section 47(1) provides powers for the secretary of state to extend or modify the authorisation provisions. They can provide for any directed surveillance 'to be treated for the purposes of this Part as intrusive surveillance'. Under s 47(2), this power is subject to the negative resolution procedure, but clearly that does not provide the same safeguards as the full parliamentary process would do.

'Directed' surveillance may be authorised on the grounds under s 28. The grounds include 'the interests of national security, for the purpose of preventing or detecting crime or of preventing disorder, in the interests of the economic well-being of the UK, in the interests of public safety; for the purpose of protecting public health; for the purpose of assessing or collecting any tax, duty . . . or other . . . charge payable to a government department'; or for any other 'purpose specified for the purposes of this sub-section by an order made by the Secretary of State'. This order must be approved by Parliament. Proportionality requirements are introduced under s 28(2) to the effect that the authorising person must believe that the authorisation or authorised conduct is 'proportionate to what is sought to be achieved by carrying it out'.

The authorisation for directed surveillance is granted by a 'designated person' under s 28. Under s 30, such persons are 'the individuals holding such offices, ranks or positions with relevant public authorities as are prescribed for the purposes of this

---

101 Such an underpinning can be created, by order of the Secretary of State, under s 47.

sub-section by an order' made by the Secretary of State. The Secretary of State can himself be a designated person under s 30(2). The 'relevant public authorities' (set out in Sched 1) include the police, the security and intelligence services, Customs and Excise, Inland Revenue, the armed forces, the Departments of Health; Social Security; Trade and Industry; Environment, Transport and the Regions. Further authorities can be designated by order of the Secretary of State. The prescribed persons in the relevant public authorities are now set out in the Regulation of Investigatory Powers Act 2000 (Prescription of Offices, Ranks and Positions) Order 2000.[102] In police forces, the pre-scribed office is that of superintendent; in urgent cases, it is that of inspector. The code of practice, para 5.7 recommends that authorising officers should not 'be responsible for authorising operations in which they are directly involved, although it is recognised that this may sometimes be unavoidable ...'. The Protection of Freedoms Act 2012 created a significant additional protection by inserting a new section into Part II of RIPA, s32A, which provides that an authorisation under s 28 does not have effect until there has been judicial confirmation that the s 28(2) conditions have been met.

Under s 43, written authorisations cease to have effect after three months, although they may be renewed for additional three-month periods (security or intelligence ser-vice authorisations may be renewed for six months). Urgent authorisations cease to have effect after 72 hours unless they are renewed either orally (if the urgency sub-sists) by a person whose entitlement to act is not confined to urgent cases, or in writ-ing. Authorisations cannot be granted orally except in urgent cases and by a person whose entitlement to act is not confined to such cases. Under s 43(3)(b) 'in a case not falling within paragraph (a) in which the authorisation is for the conduct or the use of a covert human intelligence source', the period is 12 months from its grant or last renewal. In a case falling outside s 43(3)(a) or (b), the period is three months under s 43(3)(c). Under s 44(5)(a), when an authorisation for the carrying out of directed surveillance is granted by a member of any of the intelligence services and renewed by an instrument 'endorsed under the hand of the person renewing [it] with a statement that the renewal is believed to be necessary on grounds falling within section 32(3)(a) or (c), the authorisation (unless renewed again) shall cease to have effect at the end of the period of six months'. A chief surveillance commissioner, who is assisted by assistant commissioners, has a general oversight role in relation to this regime, under s 62 (see below).

Other surveillance

Under s 47, the secretary of state may also by order 'apply this Part, with such modifica-tions as he thinks fit, to any . . . surveillance that is neither directed nor intrusive'. The power is intended to afford, if necessary, a statutory basis for the use of other powers which may be found to have fallen outside this Act. The compatibility of this the legal basis for the powers with the Convention is questionable, partly because, it is suggested, it is so uncertain and so dependent on the exercise of executive power. The term 'such modifications' implies that lesser safeguards than those available for directed surveil-lance might be adopted, a possibility could have Art 8 implications.

102 SI 2000/2417.

Sensitive information

There are certain safeguards relating to the type of information that can be gathered using directed or intrusive surveillance, but the relevant rules appear only in the 2014 code of practice, not in the Act itself. Paragraph 4 relates to certain types of confidential information: confidential personal information (relating to physical or mental health or to spiritual counselling), matters subject to legal privilege and confidential journalistic material. Under para 4.1, 'particular care must be taken' if the subject 'might reasonably expect a high degree of privacy'. Under para 4.27, the code of practice such information should be reported to the relevant commissioner or inspector.

The use and storage of information obtained by surveillance techniques is governed as far as the police are concerned by the Data Protection Act.[103] The surveillance commissioners also have power, when quashing authorisations of intrusive surveillance under s 37, to order the destruction of records. Storage and retention of police information are also governed by a detailed ACPO Code[104] which instructs on the applicability of data protection principles to such information. As indicated above, concerns have been raised regarding record keeping by the security service, bearing in mind the fact that it does not have to comply with the Data Protection Act 1998, even in its criminal function.[105] Under the 1998 Act, in relation to personal information, the police do not have to comply with the fair and lawful processing provisions of the first data protection principle,[106] subject access requests, or restrictions on disclosure of personal information, if to do so would be likely to prejudice the prevention and detection of crime or the apprehension and prosecution of offenders. These are not blanket exemptions; they should be considered in their application to individual cases. But it is unclear that careful scrutiny on this basis occurs.[107] The ACPO Code of Practice is therefore of significance since it provides greater clarity and safeguards a significant aspect of privacy. But it is argued that such a significant task should not be undertaken by quasi-legislation.[108]

The RIPA codes of practice on covert surveillance and interception of communications

As discussed above, the current codes of practice apply to every authorisation of covert surveillance and interference with property or interception of communications carried out under s 5 of the Intelligence Services Act 1994, Part III of the Police Act 1997 or Parts I or II of the Regulation of Investigatory Powers Act 2000 by public authorities. There are four RIPA codes of practice, of which the most relevant to this chapter are those relating to covert surveillance and property interference and interception

---

103 See Chapter 10.
104 ACPO 'Data Protection: Manual of Guidance' 2012.
105 See pp 765–66.
106 Except in relation to 'sensitive' data.
107 See e.g., Foster, S 'Classification of prisoners, access to reasons and confidentiality' (2004) 9(2) Cov LJ 98; see also *Justice* 'Under Surveillance: Covert Policing and Human Rights Standards,' 1998, Chapter 4, esp pp 92–95.
108 See Chapter 12, p 835 *et seq* for analogous discussion in relation to the PACE Codes.

of communications. The codes are made and set before Parliament pursuant to s 71 RIPA.[109]

The relationship between the current codes of practice and the statutes is significant. The statutes grant broad discretionary powers to conduct intrusive surveillance and interfere with property to senior law enforcement officials, but seeks to constrain and structure these powers in two main ways. First, there are general precedent conditions for the exercise of such powers, the most significant being the requirement that the action is likely to be of substantial value in preventing or detecting serious crime. Secondly, there are specific countervailing provisions intended to protect privacy and confidentiality. Parts I and II RIPA and the other provisions mentioned above provide the key powers, but the code of practice, a set of quasi-legal rules, provides a due process underpinning. The statutory provisions, together with the code provisions, could be viewed as providing a detailed domestic scheme satisfying the demands of Art 8. But this view fails to take account of the rule of law implications of placing a number of key protective provisions on a quasi-legislative basis within what Baldwin has termed 'tertiary rules', or government by circular.[110]

In common with many of the codes accompanying 'state power' legislation discussed in this book,[111] the code provisions are not on their face discretionary; they are in general phrased in the precise terms of mandatory instructions. Nevertheless, no formal sanction, apart from an internal disciplinary one, is provided for their breach (s 72(2) RIPA).[112] This is also true of the statutory provisions. However, they cloak otherwise tortious actions with authority, while the mere fact that they are statutory may appear to give them greater weight than the code provisions in the eyes of those to whom they are directed, and of the judiciary. If the provisions were not followed, it would be, theoretically, an internal disciplinary matter and in practice, police officers might pay more attention to this than to the theoretical possibility of being sued. But, as Chapter 14 points out, the same sanction is used for breach of the PACE codes and does not appear to be effective, taking into account the very few disciplinary charges laid for their breach.[113] Thus, senior law enforcement officials are in effect given at least a partial discretion as to whether to follow the code rules and thus whether to respect the Art 8 rights which they reflect.[114] As pointed out in Chapter 1, the concept of a right

---

109 The others are: the Covert Human Intelligence Sources Code of Practice; Interception of Communications Code of Practice; The Acquisition and Disclosure of Communications data Code of Practice.
110 See Baldwin, R, *Rules and Government*, 1995, Clarendon.
111 The Codes of Practice made under the Police and Criminal Evidence Act 1984 considered in Chapters 12 and 13 were the forerunners of the Codes adopted under the Regulation of Investigatory Powers Act 2000.
112 On the model provided by the PACE Codes (adopted for all the Codes mentioned in this book) it is admissible in evidence under s 72(3). It should be taken into account by courts, the single tribunal and relevant Commissioners under s 72(4).
113 See p 1013 *et seq*.
114 Ronald Dworkin has argued that if an official's decision whether to comply with a given rule is final and unreviewable, he is endowed with a form of discretion (*Taking Rights Seriously*, 1977, p 69). In practice, decisions taken by police officers in relation to the provisions of the Codes of Practice discussed in this book (see, in particular, Chapter 11, p 884 and Chapter 13, p 1010 *et seq*) are in general unlikely to be considered in courts or in police disciplinary proceedings. In a minority of instances, however, such provisions may be considered in relation to exclusion of evidence. Even

precludes the idea of an open-ended discretion to infringe it in the pursuit of competing interests.[115] It is however possible that the principle from that intrusive measures must be Art 8 compliant might come to influence this position.[116]

Unless rigorous, independent review of rule-compliance is available, the code rules are, in effect, largely discretionary, and the rights protected by them, to an extent, illusory. This is a concern in respect of the statutory provisions, but it arises *a fortiori* in respect of the Code made under s 71 RIPA. It is suggested below that the single tribunal system has recently become generally effective, and that since no clear parliamentary or administrative means of seeking to enhance rule compliance is available, recourse to such a court-based remedy under the influence of the HRA is of particular significance in this context.

4 Accountability

The Intelligence and Security Committee

The Security Services Act 1989 provided for no real form of parliamentary oversight of the security service.[117] But the Intelligence Services Act 1994 set up, under s 10, the Intelligence and Security Committee (ISC), to oversee the 'expenditure, administration and policy' of MI5, MI6 and GCHQ.[118] Operational matters were omitted from their remit. The committee has access to a wider range of agency activities and to highly classified information. Its cross-party membership of nine from both Houses is appointed by the Prime Minister after consultation with the leader of the opposition.[119] The committee is supported by a clerk and secretariat in the Cabinet Office and can employ an investigator to pursue specific matters in greater detail. The ISC has undergone significant recent reform under Part 1 of the Justice and Security Act 2013, and its remit now extends to consideration of material from all government departments relating to intelligence or security matters (2013 Act, s 2(2)).

Thus, state surveillance activity is, to an extent, accountable to Parliament. The committee's reports may not, however, be presented to Parliament without consulting the Prime Minister, who may censor a report on broad grounds – it need not be damaging to national security, merely to the continued discharge of the functions of the services (2013 Act, s 3(4); Sched 1, para 5). By s 3(5), the ISC's report to Parliament must contain a statement as to whether any matter has been excluded from the report. After deletions of sensitive material, the reports are placed before Parliament. Appointment to the committee is by the Prime Minister (s 1(4)(a)).

---

then, the 'sanction' of such exclusion is unlikely to be used in respect of most forms of non-confession evidence, the form of evidence to which the provisions of the RIPA Code are most likely to relate. See, generally, Davis, KC, *Discretionary Justice*, 1980, Greenwood, pp 84–88.

115 See pp 19–20. Dworkin argues that it only makes sense to denote an interest as a right if it will generally win any battle with competing societal considerations: see *op cit*, p 191.

116 See eg *Wainwright v UK* (2007) 44 EHRR 40.

117 See further Leigh, I and Lustgarten, L, *In From the Cold: National Security and Parliamentary Democracy*, 1994.

118 For discussion of the introduction of the Committee in 1994 see Leigh and Lustgarten, *ibid.*

119 Section 1(2).

As the committee is not a select committee, it has no powers to compel witnesses to appear before it. But in practice it has exercised greater powers than a select committee: in its inquiry into GCHQ's bulk surveillance operation in the wake of the Snowden affair it was able to obtain papers from former administrations and official advice to ministers, both of which are forbidden to select committees. After each general election the Prime Minister nominates the nine parliamentarians to the committee, in consultation with the leader of the opposition (s 1(4)); the nominees are then appointed by the House of Parliament from which they are drawn (s 1(3)). Members are mainly from the House of Commons, but at least one must be from the House of Lords (s 1(2)). Serving ministers are not allowed to be members (s 1(4)(b)), but several members have previously held ministerial positions. Details of the membership of the most recent committee, including its final report and the government's response, are on its web page.[120]

The members of the committee are notified that s 1 of the Official Secrets Act will apply to them as though they were members of the services themselves and therefore they will commit a criminal offence if they disclose any information or document they have obtained as a result of their work. They would have no defence that the disclosure revealed a serious abuse of power which could not be otherwise addressed, or that the information was already in the public domain. The 2013 Act significantly enhanced the committee's power to require the agencies to provide information, which is now subject only to a veto by the secretary of state (Sched 1 para 4(2)(b)) rather than by agency heads, as was previously the case.[121]

It was clear at its inception that the extent to which the work of the committee was likely to have a real impact on the agencies depended on its appointees and on the way they interpreted their role. The initial 1996–97 Report of the Intelligence and Security Committee made no recommendations as to independence at all, in contrast to the modern emphasis on its independent status, particularly after the 2013 Act.

The Commissioners

The role of the Interception of Communications Commissioner

The Commissioner is a senior judge appointed by the Prime Minister on a part-time basis to monitor the warrant procedure and to consider complaints.[122] He had a duty under s 8(1)(a) of the 1985 Act, which was continued under s 57(2)(a) of the RIPA, to keep the warrant procedure under review. Apart from the statutory limitations of his powers, the practical constraints on them have been overwhelming. He had no staff and carried out the checking procedure personally on a part time basis. Clearly, as he accepts, these constraints precluded consideration of every warrant that is brought to his attention. His powers were very limited. He could not order that warrants should be quashed or that the material obtained should be destroyed; under s 8(9) he could merely report a contravention of ss 2–5 to the Prime Minister, which had not already been the

---

120 http://isc.independent.gov.uk/.
121 Intelligence Services Act 1994, Sched 3, para 3(2).
122 It may be noted that the Interception of Communications Commissioner claims not to be a public body under the Freedom of Information Act 2000.

subject of a tribunal report, or a contravention of s 6 which covered destruction of material, and he had to prepare an annual report for the Prime Minister under s 8(6).

Both the commissioner's powers and support were expanded under RIPA, under ss 57[123] and 58; however, his complaints role has been taken over by the single tribunal (see below). His powers now extend beyond review of warrants to the acquisition and disclosure of communications data, and the adequacy of arrangements for safeguards relating to use that is made of interception material. The commissioner is also now supported by the head of the Interception of Communications Commissioner Office (IOCCO) and a team of nine inspectors and two secretarial staff.[124] The commissioner is required to issue a half-yearly report to the Prime Minister as to the exercise of his statutory functions (s 58(4)) and these reports must be laid before Parliament (s 58(6)).

Although various individuals involved in state surveillance and operating communications networks are required to provide the commissioner with the information needed to carry out his task, he has no effective means of checking that information has not been withheld. His office is empowered to conduct inspections of warrants issued, renewed, modified or cancelled since the last visit, and check a sample of them, as well as interview individuals involved in the interception of communications; however, he has no means of knowing whether the unauthorised interception has not in fact been disclosed to him.

The remit of the commissioner gives him the opportunity to note that unauthorised surveillance had occurred, but only when he was informed of it by the agencies concerned. In his 2015 report the commissioner stated: 'The total number of interception errors reported to my office during 2014 was 60, three more than in 2013'.[125] He found that '78% of the errors reported fell into 3 key categories: Section 15/16 safeguards breaches; failure to cancel interception; or interception of the incorrect communications address.'[126] He provides examples of some of the most common safeguard breaches, the most serious of which was in relation to unauthorised searches of communications data:

> In one very serious case last year an employee at GCHQ deliberately undertook a number of unauthorised searches for related communications data. The employee was immediately suspended from duty on discovery of the illegitimate searches and a full investigation was launched. This abuse of the systems amounted to gross misconduct and the individual's employment was terminated and vetting status withdrawn.[127]

The Intelligence Services Commissioner

The commissioner is supposed to provide oversight of the procedure, but only after the event. At present, the same commissioner operates as commissioner in respect of all

---

123 Under s 57(2), 'Subject to subsection (5), the Interception of Communications Commissioner shall keep under review the exercise and performance by the Secretary of State of the powers and duties conferred or imposed on him by or under sections 1 to 11'.
124 'Report of the Interception of Communications Commissioner', HC 1113, SG/2015/28, para 2.18.
125 *Ibid*, para 6.86.
126 *Ibid*, para 6.89.
127 *Ibid*, para 6.92.

three agencies, and can be re-appointed to continue his role as 'the Intelligence Services Commissioner' under s 59 RIPA. Section 59 of the Act provides for the Prime Minister to appoint the commissioner, who must hold or have held high judicial office.[128] He or she is appointed for a period of three years with the possibility of re-appointment. His job is to keep under review the issue of warrants by the secretary of state authorising intrusive surveillance (e.g., eavesdropping) and interference with property in order to make sure that the secretary of state was right to issue them. Like the Interception of Communications Commissioner, the Intelligence Services Commissioner reviews warrant applications and visits the security service and other agencies to discuss any case he wishes to examine in more detail. He must be given access to whatever documents and information he needs and at the end of each reporting year he submits a report to the Prime Minister;[129] it is subsequently laid before Parliament and published. The Intelligence Services Commissioner is also responsible for reviewing the internally authorised use of directed surveillance (the covert monitoring of targets' movements, conversations and other activities) and of covert human intelligence sources (i.e. agents) to check that the agencies are acting in accordance with the requirements of the law.

The oversight is, however, limited. The commissioner can only oversee the issuance of warrants under ss 5 and 6 of the 1994 Act; he cannot order that they should be quashed; nor can he order an operation against a particular group to cease. The commissioner cannot address instances in which no warrant was necessary, since the procedure in question is not unlawful. The remit of the commissioner precludes consideration of unauthorised actions since he can only consider whether a warrant was properly authorised. If an action does not require a warrant, such a question becomes irrelevant. This is also true of actions which are unlawful and unauthorised by warrant, such as burgling a property.

The Chief Surveillance Commissioner

The Chief Surveillance Commissioner's role mirrors that of the Interceptions of Communications Commissioner; however, his role concerns surveillance activities conducted in relation to more ordinary crime, and not necessarily in relation to terrorism or other activities having a potential impact on national security. The office of commissioner is established by s 91 of the Police Act 1997. Assistant surveillance commissioners can be appointed under s 63 of the RIPA to aid the Chief Surveillance Commissioner. Such aid is clearly needed since the commissioner provides oversight, not only of police surveillance, but also of surveillance carried out by all the persons covered by Part II of the RIPA. Thus, the oversight role of the surveillance commissioners is broader than their role in relation to authorisations, since the latter relates only to the police and customs, while the former covers other public authorities and the Home Secretary's authorising role under s 41. Thus, the role of the surveillance commissioners overlaps with that of the Intelligence Services Commissioner who has an oversight role which, as indicated above, covers, *inter alia*, surveillance carried out by those services.

---

128 Within the meaning of the Appellate Jurisdiction Act 1876.
129 See 'Report of the Intelligence Commissioner for 2014,' 25 June 2015, HC 225, SG/2015/74.

Under s 107 of the Police Act 1997, the Chief Surveillance Commissioner has reporting duties similar to those of the Interception of Communications Commissioner. (His duty under s 106, to report to the Prime Minister if an appeal is allowed and where a finding in favour of a complainant is made by a commissioner, was repealed under Sched 4 to the 2000 Act.) He must make an annual report on the discharge of his functions.[130] The report must be presented to Parliament and published as a command paper. The Prime Minister may exclude matters from the report under s 107(4) of the Act if it appears to him that it contains matter 'prejudicial to the prevention and detection of serious crime' or to the discharge of the functions of a police authority, the service authorities for the National Criminal Intelligence Service or the duties of the Commissioner for Customs and Excise.

The single tribunal under RIPA

Taking the Interception of Communications Act 1985 as a model, the Security Services Act 1989 set up a commissioner under s 4 and a tribunal under s 5 as a means of oversight for MI5 (in Scheds 1 and 2). The Intelligence Services Act 1994 adopted the same model for MI6 and GCHQ (ss 8 and 9 and Scheds 1 and 2). However, the complaints procedure provided under these Acts was strongly criticised for being ineffective and complaints were rarely upheld.[131] The current single tribunal, set up under s 65 of the RIPA,[132] has taken over from the Interception of Communications Tribunal and the Intelligence and Security Services Tribunals; it has also taken over the complaints role of the commissioners set up under Part III of the 1997 Act, the role of commissioners in hearing complaints under the Police Act 1997 s 102, and Sched 7 (discussed above) and acquired a role in considering surveillance undertaken by other public authorities. The tribunal's creation was therefore a development of immense significance, since it provided a central mechanism protecting citizens against abuse of state surveillance powers. As discussed below, the tribunal has recently decided a number of significant surveillance cases in which it has found that the agencies have acted unlawfully and contrary to the guarantees of Art 8.

---

130   See 'Annual report of the Chief Surveillance Commissioner to the Prime Minister and to the Scottish Ministers for 2013–14', 4 September 2014, HC 343, SG/2014/92.

131   Gill found: 'this structure . . . has been constructed neither for elegance nor impact' (Gill, P, *Policing Politics: Security Intelligence and the Liberal Democratic State*, 1994, p 295). Lustgarten and Leigh summed up the problem: 'in so far as the government believed that by creating these new structures it would reassure the public that all is well it seriously miscalculated' *In From the Cold: National Security and Parliamentary Democracy*, 1994) p 439. The Report of the Interception of Communications Commissioner, Cm 4001, 1997, stated that since it was established in 1986, the tribunal had received 568 complaints and that none had ever been upheld.

132   Schedule 3 governs the membership of the single tribunal. Members must have held 'high judicial office' within the meaning of Part 3 of the Constitutional Reform Act 2005, or a person who meets the judicial eligibility condition on a seven-year basis; in Scotland and Northern Ireland they must be practitioners of at least seven years' standing. Thus, they need not be judges, although the President must be a judge. Its members are remunerated by the Secretary of State, but can be removed from office only on an address to the Queen by both Houses of Parliament under Sched 3, para 1(5). These arrangements afford the tribunal a measure of independence from the executive.

However, there is a key limitation to the tribunal in that there is no duty placed upon on the agencies to disclose to an individual the fact that an operation has occurred after it is over, and service personnel who feel that they had been required to act improperly in bugging or searching a person's property are unlikely to disclose the matter. Furthermore, as discussed in Chapter 8, s 1 of the Official Secrets Act 1989 prevents members or former members of the security and intelligence services disclosing anything at all about the operation of those services. These provisions also apply to anyone who is notified that he or she is subject to the provisions of the section. Similarly, s 4(3) of the Official Secrets Act 1989 prohibits disclosure of information obtained by, or relating to, the issue of a warrant under the Regulation of Investigatory Powers Act 2000 or the Intelligence Services Act 1994. Most individuals will therefore have no means of knowing that surveillance has occurred and therefore will be unlikely to bring a complaint. If an individual brings a speculative complaint to the tribunal, uncertain whether surveillance or intrusion has occurred, the result may leave him or her none the wiser. An individual is therefore normally only able to bring complaints or proceedings to the tribunal only if she has become aware of the surveillance due to criminal proceedings.

This position is contrary to the recommendation of the Data Protection Working Party for the European Commission, which said in May 1999 that a 'person under surveillance [should] be informed of this as soon as possible'.[133] The UK position also contrasts with the approach in other European countries, such as Germany[134] or Denmark,[135] in which the police and the other state agencies have a duty to inform him or her of the interception, after it is over. The lack of such a duty was challenged before both the tribunal and Strasbourg Court in the *Kennedy* litigation.[136] The claimant argued, unsuccessfully, that the lack of a notification duty was incompatible with Art 8.[137] It was found by both the tribunal[138] and ECtHR[139] that the safeguards provided by RIPA, including the tribunal, were sufficiently effective and therefore that there was no violation (see below for a full discussion of *Kennedy*).

A further limitation is placed on complaints relating to interceptions. Section 67(5) provides that unless the tribunal in the circumstances considers it 'equitable' to do so, such complaints will not be considered if made more than one year after the conduct in question took place. Otherwise, conduct under s 65(5) can be considered whenever it occurred. Thus, pre-commencement surveillance can be brought before the tribunal.

---

133 Statewatch 'FU-FBI telecommunications surveillance plan: Commission working party' (1999) Vol 9 Nos 3 and 4. See further as regards the duty to notify in EU law and under the ECHR: DeHert, D and Boehm, F 'The right of notification after surveillance is over: ready for recognition?' (2012) *Digital Enlightenment Yearbook* 19.

134 See *Klass v Federal Republic of Germany* (1978) 2 EHRR 214. Germany's current bugging law contains this requirement.

135 Criminal Procedure Code, para 788.

136 See *Kennedy and another* IPT/01/62 & 77, 23 January 2003; *Kennedy v Security Services, GCHQ and the Metropolitan Police* IPT/01/62, 9 December 2004; *Kennedy v UK* (2011) 52 EHRR 4.

137 *Kennedy v Security Services, GCHQ and the Metropolitan Police* IPT/01/62, 9 December 2004.

138 *Ibid.*

139 *Op cit*, fn 136.

Jurisdiction of the tribunal

Under s 65(2), the tribunal has three main functions and a potential fourth one. First, challenges to surveillance on Convention grounds by certain bodies or to interception by all bodies must be brought within it. In the words of the sub-section, 'it will be the only appropriate tribunal for the purposes of section 7 of the HRA 1998 in relation to any proceedings under sub-section (1)(a) of that section (proceedings for actions incompatible with Convention rights) which fall within sub-section 3 of this section'. Under s 65(3), they are proceedings against any of the intelligence services 'or against any other person in respect of any conduct, or proposed conduct, by or on behalf of any of those services' or 'relating to the taking place in any challengeable circumstances of any conduct falling within subsection (5)'.

Section 65(5) applies to 'conduct . . . (whenever it occurred) by or on behalf of any of the intelligence services; in connection with the interception of communications in the course of their transmission by means of a postal service or telecommunication system; conduct to which . . . Part II applies, the carrying out of surveillance by a foreign police or customs officer; any entry on or interference with property or any interference with wireless telegraphy'. Section 65(6) introduces a significant limitation in providing: 'for the purposes only of subsection (3)', conduct to which Part II applies, an entry on or interference with property or an interference with wireless telegraphy is not conduct falling within sub-section (5) 'unless it is conduct by or on behalf of a person holding any office, rank or position with (a) any of the intelligence services; (b) any of Her Majesty's forces; (c) any police force; (d) the Serious Organised Crime Agency; (e) the Scottish Crime and Drug Enforcement Agency; or (f) the Commissioners of Customs and Excise . . .'. In other words, as indicated above, the intention is that surveillance by these bodies can be challenged only in the tribunal where it is argued that they have breached a Convention right.

Secondly, the tribunal is the appropriate forum for complaints if, under s 65(4), 'it is a complaint by a person who is aggrieved by any conduct falling within subsection (5) which he believes to have taken place in relation to him, to any of his property, to any communications sent by or to him, or intended for him, or to his use of any postal service, telecommunications service or telecommunication system; and to have taken place in challengeable circumstances or to have been carried out by or on behalf of any of the intelligence services'. Section 65(7) and (8) apply in relation to both s 65(3) and (4). Section 65(7) defines 'challengeable circumstances' as conduct which '(a) takes place with the authority, or purported authority, of anything falling within subsection (8); or (b) the circumstances are such that (whether or not there is such authority) it would not have been appropriate for the conduct to take place without it, or at least without proper consideration having been given to whether such authority should be sought'. Conduct also takes place in challengeable circumstances if it takes place, or purports to take place, as part of a collaboration with a foreign security operation (s 65(7A); s 76A).

Thus, in its complaints and 'proceedings' jurisdiction, the tribunal can consider unauthorised interception. In relation to complaints, the term used under s 67(3)(b) is 'investigate the authority' which does not appear to confine the tribunal, bearing in mind the meaning of challengeable circumstances', to merely considering whether the authority (if it exists) was properly given. Section 65(8) covers: interception warrants under the Acts of 1985 or 2000, an authorisation under Part II of the 2000 Act, a permission of the Secretary of State under Sched 2 (relating to powers to obtain data protected by encryption), or an authorisation under s 93 of the Police Act 1997.

Thirdly, the tribunal has jurisdiction (s 65(2)(c)) to determine a reference to them by a person that he has suffered detriment as a consequence 'of any prohibition or restriction' under s 17 (the exclusion of evidence section) on his relying on any matter in, or for the purposes of, civil proceedings. It is notable that no means is provided of seeking redress for detriment arising when evidence is excluded in *criminal* proceedings.[140] Finally, under s 65(2)(d), the secretary of state can also, by order, allocate other proceedings to the tribunal but a draft of the order must have been approved by a resolution of each House of Parliament.[141]

Procedure

The tribunal is modelled on the Special Immigration Appeals Commission (SIAC),[142] which in turn provided the model for the tribunal set up under the Northern Ireland Act 1998.[143] The Investigatory Powers Tribunal Rules[144] came into force on the same date as did the HRA.[145] The current rules follow the old practices in various respects. Under s 68, the tribunal is entitled to determine its own procedure, subject to these rules. By rule 9(6) *all* hearings were to be held in secret; however, the tribunal has declared this rule ultra vires in relation to s 69 RIPA (by which the secretary of state is authorised to create the rules) on the basis that it was a blanket rule prohibiting even open hearings regarding points of legal procedure. The tribunal found that legal argument conducted for the sole purpose of ascertaining what the law is did not involve the risk of disclosure of any sensitive information.[146]

The rules envisage the possibility of an oral hearing, but there is no right to such a hearing.[147] The rules allow for the possibility of separate oral hearings; the applicant and the representatives of the public authority will not confront each other.[148] Under s 68(6) and (7)(i) 'every person by whom or on whose application there has been granted any authorisation under Part II . . . must disclose or provide to the Tribunal all such documents and information as the tribunal may require [in the exercise *inter alia* of

---

140 See *R v Preston* [1993] 4 All ER 638 p 686 in which the appellants may have suffered detriment due to the exclusion of material derived from phone tapping under the predecessor of s 17, s 9 of the 1985 Act.

141 Section 66(3).

142 Set up under s 1 of the Special Immigration Appeals Act 1997 in response to the findings in *Chahal v UK* (1997) 23 EHRR 413.

143 Under s 90.

144 SI 2000/2665.

145 2 October 2000.

146 In *Kennedy* (ipt/01/62) and *British-Irish Rights Watch & Others* (ipt/01/77).

147 Rule 9(2): 'The Tribunal shall be under no duty to hold oral hearings but may do so in accordance with this rule (and not otherwise).' Rule 9(3): 'The Tribunal may hold oral hearings at which the complainant may make representations, give evidence and call witnesses.'

148 Rule 9(4): 'The Tribunal may hold *separate* oral hearings which the person whose conduct is the subject of the complaint, the public authority against whom s 7 proceedings are brought . . . may be required to attend and at which that person or authority may make representations, give evidence and call witnesses' (emphasis added).

its jurisdiction under s 65(2)(a)]'. But information given at the separate hearing can be withheld from the applicant unless the person providing it consents to its disclosure.[149]

The tribunal cannot publish its judgment in entirety; by rule 13(2), where determination is made in favour of the complainant the tribunal can provide him with a summary of that determination including any findings of fact, but not the full reasoning for that finding.[150] Furthermore rule 13(2) is subject to the general rule that disclosure of the determination and finding of fact are 'contrary to the public interest, or prejudicial to national security . . . or the continued discharge of the functions of any of the intelligence services' (rule 6(1)). The tribunal has established that it is entitled to publish detailed reasons for its rulings on questions of law concerning procedure and practice.[151]

Where there is no finding in favour of the complainant because the tribunal finds that no warrant or authorisation exists and that apparently no surveillance or interception is occurring, or that proper authorisation occurred, it merely informs the complainant that the complaint has not been upheld. The complainant who suspects, for example, that his or her phone or e-mails are being tapped is then left not knowing whether in fact tapping is occurring. But if the complaint is upheld, the complainant will know that tapping/surveillance was occurring but unauthorised. This is an improvement on the old position since previously the fact that a complaint was not upheld could still mean that unauthorised tapping was occurring. For example, on 6 December 1991, Alison Halford complained to the Interception of Communications Tribunal in respect of the suspected tapping of her home and office telephones.[152] From the circumstances, it appeared that tapping was probably occurring. She was informed on 21 February 1992, without any reason given, that the complaint had not been upheld: no contravention of ss 2–5 of the Interception of Communications Act 1985 had been found. It later confirmed by letter that it could not specify whether any interception had in fact taken place. She was left in ignorance as to whether an intercept had indeed been authorised, whether one was in place, although unauthorised, or whether no interception was occurring.[153] Had it been authorised it is inconceivable, bearing in mind the circumstances, for it to have been authorised properly.

In its 'proceedings' under s 65(2)(a), the tribunal uses 'the principles applicable by a court on an application for judicial review'. Under the HRA it therefore must apply the principles a court bound by s 6 of the HRA would apply on such an application. The proportionality requirements under the RIPA should be strictly scrutinised. But one problem is, as Leigh and Lustgarten have argued, that the procedure may

---

149 Under Rule 2, the tribunal may not disclose to the complainant or any other person any information disclosed or provided to the tribunal in the course of [an oral hearing] without the consent of the person who provided it.

150 RIPA, s 68(4). This matter was covered by the 1985 Act, s 7(4)(1) and Sched 1, para 4(2).

151 Ibid.

152 See the facts of *Halford v UK* (1997) 24 EHRR 523, p 800 above.

153 Lord Nolan, the previous Commissioner, has defended the failure to inform complainants as to whether an intercept has occurred on this basis: 'If the tribunal were able to tell a complainant that he or she had not been the subject of legitimate interception, silence or any equivocal answer on another occasion might be interpreted as an implication that interception had taken place. Furthermore a positive answer would allow criminals or terrorists to know whether they were subject to interception or not' (Report of the Commissioner under the Interception of Communications Act 1998, Cm 4364, published June 1999, p 2, para 13 and p 11).

be unsuitable as a means of conducting such scrutiny due to its inefficacy in a fact-finding role.[154] Clearly, this problem is likely to be exacerbated by the non-disclosure of relevant information. However, as discussed below, a number of successful declarations of unlawful surveillance activity contrary to Art 8 ECHR indicate that the tribunal is no longer acting in a tokenistic fashion to merely give the appearance of judicial oversight, but has created, to an extent, judicial accountability comparable to that of other courts.

Remedies

The remedial powers of the current tribunal are similar to those of the old.[155] Under s 67(7), 'the Tribunal . . . shall have power to make any such award of compensation or other order as they think fit; [subject to the power of the Secretary of State to make rules under section 69(2)(h)] . . . and . . . may make an order quashing or cancelling any warrant or authorisation; and an order requiring the destruction of any records of information which has been obtained in exercise of any power conferred by a warrant or authorisation; or is held by any public authority in relation to any person' (subject to s 69 orders). Thus the award of remedies continues to be discretionary; the successful complainant or applicant could be left remediless. The tribunal does not have the power to make a declaration of incompatibility.[156] If the tribunal finds in favour of an applicant, a report does not automatically go to the Prime Minister under s 68(5); it would do so only if the secretary of state bore some responsibility in the matter.

Recourse to the courts from the tribunal

The RIPA seeks to make it impossible for a member of the public who is dissatisfied with the outcome of the tribunal procedure to seek a remedy in the courts. The Act, like the 1985, 1989, 1994 and 1997 Acts, contains a post-*Anisminic* ouster clause. Section 67(8) provides: 'Except to such extent as the Secretary of State may by order otherwise provide, determinations, awards, orders and other decisions of the tribunal (including decisions as to whether they have jurisdiction) shall not be subject to appeal or be liable to be questioned in any court.'[157] The upshot is, at present, that the citizen cannot challenge a finding as to interception rather than surveillance outside the tribunal since both s 17 and s 67(8) stand in the way of so doing. Of course, a citizen may in a sense 'appeal' a tribunal decision by raising the issue complained of at Strasbourg. A citizen seeking to challenge a tribunal decision in respect of surveillance would be unaffected by s 17, but would have to seek to circumvent s 67(8).

---

154 See Leigh, I and Lustgarten, L, 'Making rights real: the courts, remedies and the Human Rights Act' (1999) 158 CLJ 509.

155 Under the 1985 Act, s 7(5), the tribunal could order quashing of the warrant, destruction of material obtained and payment of compensation to the victim.

156 See the HRA 1998, s 4(5), discussed in Chapter 4, p 170.

157 Section 67(8) by an Order of the Secretary of State. It is possible that a tribunal or other body might be established to hear appeals. Under s 67(9), the Secretary of State was under a duty to establish such a body to hear appeals relating to the exercise of the tribunal's jurisdiction under s 65(2)(c) or (d), but not, significantly, in relation to the broader and much more important jurisdiction under s 65(2)(a) or (b).

Under s 3 of the HRA it is conceivable that s 67(8) could be interpreted in an application for leave under Order 53[158] in accordance with the Convention in such a way as to allow review. The argument for seeking to circumvent s 67(8) would depend upon the extent to which the tribunal appeared to meet Convention requirements, considered below. The courts have not so far circumvented such post-*Anisminic*[159] clauses. It could be argued that the wording of s 67(8) cannot be intended to be taken literally. The courts could rely on *Anisminic* itself in seeking to satisfy s 6 of the HRA, in that since the word 'decision' is used in relation to tribunal findings themselves, and in relation to its jurisdiction, the argument is open that any decision tainted by an error of law is a nullity; and therefore the ouster clause cannot bite on it. However this argument has not been made over the 15 years that the tribunal has been in operation, so it remains only a theoretical possibility.

Since the tribunal can determine its own jurisdiction under s 67(8), and it is bound by s 6 of the HRA, argument could also be raised before it that, at least in respect of the circumstances of certain claims, it does not provide a fair hearing under Art 6, due *inter alia* to orders made under s 69, and that therefore its duty under s 6 requires it to declare that its jurisdiction does not cover such claims.

The influence of the HRA

The tribunal is bound by all the ECHR rights, including Art 6, under s 6 of the HRA. There was initially uncertainty as to the applicability of Art 6, since it was considered to be unclear that its findings amounted to a 'determination of civil rights and obligations' under Art 6(1). In the seminal *Kennedy* decision[160] the tribunal found that the right to apply to the tribunal in s 65 was founded upon common law and statutory rights and obligations which could fairly be described as 'civil rights and obligations'. The tribunal was influenced in this finding by the fact that '[f]or all practical purposes the Tribunal is . . . the only forum for the effective investigation and determination of complaints and for granting redress for them where appropriate ...'. It concluded as follows:

> [V]iewing the concept of determination of 'civil rights' in the round and in the light of the Strasbourg decisions, the Tribunal conclude that RIPA, which puts all interception, surveillance and similar intelligence gathering powers on a statutory footing, confers, as part of that special framework, additional 'civil rights' on persons affected by the unlawful exercise of those powers.[161]

The influence of Art 6 has seen an increase in the transparency of the tribunal's legal determinations where such transparency cannot reasonably be deemed contrary to 'the

---

158 Of the Rules of the Supreme Court and the Supreme Court Act 1981, s 31.
159 In *Anisminic v Foreign Compensation Commission* [1969] 2 AC 147 the House of Lords refused to accept that the jurisdiction of the courts was entirely ousted on the basis that the Commission had acted outside its powers. Therefore, it had not made a determination; it had made a purported determination – i.e., a nullity. The ouster clause under the RIPA seeks to avoid this possibility, since it provides that the jurisdiction of the tribunal cannot be questioned in any court.
160 *Kennedy and another* IPT/01/62 & 77, 23 January 2003.
161 *Ibid*, para 108.

public interest, or prejudicial to national security . . . or the continued discharge of the functions of any of the intelligence services' (rule 6(1)). The influence of the ECHR is therefore of a strictly procedural nature. However, recent case law may be adopting a stronger approach to the evaluation of national determinations that state surveillance is necessary in the interests of national security. This question is considered in detail below.

5 The ECHR and surveillance powers in domestic proceedings

The discussion below considers the extent to which aspects of RIPA Parts I and II, and surveillance under the Police Act 1997 are compatible with Art 8. The RIPA framework was considered in detail by the Strasbourg Court in *Kennedy v UK*[162] which largely found it to be compatible with the requirements of Art 8.[163] The section therefore begins with an outline of the facts and claims in *Kennedy* since, as the definitive case on the compatibility of RIPA with the ECHR rights, the Court's findings are relevant at each stage of the Art 8 analysis.

The facts and claims in Kennedy v UK

In *Kennedy v UK* the applicant claimed that he had been subject to unlawful police surveillance that had caused him to feel intimidated and, he alleged, had interfered with the operation of his business.[164] The background to his complaint was that in 1990 he had been charged with the murder of a cell-mate (Mr Quinn), which he claimed was a miscarriage of justice. The murder occurred in circumstances that had raised suspicions, widely reported in the media, of police involvement in the killing and an attempted cover up. Upon his release, in 1996, Kennedy became active in campaigning against miscarriages of justice. In the following years, in which his business began to suffer financially, he became convinced that the police were monitoring his phone calls in an attempt to undermine his business.

In 2001 Kennedy brought a complaint about suspected surveillance to the recently established RIPA tribunal.[165] He complained that his communications were being intercepted in 'challengeable circumstances', within the meaning of s 65(7) RIPA. He also complained that there was an unlawful interference with his Art 8 right. He claimed that any warrant under RIPA Part I or its predecessor, and surveillance thus authorised, was unjustified in terms of the provisions in RIPA or Art 8(2). On 17 January 2005 the tribunal notified him that no determination had been made in his favour in respect of his complaints, which, as discussed above, could be taken to mean either that there had been no interception or that any interception that had taken place was lawful. He therefore decided to take his case to Strasbourg, re-raising his claims under Art 8.[166]

---

162 (2011) 52 EHRR 4.
163 Para 170.
164 Para 5 *et seq.*
165 Para 9.
166 He also claimed, unsuccessfully, of violations of Arts 6 (paras 171–191) and 13 (paras 192–198), but his claims as regards these Articles claims are beyond the scope of this section.

Interference with the guarantees of Art 8

It was common ground between the parties in *Kennedy* that the interception of communications interfered with the applicant's Art 8(1) rights to respect for private life, the home and correspondence. In a number of cases, Strasbourg has found that the collection of information about an individual by the state without his or her consent will, in principle, interfere with the right to respect for private life[167] and it has contemplated the possibility that compiling and retaining the information will also do so.[168] The use of listening devices has been found to create an interference with the Art 8(1) guarantee.[169] Systematic or even indirect targeting of an individual is also very likely to involve such an interference.[170]

However, in the case of secret surveillance that has neither been confirmed nor denied an important initial step is to establish that a complainant has sufficient basis for arguing that he has reasonable grounds for suspecting that an interference with his Art 8(1) right has in fact occurred. The Strasbourg Court found in *Klass*[171] that the *possibility* that an interception was occurring could infringe Art 8, and this was also accepted in *Kennedy v UK*. In *Klass*, the Court said: 'in the mere existence of the legislation itself there is involved, for all those to whom the legislation could be applied, a menace of surveillance; this menace necessarily strikes at freedom of communication between users of the postal and telecommunications services . . .'.[172] As the Court explained in *Halford v UK*,[173] under the Convention the issue is whether, on the particular facts, the essence of the complaint concerned the actual application to her of the measures of surveillance or that her Art 8 rights were menaced by the very existence of the law and practice permitting such measures. A significant limitation upon the test in *Klass* is that there must be a 'reasonable likelihood' that the measures had been applied.[174] In *Kennedy* it was accepted that in light of the broad powers to intercept communications under RIPA, the applicant's allegation that any interception was taking place without lawful basis in order to intimidate him was sufficient to meet the test for interference with Art 8(1).[175]

In accordance with the law

In the surveillance context the 'prescribed by law' ECHR requirement has assumed a particular significance and it is frequently the case that when an interference is found to be in accordance with the law the Court either fails to consider the further stage

---

167 See: *Murray v UK* A 300 (1994), paras 84, 85; *McVeigh v UK* (1981) 25 DR 15, p 49.
168 See *G, H and I v UK* 15 EHRR CD 41 (application of first and third applicants failed on the basis that they had not shown sufficient likelihood that such compiling or retention had occurred).
169 See *Govell v UK* (1997) 4 EHRLR 438; *Khan v UK* Appl No 35394/97 (declared admissible on 20 April 1999) (1999) 27 EHRR CD 58; judgment of the Court: 8 BHRC 310.
170 *Harman and Hewitt v UK* (1992) 14 EHRR 657.
171 (1978) 2 EHRR 214.
172 *Ibid*, para 41.
173 (1997) 24 EHRR 523.
174 *Kennedy v UK* (2011) 52 EHRR 4 para 122.
175 *Ibid*, para 128.

of necessity as a separate issue or performs only a superficial analysis.[176] The Court's approach has been subject to criticism on the basis that it tends towards a less rigorous evaluation of the justification for the interference under Art 8(2). In his dissenting judgment in *Malone v UK*, Judge Pettiti found that the 'major importance of the issue at stake' as regards state surveillance required 'a fuller analysis' than was conducted under the prescribed by law requirement.[177]

As indicated above, state interference with the Art 8 guarantees must be in accordance with the law, under para 2. The ECHR had previously found violations of Art 8 in relation to the pre-RIPA regime on this basis. In *Halford v UK*,[178] the interception of the internal office telephone was clearly not in accordance with the law since domestic law provided no regulation at all of such interception, and therefore the Court found a breach of Art 8.

The prescribed by law requirement covers not only the existence of national law, but its quality. It must be asked whether the measure is 'compatible with the rule of law . . . there must be a measure of legal protection in domestic law against arbitrary interferences by public authorities with [the right to respect for private life under Art 8(1)]. Especially where a power of the executive is exercised in secret, the risks of arbitrariness are evident.'[179] In *Kopp v Switzerland*[180] the Court clearly stated that the essential requirements of a national legal basis are those of accessibility and foreseeability so that, in this context, the citizen is sufficiently aware of the circumstances allowing interception. It must be clear as to the 'circumstances in and conditions on which public authorities are empowered to resort to any such secret measures'.[181]

In *Kruslin v France*,[182] a basis in law was found for interception but it was not found to be of sufficient quality owing to its imprecision, which was found to fail to satisfy the requirement of foreseeability.[183] Similarly, in *Kopp v Switzerland*, which was also concerned with crime, not national security, the Court said: 'interception . . . constitutes a particularly serious interference with private life and correspondence and must accordingly be based on a "law" that is particularly precise'.[184] In another case outside the realm of national security or economic well-being, *Valenzuela v Spain*,[185] the Court also found that the legal basis available for interception did not satisfy the requirements of foreseeability. In particular, the conditions necessary under the Convention to satisfy that requirement, including the nature of the offences which might give rise to an intercept order, were not included in the relevant provisions.[186] In *Weber v Germany*[187] the

---

176 See for discussion e.g., Murphy, M 'A shift in the approach of the European Court of Human Rights in Surveillance cases: a rejuvenation of necessity' (2014) EHRLR 507.

177 Concurring opinion of Judge Pettiti in *Malone v UK* (1984) 7 EHRR 14.

178 (1997) 24 EHRR 523.

179 *Malone v UK*, *op cit*, para 67. The Court reaffirmed this in *Halford v UK* (1997) 24 EHRR 523 above: 'this expression . . . relates to the quality [of domestic law], requiring it to be compatible with the rule of law' (para 49).

180 (1999) 27 EHRR 91, paras 70–71.

181 *Halford v UK* (1997) 24 EHRR 523, para 49.

182 (1990) 12 EHRR 528.

183 *Ibid*, para 30. See also *Huvig v France* (1990) 12 EHRR 528, para 29.

184 (1999) 27 EHRR 91, para 44.

185 (1998) 28 EHRR 483.

186 *Ibid*, para 75.

187 *Weber v Germany* (2008) 46 EHRR SE5.

Court found that 'the domestic law must be sufficiently clear in its terms to give citizens an adequate indication as to the circumstances in which and the conditions on which public authorities are empowered to resort to any such measures'.[188] The Court derived a number of specific elements that must be present in surveillance law if it is to satisfy this requirement:

> the nature of the offences which may give rise to an interception order; a definition of the categories of people liable to have their telephones tapped; a limit on the duration of telephone tapping; the procedure to be followed for examining, using and storing the data obtained; the precautions to be taken when communicating the data to other parties; and the circumstances in which recordings may or must be erased or the tapes destroyed.[189]

In *Kennedy*, the Court evaluated the RIPA regime as a legal basis for UK surveillance activity using the *Weber* criteria. The Court found that foreseeability of surveillance in relation to particular categories of offence must be balanced against the state's need to maintain the secrecy of state surveillance operations.[190] In light of this it was found that the grounds that the secretary of state should take into account when issuing a warrant under s 5 RIPA (national security, prevention or detecting of serious crime, economic well-being of the UK) were sufficiently clear.[191] The Court found that the category of persons whose communications would be intercepted in practice was sufficiently clear for similar reasons. It also found that the warrant itself was sufficiently specific, since it identified one individual or property as the subject of the warrant, rather than permitting indiscriminate collation of data.[192]

The Court arrived at a similar conclusion as regards the duration of telephone tapping since RIPA, 'clearly stipulates, first, the period after which an interception warrant will expire and, second, the conditions under which a warrant can be renewed'.[193] As regards the procedure for examining, using and storing intercept material, it was noted that, under RIPA, an intercepting agency could access all intercept material collected, but that since 'interception warrants . . . under RIPA relate to one person or one set of premises only'[194] the power to access such material was sufficiently limited.

The Court also found that the general safeguards for the processing and communication of intercept material provided by the Secretary of State's duties under s 15 RIPA (to put in place arrangements to secure any data obtained from interception) was established with sufficient clarity, taking into account the further details of such arrangements provided by the code of practice. The Court noted in particular that 'the Code strictly limits the number of persons to whom intercept material can be disclosed, imposing a requirement for the appropriate level of security clearance as well as a requirement to

---

188 *Ibid*, para 93.
189 *Ibid*, paras 93–95.
190 *Kennedy v UK* (2011)52 EHRR 4, para 156.
191 *Ibid*, para 159.
192 *Ibid*, para 160.
193 *Ibid*, para 161.
194 *Ibid*, para 162. *Cf Liberty and Others* IPT/13/77/H, judgment of 5 December 2014, para 64.

communicate data only where there is a "need to know" '.[195] The Court has found a violation on the basis that safeguards were defective in *Draksas v Lithuania*.[196]

The requirement that intercept material be destroyed when no longer necessary was found to be satisfied by s 15(3) RIPA and the code of practice.[197] Similarly, the procedures for recording and reviewing of interception warrants, provided for in the code of practice, were found to be sufficient;[198] the Court found that such procedures were especially important as they provided the basis for the oversight provided by the Commission and tribunal.[199] As regards the tribunal, the Court found that its extensive jurisdiction and ability to hear any complaint where unlawful interception was suspected, created an effective form of judicial oversight, despite the lack of a duty to notify individuals that a warrant for interception had been issued.[200]

The Court concluded in *Kennedy* as follows:

> In the circumstances, the Court considers that the domestic law on interception of internal communications together with the clarifications brought by the publication of the Code indicate with sufficient clarity the procedures for the authorisation and processing of interception warrants as well as the processing, communicating and destruction of intercept material collected . . . Having regard to the safeguards against abuse in the procedures as well as the more general safeguards offered by the supervision of the Commissioner and the review of the [tribunal], the impugned surveillance measures, insofar as they may have been applied to the applicant in the circumstances outlined in the present case, are justified under Art 8 § 2.[201]

The *Kennedy* case therefore established that the general legal framework of RIPA was compatible with Art 8.

The reasoning in *Kennedy* was applied in *Re RA* in relation to covert surveillance.[202] R, who had been detained by the police, requested that they provide an assurance that consultations with his solicitor would not be monitored by covert surveillance. When the police refused to give such an assurance he sought a declaration that the use of covert surveillance to monitor consultations with his solicitor in the police station would be unlawful. R claimed that the terminology of 'exceptional and compelling circumstances' for making an authorisation under the revised code was not sufficiently clearly defined, and that there was no adequate guidance as to how legally privileged confidential information was secured and destroyed.

The High Court dismissed his application on the basis that it was clearly established that a surveillance operation that was likely to reveal matters covered by legal privilege could be properly authorised only where it was justified as a proportionate response to

---

195 *Ibid*, para 163.
196 Appl 36662/04, judgment of 31 July 2012.
197 In other words, that intercept material must be destroyed as soon as there are no longer any grounds, under s 5(3) RIPA (national security etc), for retaining it.
198 *Kennedy v UK, op cit*, paras 164–168.
199 *Ibid.*
200 *Ibid*, para 167.
201 *Ibid*, para 168.
202 *RA's Application for Judicial Review, Re* [2010] NIQB 99.

a high degree of risk of harm to another or to national security and the 'potential useful-ness of the surveillance was demonstrably shown'.[203] It was found that the wording of the revised code, taking into account the oversight provided by the Surveillance Com-missioner, and the ultimate protection provided by the Investigatory Powers Tribunal, provided an adequate safeguard.[204] The judge reached the same conclusion as regards the guidelines relating to the retention, storage and destruction of such data, again noting the commissioner's involvement in overseeing the regime.[205] However, the judge also found that the statutory regime under Part I RIPA was more detailed, prescriptive and precise than that governing covert surveillance.[206]

The tribunal applied *Kennedy* in the extremely significant *Liberty*[207] litigation as regards the legal basis for the issuance of controversial warrants for the bulk interception of commu-nications data, that legitimised the siphoning of large amounts of telecommunications data by GCHQ. The existence of this operation was revealed in files leaked by Edward Snowden and the challenge was brought by several campaign groups, including Liberty. Bulk warrants were found to be lawful only when they comply strictly with the RIPA framework. It was found that the material could only be *accessed* lawfully if it is necessary (on the s 5(3) grounds: interests of national security etc) and proportionate and, after being accessed, was then subject to the same rules of limited data retention, destruction, processing, storage and review to which other forms of intercept material was subject.[208] The tribunal found that the difference between the bulk warrant and other warrants designed to acquire surveillance material is that at the *point of interception* there is no differentiation between material that would be intercepted lawfully or unlawfully. The tribunal found that it was neither neces-sary nor possible to effect such a differentiation at the interception stage.[209] The tribunal also found, significantly, that judicial authorisation of such warrants was not required by Art 8.[210]

The tribunal subsequently found that the retention of intercept material relating to two claimants was unlawful.[211] The complained of interception in that case concerned a bulk interception warrant relating, in particular, to e-mail correspondence of the claim-ants.[212] The tribunal was not permitted to disclose full details of the surveillance opera-tion, but it was able to disclose the fact that e-mail correspondence of the claimants had been unlawfully retained by GCHQ.[213]

Legitimate aim and necessary in a democratic society

If an interference is 'in accordance with the law', it must have a legitimate aim. The legitimate aims under Art 8(2), are very broad and echo those used under s 5(3). Thus, this requirement is readily satisfied in the surveillance context.

---

203 *Ibid*, [17]. See *Covert surveillance and property interference* 2014 para 4.12.
204 *Ibid*, [17]–[18]. Applying *Kennedy v United Kingdom* (2011) 52 EHRR 4.
205 *Ibid*, [24].
206 *Ibid*.
207 *Liberty & Others vs. the Security Service, SIS, GCHQ*, IPT/13/77/H, 5 December 2015.
208 *Ibid*, para 160.
209 *Ibid*, paras 94–95, 101.
210 *Ibid*, para 116(vi).
211 *Liberty and others v SSHD* [2015] UKIPTrib 13_77-H_2.
212 *Ibid*, paras 14–15.
213 *Ibid*.

The Court has interpreted 'necessary in a democratic society' as meaning: 'an interference corresponds to a pressing social need and, in particular, that it is proportionate to the legitimate aim pursued'.[214] The scrutiny of proportionality in a particular instance, as Chapters 2 and 4 indicated, is strongly linked to the extent of the margin of appreciation conceded to the state. In relation to the aim of national security and prevention of serious crime, the Court has allowed a very wide margin to the state.[215] It is less wide in relation to the prevention of crime in general and arguably also in respect of the other grounds. While the margin of appreciation should be irrelevant in domestic determinations of proportionality, in practice a broad margin of appreciation at Strasbourg tends to result in a deferential judicial analysis of proportionality by domestic judges.[216]

The tribunal has generally avoided close consideration of the necessity and proportionality of surveillance, which is believed to be necessary on grounds of the prevention of serious crime or a threat to national security. However, the tribunal has closely scrutinised the proportionality of authorisations relating to directed surveillance where such grounds are not raised. In *Paton v Poole Borough Council*[217] a complaint was brought by Ms Paton against the use of surveillance consisting of having an education officer watch her and her property for 22 days from the street (both in drive-by sightings of the property and from a parked car) including following her, and her children, on a short drive to a school. The use of covert surveillance was authorised in order to determine whether Ms Paton had supplied a fraudulent address so that she could enrol her children in a favourable school.[218]

The complainants argued that the authorisation of such surveillance was unnecessary to demonstrate that Ms Paton had provided a fraudulent address. The tribunal agreed, especially as regards the surveillance regarding her children.[219] The tribunal found that the council had failed to consider whether a less intrusive measures of establishing the veracity of Ms Paton's claim than covert surveillance were available.[220] As regards proportionality, the complainants argued that the fundamental nature of the intrusion into their private lives outweighed the public interest in preventing or detecting the giving of a false address to the council to gain a school place, and that the extent of the surveillance operation (for a prolonged period and including children) was not rationally connected to that public interest and were a disproportionate means for achieving it.[221] The tribunal accepted that the inclusion of Ms Paton's children and the lack of consideration given to the fact that investigation of the offence would necessarily result in placing them under surveillance, was disproportionate and thus an interference with the complainant's Art 8 right.[222]

---

214 *Olsson v Sweden* A 130 (1988), para 67.
215 See e.g., in the counter-terrorism context: DeHert, D, and Boehm, F, 'The right of notification after surveillance is over: ready for recognition?' (2012) *Digital Enlightenment Yearbook* 19 at 26.
216 See e.g., Keene, D, 'Principles of Deference under the Human Rights Act', in Fenwick, Phillipson and Masterman (eds), *Judicial Reasoning under the Human Rights Act*, CUP, Cambridge.
217 IPT/09/01/C, 29 July 2010.
218 *Ibid*, para 13.
219 *Ibid*, para 68.
220 *Ibid*, para 69.
221 *Ibid*, para 72.
222 *Ibid*, para 73.

6 The Investigatory Powers Bill 2015

New powers to collect data were referred to briefly in the 2015 Queen's speech and will arise under the Investigatory Powers Bill 2015–16. The bill was to cover powers that would have arisen under the Communications and Data Bill, often referred to as the 'snoopers' charter', and the Data Retention and Investigatory Powers Act 2014 (which was disapplied in so far as it was incompatible with EU law, although the disapplication was delayed).[223] The new bill goes much further than requiring private companies to retain communications data, and will increase the security services' warranted powers for the mass interception of the content of communications.

The new legislation will require data communications companies to store the details of messages sent on social media and gaming, voice calls made over the internet, e-mails and phone calls – known collectively as metadata – for 12 months (replacing s 1(5) Data Retention and Investigatory Powers Act 2014). It will probably require that the information is stored in a common format data in vast databases; the security services and police would be able to access this meta-data, albeit with the permission of a judge, in the interests of investigating criminal or terrorist-related activity. The bill aims to address the fact that terrorist and other organised criminal groups are increasingly exploiting available communications technology in a range of sophisticated ways; for instance, by using encryption, and communicating via platforms such as WhatsApp and Snapchat.

The Bill is likely to reflect recommendations by the Intelligence and Security Committee (ISC),[224] and possibly also the Independent Terrorism Legislation Reviewer, David Anderson,[225] who have both recently issued special reports on the legal framework for data retention and investigatory powers. Their recommendation is that the current legal framework for surveillance and communications data collation by public authorities and private companies should be replaced by a new comprehensive Act of Parliament.

The ISC's proposal for the new bill is that it 'must clearly set out the intrusive powers available to the Agencies, the purposes for which they may use them, and the authorisation required before they may do so'.[226] The ISC's report proposed that the most intrusive activities should continue to be authorised by ministers, not by judges.[227] That was viewed as justified on the basis that ministers are able to take into account the wider context of each warrant application and the risks involved. The terrorism legislation reviewer, David Anderson, on the other hand, proposed radically extending judicial authorisation and the scope of the reconstituted tribunal's powers generally in order to ensure that access to surveillance material and communications data generally is only

---

223 Until 31 March 2016. See *R (Davis) v Secretary of State for the Home Department* [2015] EWHC 2092 (Admin). The decision followed the ECJ's finding that Directive 2006/24 was invalid in *Digital Rights Ireland Ltd v Minister for Communications, Marine and Natural Resources* (C-293/12) [2015] QB 127.

224 Intelligence and Security Committee 'Privacy and Security: A Modern and Transparent Legal Framework,' HC 1075, 12 March 2015.

225 Anderson, D, 'A question of trust: report of the investigatory powers review,' June 2015; see at https://terrorismlegislationreviewer.independent.gov.uk.

226 *Op cit*, p 2.

227 *Ibid*, p 75, para FF.

warranted in accordance with the requirements of Art 8.[228] It remains to be seen which view will prevail in the final bill.

7 Conclusion

The democratic values enshrined in the Convention demand that citizens in a democracy should be able to feel confident that surveillance and interception by the state is undertaken for appropriate ends, by proportionate means and with respect for privacy. The HRA aroused the expectation, not only that a new comprehensive statutory basis for invasion of privacy would be introduced, but that it would be underpinned by Convention principles.[229] It is contended that the RIPA framework, unlike its predecessors, does not merely create an appearance of lawfulness and proportionality but rather creates a degree of genuine judicial scrutiny. Judicial evaluation of state surveillance operations in terms of their compatibility with the Art 8 requirements of lawfulness, necessity and proportionality occurs, in the single tribunal, albeit generally without public disclosure of its reasoning. The tribunal operates like a court in many respects; it can award damages and make findings as regards unlawful activity. However, a striking feature of the RIPA is the determination evinced under it to prevent citizens invoking Convention rights in the ordinary courts against state bodies in respect of the profound threat to privacy represented by state surveillance.[230]

The imperfect nature of the extra-judicial elements of the RIPA framework was starkly revealed by the documents leaked by Edward Snowden in 2013. Surveillance by means of either bulk interception of communications data or by automatic storage of such data represents a threat to privacy on a scale much greater than was contemplated when RIPA was passed. There is therefore broad agreement that a comprehensive framework governing surveillance and communications data acquisition in general is now necessary. The new Investigatory Powers Bill will seek to provide a clear legal basis for the collation of communications data, and it is expected that it will repeal RIPA. However, it remains to be seen whether it will also address the failures of accountability that resulted in the British public learning about the existence of GCHQ's bulk-surveillance operation from a foreign source. The task of subjecting surveillance operations to judicial evaluation of their lawfulness and proportionality should therefore be expanded in the new bill if it is to fully meet the requirements of Art 8, particularly in relation to the authorisation of exceptional surveillance measures, in particular the bulk-interception of communications.

228 *Op cit* para 36.
229 This was the expectation of the Justice report, *Under Surveillance*, 1998.
230 For further discussion, see Akdeniz, Y, Taylor, N, and Walker, C, 'RIPA (1): State surveillance in the age of information and rights' [2001] Crim LR 73.

Part IV

Personal liberty

Part IV considers the extent to which agents of the state have the power to interfere with individual liberty and freedom of movement in the name of the prevention of crime, in order to counter terrorism, and to preserve national security. Chapters 12, 13 and 14 consider police powers and safeguards for suspects. Chapter 15 covers a range of counter-terrorism provisions, including non-trial-based measures, and special terrorism offences, introduced to address the threat of terrorism, especially post 9/11, and 7/7, and in particular the threat represented by Islamic or extreme right-wing terrorism.

In the case of police powers to stop, search, arrest, detain and question, it can be said that there has been a marked tendency to increase the discretion of the police to interfere with liberty, stemming mainly from the changes made by the Police and Criminal Evidence Act 1984, the Criminal Justice and Public Order Act 1994, the Terrorism Act 2000, the Serious and Organised Crime Act 2005. The ordinary courts over the past 15 years, after the HRA came into force, have had the opportunity to apply the ECHR (in particular Art 5, the right to liberty and security) directly to considerations of police uses of coercive power in the contexts in question, usually in judicial review proceedings, or in the course of the criminal process. But, clearly, prior to the inception of the the Human Rights Act 1998 (HRA), the judges and Parliament already had common law principles of protection for liberty in mind in relation to the exercise of police powers. Thus in relation to the commonly used powers – particularly powers used in the context of street policing – the HRA was always likely to have a muted impact. Nevertheless, the HRA has to an extent proved a corrective to the authoritarian tendency of the statutory schemes and has at times provided a check on the arbitrary use of state power, as have common law rights-based principles.

In the case of counter-terrorist powers, considered in Chapter 15, complex statutory schemes put in place under previous Conservative governments were built upon and extended by the Labour governments of 1987–2010. The wide range of counter-terror measures then in existence were added to and previous non-trial-based measures were used as models, by the Coalition government 2010–15, and now by the Conservative government, with the result that a very wide range of broad counter-terror powers is now in existence in 2016, although certain of the most repressive ones are no longer in place, partly due to the impact of the ECHR. Clear tensions can be discerned between a number of the statutory provisions considered in Chapter 15 and the ECHR scheduled in the Human Rights Act. That includes provisions arising from the Terrorism Act 2000 as amended, the Prevention of Terrorism Act 2005, the Terrorism Act 2006, the Terrorism Prevention and Investigation Measures Act (TPIMA) 2011, the Counter-Terrorism and Security Act 2015. As will be discussed, the Anti-Terrorism, Crime and Security

Act 2001 Part 4, which allowed for the detention without trial for non-British citizens suspected of terrorism, with appeal to the Special Immigration Appeals Commission (SIAC, discussed in Chapter 15) represented the culmination of the previous Labour government's tendency to introduce provisions in severe tension with human rights' values. It was only possible to declare the 2001 Bill compatible with the Convention by derogating from Art 5 in respect of Part 4. That detention scheme was abandoned since it was found by the House of Lords to contravene the European Convention on Human Rights, Articles 5 and 14, in the seminal decision in *A and Others v Secretary of State for the Home Dept.*[1] The derogation was not found to be justified since it went further than demanded by the exigencies of the situation. The ECHR also had an impact in ameliorating control orders under the Prevention of Terrorism Act 2005, and on their replacement under the Terrorism Prevention and Investigation Measures Act (TPIMA) 2011 (TPIMs). Under the Conservative government from 2015 onwards control orders have not been reintroduced; reliance is still being placed on more human rights-compatible TPIMs, but they have recently been re-strengthened under the Counter-terrorism and Security Act 2015.

The Labour government that took power in 1987 embarked on a programme of constitutional reform which included introducing the HRA; the Coalition government from 2010–15 did not seek to repeal the HRA, despite the Conservative stance on that issue, as discussed in Chapter 3;[2] the current Conservative government, which took office in 2015, intends to introduce a British Bill of Rights, which will still protect all the ECHR rights. But more significant than these measures is the dominance of the executive over Parliament. That tends to mean that provisions invading personal liberty can be introduced, especially in the area of counter-terrorism, without a very significant parliamentary check. The HRA is aimed at the responsibility of the state (in the form of public authorities), not at non-state actors such as terrorist groups. Serious crime and acts of terrorism may amount to rights violations;[3] whether that is the case or not it is irrelevant to the impact on the victim that harms caused by terrorism or crime are caused by non-state actors. Even if such harms are not addressed via human rights' law, protection is offered to victims and potential victims via criminal laws and counter-terror laws enforced by the police and other state agents deploying the powers discussed below.

Against that back-drop, the following chapters trace the responses of Parliament and the judges to the need to balance the needs of crime control, of national security, of potential victims of crime or terrorist attacks, with the interest of citizens generally and suspects in personal liberty and due process.

---

1 (2004) UKHL 56; [2005] 2 AC 68; [2005] 2 WLR 87; [2005] 3 All ER 169. See Chapter 15, pp 1027–28.
2 See Chapter 3, p 124–26.
3 See H Duffy 'The "War on Terror" and the Framework of International Law' 2nd edn, 2015, pp487–489.

Chapter 12

Police powers of stop, search, arrest, detention

1 Introduction

Crime control and due process

The exercise of police powers such as arrest and detention represents an invasion of personal liberty and privacy that is most frequently justified in the interests of personal safety and security, the prevention and detection of crime or of terrorist activity. However, the interest in personal liberty necessitates that such powers should be strictly regulated. Here it may appear that the conflict between due process and police powers creating crime control comes into sharp relief. The rights-based due process model seeks to recognise the 'primacy of the individual and the complementary concept of limitation of official power'.[1] It calls for the police to be subject to tightly defined and rigorous control and for clear, legally guaranteed safeguards for suspects, with clear remedies for abuse through the courts.[2] In contrast, the crime control model values a 'quick, accurate and efficient administrative fact-finding role . . . over slow, inefficient, and less accurate judicial trials' in order to achieve 'the dominant goal of repressing crime'.[3] However, the goals of crime control and of due process are not ultimately divergent since both are aimed at preserving personal security, safety and liberty by bringing the guilty into a criminal process regulated as would be expected in a democracy, while discarding the innocent as rapidly as possible from it. Thus, while the discussion below relies on notions of due process and of crime control, the degree to which their aims are *not* in conflict should be borne in mind.

---

1 Packer, H, *The Limits of the Criminal Sanction*, 1968, Stanford University Press. As Walker puts it: 'The primacy of individual autonomy and rights is central to the due process model', *Miscarriages of Justice*, 1999, p 39.
2 See further Baldwin, R, 'Taking rules to excess: police powers and the Police and Criminal Evidence Bill 1984', in Brenton, M and Jones, C (eds), *The Year Book of Social Policy in Britain 1984–85*, 1985, Routledge, pp 9–29; Jones, P, 'Police powers and political accountability: the Royal Commission on Criminal Procedure'; Hillyard, P, 'From Belfast to Britain: some critical comments on the Royal Commission on Criminal Procedure', both in *Politics and Power*, Vol 4, 1981; Jefferson, T, 'Policing the miners: law, politics and accountability', in Brenton, M and Ungerson, C (eds), *The Year Book of Social Policy in Britain 1985–86*, 1986, pp 265–86.
3 Packer, *ibid*, (1968).

Current analysis of aspects of the criminal justice system continues to rely quite heavily on the two familiar models of crime control and due process.[4] But while a rhetorical commitment to due process is still evident,[5] there is a perception that the law in practice does not always currently reflect this model. Sanders and Young have found: 'Police and Court officials need not abuse the law to subvert the principles of justice; they need only use it.'[6] However, as a number of scholars have argued, the impact of externally imposed rules on actual police practice is at times limited, variable and uncertain;[7] in particular, researchers have highlighted the problems of rule-evasion – the avoidance of apparent safeguards through the use of informal practices[8] – and of deterring such practices.[9]

The Police and Criminal Evidence Act 1984: context[10]

Before the inception of the Police and Criminal Evidence Act 1984 (PACE), police powers arose from a mixture of common law and statute. PACE was introduced in order

4　Packer, *ibid* e.g., the two models are extensively relied on in Walker, C and Starmer, K (eds), *Miscarriages of Justice*, 1999. For discussion and criticism of the two models, see Sanders and Young, *Criminal Justice*, 2010, Chapter 1.

5　See, e.g., *Legislation Against Terrorism: A Consultation Paper*, Cm 4178, 1998, esp para 8 of the Introduction.

6　Sanders and Young, *op cit*, fn 4, p 20, 2nd edn, 2000. (Current edn 2010.)

7　See: the PSI Report's distinction between Presentational, Inhibitory and Working Rules; Dixon, D, *Law and Policing: Legal Regulation and Police Practices*, 1997, Clarendon.

8　See, e.g., Goldsmith, A, 'Taking police culture seriously: police discretion and the limits of the law' (1990) Policing and Society Vol 1, pp 91–114.

9　There is some evidence that use of exclusion of evidence may encourage police officers to observe suspects' rights. See Orfield, JR, 'The exclusionary rule and deterrence: an empirical study of Chicago narcotics officers' (1987) 54 U Chicago L Rev 1016–69. In the context of PACE, this finding receives some support from research by Sanders, Bridges, Mulvaney and Crozier entitled 'Advice and assistance at police stations', November 1989; it was thought that unlawful denials of legal advice had been discouraged by the ruling in *R v Samuel* [1988] 2 All ER 135 (see p 931 *et seq*, below). The research found that in 1987, before the ruling, delay was authorised in around 50% of applicable cases; in 1990–91, in only one case out of 10,000. Such evidence cannot, however, be treated as conclusive of the issue; apart from other factors, police officers will be aware that the question of exclusion of evidence is unlikely to arise since the case is unlikely to come to a full trial; even if it does arise, a conviction may still be obtained. Any deterrent effect is therefore likely to be undermined

10　For comment on PACE and the Terrorism Act 2000, and on the relevant provisions under the Criminal Justice and Public Order Act 1994, see: Zander, M, *Zander on PACE: The Police and Criminal Evidence Act 1984* 2015; Stone, R, *The Law of Entry, Search and Seizure*, 5th edn, 2012; Sanders, A and Young, R, *Criminal Justice*, 4th edn, 2010; Bailey, S, Taylor, N, *Bailey, Harris and Jones: Civil Liberties: Cases and Materials*, 6th edn, 2009, Chapter 2; Clark, D, *Bevan and Lidstone's The Investigation of Crime*, 2004; Ashworth, A, *The Criminal Process*, 3rd edn, 2005; Feldman, D, *Civil Liberties and Human Rights in England and Wales*, 2nd edn, 2002, Chapters 5 and 9. For background reading, see: Hewitt, P, *The Abuse of Power*, 1982, Chapter 3; Lustgarten, L, *The Governance of Police*, 1986, Sweet and Maxwell; Leigh, LH, *Police Powers in England and Wales*, 2nd edn, 1985, Butterworths; Robilliard, J and McEwan, J, *Police Powers and the Individual*, 1986, Blackwell; Benyon, J and Bourn, CJ, *The Police: Powers, Procedures and Proprieties*, 1986, Pergamon. For very early comment on the Police and Criminal Evidence Act, see [1985] PL 388; [1985] Crim LR 535. See also: McConville, M, Sanders, A and Leng, R, *The Case for the Prosecution*, 1991, Routledge; Reiner, R and Leigh, LH, 'Police powers', in McCrudden, C and Chambers, G (eds), *Individual Rights and the Law in Britain*, 1994, Clarendon; Klug, F, Starmer, K and Weir, S, *The Three Pillars of Liberty*, 1996.

to provide clear and general police powers, but these were supposed to be balanced by greater safeguards for suspects which took into account the need to ensure that miscarriages of justice[11] would not recur. The Royal Commission on Criminal Procedure,[12] whose report influenced PACE, was established largely in response to the inadequacies of safeguards for suspects which were exposed in the *Confait* report.[13]

The result was a statutory scheme in which the broad discretionary powers granted were to be balanced by three central structuring constraints. First, there were general precedent conditions for the exercise of such powers, the most common and significant being the requirement of reasonable suspicion or belief. Second, there was the provision of specific countervailing due process rights, in particular a general right of custodial access to legal advice, in most cases laid down in, or underpinned by, quasi- and non-legal rules – the codes of practice and notes for guidance made under PACE.[14] Thirdly the discretionary powers of the police were to be subject to bureaucratic oversight and control. Redress for breaches of the due process safeguards was largely to be within the disciplinary rather than the judicial sphere: breach of the codes at the inception of PACE constituted *automatically* a breach of the police disciplinary Code.[15] That is no longer the case, as discussed below, although breach of the codes can be taken into account in disciplinary proceedings.

Throughout the eighties the drift towards further crime control but combined with increased managerialism continued. Notwithstanding the discovery of further miscarriages of justice – the cases of the *Birmingham Six*,[16] the *Guildford Four*,[17] *Judith Ward*,[18] *Stefan Kiszko*,[19] the *Tottenham Three*,[20] the *Maguire Seven*[21] – and the renewal of due process concerns, the subsequent establishment of another Royal Commission under Lord Runciman in 1992[22] was focused on further measures that could be introduced to improve the efficacy of the criminal justice system in terms of securing the conviction of the guilty and the acquittal of the innocent.[23] Once again, a royal commission was seeking to reconcile potentially conflicting aims – concern to protect due process, but also to further crime control. However, as a number of commentators have observed, not only was the former part of this remit largely swallowed up in

11 See Report of the Inquiry by the Hon Sir Henry Fisher, HC 90 of 1977–78.
12 Royal Commission on Criminal Procedure Report, Cmnd 8092, 1981 (RCCP Report).
13 Report of the Inquiry by the Hon Sir Henry Fisher, HC 90 of 1977–78.
14 PACE 1984, s 66, Codes of Practice.
15 *Ibid*, s 67(8).
16 See *R v McIlkenny and Others* [1992] 2 All ER 417.
17 See May, J (Sir), *Report of the Inquiry into the Circumstances Surrounding the Convictions Arising out of the Bomb Attacks at Guildford and Woolwich in 1974, Final Report*, 1993–94 HC 449, Chapter 17.
18 *R v Ward* (1992) 96 Cr App R 1.
19 (1992) *The Times*, 18 February.
20 (1991) *The Times*, 9 December.
21 See *R v Maguire* [1992] 2 All ER 433.
22 Runciman Report, Cm 2263, 1993, Chapter 1, para 5; Royal Commission on Criminal Procedure chaired by Lord Runciman; it was announced by the Home Secretary on 14 March 1991, HC Deb Vol 187 col 1109. It reported on 6 July 1993; see (1993) 143 NLJ 933–96 for a summary of its recommendations in respect of police investigations, safeguards for suspects, the right to silence and confession evidence.
23 Effectiveness in securing 'the conviction of those guilty of criminal offences and the acquittal of those who are innocent', Runciman Report, *ibid*, Chapter 1, para 5.

the latter,[24] it failed to articulate a principled account of investigative procedures. It may be said that since 1979 two opposing forces have been at work in the context of criminal justice. On the one hand there has been periodic concern about due process safeguards, particularly in the wake of miscarriages of justice. But on the other the dominant drive has been a political and legislative drift towards crime control values, and powers to counter terrorist activity, especially post-9/11. That drift has also been accompanied by an increase in managerialism, linked to an extent to preserving due process, as exemplified in the increasingly complex provisions of the PACE codes of practice, as discussed below.

The structure of the PACE rules

At present, the rules governing the exercise of police powers are largely, not wholly, contained in the scheme created under PACE, as amended, which is made up of rules deriving from the Act itself, from the codes of practice made under it, and the notes for guidance contained in the codes. It is also influenced by Home Office circulars. The difference in status between these four levels and the significance of adopting this four-tiered approach is considered below. (It should be emphasised at this point that a number of significant police powers are not contained in PACE, as will be indicated.) The PACE pre-trial scheme must be examined in conjunction with the scheme that was created under the Terrorism Act 2000, as amended, with a view to creating at certain points a lesser level of protection for terrorist suspects.

PACE and the codes of practice

Until 2006 there were six codes of practice: Code A, covering stop and search procedures, Code B, covering searching of premises, Code C, covering interviewing and conditions of detention, Code D, covering identification methods and Code E, covering tape recording. Code F covering visual recording of interviews was introduced in 2004, a new version coming into force in 2006. Thus, each covers a particular area of PACE, although not all areas were covered: arrest, for example, was, until 2006, governed only by statutory provisions. The codes have gone through a number of revisions post-PACE, becoming steadily longer and more cumbersome in the process (Code C, for example, now runs to nearly 80 pages). In 2006 new, revised versions of the existing codes came into force and two new codes were also added: Code G covering arrest was introduced, as was a special new Code H. It was introduced to govern the rights of terrorist suspects in police questioning and detention, meaning that the provisions of Code C relating to such suspects were removed, reappearing in a revised form in Code H. There are still as of 2015 eight codes in force, which have been periodically revised.

If safeguards for suspects are taken seriously then why do they largely appear in the codes rather than in PACE itself? It may be asked why all of the stop and search Code rules, for example, were not merely made part of the Act. The answer may partly lie in the need for some flexibility in making changes. The codes are frequently amended. However, it is also probable that the government did not want to create rules that might

---

24 See Sanders, A and Young, R, 'The RCCJ' [1994] 14 OJLS 435; Walker, C and Starmer, K (eds), *Miscarriages of Justice*, 1999, especially p 57.

give rise to liability on the part of the police if they were broken; rules that could operate at a lower level of visibility than statutory ones may have appeared more attractive. It has for some time been apparent that the police powers were contained in PACE, as amended, and other statutes, while suspects' rights were largely, not wholly, contained in the non-statutory codes. That tendency has only become more marked post-PACE. The proliferation of code provisions has not been accompanied by any determination to deal with their very doubtful legal status.[25] At the same time certain safeguards of particular significance have always remained in the statute, in particular the provisions governing time limits on police detention. It is hard to escape the conclusion that most of the safeguards, in particular those surrounding the questioning of suspects (discussed in Chapter 13), contained mainly in Codes C and H, are viewed as of less significance.

Section 67(10) of PACE makes clear the intended distinction between Act and codes in providing that no civil or criminal liability will arise from a breach of the codes. But the question of civil liability in respect of a breach of PACE, as opposed to the codes, is not without difficulty. Liability will arise where a police power is needed in order to render an act non-tortious that would otherwise be tortious. For example, an arrest would give rise to liability for false imprisonment if no power to arrest arose. Certain PACE rules have been treated by the courts as mandatory and therefore adherence to them is necessary in order to render the act in question lawful, as will be discussed below. So breach of certain PACE rules will give rise to civil liability because they operate in the context of existing areas of tortious liability, as discussed in Chapter 14, whereas breach of the Codes cannot give rise to liability, even within that context. To that extent they are somewhat parasitic.

This distinction is of significance in relation to the stop and search, search of premises, arrest and detention provisions of Parts I–IV of PACE,[26] in comparison with the Code provisions in those areas, in Codes A, B and G. However, this distinction does not seem to have any significance as far as the interviewing provisions of Part V are concerned. The most important statutory safeguard for interviewing, the entitlement to legal advice, has not been affected by the availability of tortious remedies.[27] Thus statutory and code provisions concerned with safeguards for suspects in police interviewing are in an equally weak position in the sense that a clear remedy is not available if they are breached. However, following the Strasbourg Court's decision in *Salduz v Turkey*[28] holding that Art 6 contains an implied right to custodial legal advice necessary to protect

---

25   In *Delaney* (1989) 88 Cr App R 338; (1988) *The Times*, 20 August, CA, the status of the codes was considered. It was held that the mere fact that there had been a breach of the Codes of Practice did not of itself mean that evidence had to be rejected. Section 67(11) of the Act provides that 'if any provision of such Code appears to the court . . . to be relevant to any question arising in the proceedings, it shall be taken into account in determining that question'.

26   In that respect, such claims are significant. For discussion of the use of tortious claims in this context, see Chapter 14, p 1003 *et seq.*

27   The question whether an unlawful denial of access to legal advice amounts to a breach of statutory duty was considered in an unreported case, 26 October 1985, QB (Rose J), which is cited by Clayton, R and Tomlinson, H in *Civil Actions Against the Police*, 1st edn, 1992, p 359. It was held that the application would be refused even if jurisdiction to make the order sought existed as it would 'cause hindrance to police inquiries'.

28   [2007] ECHR 36391/02.

the rights of the defence a further avenue of challenge opened up under the HRA.[29] The context in which breaches of the interviewing provisions *has* been considered is that of exclusion of evidence, discussed in Chapter 14.[30] In that context, the courts have not drawn a clear distinction between the provisions of the Act or of the codes, except to require that breach of a code provision should be of a substantial and significant nature[31] if exclusion of evidence is to be considered.

Notes for guidance

The notes for guidance are contained in the codes but are not part of them.[32] They were apparently intended, as their name suggests, to be used merely as interpretative provisions and, it appears, to have no legal status at all. However, as will be seen, they contain some very significant provisions, although it is unclear what the consequences of breach of a note are. Evidence tainted by breach of a note for guidance is unlikely to be excluded since, unlike Code provisions, s 67(11) of PACE does not require a court to take the notes into account in determining any question.[33] However, in *DPP v Blake*,[34] the Divisional Court impliedly accepted that a note for guidance should be considered in relation to exclusion of evidence if it can be argued that it merely amplifies a particular code provision and can therefore be of assistance in determining whether breach of such a provision has occurred. Moreover, certain notes need not merely be considered in conjunction with the code paragraph they derive from; the ruling in *DPP v Rouse* and *DPP v Davis*[35] that they can sometimes be used as an aid to the interpretation of Code C as a whole extended their potential impact. Thus the courts have partially made up for another deficiency of the codes.

It may be said that the notes are of a very uncertain legal status but that their importance has been recognised in certain decisions as to admission of evidence. These decisions clearly raise the question why important safeguards were placed in the notes at all.

Obstruction or assault on a police officer in the course of his duty

A number of the powers discussed below may be discussed within the contexts of the offences of assault on or obstruction of an officer in the course of his duty. The formal position remains unchanged – police officers have no right to detain and search or question

---

29 See *Cadder v Lord Advocate* [2010] UKSC 43.
30 See p 963 *et seq*.
31 Breach of a code provision is quite frequently taken into account in determining whether or not a confession should be excluded, usually under PACE, s 78. Breach of a code provision will not lead to automatic exclusion of an interview obtained thereby, but a substantial and significant breach may be the first step on the way to its exclusion (see *Walsh* [1989] Crim LR 822, CA, transcript from LEXIS). See also Chapter 14, p 982 *et seq*.
32 *Keenan* [1989] 3 All ER 598, CA.
33 PACE 1984, s 67(11) provides: 'In all criminal and civil proceedings any such code shall be admissible in evidence; and if any provision of such a code appears to the court or tribunal conducting the proceedings to be relevant to any question arising in the proceedings it shall be taken into account in determining that question.'
34 [1989] 1 WLR 432, CA.
35 (1992) Cr App R 185.

a person in the absence of specific statutory powers allowing them to do so. While it might be considered desirable on the one hand that the police should be able to make contact with citizens in order to make general inquiries without invoking any specific powers, on the other, citizens should not in law be bound to reply to such inquiries. Thus neither refusing to answer police questions nor advising another not to answer will constitute obstruction.[36] A police officer can ask a citizen to refrain from doing something, but in general, the citizen may refuse if the action is not in itself unlawful. If this were not the case, there would be little need for other specific powers; an officer could, for example, merely ask a person to submit to a search and if he refused, warn him that he could be charged with obstruction.

However, some otherwise lawful behaviour, including failure to obey a police officer, may bring a citizen within the ambit of the offence of obstruction of a constable which arises under s 89(2) of the Police Act 1996 (formerly under s 51(3) of the Police Act 1964), and therefore, the way it has been interpreted determines the borderline between legitimate and illegitimate disobedience to police instructions or requests.[37] Section 89(2) creates an area of liability independent of any other substantive offence. Behaviour is criminalised in relation to police officers which would not give rise to criminal liability if directed at any other group of persons. Thus, some contacts between police officer and citizen may result in the creation of liability where, otherwise, none would have existed.[38]

Following *Rice v Connolly*,[39] three tests must be satisfied if liability for this offence is to be made out. First, it must be shown that the constable was in the execution of his or her duty. Actions outside an officer's duty would seem to include any action which is unlawful or contrary to Home Office circulars[40] or the codes of practice. Secondly, it must be shown that the defendant did an act which made it more difficult for the officer to carry out her or his duty. Third it must, finally, be shown, following *Lewis v Cox*,[41] that the defendant behaved wilfully in the sense that he acted deliberately with the knowledge and intention that he would obstruct the police officer. A defendant may be 'wilful' even though his purpose is to pursue some private objective of his own, rather than to obstruct the officer, so long as his act is deliberate and he realises that it will in fact impede the officer. This will be the case, according to *Hills v Ellis*, even if the purpose of the defendant is to help the officer.[42] If a person physically resists an arrest or stop in the belief that it is unlawful, he may incur liability under the offence of assault on a constable in the execution of duty which now arises under s 89(1) of the Police Act 1996. Liability may arise even though the defendant is unaware that the person he is assaulting is a police officer.[43]

---

36 *Rice v Connelly* [1966] 2 QB 414. *Green v DPP* (1991) 155 JP 816.
37 See *Home Secretary ex p Westminster Press Ltd* (1991) the *Guardian*, 12 February; *Secretary of State for the Home Dept ex p Lancashire Police Authority* (1992) *The Times*, 26 May.
38 This point was made in Wolchover, D and Heaton-Armstrong, A, 'The questioning Code revamped' [1991] Crim LR 232, with reference to the revision of Code C.
39 [1966] 2 QB 414; [1966] All ER 649; [1966] 3 WLR 17, DC.
40 In *Collins v Wilcock* [1984] 3 All ER 374; [1984] 1 WLR 1172 a police officer wrongly interpreted a Home Office circular; her actions in reliance on the incorrect interpretation were held to be outside the execution of her duty.
41 (1985) Cr App R 1.
42 *Hills v Ellis* [1983] QB 680. See also *Wilmott v Atack* [1977] QB 498; [1976] 3 All ER 794.
43 *Forbes* (1865) 10 Cox CC 362; for criticism, see Williams, G *Textbook of Criminal Law*, 1983, p 200.

2 Stop and search powers

Introduction[44]

The PACE stop and search powers were intended to maintain a fair balance between the interests of individuals and society, as represented by the police, in personal security and crime control, and the interest of the citizen in personal liberty. Under the due process model, detention short of arrest – usually, although not invariably, exercised in the form of stop and search powers – should be based on reasonable suspicion relating to the specific actions of an individual. Under the crime control model, such detention is viewed as an investigative tool which should be based on general police experience; inhibitory rules should be kept to a minimum in order to allow police officers to act on instinct; police discretion should be the guiding principle. The use of such powers is currently viewed as a necessary part of effective modern policing. It has been argued that much policing is reactive; it is initiated by civilians[45] and therefore the nature of stop and search powers assumes less significance, but this argument is clearly open to question.[46] At the present time the growth of intelligence-led policing[47] especially in the context of terrorism, has led to a more proactive stance, which is tending to enhance the importance and use of stop and search powers. The powers represent less of an infringement of liberty than an arrest, but on the other hand their exercise may create a sense of grievance and of violation of personal privacy.[48] Such feelings may contribute to the alienation of the police from the community, leading to a breakdown in law and order expressed in its most extreme form in rioting,[49] and otherwise in a general lack of cooperation with the police, affecting the acquisition of intelligence. Thus, the extensiveness of stop and search powers may tell us something about the extent to which UK society values individual liberty; too great an infringement of liberty may be as likely to result ultimately in less effective crime control as in too great a restriction of police powers.

The use of these powers remains a contentious matter that continues to attract public attention, especially as it has frequently been suggested that they may be used in a

44 For further comment on PACE and the Terrorism Act 2000, and on the relevant provisions under the Criminal Justice and Public Order Act 1994, see for example Sanders, A and Young, R, *Criminal Justice*, 4th edn, 2010, Zander, M, *Zander on PACE: The Police and Criminal Evidence Act 1984*, 2015.

45 See Shapland, J and Vagg, J, *Policing by the Public*, 1988, Routledge.

46 In 1993–94, 24% of arrests resulted from proactive policing including stopping and searching: Phillips, C and Brown, D, *Home Office Research Study No 185*, 1998. Contemporary stopping and searching appears to play a lesser part in arrests (see n 53 below and associated text).

47 See Sanders, A and Young, R, Burton, M, *Criminal Justice*, 4th edn, 2010, Chapter 2; Ashworth, A, *The Criminal Process*, 3rd edn, 2005; Feldman, D, *Civil Liberties and Human Rights in England and Wales*, 2nd edn, 2002, Chapters 5 and 9; Zander, M, *The Police and Criminal Evidence Act 1984*, 2015; *Home Office Stop and Search Manual*, 2005; Lustgarten, L, 'The future of stop and search' [2003] Crim LR 603.

48 See for discussion Miller, J. (2010) 'Stop and Search in England: A Reformed Tactic or Business as Usual?' *British Journal of Criminology*, 50, 5: 954–74.

49 See, on this point, Lord Scarman, *The Brixton Disorders*, Cmnd 8427, 1981; McConville, M, 'Search of persons and premises' [1983] Crim LR 604–14.

discriminatory fashion.[50] It now appears incontrovertible that racial discrimination – or a form of racial profiling – continues to affect their use, as recently confirmed by the Equality and Human Rights Commission in its 2015 report *Stop and Think*, and by the 2013 HMIC study.[51] The Commission in that report detailed, for example, that an Afro-Caribbean male was six times more likely to be stopped and searched under PACE than a white comparator. A similar pattern of disproportionate stops and searches had been evident for some time. Initially, there was evidence that the use of these powers was regulated as intended. However, the police soon discovered that consensual searches[52] fell outside of the scope of PACE and thus there was no need to follow the procedural safeguards, although under Code A that position has changed in formal terms, as discussed below.

The recorded use of stop and search more than trebled after PACE came into force in 1986 and, as indicated below, a large number of further powers have been introduced in the post-PACE period. One factor influencing the rise in their use may have been the introduction of 'zero tolerance' policies in the mid-1990s. The efficacy of such powers is debatable. Between 2004 and 2015 the arrest rate following a stop and search remained between 9% and 13% of all encounters.[53] These figures do not include stops that did not lead to a search, or voluntary stops, and therefore the percentage of stops leading to an arrest must be lower than this. There are, of course, other methods of measuring the crime control value of stop and search powers; in particular, they have some value in terms of information-gathering and, more controversially, as a means of asserting police authority on the streets.

This proliferation of usage and of powers post-PACE was not accompanied by a full official review of their crime control value or adverse due process impact[54] until the issues were raised in relation to the *Lawrence* case in the MacPherson Report in 1999.[55] MacPherson identified the practice of stop and account as one of the drivers in friction between the police and minority communities. The report recommended that such encounters be recorded. More recently, concern over the alleged misuse of stop and search powers has led to two important inquiries, one by the HMIC and the other by the EHRC – both mentioned above. However, while the use of such powers has been subject to greater scrutiny by some actors in the criminal justice process[56] this has not been matched by the courts. In fact, control by the courts remains largely as it has always been, that is rather permissive. For instance, in *R (Rutherford) v Independent*

---

50 See Bowling, B and Phillips, C, 'Disproportionate and Discriminatory:Reviewing the Evidence on Police Stop and Search' (2007) 70(6) MLR 936–61; Equality and Human Rights Commission (2012) *Race Disproportionality in Stops and Searches under Section 60 of the Criminal Justice and Public Order Act 1994*. EHRC Briefing Paper No 5. Manchester: Equality and Human Rights Commission; http://www.equalityhumanrights.com/publications/our-research/briefing-papers.

51 20 October 2015. See also 'Stop and Search Powers: Are the police using them effectively and fairly?', HMIC 2013.

52 Coleman,C, 'Consent and the Legal Regulation of Policing' (1990) 17 Journal of Law and Society 345, 363. Now prohibited under Code A para 1.5 PACE.

53 The full data, current and historical, can be browsed at https://data.police.uk/data/stop-and-search/.

54 They were outside the remit of the Runciman Royal Commission.

55 Cm 4262-I. (1999); https://www.gov.uk/government/uploads/system/uploads/attachment_data/file/277111/4262.pdf.

56 See for discussion, Miller, J. (2010) 'Stop and Search in England: A Reformed Tactic or Business as Usual?' *British Journal of Criminology*, 50, 5: 954–74; Ellis, D. (2010) 'Stop and Search: Disproportionality, Discretion and Generalisation', *Police Journal*, 83, 3: 199–216.

Police Complaints Commission[57] it was held that there is no requirement for an officer to be aware of the legal origin of a power they purport to be exercising for it to be lawful. We shall return to further instances below.

The PACE stop and search power

There was no general power at common law to detain without the subject's consent in the absence of specific statutory authority.[58] Instead, there was a miscellany of such powers, many of which were superseded by PACE. A large number, however, such as the power to search for firearms under s 47 of the Firearms Act 1968, continued to subsist alongside the PACE power. The Phillips Royal Commission, whose report influenced PACE,[59] recommended the introduction of a new national power, but accepted the need to maintain a balance between the interest of society as represented by the police in crime control, and the interest of the citizen in personal liberty and privacy. This balance was sought to be achieved partly by introducing a reasonable suspicion element into the PACE powers described by the report as the 'principal safeguard'.[60] However, crucially the power was to be surrounded by record-keeping requirements, a scrutiny duty by superior officers, a publication requirement and the provision of a record of the stop and search to be given to the subject of the search.[61] This balanced approach of bureaucracy and due process was thought to be the most effective way of ensuring the lawful use of the new power.

Thus under s 1 of PACE for the first time a general power to stop[62] and search persons (s 1(1)) or vehicles (s 1(2))[63] was conferred on police constables. It arises if the constable forms the reasonable suspicion that stolen goods, or prohibited articles (including offensive weapons)[64] will be found by searching the suspect. It may be that the suspect appears to be in innocent possession of the goods or articles; this does not affect the power to stop, although it would affect the power to arrest; in this sense, the power to stop is broader than the arrest power. Section 4 of PACE enables the police to use their powers under the Road Traffic Act 1988 to set up roadblocks and to stop and search any vehicle to see whether it contains a wanted person.

---

57 [2010] EWHC 2881 (Admin), [18] Ouseley J.
58 For a full list of the powers arising from 16 statutes, see RCCP Report 1981.
59 Cmnd 8092 (1981).
60 Above, para 3.25.
61 Above, para 3.26.
62 It should be noted that the police do not need to search the suspect once he or she has been stopped; they may decide not to. Nevertheless, reasonable suspicion that stolen goods or articles are being carried must arise before the stop can be made. Under Code A 2.11: 'There is no power to stop or detain a person in order to find grounds for a search.'
63 A power to stop vehicles which is not dependent on reasonable suspicion arises under s 163 of the Road Traffic Act 1988. PACE 1984, s 4 regulates it when it is used as the basis for a general road check.
64 Under s 1(7), the articles are '(a) offensive weapons or (b) articles (i) made or adapted for use in the course of or in connection with an offence to which this sub-paragraph applies; or (ii) intended by the person having it with him for such use by him or by some other person'. Under s 1(8), the offences to which s 1(7)(b)(i) above applies are: '(a) burglary; (b) theft; (c) offences under s 12 of the Theft Act 1968; (d) offences under s 15 of that Act.' Section 1(8A) applies 'to [any article which falls within] s 139 of the Criminal Justice Act 1988'. Under s 1(9), offensive weapon means 'any article (a) made or adapted for use for causing injury to persons or (b) intended by the person having it with him for such use by him or by some other person.'

Under s 1(6), if an article is found that appears to be stolen or prohibited, the officer can seize it. The s 1 power may be exercised in any place to which the public, or a section of it, have access (s 1(1)(a)) or in any other place 'to which people have ready access at the time when [the constable] proposes to exercise the power but which is not a dwelling' (s 1(1)(b)). Powers to enter a dwelling arise under ss 17 and 18, but an officer can search a suspect in a garden or yard or other land 'occupied with or used for the purposes of a dwelling' (assuming, of course, that the provision of s 1 as to reasonable suspicion is fulfilled) if it appears that the person does not reside in the dwelling or have the permission of the owner to be there (s 1(4)).

This general power to stop, search and seize is balanced in two ways. First, the concept of reasonable suspicion allows it to be exercised only when a fairly high level of suspicion exists. Secondly, under s 2, the police officer must provide the person to be searched with certain information. These requirements are discussed below.

Power to search for drugs

Section 23 of the Misuse of Drugs Act 1971 provides a stop and search power that is very frequently invoked. Under s 23, a constable may stop and search a person whom the constable has reasonable grounds to suspect is in possession of a controlled drug. This power may be exercised anywhere, unlike the power under s 1 of PACE; thus, persons on private premises may be searched once police officers are lawfully on the premises. The provisions as to reasonable suspicion will be interpreted in accordance with Code A. Code A and ss 2 and 3 of PACE apply to this power as they do to all the other statutory stop and search powers unless specific exceptions are made (see below).

Reasonable suspicion

Reasonable suspicion is a flexible, broad and uncertain concept that has long been recognised as a weak condition precedent.[65] It is, for example, a less stringent standard than 'reasonable grounds for believing'.[66] Code of Practice A on Stop and Search and applying to *all* statutory search powers, sets out to explain what it means. Paragraphs 2.2–2.11 Code A apply to searches dependent on reasonable suspicion. Paragraph 2.2 requires officers to be able to provide an explanation of the basis for their suspicion by reference to intelligence, information about a person or, failing that, their specific behaviour. Under para 2.2(i) the officer must have a genuine suspicion that the object that they are searching for will be found. Paragraph 2.2B not only explains the objective nature of reasonable suspicion, but forbids stereotyping in arriving at such suspicion: 'generalisations or stereotypical images that certain groups or categories of people are more likely to be involved in criminal activity cannot form the basis of a reasonable suspicion'. No doubt that provision is intended to deter the police from targeting Muslims in the wake of 9/11 and 7/7. Paragraph 2.4 provides: 'reasonable suspicion should normally be linked to accurate and current intelligence or information'. The reason is

65   *Commissioner of the Metropolitan Police v Rassi* [2008] EWCA Civ 1237, [20] Clarke MR.
66   See for example s 38(1) PACE governing bail following charge.

simple, as para 2.4A makes clear: 'Searches based on accurate and current intelligence or information are more likely to be effective.'

The most significant change brought about when Code A was revised in 1991 was the omission of the requirement that the suspicion should be of the same level as that necessary to effect an arrest.[67] The original intention behind including this provision was to stress the high level of suspicion required before a stop and search could take place; this change, therefore, tended to remove some of that emphasis and could be taken to imply that there are two levels of suspicion, the level required under Code A being the lower. However, although this omission may convey such a message to police officers, it may not make much difference to the way the police actually operate stop and search.

When Code A was revised in 1997,[68] some departure from the 'objective grounds for suspicion' stance was effected, and this was carried through into later versions. Paragraph 2.2(ii) requires that an officer has an objective basis for a suspicion. Paragraph 2.8A further provides that 'All police officers must recognise that searches are more likely to be effective, legitimate and secure public confidence when their reasonable grounds for suspicion are based on a range of objective factors.' Even under s 60 Criminal Justice and Public Order Act 1994 (CJPOA), discussed below, the selection of members of an available population for stopping and searching must be conducted on the basis of an objective assessment.

In practice, despite the wordy strictures of Code A, there is little evidence that reasonable suspicion acts as a constraint if police officers wish to stop and search without it.[69] Research in the area suggests that there is a tendency to view reasonable suspicion as a flexible concept that may denote a very low level of suspicion.[70] Research by both academics and HMIC has shown that the reasonable suspicion requirement is frequently absent despite the strictures of Code A.[71]

The case law is extremely meagre and unhelpful, but suggests that a highly imprecise and inconsistent standard is maintained. In *Slade*,[72] the suspect was close to the house of a well-known drug dealer; on noticing the officer, he put his hand in his pocket and smiled. This was found to constitute reasonable suspicion. However, in *Black v DPP*,[73] the fact of visiting a well-known drug dealer was found to be insufficient as the basis for finding reasonable suspicion. In *Francis*[74] the police purported to have reasonable suspicion to stop and search on the basis that the person in question was driving in an area known for drug use, with a passenger. The person had been stopped previously and her passenger at the time had been found to be in possession of drugs. Reasonable suspicion was not found to be established. This handful of cases clearly does very little to define the concept of reasonable suspicion, although it could be taken to indicate that extremely vague and broad bases for suspicion will not be sufficient.

67 Previously contained in Annex B, para 4 of Code A.
68 SI 1997/1159.
69 See Foster, J, 'Police Cultures', in Newburn, T, (ed), *The Handbook of Policing*, 2003, Willan.
70 See Dixon (1989) 17 Int J Soc Law 185–206.
71 See the HMIC Report (n 51 above) *opt cit* fn 64.
72 LEXIS CO/1678/96 (1996).
73 (1995) unreported, 11 May.
74 (1992) LEXIS CO/1434/91.

Counter-terrorist stop and search powers[75]

Section 47A of the Terrorism Act 2000 (TA) provides a power to stop and search without reasonable suspicion once an authorisation has been given.[76] This more focused power replaced the now repealed s 44 power, discussed below. Section 44 was repealed under the Protection of Freedoms Act 2012 s 59, after the *Gillan* case, below, was heard at Strasbourg. It was replaced by the narrower provision under s 47A of the 2000 Act as amended by the 2012 Act. Section 47A only allows searches for items that could be related to terrorism and the authorisation procedure is more tightly controlled, allowing authorisation only in relation to the specified area or place that is no greater than is necessary to prevent an act of terrorism.

Section 43 TA provides a further power that, unlike the s 1 PACE power, is not based on reasonable suspicion that a person is carrying an item, but on reasonable suspicion of being a terrorist.

Section 43 TA provides:

> A constable may stop and search a person whom he reasonably suspects to be a terrorist to discover whether he has in his possession anything which may constitute evidence that he is a terrorist.

'Being a terrorist' is not in itself an offence under the TA (unless the 'terrorist' group in question is also proscribed), although some, but not all, actions falling within the definition of terrorism in s 1 of the TA are coterminous with existing offences.[77] Therefore, this power is not dependent on suspicion of commission of an offence or of carrying prohibited articles, but it is narrower than the repealed s 44 power.

These powers are not entirely new; they are based on powers provided under the previous counter-terrorist legislation. The powers under ss 43 and 47A of the TA are partly based on the previous powers and, as Chapter 15 explains, they can potentially be applied to a

---

75 See for discussion, Parmar, A. (2011) 'Stop and Search in London: Counter-terrorist or Counter-productive?' *Policing and Society*, 21, 4: 369–82.
76 47A Searches in specified areas or places
    (1) A senior police officer may give an authorisation under subsection (2) or (3) in relation to a specified area or place if the officer –
        (a) reasonably suspects that an act of terrorism will take place; and
        (b) reasonably considers that –
            (i) the authorisation is necessary to prevent such an act;
            (ii) the specified area or place is no greater than is necessary to prevent such an act; and
            (iii) the duration of the authorisation is no longer than is necessary to prevent such an act.
    (2) An authorisation under this subsection authorises any constable in uniform to stop a vehicle in the specified area or place and to search –
        (a) the vehicle;
        (b) the driver of the vehicle;
        (c) a passenger in the vehicle;
        (d) anything in or on the vehicle or carried by the driver or a passenger.
    (3) An authorisation under this subsection authorises any constable in uniform to stop a pedestrian in the specified area or place and to search –
        (a) the pedestrian;
        (b) anything carried by the pedestrian.
77 See Chapter 15, p 1050.

wider range of people under s 1 TA owing to the very broad definition of 'terrorism' that s 1 TA introduced.[78] It may be noted that under s 116(2) of the TA, the powers conferred under the Act to stop persons are deemed to include powers to stop vehicles, and it is an offence to fail to stop a vehicle.

The unreformed section 44 – stop and search without reasonable suspicion

The old s 44 power was viewed as controversial with good reason. It not only arose independently of reasonable suspicion relating to objects suspected of being carried, or of reasonable grounds to believe that acts of terrorism might have occurred in the area covered by the authorisation, but it was an offence in itself to refuse to comply with the search. It is not an offence under PACE to refuse to comply with a s 1 search, or to obstruct it, although to do so would probably amount to the offence of obstructing a constable under s 89(2) of the Police Act 1996.[79] The provisions were challenged domestically in *R (on the application of Gillan) v Commissioner of Police for the Metropolis*[80] on the grounds *inter alia* that a stop and search amounted to a deprivation of liberty under Art 5 ECHR, scheduled in the HRA. Lord Bingham, who gave the leading judgment, sought to determine firstly whether the stops and searches were 'a deprivation of liberty' in Art 5(1) terms. He found:

> the clearest exposition of principle by the Strasbourg Court is to be found in *Guzzardi v Italy*,[81] an exposition repeatedly cited in later cases. In paragraphs 92–93 the Court observed: 'The Court recalls that in proclaiming the "right to liberty", paragraph 1 of Art 5 is contemplating the physical liberty of the person; its aim is to ensure that no one should be dispossessed of this liberty in an arbitrary fashion. As was pointed out by those appearing before the Court, the paragraph is not concerned with mere restrictions on liberty of movement; such restrictions are governed by Article 2 of Protocol No 4 which has not been ratified by Italy. In order to determine whether someone has been "deprived of his liberty" within the meaning of Art 5, the starting point must be his concrete situation and account must be taken of a whole range of criteria such as the type, duration, effects and manner of implementation of the measure in question. . . . The difference between deprivation of and restriction upon liberty is nonetheless merely one of degree or intensity, and not one of nature or substance.'

Lord Bingham found (in para 25) that there was no deprivation of liberty in Art 5(1) terms.

He found that it was ' accordingly clear', as was held in *HL v United Kingdom*,[82] that: 'in order to determine whether there has been a deprivation of liberty, the starting-point must be the concrete situation of the individual concerned and account must be taken of

---

78 See Chapter 15, p 1049 *et seq.*
79 Reproducing the Police Act 1964, s 51(3).
80 [2006] UKHL 12.
81 (1980) 3 EHRR 333.
82 (2004) 40 EHRR 761, at para 89.

a whole range of factors arising in a particular case such as the type, duration, effects and manner of implementation of the measure in question'. When a person is stopped and searched under ss 44–45 the procedure has the features on which the appellants rely. On the other hand, the procedure will ordinarily be relatively brief. The person stopped will not be arrested, handcuffed, confined or removed to any different place. I do not think, in the absence of special circumstances, such a person should be regarded as being detained in the sense of confined or kept in custody, but more properly of being detained in the sense of kept from proceeding or kept waiting. There is no deprivation of liberty. That was regarded by the Court of Appeal as 'the better view' (para 46), and I agree.

These findings left some leeway, but not very much, for finding that in different circumstances Art 5(1) would be engaged. Lord Bingham went on to consider the question whether, had there been a deprivation of liberty, it would have been justified as within Art 5(1)(b). He found that the statutory regime and the authorisation itself were 'prescribed by law' and that:

> the respondents bring themselves within the exception, for the public are in my opinion subject to a clear obligation not to obstruct a constable exercising a lawful power to stop and search for articles which could be used for terrorism and any detention is in order to secure effective fulfilment of that obligation.

The provisions were subsequently challenged before the European Court of Human Rights, where the Court considered the application primarily under Art 8, finding a violation of that provision on the basis that s 44 left so broad a discretion to the police that it was not 'in accordance with the law'.[83] The Strasbourg judges found that the powers vested in the police under ss 44–47 of the Act could not be regarded as 'in accordance with the law' because the power dispensed with the condition of reasonable suspicion: 'The powers of authorisation and confirmation as well as those of stop and search under sections 44 and 45 of the 2000 Act are neither sufficiently circumscribed nor subject to adequate legal safeguards against abuse', the Court ruled. The judges pointed, in particular, to the breadth of the discretion conferred on the individual police officer whose decision to stop somebody could be 'based exclusively on the "hunch" or "professional intuition" of the officer concerned'. The Court continued: 'There is a clear risk of arbitrariness in the grant of such a broad discretion to the police officer.' The Court did not find a breach of Art 5, but it nevertheless noted that the use of stop and search powers came with an element of coercion that 'is indicative of a deprivation of liberty within the meaning of Art 5(1)'.[84] In *Gillan*, in demanding alignment of UK anti-terrorism stop and search powers with the Art 8 standards, the Strasbourg decision offered a much-needed check upon the excessively broad police discretion provided by s 44. *Gillan* provides an important instance in which Strasbourg upheld higher human rights standards than the domestic judiciary, under the HRA, had done. The decision led to the repeal of s 44, as indicated above. A future challenge to stop and search powers under Art 5 therefore remains a possibility, albeit a slim one, but it is possible under Art 8 (see below).

83 *Gillan v UK* [2010] ECHR 4158/05.
84 Above at [57].

Other powers – ports and border controls

Schedule 7 Terrorism Act 2000 (as amended by the Anti-social Behaviour, Crime and Policing Act 2014) provides another somewhat similar stop and search power, which at its core allows for questioning. It allows for the detention of persons for a maximum of six hours at borders and ports without reasonable suspicion that he/she has been involved in terrorism-related activity. Schedule 7 gives 'examining officers' at ports and airports, along with international rail services in the UK, the power to stop, search, question, detain and examine an individual in order to determine whether or not a person is concerned in the commission, preparation or instigation of an act of terrorism. The officer can also require the production of documents. The examining officer does not need to have any reasonable suspicion that the person has been or is concerned in terrorism-related activity in order to question or examine an individual under this power. Under para 8 the person detained can be searched. Items, including electronic equipment, can be seized and retained for up to seven days if there is a belief (which does not need to be a reasonable belief) that the item might be needed in relation to criminal proceedings or deportation (para 11). It is an offence not to comply with the examination. Officers can ask for information and documents; if the person being questioned deliberately (i.e. not due to language difficulties etc) fails to comply, they commit an offence under para 18(1) Sched 7 TA.

Examining officers use the code of practice for the use of Schedule 7 of the Terrorism Act 2000 powers at ports (the code issued pursuant to para 6(1) of Sched 14 to the Terrorism Act 2000 (2009)). It provides guidance on the application and interpretation of Sched 7 powers. The code of practice provides guidance for examining officers (defined as a constable, immigration officer or customs officer) in relation to the application and interpretation of their powers under Sched 7 of the Terrorism Act 2000. The code is intended to be used by examining officers, their supervisors and managers and others who may have an interest in the exercise of these powers. The code provides that an examining officer should 'make every reasonable effort to exercise the power in such a way as to minimise causing embarrassment or offence to a person who is being questioned'. The power must be 'used proportionately, reasonably, with respect and without unlawful discrimination'. Furthermore, examining officers should take particular care to ensure that the selection of persons is not 'solely based on their perceived ethnic background or religion' and 'a person's perceived ethnic background or religion must not be used alone or in combination with each other as the sole reason for selecting the person for examination.' While the examining officer can stop a person without any suspicion, the code makes it clear that decisions should not be arbitrary but based on the nature of the threat posed, including information on the origin or location of terrorist groups, and the trends of travel patterns of those linked to terrorist activity.

In *Beghal*[85] the Supreme Court considered a challenge to the use of the power under Sched 7 to the Terrorism Act 2000. As indicated, it allows a police or immigration officer to question a person at a port or in the border area whom he believes to be entering or leaving the United Kingdom or travelling by air within it. The object of the questioning is to determine whether the person 'appears to be' a terrorist within

---

85   [2015] UKSC 49.

the meaning of that part of the Act. But the officer does not have to have grounds for suspecting that he does. The claimant was stopped and questioned for an hour and three quarters on returning to this country from a visit to her husband in France where he was in custody in relation to terrorist offences. She was prosecuted for refusing to answer some of the questions. By a majority, Lord Kerr dissenting, the Supreme Court declined to hold that the prosecution was an unjustified interference with her Art 8 or Art 5 ECHR rights, as scheduled in the HRA. Lord Hughes (with whom Lord Hodge agreed) pointed out that there is a distinction between port controls and street searches in the sense that the former are a lesser intrusion than the latter since there is an expectation that people will be searched at airports, for the safety of all. Lord Hughes listed a number of effective safeguards that he considered sufficient to meet the requirement of legality:

> They include: (i) the restriction to those passing into and out of the country; (ii) the restriction to the statutory purpose; (iii) the restriction to specially trained and accredited police officers; (iv) the restrictions on the duration of questioning; (v) the restrictions on the type of search; (vi) the requirement to give explanatory notice to those questioned . . .; (vii) the requirement to permit consultation with a solicitor and the notification of a third party; (viii) the requirement for records to be kept; (ix) the availability of judicial review . . . if bad faith or collateral purpose is alleged, and also via the principle of legitimate expectation where a breach of the code of practice or of the several restrictions listed above is in issue.[86]

Lord Neuberger and Lord Dyson agreed, adding that as to the question whether the legality principle was satisfied, 'one must look not only at the provisions of the statute or other relevant instrument which gives rise to the system in question but also at how that system actually works in practice'.[87] They found that there were key differences from the s 44 scheme at issue in *Gillan*: the Sched 7 powers were more foreseeable and less arbitrary.[88] On that basis para 2 of Art 8 was found to be satisfied. As regards Art 5 it was found that 'To the extent that there was any deprivation of liberty in the present case, it seems clear that it was for no longer than was necessary for the completion of the process. There was no requirement to attend a police station. Accordingly, there was in this case no breach of article 5.'[89]

Similarly, in August 2013 the partner (David Miranda) of a *Guardian* journalist (Glenn Greenwald), who had been involved in revelations as to NSA surveillance was detained for nine hours under Sched 7 at Heathrow airport, (the information was passed in encrypted form to Greenwald by the whistleblower Snowden). A series of port circulation sheets (PCS) were circulated to counter-terrorism police alerting them that the claimant was 'likely to be involved in espionage activity which has the potential to act against the interests of UK national security', and requesting them to establish the nature of his activity, and assess the risk that he posed to UK national security. Miranda was released but electronic equipment was seized, including his mobile phone, laptop,

86 Above at [43].
87 Above at [86].
88 Above at [87].
89 Above at [56].

camera, memory sticks. The stop may have been requested by US intelligence, and may have been intended to intimidate Greenwald, but it is also possible that information was being sought that could have been linked to the whistle-blowing as to the NSA and GCHQ (the *Guardian* had published stories on GCHQ). According to a statement from the Intelligence, Security and Resilience Director in the Cabinet Office, the encrypted data contained in the external hard drive taken from the claimant contained approximately 58,000 highly classified UK intelligence documents. Many were classified 'secret' or 'top secret'.

Miranda's detention lasted for the full nine hours, which was very unusual. Also he had not arrived from a country in which terrorist activity was prevalent. Thus his detention had an appearance of arbitrariness. His partner Glenn Greenwald raised the concern in *the Guardian* that the detention represented an attempt at intimidation, given Greenwald's revelations as regards NSA surveillance. Miranda was not himself a journalist but the detention raised concerns about the use of Sched 7 to intimidate journalists, and to undermine the confidentiality of journalistic information. A *Guardian* editorial argued that: 'Mr Miranda's detention was part security service fishing trip, part police harassment exercise and part government warning signal to journalists and whistleblowers.'[90]

The detention of Miranda raises in particular the question whether further safeguards against an arbitrary use of the power are required, given that his detention appeared to be unlinked to terrorist-related activity, although the material he was carrying appeared to have a link to national security. The challenge to the use of the power and to the power itself in relation to the ECHR failed in the High Court,[91] and the case was appealed to the Court of Appeal.[92] The Court of Appeal noted that Sched 7 allows travellers to be questioned to find out whether they appear to be terrorists. They have no right to remain silent or receive legal advice and they may be detained for up to nine hours. The Court found that the use of the power of detention against Miranda was in itself lawful. But the Court found that powers themselves contained in Sched 7 of the Terrorism Act 2000 and based on the broad definition of terrorism in s 1 of the Act were flawed if used in respect of journalistic information or material. It was found that since the powers could be used in that instance, they were incompatible with Art 10, providing a right to freedom of expression of the European Convention on Human Rights, as discussed in Chapter 2, on the basis that Art 10(2) was not satisfied since the power was not found to be 'prescribed by law'. The judgment continued: 'If journalists and their sources can have no expectation of confidentiality, they may decide against providing information on sensitive matters of public interest.' The Court of Appeal ruling rejected the broad definition of terrorism advanced by government lawyers. The correct legal definition of terrorism, the Court of Appeal found, would be capable of excluding journalists since it should 'require some intention to cause a serious threat to public safety such as endangering life'.

An application to Strasbourg challenging the compatibility of Sched 7 has been made in another case, *Malik v UK*,[93] and found admissible. Should the Strasbourg Court find

---

90 *The Guardian* 20.8.13.
91 *David Miranda v Secretary of State for the Home Department, the Commissioner of Police for the Metropolis and three interveners* [2014] EWHC 255 (Admin).
92 19 Jan 2016 – Neutral Citation Number: [2016] EWCA Civ 6. Case No: C1/2014/0607.
93 *Malik v United Kingdom* (Admissibility), no.32968/11 (28 May 2013).

against the UK, which seems quite possible, then that power, too, will have to be reformed. But that may occur in any event as a result of *Miranda*, in relation to journalistic material, unless the Supreme Court overturns the Court of Appeal.

Special powers to prevent anticipated local violence

Section 60 of the Criminal Justice and Public Order Act 1994 provides police officers with a further stop and search power that does not depend on showing reasonable suspicion of particular wrongdoing on the part of an individual. An officer of at least the rank of inspector can authorise the stop and search of any person or vehicle within a particular locality if he or she reasonably believes that incidents involving 'serious violence' may take place in that area and that authorisation is expedient in order to prevent their occurrence. The authorisation may apply to a period not exceeding 24 hours, but it can be renewed for a further 24 hours if such an authorisation is in force. An officer may stop anyone within the specified locality in order to look for offensive weapons or dangerous instruments, whether or not there any grounds for suspecting that such articles are being carried. In contrast to s 1 of PACE, failure to stop is an offence under s 60(8).

In *R (Roberts) v The Commissioner of the Metropolitan Police*[94] the applicant challenged the use of s 60 under the HRA. The application arose from a fracas over a bus fare. A ticket inspector discovered that the applicant, Ms Roberts, had insufficient funds to cover the cost of her journey. The police were called when Ms Roberts became agitated and was asked to leave the bus in Haringey. At that time Haringey had been blighted by inter-gang fighting using knives. Consequently, an inspector had authorised the use of power to stop and search for weapons under s 60 Criminal Justice and Public Order Act 1994 (CJPO). PC Reid decided to search the claimant using this power. The applicant refused to be searched, kept a firm hold of her bag and attempted to walk away. At this point the PC told the applicant she was to be detained and when she again resisted, with the assistance of other officers, she was handcuffed and pinned to the ground. Her bag was then searched, and on discovering bank cards in her maiden name and her son's name she was arrested on suspicion of handling stolen goods. At first instance Moses LJ concluded that there had been no deprivation of liberty under Art 5 during this process and, moreover, that the claimant not resisted the stop and search would have lasted only a few minutes. The case reached the Supreme Court in 2015[95] where the appeal was argued and decided on the basis of Art 8 (the other claims based on the ECHR having been dropped). Lady Hale and Lord Reed gave the judgment of the Court. It was common ground in the appeal that the power created an interference with the right to respect for private life under Art 8(1), but it was accepted that it pursued a legitimate aim that was capable of justification under Art 8(2). It was admitted that the interference with Mrs Roberts' rights was, in the circumstances, proportionate to the legitimate aim of preventing crime, so her claim only turned on the issue of whether the exercise of the power was found to also satisfy Art 8(2) by being 'in accordance with the law'.

94 The facts are set out in brief at [2012] EWHC 1977 (Admin) [37]-[42].
95 [2015] UKSC 79.

Gillan which, as indicated above, concerned a fairly similar stop and search power, had already established, in conjunction with *Colon v The Netherlands*[96] that 'suspicion-less' powers could fail the requirement of lawfulness under Art 8(2). The power had to be operated in a manner that was compatible with the ECHR rights of any individual and was free of discrimination.[97] The Court noted that it is often important to the effectiveness of such powers that they needed to be exercised randomly and unpredictably. Lord Reed said on this:

> It must be borne in mind that many of these gangs [involved in violence] are largely composed of young people from black and minority ethnic groups. While there is a concern that members of these groups should not be disproportionately targeted, it is members of these groups who will benefit most from the reduction in violence, serious injury and death that may result from the use of such powers. Put bluntly, it is mostly young black lives that will be saved if there is less gang violence in London and some other cities.[98]

The question was whether the legal framework applicable to the exercise of the s 60 power permitted the court to examine fully the propriety of its exercise of the power.[99] The Court then went on to examine the power, concluding that it was surrounded by sufficient safeguards that rendered it compatible with Art 8(2). There were procedural safeguards governing how the power could be invoked, there were supervisory safeguards and the exercise of the power itself was subject to procedural strictures and a record keeping duty.[100] That differentiated it sufficiently, it was found, from the s 44 TA power at issue in *Gillan*.

Use of the counter-terrorist, and special powers

It is notable that no judicial body is involved in the pre-search supervision of the counter-terrorist and special powers. They are subject to executive supervision only, either by the police themselves or, in the case of s 47A TA, by the Home Secretary. These powers discard a key due process safeguard and therefore might be justified only if they are likely to have real value in terms of curbing criminal or terrorist activity. Section 60 CJPOA, which may allow near-random stopping once an authorisation is in force, may, as indicated, result not in arrests for offences of serious violence, but for drug-related or other, more minor offences. It has often been observed that arrests may well be entirely unrelated to the reason for the original encounter with the police. These powers are therefore objectionable in the sense that they have been adopted apparently in response to near-crisis situations, whereas they may be used in situations that would not alone have justified their adoption. Since the wide powers under s 60 of the 1994 Act and s 47A of the Act of 2000 are not subject to limitation flowing from the concept of reasonable suspicion, they represent a departure from the principle that only an individual who has given rise to such suspicion due to his or her actions should suffer the infringement

---

96 (2012) 55 EHRR SE45.
97 [2015] UKSC 79, [42].
98 Above at [41].
99 Above at [15]–[26].
100 Above at [44]–[46].

of liberty represented by a stop and search. On the other hand, the powers can be supported on the basis, as the Supreme Court pointed out in *Roberts*, that to prevent knife crime (and this would also apply to terrorist activity) the police have to be able to act swiftly and unpredictably.

Voluntary searches

Until 2003 consensual searches were permissible but the apparently voluntary basis of a large number of searches continued to be questionable.[101] Inconsistency of practice between forces was readily apparent.[102] Although such searches were prohibited in Code A para 1.5 – and that is still the case in the 2014 edition – it is possible that they are still continuing. Persons may be intimidated by police authority and may submit to a search where no power to search in fact exists. Such searches may come to light only if the suspect later raises the argument that the police had no power to search, or if the suspect resists and is charged with assaulting an officer in the course of his duty.[103]

Code A does not, in general, affect ordinary consensual contact between police officer and citizen; officers can ask members of the public to stop and can ask them questions and, at least theoretically, the citizen can refuse. Prior to 2003 'voluntary' searches were possible. However, the voluntariness of such contacts was frequently doubtful: some people might 'consent' to a search in the sense of offering no resistance to it, owing to uncertainty as to the basis or extent of the police power in question.[104] The search could then be classified as voluntary and subsequently it would be difficult, if not impossible, to determine whether such classification was justifiable.

When from 2003 'voluntary' stops and searches were forbidden, under para 1.5, that appeared to solve the problem, but there are loopholes in the provision in practice. It appears to apply only to searches and not to stops – thus voluntary stops are still possible, even if they lead to 'consensual' detention for a period of time. This appears to be implicit in para 4.12 Code A which now provides (2014 version): 'There is no national requirement for an officer who requests a person in a public place to account for themselves' or to make a record. A stop cannot occur in order to find the grounds for a search, under Code A para 2.11, but since this provision is virtually unenforceable, as discussed below, it appears probable that the continued availability of voluntary stops significantly undermines the prohibition on voluntary searches.

If a search occurred on an apparently consensual basis where no power arose to search, because reasonable suspicion was required and was not present, para 1.5 would be breached, but no liability could arise in respect of the Code breach. However, if

---

101   Dixon, D, Coleman, C and Bottomley, K, 'Consent and the legal regulation of policing' (1990) 17 JLS 345.

102   Certain forces, such as Bedfordshire, used a separate consent form for voluntary searches, but such practice was by no means universal. See 'Modernising the tactic: improving the use of stop and search', *Policing and Reducing Crime: Briefing Note No 2*, November 1999.

103   See *Osman v Director of Public Prosecutions* (1999) *The Times*, 29 September, judgment of 1 July 1999, in which Sedley LJ indicated that an initial passive response to a search would not entitle officers to assume that the subject was consenting to it.

104   For further discussion of this point, see Dixon et al, 'Consent and the legal regulation of policing' (1990) 17 JLS 245–362.

the situation was viewed as one of searching without a power to do so (under e.g., s 1 PACE), which is the better view, then liability might arise, for trespass to the person or – if an item was seized – to goods. However, if a person was asked to turn out his pockets and did so voluntarily without physical contact with the police officers, no liability would arise, unless an item was seized. There would also be the practical difficulty of establishing a breach, bearing in mind the low level of suspicion required. However, the requirements of ss 2 and 3 (below) elaborated in Code A would have to be followed. Thus if an item was found and seized during a 'voluntary' search, it could lead to an arrest and conviction but it is unclear that redress would be available in respect of the police action.

Use of force

The use of force in order to carry out a stop and search is permitted under s 117 of PACE, which provides: 'the officer may use reasonable force, if necessary, in the exercise of the [PACE] power'. The TA provides an equivalent provision in s 114(2). But, under Art 3 ECHR, the use of force must be strictly in proportion to the conduct of the detainee; this is discussed further below in respect of forcible arrest.[105] The lawfulness of the initial detention would then have to be considered, bearing in mind the arguments above.

Procedural requirements for stop and search powers

Under s 2(1) of PACE, the procedural safeguards it sets out, together with those under s 3, apply to the PACE power and to powers under any other statutory provisions. All other statutory powers of search are also subject to the same procedural require-ments under Code A as those relating to the powers under s 1 of PACE, apart – where relevant – from the Code A provisions relating to reasonable suspicion (Code A, para 2). The special counter-terrorism powers are subject to such requirements, apart from searches carried out for the purposes of examination under Sched 7 to the Terrorism Act 2000 which are covered by Code H of PACE.[106]

An element of due process is introduced into all these statutory stop and search pow-ers by the information giving and recording requirements under ss 2 and 3 of PACE and Code of Practice A, paras 3 and 4. Under s 2(3) PACE, the constable must give the suspect certain information before the search begins, including 'his name and the name of the police station to which he is attached; the object of the proposed search; the constable's grounds for proposing to make it'. In *R v Bristol*[107] the Court of Appeal had to consider whether the arresting officer had complied with the provisions of s 2 PACE when searching for drugs. The officer had failed to give his name or station as required by s 2. There had been no evidence that a police officer had taken all reasonable steps to bring his name and police station to the attention of the defendant before searching him; and it followed that the search carried out under the Misuse of Drugs Act 1971 was unlawful, given that it had not complied with s 2. The search was thus unlawful

---

105 See p 893.
106 See p 836.
107 [2007] EWCA Crim 3214.

and it was found that the case should not have been put before a jury. It followed that the defendant was not guilty of intentionally obstructing a search under the 1971 Act. The conviction was quashed.

Under s 3, the officer must make a record of the search, either on the spot if that is practicable or as soon as it is practicable. The subject of the search can obtain a copy of the search record later on from the police station. Code A, para 3.8 also covers the information-giving requirement, and para 4 covers search records. General guidance as to the conduct of the search is contained in Code A, paras 3.1–3.7; they require the officer to complete the search speedily, to minimise embarrassment and to seek cooperation.

The statutory and code information-giving and record-keeping requirements give the impression of creating due process-based controls since they mean that the citizen can make a complaint and the police station will have a record of the number of stops being carried out. These procedural requirements are supposed to inject some accountability into stopping and searching, but in so far as they rely on Code A, they are effectively virtually unenforceable. Crucially, an officer under the revised Code A (para 4.2) needs only to provide a receipt unless a full record of the encounter is asked for. The status of the ss 2 and 3 PACE requirements is considered below.

Redress for breaches of the stop and search rules; reliance on ECHR challenges

A search would be unlawful if no reasonable suspicion arose in the circumstances – as required by the statutory provision that the police officers purported to be relying on, or if the police purported to act under an authorisation which was not in fact in force. A search would also be unlawful if one of the *mandatory* statutory procedural requirements was not complied with.

Engagement of Art 5(1)

Article 5 provides a guarantee of 'liberty and security of person'. Following *Gillan* it does not appear to be necessary, except in exceptional circumstances (possibly where a stop and search was particularly prolonged) to show that an exception to Art 5 applies, since Art 5(1) is not, apparently, engaged. However, as discussed above, that question may still be open, especially in circumstances differing from those applicable in *Gillan* and in *Roberts*.

The reliance in *Gillan* on *Guzzardi* in the House of Lords (see above) was doubtful, since the question in *Guzzardi* was whether restrictions on freedom of movement were sufficient to amount to deprivation of liberty. *Guzzardi* was detained on an island and therefore had some freedom of movement; the Court thought that his detention was somewhat akin to that experienced by someone in an open prison. In contrast, Gillan and Quinton were completely detained – i.e. they could not move appreciably from the spot on which they were stopped and searched. Had they sought to do so they would probably have been arrested for the offence encapsulated in s 47 – that of failing to stop when ordered to do so. The applicants in *Austin v Commissioner of the Metropolitan Police*[108] fared no better than those in *Gillan*, domestically. Despite being 'kettled', that is

---

108 [2009] UKHL 5, [34].

corralled under police supervision on the threat of arrest for some hours, the House of Lords and ultimately the Grand Chamber of the European Court[109] held that there had been no deprivation of liberty. It was found that Art 5 contained an implied limitation that covered such public order situations. Equally, in *Roberts* Art 5 had no application. Only in *Re Canning*'s *Application*[110] did Girvan LJ indicate, albeit *obiter*, that Art 5 might be engaged due to use of the power under ss 21 and 24 of the Justice and Security Act (NI) (2007) where the conditions of its use approximated to arrest. The powers under the Act in Northern Ireland which had been used to stop and question the applicant up to 100 times were found to be incompatible with his right to respect for private life under Art 8 ECHR due to lack of regulation of the use of the power.

The cases of *Gillan* and *Roberts* are readily distinguishable from that of *Guzzardi*. The question in their case was that of *duration of time*, not, on its face, of deprivation of liberty. They involve situations where, in common parlance, they had clearly been deprived of liberty in the sense of being unable to move from one spot, under threat of arrest, whereas Guzzardi was able to move around the island; the question was whether the restraints on his movement amounted to a deprivation of liberty in Art 5 terms. It appears then that in general stop and search does not engage Art 5(1).

Application of Art 5(1)(b)

But even assuming that Art 5 had been found to be engaged in *Gillan* or *Roberts'* an exception could probably be established in most instances. In *Gillan* Lord Bingham found that Art 5(1)(b) would have applied. Deprivation of liberty can occur only on a basis of law and in certain specified circumstances, including, under Art 5(1)(b), the detention of a person in order to secure the fulfilment of any obligation prescribed by law. Article 5(1)(c) provides an exception in respect of the 'lawful detention of a person effected for the purpose of bringing him before the competent legal authority on reasonable suspicion of having committed an offence' but this exception appears to apply to arrest rather than to stop and search. That was the view taken in *Gillan*. Section 1 PACE requires suspicion as to carriage of an article, not as to an offence; it is clearly aimed at gathering evidence of offences and its requirements are not fully coterminous with the relevant range of offences. Carrying certain of the articles that fall within s 1 of PACE is not an offence[111] even if the carrier can be said to 'possess' them, although the officer also requires suspicion as to *mens rea*, while carriage of prohibited articles without sufficient 'possession' will clearly not constitute an offence. That provision clearly allows searches that could not be covered by Art 5(1)(c).

Thus Art 5(1)(b) could cover potentially temporary detention for the purposes of a search. The provision under Art 5(1)(b) raises difficulties of interpretation and is clearly not so straightforward as the form of detention permitted under Art 5(1)(c). On its face, its broad wording appears to allow arbitrary detention on a broader basis than that permitted based on the requirements of reasonable suspicion or authorisation that PACE, other statutory powers and the TA depend upon, and without intervention by a court. At

---

109 *Austin v UK* Judgment of 15 March 2012 Applications nos. 39692/09, 40713/09 and 41008/09.
110 [2012] NIQB 49.
111 Under s 1(7)(b), such articles could include credit cards or keys.

first glimpse it gives the impression of representing a scheme that affords less weight to due process than the current domestic one.

However, Art 5(1)(b) has received a restrictive interpretation at Strasbourg. In *Lawless*,[112] it was found that a specific and concrete obligation must be identified; once it has been, detention can in principle be used to secure its fulfilment. It is probable that the term 'obligation' could apply to the current statutory provisions – if Art 5(1), exceptionally, was found to be engaged. The requirements are to submit to a search, and, apart from the power under s 163 of the Road Traffic Act, to remain under police detention for the period of time necessary to allow it to be carried out. Following this interpretation, the PACE, CJPOA and TA stop and search provisions are probably compatible with Art 5(1)(b). In *McVeigh, O'Neill and Evans*[113] a requirement to submit to an examination on arrival in the UK was found not to violate Art 5(1)(b) since it was sufficiently specific and concrete, but the Commission emphasised that this was found on the basis that the obligation in question only arose in limited circumstances and had a limited purpose – to combat terrorism. The PACE powers, the Misuse of Drugs Act power and, arguably, the power arising under s 43 of the TA, which is a permanent power, not one adopted temporarily to meet an emergency as in *McVeigh*, could not readily be said to arise in limited circumstances but the obligation would probably be found to arise since they are founded upon a requirement of reasonable suspicion. The CJPOA and other TA powers have more limited purposes in the sense that the place in which they can be exercised is circumscribed either by its nature (as in port or border controls) or by the authorisation given, which is based on the need for special powers. Whether any particular authorisation would be viewed as rendering the obligation in question sufficiently specific would be open to question, depending on the factual situation.

The exercise of the powers under s 60 CJPOA and s 44 TA appears to be compatible with Art 5(1)(b). The power under s 163 of the Road Traffic Act (RTA) also appears to be compatible with Art 5(1)(b) since it is exercised in respect of a specific obligation, as explained in *McVeigh*. The obligation may be viewed as one inherent in the use of a vehicle on the roads. The power probably carries with it, impliedly, the power to detain for a short period.[114] The offence under the RTA of failing to stop would probably be committed if the response to the stop was to brake and pause for an instant before driving on. It appears, after *Gillan* that Art 5 is not normally engaged by the use of this power, but that if it were engaged, it would usually fall within the exception.

Tortious remedies

A citizen who submitted to a search where no power arose to search in the circumstances would have a remedy in trespass to the person. If a search is conducted unlawfully, the citizen is entitled to resist and to sue for assault. But in many instances, and especially where a search is conducted under one of the provisions that do not require reasonable

---

112 Report of 19 December 1959, B1 (1960–61) p 64; judgment of 1 July 1961, A 3 (1960–61); (1961) 1 EHRR 15.

113 See *McVeigh, O'Neill and Evans* (1981) 5 EHRR 71; the obligation imposed was a requirement to 'submit to examination'. In *Reyntjens v France* Appl No 16810/90 (1992) unreported, the obligation was to submit to an identity check.

114 This may be suggested by the findings in *Lodwick v Sanders* [1985] 1 WLR 382.

suspicion, the citizen has no means of knowing that the search is unlawful. A citizen who believed that there could be no grounds for a search and therefore resisted it would be taking a risk. Resistance to an authorised TA or CJPOA search could incur criminal liability, not only, in all probability, in respect of obstruction or assault of a constable,[115] but under the special TA or CJPOA search-related offences as well. Article 5 arguments, possibly combined with Art 14 ones, could be raised under s 7(1)(b) HRA in the context of a civil action for false imprisonment or trespass to the person, although given the lack of success of the applicant in *Roberts* on these grounds, that must be doubtful. Clearly, *Gillan* has not encouraged such argument, but *Gillan* did not rule out the possibility that in certain circumstances Art 5 could be engaged by a stop and search, or that Art 5 read with Art 14 would not be breached in certain circumstances by a discriminatory use of the stop and search power. If Art 5 alone or read with Art 14 was found to be breached, the options of extending an existing tort in order to cover the instance in question could arise, or of merely affording a remedy under s 8 HRA. A racially discriminatory stop and search would also be tortious under the Equality Act 2010. If there was a doubt as to the ambit of the tort in question, suggesting that in the particular instance it might be inapplicable, it could be argued that it should be extended to cover the breach of Art 5 in question. If Code A had been breached during a stop and search that in itself would not give rise to any civil liability, but the breach could be relied upon as part of an argument that Art 5 itself had been breached. The use of tort actions in this context is discussed further in Chapter 14.

There is no provision under the TA, PACE or Code A to the express effect that if the *procedural* requirements are not complied with, the search will be unlawful. As indicated, a number of due process requirements are contained only in Codes[116] and, therefore, their breach cannot give rise to civil liability,[117] although breach of certain of the *statutory* procedural requirements will render searches unlawful, as will breach of the statutory powers. It has been held that a failure to make a written record of the search in breach of s 3 will not render it unlawful,[118] whereas a failure to give the grounds for it will do so, following *Fenelley*[119] and *Samuel v Comr of Police for the Metropolis*,[120] as will a failure to comply with the duties to provide identification under s 2(3), following *Osman v Director of Public Prosecutions*.[121] In *Osman*, proper authorisation had been given for the police to search members of the public entering a park under s 60(4) and (5) of the CJPOA 1994. When the defendant was searched, police officers failed to comply with s 2; the search was resisted and the defendant charged with assaulting an officer in the execution of his duty. It was found on appeal that it was plain from

---

115 Offences arising under the Police Act 1996, s 89(1) and (2).

116 Code A made under PACE 1984, s 66 and the TA Code made under the TA, ss 96 and 98 in respect of Northern Ireland and the Code introduced under Sched 14 in respect of the UK. See pp 836–37 above.

117 Under PACE 1984, s 67(10). The TA Codes have the same status as the PACE Codes; under Sched 14, para 6(2) 'The failure by an officer to observe a provision of a code shall not of itself make him liable to criminal or civil proceedings', but under sub-para (3) 'A code (a) shall be admissible in evidence in criminal and civil proceedings, and (b) shall be taken into account by a court or tribunal in any case in which it appears to the court or tribunal to be relevant'.

118 *Basher v DPP* (1993) unreported, 2 March.

119 [1989] Crim LR 142.

120 (1999) unreported, 3 March.

121 1999) *The Times*, 29 September, judgment of 1 July 1999.

the mandatory words of s 2 that any search initiated without prior compliance with the duties set out in s 2 would mean that no officer was actually assaulted in the execution of his duty, since any search of a person might be a trespass requiring proper justification in law; the breach of s 2(3) meant that the search was unlawful and therefore not in the execution of their duty. The facts that the officers were clearly local and that numbers could have been obtained from their uniforms were found to be insufficient to avoid the finding of unlawfulness.[122] The strict interpretation of the information-giving duties evident in *Fenelley* and *Osman* was equally apparent in *Lineham v DPP*[123] in the context of a search of premises.

Exclusion of the products of the search from evidence; trial remedies

The PACE and TA Codes are admissible in evidence.[124] It would be possible for a defendant who claims that a search was conducted improperly or unlawfully to seek the limited form of redress represented by exclusion of evidence which has been obtained after a breach of ss 2 or 3 PACE and/or Code A. A stop and search is most likely to produce physical evidence such as drugs or perhaps a weapon, but the courts are very reluctant to exclude such evidence unless there has been deliberate illegality because it is less likely to be unreliable than confession or identification evidence.[125] Thus, the mechanism of exclusion of evidence as a form of redress for breach of a code provision, which has operated to underpin Codes C and D, is not as appropriate in relation to Code A, although an effective sanction is clearly needed.

This weakness is further exacerbated in relation to breaches of the notes for guidance rather than of Code A itself; and since the notes do not have the same legal status as code provisions, they are more likely to be ignored by officers. What would be the position if, for example, a police officer required a Muslim woman to remove a veil in public view in breach of Note for Guidance 4 Code A? A judge might well be minded to view breach of a note for guidance as of insufficient significance to lead to exclusion of any identification evidence obtained.

Article 6 arguments would be available where a breach of Art 5 was alleged that might affect the fairness of the trial; they could be raised in respect of admission of evidence obtained after a breach of Art 5, or in respect of an argument for abuse of process; these possibilities are considered further in Chapter 14. Again, *Gillan* has not encouraged such argument, but, as mentioned, *Gillan* did not rule out the possibility that in certain circumstances Art 5 could be engaged by a stop and search, or that Art 5 read with Art

---

122   The Crown Court had found that there had been a breach of the 1984 Act, s 2(3)(a), but given the fact that the officers were clearly local police officers policing a local event in broad daylight, as expeditiously as possible, and because numbers could readily be obtained from the officers' uniforms, the breach was not so serious as to render the search unlawful. These findings would clearly have undermined s 2(3).

123   (1999) unreported, judgment of 8 October. Laws LJ found that police officers who conducted a search under PACE 1984, s 18 had not been acting in the execution of their duty because they had failed to inform the appellant so far as possible as to the reason why they intended to search the premises.

124   PACE 1984, s 67(11); TA, Sched 14, para 6(3).

125   See the pre-PACE ruling of the House of Lords in *Fox* [1986] AC 281; see also *Thomas* [1990] Crim LR 269 and *Khan* [1996] 3 All ER 289; *cf Fenelley* [1989] Crim LR 142. See further Chapter 14, p 991 *et seq*.

14 could be breached in certain circumstances by a discriminatory use of the stop and search power. These arguments could be raised at trial in respect of failing to stop, either under one of the specific offences under the relevant statute or under s 89(1) or (2) of the Police Act 1996. Further possibilities are considered in respect of arrests in breach of Art 5, below.

Where searches are conducted in contravention of the requirements of PACE itself the courts have been unusually firm in punishing transgressions. In addition to *Bristol*, discussed above, the Divisional Court noted in *Osman* that 'a search is a serious interference with [a person's] liberty . . . all proper safeguards must be followed.'[126] A failure to comply with s 2 renders the search unlawful. The question in both *Bristol* and *Osman* was not one of admissibility of the evidence but rather whether or not the officers had been acting in the execution of their duty when they conducted the search. As they were not the convictions in both cases were dropped.

Disciplinary action

Disciplinary action, the other form of redress for breach of a code provision, may be even less effective in relation to Code A than Codes C, D and E, which largely govern interrogation and identification, because stop and search powers are exercised away from the police station, at a low level of visibility. Moreover, if a police officer decides that a search can be called voluntary, he need not give his name or number and therefore it will be almost impossible to bring a complaint against him. Thus, it is fair to say that in so far as the balance between police powers and individual rights is supposed to be maintained by the Code A provisions, it is largely dependent on voluntary adherence to them. The police are bound by the Convention rights under s 6 HRA and therefore argument that a right had been breached could be raised in disciplinary proceedings, although it would not be conclusive. This is discussed further in Chapter 14.

3 Police powers of entry and search[127]

In the US, the Fourth Amendment to the Constitution guarantees freedom from unreasonable search and seizure by the police, thus recognising the invasion of privacy that a search of premises represents. A search without a warrant will normally[128] be unreasonable; therefore, an independent check is usually available on the search power. In contrast, the common law in Britain, despite some rulings asserting the importance of protecting the citizen

---

126 *Osman* cited above n 121.

127 For discussion of this area, see: Zander, M, *Zander on PACE: The Police and Criminal Evidence Act 1984*, 2015; R Stone *The Law of Entry, Search and Seizure*, 5th edn, 2012; Sanders, A and Young, R, *Criminal Justice*, 4th edn, 2010; Bailey, Taylor, N, *Bailey, Harris and Jones: Civil Liberties: Cases and Materials*, 6th edn, 2009, Chapter 2; for background, see: Feldman, D, *The Law Relating to Entry, Search and Seizure*, 1986; Clark, D, *Bevan and Lidstone's The Investigation of Crime*, 2004, Lexis-Nexis UK; Clayton, R and Tomlinson, H, *Civil Actions Against the Police*, 2nd edn, 2005, Sweet and Maxwell, Chapter 7; Ashworth, A, *The Criminal Process*, 3rd edn, 2005, OUP; Feldman, D, *Civil Liberties and Human Rights in England and Wales*, 2nd edn, 2002, Chapters 5 and 9.

128 *Coolidge v New Hampshire* (1973) 403 US 443: exception accepted where evidence might otherwise be destroyed.

from the invasion of private property,[129] allowed search and seizure on wide grounds, going beyond those authorised by statute.[130] Thus, the common law did not provide full protection for the citizen, and the Police and Criminal Evidence Act 1984 (PACE) went some way to remedy this by placing powers of entry, search and seizure on a clearer basis and ensuring that the person whose premises are searched understands the basis of the search and can complain as to its conduct if necessary. Whether the procedures actually do provide sufficient protection for the privacy interests of the subject of the search is the question to be examined by this section. PACE provides for procedures to be followed where statutory applications for search warrants are made, under PACE itself or other statutes,[131] including post-PACE provisions; it also provides non-warrant-based powers of entry, search and seizure. In this respect it strongly resembles the provisions regarding stop and search in PACE, discussed above. On the stop and search model, the procedures to be followed in exercising entry and search powers and the safeguards for suspects and others are partly in a code of practice – Code B (2013 version).

Entry without warrant

Powers under the Police and Criminal Evidence Act (PACE)

The power to enter premises without warrant conferred by PACE, as amended, is balanced in a manner similar to the method employed in respect of stop and search. A power of entry arises under s 18 if a person has been arrested for an indictable offence and the intention is to search the person's premises immediately after arrest:

> a constable may enter and search any premises occupied or controlled by a person who is under arrest for an indictable offence, if he has reasonable grounds for suspecting that there is on the premises evidence, other than items subject to legal privilege, that relates:
>
> (a) to that offence; or
> (b) to some other arrestable offence which is connected with or similar to that offence.

The power can be exercised under s 17 to: execute a warrant of arrest arising out of criminal proceedings; where an officer wants to arrest a person suspected of an indictable offence; to recapture someone unlawfully at large (such as, for example, an escapee from a prison, court or mental hospital); to save life or limb or prevent serious damage to property. This provision regarding criminal proceedings allows an entry to be made to search for someone wanted under a warrant for non-payment of a fine. Apart from the life or limb or serious damage provisions, a constable can only exercise the powers if he or she has reasonable grounds for believing that the person in question is on the premises.

---

129 See, e.g., rulings in *Entinck v Carrington* (1765) 19 St Tr 1029; *Morris v Beardmore* [1981] AC 446; [1980] 2 All ER 753.
130 The ruling in *Ghani v Jones* [1970] 1 QB 693 authorised seizure of a wide range of material once officers were lawfully on premises. *Thomas v Sawkins* [1935] 2 KB 249 allowed a wide power to enter premises to prevent crime
131 For example, powers under s 23 Misuse of Drugs Act 1971 or Terrorism Act 2000, Sched 5, para 1.

Thus, the power is subject to some significant limitations; in particular it does not arise in respect of an arrest for a non-indictable offence. If a search is considered necessary in situations in which s 17 or s 18 are inapplicable after an arrest, a search warrant would have to be obtained unless the provisions of s 32 applied. Section 32(2)(b) allows a search of premises after arrest, if there are reasonable grounds for thinking that the arrestee, who has been arrested for an indictable offence, may present a danger to himself or others if the arrestee was arrested on those premises or was on them immediately before the arrest.

Search powers under the Terrorism Act 2000

The provisions for warrantless search of premises under PACE after arrest are wide enough to cover many circumstances in which police officers might wish to search for items relating to a terrorist investigation. But they are supplemented by special powers under warrant that are discussed below and also, in an emergency, by a power in the Terrorism Act 2000, Sched 5, para 3. Sections 33–36 of the Terrorism Act 2000 allow police officers of at least the rank of superintendent, engaged in a terrorism investigation, to establish in certain circumstances a police cordon around an area. Under s 33(1) 'An area is a cordoned area for the purposes of this Act if it is designated under this section. (2) A designation may be made only if the person making it considers it expedient for the purposes of a terrorist investigation.' Once the cordon is in place Sched 5, para 3 gives a power of search. It must be authorised in writing by an officer of at least the rank of superintendent who must have reasonable grounds for believing that material that would be of substantial value to the investigation, and that is not excluded or special material or material covered by legal privilege (see below), is on specified premises within the cordon. The power is exercised by a constable who may enter and search premises and may seize items not protected by legal privilege if he has reasonable grounds for believing that they will be of substantial value to the investigation. Under para 3(1): 'Subject to sub-paragraph (2), a police officer of at least the rank of superintendent may by a written authority signed by him authorise a search of specified premises which are wholly or partly within a cordoned area.' Under para 3(2) 'A constable who is not of the rank required by sub-paragraph (1) may give an authorisation under this paragraph if he considers it necessary by reason of urgency.' There is evidence that the use of special search powers without the need to rely on reasonable suspicion or on a warrant have some value in terrorist investigations.[132] Nevertheless, the use of such powers represents an invasion of liberty which requires a strong and clear justification rather than a reliance on an uncertain phrase such as 'expedient'.

Search powers under the Police Act 1997

As discussed below, this Act places police powers of surveillance on a statutory basis. It also provides powers of entry, search and seizure. An authorisation may be issued if the search is believed to be necessary because it will be of substantial value in the prevention

---

132 See Walker, C, *The Prevention of Terrorism*, 2nd edn, 1992 p 195.

and detection of serious crime and the objective cannot reasonably be achieved by other means (s 93(2)). Under s 93(4)

> For the purposes of subsection (2), conduct which constitutes one or more offences shall be regarded as serious crime if, and only if –
>
> > (a) it involves the use of violence, results in substantial financial gain or is conduct by a large number of persons in pursuit of a common purpose, or
> > (b) the offence or one of the offences is an offence for which a person who has attained the age of twenty-one and has no previous convictions could reasonably be expected to be sentenced to imprisonment for a term of three years or more.

The main check on these extensive powers is provided by the special commissioners appointed from the senior judiciary (s 91(1)). Where the entry and search contemplated is of a dwelling house, prior approval by the commissioner is necessary, but this requirement is waived where the authorising officer believes that the search is urgent (s 94(2)). Since the belief does not need to be based on reasonable grounds, such a safeguard may have little impact in practice. These controversial extensions of the police powers of entry under the 1997 Act are therefore subject to very limited independent oversight and, unlike the s 18 power, they may be divorced from the needs of an immediate criminal investigation. These powers may in future be covered in the Investigatory Powers Bill 2015–16, currently before Parliament.[133]

Search warrants

Searching of premises other than under ss 17 and 18 can also occur if a search warrant is issued under s 8 of PACE, as amended, by a magistrate or if a warrant is applied for under other statutory powers, including post-PACE powers. Applications for all warrants by police officers, and the execution of the warrant must comply with the procedures set out in ss 15 and 16 of PACE. The application for the warrant must be supported, under s 15(3), by an 'Information' in writing. It must specify the enactment under which it is issued, the premises to be searched[134] and the articles or persons to be sought (s 15(6)). Section 8(1C) provides that multiple entry can be authorised. Previously, the warrant authorised entry to premises on one occasion only.

Section 16 governs the procedure to be followed in executing the warrant. The warrant must be produced to the occupier (although it seems that this need not be at the time of entry if impracticable in the circumstances)[135] under s 16(5)(b) and (c) and must identify the articles to be sought, although once the officer is on the premises, other articles may be seized under s 19 if they appear to relate to any other offence. The warrant does not necessarily allow for a general search of the premises[136] since the search can only

---

133 See further Chapter 11.
134 *Southwestern Magistrates' Court ex p Cofie* [1997] 1 WLR 885.
135 *Longman* [1988] 1 WLR 619, CA; for comment, see Stevens, R, *Justice of the Peace*, 1988, p 551.
136 See *Chief Constable of Warwick Constabulary ex p Fitzpatrick* [1999] 1 WLR 564.

be for the purpose for which the warrant was issued (s 16(8)). The extensiveness of the search depends upon that purpose.

Under s 16, the copy of the warrant issued to the subject of the search must identify the articles or persons sought and the offence suspected, but need not specify the grounds on which it was issued or give the name of the constable conducting the search. A warrant, like the notice of powers and rights (discussed below), therefore provides the occupier with limited information. Moreover, as noted above, it need not be produced to the occupier before the search begins if the purpose of the search might be frustrated by such production.[137] However, within these limitations, the courts seem prepared to take a strict view of the importance of complying with this safeguard. In *Chief Constable of Lancashire ex p Parker and McGrath*[138] police officers conducted a search of the applicant's premises in the execution of a search warrant issued under s 8 of PACE. However, after the warrant had been signed by the judge, the police detached part of it and reattached it to the other original documents. In purported compliance with s 16 of PACE, the police produced all these documents to the applicants. Thus, the police did not produce the whole of the original warrant and moreover, did not supply one of the documents constituting the warrant. The applicants applied for judicial review of both the issue and the execution of the warrants. It was determined that s 16(5)(b) of PACE had been breached in that the warrant produced to the applicants was not the original warrant as seen and approved by the judge and a declaration was granted to that effect. The police had admitted that there was a breach of the requirement under s 16(5)(c) that a copy of the warrant should be supplied to the occupier of the premises.

A warrant under s 8 will only be issued if there are reasonable grounds for believing that an indictable offence has been committed and where the material is likely to be of substantial value to the investigation of the offence and that will be admissible evidence at trial. A large number of other statutes also provide for the issuing of warrants to the police and to other public officials. Special provisions arise, *inter alia*, under s 27 of the Drug Trafficking Act 1994, s 2(4) of the Criminal Justice Act 1987 (in relation to serious fraud) and in relation to the security and intelligence services under the Intelligence Services Act 1994. A warrant authorising the police to search premises does not of itself authorise officers to search persons on the premises. The Home Office circular on PACE stated that such persons could be searched only if a specific power to do so arose under the warrant (for example, warrants issued under s 23 of the Misuse of Drugs Act 1971).

A wide power to search premises also arose under Sched 7, para 2 of the Prevention of Terrorism (Temporary Provisions) Act 1989[139] which, in contrast to the warrant power under PACE, was not dependent on the need to allege a specific offence and could therefore take place at a very early stage in the investigation. This power was reproduced in the Terrorism Act 2000, Sched 5, which applies to a wider range of groups. A justice of the peace must be satisfied that a terrorist investigation is being carried out and that there are reasonable grounds for believing that there is material that is likely to be of substantial value to the investigation. Also, it must appear that it is

---

137 *Longman* [1988] 1 WLR 619, CA.
138 (1992) 142 NLJ 635.
139 See Walker, C, *The Prevention of Terrorism*, 2nd edn, 1992, pp 185–97.

impracticable to gain entry to the premises with consent and that immediate entry to the premises is necessary. A warrant could also be issued under s 15(1) of the PTA in order to allow entry to premises to effect an arrest under s 14(1)(b). This power was thought necessary since the general PACE powers would not be applicable due to the broad nature of s 14(1)(b).[140] It was continued in the Terrorism Act 2000, Sched 5.

Power to enter premises at common law

Section 17(5) PACE abolished all common law powers to enter premises, subject to s 17(6), which preserves powers to enter without consent to deal with or prevent a breach of the peace. At common law, a power to enter premises in order to prevent crime arises from the much criticised case of *Thomas v Sawkins*.[141] Lord Hewart CJ contemplated that a police officer would have the right to enter private premises when 'he has reasonable grounds for believing that an offence is imminent or is likely to be committed'. This judgment received some endorsement from the provision of s 17(5) and (6); common law powers to enter were only preserved to deal with or prevent a breach of the peace; this narrowed down the power of entry, since it did not arise in respect of any offence. *Thomas v Sawkins* arose in the context of a public meeting held on private premises, but common law powers are not confined to such circumstances; in *McGowan v Chief Constable of Kingston on Hull*[142] it was found that police officers were entitled to enter and remain on private premises when they feared a breach of the peace arising from a private quarrel. The powers are even broader than s 17(6) would appear, on its face, to indicate: in *R (on the application of Rottnam) v Commissioner of Police for the Metropolis*[143] the House of Lords found that s 17 was concerned with powers to enter to arrest and that it did not limit the common law power to enter premises without consent *after* arrest.

Voluntary searches

Code of Practice B made under PACE, which governs powers of entry, search and seizure, makes special provision for voluntary searches. Paragraph 4 of Code B as originally drafted provided that a search of premises could take place with the consent of the occupier, and provided under para 4(2) that he must be informed that he need not consent to the search; in requiring that the consent should be in writing, it recognised that there might sometimes be a doubt as to the reality of such consent and went some way towards resolving that doubt. Under sub-para 5.1 the officer concerned must ensure that the consent is being sought from the correct person, whereas previously this problem was only addressed in a note for guidance (4A), and then only in respect of lodgings. Sub-paragraph 5.3 provides that the search must cease if the consent is withdrawn during it and also contains an express provision against using duress to obtain consent.[144]

---

140 See p 600.
141 [1935] 2 KB 249; for criticism, see Goodhart, ALG (1947) 6 CLJ 222; see further Chapter 9, p 600.
142 [1968] Crim LR 34. But see the ruling in *McLeod v UK* (1998) 27 EHRR 493.
143 [2002] 2 All ER 865.
144 For criticism of these provisions, see Bevan, K and Palmer, C, *Bevan and Lidstone's The Investigation of Crime*, 1996, pp 117–21.

However, it may be doubted whether these provisions have had much effect on ensuring that use of consensual search is not abused because it is not always made clear to occupiers that they can withhold consent.

Power of seizure

At common law prior to PACE, a wide power of seizure had developed where a search was not under warrant. Articles could be seized so long as they either implicated the owner or occupier in any offence or implicated third parties in the offence for which the search was conducted.[145] However, the power of seizure under PACE is even wider than this. Under s 8(2), a constable may seize and retain anything for which a search has been authorised. Section 8(2) provides that: 'A constable may seize and retain anything for which a search has been authorised under sub-section (1) above.' The power of seizure without warrant under the power of entry and search after arrest is governed by s 18(2), which provides that: 'A constable may seize and retain anything for which he may search under sub-section (1) above.' This power is greatly widened, however, by the further power of seizure arising under s 19:

> The constable may seize anything which is on the premises if he has reasonable grounds for believing:
>
> (a) that it has been obtained in consequence of the commission of an offence; and
> (b) that it is necessary to seize it in order to prevent it being concealed, lost, damaged, altered or destroyed.

The constable may seize anything that is on the premises if he has reasonable grounds for believing that:

> (a) it is evidence in relation to an offence which he is investigating or any other offence; and
> (b) it is necessary to seize it in order to prevent the evidence being concealed, lost, altered or destroyed.

Under s 22(1), anything that has been so seized may be retained 'so long as is necessary in all the circumstances'. It was made clear in *Chief Constable of Lancashire ex p Parker and McGrath*[146] that the above provisions assume that the search itself is lawful; in other words, material seized during an unlawful search cannot be retained and, if it is, an action for trespass to goods may arise. It was accepted in this instance that the search was unlawful (see below), but the chief constable contended that the material seized could nevertheless be retained. This argument was put forward under the provision of s 22(2)(a), which allows the retention of 'anything seized for the purposes of a criminal investigation'. The chief constable maintained that these words would be superfluous

---

145 *Ghani v Jones* [1970] 1 QB 693; *Garfinkel v MPC* [1972] Crim LR 44.
146 [1993] 2 WLR 428; [1993] 1 All ER 56; (1992) 142 NLJ 635.

unless denoting a general power to retain unlawfully seized material. However, it was held that the sub-section could not bear the weight sought to be placed upon it: it was merely intended to give examples of matters falling within the general provision of s 22(1). Therefore. the police were not entitled to retain the material seized.

Excluded or special procedure material or material covered by legal privilege

Under s 9, excluded or special procedure material or material covered by legal privilege cannot be seized during a search not under warrant and it is exempt from the s 8 search warrant procedure under s 8(1). However, the police may gain access to excluded or special procedure material by making an application to a circuit judge in accordance with Sched 1 or, in the case of special procedure material only, to a magistrate for a search warrant. Access to excluded material may only be granted where it could have been obtained under the previous law relating to such material. Excluded material is defined under s 11 to consist of material held on a confidential basis, personal records,[147] samples of human tissue or tissue fluid held in confidence and journalistic material held in confidence. Personal records include records held by schools, universities, probation officers and social workers. 'Special procedure material' defined under s 14 operates as a catch-all category which is, it seems, frequently used to cover confidential material that does not qualify as personal records or journalistic material.[148] A production order will not be made unless there is reasonable suspicion that a serious arrestable offence has been committed, the material is likely to be of substantial value to the investigation and admissible at trial. It should be noted that when inquiries relating to terrorist offences are made, Sched 7, para 3 of the Prevention of Terrorism (Temporary Provisions) Act 1989 (PTA) previously allowed access to both special procedure and excluded material. This power is reproduced in Sched 5 to the Terrorism Act 2000 which allows for orders to be made in relation to obtaining access to such material. The judge only needs to be satisfied that there is a terrorist investigation in being, that the material would substantially assist it and that it is in the public interest that it should be produced. It is clear that once the first two requirements are satisfied, it would be hard to show that the third was not.

The ruling in *Guildhall Magistrates' Court ex p Primlacks Holdings Co (Panama) Ltd*[149] made it clear that a magistrate must satisfy him or herself that there were reasonable grounds for believing that the items covered by the warrant did not include material subject to the special protection. The magistrates had issued search warrants authorising the search of two solicitors' firms. Judicial review of the magistrates' decision to issue a warrant was successfully sought; it was found that the magistrate had merely accepted the police officer's view that s 8(1) was satisfied rather than independently considering the matter.

The strongest protection extends to items subject to legal privilege, since they cannot be searched for or seized by police officers and, therefore, the meaning of 'legal

---

147 Defined in s 12.
148 For comment on these provisions, see Stone, R, 'PACE: Special Procedures and Legal Privilege' [1988] Crim LR 498.
149 [1989] 2 WLR 841.

privilege' is crucial. Under s 10, it will cover communications between client and solicitor connected with giving advice or with legal proceedings. However, if items are held with the intention of furthering a criminal purpose they will not, under s 10(2), attract legal privilege. It seems that this will include the situation where the solicitor unknowingly furthers the criminal purpose of the client or a third party. In *Crown Court at Snaresbrook ex p DPP*[150] it was found that only the solicitor's intentions regarding the criminal purpose were relevant, but the House of Lords in *Central Criminal Court ex p Francis and Francis*[151] rejected this interpretation in finding that material that figures in the criminal intentions of persons other than solicitor or client will not be privileged. A judge must give full consideration to the question whether particular documents have lost legal privilege.[152]

This interpretation of s 10(2) was adopted on the basis that, otherwise, the efforts of the police in detecting crime might be hampered, but it may be argued that it gives insufficient weight to the need to protect the special relationship between solicitor and client and, as argued below, is arguably vulnerable to challenge under the HRA.

Powers of seizure under the Criminal Justice and Police Act 2001

The Criminal Justice and Police Act 2001 (CJP) extended the power of seizure very significantly. The further powers of seizure it provides in s 50 apply to police powers of search under PACE and also to powers of seizure arising under a range of other statutes and applicable to bodies other than police officers, as set out in Sched 1 to the CJP. The power of seizure under s 50(1) depends on three conditions. The officer in question must lawfully be on the premises. Once there, if he finds something that he has reasonable grounds for thinking is something he is authorised to seize, and it is not reasonably practicable at the time to determine whether what he has found *is* something he is authorised to seize, he can seize as much of it as is necessary to make that determination. A further power of seizure under s 50(2) allows the person in question to seize material that he has no power to seize but that is attached to an object he does have the power to seize, if it is not reasonably practicable to separate the two.

This provision is significant since, *inter alia*, it allows police officers to remove items from premises even where they are not certain that – apart from s 50 – they have the power to do so. Thus a number of items can now be seized from premises although no power of seizure – apart from that arising under s 50 – in fact arises.

As indicated above, the seizure of excluded or special procedure material is restricted, while material covered by legal privilege cannot be seized. Most significantly, s 50 may serve to undermine these protections for certain material since, where such material is part of other material and cannot practicably be separated, it can be seized. It can also be seized where a police officer takes the view on reasonable grounds that it is something that he has the power to seize, although it turns out later that it falls within one of the special categories.

---

150 [1988] QB 532; [1988] 1 All ER 315.
151 [1989] AC 346; [1988] 3 All ER 375. For comment, see Stevenson (1989) Law Soc Gazette, 1 February, p 26.
152 *R v Southampton Crown Court ex p J and P* [1993] Crim LR 962.

Special provisions are made for the return of excluded or special procedure material or material covered by legal privilege. For obvious reasons, these provisions are most significant in relation to material covered by legal privilege since they could aid in undermining the privilege. Under s 54 such material must be returned unless it falls within s 54(2). Section 54(2) covers a legally privileged item comprised in other material. Such an item will fall within that sub-section if the retention of the rest of the property would be lawful and it is not reasonably practicable to separate the legally privileged item from the rest of the property without prejudicing the use of the rest of that property. Section 57(3) provides that ss 53–56 do not authorise the retention of property where its retention would not be authorised apart from the provisions of Part 2 of the CJP. Under s 62 inextricably linked property cannot be examined or copied but under sub-s (4) can be used to the extent that its use facilitates the use of property in which the inextricably linked property is comprised.

The provisions of ss 57 and 62, taken together with the provisions of ss 54 and 55, appear to create two categories of property. Property within the first can be retained as it would have been but for the CJP. Property within the second is not subject to an obligation to return but cannot be treated as it would have been had it fallen within the first category. It can be used to a limited extent in accordance with s 62(4). Section 62 makes it clear that s 62(4) applies to excluded or special procedure material or material covered by legal privilege that has not been returned since it is comprised in other lawfully held property.

Thus, ss 50, 54 and 55 taken together do provide avenues to the seizure and non-return of the specially protected material. The provisions thus circumvent the limitations placed on the seizure of excluded or special procedure material and, most importantly of all, provide an avenue to the seizure and use of legally privileged material. It can be said that for the first time legally privileged material has lost part of the protection it was accorded under the common law and under PACE.

These wide powers are 'balanced' by the provisions of ss 52–61, which provide a number of safeguards. Notice must be given to persons whose property has been seized under s 52, and under s 59 he or she can apply to the 'appropriate judicial authority' for the return of the whole or part of the seized property, on the ground that there was no power to seize, or that excluded or special procedure material, or legally privileged material, is not comprised in other property as provided for in ss 54 and 55. Under s 60 a duty to secure the property arises which includes the obligation under s 61 to prevent *inter alia*, copying of it. But despite these safeguards, it is unclear that these powers, especially to seize and use legally privileged material, are fully compatible with the requirements of the ECHR under the HRA, as considered further below.

Procedural safeguards for searches under Code of Practice B

Code of Practice B has progressively been revised to allow for an increase in the amount of information to be conveyed to owners of property to be searched by use of a standard form, the notice of powers and rights (para 6.7). It covers certain information including specification of the type of search in question, a summary of the powers of search and seizure arising under PACE and the rights of the subjects of searches. This notice must normally be given to the subject of the search before it begins, but under para 6.8 need not be if to do so would lead to frustration of the object of the search or danger to the police officers concerned or to others. These exceptions also apply under para 6.8 to leaving a copy of the warrant where the search is made under warrant. As explained above, s 18(4) provides that premises occupied or controlled by a person arrested for an arrestable offence[153] may be searched after the arrest if an officer of the rank of inspector or above gives authority in writing. Under para 4.3, the authority should normally be given on the notice of powers and rights. This clears up previous confusion[154] as to the form the authority should take.

Under current paras 6.7–6.8 the subjects of all searches, regardless of the status of the search, must receive a copy of the notice of powers and rights and, under para 6.8, where a consensual search has taken place but the occupier is absent, the notice should be endorsed with the name, number and station of the officer concerned. Oddly enough, it is not stated expressly that this information must be added to the notice where the subject of a consensual search is *present*. Sub-paragraph 6.5 provides that officers must identify themselves except in the case of inquiries linked to terrorism or where this might endanger them (para 2.9), but this provision appears to apply only to non-consensual searches due to the heading of that section. It might be thought that a person who voluntarily allows police officers to come onto his or her premises does not need the information mentioned, but this is to ignore the possibility that such a person might wish to withdraw consent during the search but might feel too intimidated to do so.

The power to search and seize is balanced by the need to convey certain information to the subject of the search in question, thereby rendering officers (at least theoretically) accountable for searches carried out. However, it is arguable that the provisions are partly of a merely presentational nature: they ensure that a large amount of information is conveyed to the occupier and make an attempt to ensure that community relations are not adversely affected by the operation of the search power,[155] but do not go into very much detail about the way the search should be conducted. Code B para 6 does set out certain provisions as to the conduct of searches, including that they must take place at 'a reasonable hour', but what this means in practice is no clearer than the injunction contained in para 6.10 to the effect that the search must be conducted with 'due consideration' for the privacy of the occupier. The question of the meaning of a 'reasonable hour' was raised in *Kent Pharmaceuticals Ltd v Director of the SFO*,[156] and the Divisional Court took the view that a search of premises at 6.00 am was at a reasonable hour, partly because the members of the household would be more likely to be present, bearing in mind the time at which people normally leave for work. It was fairly recently reiterated that it can include 6am in the morning even where no evidence is proffered as to a particular need to search at that time.[157] A prohibition on the non-urgent entry and search of property at night by state agents – perhaps one of the most unpleasant invasions of privacy possible – requires a clearer and more certain basis in law. This view

---

153 See *Khan v Metropolitan Police Commissioner* [2008] EWCA 723: the premises to which the s 18 power relate must be those occupied or controlled by the person who has been arrested; it is not enough for the police to have a reasonable belief in that occupation or control.

154 In *Badham* [1987] Crim LR 202 it was held that merely writing down confirmation of an oral authorisation was insufficient.

155 There is provision under para 3.5 for informing the local police community relations officer before a search of premises takes place if it is thought that it might adversely affect the relationship between the police and the community, subject to the proviso that in cases of urgency it can be performed after the search has taken place.

156 [2002] EWHC 3023.

157 *Redknapp v London Police Commissioner* [2009] 1 All ER 229.

of 'reasonable' is clearly open to doubt and the application of the search powers at that hour is, it is suggested, in doubtful compliance with Art 8.

In other words, the regulation of the search power under Code B emphasises the provision of information to the owner of premises so that officers can be rendered accountable for searches made, rather than making detailed provision regulating circumstances relating to the nature of the search itself in order to minimise the invasion of privacy represented by such searches. Clearly, however, Art 8 must be adhered to in respect of the conduct of searches, reflected in Code B para 6.10.

In contrast, searches made in order to gain evidence relating to civil proceedings, under orders known as *Anton Piller* orders,[158] must observe a number of safeguards: they must be organised on weekdays in office hours so that legal advice can be obtained before the search begins; the defendant must be allowed to check the list of items to be seized before items can be removed and, in some circumstances, an independent solicitor experienced in the execution of such orders must be present, instructed and paid for by the plaintiff.[159] It may be argued that there is a greater public interest in the prevention of crime than in ensuring that evidence is obtained by a party to civil proceedings, and therefore the police need at times to make an immediate search of premises, but the power to do so without judicial intervention should, it is submitted, be narrowed down to instances where the urgency of the search was demonstrable.

Impact of the HRA and police accountability

The PACE search and seizure provisions are clearly intended to make lawful actions that would otherwise amount to trespass to property and to goods only in very specific circumstances and only where a certain procedure has been followed. Invasion of a person's home has traditionally been viewed as an infringement of liberty that should be allowed only under tightly controlled conditions and in the exercise of a specific legal power. Article 8 ECHR under the HRA affords specific expression to these values. But it also goes further, and under ss 6 and 8 HRA a public authority is acting unlawfully and is liable to pay compensation for a breach of Art 8 in conducting a search of premises,[160] even where pre-HRA, no liability would have arisen in tort. The PACE provisions suggest some determination to strike a reasonable balance between the perceived need to confer on the police a general power to search property and the need to protect the privacy of the citizen. It is less clear that this is true of the TA and CJP provisions.

Breaches of Code of Practice B

Although Code B plays a part in creating safeguards for individual privacy, breaches of Code B will not attract tortious liability[161] and, unlike Codes C, D and E, exclusion of

---

158 From *Anton Piller KG v Manufacturing Processes Ltd* [1976] Ch 55; [1976] 1 All ER 779, CA.

159 These conditions, and others, were laid down in *Universal Thermosensors Ltd v Hibben* (1992) 142 NLJ 195. For discussion of the concern created by such orders prior to this decision, see (1990) 106 LQR 601.

160 See, e.g., *Keegan v United Kingdom* (2003) App 28867/03. The decision concerned the obtaining of compensation in the European Court of Human Rights for breach of Art 8 and Art 13 following a police search.

161 PACE 1984, s 67(10).

evidence will rarely operate as a form of redress because the courts are very reluctant to exclude physical evidence, and therefore it can have little impact on Code B provisions.

Reliance on Art 8

Article 8 values are reflected in this scheme to an extent and are capable of influencing it quite strongly due to the use of arguments under s 7(1)(b) of the HRA, either raised in criminal proceedings, in civil actions against the police for trespass, trespass to goods or for conversion, or as freestanding actions under s 7(1)(a) of the HRA. Article 8-based arguments have applicability here in relation to the level of intrusiveness represented by a search; the proportionality of the search to the aim of preventing crime can be raised. It can be argued that whether or not a basis in law for an entry to property is established, rendering the action non-trespassory, various features of the police actions might amount to infringements of Art 8. Where it is clear that a legal basis for the entry itself is likely to be established, a free-standing action can be brought against the police as a public authority under s 7(1)(a), arguing that although the entry had such a basis, such features amounted to a breach of Art 8.

The European Court of Human Rights has found that entry, search and seizure can create interferences with all the Art 8 guarantees, apart from that of the right to respect for family life.[162] Search for and seizure of documents is covered by the term 'correspondence' and the documents do not have to be personal in nature.[163] Such interferences can be justified only if they are in accordance with the law (Art 8(2)). This requirement covers not only the existence of national law, but its quality.[164] The statutory and common law powers probably meet this requirement[165] and have the legitimate aim of preventing crime or protecting national security.

It must further be shown that the interference 'corresponds to a pressing social need and, in particular, that it is proportionate to the legitimate aim pursued'.[166] It was found in the context of intercept warrants in *Klass v FRG*[167] that judicial or administrative authority for warrants would provide a degree of independent oversight: sufficient safeguards against abuse were available. This requirement was also stressed in *Kopp v Switzerland*.[168] It could be argued that the arrangements whereby magistrates issue search warrants might fail to meet this requirement since, although in appearance an independent judicial check is available before the event, the 'check' may be almost a formality in reality. These provisions provide a scheme that is reasonably sound in theory, but that is dependent on magistrates observing its requirements. Research suggests that, in practice, some magistrates make little or no attempt to ascertain whether the information a warrant contains may be relied upon, while it seems possible that magistrates who do take a rigorous approach to the procedure and refuse to grant warrants are not

---

162 See *Funke v France* (1993) 16 EHRR 297; *Mialhe v France* (1993) 16 EHRR 332.
163 See *Niemetz v Germany* A 251-B (1992).
164 *Kopp v Switzerland* (1999) 27 EHRR 91, paras 70–71.
165 In *McLeod v UK* (1998) 27 EHRR 493 powers to enter to prevent a breach of the peace were found to meet this requirement (paras 38–45).
166 *Olsson v Sweden* A 130 (1988), para 67.
167 (1978) 2 EHRR 214.
168 (1999) 27 EHRR 91.

approached again. It might be considered, therefore, that a breach of Art 8 might be established in respect of the practice of certain magistrates. It may be noted, however, that this argument failed in the Scottish case of *Birse v HM Advocate*.[169]

It is also arguable that the decision of the House of Lords in *Central Criminal Court ex p Francis and Francis*[170] regarding material subject to legal professional privilege may require re-consideration in relation to Art 8. As indicated above, the House of Lords found that privilege is lost when the material is innocently held, but is for a third party's criminal purpose. The approach in *Niemetz v Germany*[171] was to the effect that a search of a lawyer's office had led to a breach of Art 8 since it was disproportionate to the aims of preventing crime and of protecting the rights of others. That decision also raises questions about the provisions of Part 2 of the CJP. Since the CJP was accompanied by a declaration of its compatibility with the Convention rights, legal advice to the government was to the effect that Part 2 was compatible with Art 8. Clearly, this advice could subsequently be found to be flawed; the judiciary remain entirely free (in the higher courts, as Chapter 4 explained) to make a declaration of incompatibility between one or more of the Part 2 provisions and Art 8.

Clearly it could be argued that the limitations placed on the seizure and the use of legally privileged material by Part 2 may represent a proportionate response to the aim of preventing crime under Art 8(2). In other words, an interference with the Art 8 rights represented by the existence of legislation or in any particular instance could be viewed as relatively minimal, consistent with the need to serve that aim. On the other hand, the use of Part 2 provisions in practice may undermine the relationship between client and solicitor. The attitude of the courts in this context as indicated in decisions such as *Kent Pharmaceuticals Ltd v Director of the SFO* does not at present demonstrate a clear determination to afford the Convention rights real efficacy.

4 Powers of arrest

Introduction[172]

Under traditional common law doctrine an arrest occurs at the point when liberty ceases. Quite what an arrest is has not been defined by PACE and remains a common law concept. Indeed, it is clearly one that the courts continue to struggle with.[173] A person has been arrested when, if he tried to exercise his liberty to go where he will, he would be

---

169 Unreported, 13 April 2000. TLR 28/6/2000.
170 [1989] AC 346; [1988] 3 All ER 375. For comment, see Stevenson (1989) Law Soc Gazette, 1 February, p 26.
171 [1992] ECHR 13710/88.
172 For comment on arrest powers, see Zander, M, *Zander on PACE: The Police and Criminal Evidence Act 1984* 2015; Sanders, A and Young, R, *Criminal Justice*, 4th edn, 2010; Bailey, Taylor, N, *Bailey, Harris and Jones: Civil Liberties: Cases and Materials*, 6th edn, 2009, Chapter 2; Ashworth, A, *The Criminal Process*, 3rd edn, 2005; Feldman, D, *Civil Liberties and Human Rights in England and Wales*, 2nd edn, 2002, Chapters 5 and 9; Clark, D, *Bevan and Lidstone's The Investigation of Crime*, 2004; Starmer, K and Hopkins, A *Human Rights in the Investigation of Crime* (2007), OUP; Ayres, M, Murray, L and Fiti, R (2003) *Arrests for Notifiable Offences*, Home Office Paper 17/03; Healy, P, 'Investigative Detention in Canada' [2005] Crim LR 98 at p 105.
173 See *R v Iqbal* [2011] EWCA Crim 273.

prevented from doing so.[174] Some forms of detention are not deprivations of liberty. For whilst an arrest involves a deprivation of liberty, not every deprivation of liberty is an arrest. The common law has long recognised that deprivations of liberty short of arrest can lawfully occur (*Albert v Lavin*).[175] This was reaffirmed by the House of Lords in *R (on the application of Laporte) (FC) v Chief Constable of Gloucestershire*.[176]

Arrest may often be the first formal stage in the criminal process. It does not need to be; the process could begin with a consensual interview with the suspect, perhaps in his or her own home, followed by a summons to appear at the magistrates' court. It appears that arrests are sometimes effected unnecessarily; this contention is supported by the pre-PACE variation in practice regarding arrest between police areas,[177] which does not seem to be explicable on the ground of necessity, but seems to be attributable to different policies in the different areas. Any arrest represents a serious curtailment of liberty; therefore, use of the arrest power requires careful regulation. An arrest, in common with the exercise of other police powers, is seen as prima facie illegal, necessitating justification under a specific legal power. If an arrest is effected where no arrest power arises, a civil action for false imprisonment will lie.

Despite the need for clarity and precision, such powers were, pre-PACE, granted piecemeal, with the result that prior to PACE, they were contained in a mass of common law and statutory provisions. No consistent rationale could be discerned for the grant or lack of powers, and there were a number of gaps and anomalies. For example, the Criminal Law Act 1967 gave a power of arrest without warrant where the offence in question arose under statute and carried a sentence of five years. Thus, no power of arrest arose in respect of common law offences carrying such a sentence. This situation was detrimental to civil liberties owing to the uncertainty of the powers, but it may also have been detrimental in crime control terms since officers may have been deterred from effecting an arrest where one was necessary. The powers are now contained largely in PACE, as amended, but common law powers remain, while a number of statutes create a specific power of arrest which often overlaps with the PACE powers. The PACE arrest power is very broad, as explained below. Aside from PACE, a number of very broad and imprecisely defined offences exist to which arrest powers attach, such as s 5 Public Order Act 1986 or certain terrorism offences; the existence of such offences affords the police a great deal of leeway as to whether or not to arrest. Thus, the clarification of the arrest power that occurred under PACE has not led to any curbing of the ability of the police to interfere with liberty, quite the reverse.

The due process and crime control views of arrest and detention are diametrically opposed. Under the due process model, arrest should be based on a strong and

---

174 See *Shabaan Bin Hussein v Chong Fook Kam* [1970] AC 942 at p 949. In *Lewis v CC of the South Wales Constab* [1991] 1 All ER 206 the traditional position was re-stated – that arrest is not a legal concept, but a factual situation, at pp 209–10.

175 [1982] AC 546.

176 [2006] UKHL 55, para 39; CA: *R (on the application of Laporte) v CC of Gloucester Constab* [2004] EWCA Civ 1639.

177 E.g., in 1976 in Cleveland, 1% of persons were summonsed for an indictable offence, whereas in Derbyshire, 76% of suspects were, as were 40% of suspects in West Yorkshire and North Wales: Royal Commission Report 1981, Cmnd 8092, para 3.72. See further Bailey, SH and Gunn, MJ, *Smith and Bailey on the Modern English Legal System*, 1991, Sweet and Maxwell, pp 630–32.

established suspicion that the individual has committed a specific offence, since arrest and subsequent detention represent a severe infringement of individual rights. No one should be arrested except on evidence that they may have committed an offence or are about to. Due process demands that any arrest is supervised by a judicial officer who exercises a mediating influence between the citizen and the state, ensuring that the principle of legality is respected. Under the crime-control model, arrest and detention need not be sanctioned merely in relation to specific offences, but should be both an investigative tool and a means of asserting police authority over persons with a criminal record or of doubtful character, with a view to creating a general deterrent effect. Under this model, reasonable suspicion is viewed as a needless irrelevancy, an inhibitory rule standing in the way of an important police function. There is some evidence, discussed below, that English law has drifted towards the crime and control model driven not only by the attitude of the police in general towards their powers of arrest but also by the (at times) fairly deferential attitude of English judges towards police decisions on the ground.[178]

The body of research into the use of arrest and detention powers is to an extent conflicting, one school of analysis suggesting that the procedural due process elements that were supposed to create restraints on the powers largely fail to do so in practice in a number of respects. A partially opposed view agrees as to 'the limited effectiveness of PACE's control mechanisms, including routinisation of supervisory controls', but suggests that 'the potential exists for [the PACE reforms] to be given more (or less) substance'.[179] It will be argued below that such potential is being realised to an extent under the impact of the HRA, but that its influence is variable, especially as between the conventional and counter-terrorist schemes. While the conventional scheme shows a formal adherence to due process, which appears to have a subtle impact in practice, especially as regards controls on detention, the counter-terrorist scheme adheres, formally, to a lower standard, thereby providing greater leeway for departure from due process without necessarily breaching the rules.

At common law – power to arrest for breach of peace

PACE has not affected the power to arrest that arises at common law for breach of the peace.[180] Factors present in a situation in which breach of the peace occurs may also give rise to arrest powers under PACE, but may extend further than they do owing to the wide definition of breach of the peace. The leading case is *Howell*,[181] in which it was found that breach of the peace will arise if violence to persons or property, either actual or apprehended, occurs. Threatening words are not in themselves a breach of the peace, but they may lead a police officer to apprehend that a breach will arise. Where a breach of the peace is threatened by some members of a group, the police may be justified in

---

178 See *Alanov v Chief Constable of Sussex* [2012] EWCA Civ 234 reversing a highly deferential decision of a county court judge.
179 Dixon, in Walker and Starmer, *Miscarriages of Justice* (1999), p 67.
180 *Laporte v Commissioner of the Metropolitan Police* [2014] EWHC 3574 QB.
181 [1982] QB 416; [1981] 3 All ER 383, CA; for comment, see Williams (1982) 146 JPN 199–200, 217–19.

detaining all of them.[182] A police officer or any other person may arrest if a breach of the peace is in being or apprehended,[183] but not when it has been terminated, unless there is reason to believe that it may be renewed.[184] In *Humphries v Connor*,[185] Fitzgerald J summarised a constable's duty as follows:

> With respect to a constable, I agree that his primary duty is to preserve the peace; and he may for that purpose interfere, and, in the case of an affray, arrest the wrong-doer; or, if a breach of the peace is imminent, may, if necessary, arrest those who are about to commit it, if it cannot otherwise be prevented.

A temporary detention effected in order to prevent a breach of the peace need not amount to an arrest. However, in order to effect such detention, short of arrest, a breach of the peace must be imminent in the same way as would be required to justify an arrest. In other words, the requirements are *not* diminished where the action that is taken falls short of an arrest. Lord Bingham so found in *R (on the application of Laporte) (FC) (Original Appellant and Cross-respondent) v Chief Constable of Gloucestershire*:[186]

> there is a power and duty resting on constable and private citizen alike to prevent a breach of the peace which reasonably appears to be about to be committed. That is the test laid down in *Albert v Lavin*,[187] which means what it says. It refers to an event which is imminent, on the point of happening. The test is the same whether the intervention is by arrest or (as in *Humphries v Connor, King v Hodges*[188] and *Albert v Lavin* itself) by action short of arrest. There is nothing in domestic authority to support the proposition that action short of arrest may be taken when a breach of the peace is not so imminent as would be necessary to justify an arrest.

In *Laporte*, in relation to the detention of protesters on a coach that had been turned back by the police from an anti-war demonstration, the chief constable did not think a breach of the peace was so imminent as to justify an arrest. Therefore, the House of Lords found, it could not justify a detention short of arrest. Also action is only permitted to prevent a breach of the peace 'by the person arrested',[189] or against 'the person

---

182 *Austin v Commissioner of Police of the Metropolis* [2005] HRLR 20. 3,000 people were detained for seven hours in London during a May Day demonstration; it was held that the actions of the police were lawful on the basis that a breach of the peace was apprehended on the part of some members of the group.

183 Following *Foulkes* [1998] 3 All ER 705, the breach must be imminent.

184 For commentary on this point and on breach of the peace generally, see Williams, G, [1954] Crim LR 578. The view that there is no power to arrest once a breach of the peace is over was put forward in the Commentary on *Podger* [1979] Crim LR 524 and endorsed *obiter* in *Howell* [1982] QB 416; [1981] 3 All ER 383, CA. See Chapter 9, pp 642 *et seq*. For full discussion of the use of breach of the peace.

185 (1864) 17 ICLR 1, 8–9.

186 [2006] UKHL 55, para 39. CA: *R (on the application of Laporte) v CC of Gloucester Constab* [2004] EWCA Civ 1639.

187 [1982] AC 546.

188 [1974] Crim LR 424.

189 *R v Howell*, above, n 181, at p 426.

who is . . . threatening to break the peace'.[190] That condition was also unfulfilled in the circumstances in *Laporte* as there was no reason to believe that all the protesters would breach the peace. Thus the detention in *Laporte* was unlawful. *Laporte* is the most recent and authoritative pronouncement on arrest or detention where breach of the peace is apprehended.

Power of arrest with warrant

This power does not arise under PACE. There are a large number of statutory provisions allowing an arrest warrant to be issued, of which the most significant is that arising under s 1 of the Magistrates' Courts Act 1980.[191] Under this power, a warrant may be issued if a person aged at least 17 is suspected of an offence that is indictable or punishable with imprisonment or of any other offence and no satisfactory address is known allowing a summons to be served. This provision therefore limits the circumstances under which a warrant can be sought as an alternative to using the non-warrant power under PACE, and as the police have such broad powers of arrest under PACE, arrest in reliance on a warrant is used even less under PACE than it was previously.

Under PACE: power of arrest without warrant

Prior to PACE, only certain offences were arrestable without a warrant, under the Criminal Law Act 1967. PACE, as amended in 2005, broadened the category of arrestable offences. Under s 24 a person can be arrested by a constable on reasonable suspicion of being in the act of committing (s 24(1)(d)), having committed (s 24(2)), or being about to commit (s 24(1)(c)), an offence – any offence. Thus this power now allows an officer to arrest for any offence so long as reasonable suspicion can be shown. Under s 24 the previous difference between arrestable and non-arrestable offences has been abolished: all offences are arrestable so long as certain other conditions are also satisfied. As PACE Code G notes, the decision to arrest 'is an operational one at the discretion of the individual constable'.[192] A person can also be arrested by a constable if in the act of committing (s 24(1)(b)), having committed, (s 24)(3)(a)) or being about to commit (s 24(1)(a)), an offence. In other words, the officer can arrest on a hunch so long as it turns out to be justified. This possibility may tend to undermine the reasonable suspicion requirement since police officers are aware that the likelihood of being called to account for the false arrest is not high. The changes of 2005 had the effect of creating 'a single code of arrest powers. . . applicable to all offences'.[193]

This broad power is apparently balanced by a further requirement: in order to arrest under s 24, two steps must be taken: first, there must be reasonable suspicion relating to the offence in question, unless s 24(1)(b), s 24(3)(a) or s 24(1)(a) applies (the 'hunch' provisions). Second, there must be reasonable grounds for thinking that one of the arrest conditions is satisfied. The need for the officer to have reasonable suspicion relating to

---

190 *Albert v Lavin*, above, *per* Lord Diplock, p 565.
191 See [1962] Crim LR 520, p 597 for comment on these powers.
192 PACE Code G, para 2.4.
193 *Hayes v Chief Constable of Merseyside* [2011] EWCA Crim 911, para 14.

the offence in question *and* as to the further requirement (previously – general arrest conditions) was emphasised on appeal in *Edwards v DPP*[194] in relation to (old) s 25, but the decision is now applicable to s 24.

The further requirements, which are alternatives, are, under s 24(5):

(a) to enable the name of the person in question to be ascertained (in the case where the constable does not know and cannot readily ascertain the person's name or where the constable has reasonable grounds for doubting whether a name given by the person as his name is his real name;

(b) correspondingly as regards the person's address;

(c) to prevent the person in question:

(i)   causing physical injury to himself or any other person;
(ii) suffering physical injury;
(iii) causing loss of or damage to property;
(iv) committing an offence against public decency; or
(v)   causing an unlawful obstruction of the highway;

(d) to protect a child or other vulnerable person from the person in question.

Crucially, two alternative requirements were added in 2005 to s 24. The police also have the further options of showing that the arrest is needed to allow the prompt and effective investigation of the suspected offence in question, or to prevent prosecution of the offence from being hindered by the suspect's disappearance (s 24(5)(e) and(f)). These two requirements greatly broadened the ambit of this power.

An ordinary citizen has more limited powers: he or she can arrest under s 24A in the same way, in respect of indictable offences, with the omission of the possibility of arresting where the offence is about to be committed. The reasons are more limited than under s 24(5). Under s 24A they are to prevent the person in question:

(i)   causing physical injury to himself or any other person;
(ii) suffering physical injury;
(iii) causing loss of or damage to property; or
(iv) making off before a constable can assume responsibility for him.

Although Code G exhorts the police to use arrest as a last resort, in practice arrest under s 24 is likely to be resorted to quite readily, following the practices already established under (old) ss 25 and 24. A key potentially limiting requirement under s 24, as under the previous s 25, is the need to show 'reasonable grounds' for suspicion in relation to the s 24(5) requirements. The phrase suggests that a clear, objective basis for forming the view in question should exist. The decision in *Edwards v DPP* suggests that the courts appreciate the constitutional significance of upholding the requirements under the general arrest conditions. In *Edwards*, an officer arrested the appellant in the course of a struggle, stating that the arrest was 'for obstruction'. Since no power of arrest arises in respect of obstruction, the arrest must have been under

---

194 (1993) 97 Cr App R 301; (1993) *The Times*, 29 March.

s 25. However, it was found to be necessary to demonstrate that the officer had the general arrest conditions in mind when arresting. This might have been inferred, but the express reference to obstruction was thought to preclude an inference that he had other matters in mind. But where it appears that one of the conditions is contemplated, the reasonable grounds for suspicion do not appear to create an exacting standard. In *G v DPP*[195] a belief that an address was false, based on a general assumption that people who commit offences give false details, was accepted as based on reasonable grounds. On this interpretation, the s 24(5) requirements are unlikely to be acting as curbs on the arrest power: once an offence is suspected, it would seem that one of them would be almost automatically fulfilled. The two added requirements clearly enhance this possibility.

Counter-terrorist powers

There are two powers of arrest under the Terrorism Act 2000. The power of arrest under s 41 TA is, first, in respect of reasonable suspicion of having committed certain terrorist offences, when read in conjunction with s 40(1)(a). Under s 40(1)(a): 'In this Part a "terrorist" means a person who has committed [certain TA] offences.'[196] This definition is not exclusive; its other part is dependent upon s 40(1)(b). Section 40(1)(b) defines a terrorist as 'a person who is or has been concerned in the preparation or instigation of acts of terrorism'. Thus s 41 read with s 40(1)(b) allows, second, for an arrest, not in respect of a specific offence but on suspicion of 'being a terrorist' in the sense indicated. The broader and more uncertain a power of arrest, the more it may come into tension with Art 5. In considering the exceptional circumstances in which liberty can be taken away under Art 5, the requirements connoted by the general provision that they must have a basis in law under Art 5(1) are also implied into the 'prescribed by law' rubric of each sub-paragraph.[197]

   Arrests can obviously be made in respect of the terrorist offences under the Terrorism Act 2000 under s 24 of PACE. But if an arrest is effected under s 41 TA, as opposed to s 24 of PACE, this has an effect on the length of detention, as discussed below. From a constable's point of view it would probably be preferable to arrest under the TA rather than s 24 PACE, since the extra requirements under s 24(5) would not apply.

   The ordinary arrest powers under PACE or under the first power of s 41 of the TA, read with s 40(1)(a), almost certainly cover many arrests that could be undertaken under the second power covered by s 41 and s 40(1)(b) since there are a range of very broad terrorism offences. Police discretion is obviously particularly wide where no reasonable suspicion of any particular offence is necessary in order to arrest. This second power is clearly aimed at allowing arrest as a stage in the investigation, not as the culmination of it, and it may therefore be said to be firmly based on the crime control model that views the purpose of arrest as a means of furthering general investigative goals. It therefore represents a clear departure from the traditional due process view of arrest taken by Phillips in 1981 as justified only after the investigation has uncovered

---

195 [1989] Crim LR 150. For comment, see [1993] Crim LR 567.
196 This includes offences under any of ss 11, 12, 15–18, 54 and 56–63.
197 *Winterwerp v Netherlands* A 33 (1979), para 39.

sufficient evidence. The power was severely criticised when its predecessor was used in the context of Irish terrorism; it was after 2000 transplanted into a different context and afforded a wider application.

Section 41 TA read with s 40(1)(b) largely reproduces s 14(1)(b) of the Prevention of Terrorism (Temporary Provisions) Act 1989 (PTA)). The government, in its 1998 consultation paper on terrorism,[198] acknowledged the criticisms which s 14(1)(b) had attracted:

> if the police have proper cause to suspect that a person is actively engaged in terrorism, they must have sufficient information to justify an arrest under PACE . . . the absence of any requirement for reasonable suspicion of a specific offence effectively allows the police free rein to arrest whomsoever they wish without necessarily having good reason, including those who should not be arrested at all.[199]

However, the government took the view that although the ordinary powers of arrest were extensive, they were insufficient to deal with the sophisticated evasion techniques of terrorists.[200] This claim may be applicable to those who are most likely in practice to be arrested under the TA, although the wide range of broad TA offences must be borne in mind, many based, as indicated in Chapter 15, on a minimal *actus reus* and requiring no proof of *mens rea*.

The continuation of this power is thus controversial. Under s 14(1)(b), a constable had to have reasonable grounds for suspecting that a person was concerned in the preparation or instigation of acts of terrorism connected with the affairs of Northern Ireland or 'any other act of terrorism except those connected solely with the affairs of the UK or a part of the UK' in order to arrest. Under s 41 TA and s 40(1)(b), the qualifying words are omitted. In other words, the arrest power has been since 2000 applicable to non-Irish UK domestic groups who can be viewed as terrorist groups, including groups such as environmental activists threatening direct action. As the author suggested in 2000 might occur,[201] there is some evidence that the arrest power is being used in respect of groups such as animal rights activists[202] since they fall within the s 1 TA definition. In practice, since s 14(1)(b) did not require suspicion relating to an offence, it was used for investigation, questioning and general intelligence gathering that may be conducted, it has been said, for the purpose of 'isolating and identifying the urban guerrillas and then detaching them from the supportive or ambivalent community'.[203]

Owing to its departure from due process principle in failing to require arrest for a particular offence, the reproduction of s 14(1)(b) of the PTA in ss 41 and 40(1)(b) of the TA rendered the arrest power vulnerable to a challenge under Art 5 of the Convention, which in para 5(1)(c) encapsulates that principle. The test under Art 5(1)(c) relies on

---

198 *Legislation Against Terrorism: A Consultation Paper*, Cm 4178, 1998.
199 *Ibid*, para 7.5.
200 Since they are 'skilled in, and dedicated to, evading detection . . . terrorist crime is often quite different [from serious non-terrorist crime] both in terms of the sophistication of the techniques deployed and the (potential) harm caused': *ibid*, para 7.8.
201 See Fenwick, H, *New Labour, Freedom and the Human Rights Act*, 2000, Chapter 3, pp 79–80.
202 CAMPAC, *Terrorising Minority Communities: anti-terrorism powers, their use and abuse*, 2003.
203 Lowry (1976–77) 8–9 col *Human Rights L Rev* 185, p 210.

reasonable suspicion regarding an offence and therefore calls into question s 41 of the TA, in so far as it relates to suspicion that a person is a terrorist in the sense of (under s 40(1)(b)) being concerned in the commission, preparation, or instigation of an act of terrorism. Section 41 therefore allows for arrest without reasonable suspicion that a particular offence has been committed. The compatibility of s 41 and Art 5(1)(c) depends on the interpretation afforded to *Brogan and Others v UK*.[204] The case concerned the previous EPA provision, which was largely reproduced in s 41 TA, read with s 40(1)(b). The Court applied two tests to the basis for the arrests in finding that the power of arrest was justified within Art 5(1)(c). First, the definition of acts of terrorism was 'well in keeping with the idea of an offence'.[205] Secondly, after arrest, the applicants were asked about specific offences. Thus, 'the Court decided the point on the basis that involvement in "acts of terrorism" indirectly meant the commission of specific criminal offences under Northern Irish law, which would appear to be the better approach on the facts'.[206]

On either test, arrests under s 41 read with s 40(1)(b) might be in a more doubtful position. The definition of terrorism relevant in *Brogan* was identical to the s 20 PTA definition – the use of violence for political ends. The current definition under s 1 of the TA, discussed in Chapter 15, is far wider: it covers the use or threat, 'for the purpose of advancing a political, religious or ideological cause', of action, designed to influence the government or intimidate the public, which involves serious violence against any person or serious damage to property, or is designed to seriously disrupt an electronic system, or endangers life, or creates a serious risk to health or safety. Unlike the previous one, this definition may cover matters, such as threatening to hack into a computer system, or to destroy genetically modified crops, which do not clearly correspond to existing offences and therefore might not be viewed so readily as 'in keeping with the idea of an offence'. The application of the second test would partly depend in practice on the particular instance which arose before a domestic court. If a person was arrested under s 41 as part of an investigation and was not asked about specific offences on arrest, the connection with the basis of the arrest, bearing in mind the width of the s 1 TA definition, might be viewed as too tenuous to be termed an arrest on reasonable suspicion of an offence. Moreover, the purpose of such an arrest would not appear to be in accordance with the Art 5 requirement, since it would not be to 'bring [the suspect] before the competent legal authority'.

This suggestion, the government at the time rejected it, coming to the view, which is evaluated below, that this arrest power is compatible with Art 5(1)(c).[207] However, Lord Carlile, the government's previous independent reviewer of terrorist law and policy, supported the introduction of this offence, and it was introduced under the Terrorism Act 2006, ss 1 and 5. Since an arrest can now occur for those offences, which replicate the wording under s 40(1)(b), it may be being less frequently invoked. Since arrest for preparatory offences is now possible, ss 41 and 40(1)(a) of the TA are tending to avoid incompatibility with Art 5 since it is less necessary to rely on s 40(1)(b).

204 Judgment of 29 November 1988 (1989) Series A 145-B (1989) 11 EHHR 117.
205 Para 51.
206 Harris, D, O'Boyle, K and Warbrick, C, *Law of The European Convention on Human Rights*, 1995, p 116 (Current edn, 2014).
207 *Ibid*, para 7.14.

Other statutory powers of arrest

If a statute creates any offence, then obviously the arrest power under s 24 is applicable so long as one or more of the requirements under s 24(5) is satisfied. Section 11 of the Public Order Act 1986 and s 89 of the Police Act 1996 provide examples of such offences. However, certain statutes expressly create specific powers of arrest which are not dependent on ss 24 or 25, such as ss 12 and 14 of the Public Order Act. In such cases, the procedure under s 28 of PACE (which is discussed below) will still apply.

Reasonable suspicion

Level of suspicion

Apart from the second arrest power under s 41 TA, and the s 24 provisions relating to involvement or attempted involvement in an offence, as opposed to suspected involvement, the powers discussed depend on the concept of reasonable suspicion relating to an offence. Art 5(1)(c) of the Convention sets out one of the circumstances in which an individual can be detained. It permits the lawful arrest or detention of a person effected for the purpose of bringing him before the competent legal authority on reasonable suspicion of having committed an offence, or where it is reasonably considered that an arrest is necessary to prevent the person in question from committing an offence or fleeing after having done so. In requiring arrest only for specific offences, and not for general crime control purposes, Art 5(1)(c) adheres closely to the due process model of arrest indicated above. Section 24 of PACE (apart from the 'hunch' provisions) and s 41 TA (in so far as it relates to certain specific terrorist offences under s 40(1)(a)) appear prima facie to comply with Art 5(1)(c) owing to their requirements of reasonable suspicion.

The idea behind the concept of reasonable suspicion is that an arrest should take place at quite a late stage in the investigation;[208] this limits the number of arrests and makes it less likely that a person will be wrongfully arrested. It may be interpreted in accordance with the provisions as to reasonable suspicion under Code A, although, as will be discussed below, the courts have not relied on Code A in ruling on the lawfulness of arrests. Annex B, para 4 of original Code A stated that the level of suspicion for a stop would be 'no less' than that needed for arrest. Although this provision is omitted from the current revision of Code A, it would seem that in principle, the Code A, provisions should be relevant to arrests if the codes and statute are to be treated as a harmonious whole. Moreover, it would appear strange if a more rigorous test could be applied to the reasonable suspicion necessary to effect a stop than that necessary to effect an arrest. It would seem that a future revision of the codes might usefully state that the concept of reasonable suspicion in Code A applies to arrest as well; if so, it would at least deter the use of race-based factors as the basis of reasonable suspicion.

---

208 See the Phillips Royal Commission Report, Cmnd 8092 (1981).

In 2012 Code G was amended to take into account decisions of the courts since it was originally promulgated in 2005. Code G therefore goes some way to reinforcing the necessity requirement and ensuring that this criterion is not simply presentational.[209] The objective nature of suspicion required for most arrests, and now reflected in Code G, is echoed in various decisions on the suspicion needed for an arrest. In *Dallison v Caffrey*[210] Lord Diplock said the test was whether 'a reasonable man assumed to know the law and possessed of the information which in fact was possessed by the defendant would believe there were [reasonable grounds]'. Thus, it is not enough for a police officer to have a hunch that a person has committed or is about to commit an offence; there must be a clear basis for this suspicion which relates to the particular person in question and which would also be apparent to an objective observer. If an officer only has a hunch – mere suspicion as opposed to reasonable suspicion – he or she might continue to observe the person in question, but could not arrest until the suspicion had increased and could be termed 'reasonable suspicion'. Clearly, the officer could, however, arrest under the relevant provisions of s 24, if prepared to take the risk that the hunch might turn out to be incorrect.

However, this concept of reasonable suspicion still leaves a great deal of leeway to officers to arrest where suspicion relating to the particular person is at a low level, but they want to further the investigation by gathering information. At present, the courts seem prepared to allow police officers such leeway and it should be noted that PACE endorses a reasonably low level of suspicion owing to the distinction it maintains between belief and suspicion, suspicion being the lower standard.[211] The decision in *Ward v Chief Constable of Somerset and Avon Constabulary*[212] suggests that a high level of suspicion is not required, and this can also be said of *Castorina v Chief Constable of Surrey*.[213] Detectives were investigating a burglary of a company's premises and on reasonable grounds came to the conclusion that it was an 'inside job'. The managing director told them that a certain employee had recently been dismissed and that the documents taken would be useful to someone with a grudge. However, she also said that she would not have expected the particular employee to commit a burglary. The detectives then arrested the employee, having found that she had no previous criminal record. She was detained for nearly four hours and then released without charge. She claimed damages for false imprisonment and was awarded £4,500. The judge considered that it was necessary to find that the detectives had had 'an honest belief founded on a reasonable suspicion

---

209 *Richardson v Chief Constable of the West Midlands* [2011] EWCA 773 QB.
210 [1964] 3 WLR 385. See also *Shabaan Bin Hussein v Chong Fook Kam* [1970] AC 942, esp at p 948.
211 Section 17(2)(a) requires belief, not suspicion, that a suspect whom an officer is seeking is on premises; similarly, powers of seizure under s 19(2) depend on belief in certain matters. The difference between belief and suspicion and the lesser force of the word 'suspect' was accepted as an important distinction by the House of Lords in *Wills v Bowley* [1983] 1 AC 57, p 103, HL. See also *Johnson v Whitehouse* [1984] RTR 38, which was to the same effect.
212 (1986) *The Times*, 26 June; cf *Monaghan v Corbett* (1983) 147 JP 545, DC (however, although this demonstrated a different approach, the restriction it imposed may not be warranted: see *DPP v Wilson* [1991] Crim LR 441, DC).
213 [1996] LG Rev Rep 241; (1988) 138 NLJ 180, transcript from LEXIS.

leading an ordinary cautious man to the conclusion that the person arrested was guilty of the offence'.

However, the Court of Appeal overturned the award on the basis that the test applied by the judge had been too severe. It was held that the question of honest belief was irrelevant; the issue of reasonable suspicion had nothing to do with the officer's subjective state of mind. The question was whether there was reasonable cause to suspect the plaintiff of burglary. Given that certain factors could be identified, including inside knowledge of the company's affairs and the motive of the plaintiff, it appeared that there was sufficient basis for the detectives to have reasonable grounds for suspicion.

Castorina may be compared with the findings of the Strasbourg Court in *Fox, Campbell and Hartley v UK*.[214] The applicants had been arrested in accordance with s 11 of the Northern Ireland (Emergency Provisions) Act 1978, which required only suspicion, not reasonable suspicion. The only evidence put forward by the government for the presence of reasonable suspicion was that the applicants had convictions for terrorist offences and that when arrested, they were asked about particular terrorist acts. The government said that further evidence could not be disclosed for fear of endangering life. The Court found that although allowance could be made for the difficulties of evidence gathering in an emergency situation, reasonable suspicion that 'arises from facts or information that would satisfy an objective observer that the person concerned may have committed the offence'[215] had not been established. Moreover, 'the exigencies of dealing with terrorist crime cannot justify stretching the notion of reasonableness to the point where the essence of the safeguard secured by Art 5(1)(c) is impaired'.[216] The arrests in question could not, therefore, be justified. In *Murray v UK*[217] this test was viewed as a lower standard for reasonable suspicion, applicable in terrorist cases, but it was again emphasised that an objective standard of reasonable suspicion was required,[218] although the information grounding the suspicion might acceptably remain confidential in the exigencies of a situation such as that pertaining at the time of the arrest in question, in Northern Ireland.[219] It is debatable whether the UK courts are in general applying a test of reasonable suspicion under PACE or the TA that reaches the standards which the European Court had in mind, especially where terrorism is not in question. The departure which the HRA has brought about is to encourage stricter judicial scrutiny of decisions to arrest.

The European Court of Human Rights in *O'Hara v UK*[220] commented on the nature of the reasonable suspicion required to satisfy Art 5(1)(c). The Court found that it requires the existence of some facts or information that would satisfy an objective observer that *the person concerned* may have committed the offence. However, the Court also accepted that the reasonable suspicion at the time of arrest need not be of the same level as that necessary to bring a charge.[221] As mentioned above, this statement accords with

214   A 182 (1990); 13 EHRR 157.
215   *Ibid*, para 32.
216   *Ibid*, para 32.
217   [1994] EHRR 193.
218   Para 50.
219   Paras 58–59
220   (2002) 34 EHRR 32.
221   *Ibid*, paras 34, 36.

the test under Code A and that under Code G. Unsurprisingly, it confirms the need for an objective test, but otherwise has effected no radical change in the stance of the courts in relation to this concept.

Reasonable suspicion and police working rules

As Sanders and Young observe, commenting on *Castorina*, 'The decision gives the police considerable freedom to follow crime control norms, in that it allows them to arrest on little hard evidence'.[222] In practice, the concept of reasonable suspicion is interpreted very flexibly by the police, as it is in respect of stop and search powers. Doubtful grounds often appear to be sufficient to provide reasonable grounds to justify deprivation of liberty. Only in exceptional instances will an officer's use of this power be found to have been wrongful. The courts tend to be reluctant to interfere with the police interpretation and use of the arrest power. Post-PACE decisions, including *Castorina*, leave a great deal of leeway to officers to arrest where suspicion relating to the particular person or persons arrested is at a low level. Hearsay evidence is sufficient.[223]

Research into the use of arrest suggests that in practice, the concept of reasonable suspicion is deployed flexibly by the police. A wealth of academic research and analysis has established that the need for reasonable suspicion provides little protection against wrongful arrest. Very doubtful grounds often appear to be sufficient to provide reasonable grounds to justify deprivation of liberty. Further, only in exceptional instances will an officer's use of this power be found to have been wrongful; the courts are quite ready to find that these somewhat hazy tests have been satisfied.[224]

Sanders and Young speak of appearing 'suspicious' as being 'a key working rule' in arrests and stops, and observe that association with other criminals is also often the basis for arrest even where the police are 'entirely without reasonable suspicion', since the object is to obtain statements against associates.[225] The courts appear to be fairly reluctant to interfere with the police interpretation and use of the arrest power. The post-PACE decisions discussed leave a great deal of leeway to officers to arrest where suspicion relating to the particular person is at a low level, but they want to further the investigation by gathering information.[226] As a number of commentators have pointed out, arrest became under PACE avowedly no longer the culmination of the investigative process but an integral part of it.[227] The strong evidence founding the charge that

---

222 Sanders and Young, 2nd edn, 2000, *op cit*, fn 10, at p 86.
223 *Clarke v Chief Constable of North Wales* [2000] All ER (D) 77.
224 See McConville, Sanders and Leng, *op cit*, fn 10; Sanders and Young, *op cit*, fn 2, (2010), Chapter 3; Ryan, C and Williams, K, 'Police discretion' [1986] Public Law 285, and Clayton and Tomlinson, (1988) Law Soc Gazette, 7 September, p 22.
225 Sanders and Young, *op cit*, fn 10, (2010), pp 143–48 esp at 144, based on research undertaken by Leng (Royal Commission on Criminal Justice Research Study No 10), 1993.
226 See *Ward v Chief Constable of Somerset and Avon Constabulary* (1986) *The Times*, 26 June; *Castorina v Chief Constable of Surrey* (1988) NLJ 180, transcript from LEXIS.
227 Sanders and Young, *op cit*, fn 10, (2007) (3rd edn) at pp 138–50; Ewing, KD and Gearty, CA, *Freedom under Thatcher*, 1989, p 24.

used to be obtained, it has been suggested,[228] prior to arrest, thus ensuring that innocent persons were unlikely to be arrested and that the infringement of liberty of a person innocent in the eyes of the law was kept to a minimum, tended after PACE to be found in the form of a confession, after arrest. PACE also confirmed the movement away from judicial supervision of arrest, by means of the warrant procedure, which had already begun pre-PACE.

Arresting officer must form reasonable suspicion

If there is no evidence that the arresting officer thought that an offence had been committed, even if objectively speaking there are reasonable grounds for suspicion, the arrest will be unlawful (*Chapman v DPP*).[229] If the arresting officer considers that there is no possibility that a charge will be brought the arrest will be unlawful since it would not be for a proper purpose: *Plange v Chief Constable of South Humberside Police.*[230] The reasonable suspicion must be formed by the arresting officer himself or herself. The executive discretion to arrest vests in the individual officer and not his/her superiors.[231] In *O'Hara v Chief Constable of the RUC*,[232] a decision on s 12(1) of the Prevention of Terrorism Act 1989, the House of Lords found that a constable could form a suspicion based on what he had been informed of previously as part of a briefing by a superior officer, or otherwise. The question to be asked was whether a reasonable man would personally have formed the suspicion after receiving the relevant information. It was not enough for the arresting officer to have been instructed by a superior officer to arrest; his own personal knowledge must provide him with the necessary reasonable suspicion. In the instant case, the arresting officer had sufficient personal knowledge of matters, which it was found provided a basis for reasonable suspicion. The House of Lords stated that these findings applied to arrest powers other than the one arising under s 12. A belief that a superior officer probably had the information would not be sufficient.[233] The Court of Appeal has found, following *O'Hara*, that reasonable suspicion based on an entry in the police national computer is sufficient.[234] The European Court of Human Rights in *O'Hara v UK*[235] has found that the approach taken in *O'Hara* is in accordance with the demands of Art 5. The Court accepted that the reasonable suspicion must be formed personally by the arresting officer, but could be based on information from other sources.

Arresting on a 'hunch'

As indicated, under s 24 it is not always necessary to show that reasonable suspicion exists. If an offence is *in fact* being committed or has been committed or is about to be

---

228 Ewing and Gearty, *ibid*, p 25.
229 (1988) 890 Cr App R 190.
230 (1992) *The Times*, 23 March.
231 *Holgate-Mohammed v Duke* [1984] AC 437, 446 Lord Diplock.
232 [1997] 2 WLR 1; [1997] 1 All ER 129.
233 *Commissioner of Police of the Metropolis v Raissi* [2008] EWCA 1237.
234 *Hough v Chief Constable of Staffordshire*, 16 January 2001, unreported.
235 (2002) 34 EHRR 32.

committed, a constable can arrest even if he or she is just acting on a hunch which luckily turns out to be justified. Of course, if an officer arrests without reasonable suspicion, he or she is taking a risk. That provision was included because it might seem strange if a person could found an action for false imprisonment on the basis that although he was committing an offence, he should not have been arrested for it. However, if it cannot be established that the offence was committed or was about to be committed, it is not enough to show that reasonable grounds for suspicion did in fact exist although the officer did not know of them. In *Siddiqui v Swain*[236] the Divisional Court held that the words 'reasonable grounds to suspect' used in s 8(5) of the Road Traffic Act 1972 include the requirement that the officer should *actually* suspect. This approach was also adopted in *Chapman v DPP*.[237] Article 5(1)(c) also calls into question the provision under s 24 of PACE allowing for arrest without reasonable suspicion so long as a 'hunch' turns out to be justified (s 24(4)(a), (5)(a) and (7)(a)). Sanders and Young call this possibility a 'classic crime control norm since the ends are regarded as justifying the means'.[238] Such an arrest would appear to be unlawful under s 6 of the HRA where effected by a police constable since no exception under Art 5 appears to allow for it.

Purpose of the arrest

In *Castorina* Purchas LJ also ruled that once reasonable suspicion arises, officers have a discretion as to whether to arrest or do something else, such as making further inquiries, but that this discretion can be attacked on *Wednesbury* principles.[239] In making this ruling, Purchas J relied on the ruling of the House of Lords in *Holgate-Mohammed v Duke*.[240] The House of Lords had confirmed that in addition to showing that the relevant statutory conditions are satisfied, the exercise of statutory powers by officers must not offend against *Wednesbury* principles; officers must not take irrelevant factors into account or fail to have regard to relevant ones; an exercise of discretion must not be so unreasonable that no reasonable officer could have exercised it in the manner in question. Thus, an arrest will be found to be unlawful if no reasonable person looking at the circumstances could have considered that an arrest should be effected, if the decision is based on irrelevant considerations and if it is not made in good faith and for a proper purpose.[241]

It was found in *Castorina* that no breach of these principles had occurred and, as reasonable grounds for making the arrest were found, the first instance judge had erred in ruling that further inquiries should have been made before arresting. The need to make further inquiries would be relevant to the first stage – arriving at reasonable suspicion – but not to the second – determining whether to make an arrest. That it must be relevant to the first is axiomatic: an investigation passes through many stages, from the first, in which a vague suspicion relating to a particular person arises, up until the point

236 [1979] RTR 454.
237 (1988) Cr App R 190; [1988] Crim LR 843.
238 Sanders and Young, *Criminal Justice*, 1st edn, 1994, p 76.
239 *Associated Provincial Picture Houses Ltd v Wednesbury Corpn* [1948] 1 KB 223; [1948] 2 All ER 680, CA.
240 [1984] 1 AC 437; [1984] 1 All ER 1054, HL.
241 For discussion of police discretion in this respect, see [1986] PL 285.

when that person's guilt is established beyond reasonable doubt. At some point in that process, reasonable suspicion giving rise to a discretion as to whether to effect an arrest arises; thus, there must be a point in the early stages at which it is possible to say that more inquiries should have been made, more evidence gathered, before the arrest could lawfully take place. The courts appear prepared to accept that arrest at quite an early stage in this process may be said to be based on reasonable grounds. The application of *Wednesbury* principles left little leeway for challenge to the decision to arrest, so it may be said that the interest of the citizen in his or her personal liberty was not being accorded sufficient weight under the pre-HRA tests.[242]

Auld LJ in the post-HRA case of *Al Fayed v Commissioner of Police for the Metropolis*[243] reaffirmed that *Castorina* involves asking three questions and that in determining all *Castorina* questions the state of mind is that of the arresting officer, subjective as to the first question, the fact of his suspicion, and objective as to the second and third questions, whether he had reasonable grounds for it and whether he exercised his discretionary power of arrest with *Wednesbury* reasonableness. It is for the police to establish the first two *Castorina* requirements, namely that an arresting officer suspected that the claimant had committed an arrestable offence and that he had reasonable grounds for his suspicion.[244] If the police establish those requirements, the arrest is lawful unless the claimant can establish on *Wednesbury* principles that the arresting officer's exercise or non-exercise of his power of arrest was unreasonable, the third *Castorina* question.[245]

Article 5 considerations are able to limit the application of the broad *Wednesbury* principle.[246] Under the HRA, courts also have to consider whether the Convention rights have been adhered to; it is not enough to ask whether the decision to arrest was reasonable. The *purpose* of the arrest should also be in compliance with Art 5(1)(c), even where reasonable suspicion is established, in that it should be effected in order to 'bring [the suspect] before the competent legal authority', although this does not mean that every arrest must lead to a charge.[247] In the individual circumstances of a case, a breach of Art 5(1)(c) might be found where, although reasonable suspicion was present on the facts, the arrest discretion was not exercised in accordance with Art 5(1)(c) since the purpose of the arrest was in reality for general information-gathering ends. This might occur where, although there were, objectively, reasonable grounds for suspicion, the

---

242 See further as to reasonable grounds for suspicion, Clayton, R and Tomlinson, H, 'Arrest and reasonable suspicion' (1988) Law Soc Gazette, 7 September, p 22; Dixon, D, Bottomley, K and Coleman, C, 'Reality and rules in the construction and regulation of police suspicion' (1989) 17 Int J Soc Law, 185–206; Sanders and Young, *Criminal Justice*, 2007, Chapter 3.4.

243 [2004] EWCA Civ 1579, at para 83.

244 *Holgate Mohammed, per* Lord Diplock at p 441F–H, and *Plange, per* Parker LJ.

245 *Holgate-Mohammed, per* Lord Diplock at p 446A–D; *Plange, per* Parker LJ; and *Cumming, per* Latham LJ at para 26.

246 See the House of Lords in *R v SSHD ex p Bugdaycay* [1987] AC 514; *R v SSHD ex p Brind* [1991] 1 AC 696, see, e.g., *per* Lord Bridge of Harwich, at pp 748F–747B. See *Cumming*, paras 43 and 44: 'it seems to me that it is necessary to bear in mind that the right to liberty under Art 5 was engaged and that any decision to arrest had to take into account the importance of this right even though the Human Rights Act was not in force at the time . . . The court must consider with care whether or not the decision to arrest was one which no police officer, applying his mind to the matter could reasonably take bearing in mind the effect on the appellants' right to liberty.'

247 *K-F v Germany* (1997) 26 EHRR 390.

arresting officer had no belief in the guilt of the suspect. In such an instance, the arrest would be unlawful under s 6 of the HRA, not merely *Wednesbury* unreasonable. A breach might also be established where the arrest was unnecessary in order to further the purpose in question. For example, if the suspect was cooperative, there would appear to be no need to arrest her since the purpose under Art 5(1)(c) could be served by interviewing her in her own home. That purpose would not appear to cover an arrest undertaken merely for the purpose of interviewing such a suspect in the police station.[248] It was found, however, in *Chalkley and Jeffries*,[249] that the existence of a collateral motive for an arrest would not necessarily render it unlawful. Under the HRA, a domestic court has to consider whether Art 5 is satisfied by an arrest with a 'mixed' purpose.

Necessity

Section 24 of PACE requires that an arrest be necessary. The necessity requirement was considered in *Richardson*.[250] The claimant was a school teacher who was alleged to have assaulted a pupil. Richardson attended the police station both voluntarily and by appointment for interview; he was accompanied by his solicitor on both occasions. On arrival for his appointment Richardson was arrested by the police in line with their express intentions indicated during the first interview. The arrest was considered necessary by the arresting officer 'to allow the prompt and effective investigation of the offence or the conduct of the person in question' (s 24(5)(e)). The officer feared that Richardson might leave the interview before its conclusion. Slade J held however that this fear was misplaced, there being no evidence that Richardson would behave as the police feared. Consequently the officer had no basis for believing that the arrest was necessary. Indeed, the police had failed to evaluate the question of necessity correctly and on that basis the arrest had been *Wednesbury* unreasonable.[251] It was not acceptable for the police to operate a blanket policy that required everyone voluntarily attending an interview at a police station to be arrested. The necessity requirement required officers to make an individual consideration of necessity in the circumstances of each case. Therefore a decision that a suspect might leave a voluntary interview before its conclusion must be based on evidence rather than a policy to pre-emptively arrest.

In the subsequent case of *Hayes* the Court of Appeal set down a two-stage test for necessity.[252] Hayes, a petty drugs dealer, was alleged to have intimidated a drugs user and to have committed common assault. It was arranged by the police with the claimant that he would meet them at Liverpool Lime Station. On arrival at the station Hayes was arrested. In considering the lawfulness of the arrest the Court of Appeal developed a two-stage test. First, an officer has to form a belief that the arrest was necessary within the terms of s 24(5) of PACE and, second, this belief has to be objectively identified. This belief, it was found, had to be determined on the facts that the officer had been aware of the time of the arrest. On the facts of the case before the Court it was not clear that such an objective belief existed; however, this did not stop the Court of Appeal

248   *Cf Holgate-Mohammed v Duke* [1984] AC 437.
249   [1998] 2 All ER 155.
250   *Richardson v Chief Constable of West Midlands Police* [2011] EWHC 773 (QB).
251   *Ibid*, [70]–[71].
252   *Hayes v Chief Constable of Merseyside Police* [2011] EWCA Civ 911, [30].

from deciding that it did exist. Following the revision of Code G in 2012 it is now clear that where an officer is intending to interview a suspect the officer must begin with a consideration of whether voluntary attendance is a practical alternative to the arrest of the suspect. It must be made clear to the suspect that he will not be arrested if he voluntarily attends. When the suspect presents himself at the police station he cannot be arrested unless new information comes to light. Moreover, if the suspect leaves the interview then the position can be reconsidered, although the possibility that he may do so is not in itself a ground for arrest before the interview commences.

Procedural elements of a valid arrest[253]

Informing the arrestee

For an arrest to be made validly, not only must the power of arrest exist, whatever its source, but the procedural elements must be complied with. The fact that a power of arrest arises will not alone make the arrest lawful. These elements are of crucial importance owing to the consequences that may flow from a lawful arrest that will not flow from an unlawful one.[254] Such consequences include the right of the officer to use force in effecting it under s 117 of PACE or s 114 of the TA, if necessary, and the loss of liberty inherent in an arrest. If an arrest has not occurred, the citizen is free to go wherever she will and any attempt to prevent her doing so will be unlawful.[255] It is therefore important to convey the fact of the arrest to the arrestee and to mark the point at which the arrest comes into being and general liberty ceases. At common law, there had to be a physical detention or a touching of the arrestee to convey the fact of detention, unless he or she made this unnecessary by submitting to it;[256] the fact of arrest had to be made clear[257] and the reason for it had to be made known.[258] Merely taking a person into custody does not constitute an arrest unless the person is informed of the charge or the suspicions that form the basis of the arrest.[259] Some degree of specificity is necessary.[260]

But it appears that conveying to the person in question the fact that a deprivation of liberty has occurred need not be taken to imply, necessarily, that an arrest has occurred. This follows from the decision in *Laporte*.[261] An arrest is the lawful apprehension of a person in order to bring him to a police station; a temporary deprivation of liberty, short of arrest, can be for some different purpose, such as transferring the person from

---

253 The term 'valid arrest' is open to attack on the ground that there can be no such thing as an invalid arrest. However, a valid arrest may be contrasted with a purported arrest and that is the sense in which it is used in this section.

254 The question as to the difference between a valid and invalid arrest has been much debated; see Lidstone, KW [1978] Crim LR 332; Clark and Feldman [1979] Crim LR 702; Zander, M (1977) NLJ 352; Smith, JC [1977] Crim LR 293.

255 *Rice v Connolly* [1966] 2 QB 414; *Kenlin v Gardner* [1967] 2 QB 510 (see above, p 839 in relation to obstruction of or assault on a police officer in the course of his duty).

256 *Hart v Chief Constable of Kent* [1983] RTR 484.

257 *Alderson v Booth* [1969] 3 QB 216.

258 *Christie v Leachinsky* [1947] AC 573; [1947] 1 All ER 567, HL.

259 *Shields (by his litigation friend, Rebecca Shields) v Chief Constable of Merseyside Police* [2010] EWCA Civ 1281, [15].

260 *Murray v United Kingdom* [1994] ECHR 14310/88, [76]. See also *R v Iqbal* [2011] All ER (D) 138 (Jan).

261 [2006] UKHL 55.

one area to another, in order to prevent a breach of the peace. So since it appears that the police have the power at common law to deprive a person of liberty without perpetrating an arrest, it appears that indicating to the person by words or action that a deprivation of liberty has occurred could be interpreted as indicating that either a power of arrest or of a temporary detention is being invoked. It also follows from the stop and search case law discussed above that it can be indicated to a person that they are not lawfully free to leave the spot for a short period of time, but that they are not under arrest or deprived of liberty. Presumably, in all these instances, since the police are acting within their powers, resistance to the detention would be unlawful. Clearly, the citizen is left in an uncertain position in relation to deprivation of liberty. As discussed below, the *reason* for the arrest has to be conveyed to the person. So it could be argued that an arrest occurs when a deprivation of liberty occurs *and* the reason is given. But even that suggestion does not capture the notion of an arrest, since the reason need only be given if it is practicable to do; also a reason need not be given if the arrest is for breach of the peace rather than an offence.[262] Reasons are of course important because as Sedley LJ noted in *Taylor*:[263]

> The practical reasons historically given by our courts for the requirement which is reflected in article 5(2) have a good deal to do with giving the suspect an immediate opportunity of explanation or self-exculpation. With PACE procedures which for good reason discourage dialogue before interview, this is less important than perhaps it once was. The real underpinning of the Convention right is the simple one of respect for the dignity of the individual: if the state is taking away your liberty, you are entitled to know why.

The common law safeguards have been modified and strengthened by s 28 of PACE, which provides that both the fact of and the reason for the arrest must be made known at the time or as soon as practicable afterwards. This is further re-enforced by Art 5(2) ECHR. Conveying the reason for the arrest does not involve using a particular form of words,[264] but it appears that reasonable detail must be given so that the arrestee will be in a position to give a convincing denial and therefore be more speedily released from detention.[265] Given the infringement of liberty represented by an arrest and the need, therefore, to restore liberty as soon as possible, consistent with the needs of the investigation, it is unfortunate that s 28 did not make it clear that a reasonable degree of detail should be given. In *Wilson v Chief Constable of Lancashire Constabulary*[266] the arrestee was not given enough information to enable him to challenge the arrest, rendering the arrest unlawful. Code G makes further provision for informing the arrestee. Under

---

262 See *Williamson v CC of Great Midlands* [2004] 1 WLR 14; the Court of Appeal stated that it would be good practice for a person in this position to be treated as if subject to the PACE provisions.

263 *Taylor v Thames Valley Police* [2004] EWCA Civ 858, [58].

264 The Court of Appeal confirmed this in *Brosch* [1988] Crim LR 743. In *Abassey and Others v Metropolitan Police Comr* [1990] 1 WLR 385, it was found that there was no need for precise or technical language in conveying the reason for the arrest; the question whether the reason had been given was a matter for the jury. See also *Nicholas v Parsonage* [1987] RTR 199, and Chapter 2, p 55.

265 *Murphy v Oxford*, 15 February 1985, unreported, CA. This is out of line with the CA decision in *Abassey* [1990] 1 WLR 385, in which *Murphy* unfortunately was not considered.

266 [1997] COD 422; WL 1103678.

para 2.2 Code G officers need to inform the suspect of the fact of the arrest even if it is obvious. Further, significantly, information as to the relevant circumstances of the arrest relating to *both* elements of s 24 must be given. But if the reason for the arrest was given in terms of the offence arrested for, as appears to be required by s 28, but no reason was given relating to the requirements of s 24(5) as required by Code G, it would appear that the arrest would still be lawful.

Informing promptly

However, the reason for the arrest need only be made known as soon as practicable. The meaning and implications of this provision were considered in *DPP v Hawkins*.[267] A police officer took hold of the defendant to arrest him, but did not give the reason. The youth struggled and was therefore later charged with assaulting an officer in the execution of his duty. The question that arose was whether the officer was in the execution of his duty since he had failed to give the reason for the arrest. If the arrest was thereby rendered invalid, he could not be in the execution of his duty, since it could not include effecting an unlawful arrest. It was determined in the Court of Appeal that the arrest became unlawful when the time came at which it was practicable to inform the defendant of the reason but he was not so informed. This occurred at the police station or perhaps in the police car, but did not occur earlier because of the defendant's behaviour. However, the arrest did not become retrospectively unlawful and therefore did not affect acts done before its unlawfulness came into being, which thus remained acts done in the execution of duty. Thus, the police have a certain leeway as to informing the arrestee; the arrest will not be affected, nor will other acts arising from it, until the time when it would be practicable to inform of the reason for it has come and gone.

Some delay in informing of the arrest will not create incompatibility with Art 5(2), which provides that a person must be informed promptly of the reason for arrest, and corresponds to s 28 of PACE. In *Fox, Campbell and Hartley v UK*[268] the applicants, who were arrested on suspicion of terrorist offences, were not informed of the reason for the arrest at the time of it, but were told that they were being arrested under a particular statutory provision. Clearly, this could not convey the reason to them at that time. At a later point, during interrogation, they were asked about specific criminal offences. The European Court of Human Rights found that Art 5(2) was not satisfied at the time of the arrest, but that this breach was healed by the later indications made during interrogation of the offences for which they had been arrested. In *Murray v UK*,[269] soldiers occupied a woman's house, thus clearly taking her into detention, but did not inform her of the fact of arrest for half an hour. The House of Lords had found that the delay in giving the requisite information was acceptable because of the alarm which the fact of arrest, if known, might have aroused in the particular circumstances – the unsettled situation in Northern Ireland.[270] The European Court of Human Rights found no breach of Art 5(2); Mrs Murray was eventually informed during interrogation of the reason for the arrest and, in the circumstances, it was found acceptable to allow an interval of a few hours

267 [1988] 1 WLR 1166; [1988] 3 All ER 673, DC; see also *Brosch* [1988] Crim LR 743, CA.
268 (1990) A 182; 13 EHRR 157.
269 *Murray v UK* (1994) 19 EHRR 193.
270 *Murray v Ministry of Defence* [1988] All ER 521, HL; for comment, see Williams (1991) 54 MLR 408.

between the arrest and the point when she was informed of the reason for it. (The claim also made, that Art 8 had been breached, was dismissed. The violation of privacy fell within the exception under Art 8(2) in respect of the prevention of crime and was found to be necessary and proportionate to the aims of that exception.)

If the word 'practicable' in s 28 is interpreted in accordance with the interpretation of Art 5(3) in both *Murray* and *Fox* it seems that, depending on the circumstances, a certain amount of leeway is created in respect of informing the arrestee. On somewhat doubtful grounds, the Convention has allowed some departure from the principle that there should be a clear demarcation between the point at which the citizen is at liberty and the point at which her liberty is restrained.

Consensual detainment

Apart from situations in which reasonable suspicion relating to an offence arises, there is nothing to prevent a police officer asking any person to come to the police station to answer questions (s 29 PACE). There is no legal power to do so, but equally, there is no power to prevent such a request being made. The citizen is entitled to ask whether he or she is being arrested and, if not, to refuse. However, if he or she consents, no action for false imprisonment can arise. This creates something of a grey area, since the citizen may not realise that he or she does not need to comply with the request. The government refused to include a provision in PACE requiring the police to inform citizens of the fact that they are not under arrest. However, when a suspect is cautioned he must also be told that he is free to leave if he is not under arrest (para 3.21 Code C). This is repeated in Code G (para 2.9, notes 2F and 2G).

Use of force[271]

The police may use reasonable force so long as they are within one of the powers allowed for under the PACE scheme. This is provided for under s 3 of the Criminal Law Act 1967 and s 117 of PACE 1984. Section 3 is in one sense wider than s 117, since it authorises the use of force by any person, although only in relation to making an arrest or preventing crime. The prevention of crime would include resistance to an unlawful arrest. Section 117 only applies to police officers and then only in relation to provisions under PACE which do not provide that the consent of someone other than a constable is required. Section 114 TA provides an equivalent provision in respect of the TA powers. Force may include as a last resort the use of firearms. Section 117 provides that 'the officer may use reasonable force, if necessary, in the exercise of the [PACE] power'. Excessive force can raise issues under Article 3 ECHR. The ECtHR has consistently held that recourse to physical force by the police where 'this has not been made strictly necessary by an individual's own conduct diminishes human dignity and is in principle an infringement of the rights set forth in Article 3'.[272] Any such allegation must be proved beyond reasonable doubt. Nonetheless, in certain situations presumptions of facts may

271 For consideration of the use of force, see [1982] Crim LR 475; *Report of Commissioner of Police of the Metropolis for 1983*, Cmnd 9268; Waddington, PAJ, *The Strong Arm of the Law*, Clarendon, 1991.

272 *Belenko v Russia* (2011) ECHR 35330/5, para 46.

arise particularly in cases of arrest and/or custody.[273] In those circumstances the burden switches to the respondent government to provide convincing arguments that the force used was not excessive.[274] These principles are of course applicable under the HRA.[275]

5 Detention in police custody

Introduction

As discussed in Chapter 2, Article 5(1) of the Convention provides a right to liberty subject to certain exceptions which must have a basis in law. Not only must an exception apply, but the requirements under Art 5(2), (3) and (4) must also be met. The current domestic arrest and detention scheme for non-terrorist suspects is, as one would expect, largely coterminous, formally speaking, with these provisions, and in some respects may afford a higher – or, at least, clearer – value to due process. The current statutory scheme is, as Toulson LJ said in *Shields*,[276] one that 'takes into account the principle of Art 5 which therefore do not require separate consideration'. However breaches of Art 5 are most likely to be established in respect of the special counter-terrorist arrest and detention powers available under the Terrorism Act 2000, as amended in 2012. At present detention in police custody for two weeks is possible, as discussed below.

A procedure prescribed by law

The first and most essential requirement of Art 5 is that a person's detention is in accordance with a procedure 'prescribed by law'. In the case of *Khudoyorov v Russia* the Strasbourg Court noted 'that where deprivation of liberty is concerned, it is particularly important that the general principle of legal certainty be satisfied'.[277] This means that the procedure should be in accordance with national law and with recognised Convention standards, including Convention principles, and should not be arbitrary. Moreover, any detention authorised by the law must be executed in a proportionate manner.[278] Thus, where one of the Art 5(1) exceptions applies to a person's detention, this requirement also has to be satisfied. The procedure covers the arrest provisions[279] and the procedure adopted by a court in authorisations of detention.[280]

Time limits on detention after arrest under PACE

The position under the law prior to the 1984 Act with regard to detention before charge and committal before a magistrate was very uncertain. Prior to PACE, the police had no clearly defined power to hold a person for questioning. The detention scheme governed

---

273 *Salman v Turkey* (2000) ECHR 21986/95, para 108.
274 *Zelilof v Greece* (2007) ECHR 170601/03, para 47.
275 *ZH v Commissioner of the Metropolitan Police* [2012] EHWC 604 (Admin).
276 [2010] EWCA Civ 1281, [13].
277 [2005] ECHR 6847/02, [125].
278 *Vasilva v Denmark* [2003] ECHR 52792/99.
279 *Fox, Campbell and Hartley v UK*, Appl No 182; (1990) 13 EHRR 157.
280 *Weston v UK* (also known as *H v UK*) (1981) 3 EHRR 402; *Van der Leer v Netherlands* A 170-A (1990).

by Part IV of PACE put such a power on a more certain basis in accordance with the Phillips recommendations,[281] that the purpose of the detention is to obtain a confession.[282] This was foreshadowed in the developing common law recognition that detention was for the purpose of questioning.[283]

Phillips did not, however, envisage that the decision to arrest would become, in effect, the decision to detain. This is reflected in the role of the custody officer under s 37 of PACE. The custody officer (under s 37 PACE) or the public prosecutor (under s 37B PACE, and see *DPP Guidance on Charging* 2013) will decide whether there is sufficient evidence to charge the suspect with the offence at this point. If not, the suspect should be released with or without bail, unless there are reasonable grounds for believing that detention is necessary 'To secure or preserve evidence relating to an offence for which he is under arrest or to obtain such evidence by questioning him'.[284] The second ground is the most frequently used. In theory, the custody officer could refuse to accept the arrestee into detention. In practice this is extremely rare, if not unknown; the custody officer almost always simply rubber-stamps the arresting officer's decision that the suspect should be detained.[285] In *DPP v L*[286] it was held that the custody officer is under no obligation to determine the legality of an arrest. Custody officers appear to disregard the requirement to consider whether the detainee should be charged at the 'booking in' stage, with the necessity requirement under s 37(2) becoming in practice synonymous with convenience. Thus, although s 37(3) appears to protect due process since it provides that the custody officer must be satisfied that there are reasonable grounds for the detention,[287] in practice it does not appear to affect police working practices.

Under s 41, the detention can be for up to 24 hours, but in the case of a person in police custody for a serious arrestable offence (defined in s 116) it can extend to 96 hours. Part IV of PACE does not apply to detention under the Terrorism Act 2000, as amended, (below) or to detention by immigration officers.[288] Under s 42(1), a police officer of the rank of superintendent or above can sanction detention for up to 36 hours if three conditions apply: he or she has reasonable grounds for believing that either the detention is necessary to secure or preserve evidence relating to an offence for which the detainee is under arrest or to obtain such evidence by questioning him; an offence for which the detainee is under arrest is a serious arrestable offence; and the investigation is being conducted diligently and expeditiously. However, it appears that the requirement that the custody officer has 'reasonable grounds' for doing so does not in practice inhibit the authorisation of further detention. After 36 hours, detention can no longer be authorised by the police alone. Under s 43(1), the application for authorisation must be supported by information and brought before a magistrates' court, which

---

281 See Phillips Royal Commission, Cmnd 8092 (1981).
282 Part IV, s 37(2).
283 *Mohammed-Holgate v Duke* [1984] QB 209.
284 Section 37(2). See also the reasons for continued detention after charge under s 38.
285 See Dixon, D et al, 'Safeguarding the rights of suspects in police custody', 1 *Policing and Society* 115, p 130.
286 [1999] Crim L Rev 752.
287 Under s 45A, PACE allows regulation to be made allowing the decision under s 37 to be taken by means of video-conference.
288 PACE 1984, s 51.

can authorise detention under s 44 for up to 96 hours if the conditions are met as set out above. Detention must be reviewed periodically;[289] in the case of a person who has been arrested and charged, the review must by the custody officer; in the case of a person arrested but not yet charged, by an officer of at least the rank of inspector. The detainee or his solicitor (if available) has the right to make written or oral representations.[290]

Research suggests, however, that these reviews are not treated as genuine investigations into the grounds for continuing the detention, but as routinised procedures requiring a merely formal adherence.[291] The powers of detention are very significant, but they are intended to embody the principle that a detained person should normally be charged within 24 hours and then either released or brought before a magistrate. They are supposed to be balanced by all the safeguards created by Part V of PACE and Codes of Practice C, E (and F, although visual recording is not a requirement). It may be noted that a person unlawfully detained can apply for a writ of habeas corpus in order to secure release from detention, and this remedy is preserved in s 51(d). Its usefulness in practice is, however, very limited since the courts have developed a practice of adjourning applications for 24 hours in order to allow the police to present their case. Thus, detention can continue for that time, allowing the police to carry out questioning or other procedures in the meantime.

Detention under the Terrorism Act 2000, as amended

The detention scheme adopted in respect of terrorist suspects allowed for the suspect to be detained for longer periods than for non-terrorist suspects, and for a lower level of due process safeguards to be applicable during detention. The detention scheme for terrorist suspects has been through a number of revisions, as discussed below, which have been driven on the one hand by due process demands imposed in effect by the European Court of Human Rights and on the other by governmental crime control and national security concerns; the law has been subject to continual change. Essentially, the period of detention has become incrementally longer, but it is subject to judicial authorisation. Under the Protection of Freedoms Act 2012 s 57 a suspect may now be detained for up to 14 days.

Detention with judicial authorisation

Prior to the inception of the TA, if a person was arrested under s 14 of the PTA, as opposed to s 24 of PACE, whether the arrest was for an offence or on suspicion of being a terrorist, the detention provisions under PACE did not apply. The arrestee could be detained for up to 48 hours following arrest (s 14(4)) of the PTA) but this period could be extended by the Secretary of State by further periods not exceeding five days in all (s 14(5) of the PTA). Thus, the whole detention could be for seven days and, in contrast to the PACE provisions, the courts were not involved in the authorising process; it occurred at a low level of visibility as an administrative decision.

---

289 Under s 40(1)(b).
290 Under s 40(12) and (13).
291 Dixon, D et al, 'Safeguarding the rights of suspects in police custody', 1 Policing and Society 115, pp 130–31.

The similar provision under the PTA 1984 was found to be in breach of Art 5(3) in *Brogan v UK*.[292] Article 5(3) confers a right to be brought promptly before the judicial authorities; in other words, not to be held for long periods without a hearing. It covers both arrest and detention. There will be some allowable delay in both situations; the question is therefore what is meant by 'promptly'. Its meaning was considered in *Brogan* in relation to the arrest and detention of the applicants considered above, arising by virtue of the special powers under s 12 of the PTA. The UK had entered a derogation under Art 15 against the applicability of Art 5(3) to Northern Ireland, but withdrew that derogation in August 1984. Two months later, the *Brogan* case was filed. The applicants complained, *inter alia*, of the length of time they were held in detention without coming before a judge, on the basis that it could not be termed prompt. The Court took into account the need for special measures to combat terrorism; such measures had to be balanced against individual rights. However, it found that detention for four days and six hours was too long on the ground that holding a person for longer than four days without judicial authorisation was a violation of the requirement that persons should be brought promptly before a judicial officer. The Court did not specify how long was acceptable; previously, the Commission had seen four days as the limit. The government made no move to comply with this decision; instead, it entered a derogation under Art 15 to Art 5(3).

This derogation was challenged unsuccessfully in *Brannigan and McBride v UK*.[293] The European Court of Human Rights found that the derogation was justified since the state of public emergency in Northern Ireland warranted exceptional measures. The Court found: 'a wide margin of appreciation [on the question] of the presence of an emergency . . . and on the nature and scope of derogations necessary to avert it [should be allowed]'.[294] Among the government contentions uncritically accepted by the Court was one to the effect that in the particular situation, the judiciary should not be permitted a role in protecting the liberty of detainees. As Judge Walsh pointed out in his dissenting opinion, this was precisely a role that the public would expect a judge to have. *Brannigan* might appear a doubtful decision because the derogation was entered after the decision in *Brogan*, although it might also be said that states should not be encouraged to enter derogations too readily on 'insurance' grounds in order to pre-empt claims. Arguably, although there was a state of emergency in 1989, the UK had chosen not to enter a derogation even though one would have been warranted. Whatever the merits of this argument in the particular situation, it is questionable whether the exigencies of the situation did require detention of six days without recourse to independent review. Possibly it was assumed on insufficient grounds that such review would prejudice the legitimate purpose of the investigation.

The *Brogan* decision clearly presented the government with a difficulty in formulating the Terrorism Act 2000. Although the HRA continued the derogation entered in *Brogan*, under s 14(1)(a) HRA, for a time, it was vulnerable to challenge at Strasbourg at some future point, in the light of the new settlement in Northern Ireland. The government put forward various justifications for producing new terrorist legislation in 2000,

---

292 Judgment of 29 November 1988; (1989) 11 EHRR 117; A 145.
293 Series A, 258-B (1993); (1993) 17 EHRR 594. See also Chapter 2, p 96.
294 Para 207.

but it recognised that it might be in difficulties in arguing that a state of emergency sufficient to support the derogation could be said to exist post-2000.[295] Its solution, in the TA, was to make provision for judicial authorisation of detention, rather than to decrease the length of time during which terrorist suspects could be detained, harmonising it with the PACE period. In deciding on these arrangements, including the retention of the possibility of up to seven days' detention, the government rejected the suggestion of Lord Lloyd that once there was a lasting peace in Northern Ireland, it ought to be possible to reduce the maximum period for which a suspect could be detained under the new legislation to a total of four days – two days on the authority of the police and two days with judicial authorisation.

The maximum period of detention, applicable to a person arrested under s 41 of the TA, was seven days; it was extended to 14 days by amendment to s 41(7) and Sched 8 TA under the Criminal Justice Act 2003, and then, after the July 2005 bombings in London, it was extended again by further amendment under the Terrorism Act 2006, to 28 days. In 2008 the then Labour government sought unsuccessfully to increase the time limit to 42 days. Parliament periodically reviewed the 28-day-limit, however, until the Coalition government (2010–15) asked Parliament (in s 57 of the Protection of Freedoms Act 2012) to amend the period to 14 days. That position has not been changed under the current Conservative government from 2015 onwards. Thus terrorism suspects can be held in detention for two weeks, in strong contrast to non-terrorist suspects, who can only be held for 96 hours, even for the most serious offences.

After 48 hours of detention judicial approval is needed. Paragraph 29, Sched 8 TA provides that the detention must be under a warrant issued by a 'judicial authority'.[296] Under para 32, the warrant may be issued if there are reasonable grounds for believing that 'the detention of the person to whom the application relates is necessary to obtain relevant evidence whether by questioning him or otherwise or to preserve relevant evidence'. The detainee or his solicitor has the right to make written or oral representations under para 33(1). Thus, authorisation may not be merely 'on the papers'. Such a possibility might not have satisfied the aim of achieving compliance with Art 5(3), despite the involvement of a judicial figure. Judicial authorisation meant that the derogation was no longer needed, and it was lifted on 19 March 2001.

Detention authorised by police alone

The provisions provide for a twin-track system of detention, one dependent on the judicial authority and one on the police themselves. The police can detain a person on their own authority for 48 hours under s 41(3) which provides:

> *Subject to* subsections (4) to (7), a person detained under this section shall (unless detained under any other power) be released not later than the end of the period of 48 hours beginning –

---

295 See *Legislation Against Terrorism* (1988) Cm 4178, para 8.2.
296 Para 29(4) provides: 'In this Part "judicial authority" means (a) in England and Wales, the Senior District Judge (Chief Magistrate) or his deputy, or a District Judge (Magistrates' Courts) who is designated for the purpose of this Part by the Lord Chancellor, (b) in Scotland, the sheriff, and (c) in Northern Ireland, a county court judge, or a resident magistrate who is designated for the purpose of this Part by the Lord Chancellor.'

(a) with the time of his arrest under this section, or

(b) if he was being detained under Schedule 7 when he was arrested under this
     section, with the time when his examination under that Schedule began
     (emphasis added).

Section 41(4)–(7) of the TA appears to provide certain possibilities of continuing the
detention beyond 48 hours, over and above the possibility of extension under judicial
authorisation. Section 41(6) provides that if an application for an extension of detention is made, or under s 41(5), it is intended that it will be made, detention can continue
while it is pending. This impliedly means that the police can continue to detain for more
than 48 hours so long as an application is being made or is about to be made, even if it
is subsequently refused. The application need not be made during the 48 hours; under
Sched 8, Part III, para 30 it may be made within six hours of the end of that period.

     If, for example, towards the end of 54 hours in detention (a possibility under the
TA, as indicated above) the police decided to apply for an extension of detention, they
would have the power under s 41(5) to continue the detention while the application was
being made and then under s 41(6) while the hearing was occurring. This possibility
does not appear to accord with *Brogan* and *Brannigan* since there is no possibility of
judicial authorisation of detention.

     The 48-hour period is also subject to s 41(4), which provides: 'If on a review of a
person's detention under Part II of Schedule 8 the review officer does not authorise
continued detention, the person shall (unless detained in accordance with sub-sections
(5) or (6) or under any other power) be released.' The reviews have to occur every
12 hours. This is not well expressed but is intended to mean that within the 48-hour
period the review officer (this must be an officer of at least the rank of superintendent
after the first 12 hours) can continue the detention periodically, at 12-hour intervals, so
long as the review conditions (which are the same as the warrant conditions) continue
to apply. No express time limit is placed on the total period which the review officer
can authorise. Clearly, s 41(4) should be interpreted to mean that *within* the 48-hour
period there must be periodic reviews (subject to the provisions for delaying reviews).
The provision could be viewed as detracting from the certainty of the 48-hour deadline.
The stricter interpretation accords with the government's intention as expressed in the
Consultation Paper.[297] If, in practice, s 41(4) was interpreted on occasion to allow some
detentions on the authority of the review officer only, beyond 48 hours, such detentions would obviously be more likely than those under the previous provisions to create
breaches of Art 5(3).

     As part of the port and border controls regime, Sched 5 to the PTA provided a further
power of detention in allowing a person to be detained for 12 hours before examination at ports of entry into Britain or Northern Ireland. The period can be extended to
24 hours if the person is suspected of involvement in the commission, preparation or
instigation of acts of terrorism. These provisions are partially reproduced in Sched 7 of
the TA.

     Clearly, the PACE and TA detention schemes differ quite radically in due pro-
cess terms, despite the fact that many of those who are potentially subject to the TA
scheme represent a far more divergent group than the previous one which fell within

---

297 *Legislation Against Terrorism* (1988) Cm 4178.

the term 'terrorist'. Even within that previous group, as a number of the most famous miscarriage of justice cases imply, those who were designated terrorist suspects, such as *Judith Ward*,[298] were often remarkably ill-suited to the draconian terrorist regime to which they were subjected. The group covered by s 1 TA remains in theory diverse and the width of s 1 in terms of potentially covering journalistic material, has recently been criticised.[299] But in so far as the special terrorist stop and search and detention provisions are used in practice to combat groups and individuals creating the most serious terrorist threats, they can be justified on the basis that the need to maintain security and personal safety benefits the whole community, and aids in creating a climate in which in the long run due process is more likely to be respected. In the current terrorism climate, after the atrocities in Paris in November 2015, use of arrest and detention in the terrorism context partly for intelligence-gathering purposes, may be warranted.

Treatment in detention

The role of the custody officer

The general use of custody officers provided for under s 36 is a key feature of the scheme for detention, treatment and questioning created under Parts IV and V of PACE. The custody officer's role is to underpin the other safeguards by ensuring that the suspect is treated in accordance with PACE and the codes and by generally overseeing all aspects of his or her treatment. Use of custody officers was intended to ensure that somebody independent of the investigating officer could keep a check on what was occurring. The scheme was not a new idea; in certain police stations an officer was already fulfilling this role, but PACE clarified the duties of custody officers and ensured that most stations have one. Thus, best practice was placed on a statutory basis. Under s 39(1) PACE the custody officer is under a duty to ensure that detainees are treated in accordance with the provisions of that Act and any code of practice.[300]

However, the efficacy of the custody officer scheme may be called into question. It may not always be in operation: in non-designated police stations, there must simply be someone who can act as custody officer if the need arises and in designated police stations, there need not always be a custody officer on duty. The ruling in *Vince and Another v Chief Constable of Dorset*[301] made it clear that s 36 does not require that a custody officer must always be present. The plaintiffs (acting for members of the joint branch board of the Police Federation of England and Wales of the Dorset Police) sought a declaration that by virtue of s 36(1) of PACE a custody officer should normally be available in a police station. However, it was found that s 36(1) clearly provided that the chief constable had a duty to appoint one custody officer for each designated police station and a power to appoint more in his discretion which had to be reasonably exercised. It was found that there had been no breach by the chief constable, implying that a decision that a custody officer need not always be on duty is a reasonable one. It may

298   *Ward* (1992) 98 Cr App R 1.
299   See the *Miranda* case in 2016, pp 849–50, above.
300   *D v Chief Constable of Merseyside* [2015] EWCA Civ 114.
301   (1992) *The Times*, 7 September.

be argued that this case exposes a weakness in one of the central safeguards provided under PACE. That was referred to by Steyn LJ, who commented at the time that the Royal Commission on Criminal Procedure[302] might wish to consider this loophole in the PACE provisions. But no change occurred.

The custody officer may not always be able to take a stance independent of that of the investigating officer. This weakness in the scheme arises from the lowly rank of the custody officer; under s 38(3), the officer need only be of the rank of sergeant and may therefore be of a lower rank than the investigating officer, making it very difficult to take an independent line on the treatment of the suspect. If the two disagree, the custody officer must refer up the line of authority (s 39(6)); there is no provision allowing the custody officer to overrule the investigating officer. Thus, there is a danger that the custody officer will merely rubber-stamp the decisions of the investigating officer; whether this occurs in practice may largely depend on the attitude of the superior officers in a particular force to the provisions of the PACE scheme.

Vulnerable groups

Throughout the Codes, including Code H, the Code governing the treatment of terrorist suspects in detention, recognition is given to the special needs of certain vulnerable groups: juveniles, the mentally disordered or handicapped, those not proficient in English, the hearing impaired or the visually handicapped. Juveniles and the mentally handicapped or disordered should be attended by an 'appropriate adult'. Juveniles are those under 18 and consequently the treatment of 17 years old persons as adults as required by s 37(15) PACE and Code C (1.5) was both counterproductive and unlawful.[303] Paragraph 1.5A now commands the police to treat detainees as juveniles when this may be in doubt. The Codes, particularly Codes C and H, contain more detailed provisions regarding the role of appropriate adults.

Under para 1, Code C or Code H the 'appropriate' adult in the case of a juvenile will be the parent or guardian, a social worker or another adult who is not a police officer. The suspect should be informed by the custody officer that the appropriate adult is there to assist and advise him and can be consulted with privately (para 3.18 Code C, para 3.19 Code H). However, research has suggested that this requirement is not always observed and that in any event, appropriate adults may be unclear as to the role they are supposed to play.[304]

In the case of a mentally disordered or handicapped detainee, the appropriate adult under para 1 will be a relative, guardian, other person responsible for his or her welfare or an adult who is not a police officer.[305] The custody officer must as soon as practicable inform the appropriate adult of the grounds for the person's detention and ask the adult to come to the police station to see him or her. If a person appears physically or mentally

---

302 That was on the basis that it was set up (in 1992) after the miscarriage of justice which occurred in the case of the *Birmingham Six*. See p 835 above.
303 *R (C) v Home Secretary* [2013] EWHC 982 (Admin), [94].
304 See Softley, P, 'Police interrogation: an observational study in four police stations' (1985) Policing Today 119.
305 Para 1.7; Code H, para 1.13.

ill, the custody officer can ensure that he or she receives appropriate clinical attention, or, in urgent cases, can send the person to hospital or call the nearest available medical practitioner.[306]

Experience has shown that mentally handicapped or disordered persons are very likely to make an untrue or exaggerated confession and therefore it is particularly important that all the safeguards available should be in place when such a person is interviewed. Consequently PACE Code C requires the corroboration of admitted facts where possible because of the dangers of unreliability. However, there is provision for urgent interviewing of such persons without the appropriate adult if an officer of the rank of superintendent or above considers that delay will involve an immediate risk of harm to persons or serious loss of or serious damage to, property.[307] The main defect in the provisions relating to the mentally handicapped or disordered is that they rely on the ability of officers who will have had little or no training in the field to make the judgment that a person is mentally disordered.[308] It would seem essential that custody officers at least should have special training in this regard. Various provisions are also available for the protection of members of the other vulnerable groups mentioned. A blind or visually handicapped person must have independent help in reading documentation.[309]

Conditions of detention

Code H, governing the conditions of detention for terrorist suspects, is of particular significance since such suspects may be in detention for up to 14 days. Code H, as opposed to the statutory provisions, governs the physical treatment of terrorist suspects, the provision of medical care and the issue of mental illness. Physical treatment of detainees is governed by paras 8 and 9 of Codes C and H, and it is intended that they should be provided with basic physical care. Paragraphs 8 and 9 embody the principle that the detainee's physical safety should be ensured and his basic physical needs met. Persons detained should be visited every hour but, where possible, juveniles should be visited 'more frequently';[310] those who are drunk should be visited every half hour. The paragraphs do, however, allow more than one detainee to be placed in the same cell if it is impracticable to do otherwise (para 8.1) and although a juvenile must not be placed in a cell with an adult, no clear provision for frequent checks on juveniles in police cells is made. Paragraph 8 provides that cells should be adequately heated, cleaned, lit and ventilated and that three meals should be offered in any 24-hour period. A juvenile will only be placed in a police cell if no other secure accommodation is available and the custody officer considers that it is not practicable to supervise him if he is not placed in a cell. No additional restraints should be used within a locked cell unless absolutely necessary and then only approved restraints (para 8.2). Reasonable force may be used if

---

306 Code C, para 9.5; Code H, para 9.6.
307 See Codes C and H, para 11.(1).
308 Codes C and H, Annex E, para 1, provide that if an officer 'has any suspicion or is told in good faith that a person of any age, whether or not in custody, may be suffering from medical disorder or is mentally handicapped or cannot understand the significance of questions put to him or his replies, then he shall be treated as mentally disordered or otherwise mentally vulnerable.'
309 Para 3.17; Code H 3.18.
310 Codes C and H, Note 9B.

necessary (para 1), by designated persons where a police officer would also have that power. Under para 9, if a person appears mentally or physically ill or injured, or does not respond normally to questions or conversation (other than through drunkenness alone), or otherwise appears to need medical attention, the custody officer must immediately call the police surgeon (or, in urgent cases, send the person to hospital or call the nearest available medical practitioner).

Code H, like Code C, makes reference to allowing outdoor exercise, but the provisions are more detailed (Code H, para 8.7); Code H, unlike Code C, provides for facilities for detainees to conduct religious observance – in para 8.8. Code H also makes some further provision for medical treatment, requiring in para 9.1 that detainees held for more than 96 hours must be visited by a healthcare professional at least once every 24 hours. This provides a further check, over and above the provisions of para 9 for clinical treatment.

Treatment of a detainee can engage Art 3, which provides a guarantee against torture or inhuman or degrading treatment.[311] Indeed, the provisions of the Codes C and H play an important role in ensuring that the dignity of detainees is respected.[312] Article 3 could be engaged due to the conditions of detention or where physical force is used in the course of an arrest and detention. In *Ribbitsch v Austria*[313] the Court said: 'any recourse to physical force which has not been made strictly necessary by his own conduct diminishes human dignity and is in principle an infringement of the right set forth in Article 3'.[314] Force may only be used where it is strictly required to restrain the detainee and the force used must go no further, in terms of causing injury or humiliation, than is strictly necessary to achieve the purpose of restraint. The use of force in cases involving members of vulnerable groups (e.g., the young, the mentally impaired and the elderly) will be subject to strict scrutiny.[315] Indeed, the police have a duty following s 6 HRA to provide protective measures and to prevent the ill-treatment of vulnerable individuals.

Article 3 treatment may arise in respect of a number of other aspects of detention. Failure to obtain medical treatment after a forcible arrest was found to infringe Art 3 in *Hurtado v Switzerland*.[316] In the *Greek* case,[317] the conditions of detention were found to amount to inhuman treatment owing to inadequate food, sleeping arrangements, heating and sanitary facilities combined with overcrowding and inadequate provision for external contacts. It was also found that conduct that grossly humiliates may amount to degrading treatment contrary to Art 3. Such treatment may include racially discriminatory and, probably, sexually discriminatory arrests and treatment in detention;[318] such

---

311 Art 3 treatment may be justifiable where its object is to satisfy the demands of Art 2, the right to life: *Herczegfalvy v Austria* A 244 (1992).

312 *Nemtsov v Russia* [2014] ECHR 1774/11, [117]–[121].

313 (1996) 21 EHRR 573.

314 See *Selmouni v France* (2000) 29 EHRR 403 for an example of particularly egregious custodial treatment amounting to torture within the terms of Article 3 ECHR.

315 *ZH v Hungary* [2012] ECHR 28973/11, [29].

316 A 280-A (1994) Com Rep.

317 12 YB 1 (1969) Com Rep.

318 See *East African Asians* cases (1973) 3 EHRR 76. See also *Lustig-Prean and Beckett v UK* (1999) 29 EHRR 548, and *Smith and Grady v UK* (2000) 29 EHRR 493, which suggested that grossly humiliating, intrusive interrogation could, if of an extreme and prolonged nature, amount to a breach of Art 3. See further, Chapter 5.

treatment might be found to fall more readily within Art 3 in a non-terrorist context.[319] Where discrimination is a factor, Art 14 would also be engaged. Moreover, in cases involving allegations of racism an additional duty rests upon the state to uncover any racial motive, and especially to question whether such prejudice played any role in the alleged custodial abuse.[320]

Equally, Art 3 will apply where the police seek to induce evidence through physical or psychological pressure. Thus the ECtHR held in *Tarasov v Ukraine*[321] that torture had occurred when the applicant was subject to suffocation, electrocution and beatings with the intention to securing a confession. In fact, the *threat* of such treatments can infringe Art 3. Thus in *Gäfgen v Germany*[322] the applicant, who had been arrested on suspicion of child kidnapping, was threatened with violence up to, and including, torture during his interrogation. Throughout he was handcuffed and thus particularly vulnerable. In the circumstances of the cases the Court held that the treatment did not amount to torture but was inhuman treatment. The fact that the officers believed that their actions were necessary to save the life of a child was not exculpatory. Article 3 is an absolute right. Confessions that are induced as a consequence of torture will render the trial as a whole unfair, irrespective of their probative worth.[323] However confessions that are given as a consequence of inhuman or degrading treatment will not render the trial unfair as a whole, and provided they are not relied upon directly in proceedings, will not affect the fairness of the trial in the same way as torture does. Where Art 3 is inapplicable, since the treatment does not reach the level of severity the article envisages, a breach of Art 8 might be established in respect of treatment invasive of privacy in police detention.[324]

Searches of detained persons

Detained persons may not automatically be searched, but the power to search arrestees under s 32(1) of PACE is quite wide. It arises under s 32(1) if the suspect has been arrested somewhere other than a police station and a constable has reasonable grounds to suspect that an arrestee has anything on him which might be evidence relating to an offence or might be used to help him escape from custody, or that he may present a danger to himself or others. The much wider power arises under s 32(2) and allows search, again on reasonable grounds, for anything that might be evidence of an offence or which could help to effect an escape from lawful custody. The nature of the search must relate to the article it is suspected may be found; if it is a large item, the search may not involve more than removal of a coat. Such searching may occur routinely, but it must be possible to point to objectively justified grounds in each case that must not go

---

319　In *McFeeley v UK* (1980) 20 DR 44, intimate body searches in a terrorist context did not give rise to a breach of Art 3, but it has been suggested (see Harris, O'Boyle and Warbrick, Harris, D, O'Boyle, K and Warbrick, C, *Law of The European Convention on Human Rights*, 1995, p 83) that this finding might not apply in a non-terrorist context.
320　*Cobzaru v Romania* [2007] ECHR 48254/99, para 90. See further, Chapter 5.
321　[2013] ECHR 07416/03.
322　[2010] ECHR 22978/05.
323　*Harutyunyan v Armenia* (2007) ECHR 36549/03, [63].
324　*Jaeger v Estonia* (2014) ECHR 1574/13.

beyond those specified.[325] There is no requirement for believing that the arrestee presents a danger to himself or others.[326] A power of search also arises under s 54, as amended, allowing search to ascertain property the detainee has with him or her, which will apply if someone has been arrested at the police station or brought there after being arrested elsewhere. The custody officer must determine whether it is necessary to conduct a search for this purpose.

Intimate searches, bodily samples, swabs and impressions

Under s 55 PACE, an intimate search can only be ordered if an officer of the rank of superintendent or above has reasonable grounds for believing that an article that could cause physical injury to a detained person or others at the police station has been concealed or that the person has concealed a Class A drug that he intends to supply to another or to export. Even if such suspicion arises, the search should not be carried out unless there is no other means of removing the object. Before it can be carried out, the reasons for undertaking it must be explained to the suspect and a reminder given of the entitlement to legal advice. An intimate search at a police station may only be carried out by a registered medical practitioner or registered nurse unless, under Codes C and H Annex A, the authorising officer considers, in the case of a concealed object that could cause injury, that it is not practicable to wait, in which case a police officer of the same sex as the suspect can carry it out. Under Codes C and H an intimate search at a police station of a juvenile or a mentally disordered or mentally handicapped person must take place only in the presence of the appropriate adult of the same sex, unless the suspect requests otherwise.[327] Codes C and H Annex A provide that an intimate search must be conducted with proper regard to the 'sensitivity and vulnerability' of the suspect. It must take place in a completely private room in the presence of two persons of the same sex as the detainee. Children in custody are 'vulnerable and special care is required to protect their interest and well-being'.[328] It is incumbent on the police to consider alternative and less intrusive measures in such cases.

Codes C and H Annex A also make provision for strip searches. They must also be conducted with proper regard to the 'sensitivity and vulnerability' of the suspect, must not be used routinely, must take place in a private room and must be conducted by two officers of the same sex as the detainee. The suspect is required to expose first the upper half of his body and then the lower but not normally to stand completely naked. Bodily orifices are not to be touched. Searches should not be carried out routinely, but only if necessary to remove an article that the officer reasonably considers the detainee might have concealed.

Evidence obtained from the suspect himself can identify the suspect as the person who committed the offence in question, or can demonstrate that he is innocent of it. Identification procedures are largely governed by the provisions of Code D (2011

---

325 *Eet* [1983] Crim LR 806.
326 *Lord Hanningfield v Constable of Essex* [2013] 1 WLR 3632, [11].
327 Under Codes C and H Annex A, para 5 in the case of a juvenile, the search may take place in the absence of the appropriate adult only if the juvenile signifies in the presence of the appropriate adult that he prefers the search to be done in his absence and the appropriate adult agrees.
328 *Davis v Chief Constable of Merseyside* [2015] EWCS Civ 114, para 44, Pitchford LJ.

edition) which has, as its overall aim, the creation of safeguards against wrongful identification, bearing in mind that mistaken identification can be a very significant cause of
wrongful convictions.[329] Code D, together with Codes C and H, Annex A, contains provisions that are intended to safeguard vulnerable groups and to ensure that the invasion of
privacy represented by some methods of identification is kept to a minimum consistent
with PACE and the codes' overall aim. Many of the procedures will only take place
with the suspect's consent, although if consent is not forthcoming, this may be used
in evidence against him or her.[330] In the case of a mentally handicapped or disordered
person, consent given out of the presence of the 'appropriate adult' will not be treated
as true consent while the consent of a juvenile alone will not be treated as valid if the
adult does not also consent.[331]

Bodily samples, swabs and impressions may be taken in respect of recordable
offences. The relevant provisions are ss 62 and 63 PACE, as amended, and the Terrorism Act 2000, Sched 8. Intimate samples may be taken if the officer has reasonable
grounds to believe that such an impression or sample will tend to confirm or disprove
the suspect's involvement in the offence and with the suspect's written consent. But the
suspect must be warned that if they refuse without good cause the refusal may be used
against them at trial.[332] The suspect must be warned using the warning as set out in
Code D. He must also be reminded of his entitlement to have free legal advice and the
reminder must be noted in the custody record. Intimate samples[333] may only be taken
under s 62 PACE, as amended, or under the Terrorism Act 2000, Sched 8 para 12, by a
registered medical or dental practitioner or registered nurse, whereas non-intimate samples[334] may be taken by a police officer. They may be taken without consent if an officer
of the rank of inspector or above has reasonable grounds for believing that the sample
will tend to confirm or disprove his involvement in it.[335]

6 Conclusions

In this context it may be concluded that, apart from the passing of the HRA, and the
impact of decisions at Strasbourg, there has been a drift towards more repressive measures post-PACE although some effort has been made to buttress due process values in
relation to the police powers considered, partly in the codes of practice. Indeed, it may
be said that in certain respects, especially in relation to the police counter-terror powers
discussed, the beneficial impact of the HRA was largely unintended by its New Labour

---

329 The Criminal Law Revision Committee 1972 considered that wrongful identification was the greatest
cause of wrongful convictions (para 196)
330 Codes C and H, Annex A, para 2B.
331 Code D, para 2.12.
332 For non-terrorist suspects, s 62 PACE governs the taking of intimate samples and s 63 PACE covers
the taking of non-intimate samples. Terrorist suspects are governed by the Terrorism Act 2000, Sched
8, paras 10–13 in respect of intimate and non-intimate samples.
333 'Blood, semen or any other tissue fluid, urine, saliva or pubic hair or a swab taken from a person's body
orifice' (PACE, s 65).
334 Including hair other than pubic hair or a sample taken from a nail or from under a nail or a skin impression (PACE, s 65, as amended by CJPOA 1994, s 80(5)(b)).
335 See PACE s 63, as amended and Code D paras 6.5–6.9. The Terrorism Act 2000 Sched 8 para 10 covers
non-intimate samples taken from terrorist suspects.

architects. In the Protection of Freedoms Act 2012, however, certain especially repressive and misused stop and search and detention measures were repealed or modified, as considered above. The current climate, in which in 2016 it can be said that the repeal of the HRA appears to be fairly imminent, is no more propitious in due process terms than it has been in general in the post-PACE years. On the other hand, pressure on the police has mounted, partly due to the rise of the threat of terrorist incidents, especially between 2013 and 2016, meaning that there is a temptation to balance observance of due process against the need to preserve security and personal safety in the face of that threat.

Chapter 13 proceeds to consider the most significant stage in the process of the exercise of police powers – the interviewing of suspects, and the safeguards surrounding such interviewing. Chapter 14 proceeds to consider challenges to the police where misuse or abuse of power in relation to one of the stages of processing the suspect, possibly beginning with a stop and search, is alleged.

Police questioning and safeguards for suspects

This chapter has been updated and revised for this edition by Richard Edwards, Senior Lecturer in Law, University of Exeter, with some input in 2015 from Helen Fenwick.

1 Introduction[1]

In crime control terms, the police interview occupies a central position in the criminal justice system; it represents an effective use of resources, since if a confession becomes available, the criminal process is likely to be accelerated.[2] In particular, since *mens rea* is a requirement of most offences, admissions provide the most readily available means of establishing the state of mind of the suspect at the relevant time. The interview may, in effect, replace the trial, since its results may play a key part in the pre-trial risk-balancing and negotiating process in which the suspect decides whether or not to plead guilty. Clearly, the stronger the risk of a conviction that would be unaccompanied by a sentence discount, the less likely it is that he or she will plead not guilty.[3] If the suspect has confessed or made some admissions, he may feel that there is no point in pleading not guilty even if the admissions are false, exaggerated or misleading. The interview may also frequently play a part in general criminal intelligence gathering.[4] On their face, the crime control advantages of the interview are readily apparent although, clearly, if an intimidating atmosphere and a lack of due process safeguards lead a suspect to make false admissions that cannot advance crime control ends.

From a due process perspective the police interview is largely unjustifiable, since its *raison d'être* is to secure admissions that probably would not otherwise be secured; it therefore undermines the privilege against self-incrimination. This due process norm

---

1 For further comment, particularly on the 1984 Act and on the relevant provisions under the Criminal Justice and Public Order Act 1994, as amended, see: Sanders, A and Young, R, Burton, M *Criminal Justice*, 4td edn, 2010; M Davies *Davies, Croall & Tyrer on Criminal Justice*, 5th edn (2015) Part B; Baily, S, Taylor, N, *Bailey, Harris and Jones: Civil Liberties: Cases and Materials & Commentary*, 2009, Part 2, Chapter 4.7 and 4.8; Feldman. D, *Civil Liberties and Human Rights in England and Wales*, 2nd edn, 2002, Chapters 5 and 9; R Stone *Textbook on Civil Liberties and Human Rights*, 10th edn (2014), Chapter 4; Clark, D *Bevan and Lidstone's the Investigation of Crime*, 2004; Levenson, H and Fairweather, F, *Police Powers*, 1990; McConville, M, Sanders, A and Leng, R, *The Case for the Prosecution*, 1991; Zander, M, *Zander on PACE* (2015); Reiner, R and Leigh, LH, 'Police powers', in McCrudden, C and Chambers, G (eds), *Individual Rights and the Law in Britain*, 1994; Klug, F, Starmer, K and Weir, S, *The Three Pillars of Liberty*, 1996.
2 See McConville, M (1993) RCCJ Research Study No 13, 1993; Baldwin, J, 'Police interview techniques; establishing truth of proof' (1993) 33 Br J Criminology 325.
3 See Sanders, Young and Burton, *Criminal Justice*, 4th edn, 2010, Chapter 8, Part 2.
4 Maguire and Morris, RCCJ Research Study No 5, 1992.

traditionally underpinned criminal justice practice,[5] but it was gradually abandoned until it became accepted in the pre-PACE years that the purpose of the interrogation was to obtain admissions.[6] The precarious position of the interview from this perspective explains, it is suggested, why it seemed necessary, when PACE placed police interrogations on a formal basis, to infuse due process elements into them. Such elements are intended to detract from any impression that the confession is involuntary. The police, however, remain the gatekeepers to these safeguards, which seem to run counter to their crime control concerns, and therefore they may not be observed or, more subtly, the weaknesses and loopholes in the interviewing scheme will be discovered and explored.

PACE strongly reflects this uneasy compromise between crime control and due process: the detainee can be detained for the purposes of obtaining a confession under s 37(2), but a number of safeguards were created that are influenced by due process concerns to lessen the coerciveness of the interview and to ensure its integrity and reliability so that it can be used as evidence. The extensive and complex rules of Codes of Practice C, E, F, H, which appear to surround police interviews with a range of safeguards, afford the interview an appearance of due process. A number of flaws, however, in due process terms, were built into the scheme when it was first introduced. Most significantly, there are no sanctions for breach of the interviewing rules, including those arising under PACE itself, apart from the possibility of disciplinary action.[7] There is uncertainty as to when an exchange with police becomes an interview so as to attract all the safeguards. There is scope for interviewing away from the police station, thereby evading the most significant safeguards, those of access to legal advice and audio-recording. Virtually no guidance is given as to the acceptable limits of 'persuasive' interviewing, so long as it is not oppressive or likely to render admissions unreliable. This is particularly a matter of concern in respect of the questioning of terrorist suspects, especially bearing in mind the length of the detention to which they can be subjected – up to 14 days at present. As discussed below, the level of protection for due process is lower at a number of points than for non-terrorist suspects. Code H (latest edition, 2014), which governs their treatment in police questioning, does recognise to an extent that such lengthy detention has particular implications in terms of its mental impact,[8] but, although there are a number of provisions for obtaining medical aid in respect of such suspects, the problem of relying on admissions made after a lengthy period of detention are not, it is argued, afforded sufficient recognition.[9]

Under Art 6 ECHR, scheduled in the HRA, the European Court of Human Rights has developed the concept of the fairness of the trial 'as a whole', allowing for consideration of custodial treatment in a broad sense. In *Saidi v France*[10] the Court said that its role was to determine 'whether the proceedings in their entirety . . . were fair'.[11] In

---

5   The 1912 Judges' Rules did not allow police interrogation, although the police could invite and receive voluntary statements.

6   *Holgate-Mohammed v Duke* [1984] 1 AC 437; [1984] 1 All ER 1054.

7   This possibility became even more remote when PACE, s 67(8), rendering breach of the Codes automatically a breach of the police Disciplinary Code, was repealed in 1994 by the Police and Magistrates' Courts Act 1994, s 37 and Sched 9.

8   See also Chapter 12, p 902.

9   See pp 1259–62.

10   (1994) 17 EHRR 251.

11   Para 43.

Barbéra, Messegué and Jabardo,[12] the trial taken as a whole could not be said to be fair. This was partly due to features of the treatment of the defendants pre-trial, taken cumulatively. They were held for a substantial period of time incommunicado and when they confessed to the police they did not have legal assistance. Nevertheless, their confessions were significant in later questioning by examining judges. The unfair pre-trial treatment clearly had a tendency to render the trial unfair, although it is improbable that such a tendency would have been found without the unfairness at the hearing itself.[13] Nevertheless, the findings in *Barbéra* are significant, since they emphasise the need to consider the whole criminal process, *including* any custodial period, in determining fairness. In *Ambrose v Harris*[14] the Supreme Court found, relying on the relevant Art 6 jurisprudence, that the right of access to legal advice should arise from the point at which a person was being questioned as a suspect.

Various means of redress arise in respect of unfairness or oppression in police questioning, as discussed in Chapter 14. It might be appropriate where the pre-trial custodial treatment, including the manner of questioning, had had a cumulatively harsh effect, to stay the prosecution for abuse of process; or exclusion of admissions obtained during, or as a result of, a course of harsh or adverse treatment might be appropriate in order to satisfy Art 6. If the treatment was oppressive or rendered the admissions unreliable, s 76 PACE would apply, to exclude them.[15] Civil actions may be brought against the police, including claims for damages in respect of breaches of the ECHR rights under the HRA s 8.[16]

This chapter does not concentrate only on questioning of suspects inside the police station because contact between police and suspect takes place a long time before the police station is reached, and this has been recognised in the provisions of Part V of PACE and Codes of Practice C and H (last revised in 2014), which govern treatment of suspects and interviewing, but have some application outside as well as inside the police station. It should be noted that many of the key provisions relating to interviewing are contained in Codes C or H rather than in PACE itself. The most crucial events during a person's contact with police will probably be the interviews, and therefore this section will concentrate on the safeguards available, which are intended to ensure that interviews are fairly conducted and are properly recorded wherever they take place. This chapter examines selected key aspects of the interviewing scheme by considering the points at which the various safeguards must be in place; the conduct of the interview; the means of recording the interview. It then goes on to consider the right of access to legal advice, the curtailed right to silence and its relationship with the legal advice scheme. The effect of flaws in the pre-trial procedures discussed here on the fairness of the trial is considered in this chapter.

The PACE codes and police questioning

Under the pre-PACE rules, safeguards for the interview were governed largely by the Judges' Rules and Administrative Directions to the Police[17] and s 62 of the Criminal

---

12 A 14 6(2) (1989).
13 There were 'unexpected changes' in the membership of the court, the hearing was brief; most importantly, there was a failure to adduce and discuss evidence orally in the accused's presence.
14 [2011] UKSC 43.
15 See p 976 *et seq.*
16 See Chapter 14, pp 1006–7.
17 E.g., Home Office Circular 89/1978, Appendices A and B.

Law Act 1977. The latter provided for access to a solicitor (although it was frequently ignored). The former provided, *inter alia*, for the issuing of cautions when a person was charged (not necessarily when he was arrested) and for the exclusion in evidence of statements and confessions that were not 'voluntary' (see below). Under PACE, those rules were replaced by rules contained either in the Act itself or in Code of Practice C. The original interviewing scheme under Code C was revised in 1991 (and at a number of points subsequently) and improved by the introduction of tape recording under Code E.[18] The revisions, culminating in the 2014 one were, it is suggested, concerned mainly with improving the scheme's due process elements, albeit in a manner best described as superficial: the rules became more complex in order to deal with police evasion of them, but their fundamental flaws were hardly addressed. Despite the relationship a number of commentators had observed to exist between coerced confessions and miscarriages of justice,[19] the recommendations made by the 1993 Runciman Royal Commission on Criminal Procedure, which might, minor as they were, have continued the improvements undertaken in 1991, were largely ignored in subsequent revisions.[20] Under the Major government, the disciplinary sanction for breaching the codes was removed under s 37(f) of the Police and Magistrates Court Act 1994, and the right to silence was curtailed under ss 34–37 of the CJPOA 1994. Largely as a consequence of the changes introduced under the CJPOA, the PACE codes were revised in 1995; that revision, unlike the previous one, appeared to have a dual aim: it seemed to be intended to have some weak due process impact in eradicating loopholes, but it also introduced various provisions in order to give effect to the curtailment of the right to silence. These changes indicated a move away from the rather ineffectual attempts previously undertaken to protect the due process elements in the interviewing process.

Vulnerable groups and police questioning

Throughout Codes C and H (2014 versions), recognition is given to the special needs of certain vulnerable groups in police interviews: juveniles, the mentally disordered or handicapped, those not proficient in English, the hearing impaired or the visually handicapped. Juveniles and the mentally handicapped or disordered should be attended by an 'appropriate adult'. The role of the appropriate adult has received greater recognition in the later versions of Code C. Under Note 1F of Codes C and H, the solicitor should not be the appropriate adult; this provision was included in response to some evidence that the police had been treating the solicitor as the appropriate adult, thereby producing a conflict of interests.[21] It was thought that the roles of legal adviser and appropriate adult differed; the same person could not therefore fulfil both. It should be noted that the juvenile can be interviewed without the presence of an appropriate adult if an officer of

---

18 Most recent edition of Code E, revised 2016.
19 See Walker, *Miscarriages of Justice*, 1999, p 54.
20 E.g., the Runciman Report, Chapter 4, para 23 put forward a recommendation to retain the right to silence, in the context of improved safeguards for suspects, taking into account recommendations intended to lead to improvement in the quality of custodial legal advice. The Report made other proposals for improvement of the interviewing scheme including the video taping of a waiver of legal advice (Proposal 57) and a special warning to juries regarding uncorroborated confessions (Chapter 4, paras 56–87).
21 LAG Bulletin, November 1989.

the rank of superintendent or above considers that delay will involve an immediate risk of harm to persons or serious loss of or serious damage to property.[22] At various points to be discussed, the particular vulnerability of juveniles is recognised, but although this is to be welcomed, research suggests that the treatment of juveniles, particularly during interviews, is still sometimes unsatisfactory.[23]

The notification of rights must be given in the presence of the adult,[24] which may mean repeating the notification, but if the suspect wants legal advice, this should not be delayed until the adult arrives.[25] The appropriate adult who is present at an interview should be informed that he or she is not expected to act simply as an observer; and also that the purposes of being present are, first, to advise the person being interviewed and to observe whether or not the interview is being conducted properly and fairly and, second, to facilitate communication with the person being interviewed.[26]

It will be found in discussion in this chapter of unreliable confessions, that mentally handicapped or disordered persons are more likely to make an untrue or exaggerated confession and therefore it is particularly important that all the safeguards available should be in place when such a person is interviewed. However, there is provision for urgent interviewing of such persons without the appropriate adult if an officer of the rank of superintendent or above considers that delay will involve an immediate risk of harm to persons or serious loss of, or serious damage to, property.[27] A deaf or speech-handicapped person, or someone who has difficulty understanding English, must only be interviewed in the presence of an interpreter,[28] but this may be waived in the case of urgent interviewing under Annex C.

Terrorist suspects

The interviewing scheme had, from its inception, created a twin-track system under PACE, the counter-terrorist legislation and the codes, that is, one in which terrorist suspects were exposed to a regime adhering to a lower level of due process than that applicable in respect of 'ordinary' suspects. This regime afforded the coercive elements of the scheme greater rein both formally and informally. Most obviously terrorist suspects could be exposed to a much longer period of detention, which allowed greater scope for prolonged pressure during interrogation. The interviewing regime for such suspects was also less protective. The counter-terrorist scheme introduced by the then Labour government under the Terrorism Act 2000 (TA), its codes of practice and the subsequent revisions of Codes C and E not only confirmed and extended the twin-track system, but applied it to a much wider and more diverse range of suspects.[29] The twin-track system

---

22　See Codes C and H, para 11.18: urgent interviews.
23　Evans, R, 'The conduct of police interviews with juveniles' (1993) Home Office Research Study No 8. On the treatment of juveniles generally, see Dixon, D, 'Juvenile suspects and PACE', in Freestone, D (ed), *Children and the Law*, 1990, Hull University Press, pp 107–29.
24　Para 3.17 (Code H, para 3.18).
25　This used not to be the case: Note 3G and Annex E, Note E2. Now Code C, para 6.5A and Code H, para 6.6 imply that it is.
26　See Code C, para 11.17; Code H, para 11.10.
27　See Codes C, para 11.18, and H, para 11.11.
28　Para 13.
29　See Chapter 15.

was then placed on a more formal basis, under Code H, while at the same time the detention period for terrorist suspects was extended to 14 days[30] – although clearly most suspects will not stay in detention for all of that period. Code H was introduced in 2006, and subsequently revised, most recently in 2014, applying only to terrorist suspects. It covers a number of aspects of the questioning and detention of such suspects, while non-terrorist suspects continue to be covered by Code C. However, Code H replicates much of Code C.

Notification of rights

When the detainee arrives at the police station, he or she will be 'booked in'. The crucial nature of this stage in the proceedings is made clear below in relation to the discussion of the legal advice provisions. Under para 3 of Codes C and H, a person must be informed orally and by written notice of four rights on arrival at the police station after arrest: the right, arising under s 56 of PACE, to have someone informed of his detention;[31] the right to consult a solicitor and the fact that independent legal advice is available free of charge; the right to consult the other codes of practice, and the modified right to silence as embodied in the caution.

2 Police interviews

Interviews may be formal or informal. They may consist of questioning in the street, before arrest. Street interviewing is quite common,[32] while the key due process safeguards of access to legal advice and audio recording continue to be reserved for formal interviews within the police station. The caution which, as suggested below, serves both crime control and due process purposes, can be, and in most instances should be, used outside as well as inside the police station, with the result that the suspect is warned of the dangers of failing to speak before the key safeguards can be in place. Due process protection outside the police station is minimal; it consists only of contemporaneous note-taking under caution if an interview is occurring or accurate non-contemporaneous note-taking if the exchange is not an interview. Relevant non-interview exchanges with juveniles and mentally disordered persons may be admissible in evidence even though no adult is present.

Not only, therefore, is due process virtually abandoned in relation to out of police station exchanges and interviews, they may also have a structural formative influence on formal interviews and ultimately on the outcome of the process,[33] thereby undermin-

---

30 See Chapter 12, pp 901–04.

31 Under para 5.1, if the person cannot be contacted, the person in charge of detention or of the investigation has discretion to allow further attempts until the information has been conveyed (see Note 5C to Codes C and H). Section 56 PACE is subject to exceptions, similar to those under s 58 in respect of access to legal advice; for those s 58 exceptions, see pp 1216–17 below.

32 See Brown, Ellis and Larcombe, *Home Office Research Study No 129*, 1993; the study showed that questioning or unsolicited comment occurred outside the station in 24% of cases. The Runciman Royal Commission found that around 10% of interviews took place outside the police station: RCCJ Report, Cm 2263, 1993; see also Sanders and Young, *Criminal Justice*, 2007, pp 259–63.

33 See *James* [1996] Crim LR 650.

ing the protection available for such interviews. Suspects may feel, rightly or wrongly, that they have already prejudiced their position too far during informal exchanges to attempt to retrieve it in a formal taped interview; therefore, any confession made in such an interview – or any ill-considered silence – may not be truly voluntary. Thus, it is extremely important to determine how far the scheme leaves scope for exchanges to occur before the police station is reached.

From both a due process and a crime control perspective, it would not be appropriate to address the leeway in the scheme for informal interviewing by requiring that, where sufficient suspicion is present, suspects should always be arrested and taken to the police station before any exchange occurs. In crime control terms, this might not represent an efficient use of resources since some unnecessary arrests would be made. In due process terms, there are some disadvantages in police station interviewing: the element of detention is coercive and the fact of detention may lead suspects to make admissions in order to leave it. Rather, the due process 'deficit' in street exchanges may be addressed, to an extent, by applying stronger safeguards to such interviewing[34] and, as discussed in this chapter, by giving careful consideration, under Art 6, to the admission of such exchanges as evidence.

The most significant safeguards available for interviews under PACE, the TA and Codes C, E and H include contemporaneous noting down of the interview or audio-recording, the ability to verify and sign the notes of the interview as a correct record, the legal advice provisions and, where appropriate, the presence of an adult. One of the most important issues in relation to these safeguards and reflected in the 2014 revision of Code C, is the question when they come into play. There may be a number of stages in a particular investigation beginning with first contact between police and suspect and perhaps ending with the charge. At various points the safeguards mentioned have to come into play and two factors can be identified that decide which safeguards should be in place at a particular time. First, it must be asked whether an exchange between police and suspect can be termed an 'interview' and second, whether it took place inside the police station or was lawfully conducted outside it.

Interviews and non-interviews[35]

Code C creates a complex scheme in relation to the difference between interviews and non-interviews, and, to add to the complexity, Code H creates a scheme that differs from it in various significant respects. The correct interpretation of the term 'interview' under the original Code C scheme was highly significant because the relevant safeguards were unavailable unless an exchange[36] between police officer and suspect was designated an interview. The term therefore tended to be given a wide interpretation[37] and eventually the definition given to it by the Court of Appeal in *Matthews*[38] – 'any discussion

---

34 Using hand-held tape recorders and notifying the suspect of the right of access to legal advice as part of the caution.

35 See Fenwick, H, 'Confessions, recording rules and miscarriages of justice' [1993] Crim LR 174–84.

36 'Exchange' will be used throughout this section to denote any verbal interaction between suspect and police officer, including unsolicited admissions.

37 The Court of Appeal in *Absolam* (1989) 88 Cr App R 332 defined it as 'a series of questions directed by the police to a suspect with a view to obtaining admissions'. This definition was quite wide in that it obviously included informal questioning.

38 [1990] Cr App R 43; [1990] Crim LR 190, CA, transcript from LEXIS.

or talk between suspect and police officer' – brought within its ambit many exchanges far removed from formal interviews. It also covered many interviewees, as it spoke in terms of 'suspects', not arrestees. However, it was qualified by the ruling in *Scott*[39] that unsolicited admissions cannot amount to 'interviews' and by the ruling in *Marsh*[40] to the same effect as regards 'genuine requests' from the police for information. In *Marsh*, police officers investigating a burglary suddenly came across wraps of papers and asked the appellant about them; the questions and answers were admissible although no caution had been given because, until that point, the officers had had no reason to suspect her of any drug-related offence. The ruling in *Marsh* bears some resemblance to that in *Maguire*[41] which pre-dated *Matthews*. It was determined that questioning an arrestee near the scene of the crime apparently in order to elicit an innocent explanation did not constitute an interview. Thus, the original interpretation of an interview created some leeway – but not much – for gathering (or apparently gathering) admissions in informal situations before any safeguards were in place.

In one respect, distinguishing between interviews and non-interviews is not as crucial under the current scheme as it was previously: under Code C, para 11.13 as revised, any comments relevant to the offence made by a suspected person outside the context of an interview must be accurately recorded[42] and then verified and signed by the suspect. However, making such a distinction is still highly significant because it remains the first step towards bringing the other safeguards into play. Code H does not contain an equivalent of para 11.13; it merely provides in Note 11 E that significant statements (Code H para 11.4) outside the context of the interview must be 'recorded' and in the interview shall put to them any significant statement or silence outside the context of the interview (Code H para 11.4).

A definition of the term 'interview' is now contained in Code C, para 11.1A, which reads in part: 'An interview is the questioning of a person regarding his involvement or suspected involvement in a criminal offence or offences which by virtue of para 10.1 of Code C must be carried out under caution.' In contrast, Code H provides in para 11.1: 'An interview is the questioning of a person arrested on suspicion of being a terrorist, which under para 10.1 must be carried out under caution.'

Code C paragraph 10.1 reads:

A person whom there are grounds to suspect of an offence must be cautioned before any questions about it (or further questions if it is his answers to previous questions which provide the grounds for suspicion) are put to him regarding his involvement or suspected involvement in that offence if his answers or his silence (i.e. failure or refusal to answer a question or to answer satisfactorily) may be given in evidence to a court in a prosecution. He therefore need not be cautioned if questions are put to him for other purposes, eg (a) solely to establish their identity or ownership of

39   [1991] Crim LR 56, CA. See also *Younis* [1990] Crim LR 425, CA.
40   [1991] Crim LR 455.
41   (1990) 90 Cr App R 115; [1989] Crim LR 815, CA.
42   It may be noted that the weight actually given to this provision may depend on the question of whether its breach may be described as substantial and significant (see below, Chapter 14, p 982); in this respect it is disturbing to note a first instance decision in which it was found that it should not be so described: *Oransaye* [1993] Crim LR 772.

any vehicle; (b) to obtain information in accordance with any relevant statutory requirement, see *paragraph 10.9*; (c) in furtherance of the proper and effective conduct of a search.

Code H, para 10.1 reads:

A person whom there are grounds to suspect of an offence must be cautioned before any questions about an offence, or further questions if the answers provide the grounds for suspicion are put to them, if either the suspect's answers or silence . . . may be given in evidence to a court in a prosecution.

The differences between the Code H and C definitions of an interview are considered below. It may be noted that the list of examples of instances under Code C, para 10.1 in which no caution would be necessary is not exhaustive. No such definition appeared in the original code, but Note 12A read: 'The purpose of any interview is to obtain from the person concerned his explanation of the facts and not necessarily to obtain an admission.' The current definition obviously differs from this considerably and differs even more from the definition of an interview contained in *Matthews*.[43] It echoes the rulings of the Court of Appeal in *Maguire*[44] and *Marsh*[45] in attempting to draw a distinction between questioning a person regarding suspected involvement in an offence and questioning for other purposes. It appears that cautioning would not be required if the information obtained is in fact relevant to the offence, but the questioning was not directed towards uncovering such information. Such an interpretation would be in conformity with the ruling in *Marsh* that the level of suspicion excited in police officers present at the scene determines when an exchange becomes an interview. This approach is readily justifiable. However, para 11.1A combined with para 10.1 does not make it sufficiently clear that where an explanation of the facts does relate to suspected involvement in an offence and is either perceived to do so by the officer concerned or would be by the ordinary reasonable officer,[46] an interview will take place.

Where the level of suspicion clearly falls within para 10.1 of both codes as, of course, it will do after arrest, the use of the term 'questioning' in Code C, para 11.1A, and in Code H, para 11.1, nevertheless impliedly excludes instances where nothing definable as questioning has taken place. This is the correct interpretation where the police have apparently merely recorded what was said, according to the Court of Appeal in *Menard*.[47] Both paragraphs may also exclude chats or discussions between suspect and police officer or statements or commands that happen to elicit an incriminating response.[48] The definition from *Matthews* is now enshrined in para 11.13 and is not therefore inconsistent with para 11.1A. In other words, the *Matthews* definition applies

43 [1990] Crim LR 190.
44 (1990) 90 Cr App R 115; [1989] Crim LR 815.
45 [1991] Crim LR 455.
46 This qualification should, it is argued, be introduced to take account of the situation which arose in *Sparks* [1991] Crim LR 128; the officer who questioned the appellant apparently did not recognise the significance of the admissions made and therefore did not consider it necessary to caution him.
47 [1995] Cr App R 306.
48 See *Absolam* (1989) 88 Cr App R 332.

to most exchanges between suspect and police officer, but para 11.1A applies to certain particularly important ones labelled 'interviews'. This interpretation is supported by the wording of para 11.13: 'a written record shall also be made of any comments made by a suspected person, including unsolicited comments which are outside the context of an interview but which might be relevant to the offence . . .', thus implying that comments relevant to the offence other than unsolicited comments will not invariably be part of an interview. These comments are also applicable to the scheme under Code H, which also accepts in para 11.4 and Note 11E that significant statements may be made outside the context of an interview.

Interviews inside and outside the police station

Under s 30 PACE, as amended,[49] the suspect if arrested outside the police station, must be taken to the police station as soon as practicable after arrest. Under para 11.1 of Code C and Code H, para 11.2 the suspect should be taken to the station (or a designated place of detention in the case of terrorist suspects) once the decision to arrest has been made, unless certain exceptions apply. As discussed below, these provisions provide scope for informal interviewing outside the place where most of the due process safeguards are available. The unseasoned suspect interviewed outside the police station will still be unaware of the right to legal advice[50] and it is also at present unlikely that the interview would be tape recorded: Code E does not envisage tape recording taking place anywhere but inside the police station.[51] In some circumstances suspects are not, however, disadvantaged by these differences, thanks to the provisions of para 11.1, introduced by the 1991 revision (and included in subsequent revisions, including the 2014 one), which reads: 'Following a decision to arrest a suspect he must not be interviewed about the relevant offence except at a police station [except in certain instances specified in 11.1(a), (b) and (c) which call for urgent interviewing].'

Paragraph 11.1 could merely have read: 'A suspect must not be interviewed about the relevant offence except at a police station . . .'. Clearly, it was designed to allow *some* interviewing outside the police station owing to its requirement of a higher level of suspicion than that denoted by para 11.1A and para 10.1. It implies that a police officer should categorise someone either as possibly involved in an offence or as on the verge of arrest; so long as the first category is applicable, questioning can continue. This category was presumably intended to include persons under caution, because a caution must be given 'when there are grounds to suspect (him) of an offence'.[52] Obviously, these categories tend to merge into each other. However, it is difficult to be certain in retrospect as to which applied, although the police may find it difficult where there are very strong grounds for suspicion to support a claim that interviewing could continue because the decision to arrest had not been taken. It is clear that the problems associated

49 The Criminal Justice Act 2003 inserted s 30A into s 30, allowing an arrested person to be released on bail at any point before the police station is reached.

50 This is governed by para 3.1, which is expressed to apply only to persons in the police station.

51 Code E, para 3.1 states: 'audio recording shall be used for any interview . . . except when the interview takes place elsewhere than at a police station'. Some police forces have experimented with hand held tape recorders used outside the police station, but at present this is by no means common practice.

52 Codes C and H, para 10.1.

with exchanges between suspect and officer still remain, and it is evident that a significant number of suspects are still interviewed outside the police station.[53]

Most significantly, since suspects not at the police station can be interviewed, without having had an opportunity to consult a solicitor, they are not protected by the provision of s 34(2A) of the CJPOA (see below): adverse inferences can be drawn if they remain silent. Further, s 34(2A) does not affect the position of suspects who make admissions despite not having had that opportunity. This is because they are technically free to leave and seek legal advice before being arrested. Section 34(2A) only applies inside the police station or other place of detention. But this position is flawed in two respects. First, many suspects may not realise that they could leave, and may reply to questions in the street or police car, before being arrested, without realising that they could have legal advice. Once arrested the person in question is no longer free to leave, but might reply to questions or even volunteer admissions in the police car, on the way to the station, again without realising that he is entitled to have legal advice once the police station is reached. The second situation arguably leads to an infringement of Art 6, even though s 34(2A) appears to condone it – as discussed below.[54]

Where the level of suspicion would obviously justify an arrest, a police officer who is eager to keep a suspect out of the police station for the time being might be able to invoke one of the more broadly worded exceptions allowing urgent interviewing in order to avert certain specified risks. The first exception under para 11.1(a), allowing interviewing to take place at once where delay might lead to interference with evidence, could be interpreted very broadly and could apply whenever there was some likelihood that evidence connected with any offence but not immediately obtainable was in existence. Even if there were no others involved in the offence who had not been apprehended, it could be argued that the evidence was at risk from the moment of arrest because news of the arrest might become known to persons with a motive for concealing it. This argument could also apply to the exception under (c) with the proviso that it will apply to a narrower range of offences. Once an arrest has occurred, the provision of s 30(1) PACE that the suspect must be taken to the police station by the constable as soon as practicable applies. Under s 30(1), the police can delay doing so if the suspect is needed elsewhere to carry out investigations that it is reasonable to carry out immediately. The key words in s 30 are obviously 'as soon as practicable'. Thus, further leeway for informal interviewing *after* arrest is created.

Once the suspect is inside the police station under arrest or under caution,[55] any interview[56] (using this term to connote an exchange which falls within para 11.1A) should usually be audio-recorded under Code E, but there is an exception in respect of terrorist suspects, which is considered below. Many of the criticisms advanced above could also be applied under Code H. Under that Code an interview only occurs after the suspect is *arrested*. After that point he should be taken to a place designated for detention under

---

53 Brown, Ellis and Larcombe, *Home Office Research Study No 129*. The study showed that questioning and/or unsolicited comments occurred in 24% of cases. Questioning occurred in 10% of cases.
54 See pp 1213–14.
55 Under para 3.1 of Code E, once a volunteer becomes a suspect (i.e., at the point when he should be cautioned) the rest of the interview should be tape recorded.
56 Under Code E para 3.1(a), an interview with a person suspected of an offence triable only summarily need not be taped.

TA, Sched 8, para 1, following Code H, para 11.2, unless one of the urgent interviewing exceptions apply (the exceptions are the same as those under Code C para 11.1). This means that any informal exchanges prior to the point of arrest, which might well be viewed as interviews if covered by Code C, will not count as interviews and therefore will not attract the safeguards. Admissions are made before being cautioned, even if the suspect is being directly questioned about the offence, but is not under arrest, would be admissible in evidence. No contemporaneous recording of such admissions would be necessary so long as a record was made later.

Varying levels of protection for exchanges

It is now possible to identify the points at which the safeguards will be brought to bear and it is apparent not only that there are three levels of protection available, but that they vary as between terrorist and non-terrorist suspects:

(1) Inside or outside the police station, if the exchange cannot be (or at times is not) labelled an 'interview', even though it may be relevant to the offence, it seems that the level of protection provided by Code C, para 11.13 only will apply (for Code H, only the protection of Note 11E and para 11.4). This will be the case even where the suspect is an arrestee or a volunteer under caution.

(2) If an interview of a non-terrorist suspect takes place outside the police station and falls outside the Code C, para 11.1 prohibition and within the leeway created by s 30(1) PACE, the verifying and recording provisions under paras 11.11 and 11.7 will apply, with the proviso that contemporaneous recording is likely to be viewed as impracticable.[57] What is impracticable does not connote something that is extremely difficult, but must involve more than mere inconvenience.[58] Where appropriate, an adult must be present, which probably means that interviews requiring an appropriate adult would have to take place at the station.[59] Notification of the right of access to legal advice will not occur, although adverse inferences could be drawn if the suspect remains silent.

> If an interview of a non-terrorist suspect takes place outside the police station and falls outside the Code H, para 11.2 prohibition and within the leeway created by s 30(1) PACE, the verifying and recording provisions under the TA Code for detention of terrorist suspects will apply. Otherwise everything said above as regards interviews outside the station under Code C is applicable. It should be noted in particular that notification of the right of access to legal advice will not occur, although the suspect is not free to leave since he will be under arrest, and adverse inferences could be drawn under s 34(2A) CJPOA if the suspect remains silent. It is readily arguable, as mentioned above, that this position does not accord with the demands of Art 6.

57 The mere fact that an interview is conducted in the street may not be enough to support an assertion that it could not be contemporaneously recorded. This seems to follow from the decision in *Fogah* [1989] Crim LR 141.
58 *Parchment* [1989] Crim LR 290. Note-taking while the suspect was dressing and showing the officers round his flat was held to be impracticable.
59 Code C, para 11.15; Code H, para 11.9.

(3) As far as non-terrorist suspects are concerned, inside the police station, if the person in question is an arrestee or a volunteer under caution and the exchange is an interview, all the available safeguards, including access to legal advice and tape recording, will apply.[60] As far as terrorist suspects are concerned, inside the designated place of detention, if the person in question is an arrestee the exchange will be an interview if the other aspects of para 11.1 apply; therefore all the available safeguards, including access to legal advice, will apply. The provisions as to audio-recording in Code E will not apply (Code E, para 3.2) as audio-recording of such interviews is governed by a separate code of practice.[61] If the suspect is a volunteer he or she appears to be entitled to have access to legal advice, under Code H, Note 1A, but the exchange will not be an interview and therefore, it appears that the other safeguards, including the presence of an appropriate adult, will not apply. Also, although the suspect can have access to legal advice (albeit only under a note), he or she does not appear to have a right to have the adviser present when questioned.

Thus, wide but uncertain scope still remains for interviewing outside the police station and for gathering admissions outside the context of an interview. The main objection to this scheme, apart from its complexity,[62] is that the degree of protection available is too dependent on factors irrelevant to the level of suspicion in question. It may be pure chance, or something more sinister, which dictates whether a volunteer under caution is interviewed inside or outside the police station or whether or not an exchange with an arrestee can successfully be characterised or disguised as a non-interview. Bearing in mind that unreliable confessions may be most likely to emerge from informal exchanges, it is argued that the mechanisms triggering off the main safeguards – para 11.1A and para 11.1 – are deficient both in creating large areas of uncertainty as to the level of protection called for at various points and in allowing the minimal level of protection under Code C, para 11.13 to operate in too many contexts. The greater leeway within the Code H scheme for questioning suspects before arrest and therefore outside the context of an interview is a matter of particular concern, given the diversity of terrorist suspects, and the particular propensity of terrorist cases to miscarry.

Recording methods

Audio recording

Section 60 of PACE allowed for the issuing of a Code of Practice in connection with tape recording of interviews, and this was accomplished by means of Code of Practice E.

---

60 Unless under Code E, para 3.3A, it would not be reasonably practicable to tape the interview owing to failure of the recording equipment or non-availability of an interview room or recorder. Note 3B of Code E provides that if necessary, an officer must be able to justify the decision not to delay the interview.

61 The Terrorism Act 2000 and the Counter-Terrorism Act 2008 make separate provisions for a Code of Practice for the video recording with sound of interviews of persons detained under s 41 of, or Sched 7 to, the 2000 Act and certain post-charge interviews.

62 The need to adopt a commonsense approach to the rules was expressed in *Marsh* [1991] Crim LR 455 by Bingham LJ in relation to the original scheme. However, the current scheme does not lend itself readily to a simple interpretation. See especially the comments of McCullough J in *Cox* [1993] Crim LR 382 regarding Note 11A.

Once the non-terrorist suspect is inside the police station under arrest or under caution,[63] any interview (that is, an exchange which falls within para 11.1A of Code C) with a person who has been cautioned in respect of an indictable or 'either way' offence[64] should be audio recorded under Code of Practice E (last revised in 2016). Initial resistance by the police gave way to a recognition of the advantages of audio recording, which seems to be generally accepted[65] as reflecting a truer picture of an interview than note-taking[66] and the jury are in one sense even *better* placed than they would have been had they been present at the interview because they may be allowed to take the tape recordings into the jury room[67] to replay as necessary.[68]

However, exchanges may occur between formal interviews, when the tape is switched off, which affect the formal interview and although they should be recorded in writing under para 11.13, the record may not cover everything that was said, and the facts recorded by the police officers may be disputed by the suspects. In other words, leeway for falsely imputing admissions to the suspect is still apparent.[69]

Audio recording of interviews with terrorist suspects was made mandatory by Sched 7, para 9 to the TA, which provides for the audio recording of any interview by a constable of a person detained under s 41 and Sched 7 to the TA. Audio or video recording is dealt with by a code of practice for suspects arrested under TA, s 41 or detained under TA, Sched 7, issued by the secretary of state.[70]

Video recording

The recording of police interviews is one of the most rapidly developing areas of policing. The possibility that the introduction of tape recording,[71] replacing contemporaneous note-taking,[72] would eventually be overtaken by videotaping has been under consideration

---

63 Under para 3.1 of Code E.

64 Under Code E para 3.1(a), although under Note 3A it can be recorded at police discretion.

65 See Wills, McLeod and Nash, *The Tape Recording of Police Interviews with Suspects*, 2nd Interim Report, Home Office Research Study No 97, 1988. The study found that police officers and prosecutors generally welcomed audio-recording, since it is a faster recording method and renders them less vulnerable to allegations of 'verballing'.

66 Research conducted by Baldwin and Bedward of the Institute of Judicial Administration, University of Birmingham, on summaries made of tape recorded interviews found that the summaries were often of a very poor quality and presented a distorted picture of what occurred during the interview. However, they also found that the police were aware of this problem and were beginning to address it. See [1991] Crim LR 671.

67 *Emmerson* [1991] Crim LR 194. In *Riaz and Burke* [1991] Crim LR 366, the Court of Appeal held (in instances where the jury had not already heard the tapes) that better practice would be to reassemble the court and play the tapes in open court.

68 This permission was expressed to extend only to those parts of the tapes which had been heard in open court; other material would have to be edited out.

69 See *Dunn* (1990) 91 Cr App Rep 237.

70 Schedule 8, para 3(1) and (7).

71 Governed by Code of Practice E, which came into force on 29 July 1988.

72 Originally governed by Code C, para 11.3 and under revised Code C by para 11.5. Audio-recording has not entirely replaced contemporaneous note-taking, first because it does not apply to all interviews (see Code E, para 3.1) and secondly, because contemporaneous note-taking applies to interviews outside the police station where practicable, whereas audio-recording is at present only required inside it (Code E, para 3.1).

for some time[73] and Code F, which governs visual recording, was revised in 2013, but there is still no statutory requirement under PACE to visually record interviews. Video-taping of police interviews was until fairly recently at the experimental stage; the Home Office made it clear as long ago as 1991 that it supported its introduction[74] as a step in the direction of preventing miscarriages of justice. Commentators have given video-taped interviews a cautious welcome;[75] criticism has largely been directed towards the difficulty of ensuring that they are not subverted by 'informal' contacts between police and suspect,[76] rather than at the quality of the recordings.[77] Arguably, such difficulties are endemic in the interviewing scheme as currently conceived, regardless of the recording technique used. The Terrorism Act 2000 and the Counter-Terrorism Act 2008 make separate provisions for a code of practice for the video recording with sound of: interviews of persons detained under s 41 of, or Sched 7 to, the 2000 Act, and post-charge questioning of persons authorised under s 22 or s 23 of the 2008 Act.

Interviewing techniques

There seems to be a tendency in some quarters to see developments in recording techniques as going a long way towards solving the problem of unreliable confessions.[78] However, there is a danger that other relevant issues will be obscured. It is important not to over-emphasise the value of recording techniques at the expense of provisions that may have a more direct effect on their reliability. Video-taping is to be welcomed as providing a fuller picture of an interview than audio-recording, and as a means of inhibiting the use of intimidatory tactics, at least in the formal interview, but arguably its value should not be over-stressed. There is clearly a difference between the reliability of admissions and the reliability of the *record* of them.[79] In contrast to the success of the scheme in this direction, there has been little development in the area of provisions able

73 Video recording of interviews as opposed to audio taping was one of the possibilities considered by the Royal Commission on Criminal Procedure chaired by Lord Runciman. See (1991) 141 NLJ 1512 for a brief interim report by John Baldwin of a study of video taping experiments that took place in four police stations. For some time, the police had been able to video tape a confession if they first obtained the consent of the accused: *Li Shu-Ling* [1989] Crim LR 58, PC. The Runciman Royal Commission proposed that further research into the use of video taping for interviews should be carried out (Proposal 70). Video-taping is still not mandatory but is being used on a voluntary basis.

74 In response to a request from Sir John Farr MP for video taping of all police interviews in order to prevent miscarriages of justice, John Patten, then Secretary of State for the Home Office, indicated that this course would be considered after the results of a pilot project conducted for the Association of Chief Police Officers in conjunction with the Home Office were known. HC Deb Vol 200 col 391, 5 December 1991.

75 See, e.g., Barnes, M, 'One experience of video recorded interviews' [1993] Crim LR 444.

76 See McConville, M, 'Video taping interrogations: police behaviour on and off camera' [1992] Crim LR 532.

77 However, quality has been questioned: see John Baldwin's interim report of experiments with video taping of interviews, which found that there were fairly serious or very serious problems with video taping in over 20% of the recordings. These included poor picture or sound quality or camera malfunction (see (1991) 141 NLJ 1512).

78 When Kenneth Baker, the then Home Secretary, announced the inception of the Royal Commission on Criminal Procedure, he suggested that recent improvements in the provision for recording of police interviews would prevent miscarriages of justice in future: HC Deb Vol 187 col 1109, 14 March 1991.

79 See the discussion of *Paris* (1993) 97 Cr appl R 99 in Chapter 14, p 975.

to *affect* what occurred; PACE does not attempt to regulate the conduct of the interview except in so far as such regulation can be implied from the provision of s 76 that confessions obtained by oppression[80] or in circumstances likely to render them unreliable will be inadmissible. PACE forbids oppressive interviewing in Code C, para 11.5[81] and Code H, para 11.6; some very general guidance as to interviewing mentally disordered or handicapped suspects is given in Codes C and H, Note 11C. No such provision is duplicated in PACE itself although, as indicated in Chapter 14, oppression is defined under s 76(8) PACE as including Article 3 treatment, and under s 76(2)(a) a confession obtained by oppression is subject to an absolute exclusionary rule.

Obviously, the provisions governing detention and the physical comfort of the detainee[82] have relevance in this context; they provide the setting for the interrogation and remove from the situation some of the reasons why a suspect might make an unreliable confession. Provisions relating to medical treatment and to assessing the detainee's mental and physical condition are also relevant,[83] especially in relation to terrorist suspects, who may be detained for up to 14 days. But, once their limits have been set, they cannot influence what occurs next, and it seems that the use of intimidation, haranguing and indirect threats is still quite common, especially in interviews with juveniles.[84] The Runciman Royal Commission proposed that the role of the appropriate adult should be reviewed[85] and that officers should receive training in the role a solicitor would be expected to play,[86] but did not make general proposals as to outlawing or regulating use of certain interviewing techniques.[87] Such proposals would be particularly relevant after the evidence of use of bullying techniques in interrogations that arose from the post-PACE case of *Paris, Abdullah and Miller* (the Cardiff Three).[88] In fact, such techniques may have been replaced to an extent by a more subtle 'investigative approach',[89] but that is no substitute for specific guidance under Code C as to improper techniques. The significant increase in the period for which terrorism suspects can be detained – currently up to 14 days – makes it even more imperative that consideration should be given to ensuring the reliability of admissions made, especially as terrorist suspects tend to differ from each other so markedly: some may have been trained to

80 Misleading statements made during an interview distorting the state of the evidence against the defendant or hectoring and bullying may well lead to exclusion of any confession obtained under either s 76 or s 78. See *Mason* [1987] Crim LR 119; [1987] 3 All ER 481, CA; *Beales* [1991] Crim LR 118; *Blake* [1991] Crim LR 119; *Heron* (1993) unreported, in Chapter 14.

81 Code C, para 11.5 and Code H, para 11.6 provide: 'No police officer may try to obtain answers to questions or to elicit a statement by the use of oppression.'

82 Paras 8 and 9 of Code C and Code H; para 12.8, 12B, 12C regulates the physical conditions in the interview room.

83 See Chapter 12, pp 901–04. See Code H, governing the treatment of terrorist suspects, paras 8 and 9.

84 See Evans, R, 'The Conduct of Police Interviews with Juveniles', *Home Office Research Study No 8*, 1993. See (1994) 144 NLJ 120 and (1994) 144 NLJ 203 for criticism of a variety of interview techniques.

85 Proposal 72.

86 Proposal 64.

87 See Baldwin, J, 'The Royal Commission, Power and Police Interviews' (1993) 143 NLJ 1194 for criticism of the failure of the Royal Commission in this respect. See also Reiner, R, 'The Royal Commission on Criminal Justice (1) Investigative Powers and Safeguards for Suspects' [1993] Crim LR 808.

88 (1993) 97 Cr App R 99.

89 Baldwin notes ((1993) 143 NLJ 1195 and 1197) that 1993 training manuals for police interviewers advocate this approach. It is advocated in the Interviewer's Rule Book.

withstand interrogation (for example, that may have occurred if they have trained with Isis or similar groups, abroad), while others may be completely inexperienced in criminal justice terms.

The lack of provision in PACE and the TA as regards interviewing techniques encourages resort to the HRA. On its face, the Convention does not bear upon this issue, except in so far as Art 3 covers oppressive interviewing. But, as indicated above, the general requirements of fairness under Art 6 will allow consideration of interviewing techniques as part of the fairness of the criminal process as a whole.

The failure to regulate interviewing techniques is a significant gap in the PACE and TA schemes, bearing in mind the established likelihood of a link between coercive questioning and unreliable confessions.[90] Although there has been a movement from such questioning towards so-called ethical techniques,[91] it cannot be assumed that interviewing will not at times verge on the oppressive and abusive. As discussed above, the Equality Act 2010 provides a means of redress in respect of racial abuse or racially discriminatory treatment by police, which will also cover interviewing. This possibility also exists in respect of other protected grounds covering other forms of discriminatory treatment, including adverse treatment in police custody that is gender-related or homophobic.[92]

3 The right of access to legal advice

Introduction

There is general agreement that the most significant protection for due process introduced for the first time by PACE[93] was that of the right of access to legal advice.[94] But this right is far from absolute. It is subject to a number of formal exceptions, which are somewhat broader in terrorist cases, and it is dependent on a formal request to exercise it. It is also limited to interviewing in police stations, and may be subverted informally in a variety of ways. Nevertheless, its impact in due process terms should not be under-estimated. Access to legal advice has an impact in upholding due process which

---

90 See Justice, *Unreliable Evidence? Confessions and the Safety of Convictions*, 1994.

91 Home Office Central Planning and Training Unit, The Interviewer's Rule Book, 1992; Home Office Circular 7/1993 'Investigative interviewing'.

92 Bearing in mind the 'dualist' impact of international law in the UK, this means that Protocol 12 (see Chapter 2, p 93) does not provide a remedy for such treatment domestically, and it is now unlikely that it will eventually be received into domestic law under the HRA. See further Chapter 5, p 271.

93 The Criminal Law Act 1977, s 62 declared a narrow entitlement to have one reasonably named person informed of the arrest. It did not provide that the arrestee must be informed of this right, nor did it provide any sanction for non-compliance by a police officer. That statutory form of this right gave it no greater force than the non-statutory Judges' Rules (rules of practice for the guidance of the police: see *Practice Note* [1984] 1 All ER 237; 1 WLR 152). The Judges' Rules upheld the right of the suspect/arrestee in the police station to communicate with/consult a solicitor, but permitted the withholding of such access 'lest unreasonable delay or hindrance is caused to the process of investigation or the administration of justice'. Any officer, in relation to a person detained for any offence, could deny access to legal advice on these broad grounds; see *Lemsatef* [1977] 1 WLR 812; [1977] 2 All ER 835.

94 See, e.g., Sanders and Young, *Criminal Justice*, 3rd edn, 2007, Chapter 4.5; Dixon, D, *Miscarriages of Justice*, 1999, p 67. The research studies mentioned in this chapter do not question the value of the legal right of access *per se*, although they do question its quality and the responses of the police.

encompasses, but goes beyond, advising on making 'no comment' answers. How far it has such an impact in practice is debatable. The impact varies, depending on the contact with the suspect and the expertise of the adviser.[95]

The legal adviser may help the suspect to maintain silence where advice alone – in the absence of the adviser – might not be enough. It should be recognised, however, that the key question is not whether the presence of a legal adviser means that the detainee remains silent, but whether it means that he or she is unlikely to make an unreliable confession. Further, assuming for the moment an inverse correlation between a legal adviser's presence and an unreliable confession, what contribution to it, if any, is made by the right to silence in its current modified form? Obviously, the detainee will not make such a confession if he remains silent, but that is a highly dubious strategy given that adverse inferences may be drawn against him at trial. In any event, it is an ineffective[96] way of tackling the risk of such confessions and the damage they cause in crime control and due process terms; the real concern here is with the question whether the legal adviser will enable the detainee to maintain a selective silence when under pressure from police, where otherwise unreliable admissions might be made.

Rights of access to legal advice

The right of access to legal advice is really a bundle of rights. Both PACE and the Terrorism Act 2000 entitle a suspect to consult an adviser privately.[97] The statutory entitlement is therefore both to access to legal advice and to the preservation of the confidentiality of solicitor/client consultation,[98] a matter reflecting common law fair trial principles and which is also viewed as of great significance at Strasbourg, under Art 6, as scheduled in the HRA.[99] The access to legal advice is available under a publicly funded scheme;[100] under Codes C and H the suspect is entitled to be informed of this right;[101] given, if necessary, the name of the duty solicitor,[102] and be permitted to have the solicitor present during questioning.[103] The right to have a solicitor present in the interview is arguably the most significant right. Under Code C Note 6B (included from 2008) if a detainee wishes to pay for legal advice, he or she should be given an

---

95   See (2011) Issue 1 Crim LR Editorial: January 2011 'Legal Advice in Police Stations – 25 Years On', at 1; 'The Justice Lottery? Police Station Advice 25 Years on from PACE *Pascoe Pleasence*' Vicky Kemp and Nigel J. Balmer (2011) Issue 1 Crim LR 3; 'The Right to Legal Advice in the Police Station: Past, Present and Future' Layla Skinns (2011) Issue 1 Crim LR 19.

96   The Sanders research (1989) found that only 2.4% of suspects exercised their right to silence as against 54.1% who made admissions (the others denied the offence) (1989, p 136).

97   PACE, s 58(1): 'A person in police detention shall be entitled, if he so requests, to consult a solicitor privately at any time.' For TA suspects, this right also arises under the TA, Sched 8, para 7.

98   In *R v Grant* [2005] EWCA Crim 1089 the police conducted covert surveillance of the suspect's conversations with his solicitor. That was found to undermine the rule of law so seriously that the prosecution was stayed on grounds of abuse of process. But see below p 960 in relation to exceptions to the privacy requirement in relation to terrorism suspects.

99   See below p 960.

100 See Legal Aid, Sentencing and Punishment of Offenders Act 2012.

101 Codes C and H, para 3.1(ii).

102 Codes C and H, Note 6B. When a detainee asks for free legal advice, the Defence Solicitor Call Centre (DSCC) must be informed of the request..

103 Code C, para 6.8 unless one of the exceptions in para 6.6 applies; Code H, para 6.9.

opportunity to consult a specific solicitor or one from the same firm. If advice is not available by that means, and where advice is publicly funded, it is initially by a phone call to a Defence Solicitor Call Centre (DSCC). The DSCC will decide whether advice should be limited to telephone advice or in person, at the station.

The right of custodial access to legal advice is also protected by Art 6 of the European Convention on Human Rights, scheduled in the HRA. Article 6(3)(c) provides that everyone charged with a criminal offence has the right to defend himself through legal assistance of his own choosing.[104] Access to legal advice in pre-trial questioning, as opposed to such access for the purposes of the trial, was recognised by the European Court in *Salduz v Turkey*[105] where it held that Art 6(3)(c) contains an implied right to custodial legal advice necessary to protect the rights of the defence[106]. Such a right was necessary because, as the Court noted, it contributed 'to the prevention of miscarriages of justice and the fulfilment of the aims of art 6, notably equality of arms between the investigating or prosecuting authorities and the accused'[107].

In *Cadder v Lord Advocate*[108] the appellant was detained on suspicion of serious assault by Glaswegian police under the Criminal Procedure (Scotland) Act 1995. He was subsequently interviewed under caution where he made number of incriminating remarks without the benefit of legal advice. Section 15 of the Criminal Procedure (Scotland) Act 1995 required that only his presence in custody be intimated to a solicitor. He was subsequently indicted and tried at the Sherriff's Court where his taped-recorded admissions were led in evidence. The appellant brought an appeal to the UK Supreme Court under a devolution minute arguing that the use of the confession by the Lord Advocate was, following *Salduz*, incompatible with Art 6 and Art 6(3)(c). In a landmark judgment the Supreme Court agreed, Lord Hope concluding that unless 'there are compelling reasons for restricting the right, a person who is detained has access to advice from a lawyer before he is subjected to police questioning.'[109] In *Ambrose v Harris*[110] the Supreme Court held, reviewing the Art 6 jurisprudence, that the right to legal advice should arise as soon as a person is being questioned as a suspect. However, if evidence was obtained prior to the suspect having access to legal advice the question whether it would be admissible would depend on whether the trial overall would be fair if it was admitted.

In *R (Elosta) v Commissioner of Police of the Metropolis*[111] the question arose as to whether the regime contained in Sched 7 TA contained a right for a detainee to have a solicitor present during an examination. Elosta had entered the UK from Saudi Arabia and was detained under Sched 7 TA at Heathrow Airport. He was allowed to converse with a solicitor on the telephone but the police refused to delay the examination until a solicitor arrived in person at the airport. Subsequently, in the Divisional Court the Commissioner sought to argue that there was no right to consult with a solicitor in person

---

104 See Chapter 2, pp 63–64.
105 [2007] ECHR 36391/02.
106 Para 55.
107 Para 52.
108 2010] UKSC 43.
109 Para 48.
110 [2011] UKSC 43.
111 [2013] EWHC 3397 (Admin).

because the applicant had not been detained at a police station. Bean J disagreed, concluding that there was in fact such a right to a face-to-face consultation.[112] The law here was subsequently changed in the Anti-Social Behaviour, Crime and Policing Act 2014 Sched 9 para 5 to provide for consultation wherever the detention occurs. Moreover, the right for a detainee to consult a solicitor 'privately and at any time' under Sched 8 para.7 is expressed in practically identical terms to the right under PACE s 58(1): 'The detainee has the choice. The right may be exercised at any time during the period of detention and may be exercised repeatedly, although not in a manner which frustrates the proper purpose of the examination.' If the solicitor attends in person he may be present during the interview, since that is what the House of Lords in *Ex p Begley*[113] held to be the effect of the identical wording of s 58 of PACE. A reasonable delay to await the arrival of a solicitor may be required, but the detainee is not entitled to exercise that right in such a way as to frustrate the proper purpose of the examination.'[114] Finally, Bean J noted the importance of having a solicitor present during Sched 7 interrogations for there may well be circumstances in which a detainee may seek advice not only on whether he is obliged to answer a particular question, but on the legal consequences of refusing to do so.[115]

Access to legal advice where adverse inferences may be drawn from silence

Even before *Salduz*, in *Murray (John) v UK*[116] the Court held that Art 6(1) and (3)(c) had been breached by the denial of custodial access to a lawyer for 48 hours, since such access was essential where there was a likelihood that adverse inferences would be drawn from silence. It found that where such inferences could be drawn, Art 6 would normally require that the accused should be allowed to benefit from the assistance of a lawyer in the initial stages of police interrogation, although that right might be subject to restrictions for good cause.

These findings were confirmed in *Averill v UK*.[117] The applicant was denied access to a solicitor during the first 24 hours of interrogation; he was then allowed to consult a solicitor, but the solicitor was not allowed to be present during subsequent interviews. The provisions governing access to a solicitor were contained in s 45 of the EPA 1991. Adverse inferences were drawn from his silence at trial under Art 3 of the Criminal Evidence (Northern Ireland) Order 1988. The Court found that no breach of Art 6(1) had occurred; he had been subject to 'indirect compulsion', due to the probability that adverse inferences would be drawn if he remained silent, but that in itself was not decisive.[118] The drawing of adverse inferences, it was found, did not render the trial unfair since the presence of incriminating fibres found on his clothing called for an

---

112 Para 34.
113 [1997] 1 WLR 1475.
114 Para 54.
115 Para 51.
116 (1996) 22 EHRR 29.
117 (2001) 31 EHRR 36; (2000) *The Times*, 20 June. See also *Magee v UK* (2001) 31 EHRR 35; (2000) *The Times*, 20 June.
118 Para 48.

explanation from him. Further, the drawing of adverse inferences was only one factor in the finding that the charges were proved. However, the Court did find a breach of Art 6(3)(c) read with Art 6(1) on the basis – which it noted in *Murray* – that, bearing in mind the scheme contained in the 1998 Order, it is of 'paramount importance for the rights of the defence that an accused has access to a lawyer at the initial stages of police interrogation'.[119] This was because, under the scheme, the accused is confronted with a dilemma from the outset. If he remains silent, adverse inferences may be drawn. If he breaks his silence, his defence may be prejudiced. In order to deal with this dilemma, the Court found, legal advice is needed at the initial stages of the interrogation.[120] Thus, a right of access to legal advice in custodial questioning may be implied into Art 6(3)(c) when read with Art 6(1) where the drawing of adverse inferences is a relevant issue.

Murray required a domestic answer, bearing in mind the curtailment of the right to silence that had occurred under ss 34–37 Criminal Justice and Public Order Act 1994, discussed fully below. Under s 34:

> where . . . evidence is given that the accused . . . (a) on being questioned under caution by a constable trying to discover whether or by whom the offence had been committed, failed to mention any fact relied on in his defence . . . or (b) on being charged . . . or on officially being informed that he might be prosecuted . . . failed to mention any such fact, being a fact which in the circumstances existing at the time the accused could reasonably have been expected to mention when so questioned, charged or informed . . . sub-s (2) below applies.

Under s 34(2)(d), the court or jury 'in determining whether the accused is guilty of the offence charged may draw such inferences as appear proper'. The Code C, para 10.5 caution, originally introduced in the 2003 version of Code C, reflected this curtailment of the right to silence in warning the suspect that adverse inferences could be drawn. The response to *Murray* was eventually provided by s 58 of the Youth Justice and Criminal Evidence Act 1999 (which came into force in 2003). Section 58 inserted s 34(2A) into the CJPOA to provide essentially that adverse inferences shall not be drawn from a suspect's silence under caution before or after charge at an authorised place of detention if he has not been allowed an *opportunity* to consult a solicitor before that point (emphasis added).

Codes C and H reflect s 34(2A) in the sense that they provide in Annex C that a restriction on drawing adverse inferences applies when the suspect has not had an opportunity to have access to legal advice. The restriction is reflected in the use of the Annex C para 2 caution, encapsulating the traditional right to silence, which must be used where an opportunity to have legal advice has not been given. Thus s 34(2A) CJPOA is likely to encourage the police to afford access to legal advice. To an extent, s 34(2A) and the current version of Code C reflect *Murray* rather than *Brennan*. At the point when the caution is given it is, of course, not possible to know whether or not adverse inferences will in fact be drawn at trial, and yet the suspect has the right to remain silent without risk. This position accords with Art 6, following *Murray*.

---

119 Para 59.
120 Para 57.

The scheme under ss 34, 36 and 37 of the CJPOA is similar to the scheme under the 1988 Order, so the findings in *Murray* and *Averill* appear to cover all police interviews under the Code C para 10.5 caution, since once the caution has been given, it is clear that adverse inferences may be drawn from silence. However, the limitations on access to legal advice and certain of the formal and informal loopholes in the access discussed below arguably may not fully accord with the requirements of Art 6(3)(c) in conjunction with Art 6(1) as interpreted in *Murray* and *Averill*. Section 34(2A) also excludes questioning under caution at somewhere other than an authorised place of detention. Thus it does not apply to silences occurring in out of police station interviews (which will be prior to the point of notification of the availability of legal advice). The rationale is that in such interviews the suspect who has not been arrested is free to leave and could go to seek legal advice. However, the less experienced suspect may not realise that this is the case. As explained above, Code C allows for informal interviews outside the police station, under caution. Theoretically, then, such an interview, in which a suspect had remained silent and arguably had not had a true opportunity to consult a solicitor, could be adduced in evidence and s 34(2A) would not prevent the drawing of adverse inferences. Such a possibility would not appear to accord fully with the Art 6 jurisprudence since the suspect was confronted with a dilemma once cautioned, but could not avail himself of legal advice. It is suggested that the objections, based on *Murray* and *Averill*, to the drawing of adverse inferences from such silences cannot be fully met by the provision of para 11.4 of Codes C and H to the effect that any significant silence or statement outside the police station should be put to the suspect at the beginning of an interview at the police station.

Under the current domestic provisions discussed below there are instances when suspects will be interviewed in the knowledge that adverse inferences may be drawn from silence, but access to legal advice will not be available, although not formally denied. As Chapter 14 will point out, the Court in *Teixeira de Castro v Portugal*[121] found that certain pre-trial procedures render a fair trial almost impossible and therefore curb the discretion of the Court in its response.[122] This finding was not made in the context of custodial legal advice but could be applied to s 78 of PACE, in support of an argument that the exclusionary discretion embodied under the section should be used to exclude interviews where, informally, no access to legal advice was made available before or during the police interview which is proffered in evidence although the suspect was aware that adverse inferences might be drawn from silence.[123] It would be arguable that such an interview should be excluded from evidence under s 78, following *Ambrose*, *Murray* and *Averill*, on the basis that otherwise Art 6(1) would not appear to be satisfied.

Formal exceptions, limitations and informal subversion

The rights of access to legal advice are limited in formal and informal fashion. The formal PACE and TA exceptions are narrowly drawn and, as indicated below, have received a narrow interpretation. This cannot, however, be said of the formal Code C

---

121 (1998) 28 EHHR 101.
122 See pp 1291–94.
123 Under PACE 1984, Code C, this would include all interviews since, as indicated above, under para 11.1.A the definition of an interview is an exchange regarding involvement in criminal activity which is required to be under caution.

and H exceptions. Further, the factor which previously motivated the police to delay (or refuse) access to legal advice remains unchanged: the suspect still has the right to remain silent and the legal adviser may advise him or her to exercise it in the particular circumstances of the case, despite the risk that adverse inferences may be drawn later at court. Even if the solicitor does not advise silence, the police may think that they are more likely to obtain incriminating admissions from detainees in the absence of a solicitor and therefore at times may deny the access to one envisaged by s 58. Quite a large body of research suggests that the police prefer to interview suspects who have not had advice and without an adviser present.[124] Research confirms that the possibility of formally delaying access to legal advice is almost certainly not as significant as the more informal police influence on the notification and delivery of advice and on securing the presence of the adviser.[125] This may be due in part to the determination shown by the Court of Appeal to protect this due process right by restrictive interpretation of the formal exceptions under s 58(8) of PACE in a key decision.[126] However, there are a number of loopholes in the legal advice scheme that may allow for less formal methods of evading its provisions and it may be that the suspects who are thereby most disadvantaged are those most in need of legal advice. A number of formal and informal methods of evading the scheme are available and certain key methods are identified below.

As the discussion below explains, Codes C and H provide that in respect of formal denials the restriction on drawing adverse inferences applies, and the suspect should be cautioned accordingly, under Annex C para 2 of both Codes (the traditional pre-1994 caution). But in respect of other instances in which legal advice is not afforded, the Codes provide expressly or impliedly that the restriction does not apply and therefore the suspect is warned via the caution that if he remains silent adverse inferences may be drawn.

Similarly, the right recognised by the European Court in *Salduz* is subject to limits. Thus as the Court noted the right to custodial advice 'has so far been considered capable of being subject to restrictions for good cause . . . the question, in each case, has therefore been whether the restriction was justified and, if so, whether, in the light of the entirety of the proceedings, it has not deprived the accused of a fair hearing, for even a justified restriction is capable of doing so in certain circumstances.'[127]

Delaying access – harm-based exceptions

Non-terrorist suspects

The most direct method of delaying legal advice involves invoking one of the s 58(8) PACE exceptions. The exceptions come into operation if the suspect is in police

---

124 The research undertaken by Sanders et al, *Advice and Assistance at Police Stations*, November 1989; Brown, *PACE Ten Years On: A Review of the Research*, Home Office Research Study 155, 1997, p 77.

125 The research undertaken by Sanders et al, *ibid*, put the figure at around 2%. In comparison, Brown, *ibid*, found that approximately 35% of suspects may have been influenced against advice by the police. The government's *Consultation Paper on Terrorism* (1998) stated that it was not aware of any formal denial in terrorist cases over the last two years in Britain (para 8.31).

126 *R v Samuel* [1988] 2 All ER 135; [1988] 2 WLR 920.

127 Para 52.

detention for an indictable offence. It used to be the case that the exceptions applied in respect of 'serious arrestable offences'. The concept of an arrestable offence under s 24 was abolished in 2005 when PACE was amended, so s 58(8) has now broadened to cover indictable offences.[128] Section 58(8) allows an officer of at least the rank of superintendent to authorise delay, in respect of a suspect in detention for an indictable offence. If both these conditions are fulfilled, access, if requested, can be delayed for up to 36 hours, under s 58(8) which provides:

An officer may only authorise delay where he has reasonable grounds for believing that the exercise of the right . . . (a) will lead to interference with or harm to evidence connected with an indictable offence or interference with or physical injury to other persons; or (b) will lead to the alerting of other persons suspected of having committed such an offence but not yet arrested for it; or (c) will hinder the recovery of any property obtained as a result of such an offence.

Under sub-s (8A), delay can also be authorised:

where the indictable offence is a drug trafficking offence and the officer has reasonable grounds for believing (a) that the detained person has benefited from drug trafficking and (b) that the recovery of the value of that person's proceeds of drug trafficking will be hindered by the exercise of the right.

A further exception was added (s 58(8A) and (8B)) relating to confiscation orders under Part 2 of the Proceeds of Crime Act 2002. Delay is permitted where the detainee has benefited from the offence, and it is considered on reasonable grounds that recovery of the benefit would be hindered if the solicitor is contacted.

In other words, the officer must believe on reasonable grounds that exercise of the right at the time when the person in police detention desires to exercise it will lead to the solicitor acting as a channel of communication between the detainee and others – alerting them or hindering the recovery of stolen property or the products of drug trafficking, or the benefits of crime. These exceptions are repeated in Annex B of Code C, which also provides that if the exception is invoked the suspect must be allowed to choose another solicitor.

The leading case determining the scope of the s 58 exceptions is *Samuel*.[129] The appellant was arrested on suspicion of armed robbery and, after questioning at the police station, asked to see a solicitor. The request was refused, apparently on the grounds that other suspects might be warned[130] and that recovery of the outstanding stolen money might thereby be hindered.[131] The appellant subsequently confessed to the robbery and was later convicted. On appeal, the defence argued that the refusal of access was not justifiable under s 58(8) and that therefore, the confession

128 A serious arrestable offence was defined in s 116. The amendment was made to s 58(6) by the Serious and Organised Crime Act 2005 Sched 7(3), para 43 (10)(b). The Criminal Justice Act 1988, s 99 extended the exceptions to drug trafficking offences.
129 [1988] QB 615; [1988] 2 All ER 135; [1988] 2 WLR 920, CA.
130 Section 58(8)(b).
131 Section 58(8)(c).

obtained should not have been admitted into evidence as it had been obtained through impropriety. The Court of Appeal considered the use of the word 'will' in s 58(8), which suggests that the police officer must be virtually certain that a solicitor, if contacted, will thereafter either commit a criminal offence or unwittingly pass on a coded message to criminals. It must be asked, first, whether he did believe this and second, whether he believed it on reasonable grounds. The Court considered that only in the remote contingency that evidence could be produced as to the corruption of a particular solicitor would a police officer be able to assert a reasonable belief that a solicitor would commit a criminal offence. They went on to hold that showing a reasonable belief that a solicitor would inadvertently alert other criminals would also be a formidable task; such a belief could only reasonably be held if the suspect in question was a particularly resourceful and sophisticated criminal or if there was evidence that the solicitor sought to be consulted was particularly inexperienced or naïve. It was found that as no evidence as to the naivety or corruption of the solicitor in question had been advanced it could not be accepted that the necessary reasonable belief had existed. The police had made no attempt to consider the real likelihood that the solicitor in question would be utilised in this way; in fact, it was apparent that the true motive behind the denial of access was a desire to gain a further opportunity to break down the detainee's silence. It should be noted that Code C expressly disallows denial of access to a solicitor on the ground that he or she will advise the suspect to remain silent.[132]

This interpretation of s 58(8) greatly narrowed its scope, since it means that the police are no longer able to make a general, unsubstantiated assertion that it was thought that others might be alerted if a solicitor was contacted. The authorising officer has to show, on very specific grounds, why this was thought to be the case. This has meant that the exceptions are very rarely invoked; the change to allow them to operate in respect of indictable offences is unlikely to have any significant impact in encouraging police to invoke them since the central difficulty of showing that a specific solicitor would act dishonestly or naively in the ways indicated still remains. Code C reflects the s 58 exceptions in para 6.6, and they are repeated in Annex B. If an exception is invoked the restriction on drawing adverse inferences applies under CJPOA, s 34(2)(A), and this is stated in Code C, para 6.6(b). The question of exclusion of a confession where an exception is improperly invoked is considered in Chapter 13.[133]

Terrorist suspects

Under the TA 2000, as amended, the access can be delayed for up to 48 hours (see Sched 8, para 8(2)) on the grounds for delay mentioned above, with additional ones relating to terrorism. The right can be delayed if a superintendent reasonably believes that communication with an adviser will lead to interference with the gathering of information about the commission, preparation, or instigation of acts of terrorism or make it more difficult to prevent an act of terrorism or apprehend and prosecute the perpetrators of any such act. Delay can be for 48 hours, which is also the period of time for which the suspect can be detained on police authority alone, without recourse to judicial authorisation.[134]

---

132 Codes C and H, Annex B, para 4.
133 See pp 983–84.
134 See Chapter 13, pp 922–24.

The TA harmonises the arrangements for delay in Northern Ireland with those in England and Wales, in that once access has been granted, it will not then be withheld.[135] The arrangements in Scotland under the TA allow for delay under Sched 8, para 16(7) if, under para 17(3), delay is 'in the interests of the investigation or prevention of crime, or in recovering property criminally obtained, or in confiscating the proceeds of an offence, or of the apprehension, prosecution or conviction of offenders'. In all three jurisdictions, when a review officer authorises continued detention under Sched 8 of the TA he must remind the detainee of his rights to contact a friend or relative and to consult a solicitor[136] and, if applicable, of the fact of their being delayed. The officer must also consider whether the reason or reasons for which the delay was authorised continue to subsist and, if not, he must inform the officer who authorised the delay of his opinion. However, there is no provision allowing the review officer to override the view of the officer who originally authorised delay. The TA provisions largely continue the previous counter-terrorism regime, and therefore do not address the concerns of those who view confessions obtained after 24 hours in detention as inherently fallible,[137] particularly where the detainee has also been held without access to legal advice and incommunicado.[138]

The wider possibilities of delaying access under the TA in relation to the terrorist, as opposed to the conventional suspect, are open to question under Art 6, as discussed below. Code H reflects the TA exceptions in para 6.7(iii), and they are repeated in Annex B. If an exception is invoked the restriction on drawing adverse inferences applies under CJPOA, s 34(2)(A), and this is stated in Code H in para 6.7(b).

Further formal exceptions under Codes C and H[139]

Harm-based exceptions

As indicated, para 6.6(b) of both Codes C and H reflects the TA and PACE exceptions to an extent. Those exceptions are repeated word for word in Annex B of both Codes. But

---

135 Under the EPA and its codes, the powers to delay access were broadly the same as under the PTA, but also, once the police had allowed access, further delays could be imposed and there was no right to have advisers present in interviews.

136 Under Sched 8, para 27. These rights arise under paras 6 and 7 of Sched 8.

137 See, e.g., Walker, *Miscarriages of Justice*, 1999, pp 18, 39.

138 See p 910. The exceptions to the right to have someone informed of detention are similar to those allowing delay in providing access to legal advice.

139 Code C, para 6.6 provides: A detainee who wants legal advice may not be interviewed or continue to be interviewed until they have received such advice unless:

  (a) *Annex B* applies, when the restriction on drawing adverse inferences from silence in *Annex C* will apply because the detainee is not allowed an opportunity to consult a solicitor; or

  (b) an officer of superintendent rank or above has reasonable grounds for believing that:

  (i) the consequent delay might: lead to interference with, or harm to, evidence connected with an offence; lead to interference with, or physical harm to, other people; lead to serious loss of, or damage to, property; lead to alerting other people suspected of having committed an offence but not yet arrested for it; hinder the recovery of property obtained in consequence of the commission of an offence. See *Note 6A*

  (ii) when a solicitor, including a duty solicitor, has been contacted and has agreed to attend, awaiting their arrival would cause unreasonable delay to the process of investigation. Note:

the wording of para 6.6 (b) (para 6.7(b) in Code H) is significantly different and broader. Under para 6.6(b), a power to proceed with the interview, although the suspect has not had advice, arises if an officer of superintendent rank or above has reasonable grounds for believing that delay would: lead to interference with or harm to evidence connected with an offence; lead to interference with or harm to other people or serious loss of or damage to property, or hinder the recovery of property obtained in consequence of the commission of an offence; or lead to the alerting of people suspected of having committed an offence but not yet arrested for it. The para 6.6 provisions are not dependent on the offence in question being an indictable one. These exceptions are significantly broader than those contained in PACE or the TA and repeated in Annex B of both Codes. However, the curbing effect of the *Samuel* argument would still apply: it would still have to be shown that a particular adviser would be likely to act as a channel of communication with others or act dishonestly in some other fashion in relation to the harm envisaged. The restriction on drawing adverse inferences from silence applies if one of these exceptions is invoked.

Unavailability of nominated solicitor or delay

Further powers to delay access and to interview the suspect without his having had legal advice arise under Codes C and H. Code C, para 6.6(b)(ii) provides that the interview can be started although the suspect has not received advice if 'a solicitor has agreed to attend, and awaiting his arrival would cause unreasonable delay to the process of the investigation'. This is repeated in Annex B. Code H contains the same exception in para 6.7. The restriction on drawing adverse inferences from silence applies. But even where the restriction on drawing adverse inferences applies, it is clear that there should be good cause for the delay in obtaining advice, following *Murray*. That requirement may not be satisfied by these grounds for proceeding with the interview, although advice has not been obtained, since the use of the word 'unreasonable' means that the test is broad and imprecise and could offer leeway to the police to invoke it in a wide range of circumstances

Sub-paragraph 6.6(c) Code C and 6.7 (c) Code H provide a further exception: that the detainee can be interviewed without legal advice if the nominated solicitor is unavailable and, notification of the duty solicitor scheme is given but the suspect does not want to see the duty solicitor. In these instances the restriction on drawing adverse inferences from silence does *not* apply on the basis that the suspect has had an opportunity to have advice.

Consent to forgo advice

The detainee who has decided to have advice can nevertheless change his or her mind; this is provided for by para 6.6(d) of both codes, if the consent is given in writing or

---

In these cases the restriction on drawing adverse inferences from silence in *Annex C* will apply because the detainee is not allowed an opportunity to consult a solicitor.

(c) the solicitor the detainee has nominated or selected from a list:

    (i) cannot be contacted;

    (ii) has previously indicated they do not wish to be contacted; or

    (iii) having been contacted, has declined to attend; and the detainee has been advised of the Duty Solicitor Scheme but has declined to ask for the duty solicitor; in these circumstances the interview may be started or continued without further delay provided an officer of inspector rank or above has agreed to the interview proceeding. Note: The restriction on drawing adverse inferences from silence in *Annex C* will not apply because the detainee is allowed an opportunity to consult the duty solicitor.

on tape and an officer of the rank of inspector or above has inquired into the reason for the change of mind and gives authority for the interview to proceed.[140] However, there is some leeway allowing police officers to engineer a change of heart.[141] No limitations were placed on the reasons for giving such consent, thus creating a flaw in the legal advice provisions. In particular, if the consent may be based on a police misrepresentation, ought it to be treated as genuine?

The first instance decision in *Vernon*[142] suggested that the consent must be genuine; in other words, it must not be based on misleading information given by the police. The defendant consented to be interviewed under the misapprehension that if her own solicitor was unavailable, there was no alternative means of obtaining advice; the confession so obtained was excluded. Andrew J held that as her consent to the interview was given under the misapprehension that otherwise, the interview would be delayed till the morning, this could not be termed true consent: had she known of the availability of the duty solicitor, she would have withheld her consent. Thus, the relevant Code C para had been breached. This ruling suggests that although the exceptions under paras 6.6(c) and (d) are expressed disjunctively, they should be read together; if a detainee has fallen within para 6.6(c) by nominating a solicitor and being disappointed, he or she should then be informed of the alternative. It would not seem to accord with the drafter's intention to treat the consent of such a person in the same way as that of a detainee who has decided against having a solicitor at all.

The ruling of the Court of Appeal in *Hughes*,[143] however, suggested that if the police misled the suspect without bad faith, a resultant consent would be treated as genuine. The appellant, disappointed of obtaining advice from his own solicitor, inquired about the duty solicitor scheme but was informed, erroneously (but in good faith), that no solicitor was available. Under this misapprehension, he gave consent to be interviewed and the Court of Appeal took the view that his consent was not thereby vitiated.

As indicated, under the current 2014 version of Codes C and H, once the suspect has changed his mind about having advice, the interview can proceed subject to the need to

---

140 Code C, para 6.6
    (d) The detainee changes his mind about wanting a solicitor present at the interview and states that they no longer wish to speak to a solicitor. In these circumstances, the interview may be started or continued without delay provided that:
        (i) an officer of inspector rank or above: speaks to the detainee to enquire about the reasons for their change of mind (see *Note 6K*), and makes, or directs the making of, reasonable efforts to ascertain the solicitor's expected time of arrival and to inform the solicitor that the suspect has stated that they wish to change their mind and the reason (if given);
        (ii) the detainee's reason for their change of mind (if given) and the outcome of the action in
           (i) are recorded in the custody record;
        (iii) the detainee, after being informed of the outcome of the action in
           (i) above, confirms in writing that they want the interview to proceed without speaking or further speaking to a solicitor or (as the case may be) without a solicitor being present and do not wish to wait for a solicitor by signing an entry to this effect in the custody record;
        (iv) an officer of inspector rank or above is satisfied that it is proper for the interview to proceed in these circumstances . . . at any time during the interview, the detainee may again ask for legal advice and that if they do, a break will be taken to allow them to speak to the solicitor, unless *paragraph 6.6(a), (b), or (c)* applies.
141 See further Sanders, Young, Burton *Criminal Justice*, 4th edn, 2010, pp 235–239.
142 [1988] Crim LR 445.
143 [1988] Crim LR 519, CA, transcript from LEXIS.

obtain the permission of an officer of the rank of inspector or above. The requirement that the inspector enquires into the reason for the change of mind provides, however, a partial safeguard against pressure from police. The restriction on drawing adverse inferences does not apply since the suspect has apparently consented to forego advice.

Debarring solicitors' representatives

As already noted, s 58(1) entitles the detainee to consult a solicitor at any time. If an accredited or probationary representatives is sent, under Code C, para 6.12 a person should be treated as a 'solicitor' in terms of access to the client. But they can be disallowed access if an officer of the rank of Inspector or above considers that allowing it would 'hinder the investigation of crime' (para 6.12A). The Court of Appeal found in *Chief Constable of Avon ex p Robinson*,[144] that access to such representatives could be denied in a wide range of circumstances. The chief constable had issued instructions that the character and antecedents of certain unqualified clerks employed by the applicant – a solicitor – were such as to make their presence at police interviews with suspects undesirable.

The Court of Appeal considered the scope of the express exception to para 6.9: 'the clerk shall be admitted unless an officer of the rank of inspector or above considers that such a visit will hinder the investigation of crime'. (Similar wording is now used in para 6.12A.) It was held that the investigating officers had been entitled in each instance to invoke the exception because they had known of the criminal activities of the clerks. They had been informed of such activities by the chief constable, but he had not imposed a blanket ban on the clerks; the discretion to debar the clerks had been left with the officers concerned. Accordingly, there had been no breach of para 6.9 and the application would therefore be refused. May LJ, in a lengthy *dictum*, also considered that there was an implied requirement under para 6.9 that a clerk be capable of giving advice on behalf of the solicitor and therefore a police officer would be entitled to exclude a clerk if he appeared incapable of giving advice owing to his age, appearance, mental capacity or known background.

The concern as to the possible effects of employing these untrained clerks was understandable, but the result of this decision was to confer a very wide power on the police to exclude clerks. However, in *R (Thompson) v Chief Constable of Northumbria Constabulary*[145] it was found that a 'blanket ban' on such persons was not permissible and must be decided case by case.

Further provisions relate to exclusion from the interview of solicitors, which also apply to their representatives. Under para 6.10, the solicitor may be excluded from the interview if his or her conduct is such that the investigating officer is unable properly to question the suspect. Under para 6.19 a record must be made if a detainee asks for legal advice and an interview is begun without it, or the solicitor or representative has been required to leave the interview. Nothing is said about applying the restriction on drawing adverse inferences, despite the fact that the detainee may not in fact obtain an opportunity to have legal advice. Again this is an instance in which, it is argued, s 34(2A) should be applied, adopting a broad interpretation based on the Art 6 jurisprudence, so that such inferences should not be drawn.

144 [1989] All ER 15; [1989] 1 WLR 793.
145 [2001] 4 All ER 354.

Disallowing private consultation for terrorist suspects

There is an extra exception in Code H under para 6.5, based on TA, Sched 8, para 9. The detainee can be forbidden a private consultation with the solicitor if an officer of the rank of commander or assistant chief constable gives authority for this on the basis that otherwise the consequences set out in the TA, Sched 8, para 8(4) or (5) might reasonably be expected to arise. Those are the consequences allowing for delay in access to legal advice. This provision is in doubtful conformity with Art 6 since in a number of cases the Strasbourg Court has stressed the importance of maintaining the confidentiality of solicitor/client consultation (*Brennan v UK*; *S v Switzerland*).[146] In *R (La Rose) v Commissioner of Police of the Metropolis*[147] the applicant was forced to obtain telephone advice using a phone on the custody officer's desk, while other officers were in the room. It appeared that confidentiality may have been impaired and he was inhibited in his consultation with the solicitor as a result. However, the Divisional Court found no breach of his Art 6 rights. Since it was unclear that there was a pressing reason to use a phone in a situation in which the applicant could be over heard, it is likely that the Strasbourg Court would take a different view. The exception based on TA, Sched 8, para 9 does relate to pressing reasons. But, on *Samuel* lines, and taking account of the Art 6 jurisprudence on confidentiality, it is argued that there should be a basis for considering that one of the harmful consequences envisaged in Sched 8 would arise.

Conclusions

Clearly, the curtailment of the right to silence discussed is tending to affect the nature of custodial legal advice. It has affected the role of the legal adviser in the police station; that role was already, it seemed, interpreted in a variety of ways by advisers, but in circumstances where silence would previously have been advised by most of them it seems possible that, at present, it may not be.[148] It appears that the difficulty of advising the client as to when to remain silent and when not to take the risk of so doing may mean that some inexperienced advisers tend to adopt the role of referee or counsellor rather than that of legal adviser.[149] More experienced advisers will, however, be of great value to the client, since they will be able to advise on the risks of staying silent, which may be much greater in response to certain questions than to others.[150] The main studies in this area[151] recognised that interviews may be a means of constructing or creating truth rather than discovering it, but their concern was more with the causal relationship between the presence of a legal adviser and exercise of the right to silence than with

---

146 *S v Switzerland* 28 November 1991; *Brennan v UK* (2002) 34 RHRR 18.

147 [2001] EWHC 553 (Admin).

148 See Bucke et al, *The Right of Silence: The Impact of the CJPOA 1994*, Home Office Research Study No 199, 2000.

149 See 'The Right to Legal Advice in the Police Station: Past, Present and Future' Layla Skinns (2011) Issue 1 Crim LR 19.

150 For further discussion, see Fenwick, H, 'Curtailing the Right to Silence, Access to Legal Advice and Section 78' [1995] Crim LR 132; Jackson, M, 'Interpreting the silence provisions: The Northern Ireland cases' [1995] Crim LR 587.

151 The Sanders research (1989), the Home Office Study by Brown (1997) and the study by Bucke et al (2000).

the relationship between such presence and the making of an unreliable confession. This issue was touched on in the study by Dixon,[152] which found that legal advisers were more likely to advise silence at least temporarily if the client was in a confused or emotional state[153] or had been bullied or deceived.[154] A further study, conducted for the Royal Commission on Criminal Justice[155] found, not surprisingly, that the relationship between legal advice and the right to silence was affected by the quality of the advice given. McConville found that the presence of some legal advisers in interviews may have had a detrimental impact on suspects: 'Lacking any clear understanding of their role in the process, some advisers simply become part of the machine which confronts the suspect.'[156] The suggestions that advisers are reluctant to adopt an adversarial stance were given credence by the two post-PACE cases of oppression which arose in respect of tape-recorded interviews with an adviser present.[157] The advisers must operate on police territory and may, as Dixon puts it, deal with the resultant pressures by making 'some positive adaptation'.[158] However, it has also been pointed out that intervention is not called for in around one-quarter of interviews, that advisers usually intervene when it is called for but, in half of such cases, do not do so as often as is needed.[159]

Moreover, the presence of the adviser may sometimes be a potent factor discouraging use of improper tactics,[160] and may help to alter the balance of power between interviewer and interviewee, thus tending to create a climate in which an unreliable confession is less likely to be uttered. Reassurance deriving from the presence of a solicitor is not merely valuable in terms of the reliability of the confession; it may serve to make the whole experience of police detention less traumatic and daunting. In theory, the solicitor will intervene if the interview is conducted in an intimidatory fashion or if other improper tactics are used.

Exclusion of admissions obtained after a breach of the legal advice provisions may have encouraged police officers to adhere to the scheme. However, most of the methods of evading the legal advice provisions considered here tend to consist of rule evasion as opposed to rule breaking. Courts tend to prefer the defence to point to a specific breach of a code provision before deciding whether to invoke s 78 to exclude admissions.[161] However, the disapproval of persuading an inexperienced suspect to forgo advice

---

152 See Dixon, D, 'Common sense, legal advice and the right to silence' [1991] PL 233.
153 *Ibid*, p 244.
154 *Ibid*, pp 246 and 247.
155 The study by Hodgson and McConville took place over an eight-month period during which the researchers followed suspects and advisers into 180 interrogations; see (1993) 143 NLJ 659.
156 McConville, M and Hodgson, J, *Custodial Legal Advice and the Right to Silence*, Royal Commission Study No 13.
157 *R v Paris* (1993) 97 Cr App R 99; *Heron* (1993) unreported, judgment of Mitchell J, 1 November 1993.
158 Dixon, D, 'Common sense, legal advice and the right to silence' [1991] PL 233 at pp 236–37.
159 Bridges, L and Choongh, S, *Improving Police Station Legal Advice*, 1998, The Law Society.
160 One of the conclusions of the Sanders research (1989), p 150, was that suspects who did not receive advice or whose solicitors did not attend the interrogation would have been greatly assisted had the solicitor been present. Two examples are given, pp 138 and 139, of forceful or threatening questioning which produced a possibly unreliable confession from an easily intimidated suspect in the absence of a solicitor. This finding received some support from Dixon's study (Dixon, D, 'Common sense, legal advice and the right to silence' [1991] PL 233). See also Bucke et al, 2000. See also Sanders and Young, *Criminal Justice*, 3rd edn, 2007, Chapter 4.5 at pp 208–09.
161 See, e.g., *Keenan* [1989] 3 WLR 1193.

expressed in *Beycan*[162] and the decision in *Ambrose* as to the importance of legal advice under Art 6 may indicate that there may be a willingness on the part of the judiciary to consider rule evasion in this context.

If Art 6 is concerned with the objective reliability of the interview in influencing the integrity and fairness of the trial, it appears that, following *Ambrose*, unless the defendant made a clear, positive (albeit possibly misguided) decision not to have custodial advice, the admission into evidence of an interview under caution without such advice, whatever the reason for the failure, might affect the fairness of the trial. It is unclear that the fact that a vulnerable defendant (for example, on the verge of mental handicap) had waived advice, or had received brief telephone advice only, would be sufficient where it could be said that the trial, objectively speaking, might be rendered unfair by the admission of the interview. Similar arguments could perhaps also be raised where the adviser attends the station to see a mentally vulnerable suspect or one with a poor command of English, but the advice obtained is clearly inadequate.[163] When the Strasbourg Court spoke in *Murray* of the need for legal advice where adverse inferences were to be drawn from silence, it may be suggested that it had in mind – taking into account the general need for the rights to be genuinely efficacious, not illusory – the notion of sound, adversarial advice.

4 The right to silence

Introduction

There is general academic agreement that, as Sanders and Young have put it, 'it is over the right of silence that due process and crime control principles clash most fundamentally'.[164] The right to silence, in the sense of the immunity of an accused person from having adverse inferences drawn from failure to answer questions during police questioning, is central to the due process model. In contrast, adherence to crime control principles logically demands not only that such inferences should be drawn, but that, in some or all circumstances, refusal to answer police questions should be an offence in itself, on the ground that innocent persons would not thereby be disadvantaged and the burden on the prosecution would be eased.

Within the due process camp, retention of the right to silence was advocated on the grounds of its value in protecting suspects and also on the basis that it symbolises the presumption of innocence. In the crime control camp abolition was often advocated on the ground that only the guilty have something to hide; the innocent need fear nothing from speaking.[165] But one group of abolitionists departed from a classic crime control stance in arguing for an 'exchange' or trade-off between the PACE suspects' rights and the right to silence.[166] Since the inception of PACE, which adopted the due process

---

162 [1990] Crim LR 185.
163 See (2011) Issue 1 Crim LR Editorial: January 2011 'Legal Advice in Police Stations – 25 Years On', at 1; 'The Justice Lottery? Police Station Advice 25 Years on from PACE *Pascoe Pleasence*' Vicky Kemp and Nigel J. Balmer (2011) Issue 1 Crim LR 3.
164 *Criminal Justice*, 3rd edn, 2007, p 223.
165 See Greer, S, 'The Right of Silence: A Review of the Current Debate', (1990) 53 MLR 709.
166 See Greer, *Ibid*

stance,[167] there has been a clear movement towards the crime control position, on the basis of exchanging enhanced suspects' rights for curtailment of the right to silence. Curtailment of the right was effected under the CJPOA 1994, ss 34–37, but subsequent jurisprudence under Art 6 of the European Convention on Human Rights has led, as will be discussed, to a partial return to the original due process position.

Article 6 of the Convention contrasts with Art 14(3) of the International Covenant on Civil and Political Rights and with Art 34(1) of the South African Bill of Rights in that it does not expressly forbid using compulsion to obtain confessions.[168] The expectation under Art 6(2) that the state bears the burden of establishing guilt impliedly requires that the accused should not be expected to provide involuntary assistance by way of a confession. Thus, the presumption of innocence under Art 6(2) is closely linked to the right to freedom from self-incrimination that the Court has found to be covered by the right to a fair hearing under Art 6(1).[169]

Article 6(2) further impliedly requires that when carrying out their duties, members of a court should not start with the preconceived idea that the accused has committed the offence charged; the burden of proof is on the prosecution, and any doubt should benefit the accused. These matters are at issue when silence under interrogation by law enforcement bodies is penalised by a formal penalty or by drawing adverse inferences from it. The Court has drawn a distinction between these matters, although it recognised in *Murray (John) v UK*[170] that they were not entirely distinct, since adverse inference-drawing is clearly a form of penalty; it was termed 'indirect compulsion'.

Curtailment of the right

The right to silence was abrogated in 1988 in Northern Ireland in terms of allowing adverse inferences to be drawn from silence at trial.[171] But, post-PACE, the right was retained for most suspects, including terrorist suspects, in England and Wales until it was curtailed or undermined, although not abolished, under ss 34, 36 and 37 of the CJPOA 1994. The right, in the sense of an immunity from criminal sanctions due to a refusal to answer questions under suspicion, still exists as far as the majority of suspects are concerned.[172]

The majority of the Runciman Royal Commission agreed with the Phillips Commission in recommending that the right to silence should be retained, although it considered that provision to deal with so called 'ambush' defences (defences sprung on the prosecution at the last minute by a defendant who has hitherto remained silent as to his or her defence) should be introduced.[173] The Commission's recommendation was based not on

---

167   The only recognition given to this right in PACE was in Code C, in the wording of the caution, para 10.4 (now 10.5, 2014 edition of Code C).

168   It may be noted that the UN Human Rights Committee has already expressed concerns regarding the compatibility of the CJPOA 1994, ss 34, 36 and 37 with Art 14(3).

169   *Funke v France* (1993) 16 EHRR 297.

170   (1996) 22 EHRR 29. For comment, see Munday, R, 'Inferences from silence and European Human Rights Law' [1996] Crim LR 370.

171   Criminal Evidence (Northern Ireland) Order 1988, SI 1988/1987 NI 20 1988.

172   See below pp 1249 *et seq.* for a number of statutory provisions which penalise silence.

173   RCCJ Report, p 84, para 2.

a 'symbolic' but an 'instrumental retentionist' approach;[174] it arose from a concern that otherwise, a risk of miscarriages of justice might arise.[175] Given that the Commission was convened in the wake of a number of miscarriages of justice, it might have been expected that the government of the time would give these findings some weight.

The then Home Secretary, however, took what could be termed an exchange abolitionist approach[176] – suspects have greater rights than they did in pre-PACE days and therefore do not need the right to silence. In other words, the right could be curtailed in exchange for the enhanced suspects' rights available under PACE and Codes C and E. Since curtailment of the right was unlikely to have any effect at all on the crime rate, it seems most likely that it was undertaken not in order to gain genuine crime control advantage, but in order to give the impression that such advantage might be gained. The conviction rate was unaffected since the change had an impact only on the small number of criminals who are detected and who would otherwise have remained silent. While it may have had some influence on decisions to plead guilty, its main effect has probably been on that tiny percentage of cases that come to court[177] in which the defendant has remained silent and has pleaded not guilty. The academic consensus was that the advantages in terms of crime control are doubtful, whereas the risk of miscarriages of justice may have been increased.[178] At the same time it was acknowledged, prior to curtailment, that 'the reality of the right to silence is much closer [in practice] to the crime control model than it might first appear',[179] partly due to informal inference drawing by juries and magistrates.[180]

Thus, it is fair to say that prior to the CJPOA changes, the right to silence did not necessarily have a significant impact on the conduct of the interview or ensure that a suspect had a bulwark against giving in to pressure to speak. In fact, few suspects refused to answer questions[181] and, as discussed above, silence was not routinely advised by solicitors. One of the key reasons for retaining the right to silence is that the suspect may be under stress and unable to assess the situation clearly; he or she may have a number of reasons for reluctance to speak, including fear of incriminating another and uncertainty as to the legal significance of various facts. It may also be argued that the right should be reinstated in full in order to guard against the possibility that the suspect will concoct a confession in order to escape the pressure of the interrogation. A juvenile suspect in the *Silcott* case,[182] questioned about the murder of police officer Blakelock by a riotous

---

174 See Greer, S, 'The Right of Silence: A Review of the Current Debate' (1990) 53 MLR 709.

175 Runciman, RCCJ Report, p 55.

176 Greer, 1990, p 719.

177 Over 74% of defendants to be tried in magistrates' courts plead guilty; for Crown Court defendants the figure is 61.5%: Crown Prosecution Service Annual Report 04–05. See further Sanders and Young, *Criminal Justice*, 2007, Chapter 8 (current edn 2010).

178 See Zander, M, *The Police and Criminal Evidence Act 1984*, 1995, pp 303–23 (current edn, 2003); Fenwick, H, 'Curtailing the Right to Silence, Access to Legal Advice and Section 78' [1995] Crim LR 132; Jackson, M, 'Interpreting the silence provisions: The Northern Ireland cases' [1995] Crim LR 587; Pattenden, R, 'Inference from Silence' [1995] Crim LR 602–11.

179 Sanders and Young, *Criminal Justice*, 1994, p 193 (current edn, 2010).

180 Zander and Henderson, *Crown Court Study*, RCCJ Research Study No 19, 1993.

181 See Leng, *The Right to Silence in Police Interrogation*, Home Office Research Study No 10, 1993. Only 4.5% of suspects exercised their right to silence.

182 (1991) *The Times*, 9 December.

mob, made up a detailed confession based on suggestions put to him by police officers, although it was later found that he could not have been present at the scene. This suspect made the confession despite his right to exercise silence, suggesting that the right to silence alone will not benefit such suggestible detainees. However, as argued above, the right to silence in conjunction with advice from an experienced solicitor would seem to provide a surer safeguard against false confessions than either silence or legal advice alone. In other words, the pressure on the suspect in police interviews was already high prior to curtailment of the right, and did not appear to be compensated for by other factors such as audio-recording and access to legal advice. Thus, the large body of writing on the right to silence generally came down on the side of its retention.[183]

Section 34(1) of the CJPOA 1994 curtailed the 'right to silence' in police interviews; it provides:

> where . . . evidence is given that the accused . . . (a) on being questioned under caution by a constable trying to discover whether or by whom the offence had been committed, failed to mention any fact relied on in his defence . . . or (b) on being charged . . . or on officially being informed that he might be prosecuted . . . failed to mention any such fact, being a fact which in the circumstances existing at the time the accused could reasonably have been expected to mention when so questioned, charged or informed . . . sub-ss (2) below applies.

Under s 34(2)(d), the court or jury 'in determining whether the accused is guilty of the offence charged may draw such inferences as appear proper'. The difference between sub-ss (1)(a) and (b) is of interest. It is notable that sub-s (1)(b) makes no mention of questioning. It implies that an inference of guilt may be drawn from the failure of the accused to volunteer information when charged. Sections 36 and 37 of the 1994 Act provide that adverse inferences may be drawn from a failure to account for possession of substances or objects, or presence at a particular place. Under 38(4), the conviction cannot be based on silence alone; the burden of proof remains throughout on the prosecution to prove its case; in effect, a silence will be only one factor which can be used to make out the case. Under s 34 the prosecution have to identify a fact relied on in his defence that he did not mention under questioning.

Under all these provisions, there is still a right to remain silent so long as the accused is prepared to take the risk that so doing may have an adverse impact on his defence, if the case comes to trial. The caution under Code C, para 10.4 was accordingly revised in 1995 (and the 2014 version of Code C para 10.5 still uses these words) to read: 'You do not have to say anything. But it may harm your defence if you do not mention when questioned something which you later rely on in court. Anything you do say may be given in evidence.' In contrast to the old caution, this one has a dual and contradictory effect: it can no longer be seen simply as a safeguard; it must also be seen as part of the coerciveness inherent in the police interviewing and detention powers. Further special

183 See *Report of the Home Office Working Group on the Right to Silence*, 1989 (in favour of modification of the right). For criticism of the report, see Zuckerman, (1989) Crim LR 855. For review of the debate, see Greer (1990); Coldrey (1991) 20 Anglo-Am L Rev 27. In favour of modification of the right, see Williams (1987) 137 NLJ 1107; editorial (1988) Police Review, 29 April.

cautions were adopted under para 10.10 of Code C in order to take account, respectively, of the provisions of ss 36 and 37 of the 1994 Act.

It is implicit in all three CJPOA sections – ss 34, 36, 37 – that inferences may only be drawn if a sound explanation for the silence is not put forward. Although staying silent carries risks, it may be, depending on the circumstances, less risky than making ill-considered admissions since silence, unlike admissions, must be corroborated.[184] However, as the Runciman Commission pointed out, the caution is likely to put most pressure on vulnerable suspects.[185] The suspect most likely to be unable to evaluate the riskiness of silence is precisely the type of suspect who needs the protection originally afforded by the right. Vulnerable persons interviewed outside the police station may be confused by the caution and without the benefit of legal advice may be pressurised into making inaccurate and ill-considered admissions and perhaps into mentioning matters they have not been questioned about.[186] Thus, although it may be argued that in a number of circumstances it may not be 'proper' for a jury to be directed to draw adverse inferences from silence or that it was not reasonable in the circumstances existing at the time to expect the suspect to speak, this will not benefit the suspect who does in fact speak in response to the current caution. Ironically, it is probably the seasoned criminal who understands the operation of s 34 of the CJPOA and may be able to predict that silence may not be a more risky strategy than it was previously, who has not been disadvantaged by the change.[187]

The case law on s 34 of the CJPOA establishes, following *R v Cowan*,[188] that the jury should only consider drawing inferences under s 34 if a prima facie case to answer has been made out by the prosecution. It has also been made clear that where the prosecution do not seek to rely on a silence, the judge should direct the jury positively not to draw inferences.[189] Inferences may only be drawn if a sound explanation for remaining silent is not proffered;[190] it cannot be inferred that the reason for silence was the need to concoct a false explanation if the real and innocent reason for silence is put forward, so long as the reason is plausible. A number of circumstances can be taken into account. In *Argent*,[191] the Court of Appeal found that when considering whether, in the circumstances existing at the time, the defendant could reasonably have been expected to mention the fact he now relies on, the Court should take into account matters such as the defendant's age, health, experience, mental capacity, sobriety, tiredness, personality and legal advice. It is a matter for the jury to resolve whether, bearing these matters in mind, the defendant could have been expected to mention the fact in question, although the judge may give them guidance. Any restrictive impact of these findings is doubtful;

---

184 CJPOA 1994, s 38(3).
185 RCCJ Report, para 4.50.
186 It was found in *Nicholson* [1999] Crim LR 61 that if the police have not asked about facts, adverse inferences should not be drawn against the defendant if he does not state those facts.
187 See Moston, S and Williamson, T, 'The extent of silence in police stations', in Greer and Morgan (eds), *The Right to Silence Debate*, 1990, Bristol Centre for Criminal Justice.
188 [1996] 1 Cr App R 1.
189 *R v McGarry* [1998] 3 All ER 805.
190 This is implicit in *R v Cowan* [1996] 1 Cr App R 1; see also *R v Argent* [1997] Cr App R 27.
191 [1997] 2 Cr App R 27; (1996) *The Times*, 19 December. See Broome, K, 'An inference of guilt' (1997) 141 SJ 202.

in *R v Friend*[192] adverse inferences were drawn under s 35 against a defendant aged 14, with a mental age of nine.

The case law on s 34 CJPOA suggests that the courts are not on the whole taking a restrictive approach. In *Murray v DPP*,[193] which was decided on the 1988 Northern Ireland Order, but is clearly applicable to s 34, the House of Lords found that silence allows the drawing, not only of specific inferences from failure to mention particular facts, but also of the inference that the defendant is guilty. The question of what counts as a 'fact' under s 34 that the defendant did not mention in police questioning but which he could be said to be relying on in his defence has also been given a broad interpretation. The House of Lords found in *Webber*[194] that even if the defendant does not give evidence at trial, he can be said to be relying on a fact when counsel for the defence, acting on his client's instructions, puts a specific and positive case to prosecution witnesses.

The restriction on drawing adverse inferences

Under the Blair Labour government, and subsequent governments, the CJPOA provisions were retained, but it was already clear that the curtailment of the right to silence under CJPOA 1994, ss 34, 36 or 37 was in some tension with the demands of Art 6 of the European Convention on Human Rights. Depending on the particular circumstances of a case, the curtailment had the potential to lead to a breach of Art 6 on the basis that it infringes the presumption of innocence under Art 6(2) and the right to freedom from self-incrimination.[195] Consideration of the judgments in *Saunders v UK*[196] and *Murray (John) v UK* reveals that it is only where a penalty formally attaches to silence, and the interview may then be used in evidence, that a breach of Art 6 is almost *bound* to be established, but that where adverse inferences can be drawn from the silence at trial, a breach is likely to be established if the suspect has been denied access to legal advice before being questioned under caution. *Saunders v UK* concerned the sanction for refusing to answer questions in serious fraud investigations under s 437 of the Companies Act 1985. Acting under s 437, inspectors of the Department of Trade and Industry had interviewed Saunders regarding allegations of fraud. He was forced to answer the questions put to him and therefore lost his privilege against self-incrimination, which he argued was unfair and amounted to an abuse of process. The interviews were admitted in evidence under s 431(5) of the Companies Act and he was convicted.[197] The Strasbourg Court found that the applicant's right to freedom from self-incrimination under Art 6(1) had been infringed due to the threatened imposition of a penalty for remaining silent and the subsequent admission of the interviews into evidence. This finding was

---

192 [1997] 1 WLR 1433.
193 [1994] 1 WLR 1.
194 [2004] UKHL 1.
195 See the comments of the Court of Appeal in *Birchall* [1999] Crim LR 311; see also the study by Bucke et al, *The Right of Silence: The impact of the CJPOA 1994*, Home Office Research Study No 199, 2000.
196 (1997) 23 EHRR 313; Appl No 19187/91, Com Rep, paras 69–75.
197 His appeal on grounds of abuse of process and on the basis that the interviews should not have been admitted into evidence under s 78 was rejected: *R v Saunders and Others* [1996] 1 Cr App R 463.

based on the special compulsive regime applicable to Department of Trade and Industry inspections, but the key issue was the use made of the material obtained in court.

But in *O'Halloran v UK*[198] the applicants had been required to state under the Road Traffic Act 1988 s 172 who had been driving a vehicle at a particular time. One had done so but argued that the admission should have been inadmissible. The other did not and argued that he had been punished more severely than he would have been had he been punished for speeding. The Strasbourg Court found no breach of Art 6 in respect of the compulsion to make admissions, in the circumstances, given the limited information being required, and taking account of obligations inherent in choosing to drive cars, and to accept therefore the regulatory regime governing driving. However, that decision applied in the special circumstances of the regulatory regime relating to road traffic, and does not necessarily indicate a retreat from the broader decision in *Saunders*.

The decision in *Murray (John) v UK*[199] may be contrasted with that in *Saunders* since it made it clear that, depending on the circumstances of a case, Art 6 takes a different stance towards imposing a formal penalty on silence and drawing adverse inferences from it. Murray was arrested under the previous relevant provision – the Prevention of Terrorism (Temporary Provisions) Act 1989 – and taken to the police station. A detective superintendent, pursuant to the Northern Ireland (Emergency Provisions) Act 1987, decided to delay access to a solicitor for 48 hours. While being interviewed, Murray repeatedly stated that he had 'nothing to say'. After he had seen his solicitor, he stated that he had been advised not to answer the questions. As indicated above, the Criminal Evidence (Northern Ireland) Order 1988 enables a court in any criminal trial to exercise discretion to draw adverse inferences from an accused's failure to mention a fact during police questioning. Such inferences were drawn from Murray's silence in the police interviews once the prosecution had established a prima facie case against him, and he was convicted. The subsequent decisions in *Averill v UK* and *Brennan v UK*[200] were discussed above, and confirmed the finding in *Murray*, although *Brennan* took a somewhat more restrictive view of the circumstances in which a breach of Art 6 would arise.

The Strasbourg Court emphasised that its decision in *Murray* was confined to the particular facts of the case in finding that no breach of Art 6(1) or (2) had occurred where adverse inferences had been drawn at trial from the applicant's refusal to give evidence, taking into account the degree of compulsion exerted on the applicant and the weight of the evidence against him. The Court placed emphasis on the fact that he had been able to remain silent; also, given the strength of the evidence against him, the matter of drawing inferences was one of common sense that could not be regarded as unfair.[201] But, crucially, the Court did find that Art 6(1) and (3)(c) had been breached by the denial of custodial access to a lawyer for 48 hours, since it found that such access was essential where there was a likelihood that adverse inferences would be drawn from silence. In effect, therefore, the Court adopted something close to an exchange abolitionist approach.[202] The distinction it drew, impliedly, between direct and indirect

198 (2008) 46 EHRR 21.
199 (1996) 22 EHRR 29.
200 (2002) 34 EHRR 18.
201 Para 54.
202 See Greer, S (1990) 53 MLR 709.

compulsion flowing from the risk of adverse inference drawing and criminal penalties respectively, was not explicated and rests, it is suggested, on doubtful premises.

The regime under the 1988 Order is, in essentials, the same as that under s 34 of the CJPOA, which therefore became vulnerable to challenge under the HRA. The question of affording access to legal advice before questioning the suspect if adverse inferences might be drawn from silence had to be addressed; this has already been discussed above, and is considered further below. There were other aspects of *Murray*, relating specifically to the privilege against self-incrimination. As indicated, the findings in *Murray* were carefully confined to the particular facts of the case, and therefore must be treated with caution. But it is clear that the right to freedom from self-incrimination cannot be viewed as absolute under Art 6. Drawing adverse inferences from silence in police interviewing does not necessarily breach Art 6(2), but the greater the reliance placed on such inferences at the trial, the greater the likelihood that a breach will occur. The Court said that it would be incompatible with Art 6(1) and (2) 'to base a conviction solely or mainly on the accused's silence or refusal to answer questions'. As already noted, under s 38(3) of the CJPOA, a conviction cannot be based 'solely' on silence. Article 6(1) and (2) might therefore be found to be breached in circumstances differing from those applicable in *Murray*, including those in which the evidence against the defendant was less overwhelming. A domestic judge would not satisfy Art 6 if he directed a jury that the drawing of adverse inferences could play a major part in a conviction. Further, in *Murray*, there was no jury: the case was decided by a 'Diplock' court. Therefore, the evidence was weighed up by a professional who had the expertise to determine how much weight to give to aspects of it, including the 'no comment' interviews.

Murray made it clear that drawing adverse inferences from silence when the defendant had not had access to legal advice prior to the failure to reply to questioning will breach Art 6; as indicated above, s 58 of the Youth Justice and Criminal Evidence Act 1999 addressed that finding by inserting s 34(2A) into the CJPOA.[203] The amendments provide that if the defendant was at an authorised place of detention and had not had an opportunity of consulting a solicitor at the time of the failure to mention the fact in question, inferences cannot be drawn. This was a very significant change to the interviewing scheme; a number of the implications of this change were considered

---

203 The Criminal Justice and Public Order Act 1994 (CJPOA) now contains 34(2)(A) which provides:
   Where the accused was at an authorised place of detention at the time of the failure [to mention any fact relied on in his defence when questioned under caution] subsections (1) and (2) above [allowing adverse inferences to be drawn from the failure to answer] do not apply if he had not been allowed an opportunity to consult a solicitor prior to being questioned, charged or informed as mentioned in subsection (1) above.
      (3) In section 36 (effect of accused's failure or refusal to account for objects, substances or marks), after subsection (4) there shall be inserted –
      (4A) Where the accused was at an authorised place of detention at the time of the failure or refusal, subsections (1) and (2) above do not apply if he had not been allowed an opportunity to consult a solicitor prior to the request being made.
      (4) In section 37 (effect of accused's failure or refusal to account for presence at a particular place), after subsection (3) there shall be inserted –
      (3A) Where the accused was at an authorised place of detention at the time of the failure or refusal, subsections (1) and (2) do not apply if he had not been allowed an opportunity to consult a solicitor prior to the request being made.

above in relation to the custodial right of access to legal advice.[204] Once s 34(2A) came into force in 2003 no adverse inference could be drawn from silence unless the suspect was under caution (s 34(1)(A) of the CJPOA 1994), and he had had the opportunity of having legal advice. In that instance under s 34(2A) of the CJPOA, no inferences may be drawn from silence. It is notable that s 34(2A) does not provide that such a silence will be inadmissible. Informal inference drawing, which appeared to occur prior to the introduction of ss 34, 36 and 37 of the CJPOA, could therefore still occur. Further, s 34(2A) of the CJPOA does not cover the defendant who has not had legal advice but makes admissions in response to the new caution or (prima facie) the defendant who fails to obtain advice, although no formal denial of an opportunity to consult a solicitor occurs. These very significant matters are discussed further below.

As a result of this development Code C was amended in 2003 to introduce the possibility of using one of two cautions (and that is still the case under the 2014 version of Code C). The caution originally introduced in 1995 still applies, reflecting the curtailment of the right to silence. It is used where an opportunity to have access to legal advice has been given or is about to be given, and is in the following terms: 'You do not have to say anything. But it may harm your defence if you do not mention when questioned something which you later rely on in court. Anything you do say may be given in evidence.'[205] Minor deviations do not constitute a breach of this requirement, provided that the sense of the caution is preserved. The caution must be repeated during the interview if there is any doubt as to whether the detainee realises that it still applies. If a juvenile or a person who is mentally disordered or mentally handicapped is cautioned in the absence of the appropriate adult, the caution must be repeated in the adult's presence.[206] The change to the caution that occurred to reflect s 34 of the CJPOA 1994, discussed further below, means that the suspect is warned that refusing to answer questions may lead to the drawing of adverse inferences in court. Importantly, Codes C and H restrict the circumstances in which inferences can be drawn. Code C, para 10.11 provides:

> For an inference to be drawn when a suspect fails or refuses to answer a question about one of these matters or to answer it satisfactorily, the suspect must first be told in ordinary language:
> (a) what offence is being investigated;
> (b) what fact they are being asked to account for;
> (c) this fact may be due to them taking part in the commission of the offence;
> (d) a court may draw a proper inference if they fail or refuse to account for this fact;
> (e) a record is being made of the interview.

Code H para 10.10 is in the same terms. But Code C, and Code H (Annex C) also provide for a restriction on drawing adverse inferences from silence of the suspect. The provisions of ss 34, 36 and 37 of the Criminal Justice and Public Order Act 1994 are made subject to an overriding restriction, following from s 34(2A), which means that

---

204 See pp 927–29.
205 Code C, para 10.5; Code H, para 10.4.
206 Code H, para 10.11; Code C, para 10.12.

a court or jury is not allowed to draw adverse inferences from a person's silence, if the suspect:

(a) is detained at a police station and before being interviewed
    (i) has asked for legal advice;
    (ii) has not been allowed an opportunity to consult a solicitor; and
    (iii) has not changed their mind about wanting legal advice.

This restriction on drawing adverse inferences from silence is reflected in the second, alternative caution in Annex C, para 2. This is the old caution reflecting the full right to silence prior to its curtailment: 'You do not have to say anything but anything you do say may be given in evidence.' The police must use it *within* the police station when it is clear that the suspect has had an *opportunity* to have access to legal advice (emphasis added).[207] These restrictions on this partial restoration of the full right of silence are significant. In particular, the term 'opportunity' should be noted – it is not necessary that the suspect should actually have obtained access to legal advice. This change clearly reflects an exchange abolitionist approach: the suspect is in effect entitled to the full right to silence or to access to legal advice, but not to both. This is objectionable in due process terms since the two entitlements, as discussed above, tend to be most valuable in conjunction with each other.

The position of the suspect may change; he or she may be able to be silent without risk in one interview, but pressured to speak in a subsequent one. This is provided for in Annex C para 3 of both Codes:

> Whenever the restriction on drawing adverse inferences from silence (para 10.4) either begins to apply or ceases to apply after a caution has already been given, the person shall be re-cautioned in the appropriate terms. The changed position on drawing inferences and the fact that the previous caution no longer applies shall also be explained to him in ordinary language.

The loopholes in the provision for restricting the circumstances in which adverse inferences can be drawn were canvassed above, in relation to rights of access to legal advice. Suffice to say here that the suspect may well be cautioned that such inferences may be drawn in circumstances in which he has had no *true* opportunity to have access to legal advice. Given that the case is unlikely to come to court, the police are unlikely to be called to account, in any sense, in such circumstances, even assuming that what occurred in the police station could be unravelled sufficiently to demonstrate that no such opportunity in fact occurred. The restriction on drawing adverse inferences appears to adhere to the due process demands of Art 6 but, it is argued, falls short of them in practice.

---

207 Under Codes C and H, Annex C, para 2: Whenever a requirement to administer a caution arises and at the time it is given the restriction on drawing adverse inferences from silence applies, the caution shall be [in those terms].

Relying on legal advice in remaining silent

In applying ss 34, 36 and 37 it was noted above that if a sound explanation for remaining silent is given, the jury should be directed that if they accept the explanation they should not draw adverse inferences. (Clearly, they might informally draw them, as they almost certainly did in many instances prior to the 1994 changes.) The explanation often given for remaining silent is that the legal adviser advised silence, or at least a selective silence. This explanation has given rise to a problem that is still bedeviling the UK courts, and it is argued that they still have not dealt with it satisfactorily in Art 6 terms, despite more than one trip to Strasbourg, pre-HRA. From a crime control perspective the concern is that allowing this explanation would drive a coach and horses through the CJPOA provisions: legal advisers could merely advise silence in almost all circumstances, and so doing would normally preclude the drawing of adverse inferences.

But from a due process perspective, accepting the drawing of adverse inferences when the solicitor has advised silence is equally problematic. The solicitor is there in the police station to represent the interests of his or her client; he or she may consider that the best recourse for the client is silence, if, for example, the client has been pressurised or intimidated, or is unable to cope with the questioning. A number of studies have shown that many suspects may not realise that they are being led by police into admitting to having the *mens rea* of the offence in question, since, for example, the use of the word 'reckless' might appear to mean colloquially something rather different from its technical, legal, sense.[208] The police may have disclosed only part of their case against the suspect and that part may in itself be misleading.[209] In *Argent* the Court of Appeal rejected the argument that it was reasonable in the circumstances for the suspect to have stayed silent, on legal advice, when the police had not disclosed an outline of their case. So the solicitor, in seeking to further the best interests of the client, is clearly placed in a dilemma: if she advises silence this may turn out to be to the client's disadvantage. So the solicitor may be forced to advise a client to talk against her better judgment, for fear of the penalty attaching to silence later on. The domestic courts have tended to adopt the crime control stance in dealing with this issue.

The decision in *Condron and Another*,[210] in relation to the treatment in court of legal advice to stay silent, was later found at Strasbourg to have led to a breach of Art 6. The appellants were to be questioned by police at the police station on suspicion of being involved in the supply and possession of heroin. The police surgeon found that they were fit to be interviewed, but their solicitor considered that they were unfit, since they were suffering withdrawal symptoms, and so advised them not to answer any questions. They relied on that advice during the interview and remained silent. At trial, the defence involved reliance on facts that had not been mentioned in the course of the interview and thus potentially fell within s 34 of the CJPOA. The judge held a *voir dire* (a trial within a trial) and rejected argument under s 78[211] that the no comment interview should be excluded as unfair because they were unfit to be interviewed. Argument that

---

208 See McConville, M and Baldwin, J, *Custodial Legal Advice and the Right to Silence*, RCCJ Research Study No 16.
209 See *Rosenberg* (2006) EWCA Crim 6.
210 [1997] 1 Cr App R 185.
211 See pp 979 *et seq.*

it would be improper to allow an inference to be drawn under s 34 because in making no comment they had only followed the bona fide advice of their solicitor was also rejected. The interviews were admitted and the prosecution then argued that they could reasonably have been expected to mention at interview the facts they now relied on in their defence; they were cross-examined on their failure to mention such facts. They gave the explanation that they had relied on the solicitor's advice. In summing up, the judge directed the jury that they must determine whether any adverse inferences should be drawn from the failure of the defendants to mention the facts in question during the police interview. The judge did not explain that the inferences could only be drawn if, despite the explanation, the jury concluded that the silence could only sensibly be attributed to the defendants having no satisfactory explanation to give. Thus, it is possible that the jury may have drawn adverse inferences despite accepting the defendants' explanations.

The appellants were convicted and argued on appeal that the jury should not have been directed that they could draw adverse inferences from the refusal to answer questions since they had followed the advice of their solicitor in so refusing. The Court of Appeal took into account an earlier case, *Cowan and Others*,[212] which concerned the position of defendants failing to testify in court under s 35, and applied the principles enunciated to police questioning. The principles were as follows. A jury cannot infer guilt from silence alone (s 38(3)), so that the jury should only consider drawing inferences if a prima facie case to answer has been made out by the prosecution. Also, the burden of proof remains throughout on the prosecution to prove their case; in effect, a silence will be only one factor that can be used to make out the case. Inferences can be drawn if the only sensible explanation of silence was that the suspect had no explanation, or none that would stand up to cross-examination. The judge's direction was criticised in that it did not make this clear. The Court then considered the procedure to be followed in relation to s 34, where silence is on legal advice. The jury may draw an adverse inference from the failure unless the accused gives the reason for the advice being given. The reason for the advice is legally privileged, since it is part of a communication between solicitor and client, but once the client gives evidence of the nature of the advice, that will probably amount to a waiver of privilege so that the solicitor and/or client can then be asked about the reasons for the advice in court. The Court found that if an accused gives as the reason for not answering questions in a police interview that he has been advised not to do so, this assertion without more will not amount to a sufficient reason for not mentioning relevant matters that may later be relied on in defence. The convictions were upheld on the basis of the overwhelming evidence of drug supply, despite the flaw in the summing up.

It was made clear in *Bowden*[213] that explaining the grounds for the advice will amount to a waiver of legal privilege. Therefore, the prosecution can cross-examine the adviser on what was said to the suspect with a view to discovering discrepancies between the grounds put forward at trial and those discussed in the police station. The effect of these two decisions is to place the defendant and adviser in an invidious position. The adviser may be reluctant to advise silence even where there seem to be good reasons for doing

---

212 [1996] QB 373; [1995] 4 All ER 939.
213 (1999) *The Times*, 25 February.

so.[214] If the adviser advises silence, it may well appear to the defendant that that in itself is a sound reason for remaining silent. But that reason will not be accepted by a court. The adviser can either refuse to waive legal privilege and accept that adverse inferences will be drawn from the silence, or he can waive it and hope that the reasons given for the advice will be accepted in order to discourage the drawing of inferences. There may also be other confidential matters that the adviser does not wish to be asked about. It has been pointed out that solicitors may breach their professional code of conduct if they act for a client when they may be a material witness in the court case.[215] But if there is an arguably sound reason for advising silence, the jury should be directed, following the findings of the Court of Appeal in *Condron*, that if they view the reason as sound, they should not draw adverse inferences.

It was found at Strasbourg that the applicants in *Condron v UK*[216] had failed to receive a fair trial under Art 6 on the basis that the appeal court should not have found that the conviction was safe, despite the erroneous direction of the judge to the jury. Since the Court could not know what part the drawing of adverse inferences played in the jury's decision, it should have allowed the appeal. That decision impliedly confirms that juries should be directed that they should not draw adverse inferences when silence has been advised in the police interview, except in certain circumstances. The Court found that where a defendant refuses to answer questions on legal advice, the jury should not be directed to draw an adverse inference from the silence unless they were first told that they should only do so if they considered that the silence could only sensibly be attributed to the suspect having no good answer to the questions. The Court was not, however sympathetic towards the dilemma that the applicants and solicitor were placed in (para 60):

The court would observe at this juncture that the fact that the applicants were subjected to cross-examination on the content of their solicitor's advice cannot be said to raise an issue of fairness under Art 6 of the Convention. They were under no compulsion to disclose the advice given, other than the indirect compulsion to avoid the reason for their silence remaining at the level of a bare explanation. The applicants chose to make the content of their solicitor's advice a live issue as part of their defence.

The indirect compulsion in question was in fact quite significant if they had to demonstrate in the domestic court that their reliance on the advice was reasonable. The decision affects the role of trial judges; it does not give guidance on, *inter alia*, the question when a no comment interview, based on legal advice, should be excluded from evidence. It still leaves advisers in a state of some uncertainty as to when to advise a suspect to remain silent. However, it makes it somewhat easier for the solicitor to advise silence and safer for the client to rely on that advice.

The European Court of Human Rights confirmed its ruling in *Condron* in *Beckles v United Kingdom*.[217] The victim had gone to a flat where he was allegedly robbed by the defendant and others, prevented from leaving, and then thrown out of the window, sustaining very severe injuries. When arrested the defendant said that the victim 'wasn't pushed, he jumped' but, after seeing his solicitor, refused to answer any questions when

214 See, as to the difficulties facing advisers, Cape, E, 'Advising on silence' (1999) LAG, 14 June.
215 Tregilgas-Davey, M, 'Adverse inferences and the no-comment interview' [1997] 141 SJ 500; *The Guide to the Professional Conduct of Solicitors*, 1996, para 21.12.
216 [2001] 31 EHRR 1, Appl No 35718/97; [2000] Crim LR 679.
217 (2002) 36 EHRR 162.

interviewed. The judge did not direct the jury that they should not draw adverse inferences from the defendant's silence during the interview with the police if they considered that his silence was attributable to legal advice rather than to having no sensible answer to the questions. He was convicted of two counts of robbery, one count of false imprisonment and one count of attempted murder for which he was sentenced to a total of 15 years' imprisonment. The Court found that there had been a violation of Art 6(1) of the European Convention of Human Rights as to the trial judge's directions to the jury. The misdirection concerned the instruction to the jury as to their right, under s 34 of the 1994 Act, to draw adverse inferences from the defendant's silence during an interview with police. The Court had found that the jury should have been directed that if they considered that the defendant had genuinely remained silent on legal advice they should consider refusing to draw an adverse inference from his silence.

After *Beckles v UK*, the case was referred back to the Court of Appeal. In *R v Beckles*[218] it was argued that there had been a misdirection to the jury as to their right, under s 34 of the Criminal Justice and Public Order Act 1994, to draw adverse inferences from the defendant's silence during an interview with police. Lord Woolf found that in a case where a solicitor's advice was relied upon by the defendant in the police interview, the ultimate question for the jury, under s 34, remained whether the facts relied on at the trial were facts which the defendant could reasonably have been expected to mention at interview. If the jury considered that the defendant had genuinely relied on the advice, that was not necessarily the end of the matter. If it was possible to say that the defendant had genuinely acted upon the advice, but had done so because it suited his purpose, that might mean that he had acted unreasonably in not mentioning the facts. The jury had to make a determination on his reasonableness in not mentioning the facts. If they concluded that he had been acting unreasonably they could draw an adverse inference from the failure to mention the facts. The trial judge had not directed the jury to consider the reasonableness or the genuineness of the defendant's reliance on his solicitor's advice as the reason why he did not answer questions in interview. It was found that that misdirection made the defendant's conviction unsafe. The appeal was allowed and a retrial was ordered. Thus Lord Woolf purported to take account of the Strasbourg decision in his findings. However, the emphasis on, in a sense, justifying the silence – even where it was genuinely in reliance on the legal advice – represents some departure from the ECHR decision. *Beckles* is indicative of a Court of Appeal tendency, after *Condron v UK*, to take an unsympathetic stance towards defendants who rely on legal advice in remaining silent.[219]

Since *Beckles* s 34 has remained a somewhat difficult and confusing area of law, and the problems are evident in the decision in *R v Bresa*.[220] At present the circumstances in which adverse inference drawing will create a breach of Art 6 still remain somewhat uncertain,[221] except in the instance in which access to legal advice is also denied. It is clear that affording a suspect an opportunity to have access to legal advice before being

218 [2004] EWCA 2766.
219 See *R v Inman* [2002] EWCA 1950; *R v Chenia* [2003] 2 Cr App 6; *R v Hoare and Pierce* [2004] EWCA Crim 784; *R v Howell* [2003] Crim LR 405; *R v Turner* [2004] 1 All ER 1025.
220 [2005] EWCA Crim 1414.
221 See further Birch, D, 'Suffering in silence: a cost–benefit analysis of s 34 of the CJPOA' [1999] Crim LR 769; Cape, E, *Defending Suspects at Police Stations*, 4th edn, 2003.

questioned under caution is a necessary but not sufficient condition in Art 6 terms, for the drawing of adverse inferences, and s 34(2A) caters for that requirement. But, equally clearly, Art 6 will not necessarily be satisfied where adverse inferences are drawn after a defendant has had such access prior to that point and has remained silent. Cases such as *Condron* or *Bowden*, where the defendants had had legal advice and had acted on it in remaining silent, will have to be considered on their particular facts, in relation to the Art 6 requirements. Such cases obviously differ from *Murray* on the issue of the relationship between silence and legal advice. In *Condron* the defendants acted on legal advice in refusing to answer questions; in *Murray* a breach of Art 6(1) was found on the basis of inference-drawing in the absence of legal advice (not on the basis of inference-drawing *per se*). In *Condron*, the fact of having legal advice was not to the defendants' advantage, possibly the reverse, since in a sense they may have been misled into remaining silent. When will a breach of Art 6(1) arise if adverse inferences are drawn in that context – where the apparent explanation for silence was that it was on legal advice, following the domestic decision in *Beckles*? It must be borne in mind that a solicitor in the police station might need to seek to make a determination as to this question, in order to decide whether or not to advise silence. If it was fairly obvious to the solicitor that the detainee had no innocent explanation of his actions to give, it would appear to be unwise to advise silence since a court might at trial decide that remaining silent was unreasonable.

It might be appropriate to advise silence if it was unclear whether or not the advice would accord with a reasonable explanation for silence, and the defendant could not be expected – due to his or her low intelligence, youth or other vulnerability – to decide to whether to speak or remain silent without the advice. It might also be safe to advise silence where the police had disclosed little of the case against the suspect before interviewing him under caution. To hold otherwise might be viewed as undermining the value attached in *Murray* to granting access to legal advice where adverse inferences would be drawn from silence.[222] The principle from *Murray* clearly rests impliedly on the value of such advice, while the domestic decision in *Beckles* accords that value a lesser weight. This is an instance in which the domestic courts are arguably failing to use the HRA in a way which ensures at least as much rights-protection as could be delivered at Strasbourg. Their consistently crime control-based stance has led them to disregard the values associated with the presumption of innocence and the privilege against self-incrimination which underpinned the traditional right to silence.

Penalising silence and the privilege against self-incrimination

Prior to the inception of the CJPOA, the right to silence was abolished in certain specific circumstances under a number of provisions that made failing to answer questions an offence. The provisions included: s 172 of the Road Traffic Act 1988, as amended; s 2 of the Criminal Justice Act 1987; ss 177 and 178 of the Financial Services Act 1986; ss 236 and 433 of the Insolvency Act 1986; s 437 of the Companies Act 1985; the Banking Act 1987 and the Friendly Societies Act 1992. These provisions, apart from s 172

---

222 It may be noted that such a finding would involve a departure from the current position under UK law as set out in *Condron* [1997] 1 Cr App R 185 and confirmed in *Bowden* (1999) *The Times*, 25 February.

of the RTA, were amended in 1999, as explained below. Thus, in a number of specific instances, the right to silence, in the sense of penalising silence in criminal investigations, had already been eroded until it reached the point where it could be said to have virtually disappeared in those contexts.[223] If, for example, inquiries were made into a failed business, its owner could receive a 's 2 notice' from the Serious Fraud Office issued under the Criminal Justice Act 1987 which meant that a criminal offence would be committed if he or she did not attend for interview and answer questions (*Director of the Serious Fraud Office ex p Smith*).[224] Also, if the company was being investigated, a refusal to answer questions under s 432(2) of the Companies Act 1985 attracted criminal liability.

In *Saunders v UK*[225] (mentioned above) the European Court of Human Rights held that the use of formal coercion to obtain statements from persons would be clearly incompatible with Art 6 if the statement is then used against him or her in criminal proceedings. The Court was clear that public interest considerations such as the pursuit of fraudulent activity within companies could not be employed to deny the essence of the privilege against self-incrimination. This became a clear and consistent line in the Court's jurisprudence[226] until qualified in *Jalloh v Germany*[227] where the court held that a balancing test was applicable: 'In order to determine whether the applicant's right not to incriminate himself has been violated, the court will have regard, in turn, to the following factors: the nature and degree of compulsion used to obtain the evidence; the weight of the public interest in the investigation and punishment of the offence at issue; the existence of any relevant safeguards in the procedure; and the use to which any material so obtained is put.'[228] This new approach marked a significant departure in the Court's previous approach, bringing the interpretation of the right into harmony with the approach of British judges.

Section 172 of the Road Traffic Act 1988 makes it an offence for motorists not to tell police who was driving their vehicle at the time of an alleged offence. The coerced statement can then be used in evidence at trial for the RTA offence in question. The provision on its face contravenes the right against self-incrimination, and this was found to be the case in Scotland in *Stott v Brown*.[229] The defendant encountered the police officers after parking her car and was suspected of driving while intoxicated; she was asked under s 172 to reveal the name of the person driving the car at the relevant time. On pain of the penalty under s 172 she did so, revealing that she had been driving, and was convicted of driving while intoxicated, after the coerced statement was admitted into evidence. Her conviction was overturned on appeal owing to the finding that s 172 contravened Art 6. The ruling of the Edinburgh High Court is of interest since the court rendered s 172, effectively, nugatory. This stance was taken on the basis of the requirements of the Scotland Act, which differ from those of s 6 of the HRA since they do not

223 See *Re London United Investments* [1992] 2 All ER 842; *Ex p Nadir* (1990) *The Times*, 5 November; *Bishopsgate Investment Management Ltd v Maxwell* [1992] 2 All ER 856, CA.
224 [1993] AC 1; [1992] 3 WLR 66; see also *AT & T Istel Ltd v Tulley* [1992] 3 All ER 523, HL.
225 (1997) 23 EHRR 313; Appl No 19187/91, Com Rep, paras 69–75.
226 See for *Heaney and McGuinness v Ireland* [2000] ECHR 34720/97.
227 [2006] ECHR 54810/00.
228 Para 90.
229 2000 SLT 379; see [2000] J CIV LIB 193.

include the possibility envisaged under s 6(2)(b) that the authority was 'acting so as to give effect to or enforce those provisions [of incompatible primary legislation]'.

As Chapter 4 explained, the ruling of the Edinburgh High Court was overturned by the Privy Council: *Brown v Stott*.[230] The Privy Council did not find it necessary to declare that s 172 is incompatible with Art 6(1) or (2). They reached the decision that the two were compatible, despite the findings in *Saunders v UK*, on the basis that the requirements of Art 6 admit of implied restriction. The restriction, Lord Hope said, must have a legitimate aim in the public interest. It was found that this was the case, bearing in mind the need to promote road safety. If so, he went on to ask, 'is there a reasonable relationship of proportionality between the means employed and the aim sought to be realised?' He found that the answer to the question, in terms of limiting the right not to incriminate oneself under Art 6(1), was in the affirmative since the section demands a response to a single question, and does not allow prolonged questioning, as in *Saunders*. The decision in *Brown* rested on the finding that coercing a statement from the defendant was not a disproportionate response to the legitimate aim of seeking to address the problem of road safety.

In *O'Halloran v United Kingdom*[231] the applicants had been convicted in domestic proceedings using statements obtained under s 172. In *O'Halloran* the European Court was required to consider whether the privilege against self-incrimination was infringed when the registered keeper of a vehicle caught by a speed camera was asked to provide the name and address of the driver on pain of a penalty. The Court applied the balancing test that it had elucidated in *Jalloh*, concluding that the regime established by the Road Traffic Act was a regulatory one imposed in the public interest, the questioning and thus the applied pressure likely to be very short lived, the penalty moderate and non-custodial and the identity of the driver but on element in proving the offence of speeding. Thus the Court found that there was no infringement of the privilege against self-incrimination.

Of course, these cases re-open the whole question of the compatibility of penalising silence in other contexts. If it can be argued that the requirement of s 172 is in proportion to the problem it seeks to address, it might be argued equally that where the legitimate aim in question is even more pressing, as in the case of combating terrorism, a more intrusive provision, allowing for more prolonged questioning, could be viewed as a proportionate legislative response.

---

230 [2001] 2 WLR 817. See Chapter 4, p 230.
231 [2007] ECHR 15809/02.

Chapter 14

Redress for police malpractice

This chapter has been updated and revised for this edition by Richard Edwards, Senior Lecturer in Law at the University of Exeter, UK, with some input in 2015 from Helen Fenwick.

1 Introduction

Chapters 12 and 13 were concerned with the question of the balance to be struck between the exercise of powers by the police in conducting an investigation on the one hand and safeguards for the suspect against abuse or misuse of power on the other. As we have seen, the statutory rules, including in particular those under the Police and Criminal Evidence Act 1984 (PACE), the Criminal Justice and Public Order Act 1994 (CJPOA), the Criminal Justice and Police Act 2001 (CJP) and the Terrorism Act 2000 as amended (TA) contain, on the one hand, provisions intended to secure suspects' rights, such as s 58 of PACE, while on the other they create or extend a statutory basis for the exercise of police powers, which frequently enhances those powers.[1] Thus, the rules can be viewed as reflecting the two different models of crime control and due process, and since the approach and aims of those models is to an extent conflicting, the statutes in question and their application in practice reflect the resulting inevitable tension. Those rules have as a background the ordinary criminal and civil law in relation to the use of force by any person, including the police. The police are able to act in ways that, if not cloaked in statutory authority, would amount to crimes and torts. In particular, they can use 'reasonable force'[2] in carrying out policing duties. But if excessive and disproportionate force is used, causing injury or even death, a means of redress should be available. But again due process concerns appear in this instance to clash with the crime control one that the police should not be over-hampered by concerns as to prosecutions, civil actions or disciplinary proceedings when they need to take decisions as to the degree of force needed in the heat of the moment. The balance struck by those means of redress between the two principles is considered below, and it is argued that over-concern to avoid interference in police freedom of action in conducting policing has allowed abuses of power to go unaddressed by the various systems, including prosecutions, that could be deployed to curb them.

Redress for breaches of the rules governing the exercise of police powers; influence of the ECHR

The relevant statutory and Code provisions declare that certain standards for the conduct of criminal and terrorist investigations must be maintained; in order to do so a

---

1 Such as PACE 1984, s 24 and TA, s 41.
2 See Chapter 12, pp 893–94.

complex, not to say cumbersome, domestic scheme is currently in place, part of it post-dating the Human Rights Act (HRA). It is one that has become incrementally more extensive post-PACE, especially if the PACE code provisions are taken into account. Under the European Convention on Human Rights, another scheme setting standards for criminal justice is apparent. Clearly, the two schemes are very different. Not only is the domestic scheme far more detailed, but also they have different starting points. One – the domestic scheme – essentially sets out police powers and then provides for restrictions on them, and for safeguards for suspects during their exercise. The other – the ECHR – sets out fundamental rights and then, in the case of the right to liberty under Art 5, the guarantee of a fair trial under Art 6, the right to life under Art 2 and the right to be free of torture, inhuman or degrading treatment under Art 3, leaves them unqualified or qualified only by narrow exceptions.[3] Article 5 may be said to create exceptions that correspond to aspects of domestic police powers, but not all police powers are recognised on the face of the Art 5 provisions. However, the higher courts in the UK, and the Strasbourg Court, have created certain implied exceptions to Art 5 on the basis that an exercise of police powers does not create 'a deprivation of liberty', so Art 5 is not engaged.[4]

Nevertheless, it can be said that both schemes set standards for administering criminal justice, but the standards of the domestic scheme and those recognised under the Convention are not necessarily the same. Each scheme does two things. First it sets certain standards for respecting suspects' rights. Second it then provides – most clearly under Art 13 ECHR and s 7 HRA – for some methods of redress if the standards are breached. Unsurprisingly, the domestic scheme prescribes in more detail the forms of redress that are potentially available, especially in relation to the question of exclusion of evidence. The international scheme provides the basic safeguard that the remedies should be effective.

The HRA, which brings the two schemes into juxtaposition, or perhaps confrontation, demands, under s 6, that each person or body administering the domestic scheme should, unless primary legislation using very clear words provides otherwise, abide by the Convention rights. It also provides under s 3(1) that, in so far as the domestic scheme is statute or code-based, it should, if interpretation will so allow, be rendered compatible with the requirements of the other. The judges' interpretation of the ECHR under the HRA has been intended in general to provide at least the same protection for rights as Strasbourg would in the pre-trial context with which Chapters 12 and 13 have been concerned. This point is pursued below.

It may be said, then, that the HRA provides mechanisms for asking, first, whether the standards expressed by the domestic scheme are in conformity with the Convention rights. That was the question addressed by Chapters 12 and 13. Second, it ensures that the question is asked whether the means of redress provided for breach of those standards are in conformity with what the Convention demands in terms of an effective remedy. That question is addressed in this chapter. This latter question has three facets. It asks: (a) if the rules creating the domestic standards *themselves* are not in conformity, what can be done to rectify that by reliance on the Convention

3 See Chapter 2, pp 42 *et seq.*
4 See Chapter 2, p 51 *et seq.*

and the HRA; (b) what domestic means of redress are available for breach of the standards set for the criminal justice system and considered in Chapters 12 and 13, and do they provide an effective remedy in Convention terms; (c) if the police do not abide by those standards, does the Convention under the HRA add anything to what can be done under the other current domestic provisions to provide redress? It will be argued that it is in respect of redress that the domestic scheme reveals certain flaws, but that in both legal and practical terms reliance on the ECHR under the HRA, and at Strasbourg, has had a variable impact, only making up for deficiencies to an extent.

Various methods of challenging the police

There are a number of domestic methods of providing redress if the police fail to abide by the standards set by the various rules governing the aspects of the exercise of police powers considered in the previous two chapters:[5] the police complaints and disciplinary process; prosecutions of the police; civil actions (under established tort law and under ss 7(1)(a) and 8 HRA which create a statutory tort); judicial review of police actions; trial 'remedies', including stays for abuse of process and exclusion of evidence. The police complaints process and exclusion of evidence have been found to fail to provide an effective remedy for breaches of the Convention rights at Strasbourg;[6] the complaints and disciplinary process has since been reformed, and in 2016 is about to undergo further reform. Civil actions will provide such a remedy, but are not applicable to many breaches of the scheme. Stays for abuse of process are rarely used and would not be used in respect of some breaches of Convention rights – a matter that is explored below. Prosecutions of the police are very rare and can only indirectly protect Convention rights.[7]

Typically, the question of redress may arise as follows: an investigation may not, at certain points, reach the standards set by the statutory scheme and codes; it may at the same time breach one or more of the Convention rights. The police may sometimes feel hampered by all the PACE and code provisions; they may consider, for example, that they are close to obtaining a confession from a detainee, but that, in order to obtain it,

---

5 For further discussion and texts referred to below, see: Sanders, A and Young, R, *Criminal Justice*, 4th edn, 2010; Bailey, Taylor, N, *Bailey, Harris and Jones: Civil Liberties: Cases and Materials*, 6th edn, 2009, Chapter 2; Zander, M, *Zander on PACE: The Police and Criminal Evidence Act 1984*, 2015; Clark, D, *Bevan and Lidstone's The Investigation of Crime*, 2004; Ashworth, A, *The Criminal Process*, 3rd edn, 2005; Feldman, D, *Civil Liberties and Human Rights in England and Wales*, 2nd edn, 2002, Chapters 5 and 9; See Ormerod, D and Birch, D, 'The evolution of the discretionary exclusion of evidence' [2004] Crim LR 767. For background see also: Maher, G, *A Theory of Criminal Process*, 2000, Hart; McConville, M, Sanders, A and Leng, R, *The Case for the Prosecution*, 1991; Reiner, R and Leigh, I, 'Police powers', in McCrudden, C and Chambers, G (eds), *Individual Rights and the Law in Britain*, 1994; Klug, F, Starmer, K and Weir, S, *The Three Pillars of Liberty: Political Rights and Freedoms in the UK*, 1996; Sharpe, S, *Judicial Discretion and Criminal Investigations*, 1998, Sweet and Maxwell; Nobles, R and Schiff, D, 'Due process and Dirty Harry dilemmas: criminal appeals and the Human Rights Act' [2001] 64(6) MLR pp 911–22; Ashworth, A, 'Criminal Justice Reform' [2004] Crim LR 516.

6 In *Khan v UK* (2000) 8 BHRC 310, paras 44–47.

7 Since no criminal liability is created under the HRA 1998.

they need to bend or break the interviewing rules. Similarly, police officers may purport to act within a power, such as the power to arrest or search premises, where no power to do so arises. In such circumstances, certain remedies are available: a civil action leading to an award of damages, if successful, or a complaint leading to disciplinary action against the officers involved, if upheld. However, as already noted in Chapter 12, civil actions are not available for breach of the codes and will be inapplicable to some breaches of PACE itself, such as an improper denial of access to legal advice. Sections 7 and 8 HRA to an extent fill a gap, since a remedy in damages for breach of the Convention rights in the criminal justice system pre-trial may now be available (although damages are not necessarily awarded under the HRA; a declaration of the breach may be the only remedy).[8] If aspects of the domestic scheme, including code provisions, are coterminous with the Convention rights, they have in some circumstances received a remedial underpinning under the HRA, where breach of such provisions would not previously have attracted a tortious remedy. However, that remedy does not appear to be available in respect of breaches of Art 6, including failures of access to custodial legal advice, since it appears to be assumed that the remedy would be provided in the trial itself. Further, a number of breaches of the codes or statutory rules are not coterminous with a Convention right, and so no remedy would be available under the HRA if they were breached.

Police disciplinary action is applicable to breaches of both PACE itself and the codes, but at present it is arguable that, despite reform, it still does not represent a fully effective remedy. Apart from these two remedies, a further means of redress exists, represented by the use of exclusion of evidence, and it is in that context that many breaches of PACE and the codes have in fact been considered. ECHR-based arguments raised under s 7(1)(b) of the HRA may often be put forward in respect of exclusion of evidence. But not only is such exclusion irrelevant in the vast majority of cases since the suspect will plead guilty, but it cannot be viewed, even where the case does come to trial, as an effective remedy for breaches of the Convention rights, for reasons to be considered below. Possibly it could be viewed as to an extent an effective remedy for breaches of the statutory and Code-based scheme itself, rather than for breach of the ECHR. As will be found below, the extensive consideration that the rules governing the exercise of police powers have had post-PACE, and during the HRA era, in the context of exclusion of evidence explains why consideration of that area forms the bulk of the discussion in this chapter.

Efficacy of the methods of redress?

The key contention of this chapter is that no sufficient or effective means of redress are available in respect of certain misuses of police powers, although the HRA has enhanced the remedial scheme to an extent. Therefore, the safeguards considered in Chapters 12 and 13 are not fully underpinned by the scheme providing the means of redress. Clearly, even if such a scheme were available in the form, for example, of a fully independent and clearly effective police complaints and disciplinary system,

---

8   See Chapter 4, pp 207–11.

police internal practices and culture would still have an impact on the delivery of the safeguards. But, as Chapters 12 and 13 argued, externally imposed rules can affect that culture. If the enforcement of those rules is fairly weak, as this chapter contends, their impact on institutional practices is bound to be diminished.

This reading of the domestic and Convention provisions addresses significant matters, and is the main concern of this chapter, but alone it would be, it is suggested, inadequate. At the end of the chapter it will be possible to discern that the Convention under the HRA has been having least some impact in terms of reviving and reaffirming a concern for due process which has gradually been eroded in the post-PACE years. In other words, a return to those values expressed quite strongly by PACE and less so in the later legislation has become apparent in the HRA era to an extent. But such an account should also be influenced by a victim-oriented perspective. By concentrating only on due process concerns, that perspective could be ignored: the implication could be that where a choice had to be made legislatively, judicially or executively (and the latter term, of course, includes the police themselves), the demands of due process and crime control would provide the parameters of the debate. Thus, this chapter will argue for a more developed conception of the criminal justice system, one that recognises the values of privacy, security and equality as well as those of due process.

2 The Human Rights Act and trial remedies

Requirements of Art 6

As Chapter 2 indicated, Art 6 is seen as a central Convention article that holds a preeminent position in the Convention jurisprudence since the right it protects is so fundamentally important in a democratic society. It expresses a 'fundamental principle of the rule of law'[9] and is to be interpreted broadly.[10] The Strasbourg Court has tended to take an increasingly interventionist stance towards the right to a fair trial, although the Court continues to adhere to the principle that the assessment of evidence is for the national court.[11] Apart from the right to be presumed innocent under Art 6(2), the guarantee of the access to legal advice and the other minimal guarantees of para 6(3), the Court has found that a number of rights are implicit in the term a 'fair hearing',[12] including access to custodial legal advice.[13] The principle of 'equality of arms' – equality between defence and prosecution – arising from Art 6(1) affects all aspects of a hearing, therefore overlapping with its expression under Art 6(3).

Duties of the courts under the HRA

The domestic courts (save for the s 6(2) HRA proviso concerning incompatible legislation which has not been relied on expressly by successive Parliaments in the HRA era) fail to satisfy s 6 of the HRA if they act incompatibly with the Convention rights, since

---

9 *Salabiaku v France* (1988) 13 EHRR 379.
10 *Delcourt v Belgium* (1970) 1 EHRR 355.
11 *Khan v UK* (2000) 8 BHRC 310.
12 See Chapter 2, p 57 *et seq.*
13 See Chapter 13, p 924.

they are themselves public authorities. The position appears to be that wherever a court has a discretion in the course of criminal procedure, a decision regarding its use of that discretion will amount to an 'act' within the meaning s 6 of the HRA.[14] As Chapter 4 explains, s 7 allows a victim of an alleged violation, or proposed violation, of a Convention guarantee to rely on the right in litigation, and to argue in particular that he would be a victim of an unlawful act if the act proposed is undertaken. Section 8 allows courts to grant such remedies as seem to them just and convenient for such violations.[15]

It is not enough for breaches of Art 6 by courts to be remedied only through the appeal process. The House of Lords in the leading pre-HRA decision, *R v DPP ex p Kebilene and Others*[16] found in considering Art 6, that the domestic court is not, of necessity, in the same position as the Strasbourg Court: 'it was inevitable that the European Court would conduct a retrospective review of [whether a trial was fair or unfair in Art 6(1) terms] in the national court', but that in the domestic court, this matter could be considered before completion of a trial. In other words, the Strasbourg Court could consider the whole pre-trial and trial process and come to a determination as to its fairness under Art 6(1). The domestic court would have to consider, during pre-trial hearings, the trial process, or on appeal, not only whether an actual or potential breach had occurred, but also whether Art 6 would be breached owing to its own regulation of the process.

The defendant might, for example, raise the argument that if the court failed to exclude evidence, Art 6(1) would be breached and that, therefore, ss 6, 7 and 8 HRA would require that the evidence should be excluded in order to avoid the breach. In responding, a court might, of course, find, erroneously, that its particular decision during the criminal procedure would not breach Art 6, in which case the issue could be raised on appeal.

In accordance with the Strasbourg jurisprudence and s 6 of the HRA, the appeal court is itself bound by Art 6.[17] The test for criminal appeals from the Crown Court is simply whether the conviction is 'unsafe'.[18] When the HRA first entered into force the courts flirted with a more expansive role for fairness.[19] That was hardly surprising. The HRA contains an articulated fair trial guarantee that could be expected to assist the more nuanced development of fairness in appellate reasoning. Indeed, there was some evidence of this initially happening; in a series of *obiter dicta* some judges adopted an absolute approach to trial fairness when disposing of appeals.[20] It was said that it is repugnant to the law that a person be tried and condemned to punishment where it

---

14 This is the stance of the Strasbourg Court: see *Z v Finland* (1997) 25 EHRR 371.
15 See Chapter 4, p 187.
16 [1999] 3 WLR 972.
17 *Delcourt v Belgium* A 11 (1970).
18 The Criminal Appeals Act 1968, s 2(1), as amended by the Criminal Appeals Act 1995. This provision allows the conviction to stand despite, e.g., a misdirection of the judge.
19 *R v A (No 2)* [2001] UKHL 25, [30].
20 Similarly, in *R v A (No 2)* Lord Steyn concluded that 'it is well established that the guarantee of a fair trial under article 6 is absolute: a conviction obtained in breach of it cannot stand.' Later in *R v H* Lord Bingham affirmed the cardinal importance of the right to a fair trial: 'it is axiomatic that a person charged with having committed a criminal offence should receive a fair trial and that, if he cannot be tried fairly for that offence, he should not be tried for it at all.' *R v H* [2004] UKHL 3, [10].

is impossible to vouch for the fairness of the trial[21] since if the criminal justice system is to maintain its moral integrity it must punish only those whose guilt has been established by a fair trial. Consequently, it would seem axiomatic that where a defendant is punished without a fair trial a miscarriage of justice will occur.[22] Thus in *Forbes* Lord Bingham observed that where an appellate court concludes that 'a defendant's right to a fair trial has been infringed, a conviction will be held to be unsafe'.[23] In *Togher* Lord Woolf observed that 'if the defendant has been denied a fair trial it will almost be inevitable that the conviction will be regarded as unsafe'.[24]

However, this absolutist approach under the HRA was not universal, and other views were more qualified. Since the initial robustness, the certainties of broad principle have been quietly discarded[25] but a more nuanced approach is also somewhat more victim-oriented. It is important to bear in mind that while the ECHR and HRA are addressed to state actors (termed 'public authorities' under the HRA), the actions of non-state actors within the area of Convention rights, such as the right to life, may also be the responsibility of the state in the sense that in so far as it can prevent infringements of the rights by such actors it may be deemed to have a duty to do so.[26] Thus, other interests, in particular the need to punish the manifestly guilty but unfairly tried, often negate the high-sounding principles and absolute promises of general *dicta*. For example, in *Davis* Mantell LJ concluded that it was unhelpful 'to deal in presumptions . . . the effect of any unfairness upon the safety of the conviction will vary according to its nature and degree'.[27] Then in *Lambert* Lord Hope noted that even if a Convention-compatible direction had been given to the jury the appeal would have been dismissed as the conviction was safe.[28] Thus the preponderance of guilt was allowed to outweigh the unfairness caused by the infringement of the presumption of innocence. In *Cadder*[29] the Supreme Court confirmed after *Salduz*[30] that Art 6 requires that a person who has been detained by the police has the right to have access to a lawyer prior to being interviewed, unless in the particular circumstances of the case there are compelling reasons to restrict that right. It was thus held that the current law in Scotland breaches the right to a fair trial under Art 6 ECHR. The Court also held that although the right to legal advice had been denied it did not automatically follow that the conviction would be quashed. A reversal of the conviction would only be appropriate, it was found, if either there was insufficient evidence to support the conviction, the evidence of the unlawful police interview notwithstanding, or there was a real possibility that the jury would have reached a different verdict in the absence of the impugned evidence. Such cases reflect the impact

21   *R v Hines* [1997] 3 NZLR 529, 562 Thomas J.
22   *McInnes v Lord Advocate* [2010] UKSC 7, [23] Lord Hope.
23   *R v Forbes* [2001] UKHL 40, [24].
24   *R v Togher* [2001] 1 Cr App Rep 457.
25   See: Laura Hoyano 'What is Balanced on the Scales of Justice? In Search of the Essence of the Right to a Fair Trial' Crim LR [2014] 4–29; Denis [2003] CLP 201; Taylor and Ormerod 'Mind the Gap' [2004] Crim LR 266.
26   See *Osman v UK* [1998] ECHR 101; but see also Gearty, C, 'Unravelling Osman' (2001) 64 MLR 159.
27   *R v Davis* [2001] 1 Cr App R 8. *Davis*, in many senses, represents the typical approach of the Court of Appeal to its work.
28   *R v Lambert* [2001] UKHL 37, [117], Lord Hope.
29   [2010] UKSC 43.
30   See p 926.

of the ECHR but also common law due process principles, representing as they do an attempt to keep the issues of safety of convictions and fairness separate.

3 Exclusion of evidence

Introduction: conflicting values

An example may illustrate the effect of exclusion of evidence. Assume that the police have arrested a man on suspicion of theft. They are fairly certain that he is guilty and think that they have a good chance of getting him to confess. However, he asks for legal advice. The police think that a solicitor may advise him not to answer some questions or may at least help him to withstand certain questioning techniques and so they tell him (untruthfully) that the duty solicitor is unavailable and that they might as well get on with the interview rather than prolong the process. They then question him for four hours without a break. Eventually, he succumbs to the pressure and makes a full confession to theft.

The police have failed to adhere to s 58 PACE and have breached Code C provisions on interviewing and access to legal advice.[31] Moreover, they have also breached, or potentially breached, an express or implied Art 6 right to custodial legal advice.[32] Some methods of redress are potentially available. The suspect could make a complaint. He could seek to bring an action against the police under s 7(1)(a) HRA for the arguable breach of Art 6 – but this method of obtaining redress is very doubtful; no domestic authority supports its availability, and even if a court accepted the argument a declaration only would probably be forthcoming. But, most significantly, the flawed interrogation may affect the trial; the trial may lead to a conviction and possibly imprisonment. The defendant may decide to plead guilty. But if he pleads not guilty, his counsel may ask the judge at the trial not to admit the confession in evidence on the basis that the interrogation which produced it was conducted unfairly.

The trial judge then has an opportunity to ensure that the original misuse of power on the part of the police is unable to affect the fairness of the trial. Unfairness is arguably less likely to occur if the judge refuses to admit the confession in evidence. The judge can hold a *voir dire* (a trial within a trial) by sending out the jury and then hearing defence and prosecution submissions on admitting the confession. If it is not admitted, the jury will never know of its existence and will determine the case on the basis of any other available evidence – and on that basis they may still find the defendant guilty. The judge is in a difficult position. On the one hand, it is apparent that the police have abused their powers; the judge does not want to condone or appear to condone such behaviour by admitting the evidence gained thereby. On the other, the prosecution case may collapse and a possibly guilty man walk free from the court if the confession is excluded. Assuming that he is guilty, that would be to the detriment of the victim of the theft and to society in general. Also, if the other evidence against the defendant is strong, it could be argued that admission of the confession if it appears to be reliable is acceptable since it would have little or no impact on the overall fairness of the trial: even if it was excluded, the defendant would probably be convicted.

31 See Chapter 13.
32 *Salduz v Turkey* (2008) 49 EHRR 421.

If the defendant did commit the theft, it might be said that the end in view – the conviction of a guilty person – justifies the means used to obtain it, but should the judge ignore the fact that the confession might not be before the court at all had the police complied with PACE and Code C? Should the judge merely consider the punishment of one defendant in isolation? If the confession is admitted, the judge is arguably making in effect a public declaration that the courts will not use their powers to uphold standards for police investigations. The result may be that in future, PACE due process standards are not adhered to and that, occasionally, an innocent citizen is convicted after a false confession has been coerced from him. The multiplicity of issues raised by examples of this nature have provoked a long-running debate among academics and lawyers as to the purpose of excluding evidence that has been obtained improperly, and a number of schools of thought have arisen, advocating different principles on which evidence should be excluded.

The crime control position is that evidence should be excluded only if it appears to be unreliable (the 'reliability' principle), that is, in the case of a confession, false or inaccurately recorded.[33] Taken to its logical conclusion, that would mean that if a true confession (able to be verified as true) has been extracted by torture, it should nevertheless be admitted. This is argued on the basis that the function of a criminal court is to determine the truth of the charges against the accused, not to inquire into alleged improprieties on the part of the police. It is not equipped to conduct such an inquiry; therefore, if evidence is excluded on the basis that impropriety occurred in the investigation, the reputation of the police officer in question will be damaged after a less than full investigation into his or her conduct. On this argument, the court in admitting evidence obtained by improper methods is not condoning them. It is acknowledging that it is not within its function to inquire into them.

Further, it can be argued from the perspective of ensuring fairness in general – to the defendant, the victim and society that even if impropriety did occur in the investigation, (although it produced a reliable confession) which the court could be viewed as disregarding or even condoning, that should not allow a guilty defendant to walk freely from the court due to the adverse impact on society and on the victim of the theft. The adverse impact on society if the factually guilty defendant is acquitted due to lack of evidence is three-fold. First, valuable resources have been wasted since the police and other bodies have processed the defendant through the criminal justice system without having any impact on controlling crime. Second, the defendant may commit further crimes, causing distress and financial loss to the victims and a general rise in insurance premiums. Third, society may lose faith in the criminal justice system if the guilty are not convicted.

From a due process stance, it has been argued that a court cannot merely inquire into the truth of the charges against a particular defendant; it must also play a part in maintaining standards in criminal investigations.[34] The court has one particular part to play in the processing of the defendant through the criminal justice system: it should not play its brief part and ignore what has gone before. If the courts are prepared to accept

---

33 See Wigmore, JH, *Treatise on Evidence*, 3rd edn, 1940, and Andrews, JA, 'Involuntary Confessions and Illegally Obtained Evidence in Criminal Cases' [1963] Crim LR 15, p 77.
34 See e.g., Cross, R (Sir), *Cross on Evidence*, 5th edn, 1979, Butterworths, pp 318–28.

evidence obtained by improper methods, the police may be encouraged to abuse their powers to the detriment of the citizen. Exclusion of evidence should be used to punish the police by depriving them of the fruits of their impropriety and to deter them from using such practices. This principle – often termed the disciplinary principle – may encompass either a deterrent or a punitive role for exclusion of evidence, although it is recognised that no clear-cut relationship between police behaviour and rejection of evidence should be envisaged.[35] Obviously the defendant may plead guilty so that any punitive or deterrent role is undermined. Since most defendants plead guilty, it may appear to a police officer that there is more to be gained than lost by placing pressure on suspects to make admissions.

The use of exclusion of evidence to punish the police has come to be viewed by most commentators as an inefficient and possibly ineffective means of protecting due process, and that led Ashworth to suggest a somewhat different principle, which he termed protective.[36] He contended that once a legal system has declared a certain standard for the conduct of investigations, the citizen obtains corresponding rights to be treated in a manner that adheres to those standards. If such rights are denied and evidence gained as a result, the court can wipe out the disadvantage to the defendant flowing from the denial by rejecting the evidence in question. If, for example, it appears that the defendant would not have made the confession if the police had afforded him access to legal advice, the judge could recreate the situation for the jury's benefit as it would have been had the access been afforded, by excluding the confession. In the eyes of the jury, the position would be as if the right had never been denied; the judge would therefore have succeeded in protecting the defendant's right of access to legal advice in the interview. It must be pointed out that use of this argument in practice became more problematic when the caution became a warning that silence may be commented on adversely in court, as discussed in Chapter 13.[37] If access to legal advice is not given, it might be argued that such a failure could *not* be causally related to the confession, since the adviser would have advised the defendant not to risk remaining silent in any event. This point will be returned to below.

An alternative but allied argument, also founded on due process values, may be termed the 'reputation' or 'integrity' principle. It can be argued that admitting the confession causes the trial to appear unfair because the court thereby appears to condone or lend itself to the original unfairness. The imprimatur of the court may be necessary in order to allow the impropriety to bear fruit. If the trial is viewed, not as a separate entity, but as the culmination of a process in which the court and the police both play their part as emanations of the state, it can be argued that the court should refuse to lend itself to the unfairness that has gone before in order to ensure that the state does not profit from its own wrong. It cannot wipe out the unfairness, but it can wipe out its consequences, thereby ensuring that the reputation of the criminal justice system is not tarnished. But it need concern itself with the police unfairness only if that unfairness did have consequences. If it concerned itself with an inconsequential breach, the reputation of the criminal justice system would also suffer since the detriment caused to

35   *Ibid*, p 328.
36   See Ashworth, A, 'Excluding Evidence as Protecting Rights' [1977] Crim LR 723.
37   See p 940 *et seq*.

society in allowing someone who has perpetrated a serious crime to walk free from the court would be perceived as entirely outweighing the detriment to the defendant caused by the breach (and of course that might be the case even if the improperly obtained admissions did have some consequences). From that perspective it may be argued that where the police have breached a Convention right, evidence thereby obtained should be excluded, partly to vindicate the right and partly to preserve the integrity of the criminal justice system.

As will be found below, the dominant principle is that of reliability; that meant that *non-confession* evidence ('real' evidence), obtained due to a police impropriety would usually be admitted. That principle influenced the pre-HRA approach of the domestic courts,[38] and remains the current approach of the domestic courts. It has been found overall to be sustainable under the HRA, as discussed below. The position as regards confession evidence is more complex, and the reliability principle has had less influence. That established position has not been strongly affected by the inception of the HRA. It means that a Court's duty under s 6 HRA allows it to take account of a breach of the Convention rights that has occurred in the pre-trial or custodial procedures and that has been instrumental in obtaining confession evidence.

The Strasbourg stance as to exclusion of evidence

Article 6(1) is silent as to the admissibility of improperly obtained evidence. The Strasbourg Court has emphasised that the assessment of evidence is for the domestic courts[39] and that Art 6 does not require any particular rules of evidence; thus, it has allowed the national authorities a wide margin of appreciation in this respect. In the context of Art 6 ECHR, an approach that balances the rights of the defendant, the victim and of society is apparent. *Al-Khawaja v UK*[40] (not a case relating to police impropriety) provides an example where guidance from the domestic court was available; the Grand Chamber allowed itself to be guided towards a position in harmony with that taken by the national court, even where that meant departing from its own previous judgment in the same case.[41] In *Al-Khawaja v UK*, as others have pointed out (for example Baroness Hale),[42] the Grand Chamber was guided by the findings of the Supreme Court in *R v Horncastle*[43] in reaching a decision on the scope of Art 6, which was contrary to its previous stance as to acceptance of hearsay evidence under Art 6 in the Chamber. The Supreme Court took a more pragmatic, less absolutist, approach to Art 6 requirements than the ECtHR had previously done, and the Grand Chamber then accepted that approach. The question was whether hearsay evidence (evidence not derived from oral testimony before the court) could be relied on as the sole or decisive evidence in securing a conviction where the victim-witness, or other witness, had died or was too

---

38 See *Chalkley* [1998] 2 Cr App R 79.
39 *Edwards v UK* A 247-B (1992).
40 *Al-Khawaja v UK* [2011] ECHR 2127 (2012) 54 EHRR 23 (Grand Chamber).
41 *Al-Khawaja v UK*, App No 26766/05(ECtHR, 20 January 2009) (Fourth Section).
42 B Hale 'Argentoratum Locutum: Is Strasbourg or the Supreme Court Supreme?' (2012) 12(1) *Human Rights Law Review* 65.
43 *R v Horncastle* [2009] UKSC 14 [2010] 2 WLR 47.

intimidated to give oral evidence. Consideration of Art 6 was fully embedded in the Supreme Court's judgment. Lord Philips found:

> I believe that those provisions strike the right balance between the imperative that a trial must be fair and the interests of victims in particular and society in general that a criminal should not be immune from conviction where a witness, who has given critical evidence in a statement that can be shown to be reliable, dies or cannot be called to give evidence for some other reason. In so concluding I have taken careful account of the Strasbourg jurisprudence. I hope that in due course the Strasbourg Court may also take account of the reasons that have led me not to apply the sole or decisive test in this case.[44]

This approach of the Supreme Court gave greater weight to the interests of victims of crime than had the Chamber. It was characterised by looking at the fairness of the proceedings as a whole in relation to the defence as well as the victim, under Art 6, rather than demanding an absolutist application of a particular rule of evidence, regardless of overall fairness, an approach that is typical of common law reasoning. The Grand Chamber found:

> It would not be correct, when reviewing questions of fairness, to apply [the rule in question] in an inflexible manner . . . To do so would transform the rule into a blunt and indiscriminate instrument that runs counter to the traditional way in which the Court approaches the issue of the overall fairness of the proceedings, namely to weigh in the balance the competing interests of the defence, the victim, and witnesses, and the public interest in the effective administration of justice.[45]

The Grand Chamber concluded:

> [V]iewing the fairness of the proceedings as a whole, the Court considers that, notwithstanding the difficulties caused to the defence by admitting the statement and the dangers of doing so, there were sufficient counterbalancing factors to conclude that the admission in evidence of ST's statement did not result in a breach of Art 6(1) read in conjunction with Art 6(3)(d) of the Convention.[46]

The Court then applied the ruling in *Al-Khawaja v UK* to *Horncastle v UK*.[47] The applicants invited the Court to modify substantially the Grand Chamber's decision in *Al-Khawaja*. In *Horncastle v UK* the Court found:

> [I]n the applicants' case the Supreme Court said that it declined to apply the so-called 'sole or decisive rule', as it was at that time understood following the judgment of the Chamber in *Al-Khawaja and Tahery*. However, this does not, of itself,

---

44   *Ibid*, para 108.
45   *Al-Khawaja v UK*, para 146.
46   *Ibid*, para 158.
47   *Horncastle v UK* App No 4184/10 (ECtHR, 16 December 2014).

lead to a violation of Art 6 of the Convention, since the Grand Chamber's subsequent judgment in that case made it clear that the admission of sole and decisive absent-witness evidence may be compatible with Art 6 if the appropriate counter-balancing measures are present.[48]

The Court proceeded to find even where or if (in relation to the different applicants) the hearsay evidence had been taken as 'decisive' in terms of the outcome, it was satisfied that there were sufficient counterbalancing factors to compensate for any difficulties caused to the defence by the admission of the statement.[49] It therefore found no breach of Art 6. *Al-Khawaja v UK* and *Horncastle v UK* provide clear examples of dialogue between the Supreme Court and the ECtHR, and indicate that the ECtHR is prepared to depart from an absolutist stance as to Art 6 requirements in favour of a balancing approach.

However, the Court has laid down rules for the exclusion of a confession where there has been deliberate maltreatment. It was found in an early decision, *Austria v Italy*,[50] that maltreatment with the aim of extracting a confession had created a breach of Art 6(2). The question of pressure on the applicant in the interview was taken into account by the Court in reaching its conclusion that Art 6 had been breached in *Saunders v UK*[51] by the admission in evidence of the coerced admissions (but that does not necessarily mean that that argument could be extended to encompass other evidence uncovered as a result of such admissions – see below).

In *Schenk v Switzerland*[52] the Strasbourg Court found no breach of Art 6(1) when an illegally obtained incriminating tape recording was admitted in evidence, and made it clear that unlawfully obtained evidence is not necessarily inadmissible. The Court found: 'While Art 6 guarantees the right to a fair trial it does not lay down any rules as to admissibility of evidence as such, which is therefore primarily a matter of regulation under national law.' The test is to ask whether the trial as a whole would be rendered unfair if the 'tainted' evidence was admitted.[53]

Although the *principle* deriving from *Schenk* has largely remained unaffected, a much more interventionist approach was adopted in a number of judgments, in particular that in *Teixeira de Castro v Portugal*.[54] The applicant, who had no criminal record and was previously unknown to the police, was introduced by a third party to two undercover police officers who told him that they wished to buy 20 grams of heroin. He bought the drugs on their behalf at a price allowing him to take a profit. He was then tried and convicted on the evidence of the officers of drug dealing and sentenced to six years' imprisonment. The Court found, by 8 votes to 1, that the entrapment by the

---

48　*Ibid*, at para 139.
49　*Ibid*, at para 142.
50　Appl No 788/60 4 YB 112 (1961).
51　(1997) 23 EHRR 313. *Saunders* is discussed in Chapter 13, pp 944–45.
52　(1988) 13 EHRR 242.
53　A 140 (1988), para 46. This test was also used in *Khan v UK* (2000) 8 BHRC 310.
54　(1998) 28 EHRR 101; [1998] Crim LR 751. See also *Van Mechelen v Netherlands* (1998) 25 EHRR 647; the findings of the Commission and Court in *Rowe and Davis* (2000) 30 EHRR 1; *Condron v UK* (2001) 31 EHRR 1.

police officers in order to secure evidence had made a fair trial impossible: 'right from the outset the applicant was definitively deprived of a fair trial'.[55]

This argument can also be applied where 'compelled' admissions, including those obtained by treatment falling within s 76, and those obtained on pain of a penalty under the TA, while not themselves used in evidence, had led to the uncovering of other evidence. In *Jalloh v Germany*[56] the forcible use of emetics against the will of the applicant produced real evidence in the form of unlawful narcotics which were later used against him at trial. The European Court of Human Rights held that the treatment fell within the scope of Art 3 as 'inhuman or degrading treatment', not torture, and the use of the derived evidence was unfair within the terms of Art 6. However, as a matter of general principle the Court left the wider question whether use of evidence obtained by 'inhuman or degrading treatment' would automatically render a trial unfair, open. The Court returned to the matter in *Gäfgen v Germany*[57] where it confirmed that admission of real evidence procured through the use of torture would be contrary to Art 6, rendering the proceedings as a whole unfair.[58] But where the unlawful treatment was classified as inhuman or degrading treatment the Court held that evidence obtained thereby should not be admitted at trial to form the basis of the conviction, but where it had no bearing on the verdict the trial as a whole would not be rendered unfair if it was admitted, under Art 6.

This distinction is, as the minority judgment noted in *Gäfgen*, open to question. First, the absolute nature of Art 3 is undermined if state agents do not have a strong incentive for compliance. Second, even where there is only indirect reliance on evidence produced in this manner it arguably weakens the integrity of the criminal justice process. It could be argued, in furtherance of a fair procedure under Art 6, that that other evidence should be excluded under s 78, but the concept of 'fairness' under that section does not encompass fairness only to the defence.

The decisions in *Brown v Stott*[59] and *O'Halloran v UK*[60] concerned compelled statements – where the defendant in relation to road traffic management was required to answer questions on pain of penalty otherwise. In both it was found that the nature of the obligation in question did not destroy the right to remain silent or the privilege against self-incrimination. The two decisions do not comport with the argument for a more absolutist approach under Art 6, since the courts in future are likely to consider the legitimate aim of the compulsion and the question whether the compulsion is in proportion to the aim in creating a minimal impact on the accused's Art 6 rights. But in more compelling circumstances where covert compulsion is apparent, the Court has shown a greater inclination to find a violation of Art 6. For example, in *Allan v UK*[61] the police had obtained permission to place an informer and listening devices in the cell of the applicant who was suspected of murder. The applicant had refused to confess during police interview. The police then coached the informer and instructed him to 'push

---

55 *Ibid*, para 39.
56 (2006) 20 BHRC 575.
57 [2010] ECHR 22978/05.
58 Above para 167.
59 [2001] 2 WLR 817.
60 [2007] ECHR 25624/02.
61 [2002] ECHR 697.

Allan for what you can get'. Allan admitted to the informer that he had been present at the time of the murder, and a witness statement from the informer was admitted as evidence. This statement and the police recordings formed the entirety of the evidence against the applicant at this subsequent trial, where he was convicted. Allan's appeal against conviction was unsuccessful. The Strasbourg Court held that the use of the informer and the evidence was incompatible with Art 6. The evidence was obtained in contravention of the privilege against self-incrimination and under compulsion on the basis that the informer was in fact an agent of the state who had manipulated Allan.

When dealing with non-confessional evidence *Khan v UK*[62] remains good law. In *Khan* a fundamental breach of Art 8 (secret recording which was not in accordance with the law) had occurred in obtaining the only evidence against the defendant, but, following *Schenk*,[63] no breach of Art 6 was found, owing to the admission of the evidence. The Court said that it was not its role to determine whether unlawfully obtained evidence should be admissible. Thus, the Court appears to adhere to two, partly conflicting views. First, if the pre-trial behaviour is such that the trial is almost bound to be unfair, a breach of Art 6 will be found. The Court has not characterised this issue as one necessarily relating to exclusion of evidence; it could relate to abuse of process. Secondly, where pre-trial practices, although consisting of a breach of another Convention right, are viewed as creating less unfairness to the accused, and the question of a breach of Art 6 arises in the form of the question of admissibility, the Court leaves the matter to the national courts. The case of *Khan v UK*[64] therefore has been utilised by the courts to support their stance in relation to non-confession evidence, under the HRA.[65]

Exclusion of evidence and abuse of process

If malpractice by police or prosecutors reaches a certain level of seriousness, the trial can be halted on the basis that to do otherwise would be an abuse of process. The House of Lords found in *Latif*[66] that in considering whether to stay the proceedings for abuse of process, the judge should weigh the public interest in ensuring that those accused of serious crimes are brought to trial, against the public interest in avoiding giving the impression, based on classic crime control norms, that courts are prepared to find that the end justifies the means. This balancing of interests may be termed the '*Latif* test'. The stance taken in *Latif* may be compared with that taken in *Mullen*[67] in which the Court of Appeal said: 'the need to discourage [blatant and very serious malpractice] . . . is a matter of public policy to which . . . very considerable weight should be attached'.

In *Warren v Attorney General of Jersey*[68] the Privy Council considered an appeal from Jersey against a conviction of conspiracy to import unlawful narcotics. At trial the defendant sought a stay on the grounds of abuse of process. The alleged abuse consisted

---

62 (2000) 8 BHRC 310; Commission decision: (1999) 27 EHRR CD 58.
63 (1988) 13 EHRR 242.
64 (2000) 8 BHRC 310.
65 See also *PG v UK* [2002] Crim LR 308.
66 [1996] 1 All ER 353.
67 [1999] 2 Cr App R 143, p 157.
68 [2012] 1 AC 22. See also the discussion in the earlier Supreme Court decision in *R v Maxwell* [2010] UKSC 48.

of the unlawful and 'reprehensible' actions of the Jersey police who had bugged the defendant's car in France without legal authority or permission. The council concluded that a court has a broad discretion to protect the integrity of its processes, although it was found that there was no abuse of process in this instance requiring the over-turning of the conviction.

In the pre-HRA case of *Chalkley*,[69] Auld LJ stated that the issue of exclusion of evidence is distinct from the question whether the prosecution should be stayed for abuse of process. He said that while the discretion to declare an abuse of process would be governed by the *Latif* balancing test referred to above, the discretion under s 78 would be governed almost entirely by the question whether the impropriety of the police or prosecutor had affected the reliability of the evidence. In other words, in exceptional circumstances, the trial might be halted to mark the court's disapproval of pre-trial malpractice; he considered that this would virtually never occur in respect of exclusion of evidence, except in the case of confessions.

The domestic approach to exclusion of evidence

The question of exclusion of non-confession evidence where there has been a police breach of statutory or code standards has been left largely up to the domestic courts by Strasbourg on the basis that the assessment of evidence in general is a matter for the national courts.[70] Domestic courts seeking to apply the Strasbourg jurisprudence under s 2 HRA have been given the message, via the case of *Khan*,[71] that a breach of Art 6 will not necessarily occur if non-confession evidence obtained in breach of a Convention right, or a domestic due process-based rule, is admitted. It may therefore be argued that the domestic courts could look to other jurisdictions for guidance as to the requirements of due process in relation to exclusion of evidence. The counter-arguments are that the HRA does not require them to do so, that other jurisdictions have developed their own rules, in accordance with their own traditions, for the assessment of evidence, as has Britain, and that therefore the domestic common law tradition of balancing due process and crime control concerns should prevail in the HRA era. It is suggested that case law in the HRA era demonstrates that that is the approach being taken. As discussed below, the courts differentiate between confession and non-confession evidence in respect of the issue of exclusion, thereby giving some endorsement to both the reliability and protective principles.

The common law pre-PACE went some way towards endorsing the crime control 'reliability' principle. However, exclusion of evidence was largely placed on a statutory basis under PACE.[72] PACE differentiates between confession and non-confession evidence, reflecting the previous common law stance. PACE contains four separate tests that can be applied to a confession to determine whether it is admissible in evidence. In theory, all four tests could be applied to a particular confession, although in practice it is

---

69 [1998] 2 Cr App R 79.
70 See pp 57–62.
71 *Khan v UK* (2000) 8 BHRC 310.
72 For general commentary once PACE had been in force for three years, see Birch, D, 'Confessions and confusions under the 1984 Act' [1989] Crim LR 95. See also Feldman, D, 'Regulating Treatment of Suspects in Police Stations: Judicial Interpretation of Detention Provisions in the Police and Criminal Evidence Act 1984' [1990] Crim LR 452.

not necessary to consider all of them, and the courts have gone some of the way towards creating a distinct role for each test. The four are: the 'oppression' test under s 76(2)(a); the 'reliability' test under s 76(2)(b); the 'fairness' test under s 78, and the residual common law discretion to exclude evidence, preserved by s 82(3). It will become apparent that there is a large area of overlap between all four tests. Section 78 can cover unreliable evidence and also evidence obtained by the use of improper methods, whether amounting to oppression or not. Equally, certain types of improper behaviour can be termed oppressive, thus falling within s 76(2)(a), but they can also be viewed as circumstances likely to render a confession unreliable, falling therefore within s 76(2)(b). In some circumstances, a confession will obviously fail one of the tests under s 76 and so there will be no need to consider the other three. In other circumstances, it may be worth considering both tests under s 76 as well as s 78. The scheme in respect of *non-confession* evidence is less complex: only ss 78 and 82(3) are applicable. Significantly, physical evidence which is discovered as a result of an inadmissible confession will be admissible under s 76(4)(a). In practice, s 78 appears to have taken over the role of s 82(3), and therefore it is rare for s 82(3) to receive separate consideration.

It is important to bear in mind that even if a confession is admitted, the jury may differ from the judge in their evaluation of the circumstances in which it was obtained. The jury may decide that they should not place weight on it due to those circumstances, thereby in effect taking the view that the judge may have erred in deciding to admit it. This rule was reaffirmed in *R v Mushtaq*;[73] it was found:

> The law is clear that where a judge has ruled on a *voir dire* that a confession is admissible the jury is fully entitled to consider all the circumstances surrounding the making of the confession to decide whether they should place any weight on it, and it is the duty of the trial judge to make this plain to them.

Section 76(2)(a) of PACE: the 'oppression' test

Section 76(2)(a) provides that where:

> it is represented to the court that the confession was or may have been obtained by oppression of the person who made it . . . the court shall not allow the confession to be given in evidence against him except in so far as the prosecution proves to the court beyond reasonable doubt that the confession (notwithstanding that it may be true) was not obtained as aforesaid.

This test is a strict one; it reflects the disciplinary and protective principles referred to above in relation to exclusion of confessions. It derives from the rule as it was at common law:[74] if it is put to the court that the confession was or may have been obtained by oppression of the person who made it, and the prosecution cannot prove beyond reasonable doubt that the police did not behave oppressively, the confession is inadmissible. The judge has no discretion in the matter. The wording derives from Art 3 of

---

73 [2005] 1 WLR 1513 at para 3.
74 *Ibrahim v The King* (1914) AC 599.

the ECHR,[75] but it is not necessary for torture or inhuman or degrading treatment to be present, as discussed below. If it is present, the confession will be excluded under this sub-section. Section 76(2)(a) accords with the Strasbourg position under Art 6. In the case of *Soylemez v Turkey*[76] the applicants were subject to physical abuse that reached the minimum level of severity required for the application of Art 3. The statements they made as a consequence formed the basis of their conviction. The resulting trial was found to be unfair within the terms of Art 6.

Underlying values

The idea behind the old common law rule on oppression, and now s 76(2)(a), is that threats of violence or other oppressive behaviour are so abhorrent that no further question as to the reliability of a confession obtained by such methods should be asked. But the principle of reliability underlies the rule, as does the principle of voluntariness. In *R v Mushtaq* Lord Hutton said:

> It is clear that there are two principal reasons underlying the rule that a confession obtained by oppression should not be admitted in evidence. One reason, which has long been stated by the judges, is that where a confession is made as a result of oppression it may well be unreliable, because the confession may have been given, not with the intention of telling the truth, but from a desire to escape the oppression imposed on, or the harm threatened to, the suspect. A further reason, stated in more recent years, is that in a civilised society a person should not be compelled to incriminate himself, and a person in custody should not be subjected by the police to ill-treatment or improper pressure in order to extract a confession.[77]

He found that these principles were in harmony with those accepted under Art 6(1): 'These two reasons also underlie the decision of the European Court of Human Rights in *Saunders v The United Kingdom*.'[78] This rule has the dual function of removing any incentive to the police to behave oppressively, and of protecting the detainee from the consequences of oppressive behaviour if it has occurred.

Under this head, once the defence has advanced a reasonable argument (*Liverpool Juvenile Court ex p R*)[79] that the confession was obtained by oppression, it will not be admitted in evidence unless the prosecution can prove that it was not so obtained. If no reasonable doubt is raised it will be admitted. The reliability of a confession obtained by oppression is irrelevant to the issue of exclusion: it matters not whether the effect of the oppression was to frighten the detainee into telling the truth or alternatively into lying in order to get out of the situation. But it is highly relevant if the confession is admitted. In *R v Mushtaq*[80] the House of Lords had to consider the appropriate

---

75 See Chapter 2, pp 46–50 for the wording of Art 3 and for Strasbourg case law on the meaning of the three terms used in it.
76 [2006] ECHR 46661/99.
77 [2005] UKHL 25 at para 7. He relied on *Wong Kam-ming v The Queen* [1980] AC 247, 261 and *Lam Chi-ming v The Queen* [1991] 2 AC 212, p 220 E–G.
78 [2005] UKHL 25 at para 8; (*Saunders* [1996] 23 EHRR 313).
79 [1987] All ER 688.
80 [2005] 1 WLR 1513.

direction to a jury, taking account of Art 6(1), where a confession alleged to have been obtained by oppression *was* admitted in evidence. The question certified by the Court of Appeal was: whether 'in view of article 6 of the Convention for the Protection of Human Rights', a judge 'is required to direct the jury, if they conclude that the alleged confession may have been [obtained by oppression] that they must disregard it'. The majority in the House of Lords answered this question in the affirmative. They found that both the judge and the jury are public authorities under s 6 HRA. Therefore it would be unlawful for the judge and jury to act in a way that was incompatible with a defendant's right against self-incrimination as implied into Art 6(1).

The judge had directed the jury that, if they were sure that the appellant's confession was true, they might rely on it even if they considered that it might have been made as a result of oppression. The majority in the House of Lords found:

> Such a direction was an invitation to the jury to act in a way that was incompatible with the appellant's right against self-incrimination under article 6(1). As such, the direction was itself incompatible with that right . . . It follows, both on the basis of section 76(2) when viewed without regard to the Convention and on the basis of the appellant's article 6(1) Convention right against self-incrimination, that the judge misdirected the jury.[81]

The Court of Appeal had referred to the last sentence of the judge's direction: 'If, on the other hand, you are sure that it is true you may rely on it, even if it was or may have been made as a result of oppression or other improper circumstances.' The Court found, and the House of Lords agreed, that the jury would have received more assistance if the second part of the sentence had been omitted. Lord Hutton said: 'the words might to some extent deflect the jury from concentrating on the question whether, if there was a reasonable possibility of oppression, it would be safe to rely on the confession as being truthful'.

This situation is not likely to arise frequently since the judge can admit confession evidence only if satisfied beyond a reasonable doubt that it was not obtained by oppression or any other improper means. If there is anything in the evidence that gives rise to a reasonable doubt, the confession must be excluded. So the direction to disregard the confession would only be relevant where, despite the judge's view that, beyond a reasonable doubt, the confession was not obtained by oppression or any other improper means, the jury decided that it was, or might have been, obtained in that way. In the instant case the trial judge had found that the evidence had not been obtained by oppression. Therefore, although the judge's direction had been at fault, the conviction was found to be safe.

Police bad faith and seriousness of the impropriety

The only evidence given in the Act as to the meaning of oppression is the non-exhaustive definition contained in s 76(8): 'In this section "oppression" includes torture, inhuman or degrading treatment and the use or threat of violence (whether or not amounting to

---

81 At paras 53 and 54, *per* Lord Rodger of Earlsferry.

torture).' The word 'includes' ought to be given its literal meaning according to the Court of Appeal in *Fulling*.[82] Therefore, it appeared that the concept of oppression might be fairly wide: the question was whether it encompassed the old common law rulings on its width. In *Fulling*, the Court of Appeal held that PACE is a codifying Act and that therefore, a court should examine the statutory language uninfluenced by pre-Act decisions. The Court then proffered its own definition of oppression: 'the exercise of authority or power in a burdensome, harsh or wrongful manner; unjust or cruel treatment of subjects, inferiors, etc; the imposition of unreasonable or unjust burdens'. It thought that oppression would almost invariably entail impropriety on the part of the interrogator.

However, the terms 'wrongful' and 'improper' used in this test could potentially cover *any* unlawful action on the part of the police. That could have been taken to mean that any breach of the Act or codes could constitute oppression. This wide possibility was briefly pursued at first instance in the early post-PACE period,[83] but has been abandoned.[84] The Court of Appeal in *Hughes*[85] held that a denial of legal advice, owing *not* to bad faith on the part of the police, but to a misunderstanding, could not amount to oppression. In *Alladice*[86] the Court of Appeal also took this view in suggesting, *obiter*, that an improper denial of legal advice, *if* accompanied by bad faith on the part of the police, would certainly amount to 'unfairness' under s 78 and probably also to oppression. In *Beales*,[87] rather heavy-handed questioning accompanied by misleading suggestions, although not on the face of it a very serious impropriety, was termed oppressive because it was obviously employed as a deliberate tactic. In *Paris*,[88] the case of the *Cardiff Three*, confessions made by one of the defendants after some 13 hours of highly pressured and hostile questioning were excluded on the ground of oppression. He was a man of limited intelligence, but the Court of Appeal thought that the questioning would have been oppressive even in relation to a suspect of normal intelligence.

This emphasis on bad faith may be criticised because, from the point of view of the detainee, it matters little if mistreatment occurs because of an administrative mix-up, an innocent misconstruction of powers or malice. Looking to the state of mind of the suspect rather than that of the oppressor would enable account to be taken of the very great difference in impact of certain conduct on a young, inexperienced suspect and on a hardened, sophisticated criminal. However, at present the courts have not shown a desire to import a subjective assessment of oppression into s 76(2)(a), although at common law such an assessment would have been warranted.[89]

On the other hand, it cannot be said that the Court of Appeal has consistently invoked s 76(2)(a) rather than s 78 when the police *have* deliberately misused their powers in obtaining a confession; in *Mason*,[90] for example, a trick played deliberately on

82 [1987] QB 426; [1987] 2 All ER 65, CA.
83 In *Davison* [1988] Crim LR 442.
84 See *Parker* [1995] Crim LR 233.
85 [1988] Crim LR 519.
86 (1988) 87 Cr App R 380, CA.
87 [1991] Crim LR 118. See, to the same effect, *Heron* (1993) unreported; forceful questioning was accompanied by lies as to the identification evidence.
88 (1993) 97 Cr App R 99; [1994] Crim LR 361, CA.
89 *Priestley* (1966) 50 Cr App R 183, CA.
90 [1987] Crim LR 119; [1987] 3 All ER 481, CA.

the appellant's solicitor led to the exclusion of the confession under s 78. In *Blake*,[91] misleading statements made to the detainee, presumably in bad faith, led to exclusion of the confession under s 76(2)(b) or s 78. Thus, apart from the requirement of bad faith, it is also necessary to show that the improper behaviour has reached a certain level of seriousness in order to show oppression.[92] However, the case law has not been entirely clear as to the level of seriousness needed. All that can be said with some certainty is that the impropriety should be of a serious nature and that bad faith appears to be a necessary, but not sufficient condition for the operation of s 76(2)(a), whereas it will probably automatically render a confession inadmissible under s 78.

Conclusions

So oppression will arise if, first, improper behaviour of a certain level of seriousness has occurred. The behaviour in *Paris* was clearly oppressive; other improper behaviour might fall only just within the category of oppressive behaviour. Second, the behaviour must be perpetrated deliberately. Improper treatment falling outside s 76(8) and of insufficient seriousness to be termed oppressive or oppressive behaviour unaccompanied by bad faith can fall within s 76(2)(b) instead if the confession was likely to have been rendered unreliable thereby. The emphasis on bad faith or the lack of it at least gives an indication as to when improper behaviour on the part of the police will lead to automatic exclusion of the confession under s 76(2)(a) and when it will merely suggest the likelihood of unreliability under s 76(2)(b). But, since s 76(2)(a) only operates to exclude confessions obtained as a result of very serious impropriety on the part of the police, meaning that confessions are very rarely excluded under the sub-section, its ability to protect due process is limited. However, its impact on due process should not be disregarded. It sets a basic standard for police behaviour, probably deterring police from forms of impropriety still relatively common in some jurisdictions.

Section 76(2)(b): the 'reliability' test

Section 76(2)(b) provides that where a confession was or may have been obtained:

> in consequence of anything said or done which was likely in the circumstances existing at the time, to render unreliable any confession which might be made by him in consequence thereof, the court shall not allow the confession to be given in evidence against him except in so far as the prosecution proves to the court beyond reasonable doubt that the confession (notwithstanding that it may be true) was not obtained as aforesaid.

The 'reliability' test of s 76(2)(b) derives from the rule as stated in *Ibrahim*[93] on inducements to confess. However, as will be seen, it represents a relaxation of that rule as it was applied in *Ibrahim*. It also works certain changes in the emphasis of the test.

---

91 [1991] All ER 481, CA.
92 See *L* [1994] Crim LR 839.
93 [1914] AC 599; see p 972, above.

The test does not reflect the full rigour of the reliability principle, which requires that a confession extracted by torture but determined to be true should be admitted in evidence.[94] Instead, it is concerned with objective reliability: the judge must consider the situation at the time the confession was made and ask whether the confession would be *likely* to be unreliable, not whether it *is* unreliable.

It is not necessary, under this section, to show that there has been any misconduct on the part of the police, but often the 'something said or done' will consist of some such misconduct. In *Harvey*,[95] a mentally ill woman of low intelligence may have been induced to confess to murder by hearing her lover's confession. Her confession was excluded as being likely to be unreliable. In *Harvey*, the 'something said or done' (the first limb of the test under s 76(2)(a)) was the confession of the lover, while the 'circumstances' (the second limb) were the defendant's emotional state, low intelligence and mental illness. The 'something said or done' cannot consist of the defendant's own mental or physical state, according to *Goldberg*.[96] In that case, the defendant was a heroin addict who confessed because he was desperate to leave the police station and obtain a 'fix'. The contention of the defence counsel that the defendant's decision to confess prompted by his addiction amounted to 'something said or done' was not accepted by the court. In *Wahab*[97] the defendant tried to negotiate the release of his family from arrest with the police by offering to confess. The police did not make the bargain but he confessed in any event, and tried later to have the confession excluded under s 76(2)(b). This was refused, partly on the ground that the confession was reliable, but also on the ground that the inducement to confess did not come from the police.

In most instances, then, the 'something said or done' will consist of some impropriety on the part of the police. Having identified such a factor, a court will go on to consider whether any circumstances existed that rendered the impropriety particularly significant. The 'circumstances' can include the particularly vulnerable state of the detainee. In *Mathias*,[98] the defendant was particularly vulnerable because he had not been afforded legal advice although an offer of immunity from prosecution had been made to him. The Court of Appeal held that the offer had placed him in great difficulty and that this was a situation in which the police should have ensured that he had legal advice. From the judgment, it appears that if an inducement to confess is offered to the detainee, the police should ensure that he or she can discuss it with a solicitor, even if the police are entitled to deny access to legal advice, on the ground that the detainee falls within s 58(8).[99] Thus in such instances s 76(2)(b) may be satisfied since the 'circumstances' will be the lack of legal advice and the 'something said or done', the inducement.

The vulnerability relied upon by the defence as a special circumstance may relate to a physical or mental state. In *Trussler*[100] the defendant, who was a drug addict and had been in custody 18 hours, had been denied legal advice and had not been afforded the

94 As advocated by Andrews [1963] Crim LR 15, p 77; see p 964 above.
95 [1988] Crim LR 241.
96 [1988] Crim LR 678.
97 [2003] 1 Cr App R 15.
98 (1989) *The Times*, 24 August.
99 See Chapter 13, p 930.
100 [1988] Crim LR 446.

rest period guaranteed by Code C, para 12. His confession was excluded as likely to be unreliable. In *Delaney*[101] the defendant was 17, had an IQ of 80 and, according to an educational psychologist, was subject to emotional arousal that would lead him to wish to bring a police interview to an end as quickly as possible. These were circumstances in which it was important to ensure that the interrogation was conducted with all propriety. In fact, the officers offered some inducement to the defendant to confess by playing down the gravity of the offence and by suggesting that, if he confessed, he would get the psychiatric help he needed. They also failed to make an accurate, contemporaneous record of the interview in breach of Code C, para 11.3 (under the version of Code C in force at the time). Failing to make the proper record was of indirect relevance to the question of reliability since it meant that the court could not assess the full extent of the suggestions held out to the defendant. Thus, in the circumstances existing at the time (the mental state of the defendant), the police impropriety did have the special significance necessary under s 76(2)(b). The decision in *Marshall*[102] was to similar effect, although it did not identify a specific breach of Code C: the defendant was on the borderline of sub-normality and therefore, after an interview accompanied by his solicitor, he should not have been re-interviewed unaccompanied about the same matters.

From the above it appears that the 'circumstances existing at the time' may be circumstances created by the police (as in *Mathias*) or may be inherent in the defendant (as in *Delaney*). Impropriety on the part of the police can go to either limb of the test, but a state inherent in the detainee (such as mental illness) can go only to the 'circumstances' limb. Thus, a single breach of the interviewing rules such as a denial of legal advice in ordinary circumstances would not, as far as the current interpretation of s 76(2)(b) is concerned, satisfy both limbs of the test. On the other hand, a doubtful breach or perhaps no breach of the interviewing rules but, rather, behaviour of doubtful propriety, such as misleading the suspect as to the need to have legal advice, might satisfy the 'something said or done' test where special circumstances were *also* present.

It must now be apparent that s 76(2)(b) could be used to exclude all confessions obtained by oppression. It may then be wondered why s 76(2)(a) exists at all. The principle lying behind the two heads of s 76 appears to be that some types of impropriety on the part of the police are so unacceptable that it would be abhorrent in a court to go on to consider the reliability of a confession gained by such methods. In other words, s 76(2)(a) can speed up a process that could be carried out under s 76(2)(b).

Causation and the two heads of s 76

The words of s 76(2): '[if] it is represented to the court that the confession was or may have been obtained [by oppression or by behaviour in circumstances conducive to unreliability]' import a causal link between the police behaviour (the 'something said or done' or the oppression) and the confession. (It should be noted that the sections could also apply to persons other than police officers.) Thus, if the police threaten the suspect with violence *after* he has confessed, that will clearly be irrelevant to the obtaining of the confession. The question of causation under s 76(2)(b) appears, on the face of it,

---

101 (1989) 8 Cr App R 338; (1988) *The Times*, 20 August, CA.
102 (1992) *The Times*, 28 December.

quite complex. From the wording of the sub-section it appears to be necessary to adopt a two-stage test, asking first whether something was said or done, likely in the circumstances to render any confession made unreliable – an objective test – and, second, whether that something actually caused the detainee to confess – a subjective test.

The relationship between ss 76 and 78

The s 76(2)(b) test for admissibility of confessions takes account of the position of inexperienced and more vulnerable detainees. In *Canale*,[103] the police breached the recording provisions and allegedly played a trick on the appellant in order to obtain the confession. Ruling that the confession should have been excluded under s 78, the Court of Appeal took into account the fact that the appellant could not be said to be vulnerable or weak-minded; it was therefore thought inappropriate to invoke s 76(2)(b).[104]

The need in most instances to identify special factors in the situation (oppression or special vulnerability) in order to invoke either head of s 76 means that breaches of the interviewing rules unaccompanied by any such factor are usually considered under s 78. Furthermore, allegedly fabricated confessions clearly cannot fall within s 76(2) owing to its requirement that something has happened to the defendant that caused *him* to confess; its terms are not therefore fulfilled if the defence alleges that no confession made by the defendant exists.

In practice, confessions are rarely excluded under either head of s 76, and s 78 is usually used instead; that may be in part because the judges strongly wish to retain a discretion as to admissibility. As indicated above, even where a confession is excluded, physical evidence found as a result of information given in it need not be, under s 76(4).[105] Therefore, it may be said that s 76 has had a limited impact in upholding due process. That stance has not changed in the HRA era – there has been no evidence post-HRA of greater judicial willingness to use the sub-sections. Section 78 operates as a catch-all section, bringing within its boundaries many confessions (and other evidence) that pass the tests contained in either head of s 76.

Section 78: the 'fairness' test[106]

Introduction

Section 78 provides:

> In any proceedings the court may refuse to allow evidence on which the prosecution proposes to rely to be given if it appears to the court that, having regard

---

103 [1990] All ER 187, CA.
104 [1990] All ER 187, CA.
105 Section 76(2)(a) was not invoked, although apparently the police deliberately breached the recording provisions. Presumably, breaches of the interviewing rules were not seen as behaviour serious enough to be termed 'oppression'.
106 See further Mirfield, P, *Silence, Confessions and Improperly Obtained Evidence*, 1997, Clarendon; Mirfield, P, 'Successive confessions and the poisonous tree' [1996] Crim LR 554; Sharpe, *Judicial Discretion and Criminal Investigation*, 1998.

to all the circumstances, including the circumstances in which the evidence was obtained, the admission of the evidence would have such an adverse effect on the fairness of the proceedings that the court ought not to admit it.[107]

Section 78 can be invoked to argue for: (a) exclusion of confessions, and is of particular pertinence if they cannot be excluded under s 76 since the behaviour relied upon to argue for exclusion does not satisfy the tests discussed under s 76; (b) exclusion of non-confession evidence, including silences. Section 78 may be invoked where police questioning met with a 'no comment' response from the defendant. Such a response cannot be considered within s 76 due to the use of the word 'confession' within that section. It would be a very distorted use of statutory language to use the term 'confession' to cover a silence. If a silence is excluded from evidence under s 78, adverse inferences obviously cannot be drawn from it (unless the jury becomes aware of it in the course of hearing other evidence) and therefore argument on this issue has arisen, although the courts have shown themselves reluctant to exclude 'no comment' interviews.[108] Where access to legal advice has been delayed, and the accused has remained silent in interviews without having had access to legal advice, a breach of Art 6(3)(c) and possibly of Art 6(1) is likely to occur if adverse inferences are then drawn at trial.[109] One method of preventing this, which has not been catered for *expressly* under domestic law,[110] is to exclude the interviews under s 78.

Section 78 confers an exclusionary *discretion* on a judge and was conceived of in part to cover the very narrow function of the old common law discretion[111] to exclude improperly obtained non-confession evidence. But it soon became established (*Mason*)[112] that s 78 also covered confessions. Under s 6 HRA domestic courts clearly have a duty to exercise their discretion under s 78 in such a way as to ensure that compliance with Art 6(1) is achieved but, as discussed below, that duty has added little to the approach to s 78 established pre-HRA. The domestic jurisprudence is far more extensive on this matter than that at Strasbourg regarding confessions under Art 6, and, despite the reluctance of the judiciary to lay down guiding principles for the application of s 78, academics in an extensive literature have identified some indications of adherence to such principle.[113] It might have been expected that the effect of Art 6 would be

---

107 For discussion of the operation of s 78, see Allen, CJW, 'Discretion and Security: excluding evidence under section 78(1) of the Police and Criminal Evidence Act 1984' [1990] 49(1) 80; Gelowitz, M, 'Section 78 of the Police and Criminal Evidence Act 1984: Middle ground or no man's land?' (1990) 106 LQR 327; May [1988] Crim LR 722; Stone, R, 'Exclusion of Evidence under section 78 of the Police and Criminal Evidence Act: Practice and Principles' (1995) 3 Web JCL 1; Sanders and Young, op. cit., fn 1, Chapter 11, Part 5; Choo, AL-T and Nash, S, 'What's the matter with s 78?' [1999] Crim LR 929–40; Hunter, M, 'Judicial Discretion: s78 in practice' (1994) Crim LR 558; Ormerod, D and Birch, D, 'The evolution of the discretionary exclusion of evidence' (2004) Crim LR 767.
108 See *Condron* [1997] 1 WLR 827.
109 See pp 1210–15. This argument is based on *Murray v UK* (1996) 22 EHRR 29, *Averill v UK* (2001) 31 EHRR 35, and *Magee v UK* (2001) 31 EHRR 35.
110 Youth Justice and Criminal Evidence Act 1999, s 58, only provides that in such circumstances adverse inferences may not be drawn.
111 See *Sang* [1980] AC 402; [1979] 2 All ER 1222, HL.
112 [1987] Crim LR 119; [1987] All ER 481, CA.
113 See: Sanders and Young, *op cit*, fn 1, (2010) Chapter 125; Allen [1990] CLJ 80; Gelowitz (1990) 106 LQR 327; May [1988] Crim LR 722; Stone (1995) 3 Web JCL 1.

to encourage the articulation of some clearer statements of principle under s 78. The difficulty of discerning consistency of principle in the decisions under s 78 only became more apparent in the later 1990s and post-HRA.[114]

Section 78 provides a discretion to exclude evidence if admitting it would render the trial unfair. In adopting this formula, it was clear that the government did not wish to import into this country a USA-type exclusionary rule. The Home Secretary informed the House of Commons[115] that the function of exclusion of evidence after police misconduct must not be disciplinary, but must be to safeguard the fairness of the trial. The idea behind this was that non-confession evidence obtained by improper means could still be admitted on the basis that police misconduct could be dealt with by internal disciplinary procedures. Similarly, confessions obtained improperly in circumstances falling outside s 76 could nevertheless be admissible in evidence, with the proviso that the trial should not thereby be rendered unfair. In fact, as will be seen, the courts have managed to create a role for s 78 that, as far as confessions are concerned, is probably rather far removed from the government's original intention. The approach adopted towards confessions tends to reflect to an extent the protective and integrity principles.

It may be noted that s 78 is not explicit as to who bears the burden of proof where a breach of the rules is alleged, but in *Vel v Owen*[116] the Divisional Court ruled that the defence should make good its objection. In *Anderson*,[117] however, the Court said that it was not entirely clear where the burden of proof lay.

In the HRA era s 78 must be applied in accordance with the courts' duty under Art 6,[118] but the courts have been very reluctant to lay down general rules for the application of the section.[119] The attempt will be made here, however, albeit tentatively, to identify some of the factors that tend to be taken into account in relation to confessions/admissions. If it is found that admitting an interview in which admissions were made *would* render the trial unfair, then not only the interview affected, but possibly any interviews subsequent to that one[120] may be excluded from evidence under s 78. Non-confession evidence will be considered separately, below.

Admissions linked to breaches of rules as to interviewing and access to legal advice

The PACE interviewing scheme, made up to a significant extent of code-based rules, as Chapter 13 made clear, may be breached or undermined in a variety of ways. There may be a clear failure to put in place one of the safeguards, such as access to legal advice or audio-recording. However, it is not always possible to identify such a clear breach

---

114 See Ormerod, D and Birch, D, 'The evolution of the discretionary exclusion of evidence' (2004) Crim LR 767.

115 1983–84, HC Deb col 1012, 29 October 1984.

116 (1987) JP 510.

117 [1993] Crim LR 447.

118 The duty flows from sections 3 and 6 HRA whereby the courts are public authorities for the purposes of the HRA, and thus must act compatibly with Convention rights. Under s 3 HRA s.78 of PACE must be read and given effect in a manner compatible with Convention rights.

119 See the comments of Auld J in *Katz* (1990) 90 Cr App R 456, CA.

120 *Ismail* [1990] Crim LR 109, CA; *cf Gillard and Barrett* (1991) 155 JP Rep 352 and *Y v DPP* [1991] Crim LR 917. Later interviews may be found to have been contaminated by earlier breaches if those breaches are of a fundamental and continuing character and the accused has not had sufficient opportunity of retracting what was said earlier: *Neill* [1994] Crim LR 441, CA.

of the rules. The failure to do so may have contributed to the decision in *Hughes*:[121] a misrepresentation as regards unavailability of legal advice made to the appellant did not involve a clear breach of a specific code provision and therefore, led to the reluctance to exclude the confession. Similarly, in *Khan*[122] it was found that while s 30(1) of PACE allowed officers to keep a suspect out of the police station for a time in order to make investigations, including a search, questioning during that time should be limited, since otherwise the provisions of the interviewing scheme would be subverted. Some of the questions that had in fact been asked went beyond what was needed for the search; however, it was found, they should not have been excluded, since the matter was 'a question of degree', although officers did not have *carte blanche* to interview suspects in such circumstances.

In contrast to this approach, there has been some willingness at first instance to consider situations where the PACE interviewing scheme seemed to have been infringed, although it was impossible to point to a clear breach.[123] The interviewing scheme lends itself to many methods of infringement, some of which may occur at a low level of visibility, but that may nevertheless be of significance. For example, there may be breach of a rule contained in a non-statutory instrument other than PACE itself or Code C;[124] there may be evasion or bending of a rule as opposed to breaking it; there are instances where the interviewing scheme itself leaves it unclear whether or not a particular safeguard should have been in place at a given stage in the process.[125] Clearly, a court may never have an opportunity to hear such argument. Infringement of this type is difficult to detect; for example, a suspect who is persuaded to forgo legal advice at the 'booking in' stage may be unaware that something has occurred to his disadvantage, unlike the suspect who has been straightforwardly refused advice. Even assuming that the suspect pleads not guilty, defence counsel may be reluctant to argue for exclusion of a confession if unable to point to a clear breach of the rules.

In *Keenan*,[126] the Court of Appeal ruled that once a breach of the rules can be identified, it will be asked whether it is substantial or significant. The Court found that a combination of breaches of the recording provisions satisfied this test. In contrast, a breach of Code C para 10.2 requiring a police officer to inform a suspect, if that is the case, that he is not under arrest, is free to go and may obtain legal advice, has been held to be insubstantial.[127] This view of para 10.2 also seems to have been implicit in the ruling of the Court of Appeal in *Joseph*,[128] although a breach of para 10.5 governing contemporaneous recording (now para 11.7, 2014 edition), in contrast was clearly found to be substantial and significant in order to merit exclusion of the confession. In *Walsh*,[129] the Court of Appeal held that what was significant and substantial would

---

121 [1988] Crim LR 519. See Chapter 14, p 935 for discussion of the decision.
122 [1993] Crim LR 54, CA.
123 See, e.g., *Vernon* [1988] Crim LR 445; *Woodall and Others* [1989] Crim LR 288.
124 The Notes for Guidance, which are not part of the Codes and therefore may in effect be said to form part of a separate instrument; Home Office Circulars; Force Standing Orders.
125 See Chapter 14, pp 914–920 (discussed in Fenwick, H, 'Confessions, recording rules and miscarriages of justice' [1993] Crim LR 174).
126 [1989] 3 WLR 1193; [1989] All ER 598, CA.
127 *Rajakuruna* [1991] Crim LR 458.
128 [1993] Crim LR 206, CA.
129 [1989] Crim LR 822; (1989) 19 Cr App R 161.

be determined by reference to the nature of the breach except in instances where the police had acted in bad faith: 'although bad faith may make substantial or significant that which might not otherwise be so, the contrary does not follow. Breaches which are themselves significant and substantial are not rendered otherwise by the good faith of the officers concerned.'

This test as to a significant and substantial breach has so far been applied only to code provisions. It seems likely that breach of rules contained in notes for guidance or Home Office circulars would fail it – assuming that a court was prepared to consider such breaches at all. The courts have been reluctant to take such rules into account in the context of exclusion of evidence or, as far as the notes are concerned, in any other context. That was the approach taken in *DPP v Billington*;[130] the Court of Appeal preferred not to consider Note 6C of Code C despite its relevance to the question before it. However, there are some patchy signs that the judiciary are prepared to react to the notes differently, perhaps owing to a perception that their legitimacy derives from their substance, as opposed to their source. In *DPP v Blake*[131] the Divisional Court impliedly accepted that a Note for Guidance can be considered if it can be argued that it amplifies a particular Code provision, and can therefore be of assistance in determining whether breach of such a provision has occurred. The question arose whether an estranged parent could be the appropriate adult at the interview of a juvenile under Code C, para 13.1;[132] that provision was interpreted in accordance with Note 13C, which at the time described the adult's expected role,[133] and it was then found that para 13.1 had been breached.[134] A variation on this view of the Notes, which nevertheless supports the argument that they are unlikely to be considered in their own right, was expressed by the Court of Appeal in relation to one of the most significant notes, Note 11A. It was taken into account on the basis that it could be seen as part of para 11.1 and could thereby acquire the status of a paragraph.[135] (Note – the references to the Code provisions are to the provisions in force at the time.)

In cases concerning such breaches, once a court has identified a significant and substantial breach of the interviewing rules, it may then take some account of the *function* of the rule in question. Rules governing access to legal advice and the right to silence provide rights that are valuable in themselves in due process terms; they also tend to place the suspect on a more equal footing with police officers during the interview. These rights are also reflected in the ECHR in Art 6(2) and (3)(c). An innocent detainee who is confused and emotionally affected by the interrogation may be less likely to make

---

130 (1988) Cr App R 68; [1988] 1 All ER 435. The court had to consider whether a desire to consult a solicitor first could properly found a refusal to furnish a specimen of breath under the Road Traffic Act 1972, s 8(7). Under the version of Code C applicable at the time it the s 8 procedure does not constitute an interview, but no weight was placed on the Note in question. The issue which fell to be determined did not concern the question of exclusion of evidence, but has a bearing upon the general question whether courts are prepared to place any reliance upon the Notes.

131 [1989] 1 WLR 432, CA.

132 Now para 11.15 under the 2014 revised Code.

133 This role is now described in para 11.17; this provision has therefore been elevated in status, indicating its importance.

134 This decision was followed in the first instance decision of *Morse* [1991] Crim LR 195; see also *DPP v Rouse* and *DPP v Davis* (1992) 94 Cr App R 185.

135 *Cox* (1993) 96 Cr App R 464; [1993] Crim LR 382; (1992) *The Times*, 2 December.

false admissions if a legal adviser is present at the interview.[136] In contrast, the verifying and recording rules may be said to be concerned mainly with the evidential integrity of admissions rather than with providing rights valuable in themselves. Categorising the interviewing rules in this way – by means of their dominant function – may be useful as a means of determining the type of unfairness that may flow from their breach.

Breach of rules aimed at ensuring that the record of an interview can be relied on at trial need not be considered under s 78 in terms of their impact on the defendant during the interview. The question is not normally whether the breach of the recording rules placed the defendant at a disadvantage during the interview. Once such a breach, of a substantial nature, has been identified, a court will be likely to react by excluding the confession on the basis that it is impossible to be sure of its *reliability*,[137] and therefore its prejudicial quality may outweigh its probative value. In other words, a jury may place reliance on an inaccurate record or believe a fabricated confession which clearly has no evidential value at all. An obvious example of such a breach is a failure to make contemporaneous notes of the interview in breach of Code C, para 11.7, allowing a challenge to the interview record by the defence on the basis that the police have fabricated all or part of it. The court then has no means of knowing which version of what was said is true, precisely the situation which Code C was designed to prevent. In such a situation, a judge may well exclude the interview record on the basis that it would be unfair to allow evidence of doubtful reliability to go before the jury. If, however, as in *Dunn*,[138] the defence has an independent witness to what occurred – usually a solicitor or solicitor's clerk – the judge may admit the confession as the defence now has a proper basis from which to challenge the police evidence.

It is fairly clear that allowing a confession that may have been partly fabricated to go before the jury may render a trial unfair. On the one hand, the jury may rely on a confession that may be entirely untrue, while on the other, if the defendant alleges that the police fabricated the confession, the prosecution can then put his character in issue and the jury may hear of his previous convictions. The jury may then tend to rely on his convictions in deciding that his guilt is established on this occasion. In both circumstances, the defendant is placed at a clear disadvantage.

If a breach of Code C has occurred which casts doubt on the accuracy of the interview record, the defence may not necessarily submit that the police have fabricated admissions; the judge may merely have to determine whether the trial will be rendered unfair if a possibly inaccurate record of an interview is admitted in evidence. There is authority to suggest that a judge in such circumstances will exclude the record,[139] presumably owing to the risk that the jury will rely on fabricated admissions.

Other forms of impropriety

Use of s 78 does not of course depend on identifying a specific breach of Code C (or any of the other rules). Anything likely to cause unfairness at trial that has occurred

---

136 The evidence as to the advantage to the detainee of having the adviser present at the interview is of a rather mixed nature; see, e.g., comment on the solicitor's role at [1993] Crim LR 368.

137 See, e.g., *Keenan* [1989] 3 WLR 1193; [1989] 3 All ER 598, CA.

138 (1990) 91 Cr App R 237; [1990] Crim LR 572, CA. See also *Heslop* [1996] Crim LR 730.

139 *Foster* [1987] Crim LR 821; *Keenan* [1989] 3 All ER 598

during the process could trigger exclusion of evidence under s 78. For example, in *R v Newell*[140] the defence advocate had prepared a statement on a form as part of a plea and case management hearing, and the trial judge allowed cross-examination at trial as to inconsistencies between that statement and the defence at trial. The Court of Appeal found that such a hearing was intended to allow the judge to be provided with information allowing him or her to manage the case. If statements on forms as part of that hearing were not to be excluded, the defence would be likely to become over-cautious in providing the information. Therefore a judge should normally exercise discretion to exclude evidence of such statements. In exceptional circumstances however such evidence could be used against the defendant.[141]

Police bad faith

In the cases considered above, it was not clear that the police had *deliberately* failed to comply with the rules; the failures in question may have arisen out of a mistake as to the application of PACE or Code C or because of an administrative error. It seems that if the police have acted deliberately, the exercise under s 78 will be far less complex. Lord Lane CJ in *Alladice*[142] stated that he would not have hesitated to hold that the confession should have been excluded had it been demonstrated that the police had acted in bad faith in breaching s 58. The lack of emphasis that he thought should in general be placed on the causal relationship in question, if bad faith on the part of the police could be demonstrated, was the most striking feature of this decision. His approach appears to involve asking only whether a breach was accompanied by bad faith. If so, that would appear to be the end of the matter: exclusion of the confession would follow almost automatically. If the breach occurred in good faith, however, a close scrutiny of the causal relationship should follow.

Using the questions of bad faith and causation as alternatives to keep a check on a too ready exclusion of confessions can be criticised because it is hard to see why an instance of bad faith on the part of the police which is not causally linked to the confession should be considered in relation to its admissibility. Deliberate denial of rights certainly gives a greater appearance of unfairness to the interrogation than an innocent denial, but if the detainee is unaffected by it, why should it affect the trial? It cannot be said that the court is associating itself with or condoning the bad faith displayed by the police in the interrogation because the link between the admissions arising and the denial of rights is missing. If, in future, the situation that arose in *Alladice* recurs, but with the added ingredient of bad faith, it is hard to see why the consequences for the future defendant should differ so greatly. The only justification appears to be that the police are 'punished' for their deliberate impropriety, but the disciplinary approach has been explicitly repudiated, in *Delaney*[143] and *Chalkley*,[144] on the basis that it is not part of the proper purpose of a criminal trial to inquire into wrongdoing on the part of the police. Nevertheless, at present, deliberate breaches of Code C will almost certainly lead

---

140 [2012] EWCA 650.
141 As it had been in *R (Firth) v Epping Justices* [2011] EWHC 388 (Admin).
142 (1988) 87 Cr App R 380
143 (1989) 88 Cr App R 339; (1988) *The Times*, 20 August, CA.
144 [1998] 2 All ER 155.

to exclusion of evidence under s 78 whether the breaches were linked to the confession or not. The Court of Appeal in *Walsh*[145] confirmed that this was the correct approach and suggested that it would be followed even if the breach was of a trivial nature. In fact, the dearth of cases on this point suggests that courts are reluctant to accept that a breach of PACE may have been perpetrated deliberately by the police; they appear to be satisfied that breaches arise due to administrative errors or incompetence rather than bad faith.

Admissions and causation under s 78

In *Samuel*,[146] the Court of Appeal found that the confession should have been excluded under s 78 because it was causally linked to the police impropriety – a failure to allow the appellant access to legal advice. In order to establish this point, the solicitor in question gave evidence that had he been present, he would have advised his client to remain silent in the last interview, whereas in fact Samuel made damaging admissions in that interview that formed the basis of the case against him. It could not be said with certainty that he would have confessed in any event: he was not, it was determined, a sophisticated criminal who was capable of judging for himself when to speak and when to remain silent. Thus – although this was not made explicit – the Court of Appeal was in effect prepared to make the judgment that a trial would be rendered unfair if a court associated itself with a breach of the PACE interrogation procedure. The Court of Appeal in *Alladice*,[147] also faced with a breach of s 58, accepted that the key factor in exercising discretion under s 78 after a breach of the interviewing rules was the causal relationship between breach and confession (and, it appeared by implication, between breach and fairness at the trial). On the basis of this factor, it was determined that the confession had been rightly admitted despite the breach of s 58 because no causal relationship between the two could be established. This finding was based partly on the defendant's evaluation of the situation (that he only wanted the solicitor to see fair play and did not require legal advice), and partly on the fact that he *had* exercised his right to silence at certain points. Therefore, it was determined that he would have made the incriminating admissions in any event – even with the benefit of legal advice. Possibly this was surprising in view of the fact that the appellant, as the court itself accepted, was an unsophisticated criminal who did in fact make admissions in the absence of a solicitor that formed the basis of the case against him.[148]

In the early post-PACE years, there was a tendency for judges to move rather rapidly from a finding that the police had breached Code C to a determination that s 78 should be invoked to exclude the confession, without explicitly considering whether a causal relationship between the breach and the confession existed.[149] Such a tendency can be

145 [1989] Crim LR 822.
146 [1988] QB 615; [1988] 2 All ER 315; [1988] 2 WLR 920, CA.
147 (1988) 87 Cr App R 380. The Court of Appeal appeared to have a similar test in mind in relation to a failure to caution in *Weerdesteyn* (1995) 1 Cr App R 405; [1995] Crim LR 239, CA.
148 See also *Dunford* (1990) 91 Cr App R 150; (1990) 140 NLJ 517, CA: the Court of Appeal determined that the criminally experienced appellant had made his own assessment of the situation in deciding to make certain admissions and legal advice would not have affected his decision; the failure to allow legal advice was not therefore causally linked to the confession.
149 See *Williams* [1989] Crim LR 66 and *Mary Quayson* [1989] Crim LR 218.

discerned in the case of *Absolam*[150] in which the Court of Appeal, in finding that 'the prosecution would not have been in receipt of these admissions if the appropriate procedures had been followed', seemed to assume that the causal relationship between the impropriety[151] and the admissions did exist. The chain of causation would have been fairly long – had the detainee been informed of his right to legal advice, he would have exercised it; had he exercised it, he would not have made the incriminating admissions – but the Court of Appeal did not make much attempt to scrutinise its links.[152] However, in *Walsh*,[153] the Court of Appeal reaffirmed the need to identify the causal relationship between the breach in question and the confession.

In this context, the curtailment of the right to silence under the CJPOA, discussed in Chapter 13,[154] is particularly significant. One result of its curtailment appears to be that it is now harder to argue that an improper denial of access to legal advice should lead to exclusion of admissions obtained under s 78. That is because the main basis for excluding confessions gained after denial of legal advice has been eroded. Prior to curtailment of the right to silence, the courts had been excluding them mainly on the ground that, had the legal adviser been present, he or she would probably have advised the client to remain silent; but if this cannot be contended, the causal relationship between breach and confession is destroyed. How far this is happening depends on the readiness of legal advisers to advise their clients to remain silent in the face of the knowledge that such silence may be commented on in court. At present, it is unclear that legal advisers are less disposed than they were previously to advise silence. However, if such a tendency did become apparent, a number of consequences might follow. The police may have been encouraged to afford access to a legal adviser; but, on the other hand, any disincentive to deny access – the result of such decisions as *Samuel* and *Absolam* – has been undermined. The balance still comes down in favour of discouraging, delaying or denying access.

If, on a *voir dire*, a court has to consider such a denial, it is harder than it was previously to contend confidently that the legal adviser would have advised the client to remain silent; the result is that the courts are finding themselves less able to uphold this particular safeguard for the suspect. Of course it might be said, in the light of a large amount of research,[155] that it was, even prior to the inception of the CJPOA, *already* becoming difficult to contend confidently that a legal adviser would have advised silence, except perhaps in cases where the client was under very obvious pressure.[156]

---

150 (1989) Cr App R 332.

151 A failure to inform Absolam of his right to legal advice in breach of Code C, para 3.1(ii).

152 Possibly, this may have arisen because the defendant had denied making the admissions in question; the court was therefore placed in the position of accepting the word of the police officer against that of the defendant – precisely the problem which Code C, para 11 was designed to prevent. The Court of Appeal, while speaking in the language of causation, may simply have had a doubt as to whether the admissions were made at all.

153 [1989] Crim LR 822.

154 See pp 949–53.

155 See, e.g., McConville, M and Hodgson, J, *Custodial Legal Advice and the Right to Silence*, 1993, Royal Commission Study No 16. See further Chapter 13, pp 949–53.

156 See Dixon's findings in this respect: [1991] PL 233, p 244: 'silence may be advised . . . when the suspect is confused or highly emotional . . . several solicitors stressed that their clients are under great pressure'.

However, that problem can be addressed by means of better training in the provision of custodial legal advice. The effect of curtailment of the right to silence, however, is probably in the long run to undermine one of the props holding up the legal advice scheme.

Unfairness

Deciding that an impropriety is causally linked to the confession does not of itself explain *why* admission of the confession will render the trial unfair, although it is perhaps reasonable to conclude that admission of a confession that is not so linked will *not* render the trial unfair. The necessary unfairness must arise through admission of the confession, in other words *after* its admission; the unfairness in the interrogation cannot therefore without more satisfy this requirement; instead, the unfairly obtained confession must be the agent which somehow creates unfairness at the trial. It must be acknowledged that at present the courts have not addressed this question. In *Samuel*, for example, the Court of Appeal merely stated:

> the appellant was denied improperly one of the most important and fundamental rights of the citizen . . . if [the trial judge] had found a breach of s 58 he would have determined that admission of evidence as to the final interview would have 'such an adverse effect on the fairness of the proceedings' that he ought not to admit it.[157]

Broadly, it could be argued that if the court refuses to take the opportunity afforded by s 78 to put right what has occurred earlier in the process, this will give an appearance of unfairness to the trial. This argument is based on the 'protective principle':[158] if admissions gained in consequence of denial of a right (in the broad sense of an entitlement) are excluded, the particular right is being protected in the sense that the defendant is being placed at trial – as far as the jury is concerned – in the position he or she would have been in had the right not been denied. If s 78 is, at least in part, concerned with ensuring fairness to the defence, it is arguable that the court should take the opportunity offered to it of upholding the standards of fairness declared by PACE. However, following an argument based on the reputation or integrity principles, if the police unfairness has had no consequences for the defendant, the court need not exclude the confession since to do so would place him in a *more* favourable position than he would have been in had the proper standard of fairness been observed.

Admittedly, both these arguments assume that the court will appear to be associating itself unfairly with the prosecution, rather than dealing even-handedly, if it admits the evidence in question and that, therefore, the court should refuse to do so. They therefore seem to beg the very question to which s 78 demands an answer. If admitting the confession despite the breach *could* be seen as fair, the court would not be associating itself with unfairness and could not be seen as lacking even-handedness. But bearing in mind the balance PACE is supposed to create between increased police powers and safeguards for suspects, it can perhaps be argued that to accept evidence deriving from an interview in which the police were able to use their powers to the full, but the defendant was unable to take advantage of an important safeguard, would not be perceived by

---

157 [1988] 2 WLR 920, p 934.
158 See Ashworth, A [1979] Crim LR 723.

most reasonable people as fair. The findings of the Privy Council in *Mohammed (Allie) v State*[159] in respect of a denial of custodial access to legal advice adopted this stance:

> The stamp of constitutionality on a citizen's rights is not meaningless: it is clear testimony that added value is attached to the protection of the right . . . Not every breach will result in a confession being excluded. But their Lordships make clear that the fact that there has been a breach of a constitutional right is a cogent factor militating in favour of the exclusion of the confession. In this way the constitutional character of the infringed right is respected and accorded a high value.

This stance receives clear, albeit indirect support from Strasbourg.[160]

It may be noted that a judge may exceptionally admit the confession after deciding to exclude it because some particular feature of the trial proceedings makes it necessary to do so in order to maintain the balance of fairness between prosecution and defence.[161] In other words, if it was clear that in some way the prosecution is at a disadvantage that could be seen as equal to that experienced by the defendant, the judge might allow the confession to be admitted. This flows from the concern of s 78 with the fairness of the proceedings rather than simply with fairness to the defence. On the other hand, it does not appear that reconsidering the decision to *admit* the confession is covered by s 78 – in the sense of telling the jury to disregard the confession – due to its focus on determining whether to admit the confession (although s 82(3) might be invoked – see below).

Exclusion of non-confession evidence – introduction[162]

The discussion has shown that the courts have continued the common law tradition within the PACE scheme of excluding confessions tainted by impropriety, but they have shown great reluctance to exclude *other* evidence that is equally tainted. A stay will be used only in relation to certain instances of gross malpractice. The threshold is extremely high and arguably not a suitable remedy in cases involving human rights. The arguments above have concentrated on exclusion of admissions, but non-confession evidence can also be excluded under s 78 (or s 82(3)), although not under s 76. Where non-confession evidence is concerned, the courts have taken a stance that differs strongly from that taken to admissions obtained in police interviews which breach PACE. The general stance taken is that improperly obtained evidence is admissible in a criminal trial subject to a discretion to exclude it. Except in one instance – that of identification evidence – the discretion is viewed as very narrow, although where the impropriety consists of some forms of trickery, it may be wider. That stance has not

---

159 [1999] 2 WLR 552 (Trinidad and Tobago); judgment delivered by Lord Steyn on 8 December 1998.
160 See pp 969–70.
161 See *Allen* [1992] Crim LR 297: having decided to exclude a conversation between police officers and the defendant because of breaches of the recording provisions, the judge reconsidered when the nature of the defence case became apparent; it placed prosecution witnesses at an unfair disadvantage if they were unable to refer to the excluded conversation. Thus, it appears that in such circumstances the original unfairness caused to the defendant may be outweighed by unfairness to the prosecution if the confession is not admitted.
162 For discussion see Gelowitz (1990) 106 LQR 327; Choo, AL-T and Nash, S, 'What's the matter with s 78?' [1999] Crim LR 929–40. Choo (1989) 9(3) LS 261; Allen [1990] CLJ 80; Choo (1993) Journal of Crim Law 195; Sharpe, *op cit*, fn 1, (1998) Chapter 2.

changed under the HRA. Pre-HRA the courts demonstrated little inclination to take a different stance where the impropriety consisted of a breach of a Convention right,[163] and, following the Strasbourg jurisprudence, it was not necessary for that approach to change under the HRA.[164]

Identification evidence

Identification evidence has been seen as particularly vulnerable and may therefore be treated in the same way as a confession obtained in breach of PACE. Arguments can be raised as to the reliability of identification evidence and also as to police impropriety in conducting identification. For example, if no reminder as to the availability of legal advice were given (Code D, para 3.17(ii), 2011 edition) before a form of identification was arranged, it could be argued that the form used had prejudiced the position of the defendant, who would have asked for a different form had he had advice. It could possibly be argued that no identification would have been made had the other form been used and that, therefore, the failure to remind the suspect of the right to advice was causally linked to the identification evidence obtained. If some doubt is raised as to the reliability of the identification owing to delay[165] or to a failure to hold an identification parade where one was practicable,[166] the identification evidence is likely to be excluded. However, in the leading decision on identification evidence, *Forbes*,[167] the House of Lords found that despite a breach of Code D, para 2.3, there had been no need to exclude the evidence.

Thus, following this decision, each case must turn on its own facts, except where bad faith is shown in conducting the identification procedure. In such an instance, it seems that the courts will react to it as they would in relation to confessions.[168] It will mean that no causal relationship between the breach and the evidence obtained need be shown and, possibly, that the breach need not be substantial and significant. It may be argued that there is a stronger case than that considered above in relation to confessions for treating bad faith shown during the identification process with particular stringency owing to the appearance of unfairness created to the defendant who may think that there has been collusion between witnesses and the police.

Other non-confession evidence

On due process grounds, the argument accepted in *Samuel*[169] as to the causal relationship between an impropriety and a confession (where bad faith is not shown) should be applied to non-confession evidence, such as a weapon or drugs found on the suspect or his premises during an improper or unlawful search. However, the stance taken by the courts is based more strongly on crime control principles, bearing in mind that physical

---

163 See the judgment of the House of Lords in *Khan* [1997] AC 558.
164 See *R v Button* [2005] EWCA Crim 516.
165 *Quinn* [1990] Crim LR 581, CA; (1990) *The Times*, 31 March.
166 *Ladlow* [1989] Crim LR 219.
167 [2001] Crim LR 649.
168 *Finley* [1993] Crim LR 50, CA.
169 [1988] QB 615.

evidence is more likely to be reliable than admissions. Where non-confession evidence is in question, the discretion under s 78 is applied very narrowly. The first instance decision in *Fennelly*[170] in which a failure to give the reason for a stop and search led to exclusion of the heroin found is out of line with the later decisions. Indeed, even if the principles developed under s 78 with respect to confession evidence were generally applied to other evidence, *Fennelly* would still be a doubtful decision since, on the facts, no causal relationship could exist between the impropriety in question and the evidence obtained.

According to *Thomas*[171] and *Quinn*,[172] physical evidence will be excluded only if obtained with deliberate illegality; the pre-PACE ruling of the House of Lords in *Fox*[173] would also lend support to this contention. In *Fox*, the police made a bona fide mistake as to their powers in effecting an unlawful arrest and the House of Lords, in determining that the physical evidence obtained was admissible, considered that the unlawful arrest was merely part of the history of the case and not the concern of the court. This stance is in accord with that taken in *Sang*[174] and confirmed as correct in *Khan (Sultan)*.[175] It appears to be in accord with the general PACE scheme, since evidence obtained as a result of an inadmissible confession will be admissible under s 76(4).

Zander has found,[176] citing, *inter alia*, *Sharpe v DPP*,[177] that the courts have rejected the 'real' evidence of intoxication in certain drink-driving cases under s 78 owing to the way in which the evidence was obtained, even where bad faith may not have been present. Zander views the Divisional Court decision in *Sharpe*, along with the decisions in cases such as *Samuel* and *Gall*[178] (on identification evidence) as affirming an abandonment of 'the amoral common law tradition of receiving non-confession evidence regardless of how it was obtained'.[179] However, it may now be said with some certainty that the 'amoral' common law tradition has continued and will continue to prevail, on the basis of the reliability principle. The inception of the HRA has not yet affected this position.[180]

The position as regards unlawfully obtained non-confession evidence, which broadly reflects the crime control stance, is, as stated pre-HRA by the House of Lords in *Khan (Sultan)*,[181] the leading case on s 78. It suggests that a narrow exclusionary discretion only is available under s 78. A bugging device had been secretly installed on the outside of a house that Khan was visiting. Khan was suspected of involvement in the importation of prohibited drugs and the tape recording obtained from the listening device clearly showed that he was so involved. The case against him rested wholly on the tape recording. The defence argued, first, that the recording was inadmissible as evidence

---

170 [1989] Crim LR 142.
171 [1990] Crim LR 269. See, to the same effect, *Wright* [1994] Crim LR 55.
172 [1990] Crim LR 581, CA.
173 [1986] AC 281; see to the same effect *DPP v Wilson* [1991] Crim LR 441. On similar facts, in *Matto v Wolverhampton Crown Court* [1987] RTR 337, physical evidence was excluded since the police had acted with *mala fides*.
174 [1980] AC 402; [1979] 2 All ER 1222, HL.
175 [1997] AC 558; [1996] 3 All ER 289.
176 Zander, *op cit*, fn 1, 2nd edn, pp 236–37.
177 (1993) JP 595.
178 (1990) 90 Cr App R 64.
179 Zander, *op cit*, fn 1, 2nd edn, p 236.
180 See p 157 *et seq* as to the Strasbourg stance, influencing the domestic courts via ss2 and 6 HRA.
181 [1996] 3 All ER 289; (1996) 146 NLJ 1024. For comment, see Carter (1997) 113 LQR 468.

because the police had had no statutory authority to place listening devices on private property and that, therefore, such placement was a trespass and, further, that admission of the recording would breach Art 8 of the European Convention on Human Rights, which protects the right to privacy. Secondly, it was argued that even if the recording was admissible, it should be excluded from evidence under s 78 because of the unfairness of admitting the evidence so. It was accepted in the Court of Appeal that trespass to the building had occurred as well as some damage to it and that there had been an invasion of privacy. However, the Court of Appeal found,[182] supporting the trial judge, that these factors were of slight significance and therefore were readily outweighed by the fact that the police had largely complied with the Home Office guidelines and that the offences involved were serious. The Court found that since the ECHR (at that time) was not part of UK law, it was of only persuasive assistance.

The House of Lords upheld the Court of Appeal. The Lords relied on the decision in *Sang*[183] to the effect that improperly obtained evidence other than 'involuntary' confessions is admissible in a criminal trial. Involuntary confessions were inadmissible on the ground that if a defendant was in some way induced to confess during a police interrogation, his confession might be unreliable. It was argued for the appellant that the recording fell within the category of involuntary confessions and therefore was outside the rule from *Sang*. The House of Lords disagreed and went on to find that *Sang* would be inapplicable only if there were a right to privacy in UK law and breach of such a right could be treated as a form of impropriety different in kind from that covered by *Sang* and so serious that it would render evidence thereby obtained inadmissible. Neither of these two principles was accepted; therefore, the recording was admissible. The decision of the House of Lords was subsequently confirmed as compatible with Art 6 by the European Court of Human Rights.[184] In *PG and JH v UK*[185] the Court found that the use of covert listening devices in a police station to obtain samples of the suspect's speech had breached Art 8 since there was no underpinning statutory basis for their use; thus the 'in accordance with the law' test of Art 8(2) was not satisfied. But such a basis now exists under the Regulation of Investigatory Powers Act 2000.[186]

Should the recording have been excluded under s 78, taking Art 8 into account? The House of Lords found that although a judge in exercising discretion under s 78 might take Art 8 into account, but an apparent breach of Art 8 would not necessarily lead him or her to conclude that the evidence in question should be excluded. The key question would be the effect of the breach upon the fairness of the proceedings. The House of Lords concluded that the circumstances in which the evidence was obtained, even if they involved a breach of Art 8, were not such as to require exclusion of the evidence. Obviously, under s 6 HRA a court would have to consider the possible breach of Art 8, but that would not mean that the evidence obtained thereby would necessarily be excluded.

182 *Khan* [1996] 3 All ER 289; (1996) 146 NLJ 1024, HL; [1995] QB 27, CA.
183 [1980] AC 402; [1979] 2 All ER 1222.
184 *Khan v United Kingdom* [2000] ECHR 35394/97.
185 (2008) 46 EHRR 51.
186 See Chapter 11, p 793 *et seq.*

This decision confirms that, apart from admissions falling within s 76 of PACE (which has partly replaced the common law concept of involuntariness), improperly obtained evidence is admissible in criminal trials subject to a discretion to exclude it. Thus, that approach does not protect due process in an absolutist sense. The House of Lords was only prepared to find that the Convention would be 'relevant' to the exercise of discretion under s 78 and further found that where a breach of the Convention was found, that would not necessarily lead a judge to conclude that evidence should be excluded. In *Chalkley*,[187] the same stance was taken. The evidence consisted of incriminating statements made by the accused that were secretly recorded by the police. Despite the impropriety of the police actions, it was found that the evidence was rightly admitted. That stance did not change with the inception of the HRA. In *AG's Reference (No 3 of 1999)*,[188] a rape case, DNA evidence against the suspect should have been destroyed but had not been, in breach of s 64 of PACE. The evidence was not admitted under s 78 and the defendant was acquitted. On a reference of the Attorney General, it was found by the House of Lords, following the *Sang* principle, that the evidence could have been admitted, despite the breach of PACE. It was not found that Art 6 affected the position, since the Court has left the assessment of evidence to the national courts. That stance was affirmed in later decisions.[189]

An argument for exclusion of evidence under s78, taking account of Art 6(1), can be raised where admitting material deriving from informers, although not illegally obtained, might affect the fairness of the trial,[190] particularly where part of the evidence and/or the identity of the informer is not disclosed to the defence.[191] The rules on disclosure under the Criminal Procedure and Investigations Act 1996 create a regime that allows sensitive material to be withheld by the prosecution so that neither the court nor the defence is aware of its existence. Where this has occurred, argument for exclusion of the material from evidence based on Art 6 demands could be raised at first instance or on appeal, relying on the general requirements of fairness under Art 6(1) and on the 'equality of arms' principle.[192]

This current interpretation of s 78 of PACE[193] means that improperly obtained non-confession evidence will rarely be excluded, whether or not the impropriety also amounted to a breach of a Convention right. In other words, the admission of evidence

---

187 [1998] 2 Cr App R 79.

188 [2001] 2 WLR 56.

189 See *Button* [2005] Crim LR 571. See further Ormerod, D, 'Trial remedies for Art 8 breaches?' [2003] Crim LR 61.

190 For detailed discussion see Justice, *Under Surveillance: Covert Policing and Human Rights Standards*, 1998, Chapter 2, especially pp 37–51, and Chapter 3, especially pp 70–74.

191 E.g., the evidence might be tainted owing to the motivation of the informer. In *Windisch v Austria* [1990] 13 EHRR 281 the Court said: 'the Convention does not preclude reliance, at the investigation stage, on sources such as anonymous informants. However, the subsequent use of their statements by the trial court to found a conviction is another matter.' But see *Edwards v UK* (1992) 15 EHRR 417 (it was found that the hearing in the CA remedied the failure of disclosure). These issues were, however, raised successfully under Art 6 in *Rowe and Davis v UK* (2000) 30 EHRR 1.

192 In *Jespers v Belgium*, Appl No 8403/78, 27 DR 61, the Commission found that under Art 6(3), the accused has the right 'to have at his disposal . . . all relevant elements that have been or could have been collected by the relevant authorities'.

193 See *Chalkley* [1998] 2 All ER 155; *Khan* [1997] AC 558 and *Shannon* [2001] 1 WLR 51.

in such circumstances need not be found to amount to a breach of Art 6. It may be said that the interpretation of s 78, post-HRA, continues to adhere to the crime control values implicit in the reliability principle, and allows a balance to be struck under s 78 between the interests of the defence, the victim and society. The domestic decision in *Khan* may be consistent with certain of the decisions on evidence obtained in breach of the interviewing or identification rules since, in such instances, it may be said that the evidence is unreliable.[194] However, *Khan* is not consistent with the decisions on excluding apparently reliable but improperly obtained confession evidence.

Thus, it seems that improperly obtained non-confession evidence will continue to be admissible subject to a narrow discretion to exclude it. This stance seems to afford encouragement to police officers to disregard suspects' rights in the pursuit of such evidence and amounts to a declaration by the courts that a conviction may be based on evidence that would not be before a court had police officers not acted unlawfully. In due process terms, a principled justification for creating a distinction between improperly obtained, but probably reliable, confession evidence and improperly obtained physical evidence is not apparent. Despite some judicial dissent including, for example, that of Loucaides J in *Khan*, the due process argument, to the effect that certain types of impropriety should lead almost automatically to exclusion of the evidence affected by them, has so far been rejected.

Evidence obtained by entrapment or other deceptions[195]

A stay of proceedings is the preferred remedy in respect of evidence obtained by entrapment rather than exclusion of evidence, and a stay is unlikely because the courts have set the bar for success so high.[196] As indicated, *Sang*[197] stated the general rule that improperly obtained evidence other than 'involuntary' confessions is admissible in a criminal trial subject to a narrow discretion to exclude it. The fact that the police have acted as agents provocateurs, entrapping the defendant into a crime he would not otherwise have committed, was not found in *Sang* to mean that the evidence gained thereby should be excluded. The position as regards tricks or undercover work by police that still prevails was stated by the Court of Appeal in *Smurthwaite*.[198] The mere fact that the evidence has been obtained in the course of an undercover operation, of necessity involving deceit, does not of itself require a judge to exclude it. Everything will depend on the particular circumstances in question. For example, how active or passive was the officer's role in obtaining the evidence? What is the nature of the evidence and is it unassailable? If the officer's role is active, the evidence will be viewed as having been obtained by entrapment or by an agent provocateur and will probably be excluded. *Smurthwaite* suggests

194 See the comments of the Court of Appeal in *Bray* (1998) 31 July, unreported, to the effect that where the impropriety does not affect the quality of the evidence, it should be admitted.
195 For discussion, see Sharpe [1994] Crim LR 793; Robertson, Crim LR 805; Heydon [1980] Crim LR 129; Birch, D 'Excluding Evidence from Entrapment: What is a "Fair Cop"?' (1994) 47 *Current Legal Problems* 73; Bradley, CM, *The Failure of the Criminal Procedure Revolution*, 1993, University of Pennsylvania Press; Choo, A L-T, *Abuse of Process and Judicial Stays of Criminal Proceedings*.
196 *R v Loosely* [2001] UKHL 53.
197 [1980] AC 402; [1979] All ER 1222, HL.
198 [1994] All ER 898; (1994) 98 Cr App R 437, CA.

that the discretion to exclude 'unfair' evidence is of a somewhat wider scope than was indicated in *Sang*.

However, in the majority of cases, evidence obtained by a deception has been admitted,[199] but where the deception 'creates' the evidence and it is not possible to say that the defendant has applied himself to the ruse, the courts will tend to exclude it.[200] In *Williams and O'Hare v DPP*,[201] police officers set up a 'virtue-testing' operation in order to see who might succumb to temptation. An insecure vehicle apparently loaded with cigarettes was left in a high crime area in order to catch would-be thieves. The resultant evidence was not excluded, since it was not found that it had been obtained by means of entrapment. The stance taken in *Smurthwaite* was confirmed by the Court of Appeal in *Shannon*,[202] although the Court took, it is suggested, a narrower view of practices amounting to entrapment. Reporters rather than undercover officers carried out a 'sting' operation in which evidence of drug dealing was obtained. Although it was arguable that the accused had, to an extent, been enticed into incriminating himself, the Court found that the evidence thereby gained could rightly be viewed as admissible.

In *Mason*,[203] the defendant had been tricked into confessing to damaging his neighbour's car by the police, who had falsely informed him and his solicitor that his fingerprints had been found on incriminating evidence. The Court of Appeal held that the confession should have been excluded under s 78: the trial judge had erred in omitting to take into account the deception practised on D's solicitor. The court appeared to view the deliberate deception practised by the police as the most significant factor without making it clear why the trial would be rendered unfair by admission of the confession gained thereby. It might have been better to have shown explicitly that the confession should be excluded on the basis that the police had acted improperly in deceiving the solicitor; the deception of the solicitor had resulted in receipt of the confession and the failure to exclude it meant that the court of first instance had, in effect, condoned the impropriety involved.

In *Christou*,[204] undercover police set up a jeweller's shop purporting to be willing to deal in stolen property and transactions with customers were recorded by means of recording equipment hidden in the shop. The police officers engaged in conversation with the defendants who came to sell recently stolen jewellery and asked them questions. They also asked the defendants to sign receipts for the jewellery. The defendants were convicted of handling stolen goods and appealed on the basis that all the evidence against them gained through the undercover operation should have been excluded either

---

199 See, e.g., *Maclean and Kosten* [1993] Crim LR 687; *Gill and Ranuana* [1991] Crim LR 358; *Edwards* [1991] Crim LR 45, CA.

200 See *Colin Stagg* (1994) unreported, but see news items in the *Guardian*, 15 September 1994, and *The Independent*, 15 September 1994; feature in *The Independent on Sunday*, 18 September 1994, p 16; see recent discussion: Cohen, N, *Observer*, 25 June 2006; *H* [1987] Crim LR 47.

201 [1993] Crim LR 775.

202 [2001] 1 WLR 51.

203 [1987] Crim LR 119; [1987] 3 All ER 481, CA; see also *Woodall and Others* [1989] Crim LR 288 in which the 'trick' consisted of allowing the detainee to think that an off-the-record interview could take place in the police station.

204 [1992] QB 979; [1992] 4 All ER 559, CA. See also *Williams and O'Hare v DPP* [1993] Crim LR 775; *Smurthwaite* [1994] 1 All ER 898, CA.

at common law under the principles enunciated in *Sang*[205] or under s 78 as obtained by deception: they would not have entered the shop had they known its true nature. This submission was rejected on the basis that the appellants had not been tricked, but had 'voluntarily applied themselves to the trick'; although specific deception had occurred, such as the request to sign the receipts, that was to be treated as part of the general deceit concerning the dishonest jeweller's shop. Therefore, the trick had not resulted in unfairness. The test for unfairness was found to be the same at common law and under s 78.

It was also submitted that the conversations were an interview within the purview of Code of Practice C; the provisions applying to interviews should, therefore, have been followed. This submission was rejected on the basis that the code provisions were intended to apply only where police officer and suspect were on an unequal footing because the officer was perceived to be in a position of authority. However, this was not to be taken as encouragement to officers to use undercover operations as a method of circumventing the code provisions. In saying this, the court clearly recognised the danger that this ruling might encourage plain clothes police officers to operate secretly using hidden tape recorders to tape admissions, in preference to arresting openly and administering a caution. However, their remarks left open the possibility that such action, if cleverly enough disguised as a genuinely necessary undercover operation, could lead to circumvention of Code C and consequent erosion of the privilege against self-incrimination.

In *Bryce*,[206] the Court of Appeal was clearly fully alive to this danger. An undercover police officer posed as the buyer of a stolen car and, in conversation with the appellant, asked him questions designed to show that the car in question was stolen. The appellant allegedly gave incriminating replies. He was then arrested, refused to comment during the tape-recorded interview, but allegedly made further admissions after the tape recorder had been turned off. He appealed against conviction on the ground that the evidence of the conversations and the interview was inadmissible under s 78. On the issue as to the admissibility of the conversation with the undercover officer, it was determined that the case differed from that of *Christou* on the following grounds: first, the questions asked went directly to the issue of dishonesty and were not necessary to the undercover operation; secondly, the possibility of concoction arose, whereas in *Christou* the conversations were taped. As to the unrecorded interview, the possibility of concoction clearly arose, owing to the suspicious willingness of the appellant to make admissions after refusing to do so during the recorded interview. Therefore, the judge at trial should have exercised discretion to exclude both the conversation and the unrecorded interview. Difficulty will arise after these two cases where it appears possible that a purported undercover operation has been used to circumvent the provisions of Code C, especially the need to caution, but the possibility of concoction does not arise, owing to the use of a hidden tape recorder. A court may have to draw a very fine line between questions asked going directly to the issue of guilt and those touching obliquely on it.

The common theme running through the cases considered is the use of a deception of one sort or another. The courts have had to draw fine lines between degrees of

---

205 [1980] AC 402; [1979] 2 All ER 1222, HL.
206 [1992] 4 All ER 567; (1992) Cr App R 230; (1992) 142 NLJ 1161, CA.

deception in determining whether or not admission of the evidence obtained would render the trial unfair. There is a judicial recognition that undercover operation are particularly useful for obtaining evidence. A rather different stance is taken, as indicated above, towards instances of secret recording in which no positive deception occurs, those in which it may be said that the role of the police is confined only to recording a conversation that would have taken place in any event. In such instances, it cannot be said that the police deception is instrumental in obtaining the evidence except in the hypothetical sense: had the defendant applied his mind to the possibility of secret recording, he might not have made the admissions in question. Passive secret recording may thus be contrasted with instances in which the police, or someone acting on their behalf, have created a situation that makes it likely that admissions will be made where otherwise they would not have been. This distinction may have led the courts to accept evidence derived from secret recordings[207] (except in the case of telephone tapping, where special rules apply[208]) more readily than evidence deriving from a 'positive' deception, since, in comparison with other forms of deception, secret recording seems to be at the lower end of the scale. Moreover, although evidence obtained from secret recordings may have the same inculpatory effect as a confession made in police custody, the courts seem to view the two methods of obtaining admissions differently. The tendency, which reflects the reliability principle, is to view secretly recorded evidence as unaffected by the manner of its acquisition, unlike admissions made to the police in an interview conducted in breach of PACE. However, although use of secret recording may be regarded as less improper than the use of a positive deception, it may involve other forms of impropriety. Thus, in focusing only or mainly on the reliability of evidence obtained, the courts have demonstrated a clear preference for crime control over due process.

As discussed above, *Teixeira de Castro v Portugal*,[209] since affirmed on numerous occasions, laid down quite a strict test in relation to evidence obtained by entrapment. Where there had been enticement by undercover officers to supply drugs, the applicant was found to have been 'definitively deprived of a fair trial'.[210] The case could be distinguished from *Ludi v Switzerland*,[211] in which no breach of Art 6 was found where a police officer had posed as a buyer in a drug deal that was already under way. The Court, therefore, did not find that undercover work of this type would inevitably affect the fairness of the trial. The test was whether the defendant could be said to be 'predisposed' to commit the offence in question. If so, unfairness would not be established. This test arguably differs slightly from the current one under UK law. As indicated above, if undercover officers give the defendant an *opportunity* to commit the offence

---

207 See, e.g., *Shaukat Ali* (1991) *The Times*, 19 February; *Chief Constable of West Yorkshire Police ex p Govell* (1994) transcript from LEXIS; *Effick* (1992) 95 Cr App R 427, CA; [1994] 3 All ER 458, HL; *Roberts* (1997) 1 Cr App R 217.

208 See *Preston* [1993] 4 All ER 638; (1994) 98 Cr App R 405, HL. See now the scheme under RIPA 2000, s 17; discussed in Chapter 11, p 817.

209 (1998) 28 EHHR 101; [1998] Crim LR 751. See also *Van Mechelen v Netherlands* (1998) 25 EHRR 647; the findings of the Commission and Court in *Rowe and Davis* (2000) 30 EHRR 1; *Condron v UK* (2001) 31 EHRR 1.

210 *Ibid*, para 39.

211 (1993) 15 EHRR 173.

where it appears that he would have committed it had the opportunity been offered by someone else, that is not entrapment; but it will amount to entrapment if they impliedly persuade him into it or otherwise can be said to instigate it. It is suggested that while *Smurthwaite*[212] is probably in harmony with the test as laid down by the Court in *Teixeira, Williams and O'Hare v DPP* is not, since it was not certain that the particular offences in question would have been committed without the intervention of those conducting the 'sting'.

However, the first domestic decision to apply *Teixeira, Nottingham CC v Mohammed Amin*,[213] gave it a restrictive interpretation in distinguishing it on somewhat narrow grounds. The respondent, who was driving an unlicensed motor vehicle, responded to a flagging down by two constables posing as members of the public; he took them to their destination, where the fare was paid over. He contended that the constables had not confined themselves to passive investigation but had incited him to commit the offence, thereby rendering the proceedings as a whole unfair. Lord Bingham found that he had not been pressured or incited into committing an offence. The basis on which it was found that flagging him down – a positive action – was not incitement to commit the offence is, it is suggested, unclear. The respondent had turned off his light, thereby indicating that he was not for hire. Similarly, in *Shannon*,[214] the Court of Appeal was unwilling to characterise the behaviour of the reporters as being that of *agents provocateurs*. But it was also found that even if their behaviour had crossed the borderline into that of an agent provocateur, it would not have been viewed as right to disturb the discretion of the judge to admit the evidence.[215] This stance was confirmed in *R v Loosely; AG's Reference (No 3 of 2000)*[216] in which, on facts bearing quite a strong resemblance to those of *Teixeira*, it was found that the judge should not have stayed the trial, applying *Teixeira*, on the basis that the defendant had been encouraged to commit the offence in question by the undercover officers. Instead, it was found that the fact of enticement to commit the offence was not enough: a number of questions should have been asked concerning the defendant's freedom of choice and the extent to which he had been pressured into supplying drugs. As to Loosely, it was found that on the facts the police officers had not instigated the offence; they had provided the opportunity for it to occur; therefore it had not been necessary to exclude the resulting evidence under s78. The House of Lords also said:

> The question raised by *Attorney General's Reference No 3 of 2000* is whether, in a case involving the commission of an offence by an accused at the instigation of undercover police officers, the judicial discretion conferred by section 78 of the Police and Criminal Evidence Act 1984 or the court's power to stay proceedings as an abuse of the court has been modified by article 6 of the European Convention of Human Rights and the jurisprudence of the European Court of Human Rights. I would answer that question in the negative. I do not discern any appreciable

212 [1994] 1 All ER 898.
213 [2000] 1 WLR 1071; [2000] Crim LR 174.
214 [2001] 1 WLR 51.
215 *Ibid*, p 73, para 50.
216 [2001] UKHL 53.

difference between the requirements of article 6, or the Strasbourg jurisprudence on article 6, and English law as it has developed in recent years.[217]

Thus, the key question appears to be whether the courts are prepared to express disapproval of certain evidence-gathering techniques by excluding the evidence in question, as *Teixeira* arguably appears to require. In *Shannon*, the Court of Appeal appeared to be determined to view *Teixeira* as an abuse of process case rather than as applicable to exclusion of evidence, on the basis that to find otherwise would create a conflict with the finding of the Court in *Schenk*.[218] On this basis, the courts are able to disregard possible conflicts between the domestic basis for excluding evidence obtained by *agent provocateurs* and the Strasbourg basis, as expressed in *Teixeira*. It is suggested that determination to retain and maximise judicial discretion, allowing for the pursuit of crime control aims untrammelled by due process constraints imported from Strasbourg, provides the true reason for taking this view of *Teixeira*.

Section 82(3): the common law discretion

Section 82(3) provides:

> Nothing in this part of the Act shall prejudice any power of a court to exclude evidence (whether by preventing questions from being put or otherwise) at its discretion.

This provision presumably preserves the whole of the common law discretion to exclude evidence, thanks to inclusion in it of the words 'or otherwise'. In practice, its role as regards exclusion of evidence is insignificant, owing to the width of s 78. However, a distinct function for s 82(3) was suggested in *Sat-Bhambra*;[219] it was held that ss 76 and 78 only operate before the evidence is led before the jury, but that s 82(3) can be invoked after that point. Similarly, Zander[220] has argued that the common law discretion to exclude evidence is covered by both s 78 and s 82(3). Thus at present, s 82(3) may have a significant role to play only in preserving the judicial function of the judge in protecting witnesses or asking the jury to disregard evidence. The judge can at any point direct the jury to disregard evidence that has already been admitted and that may be unreliable.

In *O'Leary*,[221] May LJ expressed the view that s 82(3) rather than s 78 preserves the common law discretion to exclude unreliable evidence (presumably in circumstances falling outside s 76(2)(b)). However, it is hard to see how to separate the questions of the admissibility of unreliable evidence and of unfairness at the trial. Admission of unreliable evidence will always affect the trial. In *Parris*,[222] evidence that may have

---

217   At para 30.
218   (1988) 13 EHRR 242.
219   (1988) JP Rep 365; (1988) Cr App R 55.
220   Zander, *op cit*, fn 1 2nd edn, p 210. Case law has not identified a distinction between the functions of the two sections (see, e.g., *Christou* [1992] 4 All ER 559).
221   [1988] Crim LR 827, CA.
222   (1989) 9 Cr App R 68, CA.

been fabricated by the police was excluded under s 78, not s 82(3). It appears likely that the established practice of relying on s 78 will continue as a means of excluding unreliable evidence where s 76(2)(b) cannot be invoked.

Mentally handicapped defendants: special rules

As noted above, the confession of a suspect who is mentally disordered or of low intelligence may be rendered inadmissible under s 76(2)(b) if the interrogation is not conducted with particular propriety. However, special rules will apply in the case of some mentally handicapped defendants. The confession of a mentally retarded defendant must be treated with particular caution. Under s 77, in such an instance, if the confession was not made in the presence of an independent person and if the case depends largely on the confession, the jury must be warned to exercise particular caution before convicting.

In some such instances, s 77 need not be invoked because the judge should withdraw the case from the jury. In *McKenzie*[223] the appellant, who was of subnormal intelligence and had sexual problems, was arrested and questioned about arson offences and about the killing of two elderly women. He made detailed admissions as to the arson offences and the two killings in a series of interviews. He also admitted to ten other killings that he had not committed. He appealed against his conviction for manslaughter and arson, and it was held on appeal that where the prosecution case depends wholly on confession evidence, the defendant is significantly mentally handicapped and the confessions are unconvincing, the judge should withdraw the case from the jury. When these three tests were applied in the instant case in respect of the confessions to the killings, it was found that they were satisfied, the third largely by the doubt cast on the appellant's credibility owing to his confessions to killings he could not have committed. However, the first test was not satisfied in respect of the convictions for arson. Those convictions, it was found, could therefore stand, but those for manslaughter were quashed. These rules are clearly of value as a means of affording protection to a group of persons who are least able to withstand pressure from the police and most likely to make a false confession. However, it is suggested that the second test could usefully be broadened so that it includes all those suffering from significant mental impairment at the time when the offences took place.

Conclusions: moving beyond the models of due process and crime control

It was argued in the introduction to this chapter that a more developed conception of criminal justice would take into account the interests of victims as well as the requirements of fairness to the accused. The issues of exclusion of evidence and of staying the proceedings provide a forum for considering what such a more developed conception might mean. It can be argued that where evidence which is reliable is crucial to the case, the ECHR rights of the victim should be taken into account in making a determination as to its admission or exclusion. Indeed, it is arguable that Lord Steyn's

223 [1993] 1 WLR 453; (1992) 142 NLJ 1162, CA.

triangulation of rights – taking account of the interests of the accused, the victim, and society – requires this,[224] and such triangulation has also been recognised recently at Strasbourg.[225] If, for example, in a rape case a guilty accused walks free from court, the victim's life may be profoundly disrupted owing to psychological disturbance, fear, and physical constraints, such as feeling forced to move to a different area. She is likely to be profoundly affected in the free ordering of her life by the knowledge that the rapist is at large. These experiences may occur in any event, but there is a large body of evidence to the effect that the victim's recovery is affected by the conviction of the attacker,[226] while her physical security at the point at which she is psychologically most vulnerable will be affected by the fact that he has been imprisoned. Thus, it is argued that a developed conception of criminal justice allows such considerations to be taken into account under Art 6, bearing in mind victims' interests under Arts 8, 14 and 3.

Similar considerations apply in respect of the victims of many offences. The victim of a serious violent offence may be said to suffer a violation of his or her right to security of the person and possibly to privacy and freedom of movement if an offender is acquitted, not on the basis of doubts about his or her guilt, but as a result of police impropriety. The victim of a racial attack, or the family of the victim, may experience a similar restriction. Article 2 might also be engaged. To take an extreme example: if, in the case of a trial for attempted murder, a court excluded, owing to a serious breach of Art 8, tape-recorded evidence linking a defendant with a history of domestic violence to the attempted murder of his wife, the possibility of her subsequent murder could be viewed as engaging the duty of the court under s 6 of the HRA to abide by Art 2.[227]

Such arguments clearly look like crime-control arguments and they may well lead to the same outcome. However, victim-orientated arguments should not merely be co-opted by advocates of crime control.[228] The difference is that such arguments may be viewed as based on principle, while crime-control arguments are purely consequentialist. While the crime control model would not allow for a nuanced, proportionate approach to exclusion of evidence since it would merely ask whether it was reliable, the approach that takes account of the victims' interests can be more nuanced since in some instances, the victims' interests could not be said to be engaged. Clearly, the court has a duty to uphold standards of criminal justice[229] but strands of Convention jurisprudence are emerging that may allow for those interests to be taken into account in adoption of a nuanced approach.[230] The Convention provides a growing recognition of victims' rights.[231] In particular, there is now a significant body of jurisprudence recognising

---

224 See *R v A (No2)* [2002] 1 AC 45, 65.

225 See *Al-Khawaja and Tahery v UK* [2011] ECHR 26766/05, [118].

226 See, e.g., Lees, S, *Ruling Passions, Sexual Violence, Reputation and the Law*, 1997, Open University Press; *Sexual Violence: The Reality for Women*, 1999, The Women's Press.

227 See *Osman v UK* (2000) 29 EHRR 245, discussed in Chapter 2, pp 59 and 60.

228 For discussion, see Whitty, N, Murphy, T and Livingstone, S, *Civil Liberties Law*, 2000, p 194; Young, J, *The Exclusive Society: Social Exclusion, Crime and Difference in Late Modernity*, 1999, Sage.

229 See Fenwick, H, 'Procedural rights of victims of crime: public or private ordering of the criminal justice process?' (1997) 60 MLR 317–33.

230 See *Gäfgen v Germany* [2010] ECHR 22978/05, [163] and [175].

231 See *X and Y v Netherlands* (1985) 8 EHRR 235.

rights of victims and victims' families within the criminal justice system where the state is the 'attacker'.[232] Thus, there is a case for arguing, under the HRA, that the impact of a decision to exclude evidence or stay the proceedings should be considered from a perspective that is not bounded by Art 6 concerns alone.

While due process demands that improperly obtained evidence should be excluded, that the police officers involved should be disciplined or prosecuted, and, where appropriate, that compensation should be available, it is unclear that it demands, in principle, that a person who is factually guilty of an offence should be acquitted. If evidence is excluded and, as a result, the burden of proof cannot be discharged, acquittal must clearly follow. But methods of escaping from the conflicts of interest indicated inherent in such exclusion should be sought. Acquittals of the factually guilty uphold the integrity of the criminal justice system since they demonstrate a refusal of the courts to associate themselves with a fundamental breach of rights, but they profoundly fail to address the interests of victims, also recognised at Strasbourg, their relatives, and the general societal interest in the prevention of crime. Moreover, although exclusion of evidence may have symbolic value in terms of integrity, it has not been viewed at Strasbourg as providing an effective remedy for breach of a Convention right,[233] and it clearly can have no impact on the overwhelming majority of cases in which the defendant pleads guilty. Given that, increasingly, the police know that the case is unlikely to come to trial, the deterrent effect of exclusion, such as it is, may be diminishing. Even in cases that do come to trial, exclusion of evidence can have no impact where there is other evidence which can support the conviction. Stays for abuse of process are rarely used and arguably their use is arbitrary; therefore, they are unlikely to have a significant impact on police practice.

These arguments strengthen the case for further, more radical reform of the police complaints and disciplinary system and of CPS decision-making, since so doing would tend to discourage illegality and impropriety and enhance levels of adherence to the PACE rules, including the code provisions. Arguments for exclusion of evidence on the basis of police impropriety might be raised less frequently. There is a further pragmatic reason for adopting this approach. The judges have made it clear that despite the inception of the HRA, they are wedded to the common law tradition of admitting evidence even if it has been obtained improperly. If anything, decisions such as *Forbes* and *Shannon* suggest that their determination to adhere to this tradition has been *strengthened* by the inception of the HRA. Possibly, this is another example of the common law resisting or subsuming the influence of the ECHR. Maintenance of judicial discretion to react to the facts of particular cases remains the overwhelming priority and, in furtherance of this aim, the requirements of Art 6 have been minimised. Given that this clear pattern has emerged, remedies must be sought elsewhere, while at the same time failures of police accountability should be used to press for organisational reforms. The efficacy of such other remedies is considered briefly below.

---

232 *Kaya v Turkey* (1998-I) ECtHR 297; *Akdivar v Turkey* (1997) 23 EHRR 143; *Mentes v Turkey* (1997) 27 EHRR 595; *Gulec v Turkey* (1999) 28 EHRR 121; *Cetin v Turkey* (unreported); *Tekin v Turkey* (2001) 31 EHRR 4.
233 *Khan v UK* (2000) 8 BHRC 310, paras 44–47.

4 Civil actions against the police[234]

Introduction

Traditionally, if a citizen is unlawfully detained by state agents he or she could rely on the ancient writ of habeas corpus. However, habeus corpus has little application in this context since it does not apply if the right procedure has been followed; it would be hard for the detainee to demonstrate that no reasonable suspicion for the arrest had been present. Further, detentions under PACE are usually of short duration,[235] so there would not be enough time to issue the writ. Detentions under the TA can be longer so a writ could be issued, but the problem of showing that the basis for the arrest and detention was not present still applies. Judicial review actions may be appropriate, including actions under the HRA, as discussed below. But the use of actions in tort has been more frequent, although, as discussed below, there are various obstacles, practical and legal, lying in the path of relying on such actions.

Tort actions

Relevant actions

Tort damages will be available as a result of some breaches of PACE, the TA and other relevant statutes on the basis that certain actions by persons, including, obviously, police officers, interfering in some way with others require a legal basis allowing the action (if certain rules are followed), if they are not to be tortious. If that basis is missing, then obviously tort liability will arise under existing tort actions, such as trespass to the person. As far as the police are concerned such a basis is created by the police powers discussed in Chapters 12 and 13. For example, if a police officer arrests a citizen where no reasonable suspicion arises under s 24 PACE, an action for false imprisonment is – at least in theory – available. A tort remedy for false imprisonment would also be available if the Part IV provisions governing time limits on detention were breached[236] or if a detention review failed to occur for a period of time.[237]

An action for assault and battery would be available if excessive force is used in making an arrest, where it is not warranted by the arrestee's actions. The tort of battery may be available in respect of deaths in custody[238] or in the course of a house search or arrest – and obviously criminal liability could also arise (see below). An example arose in *Ashley v*

---

234 See Clayton, R and Tomlinson, H, *Civil Actions Against the Police*, 3rd edn, 2004, Chapter 14 for examples of damages awards. See also Sanders and Young, *op cit*, fn 1, Chapter 12, Part 3.

235 See Chapter 12, pp 894–96.

236 E.g., *Edwards v Chief Constable of Avon and Somerset* (1992) 9 March, unreported; the plaintiff was detained for 8 hours, 47 minutes following a lawful arrest. The detention was wrongful because it was 'unnecessary'; compensation was awarded.

237 In *Roberts* [1999] 1 WLR 662 the review took place two hours after it should have done. The Court of Appeal found that Roberts had been falsely imprisoned during those two hours even though it was found that, had the review taken place, he would have remained in detention.

238 See J Wadham 'Investigations into deaths in police custody and the Independent Police Complaints Commission' (2004) 4 EHRLR 2004 353–61.

Chief Constable of Sussex.[239] PC Sherwood was part of a group of armed police officers who conducted a drugs raid on James Ashley's house in the early hours of the morning. Sherwood entered Ashley's bedroom, saw Ashley standing naked in the dark, since he had been woken by the noise of the raid, and shot Ashley dead. Sherwood had previously been briefed that Ashley might be dangerous and honestly believed that Ashley was about to kill him. He was then tried for murder, but was acquitted on the ground that he had acted in self-defence, based on an honest belief.[240] Ashley's family then sued the chief constable of Sussex police, claiming firstly that the organisers of the raid had acted negligently in briefing Sherwood that Ashley might be dangerous and, secondly, that Sherwood had committed the tort of battery in shooting Ashley. The chief constable admitted liability as to the first claim, offering to pay Ashley's family all the damages they sought under that head. He applied for the family's second claim under to be struck out on the basis that: (i) Sherwood's honest belief that his life was in danger meant that he did not commit a battery in shooting Ashley; and (ii) given his admission of liability and offer to pay all the damages claimed under the first claim it would be an abuse of process to allow that claim.

As regards the issue of battery the House of Lords held unanimously that Sherwood's belief that Ashley posed a lethal threat to him had to be *reasonable*, not merely honest, to find that he did not commit a tort in shooting Ashley. The majority held on the second issue that it was entirely legitimate for Ashley's family to seek to pursue their second claim in order to have it established publicly that Sherwood had acted unlawfully in killing Ashley. The case is of some interest since it demonstrates that the tests applicable in respect of self-defence in relation to tort are not necessarily the same as those under criminal law; thus the police are in effect held to a higher standard under tort.

Trespass to land or to goods will occur if the statutory provisions providing powers to search premises or seize goods are not followed. Malicious prosecution will be available where police have abused their powers in recommending prosecution to the Crown Prosecution Service. Also, one of the ancient 'malicious process torts' may be available where a malicious search or arrest has occurred, although in fact these actions are extremely rare and their continued existence is in doubt.[241] Such actions may not be brought because a claim of false imprisonment is preferred, but there is a distinction between malicious process torts and false imprisonment in that in the former case, but not the latter, all the proper procedural formalities will have been carried out. Actions for malicious prosecution are quite common, but the plaintiff carries quite a heavy burden in the need to prove that there was no reasonable or probable cause for the prosecution.[242] It may be that if the prosecution is brought on competent legal advice, this action will fail, but this is unclear.[243]

Actions in tort and police interviewing

Almost the whole of the interviewing scheme is contained mainly in Codes C, E and H rather than in PACE or the TA. Tortious remedies are irrelevant to breaches of the

---

239 [2008] UKHL 25; [2008] 1 AC 962 (HL).
240 Reliance was placed on *R v Williams (Gladstone)* [1987] 3 All ER 411.
241 See Clayton, R and Tomlinson, H, *Civil Actions Against the Police*, 1st edn, 1987, p 284. For discussion, see Winfield, *History of Conspiracy and Abuse of Legal Process*, 1921.
242 See *Glinskie v McIver* [1962] AC 726.
243 *Abbott v Refuge Assurance Co Ltd* [1962] 1 QB 632.

codes. Section 67(10) of PACE provides that no civil or criminal liability arises from a breach of the codes of practice. The same is true of the TA codes under Sched 12, para 6 to the TA. This lack of a remedy also extends to some statutory provisions, in particular the most significant statutory interviewing provision, the entitlement to legal advice, arising under both PACE and the TA. There is no tort of denial of access to legal advice, although a remedy – which could be available within the trial process – would usually be required under the HRA for such denial, following *Salduz*.[244] It might have been expected that an action for false imprisonment might lie where gross breaches of the questioning provisions had taken place, such as interviewing a person unlawfully held incommunicado: a detention in itself lawful might thereby be rendered unlawful. However, although the ruling in *Middleweek v Chief Constable of Merseyside*[245] gave some encouragement to such argument, it now seems to be ruled out by the decision in *Weldon v Home Office*[246] in the context of lawful detention in a prison.

Permission to bring claims under s 329 of the Criminal Justice Act 2003

A possible obstacle to bringing civil actions against the police is created by s 329 of the Criminal Justice Act 2003. Section 329 provides that if the claimant has been convicted of an imprisonable offence. . . 'committed on the same occasion as that on which the act is alleged to have been done', his action shall not proceed without judicial leave. Leave shall be given only in one or other of two situations: first, where there is evidence suggesting that the defendant did not believe his act of injuring the claimant was necessary to stop the crime or catch the criminal;[247] or secondly, where there is evidence suggesting that 'the defendant's act was grossly disproportionate'. This provision was introduced to protect householders who attack burglars, but obviously it also applies to the police; it has a particular application to police officers when using force to effect an arrest, so long as later on the arrestee is convicted of an imprisonable offence. Under PACE 1984 police officer may use 'reasonable force'[248] in the exercise of their powers, including arrest. But the term 'grossly disproportionate' appears to denote use of greater force. Thus in certain circumstances if the police use excessive force in arresting (and the condition as regards an imprisonable offence is later satisfied), but the evidence does not demonstrate that the force used was 'grossly disproportionate', they could be protected from a civil action, even if the force used was unreasonable, since permission to bring the action might be refused. In *Buike v Chief Constable of West Yorkshire*[249] the Court of Appeal held that at the permission application the claimant was required to show that the claim had a real prospect of success and in particular that there was a real prospect of the Court at trial concluding either that the reasonable belief as to

---

244 See p 926.
245 [1992] AC 179; [1990] 3 WLR 481.
246 [1991] WLR 340, CA.
247 Under s 329(5) the defendant did the act only because – (a) he believed that the claimant – (ii) was in the course of committing an offence, or (iii) had committed an offence immediately beforehand; and (b) he believed that the act was necessary to – (i) defend himself or another person, (ii) protect or recover property, (iii) prevent the commission or continuation of an offence.
248 See Chapter 12, p 893.
249 [2009] EWCA Civ 971.

committing an offence requirement was not met or that the defendant's conduct was grossly disproportionate.

The potentially difficult position certain claimants against the police were placed in by s 329 was ameliorated to an extent by the Court of Appeal in *Adorian v Commissioner of Police of the Metropolis*.[250] The claimant was bringing a civil action in respect of an arrest using a high degree of force that had left him severely injured (see further below). He was later charged with obstructing the police, and received a conditional discharge. He issued his claim just before the three-year limitation period ran out, but it was met with an application to strike it out pursuant to s 329 of the Criminal Justice Act 2003. The Police Commissioner argued firstly that there was 'no evidence' that the force used by his officers arresting Adorian was 'grossly disproportionate'. Secondly, he argued that in any event the requirement for prior leave under s 329 was mandatory, not directory. So the court could not give retrospective leave and Adorian should have instituted proceedings within the limitation period.

The Court of Appeal rejected both arguments, holding that the leave requirement under s 329 is merely directory, and therefore if a claimant has failed to get leave before issuing a claim, a court could grant it retrospectively. The Court also found that there was evidence of use of grossly disproportionate force. Thus, claimants seeking to bring civil actions against the police in similar circumstances who have not sought leave can have it granted retrospectively. But it is still necessary as one alternative to provide evidence either that the police had no belief in the necessity of using force to prevent commission of an offence or to apprehend the person who had committed an offence, which would be likely to prove very difficult in most circumstances. Or evidence must be available that the force used was 'grossly disproportionate', not just 'unreasonable'. That may also be difficult where no witnesses to the arrest are available, and there is no CCTV footage of the incident. Even if permission is given a court may accept that the force used was not unreasonable. In the event, it was later found in Adorian's case that the degree of force applied by the officers was reasonable, despite the severity of his injuries. Given that the claimant had resisted arrest, the higher degree of force used was found to be justified.[251]

The HRA and civil liability

Under ss 6, 7 and 8 HRA, the police can attract liability if in the exercise of discretionary powers, whether or not statute-based, they breach a Convention right. As Chapter 4 demonstrated, ss 6, 7 and 8 of the HRA require the courts to offer a remedy where a public authority violates the Convention rights,[252] unless in so doing it is acting in accordance with incompatible legislation.[253] As Chapters 12 and 13 indicated, Arts 3, 5, 8 and 14 ECHR potentially cover certain pre-trial rights of suspects. Tortious liability arises and damages can be awarded under s 8 of the HRA if one or more of these articles is found to have been breached in respect of police treatment of suspects. As indicated,

---

250 [2009] EWCA Civ 18; [2009] 1 WLR 1859.
251 High Court (Queen's Bench Division) 23 August 2011.
252 Sections 6(1), 7 and 8.
253 Section 6(2).

some custodial treatment in breach of these articles is already tortious under domestic law, and civil actions against the police have provided a fairly significant means of creating some police accountability.[254] This possibility is clearly of particular significance where domestic law currently fails to provide a tortious remedy in respect of the maltreatment of detainees. But if no pre-HRA tortious liability would arise in respect of a particular exercise of police power, despite the lack of legal authority for its exercise, then the claimant could rely on s 6 HRA and the relevant right against the police. In that way the police action could be found to be tortious, whereas pre-HRA it would probably have been non-tortious. The courts have been reluctant to allow parallel claims. Core human rights are to be protected through the HRA and not via a parallel system.[255] Thus where a Convention right covers the same ground as a tort action, the plaintiff may claim a cause of action based on breach of the right, relying on s 7(1)(a) HRA.

If ss 6, 7, 8 are relied on in respect of an alleged breach of the ECHR by police, the ambit of the right understood by reference to the jurisprudence and the width of any exceptions to it will be determinative; Strasbourg and domestic case law will be taken into account. This is in essence a question of proportionality in relation to Art 8, or a question of the content and requirements of the right in relation to Arts 2, 3, 5 and 6.[256] As a result of this possibility, the domestic courts may eventually have to reconsider their current approach to conditions of detention in terms of tortious liability. Prior to the inception of the HRA, so long as existing torts or offences, such as assault, were not committed by police, it followed from the findings in *Weldon v Home Office*[257] that no means of redress in respect of adverse conditions, other than a complaint, was available. The possible creation of liability[258] under the ECHR by means of reliance on the guarantee under Art 8 fills a gap in domestic law[259] in relation to conditions of detention. Such a course would not necessarily involve departing from the findings in *Weldon v Home Office*, since the liability would be for breach of a Convention right under s 6, using s 7(1)(a) of the HRA, not for false imprisonment. In the Scottish case of *Napier v Scottish Ministers*[260] the petitioner sought judicial review on the grounds that he was held in conditions inside HMP Barlinie that contravened Art 3 ECHR. Napier recovered damages as a consequence of that treatment since it was found to be degrading.

Damages awards

While the main aim of the award of damages in these circumstances is compensatory such awards may be of particular value owing to the willingness of the courts to accept that exemplary or punitive damages may sometimes be appropriate. Such damages are

---

254 See the Home Affairs Committee First Report 1997–98, *Police Disciplinary and Complaints Procedures* printed 16 December 1997, which noted (para 32) the 'striking' rise in the cost of civil settlements for the Metropolitan Police, from £0.47m in 1991 to £2.69m in 1996. (This figure declined owing to the decision in *Thompson*, [1997] 2 All ER 762.) The Police Action Lawyers Group and the Commission For Racial Equality attributed the rise to disillusionment with the complaints process.

255 *Watkins v Home Office* [2006] UKHL 17, [26], Lord Bingham and [64], Lord Rodger

256 See Chapter 2, p 41 *et seq.*

257 [1990] 3 All ER 672.

258 Under HRA 1998, ss 6 and 7. The HRA does not allow for the creation of new criminal liability.

259 See *Wainwright v HO* [2004] AC 406. (Discussed in Chapter 4, p 205.)

260 (2001) WL 1346975.

awarded to punish the defendant and will be available only in two instances:[261] where there has been 'oppressive, arbitrary or unconstitutional behaviour by the servants of the government' or where the profit accruing to the defendant through his conduct may be greater than the compensation awarded to the plaintiff. Only the first of these two categories will be relevant in actions against the police and, in order that such damages should be available, the term 'servant of the government' has been broadly interpreted to include police officers.[262] In *Ashley v Chief Constable of Sussex*,[263] the House of Lords found that that the principal aim of an award of compensatory damages is to compensate the claimant for loss suffered, but found that there would be no reason in principle why an award of compensatory damages should not also fulfil a vindicatory purpose – to vindicate rights.

The high jury awards of damages in the mid-1990s against the police may have reflected a public perception that the police are insufficiently accountable. For example, in *Hsu v Comr of Metropolitan Police*,[264] the plaintiff won £220,000 damages for assault and wrongful arrest at his home. One of the highest awards was made in *Treadaway v Chief Constable of West Midlands*:[265] £50,000, which included £40,000 exemplary damages, was awarded in respect of a serious assault perpetrated in order to obtain a confession. In *Goswell v Comr of Metropolitan Police*[266] the plaintiff was awarded £120,000 damages for assault, £12,000 for false imprisonment and £170,000 exemplary damages for arbitrary and oppressive behaviour. Mr Goswell, who is black, was waiting in his car when a police officer approached. Goswell complained about the lack of police activity over an arson attack on his home. He was handcuffed to and then struck by the officer; the blow left a permanent scar. Goswell was then arrested for assault and threatening behaviour. He was cleared of these charges and then brought the successful civil action. In *Hsu v Comr of Metropolitan Police*,[267] the plaintiff won £220,000 damages for assault and wrongful arrest at his home. But since the decision of the Court of Appeal in *Thompson*,[268] giving guidance as to the level of the awards, those very high awards have not been replicated.[269]

261 This limitation was imposed by the House of Lords in *Rookes v Barnard* [1964] AC 1129, p 1226. Note that the Law Commission, *Consultation Paper on Punitive Damages*, Consultation No 132, 1993, advocates, in its provisional conclusion, retention of such damages, but that they should be placed on a more principled basis.

262 *Broome v Cassell and Co* [1972] AC 1027, at 1088.

263 [2008] UKHL 25; [2008] 1 AC 962 (HL).

264 [1997] 2 All ER 762.

265 (1994) *The Times*, 25 October.

266 (1996) *The Guardian*, 27 April.

267 [1997] 2 All ER 762.

268 [1997] 2 All ER 762. The court laid down guidelines for the award of damages which took as a starting point a basic award of £500 for the first hour of unlawful detention, with decreasing amounts for subsequent hours. It was found that aggravated damages could be awarded where there were special features of the case, such as oppressive or humiliating conduct at the time of arrest. Such damages would start at around £1,000 but would not normally be more than twice the level of the basic damages. Exemplary damages should only be awarded where aggravated and basic damages together would not appear to provide a sufficient punishment. Exemplary damages would be not less than £5,000, but the total figure awarded as exemplary damages would not be expected to amount to more than the basic damages multiplied by three. The overall award should not exceed £50,000. In accordance with these guidelines, the award made in *Hsu* was reduced to £50,000.

269 See further Clayton, R and Tomlinson, H, *Civil Actions Against the Police*, 3rd edn, 2004, Chapter 14.

The HRA has not affected the quantum of damages (or the practical problems of suing the police). The level of damages awarded under the HRA is quite low, as discussed in Chapter 4.[270] For example, in *Faulkner, R (on the application of) v Secretary of State for Justice and another*[271] (not a case related to police powers) the Supreme Court gave guidance as to the level of damages that should be awarded under the HRA. The Court reduced one award of damages from £10,000 to £6,500 and, while allowing the other appeal, did not increase the £300 award originally granted.

Conclusions

The value of civil actions against the police in terms of ensuring police accountability is limited for a variety of reasons.[272] The cost factor deters the majority of potential plaintiffs from suing the police, especially now that legal aid is unavailable in most instances, unless the action is under the HRA.[273] Even where a civil action is successful, disciplinary charges are unlikely to be brought against the officers concerned, and there is a strong tendency to settle actions, which means that the police do not admit liability. For example, PC Harwood, discussed below, who allegedly killed Ian Tomlinson during the G20 protest in London in 2009, had previously been involved in an incident in which he allegedly attacked a motorist; the Metropolitan police settled the case out of court, paying compensation.[274]

The tendency to fail to follow a successful civil action with disciplinary proceedings has been justified by the police in the past on the basis of the differing standards of proof: civil claims need only be proved on the balance of probabilities while, until fairly recently, disciplinary charges had to be proved beyond reasonable doubt. That is no longer the case, and therefore disciplinary action might be expected to follow a successful civil action, although there is no statutory requirement that it must do so, even in particularly serious cases. Under the reforms of the complaints system that will arise once the Policing and Crime Bill 2015/16 becomes law, there will still be no statutory requirement that at least formal consideration should be given to the possibility of disciplinary action in that circumstance, even if no complaint is brought; such consideration could have been given by the reformed body about to become the Office for Public Conduct rather than the IPCC (as discussed below).

There is clearly something anomalous about creating a vast, complex statutory or quasi-legislative edifice (PACE, the TA, the CJP, the codes) that governs police powers and suspects' rights, but then failing to provide a remedy, apart from proceeding with a police complaint, if those rights are breached, except where that breach is coterminous with an existing area of tortious liability or where a Convention right applies. The HRA

---

270 See p 208.
271 [2013] UKSC 23.
272 It may be noted that if a civil action against a police officer is successful, he or she will not be personally liable. The Police Act 1964, s 48, provides that a chief constable will be vicariously liable in respect of torts committed by constables under his direction or control in the performance or purported performance of their functions.
273 Legal aid is governed by the Access to Justice Act 1999. Very significant cuts to the legal aid budget have occurred under the Coalition and current Conservative government.
274 See https://www.theguardian.com/uk-news/2013/aug/05/ian-tomlinson-metropolitan-police-statement.

may be having some impact in respect of police accountability since it created for the first time under ss 7(1)(a) and 8 a remedy where Convention rights were breached by the police, whether or not existing tortious liability would arise.[275] But the practical problems considered, and the low level of damages awards under the HRA limit its ability to create accountability. In general, the use of civil actions to create accountability when police officers use excessive force in various situations, including during arrests, is flawed, given the lack of legal aid, and the tendency of police forces to settle out of court, meaning that more general and far-reaching reforms, to, for example, vetting procedures of particular police forces, are not triggered. The system that should be able to deal effectively with police abuse of power and trigger such reforms is the police complaints and disciplinary system, to which this chapter now turns; but, as discussed below, that system also appears to be lacking in efficacy at present, although imminent reforms in 2016 may improve it.

5 Complaints against the police[276]

The independent element in the police complaints and disciplinary system

The police complaints and disciplinary system[277] provides a potential method of seeking to ensure that the police do not use excessive force in effecting arrests or in deploying other powers, do not abuse arrestees, and adhere to the statutory safeguards created by PACE, as amended, and the TA. A reformed system of police complaints was instigated under the Police Reform Act 2002,[278] which came into force in 2004, replacing the previous system under PACE and creating the Independent Police Complaints Commission (IPCC). The IPCC is responsible for overseeing the police complaints system in England and Wales, assessing appeals against complaints decisions and investigating serious matters involving the police, including deaths and serious injuries (DSI) following police contact. A major change programme was implemented in 2013[279] intended to

---

275 See e.g., *Caetano v Commissioner of Police for the Metropolis* [2013] EWHC 375: an application for judicial review succeeded in respect of a decision of the police to issue a caution.

276 See Sanders, A and Young, R, *Criminal Justice*, 4th edn, 2010, Chapter 12. See for background: Maguire, M, 'Complaints against the police: the British experience', in Goldsmith, A (ed), *Complaints Against the Police: A Comparative Study*, 1990, Clarendon; Greaves [1985] Crim LR; Khan (1984) 129 SJ 455; Williams [1985] Crim LR 115; Lustgarten, L, *The Governance of Police*, 1986, pp 139–40. The Runciman Commission considered that the existing arrangements probably do not command public confidence: Cm 2263, p 46; Harrison, J, *Police Misconduct: Legal Remedies*, 1987, Legal Action Group; Triennial Review of the PCA 1991–94, HC 396 (1994–95); Home Affairs Committee Fourth Report, HC 179 (1991–92); House of Commons Home Affairs Select Committee, Police Disciplinary and Complaints Procedure, First Report, HC-258–1 (1998).

277 See further R Stone *Civil Liberties and Human Rights*, 6th edn, 2006, Chapter 4.6.3; Complaints Against the Police: A Framework for a New System – available from the Home Offi ce website: www.homeoffice.gov.uk.

278 See further Stone, R, *Civil Liberties and Human Rights*, 10th edn, 2014, Chapter 4.6.3; Complaints Against the Police: A Framework for a New System – available from the Home Office website: www.homeoffice.gov.uk.

279 Statement to Parliament by the Home Secretary. HC Deb12 February 2013, vol 604, col 714–720; http://www.publications.parliament.uk/pa/cm201213/cmhansrd/cm130212/debtext/130212–0001.htm#13021255000004.

accord the IPCC the funding and capacity to investigate 'all serious and sensitive matters' involving the police, and enabling it to increase the number of cases it investigates,
from opening 109 cases in 2013–14 to 241 in 2014–15. But even taking account of
that change, the 2004 reform of the complaints system did not fully achieve its aim of
creating an independent element in the system which resulted in high quality investigations of certain complaints, so is to be followed in 2016 by a further, potentially quite
far-reaching, reform of the IPCC.

One of the aims of the reform under the 2002 Act was to make investigations more
open, timely, proportionate and fair.[280] Under Sched 3 Police Reform Act 2002, a complaint may be received in the first instance by the chief constable or the Independent
Police Complaints Commission (IPCC). It must then be determined who is the 'appropriate authority' for the purposes of the investigation (Sched 3, para 1). That is normally
the chief constable of the force in question. The chief constable then appoints an officer
to carry out a formal investigation, unless the complaint can be informally resolved.
Therefore, it is fair to say, that an issue of independence arises at the beginning of
the process. Informal resolution can only occur if the complainant consents and the
authority is satisfied that, even if the complaint is proved, no criminal or disciplinary
proceedings would be appropriate (Sched 3, para 6). Furthermore, there can be no local
resolution where the complaint involves an allegation of an infringement of either Arts
2 or 3 ECHR. More serious complaints are referred to the IPCC, as are those where
the complainant is not satisfied with the local police procedure. Where a complaint is
referred to it, the IPCC decides on the procedure (Sched 3, para 15). It can carry out the
investigation itself using its own staff where a complaint is referred to it. That is the key
difference from the previous scheme. It can also supervise or manage the investigation
by the appropriate authority and then receive a report at the end of it. The appropriate
authority can also carry out the investigation on behalf of the IPCC. If it appears once
an investigation has been completed that a criminal offence may have been committed,
the case must be referred to the CPS (Sched 3, para 24).

The key change under the 2002 reformed scheme was that the police were made
for the first time subject to external investigation. However, the IPCC's role in relation
to the investigation – as opposed to the supervision – of complaints remains limited
and the quality of its investigations has frequently been criticised, leading to the current reform of the IPCC discussed below, expected to be in place in late 2016. Many
complaints will never be referred to the IPCC but will remain in the hands of the police
force in question. Although the system contains this independent element, a number
of problems remain, even in relation to those exceptional cases in which independent
investigation by civilian investigators occurs. Institutional factors, including obstruction of the system by the police, and the possibility that civilian investigators will be
affected by police culture, are continuing to hamper the system, while at the same time
the number of complaints made continues to rise.[281] As Sanders and Young have argued,

---

280   Complaints are dealt with under the 2002 Act and Regulations made under it: The Police (Complaints
       and Misconduct) Regulations 2004, SI 2004/643. See for discussion Harrison, J and Cuneen, M, *An
       Independent Police Complaints Commission*, 2000; Goldsmith, A and Faran, S, 'Complaints against
       the police in Canada: a new approach' [1987] Crim LR 615.
281   There were 34,863 cases involving complaints in 2013–14, figures from the Independent Police Com-
       plaints Commission show. The figures show a 15% increase on the previous year – and are the highest

the IPCC is in the same position as the previous body (the PCA) since in general it relies on reports of the facts of a case, compiled by police officers. The police concerned use various techniques to discredit a complainant, constructing the case in a manner that justifies no further action.[282]

An example of the slowness of the system arises related to *Adorian v Commissioner of Police of the Metropolis*.[283] Adorian was arrested very forcibly for disorderly behaviour. It was found at the police station after his arrest that he was badly injured, and he was taken to hospital. There he was found to have very serious and multiple fractures to his leg and hip, due, it appeared to the excessive force used in arresting him. He submitted a complaint about his treatment to the Independent Police Complaints Authority but, after three years, his complaint had not been resolved and appeared to be bogged down in its bureaucracy. The Chapman Review in 2014[284] concluded that the current police disciplinary system is too complex; it found it lacked transparency and independence, with much of the system being managed by police forces themselves.

The IPCC's handling of complaints was also recently criticised by the Court of Appeal which quashed its Report on a particular complaint, in *Chief Constable of West Yorkshire v Independent Police Complaints Commission*.[285] Arguably, the facts and outcome are illustrative of the connections between police complaints and the difficulty of prosecuting the police (see further below on such prosecutions) and possibly of the ineptitude of the IPCC. But it raised quite significant issues as to the role of the IPCC. It does suggest that the IPCC are seeking to take an independent, proactive role but, in this instance, not in an effective manner, due to current statutory constraints on its role. The complaint arose after a police officer, Armstrong, stopped a motorist for alleging exceeding the speed limit; an altercation followed, resulting in Mr Sutcliffe's arrest apparently for a public order offence. During the arrest, PC Armstrong used CS spray and struck the arrestee, Mr Sutcliffe, with his police baton; he was injured by the effects of the spray and suffered an injury to his hand. Mr Sutcliffe's mother made a complaint to the West Yorkshire police as to abuse of authority and of assault; she alleged that he had sprayed her son with CS spray three times, once whilst he was handcuffed. The complaint was referred to the IPCC; a lead and deputy senior investigator of the IPCC commenced an investigation and produced a report that concluded that the complaint was upheld and that there was a case to answer in respect of an alleged 'breach of the standards of professional behaviour'. The report also made clear the investigators' view that Mr Sutcliffe's arrest was unlawful. The case was referred to the CPS for consideration of the prosecution of PC Armstrong for assault but the CPS decided there was insufficient evidence for a realistic prospect of conviction; its view was that the arrest of Mr Sutcliffe was lawful.

---

since the IPCC was established in 2004 (February 2015). A total of 37,105 complaints were recorded during 2014–15. This was a 6% increase compared to 2013/14 and represents a 62% increase since 2004–05.

282 See Sanders and Young *Criminal Justice*, 3rd edn, 2007 at 615.

283 [2009] EWCA Civ 18; [2009] 1 WLR 1859.

284 *An Independent Review of the Police Disciplinary System in England and Wales* C Chapman, October 2014.

285 [2014] EWCA Civ 1367. See also *R (on the application of Allatt) v Chief Constable of Nottinghamshire Police and IPCC* [2011] EWHC 3908 (Admin).

When the IPCC report was disclosed to PC Armstrong and Mrs Sutcliffe the chief constable commenced judicial review proceedings for its quashing on the basis that as the contents of the report exceeded the lawful limits of such a report, the report was unlawful. His complaint that the role of the PCC was purely an investigative one, and to report alleged breaches of the criminal law or police discipline to the CPS or the chief constable, as appropriate. Its function, therefore, he argued, was to decide whether there was a case to answer; it was not also to purport finally to decide the answer to that case. The IPCC submitted that its primary function was to respond to a complaint. Reliance was placed on s 10(1) of the 2002 Act, which it was said regarded the repose of public confidence in the IPCC's role as demanding that complaints were handled with appropriate vigour. The IPCC said the boundary as to the limits of expressing permissible opinion had not been crossed. The Court of Appeal found that the IPCC had exceeded their powers. The Court found that if the investigators' task was to report their opinion as to whether there was a case to answer before another tribunal, it was not their function also to purport to *decide* the very question or questions that were raised by such a case.

While the decision in this instance appears to have been correct, as regards the interpretation of the existing statutory scheme, that the IPCC did not have the power to come to the conclusions it came to, the decision indicates that the current system may not be able to command public confidence. The decision makes it clear that the IPCC's role is usually, having found a case to answer, to refer the case back to the police force in question which then can proceed to a disciplinary hearing. The Court of Appeal appeared to be eager to ensure that the IPCC did not stray into making pronouncements on the merits of the case, and very clearly left it up to the chief officer of police of the force in question to institute proceedings. In general, if it does not institute such a hearing, the IPCC may also direct it to do so, but the hearing is still retained in the hands of the police force in question. The PCC's report need not be disclosed to the complainant.[286] The decision clearly curbs the opinions of the PCC that can be expressed in reports that may lead to disciplinary procedures. The case also indicates that the system is slow and that complaints may get mired in bureaucracy; over a year and a half since the original incident in which Sutcliffe was injured, no prosecution was under way, and no disciplinary procedures had begun.

Lack of full accountability

There are a range of flaws in the police complaints and disciplinary system, which it is argued mean that police abuses of power at times tend to go unaddressed. However, some changes have already been made, which the 2016 reforms will build on. Where officers were placed under investigation with a view to disciplinary charges, they sometimes took early retirement or resigned on medical grounds; in some instance officers who had resigned, avoiding disciplinary proceedings, then rejoined the force. After the MacPherson Report[287] into the *Stephen Lawrence* case, disciplinary charges were recommended against five officers involved. All, however, retired and therefore could not face charges. The

---

286 Para 23(12) of Schedule 3 empowers the IPCC to furnish a copy of the report to the complainant.
287 Cm 4262-I, 1999.

history of PC Simon Harwood who was cleared in 2012 of killing Ian Tomlinson[288] at the G20 protests[289] in London in 2009 is illustrative of the weaknesses of the system, although no doubt it provides an extreme example. He had previously been repeatedly accused of using excessive force against members of the public; his disciplinary history, disclosed at pre-inquest hearings and pre-trial hearings, in relation to the alleged manslaughter of Tomlinson, included allegations that he perpetrated serious assaults, threatened and unlawfully arrested people over a long period of time prior to the Tomlinson case. The hearings and the IPCC Report into the death (published in 2012)[290] show that he avoided probable or upcoming disciplinary proceedings by the Metropolitan police by resigning owing to ill health, but later joining another force before moving back to the Metropolitan police. The Independent Police Complaints Commission, which investigated Tomlinson's death, said it had 'grave concerns' over the failure of the Metropolitan police's vetting procedures.[291] Its inquiries established that disciplinary proceedings brought against Harwood included 'unlawful arrest, abuse of authority and discreditable conduct'. However, most of the complaints were found to be unproven, and his disciplinary history was not disclosed in the manslaughter trial on the grounds of creating prejudice.

In relation to an incident in which Harwood had allegedly attacked a motorist, the Metropolitan police had settled out of court with the individual concerned and had paid him compensation. The IPCC report into the death of Tomlinson compiled in 2010, but published in 2012 after Harwood's trial, concluded that PC Harwood had a case to answer for gross misconduct in respect of the death.[292]

In 2012, after the trial, a police disciplinary panel found he had committed gross misconduct in respect of pushing and hitting Tomlinson on the basis that his use of force was disproportionate; but the panel decided that it did not need to investigate the issue of whether his actions led to Tomlinson's death. He was dismissed but his pension was unaffected as he had not been convicted of an offence.

However, changes were made in 2014: the Police (Conduct) (Amendment) Regulations 2014[293] prevents officers from resigning or retiring to avoid investigation for gross misconduct. Provision was made for police misconduct hearings and appeals to be held in public. Independent legally qualified chairs were introduced from January 2016, replacing senior police officers as chairs of misconduct hearing panels.

As mentioned above, there still remains a disconnection between successful civil actions against the police and disciplinary action or prosecution.[294] For example, in the

---

288 See *The Telegraph*, 19 July 2012 for a report of the trial.
289 The police were operating an overall strategic plan to begin the dispersal of demonstrators from the area of the Bank of England had commenced. Tomlinson who had been drinking heavily was in that area. PC Harwood pushed Tomlinson, who was not part of the protest and had not acted aggressively, from behind and then hit him with his baton, causing him to fall heavily to the ground and then die on the street.
290 See IPCC Report into the death of Ian Tomlinson (2012).
291 See Independent Investigation into the death of Ian Tomlinson on 1 April 2009 (2012) p 5. https://www.ipcc.gov.uk/sites/default/files/Documents/investigation_commissioner_reports/inv_rep_independent_investigation_into_the_death_of_ian_tomlinson_1.pdf.
292 IPCC Report into the death of Ian Tomlinson, published 2012, para 346.
293 SI 2014/3347.
294 *The Butler Report*, 1998, criticised the CPS for its decision-making in the *Treadaway* case; Derek Treadaway was awarded £50,000 in damages in respect of a serious assault by police officers while he was in custody: *R v DPP ex p Treadaway* (1997) *The Times*, 18 November. The CPS decided not to prosecute the officers. Treadaway successfully sought judicial review of this decision and the case was remitted for re-consideration by the CPS.

Hsu case,[295] it was found that Mr Hsu was assaulted, racially abused and falsely arrested. It was accepted that the police officers in question had lied on oath and fabricated note-book entries. Mr Hsu was awarded £200,000 damages (reduced on appeal to £35,000), but no officer was disciplined.[296]

Thus, despite evidence of police malpractice from miscarriage of justice cases such as that of the *Birmingham Six*[297] and the subsequent indications discussed above of poor practice and deliberate wrongdoing within the police service, the system for accountability remains, in essentials, flawed since the element of independence under the 2002 reforms appears to have had a limited impact in a number of instances, although improved performance occurred as a result of the 2014 the changes mentioned and an increased budget in 2013–15.[298] As Smith argues, in relation to the 2002 reforms: 'the complaints reform programme has been driven by the prevailing managerialist orthodoxy and the principal effect of the legislation will be to transfer some responsibilities for the management of police complaints to another public body which will report directly to the Home Secretary'.[299] The system also still raises various serious issues under the HRA. Arguably, it does not generate sufficient confidence that it is playing a significant part in ensuring that police officers and forces act in compliance with the Convention. In so far as the Convention rights are reflected in the safeguards for suspects contained in PACE, the TA and their associated codes, it is not fully apparent that it can ensure adherence to them. It is also not apparent, as the disciplinary history of PC Harwood suggests, that it is at present effective in dealing with allegations of excessive force used by certain officers in various policing situations.

Further IPCC reforms in 2016

The concerns expressed here as to the inefficacy of the IPCC may to an extent be addressed in reforms of the system likely to be brought about in 2016–17. The

---

295 *Thompson v Comr of Police for the Metropolis, Hsu v Comr of Police for the Metropolis* [1997] 2 All ER 762.
296 See further the Home Affairs Committee First Report (1998), Section B: 'The evidence from civil actions'. A further example, in which the disciplinary sanction was, in effect, rescinded, is provided by *Goswell v Comr of Metropolitan Police* (*The Guardian* Report, 27 April 1996). The officer who was found in that case to have perpetrated a serious assault, PC Trigg, was dismissed as a result of a complaint from Goswell. In the civil action Goswell had been awarded £120,000 for assault, £12,000 for false imprisonment and £170,000 for arbitrary and oppressive behaviour. Trigg appealed against his dismissal and was reinstated by the Home Secretary, Michael Howard. On the face of it, his reinstatement after it had been proved beyond reasonable doubt (in the disciplinary proceedings) that Trigg had perpetrated the assault in question appeared highly questionable.
297 *R v McIlkenny and Others* [1992] 2 All ER 417.
298 'The IPCC is to increase the number of cases it investigates year on year, from opening 109 cases in 2013/14 to 241 in 2014/15. The IPCC is on course to meet its target of opening between 400 and 700 independent investigations in 2015/16. The IPCC is also improving the rate at which cases are closed, closing more cases in the first six months of 2015/16 than it did throughout 2014/15': Reforming the Independent Police Complaints Commission: structure and governance: Summary of consultation responses and next steps, 15 December 2015.
299 Smith, G, 'Rethinking Police Complaints' Brit J Crminol. (2004) 44, 15–33, at p 28.

government announced plans in 2015 to reform the Commission.[300] The intention was stated to be: to deliver a stronger IPCC as 'a key part of the government's reforms of the police complaints system to ensure that complaints made against the police are responded to in a way that restores trust, builds confidence, and allows lessons to be learned. These reforms include strengthening the system's independence at a local level by giving Police and Crime Commissioners a greater role, making the system less bureaucratic and adversarial, and enhancing the IPCC's powers of investigation and remedy'. Since the body would no longer be organised as a commission, the government's proposal is to rename it the 'Office for Police Conduct' (OPC). There appeared to be agreement among those consulted by the Home Office that the commission model, as currently set out in the 2002 Act, is no longer sustainable. The reformed IPCC is intended, according to the Home Office plans, to have clear lines of accountability and decision-making, intended to ensure that the expanded IPCC can deliver more high quality investigations, and a single head.

Once the consultation was concluded, the reforms[301] were captured in the Policing and Crime Bill 2015–16, which, at the time of writing, is before Parliament, and makes a range of amendments to the 2002 Act. No change is intended in the accountability of the IPCC itself: it will remain accountable to the Home Office, not Parliament. The reforms are not radical and most complaints will still not be investigated by the OPC. The will have a somewhat stronger role in relation to complaints, but no provision is made for it to investigate all or most of them. Under cl 11 a police complaint is to be defined as 'any expression of dissatisfaction with a police force which is expressed (whether in writing or otherwise) by or on behalf of a member of the public', and under cl 14 the IPCC may direct the appropriate authority to record the complaint. The local policing body, under cl 10, may give notice that it rather than the chief officer of the force in question will handle a complaint,[302] and provision is made for the Home Secretary to make regulations as to the giving of such notice. Schedule 4 para 12 provision is made for regulations ensuring the IPCC investigate all cases involving chief officers;[303] under Part 2 provision is also made allowing the IPCC to present its own cases to disciplinary hearing panels. Schedule 4 of the Bill amends Sched 3 of the 2002 Act covering the handling of complaints. In particular, for 'record the complaint' will be substituted 'contact the complainant and seek the complainant's views on how the complaint should be handled'. The reformed IPCC will have a power to require re-investigation, under clause 15, if 'satisfied that there are compelling reasons for doing so', and a power to investigate concerns raised by whistleblowers under cl 29E(2).[304] Under cl 12 there is

300 *Reforming the Independent Police Complaints Commission: structure and governance: a consultation* (2015).

301 *Reforming the Independent Police Complaints Commission: structure and governance: Summary of consultation responses and next steps*, 15 December 2015.

302 'The local policing body that maintains a police force may give notice to the chief officer of the police force that it (rather than the chief officer) is to exercise the functions conferred on the chief officer by the provisions specified in subsection (2) or subsections (2) and (3).'

303 'The Secretary of State may by regulations provide that the Commission must investigate in accordance with paragraph 19 recordable conduct matters referred to it that relate to the conduct of a chief officer or the Deputy Commissioner of Police of the Metropolis.'

304 'The Commission may investigate any concern raised by a whistle-blower of which it becomes aware (whether because the whistle-blower has contacted the Commission or for any other reason) but only

a duty to keep the complainant and other interested persons informed of the progress of the complaint. There is also provision for the making of 'super-complaints' – more fundamental complaints as to a police force in general,[305] which can be made by a 'designated body', which means a body designated in regulations to be made by the Home Secretary (cl 19); under cl 20 the Home Secretary may make other regulations about super-complaints.

The promise that investigations will be of a higher quality appears to be intended to be addressed by regulations yet to be made; under cla 25 the secretary of state may issue guidance as to the discharge of their disciplinary functions to the bodies involved. Clause 22 is intended to make further provision to address the propensity of police officers facing a disciplinary hearing to resign by providing that if at the time of the alleged misconduct the officer was a member of a force but is no longer a member by the time of the hearing, regulations can be made under the section addressing the procedure to be followed in that circumstance. Clause 29J has the potential to create greater secrecy in relation to IPCC investigations related to concerns raised by whistleblowers in future since it makes provision for the secretary of state to make regulations disallowing publication of information by the IPCC that go beyond protecting the anonymity of whistleblowers.[306]

Conclusions

As indicated, under the 2016 reforms it is not intended that police complaints will all go directly to the new localised IPCC, but the reformed body will apparently have the power and capacity to undertake more investigations than at present. In particular, the intention is that it will be able to conduct higher quality investigations than is currently the case. These reforms appear to be long overdue and may have the potential to address in particular the problem of the over-bureaucratic, ineffectual and low quality nature of current IPCC investigations. However, it is not apparent at present that they represent the radical reform of the system that it is suggested is needed. The transparency of the system created by 2002 Act has not been improved by the 2016 amendments. It might have been more effective, rather than amending the 2002 Act, to repeal it and introduce an entirely new scheme under the 2016 Act, which did not focus mainly on the IPCC, but focused equally on those practices of police forces and police officers that appear to be obstructing the working of an effective complaints and disciplinary system. The reforms appear to leave most investigations and disciplinary hearings in the hands of the police forces concerned, as at present. It cannot fully be determined yet, since the Bill refers at a number of points to regulations to be made, without indicating what their

---

if the whistle-blower informs the Commission, before the beginning of the investigation, that he or she consents to an investigation taking place'.

305 Clause 29A: 'A designated body may make a complaint to Her Majesty's Chief Inspector of Constabulary that a feature, or combination of features, of policing in England and Wales by one or more than one police force is, or appears to be, significantly harming the interests of the public'.

306 'The Secretary of State may by regulations make provision setting out the circumstances in which the Commission is required or authorised to disclose information falling within subsection (2) (or any particular description of such information) to whistle-blowers or to other persons specified, or of a description specified, in the regulations'.

substance will be, whether they will go far enough to address fully the concerns articulated here. It is suggested, despite the rhetoric of the consultation paper, that under the Policing and Crime Bill that has emerged, some of the essential flaws in the system are likely to persist.

6 Prosecutions of the police

Police actions that are unauthorised may create criminal as well as civil liability. For example, the use of force in effecting an unlawful arrest would be an assault. The use of lethal force in such circumstances might give rise to liability for murder or manslaughter. Equally, excessive force used to effect a lawful arrest or to restrain a suspect lawfully detained might give rise to criminal liability. In practice, successful prosecutions of police officers are very rare.[307] A number of high profile cases failed to lead, ultimately, to successful prosecutions. The Home Affairs Committee noted that no convictions of police officers had arisen from the recent miscarriage of justice cases despite strong evidence of fraud or perjury on the part of some of the officers involved.[308] The number of deaths annually in police custody remains high; between 1990 and 2015, 1,544 such deaths were recorded by INQUEST (the figures included police pursuits)[309] and the failure of disciplinary charges or prosecutions in relation to complaints arising from such deaths has attracted quite severe criticism.[310] The Police Reform Act 2002 does not distinguish between complaints of criminal conduct and of unprofessional behaviour (s 12); thus it does not facilitate the use of the criminal process as distinct from the disciplinary one, where a complaint reveals that a criminal act by a police officer may have occurred.

The Crown Prosecution Service takes the decision as to prosecution, but their impartiality and independence have been questioned. It appears that the issue of independence arises at every stage in the decision-making process of the CPS in relation to the question whether to prosecute police officers where complaints appear to disclose criminal offences.[311] The CPS is, of course, independent of the police, but 'the issue is whether it exercises this independence properly'.[312] Evidence submitted in 1997 to the Home Affairs Committee regarding the matter indicated a 'lack of willingness' on the part of the CPS and DPP to prosecute. 'There is clearly bias which pervades both

307   Only about 1.5% of cases concerning the police referred to the DPP are prosecuted.
308   The Home Affairs Committee Report (note 00 above), para 24.
309   See further http://www.inquest.org.uk. See also Leigh, Johnson and Ingram, *Deaths in Police Custody*, Police Research Series Paper 26 (1998).
310   See *The Butler Report*, 1998; Kennedy, H, in Walker, C and Starmer, K (eds), *Miscarriages of Justice: A Review of Justice in Error*, 1999, p 374. Note the report in June (1999) LAG 21 regarding the inquest into the death of N Delahunty due to cocaine intoxication aggravated by police restraint. See also November (1999) LAG 6 regarding the acquittal of police officers for the death of a Mr O'Brien in custody after a restraint by a number of police officers. His death was considered in *The Butler Report*, s 6. In s 8, the report criticised the CPS system for considering prosecutions in respect of deaths in custody (including that of O'Brien) as 'inefficient and fundamentally unsound'. See above, Chapter 14, p 1014, fn 299.
311   *Ibid*, para 25.
312   See Home Affairs Committee First Report (1997–98), para 88.

the police and the CPS preventing viable prosecutions through nonsensical analysis of evidence.'[313] It is notable that the CPS initially decided against prosecuting PC Harwood in respect of the death of Ian Tomlinson in 2009 (discussed above), and only decided to proceed with the prosecution after the IPCC's Report into the death was brought to their attention.[314]

No criminal liability is created under the HRA, so that a breach of, for example, Art 3 or 8, if non-coterminous with existing offences, could not found a prosecution. But decisions as to prosecutions of the police raise a number of Convention issues that can be addressed in proceedings for judicial review of a decision not to prosecute. The burden of proof would be affected where it was alleged that Art 3 had been breached by custodial maltreatment, or, under Art 2, where a death had occurred in custody. Once it was shown that the detainee was free of the injury in question,[315] or was not already in a life-threatening condition, before arrest, the state would bear the burden of exculpating the officers involved.

7 Conclusions

A recurring theme throughout this chapter, and Chapters 12 and 13, has concerned the extent to which a 'balance' is struck between suspects' rights and police powers. The dual themes of the need for enhanced police powers but also for the introduction of rules to protect due process, are only clearly evident in the piece of legislation that is still central to police powers – the Police and Criminal Evidence Act 1984. The notion of achieving in PACE what Reiner has called 'a fundamental balance'[316] has some foundation. It may be said that on the face of it, the balance struck by PACE is fairly acceptable, at least in relation to the non-terrorist suspect, despite the increased powers of arrest and stop and search that PACE confers. Concern may be expressed as to the uncertainty of the concept of reasonable suspicion on which these powers depend but, nevertheless, taking PACE and the codes at face value, a concern to protect the rights of suspects is evident. It is, however, less clear that the later legislation, in particular the Criminal Justice and Public Order Act 1994, the Terrorism Act 2000 as amended, the Serious and Organised Crime Act 2005, and the Criminal Justice and Police Act 2001, reflects such a concern. The post-PACE legislation, then, has effected continued extensions of police powers, but has brought about only minor increases in safeguards for suspects. Those increases, including the use of judicial authorisation for the lengthy detention of terrorist suspects and the requirement of access to legal advice if adverse inferences are to be drawn from silence, were in effect imposed on the government by decisions of the European Court of Human Rights. However, obviously, the Human Rights Act introduced an express fair trial right under Art 6, along with the express guarantees under Arts 5, 3, 8, 2, into domestic law, and placed a duty on the police under s 6 to abide by those guarantees.

313 *Ibid*, para 90.
314 IPCC Report into the death of Ian Tomlinson (2012).
315 *Tomasi v France* A 241-A (1992). See also Chapter 2, p 48.
316 Reiner, R, 'The politics of the Act' [1985] PL 394, p 395.

The later legislation made no attempt to address one of the central problems inherent in the provision for safeguarding suspects' rights in PACE, the TA and the codes – the lack of effective redress for its breach. PACE itself made some provision for such redress in its exclusion of evidence scheme and in respect of police complaints (arising now under the 2002 Act, and about to be reformed in 2016) but no general, effective and full scheme of redress was created, in particular in respect of excessive use of force by police in conducting policing duties, aside from the ordinary law and the police complaints system, which, as discussed, is no longer viewed as sustainable in its current form. The Human Rights Act, as discussed, created a remedial scheme for breach of the ECHR rights, but that scheme does not cover all breaches of the rules governing suspects' rights, as this chapter has made clear. The lack of effective redress for abuse of power and breaches of the rules was a recurring theme in these chapters. It is particularly true of Codes C and H; they create a scheme that seems to make every effort to ensure fair treatment in custody and in the interview, but that operates outside the realm of general legal sanctions since breaches may be remedied (in the accepted sense of that word) only in internal disciplinary proceedings, and only rarely then. The right to legal advice, although on a statutory basis, is also in a relatively weak position. The notes for guidance, which occupy key points in the interviewing scheme, appear to be intended to have no legal status at all. Since no other effective means is available of ensuring that the rules are adhered to, the courts have stepped into the breach and have developed complex rules for the exclusion of confessions obtained in breach of the interviewing rules. Thus, in effect, exclusion of confession evidence has become one of the main methods of upholding the rights of the suspect while in custody and in the interview, according some compliance with the principle of legality that the effective guarantee of human rights requires.

But the use of exclusion of evidence as a means of redress clearly leads to an ineffective protection against police abuse of power and for suspects' rights, and as argued above may disregard the interests of victims. The detrimental impact on the victim and on the criminal justice system, in terms of placing pressure on resources if a case collapses due to exclusion of crucial evidence, renders the effects of this method, it is argued, disproportionate in some instances to the aim pursued. That is partly because exclusion of evidence is not an effective method of protecting rights: it can only operate where the case comes to court and the suspect pleads not guilty. Even then it is only likely to have effect in relation to admissions and where the breach of the provision in question can be shown to have been substantial and significant. Many code or statutory provisions relate to physical treatment or to interaction outside the police station and have no obvious linkage with the making of admissions. Police use of excessive force against persons during investigations can only be addressed by exclusion of evidence if it is linked to evidence later presented in court. If, as is often the case, the excessive use of force occurs, but is not part of an investigation leading to charges and court action, exclusion of evidence, whether oppressive behaviour did or did not occur, is irrelevant. Where non-confession evidence is obtained in breach of the PACE or TA standards, it is highly probable, as discussed, that the courts will admit it, thereby possibly encouraging laxity in relation to the rules. Thus, the police may still be inclined to break the rules in the hope of obtaining a guilty plea, or non-confession evidence, or merely on the basis that the rules fail to harmonise with police culture, or with the propensity of a few officers to use excessive force to assert their authority.

Since the rules are not underpinned by an effective remedy for their breach, as represented by exclusion of evidence, many suspects may experience a process, including interviews, that falls below the standard apparently set by the TA, PACE and the codes. If, in particular instances, this does not come to light, a doubtful guilty plea may be accepted, or a false confession may be admitted, leading to a miscarriage of justice, while on the other hand such failures may sometimes mean that reliable confession evidence cannot be accepted in court, although it would have been had the rules been observed. If confession evidence would not have been available but for oppressive questioning, it is argued on the grounds of both protection for suspects and reliability that the energies of the police should have been devoted to uncovering other evidence. Curtailment of the right to silence has to an extent exacerbated the situation, since it is likely in itself to increase the pressure on the suspect to speak and it has also undermined the safeguard that, it is suggested, has most real value in the interview: the provision of legal advice from an experienced solicitor.

There is the further problem that, as Chapters 11 and 13 have shown, the Code C, H and statutory safeguards can be evaded by operating entirely outside the PACE and TA schemes, using secret surveillance techniques,[317] as occurred in *Khan*[318] and *Chalkley*,[319] or operating undercover, as in *Amin*.[320] Thus, the safeguards for suspects can in some instances be marginalised. While such techniques are effective in crime-control terms, the concern arises that they may be used deliberately in some instances rather than arresting and interviewing a suspect, thereby triggering off all the safeguards. Such techniques are regulated by the Police Act 1997 and the Regulation of Investigatory Powers Act 2000 (RIPA). They will soon be regulated by a new statute if the Investigatory Powers Bill 2016 is enacted.[321] But a breach of either statute does not in itself give rise to liability, unless the action, if unauthorised, would create existing tortious or criminal liability. As has been discussed, the courts are not willing to use exclusion of evidence in such instances in an automatic fashion to vindicate any rights violated, partly because so doing would fail to give weight to the interests of the victim and to the public interest in crime control. But if use of exclusion of evidence is ineffective as a means of upholding rights, and accords too little weight to the interests of victims, other means of redress are needed, outside the trial process. But as discussed in this chapter those other means – civil actions and police complaints – do not provide a fully effective system either. Police complaints in particular requires further reform, which, as discussed, is intended to occur in 2016.

This chapter and Chapters 12 and 13 have focused quite closely on the role of the HRA in terms of creating a 'reinvigoration of fundamental values' in the criminal justice system.[322] It appeared possible that the inception of the HRA might herald a return to an emphasis on such values that has not been fully evident since the early 1990s. This

---

317 See Ormerod, D and Birch, D, 'The evolution of the discretionary exclusion of evidence' [2004] Crim LR 767.
318 [1996] 3 All ER 289; (1996) 146 NLJ 1024.
319 [1998] 2 Cr App R 79.
320 [2000] 1 WLR 1071; [2000] Crim LR 174.
321 See Chapter 11, p 828.
322 Walker, C, in Walker, C and Starmer, K (eds), *Miscarriages of Justice: A Review of Justice in Error*, 1999, p 62.

part has sought to suggest that, in the face of the quite wide police discretion created by the statutory provisions, particularly those of the TA, the ECHR via the HRA offers some possibilities of curbing police discretion in the interests of due process values since it allow domestic judges to look more closely and directly at standards of fairness in the criminal justice system. But in practice the impact of the ECHR under the HRA has been patchy. Indeed, it appears likely that the HRA will continue to have a diffuse and patchy effect; it is not having a radical impact on the use of the current repressive legislation or on the further powers that may be introduced to tackle terrorism. The ECHR may itself be manipulated either by the judiciary or the legislature, in the sense that in court, the Convention rights can be 'read down' in order to preserve the effect of such legislation, while the use of s 19 statements of compatibility may provide such legislation with a spurious appearance of rectitude. MPs may accept that a process of human rights auditing has occurred, allaying concerns about the provisions.

A blending of ECHR values with those of the common law is becoming especially apparent in this field, but it is suggested that those of the Convention only attain an appearance of gaining greater respect owing to the HRA, where they harmonise with values *already* held dear by the common law. It may be said that where the judiciary have traditionally established a firm opposition to due process values, as they have in respect of the admission of improperly obtained non-confession evidence, the HRA will leave that position unchanged, and it may aid in confirming the position where the judges have traditionally been sympathetic to due process, as they have been in relation to the deprivation of liberty in police detention.[323] Where police abuse their powers by using excessive force in the course of policing, although articles of the ECHR are engaged (depending on the circumstances, potentially Arts 5, 8, 3, 2), it is clear that reliance on the HRA is not likely to provide an effective remedy, and that wholesale reform of the police complaints and disciplinary system is part of the answer. As discussed, reform is to occur in 2016 but, as indicated above, it is not clear that it is of the very far-reaching nature needed.

The legislation discussed in these three chapters reflects the change in the political climate that became evident in the mid-1990s, and has continued in the first decade post-2000, and beyond. As Dixon puts it, 'The political and professional consensus about the need for criminal justice reform [in the face of discovery of a number of miscarriages of justice] had broken down . . . the.. Home Secretary encouraged renewed populist obsession with law and order . . . .'[324] It is fair to say that from the early 1990s to the present time, 2016, British political culture has been fairly hostile to due process values. Crime-control considerations and the importance of a reputation for governmental effectiveness in dealing with crime and threats of terrorism have created a climate in which repressive laws have been readily enacted, as Chapter 15 indicates. The due process potential the HRA may have had was bound to be further tempered after the 9/11 attacks, and in the face of the subsequent terrorist threats, reaching a peak in 2013–16.

---

323 See *Roberts v Chief Constable of Cheshire* [1999] 1 WLR 662.
324 In Walker, C and Starmer, K (eds), *Miscarriages of Justice: A Review of Justice in Error*, 1999, p 73.

Chapter 15

Anti-terrorism law and human rights

1 Introduction

9/11 re-shaped the counter-terrorist response in the UK. After 9/11, a war on terror was viewed, as 'not a matter of choice but a strategic imperative'.[1] Since 9/11 a range of attacks by Islamic militants have occurred in Europe, including the Madrid bombing in 2004, the London tube bombing in 2005, the Lee Rigby murder in 2013, the Paris massacre in 2015. A range of terrorist plots have been foiled in the UK, especially in the years 2012–16, and the number of arrests and prosecutions for terrorist offences reached their highest annual rate in 2013–15.[2] Thus the response has been heavily influenced post-2001 by the threat posed by extremist Islamic groups (although they do not pose the only threat), the fear of suicide-bombing and recently of multi-site attacks, as in Paris in 2015, using machine guns as well as suicide bombs.[3] The counter-terrorist measures adopted post-9/11 and again post-7/7 have tended to be of a proactive as well as a reactive nature. In other words, rather than simply charging persons with terrorist crimes and bringing them to trial, attention has turned also to targeting possible terrorist suspects – persons who may in future commit terrorist acts – and curtailing their liberty in order to prevent terrorist activity before it can occur. But proactive measures are clearly more risky and concerning in human rights terms since they are not subject to the normal due process safeguards created by the criminal justice system, and therefore miscarriages of justice may be more likely to occur. This chapter documents the counter-terrorist law and policy of successive governments from 2000–2016. The following pages evaluate a very wide range of counter-terrorist provisions, including a large number of special terrorism offences and pro-active sanctions applied outside the criminal justice system, and in so doing explores in particular their interaction with human rights,[4] especially those ECHR rights scheduled in the Human Rights Act.

The Terrorism Act 2000 remains the central measure within this scheme, but the later additions to its provisions in the Anti-Terrorism, Crime and Security Act 2001 (ATCSA), the Prevention of Terrorism Act 2005, the Terrorism Act 2006, the Counter-Terrorism

---

1 Freedman, L (ed), *Superterrorism*, 2002, Blackwell at p 44.
2 See 'Operation of police powers under the Terrorism Act 2000 and subsequent legislation', Home Office, 2016.
3 Europol warned in January 2016 that Isis was planning large-scale attacks in European capitals: see e.g., *The Times*, 26 January 2016.
4 For a lengthy discussion of such interaction globally see Duffy, H, *The 'War on Terror' and the Framework of International Law*, 2nd edn, 2015, esp 4B2 and Part 7.

Act 2008, the Justice and Security Act 2013 and the Counter-Terrorism and Security Act 2015, have tended progressively to increase the tension between the counter-terrorist measures and human rights. When over-broad provisions are applied on the basis of a low standard of due process, the human rights traditions of the UK may be undermined, possibly with a counter-productive security impact and in some instances without a rational security basis. The most obvious example was the use of indefinite detention against non-British suspected terrorists after 9/11; had that legislation still been in place prior to 7/7 it could not have been used against the suicide bombers, all of whom were British citizens.

If a democracy appears to abandon its democratic ideals too readily, including adherence to human rights and the rule of law, in the face of terrorist activity, it lays itself open to the charge that its attachment to them was always precarious and qualified. In defending the introduction of new counter-terrorism legislation, the Terrorism Act 2000, with immense potential to extend the impact of the previous legislation, Jack Straw, the then Home Secretary, claimed in 1999 that the TA was simply intended to protect democracy, and that extensive measures were needed since 'by its nature terrorism is designed to strike at the heart of our democratic values'.[5] In justifying similar, if far less wide-ranging, extensions of such legislation in the face of high levels of IRA activity during the 1970s and 1980s, Margaret Thatcher famously said in 1988: 'We do sometimes have to sacrifice a little of the freedom we cherish in order to defend ourselves from those whose aim it is to destroy that freedom altogether. . . .' That is a powerful argument, but it must fully confront the question of the extent to which counter-terrorist measures can undermine democracy in seeking to defend it: they may themselves strike at fundamental democratic values if they appear to be disproportionate to the aim of protecting them.

As will be detailed below, the post 9/11 counter-terrorist policy is not in all respects exceptional since it represents in a number of respects a continuation of previous policies relating to IRA violence. The key difference is that such powers are no longer seen as emergency measures pending a political settlement. Since the response is founded, unsurprisingly, on the view that political negotiation is not possible with groups such as Isis, the resultant significant creep in the adoption of authoritarian powers, and their normalisation, has placed a concomitant strain on human rights. But the relationship between counter-terror measures and preserving human rights is a complex one since the impact of such measures in preserving the human rights of potential victims, as an aspect of preserving security, is a central concern. In the words of the Council of Europe, the efforts of state parties need to be enhanced in 'preventing terrorism and its negative effects on the full enjoyment of human rights, in particular the right to life, both by measures to be taken at national level and through international cooperation'.[6]

This chapter focuses mainly on the central and changing characteristics of the UK's current counter-terrorist response from 2000 to 2016. As indicated, a notable aspect has been the shift from reactive (reacting to terrorist acts via criminal offences) to preventive or proactive measures (interfering in the activities of suspects via non-trial-based

5 See *The Guardian*, 14 November 1999.
6 See the Council of Europe's Additional Protocol to the Council of Europe Convention on the Prevention of Terrorism 12 March 2015, Art 1.

measures) as an aspect of the so-called 'war on terror' post-9/11. When the previous Labour government introduced a new counter-terrorist scheme in the form of the Terrorism Act 2000 (TA), it encapsulated a change in policy in that temporary, graduated measures were replaced with permanent, broadly applied ones. But the 2000 Act relied on a traditional reactive approach, that of seeking to charge terrorist suspects with offences and bring them to trial. This scheme offered quite a strong contrast to the previous one of the 1970s, 1980s and 1990s. The previous UK counter-terrorist scheme – under the Prevention of Terrorism (Temporary Provisions) Act 1989 and the Northern Ireland (Emergency Provisions) Act 1996, as amended – revealed some acceptance of the principle that emergency measures should by definition be viewed as exceptional. The TA was introduced at a time when terrorist attacks were not of the scale that they had been previously, although the government clearly had in mind an impending threat from extremist Islamic groups. The TA applied all the special terrorism offences to a far wider range of groups than had previously been the case; it was therefore a much less graduated measure than the previous ones.

The special terrorism offences on their *face*, due to over-breadth, apply potentially not only to groups that might be viewed in common parlance as 'freedom fighters' or protest groups rather than 'terrorists', but also to a very large number of persons, including ordinary citizens, such as journalists, property agents, accountants, bankers, who have some association with terrorist groups, sometimes unknowingly.[7] In practice the executive has not sought to apply the counter-terrorist sanctions to all the groups or persons that meet the statutory definitions. This is partly due, in relation to supporters of Al-Qaeda, or Isis, as discussed below, to the difficulty of uncovering evidence and of transforming security and intelligence service material into evidence that could be put forward in a criminal trial. Not only may it genuinely be of a very sensitive nature, involving, *inter alia*, informants whose lives might be put at risk,[8] but the security services may be very reluctant for it to be put forward as evidence for reasons that may not fully relate to genuine concerns of that nature.[9] Such reasons also appear to relate to the continuing refusal to allow intercept material to be put forward as evidence in a criminal trial, discussed in Chapter 11.[10]

But those are not the only reasons for the under-use of the counter-terrorist sanctions, or alternatively for their very existence as additions to the ordinary criminal law. The counter-terrorism offences documented in this chapter appear to be intended to have an effect that, to an extent, is more symbolic than actual.[11] They are viewed by government as playing an important role in signalling this society's rejection of the message of certain groups – to isolate and marginalise them,[12] to deny them some legitimacy on

---

7 See Walker, C, 'Political violence and commercial risk' (2004) 56 *Current Legal Problems* 531.

8 The questions of sensitivity and disclosure in the criminal trial (including informants), graymail and prosecutorial discretion are addressed in Lustgarten, L and Leigh, I, *In From the Cold: National Security and Parliamentary Democracy*, 1994, Chapter 11.

9 See p 1127 below.

10 See p 793.

11 See, e.g., Tushnet, M and Yackle, L, 'Symbolic Statutes and Real Laws: The Pathologies of the Antiterrorism and Effective Death Penalty Act and the Prison Litigation Reform Act', *Duke Law Journal*, Vol 47, No 1 (Oct 1997), pp 1–86; Freedman, L, 'The Coming War on Terror', in Freedman, L (ed), *Superterrorism*, 2002.

12 See, in particular p 1051 below.

the basis that they have refused to use democratic methods, resorting instead to the anti-democratic course of creating terror by using violence targeted at civilians.

But the TA, despite its immense and unprecedented scope, has been viewed since 2001 by successive governments as inadequate to address the terrorist threat post-9/11. The main change in UK anti-terrorist policy in recent years has been described as being 'the shift to intelligence-based and proactive methods [with] the primary aim of preventing terrorist attacks, rather than responding to events and attempting to solve crimes after they occur'.[13] The criminal offences under the TA provisions have been added to, especially under the Terrorism Act 2006, but also by successive non-trial-based measures which have been more controversial, since they rely on interfering proactively with the liberty of suspects before any offences have been committed, or where it appears difficult to prove that they have been committed. Broad proactive measures were introduced post-2000, in particular control orders, but they were not applied, as they would have been under a more authoritarian regime, to a large number of persons. In a fashion typical of the UK counter-terrorist response (also evident in public order and criminal justice measures), certain over-broad and arguably counter-productive draconian proactive measures were introduced, but then they were significantly under-used. Also certain of the more draconian non-trial-based measures were progressively replaced by less repressive measures. Thus, as discussed below, indefinite detention without trial under Part IV ATCSA 2001 was replaced by less repressive control orders, which in turn were replaced in 2012 by still less repressive terrorism prevention and investigation measures (TPIMs) under the Terrorism Prevention and Investigation Measures Act 2011 (a form of 'light touch' control order).

However a racheting up of the counter-terror response in the form of non-trial-based measures has recently occurred; certain new counter-terror measures were introduced in the Counter-Terrorism and Security Act 2015, including the introduction of temporary exclusion orders, new passport seizure powers, and significant strengthening of TPIMs. These measures were introduced partly to combat the threat represented by Isis[14] supporters, including in particular British citizens who have fought for or supported Isis in Syria, or who seek to travel to Iraq or Syria to do so. The rise of Isis, especially in the years 2013–16, also led to the introduction of further security measures to protect places where large numbers of people congregate and contributed to the introduction of the new measures. The potential danger returnees represent was illustrated by the Paris attacks in November 2015 which appear to have been co-ordinated by a supporter of Isis, who had been in Syria, and a number of the terrorists involved had apparently trained with Isis in Syria.[15] Isis had issued a fatwa in September 2014 urging 'its sup-

---

13 See *Civil Liberties Law: The Human Rights Act Era*, Whitty, Livingstone and Murphy, (2001), at 143. As Clive Walker puts it, 'The trend [of UK anti-terrorist policy] . . . represents a part of a fundamental switch away from reactive policing of incidents to proactive policing and management of risk': Walker, C, 'Terrorism and Criminal Justice: Past, Present and Future' [2004] Crim LR, May, 311, 314. Walker further cites Ericson, RV and Haggerty, KD, *Policing the Risk Society*, 1997, University of Toronto Press.

14 The terrorist group variously known as 'Islamic state of Iraq and Syria' (Isis) or 'Islamic State' (IS) or Da'esh.

15 Abdelhamid Abaaoud, who is thought to have left Brussels to join Isis, appeared to have returned and co-ordinated the attacks: BBC News 19 November 2015. Officials stated that the attacks in Paris were co-ordinated by Isis fighters: see e.g., the *New York Times* 14 November 2015. See also the case of Imran Khawaja from West London, who travelled from the UK to join a militant group with links to so-called Islamic State while overseas. He was pictured posing with severed heads during his six months in Syria.

porters to kill disbelievers in the west'. There is also some evidence that TPIMs have been used, not solely to combat a threat that their subjects might mount an attack in the UK, but also to prevent them travelling to support terrorism abroad (see below).

The 2015 Act also placed aspects of the 'Prevent' strategy on a statutory basis, as this chapter will discuss. Prevent focuses on the causes of terrorism; it is one of the four elements of CONTEST, the government's current counter-terrorism strategy.[16] It aims to stop people becoming terrorists or supporting terrorism – in other words, it is aimed at enabling intervention before persons who may be radicalised are drawn into terrorism. In seeking to prevent people from being drawn into terrorism and ensure they are given appropriate advice and support Prevent works with a wide range of sectors (including education, criminal justice, faith, charities, online and health) where there are risks of radicalisation and of eventually participating in terrorism.

The Prevent strategy, as it has developed, and the new measures in the 2015 Act, also address the recent call from the UN Security Council to member states to tackle the problem represented by terrorist groups operating in Iraq and Syria. It said that member states should: 'prevent and suppress the recruiting, organizing, transporting or equipping of individuals who travel to a State other than their State of residence or nationality for the purpose of the perpetration, planning or preparation of, or participation in, terrorist acts or the providing or receiving of terrorist training, and the financing of their travel and of their activities'. It went on to stress: 'the particular and urgent need to implement this resolution with respect to those foreign terrorist fighters who are associated with ISIL [Islamic State of Iraq and the Levant], ANF [Al-Nusrah Front] and other cells, affiliates, splinter groups or derivatives of Al-Qaida'; these strictures were also captured in the Additional Protocol to the Council of Europe Convention on the Prevention of Terrorism.[17]

2 Terrorism and human rights

Introduction

The provisions of counter-terror legislation come into conflict in a potentially unjustifiable fashion with a range of Convention rights.[18] Unsurprisingly, the judiciary have utilised the Human Rights Act in order to seek to impose Convention-compliance upon them. The decision of the House of Lords in *A and Others v Secretary of State for the Home Dept*[19] in 2004 marked a turning point in this respect. The stance taken by

---

He was arrested on return and later admitted preparing for acts of terrorism, attending a camp, receiving training and possessing firearms. See *R-v-Imran Khawaja, Tahir Bhatti, Asim Ali: R v Bhatti* [2015] EWCA Crim 764; sentencing remarks of Jeremy Baker J, Woolwich Crown Court, 6 February 2015.

16 See Home Office *Countering International Terrorism* (London: Cm 6888, 2006); *Pursue, Prevent, Protect, Prepare: the UK's Strategy for Countering International Terrorism* (London: Cm 7547, 2009), For discussion of 'Prevent' see Ramraj, VV, Hor, M and Roach, K (eds), *Global Anti-terrorism Law and Policy*, (2012), C Walker and J Rehman, Chapter 10.

17 UNSCR 2178; Statement by the President of the Security Council S/PRST/2014/23, 19 November 2014. See also the Council of Europe's Additional Protocol to the Convention on the Prevention of Terrorism 12 March 2015.

18 See Warbrick, C, 'The principles of the European Convention on Human Rights and the responses of states to terrorism' [2002] *European Human Rights Law Review* 287.

19 (2004) UKHL 56; [2005] 2 AC 68; [2005] 2 WLR 87; [2005] 3 All ER 169.

the judiciary in defence of Convention, international and common law human rights principles in that decision, and in other similarly seminal ones discussed below, has been of great significance in curbing some over-broad provisions. Traditionally, since terrorism has been viewed as threatening national security, the courts adopted a deferential stance.[20] The post-HRA approach of the courts continues to be affected by the extent to which national security can be said to be at stake but, as discussed below, the courts are more prepared than they were pre-HRA to take a *selectively* deferential approach, an approach that considers how far a particular decision is genuinely within a particular area of constitutional competence. This stance was taken by the House of Lords in *A and Others v Secretary of State for the Home Dept.*[21]

The courts are less likely to be deferential where national security is not genuinely at stake, and in any event they are taking their role under s 6 HRA seriously.[22] They have shown a willingness in a number of instances to take a robust approach to counter-terrorist provisions that, on their face, are in strong tension with Convention and common law principles. The HRA has been used in some instances in the courts, either to modify the provisions in question under s 3 in order to render them Convention-compliant, or, much more infrequently, to declare them incompatible with the Convention under s 4. In short, the courts have relied on the HRA in a number of instances to impose an ECHR-compliance on a range of counter-terrorist provisions that the executive alleged in Parliament had been achieved at the time of passing the provisions in question (s 19(1)(a) HRA), and which Parliament accepted had been achieved.

But Parliament has also played a significant part in imposing Convention-compliancy on provisions that were probably non-compliant as originally drafted. The Joint Committee on Human Rights has played an important advisory role in this respect. For example, this was especially the case in relation to the offence of glorification of terrorism introduced under the Terrorism Act 2006.[23] But parliamentary and judicial intervention have not fully succeeded in ensuring clear Convention compliance in respect of all aspects of the current counter-terrorist scheme. These problems of compatibility and the response of the domestic courts are considered in relation to specific provisions below.

Fair trial under Art 6(1) – proceedings before courts outside the criminal justice system

As discussed in Chapter 2, Art 6(1) provides a right to a fair and public hearing:

> In the determination of his civil rights and obligations or of any criminal charge against him, everyone is entitled to a fair and public hearing within a reasonable time

---

20 In *CCSU v Minister for the Civil Service* [1985] AC 374 the House of Lords accepted the government's claim that national security was at risk, without demanding that evidence should be put forward to support it. In the case of *Secretary of State for the Home Dept v Rehman* [2001] UKHL 47 the House of Lords accepted that it was largely for the government to determine whether a threat to national security, broadly defined, existed. Lord Steyn said: 'It is, however, self-evidently right that national courts must give great weight to the views of the executive on matters of national security' (para 31). Thus, pre-HRA, the judiciary tended to accept government claims that such a threat is self-evident or must be taken on trust.

21 (2004) UKHL 56; [2005] 2 AC 68; [2005] 2 WLR 87; [2005] 3 All ER 169.

22 See Chapter 4, p 187 *et seq.*

23 See pp 1075–80 below.

by an independent and impartial tribunal established by law . . . the press and public may be excluded from all or part of the trial in the interest of . . . national security.[24]

In the proceedings considered it appears at present that the rest of Art 6 is inapplicable since it only applies in criminal trials. Its application in criminal trials is considered in Chapters 12–14.[25]

Field of application of Art 6?

A number of the procedures made available to challenge the imposition of sanctions on persons suspected of terrorist activity, or those belonging to a proscribed organisation, are problematic in terms of their compliance with Art 6(1). They tend to place the accused person in a very weak position in the proceedings and provide a level of scrutiny falling short of that available in a criminal trial, despite the fact that significant sanctions are being imposed. In a number of respects the judicial supervision involved affords, it will be contended, a somewhat thin veneer of legitimacy to the process, which however the courts have brought more fully into accordance with the demands of Art 6.

Clearly, Art 6 applies to the proceedings considered below only if the hearings are within its field of application. The proceedings are those in the Special Immigration Appeals Commission (SIAC), in the Proscribed Organisations Appeals Commission (POAC) and control order/TPIM proceedings. As can be seen from the opening words of Art 6(1) set out above, it applies only if those procedures are viewed as the 'determination of a criminal charge' or of 'civil rights and obligations'. It might be thought that the proceedings in question *should* be viewed as criminal ones due to the sanctions that can be imposed, that the values underlying Art 6 and common law due process principles would argue against circumventing its fundamental safeguards by such devices as control orders/TPIMs (see below) or executive designation of suspects under temporary exclusion orders, as opposed to charging suspects with offences and prosecuting them. The mere designation of detention or the use of control orders/TPIMs as 'preventive', allowing the avoidance thereby of the need for a charge or for proof of an offence beyond reasonable doubt – themselves aspects of due process – arguably should not, in accordance with those values, be allowed to obscure the true nature of the situation. When obligations are imposed on a suspect under a control order/TPIM they may be experienced by the controlee as the use of sanctions as punishment. This point is perhaps even clearer in relation to proscription since on their face the proscription provisions criminalise a person who is a member of a proscribed organisation at the time when the organisation is proscribed, even though he or she had no warning that this was about to occur. Thus if POAC refuses to allow de-proscription a number of persons are automatically criminalised.[26]

However, the orthodox view apparent from the cases discussed below in the context of control order/TPIM proceedings is that the use of sanctions of a punitive nature in terms of their impact, outside the criminal process, is *not* the equivalent of a criminal charge.[27] Clearly, SIAC, the POAC and courts in control order/TPIM proceedings

---

24 See Chapter 2, p 58.
25 See in particular pp 960–63.
26 See p 1051 *et seq*.
27 See Fenwick, H, and Phillipson, G (2011) 56:4 McGill LJ 8.

are not dealing with such a charge as a matter of domestic law, although this in itself does not determine the matter since the term has an autonomous Convention meaning.[28] Their proceedings may be determinative of the question whether a deprivation of liberty under Art 5 has occurred, but the procedure is precisely not the determination of a charge and arguably if a criminal charge could have been brought it would have been. The procedures in question do, however, represent a 'determination of civil rights and obligations' under Art 6(1). That view was taken in *Secretary of State v MB*[29] in relation to proceedings very similar to those of SIAC – control order proceedings. The sanctions supervised by the courts in question, including SIAC, can be viewed, not as punishments in themselves, but as precautionary since no liability is necessarily imposed. In terms of Convention principle, this, it is argued, is a limited but orthodox perspective. It is the one accepted by the courts, executive and Parliament at present. The House of Lords in *A and Others* in 2004 left the question open whether such proceedings should be viewed as criminal or only as civil, attracting a lower level of safeguards.[30]

What is the basis for viewing the procedures in question as representing a 'determination of civil rights and obligations'? Civil rights and obligations are normally viewed as matters – broadly speaking – of private law,[31] not aspects of public law.[32] It is well established at Strasbourg that all the Convention rights are not 'civil rights' for the purposes of Art 6(1)[33] although the 'family' rights under Art 8(1) generally are viewed as 'civil rights'.[34] In *Re S and Re W (Care Orders)*[35] Lord Nicholls found:

> Although a right guaranteed by article 8 is not *in itself* a civil right within the meaning of article 6(1), the Human Rights Act has now transformed the position in this country. By virtue of the Human Rights Act article 8 rights are now part of the civil rights of parents and children for the purposes of article 6(1). This is because now, under section 6 of the Act, it is unlawful for a public authority to act inconsistently with article 8.[36]

In other words, Convention rights that would not be viewed as civil rights for Art 6 purposes at Strasbourg (due to the lack of a basis in domestic law) can now be so viewed, as a matter of domestic law, due to s 6 HRA. Clearly, Lord Nicholls was referring to Art 8 rights which might have been viewed as having such a basis anyway, but his point was that since Strasbourg requires a footing for the right in domestic law that footing has been established due to the HRA. As discussed below, the proceedings in question relate to a range of Convention rights and it has been accepted that the domestic consideration of the alleged breach of those rights does

---

28 See: *Campbell and Fell v UK* A 80 (1984); *Benham v UK* (1996) 22 EHRR 293.
29 *Secretary of State for the Home Department v MB* (2007) UKHL 46, (2008) 1 AC 440; Court of Appeal decision: [2006] EWHC 1000, [2006] HRLR 29, [2006] 8 CL 108.
30 Fn 21 above.
31 At Strasbourg they would be viewed as the determination of 'civil rights and obligations' since these are matters – broadly speaking – of private law: *Ringeisen v Austria* A 13 (1971), para 94.
32 See, e.g., *Agee v UK* No 7729/76, 7DR 164 (1976).
33 *Golder v UK* (1975) 1 EHRR 524.
34 *W v UK* A121 (1987).
35 [2002] UKHL 10.
36 At para 71.

amount to the determination of civil rights and obligations.[37] Since the proceedings are so viewed domestically they must therefore be Art 6 compliant. But only the guarantees of Art 6(1) apply; the other guarantees of Art 6 do not since they are applicable only in criminal matters.[38]

Further, as discussed in Chapter 2, Art 5(4) in any event provides a right to review of detention, whatever the basis of the detention.[39] The detainee must be able to take court proceedings in order to determine whether a detention is unlawful. This is an independent provision: even if it is determined in a particular case that the detention was lawful, there could still be a breach of Art 5(4) if no possibility of review of the lawfulness of the detention by the domestic courts arose. It is well established that proceedings for the purposes of satisfying Art 5(4) must satisfy the basic requirements of a fair trial.[40] Article 5(4) is only applicable if the proceedings relate to 'detention'; therefore its applicability would depend on the issue being determined. If, for example, the proceedings concerned obligations that affected Art 8 or 10 rights, it would appear that Art 5(4) would be inapplicable, but that Art 6(1) would continue to apply as the proceedings would concern the determination of civil rights.

The procedure for the use of closed material and the use of special advocates

The requirements of fairness, expressed or implied in Art 6(1), including those of equality of arms,[41] are applicable in the relevant proceedings. In these proceedings closed material on which the grounds for the suspicion against the applicant may be wholly or partly based, used to be completely withheld from him or her and from their legal representatives. However, it has been established that the gist of it must be disclosed.[42] Limitations on the disclosure of evidence in such proceedings always had the potential to breach Art 6(1). In *Balfour v Foreign and Commonwealth Office*[43] the Court found that once an actual or potential risk to national security had been demonstrated by a public interest immunity certificate, the Court should not exercise its right to inspect the documents. This view of national security as the exclusive domain of the executive was not adhered to in the robust approach taken to the concept in the context of deportation by SIAC in the case of *Secretary of State for the Home Dept ex p Rehman.*[44] However, the House of Lords disagreed with their findings, ruling that the threat to national security is a matter for 'executive judgment' that need not be demonstrated to the civil standard of proof.[45] It is argued that these findings were not fully in accordance with the findings of the Strasbourg Court in *Tinnelly v UK*[46] or in *Chahal v*

---

37 See Chapter 2, pp 57–60.
38 The guarantees of Art 6(2) and Art 6(3) are only applicable where the hearing is the 'determination of a criminal charge'. See further Chapter 2, pp 62–64.
39 See Chapter 2, p 57.
40 *Garcia Alva v Germany* (2001) 37 EHRR 335; *R (West) v Parole Board, R (Smith) v Parole Board (No 2)* [2005] UKHL 1, [2005] 1 WLR 350.
41 See Chapter 2, p 62.
42 *Secretary of State for the Home Department v AF and others* [2009] UKHL 28.
43 [1994] 2 All ER 588.
44 [2000] 3 WLR 1240.
45 (2001) UKHL 65 at para 22.
46 (1998) 27 EHRR 249.

UK.[47] Both, particularly *Tinnelly*, took the view that the threat to national security should be demonstrated. In *Chahal* the Court said that the remedy offered should be 'as effective as it can be' given the need, in the context in question, to rely on secret sources. Clearly, the government in closed hearings before SIAC, the POAC, or in control order proceedings, had an opportunity to demonstrate the threat to national security and to indicate that the statutory requirements in question were satisfied. The problem – before the 'gisting' requirement was established – was that the standard to which it had to show that they were satisfied, following the findings on this point in *Rehman*, were always likely to be viewed at Strasbourg as unacceptably low. The powers to exclude the applicant[48] and his/her legal representative from the proceedings when closed material was examined (without providing a gist of it) were eventually found not to meet the requirements of fairness in *A v UK*.[49] That finding was then applied in the domestic context under Art 6(1) via the HRA in *Secretary of State for the Home Department v AF and others*.[50]

The special advocates (SAs) scheme – whereby security-cleared advocates are appointed to represent the applicant – aids in ensuring that Art 6 compliance has been achieved; in relation to closed material proceedings (CMPs) where only the gist of the material is disclosed, SAs represent the suspect, having been selected from advocates with special experience of administrative and public law. The special advocates see all the closed material. They are not permitted to disclose any part of that material to those whom they represent, aside from the agreed gist.

That means that although the special advocate is able to cross-examine witnesses on the applicant's behalf, he is denied the full benefit of that right; since he does not know of all of the closed evidence against him, he cannot indicate to counsel all the points that potentially could be challenged. The claimants whose interests the SAs represent can, and in practice do, have their own lawyers too, but those lawyers are excluded from closed evidence and closed sessions. So the entitlement of the applicant to SA representation throughout the proceedings is rendered less valuable since that counsel is also prohibited from attending the closed hearings and knowing all the closed evidence against the applicant, aside from the gist.

The procedure for closed material and the use of a special advocate was designed to accord with the Canadian SA model referred to in *Chahal*, to which the ECtHR gave approval. In *Tinnelly & McElduff v UK*[51] the ECtHR referred to this procedure, as provided for at that time in the Special Immigration Appeals Commission Bill with approval as a method of seeking comply with Art 6 while also complying with the demands of national security.[52]

'Public' hearing

The hearings in SIAC are not 'public' as required under Art 6(1), but that is justifiable in the interests of national security, as Art 6(1) provides, so long as the restriction is

---

47 (1997) 23 EHRR 413 (in the context of Art 13).
48 See on this point, *Zana v Turkey* (1999) 27 EHRR 667, in which, in the context of terrorism, the applicant was not allowed to be present at the trial; a breach of Art 6 was found on this basis.
49 (2009) 49 EHRR 29 (Grand Chamber). That finding was made under Art 5(4).
50 [2009] UKHL 28.
51 (1999) 27 EHRR 249.
52 See para 52, and para 78.

proportionate to the legitimate aim pursued. However, arguably proportionality may not be satisfied since even where national security is not in issue – when, for example, the question of Art 3 treatment abroad is being considered – no provision is made for part of the proceedings to be held in public in the sense of admitting journalists to any part of them. The POAC sits in public, but is able to hear closed evidence in camera and with the applicant and their representatives excluded. Control order/TPIM proceedings can be held in private as accepted in *Secretary of State for the Home Dept v E*[53] and in *Secretary of State for the Home Dept v Rideh and J.*[54]

Use of material obtained by third party Art 3 treatment (torture or inhuman or degrading treatment) under Art 6 in non-criminal proceedings?

In *A and Others*,[55] as discussed by Thienel,[56] the House of Lords had to consider whether the court could take account of evidence that might have derived from torture perpetrated in another country. The decision is, it is argued, relevant to proceedings not only in SIAC, but also in the POAC and in control order/TPIM proceedings. In criminal proceedings s 76(2)(a) PACE would apply and the evidence could not be admitted.[57] Lord Bingham, giving the leading judgment in *A and Others*, considered that the issue was one of constitutional principle, and found that evidence obtained by torturing another human being cannot lawfully be admitted against a party to proceedings in a British court, irrespective of where, or by whom, or on whose authority the torture was inflicted.[58] But the most important aspect of the case was that of the burden of proof placed on the secretary of state where the question is raised whether the material relied on might have been obtained by third party torture.

The majority in the House found that SIAC should not admit the evidence if it concluded on a balance of probabilities that it was obtained by torture. In other words, where SIAC was left in doubt as to whether the evidence was obtained in this way, it should admit it. It was found that it would be unrealistic to expect SIAC to demand that each piece of information should be traced back to its ultimate source and the circumstances in which it was obtained investigated so that it could be proved piece by piece, that it was *not* obtained under torture. Lord Hope, in the majority, considered that the threshold should not be put that high[59] and the majority in the Lords agreed to that test.

Thus, reliance can be placed by the secretary of state on material obtained by torture if the court cannot determine on the balance of probabilities that it was so obtained. Further, the initial decision by the secretary of state to impose a TPIM or to proscribe an organisation under TA 2000, as amended in 2006, could be based on material obtained by torture. Further, if material was obtained by the use of inhuman or degrading treatment, but not torture, it could, according to this decision, be admitted and relied on. This appears to be the case even if it was proved by the applicant beyond reasonable doubt that the material was so obtained. If inhuman or degrading

---

53 [2007] EWHC 33 (Admin).
54 [2007] EWHC 804 (Admin).
55 [2005] UKHL 71.
56 See Thienel, T (2006) 17(2) Eur J Int Law, 349–67.
57 See Chapter 14, p 972 *et seq*.
58 At para 51.
59 At para 119.

treatment was perpetrated by British officials to obtain the material, then clearly the applicant could rely on Art 3 and s 7(1)(a) HRA to bring proceedings against the state. But, it appears, from *A and Others*, that he could not rely on Art 6(1) in arguing that the evidence should not be admitted.

But in *Mohamed v Secretary of State for Foreign & Commonwealth Affairs*[60] it was made clear that in certain circumstances material that could demonstrate that torture by a third party state had occurred must be disclosed. The case arose out of an application for disclosure brought by Mohamed, seeking documentation and information from the UK government in order to assist in his defence against charges likely to be brought against him by the US. Mohamed intended to claim that his confessions were false, and were made as a consequence of torture, or at least inhuman treatment. The disclosure application was based on the court's jurisdiction to order a third party to disclose documents, where that party had been involved in the wrongdoing.[61] It was alleged that the UK was involved, due to the participation of the security service, in the alleged wrongdoing. The Divisional Court then granted Mohammed access to the documents. The Foreign Secretary then issued three public interest immunity certificates. There were a further five decisions concerning the status of the 'seven redacted paragraphs' and also a decision of the District Court for the District of Columbia;[62] in it was stated that 'the [US] Government does not challenge or deny the accuracy of Binyam Mohamed's story of brutal treatment' and also (at 64):

> [Mr Mohamed's] trauma lasted for 2 long years. During that time, he was physically and psychologically tortured. His genitals were mutilated. He was deprived of sleep and food. He was summarily transported from one foreign prison to another. Captors held him in stress positions for days at a time. He was forced to listen to piercingly loud music and the screams of other prisoners while locked in a pitch-black cell. All the while, he was forced to inculpate himself and others in various plots to imperil Americans. The Government does not dispute this evidence.

The essence of the UK government's claim in the domestic courts was not that there was anything in the redacted paragraphs that would, in itself, harm the national interest, but that the inability of the government to maintain absolute confidentiality of intelligence information provided by the US would lead to a review of the intelligence-sharing arrangements between the US and the UK, which could result in those arrangements becoming less 'productive'. This claim, reasserted in various formulations in the three certificates, was rejected by the Divisional Court, which held that the seven redacted paragraphs should be made publicly available, and the Court of Appeal dismissed the secretary of state's appeal on the basis that, while the intelligence-sharing arrangements were significant, they could not in this instance override his claim since it was essential for him to be able to refer to the material in order to have a fair trial.

60 [2010] EWCA Civ 65 (10 Feb 2010).
61 *Norwich Pharmacal Co v Customs and Excise Commissioners* [1974] AC 133.
62 Civil Action No 05–1347 (GK) in *Farhi Saeed Bin Mohamed v Barack Obama*.

Freedom of expression, association and assembly under ECHR Arts 10 and 11

The Terrorism Act 2000, as amended, together with the Terrorism Act 2006, creates offences and sanctions able to stifle the expression of a range of dissenting groups and outlaw the very existence of many of them. Certain provisions potentially also prevent or curb journalistic investigation of the activities of certain of those groups. Proscription – the banning of groups deemed 'terrorist' clearly strikes at freedom of association and assembly as well as freedom of expression, taking account, *inter alia*, of the offences of belonging to a proscribed organisation and the offences relating to meetings where members of such organisations are speaking. The provisions discussed below under the TA make it a criminal offence for proscribed organisations to distribute literature, hold or speak at meetings. The offence of 'glorification' of terrorism under the TA 2006 clearly represents an infringement of freedom of expression, although potentially justifiable.

As mentioned above, control orders were imposed under the Prevention of Terrorism Act 2005, but were replaced by terrorism prevention and investigation measures (TPIMs) under the Terrorism Prevention and Investigation Measures Act 2011 (TPIMA).[63] TPIMs, like control orders, can disallow communication and association with non-approved persons, and so clearly affect freedom of expression under Art 10, and freedom of association under Art 11. If Arts 10 or 11 (or other Convention articles, such as Art 1 of the First Protocol where terrorist funding or property is involved) are relevant due to the nature of the offence in question then they can be raised under the argument that the court is under a duty due to s 6 HRA to apply the provisions compatibly with the Convention guarantees,[64] whether a defence is or is not expressly provided. They should not be raised merely as part of a defence – such as a defence of 'reasonable excuse' – since to do so turns those articles on their heads: under para 2 of each article it is for the state to prove that the interference with the right is necessary and proportionate, not for the defendant to prove that a Convention guarantee constitutes a defence to a state action.

The ability of offences under the 2000 Act, the additional offences introduced in 2001 and 2006, and the ability of TPIMs (below) to threaten expression and association is in particular the case given that the aims of some of the groups potentially affected are, broadly speaking, political ones, and so the expression in question may fall into the category of political speech.[65] The high regard in which freedom of speech and of

---

63 For discussion, see: Helen Fenwick, 'Designing ETPIMs around ECHR Review or Normalisation of "Preventive" Non-Trial-Based Executive Measures?' (2013) 76(5) *Modern Law Review* 876; Alexander Horne and Clive Walker, 'The Terrorism Prevention and Investigation Measures Act 2011: one thing but not much the other?' (2012) *Criminal Law Review* 421. See also David Anderson QC, 'Terrorism Prevention and Investigatory Measures in 2012' First Report March 2013 ('TPIMS in 2012'), paras 6.23, 11.33–38. David Anderson comments at para 1.13 of the First Report that '[t]he journey from indefinite detention (2001) through control orders (2005) to TPIMs (2011) has been in a liberalising direction'. Control orders were abandoned from 2012 onwards.

64 See Chapter 4, p 187 *et seq.*

65 See Barendt, E, *Freedom of Speech*, 1st edn, 1987, pp 20 and 23 respectively. See Meiklejohn, A, 'The First Amendment is an Absolute' (1961) Sup Ct Rev 245 and *Political Freedom* (1960), esp pp 115–24.

the press, as 'essential foundations of a democratic society'[66] is held by the Strasbourg institutions was discussed in Part II and need not be rehearsed in any detail here. As discussed, it is a marked feature of the Strasbourg Art 10 jurisprudence that clearly political speech receives a particularly high degree of protection. Where national security was raised as an issue in *Observer and Guardian Newspapers v UK*[67] the margin of appreciation conceded was broader but a violation of Art 10 was found. Where the speech directly concerns government actions – such as the previous intervention in Iraq – the stance taken is particularly robust, even where issues of national security appear to arise. In *Incal v Turkey*,[68] finding a breach of Art 10, the Court said that 'the limits of permissible criticism are wider with regard to the government than in respect of private citizens', and that the dominant position the government occupies should persuade it to display restraint in resorting to criminal proceedings. The Court found that although the argument had been raised that the measures in question were counter-terrorist, the links of the applicant to terrorism were uncertain.[69] This stance reflects values endemic in the Convention: it is clearly difficult to show that an interference with democracy-supporting speech is 'necessary in a democratic society'.[70] On the other hand, political speech that is also homophobic, racist or constitutes an attack on religious groups, such as Jews or Shia Muslims, from a Salafist speaker, would receive a very low level of protection.[71]

Determination to protect political expression is readily evident in UK courts under common law principle or the HRA, as the introduction to Part II indicated, particularly in cases where journalistic material raises political issues,[72] although deference to widely drafted primary legislation,[73] or governmental arguments from national security,[74] has resulted in the ready upholding of restrictions on directly political speech. Earlier findings to the effect that: 'The media . . . are an essential foundation of any democracy'[75] were reinforced by pronouncements in the House of Lords' decision in *Reynolds*,[76] which afforded an explicit recognition to the duty to inform the people on matters of legitimate public interest.[77]

---

66 *Observer and Guardian v United Kingdom*, judgment of 26 November 1991, Series A, no 216, pp 29–30, para 59.
67 (1991) 14 EHRR 153.
68 (2000) 29 EHRR 449.
69 The conviction of the applicant was found to be disproportionate to the aim of countering terrorism pursued.
70 Art 10(2).
71 See *Norwood v UK* 16 November 2004, Application No 23131/03 in which Art 17 (see Chapter 2, p 101) was relied on.
72 *Reynolds v Times Newspapers* [1999] 4 All ER 609; *Derbyshire County Council v Times Newspapers* [1993] AC 534.
73 *Secretary of State for Home Affairs ex p Brind* [1991] 1 AC 696.
74 *Attorney General v Guardian Newspapers (No 2)* [1990] 1 AC 109.
75 *Francome v Mirror Group Newspapers* [1984] 1 WLR 892, p 898, *per* Sir John Donaldson.
76 *Reynolds v Times Newspapers* HL [1999] 4 All ER 609, judgement of 28 October, available from the House of Lords website: www.publications.parliament.uk/pa/ld/ldjudinf.htm.
77 As Lord Nicholls put it: 'freedom to disseminate and receive information on political matters is essential to the proper functioning of the system of parliamentary democracy cherished in this country. This freedom enables those who elect representatives to Parliament to make an informed choice, regarding individuals as well as policies, and those elected to make informed decisions'.

Since press freedom in relation to political expression has clearly been recognised as having a particularly high value in UK and Convention jurisprudence, the possible inclusion of journalists in the wide net of counter-terrorist liability discussed below requires a very strong justification, particularly as it potentially extends to a range of groups covering such divergent issues as animal rights, environmental matters, abortion, the national identity of groups such as the Kurds in Turkey, and also militant fundamentalist religious beliefs. It creates dilemmas for journalists that have any association with such groups – by, for example, producing specialist publications or web-pages aimed at minority groups with some association with a proscribed group. This is true, for example, of publications aimed at the Kurdish minority in the UK, who may have some associations with the PKK.[78] *R (on the application of the Kurdistan Workers' Party and Others) v Secretary of State for the Home Dept*,[79] illustrated these problems for journalists. The case of *Gillan*, discussed in Chapter 12,[80] demonstrated that provisions aimed at terrorism can readily have an effect on the freedom of expression of those entirely uninvolved in terrorist activity but participating in or reporting on dissent. However, the activities and stance of certain groups, including Al-Qaeda and Isis, run entirely counter to the justifications for political speech, so the argument from democracy does not apply to them.

While earlier Strasbourg jurisprudence was more protective of state interests,[81] the more recent 'association' jurisprudence of the Court is more interventionist. In *Socialist Party and Others v Turkey*[82] the Court allowed only a very narrow margin of appreciation in finding that the dissolution of the Socialist party of Turkey had breached Art 11. The Court said that democracy demands that diverse political programmes should be debated, including those that call into question the way a state is currently organised. The Court did not accept that the message of the group that a federal system should be put in place, which would ensure that Kurds would be put on an equal footing with Turkish citizens generally, amounted to incitement to violence. The dissolution of the party was thus found to be disproportionate to the aim in view – the preservation of national security. That stance was in accordance with the Convention jurisprudence that has quite consistently recognised the need to protect the interests of minority and excluded groups.[83] Similar findings were made in *Sidiropoulos v Greece*.[84] The Court said that one of the most important aspects of freedom of association was that citizens should be able to form a legal group with the aim of acting collectively in their mutual interest. Similarly, in *Vogt v Germany*[85] the Court held that a woman dismissed from

---

78 See p 1038, 1074.
79 [2002] EWHC Admin 644.
80 See pp 846–47.
81 See *Glasenapp v FRG* A 104 (1986); *Kosiek v FRG* A 105 (1986); *CCSU v UK* (1988) 10 EHRR 269.
82 Judgment of 25 May 1998 (Appl No 20/1997/804/1007); (1999) 27 EHRR 51, paras 41, 47 and 50.
83 Such groups have included criminals: *Soering v UK* A 161 (1989); prisoners: *Ireland v UK* A 25 (1978), *Golder v UK* A 18 (1975); racial minorities: *East African Asians* cases 3 EHRR 76 (1973), *Hilton v UK* No 5613/72, 4 DR 177 (1976) (No breach found on facts); sexual minorities: *Dudgeon v UK* A 45 (1981), *B v France* A 232-C (1992); political minorities: *Arrowsmith v UK* No 7050/75, 19 DR 5 (1978); religious minorities: *Kokkinakis v Greece* A 260-A (1993).
84 10 July 1998 [ECtHR]. Case no 26695/95, available from the Court's website, www.dhcour.coe.fr.
85 (1995) 21 EHRR 205.

her teaching post due to her membership of an extreme left-wing group had suffered a violation of both Arts 10 and 11.

United Communist Party of Turkey v Turkey[86] concerned the United Communist Party of Turkey, TBKP, was formed in 1990. The Constitutional Court made an order dissolving the TBKP, which entailed the liquidation of the party and the transfer of its assets to the Treasury. The order was based on the inclusion in its name of the prohibited word 'communist' and the alleged encouragement of Kurdish separatism. The TBKP and its leaders applied to the Commission, complaining that the dissolution of the party infringed their right to freedom of association as guaranteed by the ECHR, Art 11. It was found that Art 11 was applicable to the present case. It was further found that the exceptions set out in Art 11(2) had to be construed strictly in relation to political parties. In that case, a political party's choice of name was in principle not able justify dissolution in the absence of other relevant and sufficient circumstances, and there was no evidence that the TBKP represented a real threat to Turkish society or the Turkish state. A scrutiny of the TBKP's programme showed that it intended to resolve the Kurdish issue through dialogue. Thus, it was penalised solely for exercising freedom of expression. In the circumstances, the drastic measure of the dissolution of the TBKP was found to be disproportionate to the aim pursued and consequently unnecessary in a democratic society. Accordingly, it was found that the measure infringed Art 11.

In relation to certain groups the infringement of Arts 10 and 11 may be proportionate to the aims pursued, but that is not necessarily the case in relation to all such groups, especially pro-democracy groups whose 'terrorist' activities only threaten autocratic regimes abroad. The 2000 Act also has the potential to threaten rights of assembly and expression of groups only doubtfully viewed in common parlance as 'terrorist', such as animal rights' or environmental activists. Proscription orders are not sought against all the groups that meet the definition of terrorism under s 1 TA; in effect, proportionality is built into the scheme via executive decisions as to which groups to proscribe or prosecute under the general counter-terrorist offences. The proscription or prosecution of members or supporters of Al-Qaeda, Isis or linked groups is obviously proportionate to the aims pursued under Arts 10 and 11, para 2, and in any event Art 17, providing that the Convention is not to be interpreted so as to imply a right 'for any state, group or person to engage in any activity . . . aimed at the destruction of any of the [Convention rights] or at their limitation to a greater extent than . . . provided for in the Convention', would apply.[87] Such groups are obviously not seeking to use legitimate democratic means in order to persuade persons of their political agenda, and therefore the invocation on their behalf of Convention rights fundamentally based on democratic values is affected. But, as argued below, certain groups have been proscribed, such as the PKK, where it is arguable that the initial proportionality inquiry carried out in effect by the Home Secretary was defective.

Counter-terrorist provisions, therefore, which potentially extend to domestic protest groups putting forward a wide range of political messages – using that term in the broad sense that Strasbourg has endorsed – interfere with the flow of information and ideas;

---

86 1998 WL 1043934 (ECHR), 4 BHRC 1; (1998) 26 EHRR 121; [1998] HRCD 247.
87 See further Chapter 2, p 101.

that can also be said of groups that do not threaten national security in the UK and that could be viewed as 'freedom fighters'. Such provisions therefore come into conflict, if taken at face value, with the expression, association, and assembly of a very wide and diverse range of groups and persons and therefore call into question their compatibility with democratic values. As discussed in Chapter 9, domestic 'protest' groups that adopt the use of direct action may create the possibilities of disorder, of harm to citizens, and damage to property.[88] They may eventually, if sufficiently resourced and well organised, threaten national security. Clearly, the state has a duty to protect citizens from their attentions. The need to give weight to such interests explains the general acceptance of the freedoms of expression, assembly and association as non-absolute rights,[89] even though it may be that direct action and more forceful protest is most likely to bring about change. Protest groups that may affect national security in another country but not in the UK may seek to use the legitimate outlets of expression and protest to further their cause in the UK. The ordinary criminal law exists, however, in order to punish members of all such groups for specific actions domestically, such as causing criminal damage, while public order law is available to control protests where harm to persons or property is a possibility. It will be argued below that the potentially chilling impact of the counter-terrorist provisions on the freedoms of expression, association and assembly can have an impact that fails to satisfy the demands of proportionality, depending on the range of persons that are affected by the provisions.

Article 3 treatment

Deporting suspected terrorists who could face Art 3 treatment abroad or an unfair trial?

The government views itself as confronted by a dilemma in respect of persons who are suspected of being international terrorists but who cannot be extradited, or deported to their country of origin, because there are grounds to think that they would there be subject to torture or inhuman and degrading treatment, since to do so would violate Art 3 of the Convention. The decision of the European Court of Human Rights in *Soering v UK*,[90] extended in *Chahal v UK*,[91] found that a breach of Art 3 will arise where a country deports a person to another country, knowing that he or she will face a substantial risk of Art 3 treatment in that other country. It should also be noted that the UK has ratified Protocols 6 and 13[92] and therefore cannot deport persons to countries where there is a real risk that the death penalty will be imposed.[93]

---

88 See pp 662, 680.

89 See the leading US case, *Hague v Committee for Industrial Organisation* 307 US 496 (1938). For further discussion, see Williams, DGT [1987] Crim LR 167.

90 (1989) 11 EHRR 439, paras 90–91.

91 (1996) 23 EHRR 413, para 74.

92 Protocol 6 prohibits the death penalty in time of peace. Protocol 13 requires member states to abolish the death penalty in all circumstances, removing the exception for time of war. See *Harris, O'Boyle and Warbrick Law of the ECHR*, 3rd edn, 2014, pp 963–965.

93 *X v Spain* D R 37 (1984) p93; *Aylor-Davis v France* (1994) 76-A DR 164; *Raidl v Austria* (1995) 82-A DR 134

It is not possible for the government to enter a derogation to Art 3 under Art 15 of the Convention.[94] If this had been possible it would have allowed the Home Secretary to deport persons to various countries, regardless of the fact that they might there be subjected to torture or other forms of Art 3 treatment. The Joint Committee on Human Rights at one point appeared to take the view that the government could have escaped from the demands of Art 3 by denouncing the whole Convention[95] and then re-entering it, at the same time entering a reservation to Art 3.[96] However, it is probable that such a reservation would have been viewed as invalid since as a matter of general international law it is accepted that reservations are not permitted to non-derogable articles.[97] Had the UK sought to take this immensely controversial course, it would almost certainly have been found to be in breach of Art 3 and would also have breached the International Covenant on Civil and Political Rights (ICCPR), which does not allow for derogation from Art 7, which covers Art 3 treatment.[98] It is also a party to the United Nations Convention Against Torture and Other Cruel, Inhuman or Degrading Treatment or Punishment 1984[99] and the European Convention for the Prevention of Torture and Inhuman and Degrading Treatment or Punishment 1987.[100]

The government has sought to escape from the effects of *Chahal* by two methods. First, it sought to have *Chahal* – in effect – overturned at Strasbourg. The government sought to overturn the *Chahal* ruling by supporting the Netherlands in *Ramzy v the Netherlands*,[101] a case that was brought by Mohammad Ramzy, an Algerian accused by

---

94   The guarantee under Art 3 is one of the non-derogable guarantees under Art 15(2).
95   Under Art 58. See 2nd Report of the Joint Committee, para 19.
96   Section 15 HRA provides powers for the Secretary of State to make designated reservations by order. Under Art 57 of the Convention this power can only be exercised at the point of ratification.
97   There is no explicit exclusion of the right to make reservations to Art 3. The matter is one of general international law: reservations may not be made which are incompatible with the object and purpose of a treaty (Vienna Convention, Art 19(c)). There is little doubt that the ECtHR would claim the right to determine this question under the ECHR (see Van Dijk and Van Hoof, *The European Convention on Human Rights: Theory and Practice*, 2nd edn, 1998, pp 774–75 and *cf* p 776 for the non-derogable provisions). It has not yet had to do so. France has a reservation with respect to Art 15: 17 YB 4 (1974). The general opinion is that this does not give France the right to derogate from a non-derogable provision, nor would it protect France from the jurisdiction of the Court to determine the question. The UN Human Rights Committee (HRC) has taken a strong position against the power of states to make reservations with respect to the non-derogable provisions of the Covenant (General Comment 24) and, in the case of torture, an absolute one, since the HRC says torture is contrary to a peremptory norm of international law. Thus, even if the UK could avoid the Art 3 duty under the ECHR by reservation, it could not do so under the ICCPR, Art 7. Obviously the UK would not be permitted to enter a reservation to the UN Convention Against Torture. It may be noted that the UN Committee Against Torture made a statement directly communicating with the state Parties (22 November 2001, 27th session) reminding them, in the light of the September 11 atrocities, that obligations under the Convention against Torture in Arts 2, 15 and 16 are non-derogable and 'must be observed in all circumstances'.
98   Art 4(2).
99   (1985) Cmnd 9593; it came into force in 1987 and it was ratified by the UK in December 1988.
100 (1991) Cm 1634; it was ratified by the UK in June 1988. For discussion, see Evans, M and Morgan, R, *Preventing Torture: A Study of the European Convention for the Prevention of Torture*, 1998. The right to freedom from torture or inhuman or degrading treatment or punishment is also recognised in Art 5 of the Universal Declaration on Human Rights and in many jurisdictions: see Clayton and Tomlinson *The Law of Human Rights*, 2000, Chapter 8, esp pp 412–29. Torture is a crime under International Law: see *R v Bow Street Stipendiary Magistrate ex p Pinochet Ugarte (No 3)* [1999] 2 WLR 827.
101 Application No 25424/05 20 July 2010.

the Dutch authorities of involvement in Islamic terrorism. He alleged that, if expelled to Algeria, he would be exposed to a real risk of treatment contrary to Art 3. But the case came to nothing when Ramzy disappeared and showed no further interest in pursuing it. However, the issue was considered in *Saadi v Italy;*[102] the Grand Chamber of the European Court of Human Rights upheld the reasoning in *Chahal*.

More fruitfully, the UK government has been seeking to conclude agreements with the countries to which it could return the suspects in question. The idea is that under the agreement the returnee would not be exposed to Art 3 treatment in the state to which he was returned. After the London transport bombings in July 2005, the Blair government signed a series of memorandums of understanding with North African and Middle Eastern countries that would allow terrorist suspects who could not be tried in Britain to be deported. The policy was continued under the Coalition government[103] and the current (post-2015) Conservative government. General agreements have been reached with *inter alia* the governments of Jordan, Libya, Algeria and Lebanon.[104]

RB, U, OO v SSHD[105] was of especial significance in relation to such agreements since the case had the potential to determine whether deportation of a particular group of suspects, and in particular of Abu Qatada, could occur. The deportation of Qatada to Jordan, attracting a very high volume of media attention, became politicised as something of a litmus test of the government's competence and determination in dealing with terrorism. The case focused on the use of diplomatic assurances to reduce the risk of Art 3 treatment, and on the real risk of treatment of Qatada in 'flagrant breach' of Art 6 in Jordan at his retrial there. The key issue raised in the appeal was to the effect that assurances in relation to individuals cannot be relied upon where there is a pattern of human rights violations in the receiving state, coupled with a culture of impunity for the state agents in the security service, and for the persons perpetrating such violations, and therefore SIAC's reliance on the diplomatic assurances that had been given against harm to Qatada in Jordan was irrational.

In two claims against Russia the Strasbourg Court had spoken of the need for assurances to 'ensure adequate protection against the risk of ill-treatment' contrary to Art 3.[106] Lord Phillips also noted that in *Mamatkulov v Turkey*[107] the assurances against ill-treatment were treated by the Court as part of the matrix that had to be considered when deciding whether there were substantial grounds for believing in the existence of a real risk of inhuman treatment. He further found that the Court had applied a similar approach in *Shamayev v Georgia and Russia*,[108] and so, he pointed out, had the United

---

102   (2008) application no 37201/06 (2009) 49 EHRR 30.

103   The Coalition Government set out its approach to MOUs in its Review of Counter-Terrorism Powers (CM 8004) published in January 2011.

104   HC 11 January 2006 col GC107.

105   *RB (Algeria) (FC) and another (Appellants) v SSHD OO (Jordan) (Original Respondent and Cross-appellant) v SSHD (Original Appellant and Cross-respondent)* [2009] UKHL 10; on appeal from: [2007] EWCA Civ 808, [2008] EWCA Civ 290.

106   *Ismoilov and others v Russia* (App No 2947/06) judgment of 12 December 2006 para 127 and *Ryabikin v Russia* (App No 8320/04) judgment of 19 June 2008 para 119.

107   (2005) 41 EHRR 494. The court said that it was unable to conclude that substantial grounds existed for believing that the applicants faced a real risk of treatment proscribed by Art 3: para 77.

108   App No 36378/02, judgment of 12 April 2005.

Nations Committee Against Torture in *Hanan Attia v Sweden*.[109] The political realities in Jordan, the bilateral diplomatic relationship with the UK, and the fact that Othman (Qatada) would have a high public profile, were, he found, the most significant factors in SIAC's assessment of the Art 3 risk, which disclosed no irrationality. Lord Hope agreed, noting the UN position to the effect that in a regime systematically practicing torture, the principle of *non-refoulement* must be strictly observed and diplomatic assurances should not be resorted to,[110] but viewing that position as indicating that the question of reliance would always be a matter of fact, dependent on particular circumstances relating to the individual in question; he relied on the finding in *Saadi*[111] to the effect that where evidence capable of proving that there are substantial grounds for believing that he would be exposed to ill-treatment is adduced by the applicant, it is for the government to dispel any doubts about it.

As regards the Art 6 issue, SIAC had found that there was a real risk that confessions would be relied on in Othman's retrial which had been obtained by treatment that breached Article 3, but their admission would be the consequence of a judicial decision, within a system at least on its face intended to exclude evidence which was not given voluntarily.[112] So SIAC had found no total denial of the right to a fair trial, but the Court of Appeal had found that SIAC had erred in law: 'The use of evidence obtained by torture is prohibited in Convention law . . . because of the connexion of the issue with article 3, a fundamental, unconditional and non-derogable prohibition'. SIAC was wrong not to recognise this crucial difference between breaches of article 6 based on this ground and breaches of article 6 based simply on defects in the trial process or . . . composition of the court.'[113] Lord Phillips did not accept the conclusion of the Court of Appeal[114] that it required a high degree of assurance that evidence obtained by torture would not be used in the proceedings in Jordan before it would be lawful to deport Othman to face those proceedings. He found that the principle at issue was that the

> state must stand firm against the conduct that has produced the evidence, but that did not require a different state to retain to the detriment of national security a terrorist suspect absent a high degree of assurance that evidence obtained by torture would not be adduced in the receiving state.[115]

This decision was then challenged at Strasbourg; the Strasbourg Court's stance in *Othman v UK*[116] echoed that of the House of Lords as far as the Art 3 issue was concerned since it considered that only in rare cases would the general situation in a country mean that no weight at all would be given to assurances. It found that its only task

---

109 17 November 2003, Communication No 199/2002.
110 Cited in *Sing v Canada (Minister of Citizenship and Immigration)* 2007 FC 361, para 136, from UN Document A/59/324.
111 (2009) 49 EHRR 30, para 129.
112 At para 422 of SIAC's judgment.
113 Paras 45, 49, Court of Appeal judgment.
114 At para 154. See further M. Garrod 'Deportation of Suspected Terrorists with 'Real Risk' of Torture: The House of Lords Decision in *Abu Qatada*' (2010) 73 MLR 631.
115 At para 153.
116 (2012) 55 EHRR; [2012] ECHR 56.

was to examine whether the assurances obtained in a particular case were sufficient to remove any real risk of ill-treatment.[117] The Court found that on the evidence the Jordanian criminal justice system lacked many of the standard, internationally recognised safeguards to prevent torture and punish its perpetrators,[118] but that the assurances under the MOU that the applicant would not be ill-treated upon return to Jordan were superior to those that the Court had previously considered in both detail and formality. They were found to have been given in good faith by the Jordanian government, at the highest levels of that government, and therefore capable of binding the state. The MOU was also found to be unique in that it had withstood the extensive examination that had been carried out by SIAC, which had had the benefit of receiving evidence adduced by both parties, including expert witnesses. The Court concluded on that basis that the applicant's return to Jordan would not expose him to a real risk of ill-treatment, meaning that no violation of Article 3 was found.[119]

In relation to Art 6 the Court found that the admission of torture-tainted evidence in Othman's trial in Jordan would be manifestly contrary, not just to the provisions of Art 6, but to the most basic international standards of a fair trial.[120] Having made that finding, the remaining two issues which the Court had to consider were: (i) whether showing a real risk of the admission of torture evidence would be sufficient; and (ii) if so, whether a flagrant denial of justice (a breach so fundamental as to amount to a nullification of the very essence of the right guaranteed by Art 6) would arise in this case.[121] The Court found that on any retrial of the applicant, it would undoubtedly be open to him to challenge the admissibility of statements made against him, alleged to have been obtained by torture. But the difficulties he would face in trying to do so many years after the event, and before the same court that had already rejected a claim of inadmissibility (and that routinely rejected all such claims), were very substantial indeed.[122] The Court therefore concluded that the applicant had discharged the burden that could be fairly imposed on him of establishing that the evidence that could be used against him was obtained by torture. So the Court, in agreement with the Court of Appeal, found that there was a real risk that the applicant's retrial would amount to a flagrant denial of justice, and therefore that his deportation to Jordan would create a breach of Art 6.[123]

Thus, the decision on the Art 6 question took a strict stance[124] since it meant that the prospective use of evidence obtained by torture would *automatically* constitute a flagrant denial of justice in a foreign state, regardless of other safeguards or of its importance to the outcome of the trial.[125] The decision on Art 3, like that of the House

---

117 Para 186.
118 Para 191.
119 Para 205.
120 Para 267.
121 Para 271.
122 Para 279.
123 Paras 280, 282.
124 See on the Art 6 issue *Gafgen v Germany* [2011] 52 EHRR 1 and *El-Haski v Belgium* App No 649/08, 25 September 2012; in *Gafgen* it was found that the risk of admission of such evidence was not viewed as *automatically* creating a flagrant denial of justice, but as raising serious issues as to the fairness of the proceedings.
125 Note: after this decision, in *Othman v SSHD* [2012] UKSIAC 15/2005_2 (12 November 2012) SIAC found that the secretary of state should not have declined to revoke the deportation order, because she

of Lords, ran contrary to the 'recurring theme in NGO advocacy that because Article 3 (ECHR/CAT) is absolute, the use of diplomatic assurances in the context of a risk of torture is wrong or prohibited'[126] since they are not an effective safeguard, the stance taken in the 2004 report to the UN General Assembly[127] by the UN Special Rapporteur on Torture.[128] The decision not only confirmed the acceptability under Art 3 of deportation with assurances against Art 3 treatment, but it impliedly also allowed deportation with assurances against a flagrant breach of Art 6, so long as they were specific enough in relation to the potential use of torture-tainted evidence. The decision in *Othman* departed from that in *Saadi* in that an executive process – the obtaining and negotiation of unenforceable assurances – was allowed to create a departure from the absolute nature of Art 3. In that sense it is redolent of a dialogic approach in that the stance taken in the House of Lords appeared to be influential at Strasbourg. The argument that the risk posed by Qatada in the UK should influence the standard of proof he would have to adduce as to the likelihood that torture-tainted evidence would be used at his trial was rejected, a far from appeasing approach that was received with intense irritation by the UK government. But nevertheless the judgment did create a compromise between fair trial values and national security since it indicated that diplomatic assurances would be valuable in reducing that likelihood.[129]

Freedom from discrimination – Article 14

A number of the powers discussed below can be challenged, and have been challenged, by reading one of the ECHR articles – most obviously Art 5 read with Art 14[130] – on the basis that certain of the provisions discussed may create discrimination on the basis of race or nationality, direct or (possibly) indirect. (The question of indirect discrimination under Art 14 is examined in Chapter 5[131].) The discrimination may be justifiable, but only if the demands of proportionality are satisfied; that would mean that there had to be a rational connection between the interference in question and the aim pursued, and that the interference went no further than necessary to achieve that end.[132] The key anti-terrorist measure adopted post-9/11 under Part IV ATCSA allowed non-British suspected international terrorists to be detained without trial. This detention scheme was

---

had not satisfied the judges that, on a retrial in Jordan, there would be no real risk that the impugned statements apparently obtained by torture would be admitted.

126 Refugee Studies Centre University of Oxford RSC Working Paper No 32, *The Use of Diplomatic Assurances in the Prevention of Prohibited Treatment* Nina Larsaeus, October 2006. See also the joint report of Amnesty International, Human Rights Watch and the International Commission of Jurists of 2 December 2005; Tribunal Record, vol 1, pp 179–223.

127 11 January 2004.

128 UN Document A/59/324.

129 The Home Secretary later sought fresh assurances that torture-tainted evidence would not be used at trial against Qatada if deported (see e.g., *The Telegraph*, 13 November 2012 'Abu Qatada's legal battle to stay in Britain'); eventually he was deported to Jordan where he stood trial and was acquitted.

130 See pp 1089–90. Art 14 provides a guarantee of non-discrimination in the context of the other rights. Even where the other article would not be breached if read alone, it may be found to be breached when read with Art 14. See Chapter 2, pp 93–94; Chapter 5, pp 269–71.

131 See p 270.

132 See Chapter 4, p 245. See also Chapter 5, pp 265, 267–68.

abandoned since, *inter alia*, it was found by the House of Lords to be discriminatory on the ground of nationality and therefore in contravention of the ECHR, Arts 5 and 14, in the seminal decision in *A and Others v Secretary of State for the Home Dept*,[133] discussed below.

3 Counter-terrorist criminal offences

Key themes

The permanent counter-terrorist scheme created by the TA 2000 under the then Labour government represented a dramatic break with the values arguably adhered to in relation to the previous scheme – that as emergency legislation the provisions should be temporary and graduated to the level and location of the threat. Ironically, the key development able to temper the excesses of the TA was the Human Rights Act (HRA), although the UK also remained bound by the ECHR at the international level. Interestingly, the consultation paper that preceded the legislation[134] appeared to assume that most of its proposals would not lead to conflicts with the Convention, under the HRA. At certain points this issue was explicitly addressed; at others the relevant Convention articles were simply not mentioned. When the then Home Secretary introduced the Terrorism Bill to Parliament in December 1999 he made a declaration of its compatibility with the Convention rights under s 19(1)(a) HRA, but obviously the courts remained at liberty to find incompatibility.[135] This was an instance in which the courts were clearly going to have the key role to play in tempering the potential of the legislation. This was apparent, bearing in mind the role played by Parliament in debating the Terrorism Bill 2000, which was circumscribed – in civil liberties' terms – due to the very large majority of the Labour government and the stance of the main opposition party. In debate on the bill of 2000 the main proposals made by the Conservative opposition were more draconian than those of the government. They included the re-introduction of internment[136] and the extension of detention by executive, not judicial, authorisation.[137] The stance of the courts was also of indirect significance in shaping the response of the executive to the TA powers.

Introduction of the Terrorism Act 2000; relationship with the previous scheme

The then Labour government published a consultation paper on the future of anti-terrorism laws in December 1998.[138] It was intended to address the question of the rationale of retaining 'emergency' anti-terrorism laws in the face of the peace process[139] in Northern Ireland and therefore to counter the argument that the Prevention of Terrorism

---

133 (2004) UKHL 56; [2005] 2 AC 68; [2005] 2 WLR 87; [2005] 3 All ER 169.
134 Cmnd 4178, prepared 17 December 1998.
135 See further Chapter 4, pp 180–83.
136 A new Sched 2 and a new clause which would have effected this was proposed: HC Debs 15 March 2000 cols 331–37. Both were defeated, Labour and Liberal Democrat MPs voting together: HC Debs 15 March 2000 col 347.
137 HC Debs 15 March 2000 col 431.
138 *Legislation against Terrorism. A Consultation Paper*, Cm 4178.
139 See the Introduction to the Paper, and in particular para 6.

Act (PTA) 1989 with its various later accretions should be repealed and not replaced. The 1998 paper was based on a report prepared by Lord Lloyd of Berwick in 1996[140] who had recommended that a new permanent anti-terrorist law should replace the temporary provisions. The policy adopted in his report formed the background to the consultation paper and in turn to the Terrorism Bill 2000. Once the Act of 2000 came into force, it repealed the PTA and Emergency Provisions Act (EPA) 1996 (which applied only to Northern Ireland).[141]

The TA has four key hallmarks. It is far more extensive, covering a much wider range of groups; it is permanent; its main provisions apply equally across the UK, although there were special transitional provisions for Northern Ireland, and it retains almost all the draconian special powers and offences adopted under the previous 'temporary' counter-terrorist scheme, while adding new incitement offences.

The justification for the TA provisions was that they were needed post-2000 to combat the threat from three groups. The first of these comprised those Irish dissident groups opposed to the peace process.[142] The second comprised 'international terrorists'. The paper noted that across the world there had been 'a rise in terrorism motivated by religious idealism'.[143] Both these groups were already covered under the existing legislation, although not all the special provisions were applied equally to international terrorism. The threat was apparently mainly from the new, third, group, on which the case for the new legislation appeared mainly to rest. This group comprised of a wide and disparate range of domestic groups other than those connected with Irish terrorism, such as animal rights or environmental activists,[144] and, possibly, anti-abortion

---

140 Lord Lloyd of Berwick's *Inquiry into legislation against terrorism* (Cmnd 3420), published in October 1996.

141 The PTA was renewed for the last time on 15 March 2000. The EPA was renewed for the last time on 24 August 2000. The special measures it provided for Northern Ireland were provided in Part VII of the Act of 2000.

142 In the paper the government found: 'there are small numbers who remain opposed to peace and wedded to violence. So, even though the context is of a general movement towards lasting peace in Northern Ireland, it is too soon to be confident that all terrorism has been abandoned' (*ibid*, para 2.3).

143 Lord Lloyd's Report drew attention to 'possible future changes in the terrorist threat' and to lives and property in the UK; 'changes which mirror what is happening across the world' (*ibid*, para 2.4). Examples were given of the rise of 'Islamic extremism' and the use of Sarin nerve gas on the Tokyo underground in 1995 by the Aum Shinrikyo religious cult, which killed 12 people and affected up to 5,500.

144 'The threat from some marginal but extreme elements of the animal rights movement continues to be of more concern to the Government [than Scottish or Welsh nationalist groups].' The paper noted that animal rights extremists have in the past sent letter bombs to the leaders of major political parties, attacked Bristol University's Senate House with a high explosive bomb, targeted a veterinary surgeon and a psychologist with car bombs and caused millions of pounds worth of damage. 'The shape of new counter-terrorist legislation needs to reflect the possible threat from indigenous groups too' (Chapter 2 of the Paper, at para 2.5). In Chapter 3 of the Paper the concerns regarding these groups are given some further substance. It is noted that in 1997 more than 800 incidents were recorded by the Animal Rights National Index (ARNI) and 'these included attacks on abattoirs, laboratories, breeders, hunts, butchers, chemists, doctors, vets, furriers, restaurants, supermarkets and other shops' which resulted in injuries although not in deaths and in damage done in 1997 estimated at more than 1.8 million (*ibid*, para 3.10). See also Home Office, Animal Rights Extremism, 2001.

groups.[145] The paper accepted that the level of violence associated with such groups was low compared with the level of IRA violence in the early 1970s. However, it argued that those groups posed a continuing threat and that other single issue groups might be set up and might use violent methods 'to impose their will on the rest of society'.[146] Thus, the paper switched the focus of concern from the need for measures to combat a high and rising level of violence to the need to be ready to combat the possibility of violence in the future. The threat of violence from environmental, animal rights' or anti-abortion activists might have appeared to be a real possibility at the time, but it had not, pre-2000, materialised on anything like the scale previously thought of as necessary to justify draconian anti-terrorist laws. Moreover, the ordinary criminal law was argu-ably adequate as a response to the activities of such groups. The paper merely provided assertions rather than evidence as to the need for special counter-terrorist measures, as opposed to a more effective use of the existing criminal law. No effort was made to analyse the need for the extension of the special provisions to a very wide range of new groups, including protest groups. The paper did not appear, for example, to draw on experience from other countries, including European ones, which were equally faced with extremist groups. The problems experienced in the US were mentioned, but the paper did not examine the efficacy of the means used to combat them. The conclusion of the government in the consultation paper was that a threat comparable to that existing in 1974 could be discerned. Obviously since that point it has become clear that the threat is not from animal rights' activists, but mainly from 'international' terrorist groups, often comprised of Islamist militants, in particular Al-Qaeda, Isis and similar groups.

The intention was that the Terrorism Act 2000 would be permanent; that had the advantage, as the paper pointed out,[147] of being 'transparent', that is, no pretence was made that the legislation would be repealed. This was a strong argument, given the spu-rious nature, indicated above, of claims that the previous legislation was temporary and passed only in response to a current emergency. But it abandoned even the pretence that temporary and regrettable emergency measures, involving an ordinarily unacceptable infringement of civil liberties, were in contemplation. The paper noted that the vast majority of criminal law is permanent, implying that this provided a reason for aban-doning the temporary nature of the counter-terrorism legislation and thereby blurring past distinctions between criminal law and special measures adopted to meet specific emergencies. No provision for the full review of the legislation was included. Therefore it was intended that the permanent powers would receive even less scrutiny than the temporary ones did. The Act failed to take account of the need for parliamentary scru-tiny to oversee the workings of the powers. The Act left their use far more overtly in executive, as opposed to parliamentary, hands. If certain of the powers were not used in practice it should have been possible to repeal them, and in fact a number of the powers

---

145 The paper speculated as to the possibility that anti-abortion groups might adopt terrorist methods in the UK: 'In the United States, for example, there is an increasing tendency by individuals and groups to resort to terrorist methods. Some of those opposed to the USA's laws on abortion have bombed clinics and attacked, and, in a number of cases, killed doctors and nursing staff employed by them. Although there have been no comparable attacks in the United Kingdom, the possibility remains that some new group or individual could operate in this way in the future' (*ibid*, para 3.12).
146 Para 3.12.
147 *Ibid*, at para 2.8.

were strikingly under-used, even post 9/11; an annual review would have provided a forum for arguing for such repeal. However, since 2000, due mainly to the activities of Islamic militant groups, especially from 2012 to 2016, repeal of the 2000 Act is not in contemplation. Instead, the rise in terrorist attacks and conspiracies, and the 7/7 suicide bombing, have led to the introduction of a range of new offences, including very early intervention offences, especially in the Terrorism Act 2006.

Extending the definition of 'terrorism' under the Terrorism Act 2000

The definition of 'terrorism' under the TA provides the foundation for a very wide range of broad special terrorism offences in the TA, and for those subsequently introduced under the Anti-Terrorism, Crime and Security Act 2001, the Terrorism Act 2006 and the Counter-terrorism Act 2008. The definition also allowed, as discussed below, for the application of special terrorism sanctions under the Prevention of Terrorism Act 2005, and later enactments, including the Counter-Terrorism Act 2015, not dependent on charging a person with a specific offence and without proof of an offence.

Defining 'terrorism'

The problem of defining terrorism has spawned an extensive literature.[148] One 1988 study identified a total of 109 different definitions in use across the world[149] and the number is far higher today. Attempts to develop a generally accepted legal definition of terrorism have failed. Golder and Williams find:[150]

> Some have likened 'the search for the legal definition of terrorism . . . [to] the quest for the Holy Grail'. Others, such as Judge Richard Baxter, formerly of the International Court of Justice, writing in 1974, have questioned the utility of a legal definition, stating: 'We have cause to regret that a legal concept of terrorism was ever inflicted upon us. The term is imprecise; it is ambiguous; and, above all it serves no operative legal purpose'.[151]

Terrorism was defined in s 20(1) of the Prevention of Terrorism (Temporary Provisions) Act 1989 as 'the use of violence for political ends and includes any use of violence

148 See, e.g., Primoritz, I, 'What is Terrorism?', in Gearty, C (ed), *Terrorism*, 1996, p 130; Butko, T 'Terrorism redefined' (2005) 18 *Peace Review* 145; Donohue, L K, 'Terrorism and the counter-terrorist discourse', in Ramraj, VV, Hor, M and Roach, K, *Global Anti-terrorism Law and Policy*, 2005; Claridge, D, 'State terrorism? Applying a definitional model' (1996) 8 *Terrorism and Political Violence* 47; Levitt, G, 'Is "Terrorism" Worth Defining?' (1986) 13 *Ohio Northern University Law Review* 97; Schmid, A and Jongman, A *Political Terrorism*, 1987, Royal Netherlands Academy of Arts and Sciences; Murphy, JF, 'Defining International Terrorism: A Way Out of the Quagmire' (1989) 19 *Israel Yearbook on Human Rights* 13, 14; Gearty, C, *Terror*, 1991. Levitt, G, 'Is "Terrorism" Worth Defining?' (1986) 13 *Ohio Northern University Law Review* 97.
149 Schmid, AP and Jongman, AJ, *Political Terrorism: A New Guide to Actors, Authors, Concepts, Databases, Theories, and Literature*, 1988, 5.
150 Golder, B and Williams, G, 'What is "Terrorism"? Problems of Legal Definition' [2004] 27(2) *UNSW Law Journal*, Vol 27(2) 271, at p 271.
151 Baxter, RR, 'A Skeptical Look at the Concept of Terrorism' (1974) 7 *Akron Law Review* 380, p 380.

for the purpose of putting the public, or any section of the public in fear'. But this did not mean that the PTA powers applied to all activities that fell within that definition. The special powers conferred applied only to 'terrorism connected with the affairs of Northern Ireland' or (in certain instances) to international terrorism. Non-Irish domestic terrorism, that is, terrorism having its origins in the affairs of any part of the United Kingdom other than Northern Ireland, was excluded from the scope of the Act. The s 20 definition of terrorism was in fact extraordinarily wide and imprecise since the use of the word 'includes' meant that the requirement of putting a section of the public in fear was not an essential ingredient of it. The terms 'violence' and 'political ends' were undefined. Arguably, therefore, 'the use of violence for political ends' could have included some direct action public protest. It is unclear whether s 20 was confined to violence against persons. The definition might therefore have been unworkable in practice had it not been for the qualified application of the powers.

The definition adopted under the Terrorism Act 2000

The broad definition adopted under s 1 of the Terrorism Act 2000 (TA),[152] as amended by s 34 Terrorism Act 2006, and s 75 Counter-terrorism Act 2008, has three main elements. 'Terrorism' means, first, 'the use or threat of action involving serious violence against any person or serious damage to property, which endangers the life of any person, or creates a serious risk to the health or safety of the public or a section of the public, or is designed seriously to interfere with or seriously to disrupt an electronic system'. Second, the use or threat must be for the purpose of advancing a 'political, religious, racial or ideological' cause. Third, the use or threat must be 'designed to influence the government or an international governmental organisation[153] or to intimidate the public or a section of the public' (s 1(1)(b)). It may be noted that the third element is not needed if firearms or explosives are used.[154] The Act applies *wherever* terrorist action takes place, under s 1(4), not just in the UK. The requirement of a threat to the established order contained in the words: 'to intimidate or coerce a government', the main limiting factor under the proposed definition, was watered down to 'influence'. Section 75 of the 2008 Act gave effect to Lord Carlile's 12th recommendation

---

152 Section 1 of the Terrorism Act, as amended, provides in full:
    (1) In this Act 'terrorism' means the use or threat of action where –
        (a) the action falls within sub-section (2),
        (b) the use or threat is designed to influence the government or an international governmental organization or to intimidate the public or a section of the public, and
        (c) the use or threat is made for the purpose of advancing a political, religious or ideological cause.
    (2) Action falls within this sub-section if it –
        (a) involves serious violence against a person,
        (b) involves serious damage to property,
        (c) endangers a person's life, other than that of the person committing the action,
        (d) creates a serious risk to the health or safety of the public or a section of the public, or
        (e) is designed seriously to interfere with or seriously to disrupt an electronic system.
153 The words 'or an international governmental organisation' were added by the Terrorism Act 2006, s 34.
154 See further: Fenwick, H, *Civil Rights: New Labour, Freedom and the Human Rights Act*, 2000, Chapter 3; Walker, C, *A Guide to the Anti-Terrorism Legislation*, 3rd edn 2014, Blackstone; Rowe, JJ, 'The Terrorism Act 2000' [2001] Crim LR 527.

in his detailed January 2007 report on the definition of terrorism,[155] which was that the definition of terrorism in s 1(1) of the 2000 Act be amended to include, in para (c), the purpose of advancing a racial cause (in addition to a political, religious or ideological cause). The s 1 definition does not in itself create a criminal offence of 'being a terrorist'. But the key point is that in its potential effect the s 1(1) definition is far wider in practice than s 20 since the TA, unlike the PTA, allows the *definition itself* to determine the application of the special powers. The then government assumed that such application would, due to the decisions of police officers, the DPP and CPS, in practice affect only certain extremist groups. But given the lack of effective, independent control over the day-to-day decision-making of such bodies, that is not, it is argued, a satisfactory position in civil liberties' terms,[156] although in practice the special terrorism offences dependent on the s 1 definition have not been used against protest groups.

The TA definition allowed the activities of a number of groups, including protest groups, previously criminal, to be re-designated – potentially – as terrorist. The definition expressly covers threats of serious disruption or damage to, for example, computer installations or public utilities. The definition is therefore potentially able to catch a number of forms of public protest. Danger to property, violence or a serious risk to safety that can be described as 'ideologically, politically, racially or religiously motivated' may arise in the context of many demonstrations and other forms of public protest, including some industrial disputes. The government stated in the consultation paper that it had 'no intention of suggesting that matters that can properly be dealt with under normal public order powers should in future be dealt with under counter-terrorist legislation'.[157] But once special arrest and detention powers are handed to the police they can be used, at their discretion, if a particular person or group falls, or appears to fall, within the TA definition. For instance, some direct action against property by anti-war, animal rights or environmental activists falls within it, on its face. The definition also allowed the previously *non-criminal* actions of a number of persons to be re-designated as terrorist in theory since the special terrorist offences, discussed below, had in a number of instances no equivalents in ordinary criminal law; they potentially apply to a wide range of persons, including those who have some contact with persons designated 'terrorist'. Thus, technically speaking, the then Home Secretary was right in stating, as he did, that the definition *itself* did not create any new offences.[158] But it potentially led to the criminalisation of the actions or omissions of a wide range of persons, many of whom did not themselves fall within the definition. The Court of Appeal found in *R v F*[159] that the term 'government' in s 1 was not limited to governments based on democracy – the 'apparent nobility' of the terrorist' cause in taking action against a repressive dictatorship would not mean that those concerned fell outside the definition. The question of the width of the definition of terrorism was considered by the Supreme Court, as discussed below, in *R v Gul (Appellant)*[160] which confirmed the finding in *R v F*, and by the Court of Appeal in *David Miranda v Secretary of State for the Home Department*.[161]

155 'The definition of terrorism' Cm 7052, 2007.
156 See for discussion C Walker (2007) PL 331
157 *Ibid*, para 3.18.
158 See the *Guardian*, 14 November 1999.
159 [2007] EWCA Crim 243.
160 [2013] UKSC 64, 23 October 2013.
161 See [2016] EWCA Civ 6. *The Guardian* 19 January 2016. See Chapter 12, pp 849–50.

Proscription

Introduction

The government stance is that the proscription – banning – of terrorist organisations contributes towards making the UK a hostile environment for terrorists and sends a clear message to the international community and to UK citizens that the UK absolutely rejects such organisations and any of their claims to legitimacy as opposition groups. Proscription is a strong and far-reaching power since it has the effect of outlawing previously lawful activity without recourse to a court, except retrospectively – after proscription has occurred. The use of proscription means that in effect the definition of terrorism is extended because a range of people become terrorist suspects, or suspects associated with terrorist activity, who do not necessarily fall within the s 1 definition themselves. Proscription under the TA 2000 as amended is a reactive measure in the sense that if criminal sanctions are to be applied a trial must occur, but it is proactive in that the initial decision to proscribe is not taken by a judicial body, but by the Home Secretary with – it is argued – a thin veneer of parliamentary oversight. As discussed below, it is a criminal offence to belong to, support, glorify or display support for a pro-scribed organisation; the Terrorism Act 2000 also allows the police to seize all the property of a proscribed organisation. Once a group is proscribed the freedom of speech, assembly and association of its members is severely curtailed, or abrogated entirely, in relation to the political, religious or ideological cause upon which the initial proscrip-tion was based. This is also true of supporters of the group who are not members of it. The proscription-related offences and the proceedings allowing for challenge to the proscription decision are also in some tension with Art 6.

Proscription may be seen as providing a legitimate means of expressing outrage at certain activities, thereby tending to prevent illegitimate expressions of public anger. It has been argued that it may discourage supporters of terrorist organisations and may signal political strength.[162] Walker has argued, in relation to the PTA and EPA provi-sions, that, prima facie proscription breaches Arts 10 and 11 of the European Conven-tion on Human Rights but that, apart from exceptions contained in those articles, Art 17 might justify it since it limits Convention guarantees to activity in harmony with its aims, and that could not be said of IRA methods.[163] Obviously it also could not be said of the methods of Isis or similar groups. As discussed above, Art 17 provides that the Convention is not to be interpreted so as to imply a right 'for any state, group or person to engage in any activity . . . aimed at the destruction of any of the [Convention rights] or at their limitation to a greater extent than . . . provided for in the Convention'. That obviously is true of Al-Qaeda, Isis, and linked groups. But a number of groups might be proscribed under the current provisions, taking s 1 TA into account, which cannot so readily be viewed as out of harmony with the aims of the Convention, and therefore the exceptions under the relevant articles would usually have to be relied on if compat-ibility between the proscription provisions and the Convention is to be found. But the current reliance on the executive to satisfy the demands of proportionality by showing restraint in taking decisions as to groups to be included in proscription orders put before Parliament can hardly be seen as a satisfactory safeguard. Unsurprisingly, Lord Carlile,

---

162 Wilkinson, P, *Terrorism and the Political State*, 1986, Macmillan, p 170.
163 Walker, C, *The Prevention of Terrorism in British Law* (1992) pp 49–50.

a former independent reviewer of counter-terrorism legislation, observed that 'the pro-scription of organisations is at best a fairly blunt instrument'.[164]

The power of proscription under the Terrorism Act, as amended in 2006

Under the Terrorism Act 2000 the very broad power of proscription, and all the pro-scription-related offences, were retained, and their impact was greatly extended. The notion of increasing the number of groups to be proscribed lay at the heart of the intro-duction of the TA. Clearly, it was intended that a range of extremist Islamic groups would be proscribed, some, but not all, linked with Al-Qaeda, and that occurred shortly after the TA came into force. Other international groups have been proscribed, some that do not appear to create a security risk within the UK itself. The amendment made by s 22 of the 2006 Act allows the Home Secretary to list names that are used as aliases by proscribed organisations.[165]

Section 3(1) TA provides: 'For the purposes of this Act an organisation is proscribed if it is listed in Schedule 2, or it operates under the same name as an organisation listed in that Schedule.' The power to add to or delete groups from the schedule is exercised under s 3(3) by the secretary of state, by order. Under s 3(4) the power may be exercised 'only if he believes that [the organisation] is concerned in terrorism'. Thus no express distinc-tion is created by the TA between organisations falling within s 1 and those which can be proscribed; the power of seeking proscription is left entirely at the Home Secretary's dis-cretion – it is entirely unregulated by the TA itself, though it is subject to the parliamentary affirmative resolution procedure. This provides the Home Secretary with an extraordinar-ily wide power, bearing in mind that Parliament has not refused an order on the occasions that one has been sought since 2000. The consequences of proscription are far more far-reaching than the consequences flowing from the possibility that a group falls within the s 1 TA definition.

The breadth of the definition of terrorism means that any armed opposition group, or any person or group that supports an armed opposition group in any part of the world, including those who oppose repressive regimes, are 'terrorists'. Section 3 permits the proscription of organisations that would normally not be proscribed in practice,

> including organisations which are fighting against undemocratic and oppressive regimes and, in particular, those which have engaged in lawful armed conflict in the exercise of the internationally recognised right to self-determination of peoples (where the United Kingdom is bound in international law to recognise the right and to refrain from offering material support to states engaged in the suppression of the exercise of the right by military or other coercive means).[166]

Support has come from the West for a number of organisations that are terrorist under the TA definition, including UNITA in Angola and the mujahidin in Afghanistan;

---

164 Carlile, 2010. *Report on the operation in 2009 of the Terrorism Act 200 and of Part 1 of the Terrorism Act 2006*, para 73.
165 See *R v Z (A-G for Northern Ireland's Reference)* [2005] UKHL 35 in which the House of Lords found that the proscription of the 'IRA' covered members of the 'Real IRA'.
166 See *R (on the application of the Kurdistan Workers' Party and Others) v Secretary of State for the Home Dept* [2002] EWHC Admin 644, at para 47.

the West also sought, prior to the Iraq war, to persuade the Shi'a in Iraq to rise against Saddam Hussein. Some of the proscribed groups are from countries where repressive regimes prevent them from exercising democratic rights and provide them with no legitimate means of pursuing their ends. In a number of instances the proscribed organisation would have had no method open to it to seek its objectives peacefully through the political system. This can be said of the Kurds, who are not recognised as a minority in Turkey and are persecuted as terrorists there, and the People's Mujahidin of Iran (Mujahidin e Khalq). In Iran anyone questioning the supremacy of the religious leader can be criminalised; widespread executions and murders against the People's Mujahidin of Iran have been documented. The question of the width of the definition of terrorism has been considered by the Supreme Court in *R v Gul (Appellant)*.[167] The questions raised by the specific case did not directly raise issues about bringing 'freedom fighters' fighting for democracy and engaging in attacks in repressive states within the definition of 'terrorism' since the non-state groups in question were not fighting to establish democracy but a theocracy. But it did raise the general question whether the definition covered all non-state actors fighting against all types of states in the context of a civil war. Mr Gul had been convicted by a jury of five counts of disseminating terrorist publications, for which he was sentenced to five years' imprisonment. The offence was created by s 2 of the Terrorism Act 2006, which defines 'terrorist publications' as including publications which are likely to be understood as a direct or indirect encouragement to the commission, preparation, or instigation of acts of terrorism (see below).

The publications at issue included videos that Mr Gul posted on YouTube showing attacks by members of al-Qaeda, the Taliban, and other proscribed groups on military targets in Chechnya, and on the coalition forces in Iraq and in Afghanistan. They also showed the use of improvised explosive devices against coalition forces, excerpts from 'martyrdom videos', and clips of attacks on civilians, including the 11 September 2001 attack on the US. These videos were accompanied by commentaries praising the bravery, and martyrdom, of those carrying out the attacks, and encouraging others to emulate them.

His appeal to the Supreme Court challenged the definition of terrorism on the basis that it included military attacks by non-state armed groups against national or international armed forces in their territory. The first aspect of Mr Gul's argument was that the UK's international obligations required it to define terrorism more narrowly in its criminal laws, as it should have the same meaning as in international law. The second aspect was that the UK could not criminalise terrorism happening abroad except so far as international law allowed. But it was found that both aspects of the international law argument faced the 'insuperable obstacle' that there is no accepted definition of terrorism in international law. Also it was found to be irrelevant for the appeal whether the UK could criminalise certain actions committed abroad, because the material in the case was disseminated in the UK.[168]

It was concluded that whether the issue was one of purely domestic law, or of domestic law read in the light of international law, there was no valid basis for reading the definition of terrorism more narrowly than the plain and natural meaning of its words suggested. So the appeal failed. However the Court did note that the current definition

167 [2013] UKSC 64, 23 October 2013.
168 Para 56.

of terrorism was 'concerningly wide'[169] although change would be a matter for Parliament. As Lord Carlile had previously pointed out, zero tolerance for terrorism, even if in a good cause, in international conventions on terrorism would make it hard for the UK government to introduce a defence relating to s 1 and applying to 'freedom fighters'.[170]

Significantly, the power of proscription is, on its face, broader even than the ambit of s 1 TA would permit. Groups that do not themselves fall within the s 1 definition, but that are in any way 'concerned' in terrorism, can be proscribed. The addition of the term 'concerned in terrorism' makes this provision wider than that under the PTA.

Parliament's approval is required for additions to, or deletions from, the list of proscribed groups, as it was under the PTA provisions.[171] Under s 3(5) a group is 'concerned in terrorism', and so is a candidate for proscription, if it: '(a) commits or participates in acts of terrorism, (b) prepares for terrorism, (c) promotes or encourages terrorism, or (d) is otherwise concerned in terrorism', and now (under the Terrorism Act 2006) if it glorifies it.[172] In other words, the group itself need not have issued threats or taken part in action covered by s 1 TA. Thus, for example, a group verbally supporting on a website the use of threats to property as part of opposition to a despotic regime could theoretically be proscribed.

The main objection to proscription is that the key decisions are in executive hands: a person can become subject to a large range of criminal offences on the basis of an executive decision. In effect a person can be criminalised by executive decision alone – with a thin veneer of parliamentary or judicial oversight – because if an organisation is proscribed any member of it commits a criminal offence purely by virtue of their status (s 2(1)(a)). Persons receive no warning that the organisation of which they are members is about to be proscribed since the Home Office policy is not to comment on whether or not a particular organisation is being considered for proscription, or to give reasons

169   Para 38.
170   'The definition of terrorism' (2007) Cmnd 7052, para 80.
171   Under s 123(4) of the Act of 2000: 'An order or regulations under any of the following provisions shall not be made, subject to sub-section (4), unless a draft has been laid before and approved by resolution of each House of Parliament . . . ' The provisions listed include s 3(3). Section 123(5) covers cases of urgency, in which case an order may be made without approval, if so it will lapse after 40 days unless approved.
172   The 2006 Act provided that encouraging terrorism included the 'unlawful glorification' of 'acts of terrorism'. The following words were added by the 2006 Act:
      (5A) The cases in which an organisation promotes or encourages terrorism for the purposes of sub-section (5)(c) include any case in which activities of the organisation–
            (a) include the unlawful glorification of the commission or preparation (whether in the past, in the future or generally) of acts of terrorism; or
            (b) are carried out in a manner that ensures that the organisation is associated with statements containing any such glorification.
      (5B) The glorification of any conduct is unlawful for the purposes of sub-section (5A) if there are persons who may become aware of it who could reasonably be expected to infer that what is being glorified, is being glorified as –
            (a) conduct that should be emulated in existing circumstances, or
            (b) conduct that is illustrative of a type of conduct that should be so emulated.
      (5C) In this section –
            'glorification' includes any form of praise or celebration, and cognate expressions are to be construed accordingly;
            'statement' includes a communication without words consisting of sounds or images or both.

for an organisation's absence from the list.[173] Persons in that position can only escape conviction in limited circumstances and on the basis of a reversed burden of proof, as discussed below. In effect, they are first criminalised and then the case against them can be inquired into – if they challenge the proscription order. The decision to proscribe is likely to be based on material from domestic and foreign intelligence and security services. Where proscription is based on confidential information available to the Home Secretary, it is difficult for organisations to mount effective appeals against it without access to such information. If an organisation is proscribed that appears to be no longer functional in the UK, the mounting of a challenge to the proscription would demonstrate that it is no longer defunct and would identify those associated with it. This position has security benefits, but it also operates as a significant deterrent to challengers, although they have immunity from prosecution in certain circumstances, as discussed below.

The implicit, tacit assumption on which the legislation rests is that the secretary of state will not proscribe certain organisations despite the fact that they meet the statutory criteria of ss 1 and 3. Thus, the relationship between the s 1 definition of terrorism and the s 3 proscription power is of interest. The very broad s 1 definition is objectionable as discussed, but it was always highly improbable that the Home Secretary would seek to proscribe all, or even the majority, of the groups falling within s 1. Sections 1 and 3 combined are convenient since they maximise executive discretion as to proscription. As political alliances change, the proscription or de-proscription of relevant groups can occur, and the lack of information available to Parliament means that no real check on the exercise of that discretion is available. The proscription of a new group in order to placate an ally or cement a new international agreement clearly arises; the possibilities of arbitrariness and injustice are apparent. Clearly, it is difficult, if not impossible, to devise a definition of terrorism that differentiates between 'good' and 'bad' terrorists – between 'terrorists' and 'freedom-fighters'. Proscription provides a somewhat clumsy means of doing so, which in effect trusts the executive to make a questionable differentiation.

Choosing the groups to proscribe

Clearly, the Home Secretary and other relevant members of the executive are bound by s 6 HRA to abide by the Convention. Articles 10 and 11 should therefore be taken into account in taking decisions to add groups to the list of those proscribed under the TA.

---

173 See, e.g., Parliamentary and Health Service Ombudsman, *Investigations Completed* July 2004–March 2005, Part Two, Home Office, A.26/05. On 17 February 2004 Ms T wrote to the Home Office and, citing the Code of Practice on Access to Government Information (superseded by the Freedom of Information Act 2000 from 1 January 2005 onwards; see Chapter 7), asked what steps the government had taken to proscribe the organisation known as the al-Aqsa Martyrs' Brigade. She also asked why the government had not listed this organisation as a proscribed terrorist group. The Home Office acknowledged the request on 30 March 2004 and replied in full on 27 April 2004. They said that the government's list of proscribed organisations was kept under constant and active review. However, they said that it was their policy not to comment on whether or not a particular organisation was being considered for proscription, or upon the reasons for an organisation's absence from the list. It was found that the Home Office had been justified in refusing to release the information sought by Ms T, under Exemption 1 of the Code – although the Ombudsman was critical of the Home Office's handling of the request.

Difficult decisions had to be taken concerning the range of 'terrorist' groups (under the s 1 TA definition) chosen initially for proscription. In 2000 under Sched 2 TA the groups listed had already been proscribed under the EPA; they were then proscribed throughout the UK.[174] But a key issue under the TA was whether all or most of the other groups falling within the s 1 definition would eventually be proscribed. There appeared to be three options for the trend of proscription over a period of time – although it is suggested that in reality there were only two.

First the current proscriptions could have been retained, merely adding further Irish splinter groups if necessary. Second, the option was open of proscribing both Irish and international terrorist groups, leaving domestic groups that fell within the s 1 definition unproscribed. Third, the possibility arose of proscribing *all* or most groups falling within the TA definition. So far, unsurprisingly, in the face of the threat from Isis and similar groups, successive governments have taken the second option, proscribing since 2000 a range of international 'terrorist' groups, including a very large number of extremist Islamic groups.[175] The fact that a group is about to be added to the list is not made known in advance; there is no consultation with the groups concerned, meaning that a person is suddenly subject to criminal sanctions by virtue of his membership of or support for a newly proscribed group. This is a desirable stance to take in security terms if the group does pose a threat to the security of the UK, but it has significant Convention implications; this point is returned to below. This position means that groups that fall within s 1 TA but are unproscribed can be dealt with for a time under the general TA provisions, particularly under s 56, the offence of directing a terrorist organisation. But at any point, without warning, the group can be proscribed, meaning that the proscription-based offences can also be utilised.

In considering which international terrorist organisations should be subject to proscription, the Home Secretary takes the following five factors into account: (1) the nature and scale of an organisation's activities; (2) the specific threat that it poses to the UK; (3) the specific threat that it poses to British nationals overseas; (4) the extent of the organisation's presence in the UK; and (5) the need to support other members of the international community in the global fight against terrorism.[176] But despite factor (5), the fact that an organisation is added to the EU's list of recognised terrorist groups or designated by the US as a 'foreign terrorist organisation' does not necessarily mean that the group will be proscribed as a terrorist organisation by the UK government.[177] On

---

174   The following groups are listed in Sched 2: The Irish Republican Army, Cumann nam Ban, Fianna nah Eireann, The Red Hand Commando, Saor Eire, The Ulster Freedom Fighters, The Ulster Volunteer Force, The Irish National Liberation Army, The Irish People's Liberation Organisation, The Ulster Defence Association, The Loyalist Volunteer Force, The Continuity Army Council, The Orange Volunteers, The Red Hand Defenders.

175   67 groups are proscribed. Al-Qaeda, Isis and the associated groups are of course proscribed, along with a number of other groups not linked to it, including the PKK and various groups associated with Northern Ireland, as indicated above.

176   See HL Debs vol 613 col 252, 16 May 2000; Home Office Press Release, 28 February 2001; these factors have continued to be reiterated: see, e.g., Parliamentary and Health Service Ombudsman, Investigations Completed July 2004–March 2005, Part Two, Home Office, A.26/05; *Home Secretary To Ban Terror Groups*, Home Office Press Release 17 July 2006. See also resolution 2253 (2015) under Chapter VII of the United Nations Charter.

177   E.g., the al-Aqsa Martyrs' Brigade was added to the European Union's list of recognised terrorist groups in June 2002 but was not at that point proscribed in the UK.

the other hand, a group may be proscribed in the UK but not in, for example, Germany, meaning that if a member of the group travels to Britain he or she commits a criminal offence as soon as he or she arrives in the UK. Quite a large number of groups have been added to the list since the 2000 Act was introduced; in 2016 67 organisations are proscribed of which 14 have their origins in Northern Ireland and/or Ireland, while the rest are international terrorist organisations, within the s 1 TA definition. The list of organisations has had to be added to fairly recently when groups banned under one name reformed under another. So for example, the government laid orders, in January 2010 and November 2011, which provide that Al Muhajiroun, Islam4UK, Call to Submission, Islamic Path, London School of Sharia and Muslims Against Crusades should be treated as alternative names for the organisation that is already proscribed under the names Al Ghurabaa and The Saved Sect. The government laid an order, in June 2014 recognising Need4Khilafah, the Shariah Project and the Islamic Dawah Association as the same as the organisation proscribed as Al Ghurabaa and The Saved Sect, which is also known as Al Muhajiroun. In terms of doubtful decisions, the example of the Iran opposition group commonly known as the PMOI is relevant; the case for proscription of the PMOI appeared doubtful. Lord Carlile in his 2006 Report on the operation of the TA singled out the PMOI:

> They claim to have disarmed in 2003 to become a political organisation dedicated to the reform of government in Iran. They certainly have significant Parliamentary support across parties at Westminster. I am sure that [the working group existing within the government service at which all the interested parties meet and scrutinise proscriptions] will give serious examination to whether the PMOI really should remain proscribed.[178]

Eventually the Mujaheddin e Khalq (MeK), also known as the Peoples' Mujaheddin of Iran (PMOI), was removed from the list of proscribed groups in June 2008 as a result of judgments of the POAC and the Court of Appeal.[179] The PMOI describes itself as a broad-based popular resistance movement committed to the establishment of a democratic, secular and pluralist government in Iran, which would respect human rights and the internationally recognised norms of state behaviour. It stated that it had sought to achieve its aims through the political system, but it had been denied access to it through brutal suppression at the hands of the Iranian regime. It said that it had therefore been driven to resort to armed struggle in Iran. It was argued on its behalf that the secretary of state had unfairly discriminated against it by including the PMOI in a list with organisations such as Al-Qaeda. The PMOI was recognised by the secretary of state to be democratic in its aims.

The decision to proscribe a range of international terrorist groups, *not* all those that fall within the s 1 definition, means that while the members of certain domestic activist or protest groups have, in effect, been re-defined as 'terrorists', the groups

---

178 Report on the Operation in 2005 of the Terrorism Act 2000 by Lord Carlile of Berriew QC, at para 43. In 2001 he was appointed as Independent Reviewer of the Terrorism Act 2000. His reports can be found at www.homeoffice.gov.uk. The current reviewer is David Anderson QC.

179 *Secretary of State for the Home Dept v Lord Alton* (2008) EWCA Civ 443, Judgment 30 November 2007.

remain openly able to engage in various public activities such as advertising for members, fund-raising, holding marches or possibly even putting up members to stand for elections.[180]

The attention of the then Labour government post-2001 was on the threat posed by groups associated with Al-Qaeda. The proscription of a range of animal rights, anti-abortion, or environmental groups falling within s 3 TA was not high on the political agenda. It is suggested that the then Labour government never seriously intended that all those groups covered by s 1 TA would be proscribed, and successive governments have not sought to proscribe the majority of the groups falling within that definition At the same time the provisions were of value since they left open the possibility that in extreme and possible future circumstances, such as the mounting of a violent campaign by an anti-abortion activist group in the UK, they could be utilised. The threat of proscription may also be of some value in deterring groups from adopting methods other than recognised democratic ones to push their political agenda.

Offence of belonging to a proscribed organisation

Section 11 of the 2000 Act makes it an offence to belong to a proscribed organisation.[181] Under s 11(1) a person commits an offence if he belongs or professes to belong to a proscribed organisation; a maximum penalty of ten years' imprisonment is imposed. It is notable that there is no *mens rea* requirement. There is a limited defence under s 11(2):

> it is a defence for a person charged with an offence under sub-section (1) to prove that the organisation was not proscribed on the last (or only) occasion on which he became a member or began to profess to be a member, and that he has not taken part in the activities of the organisation at any time while it was proscribed.

Section 11 in effect comes close to imposing a reverse burden of proof on the defendant once the prosecution has discharged its burden in showing that he was a member of a proscribed organisation, even if he was unaware that it had been proscribed (and as indicated above organisations are constantly added to the list of proscribed organisations and the members are given no warning of this beforehand). The burden of proof is then placed on him to prove that it was not proscribed when he was a member, under s 11(2). This appears to infringe the presumption of innocence under Art 6(2), discussed above, and in Chapters 2 and 13,[182] since it places a burden on a defendant who has arguably not engaged in any blameworthy conduct to disprove a substantial element of the offence. However, as mentioned in Chapter 4, the UK courts have engaged in 'reading down' under s 3 HRA of legal burdens to evidential ones in order

---

180 All these activities might in certain respects fall within the terrorist offences discussed below, but they do not in themselves either constitute offences or lead almost inevitably to liability under the proscription-related offences.

181 Previously this was provided for under s 2(1)(a) of the PTA.

182 See pp 62–63 and p 944 *et seq.*

to seek to create compliance with Art 6(2).[183] Thus they have sought to give effect to the fundamental right encapsulated in Art 6(2),[184] and long recognised under common law principle.[185]

This issue was raised in *Attorney General's Reference (No 4 of 2002)*.[186] Lord Bingham, giving the opinion of the House, found that a person who had not engaged in any blameworthy conduct could come within s 11(1) and that the presumption of innocence was infringed by requiring him or her to disprove involvement in the organisation at the time in question. He said that there was a real risk that a person who was innocent of any blameworthy or properly criminal conduct, but who was unable to establish a defence under s 11(2), might fall within s 11(1), thereby resulting in a clear breach of the presumption of innocence and an unfair conviction. He found that, bearing in mind the difficulties a defendant would have in proving the matters contained in s 11(2), and the serious consequences for the defendant in failing to do so, the imposition of a legal burden upon the defendant was not a proportionate and justifiable legislative response to the threat of terrorism. Further, it was found that while security considerations always carried weight, they did not absolve member states from their duty to ensure that basic standards of fairness were observed; and that since s 11(2) impermissibly infringed the presumption of innocence, it was appropriate, pursuant to s 3 of the Human Rights Act 1998, to read down s 11(2) so as to impose on the defendant an evidential burden only, even though that was not Parliament's intention when enacting the sub-section.[187]

Thus a majority of the House of Lords relied on s 3 to read the word 'prove' as though it meant 'adduce sufficient evidence to raise an issue in the case'. Thus the Lords ameliorated the difficulty facing defendants in proving their innocence in relation to s 11 and created a compatibility with Art 6(2) ECHR that was not previously present. The decision has implications for a number of the counter-terrorism offences discussed below. However it is not a defence to prove that the defendant did not know that the organisation was proscribed or that it was engaged in activities covered by ss 1(1) and 3 of the Act: *R v Hundal (Avtar Singh); R v Dhaliwal (Kesar Singh)*.[188]

---

183 See further on 'reading down' under s3: p 149 *et seq*. For further discussion, see: Tadros, V and Tierney, S, 'The Presumption of Innocence and the Human Rights Act' (2004) 67 MLR 402, at p 403; Simester, AP and Sullivan, GR, *Criminal Law: Theory and Doctrine*, 2nd edn, 2004, Hart, esp p 69; Dennis, I, 'Reverse Onuses and the Presumption of Innocence: In Search of Principle' [2005] CLR 901; Dingwall, G, 'Statutory Exceptions, Burdens of Proof and the Human Rights Act 1998' (2002) 65 MLR 40; Ashworth, A, 'Four Threats to the Presumption of Innocence' (2006) 10 *International Journal of Evidence and Proof* 241; Ashworth, A, 'Criminal Justice Reform: Principles, Human Rights and Public Protection' [2004] Crim LR 516.

184 See Chapter 2, pp 62–63.

185 See *Woolmington* [1935] AC 462, pp 481–82. See further Ashworth, A and Blake, M, 'The Presumption of Innocence in English Criminal Law' [1996] CLR 306.

186 [2004] UKHL 43; [2005] 1 AC 264; [2005] 1 All ER 237. The House of Lords took account of *R v Lambert* [2002] 2 AC 545, HL(E), *R v A (No 2)* [2002] 1 AC 45, HL(E), *R v Johnstone* [2003] 1 WLR 1736, HL(E), *Ghaidan v Godin-Mendoza* [2004] 2 AC 557, HL(E).

187 At paras 48–53, 55 and 56.

188 2004 WL 62035 (CA (Crim Div)), [2004] 2 Cr App R 19, [2004] 2 Cr App R (S) 64 (2004), *The Times*, 13 February, 62,035 [2004] EWCA Crim 389.

Symbols of allegiance to a proscribed group; meetings

If proscription is at least partly of symbolic value, as an affirmation of society's rejection of the value of associating with certain groups, then it follows that visible signs of allegiance to those groups will also be banned. Therefore there are a number of further offences relating to badges, symbols and meetings. Under s 12(1) TA it is an offence to solicit support, other than money or other property, for a proscribed organisation.[189] This offence now overlaps with the offence of indirectly (including glorifying) or directly encouraging terrorism under the Terrorism Act 2006 (below). It is also an offence under s 12(2) for a person to arrange, manage or assist in arranging or managing a meeting that he knows is: '(a) to support a proscribed organisation, (b) to further the activities of a proscribed organisation, or (c) to be addressed by a person who belongs or professes to belong to a proscribed organisation'. It is an offence under s 12(3)(a) TA to address such a meeting in order to encourage support for a proscribed organisation or 'further its activities'. These are broadly drawn offences, although they do include a *mens rea* ingredient. Their impact on speech, association and assembly is clearly far-reaching, bearing in mind the wide range of meetings, including very small, informal ones, covered.

The fact that the majority of speakers at a meeting were opposed to the methods or aims of a proscribed group would not affect the liability of the organiser so long as s/he was aware that a speaker was a member, or professed member, of such an organisation, speaking in support of it. A meeting is defined as one at which three or more persons are present and there is no need for it to be open to the public. A narrow defence is provided under s 12(4) in relation to private meetings only if the defendant can show that he had no reasonable cause to believe that the address as mentioned in s 12(2)(c) was to support a proscribed organisation. Section 12(4) is covered by s 118, meaning that if the accused puts forward evidence sufficient to raise a doubt as to whether he or she had no cause to believe that the address would be in support of such an organisation, the court or jury must assume that the defence is satisfied unless the prosecution proves beyond reasonable doubt that it is not. The maximum punishment for this offence is ten years' imprisonment. The problem is that s 12(4) is narrowly drawn; a person who assisted in arranging a public meeting, even if of only three people, not knowing that the member of the proscribed organisation would speak in support of the organisation, would commit an offence.

Restrictions on the use of badges or uniforms as signals of support for certain organisations are intended to have the dual effect of preventing communication – by those means – of the political message associated with the organisation, and of tending to minimise the impression that the organisation is supported, thereby denying reassurance to its members, lowering their morale and preventing them from arousing public support. Under s 13 TA it is an offence to 'wear any item which arouses a reasonable apprehension that a person is a member or supporter of a proscribed organisation',[190] and it is an offence to wear an item of clothing, or wear, carry or display an article, 'in such a way or in such circumstances as to arouse reasonable suspicion [that the person in question] is a member or supporter of a proscribed organisation'. Again it is notable

---

189   Previously this was provided for under s 2(1)(a) PTA.
190   Previously this was provided for under s 3 PTA.

that no element of *mens rea* is included. The offence can be established on the basis of proof of reasonable suspicion alone and no defence is provided.

An overlapping offence arises under s 1 of the Public Order Act 1936: it is an offence to wear a uniform signifying association with any political organisation or with the promotion of any political object. Section 1 was invoked in *Whelan v DPP*[191] against leaders of a Provisional IRA protest march against internment in Northern Ireland, all of whom wore black berets while some wore dark glasses, dark clothing and carried Irish flags. It was found that, first, something must be 'worn' as apparel and second, that it must be a uniform. Something might amount to a uniform if worn by a number of persons in order to signify their association with each other or if commonly used by a certain organisation. By this means, the third requirement that the uniform must signal the wearer's association with a particular political organisation could also be satisfied. Alternatively, it might be satisfied by consideration of the occasion on which the uniform was worn without the need to refer to the past history of the organisation. It was found that the items worn could amount to a uniform; this decision therefore greatly diminished the distinction between this offence and that under the PTA. The justification for retention of the PTA provisions in the TA is therefore doubtful due to the overlap between the two offences.

The decision of the House of Lords in *Attorney General's Reference (No 4 of 2002)*[192] is arguably relevant to a number of these offences since, apart from s 12(4), they are not covered by s 118. But it may be problematic to apply the House of Lords' decision where no defences are available. In that case, as discussed above, Lord Bingham found that a person who had not engaged in any blameworthy conduct could commit an offence under the Act and that the presumption of innocence was infringed by requiring him or her to disprove a significant element of the offence. Since the Lords found that this burden placed on the accused impermissibly infringed the presumption of innocence, they employed s 3 HRA to read down the relevant section so as to impose on the defendant an evidential burden only. A number of these offences allow for the criminalisation of the defendant despite the fact that arguably his or her conduct was not blameworthy.

As discussed, a person who is accused of being a member of a proscribed organisation under s 11 has a defence if he can raise the possibility that he was not a member of it at the time when it was proscribed. The burden then passes to the prosecution to prove beyond reasonable doubt that he was a member of it at the relevant time. It is not a defence under s 13 to prove that at the time when the support was accorded to the organisation by the defendant, it was not proscribed, but that requirement could be read into the offence. In order to prevent anomalies arising, s 13 should be interpreted compatibly with s 11; the word 'currently' could be implied into the section before the word 'proscribed'. It is not a defence under either s 11 or s 13 that the defendant did not know that the organisation had been proscribed at the time in question. Thus the defendant under s 13 in that position must seek to disprove that the organisation was proscribed at the time, unless a court was prepared to read the word 'knowingly' into s 13.

A number of objections of principle arise in respect of the application of the proscription-related offences to a wider range of groups. The key objection is that, by

191 [1975] QB 864.
192 [2005] 1 AC 264; [2005] 1 All ER 237.

making it possible to proscribe a wide range of groups, the legislation at least in theory potentially curtails proscription-related activities that previously would not have been conceived of as related to terrorism. Some examples are illustrative of the broad potential of the TA, which however has not been fully exploited. It is an offence to wear a badge expressing support for the PKK, a group supporting establishment of a Kurdish state, or to carry a leaflet that arouses reasonable suspicion that such support was being expressed, and this would be the case even if the leaflet was in fact that of a similar but non-proscribed group. If a person who opposed the use of violence to further the cause of animal rights organised a meeting to express such views in private with two other people, one of whom was a member of a proscribed animal rights group, who spoke in its favour, she could commit an offence carrying a maximum penalty of ten years' imprisonment. A group which did not itself engage in terrorism but which, for example, expressed support during one of its assemblies for the 'serious disruption' of a computer system could be proscribed as falling within the terms of ss 1 and 3 combined. If, during a march, members of a group opposed to the introduction of GM crops wore badges expressing support for a proscribed environmental activist group, they would commit an offence. They would also attract criminal liability if they carried leaflets that aroused reasonable suspicion that such support was being expressed.

These proscription-linked offences strike directly at freedom of political expression, which, as indicated above, is viewed as one of the 'essential foundations of a democratic society', so that exceptions to it 'must be narrowly interpreted and the necessity for any restrictions . . . convincingly established'.[193] The use of these offences is prima facie an interference with the guarantee under Art 10 since all, including the wearing of an item, or organising a meeting at which a member of a proscribed organisation is speaking, involve or relate to exercises of expression. Such offences include those of wearing any item that arouses a reasonable apprehension that a person is a member or supporter of a proscribed organisation, of organising a meeting at which a member of a proscribed organisation is speaking, and that of soliciting support for such an organisation. In particular, the provision of s 12 regarding meetings affords very little recognition to the value of peaceful protest and assembly. Strasbourg, as indicated above, affords that value pre-eminence in a democracy.[194] Charging a member of an assembly with one of these offences would clearly, therefore, amount to an interference with the Art 10 or 11 guarantees. The domestic court would be expected to observe the same or higher standards than Strasbourg in scrutinising the need for the interference, bearing in mind the narrow margin of appreciation afforded to states in respect of interference with political speech, especially where it concerns criticism directed at the government itself.[195]

Obviously, the view taken of the necessity and proportionality of the interference would depend on the particular circumstances behind the charging of the offence in the instance before the court. But to take the example used above of a person making arrangements to meet privately with two others and hearing a member of a proscribed

---

193 *Observer and Guardian v United Kingdom* judgment of 26 November 1991, Series A no 216, pp 29–30, para 59.

194 See *Ezelin v France* (1991) 14 EHRR 362. On political expression generally, see *Castells v Spain* A 236, p 23, para 43; judgment of 23 April 1992.

195 See *Incal v Turkey* (2000) 29 EHRR 449 and see above, pp 1035–39.

group speak: it might be problematic to find that the necessity for the interference with freedom of expression in a democratic society had been convincingly established. This offence is especially pernicious in terms of freedom of expression since the meeting in question might be entirely peaceful: liability would indirectly relate to the *content* of the speech of at least one of the speakers. Since no defences are provided on which s 3 HRA could bite, a declaration of incompatibility between the relevant section and Arts 10 and 11 might have to be made. However, a court could instead rely on s 6 HRA on the argument that the offence has to be applied in a manner that ensures that the demands of necessity and proportionality are satisfied, an argument that has been used post-HRA in the public protest context, as Chapter 9 notes.[196] Account could be taken of the necessity and proportionality of charging the defendant with a criminal offence in the first place. The threat posed by the proscribed group could be taken into account and obviously the second paragraphs of Arts 10 or 11 would be likely to be satisfied (and Art 17 would apply) if groups or persons supportive of Isis or similar/linked groups were convicted of one of the various available offences discussed.

Fund-raising; terrorist property; commercial risks

Further criminal offences, punishable by up to 14 years' imprisonment, exist under s 15 in relation to fund-raising for the purposes of terrorism, under s 16 in relation to the use or possession of money or other property for the purposes of terrorism, under s 17 in relation to arrangements to make money or property available for the purposes of terrorism (funding arrangements), and under s 18 in relation to arrangements facilitating the retention or control of terrorist property by concealment, removal, transfer etc (money laundering). These offences are not limited to proscribed organisations, but s 14 defines 'terrorist property' as including any resources of a proscribed organisation and s 1(5) provides that action 'for the purposes of terrorism' includes action taken for the benefit of a proscribed organisation. Pursuant to s 19 it is an offence to fail to disclose any belief or suspicion that another person has committed an offence under any of ss 15–18 if that belief or suspicion is based on information that comes to a person's attention in the course of a trade, profession, business or employment. These offences, affecting businesses, are discussed further below in relation to the general terrorism offences.[197]

Challenges to proscription; deproscription

Under the previous scheme if an organisation was proscribed on insufficient grounds there was little possibility of challenge to the order. There was no right of appeal against proscription, and judicial review, while theoretically available, was likely to create extremely limited scrutiny. In *McEldowney v Forde*[198] an order was made under statutory instrument banning republican clubs or any like organisation, thus potentially outlawing all Nationalist political parties. Nevertheless, the House of Lords preferred

---

196 See pp 668, 675.
197 See pp 1069–70.
198 [1971] AC 632.

not to intervene, Lord Diplock stating that he would do so only if proscription were extended to bodies obviously distanced from Republican views.

As mentioned above, the TA set up, under s 5, the Proscribed Organisations Appeal Commission (POAC). It is modelled on the Special Immigration Appeals Commission, which also provided the model for the tribunal set up under the Regulation of Investigatory Powers Act 2000, discussed in Chapter 11.[199] The Commission also appears to have certain parallels with the Security and Intelligence Services Tribunals, also discussed in Chapter 11. Rules have been made under s 9 providing that the POAC is the forum in which proceedings under s 7 HRA can be brought.[200]

Under s 4, if an individual is affected by proscription, or an organisation considers that it should not have been proscribed, the first step is to ask the secretary of state to deproscribe.

Appeals to the POAC

If the Secretary of State refuses to deproscribe, then the organisation or individual may appeal to the POAC as set out in s 5 and Sched 3.[201] The Commission has to apply Convention principles as a court would in judicial review proceedings, due to s 6 HRA.[202] Under s 5(3): the Commission must allow an appeal against a refusal to deproscribe an organisation if it 'considers that the decision to refuse was flawed when considered in the light of the principles applicable on an application for judicial review'. The POAC itself, as a public authority, must apply the Convention rights in its adjudications and therefore, in relation to the question of deproscription, it should take the relevant Convention rights into account.

The procedure before the POAC is far removed from that which would be applicable in an ordinary court in a criminal trial. Under Sched 3, para 5(1) the Lord Chancellor has the power to make rules regulating the exercise of the right of appeal to the Commission and prescribing practice and procedure to be followed in its proceedings. Its members are appointed by the Lord Chancellor; three of them must attend the proceedings and one must be a person who holds or has held high judicial office. Under powers in Sched 3 the Lord Chancellor has the power to make rules providing that proceedings may be determined without an oral hearing in specified circumstances; provision may be made regarding the burden of proof; full particulars of the reasons for proscription

---

199   At p 795 *et seq.*

200   Under the Proscribed Organisations Appeal Commission (Human Rights Act Proceedings) Rules 2001, POAC is the appropriate tribunal for the purposes of s 7 HRA in relation to any proceedings under s 7(1)(a) against the Secretary of State in respect of a refusal by him to exercise his power of deproscription under s 3(3)(b).

201   It may be noted that under s 10 TA immunity from criminal proceedings is conferred upon a person who seeks deproscription by way of application or appeal under ss 4 or 5, either on behalf of the proscribed organisation or as the person affected. Clearly, otherwise, such a person would be discouraged from pursuing either course, or from instituting proceedings under s 7 of the Human Rights Act, by the risk of prosecution for certain offences, for example the offence of membership of a proscribed organisation. Section 10 provides that evidence of anything done, and any document submitted for these proceedings, cannot be relied on in criminal proceedings for such an offence except as part of the defence case.

202   See Chapter 4, p 187 *et seq.*

or refusal to deproscribe may be withheld from the organisation or applicant concerned; the Commission may exclude persons, including legal representatives, from all or part of the proceedings and permit proceedings for leave to appeal to a court under s 6 to be determined by a single member.

The current rules make provision, *inter alia*, for the appointment of a special advocate to represent the interests of the appellant in the proceedings, in particular in any proceedings from which the appellant and his representative are excluded. The POAC sits in public in central London, but is able to hear closed evidence in camera and with the applicant and their representatives excluded. POAC considers all the evidence upon which the secretary of state relies in support of his grounds for opposing the appeal, including some evidence that by statute or on general grounds of public interest cannot be disclosed to the appellant or his representative, with the POAC sitting in private for that purpose. Thus, although the procedure may appear adversarial, its procedural limitations are likely to handicap one side, meaning that the Commission may be unable to discharge its fact-finding role effectively.[203] This procedure was clearly designed to keep de-proscription claims, for the most part, out of the ordinary courts.

Bearing these comments in mind, a further feature of the proceedings is significant. By s 18(1)(f) of the Regulation of Investigatory Powers Act 2000 the normal prohibition on the receipt of evidence based on intercepted communications does not apply to the POAC.[204] Thus, the Commission may take its decision on the basis of secret intercept material. But such evidence cannot be disclosed to the organisation concerned, its legal representatives or the applicant under para 8(2). Therefore the applicant or the legal representatives would have no means of challenging it or of bringing forward other evidence that might be relevant to it. If the Commission finds in favour of an applicant and makes an order to that effect, this has the effect of requiring the Secretary of State either to lay a draft deproscription order before Parliament or to make a deproscription order on the basis of the urgency procedure. Such a finding is to be treated, under s 9(4)(b), as determining that 'an action of the Secretary of State is incompatible with a Convention right'. The powers of POAC and the consequences of its allowing an appeal are set out in s 5(3)–(5).[205] Under s 7, if an appeal to the POAC is successful, and an order has been made deproscribing the organisation, anyone convicted of one of the offences listed in sub-s (1)(c) in respect of the organisation, may appeal against his conviction to the Court of Appeal or Crown Court that must allow the appeal,[206] so long

---

203 For discussion of the similar limitations in respect of the Tribunal set up under the Regulation of Investigatory Powers Act 2000, see Chapter 11, p 814 *et seq.*

204 Previously, under Sched 3, para 8, s 9(1) of the Interception of Communications Act 1985 'shall not apply in relation to (a) proceedings before the Commission, or (b) proceedings arising out of proceedings to which paragraph (a) applies'. For discussion of the equivalent provisions under the Regulation of Investigatory Powers Act 2000, see Chapter 11, p 819.

205 (4) Where the Commission allows an appeal under this section by or in respect of an organisation, it may make an order under this sub-section. (5) Where an order is made under sub-section (4) the Secretary of State shall as soon as is reasonably practicable – (a) lay before Parliament, in accordance with section 123(4), the draft of an order under section 3(3)(b) removing the organisation from the list in Schedule 2; or (b) make an order removing the organisation from the list in Schedule 2 in pursuance of section 123(5).

206 Under s 7(2), once deproscription has occurred, if the convicted person appeals to the Court of Appeal under s 1 of the Criminal Appeal Act 1968 (appeal against conviction on indictment) 'the court shall allow the appeal'.

as the offence was committed after the date of the refusal to deproscribe. This provision covers members of the organisation itself, and persons who have been convicted of proscription-related offences at a point after a refusal to de-proscribe, who have already exhausted ordinary avenues of appeal.

If the POAC finds against the applicant, s 6 of the TA 2000 allows a further appeal from its decision to a court, on a point of law, if leave is given by the POAC or where POAC refuses permission, the Court of Appeal. The Act does not contain an ouster clause.

Judicial review of POAC decisions or appeals from POAC on points of law

Judicial review can be sought of decisions taken under the TA. The courts are able to apply the Convention rights in judicial review proceedings or on an appeal on a point of law to a court against a refusal to de-proscribe. The procedural rules for appeals from POAC to the Court of Appeal require that the Court of Appeal must secure that information is not disclosed contrary to the interests of national security. This enables the Court of Appeal, like POAC, to exclude any party (other than the Secretary of State) and his representative from the proceedings on the appeal.[207] Various Convention points can be raised in these proceedings.

It could be argued that the POAC does not meet the requisite standards of independence under Art 13 or under Art 6(1) ECHR since, *inter alia*, the Lord Chancellor appoints its members. Thus it could be considered whether the POAC provides an effective remedy for the citizen. (As regards Art 13 this argument would probably have to be raised at Strasbourg since Art 13 was not included in Sched 1 HRA.[208]) The ability of the Lord Chancellor to regulate its procedure is also relevant. This argument depends on the view taken of the role of the Lord Chancellor, and in particular whether it could be said that in appointing the POAC and regulating it he should be viewed as acting as part of the executive. It is suggested that the appointments procedure for the POAC complies with the Art 6 impartiality and independence requirements in these respects,[209] but that it is debatable whether that is the case in relation to the possibilities provided for under the Act for the determination of its procedure by the Lord Chancellor.

It could also be argued that the POAC fails to comply with the fair trial provisions of Art 6(1) since the applicant may be in such a weak position before it. As discussed above, Art 6 guarantees a fair hearing in the determination of civil rights and obligations or a criminal charge.[210] The Art 6(1) requirements are discussed further in Chapters 2, 13 and 14.[211] It could be argued that the POAC's appeal function should be viewed as the 'determination of a criminal charge' since proscription of an organisation creates the possibility of imposing criminal liability on a range of persons including existing members of the newly-proscribed organisation. However, at present it is assumed that the POAC is determining civil rights and obligations only.

---

207   The Court of Appeal (Appeals from Proscribed Organisations Appeal Commission) Rules 2002.
208   See *Govell v UK* (1997) 4 EHRLR 438, and see Chapter 2 at pp 92–93.
209   See *Campbell and Fell v UK* A 80 (1984).
210   For further discussion as to the field of application of Art 6, see Chapter 2, pp 58–60.
211   See, in particular, pp 961–62, 966 *et seq*.

Various features of decisions to proscribe and of the proscription scheme itself raise further Convention issues under Arts 10 and 11, as discussed in the human rights section of this chapter, above. Under the HRA the compatibility of the proscription of a range of groups with Arts 10 and 11 is problematic since the complete outlawing of a group constitutes prima facie a breach of those articles. In findings as to proscription, therefore, the focus must be on the demands of para 2 of those articles, unless Art 17 applies.[212] As discussed in Chapter 2, state interference with the Arts 10 and 11 guarantees must be pre-scribed by law, have a legitimate aim, be necessary in a democratic society and be applied in a non-discriminatory fashion if it is to be justified. It can almost certainly be assumed that the exercise of the proscription power can be viewed domestically as prescribed by law since it is enshrined in primary legislation, and Parliament must approve proscription orders, although the 'quality' of proscription decisions is arguably open to question.[213]

In freedom of expression cases Strasbourg's main concern has unsurprisingly been with the 'necessary in a democratic society' requirement. In *Sidiropoulos v Greece*[214] the Court considered the outlawing in Greece of an association called the Home of Mac-edonian Civilisation, which had been formed in Macedonia. The authorities refused to register it, on the basis that it was viewed as intended to undermine Greece's national integrity, contrary to Greek law, since it intended to publicise the idea that there is a Macedonian minority in Greece. The Court indicated the stance it would take towards the aims of the state authorities – the preservation of national security and the preven-tion of disorder – in this context. They were found to be legitimate, but the means used to further them – disallowing the registration of the group and therefore outlawing it – was found to be disproportionate to them and therefore unnecessary in a demo-cratic society. Thus, proscription of a particular group, depending on the extent to which there was evidence that it threatened national security and public order, might be found domestically to violate these two articles. Where, for example, a group presenting no risk to national security in the UK itself had been proscribed on the basis of its action in seeking to combat an oppressive regime in another state or in providing support for another group operating against such a regime, it could be found that proscription was disproportionate to the aims in view.

Special terrorism offences

Introduction

Virtually all the extensive range of special terrorist offences were retained under the TA, so they could apply to the vast range of groups which could, potentially, fall within the s 1 definition.

The TA provides a very extensive portfolio of counter-terrorist offences since it adopted EPA offences that had previously not been applied in the UK generally. The extensive range of offences of an early-stage, preparatory nature were added to under ATCSA 2001 and the Terrorism Act 2006. The Terrorism Act 2006 introduced in

---

212 See Chapter 2, pp 64–65.
213 See Chapter 2, pp 65–66.
214 No 57/1997/841/1047 10 July 1998.

particular two new and very broadly defined offences of preparation of terrorist acts under s 5 and of glorifying terrorism under s 1. The range of offences based on failing to give information or relating to property draw ordinary citizens, including the commercial sector, into the scheme. Clearly, the groups affected by the proscription scheme can also be affected by the general terrorism offences. The very wide range of terrorist offences now available, and their far-reaching impact, highlights the potentially immensely broad scope of s 1 TA, and its partially symbolic rather than actual import. In examining the current incrementally extended range of offences, it must be remembered that they are of course *additional* to the provisions of the ordinary criminal law. Violent terrorist acts obviously infringe a number of criminal law provisions, without the need for recourse to the special terrorism offences. If one of the 7/7 suicide bombers in London had survived he could have been charged with a number of criminal offences, beginning with murder. But obviously the threat of suicide attacks provides a justification for including very early intervention offences.

The offences discussed below were originally developed in the context of the PTA or EPA. At the time MPs obviously could not know that in 2000 they would be asked to apply all those offences to a wide range of groups, some of which, in terms of their ability to create a serious threat to life and their willingness to do so, cannot be compared with the IRA, although some present a more serious threat. Moreover, certain of these offences appeared only in the EPA, partly on the basis, as indicated above, that the threat was greatest in Northern Ireland and that without some apparently strong justification, they should not be included in the PTA. All the special terrorist offences, which have no equivalents in ordinary criminal law, can be applied to persons falling within s 1 TA, and also to persons falling outside s 1 but in some way dealing with or associated with persons who do fall within the definition. The use of the stop and search power under s 44 TA (now repealed), discussed in Chapter 12, in relation to reporters and protesters, is indicative of the possibility of applying terrorism offences in the public protest context, as was its use against a peace activist attempting an anti-war protest at the Labour party conference in 2005.[215] A number of the offences create prima facie infringements of certain of the Convention rights, albeit potentially justifiable, most notably Arts 10, 11, 6 and 5, scheduled in the HRA.

Directing a terrorist organisation

Section 56 TA 2000 makes it an offence to direct 'at any level' a terrorist organisation. Thus, the leaders, and all with some authority within the vast range of groups within the UK that may fall within the s 1 definition, are liable to a sentence of life imprisonment simply by virtue of their position. It does not appear to cover minor figures in the organisation.[216] The maximum sentence that can be given on conviction for the offence

---

215 Walter Wolfgang, a well-known peace activist, currently vice president of the Campaign for Nuclear Disarmament (CND), vice chair of Labour CND and a supporter of the Stop the War Coalition, was ejected from the Labour Party conference for protesting against the Iraq war; when he attempted to re-enter the conference later the same day, his pass showed that he had been removed previously, and he was briefly held by police under s 44 of the Terrorism Act.
216 HC Debs vol 187 col 404, 6.3 1991. See Walker, C and Reid, K, 'The Offence of directing Terrorist Organisations' (1993) Crim LR 669 on the previous equivalent offence under the EPA.

is life imprisonment. This offence has the advantage that it can be used to disrupt groups falling within s 1 TA even though they have not (yet) been proscribed. The police and prosecuting authorities have so far shown discretion in seeking to use this offence, and have not applied it to the leaders of e.g., protest groups advocating direct action, but it is unsatisfactory that the leaders of such groups should be placed in a precarious position in relation to the criminal law, one that is merely dependent on forbearance.

The offence under s 56 of the TA to direct 'at any level' a terrorist organisation is not confined to proscribed groups. If a relatively minor figure in an organisation which met the wide definition of terrorism under s 1, but was within its less serious aspects, was charged with this offence, a court which found that this interference with Art 11 was disproportionate to the aims pursued could interpret the terms used in s 56, especially 'directing' and 'at any level' under s 3 HRA so as to exclude such figures from the ambit of the section. For example, taking the terms together it could be argued that the term 'directing' qualifies 'at any level' so that only figures at the highest level within the *leadership* sector of the organisation are covered.

Preparatory and possession offences

A number of offences introduced under the Terrorism Acts 2000 and 2006, and in the ATCSA, and Counter-terrorism Act 2008 cover activities ancillary to terrorism; certain of them are broadly of a preparatory nature; some are aimed at terrorist conspiracies and at fund-raising and other activities of terrorist groups ancillary to acts of terrorism; some are aimed at businesses and ordinary citizens. These offences disrupt terrorist funding activities, and are of value in relation to the threat of suicide bombing since they can allow for the arrest of terrorists at an early planning stage, but a number of them were so broadly drawn as to fail initially to achieve Convention compliance.

As mentioned above, a large number of further criminal offences, not limited to proscribed organisations, and punishable by up to 14 years' imprisonment, exist under ss 14–18 TA in relation to fund-raising for the purposes of terrorism; the use or possession of money or other property for the purposes of terrorism; arrangements to make money or property available for the purposes of terrorism (funding arrangements), and under s 18 in relation to arrangements facilitating the retention or control of terrorist property by concealment, removal, transfer, etc (money laundering). The offences provided under ss 14–18 impose a range of significant responsibilities on members of the public; s 18 is broadly defined and could cover, for example, a property agent collecting rent from premises unaware that the ultimate beneficiary of the profits was a company operating for the benefit of a terrorist organisation. If charged, the statutory defence made available under s 18(2) would place a reverse burden upon him to show 'that he did not know and had no reasonable cause to suspect that the arrangement related to terrorist property'. However, if this occurred, following *Attorney General's Reference (No 4 of 2002)*,[217] discussed above, the burden should be read down under s 3 HRA to an evidential burden only in order to ensure compliance with Art 6(2).

Section 34 of the Counter-terrorism Act 2008 replaced s 23 of the 2000 Act (forfeiture: terrorist property offences), which deals with the power of a court to order the

217 [2004] UKHL 43; [2005] 1 AC 264; [2005] 1 All ER 237.

forfeiture of money or other property from a person convicted of offences under ss 15–18 of that Act ('terrorist finance' offences). The principal change made to s 23 is that the court may make a forfeiture order in respect of money or other property that had been used for the purposes of terrorism. So, for example, the court could order the forfeiture of a flat that was used for the assembly of bomb-making materials.

Section 35 of the 2008 Act inserted a new s 23A into the 2000 Act. It allows the court which convicts a person of certain offences to order the forfeiture of money or other property in the possession or under the control of the convicted person at the time of the offence, and which either had been used for the purposes of terrorism or was intended by that person to be used for those purposes, or that the court believed would be used for the purposes of terrorism unless forfeited. The offences in respect of which this power of forfeiture is available are certain offences under the 2000 Act and the Terrorism Act 2006 (but not the terrorist finance offences, which are covered by new s 23), and, in England and Wales and in Scotland (but not in Northern Ireland), offences falling within Sched 2 that the court determines have a terrorist connection (as defined in s 93) under ss 30 or 31.

Section 57 TA criminalises the 'possession of an article in circumstances which give rise to a reasonable suspicion that [it] is for a purpose connected with the commission, preparation or instigation of an act of terrorism'; the offence carries a ten-year jail sentence under s 57. As discussed above, s 57 only imposes an evidential, not a legal burden, on the defendant, in order to satisfy Art 6(2): s 118 of the Act applies to s 57 and provides that if the defendant adduces evidence that is sufficient to raise an issue with respect to the matter, the court or jury shall assume that the defence is satisfied unless the prosecution proves beyond reasonable doubt that it is not.

These offences of possession of information or objects were added to under the Terrorism Act 2006, which introduced a range of offences of 'acts preparatory to terrorism'. The offences were aimed at those planning acts of terrorism in a manner not already covered by the existing offences. Section 5 prohibits anyone from engaging in any conduct in preparation for an intended act of terrorism. The offence requires intention, but the *actus reus* is exceptionally broad. Under s 5:

(1) A person commits an offence if, with the intention of–

    (a) committing acts of terrorism, or

    (b) assisting another to commit such acts, he engages in any conduct in preparation for giving effect to his intention.

(2) It is irrelevant for the purposes of sub-section (1) whether the intention and preparations relate to one or more particular acts of terrorism, acts of terrorism of a particular description or acts of terrorism generally.

Under s 5(3) the maximum penalty is life imprisonment. Section 5 was obviously intended to be a catch-all offence able to allow intervention in relation to would-be terrorists at a very early stage, before any conduct linked to the actual preparation of a terrorist act has occurred. For example, visiting a 'jihadist' website could be covered so long as the requisite intention could be shown. This offence overlaps to an extent with the proscription offences, but it obviates the need to show membership of Isis, Al-Qaeda or a related organisation.

Section 5 is clearly aimed at criminalising supporters of Al-Qaeda or similar groups largely on the basis of that support, but the person in question must have the intention of committing or assisting in the commission of a 'terrorist' act, although that need not be a specific act. Presumably that term would be defined by reference to s 1 TA. The addition of 'acts of terrorism generally' brings this offence closer to 'thought crime'[218] but such 'pre-crime' offences can be justified due to the magnitude of the harms they are intended to prevent, including multi-site attacks similar to those in Paris in November 2015. Lord Carlile, the then government reviewer of the TA, supported the introduction of this offence, allowing for very early intervention in preparatory activity, on the basis that: 'there is clear evidence that such an offence would provide for some cases a way of dealing with suspects more acceptable in perceptual terms than control orders. It is better that sanctions should follow conviction of crime rather than mere administrative decisions'.[219] This is clearly laudable in principle, especially as the control orders, (now TPIMs' scheme) as discussed below, is over-broad in human rights terms but under-inclusive in security terms – since the orders do not at the moment include detention. But as the widest offence introduced so far in the counter-terrorist scheme, it again relies heavily on executive discretion in deploying it.

A number of new offences relating to materials that could be used in an attack were also introduced in the 2006 Act.[220] Section 12 TA 2006 extends the ban on trespassing in specified locations imposed by the Serious and Organised Crime and Police Act 2005, to cover any nuclear site. Section 6 prohibits anyone from training others in terrorist activities, or from receiving training and carries a maximum penalty of ten years' imprisonment. A further new offence of 'terrorist training' was introduced under the 2006 Act to be added to the existing offence under s 54 Terrorism Act 2000; under s 54 those who give or receive training in the making or use of weapons or explosives, or recruit persons for this purpose, are liable to ten years in prison. Section 8 prohibits anyone from being at a place where training is going on (whether in the UK or abroad), provided the person knew or reasonably believed that training was happening. The offence carries a maximum penalty of ten years' imprisonment. That offence is much broader in that s 8 makes it an offence merely to be in attendance at any place in the world where such instruction is taking place. Lord Carlile has pointed out that this would leave open the possibility of prosecuting journalists reporting in the public interest from camps of fighting groups revolting against despotic regimes.[221] But the offence is of value in relation to persons who have left Britain to fight with Isis, but then return to the UK, having received weapons training.

---

218 See Macdonald, S, 'Prosecuting suspected terrorists: Precursor crimes, intercept evidence and the priority of security', in Jarvis, L and Lister, M (eds), *Critical Perspectives on Counter-Terrorism*, 2015, Routledge, pp 130–149

219 Report on the Operation in 2005 of the Terrorism Act 2000, May 2006, at para 33.

220 Section 9 prohibits the making or possession of any radioactive device (i.e. a 'dirty' bomb). The maximum penalty is life imprisonment. Section 10 prohibits using radioactive materials or a radioactive device in a terrorist attack, and the sabotage of nuclear facilities which causes a radioactive leak. The maximum penalty is life imprisonment. Section 11 covers terrorist threats relating to devices, materials or facilities; it prohibits anyone from making threats to demand that they be given radioactive materials. The maximum penalty is life imprisonment.

221 *Ibid*, fn 219 (2006).

Positive obligations to report information[222]

A very wide range of other people, including ordinary citizens, banks and businesses, who are not part of any of the groups covered by s 1 TA, are potentially criminalised under various offences relating to the reporting of information. The government considered that its existence gave a 'clear signal' to citizens regarding the abhorrence of terrorism, and included it in the Act, in s 19, in a somewhat modified and narrowed form. Suspicions arising in home life were no longer covered, but the offence is nevertheless of extremely wide application.[223] Section 19 goes well beyond requiring banks and other businesses to report any suspicion they might have that someone is laundering terrorist money or committing any of the other terrorist offences in ss 15–18. It applies to all employees or employers and means that if, during the course of their work, a person comes across information about, or becomes suspicious of, someone whom she suspects may be using money or property to contribute to the causes of terrorism, she will commit a criminal offence carrying a maximum penalty of five years' imprisonment if she does not report them.

Section 38B, inserted by s 117 ATCSA, creates a much broader provision. Section 38B makes it an offence, subject to an unexplicated defence of reasonable excuse, for *any* person to fail to disclose to a police officer any information that he knows or believes *might* be of material assistance in preventing an act of terrorism or securing the apprehension or conviction of a person involved in such an act.[224]

ATCSA 2001 also inserted ss 21A and 21B into TA 2000, placing new responsibilities on the regulated financial sector.[225] This is a stricter duty, applied instead of, rather than in addition to, the duty under s 19. Section 21A provides that if a person believes

---

222   See further Walker, C, *The Anti-Terrorism Legislation*, 2014)
223   Section19(1) provides:
    this section applies where a person –
    (a) believes or suspects that another person has committed an offence under any of sections 15 to 18, and
    (b) bases his belief or suspicion on information which comes to his attention in the course of a trade, profession, business or employment.
    (2) The person commits an offence if he does not disclose to a constable as soon as is reasonably practicable –
    (a) his belief or suspicion, and
    (b) the information on which it is based'.
    Sub-section (5) preserves the exemption in respect of legal advisers' privileged material.
224   Section 38B provides: Information about acts of terrorism (1) This section applies where a person has information which he knows or believes might be of material assistance –
    (a) in preventing the commission by another person of an act of terrorism, or
    (b) in securing the apprehension, prosecution or conviction of another person, in the United Kingdom, for an offence involving the commission, preparation or instigation of an act of terrorism.
    (2) The person commits an offence if he does not disclose the information as soon as reasonably practicable in accordance with sub-section (3) ...
    (4) It is a defence for a person charged with an offence under sub-section (2) to prove that he had a reasonable excuse for not making the disclosure.
225   As defined in new Sched 3A. Supervisory authorities include: the Bank of England; the Financial Services Authority; the Council of Lloyd's; the Director General of Fair Trading; a body which is a designated professional body for the purposes of Part 20 of the Financial Services and Markets Act 2000; The Secretary of State; The Treasury. There are increasing concerns in banks and businesses in the regulated sector about the difficulties of compliance.

or suspects or has reasonable grounds for knowing or suspecting that another person has committed an offence under any of ss 15–18, and the basis for the belief or suspicion came to him in the course of a business in the regulated sector, he will commit an offence if he does not disclose the information in question to a constable or nominated officer as soon as is reasonably practicable. Under s 21A(5) he has a defence of reasonable excuse for not disclosing the information or other matter, or he can raise legal professional privilege.

Journalists are among the groups of ordinary citizens affected by these duties of disclosure of information. Sections 19 and 38B could potentially curb journalistic investigation into the activities of a very wide range of groups, since journalists are unlikely to be prepared to incur the risk of a lengthy prison sentence. The offence also potentially places journalists investigating, or in some way associated with, the activities of certain groups, such as the PKK or Teyrebaz Azadiye Kurdistan, in a very difficult position, especially where they have contacts within the group. It would appear almost impossible for any investigative journalism to occur in such circumstances, without risk of incurring a five-year prison sentence. The provision requiring the surrender of information might mean that the identity of sources could not be protected. The two offences may be having a strong deterrent effect on investigative journalism in relation to extremist groups. This may be having the counter-productive effect of helping to keep the activities of the more secretive of such groups out of the public eye.

These provisions may accord insufficient recognition to the role of the media in investigating matters of public interest and informing the public. Strasbourg, as indicated in Part 2 of this chapter, and in the Introduction to Part II of this book, gives pre-eminence to the role of the press in a democracy.[226] Restrictions placed on the press in performing this vital role have been subjected to the strictest scrutiny.[227] Charging a journalist with these offences would clearly, therefore, amount to an interference with the Art 10 guarantee. The domestic court would be expected to observe the same or (arguably) higher standards than Strasbourg (based on common law recognition of the value of freedom of expression) in scrutinising the need for the interference, bearing in mind the narrow margin of appreciation afforded to states in respect of interference with political speech, especially where it concerns criticism directed at the government itself.[228] The Divisional Court in *Ex p Kebilene*[229] indicated the strictness of the standards which domestic courts are capable of applying, albeit in relation to Art 6(2) rather than Art 10.

Defences are provided in relation to these offences which – apart from that of s 21A – appear to be aimed, *inter alia*, at journalists. The s 21A defence would be relevant in relation to the presumption of innocence. All three offences provide: 'it is a defence for a person charged with an offence under [the relevant sub-section] to prove that he had a reasonable excuse for not making the disclosure'. Under ss 19 and 38B this defence would allow a journalist to raise Art 10 points under the HRA. The defence

226 *Castells v Spain*, judgment of 23 April 1992, Series A no 236, p 23, para 43.
227 *Goodwin v UK* (1996) 22 EHRR 123.
228 *Incal v Turkey* (2000) 29 EHRR 449 (above, p 1062).
229 [1999] 4 All ER 801.

of 'reasonable excuse' under ss 19 and 38B could be afforded a wide interpretation in order to protect investigative journalism. Section 21A and ss 19 and 38B all have to be interpreted compatibly with Art 6(2), as discussed above. Section 118 eases the burden of proof on defendants, in accordance with the presumption of innocence under Art 6(2), as discussed above, but it does not cover s 19, or s 38B or s 21A. However, the decision of the House of Lords in *Sheldrake v DPP; Attorney General's Reference (No 4 of 2002)*[230] is relevant. First, it may be noted that requiring a journalist to prove reasonable excuse stands Art 10 on its head since freedom of expression is not viewed as a defence under Art 10; the justification for the interference operates in a sense as a defence negating the potential breach. Second, following the House of Lords' decision the defences in question could be read down so as to impose on the defendant an evidential burden only. The Court of Appeal in *R v Keogh*[231] accepted that the principle from *Attorney General's Reference* must be applied in a wide range of situations. Given the burden that is being placed on groups of citizens, including those working in the financial sector, by these offences, it is arguable that requiring a defendant to prove a defence of reasonable excuse could be viewed as requiring him to disprove a substantial element of the offence, so as to engage the principle from *Attorney General's Reference*.

A further wide range of citizens and businesses can be criminalised under the provision relating to the collection of information. Section 58(1) provides: 'A person commits an offence if (a) he collects or makes a record of information of a kind likely to be useful to a person committing or preparing an act of terrorism, or (b) he possesses a document or record containing information of that kind.'

This is another extremely wide offence, particularly since, in common with the one arising under s 56, it lacks any requirement of knowledge regarding the nature of the information, or any requirement that the person intended to use it in order to further the aims of terrorism. It could catch, for example, a journalist, or an accountant who had records of information relating to funding activities of terrorist groups abroad that could be useful to a group within s 1. However, a defence of proving that 'he had a reasonable excuse for his action or possession' is provided. It was apparent from *R (on the application of the Kurdistan Workers' Party and Others) v Secretary of State for the Home Department*[232] that persons, including journalists, were placed in a difficult position in working for Kurdish organisations in the UK since it was very difficult to ensure that the PKK was excluded from their networks, and journalists who were in possession of information relating to the PKK were placed in an impossible position. The deterrent effect on journalism in such circumstances is clearly severe, especially as the maximum penalty is imprisonment for ten years. Section 58, however, only imposes an evidential, not a legal, burden on the defendant, in order to satisfy Art 6(2): s 118 of the Act, as discussed above, applies to s 58 and provides that if the defendant adduces evidence which is sufficient to raise an issue with respect to the matter the court or jury shall

230 [2005] 1 AC 264; [2005] 1 All ER 237.
231 [2007] All ER (D) 105 (Mar); [2007] EWCA Crim 528, 7 March 2007.
232 [2002] EWHC Admin 644.

assume that the defence is satisfied unless the prosecution proves beyond reasonable doubt that it is not.

Inciting terrorism abroad and encouraging/glorifying terrorism

The TA not only applied the old PTA and EPA offences to a much wider range of groups, it also created new offences of inciting terrorism abroad, which apply under ss 59, 60 and 61 to England and Wales, Northern Ireland and Scotland, respectively. Under s 59(1) 'A person commits an offence if (a) he incites another person to commit an act of terrorism wholly or partly outside the United Kingdom, and (b) the act would, if committed in England and Wales, constitute one of the offences listed in sub-section (2).' Under s 59(2) the offences are the more serious offences against the person: murder, an offence under ss 18, 23, 24, 28 or 29 of the Offences against the Person Act 1861 (OAPA) and an offence under s 1(2) of the Criminal Damage Act 1971. Under s 59(3), the penalty for conviction under this section will be the penalty 'to which he would be liable on conviction of the offence listed in sub-section (2) which corresponds to the act which he incites'. Sections 60 and 61 create equivalent provisions relating to Scotland and Northern Ireland.

It means that a person who encouraged another to assassinate a dictator of an oppressive regime would commit an offence punishable with a mandatory sentence of life imprisonment. The offence might also be committed during a demonstration at which words spoken denouncing such a dictator could be construed as amounting to incitement to assassinate him. Section 59 also creates doubtful distinctions between offences. Sometimes very little separates the person who commits grievous bodily harm (s 18 of the OAPA) from the person who commits serious bodily harm (s 20 OAPA), and this is more clearly the case where the attack need not in fact have been committed. But the s 20 offence is not listed in s 59(2). Therefore, determination that a person is subject to a penalty of a maximum of life imprisonment or to no penalty at all may rest on a very fine distinction.

The incitement provisions under ss 59, 60 and 61 on their face afford little recognition to the value of protest and assembly. They are unconfined to members of proscribed groups. Taking the example used above of charging the offence in respect of persons at a public meeting denouncing a terrorist dictator, a court which viewed the interference with freedom of expression as, in the circumstances, disproportionate to the aims in view, could take the opportunity of construing the wording of the provisions very strictly. In particular, where there was leeway to do so, on a very strict interpretation of the application of certain of the offences listed in s 59(2), it might be found that incitement merely of lesser, similar, but unlisted offences had occurred.

This incitement offence is aimed at incitement of specific and serious acts of violence. The offence of indirect encouragement of acts of terrorism which includes the glorification of such acts – a much broader offence – was introduced in the Terrorism Act 2006. It is not confined to glorifying acts of terrorist violence that also amount to serious criminal offences, and it does not require *incitement* since it includes the condoning of acts that have already occurred. The Act was drafted in the aftermath of the

7 July 2005 London bombings. The offence was intended to apply to figures such as Omar Bakri Muhammad who had received a great deal of publicity for his reaction to the London bombing. There had been other statements, made by a number of controversial figures, including Muslim clerics such as Abu Qutada and Abu Hamza al-Masri about the 11 September 2001 attacks and attacks on US and UK forces in Iraq.

The concept of 'glorification' is imprecise; apparently modelled on the Spanish law of *apologia de terrorismo*, it is based on the principle, already established as acceptable in UK law, but not in such a broad fashion, of criminalising persons for what they say rather than what they do. As the Joint Committee on Human Rights put it in its report on the Terrorism Bill 2006[233] in relation to the two offences – the existing offence of incitement and the new offence of glorification: 'the law already outlaws incitement to commit a particular terrorist act, such as the statement "Please will you go and blow up a tube train on 7 July in London?" but not a generalised incitement to terrorist acts such as "We encourage everybody to go and blow up tube trains".'[234] The Committee also noted that the offence overlapped with existing criminal offences that had been used in this context,[235] including the very broad offence of soliciting to murder. They noted that in *R v El-Faisal*,[236] for example, in 2004, the Court of Appeal had upheld the convictions of a minister of Islam for soliciting murder under s 4 Offences Against the Person Act 1861 and for incitement to racial hatred under the Public Order Act 1986, for having made audio tapes urging Muslims to fight and kill, among others, Jews, Christians, Americans, Hindus and other 'unbelievers'.[237] They also noted that the Muslim cleric Abu Hamza Al-Masri was charged in 2004 with solicitation to murder for soliciting or encouraging others at a public meeting to kill non-believers in the Muslim faith, and with incitement to racial hatred. The Committee considered therefore that the strict necessity for a new offence might be thought to be questionable, but accepted that there was some uncertainty about the scope of the existing offences.

Section 1(1) prohibits the publishing of:

> a statement that is likely to be understood by some or all of the members of the public to whom it is published as a direct or indirect encouragement or other

---

233 Report on the Prevention of Terrorism Bill (2005–6) HL Paper 75–1, HC 561–1.
234 Report on the Prevention of Terrorism Bill (2005–6) at para 21.
235 *Ibid* at paras 23 and 24.
236 [2004] EWCA Crim 456.
237 They noted that in the course of its judgment the Court of Appeal explained the very great width of the offence of soliciting to murder. The offence of soliciting to murder is contained in s 4 of the 1861 Act which states: 'Whosoever shall solicit, encourage, persuade or endeavour to persuade, or shall propose to any person, to murder any other person, whether he be a subject of her Majesty or not, and whether he be within the Queen's dominions or not, shall be guilty of a misdemeanour, and being convicted thereof shall be liable to imprisonment for life.' The scope of the behaviour sufficient to constitute the offence was classically identified as follows in *R v Most* (1881) 7 QBD 244, *per* Huddleston B at 258: '"solicit" that is defined to be, to importune, to entreat, to implore, to ask, to attempt to try to obtain; "encourage", which is to intimate, to incite to anything, to give courage to, to inspirit, to embolden, to raise confidence, to make confident; "persuade" which is to bring any particular opinion, to influence by argument or expostulation. . . .'.

inducement to them to the commission, preparation or instigation of acts of terrorism or Convention offences.

Statements of indirect encouragement include every statement that glorifies the commission or preparation (whether in the past, in the future or generally) of such acts or offences. But this very broad provision of s 1 is qualified in a number of respects by s 1(2). A person commits an offence under s 1(2)(a) if:

> he publishes a statement to which this section applies or causes another to publish such a statement on his behalf; and

> (b) at the time he does so, he intends the statement to be understood as mentioned in sub-section (1) or is reckless as to whether or not it is likely to be so understood.

> (3) For the purposes of this section the statements that are likely to be understood by members of the public as indirectly encouraging the commission or preparation of acts of terrorism or Convention offences include every statement which –

> (a) glorifies the commission or preparation (whether in the past, in the future or generally) of such acts or offences; and
> (b) is a statement from which those members of the public could reasonably be expected to infer that what is being glorified is being glorified as conduct that should be emulated by them in existing circumstances.

The statement indirectly or directly encouraging terrorism is to be taken as a whole and looked at in all the circumstances in which it was made (sub-s (4)). It is not necessary to show that anyone was actually 'encouraged or induced' to commit any relevant offence by the statement (sub-s (5)). The words 'by *them* in *existing* circumstances'[238] do narrow the scope of the offence since they require that members of the audience *themselves* might commit the acts of terrorism. Also they indicate that it would not suffice to show that the acts being glorified are acts that might be committed many years in the future by an audience member. Equally, it must be possible for the audience to emulate such acts in the present context; it is not enough for the speaker to glorify past acts, such as the Crusades. But those limiting words appear only to be intended to apply to indirect encouragement by means of glorification; they do not appear to apply to *other* forms of encouragement, although possibly s 3 HRA could be used to extend them to the offence generally. There is a defence of innocent publication, where the statement is published electronically, a defence intended to benefit those who run websites, on which such statements might be published without their knowledge or consent (sub-s (6)). Section 2 prohibits the dissemination of a publication that is either (a) likely to be understood as directly or indirectly encouraging terrorism, or (b) includes information which is likely to be understood as being useful in

---

238 The words 'by them' were added by the government by amendment at report stage in the Commons to cl 1(4)(b).

the commission or preparation of an act of terrorism. The maximum penalty for both offences is seven years' imprisonment.

The Joint Committee on Human Rights considered that the offence might be compatible with Art 10, under the existing Strasbourg case law. It found that restrictions on *indirect* incitement to commit violent terrorist offences are capable in principle of being compatible with Art 10,[239] provided that they are necessary, defined with sufficient precision to satisfy the requirements of legal certainty, and proportionate to the legitimate aims of national security, public safety, the prevention of crime and the protection of the rights of others.[240] In terms of necessity, whilst the Committee thought that general statements encouraging terrorism might well fall within the existing law on soliciting murder,[241] it accepted that 'there is some uncertainty about the scope of the existing offences'. It found that:

> A clarification of the law is therefore in principle justifiable, even if it overlaps to some extent with other existing offences. We therefore accept, on balance, that the case has been made out by the Government that there is a need for a new, narrowly defined criminal offence of indirect incitement to terrorist acts.[242]

A very significant concern of the Committee was as to the imprecision of the new offence: 'The legal certainty concern is that terms such as glorification, praise and celebration are too vague to form part of a criminal offence which can be committed by speaking.' The Committee pointed out that the Home Secretary rested upon a distinction between: 'encouraging and glorifying on the one hand and explaining or understanding on the other. The last two, he says would not be caught by the new offence, because they do not amount to encouraging, glorifying, praising or celebrating.'[243] The Committee was unconvinced by this reasoning on the basis that no 'bright line' distinction can be drawn consonant with legal certainty, between glorifying and explaining in this context:

> In our view, the difficulty with the Home Secretary's response is that his distinction is not self-executing: the content of comments and remarks will have to be carefully analysed in each case, including the context in which they were spoken, and there will be enormous scope for disagreement between reasonable people as to whether a particular comment is merely an explanation or an expression of understanding or goes further and amounts to encouragement, praise or glorification. The point is made by the vast range of reaction to the comments of both Cherie Booth QC and Jenny Tonge MP about suicide bombers. Some reasonable people thought they fell on one side of the Home Secretary's line, other reasonable people thought they fell on the other.[244]

---

239 Report on the Prevention of Terrorism Bill (2005–6) HL Paper 75–1, HC 561–1. The Committee gave the example of *Hogefeld v Germany*, Appl No 35402/97 (20 January 2000).
240 Report on the Prevention of Terrorism Bill (2005–6) at para 20.
241 Under the Offences Against the Person Act 1861, s 4.
242 Report on the Prevention of Terrorism Bill (2005–6) HL Paper 75–1, HC 561–1, at para 25.
243 *Ibid*, at para 27.
244 *Ibid*, at para 28.

The Committee also considered that the offence was over-broad. The offence relies on the very broad definition of 'terrorism' in the 2000 Terrorism Act, which is discussed above. As indicated above, the definition under s 1 TA covers the use or threat, 'for the purpose of advancing a political, religious or ideological cause', of action anywhere in the world 'designed to influence a government or to intimidate the public or a section of the public', which involves serious damage to property. The offence makes it criminal to vocalise support for armed opposition to regimes viewed by the speaker and by others in the international community as tyrannous and illegitimate. Since 'terrorist' acts are defined so broadly under s 1 TA, it is not necessary that the acts glorified could threaten life. It includes, on its face, the glorification of threats to damage property abroad in furtherance of the cause of a group fighting to establish a democratic regime in an oppressive state, since that action is covered by s 1 TA. The law is also drafted very broadly to include the 'glorification' of 'acts of terrorism' in the past. It is reasonably clear, however, that although the offence covers such speech, it was not intended for use against those speaking to condone or in defence of actions of groups operating only abroad, such as the PMOI in Iran who are 'terrorists' within s 1 TA, but could probably be regarded as 'freedom fighters'. But obviously it hands a very broad discretion to the executive as to its application.

Intent or recklessness as to the statement being understood by the audience as mentioned in s 1(2) is required for an offence to be committed. Thus, the offence can be committed by means of subjective recklessness or oblique intent. So even if the defendant has no intention of inciting people to support or condone terrorist actions, he/she could still be committing an offence so long as members of the public might reasonably regard it as direct or indirect encouragement, if he adverts to that possibility. It is also possible that the offence could prove to be discriminatory in its application, raising questions as to its impact under Arts 10 and 14 combined. Arguably, certain statements made by Muslims could be regarded as 'glorification' if addressed to a Muslim audience, but not if addressed to a non-Muslim audience, due to the requirement under s 1(3)(b) that the audience 'could reasonably be expected to infer that what is being glorified is conduct that should be emulated by them in existing circumstances'. The incitement offence, together with the offence of indirect encouragement of terrorism, have been employed on a number of occasions, especially in relation to postings on social media, against those seeking to encourage others to take part in terrorist acts, including murder. For example, they were employed in 2007 as part of a long-term proactive investigation into radicalisation of Muslims. A number of persons associated with the extremist Islamic group al-Ghurabaa, including Abu Izadeen, were arrested on grounds of incitement in April 2007. A further three persons stood trial on incitement charges in April 2007.[245] In 2012 in *R v Ahmed Faraz*[246] a man referred to in the press as 'the terrorists' favourite bookseller' successfully challenged seven convictions for disseminating 'terrorist publications' (books and DVDs) under s 2 of the Terrorism Act 2006. But the convictions were successfully challenged only on the ground that prejudicial material had gone before the jury. The defendant had argued in relation to freedom of expression that in dealing with publications

---

245 See *The Guardian* report, 25 April 2007, p 4.
246 [2012] EWCA Crim 2820.

expressing 'political or religious ideas' it should not be possible to convict someone on the basis they were merely *reckless* as to whether the publication was likely to encourage terrorism. Actual intent should be required. He also argued that publication of a 'legitimate expression of a political or religious view' should not be an offence. His arguments did not reflect the position under Art 10, as the Court of Appeal found: the mere fact that a publication reflected a religious view would not mean that a conviction in respect of it could not be justified under Art 10(2) (or at common law) if it also encouraged terrorist acts. The Court also considered that the directions given by the judge in respect of the offence were compatible with Art 10. Since then a number of persons, including persons associated with or praising groups linked to Al Qaeda or Isis, have been found guilty of this offence.[247]

4 The changing nature of 'emergency' executive non-trial-based measures post 9/11

Introduction

This part of this chapter considers the use of measures designed to curb the activities . of terrorist suspects, without reliance on a criminal trial. It examines the transition in 2005 from detention without trial to control orders, and in 2012 from control orders to more ECHR-compliant 'terrorism prevention and investigation measures' (TPIMs) under the Terrorism Prevention and Investigation Measures Act 2011 (TPIMA). It argues that the interaction between security and liberty over the post 9/11 years has the appearance of a dialogue between courts and the executive that has resulted in a diminution in the repressive character of non-trial based preventive measures. The 15 years that have passed since the catastrophic terrorist strike of 9/11 have seen a complex interaction between human rights and non-trial based counter-terrorist measures in the UK, leading to modification of such measures, rendering them more human rights compliant.

In order to seek to demonstrate that a movement towards normalisation of 'preventive' non-trial-based measures[248] has occurred, it is suggested that three phases, broadly speaking, could be identified to date in the post-9/11 response in the UK.

---

247 For example, in 2015 in *R v Alaa Esayed* (BBC News, 11.6.15) the defendant came to the attention of the police due to the nature and volume of material she was posting on her Twitter and Instagram accounts. Examination of the accounts revealed a large number of messages posted (on occasion in excess of 50 a day) which indicated a support for IS and their actions in Syria and Iraq. A review of the messages revealed that she was in fact encouraging others to engage in such acts. She pleaded guilty to the s 1 offence.

248 See generally for discussion of 'preventive' measures in the UK: Zedner, L, 'Preventive Justice or Pre-punishment? The Case of Control Orders' (2007) 60 CLP 174; Walker, C, *Terrorism and the Law*, 2011, OUP, Ch 7. See generally as regards preventive measures: Paust, J, 'Survey of Possible Responses to International Terrorism, Prevention, Punishment and Cooperative Action' (1975) 5(2) Georgia Journal of International and Comparative Law 431; Ruddock, P, 'Law as a Preventative Weapon Against Terrorism', in Lynch, A, Macdonald E and Williams, G (eds), *Law and Liberty in the War on Terror*, 2008, Sydney; Elias, SB, 'Rethinking "Preventive Detention" from a Comparative Perspective: Three Frameworks for Detaining Terrorist Suspects' (2010) 41 Columbia Human Rights Law Review 99.

The first phase – indefinite detention without trial

Introduction

Since 9/11 the UK government has sought to restrict the physical liberty of those that it considers to be a security threat. Initially, these measures were without doubt the most draconian since the use of internment during the Troubles in Northern Ireland. As part of its legislative response to the attacks on New York and Washington on 11 September 2001 the UK government took the decision to seek to introduce detention without trial for foreign nationals suspected of being 'international terrorists' who could not be deported due to the risk they would face of Art 3 treatment in the receiving country (see above). In general, non-British citizens who present a risk to national security can be deported.[249] The government achieved its aim when Parliament passed the Anti-Terrorism, Crime and Security Act 2001 (ATCSA). Part 4 of the Act contained the detention without trial provisions. Part 4 created conflicts with a number of the guarantees of the European Convention on Human Rights received into domestic law under the Human Rights Act 1998. The Part 4 scheme could not be reconciled with the fundamental guarantee of liberty of the person under Art 5, so the government was forced to derogate from Art 5.

Part 4 was eventually repealed in 2005, as discussed below, after the House of Lords found that it was a disproportionate response to the emergency and conflicted with Arts 5 and 14 of the Convention read together. However, Part 4 is discussed in some detail below, partly in order to provide the context and background, not only for the control orders scheme under the Prevention of Terrorism Act 2005, which initially succeeded it, but also for the terrorism prevention and investigation measures (TPIMS) made under the Terrorism Prevention and Investigation Measures Act 2011. Moreover, Part 4 forms part of a very significant chapter in the UK's history of interaction between human rights and counter-terrorist measures.

Introduction of part 4 ATCSA, and the derogation order

The ATCSA builds upon the Terrorism Act 2000 (TA), which as indicated above already provided an extremely extensive range of coercive and investigatory powers. In introducing the ATCSA, however, the government claimed that, despite the range of offences it offered, the TA did not provide it with sufficient powers. It stated that as a response to 9/11 it needed a power to detain non-British citizens suspected of international terrorism, without trial. Thus, before the TA had been in force for one year, it came to be viewed as inadequate. The problem faced by the government after 9/11 was presented to Parliament and a number of parliamentary committees[250] in the following terms: a dilemma had arisen in respect of persons suspected of being international terrorists but who could not be placed on trial due to the sensitivity of the evidence and the high standard of proof, and often could not be extradited, or deported to their country of

---

249 See pp 1039–40. For comment, see Walker, C, 'The Treatment of Foreign Terror Suspects' (2007) 70(3) MLR 427.
250 Home Affairs Select Committee, *The Anti-Terrorism, Crime and Security Bill* (HC (2001–02) 351, 10 November 2001), First Report.

origin, or another country, because there were grounds to think that they would there be subject to torture or inhuman and degrading treatment, in breach of Art 3 of the European Convention. However, characterising the problem in this fashion ignored the fact that the security problem was created by British extremist Muslims linked to Al-Qaeda, as well as non-British citizens.

The dilemma arose in part due to the decision of the European Court of Human Rights in *Chahal v UK*,[251] in which it found that a breach of Art 3 will arise where a country deports a person to another country, knowing that he or she will face a substantial risk of Art 3 treatment in that other country.[252] Mr Chahal was an Indian citizen who had been granted indefinite leave to remain in the UK but his activities as a Sikh separatist brought him to the notice of the authorities; the Home Secretary at the time decided that he should be deported because his continued presence was not conducive to the public good for reasons of a political nature, namely the international fight against terrorism. He resisted deportation on the ground (among others) that, if returned to India, he faced a real risk of death, or of torture in custody contrary to Art 3 of the European Convention which provides that 'No one shall be subjected to torture or to inhuman or degrading treatment or punishment.'

Before the European Court the UK contended that the effect of Art 3 should be qualified in a case where a state sought to deport a non-national on grounds of national security. The Court, affirming a unanimous decision of the Commission, rejected that argument. It said:[253]

> Article 3 enshrines one of the most fundamental values of democratic society. The Court is well aware of the immense difficulties faced by states in modern times in protecting their communities from terrorist violence. However, even in these circumstances, the Convention prohibits in absolute terms torture or inhuman or degrading treatment or punishment, irrespective of the victim's conduct. Unlike most of the substantive clauses of the convention and of Protocols Nos. 1 and 4, Article 3 makes no provision for exceptions and no derogation from it is permissible under Article 15 even in the event of a public emergency threatening the life of the nation.
>
> The prohibition provided by Article 3 against ill-treatment is equally absolute in expulsion cases. Thus, whenever substantial grounds have been shown for believing that an individual would face a real risk of being subjected to treatment contrary to Article 3 if removed to another state, the responsibility of the contracting state to safeguard him or her against such treatment is engaged in the event of expulsion. In these circumstances, the activities of the individual in question, however undesirable or dangerous, cannot be a material consideration. The protection afforded by Article 3 is thus wider than that provided by Articles 32 and 33 of the United Nations 1951 Convention on the Status of Refugees.

The Court went on to consider whether Mr Chahal's detention, which had lasted for a number of years, had exceeded the period permissible under Art 5(1)(f). The Court,

---

251 (1996) 23 EHRR 413.
252 *Ibid*, at para 74.
253 *Ibid*, in paras 79–80 of its judgment.

differing from the unanimous decision of the Commission, held that it had not. But it reasserted[254] that 'any deprivation of liberty under Art 5(1)(f) is justified only for as long as deportation proceedings are in progress'. In a case like Mr Chahal's, where deportation proceedings were precluded by Art 3, Art 5(1)(f) would not sanction detention because the non-national would not be 'a person against whom action is being taken with a view to deportation'. A person who commits a serious crime under the criminal law of this country may of course, whether a national or a non-national, be charged, tried and, if convicted, imprisoned. But a non-national who faces the prospect of torture or inhuman treatment if returned to his own country, and who cannot be deported to any third country, and is not charged with any crime, may not under Art 5(1)(f) of the Convention be detained in the UK even if judged to be a threat to national security.

Thus Article 3 imposes an absolute obligation on signatory states not to deport persons where they are at risk of Art 3 treatment in the receiving country.[255] As a matter of domestic law, it is clear that the power to place persons in immigration detention prior to deportation[256] is limited to such time as is reasonable to allow the process of deportation to be carried out, and that deportation should follow promptly after the making of the order: *R v Governor of Durham prison ex p Singh*.[257] Thus the available powers of detention prior to deportation did not provide the government with a solution since the suspected terrorists in question could not be deported within a reasonable time or, in some instances, at all.

The government's preferred solution to the dilemma was to introduce detention without trial for suspected non-national terrorists even where they could not be deported. But it considered that the new provisions would be incompatible with Art 5(1) of the European Convention on Human Rights, which protects the right to liberty and security of the person, afforded further effect in domestic law under the HRA. Although there is an exception under Art 5(1)(f) allowing for detention of 'a person against whom action is being taken with a view to deportation or extradition', it was clear, following *Chahal*, that it would not cover the lengthy detentions envisaged during which deportation proceedings would not be in being.[258]

Therefore, in order to introduce the new provisions it was necessary to derogate from Art 5(1). Before giving notice to the Secretary-General the government made an order under s 14 HRA, the Human Rights Act (Designated Derogation) Order 2001[259] setting out the derogation from Art 5(1). The derogation itself was expressed to subsist until it was withdrawn, but for HRA purposes it was to cease to have effect after five years unless its extension was approved by the positive resolution procedure in both Houses

---

254 At para 113.
255 Further, the UK has ratified Protocols 6 and 13 (see Chapter 2, pp 30–31) of the Convention and therefore cannot deport persons to countries where there is a real risk that the death penalty will be imposed. See *X v Spain*, DR 37 (1984) p 93; *Aylor-Davis v France* (1994) 76-A DR 164; *Raidl v Austria* (1995) 82-A DR 134. Protocol 6 prohibits the death penalty in time of peace; Protocol 13 prohibits it generally.
256 Under the Immigration Act 1971, Sched 3, para 1.
257 [1984] 1 WLR 704.
258 At para 113. In order to detain, deportation proceedings should be in being and it should be clear that they are being prosecuted with due diligence.
259 SI 2001/3644. It was laid before Parliament on 12 November 2001, coming into effect on the following day. It designated the proposed derogation as one that was to have immediate effect.

of Parliament.[260] The schedule to the derogation order, which took the form of a draft letter to the Secretary-General, pointed out that the UN Security Council recognised the 9/11 attacks as a threat to international security and required states in Resolution 1373 to take measures to prevent terrorist attacks, which would include denying a safe haven to those who plan, support or commit such acts. The schedule argued that on this basis there was a domestic public emergency, which was especially present since there were foreign nationals in the UK who threatened its national security. Therefore, it argued, the measures in Part 4 of ATCSA were clearly and strictly required by the very grave nature of the situation. The government also derogated from Art 9 of the International Covenant on Civil and Political Rights as a further method of safeguarding the new measures from challenge.[261]

The Part 4 detention provisions

Detention under Part 4 ATCSA depended on certification by the Home Secretary as – in effect – a substitute for a trial. Under s 21(1) the Home Secretary could issue a certificate in respect of a person on the basis of (a) a reasonable belief that the person's presence in the UK was a 'risk to national security' and (b) reasonable suspicion that he or she was a terrorist. It may be noted that as a result of the decision in *Rehman v Secretary of State for the Home Dept*[262] the Home Secretary was accorded, as discussed below, a broad latitude in determining when a risk to national security arises.

Under s 21(2) ATCSA a 'terrorist' was a person who was or had been 'concerned in the commission, preparation or instigation of acts of international terrorism' or was (b) a member of or belonged to an international terrorist group or (c) had 'links' with such a group. Under s 21(4) such links would exist only if the person supported or assisted the international terrorist group. 'Terrorism' was afforded the meaning given to it in s 1(1) of the TA.[263] Thus the TA and ATCSA had to be read together. The detention provisions in the 2001 Act clearly did not apply to all those persons who fell within the definition in s 1(1) TA; the power to detain only applied to 'suspected international terrorists' who were non-British citizens. Under s 21(5) ATCSA a 'suspected international terrorist' was a person who fell within the definition of terrorism in s 1 of the TA 2000 and who had been certified under s 21(1).

It was crucial that the definition of a 'suspected international terrorist' should be precise since such a person could be subjected to lengthy – perhaps indefinite – detention without trial. But, as indicated above, the definition of 'terrorism' under s 1 TA, on which it was centrally based, is itself immensely broad and imprecise. No full definition of an 'international' terrorist was contained in the Act, but s 21(3) provided that an international terrorist group 'is a group subject to the control or influence of persons outside the UK' and 'the Home Secretary suspects' (not qualified by 'reasonably') 'that it is concerned in the commission, preparation and instigation of acts of terrorism'. Further,

---

260 Section 16 HRA.
261 Under Art 4(1) of the Covenant: see *UK Derogation under the ICCPR*, 18 Dec 2001. See further, Michaelsen, C, 'Derogating from International Human Rights Obligations in the "War Against Terrorism"? – A British–Australian Perspective' [2005] 17 (1–2) Terrorism and Political Violence 131–55.
262 [2001] 3 WLR 877.
263 Section 21(5).

a person could be termed a 'suspected international terrorist' on the basis that he or she had 'links' with an international terrorist group.

The power of certification could be exercised in respect of persons who, under s 22, could be subject to various immigration controls,[264] thus excluding British citizens from the scheme, however far they posed a risk to national security. Under s 23(1) persons falling within s 21 could be:

> detained under a provision specified in sub-section (2) despite the fact that his removal or departure from the UK is prevented (whether temporarily or indefinitely) by (a) a point of law which wholly or partly relates to an international agreement or (b) a practical consideration.

Section 23(2) referred to Sched 2, para 16 of the 1971 Act (detention of persons liable to examination or removal) and Sched 3, para 2 of that Act (detention pending deportation). No definition or explanation of the terms used in s 23(1) was offered. Provision under (a) had to be taken to relate to Art 3 and Protocol 6 of the European Convention on Human Rights, while the 'practical consideration' covered, *inter alia*, a failure to identify a country that would take the person.

The Part 4 provisions went beyond answering to the dilemma the government claimed to be addressing.[265] The scheme covered, on its face, a range of persons unconnected with Al-Qaeda – the terrorist group that was almost certainly responsible for the 9/11 attacks. It appeared to cover those who posed a threat only to other countries, such as Tamil Tigers, and also those who merely had 'links' with such groups. In theory, the scheme could have covered a Kurd who supported the PKK and had come to Britain to hand out leaflets about them, or even a non-British citizen fund-raising in support of a non-proscribed activist environmental group advocating direct action abroad. In fact the first of these persons could have been arrested and charged with one of the proscription-linked offences under the TA.[266] The second arguably would not have committed any existing offence. Therefore, disturbingly enough, ss 21 and 23 not only allowed for the detention of those who – apparently – could not be brought to trial due to the sensitivity of the evidence, but also of those who could not have been brought to trial in any event.

Even accepting the necessity of introducing detention without trial, the separate question arose of the proportionality between the emergency situation and the detention scheme in Part 4.[267] Bearing in mind the doubts that have been expressed as to the existence of a public emergency, it is fair to argue that if one existed it appeared to be one that only marginally fell within that term. Therefore, it is suggested, the government

---

264 In terms of: a refusal of leave to enter or remain, or a variation of a limited leave to enter or remain in the UK under ss 3–3B Immigration Act 1971 or to a recommendation to deport under s 3(6) of that Act, or a decision to deport or an order to deport under s 5(1), refusal to revoke a deportation order, a cancellation of leave to remain, a direction of removal under paras 8–10 or 12–14 of that Act or a direction of removal under s 10 of the Immigration and Asylum Act 1999 or the giving of a notice of a decision to deport under the 1999 Act.

265 Fifth Report of the Joint Committee on Human Rights (2001), para 6.

266 Section 12(1) TA would provide the obvious one.

267 The tests of *both* necessity and proportionality must be satisfied: *Lawless v Ireland* A 3 (1961); *De Becker v Belgium* B4 (1962), at para 271.

should have viewed itself as circumscribed in its choice of the measures to be taken. Among the possible measures that could have been adopted the less repressive ones should have been chosen. The choice in fact made failed, it is argued, to satisfy the requirements of proportionality due to the use of extraordinarily broad definitions, of 'terrorism', and of national security, on which the power of certification depended. The scheme was over-inclusive since on its face it covered persons who were suspected of being part of or linked to international terrorist organisations but who had no links with Al-Qaeda. The 'emergency' was apparently imminent due to the 9/11 attacks. Therefore a measure allowing for the detention without trial of those who were unconnected in any way to those involved in the attacks appeared to be disproportionate to the demands of the post-9/11 situation. But it was also under-inclusive: it could not have covered the 7/7 London suicide bombers since they were British citizens.

The role of the Special Immigration Appeals Commission

The Special Immigration Appeals Commission (SIAC), established under s 1 of the Special Immigration Appeals Commission Act 1997 (SIACA), played a crucial role in this scheme since in most instances it represented the only means of challenging the decision to detain. Under s 21(8) ATCSA the Secretary of State's decision in connection with certification could only be questioned under ss 25 or 26, which dealt with challenges to the certificate or reviews of it by SIAC. There were two methods of judicial control enshrined in Part 4. Under s 25 a detainee could appeal to SIAC which had the power to cancel the certificate of the Home Secretary if it found that there were no reasonable grounds for a belief or suspicion of the kind referred to in s 21(1)(a) or (b), or that for 'some other reason' the certificate should not have been issued. The Commission could allow the appeal and cancel the certificate, but the Home Secretary could then issue a further certificate under s 27(9). There was also a distinct power of review of the certificate, which was not instigated by the applicant and which had to occur in SIAC.

The procedure in SIAC is described above.[268] Clearly, the position of the applicant is weak before SIAC. The extent to which the evidence can genuinely be tested is questionable. As White put it in relation to this type of tribunal: it 'attempts to create an adversarial forum where one of the parties is severely hampered in presenting his or her case'.[269] This was of particular concern in relation to Part 4 since it allowed for a power of indefinite detention, demanding greater judicial scrutiny of the basis for the suspicion.

The question of the compliance of such proceedings with Art 6 is considered below in relation to control order proceedings. But control orders obligations do not at present include detention, so the SIAC proceedings in relation to Part 4 raised greater concerns, and at the time even the gist of the case against him could be withheld from the suspect (see further on the current position on 'gisting' below).

---

268 See pp 1031–32, above. See also SI 1998/1881, amended by SI 2000/1849.
269 For discussion, see White, C, 'Security Vetting, Discrimination and the Right to a Fair Trial' [1999] PL 406–18, at p 413. See also Walker, C, *The Prevention of Terrorism* (1986) p 82; he advocated an inquisitorial system for such tribunals.

The challenge to the derogation and the Part 4 scheme in A and Others[270]

The detention powers were used immediately to detain 11 persons in Belmarsh Prison in London. Two of them stated that they were prepared to leave the country and did so.[271] A further five persons were later detained. In the 11 cases determined by SIAC following appeal against certification, the Home Secretary's decision to certify was upheld in all but one of them; the Court of Appeal agreed with SIAC's decision in all instances.[272] The result was therefore that one detainee was released, while the powers were still in force, on the ground that the evidence against him did not satisfy the 'reasonable suspicion' test of s 21 and he was released on bail, on strict conditions, in April 2004. One of the detainees was transferred to Broadmoor Hospital on grounds of mental illness in July 2002. The Home Secretary revoked his certification of another in September 2004, and he was released without conditions.

The decision in *A and Others v Secretary of State for the Home Dept*[273] eventually led to the abandonment of the scheme after it was declared incompatible with Arts 5 and 14 under s 4 HRA by the House of Lords in 2004. The detainees challenged the designated derogation and the detention scheme in relation to the Convention rights scheduled in the HRA. Lord Bingham reviewed the Strasbourg authorities in relation to the question whether an emergency was in being as required by Art 15.[274] He relied in particular on *Lawless v Ireland (No 3)*[275] in which grave loss of life caused by terrorism had not occurred, so the threat to security was implied. He noted that it had never been disavowed and that the House was required by s 2(1) HRA to take it into account. He said that the decision might be explained as showing the breadth of the margin of appreciation accorded by the Court to national authorities. But he found that if it was open to the Irish government in *Lawless* to conclude that there was a public emergency threatening the life of the Irish nation, then the British government could not be faulted for reaching that conclusion in the much more dangerous situation which arose after 9/11. Thirdly, as discussed further in Chapter 4, he accepted that great weight should be given to the judgment of the Home Secretary, his colleagues and Parliament on the question of an emergency, because they were called on to exercise a pre-eminently political judgment.[276]

---

270 For comment on *A and Others*, see: '*A v Secretary of State for the Home Department* Introduction' [2005] 68(4) MLR 654; Hickman, T, 'Between Human Rights and the Rule of Law: Indefinite Detention and the Derogation Model of Constitutionalism' (2005) 68(4) MLR 655–68; Hiebert, J, 'Parliamentary Review of Terrorism Measures' (2005) 68(4) MLR 676–80.

271 See the *Guardian*, 15 April 2002.

272 See *M v Secretary of State for the Home Dept* SIAC – SC/15/2002; CA 2004 EWCA Civ 324.

273 (2004) UKHL 56; [2005] 2 AC 68; [2005] 2 WLR 87; [2005] 3 All ER 169.

274 At para 28. He said: 'The European Court decisions in *Ireland v United Kingdom* (1978) 2 EHRR 25; *Brannigan and McBride v United Kingdom* (1993) 17 EHRR 539; *Aksoy v Turkey* (1996) 23 EHRR 553 and *Marshall v United Kingdom* (10 July 2001, Appl No 41571/98) seem to me to be, with respect, clearly right. In each case the member state had actually experienced widespread loss of life caused by an armed body dedicated to destroying the territorial integrity of the state. To hold that the Art 15 test was not satisfied in such circumstances, if a response beyond that provided by the ordinary course of law was required, would have been perverse.'

275 (1961) 1 EHRR 15.

276 At para 29. For further discussion of *A, see* Chapter 4, pp 244–46.

The majority of the House of Lords agreed (Lord Hoffmann dissenting on this point), and so concluded that it was open to the government to find that there was a state of emergency within the terms of Art 15; that was viewed by the majority as a largely political judgment. Taking into account the breadth of the definition of an emergency under Art 15, and the fact that the domestic courts had to assess, on the basis of very sensitive intelligence, not an overt but a covert, implicit and speculatively imminent state of emergency, it was unsurprising that they concluded that one was in existence in the UK

The second question to be asked under Art 15 is whether the derogation applies 'only to the extent strictly required by the exigencies of the situation'. That was a more problematic issue. The Joint Committee on Human Rights had concluded that even if the requisite state of emergency existed, it doubted whether the measures in the 2001 Bill could be said to be strictly required, bearing in mind the array of measures already available to be used against terrorism, and the fact that no other European country had derogated from Art 5.[277] Other legal opinion on this issue was quite firmly to the effect that the detention scheme was unjustified on the basis that it went further than was required by the exigencies of the situation.[278]

The Lords were prepared to adopt a strict scrutiny of the measures taken and so accepted, as discussed in Chapter 4, that a strict proportionality test should be adopted.[279] Lord Bingham said:

> the appellants are in my opinion entitled to invite the courts to review, on proportionality grounds, the Derogation Order and the compatibility with the Convention of section 23 and the courts are not effectively precluded by any doctrine of deference from scrutinising the issues raised.[280]

On the question of proportionality under Art 15 – that the measures went no further than required by the exigencies of the situation – the Lords made the point that ss 21 and 23 ATCSA did not rationally address the threat to the security of the UK presented by Al-Qaeda terrorists and their supporters because (a) they did not address the threat presented by UK nationals, (b) they permitted foreign nationals suspected of being Al-Qaeda terrorists or their supporters to pursue their activities abroad if there was any country to which they were able to go, and (c) the sections permitted, on their face, the certification and detention of persons who were not suspected of presenting any threat to the security of the UK as Al-Qaeda terrorists or supporters.

Further, they found that if the threat presented to the security of the UK by UK nationals suspected of being Al-Qaeda terrorists, or their supporters, could be addressed without infringing their right to personal liberty, it had not been shown why similar

---

277 Second Report, para 30.
278 David Pannick wrote a legal Opinion for *Liberty*; David Anderson QC and Jemima Stratford wrote one for the group JUSTICE on this issue (Memorandum from Justice). Both came to the conclusion, on different grounds, that the derogation was unjustified. The Opinion for JUSTICE considered that Part 4 went beyond what was strictly required by the exigencies of the situation in covering a wide range of suspected international terrorists.
279 See pp 245–46.
280 At para 42.

measures could not adequately address the threat presented by foreign nationals. So the Part 4 measures allowed both for the detention of those presenting no direct threat to the United Kingdom and for the non-detention or the release of those who – allegedly – did. The House of Lords accepted that such a 'paradoxical conclusion was hard to reconcile with the strict exigencies of the situation'. The key problem, they found, was that the choice of an immigration measure to address a security problem had had the inevitable result of failing adequately to address that problem. The Lords found the conclusion that the derogation order and s 23 were, in Convention terms, disproportionate to the aims pursued, to be irresistible.

The Lords then turned to the question of discrimination under Art 14. The UK had not derogated from Art 14 of the European Convention (or from Art 26 of the ICCPR, which corresponds to it). The Attorney General did not submit in the House of Lords that there had been an implied derogation from Art 14. The appellants argued that in providing for the detention of suspected international terrorists who were not UK nationals, but not for the detention of suspected international terrorists who were UK nationals, s 23 unlawfully discriminated against them as non-UK nationals in breach of Art 14.

Lord Bingham found that the question to be asked under Art 14 was whether persons in an analogous or relevantly similar situation enjoyed preferential treatment, without reasonable or objective justification for the distinction, and whether and to what extent differences in otherwise similar situations would justify a different treatment in law.[281] He relied in particular on *R (S) v Chief Constable of the South Yorkshire Police*[282] from which he considered that the questions to be asked were:

> (1) Do the facts fall within the ambit of one or more of the Convention rights? (2) Was there a difference in treatment in respect of that right between the complainant and others put forward for comparison? (3) If so, was the difference in treatment on one or more of the proscribed grounds under article 14? (4) Were those others in an analogous situation? (5) Was the difference in treatment objectively justifiable in the sense that it had a legitimate aim and bore a reasonable relationship of proportionality to that aim?

The facts were found to fall within Art 5; difference of treatment had been accorded to the applicants and their comparators since the applicants had been detained; the treatment related to an impliedly proscribed ground – that of nationality. The appellants' chosen comparators were suspected international terrorists who were UK nationals. The appellants pointed out that they shared with this group the important characteristics (a) of being suspected international terrorists and (b) of being irremovable from the UK (due to

---

281   At para 50. Lord Bingham relied on: *Stubbings v United Kingdom* (1996) 23 EHRR 213, para 70. He said that the parties were agreed that in domestic law, seeking to give effect to the Convention, the correct approach was to pose the questions formulated by Grosz, Beatson and Duffy, *Human Rights: The 1998 Act and the European Convention* (2000), para C14–08, substantially adopted by Brooke LJ in *Wandsworth London Borough Council v Michalak* [2002] EWCA Civ 271, [2003] 1 WLR 617, para 20, and refined in the later cases of *R (Carson) v Secretary of State for Work and Pensions* [2002] EWHC 978 (Admin), [2002] 3 All ER 994, para 52, [2003] EWCA Civ 797, [2003] 3 All ER 577, paras 56–61, *Ghaidan v Godin-Mendoza* [2004] UKHL 30, [2004] 3 WLR 113, paras 133–34.

282   [2004] UKHL 39, [2004] 1 WLR 2196 para 42.

the effect of *Chahal*). The Lords accepted this. Suspected international terrorists who are UK nationals were, it was found, in a situation analogous with the appellants because, in the present context, they shared the most relevant characteristics of the appellants.

The measure taken might have been viewed as reasonable and justified in an immigration context, but not in a security one since the threat came from both nationals and non-nationals. Lord Bingham found on this point:

> Article 15 requires any derogating measures to go no further than is strictly required by the exigencies of the situation and the prohibition of discrimination on grounds of nationality or immigration status has not been the subject of derogation. Art 14 remains in full force. Any discriminatory measure inevitably affects a smaller rather than a larger group, but cannot be justified on the ground that more people would be adversely affected if the measure were applied generally. What has to be justified is not the measure in issue but the difference in treatment between one person or group and another. What cannot be justified here is the decision to detain one group of suspected international terrorists, defined by nationality or immigration status, and not another. To do so was a violation of article 14. It was also a violation of article 26 of the ICCPR and so inconsistent with the United Kingdom's other obligations under international law within the meaning of article 15 of the European Convention.[283]

So since the different treatment could not be justified, the scheme was found to violate Arts 14 and 5 read together on the basis of differentiating between groups of suspected international terrorists on the basis of nationality – that was found to be the key weakness of the scheme. The derogation order was quashed and a declaration of incompatibility between Arts 14 and 5 and s 23 was made. Since, in contrast with the position in Canada,[284] under the HRA judges cannot strike down provisions that conflict with fundamental rights, the detainees remained in Belmarsh while the government decided how to respond to the decision, and the new legislation was prepared. But as discussed in Chapter 4, declarations of incompatibility place a lot of pressure on the government to respond, under s 10 HRA.[285] That is especially the case when, as in this instance, a declaration is made by a unanimous nine-member House of Lords. The government accepted that it could no longer sustain the scheme. It could theoretically have continued it, as the HRA allows, in the face of an admitted violation of Art 5 (since the derogation order had been quashed) and of Arts 5 and 14 read together – but it bowed to the pressure and accepted that Part 4 must be repealed. It was replaced by the control orders scheme, discussed below.

---

283 At para 68.
284 In a similar decision, *Charkaouri v Canada*, 24 February 2007, [2007] 1 S.C.R. 350, Canada's Supreme Court unanimously struck down the use of secret testimony to imprison and deport foreigners as possible terrorist suspects, ruling that the procedures violated Canada's Charter of Rights and Freedoms. The six men were detained without trial under a 'security certificate'. The ruling was hailed as a victory for civil rights as an aspect of dismantling what has been termed 'Canada's Guantanamo North'. However, although the Canadian Supreme Court can strike down statutory provisions, unlike the House of Lords, the detainees in the UK reached a position of legal certainty earlier.
285 See pp 178–79.

From control orders to TPIMs

The second and third phases in the preventive non-trial-based strategy were represented by control orders which then gave way to TPIMs. Once the Part 4 ACTSA scheme was abandoned the preventive strategy re-emerged in the form of control orders under the Prevention of Terrorism Act 2005 (PTA).[286] But their repressive nature indicated implicit reliance on a down-graded, attenuated version of Art 5, able to accommodate to the needs of the crisis.[287] Although the courts' response meant that the control orders' scheme had to be modified to achieve greater ECHR-compatibility, albeit this time without rejecting it wholesale,[288] the courts partially acquiesced, it will be argued, in the notion of such accommodation.

The control orders scheme

Control orders were introduced under the Prevention of Terrorism Act 2005 (PTA) as a replacement for the abandoned and repealed Part 4 ATCSA scheme. The scheme drew a fundamental distinction between derogating and non-derogating orders. Non-derogating orders, imposing obligations short of detention, such as curfews, semi-house arrest and tagging, were considered not to breach Art 5, and therefore no derogation order was thought to be needed. The non-derogating control orders scheme thus appeared to be less invasive of human rights than Part 4. At their most stringent, however, control orders were able to allow for detention without trial (either full house arrest or in prison) and would have required a derogation; they were termed derogating control orders. However, the derogating orders were never introduced. Nevertheless, control orders were controversial in human rights terms, since, like Part 4 ATCSA, they relied on interfering proactively with the liberty of suspects before any offences had been committed, or where it appeared difficult to prove that they have been committed.

Section 1(1) PTA defined a 'control order': 'In this Act "control order" means an order against an individual that imposes obligations on him for purposes connected with protecting members of the public from a risk of terrorism.' The orders could be applied to British and non-British suspects alike. Under s 1(3) a control order made against an individual could impose *any* obligations that the Secretary of State or the court considered necessary for purposes connected with preventing or restricting involvement by that individual in terrorism-related activity.

Control orders were preventative. They placed one or more obligations upon an individual in order to prevent, restrict or disrupt involvement in terrorism-related activity. A range of obligations could be imposed to address the risk viewed as posed by the individual concerned, including an 18-hour curfew, restrictions on the use of communication equipment; restrictions on the people that the individual can associate with; travel restrictions; electronic tagging; the suspect's house could be subject to a search at any

---

286 For a detailed account of the control orders regime see generally: Walker, C, 'Keeping Control of Terrorists Without Losing Control of Constitutionalism' (2007) 59 Stanford Law Review 1395.

287 See the discussion of early 'heavy touch' control orders below. See also Fenwick, H, 'Recalibrating ECHR Rights, and The Role of The Human Rights Act Post 9/11: Reasserting International Human Rights Norms in the "War On Terror"?' (2010) 63 CLP 153.

288 See in particular *Secretary of State for the Home Department v AP* [2010] 3 WLR 51, discussed below.

time; communication with any person could be disallowed unless approved; prohibitions were placed on electronic communication.

Under s 2 PTA the Home Secretary could make a control order that imposed non-derogating obligations (obligations that apparently did not require a derogation from Art 5, guaranteeing the fundamental right to liberty, or from any other Convention guarantee)[289] if he had reasonable grounds for suspecting that an individual was involved in 'terrorist-related activity' (s 1(9)).

Permission was needed by a court to make a non-derogating control order, under s 3(1) PTA, unless the order was urgent or the person was detained under Part 4. If an order was made without the court's permission, the Secretary of State had to (within seven days) apply to the court, and the function of the court on the application was to consider whether the decision of the Secretary of State to make the order that he did was obviously flawed (s 3(3)). Under s 3(2) when the Secretary of State made an application for permission to make a non-derogating control order against an individual, the function of the court was to consider whether the secretary of state's decision that there were grounds to make that order was obviously flawed.

As challenges to the control orders scheme were heard in the courts, modifications occurred to the scheme, which brought it into closer compliance with both Arts 5 and 6, meaning that the scheme itself became in various respects, less repressive. In particular, it was found that 18 hours' house detention a day, combined with other restrictions would breach Art 5, so shorter periods had to be imposed.[290] It was also found that in the judicial review proceedings considering the imposition of the control order, the gist of the case against him had to be disclosed to the controlee, as mentioned above.[291] To an extent, the control orders scheme incrementally accommodated Arts 5 and 6 rather than the other way round.

The control orders saga could therefore be characterised as representing a new phase in the preventive strategy, during which a scheme in 2005 compatible with the ECHR only on the basis of presupposing a narrow interpretation of Art 5,[292] was transmuted into a modified version of itself by 2011 that came closer to achieving such compatibility. However since significant interferences with liberty[293] without trial – although not as significant as originally imposed – had been accepted by the courts as compatible with Art 5, such interferences could then be viewed as having received judicial imprimatur.

Introduction of TPIMs

The process of an apparent return to 'business as usual' in human rights' terms in which control orders and their review were modified in the courts by reference to the ECHR,

---

289 See discussion of Art 5 in Chapter 2, pp 51–57.
290 See in particular the decisions in *Secretary of State for the Home Department v JJ* [2007] 3 WLR 642. See e.g., *Secretary of State for the Home Department v B and C* [2010] 1 WLR 1542.
291 See p 1032. This was determined in *A v United Kingdom* (2009) 49 EHRR 29 (Grand Chamber) and *Secretary of State for the Home Department v AF (No 3)* [2007] 3 WLR 681.
292 This was apparent in relation to the early control orders which were then found to create a deprivation of liberty under Art 5: *Secretary of State for the Home Department v JJ* [2007] 3 WLR 642.
293 They included some acceptance of up to 16 hours a day house detention: *Secretary of State for the Home Department v JJ* [2007] 3 WLR 642 [105]. That could be combined with forced relocation where no special features particularly 'destructive of family life' arose: *Secretary of State for the Home Department v AP* [2011] 3 WLR 53 [19]–[24].

might be said to have led to the third, current phase in which non-trial-based preventive measures appear to have become 'normalised'. The modifications of control orders, directed towards compliance with Art 5, meant that their abandonment,[294] and the transition in 2012 to still more Art 5-compliant TPIMs under the Terrorism Prevention and Investigation Measures Act 2011, was of a less dramatic nature than the then Coalition government claimed. The introduction of TPIMs as 'lighter touch' control orders apparently formed part of a process of reaffirming a commitment to liberty under the government post-2010.[295] That might also be said of the abandonment of the very broad power of suspicion-less stop and search under s 44 Terrorism Act 2000 (TA),[296] which was replaced by ss 60–63 of the Protection of Freedoms Act 2012.[297] Under the Conservative government from 2015 onwards control orders have not been reintroduced; reliance is still being placed on TPIMs. However, they have been somewhat strengthened under the Counter-terrorism and Security Act 2015 (CTSA), as discussed below.

Purpose of the TPIMs scheme

Post 9/11 the rise of 'neighbour' or 'home grown' terrorism in the UK became more apparent.[298] Thus measures suitable for use against nationals deemed a security risk where prosecution is viewed as problematic,[299] or – more rarely – against non-nationals,[300] continue to be perceived as necessary. Since the model used for control

294 Both Houses of Parliament voted to renew Control Orders for another year in 2010 despite a highly critical report on renewal from the JCHR ('Counter-Terrorism Policy and Human Rights' HL 64, HC 395 (2010)) pointing to the grave incursions into human rights norms they represented. See also HC Deb vol 717 col 506 1 March 2010, and HL Deb vol 717 col 1545 3 March 2010. In March 2011 Parliament voted to renew the PTA until December 2011. TPIMA, s 1 also provided for repeal of the PTA.

295 See HC Deb vol 524 col 205, 1 March 2011. See further e.g., McVeigh, K, 'Nick Clegg Scraps Control Orders' *The Guardian*, 2 January 2011, at http://www.guardian.co.uk/politics/2011/jan/02/nick-clegg-scrap-control-orders.

296 Repealed under Protection of Freedoms Act 2012, s 59.

297 Section 61 inserted s 47A into the TA, creating a more tightly worded power. It might also be noted that a consultation on Sched 7 TA has occurred which might lead to reform of that heavily executive-dominated process to create clearer human rights compliance, although no commitment to such reform is as yet evident. See: 'Review of the Operation of Schedule 7 Terrorism Act 2000 A public consultation' Home Office, September 2012, at https://www.gov.uk/government/uploads/system/uploads/attachment_data/file/157896/consultation-document.pdf.

298 For example, British nationals perpetrated the 7/7 bombing. See Beutel, AJ, 'Radicalization and Home-grown Terrorism in Western Muslim Communities' Minaret of Freedom Institute, 30 August 2007, 'Home-grown' terrorism may currently be linked to a change in strategy by Al Qaeda and linked groups, whereby more spectacular, complex operations that can be fairly readily detected by Western intelligence agencies are to be abandoned in favour of more minor strikes by small groups against soft targets such as high profile sporting events or shopping centres, where security is weak, as occurred in Paris in November 2015.

299 Prosecutions are viewed as problematic partly because security material would have to be presented in a criminal trial, which might jeopardise operations, put informers at risk or breach agreements with other Security Services.

300 Detention/imposition of strict bail conditions followed by deportation and attempts at deportation, with assurances where necessary, provides an alternative non-trial-based process in relation to suspect non-nationals. Detention or stringent bail conditions can be imposed if deportation can be seen as imminent, while assurances are negotiated, since the exception under Art 5(1)(f) ECHR is viewed as applicable: *R (on the application of Hardial Singh) v Governor of Durham Prison* [1984] WLR 704. See in relation

orders had not been found in itself to breach Art 5, as it apparently had the ability to impose restrictions falling just outside Art 5(1), which were credited with success in security terms,[301] it was continued under the Coalition government and Conservative government with modifications, in the form of TPIMs. Continued use of preventive non-trial-based measures had received the support of the Counter-terror Review 2011.[302]

This model may be termed preventive as opposed to punitive, in the sense that it relies on targeting terrorist suspects to curtail their liberty without the need for a trial, by imposing specific restrictions on them, related to the particular types of activity it is thought that they might engage in, with the aim of preventing future terrorist activity before it occurs. Since reliance on TPIMs has essentially the same purpose as control orders had, TPIMA relies heavily on the control orders model.

Imposition of TPIMs

TPIMs can be imposed by the Home Secretary[303] on an individual if certain conditions are met, and then subjected to review by a court.[304] Those conditions (A to E) are set out at s 3(1)-(6) TPIMA. Under s 3(1) TPIMA the standard of proof required under Condition A is low: it relies on asking only whether 'the Secretary of State reasonably believes that the individual is, or has been, involved in terrorism-related activity' (TRA).[305] That was a slightly higher standard than that which was required for control orders under the PTA, which relied only on the 'reasonable grounds for suspicion' standard. (The

---

to deportation with executive assurances where a breach of Art 3 might occur in the receiving country *RB (Algeria) v Secretary of State for the Home Department* [2009] 2 WLR 512; also *Othman v UK* (2012) 55 EHRR 1. See further Walker, C, 'The Treatment of Foreign Terrorist Suspects' (2007) 70 MLR 427.

301 See Anderson, D, 'Control Orders in 2011,' Final Report, March 2012, paras 6.7–6.8; at http://www. official-documents.gov.uk/document/other/9780108511417/9780108511417.pdf; see also as regard TPIMs, 'TPIMS in 2012', n 34 above, para 11.7. See also Lord Carlile of Berriew QC 'Sixth Report of the Independent Reviewer Pursuant to s 14(3) of the Prevention of Terrorism Act 2006', 6 February 2011, para 13.

302 See the government review of counter-terrorism powers: Review of Counter-Terrorism and Security Powers Home Office, Report Cm 8004 (2011) which concluded that control orders should be abandoned but such measures should be maintained.

303 Under TPIMA, s 2(1) : 'The Secretary of State may by notice (a "TPIM notice") impose specified terrorism prevention and investigation measures on an individual if conditions A to E are met'.

304 Under TPIMA, s 9(2) (discussed below) the court, on the full hearing on the order, has to decide whether the Secretary of State's decision is 'flawed', applying judicial review principles, which include compliance with Convention rights. This echoes the position regarding control orders.

305 Terrorism-related activity is defined in TPIMA, s 4(1); the definition is very broad, as it was under the PTA. It covers inter alia encouragement of the preparation of such acts: 'involvement in terrorism related activity is any one or more of the following (a) the commission, preparation or instigation of acts of terrorism; (b) conduct which facilitates the commission, preparation or instigation of such acts, or which is intended to do so; (c) conduct which gives encouragement to the commission, preparation or instigation of such acts, or which is intended to do so; (d) conduct which gives support or assistance to individuals who are known or believed by the individual concerned to be involved in conduct falling within (a)-(c) and for the purposes of this subsection it is immaterial whether the acts of terrorism in question are specific acts of terrorism or acts of terrorism generally.' Under s 4(2) it is immaterial whether the involvement in the activity took place before or after the passing of TPIMA. Under both PTA, s 15(1) and TPIMA, s 30(1) 'terrorism' has the same meaning as in the Terrorism Act 2000 s 1(1).

standard was raised to the civil standard in 2015, as indicated below.) However, in practice it appeared that the higher level of suspicion was not likely to make a significant difference to the ability of the Home Secretary to impose TPIM notices.[306] Condition B, discussed below, concerns the (misleading) requirement that the terrorist activity in question must be 'new' to impose the measure. Condition E requires imposition of a TPIM (or ETPIM) by a court *unless* the case is deemed urgent[307] – as will normally be the case. Under s 3(3) TPIMA. Condition C is that the Secretary of State reasonably considers that it is necessary for a TPIM to be imposed 'for purposes connected with protecting members of the public from a risk of terrorism'. Condition D (s 3(4)) provides that the Secretary of State must reasonably consider that it is necessary for the specified terrorism prevention and investigation measures to be imposed on the individual 'for purposes connected with preventing or restricting the individual's involvement in terrorism-related activity'.

In *Secretary of State for the Home Department v CC, CF*[308] it was confirmed that the requirement in TPIMA of showing reasonable belief imposes a higher threshold than that which previously applied under the PTA. Reliance was placed on *A and Others v Secretary of State for the Home Department*[309] in which Laws LJ said: 'Belief is a state of mind by which the person in question thinks that X is the case. Suspicion is a state of mind by which the person in question thinks that X may be the case'.[310] In *Secretary of State for Home Department v BM*,[311] and in *CC, CF*, the argument was rejected that under TPIMA the standard of proof is *higher* than 'the reasonable belief' standard in that the foundation of past facts upon which the belief is predicated must be proved on the balance of probabilities.[312]

Time periods under TPIMs

A TPIM notice can only be imposed for a two-year maximum period,[313] although a fresh TPIM can then be imposed if a reasonable belief can be shown that 'new'

---

306 All the suspects at that time on control orders were transferred to TPIMs, so the material supporting the level of suspicion previously applicable was also deemed to be sufficient under the slightly higher standard.

307 Condition E is that the court must give permission for the imposition of the TPIM, but under s 3(5)(b) permission is not needed if the Secretary of State 'reasonably considers' that the case is urgent.

308 [2012] EWHC 2837.

309 [2005] 1 WLR 414.

310 *Ibid*, [229]; *R v Saik* [2006] 2 WLR 993 was also referred to, in which Lord Brown observed that 'to suspect something to be so is by no means to believe it to be so: it is to believe only that it may be so' [120].

311 [2012] 1 WLR 2734.

312 *Ibid*, at [25]. It was found in BM, which was relied on in CC,*CF*, that 'to found a reasonable belief that a subject is or has been involved in TRA and that a TPIM is necessary does not involve the requirement to establish involvement in specific TRA to any higher standard than that which can properly give rise to such a belief. No doubt some facts which go to forming the belief will be clearly established, others may be based on an assessment of the various pieces of evidence available' [34].

313 It can be imposed for one year initially; it may only be imposed for a further year if Conditions A,C,D are met: so it is not necessary for suspicion of new TRA to be present – s 5(1),(2),(3). Where a TPIM has expired it can be 'revived' (s 13(6)) without an application to a Court if it has not been revoked, or extended under s 5 (s 13(6)), and can be revived regardless of revocation or extension if an application

terrorism-related activity has occurred after the imposition of the first notice,[314] or, if two or more TPIM notices have been in force, the 'new' TRA must have occurred after the coming into force of the most recent notice.[315] These time periods under TPIMA differentiate the scheme significantly from the control orders one in which the orders could be renewed indefinitely. However, the term 'new' (in Condition B) is otiose under TPIMA if no TPIM notice has ever been in force against the individual since the TRA can have occurred 'at any time' before or after the coming into force of TPIMA,[316] and it is *not* a requirement that if a person has been subjected to a control order previously, the new TRA should have occurred since the order was imposed.[317] That position obviously made it easy to transfer all the controlees to TPIMs in January 2012. As Collins J observed in *Secretary of State for the Home Department v BM*,[318] 'new' is therefore a somewhat 'odd adjective' to use.[319] However, he pointed out that the *age* of the terrorism-related activity is relevant in considering whether Condition *C* is satisfied since an order will not be necessary unless there is a need to protect the public from a risk of terrorism.[320] In other words, if there has been a very significant time lapse between the point at which the TPIM is being considered and the suspected TRA, Condition C might not be satisfied since the *current* need to protect the public might not appear to be established.

David Anderson QC, the current government appointed Independent Reviewer of Terrorism Legislation, has found that the two-year limit for TPIMs could have positive results, 'in terms of concentrating minds on the need for serious efforts to prosecute, deport or de-radicalise controlled persons'.[321] That is a clear improvement on the position under control orders.

TPIM restrictions affecting association, communication, movement, property

The obligations that can be imposed under TPIMs are less onerous than those that could be imposed under control orders, in a range of respects, but they were recently strengthened under the CTSA 2015, minimising a number of the differences between control orders and TPIMs. Greater access to electronic communications is allowed since a

---

to court has been made (s 13(7)); it can be revived regardless of it being extended under s 5: s 13(7), s 6(1)(b). Also a TPIM notice may be revoked (s 13(2)) and later renewed when a TPIM subject is taken into custody when he/she has been charged with a criminal offence, meaning that the clock can be stopped: the two-year period could thus be somewhat lengthened, even if the charge is then dropped.

314   TPIMA, ss 3(2), (6)(b).
315   TIPMA, ss 3(2), (6)(c).
316   TPIMA, s 3(6)(a).
317   This follows from s 3(6)(a) and para 4 of Sched 8 which provides that the Secretary of State's powers under the 2011 Act 'are not affected by a control order having been made in relation to that individual'; provided the conditions set out in s 3 are satisfied, the Secretary of State is entitled to impose measures by a TPIM notice on an individual in respect of activities which wholly or in part founded the making of the control order. See *Secretary of State for the Home Department v AM* [2012] EWHC 1854 (Admin) per Mitting J. [13]; *Secretary of State for the Home Department v CC and CF* [2012] WLR(D) 283, [21].
318   [2012] 1 WLR 2734.
319   *Ibid*, at [16].
320   *Ibid*, at [15].
321   In his Report 'Control Orders in 2011', para 6.34.

minimum level of access is specified.[322] The option to prevent travel abroad is retained under TPIMA,[323] as is the option to require daily reporting to the police.[324] The option to prevent transfer of funds abroad under the PTA is replaced by an option under TPIMA to place restrictions on transfers of property and requirements to disclose details of property.[325] TPIMA includes requirements to cooperate with measures allowing communications, movement (via electronic tagging) or other activities to be monitored.[326] The TPIM subject can also be required to seek prior permission from the secretary of state before meeting or communicating with 'specified persons or specified descriptions of persons'[327] and can be subjected to a requirement not to carry out specified work or studies.[328]

A suspect under a standard TPIM notice can be required to seek prior permission from the Secretary of State before meeting or communicating with 'specified persons or specified descriptions of persons'.[329] Thus, under a TPIM notice a suspect can be barred from any communication or association with specific people. The secretary of state can also impose a requirement not to carry out specified work or studies,[330] and the individual can be required to cooperate with measures allowing communications, movement (via electronic tagging) or other activities to be monitored.[331] These restrictions, including limitations on electronic means of communication, affect the qualified ECHR rights in Arts 8–11, but they have tended to be upheld by the courts as necessary and proportionate interferences with those rights.[332] However, some of them could also be taken into account under a holistic evaluation of the deprivation of liberty concept under Art 5(1).[333]

The 'deprivation of liberty' jurisprudence underlying the design of obligations imposed under control orders and TPIMs

Under the PTA *any* obligations that the secretary of state considered necessary for the purpose of preventing or restricting involvement in terrorism-related activity could

---

322 The 2011 Act provides in Sched 1 para 7(1): 'The Secretary of State must allow the individual to possess and use (at least) one of each of the following descriptions of device (subject to any conditions on such use as may be specified under sub-para (2)(b)) – 3(a) a telephone operated by connection to a fixed line; 3(b) a computer that provides access to the internet by connection to a fixed line (including any apparatus necessary for that purpose); 3(c) a mobile telephone that does not provide access to the internet'.
323 Without permission of the Secretary of State (TPIMA, Sched 1 para 2). CTSA increased the sentence for breaching the restriction from 5 to 10 years.
324 TPIMA, Sched 1 para 10.
325 TPIMA, Sched 1 para 6.
326 TPIMA, Sched 1 para 12.
327 TPIMA, Sched 1 para 8(2)(a).
328 TPIMA, Sched 1 para 9.
329 TPIMA, Sched 1 para 8(2)(a).
330 TPIMA, Sched 1 para 9.
331 TPIMA, Sched 1 para 12.
332 For example in *AM v Secretary of State for the Home Department* [2011] EWHC 2486 (Admin) the High Court upheld control order conditions that included bans on any internet access at the individual's home and on the use of USB memory sticks to transfer any data from his home to his university, restrictions on his access to the internet at university and when visiting his parents.
333 See *Secretary of State for the Home Department v AP* [2011] 3 WLR 51; the Supreme Court found that the fact that a restriction affects a qualified right, in that case Art 8, does not preclude it from being viewed as also relevant to analysis under Art 5(1). In *Guzzardi* [1980] 3 EHRR 333, relied on in *AP*, lack of social contacts was taken into account in finding a deprivation of liberty ([50]). This could now include e.g., limitations on use of the internet, preventing access to social media.

be imposed,[334] with the implied requirement that they did not breach Art 5 ECHR.[335] Under TPIMA, however, the obligations are specified in Sched 1. Under TPIMA the obligations are also more limited; they are clearly designed to ensure that Art 5 is very unlikely to be breached, taking account of the control orders case law.

The autonomous Strasbourg concept of deprivation of liberty under Art 5(1)[336] creates a deliberate disconnect between the commonly understood idea of taking liberty away, and the idea of an intensified 'deprivation' of it which requires justification within the specified and narrow exceptions under Art 5. That disconnect opens up an imprecise area for state action interfering with liberty which measures of the type of control orders or TPIMs can inhabit, although Art 5 itself contains no exception allowing for forms of executive detention to protect national security. Article 5 was designed at a time when only *paradigmatic* (obvious) deprivations of liberty – arrest, detention – were in contemplation by the drafters of the ECHR.[337] Since then a range of non-paradigm interventions have arisen, based on the control order model. Such measures may fall just short of the point at which the concept of such deprivation converges with that of an interference with movement under Protocol 4 Art 2,[338] which the UK has not ratified. No control order case has yet been decided at Strasbourg, but the leading Strasbourg decision in *Guzzardi v Italy*[339] potentially enables Art 5 to encompass such measures since it focuses on the impact of restrictions on the life the person subject to them would otherwise have been living.[340] In *Guzzardi* it was found in relation to non-paradigmatic interferences with liberty that the difference between a deprivation of and a restriction on liberty was one of degree, not of substance, and that it was for the court to assess into which category a particular case fell, taking account of a range of criteria, including the 'type, duration, effects and manner of implementation of the measure in question'.[341] The curfew of nine hours daily that had been imposed was *not* the core issue in the

---

334 The obligations listed in the PTA were, formally speaking, only illustrative, although in practice they were relied on.

335 The PTA operated subject to an implied – but unclear – restriction to the effect that the obligations imposed must not breach Art 5 ECHR. That was the apparent position, since otherwise, obviously, the orders could not be viewed as ones that did not require a derogation from that article. Certain orders were quashed on the basis that they were in fact derogating orders which the Home Secretary had had no power to make – see e.g., *Secretary of State for the Home Dept v JJ* [2007] 3 WLR 642.

336 Art 5(1) provides: 'Everyone has the right to liberty and security of person. No one shall be deprived of his liberty save in the following cases and in accordance with a procedure prescribed by law.' See Chapter 2, p 51.

337 See: van Dijk, P and van Hoof, G, *Theory and Practice of the European Court of Human Rights*, 2nd ed, 1990, Kluwer Law International, 255; Murdoch, J, 'Safeguarding the Liberty of the Person: Recent Strasbourg Jurisprudence' (1993) 42 ICLQ 494, 497–99.

338 See Bates, E, 'Anti-terrorism Control Orders: Liberty and Security Still in the Balance' (2009) 29 LS 99.

339 [1980] 3 EHRR 333.

340 *Ibid*, at [95].

341 *Ibid*, at [92]. Guzzardi was confined on a small island for 16 months within a confined area and subject to house detention for nine hours overnight daily. That meant that he had to remain in his home (where his family was allowed to reside but which was dilapidated) between 10 pm–7 am; he also had to seek permission to make phone calls or have visitors. He was ordered (although there was no physical restraint such as a fence) to remain in an area of 2.5 square kilometres. The Court noted that there were few opportunities for social contacts.

finding that the restrictions amounted to a deprivation of liberty.[342] *Ashingdane v UK*[343] re-emphasised the point made in *Guzzardi* that the core obligation of confinement should *not* be given overwhelming weight,[344] as did *Storck v Germany*.[345] Strasbourg has also found in a number of cases on supervisory house arrest that daily periods of about 12 hours curfew or house detention may fall outside the deprivation of liberty concept (*Trijonis*,[346] *Ciancimo*,[347] *Raimondo*).[348] Below, the Strasbourg understanding of that concept, especially as stated in *Guzzardi*, is contrasted with that adopted in the control orders jurisprudence.

Domestic Art 5 jurisprudence on non-derogating control orders

When non-derogating control orders were introduced they included (initially) 18 hours daily house detention/arrest (curfew) and forced relocation.[349] As the decisions briefly discussed below indicate, their use therefore could be said to have relied in effect on an implicit executive presupposition as to the need for acceptance of an attenuated or recalibrated version of Art 5. The precise limits imposed by Art 5(1) at Strasbourg, as discussed above, undeniably left some leeway, not only to put forward the scheme as a whole as compatible with the article, but also to allow for argument that the obligations imposed under individual early control orders did not overall fall within Art 5(1). But a deprivation of liberty was found by the House of Lords in *JJ*[350] due *inter alia* to the imposition of house detention for 18 hours daily and restriction of movement to specified areas.[351] The majority accepted that the difference between deprivation of and restriction on liberty was one of degree, not of substance. The court's task was to take account of a range of criteria from *Guzzardi v Italy*[352] to assess the impact of the restrictions

---

342 The Court found: 'the treatment complained of resembles detention in an open prison . . . or committal to a disciplinary unit': *Ibid* [95].

343 (1985) 7 EHRR 528.

344 *Ibid*, [41]–[42]; here confinements (a) in a closed psychiatric hospital with high security (which included barred windows, a high perimeter fence; visits to family twice in 7 years) and (b) in an open hospital with only an overnight residence requirement on three days a week were both found to create a deprivation of liberty.

345 (2006) 43 EHRR 96 at [74]; the Court found: 'the notion of deprivation of liberty within the meaning of Art 5(1) does not only comprise the objective element of a person's confinement in a particular restricted space for a not negligible length of time'. The Court went on: '..the starting-point must be the specific situation of the individual concerned and account must be taken of a whole range of factors arising in a particular case, such as the type, duration, effects and manner of implementation of the measure in question' (2006) 43 EHRR 96 at [71], [74]. See also *Nielsen v Denmark* (1989) 11 EHRR 175 at [67]; *HM v Switzerland* (2002) 38 EHRR 314 at [42], [46].

346 *Trijonis v Lithuania* (App No 2333/02) decision on admissibility 17 March 2005.

347 *Ciancimino v Italy* (1991) 70 DR 103.

348 *Raimondo v Italy* (1994) 18 EHRR 237 [39].

349 They also included random house searches, geographical restrictions, electronic tagging, bans on visits by non-approved persons, and prohibitions on electronic communication. Under s 1(3) of the 2005 Act there was no limitation on the measures that could be imposed under non-derogating control orders, except that the Home Secretary could only impose those deemed necessary to prevent TRA. See further Walker, C, 'Keeping control of terrorists without losing control of Constitutionalism' (2007) 59 Stanford LR 1395.

350 *Secretary of State for the Home Department v JJ* [2007] 3 WLR 642.

351 Restrictions also included spot searches of residences and electronic tagging.

352 [1980] 3 EHRR 333.

on the controlees in the context of the life they might otherwise have been living. *Secretary of State for the Home Department v E*[353] followed *JJ*, but Lord Bingham focused more strongly on the issue of restraint on *physical* liberty, finding that the restrictions cumulatively could not 'effect a deprivation of liberty if the core element of confinement, to which other restrictions . . . are ancillary, is insufficiently stringent'.[354] *Secretary of State for the Home Department v MB and AF*[355] gave some support to the finding of Lord Brown in *JJ* that 16 hours daily house detention appeared to be the upper limit.[356] These three decisions were interpreted by the then Labour government in various public statements to mean that the Lords had given support to the control orders scheme,[357] due to the apparent acceptability of 16 hours' house detention, combined with other restrictions, within Art 5.

However, *AP v Secretary of State for the Home Department*[358] relied on *Guzzardi* in finding that the imposition of 14 hours' daily house detention combined with forced relocation had created a deprivation of liberty since, due to the suspect's particular family circumstances, he had suffered an unusually high degree of social isolation.[359] Although this decision took a more holistic view of the deprivation of liberty concept, the Supreme Court may be said to have given its imprimatur to the use of executive measures of this type since the decision indicated that 14-hour to 16-hour periods of home detention, repeated over a long period of time, would not create a deprivation of liberty, even combined with forced relocation, *unless* the particular circumstances of the suspect relocation or other conditions satisfied the 'unusually destructive of normal life' test. When the findings in *AP* on forced relocation were applied in subsequent cases, it was found that specific relocations would not infringe Art 5, barring special circumstances,[360] and that under Art 8 the relocation obligation would usually be found to be a necessary and proportionate measure to protect the public.[361] Where particular social isolation might arise, it has been found that it could be alleviated by requiring the

---

353 [2007] 3 WLR 720.

354 *Ibid*, at [11].

355 [2007] 3 WLR 681: the Lords unanimously found that there was no deprivation of liberty in respect of 14 hours' detention, combined with a geographical restriction and a range of other restrictions. That finding should be taken in conjunction with the rejection of 18 hours' daily house detention in JJ.

356 In *JJ* at [105] Lord Brown considered that a 16 hour curfew would be acceptable. He considered that 12- or 14-hour curfews were consistent with physical liberty. But see also Lord Brown in *Secretary of State for the Home Department v AP* [2011] 53 WLR 53 at [3] in which he emphasised that this was not the majority view in *JJ*, and that curfew length was only one factor among many.

357 See: Counter Terrorism Policy and Human Rights (ninth report) Annual Renewal of Control Orders Legislation 2008 Home Office, Report Cm 7368 (2008) 4.

358 [2011] 3 WLR 51.

359 *Ibid*, at [4]. Lord Brown found that a control order with a 16-hour curfew and *a fortiori* one of 14 hours, would not be struck down as involving a deprivation of liberty, unless the other conditions imposed were 'unusually destructive of the life the controlee might otherwise have been living'.

360 In *BM v Secretary of State for the Home Department* [2011] EWHC 1969 (Admin), the High Court upheld the Secretary of State's decision to require BM to live in a city outside London. The Court considered that the relocation did amount to a serious infringement of Art 8 rights, but the Court accepted the reasons for the relocation and found that any such infringement was both necessary and proportionate.

361 E.g., in *CD v Secretary of State for the Home Department* [2011] EWHC 1273 (Admin) at [53], the relocation obligation was found to represent a necessary and proportionate measure to protect the public under Art 8.

Secretary of State to contribute to the travel costs incurred by the controlee's family in visiting him.[362]

Directly liberty-invading restrictions under TPIMA

It is clear that in the decisions discussed the domestic courts brought the application of the control orders scheme into somewhat closer compliance with Art 5, *without* rejecting the scheme as a whole,[363] thus in effect paving the way for the introduction of TPIMs, and influencing the legal design of the new measures. The obligations available, while designed to interfere with the liberty of suspects in such a way as to prevent them from engaging in forms of terrorism-related activity, nevertheless had to avoid creating, in legal terms, a 'deprivation of liberty' under Art 5(1). But a political decision was taken, *not* fully necessitated by the control orders' jurisprudence, to rely on +a less liberty-invading scheme for TPIMA which did *not* explore the limits of Art 5 tolerance, but fell well within them, as part of a much-trumpeted movement after the general election 2010 towards the restoration of liberties.[364] In pursuit of that determination the lengthier house detention requirements under control orders were relaxed, becoming only an 'overnight residence requirement', and the relocation provisions were dropped.[365] However, the relocation obligation was reinstated in 2015 as mentioned below. Thus TPIMA was at the time the result of a serious engagement with human rights arguments by the executive and Parliament that transcended the judicial engagement with them under the Human Rights Act (HRA).

The 'overnight' requirement under TPIMA is 'a requirement, applicable overnight between such hours as are specified, to remain at, or within, the specified residence'.[366] Clearly, the requirement leaves open room for interpretation of the term 'overnight'. It has been viewed by the secretary of state in imposing the early TPIM notices as a requirement for the controlled person to remain at his/her residence between the hours of 9.00 pm and 7.00 am daily. In *Secretary of State for the Home Department v BM*[367] Collins J found that 'overnight' in common parlance should be taken to bear some relationship to the hours between which most people would regard it as reasonable to assume that people might be at home, the evening having come to an end. He considered that the hours that could be specified would not extend beyond the period 9.00pm to 7.00am.[368] In *Secretary of State for the Home Department v CC, CF*[369] a challenge to

---

362 *Ibid.* The Court dismissed an appeal brought by CD against the Secretary of State's decision to refuse to remove an obligation that required him to reside away from his previous area of residence. The control order was not found to lead to a breach of Art 5.

363 See generally as regards control orders Ewing, K and Tham, J, 'The Continuing Futility of the Human Rights Act' [2008] PL 668.

364 For example, in July 2010 Theresa May suggested that the counter-terrorism review that led to the Protection of Freedom Bill would '. . . restore the ancient civil liberties that should be synonymous with the name of our country': 'Counter-terrorism powers to face government review' BBC News, 13 July 2013, at http://www.bbc.co.uk/news/10619419.

365 See Sched 1 para 1, TPIMA.

366 Sched 1 para 1(2)(c), TPIMA.

367 [2012] EWHC 714 (Admin).

368 *Ibid*, at [51]–[52].

369 [2012] EWHC 2837 (Admin).

an overnight measure covering those hours as beyond the powers accorded by TPIMA Sched 1 was rejected, applying that test.[370] Thus at present a TPIM notice can specify a ten-hour curfew, between those hours, which is well within the limits placed on house detention in the domestic control order cases and within the time limits accepted at Strasbourg, as discussed. Control orders could impose general geographical boundaries, whereas imposition of such boundaries are not available under TPIMA; instead there is a power to exclude the controlled person from particular specified places, such as streets and specified areas or descriptions of places, such as tube stations or airports.[371]

But TPIMs came to be seen as ineffective: their role in providing security came under question when two suspects absconded in 2012 and 2013 while subject to TPIM orders.[372] That led to proposals in 2013 to amend TPIMA in order to extend (and possibly strengthen) TPIMs.[373] In August 2014 there were also recommendations to reinstate control orders, mainly to combat the problem posed by British jihadis returning to Britain after fighting in Syria or Iraq for Isis.[374] When the terror threat level was raised from substantial to severe in 2014,[375] triggering the announcement of the new package of counter-terror measures, which eventually were captured in the Counter-terrorism and Security Act 2015, one of them included strengthening TPIMs[376] by *inter alia* allowing them to impose relocation, as control orders could do.[377]

370 *Ibid*, at [65].
371 TPIMA, Sched 1 para 3.
372 On 1 November 2013; see Rosa Silverman, 'Terror suspect absconds while being monitored' *Daily Telegraph*, 4 November 2013. When he disappeared, Mr Mohamed was facing charges relating to 20 alleged breaches of his TPIM order. Mohamed was an alleged associate of Ibrahim Magag, another TPIM subject who absconded on 26 December 2012. Yvette Cooper, formerly Shadow Home Secretary has said on this (see 'Cameron and Clegg seek agreement in anti-terror talks' *The Guardian*, 1 September 2014): 'There are currently no Tpims in use because the experts have warned that the police and the security services do not believe they are effective enough to be worth using' (see at http://www.theguardian.com/uk-news/2014/sep/01/cameron-clegg-anti-terror-talks-british-born-jihadis-syria-iraq).
373 The Home Affairs Committee 'Counter-terrorism' Seventeenth Report, HC 231, 30 April 2014 ('Counter-terrorism Seventeenth Report'), para 109 found that TPIMs need to be strengthened to prevent absconding; Yvette Cooper, former Shadow Home Secretary, has observed: 'We warned from the start that weakening these crucial counter-terror powers was a serious error of judgement by the Home Secretary . . . For so many TPIMs to end at once raises serious challenges for the police and security services – especially in London where most of the terror suspects are based' (Press Release, 5 November 2013; http://www.politicshome.com/uk/article/87796/sign_up_pro.html).
374 They were from Lord Carlile, the Government's independent reviewer of terrorism legislation from 2001 to 2011, Sir Bernard Hogan-Howe, Commissioner of Police of the Metropolis (speaking on LBC on 27 August 2014, as reported in the *Telegraph* 'British jihadists should be stripped of citizenship says top police officer' http://www.telegraph.co.uk/news/worldnews/middleeast/syria/11058319/British-jihadists-should-be-stripped-of-citizenship-says-top-police-officer.html.
375 On 29 August 2014 (see MI5 Press Release 'Threat level to the UK from international terrorism raised to severe' https://www.mi5.gov.uk/home/news/news-by-category/threat-level-updates/threat-level-to-the-uk-from-international-terrorism-raised-to-severe.html).
376 HC Deb Vol. 585, cols 24–6, 1 September 2014. The Government had previously stated that it intended to carry out a review of TPIMs as part of a broader review of counter-terrorism powers: JCHR 'Post-legislative scrutiny: Terrorism Prevention and Investigation Act 2011' Tenth Report of Session 2013–2014, HL 113 HC 1014, January 2014 ('TPIMA 2011'), para 82. David Cameron's Task-force for Tackling Violent Extremism had also recommended a range of changes in 2013: 'Tackling Extremism in the UK,' December 2013; https://www.gov.uk/government/uploads/system/uploads/attachment_data/file/263181/ETF_FINAL.pdf.
377 That had also been recommended earlier in 2014 by David Anderson, the current independent reviewer of terrorism legislation in his Report 'TPIMS in 2013', at p 57, recommendation 4. David Anderson

As a result, s 16 of the 2015 Act allows for the imposition of relocation on individuals subject to a TPIMs order by amending the Terrorism Prevention and Investigation Measures Act 2011. But the new relocation measure is not identical to the previous one. Section 16(1) to (5) amend para 1 of Sched 1 to TPIMA to provide that the Secretary of State may either agree a locality with an individual in which that individual must reside or require an individual to live in a residence in a locality that the secretary of state otherwise considers appropriate. If the individual has a residence at the time when the TPIM notice is imposed, the secretary of state may only require the individual to live in a residence that is more than 200 miles from those premises if the individual agrees. But the 2015 Act also increases the safeguards against the wrongful imposition of a TPIM, to an extent, by raising the standard of proof for such imposition to the civil standard (s20(1) of the 2015 Act).

CTSA also amended TPIMA to impose a new travel measure, allowing travel to be restricted outside the area where the TPIM subject lives.[378] New prohibitions relating to access to firearms and explosives were also included in CTSA, amending TPIMA.[379] In furtherance of deradicalisation the returnee could be required to attend appointments with specified persons by amendment to TPIMA under s 19 of the 2015 Act.[380] So use of a TPIM would now allow for more intensive monitoring of the suspect, and for greater disruption of activities, such as conspiracies or the transfer of funds abroad, that might be accessed by Isis-supporters.

The question of the *duration* of the interference with liberty and therefore of the cumulative effect of measures imposed over a long period of time is one of the key indicators of a deprivation of liberty at Strasbourg. This question might arise in relation to TPIM notices, since, as indicated above, those subject to them were previously subject to control orders. However the fact that TPIMs, unlike control orders, do not subsist for an indefinite period, and so an endpoint would be in sight, would obviously be relevant.

Like control orders, the obligations imposed under TPIMs are backed up by criminal sanctions. If a controlled person infringes any of the obligations imposed by, for example, leaving the residence during the controlled hours, he or she is liable to arrest and criminal charges.[381] The matter of coercion was emphasised in *Gillan v UK*[382] in the context of suspicion-less stop and search under s 44 of the Terrorism Act 2000. The Lords had found domestically that those stopped had merely been detained in the

---

also recommended an extra power to compel attendance at meetings to establish communication with subjects, recommendation 6 (p 57).

378 CTSA s 17(3) amends Sched 1 para 2 TPIMA and increases the sentence for breaching the restriction from 5 to 10 years. If the measure is breached by leaving the UK, amendment under s 17 CTSA disallows reliance on a 'reasonable excuse' for doing so.

379 CTSA s 18 amends Sched 1 para 6 TPIMA to this effect.

380 CTSA s 19 TPIMs amends Sched 1 para 10 to insert para 10A(1) 'The Secretary of State may impose a requirement for the individual – (a) to attend appointments with specified persons or persons of specified descriptions, and (b) to comply with any reasonable directions given by the Secretary of State that relate to matters about which the individual is required to attend an appointment. (2) A requirement under sub-paragraph (1)(a) is a requirement to attend appointments – (a) at specified times and places'.

381 Previously imposed under PTA, s 9(1)(4)(a); now contained in TPIMs Act 2011, s 23. The sanctions in relation to breach of conditions under TPIM notices are the same as those that were available in relation to control orders. Breach of any condition imposed under the notices is a criminal offence, punishable by up to five years' imprisonment.

382 (2010) 50 EHRR 45 [57].

sense of being 'kept from proceeding or kept waiting',[383] and so the interference with their liberty fell outside the ambit of Art 5(1). But the Strasbourg Court refused to be seduced, impliedly or expressly, by executive arguments as to the need to maintain a narrow ambit of Art 5(1) in the counter-terrorism context,[384] and contemplated a higher standard as to the liberty of the subject than the House of Lords had done,[385] finding that the use of coercion would be relevant to the question whether a deprivation of liberty had occurred.[386] The element of coercion underpinning the TPIM obligations is therefore one of the strongest indicators that they could cause a deprivation of liberty, following *Gillan*. A number of the persons currently subjected to TPIM notices have already spent periods of time in prison for breach of the obligations imposed under the control orders that they were previously subjected to.[387] It is notable in this context that CTSA also raised the penalty for a number of breaches of TPIMs from five to ten years.

The use of TPIMs appears to fall outside Art 5(1) as far as the *detention* obligation is concerned under current Strasbourg jurisprudence since it appears that up to 12 hours house detention a day does not create a deprivation of liberty.[388] But the impact of a particularly repressive combination of obligations under a specific TPIM notice, including restrictions that could also affect the materially qualified rights, would be more likely to be found to create a deprivation of liberty at Strasbourg than domestically, given that a line of authority at Strasbourg has more clearly recognised a concept of non-paradigm deprivation of liberty, *not* centrally focused on physical confinement, but in terms of coercion, duration and the impact on normal life.[389]

The reinstatement of relocation in the TPIMs scheme re-raises the possibility – already explored in relation to control orders – that particular TPIMs might risk breaching Art 5 ECHR.[390] However, its reinstatement does not necessarily mean that particular TPIMs that include relocation as one restriction placed on a suspect would breach Art 5 ECHR as a matter of domestic law if the relocation does not impose an unusual degree of social isolation on the controlee.[391] *Secretary of State for the Home Department v*

---

383 *R (on the application of Gillan) v Commissioner of Police for the Metropolis* [2006] 2 WLR 537 at [25]. See Chapter 12, pp 846–47.

384 On behalf of the government it was argued in Gillan at [55]: 'the purpose for which the police exercised their powers was not to deprive the applicants of their liberty but to conduct a limited search for specified articles'.

385 Although without finally deciding the case under Art 5, finding a breach instead under Art 8. *Ibid* at [87].

386 '[Those searched] were obliged to remain where they were and submit to the search and if they had refused they would have been liable to arrest, detention at a police station and criminal charges. This element of coercion is indicative of a deprivation of liberty within the meaning of Art 5(1)'. *Gillan v UK* (2010) 50 EHRR 45 at [57]. The Court noted in support the example of *Foka v Turkey* (App No 28940/09), 24 June 2008, at [74]–[79].

387 See JCHR 'Counter-Terrorism Policy and Human Rights' HL 37 HC 282 (2009) 40, Appendix 2 Q6.

388 See in particular *Raimondo v Italy* (1994) 18 EHRR 237; *Ciancimino v Italy* (1991) 70 DR 103.

389 See *Guzzardi v Italy* (A/39) [1981] 3 EHRR 333 Greater emphasis was placed on the cumulative impact of the range of restrictions than on physical restraint; it was made clear that where there is a curfew (which could be overnight) combined with other factors severely affecting the life the applicant otherwise would have been living, a deprivation of liberty can be found. See also *Engel v The Netherlands (No 1)* (1979–1980) 1 EHRR 647.

390 *Secretary of State for the Home Department v AP* [2010] 3 WLR 51.

391 *Secretary of State for the Home Department v AP* [2011] 2 AC 1 [15].

AP[392] found that the imposition of 14 hours' daily house detention combined with forced relocation had created a deprivation of liberty[393] since, as mentioned above, he had suffered an unusually high degree of social isolation.[394] Although this decision took a holistic view of the deprivation of liberty concept under Art 5, the Supreme Court may be said to have given its imprimatur to the use of executive measures of this type since the decision indicated that lengthy periods of home detention, repeated over a long period of time, would not create a deprivation of liberty, even combined with forced relocation, *unless* in the particular circumstances of the suspect relocation combined with other conditions satisfied the 'unusually destructive of normal life' test. Control orders could thus impose 14–16 hours' house detention combined with relocation without *necessarily* leading to a breach of Art 5. Thus, since TPIMs impose much less lengthy periods of detention, the addition of relocation is less likely to lead to such a breach.

The provision in the 2015 amendment to TPIMA specifying 200 miles as the limit on relocating a person compulsorily away from the location of their residence where they may have family or friends appears to be designed to meet the concern as to social isolation. It does leave open the possibility, however, that a suspect who does not have a residence could be relocated more than 200 miles away from family and friends. But if that did occur, but a contribution was made to travel costs of those visiting him, social isolation would be alleviated. In one instance a measure available under a TPIMs order – electronic tagging – was found to breach Article 3. In *DD v Secretary of State for the Home Department* the appellant appealed against the revival of his terrorism prevention and investigation measure and the respondent Secretary of State's decision to extend it. The appellant had psychotic and unusual beliefs that the tag was there to punish him, that it contained a camera and a bomb, and that voices and noises emanated from it. In November 2014, the court found that, although the tag had exacerbated the symptoms of the appellant's mental illness – post-traumatic stress disorder and either paranoid schizophrenia or a schizo-affective disorder, depressive type – Art.3 ECHR had not been breached. But the Administrative Court held that in these unusual circumstances the requirement that the appellant wear an electronic monitoring tag was such that it had eventually led to a breach of Art 3. Further, restrictions on the use of electronic communications had become disproportionate under Article 8 due to the serious effect on the appellant's children. Accordingly, the monitoring measures would be quashed and the electronic communication measures would be varied, but the other measures could remain as they were.

Thus it appears that a breach of Art 5 would be unlikely to arise due to the impact of the new provisions, (or, in general of Article 3) and there does appear to be evidence that the use of relocation tends to enhance security. David Anderson QC, the Independent

392 [2010] 3 WLR 51.
393 The Court relied on *Guzzardi v Italy* (A/39) [1981] 3 EHRR 333 in coming to this conclusion.
394 Lord Brown found that a control order with a 16-hour curfew and *a fortiori* one of 14 hours, would not be struck down as involving a deprivation of liberty, unless the other conditions imposed were 'unusually destructive of the life the controlee might otherwise have been living'. *Ibid* at para 4. On the specific facts the forced relocation of AP was found to satisfy the 'unusually destructive of normal life' test.

Reviewer, conducted a review for the government in 2014 in which he concluded that relocation remains extremely useful and is more effective than the power merely to exclude TPIMs subjects from particular locations.[395] He had therefore recommended that TPIMs would be more effective if relocation were reintroduced. The Joint Committee on Human Rights in its scrutiny of the 2015 Bill found: 'We . . . reluctantly accept his judgment that the changing nature of the threat justifies the reintroduction of relocation.'[396]

In a period of reliance on executive measures interfering with liberty, the question whether a 'deprivation of liberty' refers centrally to restraint on physical liberty as in house detention, to which other interferences are ancillary, or to a much more amorphous, relativistic concept, has resonance within and beyond the terrorism context,[397] but has not yet been fully resolved. The tendency currently evident in the UK to rely on non-paradigmatic interferences with liberty in order to avoid the necessity of seeking a derogation from Art 5 has exposed the imprecise standard it seems to denote.[398] The varied ways of interfering with liberty now available to the state under TPIMs render the traditional idea of focusing mainly on physical restraint outdated. Tying the deprivation of liberty concept most strongly to that one notion marginalises it in relation to measures, such as relocation or bars on entering specific spaces, which may appear less repressive but can have a profound impact on the lives that those subject to them might otherwise have been living.

Article 6 issues

The control orders jurisprudence on Art 6 to an extent mirrors that under Art 5 in terms of the journey that has been undertaken towards a greater acceptance of fair trial standards. But a number of Art 6 issues are not addressed expressly in TPIMA; rather, Art 6 compliance relies on such jurisprudence and s 3 of the HRA. In most TPIM cases the review hearing under s 9 of the TPIMA will represent the point at which court intervention occurs; it will normally arise some months after the TPIM has been imposed by the Home Secretary. At the review hearing the court must apply the judicial review principles applicable in deciding whether the decision is flawed. In using the terminology of the PTA, it is assumed that the provisions will be applied subject to the interpretation imposed on control order proceedings under s 3 HRA and Art 6(1).[399] The courts apply a more exacting standard of review, including 'intense scrutiny' of the necessity for the measures imposed.[400]

395   See his Report 'TPIMS in 2013' p. 57, recommendation 4.
396   Human Rights Joint Committee–Fifth Report Legislative Scrutiny: Counter-Terrorism and Security Bill, HL Paper 86, HC 859, published 12 January 2015, para 4.10.
397   In relation to Anti-Social Behaviour Orders, Serious Crime Prevention Orders (Serious Crime Act 2007, ss 1–41 and Scheds 1 and 2) and powers to interfere with protest: see *Austin v Commissioner of Police for the Metropolis* [2009] 1 AC 564. For comment see Fenwick, H, 'Marginalising Human Rights: Breach of the Peace, "Kettling", the Human Rights Act and Public Protest' [2009] PL 737. It is also significant within other areas of counter-terror law: under e.g., Terrorism Act 2000, Sched 7; Protection of Freedoms Act 2012, s 61. See further Chapter 12, pp 845–46.
398   As a result, Feldman has argued, in the control orders context, that a new Protocol to the Convention, setting out further specified circumstances in which liberty can justifiably be infringed may be needed: Feldman, D, 'Deprivation of Liberty in Anti-Terrorism Law' (2008) 67 CLJ 4, 8.
399   The Government in its ECHR memo on Art 6 in relation to TPIMs considers on this basis that the provisions relating to court review are compatible with Art 6; TPIMA ECHR memo, para 24–42,
400   The test from *Secretary of State for the Home Department v MB* [2006] 3 WLR 839 at [63]–[65].

The review hearing relies on closed and open material. A closed material procedure (CMP) is well established in the context of control orders/TPIMs, and has been accepted by the courts.[401] The provisions governing the procedure did not derive from the PTA, and the same is true of TPIMA. The provisions are found in the Civil Procedure Rules (CPR),[402] and that position has been unaffected by the move from control orders to the new measures, although CMP have been given a further legal basis under the Justice and Security Act 2013.[403] The PTA case law which relied on s 3 of the HRA to seek to ensure that the procedure reached Art 6 standards[404] also applies to TPIMs.[405] It is clear from *Secretary of State for the Home Department v BC and BB*[406] that Art 6(1) is engaged by proceedings in relation to a TPIM: the argument was not accepted that the obligations imposed under 'light touch' control orders – similar to the obligations under a TPIM – do not require Art 6(1) compliance.[407]

Although CMP are used, disclosure of the *essence* of the case to the suspect is required, as discussed above.[408] Thus, if the essence or gist of the case cannot be disclosed on national security grounds,[409] the TPIM notice cannot be sustained. The question of the degree of disclosure required to the suspect has not been fully resolved, and no attempt was made to resolve it in the TPIMA provisions themselves. In *AT v Secretary of State for the Home Department*[410] the Court of Appeal found that insufficient disclosure had occurred to satisfy Art 6. In *BM*[411] it was found that once some disclosure has occurred, the failure of the TPIM suspect to deal with the allegations to the extent that was

401 *Secretary of State for the Home Department v MB* [2007] 1 AC 440.
402 Part 76 CPR. The closed material is considered by the Special Advocate (SA). Provision is made for the exclusion of a relevant person and his legal representative from a hearing to secure that information is not disclosed contrary to the public interest: r 76.22. The SA may only communicate with the relevant party before closed material is served upon him or her, save with permission of the court: rr 76.2, 76.28(2). See further Chamberlain, M, 'Special Advocates and Procedural Fairness in Closed Proceedings' (2009) 28 Civil Justice Quarterly 314.
403 The Justice and Security Act 2013 makes provision for closed material proceedings (CMP) in PT II, which cover TPIM hearings (s 6), but since CMP were and are being used in this context in any event, it does not appear that it will bring about significant change; see Justice and Security Green Paper Ministry of Justice, Report Cm 8194 (2011).
404 See *Secretary of State for the Home Department v AF (No 3)* [2009] 3 WLR 74.
405 See the ECHR memorandum on the TPIM Bill as regards Art 6 para 29–42.
406 [2010] 1 WLR 1542. See also *BM v Secretary of State for the Home Department* [2011] EWCA Civ 366; Lord Justice Thomas said at [19]: 'on the open evidence, the control order could not be justified as necessary at the time it was made as the evidence was too vague and speculative'.
407 It has been found that control orders affect civil rights and obligations; therefore Art 6(1)'s requirement of a fair hearing applies: *Secretary of State for the Home Department v MB* [2008] 1 AC 440, 470F.
408 See p 1032. See *Secretary of State for the Home Department v AF (No 3)* [2009] 3 WLR 74. This matter of gisting is covered by the Justice and Security Act 2013, s 8: if the court gives permission not to disclose material, it must consider requiring the relevant person to provide a summary of the material to every other party to the proceedings.
409 Justice and Security Act 2013, s 8: '. . .but the court must ensure that such a summary does not contain material the disclosure of which would be damaging to the interests of national security'. This provision does not affect the essential principle deriving from *AF no 3* (n 412 above): it regulates its application in CMP.
410 [2012] EWCA Civ 42.
411 [2012] EWHC 714 (Admin).

possible, having regard to the disclosure given, could be taken into account in relation to the level of suspicion.[412]

Use of closed material proceedings is leaching into many other civil actions with a national security dimension,[413] despite criticism of the quality of the information relied on.[414] That expansion of their use provides an example of a trend towards habituation and normalisation of measures in tension with Art 6, as is also apparent in relation to non-trial-based measures that are able to operate outside Art 5(1).

Parliamentary scrutiny

Parliamentary scrutiny is reduced under TPIMA 2011 since, unlike the PTA, it will not expire if Parliament does not review and renew it annually, indicating the extent to which these measures have undergone normalisation. The House of Lords' Select Committee on the Constitution questioned 'whether it is constitutionally appropriate to place on a permanent basis such a scheme of extraordinary executive powers'.[415] TPIMA is time-limited to five years under s 21 but the powers can be revived under statutory instrument for further five-year periods[416] so, while it might be viewed as an emergency, last resort measure, not only is it very likely to become a familiar feature of the counter-terror landscape, but it is also unlikely to receive significant scrutiny on renewal.

The 'investigative' element of TPIMs

TPIMs were put forward as resembling control orders in their *preventive* aspect, but also as having a more genuinely significant *investigative* element – hence the use of the term 'investigation' in the title of the instrument. The term was intended to emphasise the dissimilarity between the scheme and the control orders one. The apparent stance of the Coalition government, implicit in the use of that term, was that TPIMs are more closely associated with facilitating the criminal prosecution of suspects, and are designed to further that end, rather than being viewed as an end in themselves.

The emphasis under control orders was on the isolation of the controlee, in physical and communicative terms; control orders barred suspects from employing technology – the internet, phones – to facilitate contact with certain associates, thereby preventing TRA. But such bars meant that data that could have been collected by way of electronic surveillance could not be available. Thus the use of control orders

---

412 [22]. The same approach was taken in *Secretary of State for the Home Department v CC, CF* [2012] EWHC 2837 (Admin) in which CF and CC declined to give evidence once they were made aware of the allegations against them.

413 Under the Justice and Security Act 2013.

414 Justice has found: 'intelligence material may contain second or third-hand hearsay, information from unidentified informants, or received from foreign intelligence liaisons, not to mention hypotheses, predictions and conjecture.' 'Secret Evidence' JUSTICE report, June 2009, at http://www.justice.org. uk/data/files/resources/33/Secret-Evidence-10-June-2009.pdf, para 413.

415 House of Lords Select Committee on the Constitution 'Terrorism Prevention and Investigation Measures Bill' HL 198, 14 September 2011, 5, at http://www.publications.parliament.uk/pa/ld201012/ldselect/ldconst/198/198.pdf).

416 As provided for under s 21(2)(b).

tended to be inimical to the prospects of prosecuting the controlees.[417] Interference with the suspect's use of communications technology is also a significant aspect of TPIMA. But, as discussed, the level of interference was higher under control orders than it is under TPIMs. Thus – so the argument goes – since under a TPIM the suspect is not *as* isolated from possible associates, terrorism-related activity might occur, or past occurrences of such activity might be revealed, leading to the possibility of a prosecution, although obviously any potential risk he/she represents might thereby be enhanced.

Control orders contained a specific prosecutorial review element potentially linked to investigations, which was strengthened to an extent in TPIMA s 10. Under s 8 of the PTA the relevant chief officer of police had to keep the prospects of prosecution under review, consulting the CPS as necessary. Under s 10 TPIMA there is a duty to consult the chief officer of the appropriate police force as to the prospects of prosecution[418] before imposing a TPIM.[419] The chief officer must consult the relevant prosecuting authority before responding (s 10(6)), although the duty to consult can be satisfied by a consultation that occurred previously (s 10(9)). This appears to refer to the previous consultation duty under s 8 of the PTA. The secretary of state must then inform the chief officer that the TPIM notice has been served (s 10(4)), and he or she must keep prosecution under review for the duration of the notice.[420]

Given that all the controlees were transferred on to TPIMs at the beginning of 2012, and there have been no prosecutions since then of those currently subject to TPIMs, leaving aside prosecutions for breach of TPIM conditions, the danger that the review of the possibility of prosecution is merely part of a tokenistic, routinised, presentational exercise with no genuine investigative element – as it appears to have been in relation to control orders – still remains.[421] That danger may have been exacerbated by the two-year limit on imposition of a TPIM. The possibility that the two-year limit might incentivise those looking for evidence to found a prosecution and create a stronger focus on so doing than was the case under control orders that could be renewed indefinitely appears remote: the time limit is more likely to mean that none will be found since a rational suspect is unlikely to engage in TRA as the end point of the TPIM comes closer.

The ETPIMs Bill

The inception of the more ECHR-compliant TPIMA was rapidly followed by the introduction of the Enhanced Terrorism Prevention and Investigation Measures Bill (ETPIM

---

417 Review of Counter-Terrorism Powers Lord MacDonald, Report Cm 8003, (2011) 9.

418 Under s 10(2) this means: 'whether there is evidence available that could realistically be used for the purposes of prosecuting the individual for an offence relating to terrorism'.

419 Whether by the urgent procedure or when applying to a court under TPIMA, s 6, s 10(1); ETPIM Bill, cl 2 Condition E.

420 The chief officer must: 'secure that the investigation of the individual's conduct, with a view to a prosecution of the individual for an offence relating to terrorism, is kept under review throughout the period the TPIM [or ETPIM] notice is in force' (s 10(5)).

421 See e.g., 'From "War" to Law: Liberty's Response to the Coalition Government's Review of Counter Terrorism and Security Powers' Liberty report, 2010, at http://www.liberty-human-rights.org.uk/pdfs/policy10/from-war-to-law-final-pdf-with-bookmarks.pdf.

Bill),[422] providing for enhanced measures, similar in terms of their more repressive character to control orders, but accompanied by somewhat greater safeguards, and ready to be introduced as emergency legislation. However, ETPIMs have not yet been introduced.

TPIMA makes provision in s 26 to introduce the enhanced measures if it is urgent to do so when Parliament is in recess,[423] but the ETPIM Bill would allow the measures to be relied on generally in future. It appears to have been introduced on the basis that in certain circumstances TPIMs might not be viewed as adequate to meet the demands of a heightened security threat, so ETPIMs could be needed as a supplementary measure. The Bill has received parliamentary scrutiny[424] and is available to be brought forward at any time to meet the demands of an unspecified crisis situation; the trigger that would allow it to be enacted is not indicated in the bill.[425] If passed, it would grant the Home Secretary additional powers to deal with exceptional circumstances, and ETPIMs would provide a separate, parallel regime running alongside the TPIMs scheme. The ETPIM Bill is in many respects a disturbing, even extraordinary, legislative measure.

The deputy assistant police commissioner told the ETPIM Bill Joint Committee that ETPIMs could be introduced in response to a general rising of the threat level that could be triggered either by an increase in the danger posed by terrorists or a reduction in resources for policing.[426] The government in its response to the committee[427] declined to give an exhaustive summary of the trigger circumstances, but stated that they might arise where the country faced a serious terrorist threat that the government, on the advice of the police and the security service, judged could not be managed by any other means.

Such uncertainty as to the trigger circumstance for introducing the bill underpins the concerns that have arisen that the legislation is being kept in the 'back pocket' to be introduced abruptly to be rushed through as emergency legislation, meaning that Parliament cannot debate it fully or subject the basis for introducing the bill to meaningful scrutiny.

422 See Draft Enhanced Terrorism Prevention and Investigation Measures Bill Home Office, Report Cm 8166 (2011).
423 Section 26(1) provides 'If the Secretary of State considers that it is necessary to do so by reason of urgency, the Secretary of State may make a temporary enhanced Terrorism Prevention and Investigation order [while Parliament is in recess]'. An order made under s 26 is made on the same basis and provides for certain of the same obligations as an order that could be made under the ETPIM Bill, as discussed below. No temporary ETPIMs have yet been introduced under s 26. For consideration of s 26 see e.g., TPIM Bill 2nd Reading per Lord Hunt, HC Deb vol 730, col 1139 5 October 2011.
424 The ETPIM Bill Joint Committee was set up for this purpose; see 'Draft Enhanced Terrorism Prevention and Investigation Measures Bill,' First Report, HL 70, HC 495, 27 November 2012.
425 Ibid at 3. It is to be introduced in response to 'exceptional circumstances' which 'cannot be managed by any other means'.
426 Speaking on behalf of Association of Chief Police Officers before the ETPIM Bill Joint Committee, para 8, in answer to Q39, indicating that the question of the resource-intensiveness of surveillance as opposed to use of ETPIMs could become relevant as a trigger circumstance leading to the introduction of ETPIMs. But he said that 'given the resource currently available' and the changes made to policing, the police 'are adequately managing the risk posed by people subject to TPIMs at the moment (para 21, in answer to Qs 36–39).
427 Ibid.

Conclusions

TPIMs, introduced from 2012 onwards, represented a more favourable compromise between protecting both security and liberty than control orders had done, but the enhanced version, in contrast, could reintroduce the human rights challenges they presented. It is argued that the mere 'forms of legality' that might be said to have existed in the shape of Part 4 of the ACTSA, and to a lesser extent in the form of control orders, have come to comport more closely with genuine legality, in the form of TPIMs. Court action in reliance on the ECHR in relation to control orders brought the two closer together, and parliamentary action, in passing TPIMA, brought that process closer to completion. TPIMA represents a positive development in that it has explicitly addressed Strasbourg standards, but it has done so in the form of endorsing a domestic compromise between security and liberty that is in some tension with those standards. Reliance on this domestic compromise appears to have *legitimised* the continued use of such exceptional measures, with no solution, no new exit strategy allowing for their abandonment, currently available. But overall it may be said that, as 9/11 receded, a more measured assessment of the threat occurred, conducive of a return to normality and a re-balancing in favour of human rights, largely through court action, but with some parliamentary intervention.

Temporary exclusion orders

Introduction

The idea behind these orders, introduced in the Counter-Terrorism and Security Act 2015, is that persons who have gone to Syria, or elsewhere outside the UK, to fight for or support the group Isis should not merely be allowed to return to the UK without some form of intervention before they do so, combined with providing the opportunity to manage such persons when they are allowed to return to the UK. Such interventions appear to be intended in the first instance to evaluate whether and how far such persons are likely to pose a risk to UK citizens if they return. The orders (not yet utilised 18 months after their introduction) are also intended to allow preventive action to be taken when the person in question is allowed to enter the UK, if they appear to pose a risk to UK citizens. Clearly, such persons may have become more intensely radicalised or brutalised while abroad and under the control of Isis, and may well have received weapons training. Some of those seeking to enter Britain after being in contact with Isis may be part of a planned attack in Britain.[428] For example, as mentioned above, Abdelhamid Abaaoud, the suspected mastermind behind the massacre in Paris in November 2015 was a Brussels resident who left for Syria to join Isis in 2014 before returning and coordinating the attacks.

428 See on this issue in relation to other jurisdictions: Hegghammer, T, 'Should I stay or should I go?'(2013) 107 American Political Science Review 1, 10. *Cf* Jones, SG, *The Extremist Threat to the U.S. Homeland*, 2014, RAND; Skidmore, J, 'Foreign fighter involvement in Syria', 2014, ICT; Al Qaeda Sanctions Committee, Analysis and Recommendations with regard to the Global Threat from Foreign Terrorist Fighters (New York: S/2015/358, 2015).

Removal of citizenship

Under the Immigration Act 2014 there is provision in s 66 amending the British Nation-ality Act 1981 (inserting s 4A) to allow removal of citizenship if the conduct of the person is 'seriously prejudicial to the vital interests of the UK, any of the Islands, or any British overseas territory' (s 4A(b)), but only if the citizenship status results from the per-son's naturalisation, and 'the Secretary of State has reasonable grounds for believing that the person is able, under the law of a country or territory outside the United Kingdom, to become a national of such a country or territory' (s 4A(c)).[429] Section 4A(c) overturns the findings of the Supreme Court in *Al-Jedda*[430] to the effect that a person is rendered stateless if at the time when he is stripped of his citizenship he does not have another nationality. The Court found that it was not relevant that the person in question could have attained another nationality previously and would be likely still to be able to do so.

Section 4A(c) was included in an attempt to comply with the 1954 Convention relat-ing to the Status of Stateless Persons and the 1961 Convention on the Reduction of Statelessness, but could be utilised to render a person stateless where, despite show-ing the reasonable grounds in question, the person could not in practice attain another nationality. But this provision does not affect persons whose citizenship status did not arise from naturalisation. If such a person leaves the UK to join Isis, giving rise to the possibility that he or she might return to the UK and might therefore pose a risk to UK citizens, at present the removal of citizenship provisions do not apply. The new tem-porary exclusion orders are intended as a substitute for taking that more extreme step, while still dealing with the risk such a person might be likely to pose.

Imposing temporary exclusion orders

These orders – 'temporary exclusion orders' (TEOs) – are provided for under s 2 (1) of the 2015 Act. They can be imposed on persons who have a right of abode in the UK, and are outside the UK, if the secretary of state reasonably suspects that the individual is, or has been, involved in terrorism-related activity (TRA)[431] outside the UK (s2(3)), and also reasonably considers that it is necessary to impose a TEO for purposes con-nected with protecting the public in the UK from a risk of terrorism.[432] It is notable that

---

429 Section 66: Deprivation if conduct seriously prejudicial to vital interests of the UK:
    (1) In section 40 of the British Nationality Act 1981 (deprivation of citizenship), after subsection (4) insert – '(4A) But that does not prevent the Secretary of State from making an order under subsection (2) to deprive a person of a citizenship status if (a)the citizenship status results from the person's naturalisation, (b)the Secretary of State is satisfied that the deprivation is conducive to the public good because the person, while having that citizenship status, has conducted him or herself in a manner which is seriously prejudicial to the vital interests of the United Kingdom, any of the Islands, or any British overseas territory, and (c) the Secretary of State has reasonable grounds for believing that the person is able, under the law of a country or territory outside the United Kingdom, to become a national of such a country or territory.'

430 *Al-Jedda v SSHD* [2013] UKSC 62, [2013] WLR(D) 371; Theresa May discussed this point during the second reading of the Immigration Bill: 2014 HC Deb Vol 574, col 1038, 30 January 2014.

431 Defined in s 14(4) and in Sched 1.

432 Under s 2(2) the Secretary of State may impose a temporary exclusion order on an individual if condi-tions A to E are met: '(3) Condition A is that the Secretary of State reasonably suspects that the indi-vidual is, or has been, involved in terrorism-related activity outside the United Kingdom. (4) Condition

the standard of proof needed is lower than that now needed, as discussed above, due to amendment by the 2015 Act, to impose a TPIM, which is now proof on the civil standard. The detail of the grounds for suspicion can be in closed material which the person to be subject to the TEO cannot see,[433] although he or she will be able to see a summary.

The Secretary of State must seek permission from the court (under s 3) to impose the order, unless the secretary of state considers on reasonable grounds that due to urgency the TEO should be imposed without the court's permission.[434] The court must withhold permission if the decision of the secretary of state is 'obviously flawed' (s 3(2) and (6)). The court applies judicial review principles in considering whether to give the secretary of state permission (s 4), and can consider the application in the absence of the applicant, without notification to the applicant, and without him or her being given an opportunity of making representations to the court (s 3). If an urgent temporary TEO is imposed without court permission, Sched 2 applies, providing (para 3(1)) that immediately after giving notice of the imposition of the temporary exclusion order, the Secretary of State must refer the imposition of the order to the court which must decide whether the decision to impose it is obviously flawed (s 3(2)).[435] Again the court can consider the application in the absence of the applicant, without notification, and without him or her being given an opportunity of making representations to the court (Sched 2 para 3(4)). Thus while court oversight is provided for it is limited in nature and the applicant is likely to experience difficulty in exercising it without returning to the UK.[436] TEOs might appear potentially to be incompatible with the UK's obligations under the ICCPR Art 12(4), which states that 'nobody shall be arbitrarily deprived of the right to enter his own country'. However, the standard of suspicion and the inclusion of court oversight could be relied on to argue that preventing the return of persons subject to TEOs for a period is not 'arbitrary'.

Obligations imposed by a TEO

The TEO can subsist for up to two years (s 4(3)(b)), and during the period for which it is in force the passport of the person to whom it applies is invalidated (s 4(9)). The order

---

B is that the Secretary of State reasonably considers that it is necessary, for purposes connected with protecting members of the public in the United Kingdom from a risk of terrorism, for a temporary exclusion order to be imposed on the individual. (5) Condition C is that the Secretary of State reasonably considers that the individual is outside the United Kingdom. (6) Condition D is that the individual has the right of abode in the United Kingdom'.

433 See Sched 3.
434 Section 2(7) Condition E is that –
    (a) the court gives the Secretary of State permission under section 3, or (b) the Secretary of State reasonably considers that the urgency of the case requires a temporary exclusion order to be imposed without obtaining such permission.
435 Section 3(2): The function of the court on the reference is to consider whether the urgent case decisions were obviously flawed.
436 See the comments on this point in R (Razgar) v Secretary of State for the Home Department [2002] EWHC 2554 (Admin). The Human Rights Joint Committee–Fifth Report Legislative Scrutiny: Counter-Terrorism and Security Bill, HL Paper 86, HC 859, published 12 January 2015, in paras 3.8–3.15 recommended strengthening the judicial oversight and commented on the difficulty of relying on judicial review while abroad.

can then be renewed for further periods (s4(8)). A TEO prevents the individual from returning to the UK unless their return is in accordance with a 'permit to return' issued by the secretary of state or if they are deported to the UK by the state that they are in (s 2(1)). Section 10(1) provides that it is an offence for an individual subject to a TEO to return to the UK in contravention of the TEO, without a reasonable excuse.

The individual can be given a permit to return to the UK under s 5 if he or she complies with conditions specified in the permit to return (s 5(2)). Further details about permitted obligations may be provided for in regulations, subject to the negative resolution procedure (s 13). Under s 5(3) the individual's failure to comply with a specified condition has the effect of invalidating the permit to return. If an individual fails to accept a condition to return that person could remain excluded from the UK for a long period of time (the TEO could be renewed under s 4(8)). The permit to return must also make specific provision about the time, manner and place of return (s 5(4)). If an individual applies for a permit it must be issued within a 'reasonable period' following an application (s 6(1)). But it need not be issued if the secretary of state requires the applicant to attend an interview with a police officer or immigration official and the applicant fails to attend. The notice imposing the obligations comes into force when given to the individual and continues in force until the TEO ends.[437] It is an offence to return to the UK in contravention of the restriction specified in the order without reasonable excuse (s 10(1)). One problem arising from these arrangements in the Act is that imposing an interview with a police officer or other official could potentially breach the privilege against self-incrimination implicit under Art 6 ECHR. However, the privilege is based on the charging of a person with a criminal offence, in the specific sense in which that word is used in the Art 6 jurisprudence of the Strasbourg Court. A person subject to a TEO has not necessarily become a person suspected of a criminal offence.

The 'permitted obligations' that can be imposed on an individual subject to a TEO when they have returned to the UK, are as outlined in s 9. It is an offence to fail to comply with permitted obligations on return, without reasonable excuse (s 10(3)). The obligations refer to a range of conditions under Sched 1 of the Terrorism Prevention and Investigation Measures Act (TPIMA) 2011, as referred to in the 2015 Act s 9, which take effect after return. But only the less intrusive obligations capable of being imposed under TPIMA can be imposed as specified. The more intrusive ones, including the imposition of curfews or of forced relocation, are not available as far as the 2015 Act is concerned; obviously if the requisite evidence is present, (depending on proof to the civil standard that the person has been engaged in TRA), as discussed above, a TPIM order could be imposed under the 2011 Act. The conditions in the permit could include being required to report to a police station, to attend an appointment (which could include attending de-radicalisation programmes), and to notify the police of the place of residence and as to changes of address.

Thus the obligations that can be imposed on return that could also be imposed under a TPIM are less intrusive than those that arise immediately due to the power to impose

---

437 Section 9(3): 'A notice under this section –
   (a) comes into force when given to the individual; and
   (b) is in force until the temporary exclusion order ends (unless the notice is revoked or otherwise brought to an end earlier)'.

a TEO, since the TEO prevents the return to the UK of the individual for a period of time. On the other hand, it should be pointed out that the TPIM-related obligations can be imposed on a lower standard of proof under the 2015 Act – reasonable suspicion – whereas if they were imposed by subjecting the person concerned to a TPIM, the standard would be that of the balance of probabilities.

TEOs and the ECHR

As indicated, these provisions stop short of providing for removal of citizenship when there are insufficient grounds for finding that the person in question could acquire another nationality, and the 2015 Act relied on TEOs rather than taking that further step. In security terms the intention behind them is to seek to ensure that returnees are monitored; the interview abroad before permitting return is presumably intended mainly to assess the level of risk they could pose on return. Given that it is now very dangerous and difficult to try to escape from Isis-held territory,[438] some returnees may have been allowed to travel back to the UK specifically in order to mount attacks there, as appears to have happened in relation to the Paris attacks. Even if that is not the case, persons who have left Britain to support Isis are obviously likely to pose a risk of being drawn into terrorist conspiracies on return, although it cannot be assumed that all such persons will continue to seek to support Isis domestically. The risk that returnees may therefore pose contextualises the relevant ECHR rights that TEOs engage. Space precludes consideration of the full ECHR obligations.

It appears to be assumed under the TEO provisions – although this is not made explicit – that any detention abroad or other potential violation of the ECHR resulting from the imposition of the TEO would be the responsibility of the state in question and would be under that state's laws. That possibility combined with the status of the person as a suspected terrorist, may tend to make it less likely that a host state would take responsibility for persons subject to TEOs. Presumably the UK government is seeking to reach agreement about the responsibility of potential host states towards persons subject to TEOs. If the host state concerned is not prepared to take responsibility for the person in question it might deport him or her to the UK, which in effect accepts under s 2(1) and s 7 of the 2015 Act its duty to admit its citizens if such deportation has occurred. The host state might decide to avail itself of this option, meaning that the issue of detention might not arise, engaging Art 5, although other rights might be engaged.

Article 1 (the obligation to respect human rights) of the European Convention on Human Rights sets limits on the reach of the Convention; however, the concept of 'jurisdiction' under that provision is not restricted to the national territory of the contracting states. But nevertheless, a state's jurisdictional competence remains primarily territorial. As two exceptions to territoriality a state can have jurisdiction when it exercises effective control over an area outside its national territory, or where state agents

438 Samra Kesinovic, 18, was reportedly murdered by Islamic State fighters when she tried to leave Isis-held territory to return to Austria: *New York Post*, 24 November 2015. See also 'Life under ISIS in Raqqa and Mosul: we're living in a giant prison': 'hundreds are defying a ban on leaving, often paying large sums to smugglers to get them out. Those who are caught fleeing are punished severely': *The Guardian*, 9 December 2015.

exercise authority and control on the territory of another state.[439] States' obligations to secure in such an area the Convention rights and freedoms derived from the fact that they exercised effective control there, whether that was done directly, through the state's armed forces, or through a subordinate local administration. But if the returnee was detained abroad due to the imposition of the TEO it would probably not be the case that the UK would have effective control over the area in question.

But ECHR rights, including Arts 3 and 5 ECHR, could be engaged if the host state in question was a Council of Europe state or if it was found that due to an agreement with the host state British agents were exercising executive public powers in imposing TEOs combined with conditions on the territory of another state. The government appears to assume that it does not have responsibilities to citizens detained abroad under TEOs,[440] but since it appears that British officials would probably be involved in the detention of persons subject to TEOs abroad, assuming a period of detention was needed, it is not clear that ECHR responsibilities could be evaded since their involvement could fall within the second exception to the general principle of territoriality. Further, the European Court of Human Rights held in *El Masri v The Former Yugoslav Republic of Macedonia*,[441] that the host state, if a party to the European Convention (as Turkey is, a probable host state), will have distinct responsibilities to ensure that the conduct of UK agents and officials who are within its territory is in conformity with the ECHR.

If it was found that in respect of the imposition of certain TEOs British state agents were exercising authority and control on the territory of another state any claim under Art 5 could be brought against the UK authorities under the HRA (and if it failed, at Strasbourg). If in practice the person is detained abroad due to the imposition of the TEO (quite probably in Turkey), in order to cancel their travel documents, interview them and add them to watch lists (including the authority-to-carry i.e. 'no fly' list) then the detention could potentially fall within one of the exceptions in Art 5(1). The relevant exception would probably be Art 5(1)(f) covering detention with a view to deportation. But the exception under Art 5(1)(f) allowing for detention of 'a person against whom action is being taken with a view to deportation or extradition', does not cover lengthy detentions, following *Chahal*.[442] Thus, if a lengthy detention resulted abroad it would appear that Art 5 might be breached.

The possibility that a person subject to a TEO might be detained abroad and suffer Art 3 treatment there is reflected in s 7 which provides that the secretary of state may issue a permit to return to an individual if 'the Secretary of State considers that, because of the urgency of the situation, it is expedient to issue a permit to return even though no application has been made under section 6'. The urgency could arise due to the need to ensure that Art 3 was not breached abroad. But obviously that assumes that the person in question is able to communicate effectively with British authorities while in detention in another state.

---

439 See the leading decision in *Al-Skeini and others v UK*, 7 July 2011 Application No 55721/07; see also the *Chagos Islanders* case ECtHR 4th Section, 11 December 2012.
440 Counter-Terrorism and Security Bill – Temporary Exclusion Orders', Impact Assessment: IA No: HO0144, 21 November 2014.
441 Application No 39630/09 13 December 2012.
442 (1996) 23 EHRR 413 [113]. In order to detain, deportation proceedings should be in being and it should be clear that they are being prosecuted with due diligence.

Where use of the TEO prevented a suspect from re-joining family members in Britain for a period of time, that would have obvious Art 8 ECHR implications. But the exceptions under Art 8(2) for the prevention of crime, preservation of national security and the rights of others would apply. The potentially very serious risks that such returnees could pose would mean that the test of necessity would be likely to be satisfied. In terms of proportionality the length of the period of time during which the person could not rejoin his or her family, and the reasons for extending the period, would clearly be relevant.

The question of jurisdiction and of ECHR obligations of the UK in relation to persons subject to TEOs abroad is an unsatisfactory area of this scheme. The question of satisfying both Arts 5 and 3 in respect of such imposition remains problematic, and may result in the kind of protracted and expensive litigation seen in relation to control orders.

5 Intervention to avoid the risk of being drawn into terrorism

Introduction

Part 5 of the Counter-terrorism and Security Act 2015 places the main aspects of the government's existing 'Prevent' strategy[443] on a statutory basis. The part is intended to address the risk of persons being drawn into terrorism by placing duties on certain authorities to seek to disallow – in effect – occasions of radicalisation or to provide information about that process on which the Home Secretary and police could act to intervene. The authorities include schools, councils and universities. Part 5 is aimed at disrupting pathways into terrorism and so contrasts with the aims behind the special offences discussed above, which are to punish acts of terrorism and to allow intervention at a very early stage in terrorist plots and in preparing terrorist acts. Part 5 also contrasts with the non-trial-based measures discussed as they are aimed at persons who appear to have engaged in forms of terrorist-related activity (TRA) already; Part 5 is aimed at seeking to prevent persons ever engaging in such activity. It attempts to allow intervention in a process of radicalisation that might eventually lead to engaging in TRA, but before it could be said that the person in question has become a terrorist suspect.

New 'Prevent duties' placed on universities and schools: background

The 'Prevent' strategy has previously highlighted the threat of extremism in educational establishments.[444] Opposing views have previously been expressed as to the like-

---

443 See Home Office Countering International Terrorism (London: Cm 6888, 2006); Pursue, Prevent, Protect, Prepare: the UK's Strategy for Countering International Terrorism (London: Cm 7547, 2009). See now at https://www.gov.uk/government/consultations/prevent-duty. The strategy is outlined in policy paper *2010 to 2015 Government policy: counter-terrorism*, updated 8 May 2015.

444 The Prevent Strategy: A Guide for Local Partners in England; Stopping people becoming or supporting terrorists and violent extremists (2008).

lihood that encountering radical materials might lead to radicalisation and then to acts of terrorism in relation to children and young people in such establishments.[445] But the provisions of Part 5 of the 2015 Act represented the first time 'Prevent' duties in relation to such establishments had been placed on a statutory basis.

As far as universities are concerned, this new duty has been included to answer to concerns that certain university Islamic societies have in a range of ways, including via visiting speakers, contributed to the radicalisation of students. This new duty was included in relation to students partly because a number of students who were senior members of Islamic societies have gone on to mount terror attacks, as documented in the report 'Roots of violent radicalisation' from the Home Affairs Committee.[446] For example, Abdulmutallab, the attempted bomber of flight 253, was the president of a university Islamic society[447] although the evidence that he had become radicalised *because* he had attended UCL was not established.[448] Kafeel Ahmed, who carried out the attempted Glasgow airport suicide attack, was on the executive of Queen's University Belfast ISOC; he died after driving a jeep packed with gas canisters into Glasgow airport in 2007. Waseem Mughal, convicted of inciting murder for terrorist purposes, ran the University of Leicester ISOC website. Yassin Nassari, convicted of possession for terrorist purposes, was president of the University of Westminster Harrow campus ISOC. Waheed Zaman, convicted for his role in the transatlantic liquid bomb plot, was formerly the president of London Metropolitan University's ISOC. Mohammed Naveed Bhatti, convicted for his role in Dhiren Barot's 2004 'dirty bomb' plot, was studying at Brunel University and met Barot in the university's prayer room.[449]

Clearly, the fact that about one-third of persons convicted of terrorist offences in the UK had attended university does not in itself demonstrate that attendance at university played any part in involvement in terrorism. But if they were exposed to an ideology linked to violent extremism while at university, and therefore at a fairly impressionable stage, then it is possible that such exposure might, to varying degrees depending on individual circumstances, have had an impact on them. Clearly the precise causal relation between exposure to radical preachers and radical materials at university and later involvement in terrorism would inevitably be very hard to establish. But some impact would be expected,[450] and that would tend to be even more likely to be the case in relation to school children as more impressionable, especially if their home lives excluded encountering a plurality of influences, including secular ones.

The background to these provisions as far as schools were concerned arose partly from the allegations made in 2013 that a number of schools in certain Muslim majority areas were attempting to teach an 'Islamic' curriculum and in other ways allowing pupils to be exposed to extremist influences, thereby failing to offer pupils full educational opportunities or the ability to integrate into the British way of life and putting

---

445 See Glees, A and Pope, C, 'When students turn to terror' (London: Social Affairs Unit, 2005)
446 Home Affairs Committee, Roots of violent radicalisation, Cm 1446, 6 February 2012; compare with Ramraj, VV, Hor, M and Roach, K (eds), *Global Anti-terrorism Law and Policy*, 2012, C Walker and J Rehman, Chapter 10, pp 257–60.
447 A number of radical speakers invited to UCL by Abdulmutallab's organisation spoke on UCL property.
448 Report to UCL Council of Independent Inquiry Panel (London 2010).
449 The Roots of violent radicalisation – Home Affairs Committee Cm1446 (2012).
450 See Radicalisation on British University Campuses (London, Quilliam, 2010).

them at risk of radicalisation. Certain governors and teachers were promoting 'a hard-line and politicised strand of Sunni Islam. Left unchecked, it would confine school children within an intolerant, inward-looking monoculture that would severely inhibit their participation in the life of modern Britain.'[451] In particular, the governing bodies of a number of schools were accused of using intimidatory tactics against headteach-ers of a number of the schools, in order to force their resignations, to make way for a headteacher who would acquiesce in imposing an 'Islamic' curriculum. The allegations became the subject of a parliamentary enquiry and a report in 2014.[452] The report found that governors with extreme Islamic views had succeeded in bringing about the resigna-tions of a number of headteachers in Birmingham schools by using intimidatory tactics. It also found that in a number of schools the curriculum was limited, that gender segre-gation was imposed in some lessons, and that extremist speakers[453] had been brought in to speak in school assemblies.

The new 'Prevent' duty in the 2015 Act

Against that background, ss 26–29 of the Counter-terrorism and Security Act 2015 are aimed in part at addressing the concern that some schools and universities have disre-garded the risk that children or students might be drawn towards violent extremism, or have in some instances facilitated it. Section 26 provides that a specified authority (listed in Sched 6 of the Act) must, when exercising its functions, have due regard to the need to prevent people from being drawn into terrorism (the 'Prevent' duty). Under s 26(3) the duty will not apply to certain functions of the authority.[454] Under s 29(1) the secretary of state can issue guidance to specified authorities about the exercise of their duty under s 26 and under s 30 if the secretary of state is satisfied that 'a specified authority has failed to discharge the duty imposed on it by section 26(1)', he or she 'may give directions to the authority for the purpose of enforcing the performance of that duty'.

That means that a university that does not appear to have given consideration to the possibility that particular speakers could aid in the radicalisation of students, or has dismissed it without full investigation, or which appears to have allowed such speakers to speak despite that risk, could come under a duty (via the giving of directions by the Home Secretary under s 30) not to allow specified radical speakers to come to speak at an event organised, for example, by the Islamic society and held on university premises.

---

451 See Report into allegations concerning Birmingham schools arising from the 'Trojan Horse' letter July 2014 HC 5762014 Report, para 5.1.
452 *Ibid*
453 *Ibid*, 2014 Report, para 7.25. Speakers include the following individuals: Shaykh Yusuf Estes – a speaker who has caused controversy in the past for reportedly advocating wife beating and the killing of homosexuals. Shaykh Shady al-Suleiman – a preacher who has reportedly called on God to 'destroy the enemies of Islam'. Al-Suleiman has also asked God to 'give victory to the Muslims in Afghanistan and Chechnya', to 'give victory to all the Mujahideen all over the world' and to 'prepare us for the jihad'. Ustadh Hamza Tzortis – a speaker who has reportedly said that Muslims 'reject the idea of freedom of speech and even the idea of freedom'.
454 Subsection (3) covers the possibility that specified authorities have a range of functions, or act in a vari-ety of capacities, and that it is appropriate that the exercise of only some of those functions is subject to the duty, or that a specified authority is only subject to the duty when acting in a particular capacity.

Schools have been provided with guidance as to their prevent duty;[455] under it schools and childcare providers need to have clear procedures in place for protecting children at risk of radicalisation and they have to be prepared to make a referral of an at-risk individual to the *Channel* programme. Schools are also tasked with ensuring that children are safe from terrorist and extremist material when accessing the internet in schools; schools need to ensure that suitable filtering is in place. The procedures would appear to include vetting external speakers coming to the school, checking that extremist material is not available in school libraries, and ensuring that teachers giving lessons do not contribute themselves to radicalisation of children.

The 'Prevent' duty under the 2015 Act and freedom of expression

Statutory free expression duties

Section 31 of the 2015 Act requires universities to have 'particular regard' to the duty to secure freedom of speech imposed by s 43(1) of the Education (No 2) Act 1986 (if they are subject to that duty), when carrying out the 'Prevent' duty. Subsection (2)(b) requires institutions to have particular regard to the importance of academic freedom as described in s 202(2)(a) of the Education Reform Act 1988 (if they are 'qualifying institutions' within the meaning of section 202(3) of the 1988 Act) when carrying out the 'Prevent' duty. This section also places a duty on the secretary of state to have particular regard to the freedom of speech duty and the importance of academic freedom when issuing guidance or when giving directions to these educational bodies. Other educational institutions are not covered by s 31.

Section 31 refers to the provisions that already place duties on universities to secure freedom of expression and academic freedom. The Education Reform Act 1988 s 202, applicable to pre-1992 universities, protects academic freedom within the law including the freedom to put forward new ideas. Section 202 requires that regard should be had to the need to: ensure that academic staff have freedom within the law to question and test received wisdom, and to put forward new ideas and controversial or unpopular opinions, without placing themselves in jeopardy of losing their jobs or privileges they may have at their institutions. Some post-1992 universities have adopted similar provisions in their constitutions. The Education (No 2) Act 1986, s 43 emphasises the significance of free speech for universities by imposing a legal obligation on them to promote and protect it, *within the law* and to take such steps as are reasonably practicable to secure it to members, students and employees, and also to promulgate a code of practice setting out procedures in this regard re meetings etc.[456] Section 43 appears to cover visiting speakers in the sense that allowing them to speak means that members of the university are able to hear their views. As with the provision on academic freedom, the starting point is that the relevant law, not the institutions, sets the limitations. But assuming that a speaking event did not appear to be likely to infringe, for example, provisions on hate

---

455 Protecting children from radicalisation: the prevent duty, 1 July 2015.

456 Section 43 of the Act provides that: 'persons concerned in the government of any establishment . . . shall take such steps as are reasonably practicable to ensure that freedom of speech within the law is secured for members, students and employees of the establishment and in particular states that the only constraints on the duty to secure freedom of speech are those imposed by the law.'

speech or other relevant provisions (see Part II of this book) the university is still under a duty to ensure that freedom of expression can be exercised, meaning that, for example, a speaker should not be barred from an event unless there are grounds for considering that the duty under s 26 would not be satisfied otherwise.

The s 31 duty overlaps with the duty already arising under s 6 HRA and Art 10 European Convention on Human Rights, applicable to public authorities, which include public universities and state schools. The interpretation of the term 'freedom of speech' in s 43 and in s 31 is affected by the interpretation of Art 10 ECHR protecting freedom of expression, scheduled in the HRA. HRA s 6 binds universities (but not student unions) as public authorities (as having a public function) not to interfere with freedom of expression or even to act positively secure it under Art 10(1) ECHR unless primary legislation unequivocally requires it to act incompatibly with Art 10 (s 6(2)). The same applies to the duty in respect of freedom of assembly and association under Art 11. Sections 43, 202 and 31 as statutory provisions need to be interpreted in the light of Art 10 and its associated jurisprudence, under s 3 HRA, as discussed in Chapter 4. Under s 2 HRA the Strasbourg jurisprudence on freedom of expression must be taken into account both in interpreting those provisions and applying them.

Discharging the duty in practice

In both universities and schools the duty under s 26 obviously could apply to visiting speakers, staff, students, and to a range of media associated with an event – e.g., pamphlets, social media, actual speech. The internet and social media such as Twitter or Facebook are playing a far greater role in schools and higher education institutions than even five years ago in, for example, promoting the work of societies and events, including student ones, and allowing them to create wider impact.

Under guidance issued in 2015 by the government on the 'Prevent' duty universities should have policies relating to the management of events on campus and use of premises that clearly state what is required in order for an event to take place.[457] The policies must equally apply to students, staff members and visitors. Universities have to balance this duty with their obligation to ensure freedom of speech and academic freedom. Thus universities are advised to refer to the universities UK's guidance, published in 2013. When institutions are deciding on whether to host a speaker they should pay particular attention to the views being expressed, or likely to be expressed, by considering whether they convey extremist views which could aid in drawing people into terrorism. Under the guidance, if that is the case, the event should not proceed unless it is clear that the risk can be fully mitigated by ensuring that the speaker who holds the extremist views can be challenged by someone holding opposing opinions who is part of the same event.

Article 10 and the 'Prevent' duty

A number of recent examples of expression in universities have arisen that could potentially receive very light protection under Art 10 ECHR where the representative of the

---

457 'Prevent duty guidance for Higher Education Institutions'; it is to be read alongside, the general guidance contained in the Revised Prevent Duty Guidance issued on 16 July 2015.

group in question attacks or is likely to attack other groups, such as particular racial groups, women, homosexuals, religious groups. An English Defence League speaker could be barred from speaking if for example it appeared that Muslims would have been attacked in the speech and/or on grounds of public order. On that basis the Oxford Union cancelled its invitation in 2013 to EDL founder Tommy Robinson to take part in a forthcoming debate.[458] The Islamist preacher, Abu Usamah at-Thahabi was invited to Reading University in 2013[459] to speak to the Islamic society; he had previously argued that gays should be killed; such speech would be very likely to attract criminal liability as hate speech on grounds of sexual orientation,[460] and could clearly fall within the category of expression potentially caught by the new statutory 'Prevent' duty.

The vetting of speakers by a school or university or the barring of speakers by the university or ultimately Home Secretary, under the new 'Prevent' duty, could infringe freedom of expression. It must be borne in mind that some of the speakers who have previously been banned from speaking at universities on grounds of extremism are *preachers*, not lecturers. Thus, they may not be presenting views that are open to debate since they are faith-based, and in a number of instances, when they have been accorded a platform, no debate has been allowed.[461] Where extremist speakers have been invited into certain schools or where teachers themselves have expressed extremist views, for example in assemblies, that has also been the case.[462] The views have been presented in an unchallenged way, not as part of a debate, or to be juxtaposed with conflicting views.

But – importantly – as discussed above in this chapter, and in the introduction to Part II,[463] not all expression is *equally* valued at Strasbourg, or domestically. Speech is usually valued instrumentally – in other words it is valued by reference to the classic free speech justifications. The justification arising from furthering democracy barely applies or does not apply to forms of faith-based speech aimed at attacking democracy, as Salafism/Wahabism does.[464] That could also be said of forms of ultra-orthodox

458   15 September 2013.

459   Reading University in February 2013.

460   See Chapter 7, p 435 *et seq.*

461   E.g., when York University Islamic society hosted the preacher Yusuf Chambers in 2012; Khalid Yasin invited to University of East London 15 March 2015 has said homosexuality and lesbianism are 'aberrations, they are immoralities.' He endorses the execution of gay people; Student Rights Report 2015 into extremism in UK Universities found that the majority of events with extremist speakers 'host just one orator, and rarely act as debates. Instead, they tend to function as unchallenged platforms where extreme or intolerant speakers are presented as religious or political authorities.'

462   2014 Report HC 576, *report into allegations concerning Birmingham schools.* Para 4.30: 'Some staff at Park View School invited a religious preacher known for his extremist views, Shaykh Shady Al-Suleiman, to speak with Year 10 and 11 students . . . Mr Hussain [headteacher] admitted that the school had no policy for vetting speakers'. Para 4.31: 'Staff reported that on another occasion Mr Hussain addressed an assembly in anti-American terms. This allegation is denied by Mr Hussain. I understand from an interview with a former pupil that Mr Hussain led assemblies with a similar theme some years ago. It is also alleged that he told students that 'your white teachers do not have your best interests at heart because they're [. . .] non-believers'.

463   See p 287 *et seq.* See also Chapter 2, pp 84–85.

464   See: 'Fundamentalist terror is by no means a tool of the poor against the rich, of the Third World against the West, of people against capitalism. It is not a legitimate response that can be supported by the progressive forces of the world. Its main target is the internal democratic opposition to [its] theocratic project . . . of controlling all aspects of society in the name of religion . . . When fundamentalists come to power, they silence people; they physically eliminate dissidents and they lock women "in their

Judaism, but a possible link between Jewish societies in universities, radicalisation of some students and a link to the current security threat has not been identified. Salafism/ Wahabism is openly anti-democratic and Salafists and other extremists in the West, or publishing about the position of Muslims in the West, have frequently sought to dissuade Muslims from voting in elections.[465] Further, if the maintenance of democracy is linked to accepting that minorities should be full participants in it, and should not in general be treated as second class citizens that also undermines support for Wahabi preachers/lecturers in free speech terms, since under their ideology 'unbelievers' include Christians, Jews, Shiites, Sufis, Sunni Muslims who do not accept Wahhabi doctrine, Hindus, atheists and others. Under that ideology such unbelievers should not be accepted in Muslim communities or tolerated by them.

Further, while the vetting of speakers in universities and in schools could infringe freedom of expression, Art 10 is qualified by a range of exceptions under Art 10(2), and also by Art 17 ECHR, which, as mentioned above, is intended to disallow the abuse of the rights by groups or individuals.[466] Certain speakers from the far right or extreme Islamists would readily fall within Art 17[467] and that would most obviously be the case where a clear link between discriminatory practices aimed at certain groups and promulgation of speeches and materials from certain speakers in universities or schools could be discerned. Further, certain extreme Islamist speakers have been reported to have aided in creating an intimidating atmosphere on some campuses, affecting in particular LGBT students.[468] Arguably, the impact of homophobic speakers on campus could lead to a justifiable withdrawal of an invitation to speak under 'the rights of others' exception in Art 10(2), while the dangers posed by the potential radicalisation of some students could fall within the exceptions for the prevention of crime or protection of national security.[469]

---

place," which, as we know from experience, ends up being a strait jacket' – a statement from a representative of the organization Women Living under Muslim Laws (WLUML), at the 2005 World Social Forum in Porto Alegre: quoted in Meredith Tax, *Double Bind: The Muslim Right, the Anglo-American Left, and Universal Human Rights*, 2012, Center for Secular Space, 82.

465 For example, from the blog of I Nazar Hussein: 'the outstanding Pakistani Islamic scholar, Dr. Israr Ahmad, has categorically declared that it is Haram [forbidden] for a Muslim to participate in the electoral politics of the modern secular state'. He also asks: 'can a believer vote for an idol-worshipping Hindu, or for an enemy of Islam, a liar, a drunkard, a thief, an adulterer, a moneylender, who owns shares in a bank or is a bank director etc.? Can he vote for a political party that supports the legalization of the lending of money on interest, lottery, homosexuality and abortion?' and decides that to do so would also be Haram.

466 Art 17 provides: 'Nothing in this Convention may be interpreted as implying for any State, group or person any right to engage in any activity or perform any act aimed at the destruction on any of the rights and freedoms set forth herein or at their limitation to a greater extent than is provided for in the Convention.' In *Pavel Ivanov v Russia* 20 February 2007 a speaker who had attacked Jews was disallowed reliance on Art 10 since he fell within Art 17. A similar stance was taken in *M'Bala M'Bala v. France* 20 October 2015. See Chapter 2, p 101.

467 See *Norwood v UK* 16 November 2004, Application No 23131/03. The expression of racist, sexist, homophobic views by such speakers would appear to be covered by Art 17.

468 For example, a report published by the University of Westminster Student Union LGBT Society (UWSU LGBT) in 2014 investigated how safe LGBT students feel on campus after a number of concerns were reported. It noted that students stated that the situation had been exacerbated by the invitation of homophobic speakers to the university, such as Haitham Al-Haddad.

469 The Prevent Strategy review stated that 'we believe there is unambiguous evidence to indicate that some extremist organisations, notably Hizb-ut-Tahrir, target specific universities and colleges . . . with the objective of radicalising and recruiting students' (Cm 8092 June 2011). In 2014 the government's

Local authority panels

Section 38 of the 2015 Act provides that local authorities must ensure that a panel is in place for its area for the purposes of assessing the extent to which individuals referred to the panel by the police ('identified individuals', defined in sub-s (2)) are vulnerable to being drawn into terrorism. Under s 38 certain organisations are partners of panels and have a duty to cooperate with the panel, including by providing information. The partners include governors of prisons or young offender institutions or probation officers, sixth form colleges, schools, NHS trusts. The police thus will be able to refer persons to such panels if they have been alerted in time to the fact that a process of radicalisation appears to be underway. These provisions are intended to allow early signs of radicalisation to be revealed and could also answer to the concerns of some Muslim families that the government has not done enough to prevent radicalisation of young family members, creating the risk that they might leave Britain to join Isis.

Conclusions

The provisions discussed may lead to accusations from some Muslim groups that Muslims are being stigmatised, singled out as especially vulnerable to radicalisation and involvement in terrorism. On the other hand, those (usually young) persons at most danger of being 'groomed' into believing that they should leave Britain to join Isis, or should engage in terrorist activity in the UK, tend to come from Muslim families and communities. Such families and communities have frequently stated that more should be done to *protect* children and young people from the dangers of such 'grooming'.[470] Therefore if these provisions are carefully targeted in terms of their use in practice at Isis-linked persons and groups or persons supporting the theology behind Isis, and not at Muslims who oppose militant Salafism/Wahabism, they would be expected to command support among Muslims. In relation to events held by university Islamic societies, it may be argued that the Part 5 provisions aid in safeguarding students: some Muslim students may be more at risk than non-Muslim students of encountering radicalisation attempts at events run by certain university Islamic societies, though by no means by all

---

Extremism Analysis Unit found that at least 70 events featuring extremist preachers were held on campuses; it named four London universities – Queen Mary, King's College, SOAS and Kingston University – as those which had hosted the greatest number of such events.

470   There is evidence that Muslim parents are concerned about possible radicalization of their children in schools and fear that they are being denied a broad education, limiting their life chances: for example Mr Zabar, who had a 10-year-old daughter at Oldknow School in Birmingham (one of the schools which was the subject of the 'Trohan horse letter report, note 00 above), and had complained repeatedly about radicalisation, reportedly said the claims of 'racism' and 'Islamophobia' made by Oldknow and Park View against their critics were 'insulting'. He said: 'The charge of Islamophobia is sometimes bandied around to deter people from approaching this issue. But there are many Muslim parents raising concerns and this is not about religion. It is about our children receiving a balanced all-round education and giving them what they need to live in British society today': *Daily Telegraph*, 5 April 2014. An opinion poll in 2015 carried out for Sky News by Survation found that while both Muslims and non-Muslims were most likely to see families as being responsible for preventing young people heading to Syria (44% of Muslims and 65% of non-Muslims agreed) 15% of Muslims thought the government was responsible for stopping young Muslims going to fight in Syria, 3% of Muslims thought the police were responsible, 9% cited religious leaders and 2% said schools.

such societies. If that was the case relatives would have a right to complain that universities had not recognised the problem if a student was eventually drawn into terrorism due in part to experiences at university.

It would also mean that in so far as a risk of a degree of radicalisation of some Muslim students or school children might arise, impairing, for example, their full participation in university life or in wider society before and after school or university, the Part 5 provisions could form part of efforts to safeguard their welfare by – in so far as possible – seeking to aid efforts to ensure that that did not occur.

The provisions in Part 5 for panels and for vetting speakers are not directly aimed at preventing intimidation of some groups in schools or universities (the duty in relation to panels does not apply to universities), but if implemented carefully they could aid in addressing that problem. It could curb the activities of some Islamic societies led by presidents in the Wahabi/Salafist tradition, which might create risks of intimidation on campus to certain groups of minorities, including Shia or Sufi Muslims, Jews, some Muslim women, homosexuals. Some religiously-based practices, such as gender segregation at events on school or university premises, or discouraging women/girls from speaking at events, whether as part of the audience or otherwise, are very problematic in a school or university setting, and are inimical to equality duties discussed in Chapter 5, as well as free speech values. It is argued that the Part 5 provisions may aid in ensuring that they should not be deemed 'religious practices' that can legitimately be promoted by Islamists against the policies of universities or schools. If particular speakers appear to be likely to foster or request such practices, the university or school would have a basis for banning them under the vetting provisions. In relation to young offender institutions and sixth form colleges, schools children or young persons who have been subject to those promoting such policies and influenced by them could be referred to a panel. So doing might also aid in preventing possible intimidation of e.g., non-conservative Sunni or Shia Muslim girls at school, possibly in relation to dress, where teachers or governors were Salafists/Wahabis.

Part of the narrative of Islamic militants is that Muslims *in general* are mistreated in the West, and are stigmatised or demonised. That narrative is utilised to seek to aid radicalisation and incitement to terrorist acts. Thus it is important that the Part 5 provisions are used in a manner that creates a clear differentiation between Salafists/Wahabis of a militant tendency (the ideology behind Isis), which some Muslims perceive as largely unrelated to Islam and other Muslim groups from differing or entirely different religious backgrounds.

6 Conclusions

As this chapter has demonstrated, the terrorist attacks of 9/11 and of 7/7 in London immediately placed the then Labour government's commitment to the Human Rights Act under great pressure. It appeared initially probable that as an aspect of counter-terrorist policy they would exploit the leeway created by the HRA for introducing legislation incompatible with the Convention.[471] However, even during a 'war on terror' that Britain had not 'won' after six years, the Labour government did *not* take that route in introducing counter-terrorist measures; after 9/11 they continued to rely on

---

471 See Chapter 4, p 148.

the Convention qualifications to the rights, based on proportionality, and on employing derogations, rather than the escape routes available under the HRA, via the use of rights-infringing primary legislation. After the *A and Others* decision in 2004, the option of relying on a derogation has also not been taken. That stance was continued by the Coalition government post-2010 and by the Conservative government post-2015. Thus, for example, in introducing TEOs in 2015 or reintroducing relocation to TPIMs, also in 2015, the Conservative government did not rely on s 6(2) HRA to argue that the legislation could be introduced regardless of the possibility that it might lead to ECHR breaches; nor did it rely on a derogation from Arts 5, 14 or 8.

This chapter has charted a dramatic change from the old model for counter-terrorist laws – a reactive model used in the TA 2000 – to the proactive model, introduced under the then Labour government in the ATCSA Part 4, then in the PTA 2005, and which was also relied on in introducing TPIMs and TEOs. The Terrorism Acts 2000 and 2006, the ACTSA, and the Counter-terrorism Act 2008 introduced a range of broad special offences applying to a wide range of groups. But criminal offences rely on charging persons with a specific offence and seeking to bring them to trial. Although in that sense terrorism offences are much less pernicious in human rights terms than relying on the non-trial-based measures, it must not be forgotten that the TA's broad definition of terrorism lies at the heart of the proactive measures introduced by its successors, and that it represented at the time one of the most significant extensions of 'emergency' legislation over the last 30 years.

The TA's introduction in the absence of any 'clear and present' danger evident in 2000 may be said to have provided an example of a failure of democracy to protect civil liberties. The legislation is remarkable in its abandonment of all the features that sought to make the original PTA and EPA legislation appear tolerable: its limited application, its temporary nature, annual review and scrutiny of the continuing threat. Obviously subsequent events have however provided a justification not only for its provisions, but for the additional offences introduced by later enactments. In so far, however, as the TA allows for greater breadth and unpredictability in the application of the terrorist offences, the Human Rights Act had to be looked to, to seek to prevent the departures from the rule of law it threatened, and which Parliament had not prevented.[472] In particular, the HRA has had, as discussed, a significant impact in imposing compliance with Art 6 on the TA.

The courts have also relied on the HRA in imposing rights-compliance on the range of non-trial-based proactive measures introduced post-2000. Part 4 ATCSA was modified due to court intervention on human rights grounds, and then finally abandoned after the Lords' decision in *A and others*. The control orders scheme under the 2005 Act followed a similar path, in the sense that the HRA was used in order to seek to impose Convention compliance upon it, although since it was a more nuanced scheme it was more

---

472 At a number of points in the debate on the Second Reading of the Bill in the Commons MPs noted that it did not appear to be compatible with the Convention: 'we are continuously finding as we go through the bill provisions that seem contrary to the spirit and precise provisions of the Convention and of the decisions of the Court' (HC Debs 15 March 2000 col 432). Nevertheless, all amendments which might have removed incompatibilities were overwhelmingly defeated due to the government's very large majority and the determination of the Conservative opposition to appear to be 'tougher on terrorism' than the Labour party.

open to modification. The introduction of TPIMs to replace control orders indicated, as discussed, a determination to avoid imposing highly repressive measures on suspects without a trial. The introduction of TEOs in 2015, which bear some resemblance to control orders in the sense that they are potentially both intrusive and non-trial-based, is a response to the recognition that the threat level has been rising recently due to the activities of Isis and its supporters. The use of TPIMs or control orders or TEOs, rather than charging suspects with offences actually committed, is a logical conclusion of the proactive approach.

The use of proactive alongside reactive trial-based measures appears, on its face, to represent the most effective strategy in relation to the threat of suicide bombing: the attacks in London on 7/7, in the US on 9/11 and in Paris in November 2015 were carried out by suicide bombers. Those who *plan* to die in carrying out attacks self-evidently cannot be 'punished' after the event and are unlikely to be deterred by the threat of conviction and imprisonment. However, preventive measures are only of utility in relation to those likely to carry out suicide bombings if they are *effective* in targeting the right people; over-broad preventive measures may possibly have counter-productive effects in appearing to give some credence to the narrative of extremists. Such measures should only be used where the alternative of imprisonment of those engaged in planning and preparation for such attacks, for example, on conviction for proscription-based offences, for conspiracy, or under the broad preparatory offences available, has been reviewed and is clearly not feasible. The question arises whether control orders and now TPIMs have been used (as detention might have been under Part 4 ATCSA)[473] where a prosecution could succeed instead under the criminal law or under one of the many broad offences of the Terrorism Acts of 2000 and 2006?[474] If so, is this at least partly due to a lack of devotion of resources to the bringing of a prosecution and to a preference for controlling an individual's movements on the basis of a low standard of proof because that avoids the difficulties of persuading the security services that it is possible to use some sensitive material as evidence, with appropriate safeguards, in a criminal trial? The campaigning group Justice argued in 2007 that greater effort could be devoted to seeking to bring prosecutions under the ordinary criminal law or the special terrorism offences. So doing could include relaxing the ban on the use of intercept material as evidence,[475] and making greater efforts to turn security material into evidence. While the impact of relaxing the ban on use of intercept material as evidence should not be exaggerated, it may be noted that virtually all other countries have dropped their bans, indicating that any value they had is outweighed by the value of using such material in criminal trials.

Post-2000 it became incrementally easier in the UK to fall within the legal category of a 'terrorist' suspect; as discussed, attention has turned to adopting broad definitions of such suspects, facilitating the application of sanctions outside the criminal process. Counter-terrorist law and policy has in part concentrated on widening the legal net so that greater numbers of persons can potentially be viewed as terrorist suspects, partly by adopting definitions of 'terrorist activity' that in effect broaden the basic definition of terrorism

---

473 See p 1084 *et seq.*
474 See further on this point the Draft Prevention of Terrorism Act 2005 (Continuance in Force of Sections 1 to 9) Order 2007 JUSTICE Briefing for House of Commons Debate February 2007 at paras 5–8.
475 See Chapter 11, pp 792–93.

under the TA and partly by lowering the standard of proof needed in order to apply counter-terrorist sanctions to suspects. The current broad construction of the 'terrorist suspect' depends on *both* legal developments, taken together, in contradistinction to the broadening of the definitions of terrorist offences, which has also occurred, especially in the TA 2006. But the range of special counter-terrorist and proscription offences, as well as the use of non-trial-based measures, has been under-utilised. The attempt has not remotely been made to apply all the terrorism offences and sanctions to the wide range of groups and persons that s 1 TA potentially covers. The counter-terrorist provisions create an appearance of extreme authoritarianism that is not in general borne out by the reality. The greatest concern is to seek to apply them to groups linked to Isis or Al-Qaeda, which do threaten national security. But only a tiny handful of persons were subjected to the detention without trial scheme under ATCSA, and to control orders or TPIMs. In certain instances the ordinary criminal law has been employed against terrorist attacks rather than the special counter-terrorism provisions. In particular, those conspiring with the 7/7 bombers were charged in 2007 and convicted of an offence in a criminal law statute passed in 1883.[476]

Current and future strands of counter-terrorism policy seem likely to continue to come into potential conflict with the European Convention on Human Rights, although the current government seems to be adopting a more nuanced approach in response to the human rights embarrassment that the then Labour government suffered as a result of the House of Lords' decision in *A and Others* in 2004. Nevertheless it continues to see non-trial-based measures as a central part of its counter-terrorist strategy. At present, as this chapter has shown, two parallel schemes are operating in Britain in respect of the counter-terrorist response: the use of non-trial-based measures – TPIMs and TEOs – based on certification by the Home Secretary for a tiny group of suspected terrorists, and a reactive scheme based on a range of broad special terrorism offences, but dependent on trial and conviction, potentially targeted at all suspected terrorists. Ironically, the special terrorist offences appear to be viewed by successive governments as ineffective in relation to some of those who pose the greatest security threat. The introduction of control orders/TPIMs amounts to an admission of the inability of the criminal law to deal fully with this threat. So far the current government has not sought to introduce modifications to the criminal trial itself[477] – such as allowing the use of intercept material in evidence – with a view to bringing more of those subject to TPIMs, and other suspects, to trial. There seems to be a continuing reluctance to use security material as evidence in a criminal trial, partly explaining the reliance on proactive measures outside the criminal justice system. So, despite the introduction of a range of broad terrorism

---

476 The charge against them alleged that between 1 November 2004 and 29 June 2005, they 'unlawfully and maliciously' conspired with the four 7/7 bombers – Mohammed Sidique Khan, Shezhad Tanweer, Jermaine Lindsay and Hasib Hussein – to cause 'by explosive substance explosions on the transport for London system and/or tourist attractions in London in a nature likely to endanger life or cause serious injury to property'. The alleged offence is contrary to s 3(1)(a) of the Explosive Substances Act 1883. See *The Telegraph*, 6 April 2007. The conspirators, with two acquittals, were convicted on 1 May 2007.

477 Apart from the introduction, in places, of reverse burdens of proof, as in s 57 TA – see pp 1058–9 above. The key proposals from the Newton Committee Report (the Privy Counsellor Review Committee), 18 December 2003, had that objective in mind: they were intended to allow for the use of the special terrorism and proscription offences in prosecutions against members or supporters of Al-Qaeda. At present no clear plans are apparent to allow intercept material to be made admissible in evidence (see The Use of Intercept Evidence in Terrorism Cases, Standard Note: SN/HA/5249 24 November 2011, A Horne).

offences in 2000 and since then, there seems to be little prospect of a very significant increase in the use of the criminal justice process and no prospect of a *political* solution to the current situation. Thus the executive will probably continue to rely on the use of interventions outside that process, and the courts' deployment of the Human Rights Act or of a new British Bill of Rights or 'common law principles' will continue to play a key role in creating a human rights-compliant balance between rights and security, bearing in mind that terrorist activity is damaging to the enjoyment of rights.

This chapter has sought to argue that there is a dissonance between the vast array of counter-terrorist provisions it has discussed, and the preservation of the security of the UK. The passing of two very broad anti-terrorism statutes – TA 2000 and ATCSA – did not prevent the worst terrorist atrocity in Britain in recent years – the London bombings in 2005. This chapter is arguing for a narrower targeting of the provisions – at Isis, Al-Qaeda and linked groups, and for greater efforts to prosecute their members and supporters employing, *inter alia*, the offences under the TA 2006. The use of TPIMs, which at present do not include detention, not only runs counter to a number of Convention principles, but is ineffective in security terms.[478] In 2016, in the aftermath of the atrocity in Paris in 2015, and threats of attacks in the UK,[479] the ability of terrorism to degrade and destroy the enjoyment of human rights is apparent although it must not be overstated. In 2012–16 a rise in the number of prosecutions for offences such as preparing acts of terrorism[480] or attending training abroad occurred, a welcome development in disrupting terrorist networks and in demonstrating that early stage intervention in terrorist plots via use of criminal offences is a realistic and effective security strategy. The current threat from Isis-inspired terrorism should not be exaggerated as so doing furthers one of that terrorist group's objectives – to inspire fear and divide communities. Moreover, Isis-inspired terrorism does not constitute the only form of terrorism posing a threat to UK nationals, whether within the UK or abroad, and some terrorist acts may be linked to mental illness as well as to adherence to extreme Islamism. The UK as a democracy clearly needs to continue to seek to preserve national security as well as the human rights of suspects as well as of potential victims of terrorism,[481] as it has previously sought to do, especially over the last 26 years, as discussed in this chapter, while mindful of the difficulty of ensuring the exercise of human rights in a state which is failing to preserve personal security.

478 As Justice pointed out in 2007 in its Draft Prevention of Terrorism Act 2005 (Continuance in Force of Sections 1 to 9) Order 2007 JUSTICE Briefing for House of Commons Debate February 2007, the absconding of two individuals subject to control orders – one from a psychiatric hospital and one from a mosque – raised serious questions about the use of control orders.

479 A video was released by the terrorist group Isis purporting to show the nine Paris attackers in Iraq and Syria, some time before they killed 130 people in the French capital on 13 November 2015. It also also threatens an attack on the UK – showing footage of major London sites, as well as David Cameron, the Prime Minister, and John Bercow: see *The Guardian*, 25 January 2016.

480 The most common offence for which persons have been charged with under terrorism legislation since 11 September 2001 is 'preparation for terrorist acts' (s 5 of the 2006 Act), which has accounted for 21% of all terrorism-related charges since then, and half of all terrorism-related charges in the year ending 31 March 2015. In the year ending 31 March 2015, there were 299 arrests for terrorism-related offences, an increase of 31% compared with the previous year. Of those charged following a terrorism-related arrest in the year ending 31 March 2015, 85% were charged with terrorism-related offences, the highest proportion on record, and an increase on the 64% in the previous year (Home Office Statistical bulletin 04/15, September 2015).

481 See fn 17 above.

Index